One-Stop Internet Resources

Log on to tajwwI.glencoe.com

ONLINE STUDY TOOLS

- Study Central
- Chapter Overviews
- ePuzzles and Games
- Self-Check Quizzes
- Vocabulary e-Flashcards
- Multi-Language Glossaries

ONLINE RESEARCH

- Student Web Activities
- Current Events
- Beyond the Textbook Features
- Web Resources
- State Resources

FOR TEACHERS

- Teacher Forum
- Web Activity Lesson Plans

Also Featuring a Complete Interactive Student Edition

Contents

Revolutionary War drum and fife ▶

Preparing the Declaration of Independence ▼

Contents

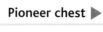

Pioneer chest ▶

Unit 4

Unit 5

◀ Civil War cannon

Unit 6

Appendix

1912 Model T Ford ▲

Features

Analyzing Primary Sources

Biography

TECHNOLOGY & History

◄ Abigail Adams

Frederick Douglass ►

America's Literature

Why It Matters

Features

▼ Molly Pitcher at the Battle of Monmouth

▼ Immigrant children learn American ways in the classroom.

SkillBuilder Handbook

Connecting to the Constitution

NATIONAL GEOGRAPHIC Geography & History

What If...

Maps, Charts, and Graphs

Maps

Unit 6

Charts and Graphs

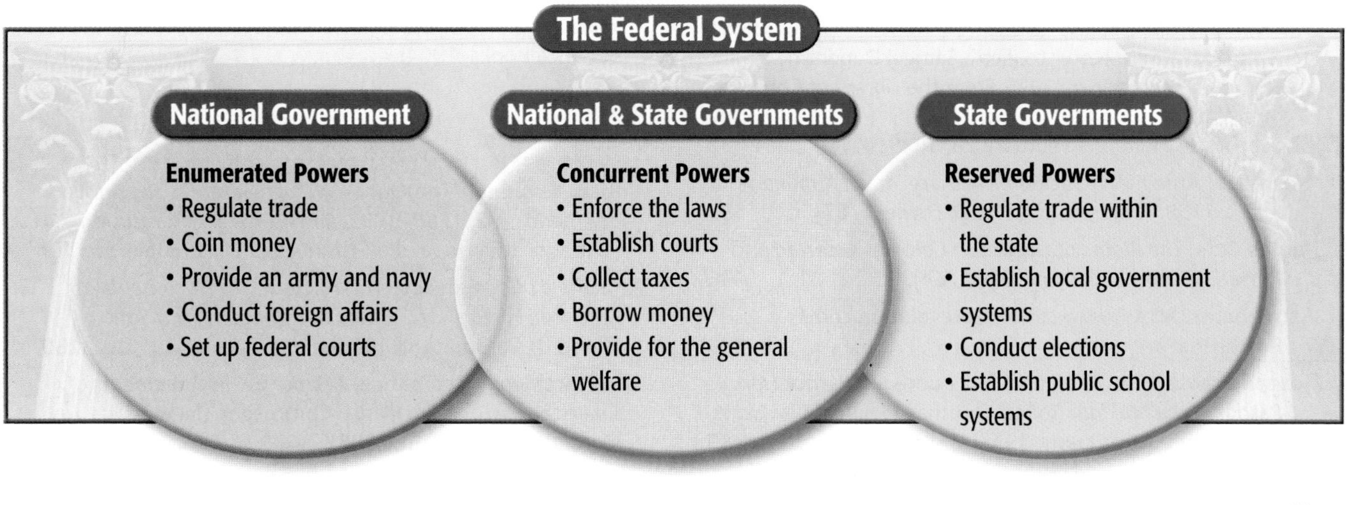

The Federal System
National Government
Enumerated Powers
• Regulate trade
• Coin money
• Provide an army and navy
• Conduct foreign affairs
• Set up federal courts
National & State Governments
Concurrent Powers
• Enforce the laws
• Establish courts
• Collect taxes
• Borrow money
• Provide for the general welfare
State Governments
Reserved Powers
• Regulate trade within the state
• Establish local government systems
• Conduct elections
• Establish public school systems

Primary Source Quotes

Primary Source Quotes

Primary Source Quotes

Primary Source Quotes

Previewing Your Textbook

Follow the reading road map through the next few pages to learn about using your textbook, *The American Journey to World War I.*

Units

Your textbook is divided into units. Each unit begins with four pages of information to help you begin your study of its topics.

WHY IT'S IMPORTANT

Each unit begins with a **preview** of important events and **Why It's Important** to read about them.

WHERE IN THE UNITED STATES?

The map shows you **where** the events in this unit happened.

PLACES TO LOCATE

Look for these important **places** as you read the unit.

TIME LINE

This time line shows you **when** the events in this unit happened. It also compares events in the United States with events in the world.

PEOPLE TO MEET

This list introduces **people** who made an impact on American history during the time period of the unit. They are highlighted throughout your text.

Chapters

Each unit of your textbook is divided into chapters. Each chapter starts by giving you some background information about what you will be reading and help with reading skills.

CHAPTER TITLE
The title tells you the **main topic** you will be reading about.

BIG IDEAS
Throughout your text the important ideas are listed at the beginning of each chapter. These are the **big themes** of history that repeat again and again.

HISTORY ONLINE
This tells you where you can go **online** to get more information.

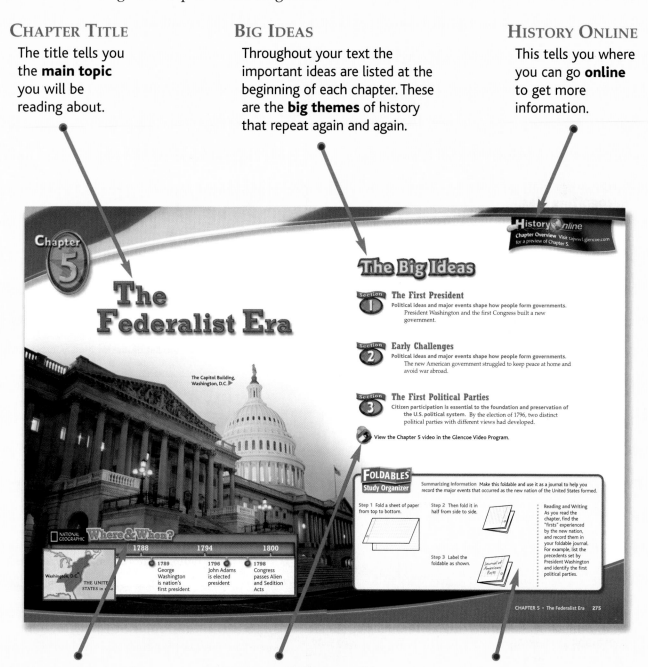

WHERE & WHEN?
Here you can see **where and when** events in this chapter happened.

GLENCOE VIDEO PROGRAM
Each **video program** highlights a unique topic in the chapter and has a Viewer's Guide.

FOLDABLES
Every chapter has a **Foldable™** that will help you organize and remember information in the chapter.

Chapter Reading Skill

Because reading about social studies is different than reading a novel or magazine, every chapter offers help with reading skills.

Chapter 5

Get Ready to Read

Recognizing Bias

1 Learn It!

Most people have feelings and ideas that affect their point of view. This viewpoint, or *bias*, influences the way they interpret events. For this reason, an idea that is stated as a fact may really be only an opinion. Recognizing bias will help you judge the accuracy of what you read. You can look for clues to help uncover bias in written form. Read the list below for hints you can use to identify bias.

- Identify the author of the statement, and examine his or her views and possible reasons for writing the material.
- Look for language that reflects an emotion or opinion—words such as *all, never, best, worst, might,* or *should.*
- Examine the writing for imbalances—focusing on one viewpoint and failing to discuss other perspectives.

READING SKILL

This shows you what reading skill you will be learning about—**Recognizing Bias.**

LEARN IT!

This explains how the skill applies to the **reading** you do every day.

READING TIP

The Reading Tip tells you more about making **connections** in your reading.

Reading Tip

One way to identify bias is to find out more about the author. Can you find information about the author that will help you understand opinions he or she may express?

276

PRACTICE IT!
Next comes an easy-to-follow **practice** activity for the reading skill.

2 Practice It!

Look at the two quotes below. Each has a different opinion about "the people." On a separate sheet of paper, restate each opinion in your own words. Discuss your conclusions with a partner.

"The people are turbulent [disorderly] and changing. . . . They seldom judge or determine right."
—*Alexander Hamilton, Federalist, page 292*

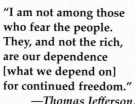
▲ Alexander Hamilton

Read to Write
Write a paragraph describing a person or event about which you feel very strongly. Now try to write a paragraph about the same person or event without including any personal opinion.

READ TO WRITE
Writing about what you read will help you remember the event.

"I am not among those who fear the people. They, and not the rich, are our dependence [what we depend on] for continued freedom."
—*Thomas Jefferson, Republican, page 293*

▲ Thomas Jefferson

READING SKILLS HANDBOOK
Located on pages 14–23 is a handbook that is full of good **reading strategies** to help you read your text. You can look back at this at any time as you read.

3 Apply It!

Look for examples of bias in comments made by key figures described in the text.

APPLY IT!
Here is an opportunity to **apply** what you have learned.

CHAPTER 5 • The Federalist Era   277

Sections

A section is a division, or part, of a chapter. The first page of the section, the Section Opener, helps you set a purpose for reading.

LOOKING BACK, LOOKING AHEAD

Read the **connection** between what you already know and what you are about to read.

CONTENT VOCABULARY

This list points out important social studies **terms** and their pronunciation.

ACADEMIC VOCABULARY

This list names other **words** you might not know that will come up in your reading.

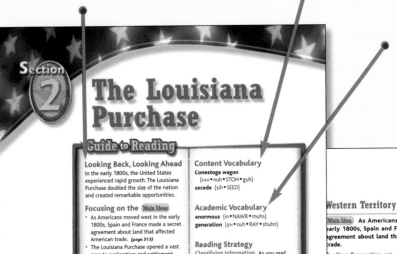

Section 2 — The Louisiana Purchase

Guide to Reading

Looking Back, Looking Ahead
In the early 1800s, the United States experienced rapid growth. The Louisiana Purchase doubled the size of the nation and created remarkable opportunities.

Focusing on the Main Ideas
- As Americans moved west in the early 1800s, Spain and France made a secret agreement about land that affected American trade. (page 313)
- The Louisiana Purchase opened a vast area to exploration and settlement. (page 314)

Locating Places
Louisiana Territory
New Orleans
St. Louis
Missouri River

Meeting People
Meriwether Lewis
William Clark
Sacagawea (SA•kuh•juh•WEE•uh)
Zebulon Pike

Content Vocabulary
Conestoga wagon (KAH•nuh•STOH•guh)
secede (sih•SEED)

Academic Vocabulary
enormous (in•NAWR•muhs)
generation (JEH•nuh•RAY•shuhn)

Reading Strategy
Classifying Information As you read the section, re-create the diagram below and describe the areas that Lewis and Clark and Zebulon Pike explored.

Explorer	Region explored
Meriwether Lewis and William Clark	
Zebulon Pike	

NATIONAL GEOGRAPHIC Who & When?

1804 — 1805 — 1806 — 1807

Oct. 1803 Senate ratifies Louisiana Purchase treaty

May 1804 Lewis and Clark begin expedition

Sep. 1806 Lewis and Clark return to St. Louis

Nov. 1806 Zebulon Pike reaches Pikes Peak

312 CHAPTER 6 • The Age of Jefferson

Western Territory

Main Idea As Americans moved west in the early 1800s, Spain and France made a secret agreement about land that affected American trade.

Reading Connection What challenges come with moving? Read to learn what the pioneers faced as they went west.

An American Story

Why did Americans risk everything they had to travel west? An English visitor, Harriet Martineau, observed:

❝ The pride and delight of Americans is in their quantity of land. . . . The possession of land is the aim of all action . . . and the cure for all social evils. . . . If a man is disappointed in politics or love, he goes and buys land. ❞
—from Society in America

Moving West During the early 1800s, more and more Americans moved west in search of land and adventure. These pioneers headed over the mountains into Kentucky and Tennessee and the less settled areas of the Northwest Territory. Most of these pioneers were farmers. They made a long and exhausting journey over the Appalachian Mountains.

Settlers loaded their household goods into Conestoga wagons (KAH•nuh•STOH•guh), sturdy vehicles topped with white canvas. For these westward-bound pioneers, two vital possessions were a rifle for protection and hunting and an ax to hack their way through the dense forests.

In 1800 the territory of the United States extended only as far west as the Mississippi River. The area to the west of the river—known as the Louisiana Territory—belonged to Spain. It was an enormous area of land, extending south to the city of New Orleans and west to the Rocky Mountains. Its northern boundaries remained undefined.

Many pioneers established farms along rivers that fed into the upper Mississippi River. The Spanish allowed Americans to sail on the lower Mississippi and trade in New Orleans. For the western farmers, this right was vital. The goods they sent downriver were unloaded in New Orleans and sent by ship to markets on the East Coast.

The French Threat In 1802 the Spanish suddenly changed their policy. They refused to allow American goods to move into or past New Orleans. That same year, President Jefferson learned that Spain and France had made a secret agreement that transferred the Louisiana Territory to France. Jefferson was alarmed. He thought French control would jeopardize American trade on the Mississippi River. He authorized Robert Livingston, the new minister to France, to negotiate for the purchase of New Orleans and other French territory.

Revolt in Santo Domingo The leader of France, Napoleon Bonaparte (nuh•POHL•yuhn BOH•nuh•PAHRT), hoped to use Santo Domingo as a Caribbean naval base from which he could control an American empire. However, a revolt in Santo Domingo ended Bonaparte's dream of a Western empire.

Inspired by the ideas of the French Revolution, enslaved Africans and other laborers in Santo Domingo rebelled against the island's plantation owners. After fierce and bitter fighting, the rebels, led by Toussaint-Louverture (TOO•SA LOO•vuhr•TYUR), declared the colony an independent republic. Toussaint set up an independent government.

In 1802 Napoleon sent troops to regain control. The French captured Toussaint but could not regain control of the island. By 1804 the French were driven out of Santo Domingo and the country regained its original name of Haiti.

Reading Check Explain Why was the Mississippi River important to western farmers?

CHAPTER 6 • The Age of Jefferson 313

FOCUSING ON THE MAIN IDEAS

Preview the **main ideas** of each section which are repeated in the reading.

AN AMERICAN STORY

Read about **real-life** Americans and what they thought and did.

Pike's Expedition Even before Lewis and Clark returned, Jefferson sent others to explore the wilderness. Lieutenant **Zebulon Pike** led two expeditions between 1805 and 1807, traveling through the upper Mississippi River valley and into the region that is now the state of Colorado. In Colorado, Pike found a snow-capped mountain he called Grand Peak. Today this mountain is known as Pikes Peak. Pike's account of his expeditions gave Americans their first detailed description of the Great Plains and the Rocky Mountains.

Federalists Plan to Secede Many Federalists opposed the Louisiana Purchase. They feared that the states carved out of the new territory would become Republican, reducing the Federalists' power. A group of Federalists in Massachusetts plotted to **secede** (sih • SEED)—withdraw—from the United States. They wanted New England to form a separate "Northern Confederacy." The plotters realized that to have any chance of success, the Northern Confederacy would have to include New York as well as New England.

MAP

Maps help you learn how **geography and history** are related.

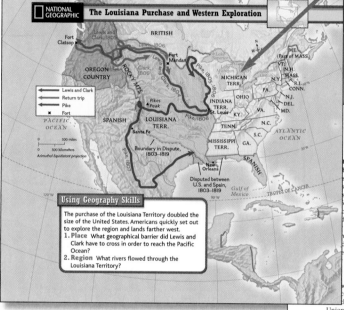

NATIONAL GEOGRAPHIC **The Louisiana Purchase and Western Exploration**

Lewis and Clark
Return trip
Pike
Fort

Using Geography Skills

The purchase of the Louisiana Territory doubled the size of the United States. Americans quickly set out to explore the region and lands farther west.
1. **Place** What geographical barrier did Lewis and Clark have to cross in order to reach the Pacific Ocean?
2. **Region** What rivers flowed through the Louisiana Territory?

...ralists Support Burr In 1804 the ...blican caucus nominated Thomas ...son for a second term as president. ...son and the Republicans, in doubt about ...s loyalty to the party, did not nominate ...r another term as vice president. Instead, ...hose George Clinton of New York. Burr ...decided to run for governor of New York.

...Federalists supported Burr as they were ...ning for a powerful ally in New York who ...d support their plan for the Northern ...deracy. Alexander Hamilton, however, ...his weight against Burr's election.

...and Hamilton Alexander Hamilton ...ever trusted Aaron Burr. Now Hamilton ...concerned about rumors that Burr had ...ly agreed to lead New York out of the Union. Hamilton called Burr "a danger... man." When ... ne election for governor, ...e blamed Hamilton and challenged him to a

duel. In July 1804, the two men—armed with pistols—met in Weehawken, New Jersey. Hamilton hated dueling and pledged not to shoot at his rival. Burr, however, did fire and aimed to hit Hamilton. Seriously wounded, Hamilton died the next day. Burr fled to avoid arrest on the charge of murder.

The Northern Confederacy Fails With Burr on the run and with almost no support in the New England states, the plans for the Northern Confederacy failed. The results of the election of 1804 showed how thoroughly the Federalists had been discredited. Jefferson and Clinton captured 162 electoral votes to 14 for the Federalist candidates Charles Pinckney and Rufus King.

Reading Check Summarize Why did France sell the Louisiana Territory to the United States?

READING CHECK

This is a **self-check** question to see if you understand the main ideas.

STUDY CENTRAL

Here you can receive **help** with homework.

History online

Study Central Need help understanding the Louisiana Purchase and its exploration? Visit tajwwl.glencoe.com and click on Study Central.

Section 2 Review

Reading Summary
Review the **Main Ideas**
* American settlers in the West depended on the use of the lower Mississippi River and the port of New Orleans to trade their farm products. That control was threatened when France gained control of the Louisiana Territory.

* After the purchase of Louisiana from the French, President Jefferson sent Lewis and Clark and others to explore the new territory.

What Did You Learn?
1. Which European countries controlled the Louisiana Territory until 1800?
2. Name the famous Native American woman who Lewis and Clark met along their journey.

Critical Thinking
3. **Organizing Information** Create a diagram like the one below that lists the benefits of acquiring the Louisiana Territory.

Benefits

4. **The Big Ideas** Why was the French port of New Orleans important to the United States?
5. **Determining Cause and Effect** How could the Lewis and Clark expedition prepare people who wanted to move west? Write a paragraph describing your conclusions.
6. **ANALYSIS** Assess What was the relationship between the Louisiana Purchase and political power? How did Jefferson's political opponents react? Write an essay explaining your assessment.

CHAPTER 6 • The Age of Jefferson **317**

SECTION REVIEW

Here you can **review** the main topics and answer questions about what you have read.

Chapter Assessment

These pages offer you a chance to check how much you remember after reading the chapter.

REVIEW CONTENT VOCABULARY

Content vocabulary is reviewed here.

REVIEW THE MAIN IDEAS

Revisit the **Main Ideas** found in your reading.

READ TO WRITE

You are reminded about the chapter **Big Ideas** here.

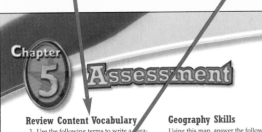

Chapter 5 Assessment

Review Content Vocabulary

1. Use the following terms to write a paragraph about the new U.S. government:
   cabinet   implied powers
   caucus   states' rights

Review the Main Ideas

Section 1 • The First President

2. Why did Hamilton want national taxes? Why did some oppose the taxes?

3. What was the importance of the Judiciary Act of 1789?

Section 2 • Early Challenges

4. What caused farmers in western Pennsylvania to revolt during the Whiskey Rebellion?

5. What was the significance of the Battle of Fallen Timbers?

Section 3 • The First Political Parties

6. According to Hamilton, what are implied powers?

7. What actions by France led to an undeclared war with the United States?

Critical Thinking

8. **Evaluate** Refer to the grievances listed in the Declaration of Independence. How were these grievances addressed in the Bill of Rights?

9. **Analyze** What did President Washington say in his Farewell Address about political parties and foreign policy?

10. **Compare and Contrast** In a brief essay, compare the positions of the Federalists and Democratic-Republicans on the national bank.

300   CHAPTER 5 • The Federalist Era

Geography Skills

Using this map, answer the following questions about the election of 1796.

NATIONAL GEOGRAPHIC   Election of 1796

Candidate	Electoral Votes	Party
John Adams	71	Federalist
Thomas Jefferson	68	Democratic-Republican

11. **Identify** How many states did John Adams win? How many did Thomas Jefferson win?

12. **Evaluate** What was the total electoral vote count for each man? What was the election result?

13. **Region** What was the distribution of votes by state? What pattern do you see?

History Online

Self-Check Quiz Visit tajwwl.glencoe.com to prepare for the Chapter 5 test.

Read to Write

14. **The Big Ideas** Government and Democracy Political ideas and major events shape how people form governments. Select an event from this chapter. Write an essay describing how people and ideas affected government through that event.

15. **Using Your FOLDABLES** Review the "American firsts" that you listed in your foldable. Using numbers, rank each first from the most important to the least important. Explain the reasons for your highest and lowest rankings.

Using Academic Vocabulary

16. Read the following sentence and then write the meaning of the underlined word. The new federal government was interested in increasing revenue in order to pay off its debts.

Building Citizenship

17. **Researching** Work in groups of four to discuss and develop answers to these questions:
   • How does the Bill of Rights reflect the principle of limited government?
   • What are two individual rights protected in the Bill of Rights?
   • Why would it be necessary to change the Constitution?

Reviewing Skills

18. **READING SKILL** **Recognizing Bias** Imagine that you were living in the United States in 1798. Write an editorial to your newspaper that demonstrates bias about your view as to whether the Alien and Sedition Acts violated the U.S. Constitution. Use details from the text and chart about the Alien and Sedition Acts on page 295.

19. **ANALYSIS SKILL** **Sequencing Information** Create a time line that lists key events in President Adams's dispute with France. Write a paragraph analyzing President Adams's handling of this dispute.

Standardized Test Practice

Select the best answer for each of the following questions.

20 Thomas Jefferson and Alexander Hamilton served as members of Washington's
   A congress.
   B judiciary.
   C cabinet.
   D military.

21 Which amendment of the Bill of Rights protects the rights of the states?
   A First Amendment
   B Fifth Amendment
   C Sixth Amendment
   D Tenth Amendment

22 The XYZ Affair dealt with problems between the United States and
   A France.
   B Spain.
   C Great Britain.
   D Canada.

23 Hamilton proposed a national tax on imports, or a(n)
   A bond.
   B impressment.
   C caucus.
   D tariff.

CHAPTER 5 • The Federalist Era   301

USING ACADEMIC VOCABULARY

Academic vocabulary is reviewed here.

REVIEW ARROWS

Look for the Review arrows that tell you are **reviewing** material you have learned before.

TEST PRACTICE

Here you **practice** answering the kinds of questions that appear on standardized tests.

Special Features

Special features supply more information about topics in a chapter or unit. They help history come alive.

AMERICA'S LITERATURE

The literature selection is connected to people or events in the chapter.

BEFORE YOU READ

Get an idea of what the literature selection is about **before** you start reading.

VOCABULARY PREVIEW

Here are words and terms that may be new to you.

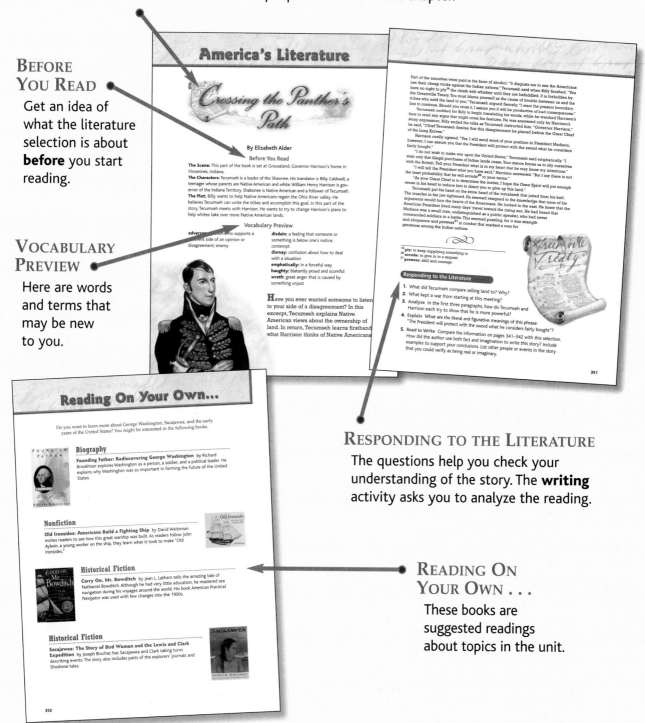

RESPONDING TO THE LITERATURE

The questions help you check your understanding of the story. The **writing** activity asks you to analyze the reading.

READING ON YOUR OWN . . .

These books are suggested readings about topics in the unit.

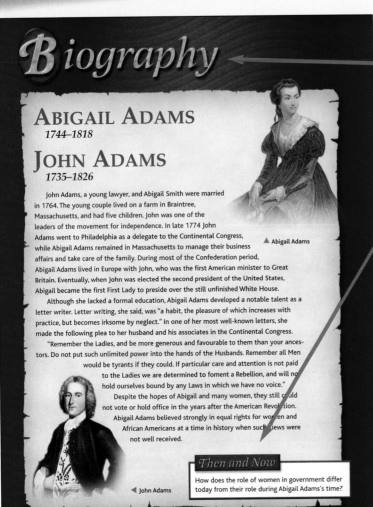

Biography

ABIGAIL ADAMS
1744–1818

JOHN ADAMS
1735–1826

John Adams, a young lawyer, and Abigail Smith were married in 1764. The young couple lived on a farm in Braintree, Massachusetts, and had five children. John was one of the leaders of the movement for independence. In late 1774 John Adams went to Philadelphia as a delegate to the Continental Congress, while Abigail Adams remained in Massachusetts to manage their business affairs and take care of the family. During most of the Confederation period, Abigail Adams lived in Europe with John, who was the first American minister to Great Britain. Eventually, when John was elected the second president of the United States, Abigail became the first First Lady to preside over the still unfinished White House.

Although she lacked a formal education, Abigail Adams developed a notable talent as a letter writer. Letter writing, she said, was "a habit, the pleasure of which increases with practice, but becomes irksome by neglect." In one of her most well-known letters, she made the following plea to her husband and his associates in the Continental Congress.

"Remember the Ladies, and be more generous and favourable to them than your ancestors. Do not put such unlimited power into the hands of the Husbands. Remember all Men would be tyrants if they could. If particular care and attention is not paid to the Ladies we are determined to foment a Rebellion, and will not hold ourselves bound by any Laws in which we have no voice."

Despite the hopes of Abigail and many women, they still could not vote or hold office in the years after the American Revolution. Abigail Adams believed strongly in equal rights for women and African Americans at a time in history when such views were not well received.

▲ Abigail Adams

◀ John Adams

294

Then and Now
How does the role of women in government differ today from their role during Abigail Adams's time?

BIOGRAPHY
Read more about important **people** and what they achieved.

THEN AND NOW
In the writing activity, you **compare** a similar situation in the past and the present.

.... take opposing ... s a result, two

... time when you ... e of your class- ... pinion? Read to ... nflict occurred ... n and Jefferson.

....

...ricans as the ... Washington did not escape criticism during his two terms as president. From time to time, harsh attacks on his policies and on his personality appeared in newspapers. One paper even called Washington "the misfortune of his country."

How Did Americans View the President?
Most attacks on Washington came from supporters of Thomas Jefferson. They were trying to discredit the policies of Washington and Hamilton by attacking the president. By 1796 Americans were beginning to divide into opposing groups and to form political parties.

In Washington's cabinet, Hamilton and Jefferson often took opposing sides. They disagreed on economic policy and foreign relations, on the power of the federal government, and on interpretations of the Constitution. Even Washington was sometimes **partisan** (PAHR• tuh•zuhn)—favoring one side of an issue. Although he believed he stood above politics, Washington usually supported Hamilton's positions.

Political Parties Emerge Like Hamilton and Jefferson, Congress and the nation at large also had differences. By the mid-1790s, two **distinct** political parties had taken shape.

The name *Federalist* had first described someone who supported ratification of the Constitution. By the 1790s the word was applied to the group of people who supported the policies of the Washington administration.

Generally, Federalists stood for a strong federal government. They admired Britain because of its stability and distrusted France because of the violent changes following the French Revolution. Federalist policies tended to favor banking and business. Federalists received the strongest support in the Northeast and from wealthy plantation owners in the South.

Efforts to turn opinion against the Federalists began seriously in late 1791 when **Philip Freneau** (frih•NOH) began publishing the *National Gazette*. Jefferson, then secretary of state, helped the newspaper get started. Later he and Madison organized people who disagreed with Hamilton.

HISTORY MAKERS
Learn how people, decisions, objects, and events **changed history.**

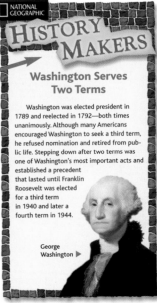

NATIONAL GEOGRAPHIC

HISTORY MAKERS

Washington Serves Two Terms

Washington was elected president in 1789 and reelected in 1792—both times unanimously. Although many Americans encouraged Washington to seek a third term, he refused nomination and retired from public life. Stepping down after two terms was one of Washington's most important acts and established a precedent that lasted until Franklin Roosevelt was elected for a third term in 1940 and later a fourth term in 1944.

George Washington ▶

CHAPTER 5 • The Federalist Era   291

Connecting to the Constitution

The Supreme Court and the Economy

Why It Matters People in the United States are free to own property; to make a profit; and to make their own choices about what to produce, buy, and sell. The Framers of the U.S. Constitution believed that economic freedom is a basic right of citizens. As a result, the Constitution laid the basis for an economy based on capitalism, or free enterprise.

Although capitalism is the basis of the American economic system, ours is a mixed economy—a system in which the government both supports and regulates private enterprise. Over the years, the American judicial system—headed by the Supreme Court—has made decisions that have encouraged business competition and private property ownership. However, the Court also has expanded the power of the government to regulate, or lay down rules for, the economy as a whole.

The Commerce Power Article I, Section 8 of the Constitution gives Congress the authority to regulate commerce. It is known as the commerce clause. Under the Articles of Confederation, each state jealously guarded its own commerce. Trade barriers among the states restricted commerce and stood in the way of a strong national economy. The Framers of the U.S. Constitution sought to avoid state rivalries by givin... ...late all forms o... affirmed... foreign...

"An unlimited p... essarily, a pow... is a limit beyon... no property ca...

◀ John Marshall

310

CONNECTING TO THE CONSTITUTION

Here you will learn about how the **Constitution** has been able to respond to challenges that the Framers never imagined.

Analyzing Primary Sources

Challenging Times

Even after the ratification of the U.S. Constitution, the leaders and citizens of this young nation faced many challenges. With an outline for how the government should work and the leadership of George Washington, people began to work together to launch this new republic.

Read the passages on pages 298 and 299 and answer the questions that follow.

Painter and President by J.L.G. Ferris ▶

Reader's Dictionary

embarking (ihm • BAHRK • ihng): setting out

integrity (ihn • TEH • gruh • tee): honesty

gallery: outdoor balcony

proclamation (PRAH • kluh • MAY • shuhn): announcement

agitated (A • juh • TAYT • ihd): upset and nervous

ungainly: awkward, clumsy

plainest manner: in a simple way

On Becoming President

Americans were happy that the hero of the American Revolution, George Washington, was elected the nation's first president. Washington expressed his feelings about becoming president in a letter.

I am **embarking** . . . on this voyage, but what returns will be made for them [Americans], Heaven alone can foretell. **Integrity** and firmness is all I can promise; these, be the voyage long or short, never shall forsake me although I may be deserted by all men.

—Letter to Henry Knox, April 1789

Washington's First Inaugural

Pennsylvania Senator William Maclay was one of the many witnesses to the nation's first presidential inauguration. He wrote about the event in his journal.

[T]he President was conducted out of the middle window into the **gallery** [overlooking Wall Street], and the oath was administered by the Chancellor [the highest judicial officer in the state of New York]. Notice that the business done was communicated to the crowd by **proclamation** . . . who gave three cheers, and repeated it on the President's bowing to them.

298 CHAPTER 5 • The Federalist Era

ANALYZING PRIMARY SOURCES

You will check your understanding of the **primary sources** and **write** a response to one or more of them.

YOU DECIDE . . .

Imagine that you can give your **opinion** when two opposing views are presented.

You Decide . . .

Independence: Yes or No?

Many American colonists joined the movement for independence. Still, many Americans did not want to break away from Great Britain.

For Independence

Many colonists in the summer of 1775 were not prepared to break away from Great Britain. The colonists resented British taxes. Because they had no representation in Parliament, as people in Great Britain did, the colonists believed that Parliament had no right to tax them. They summarized their feelings with the slogan "No taxation without representation." Most members of the Second Continental Congress wanted the right to govern themselves, but they did not want to break with the British Empire.

By 1776, however, opinion had changed. Frustrated by Britain's refusal to compromise, many Patriot leaders began to call for independence. Influential in swaying the colonists toward the idea of separating from Great Britain was Thomas Paine's pamphlet *Common Sense*, which first appeared in January 1776. Paine made an impassioned appeal:

"I have heard it asserted by some, that as America has flourished under her former connection with Great Britain, the same connection is necessary towards her future happiness. . . . I answer roundly, that America would have flourished as much, and probably much more, had no European power [taken notice of her]. . . . Everything that is right or natural pleads for separation. The blood of the slain, the weeping voice of nature cries, 'TIS TIME TO PART.'"

The Patriots believed that fighting for liberty set an example for others to follow. Ben Franklin wrote to a friend that "our cause is the cause of all mankind, and that we are fighting for their liberty in defending our own."

◀ **Thomas Paine**

158

Against Independence

The American Revolution was not only a war between the British and the Americans. It also divided Americans themselves. While American Patriots fought passionately for independence, other Americans fought just as fiercely for their British king. Americans who felt a strong sense of loyalty to the king and believed British law should be upheld came to be known as Loyalists.

Loyalists came from all parts of American society. Many Loyalists lived in Georgia, the Carolinas, and New England; the Patriots though were strong in New England and Virginia. Political differences divided communities and even split families. Benjamin Franklin's son, William, served as Royal Governor of New Jersey. When the Revolution began, William remained loyal to Britain and quarreled bitterly with his father.

Loyalists answered Paine's *Common Sense* with pamphlets of their own. One who did was Charles Inglis, a minister from New York. He wrote: "By a connection with Great Britain, our trade would still have the protection of the greatest naval power in the world." Inglis also said that if the American colonies did not give up their fight for independence, Britain would exert its great power and the result would be:

"Ruthless war, with all its aggravated horrors, will ravage our once happy land—our seacoasts and ports will be ruined, and our ships taken. Torrents of blood will be spilt, and thousands reduced to beggary and wretchedness."

YOU BE THE HISTORIAN

Give your **opinion** on the issue.

You Be The Historian

DBQ Document-Based Questions

1. What economic argument does Paine use to support separation from Great Britain?

2. What does Inglis believe will result from war with Britain?

3. Were the reasons for or against American independence convincing? Write a short letter to Inglis in which you support the Patriot or Loyalist position. Use facts to support your position.

159

GEOGRAPHY & HISTORY

Find out how **geography** has affected people and people have affected the environment.

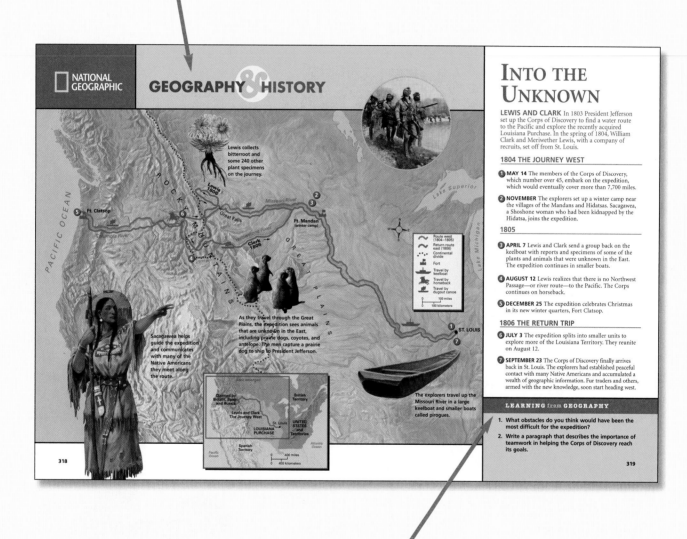

LEARNING FROM GEOGRAPHY

Evaluate in **writing** the impact of geography on people and events.

Jefferson's Policies

Main Idea Jefferson worked to limit the scope of the federal government and shift control of the federal courts away from the Federalists.

Reading Connection How should the federal government balance individual liberty with national interests? Read on to learn of changes Jefferson made to deal with this question.

In 1801, when Jefferson became president, the entire federal government consisted of only a few hundred people. This was exactly how Jefferson thought it should be. (Today nearly 3 million civilians work for the federal government.) In Jefferson's view, the national government should conduct foreign affairs and limit its domestic actions to delivering the mail, collecting customs duties, and taking a census every 10 years.

Jefferson Takes Charge When Jefferson entered office, he surrounded himself with men who shared his Republican principles. His secretary of state was his friend and fellow Virginian, James Madison. For secretary of the treasury, he chose **Albert Gallatin**, a Pennsylvanian with a strong grasp of financial matters.

Jefferson and Gallatin aimed to reduce the national debt that the Federalists had left. They scaled down military expenses by cutting the army by one-third and reducing the navy from 25 to 7 ships. By slashing spending, Jefferson and Gallatin **significantly** lowered the national debt within a few years.

Between the election and Jefferson's inauguration, Federalists in Congress passed the Judiciary Act of 1801. This act increased the number of federal judges. Outgoing President John Adams then filled many positions with Federalists.

▲ Abigail Adams in the unfinished White House

The Way It Was

Washington in 1800

The United States government moved to the new capital city of Washington, D.C., in 1800. Being located along the Potomac River, Washington was expected to emerge as a great trading city, but the plans for a great city had not proceeded very far. The president's house, with laundry sometimes

hanging in the unfinished East Room, stood in an open field with two boxlike buildings for executive offices nearby. More than a mile away, across a swamp, stood the partly built Capitol. Members of Congress lived in crowded boardinghouses. The streets were mostly muddy wagon tracks, bordered with the stumps of trees that had been recently cut. Some Americans criticized the choice of Washington as the capital. They believed that the government should move to a larger city.

308

THE WAY IT WAS

Discover how life in the United States has **changed** over more than 200 years.

Movement The ... d the way for the ... ghts movement. ... d several national ... ers—male and

... daughter of a ... w York, worked ... ance. She called ... ge training for **coeducation**—the teaching of boys and girls together.

Susan B. Anthony met Elizabeth Cady Stanton at a temperance meeting in 1851. They became lifelong friends and partners in the struggle for women's rights. For the rest of the century, Anthony and Stanton led the women's movement. They worked with other women to win the right to vote, which was granted by several states. It was not until 1920, however, that woman suffrage became a reality everywhere in the United States.

Reading Check **Explain** What is suffrage?

Why It Matters

The Seneca Falls Convention

Throughout the nation's history, women had fought side by side with the men to build a new nation and to ensure freedom. Even though the Declaration of Independence promised equality for all, the promise rang hollow for women.

Female reformers began a campaign for their own rights. In 1848 Lucretia Mott and Elizabeth Cady Stanton organized the Seneca Falls Convention. One of the resolutions demanded suffrage, or the right to vote, for women. This marked the beginning of a long, hard road to gain equal rights.

Gaining the Right to Vote, 1848–1920

The Seneca Falls Convention led to the growth of the woman suffrage movement.

Photo Gallery
Raising the Status of Women

Lucretia Mott (below) and Susan B. Anthony were leaders in the effort to allow women a greater role in American society.

"We hold these truths to be self-evident: that all men and women are created equal."
—Declaration of the
Seneca Falls Convention, 1848

1848 →	1850 →	1866 →	1869 →	1878 →	1884 →
Seneca Falls Convention	First national women's rights convention held in Worcester, Massachusetts	Susan B. Anthony forms Equal Rights Association	Women granted voting rights in Wyoming Territory	Woman suffrage amendment first introduced in U.S. Congress	Belva Lockwood runs for president

410   CHAPTER 8 • The Northeast: Building Industry

WHY IT MATTERS

Learn how particular events **influenced** the future.

Scavenger Hunt

*T*he *American Journey to World War I* contains a wealth of information. The trick is to know where to look to access all the information in the book.

If you run through this scavenger hunt exercise with your teacher or parents, you will see how the textbook is organized, and how to get the most out of your reading and study time. Let's get started!

1 How many units and how many chapters are in this book?

2 What is the title of Chapter 4, Section 3?

3 You want to quickly find all the maps in the book on the Civil War. Where are they listed?

4 What time period does Chapter 7, Section 2 cover?

5 In Chapter 4, what will the *Foldables* activity help you do?

6 What reading skill will you practice in Chapter 1?

7 What are the Big, or most important, Ideas in Chapter 2? Where can you find this information?

8 There are six Web sites in Chapter 5. The first one previews the chapter. What do the other five sites do? How are some sites similar?

9 A primary source is a document or other testimony, dating from the same period as an event. In what part of chapters 1–17 can you always find primary sources?

10 Where, in the back of the book, can you quickly find the meaning of Content Vocabulary words, such as *confederation*? What is a confederation?

READING TO LEARN

This handbook focuses on skills and strategies that can help you understand the words you read. The strategies you use to understand whole texts depend on the kind of text you are reading. In other words, you do not read a textbook the way you read a novel. You read a textbook mainly for information; you read a novel for the story and the characters. To get the most out of your reading, you need to choose the right strategy to fit the reason you are reading. This handbook can help you learn about the following reading strategies:

- how to identify new words and build your vocabulary;
- how to adjust the way you read to fit your reason for reading;
- how to use specific reading strategies to better understand what you read;
- how to use critical thinking strategies to think more deeply about what you read; and
- how to understand text structures to identify an author's ideas.

TABLE OF CONTENTS

Identifying Words and Building Vocabulary

What do you do when you come across a word you do not know as you read? Do you skip over the word? If you are reading a novel, you use the context to understand the meaning of the word. But if you are reading for information, an unfamiliar word may get in the way of your understanding. When that happens, follow the strategies below to learn how to say the word and what it means.

Reading Unfamiliar Words

Sounding Out the Word One way to figure out how to say a new word is to sound it out, syllable by syllable. Look carefully at the word's beginning, middle, and ending. For example, in the word *coagulate,* what letters make up the beginning sound or beginning syllable of the word? *Co* rhymes with *so.* Inside *coagulate,* do you see a word you already know how to pronounce? The syllable *ag* has the same sound as the *ag* in *bag,* and the syllable *u* is pronounced like the letter *u.* What letters make up the ending sound or syllable? *Late* is a familiar word you already know how to pronounce. Now try pronouncing the whole word: **co ag u late.**

Determining a Word's Meaning

Using Syntax Like all languages, the English language has rules and patterns for the way words are arranged in sentences. The way a sentence is organized is called the syntax. If English is your first language, you have known this pattern since you started using sentences. If you are learning English now, you may find that the syntax is different from the patterns you know in your first language.

In a simple sentence in English, someone or something (the subject) does something (the predicate or verb) to or with another person or thing (the object): *The soldiers attacked the enemy.* Sometimes adjectives, adverbs, and phrases are added to add details to the sentence: *The courageous young soldiers fearlessly attacked the well-entrenched enemy shortly after dawn.*

Knowing about syntax can help you figure out the meaning of an unfamiliar word. Just look at how syntax can help you figure out the following nonsense sentence: *The blizzy kwarkles sminched the flerky fleans.* Your experience with English syntax tells you that the action word, or verb, in this sentence is *sminched.* Who did the *sminching*? The *kwarkles.* What kind of *kwarkles* were they? *Blizzy.* Whom did they *sminch*? The *fleans.* What kind of *fleans* were they? *Flerky.* Even though you don't know the meaning of the words in the nonsense sentence, you can make some sense of the entire sentence by studying its syntax.

Using Context Clues You can often figure out the meaning of an unfamiliar word by looking at its context, the words and sentences that surround it. To learn new words as you read, follow these steps for using context clues.

- Look before and after the unfamiliar word for a definition or a synonym, a general topic associated with the word, a clue to what the word is similar to or different from, or an action or a description that has something to do with the word.
- Connect what you already know with what the author has written.
- Predict a possible meaning.
- Use the meaning in the sentence.
- Try again if your guess does not make sense.

Using Types of Reference Materials

Dictionaries and other reference sources can help you learn new words and how to use them. Check out these reference sources. You can find these in your local public or school library as well as on the Internet.

- A **dictionary** gives the pronunciation, the meaning or multiple meanings, and often examples of how to use the words. Some dictionaries also provide illustrations or diagrams to help define words, other forms of words, their parts of speech, and synonyms. You might also find the historical background of a word, such as its Greek, Latin, or Anglo-Saxon origins.
- A **glossary** is a word list that appears at the end—or Appendix—of a book or other written work and includes only words that are in that work. Like dictionaries, glossaries include the pronunciation and definitions of words.
- A **thesaurus** lists groups of words that have the same, or almost the same, meaning. Words with similar meanings are called synonyms. Seeing the synonyms of words can help you build your vocabulary.

Recognizing Word Meanings Across Subjects

Have you ever learned a new word in one class and then noticed it in your reading for other subjects? The word probably will not mean exactly the same thing in each class. But you can use what you know about the word's meaning to help you understand what it means in a different subject area. Look at the following example from three different subjects:

- **Social Studies:** One *product* manufactured in the southern part of the United States is cotton cloth.
- **Math:** After multiplying the numbers five and five, explain how you arrived at the *product*.
- **Science:** One *product* of photosynthesis is oxygen.

CHECKING YOUR UNDERSTANDING

The following sentence does not include real English words, but you can use what you have learned about English syntax to decode the sentence. First read the sentence. Then answer the questions that follow.

The shabs smatously graled the mul-bulowed rotfabs.

1. What is the verb in the sentence?

2. What is the subject?

3. What is the object?

Reading for a Reason

Why are you reading that paperback mystery? What do you hope to get from your American history textbook? And are you going to read either of these books in the same way that you read a restaurant menu? The point is, you read for different reasons. The reason you are reading something helps you decide on the reading strategies you use with a text. In other words, how you read will depend on why you are reading.

Knowing Your Reason for Reading

In school and in life, you will have many reasons for reading, and those reasons will lead you to a wide range of materials:

- **To learn and understand new information,** you might read news magazines, textbooks, news on the Internet, books about your favorite pastime, encyclopedia articles, primary and secondary sources for a school report, instructions on how to use a calling card, or directions for a standardized test.
- **To find specific information,** you might look at the sports section for the score of last night's game, a notice on where to register for a field trip, weather reports, bank statements, or television listings.
- **To be entertained,** you might read your favorite magazine, e-mails or letters from friends, the Sunday comics, or even novels, short stories, plays, or poems!

Adjusting How Fast You Read

How quickly or how carefully you should read a text depends on your purpose for reading it. Because there are many reasons and ways to read, think about your purpose and choose the strategy that works best. Try out these strategies:

- **Scanning** means quickly running your eyes over the material, looking for key words or phrases that point to the information you are looking for. Scan when you need to find a particular piece or type of information. For example, you might scan a newspaper for movie show times.
- **Skimming** means quickly reading a piece of writing to find its main idea or to get a general overview of it. For example, you might skim the sports section of the daily newspaper to find out how your favorite teams are doing. Or you might skim a chapter in your textbook to prepare for a test.
- **Careful reading** involves reading very slowly and paying close attention with a purpose in mind. Read carefully when you are learning new concepts, following complicated directions, or preparing to explain information to someone else.

CHECKING YOUR UNDERSTANDING

If you were working on a research paper on the American Revolution, how would you adjust the speed at which you were reading for each of the following cases?

1. You have just found a 1,200-page work that covers the entire colonial and revolutionary era of the British colonies in North America.

2. You have discovered an article in a leading history magazine that supports every point that you are trying to make.

Understanding What You Read

*R*eading without understanding is like trying to drive a car on an empty gas tank. Fortunately, there are techniques you can use to help you concentrate on and understand what you read. Skilled readers adopt a number of strategies before, during, and after reading to make sure they understand what they read.

Preparing to Read

It is important to set the stage before you read. Following these steps will make the reading process more rewarding.

Previewing If you were making a preview for a movie, you would want to let your audience know what the movie is like. When you preview a piece of writing, you are trying to get an idea about the piece. Follow these steps to preview your reading assignments.

- Look at the title and any illustrations that are included.
- Read the headings, subheadings, and anything in bold letters.
- Skim the passage to see how it is organized.
- Set a purpose for your reading.

Using What You Know You already know quite a bit about what you are going to read. You bring knowledge and personal experience to a selection. Drawing on what you learned in a previous class is called *activating prior knowledge,* and it can help you create meaning in what you read. Ask yourself, *What do I already know about this topic?*

Predicting *Predicting* requires using background and prior knowledge, as well as the ability to make educated guesses. Make educated guesses before you read and while you read to figure out what might happen in the story or article you are reading.

Reading the Text

Following these suggestions while you read will help ensure that you get the most out of your reading.

Visualizing Creating pictures in your mind as you read—called *visualizing*—is a powerful aid to understanding. As you read, set up a movie theater in your imagination. Picture the setting—city streets, the desert, or the moon. If you can visualize, selections will be more vivid, and you will recall them better later on.

Identifying Sequence When you discover the logical order of events or ideas, you are identifying *sequence.* Do you need to understand step-by-step directions? Are you reading a persuasive speech with the reasons listed in order of importance? Look for clues and signal words that will help you find the way information is organized.

Determining the Main Idea When you look for the *main idea* of a selection, you look for the most important idea. The examples, reasons, and details that further explain the main idea are called *supporting details.* Some main ideas are clearly stated within a passage—often in the first sentence of a paragraph, or sometimes in the last sentence of a passage. Other times, however, an author does not directly state the main idea. Instead, he or she provides details that help readers figure out what the main idea is.

Questioning By learning how to analyze questions, you will quickly learn where to look for information as you read. Questions vary in many ways. One of the ways that questions vary is by how explicit or implied the question is compared with the text. These types of questions fall into four categories:

- **Right there** questions can be answered based on a line from the text.
- **Think and search** questions can be answered by looking in a few different places in the text.
- **Author and you** questions can be answered by thinking about the text but that also require your prior knowledge.
- **On your own** questions cannot be answered by the text and rely on the reader.

Clarifying Clear up, or clarify, confusing or difficult passages as you read. When you realize you do not understand something, try these techniques to help you clarify the ideas. *Reread* the confusing parts slowly and carefully. *Look up* unfamiliar words. Simply *talk out* the part to yourself.

Monitoring Your Comprehension As you read, check your understanding by using the following strategies.

- **Summarize** what you read by pausing from time to time and telling yourself the main ideas of what you have just read. Answer the questions *Who? What? Where? When? Why?* and *How?* Summarizing tests your comprehension by encouraging you to clarify key points in your own words.
- **Paraphrase** what you have just read to see whether you really got the point. Paraphrasing is retelling something in your own words. If you cannot explain it clearly, you should probably reread the text.

CHECKING YOUR UNDERSTANDING

1. How does visualizing help you understand what you read in your textbook or when you read for pleasure?

2. How can you determine the main idea of a selection if the author never explicitly explains what it is?

3. Why is clarifying an important skill for you to develop?

Thinking About Your Reading

Sometimes it is important to think more deeply about what you have read so you can get the most out of what the author says. These critical thinking skills will help you go beyond what the words say and get at the important messages of your reading.

Interpreting

When you listen to your best friend talk, you do not just hear the words he or she says. You also watch your friend, listen to the tone of voice, and use what you already know about that person to put meaning to the words. In doing so, you are interpreting what your friend says. Readers do the same thing when they interpret as they read. *Interpreting* is asking yourself *What is the writer really saying here?* and then using what you know about the world to help answer that question.

Inferring

You may not realize it, but you make inferences every day. Here is an example: You run to the bus stop a little later than usual. No one is there. "I have missed the bus," you say to yourself. You might be wrong, but that is the way our minds work. You look at the evidence (you are late; no one is there) and come to a conclusion (you have missed the bus).

When you read, you go through exactly the same process because writers do not always directly state what they want you to understand. They suggest certain information by providing clues and interesting details. Whenever you combine those clues with your own background and knowledge, you are making an inference.

Drawing Conclusions

Skillful readers are always *drawing conclusions*, or figuring out much more than an author says directly. The process is like a detective solving a mystery. You combine information and evidence that the author provides to come up with a statement about the topic. Drawing conclusions helps you find connections between ideas and events and gives you a better understanding of what you are reading.

Making Connections

One way that you can remember what you have read is by making connections with the text. Your teacher often expresses these connections aloud so that you and your classmates have a model. Your teacher may also ask you to make connections with the text and share them with the class. The most common connections include:

- **Text-to-self** connections, in which you remember something from your own life that serves as a connection with what is being read. *(While reading about the Civil War, you think about a fight you had with a relative.)*
- **Text-to-world** connections, in which you remember something that is happening or has happened in the world that serves as a connection with what is being read. *(While reading about the Civil War, you remember reading a newspaper article about the civil war in Somalia.)*
- **Text-to-text** connections, in which you remember something you have read elsewhere that serves as a connection with what is being read. *(While reading about the Civil War, you recall the novel* The Red Badge of Courage.*)*

Analyzing

Analyzing, or looking at separate parts of something to understand the entire piece, is a way to think critically about written work. In analyzing persuasive *nonfiction,* you might look at the writer's reasons to see if they actually support the main point of the argument. In analyzing *informational text,* you might look at how the ideas are organized to see what is most important.

Distinguishing Fact From Opinion

Distinguishing between fact and opinion is an important reading skill. A *fact* is a statement that can be proved. An *opinion,* on the other hand, is what a writer believes on the basis of his or her personal viewpoint. Writers can support their opinions with facts, but an opinion is something that cannot be proved.

Evaluating

When you form an opinion or make a judgment about something you are reading, you are *evaluating*. If you are reading informational texts or something on the Internet, it is important to evaluate how qualified the author is to be writing about the topic and how reliable the information is that is presented. Ask yourself whether the author seems biased, whether the information is one-sided, and whether the argument presented is logical.

Synthesizing

When you *synthesize,* you combine ideas (maybe even from different sources) to come up with something new. It may be a new understanding of an important idea or a new way of combining and presenting information. For example, you might read a manual on coaching soccer, combine that information with your own experiences playing soccer, and come up with a winning plan for coaching your sister's team this spring.

CHECKING YOUR UNDERSTANDING

1. How does making connections with what you have read help you remember more?

2. How do analyzing and synthesizing differ?

3. How do facts and opinions differ? Why is it important to differentiate between the two as you study history?

Understanding Text Structure

Good writers do not just put together sentences and paragraphs in any order. They structure each piece of their writing in a specific way for a specific purpose. That pattern of organization is called text structure. When you know the text structure of a selection, you will find it easier to locate and recall an author's ideas. Here are four ways that writers organize text.

Comparison and Contrast

Comparison-and-contrast structure shows the *similarities* and *differences* among people, things, and ideas. Maybe you have overheard someone at school say something like "He is better at throwing the football, but I can run faster than he can." This student is using comparison-and-contrast structure. When writers use comparison-and-contrast structure, they often want to show you how things that seem alike are different or how things that seem different are alike.

Signal words and phrases: *similarly, on the one hand, on the other hand, in contrast to, but, however*

Cause and Effect

Just about everything that happens in life is the cause or the effect of some other event or action. Sometimes what happens is pretty minor: You do not look when you are pouring milk *(cause)*; you spill milk on the table *(effect)*. Sometimes it is a little more serious: You do not look at your math book before the big test *(cause);* you mess up on the test *(effect)*.

Writers use cause-and-effect structure to explore the reasons for something happening and to examine the results of previous events. This structure helps answer the question that everybody is always asking: *Why?* A historian might tell us why an empire rose and fell. Cause-and-effect structure is all about explaining why things are as they are.

Signal words and phrases: *so, because, as a result, therefore, for the following reasons*

Problem and Solution

How did scientists overcome the difficulty of getting a person to the moon? How will I brush my teeth when I have forgotten my toothpaste? These questions may be very different in importance, but they have one thing in common: Each identifies a problem and asks how to solve it. *Problems and solutions* are part of what makes life interesting. Problems and solutions also occur in fiction and nonfiction writing.

Signal words and phrases: *how, help, problem, obstruction, difficulty, need, attempt, have to, must*

Sequence

Take a look at three common forms of sequencing, the order in which thoughts are arranged.

- **Chronological order** refers to the order in which events take place. First, you wake up; next, you have breakfast; then, you go to school. Those events do not make much sense in any other order.
  Signal words: *first, next, then, later, finally*

- **Spatial order** tells you the order in which to look at objects. For example, consider this description of an ice-cream sundae: *At the bottom of the dish are two scoops of vanilla. The scoops are covered with fudge and topped with whipped cream and a cherry.* Your eyes follow the sundae from the bottom to the top. Spatial order is important in descriptive writing because it helps you as a reader to see an image the way the author does.
  Signal words: *above, below, behind, next to*

- **Order of importance** is going from most important to least important or the other way around. For example, a typical news article has a most important to least important structure.
  Signal words: *principal, central, important, fundamental*

CHECKING YOUR UNDERSTANDING

Read the following paragraph and answer the questions about the selection's text structure below.

The Huntington City Council recently approved an increase in the city sales tax. Recognizing the need to balance the city's budget, the council president Matt Smith noted that the council had no choice. The vote ended more than a year of preparing voters for the bad news. First, the council notified citizens that there would be a public discussion last April. Then, the council issued public statements that the vote would take place in November. Finally, the council approved the increase last week even though many residents opposed it. On one hand, the increase will increase revenues. On the other hand, more taxes could lead to fewer shoppers in the city's struggling retail stores.

1. How does the writer use comparison and contrast text structure?

2. How does the writer use problem and solution text structure?

3. What signal words show that the writer is setting the chronological order of events?

REFERENCE ATLAS

NATIONAL GEOGRAPHIC

ATLAS KEY

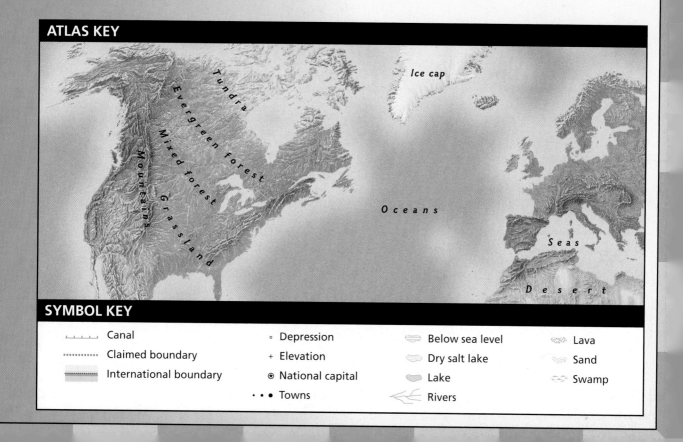

Ice cap

Tundra

Evergreen forest

Mixed forest

Mountains

Grassland

Oceans

Seas

Desert

SYMBOL KEY

⊥⊥⊥⊥ Canal	○ Depression	⬭ Below sea level	⬯ Lava
·········· Claimed boundary	+ Elevation	⬭ Dry salt lake	⬯ Sand
▓▓▓▓ International boundary	⊛ National capital	⬮ Lake	⌇ Swamp
	• • • Towns	⌇ Rivers	

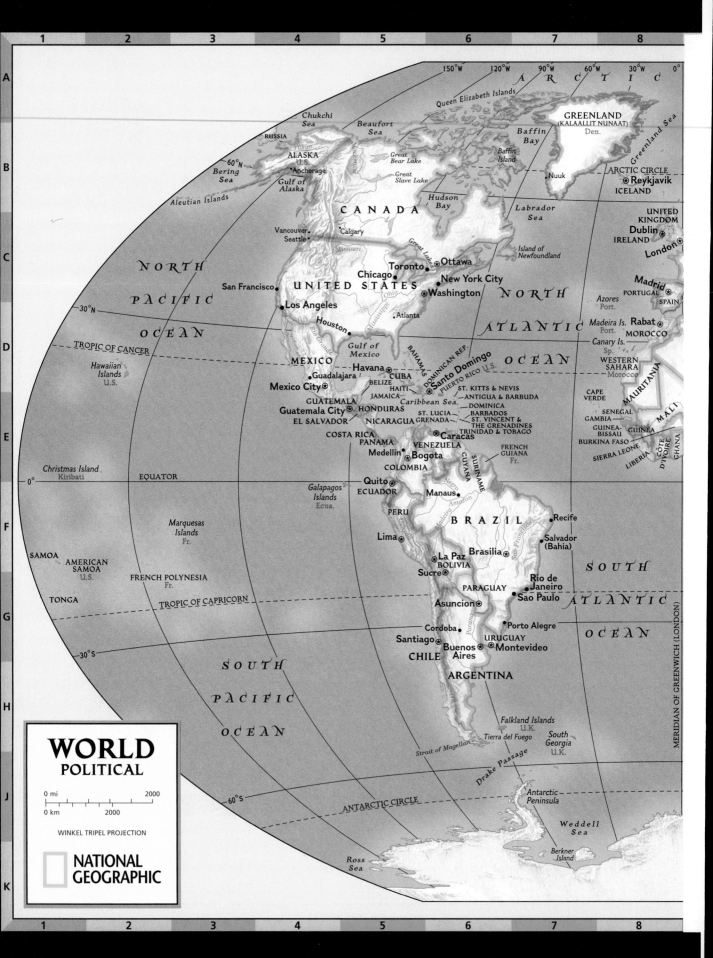

WORLD
POLITICAL

0 mi — 2000
0 km — 2000

WINKEL TRIPEL PROJECTION

NATIONAL GEOGRAPHIC

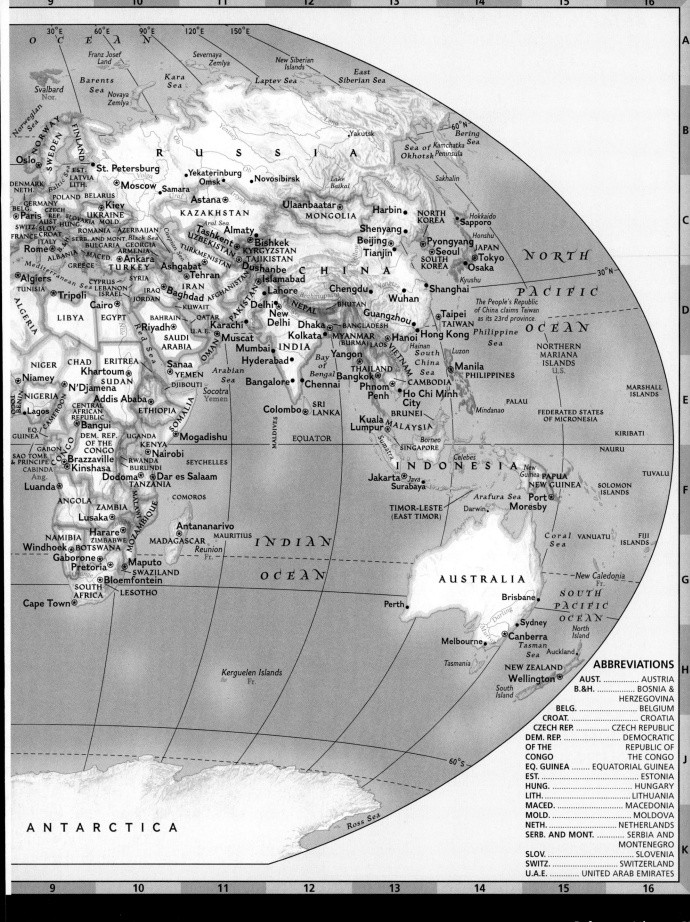

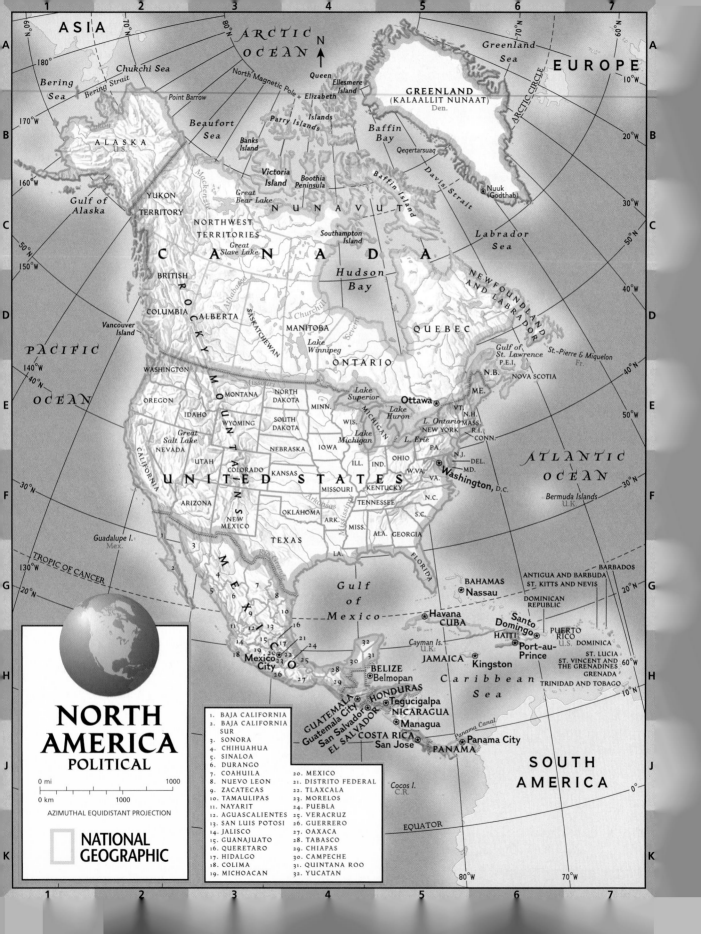

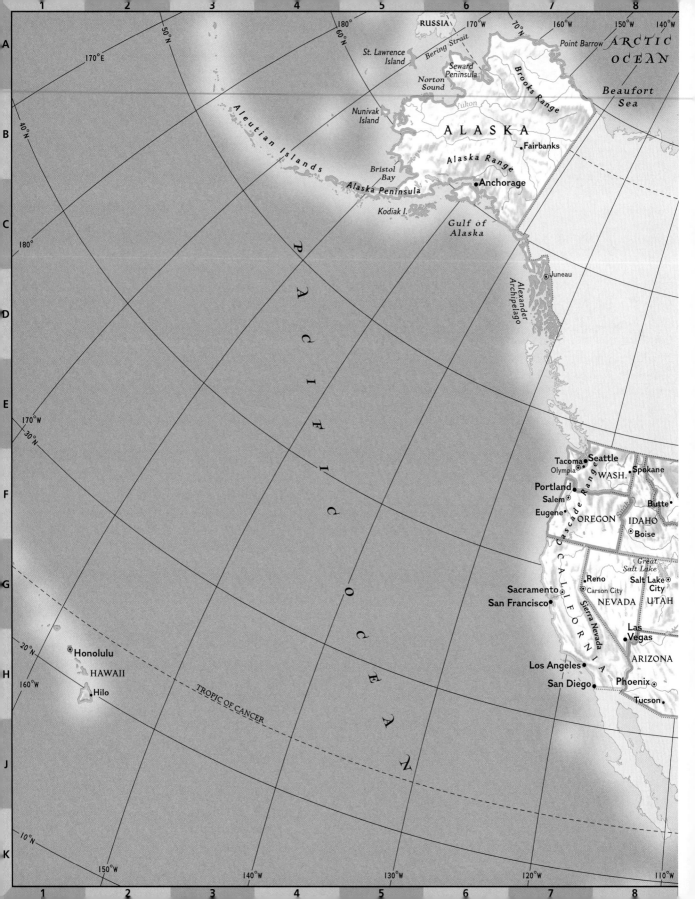

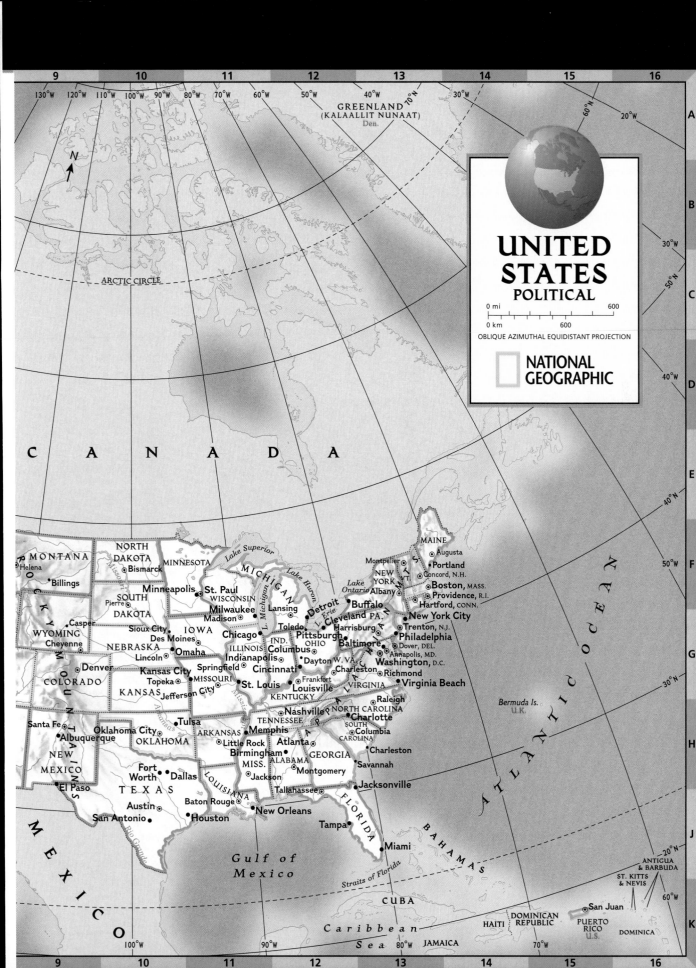

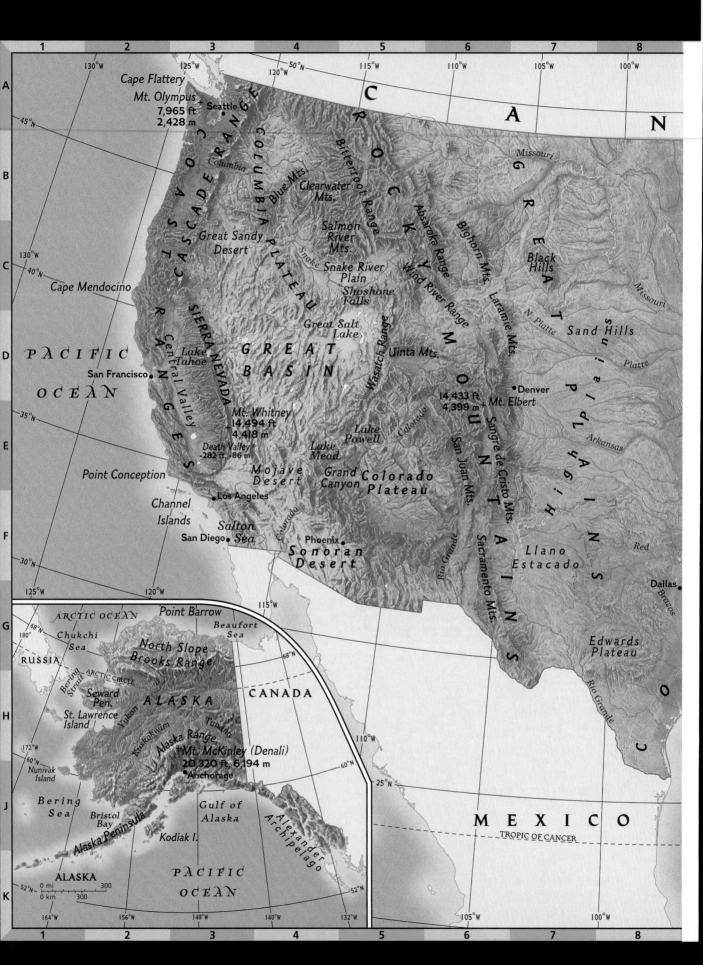

	1	2	3	4	5	6	7	8

A

B

C

D

E

F

G

H

J

K

C A N A D A

R O C K Y

M O U N T A I N S

Cape Flattery
Mt. Olympus
7,965 ft
2,428 m
Seattle

Columbia

Blue Mts.

Clearwater Mts.

Bitterroot Range

Absaroka Range

Bighorn Mts.

Missouri

Black Hills

Missouri

Great Sandy Desert

Salmon River Mts.

Snake River Plain

Snake

Shoshone Falls

Wind River Range

Laramie Mts.

N. Platte

Sand Hills

Platte

Cape Mendocino

Great Salt Lake

GREAT BASIN

Uinta Mts.

Mt. Elbert
14,433 ft
4,399 m

Denver

G R E A T   P L A I N S

High   Plains

Lake Tahoe

Wasatch Range

Colorado

San Francisco

Central Valley

SIERRA   NEVADA

Mt. Whitney
14,494 ft
4,418 m

Lake Powell

Lake Mead

San Juan Mts.

Sangre de Cristo Mts.

Arkansas

PACIFIC

OCEAN

Death Valley
-282 ft, -86 m

Mojave Desert

Grand Canyon

Colorado Plateau

Point Conception

Los Angeles

Colorado

Sacramento Mts.

Llano Estacado

Red

Channel Islands

Salton Sea

San Diego

Phoenix

Rio Grande

Sonoran Desert

Dallas

Brazos

C O

Edwards Plateau

ALASKA INSET:

ARCTIC OCEAN

Point Barrow

Beaufort Sea

Chukchi Sea

North Slope

Brooks Range

CANADA

RUSSIA

Bering Strait

ARCTIC CIRCLE

Seward Pen.

ALASKA

St. Lawrence Island

Yukon

Kuskokwim

Tanana

Alaska Range
+Mt. McKinley (Denali)
20,320 ft, 6,194 m

Anchorage

Nunivak Island

Bering Sea

Bristol Bay

Alaska Peninsula

Gulf of Alaska

Kodiak I.

Alexander Archipelago

M E X I C O

TROPIC OF CANCER

Rio Grande

ALASKA

0 mi   300
0 km   300

PACIFIC OCEAN

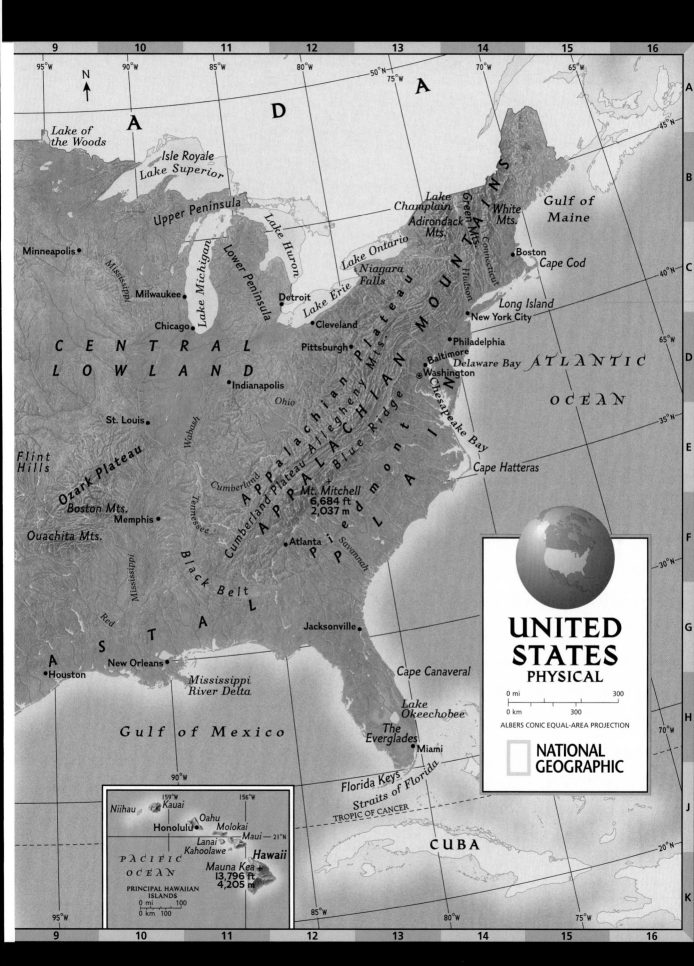

UNITED
STATES
PHYSICAL

0 mi — 300
0 km — 300
ALBERS CONIC EQUAL-AREA PROJECTION

NATIONAL
GEOGRAPHIC

Lake of the Woods
Isle Royale
Lake Superior
Upper Peninsula
Lake Huron
Lower Peninsula
Minneapolis
Mississippi
Milwaukee
Lake Michigan
Chicago
CENTRAL
LOWLAND
Indianapolis
Ohio
St. Louis
Wabash
Flint Hills
Ozark Plateau
Boston Mts.
Memphis
Tennessee
Ouachita Mts.
Mississippi
Red
Black Belt
New Orleans
Houston
Mississippi River Delta
Gulf of Mexico

Detroit
Lake Erie
Cleveland
Pittsburgh
Appalachian Plateau
Allegheny Mts.
Cumberland Plateau
APPALACHIAN
Cumberland
Blue Ridge
Mt. Mitchell
6,684 ft
2,037 m
Atlanta
Savannah
Piedmont
Niagara Falls
Lake Ontario
Lake Champlain
Adirondack Mts.
Green Mts.
White Mts.
Gulf of Maine
Boston
Cape Cod
Hudson
Connecticut
MOUNTAINS
Long Island
New York City
Philadelphia
Baltimore
Delaware Bay
Washington
Chesapeake Bay
ATLANTIC
OCEAN
Cape Hatteras

CANADA

Jacksonville
COASTAL
PLAIN
Cape Canaveral
Lake Okeechobee
The Everglades
Miami
Florida Keys
Straits of Florida
TROPIC OF CANCER
CUBA

Niihau
Kauai
Oahu
Honolulu
Molokai
Maui — 21°N
Lanai
Kahoolawe
Hawaii
Mauna Kea
13,796 ft
4,205 m
PACIFIC OCEAN
PRINCIPAL HAWAIIAN ISLANDS
0 mi — 100
0 km — 100
159°W
156°W

95°W   90°W   85°W   80°W   75°W   70°W   65°W
45°N
40°N
35°N
30°N
20°N
70°W
65°W
50°N
N

9   10   11   12   13   14   15   16
A   B   C   D   E   F   G   H   J   K

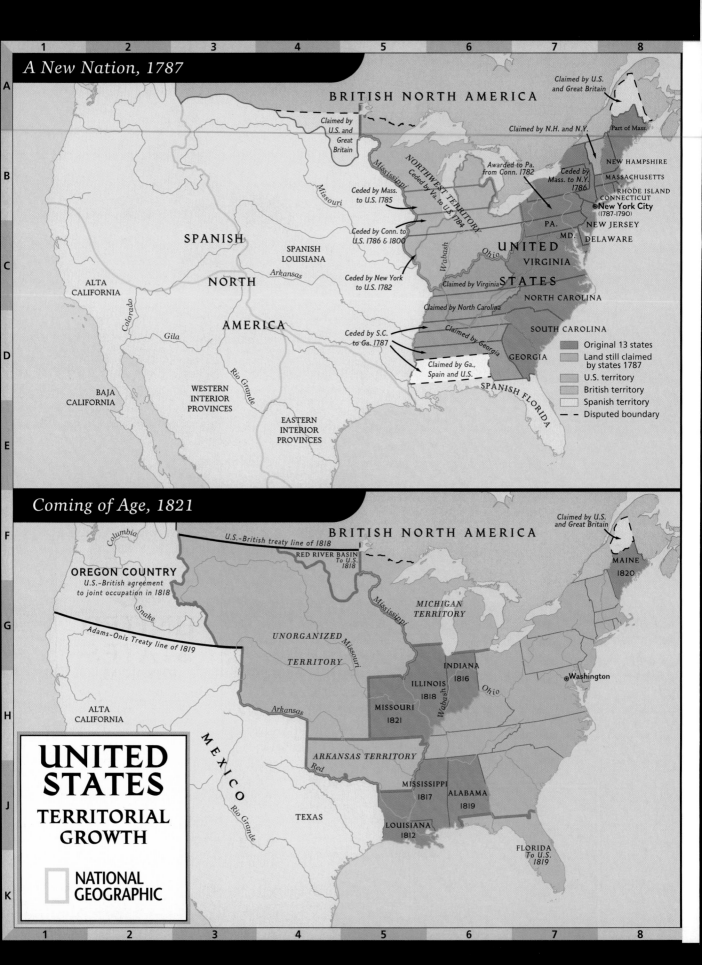

A New Nation, 1787

BRITISH NORTH AMERICA

Claimed by U.S. and Great Britain

Claimed by U.S. and Great Britain

Claimed by N.H. and N.Y.

Part of Mass.

NEW HAMPSHIRE

MASSACHUSETTS

RHODE ISLAND

CONNECTICUT

Awarded to Pa. from Conn. 1782

Ceded by Mass. to N.Y. 1786

Mississippi

NORTHWEST TERRITORY Ceded by Va. to U.S. 1784

Ceded by Mass. to U.S. 1785

Missouri

⊙ New York City (1787-1790)

NEW JERSEY

PA.

MD.

DELAWARE

SPANISH

SPANISH LOUISIANA

Ceded by Conn. to U.S. 1786 & 1800

Wabash

Ohio

UNITED

VIRGINIA

NORTH

Arkansas

Ceded by New York to U.S. 1782

STATES

ALTA CALIFORNIA

Colorado

Claimed by Virginia

NORTH CAROLINA

AMERICA

Gila

Claimed by North Carolina

SOUTH CAROLINA

Rio Grande

Ceded by S.C. to Ga. 1787

Claimed by Georgia

GEORGIA

BAJA CALIFORNIA

WESTERN INTERIOR PROVINCES

Claimed by Ga., Spain and U.S.

SPANISH FLORIDA

EASTERN INTERIOR PROVINCES

Original 13 states

Land still claimed by states 1787

U.S. territory

British territory

Spanish territory

– – – Disputed boundary

Coming of Age, 1821

Columbia

BRITISH NORTH AMERICA

Claimed by U.S. and Great Britain

U.S.–British treaty line of 1818

RED RIVER BASIN To U.S. 1818

MAINE 1820

OREGON COUNTRY

U.S.–British agreement to joint occupation in 1818

Snake

Mississippi

MICHIGAN TERRITORY

Adams–Onis Treaty line of 1819

UNORGANIZED

Missouri

INDIANA 1816

⊙ Washington

ILLINOIS 1818

Ohio

TERRITORY

ALTA CALIFORNIA

Arkansas

Wabash

MISSOURI 1821

MEXICO

ARKANSAS TERRITORY

Red

MISSISSIPPI 1817

ALABAMA 1819

Rio Grande

TEXAS

LOUISIANA 1812

FLORIDA To U.S. 1819

UNITED STATES

TERRITORIAL GROWTH

NATIONAL GEOGRAPHIC

Expanding West of the Mississippi, 1803

BRITISH NORTH AMERICA

Claimed by U.S. and Great Britain

OREGON COUNTRY
Claimed by Great Britain, Russia, Spain, and United States

Claimed by U.S. and Great Britain

VERMONT 1791

Mississippi

Missouri

INDIANA

TERRITORY

LOUISIANA PURCHASE
Purchased by U.S. in 1803 from France

OHIO 1803

Ohio

Philadelphia (1790–1800)

Washington (new capital 1800)

NEW SPAIN
(SPANISH MEXICO)

Arkansas

KENTUCKY 1792

Wabash

TENNESSEE 1796

Red

Ceded by Georgia to U.S. 1802

Rio Grande

Claimed by U.S. and Spain

MISSISSIPPI
TERR.

SPANISH FLORIDA

Claimed by U.S. and Spain

BAJA CALIFORNIA

- ▢ States previously in the Union
- ▢ States newly admitted

Coast to Coast, 1850 and beyond

BRITISH NORTH AMERICA

Treaty line of 1846

Treaty line of 1842

Treaty line of 1842

WASHINGTON 1889

MONTANA 1889

NORTH DAKOTA 1889

MINNESOTA 1858

MICHIGAN 1837

OREGON TERRITORY
Added to U.S. in 1846

MINNESOTA TERRITORY

WISCONSIN 1848

OREGON 1859

Snake

IDAHO 1890

WYOMING 1890

SOUTH DAKOTA 1889

Missouri

NEVADA 1864

UNORGANIZED

IOWA 1846

Wabash

Ohio

W. VA. 1863

Washington

UTAH TERRITORY

TERRITORY

NEBRASKA 1867

CALIFORNIA 1850

UTAH 1896

COLORADO 1876

KANSAS 1861

Arkansas

Colorado

ARIZONA 1912

NEW MEXICO
TERRITORY

OKLAHOMA 1907

ARKANSAS 1836

Gila

GADSDEN
PURCHASE
To U.S. 1853

NEW MEXICO 1912

Red

Mississippi

Rio Grande

TEXAS 1845

RUSSIA

ALASKA 1959
Purchased by U.S. 1867

MEXICO

FLORIDA 1845

HAWAII 1959
Annexed by U.S. 1898

····· States admitted after 1850

United States
States
Facts

Washington, D.C.
Population: 572,059
Land area: 61 sq. mi.

U.S. Territories

Puerto Rico
Population: 3,808,610
Land area: 3,425 sq. mi.

Guam
Population: 155,000 (est.)
Land area: 210 sq. mi.

U.S. Virgin Islands
Population: 121,000 (est.)
Land area: 134 sq. mi.

American Samoa
Population: 65,000 (est.)
Land area: 77 sq. mi.

The states are listed in the order they were admitted to the Union.

Population figures are based on U.S. Bureau of the Census for 2000. House of Representatives figures are from the Clerk of the House of Representatives. States are not drawn to scale.

1 Delaware
Year Admitted: 1787
Population: 783,600
Land area: 1,955 sq. mi.
Representatives: 1
★ Dover

2 Pennsylvania
Year Admitted: 1787
Population: 12,281,054
Land area: 44,820 sq. mi.
Representatives: 19
Harrisburg ★

3 New Jersey
Year Admitted: 1787
Population: 8,414,350
Land area: 7,419 sq. mi.
Representatives: 13
Trenton ★

9 New Hampshire
Year Admitted: 1788
Population: 1,235,786
Land area: 8,969 sq. mi.
Representatives: 2
Concord ★

10 Virginia
Year Admitted: 1788
Population: 7,078,515
Land area: 39,598 sq. mi.
Representatives: 11
Richmond ★

11 New York
Year Admitted: 1788
Population: 18,976,457
Land area: 47,224 sq. mi.
Representatives: 29
★ Albany

17 Ohio
Year Admitted: 1803
Population: 11,353,140
Land area: 40,953 sq. mi.
Representatives: 18
★ Columbus

18 Louisiana
Year Admitted: 1812
Population: 4,468,976
Land area: 43,566 sq. mi.
Representatives: 7
Baton Rouge ★

19 Indiana
Year Admitted: 1816
Population: 6,080,485
Land area: 35,870 sq. mi.
Representatives: 9
Indianapolis ★

25 Arkansas
Year Admitted: 1836
Population: 2,673,400
Land area: 52,075 sq. mi.
Representatives: 4
Little Rock ★

26 Michigan
Year Admitted: 1837
Population: 9,938,444
Land area: 56,809 sq. mi.
Representatives: 15
Lansing ★

27 Florida
Year Admitted: 1845
Population: 15,982,378
Land area: 53,997 sq. mi.
Representatives: 25
★ Tallahassee

33 Oregon
Year Admitted: 1859
Population: 3,421,399
Land area: 96,003 sq. mi.
Representatives: 5
★ Salem

34 Kansas
Year Admitted: 1861
Population: 2,688,418
Land area: 81,823 sq. mi.
Representatives: 4
Topeka ★

35 West Virginia
Year Admitted: 1863
Population: 1,808,344
Land area: 24,087 sq. mi.
Representatives: 3
★ Charleston

36 Nevada
Year Admitted: 1864
Population: 1,998,257
Land area: 109,806 sq. mi.
Representatives: 3
★ Carson City

42 Washington
Year Admitted: 1889
Population: 5,894,121
Land area: 66,582 sq. mi.
Representatives: 9
★ Olympia

43 Idaho
Year Admitted: 1890
Population: 1,293,953
Land area: 82,751 sq. mi.
Representatives: 2
★ Boise

44 Wyoming
Year Admitted: 1890
Population: 493,782
Land area: 97,105 sq. mi.
Representatives: 1
Cheyenne ★

45 Utah
Year Admitted: 1896
Population: 2,233,169
Land area: 82,168 sq. mi.
Representatives: 3
Salt Lake City ★

4 Georgia
Year Admitted: 1788
Population: 8,186,453
Land area: 57,919 sq. mi.
Representatives: 13

★ Atlanta

5 Connecticut
Year Admitted: 1788
Population: 3,405,565
Land area: 4,845 sq. mi.
Representatives: 5

★ Hartford

6 Massachusetts
Year Admitted: 1788
Population: 6,349,097
Land area: 7,838 sq. mi.
Representatives: 10

Boston ★

7 Maryland
Year Admitted: 1788
Population: 5,296,486
Land area: 9,775 sq. mi.
Representatives: 8

Annapolis ★

8 South Carolina
Year Admitted: 1788
Population: 4,012,012
Land area: 30,111 sq. mi.
Representatives: 6

Columbia
★

12 North Carolina
Year Admitted: 1789
Population: 8,049,313
Land area: 48,718 sq. mi.
Representatives: 13

★
Raleigh

13 Rhode Island
Year Admitted: 1790
Population: 1,048,319
Land area: 1,045 sq. mi.
Representatives: 2

★ Providence

14 Vermont
Year Admitted: 1791
Population: 608,827
Land area: 9,249 sq. mi.
Representatives: 1

★ Montpelier

15 Kentucky
Year Admitted: 1792
Population: 4,041,769
Land area: 39,732 sq. mi.
Representatives: 6

Frankfort
★

16 Tennessee
Year Admitted: 1796
Population: 5,689,283
Land area: 41,220 sq. mi.
Representatives: 9

★ Nashville

20 Mississippi
Year Admitted: 1817
Population: 2,844,658
Land area: 46,914 sq. mi.
Representatives: 4

★ Jackson

21 Illinois
Year Admitted: 1818
Population: 12,419,293
Land area: 55,593 sq. mi.
Representatives: 19

★ Springfield

22 Alabama
Year Admitted: 1819
Population: 4,447,100
Land area: 50,750 sq. mi.
Representatives: 7

Montgomery
★

23 Maine
Year Admitted: 1820
Population: 1,274,923
Land area: 30,865 sq. mi.
Representatives: 2

★ Augusta

24 Missouri
Year Admitted: 1821
Population: 5,595,211
Land area: 68,898 sq. mi.
Representatives: 9

Jefferson City
★

28 Texas
Year Admitted: 1845
Population: 20,851,820
Land area: 261,914 sq. mi.
Representatives: 32

Austin
★

29 Iowa
Year Admitted: 1846
Population: 2,926,324
Land area: 55,875 sq. mi.
Representatives: 5

Des Moines
★

30 Wisconsin
Year Admitted: 1848
Population: 5,363,675
Land area: 54,314 sq. mi.
Representatives: 8

Madison
★

31 California
Year Admitted: 1850
Population: 33,871,648
Land area: 155,973 sq. mi.
Representatives: 53

★
Sacramento

32 Minnesota
Year Admitted: 1858
Population: 4,919,479
Land area: 79,617 sq. mi.
Representatives: 8

Saint Paul
★

37 Nebraska
Year Admitted: 1867
Population: 1,711,263
Land area: 76,878 sq. mi.
Representatives: 3

Lincoln ★

38 Colorado
Year Admitted: 1876
Population: 4,301,261
Land area: 103,730 sq. mi.
Representatives: 7

Denver ★

39 North Dakota
Year Admitted: 1889
Population: 642,200
Land area: 68,994 sq. mi.
Representatives: 1

Bismarck
★

40 South Dakota
Year Admitted: 1889
Population: 754,844
Land area: 75,898 sq. mi.
Representatives: 1

Pierre
★

41 Montana
Year Admitted: 1889
Population: 902,195
Land area: 145,556 sq. mi.
Representatives: 1

★ Helena

46 Oklahoma
Year Admitted: 1907
Population: 3,450,654
Land area: 68,679 sq. mi.
Representatives: 5

Oklahoma City
★

47 New Mexico
Year Admitted: 1912
Population: 1,819,046
Land area: 121,365 sq. mi.
Representatives: 3

★
Santa Fe

48 Arizona
Year Admitted: 1912
Population: 5,130,632
Land area: 113,642 sq. mi.
Representatives: 8

Phoenix
★

49 Alaska
Year Admitted: 1959
Population: 626,932
Land area: 570,374 sq. mi.
Representatives: 1

Juneau ★

50 Hawaii
Year Admitted: 1959
Population: 1,211,537
Land area: 6,423 sq. mi.
Representatives: 2

Honolulu ★

NATIONAL GEOGRAPHIC

Geography Handbook

The story of the world begins with geography—the study of the earth in all of its variety. Geography describes the earth's land, water, and plant and animal life. It is the study of places and the complex relationships between people and their environment.

The resources in this handbook will help you get the most out of your textbook—and provide you with skills that you will be able to use for the rest of your life.

▼ Acadia National Park, Maine

◄ Monument Valley, Utah

The Tongass National Forest in Southeastern Alaska, ► covering nearly 17 million acres, is the single largest national forest in America.

How Do I Study Geography?

Six Essential Elements

Recently, geographers have begun to look at geography in a different way. They do this to understand how our large world is connected. They break down the study of geography into **Six Essential Elements.** You should think of these elements as categories into which to sort information you learn about the world's geography.

Being aware of these elements will help you sort what you are learning. Examples of each of the Essential Elements—detailed in maps throughout *The American Journey to World War I*—are explained here.

Element 2

Places and Regions

Place has a special meaning in geography. It means more than where a place is. It also describes what a place is like. It might describe physical characteristics such as landforms, climate, and plant or animal life. Or it might describe human characteristics, including language and way of life.

To help organize their study, geographers often group places into regions. **Regions** are united by one or more common characteristics.

Element 1

The World in Spatial Terms

Geographers first take a look at where a place is located. **Location** serves as a starting point by asking "Where is it?" Knowing the location of places helps you develop an awareness of the world around you.

Element 3

Physical Systems

When studying places and regions, geographers analyze how **physical systems**—such as hurricanes, volcanoes, and glaciers—shape the earth's surface. They also look at communities of plants and animals that depend upon one another and their surroundings for survival.

Human Systems

Geographers also examine **human systems,** or how people have shaped our world. They look at political boundary lines and why people settle in certain places. A key theme is the continual **movement** of people, ideas, and goods.

Element 5

Environment and Society

What is the relationship between people and their natural surroundings? This is what the theme of **human/environment interaction** investigates. It also shows how people affect the environment.

Element 6

The Uses of Geography

Knowledge of geography helps us understand people, places, and environments over time. Knowing how to use the tools of geography prepares you for our modern society.

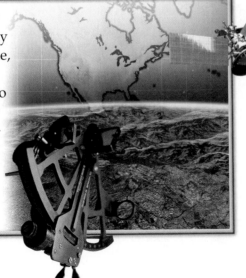

Five Themes

Some geographers study geography through five themes. The **Five Themes of Geography** are (1) location, (2) place, (3) human/environment interaction, (4) movement, and (5) regions. You will see these highlighted throughout *The American Journey to World War I.*

How Do I Use Maps and Globes?

Hemispheres

To locate a place on the earth, geographers use a system of imaginary lines that crisscross the globe. One of these lines, the **Equator,** circles the middle of the earth like a belt. It divides the earth into "half spheres," or **hemispheres.** Everything north of the Equator is in the Northern Hemisphere. Everything south of the Equator is in the Southern Hemisphere.

Another imaginary line runs from north to south. It helps divide the earth into half spheres in the other direction. Find this line—called the **Prime Meridian**—on a globe. Everything east of the Prime Meridian for 180 degrees is in the Eastern Hemisphere. Everything west of the Prime Meridian is in the Western Hemisphere.

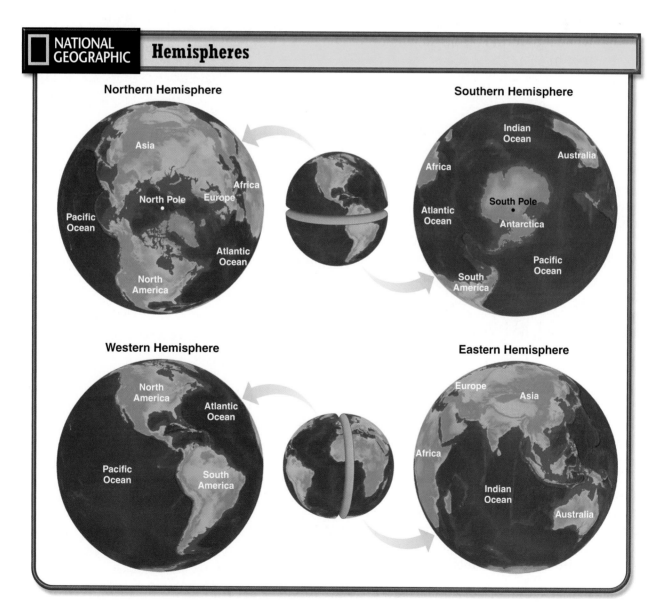

NATIONAL GEOGRAPHIC **Hemispheres**

Northern Hemisphere

Asia
Africa
Europe
North Pole
Pacific Ocean
Atlantic Ocean
North America

Southern Hemisphere

Indian Ocean
Australia
Africa
South Pole
Atlantic Ocean
Antarctica
Pacific Ocean
South America

Western Hemisphere

North America
Atlantic Ocean
Pacific Ocean
South America

Eastern Hemisphere

Europe
Asia
Africa
Indian Ocean
Australia

Understanding Latitude and Longitude

Lines on globes and maps provide information that can help you easily locate places on the earth. These lines are called **latitude** and **longitude.** They cross one another, forming a pattern called a grid system.

Latitude ▶

Lines of latitude, or **parallels,** circle the earth parallel to the **Equator** and measure the distance north or south of the Equator in degrees. The Equator is at 0° latitude, while the North Pole lies at latitude 90°N (north).

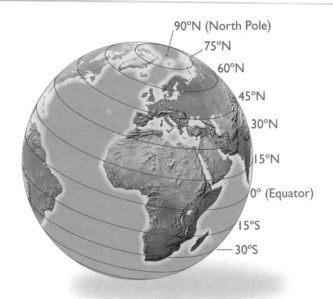

90°N (North Pole)
75°N
60°N
45°N
30°N
15°N
0° (Equator)
15°S
30°S

◀ Longitude

Lines of longitude, or **meridians,** circle the earth from the North Pole to the South Pole. These lines measure distances east or west of the starting line, which is at 0° longitude and is called the **Prime Meridian** by geographers. The Prime Meridian runs through the Royal Observatory in Greenwich, England.

45°W
30°W
15°W
0° (Prime Meridian)
45°E
30°E
15°E

Absolute Location ▶

The grid system formed by lines of latitude and longitude makes it possible to find the absolute location of a place. Only one place can be found at the point where a specific line of latitude crosses a specific line of longitude. By using degrees (°) and minutes (′)—points between degrees—people can pinpoint the precise spot where one line of latitude crosses one line of longitude—an **absolute location.**

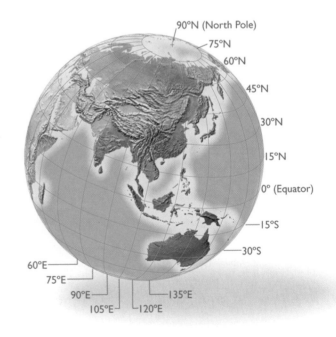

90°N (North Pole)
75°N
60°N
45°N
30°N
15°N
0° (Equator)
15°S
30°S
60°E
75°E
90°E
105°E
120°E
135°E

Parts of Maps

Map Key An important first step in reading a map is to note the map key. The **map key** explains the lines, symbols, and colors used on a map. For example, the map on this page shows the various climate regions of the United States and the different colors representing them. Cities are usually symbolized by a solid circle (•) and capitals by a star (✪). On this map, you can see the capital of Texas and the cities of Los Angeles, Seattle, New Orleans, and Chicago.

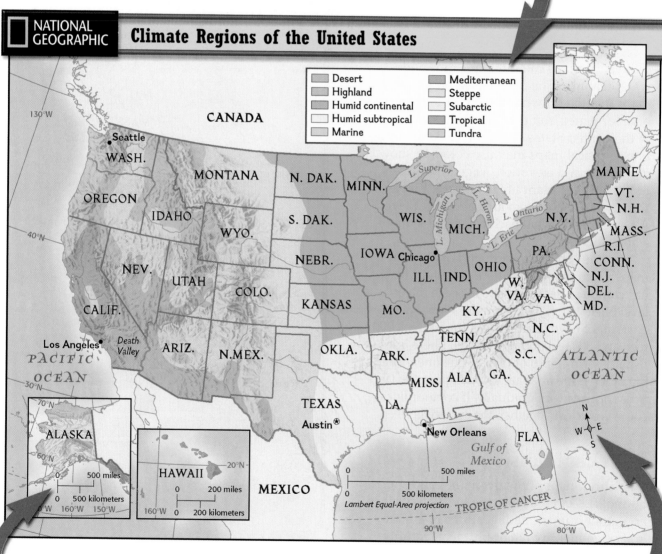

NATIONAL GEOGRAPHIC

Climate Regions of the United States

Desert
Highland
Humid continental
Humid subtropical
Marine
Mediterranean
Steppe
Subarctic
Tropical
Tundra

CANADA

130°W

Seattle

WASH.

MONTANA

OREGON

IDAHO

WYO.

N. DAK.

MINN.

S. DAK.

WIS.

L. Superior

L. Michigan

MICH.

L. Huron

L. Ontario

L. Erie

MAINE

VT.

N.H.

N.Y.

MASS.

R.I.

PA.

CONN.

N.J.

40°N

NEV.

UTAH

COLO.

NEBR.

IOWA Chicago

ILL. IND.

OHIO

DEL.

MD.

W. VA.

VA.

CALIF.

KANSAS

MO.

KY.

N.C.

Los Angeles

Death Valley

ARIZ.

N.MEX.

OKLA.

ARK.

TENN.

S.C.

PACIFIC OCEAN

30°N

MISS. ALA.

GA.

ATLANTIC OCEAN

TEXAS

LA.

Austin✪

New Orleans

FLA.

Gulf of Mexico

70°N

ALASKA

60°N

0   500 miles

0   500 kilometers

170°W   160°W   150°W

HAWAII

20°N

0   200 miles

0   200 kilometers

160°W

MEXICO

0   500 miles

0   500 kilometers

Lambert Equal-Area projection

TROPIC OF CANCER

90°W

80°W

N W E S

Scale A measuring line, often called a **scale bar,** helps you figure distance on the map. The map scale tells you what distance on the earth is represented by the measurement on the scale bar.

Compass Rose A map has a symbol that tells you where the **cardinal directions**—north, south, east, and west—are positioned.

Types of Maps

General Purpose Maps

Geographers use many different types of maps. Maps that show a wide range of general information about an area are called **general purpose maps.** Two of the most common general purpose maps are physical and political maps.

Physical Maps

Physical maps call out landforms and water features. The colors used on physical maps include brown or green for land and blue for water. You may see a physical map of the United States on pages 32–33. In addition, physical maps may use colors to show vegetation and elevation. **Vegetation** refers to the kinds of plant life in an area. **Elevation** is the height of an area above sea level. A key explains what each color and symbol stands for.

A **contour map** is a third kind of physical map. It also shows elevation. A contour map has **contour lines**—one line for each major level of elevation. For example, a low-lying area might have contour lines for 100 feet, 200 feet, and 300 feet above sea level. These lines usually form circles or ovals—one line inside the other. If the lines are spread apart, the land is flat or rises very gradually. If contour lines come very close together, the surface is steep.

Political Maps

Political maps show the names and boundaries of countries, the location of cities and other human-made features of a place, and often identify major physical features. The political map of the thirteen colonies, for example, shows the boundaries of each colony. The map also has their eastern and western boundaries—the Atlantic Ocean and the Appalachian Mountains. In addition, the map shows the three major regions and the largest colonial cities.

▲ Political Map

Special Purpose Maps

Some maps are made to present specific kinds of information. These are called **thematic** or **special purpose maps.** They usually show themes or patterns, often emphasizing one subject or theme. Special purpose maps may present climate or natural resources. They may also display historical information, such as battles or territorial changes. The map's title tells what kind of special information it shows. Colors and symbols in the map key are especially important on these types of maps. Special purpose maps are often found in books of maps called atlases.

One type of special purpose map uses colors to show population. Notice the key on the map "Population of the United States, 1820." It indicates that the states with the greatest population are in pink. The map shows these states are along the Atlantic Ocean.

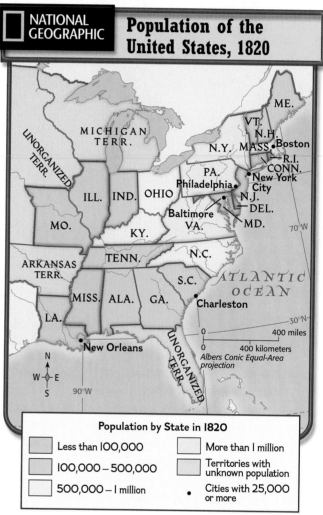

NATIONAL GEOGRAPHIC

Population of the United States, 1820

Population by State in 1820

Less than 100,000	More than 1 million
100,000 – 500,000	Territories with unknown population
500,000 – 1 million	• Cities with 25,000 or more

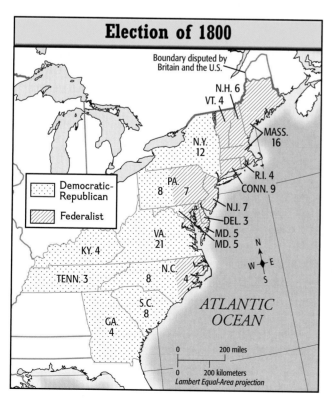

Election of 1800

Democratic-Republican

Federalist

Some special purpose maps, such as "The Election of 1800," are not in color. This map is an example of what you might find on a standardized test or in a newspaper.

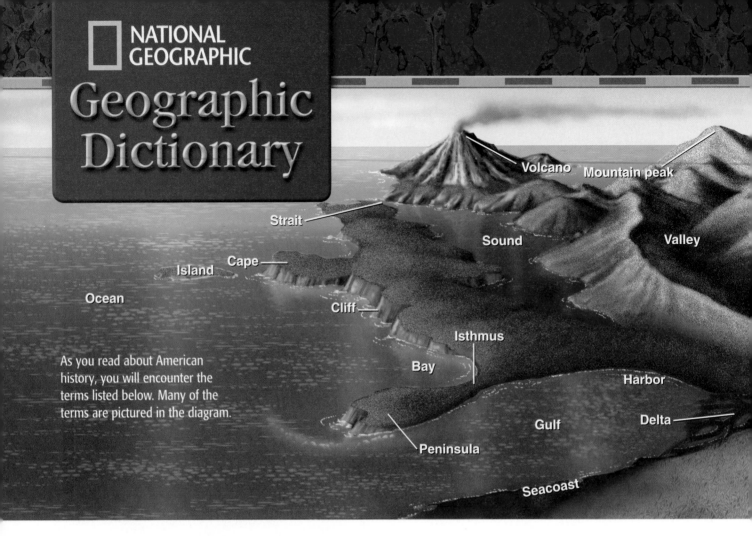

NATIONAL GEOGRAPHIC
Geographic Dictionary

Volcano   Mountain peak

Strait

Sound   Valley

Cape   Island

Ocean   Cliff

Isthmus

Bay

Harbor

As you read about American history, you will encounter the terms listed below. Many of the terms are pictured in the diagram.

Gulf   Delta

Peninsula

Seacoast

absolute location exact location of a place on the earth described by global coordinates

basin area of land drained by a given river and its branches; area of land surrounded by lands of higher elevation

bay part of a large body of water that extends into a shoreline, generally smaller than a gulf

canyon deep and narrow valley with steep walls

cape point of land that extends into a river, lake, or ocean

channel wide strait or waterway between two landmasses that lie close to each other; deep part of a river or other waterway

cliff steep, high wall of rock, earth, or ice

continent one of the seven large landmasses on the earth

cultural feature characteristic that humans have created in a place, such as language, religion, housing, and settlement pattern

delta flat, low-lying land built up from soil carried downstream by a river and deposited at its mouth

divide stretch of high land that separates river systems

downstream direction in which a river or stream flows from its source to its mouth

elevation height of land above sea level

Equator imaginary line that runs around the earth halfway between the North and South Poles; used as the starting point to measure degrees of north and south latitude

glacier large, thick body of slowly moving ice

gulf part of a large body of water that extends into a shoreline, generally larger and more deeply indented than a bay

harbor a sheltered place along a shoreline where ships can anchor safely

highland elevated land area such as a hill, mountain, or plateau

hill elevated land with sloping sides and rounded summit; generally smaller than a mountain

island land area, smaller than a continent, completely surrounded by water

isthmus narrow stretch of land connecting two larger land areas

lake a sizable inland body of water

latitude distance north or south of the Equator, measured in degrees

longitude distance east or west of the Prime Meridian, measured in degrees

lowland land, usually level, at a low elevation

map drawing of the earth shown on a flat surface

meridian one of many lines on the global grid running from the North Pole to the South Pole; used to measure degrees of longitude

mesa broad, flat-topped landform with steep sides; smaller than a plateau

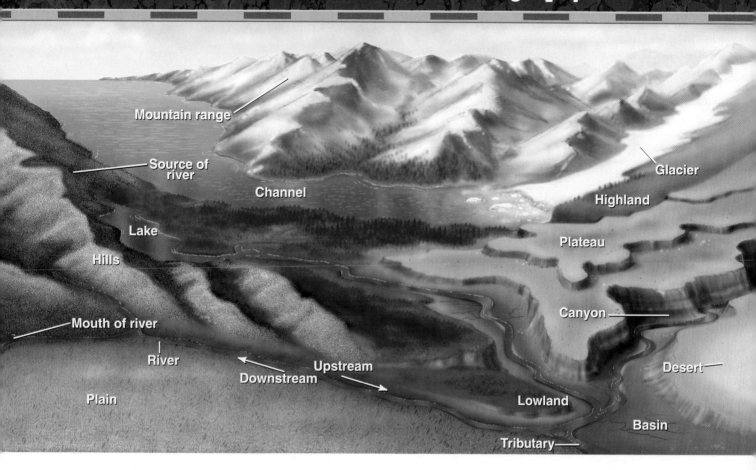

Mountain range · Source of river · Channel · Glacier · Highland · Plateau · Lake · Hills · Canyon · Mouth of river · River · Upstream · Downstream · Desert · Plain · Lowland · Basin · Tributary

mountain land with steep sides that rises sharply (1,000 feet [305 m] or more) from surrounding land; generally larger and more rugged than a hill

mountain peak pointed top of a mountain

mountain range a series of connected mountains

mouth (of a river) place where a stream or river flows into a larger body of water

ocean one of the four major bodies of salt water that surround the continents

ocean current stream of either cold or warm water that moves in a definite direction through an ocean

parallel one of many lines on the global grid that circle the earth north or south of the Equator; used to measure degrees of latitude

peninsula body of land jutting into a lake or ocean, surrounded on three sides by water

physical feature characteristic of a place occurring naturally, such as a landform, body of water, climate pattern, or resource

plain area of level land, usually at a low elevation and often covered with grasses

plateau area of flat or rolling land at a high elevation, about 300–3,000 feet (91–914 m) high

Prime Meridian line of the global grid running from the North Pole to the South Pole through Greenwich, England; starting point for measuring degrees of east and west longitude

relief changes in elevation over a given area of land

river large natural stream of water that runs through the land

sea large body of water completely or partly surrounded by land

seacoast land lying next to a sea or ocean

sea level position on land level with surface of nearby ocean or sea

sound body of water between a coastline and one or more islands off the coast

source (of a river) place where a river or stream begins, often in highlands

strait narrow stretch of water joining two larger bodies of water

tributary small river or stream that flows into a larger river or stream; a branch of the river

upstream direction opposite the flow of a river; toward the source of a river or stream

valley area of low land between hills or mountains

volcano mountain that is created as liquid rock or ash erupts from inside the earth

Tools of the Historian

A historian is a person who studies and writes about people and events of the past. Historians find out how people lived, what happened to them, and what happened around them. They look for the reasons behind events and study the effects of events.

Have you ever wondered if you could be a historian? To answer that question, you will need to find out how history is researched and written. Historians use a number of skills to research and organize information. You can learn about these skills in the next few pages. As you study this textbook, you will see that the sections listed below will help you understand geography and history.

Scientists looking for evidence of past civilizations ▶

Digging Up The Past

Historians depend on the work of archaeologists. Archaeologists are scientists who unearth the remains of the past.

What Do Archaeologists Study?

- Human and animal bones, seeds, trees
- Pottery, tools, weapons
- Mounds, pits, canals

▲ Prehistoric pottery

▲ Archaeologist at work

How Do They Gather Data?

- Surveys on foot
- Photographs taken from airplanes or satellites
- Ground-penetrating radar
- Plot locations on maps
- Dig for evidence with heavy equipment as well as shovels
- Sonar scanning to find underwater objects

How Do They Interpret Findings?

- Organize artifacts into groups based on similarities
- Compare objects in relation to other objects
- Look for evidence of changes over a period of time
- Date once-living objects by measuring carbon-14 levels
- Use microscopic and biological tests to date objects

◄ Carbon-14 dating

Do Your Own Digging

Research the library and Internet to find information on two archaeological diggings, one past and the other recent. Compare and contrast the methods used in each digging. What changes do you notice in the tools that archaeologists have used over time?

Measuring Time

Main Idea Historians use calendars to date historical events, and they use scientific methods to date artifacts.

Reading Focus Have you ever wondered what it might be like to travel back in time? Read to find out how historians learn about the past.

Calendars Historians rely on *calendars,* or dating systems, to measure time. Cultures throughout the world have developed different calendars based on important events in their history. Western nations begin their calendar with the year in which Jesus was thought to have been born. The Jewish calendar begins about 3,760 years before the Christian calendar. This is the time when Jewish tradition says the world was created. Muslims date their calendar from the time their first leader, Muhammad, left the city of Makkah for Madinah. This was A.D. 622 in the Christian calendar.

The dates in this book are based on the Western calendar. In the Western calendar, the years before the birth of Jesus are known as "B.C.," or "before Christ." The years after are called "A.D.," or *anno domini.* This phrase comes from the Latin language and means "in the year of the Lord."

▲ About A.D. 500, a Christian monk, or religious person, developed the Western way of dating events.

Dating Events To date events before the birth of Christ, or B.C., historians count backwards from A.D. 1. There is no year 0. The year before A.D. 1 is 1 B.C. (Notice that A.D. is written before the date, but B.C. is written following the date.) Therefore, a date in the 100 years before the birth of Christ lies between 100 B.C. and A.D. 1.

To date events after the birth of Christ, or A.D., historians count forward, starting at A.D. 1. A date in the first 100 years after the birth of Christ is between A.D. 1 and A.D. 100.

Dating Archaeological Finds One of the most important and difficult jobs for archaeologists is dating the artifacts that they find. Artifacts are objects made by people, such as weapons, tools, or pottery. The earliest artifacts are pieces of hard rock that were chipped into cutting or digging tools or into weapons. By examining artifacts, scientists can learn about the social and military structures of an ancient society.

◀ Ancient stone calendar

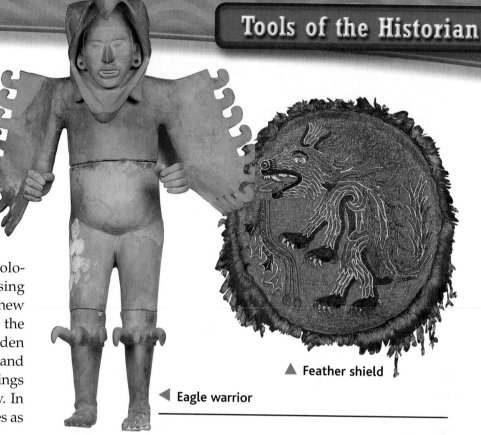

▲ **Feather shield**

◀ **Eagle warrior**

How do archaeologists determine the age of these artifacts? Early scientists correctly assumed that artifacts buried more deeply in the ground are older than those closer to the surface. In most cases, that observation is still true today.

Another way that archaeologists date artifacts is by using trees. Each year, trees form a new growth ring. Scientists count the number of rings in a wooden object, such as a house beam, and compare the pattern with the rings of a tree whose age they know. In that way, they can identify dates as far back as 3,000 years.

In 1946 an American scientist name Willard Frank Libby discovered that all living things contain a radioactive element called carbon 14. After plants, animals, and humans die, the carbon 14 gradually disappears. By measuring how much carbon 14 a skeleton or the remains of a wooden boat contain today, scientists can estimate how old an object is. This method is called radiocarbon dating.

Radiocarbon dating, however, is only accurate for dating objects that are no more than 50,000 years old. Another method of dating—thermoluminescence (THUHR•muh•LOO•muh•NEH•suhns)—helps scientists make more precise measurements back as far as 200,000 years. This method dates an object by measuring the amount of light given off by particles trapped in the soil surrounding the artifact or fossil.

New methods for analyzing remains—such as blood, hairs, and plant tissues left on rocks, tools, and weapons—give archaeologists still more information. Scientists have discovered that blood molecules can survive for millions of years. This discovery is important because it can tell us how some tools were used and the types of early animals that hunters killed. DNA is also providing new information. By analyzing the remains of plants on stone tools, for example, scientists can find out more about the history of farming.

Scientists analyze many different samples, using as many different methods as possible, because individual results may vary. Dating methods are constantly being refined to provide more accurate data.

Although scientists have developed many methods to measure the age of artifacts, what we know about early people and history will continue to change as new information and new methods of dating are discovered.

Thinking Like a Historian

1. **Identify** What do B.C. and A.D. mean? How are they used?

2. **Dating Events** What year came after 184 B.C.?

3. **Compare and Contrast** Use the Internet to find out the current year on the Jewish and Muslim calendars. Why are calendars different from culture to culture?

Organizing Time

Main Idea Historians organize history by dividing it into blocks of time.

Reading Focus Have you ever thought about the names given to events, such as "summer vacation" or "the baseball season"? Read to see how historians use names to describe different stretches of time in history.

Periods of History Historians divide history into blocks of time known as *periods,* or *eras.* For example, a period of 10 years is called a *decade.* A period of 100 years is known as a *century.* Periods are sometimes given names based on the leading events of the time span they cover.

In this book, for example, you will study American history from the nation's beginnings to the early 1900s. The first period of American history that you will be studying is the *American Revolution and the New Nation.* Other periods in the history of the United States include *National Expansion and Reform, Civil War and Reconstruction,* and *Industrialization and Progressivism.*

George Washington served as U.S. president from 1789 to 1797. ▶

▲ Many settlers headed to the West in the mid-1800s.

▼ Classroom, early 1900s

▲ Confederate soldier's cap (upper left) and Union soldier's cap (lower right), *Civil War, 1861–1865*

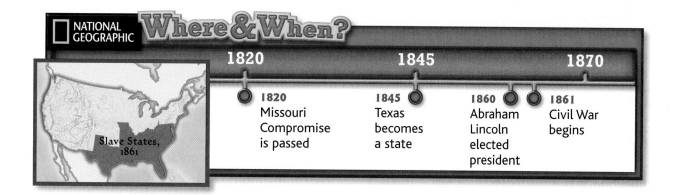

NATIONAL GEOGRAPHIC **Where & When?**

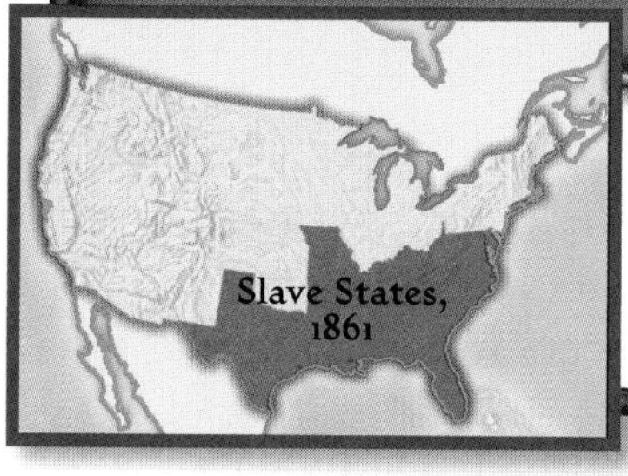

1820 | 1845 | 1870

1820 Missouri Compromise is passed

1845 Texas becomes a state

1860 Abraham Lincoln elected president

1861 Civil War begins

What Is a Time Line? Which came first: the American Civil War or World War II? Did the train come before or after the invention of the airplane? In studying the past, historians focus on *chronology,* or the order of dates in which events happened.

You might be wondering how to make sense of the flow of dates and events. An easy way is to use or make a time line. A *time line* is a diagram that shows the order of events within a period of time.

Most time lines are divided into sections in which the years are evenly spaced. In some cases, however, a spread of time may be too long to show all of the years in even spaces. To save space, a period of time may be omitted from the time line. Where this happens, a slanted or jagged line appears on the time line to show a break in the even spacing of events.

A time line also labels events. Each event on the time line appears beside the date when the event took place. Sometimes, when the exact date of an event is not known, *c.,* or *circa* (which means "about"), appears before the date.

Events and their dates often are shown on a single time line, as on the time line at the top of this page. In other cases, two or more time lines are stacked one on top of the other. These are called multilevel time lines. They help you compare events in different places at the same time period. For example, the multilevel time line on pages 520–521 shows events in the United States and in other parts of the world from 1820 to 1900. These dates lead up to and through the Civil War and include the years after the war. The skill lesson "Reading a Time Line" on page 824 will help you learn to work with time lines.

When you read a time line, you see not only when an event took place, but also what events took place before and after it. Some helpful steps will guide you in reading a time line. First, find the dates on the opposite ends of the time line. This tells you the time span. A time line that begins in 1800 and ends in 1860 has a 60-year time span. Second, study the order of events. Finally, analyze relationships among the events on the time line.

Thinking Like a Historian

1. **Reading a Time Line** Look over the time line above to get an idea of what a time line shows. When does it begin and end? What feature makes this time line different from many other time lines? Why was this feature added?
2. **Understanding a Time Line** How many years are included in each section of the time line?
3. **Making a Time Line** Create a time line using the terms B.M.B. (before my birth) and A.M.B. (after my birth). Fill in the time line with five key events that happened before and after you were born. Illustrate the time line with copies of photos from your family album.

History and Geography

Main Idea Historians try to understand how climate, landforms, and human activities have shaped past events.

Reading Focus Have you ever had a party or sports event cancelled because of bad weather? Read to find out how historians study the effects of the natural world on history.

Geography is the study of the earth and its physical features. In this text, you will discover how geography has shaped the course of events in American history. Sometimes the study of geography is broken down into five themes. *The Five Themes of Geography* are:

- **Location** Where is it?
- **Place** What is it like?
- **Human/Environment Interaction** What is the relationship between people and their surroundings?
- **Movement** How do people in one area relate to people in other areas?
- **Region** What common features bring geographical areas together?

▼ LANDSAT satellite map of San Francisco Bay area

Location

"Where is it?" In using geography, historians first look at where a place is located. Every place has an absolute location and a relative location. *Absolute location* refers to the exact spot of a place on the earth's surface. For example, the city of San Francisco, California, is located at one place and one place only. No other place on Earth has exactly the same location.

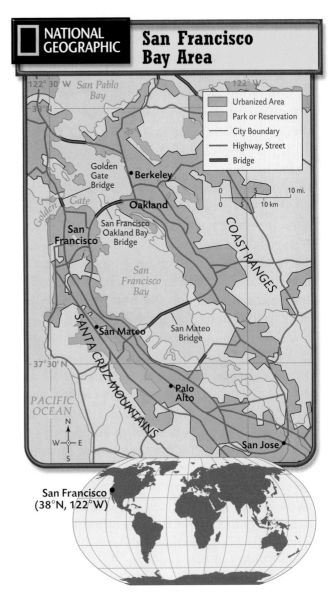

NATIONAL GEOGRAPHIC
San Francisco Bay Area

- Urbanized Area
- Park or Reservation
- City Boundary
- Highway, Street
- Bridge

San Pablo Bay
122° 30' W
122° W
Golden Gate Bridge
Berkeley
Golden Gate
Oakland
San Francisco
San Francisco Oakland Bay Bridge
San Francisco Bay
COAST RANGES
San Mateo
San Mateo Bridge
SANTA CRUZ MOUNTAINS
37° 30' N
PACIFIC OCEAN
Palo Alto
San Jose

San Francisco (38°N, 122°W)

▲ Pioneers on the Oregon Trail

Miner seeking gold ▶

The Oregon and California Trails

NATIONAL GEOGRAPHIC

Pioneer chest ▶

Relative location tells where a place is, compared with one or more other places. San Francisco is northwest of Los Angeles and southwest of Seattle. Knowing a place's relative location may help a historian understand how it was settled and how its culture developed. For example, people in California have settled in coastal areas and valleys, because inland areas have many mountains or deserts. They also have turned to the sea for food and trade.

Place

"What is it like?" *Place* describes all of the characteristics that give an area its own special quality. These can be physical features, such as mountains, waterways, climate, and plant or animal life. Places can also be described by human characteristics, such as language, religion, and architecture. For example, pioneers on the Oregon and California Trails crossed vast plains, swift rivers, high mountains, and hot deserts to reach their western destinations. When they arrived, they set up farms, homesteads, and towns.

Human/Environment Interaction

"What is the relationship between people and their surroundings?" Landforms, waterways, climate, and natural resources all have helped or hindered human activities.

People have responded to their environment, or natural surroundings, in different ways. Sometimes they have adjusted to it. For example, people throughout history have worn light clothing in hot places. At other times, people have changed their environment to meet their needs. For example, some pioneers who went westward set up farms, and others mined for gold and other minerals.

History and Geography

Movement

....

"How do people in one area affect people in other areas?" Historians answer this question with one word—*movement.* Throughout history, people, ideas, goods, and information have moved from place to place. Movement has brought the world's people closer together.

Transportation—the movement of people and goods—has allowed people to use products that are made thousands of miles away. This has increased the exchange of ideas and cultures. Communication—the movement of ideas and information—has allowed people to find out what is happening in other parts of the world. Unlike in the past, people today receive almost instant communication by radio, television, and the computer.

The movement of people to different places is called migration. Why have people migrated throughout history? Some have chosen to move to seek a better life. Others have been forced to move because of wars, famine, enslavement, or other settlers. For example, many white settlers moved into the southeastern states from the 1820s to the 1840s. They wanted the land held by Native Americans. In 1830 Congress passed the Indian Removal Act to move Native Americans west of the Mississippi River. Under pressure, the Choctaw, Creek, and Chickasaw moved. The Cherokee and the Seminole resisted but in the end many of them were forced to relocate.

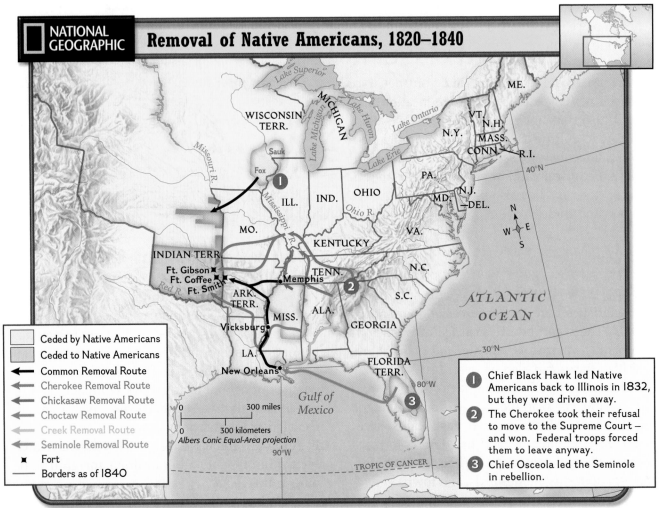

NATIONAL GEOGRAPHIC

Removal of Native Americans, 1820–1840

Legend:
- Ceded by Native Americans
- Ceded to Native Americans
- Common Removal Route
- Cherokee Removal Route
- Chickasaw Removal Route
- Choctaw Removal Route
- Creek Removal Route
- Seminole Removal Route
- ⊠ Fort
- Borders as of 1840

300 miles
300 kilometers
Albers Conic Equal-Area projection

1 Chief Black Hawk led Native Americans back to Illinois in 1832, but they were driven away.

2 The Cherokee took their refusal to move to the Supreme Court — and won. Federal troops forced them to leave anyway.

3 Chief Osceola led the Seminole in rebellion.

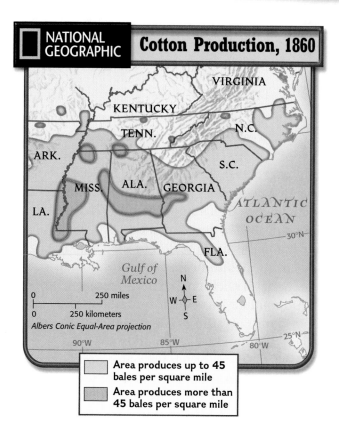

NATIONAL GEOGRAPHIC

Cotton Production, 1860

Area produces up to **45** bales per square mile

Area produces more than **45** bales per square mile

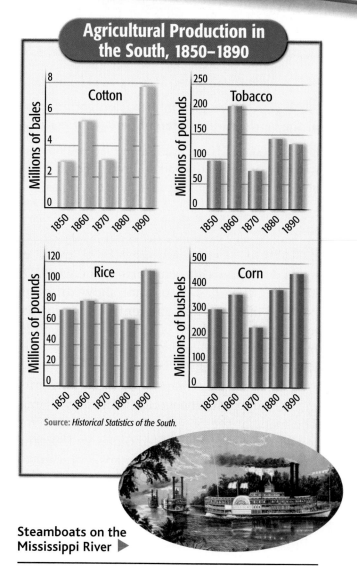

Agricultural Production in the South, 1850–1890

Cotton

Tobacco

Rice

Corn

Source: *Historical Statistics of the South.*

Steamboats on the Mississippi River ▶

Region

"What common characteristics does a certain area share?" Historians often view places or areas as regions. A *region* is an area that is defined by common features. Regions can be defined by physical features, such as mountains and rivers, or by human features, such as religion, language, or livelihood. For example, the South during the 1800s was a largely agricultural region.

Six Essential Elements

Recently geographers have begun to look at geography a different way. They break down the study of geography into *Six Essential Elements.* These elements are:

- The World in Spatial Terms
- Places and Regions
- Physical Systems
- Human Systems
- Environment and Society
- The Uses of Geography

See the information about the Six Essential Elements in the Geography Handbook on pages 39–40. Knowing these elements will help you in your study of history.

Thinking Like a Historian

1. **Identify** How are absolute location and relative location different?

2. **Analyzing Themes** What characteristics do geographers use to describe a place?

3. **Linking History and Geography** Make a list of the Five Themes of Geography. Under each theme, explain how you think geography has affected the history of your community.

What Is a Historical Atlas?

Main Idea Maps give information about areas of the world during different periods of history.

Reading Focus Have you used a map to find your way from one place to another? Read to find out how you can study certain maps for clues to the past.

....

Historical Maps An *atlas* is a book of maps that show different parts of the world. A *historical atlas* has maps that show different parts of the world at different periods in history. Maps that show political events, such as invasions, battles, and boundary changes, are called *historical maps.*

Some historical maps show how territories in a certain part of the world changed over time. The maps at the bottom of the page show the territorial size of the United States in 1800 and 1810. By comparing the two maps, you can see how the United States gradually expanded its territory westward from 1800 to 1810.

Both maps use colors to show different political areas: U.S. states, U.S. territories, foreign-ruled areas, and territories claimed but not owned by the United States. Different colored lines indicate territorial boundaries. A heavy blue line highlights areas added to the United States, and gray lines indicate present-day U.S. state boundaries. Labels on the maps present a variety of information. This data includes new states and their dates of admission to the Union, plus recently acquired U.S. territories.

Historical maps show places and events from the past. As you study history, you will use many other kinds of maps. *Thematic maps* deal with specialized information, often on a single topic such as population or land use. A *political map* shows the political boundaries or borders of a state, country, or region.

NATIONAL GEOGRAPHIC Territorial Growth, 1800–1810

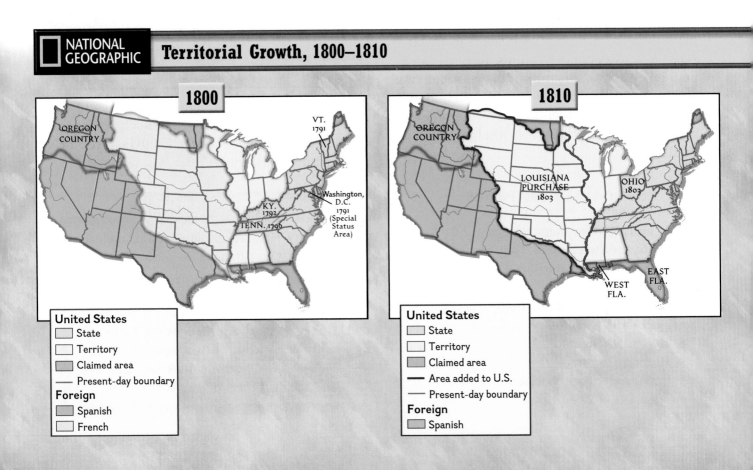

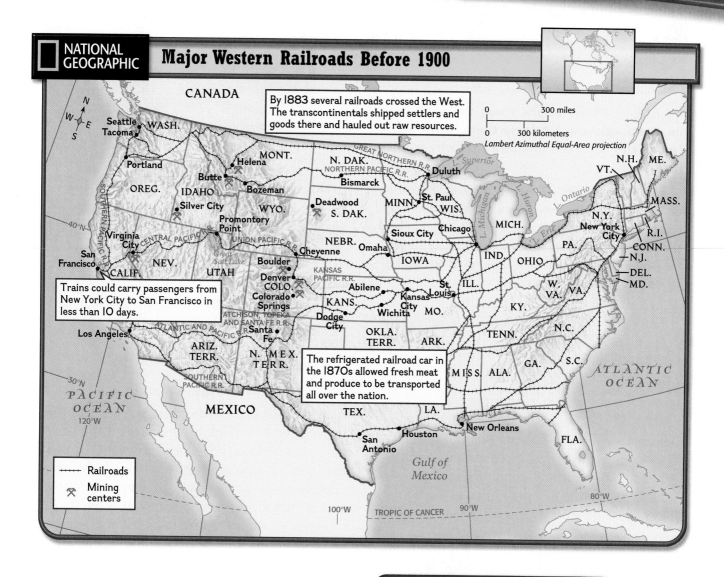

NATIONAL GEOGRAPHIC

Major Western Railroads Before 1900

By 1883 several railroads crossed the West. The transcontinentals shipped settlers and goods there and hauled out raw resources.

0   300 miles
0   300 kilometers
Lambert Azimuthal Equal-Area projection

Trains could carry passengers from New York City to San Francisco in less than 10 days.

The refrigerated railroad car in the 1870s allowed fresh meat and produce to be transported all over the nation.

++++++ Railroads
⚒ Mining centers

Historical Routes In your study of American history, you will often encounter thematic maps that show movement or routes. On some maps, lines may show *historical routes.* These are roads or courses over which people or goods have traveled all through history. Such routes are often colored or have special markings. On the map above, the black marked lines show major railroad routes in the western United States before 1900.

On maps of historical routes, the key explains what is shown on the maps. This map's key shows railroad routes and mining centers. In addition, boxes on the map provide information about railroad travel during the late 1800s.

Thinking Like a Historian

1. **Analyzing Maps** Look at the map of western railroads. Name one railroad system that extended west to the Pacific Ocean through each of these areas of the country—the North, the central part, and the South.

2. **Reading a Map Key** Look at the map of western railroads. What mining center lay on the Central Pacific Railway?

3. **Analyzing Maps** Select any chapter in your textbook. List the titles of the maps found in that chapter. Beside each map's title, state what kinds of symbols are used in each map key and what they represent.

How Does a Historian Work?

Main Idea **As historians study the past, they must ask questions to help them identify the issues and to determine how and why events happened.**

Reading Focus When preparing a report for school, do you ask questions about your topic and about the sources of information you are using? Do you ask if the sources are factual and how they relate to your subject? Read to find out the types of questions historians ask as they investigate the past.

▲ Students studying history

Asking Questions About the Past

Historians are like detectives. They look for evidence to solve problems about the past. Historians begin by asking questions, such as: Why did two particular countries go to war? What effect did their fighting have on people's lives? Such questions help historians focus on historical problems. By asking questions, historians can better identify the issues. They also can determine how and why events happened and what the effects of these events were.

Is It Fact or Opinion? Historical sources may contain facts and opinions. A *fact* can be proved, or observed; an *opinion,* on the other hand, is a personal belief or conclusion. We often hear facts and opinions mixed in everyday conversation—in advertising, in political debate, and in historical sources. Although some opinions can be supported by facts, in an argument they do not carry as much weight as facts.

▼ Native American cliff dwelling

▲ Civil War quilt

◄ Colonial revenue stamp

▼ Frederick Douglass

▲ Enslaved African Americans escaped to the North.

Sources such as letters, diaries, and speeches express personal views. This means they state what a person thinks about another person or an event. As a result, the historian must be able to separate known truth about something from what people say about it. This skill is important because it helps the historian decide whether or not the information is accurate and the historical source can be trusted.

Is It Relevant? Historians often must sift through a lot of information to find what they need. As a result, they must determine whether or not each piece of evidence is *relevant*. This means selecting only the data that helps answer their research questions. Relevant information applies directly to the topic or purpose that the historian has chosen. For example, if you are researching family life in colonial America, information about marriage and children would be relevant information. A description of colonial government or trade would not be relevant because it does not explain the type of families found in colonial America.

Is It Important? In deciding whether information is relevant, historians also must figure out what information is *essential*, or important, and what is *incidental*, or unimportant. The fact that the writer and speaker Frederick Douglass was married and had four children had little, if any, effect on his political views. However, Douglass's escape from slavery did have a lot to do with his emergence as a leader in the cause to free enslaved African Americans.

Is There Supporting Evidence? Another important task of the historian is to determine whether information in a source is *verifiable*. This means the historian must check to see if the information can be proved by other evidence that is already known to be true.

Thinking Like a Historian

Suppose you were a historian researching Gilbert Stuart and you discovered the following statement about him.

Gilbert Stuart was born in Rhode Island in 1755 and he began painting at age 13. Stuart later trained and worked as an artist in Britain. Back in America, he painted the portraits of leading Americans, including George Washington. Only Stuart could paint a true portrait. He showed the person's character, not just a face.

1. **Recognizing Fact** What in this account is a fact?

2. **Recognizing Opinion** What are opinions?

How Does a Historian Work?

Child's doll made of cornhusks ▶

Main Idea To learn about the past, historians study a variety of sources and determine whether those sources are credible and balanced.

Reading Focus Have you ever searched for clues on a treasure hunt? Read to find out how historians look for clues to create a written record about the past.

Where Is the Evidence Found? Historians generally find evidence in primary sources and secondary sources. *Primary sources* are firsthand pieces of evidence from people who saw or experienced the events described. They include written documents, such as letters, diaries, and official records. They also include spoken interviews, as well as objects such as photos, paintings, clothing, and tools. The feature Analyzing Primary Sources will give you a chance to work with primary sources throughout the text.

Secondary sources, on the other hand, often are created long after the events by people who played no part in them. Secondary sources are partially based on primary sources. They include biographies, encyclopedias, and history books—even this textbook!

Historians study secondary sources for background information and for a broader view of an event. However, to get new evidence that advances knowledge, historians must turn to the firsthand information found only in primary sources.

How Are Sources Examined? Historians *analyze,* or examine, primary and secondary sources. First, they determine who the author of a source is and what can be known about the author. Then historians consider *where* and *when* the source was created. Another important question asked by historians is *why* a source was created. Historians also ask: To what audience was the source addressed? What is known about this audience?

▼ William Clark's journal

Glass canteen, 1900 ▶

Mexican ▶
American
cowhands

Can the Sources Be Trusted? Historians examine sources for *credibility,* or truthfulness. This is because each source reflects a *point of view,* or a general attitude about people and life. The creator of a source has a point of view that selects which events are important, which people are key players, and which details are worth recording. A point of view is the particular focus a person takes when considering a problem or situation.

Being Aware of Bias Sometimes a writer's point of view is expressed as a *bias,* or an unreasoned judgment about people and events. A bias is a one-sided, unexamined view. A person who is biased has made a judgment about an event, a person, or a group without really considering the many parts of the situation. Biased speakers and writers can be detected in various ways. Their statements about certain people or groups are loaded with emotional words like *stupid, ignorant,* and *impossible,* or *great* and *wonderful.* Biased individuals also tend to use words that allow no exceptions, like *always* and *never.*

Finding a Balance Historians seek to uncover point of view and bias in historical documents and articles. They look for the ideas and facts that the author of a source emphasizes. They also think about what ideas and facts the author might be leaving out or touching on only lightly.

To make sense of the past, historians must weigh the known evidence and try to figure out what the facts are. Then they need to bring the facts together to answer the questions that interest them. In doing this, they must use their judgment. This means their own viewpoints come into play.

Historians try to be aware of point of view and bias in their sources and in themselves. Therefore, they check new sources and their own ideas against sources already known to be trustworthy. To get a balanced picture, historians study documents or articles that develop other points of view about the same situation.

▲ The Battle of the Alamo

Thinking Like a Historian

In 1836 the Texans were fighting the Mexicans to win independence. Outnumbered by the Mexican army, William Travis and about 200 other Texans fought heroically to hold a mission called the Alamo. On February 24, 1836, Travis wrote a message to the people of Texas and the United States asking for their help.

The enemy is receiving reinforcements daily & will no doubt increase to three or four thousand in four or five days. If this call is neglected I am determined to sustain myself as long as possible & die like a soldier who never forgets what is due to his honor & that of his country.

—William Barret Travis, "Appeal for Aid at the Alamo"

1. **Understand Evidence** William Travis's letter is considered a primary source. Why?

2. **Understand Evidence** Is an account of the stand at the Alamo by a modern historian a primary source? Explain.

Making Sense of the Past

Main Idea To present their findings in a clear and convincing manner, historians must place the people and events they are studying in a historical setting and discover patterns that demonstrate change and continuity through history.

Reading Focus Think about the last time you overslept and were late to school or another event. What caused you to sleep late? Perhaps you forgot to set your alarm clock the night before. Read to find out why historians research causes and effects to help make sense of history.

Interpreting History

By themselves, bits and pieces of information do not reveal the truth. Like pieces of a puzzle, they have to be put together by people using reason.

In the same way, historians must use their knowledge to give historical facts (dates, names, and events) meaning and to put them in an order that people can easily understand. Historians piece together the credible evidence and draw conclusions. They use their own thinking and knowledge of the past to *interpret,* or explain, the meaning of events. Then, they present their findings in a clear, readable, and convincing form.

Providing a Setting

Historians look at people and events of history in the matrix, or setting, of time and place. They also connect historical people and events to central issues. Central issues are main ideas, such as war and peace, the development of scientific inventions, and the forms of governments and societies. Through these links, historians can grasp the whole picture or story.

Historians also sequence events, or place events in the order in which they occurred. Sequencing helps historians organize information. From the pattern of the data, they can determine how events are related to each other. The relationship among these events can help historians identify other important ideas, such as historical importance and cause and effect.

Cause and Effect

Historical events are linked by cause and effect. A *cause* is what makes an event happen. The event that happens as a result

▲ Country school, 1800s

Drafting the Constitution, 1787 ▶

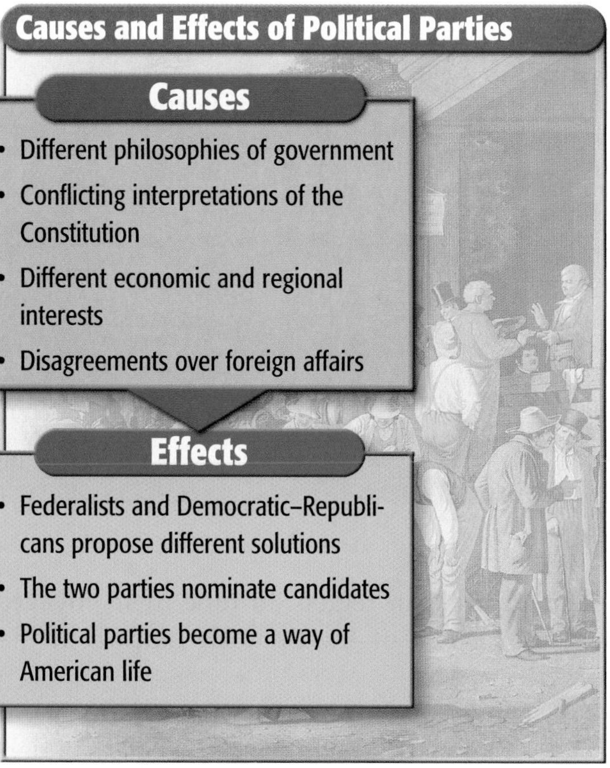

Causes and Effects of Political Parties

Causes

- Different philosophies of government
- Conflicting interpretations of the Constitution
- Different economic and regional interests
- Disagreements over foreign affairs

Effects

- Federalists and Democratic–Republicans propose different solutions
- The two parties nominate candidates
- Political parties become a way of American life

◀ Campaign poster

▼ Candidate appeals for votes

of the cause is known as an *effect*. Historians look for cause-and-effect links to explain why events happen.

Usually, one event is produced by many causes. Similarly, one event often produces several different effects. These cause-and-effect links form what is called a *cause-and-effect chain*. Because so many historical events are related, cause-and-effect chains can become very long and can include events that occur over a long period of time. The chart above shows such a chain of events.

Change and Continuity Historians look at the differences and similarities between events. History is a story of change. Therefore, historians study how events differ greatly from each other. Some historical changes have occurred quickly. For example, in A.D. 1532, Spanish conquerors toppled the vast Inca Empire in Peru, changing South America forever. Other changes take place over centuries, such as the spread of democracy or the changing role of women in many societies.

While looking at historical changes, historians also search for continuity, or the unbroken patterns in history. They study how ongoing traditions and concerns link people across time and place. For example, political actions in the United States today are based on the U.S. Constitution, which is about 220 years old. Also, the goal of passing tests in school was as important to students in America in the 1800s as it is to students today.

Thinking Like a Historian

1. **Recognizing Cause and Effect** Study the cause-and-effect chart on this page. What were some major causes of political parties? What were some important effects of political parties on American life?

2. **Applying Cause and Effect** Read an account of a recent event in your community as reported in a local newspaper. Determine at least one cause and effect of that event. Show the cause-and-effect relationship in a chart.

Making Sense of the Past

▼ Great Serpent Mound, Ohio

Main Idea To correctly interpret the past, historians must recognize that mistakes may have been made in earlier historical accounts and that the discovery of new evidence can change earlier interpretations of history.

Reading Focus Has a friend ever told you about an event, and later you heard a different version of the same event from someone else? You may have discovered that one of the accounts contained incorrect or exaggerated information or was missing details. Read to find out how historians deal with errors in and different interpretations of history.

Error and Chance in History History often has been made by chance, oversight, or error. For example, Christopher Columbus believed that his voyage in 1492 took him to the East Indies, the islands off the coast of Asia. Today the Caribbean islands are often called the West Indies. Also, the Native Americans whom Columbus met came to be called Indians.

Explorations after Columbus, however, made it clear that Columbus had not reached Asia at all. He had found a part of the globe unknown to Europeans, Asians, and Africans. In the following years, the Spanish explored most of the Caribbean region. In time their voyages led to the rise of the Spanish Empire in the Americas.

Mistakes have not only shaped historical events, they also have influenced people's understanding of the past. For example, European American settlers moving west in the 1800s discovered large human-made mounds. Biased against Native Americans, many white Americans at that time believed that some other, more advanced and ancient civilization had built the earthworks. Using scientific evidence gathered over the past 100 years, archaeologists have concluded, however, that the mounds were built by early Native American cultures.

Different Interpretations History is often called an ongoing discussion about the past. Historians argue about how to interpret the facts. What causes these differences?

Despite the efforts of the best minds, some facts are ambiguous, or not very clear to interpret. What the facts mean often depends on the historian's judgment. In addition, historians have different values and come to the evidence with different points of view. As a result, historians often arrive at different interpretations of the same event. For example, many historians see the Reformation as a result of religious causes. Others see it as a result of economic demands of a rising middle class in the cities.

▲ Columbus reaches land

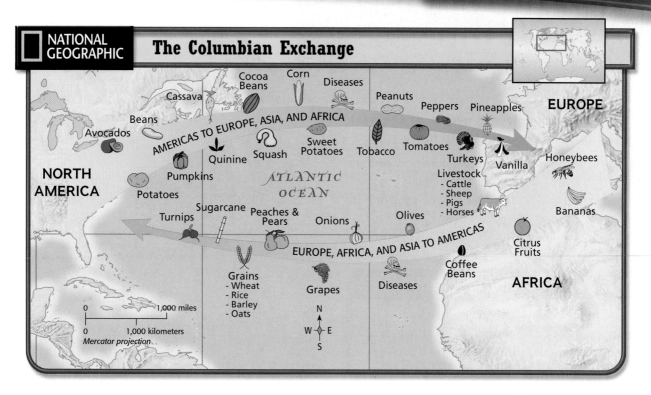

NATIONAL GEOGRAPHIC

The Columbian Exchange

The discussion among historians also continues because historians find new evidence, such as an ancient document. The new evidence leads them to question old interpretations. Sometimes historians take a new look at existing evidence and see things that others have ignored. As they do so, they may correct an earlier historian's mistake or explain events differently.

The questions that historians ask reflect the issues of the times in which they live. As a result, the historian's work is never done. There is never a final, complete version of history.

Economics and History

As part of their work, many historians investigate economies, or the ways societies produce, sell, and buy goods. They look at how economies have performed throughout history. Statistics, or mathematical data, are scarce for the economies of long ago. However, statistics for modern economies are abundant and provide historians with a wealth of information. Economists, or scientists who study economies, have developed ways to measure a modern economy's performance. These measurements are called economic indicators.

Economic indicators are statistics that tell how well an economy is doing and how well the economy is expected to do in the future. They include the number of jobless people, the rate at which prices rise and fall over periods of time, and the amount of goods and services that are made and sold.

Historians also analyze the costs and benefits of economic and political issues. This analysis requires figuring out the costs and benefits of any historical action.

Thinking Like a Historian

Christopher Columbus's arrival in the Americas brought together two worlds on opposite sides of the Atlantic Ocean. The resulting trade across the Atlantic became known as the Columbian Exchange.

Study the map of the Columbian Exchange at the top of the page. Then create a table like the one below. Next, list the costs and benefits of that exchange.

Costs	Benefits
1	1
2	2

Links Across Time

◄ Early compass

▼ European sailing ship

Main Idea The people and events of the past have left their mark on our world today.

Reading Focus How have older family members affected your life? Read to find out about some of the past-and-present links you will be studying in your text.

Unit 1 A Changing World

From about 1500 to 1800, people in many parts of the world lived through a time of far-reaching change. Thinkers developed new ideas about government and began to use scientific ideas to explore nature. Explorers traveled to other continents, and an exchange of ideas, peoples, and goods began across the globe. Today, advances in science, transportation, and communication have brought the world's peoples even closer together.

▲ Conestoga wagon

▲ Stock market

Computer and phone ▶

USA–Mexico border ▶

Unit 2 Creating a Nation

Adopted in 1788, the Constitution has endured for more than 200 years as the plan of government for the United States. Over the decades, the nation's system of courts has adapted and interpreted the Constitution to deal with the country's most important political and social issues. Many of today's issues, such as privacy rights on the Internet, were never imagined by the Constitution's eighteenth-century writers.

◀ Students viewing the original Constitution

Celebration of the ▶ Constitution's first 200 years

▲ Framers of the Constitution

Unit 3 Launching the Republic

Although presidents tried to follow Washington's advice to avoid entangling alliances, the country sometimes found itself in conflict with other nations. In today's world, presidents must also decide what to do when the actions of other nations affect the United States. For example, Iraq has large reserves of oil, but it has attacked other countries in the Middle East. Presidents have handled this problem in different ways. President George H.W. Bush led a worldwide group of countries against Iraq to stop its invasion of Kuwait. During his presidency, William Clinton used embargoes. President George W. Bush went to war against Iraq.

▲ Thomas Jefferson was an important leader of the early republic.

Links Across Time

Unit 4   The Young Republic

The new nation had three distinct geographic areas. In the North, the Industrial Revolution began and manufacturing grew increasingly more important. In the South, agriculture and the growing of cotton became king. In the West, the United States kept adding to its territorial size. Low prices for land drew people to these new territories. Settlers there supplied minerals and agricultural products to other parts of the country. Since the 1970s, the fastest-growing areas in the United States have been the South and the Southwest. Industrial growth and a pleasant climate have drawn people to this area known as the Sunbelt.

▼ Boston Harbor

◄ Plantation

Los Angeles skyline ▶

▲ Miners searching for gold

◄ Water power along the Colorado River

Unit 5 Civil War and Reconstruction

Disputes between the North and the South over slavery led to the Civil War (1861–1865). After the war, the United States ended slavery and gave once-enslaved African Americans citizenship, equal protection under the law, and the right to vote. In practice, however, civil rights were denied to African Americans. Despite obstacles, African Americans pressed for equal rights. In the late 1900s, they made advances in securing their rights under leaders such as Martin Luther King, Jr.

African American ▶ voter

▼ Martin Luther King, Jr.

Unit 6 Reshaping the Nation

By the early 1900s, many Americans had moved from farms to the cities, and thousands of immigrants poured into urban areas. A strong spirit of reform swept the country. Farmers and workers organized to improve their lot. During the second half of the 1900s, the drive for equality that had begun with African Americans spread to other groups. Migrant workers and other farm laborers joined the U.S. labor movement during the 1960s. César Chávez, a Mexican American labor leader, founded what is now the United Farm Workers of America (UFW).

Voting rights ▶ poster

◀ Young coal miners, c. 1900

▲ César Chávez

United Farm ▶ Workers

Thinking Like a Historian

As you read *The American Journey to World War I*, notice how the past affects the present. When you begin each unit, collect newspaper or magazine articles about a current event that is related to the period you are studying. Then, after completing each unit, write how you think a past event in that period is related to the current event.

A Changing World

Why It's Important

For thousands of years, the rich cultures of the Americas had remained virtually unnoticed by the rest of the world. When the Europeans began to explore in the 1400s, they soon conquered the peoples of the Americas and settled on their lands. After facing many challenges, a great new nation emerged in North America.

- New ideas about science, exploration, and trade led Europeans to explore and conquer the Americas.

- Britain's North American colonies fought for and gained their freedom.

1400   **1500**

POLITICS & ECONOMY

1492
Christopher Columbus reaches Americas

◄ Christopher Columbus

1521
Cortés defeats the Aztec

SCIENCE & SOCIETY

1542
Spanish law forbids making slaves of Native Americans

WORLD EVENTS

1420
Portuguese begin mapping Africa's coast

◄ Astrolabe

1517
Martin Luther posts Ninety-Five Theses

Defeat of the Spanish Armada ►

1519
Magellan's crew begins voyage around the world

1588
England defeats the Spanish Armada

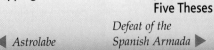

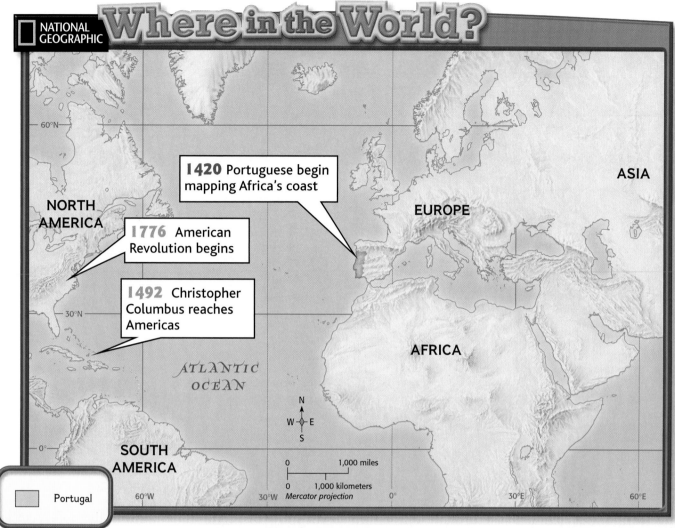

1420 Portuguese begin mapping Africa's coast

1776 American Revolution begins

1492 Christopher Columbus reaches Americas

NORTH AMERICA

EUROPE

ASIA

AFRICA

ATLANTIC OCEAN

SOUTH AMERICA

N W E S

0   1,000 miles

0   1,000 kilometers
Mercator projection

Portugal

60°N   30°N   0°   60°W   30°W   0°   30°E   60°E

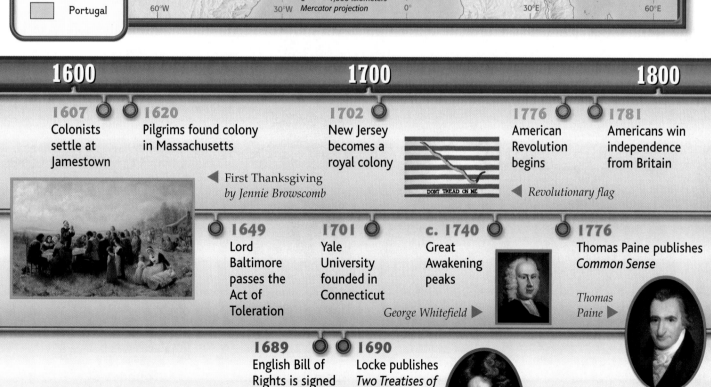

1600   **1700**   **1800**

1607 Colonists settle at Jamestown

1620 Pilgrims found colony in Massachusetts

◀ First Thanksgiving *by Jennie Browscomb*

1702 New Jersey becomes a royal colony

DONT TREAD ON ME

1776 American Revolution begins

1781 Americans win independence from Britain

Revolutionary flag

1649 Lord Baltimore passes the Act of Toleration

1701 Yale University founded in Connecticut

c. 1740 Great Awakening peaks

George Whitefield ▶

1776 Thomas Paine publishes *Common Sense*

Thomas Paine ▶

1689 English Bill of Rights is signed

1690 Locke publishes *Two Treatises of Government*

◀ *John Locke*

Places to Locate

① TENOCHTITLÁN

See *Expanding Horizons* Chapter 1

② COLUMBUS AND THE RULERS OF SPAIN

See *Expanding Horizons* Chapter 1

People to Meet

Lorenzo de' Medici
1449–1492
Italian ruler
Chapter 1, page 92

John Locke
1632–1704
English political thinker
Chapter 1, page 104

Junípero Serra
1713–1784
Spanish missionary
Chapter 2, page 118

William Penn
1644–1718
Founder of Pennsylvania
Chapter 2, page 122

③ **MAYFLOWER COMPACT**
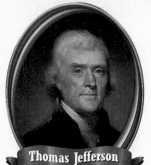
See *Road to Independence*
Chapter 2

④ **SIGNING THE DECLARATION OF INDEPENDENCE**
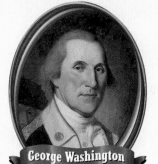
See *Road to Independence*
Chapter 2

George Washington
1732–1799
Leader of the Patriot army
Chapter 2, page 139

Thomas Jefferson
1743–1826
American political leader
Chapter 2, page 150

Benjamin Franklin
1706–1790
American scientist and patriot
Chapter 2, page 151

Abigail Adams
1744–1818
Patriot and supporter of women's rights
Chapter 2, page 155

Expanding Horizons

▼ Mission Santa Barbara
in California

NATIONAL GEOGRAPHIC

Where & When?

NORTH
AMERICA   EUROPE
                    CHINA
              INDIA
         AFRICA
SOUTH
AMERICA

1200   1450   1700

1271
Marco Polo
travels to
China

1492
Christopher
Columbus
sails to the
Americas

1521
Spanish
conquer
Aztec
Empire

1689
English Bill
of Rights
extends
rights

The Big Ideas

Age of Exploration

Exploration and trade spread ideas and goods. In the 1400s, Europeans began to explore other areas of the world. Trade increased and goods, technology, and ideas were exchanged around the world.

Rise of Modern Capitalism

Humans have created various economic systems. Our economic system is usually referred to as free enterprise, or capitalism. Capitalism is based on individual economic freedom. Capitalism developed gradually from economic and political changes in medieval and early modern Europe over hundreds of years.

The Enlightenment

World history has been shaped by significant individuals, groups, ideas, events, eras, and developments. The Scientific Revolution led to new discoveries. Using the scientific method, Europeans of the 1600s and 1700s developed new ideas about society based on reason.

 View the Chapter 1 video in the Glencoe Video Program.

Summarizing Make this foldable to help you learn about European exploration of the Americas.

Step 1 Fold the paper from the top right corner down so the edges line up. Cut off the leftover piece.

Fold a triangle. Cut off the extra edge.

Step 2 Fold the triangle in half. Unfold.

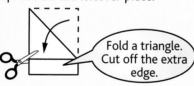

The folds will form an X dividing four equal sections.

Step 3 Cut up one fold line and stop at the middle. Draw an X on one tab and label the other three.

Step 4 Fold the X flap under the other flap and glue together.

This makes a three-sided pyramid.

Reading and Writing
As you read, ask yourself why England, France, and Spain were exploring the Americas. Write your questions under each appropriate pyramid wall.

Get Ready to Read

Previewing

1 Learn It!

If you know what to expect before reading, it will be easier to understand ideas and relationships presented in the text. Follow these steps to preview your reading assignments.

1. Look at the title and any illustrations that are included.

2. Read the headings, subheadings, and anything in bold letters.

3. Skim over the passage to see how it is organized. Is it divided into many parts?

4. Look at the graphics—pictures, maps, or diagrams. Read their titles and captions.

5. Set a purpose for your reading. Are you reading to learn something new? Are you reading to find specific information?

Reading Tip

As you preview the chapter, be sure to look over the maps, photographs, and charts.

2 Practice It!

Take some time to preview this chapter. Skim all the main heads and main ideas. With a partner, discuss your answers to these questions.

- Which part of this chapter looks the most interesting to you?
- What do you think will be covered in the next chapter?
- Are there any words in the Main Ideas that are unfamiliar to you?
- Choose one of the Reading Connection questions to discuss with your partner.

Read to Write
Use the information you have gathered through previewing to write a study outline for the chapter.

Europe Gets Ready to Explore

Main Idea New knowledge and ideas led Europeans to explore overseas.

Reading Connection Have you ever done something daring or tried something new not knowing how it would turn out? Read to learn how explorers took chances and went to new places.

Christopher Columbus ▶ in the Americas

3 Apply It!

Now that you have skimmed the chapter, write a short paragraph describing one thing you want to learn from this chapter.

Age of Exploration

Guide to Reading

Looking Back, Looking Ahead

Europeans risked dangerous ocean voyages to discover new sea routes. Today, people continue to explore the mysteries of Earth and of space.

Focusing on the Main Ideas

- New knowledge and ideas led Europeans to explore overseas. *(page 81)*
- In search of trade routes, Portuguese explorers began an era of overseas exploration. *(page 84)*
- Rivalries between countries led to increased exploration of North America. *(page 86)*

Meeting People

Marco Polo

Bartholomeu Dias
(bahr•THAH•luh•MYOO DEE•AHSH)

Vasco da Gama
(VAHS•koh dah GA•muh)

Christopher Columbus

Montezuma (MAHN•tuh•ZOO•muh)

Locating Places

Portugal (POHR•chih•guhl)

Tenochtitlán (tay•NAWCH•teet•LAHN)

Content Vocabulary

technology

astrolabe (AS•truh•LAYB)

circumnavigate
(SUHR•kuhm•NA•vuh•GAYT)

conquistador (kahn•KEES•tuh•DAWR)

pueblo (PWEH•bloh)

mission

presidio (prih•SEE•dee•OH)

encomienda (ehn•koh•mee•EHN•da)

Northwest Passage

Academic Vocabulary

culture (KUHL•chuhr)

design (dih•ZYN)

Reading Strategy

Determining Cause and Effect Use a diagram like the one below to identify three reasons Europeans increased overseas exploration.

Causes of European exploration

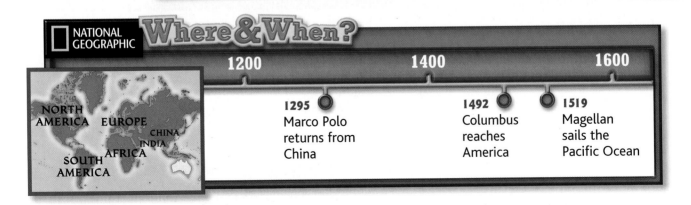

1200   1400   1600

1295
Marco Polo
returns from
China

1492
Columbus
reaches
America

1519
Magellan
sails the
Pacific Ocean

NORTH AMERICA EUROPE CHINA INDIA AFRICA SOUTH AMERICA

Europe Gets Ready to Explore

Main Idea New knowledge and ideas led Europeans to explore overseas.

Reading Connection Have you ever done something daring or tried something new not knowing how it would turn out? Read to learn how explorers took chances and went to new places.

A European Story

In 1271 **Marco Polo** set off from Europe on a great trek across Asia to China. Only 17 years old at the time, Polo journeyed with his father and uncle, both merchants from the Italian city of Venice. Traveling on camels for more than three years, the merchants crossed almost 7,000 miles (11,265 km) of mountains and deserts. Finally they reached the palace of Kublai Khan (KOO•bluh KAHN), the emperor of China. There Marco Polo spent 17 years working for the Khan and learning much about China's advanced **culture.**

When Polo returned from China in 1295, he wrote an account of the marvels of Asia, describing great riches and splendid cities. Polo's *Travels* was eagerly read in Europe and inspired a new age of exploration. Little did Polo realize the effect *Travels* would have. Nearly 200 years later his book about the East would inspire Christopher Columbus and other European explorers to sail in the opposite direction to reach the same destination.

Growth of Trade Marco Polo lived during the Middle Ages, the period in Western Europe that began with the fall of the western Roman Empire and lasted through the 1400s. During this time most Europeans knew little about India, China, or the rest of Asia. They also had no idea that the Western Hemisphere existed. Then, a dramatic series of events occurred that brought Europeans out of their isolation.

From the late 1000s to the early 1300s, Europeans fought a series of crusades, or holy wars, to free the Holy Land where Jesus had lived from the Muslims. The Muslims were followers of Islam, a religion that arose in the Middle East during the A.D. 600s. The Crusades achieved very little for Europeans, but they did increase trade between Europe and the lands to the east. During the time of the Crusades, Marco Polo made his journey. As Polo's story spread and exotic goods from the East appeared in Europe's marketplaces, more people became interested in distant lands. Merchants realized that they could make a fortune selling goods from Asia.

▲ Detail of historic map showing Marco Polo's journey

▲ Kublai Khan presents golden tablets to Marco Polo.

HISTORY MAKERS

The Compass, c. 1086

European technology improved navigation, but it was the Chinese who invented one of the more important tools for navigation: the compass. Evidence of this technology includes a Chinese document from the year 1086 that tells of sea captains relying on a "south-pointing needle" to help them find their way in foggy weather. The date on the document is more than 100 years earlier than the first recorded use of the compass in Europe.

How does a compass work? It uses a lodestone—a magnetic ore that always points in a north-south direction if allowed to freely rotate. If you know which way is north, you can determine the other directions.

▼ Compasses come in many shapes and sizes.

The Rise of Strong Nations During the 1400s, Italian merchants found it harder to get the fabled goods of the East. Political changes in Asia hindered trade between East and West. This made Asian goods more expensive. In areas of western Europe close to the Atlantic Ocean, merchants wanted to expand their businesses through foreign trade. If they could buy spices and silks from the East directly, without going through the Arab and Italian cities, they could earn huge profits. They looked for new routes to East Asia that would bypass the Mediterranean Sea and the Middle East.

Meanwhile, a new type of centralized state was emerging in western Europe. Strong monarchs had come to power in Spain, Portugal, England, and France. They began to establish national laws, courts, taxes, and armies to replace those of local lords. These ambitious kings and queens sought ways to increase trade and make their countries stronger and wealthier. They played an important role in expanding trade and interest in overseas exploration.

New Technology Advances in **technology**—the use of scientific knowledge for practical purposes—paved the way for European voyages of exploration. Maps were a problem for early navigators. By the 1400s, most educated people in Europe knew the world was round, but they only had maps of Europe and the Mediterranean. Most of these maps were inaccurate because they were drawn from the often-mistaken impressions of traders and travelers. Over time, cartographers, or mapmakers, gradually improved their skills.

Using the reports of explorers and information from Arab geographers, mapmakers made more accurate land and sea maps. These maps showed the direction of ocean currents and lines of latitude, which measured the distance north and south of the Equator. Only as sailors began to move beyond the coasts of Europe did they gain information about the actual shape of the earth. By 1500, cartography had reached the point where Europeans had fairly accurate maps of the areas they had explored.

Centers of Trade Wealthy Europeans clamored for spices, perfumes, silks, and precious stones. Merchants bought goods from Arab traders in the Middle East and sent them overland by caravan to the Mediterranean Sea, then by ship to Italian ports. The cities of Venice, Genoa, and Pisa prospered and became centers of the growing East-West trade. The expansion of trade with Asia made Italian merchants wealthy.

Better Tools and Ships Better instruments were developed for navigating the seas. Sailors could determine their latitude while at sea with an **astrolabe** (AS•truh•LAYB), an instrument that measured the position of the stars. Europeans also improved the magnetic compass, a Chinese invention the Arabs had passed on to Europe in the 1200s. The compass allowed sailors to determine their ship's location when they were far from land.

Advances in ship **design** allowed shipbuilders to build sailing vessels capable of long ocean voyages. The stern rudder and the triangular sail made it possible for ships to sail into the wind. Both of these new features came from the Arabs. In the late 1400s, the Portuguese developed the three-masted caravel. The caravel was a small vessel that sailed faster than earlier ships and carried more cargo and food supplies. It also could float in shallow water, which allowed sailors to explore inlets and to sail their ships up to the beach to make repairs.

Reading Check **Analyze** Why were Marco Polo's travels to China important?

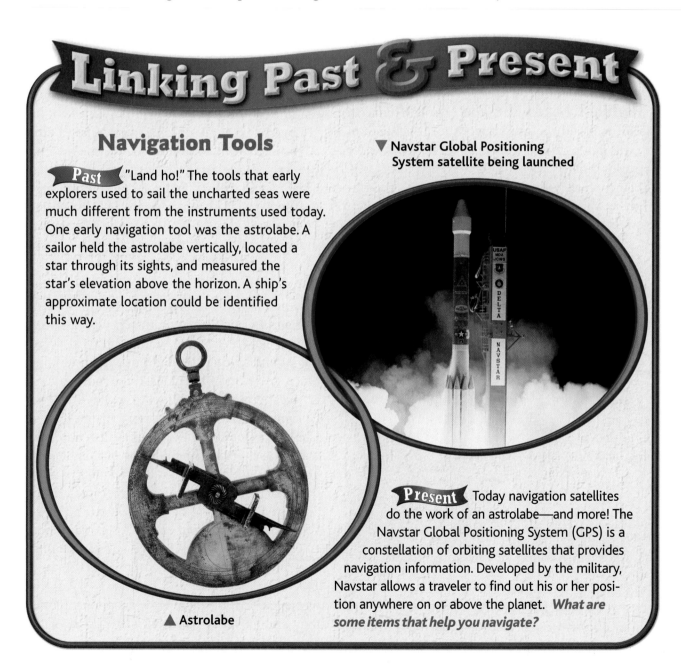

Linking Past & Present

Navigation Tools

Past "Land ho!" The tools that early explorers used to sail the uncharted seas were much different from the instruments used today. One early navigation tool was the astrolabe. A sailor held the astrolabe vertically, located a star through its sights, and measured the star's elevation above the horizon. A ship's approximate location could be identified this way.

▼ **Navstar Global Positioning System satellite being launched**

Present Today navigation satellites do the work of an astrolabe—and more! The Navstar Global Positioning System (GPS) is a constellation of orbiting satellites that provides navigation information. Developed by the military, Navstar allows a traveler to find out his or her position anywhere on or above the planet. *What are some items that help you navigate?*

▲ **Astrolabe**

Exploring the World

Main Idea In search of trade routes, Portuguese explorers began an era of overseas exploration.

Reading Connection Do you like traveling to places that you have never been? Read to see why Europeans set off to explore the Americas.

By the mid-1400s, the Italian ports faced increased competition for foreign trade. Powerful countries like **Portugal** (POHR•chih•guhl) and Spain began searching for sea routes to Asia, launching a new era of exploration. These new voyages took sailors down the west coast of Africa, which Europeans had never visited before.

Portugal Leads the Way Prince Henry of Portugal laid the groundwork for a new era of exploration. In about 1420, he set up a center for exploration on the southwestern tip of Portugal. Prince Henry brought astronomers, geographers, and mathematicians to share their knowledge with Portuguese sailors and shipbuilders.

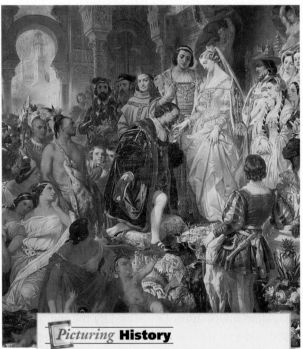

Picturing **History**

Financed by Spain's Queen Isabella, the voyages of Columbus led to an exchange of goods between Europe and the Americas.
On what island of the Americas did Columbus first land?

In early 1488, the Portuguese explorer **Bartholomeu Dias** (bahr•THAH•luh•MYOO DEE•AHSH) reached the southern tip of Africa. As Dias approached the area, he ran into a terrible storm that carried him off course and around the southern tip of Africa. Dias wrote that he had been around the "Cape of Storms." On learning of Dias's discovery, King John II renamed this southern tip of land the Cape of Good Hope—he hoped that the passage around Africa might lead to a new route to India.

The first Portuguese voyages to India were made years later. In July 1497, **Vasco da Gama** (VAHS•koh dah GA•muh) set out from Portugal with four ships. Da Gama rounded the Cape of Good Hope and visited cities along the coast of East Africa. In 1498 he reached the port of Calicut, completing the long-awaited eastern sea route to Asia.

Events moved quickly after that. Pedro Alvares Cabral, following Da Gama's route, swung so wide around Africa that he touched Brazil. By claiming land for his king, he gave Portugal a stake in the Americas. Meanwhile, Portuguese ships began to make voyages to India, returning with cargoes of goods.

Columbus Sets Sail While the Portuguese explored Africa, an Italian navigator named **Christopher Columbus** came up with a daring plan to get to Asia. He would sail west across the Atlantic Ocean. At the time, nobody knew that a great landmass blocked the route to Asia.

Desperate for money to make the trip, Columbus obtained support from Queen Isabella of Spain in 1492. The Spanish had been watching the seafaring success of neighboring Portugal with envy. They, too, wanted to share in the riches of Asian trade. Earlier in 1492, the Spanish had driven the Muslims out of Spain. They could now afford to pay for exploration.

Columbus outfitted three ships: the *Niña,* the *Pinta,* and a larger one, the *Santa María.* In 1492 they left Spain and headed west. As the weeks passed, the crew grew desperate. Finally they sighted land—a small island, part of the group now called the Bahamas.

Columbus went ashore, claimed the island for Spain, and named it San Salvador. Columbus returned to Spain in triumph. Columbus thought he was in Asia. He made three voyages to the region but never realized he had arrived in the Americas. Eventually, Europeans realized they had found two huge continents.

Magellan's Voyage The Spanish wanted to find a sea route through or around South America that would lead them to Asia. In 1519 they employed Ferdinand Magellan, a Portuguese mariner, to lead an expedition. Magellan headed west to sail around the Americas and then all the way to Asia. He sailed south along South America. Finally, he found a way around the continent—a narrow passage that today bears his name: the Strait of Magellan. After passing through the stormy strait, Magellan's expedition entered a vast sea. It was so peaceful, or pacific, that Magellan named the sea the Pacific Ocean. Magellan then headed west. His sailors nearly starved and had to eat leather, sawdust, and rats. Magellan was killed in a skirmish in the Philippines, but some of his crew continued west across the Indian Ocean, around Africa, and back to Spain. Only 18 of the more than 200 crew members completed the difficult journey. These men were the first to **circumnavigate** (SUHR•kuhm•NA•vuh•GAYT), or sail around, the world.

✓ **Reading Check** **Explain** How did the success of Portugal's voyages of exploration influence Spain?

TECHNOLOGY & History

Spanish Galleon

In the late 1500s and early 1600s, Spanish galleons carried gold and silver from the West Indies to Spain. That is not all these ships carried, however. The threat of pirates prompted the Spanish galleons to carry weapons as part of their cargo. **What powered the Spanish galleons?**

The crow's nest served as a lookout.

1 Two or three sails on the **foremast** and **mainmast** allowed the ship to "catch the wind."

2 Elaborate living quarters for the captain were placed within the high **sterncastle.** The rest of the crew slept on deck.

3 Strong hands were needed to climb the rigging into the **crow's nest,** or lookout platform.

4 Stones and bricks provided **ballast** to keep the ship from tipping over. These stones would be replaced with cargo in the Americas. Many colonial streets and sidewalks were paved with ballast stones.

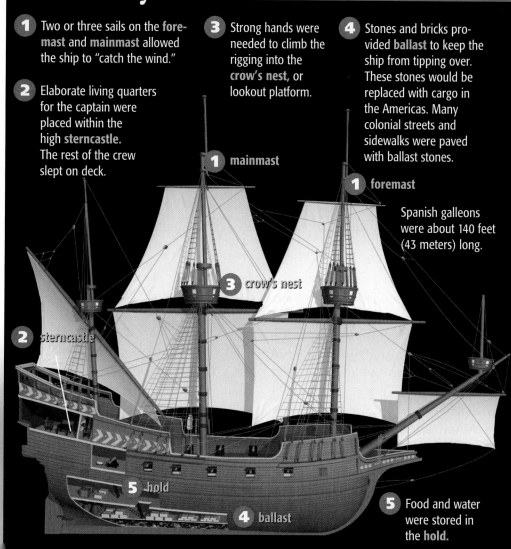

1 mainmast

1 foremast

Spanish galleons were about 140 feet (43 meters) long.

3 crow's nest

2 sterncastle

5 hold

4 ballast

5 Food and water were stored in the **hold.**

Building Empires

Main Idea Rivalries between countries led to increased exploration of North America.

Reading Connection Have you ever competed against someone for something you both wanted? Read to learn how nations competed to claim land in the Americas.

Long before the arrival of Europeans in the early 1500s, several great Native American civilizations, or highly developed societies, arose in present-day Mexico and in Central and South America. Among the largest and most advanced of these civilizations were the Aztec and Inca. Each civilization spread out over hundreds of miles, included millions of people, and established trading networks that linked different parts of the Americas.

Spanish Conquistadors

Stories of gold, silver, and kingdoms wealthy beyond belief greeted the early Spanish explorers in the Americas. The reports led them far and wide in search of fabulous riches.

Known as **conquistadors** (kahn•KEES•tuh•DAWRS), these explorers received grants from the Spanish rulers. They had the right to explore in the Americas. In exchange, they agreed to give the Spanish crown part of any gold or treasure they discovered.

Who Was Cortés?

In 1519 the Spanish conquistador Hernán Cortés landed on the east coast of what we now know as Mexico. He came with about 500 soldiers, some horses, and a few cannons. Cortés soon learned about the great Aztec Empire and the capital of **Tenochtitlán** (tay•NAWCH•teet•LAHN).

Cortés formed alliances with nearby cities against the Aztec. Then he marched into Tenochtitlán with his small army and Native American allies. The emperor **Montezuma** (MAHN•tuh•ZOO•muh)—also spelled Moctezuma—welcomed Cortés and his soldiers. However, Cortés took advantage of the Aztec's hospitality and made Montezuma his prisoner.

Cortés attacked and destroyed the Aztec capital in 1521. The Aztec Empire disintegrated, and Spain seized control of the region.

Who Was Pizarro?

Another conquistador, Francisco Pizarro, sailed down the Pacific coast of South America with about 180 Spanish soldiers. Pizarro had heard tales of the incredibly wealthy Inca Empire in present-day Peru. In 1532 Pizarro captured the Incan ruler, Atahualpa (ah•tuh•WAHL•puh), and destroyed much of the Incan army. Within a few years, Pizarro controlled most of the Inca Empire.

Why Were the Empires Conquered?

The conquistadors' victories in Mexico and Peru were quick and lasting. How could Cortés and Pizarro, with only a few hundred Spanish soldiers, conquer such mighty empires?

First, the Spanish arrived with strange weapons—guns and cannons—and fearsome animals. They rode horses and had huge, ferocious dogs. To the Native Americans, the Spanish seemed almost like gods. Second, many Native Americans hated their Aztec overlords and assisted the conquistadors.

Finally, disease played an extremely important role in the Spanish conquest. Native Americans had no immunity to the diseases the Europeans had unknowingly brought with them. Epidemics of smallpox and other diseases wiped out entire communities in the Americas and did much to weaken the resistance of the Aztec and Inca.

Searching for Gold

Mexico and Peru were rich in silver and gold. Hoping to find similar wealth to the north, conquistadors explored the southeastern and southwestern parts of North America. Juan Ponce de León made the first Spanish landing on the mainland of North America, arriving on the east coast of present-day Florida in 1513. Ponce de León failed to find gold and the legendary fountain of youth. However, his exploration led to the first Spanish settlement in what is now the United States. In 1565 the Spanish established a fort at St. Augustine, Florida.

Who Was de Vaca? Many other conquistadors led expeditions to search for quick riches. One who did was Álvar Núñez Cabeza de Vaca (kuh•BAY•zuh day VAH•kuh). De Vaca and his crew were shipwrecked on an island near present-day Texas. Stranded, Cabeza de Vaca and his companions survived by adopting the ways of the Native Americans. After several years, they set off on foot on a great 1,000-mile journey across the Southwest. Arriving in Mexico in 1536, Cabeza de Vaca related tales he had heard of seven cities with walls of emerald and streets of gold.

De Soto and Coronado In search of the cities, Hernando de Soto took a large expedition into the region north of Florida. De Soto's expedition explored parts of what are today North Carolina, Tennessee, Alabama, Arkansas, and Texas. De Soto crossed the Mississippi River in 1541, describing it as "swift, and very deep." The fabled cities of gold, however, were not to be found. Francisco Vásquez de Coronado also wanted to find the legendary "Seven Cities of Gold." After traveling through the present-day southwestern United States, the expedition realized that there was no gold.

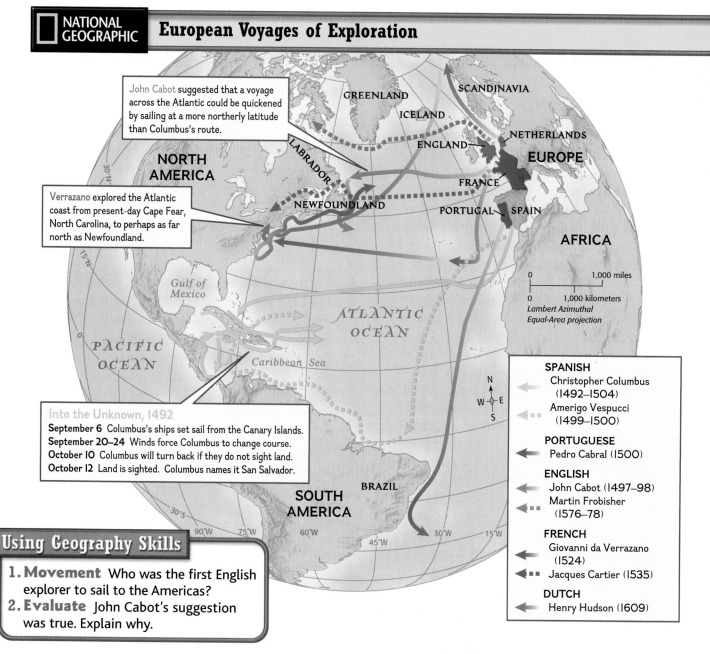

NATIONAL GEOGRAPHIC

European Voyages of Exploration

John Cabot suggested that a voyage across the Atlantic could be quickened by sailing at a more northerly latitude than Columbus's route.

Verrazano explored the Atlantic coast from present-day Cape Fear, North Carolina, to perhaps as far north as Newfoundland.

Into the Unknown, 1492
September 6 Columbus's ships set sail from the Canary Islands.
September 20–24 Winds force Columbus to change course.
October 10 Columbus will turn back if they do not sight land.
October 12 Land is sighted. Columbus names it San Salvador.

1,000 miles
1,000 kilometers
Lambert Azimuthal
Equal-Area projection

SPANISH
Christopher Columbus (1492–1504)
Amerigo Vespucci (1499–1500)

PORTUGUESE
Pedro Cabral (1500)

ENGLISH
John Cabot (1497–98)
Martin Frobisher (1576–78)

FRENCH
Giovanni da Verrazano (1524)
Jacques Cartier (1535)

DUTCH
Henry Hudson (1609)

Using Geography Skills

1. **Movement** Who was the first English explorer to sail to the Americas?
2. **Evaluate** John Cabot's suggestion was true. Explain why.

HISTORY MAKERS

The Hispanic Heritage

▲ St. Augustine, founded in 1565

The Spanish empire in the Americas included more than one-half the continental United States. The oldest surviving building in the United States is located in St. Augustine, Florida.

In what is today the southwestern United States, the Spanish founded the city of Santa Fe at about the same time the English Pilgrims were crossing the Atlantic on the *Mayflower*. By the time the United States won its independence from England, the Spanish had founded Tucson, Albuquerque, San Antonio, and San Diego.

Many elements of the Spanish culture became part of America's heritage. Spanish art forms mixed with Native American cultures to produce new styles in arts and crafts. The architecture of the Spanish missions combined the flat-roofed adobe, or sun-dried mud brick, buildings made by Native Americans with the Spanish designs of open courtyards, covered arcades, and tiled roofs.

Another important element of Spanish culture in the United States is the Spanish language. Spanish is the second most widely spoken language in the country. Many Spanish terms, such as *canyon* and *fiesta*, have been incorporated into the English language. Spanish names—Los Angeles, Mesa Verde, El Paso—fill the maps of the West and Southwest.

The Spanish also introduced horses, sheep, pigs, and beef cattle into the American Southwest. The Spanish were expert ranchers and horse breeders. The first cowboys were Spanish vaqueros.

Spain's American Empire Meanwhile, the Spanish pressed forward with establishing settlements in their new American empire. **Pueblos** (PWEH•bloh), or towns, were established as centers of trade. **Missions** were religious communities that usually included a small town, surrounding farmland, and a church. A **presidio** (prih•SEE•dee•OH), or fort, was usually built near a mission.

In the 1500s, the Spanish government granted each conquistador who settled in the Americas an *encomienda* (ehn•koh•mee•EHN•da). An *encomienda* is the right to demand taxes or labor from Native Americans living on the land. This system turned the Native Americans into slaves. Grueling labor in the fields and in the gold and silver mines took its toll. Many Native Americans died from malnutrition and disease.

A Spanish priest, Bartolomé de Las Casas, condemned the cruel treatment of the Native Americans. He pleaded for laws to protect them. Because of Las Casas's reports, in 1542 the Spanish government passed the New Laws, which forbade making slaves of Native Americans. Although not always enforced, the laws did correct the worst abuses.

French, Dutch, and English Explorations

England, France, and the Netherlands wanted to profit from trade and colonization. The voyage to Asia—either around the southern tip of Africa or around South America—was long and difficult. For this reason, the three countries hoped to discover a **Northwest Passage** to Asia—a more direct water route through the Americas.

In 1497 England hired John Cabot, an Italian-born sailor, to look for a northern route to Asia. Cabot probably landed on the coast of present-day Newfoundland. England used Cabot's voyage as the basis for its claims to North America.

In 1524 France hired an Italian, Giovanni da Verrazano, to map America's coast and find a route to Asia. Verrazano mapped from what is today North Carolina north to Newfoundland but found no path to Asia.

About ten years later, the French tried again. This time, they sent the French explorer Jacques Cartier (kahr•TYAY). Cartier sailed past Newfoundland and entered the St. Lawrence River. Hoping he had found a passage to Asia, Cartier made two more trips to map the St. Lawrence River. Cartier had heard stories about gold, but he found neither gold nor a sea route to Asia.

The Netherlands also wanted to find a passage through the Americas. They hired Henry Hudson, an English sailor, to explore. In 1609 he found a wide river in present-day New York, today known as the Hudson River. On a second voyage, sponsored by England, Hudson and his crew discovered a huge bay, now called Hudson Bay. However, he found no outlet to the Pacific.

A Trade Rivalry England and Spain also began to compete for trade. Attacks on Spanish ships and ports by such English adventurers as Sir Francis Drake angered King Philip II of Spain. He thought that Queen Elizabeth of England should punish Drake for his raids. Instead, she honored Drake with knighthood. Philip sent the Spanish Armada to conquer England, but it failed completely.

Although war between England and Spain continued until 1604, the defeat of the armada marked the end of Spanish control of the seas. Now the way was clear for England and other nations to start colonies in North America.

✓ **Reading Check** **Explain** How were the Spanish able to defeat the mighty Aztec and Inca empires?

Study Central Need help understanding the Age of Exploration? Visit tajww1.glencoe.com and click on Study Central.

Section 1 Review

Reading Summary

Review the Main Ideas

- By the late 1400s, technological and economic changes in Europe made long sea voyages possible.

- Christopher Columbus sought a sea route to Asia. Instead, he landed in the Americas.

- Spain, England, France, and the Netherlands sent explorers to the Americas in search of trade and colonies.

What Did You Learn?

1. What was the goal of Christopher Columbus's voyage in 1492?

2. What was the purpose of John Cabot's voyage?

Critical Thinking

3. **Taking Notes** Re-create the diagram below. List technological innovations mentioned in this section, and describe the effect of each on exploration.

Technology Innovation	Effect on Exploration

4. **The Big Ideas** Explain why exploration accelerated in the 1400s and 1500s.

5. **Drawing Conclusions** Why do you think the Caribbean islands that Columbus reached are often referred to as the West Indies?

6. **Analyze** Were the French or Spanish explorations more successful? Why?

7. **Descriptive Writing** Take on the role of a sailor on Columbus's first voyage to the Americas. Write a journal entry about the Caribbean islands.

8. **READING** **Previewing** Read the main ideas for Section 2. Write a paragraph describing what you think you will learn.

Rise of Modern Capitalism

Guide to Reading

Looking Back, Looking Ahead

You read how the voyages of exploration led to setting up colonies and opening new areas for trade. These changes also led to a new way of doing business and financing expeditions.

Focusing on the Main Ideas

- New ways of doing business developed to raise money to finance trade. *(page 91)*
- Nations competed to establish colonies in the Americas. *(page 94)*
- Exploration and trade led to a worldwide exchange of products, people, and ideas. *(page 95)*

Locating Places

Venice (VEH•nuhs)
Genoa (JEH•noh•uh)

Meeting People

The Medici Family (MEHD•ee•chee)
The Fugger Family (FUG•uhr)
Bartolomé de Las Casas (bahr•TOH•loh•may day lahs KAHS•ahs)

Content Vocabulary

capitalism
joint-stock company
entrepreneur (AHN•truh•pruh•NUHR)
mercantilism (MUHR•kuhn•tuh•LIH•zuhm)
bullion (BUL•yuhn)
colony
Columbian Exchange

Academic Vocabulary

assist
finance (FY•NANTS)
funds
export

Reading Strategy

Summarizing Complete a chart like the one below identifying changes in trade, banking, and settlement that occurred during this period.

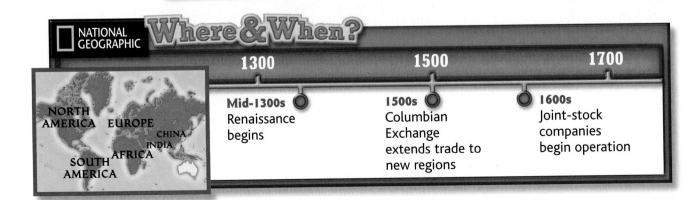

NATIONAL GEOGRAPHIC **Where & When?**

1300 — 1500 — 1700

Mid-1300s Renaissance begins

1500s Columbian Exchange extends trade to new regions

1600s Joint-stock companies begin operation

NORTH AMERICA EUROPE CHINA INDIA AFRICA SOUTH AMERICA

The Commercial Revolution

Main Idea New ways of doing business developed to raise money to finance trade.

Reading Connection Have you ever come up with a plan to raise money when you want to make an expensive purchase? Read on to find out what new ways were developed to raise money for exploration and colonization.

A European Story

In 1587 17-year-old David Baker admired the magnificent view of London from the Thames River. However, he could not begin to take pleasure in the city without walking down its busy streets. No street offered more to delight the eye or tongue than Cheapside, the city's broadest avenue, located north of London Bridge. Cheapside was filled with stalls sheltered by canopies and stocked with a tempting array of local goods as well as exotic imports such as scarves, spices, and even peacocks and apes.

How Did Capitalism Develop?

London, England, was among the cities of Europe that grew wealthy as a result of the Age of Exploration. Building empires and overseas trade expanded Europe's economy. Europe's growing population demanded more goods and services. This demand was met by Europe's increasing contacts with the rest of the world. This search for wealth led to the rise of modern **capitalism,** an economic system in which money is invested in business to make profits.

By the 1600s, the nation had replaced the city and village as the basic economic unit in Europe. Nations began competing for markets and trade goods. New business methods were developed to invest money, speed the flow of wealth, and reduce risks in commercial ventures. These changes, which came to be known as the Commercial Revolution, formed the roots of modern financial and business life.

Growth of Banking

Launching an overseas trading venture was a major undertaking. To trade goods long distance, merchants needed a lot of money. They had to buy many goods, store them in warehouses, and ship them over land and sea. They had to know what people in distant lands wanted to buy and what prices were like there. Often several years passed before a fleet finished trading overseas and returned home. Only then could the initial investment pay off. Generally, only governments and rich merchants had enough money to back such trading voyages, and even they needed financial **assistance.**

At first, merchants turned to bankers for the money to **finance** their ventures. Families like the **Medici** (MEHD•ee•chee) of Florence, Italy, and the **Fuggers** (FUG•uhrz) of Augsburg, Germany, loaned money as part of their businesses. By the 1500s, these families were so wealthy that they accepted deposits, made loans, and transferred funds over long distances. They set up branches in several European cities and made loans to European monarchs.

▲ European towns and cities grew and prospered during the 1500s and 1600s.

Biography

LORENZO DE' MEDICI
1449–1492

Renaissance means "rebirth." The years from about 1350 to 1550 in European history are called the Renaissance because a rebirth of interest in art and learning took place.

During the Renaissance, many European nations were ruled by a king or queen. However, Italy did not have a single strong monarch. The lack of a single strong ruler made it possible for a number of city-states in northern and central Italy to remain independent. Three city-states—Milan, Venice, and Florence—expanded and played important roles in Italy's political, economic, and social life.

The Medici family controlled the city of Florence. The Medicis had acquired great wealth through banking and trade. Using their wealth and personal influence, Cosimo, and later Lorenzo de' Medici, his grandson, dominated the city at a time when Florence was the cultural center of Italy.

Lorenzo de' Medici supported the arts, literature, and learning. Renaissance artists worked at his court, including Leonardo da Vinci and Michelangelo. Lorenzo helped build the Medici Library. He spent huge sums of money to buy Greek and Latin manuscripts and to have them copied. Lorenzo also worked to beautify Florence and the many Medici lands and palaces.

In political affairs, Lorenzo tried to maintain a balance of power between the Italian city-states so that no single state became too strong. He also tried to create a more unified Italy, but this effort was not successful.

"Lorenzo took the greatest delight in architecture, music, and poetry."
—**Niccolò Machiavelli**

Then and Now

Italy's wealth supported new art forms. In what way do bankers and businesspeople support the arts today?

Changes in Banking Meanwhile, many Jews fleeing persecution in Spain settled in port cities in Holland, France, and Germany. There they were granted freedom of worship and offered economic opportunities. Many Jews became financiers and investors as well as importers and shipbuilders.

By the 1600s, governments began to charter, or legally support, banks in return for the banks loaning them money. These government-backed banks accepted deposits of money and charged interest on loans. Before long, the banks began to provide other services. They issued banknotes and checks, making large payments in heavy coins a thing of the past. They acted as money changers, exchanging currencies from other countries.

What Are Joint-Stock Companies? In the 1600s, new ways of doing business developed in Europe. Individual merchants who wanted to invest in exploration often raised money by combining their resources in **joint-stock companies,** organizations that sold stock, or shares, in the venture. This enabled large and small investors to share the profits and risks of a trading voyage. If a loss occurred, investors would lose only the amount they had invested in shares. This sharing of risk provided a stable way of raising **funds** for voyages.

A few joint-stock companies became rich and powerful through government support. For example, the Netherlands entered an era of commercial prosperity upon gaining independence from Spain in 1648. Its government gave the Dutch East India Company a monopoly, or the sole right, to carry out Dutch trade with Africa and the East Indies. The Dutch government also gave the company the power to make war, to seize foreign ships, to coin money, and to set up colonies and forts. In return, the government received customs duties, or taxes on imported goods, from the company's trade.

A New Business Class As gold and silver flowed into Europe from abroad, the supply of coined money increased. At the same time, the

Picturing **History**

This picture shows a money changer and his wife at work. Trade often meant the transfer of money from place to place. *How did banks help finance trading voyages?*

nature and goals of business changed. It now came to be seen that the goal of business was to make profits. Individuals known as **entrepreneurs** (AHN•truh•pruh•NUHRZ) combined money, ideas, raw materials, and labor to make goods and profits. Profits were then used to expand the business and develop new ventures.

An entrepreneur in the cloth industry, for example, would buy wool and employ spinners to make the wool into yarn. Weavers and dyers would then be hired to turn the yarn into cloth. Because these tasks were done in the workers' homes, this system became known as the "cottage industry."

The entrepreneur would then sell the cloth on the open market for a price that brought a profit. Of course, entrepreneurs took risks when they put up capital for businesses. They could lose their investment if prices fell or if workers could not produce goods at a specified time or for a specific market.

Reading Check **Explain** What was the advantage of investing in a joint-stock company?

Government and Trade

Main Idea Nations competed to establish colonies in the Americas.

Reading Connection Suppose your family is thinking about moving to another state. What factors would influence your decision to move? Read on to find out why many Europeans migrated to the Americas.

Governments became closely involved in trade. They believed that a nation's power rested on the wealth obtained from trade. They developed national economic policies to advance trade and become as wealthy as possible.

In the 1600s, the greatest increase in trade took place in the countries bordering the Atlantic Ocean—Portugal, Spain, England, and the Netherlands—in large part because they had the largest overseas empires. Italian cities, such as **Venice** (VEH•nuhs) and **Genoa** (JEH•noh•uh), formerly the leading trade centers in Europe, found themselves cut out of overseas trade as trade routes and fortunes gradually moved westward toward the Atlantic Ocean and the Americas.

What Is Mercantilism? During the 1600s, Europe's trading nations based their policies on an economic theory known as **mercantilism** (MUHR•kuhn•tuh•LIH•zuhm). This theory held that a nation became powerful by building up its supply of **bullion** (BUL•yuhn), or gold and silver. One merchant summed up the general feeling about bullion: "[It is] the sinews of all government, it gives it its pulse, its movement. . . ." Under mercantilism, nations could gain wealth by mining gold or silver at home or overseas.

The Wealth of Nations

Many nations tried to increase their wealth and power by following the ideas of mercantilism. Putting mercantilism into practice demanded a large amount of government control.

Some economists and writers criticized mercantilism. In his book *The Wealth of Nations* (1776), economist Adam Smith described a system in which government had little to do with a nation's economy. He said individuals left on their own would work for their own self-interest:

> "Every man, as long as he does not violate the laws of justice, is left perfectly free to pursue his own interest his own way, and to bring both his industry and capital into competition with those of any other man, or order of men."

Smith set forth the basic principles of capitalism—that people are free to buy, sell, and produce what they want with little or no government restriction. Smith's ideas influenced the Founders of the United States, who limited the role of government mainly to national defense and keeping the peace.

▲ Gold bullion

DBQ Document-Based Question

Does Smith say that there are no limits on a worker "pursuing his own interest"? Explain.

How Did Mercantilism Work? Spain sent conquistadors to the Americas to seize the silver and gold mines of the Aztec and Inca Empires. Nations, however, primarily wanted to gain wealth through trade. They wanted to create a favorable balance of trade by **exporting** more goods than they imported. If a nation exported more goods than it imported, more gold and silver flowed in from other nations than went out. This greater wealth meant greater national power and more influence in the world.

Mercantilism provided great opportunities for individual merchants to make money. To increase national wealth, governments often aided businesses that produced export goods. They sold monopolies, which is the total control of an operation free of competition, to producers in certain key industries. They also set tariffs, or taxes on imported goods, to protect local industries from foreign competition.

Quest for Colonies

Mercantilism also led to increased rivalry between nations. Mercantilists believed that nations should set up overseas colonies. A **colony** is a settlement of people living in a new territory controlled by their home country. According to mercantilists, colonies are supposed to produce goods that their home country does not have. That way, the home country will not have to import those goods from other countries.

During the 1600s, several countries in Europe, such as England and Spain, competed for overseas territory that could produce wealth. They wanted to acquire colonies in the Americas that could provide valuable resources, such as gold and silver, or raw materials. The colonies would also serve as a place to sell European products.

✓ **Reading Check** **Analyze** How did mercantilism increase the wealth of countries like Spain?

Student Web Activity Visit tajww1.glencoe.com and click on Chapter 1—Student Web Activities for an activity on economic systems.

Global Exchange

Main Idea Exploration and trade led to a worldwide exchange of products, people, and ideas.

Reading Connection Think back to the last time you tried a new food or a new way of doing something. Who introduced this new food or idea to you? Read on to find out what happened when new cultures came into contact with one another.

As Europe traded with the world, a global exchange of people, goods, technology, ideas, and even diseases began. We call this transfer the **Columbian Exchange**, after Christopher Columbus.

Trade in Goods This transfer of products from continent to continent brought changes in ways of life throughout the world. Europeans planted many European and Asian grains, such as wheat, oats, barley, rye, and rice, in the Americas. They also brought new animals, such as pigs, sheep, cattle, chickens, and horses. Chickens changed the diet of many people in the Americas, and horses changed the lives of Native Americans. Horses provided a faster way to move from place to place. As a result, Native Americans in North America began hunting buffalo as their main food source.

From Native Americans, Europeans acquired food items such as corn, potatoes, tomatoes, beans, and chocolate, which they brought back to Europe. Corn was used to feed animals. Larger, healthier animals resulted in more meat, leather, and wool. The potato was also important. Europeans discovered that if they planted potatoes instead of grain, about four times as many people could live off the same amount of land.

Other American foods, such as squash, beans, and tomatoes, also made their way to Europe. Tomatoes greatly changed cooking in Italy, where tomato sauces became common. Chocolate was a popular food from Central America. By mixing it with milk and sugar, Europeans created a sweet that is still enjoyed today.

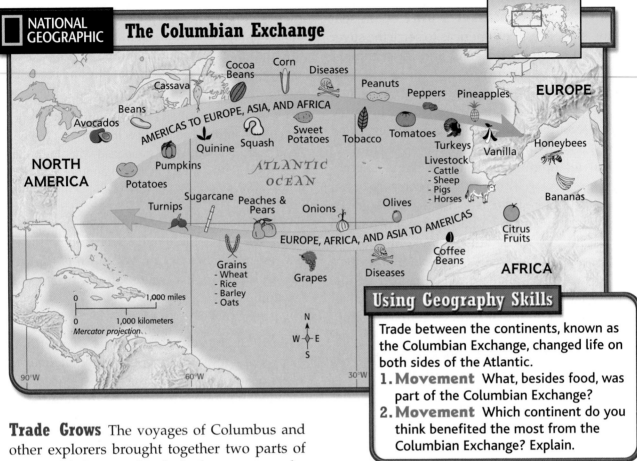

NATIONAL GEOGRAPHIC

The Columbian Exchange

AMERICAS TO EUROPE, ASIA, AND AFRICA

Cocoa Beans · Corn · Diseases · Cassava · Peanuts · Peppers · Pineapples · EUROPE · Beans · Avocados · Quinine · Squash · Sweet Potatoes · Tobacco · Tomatoes · Turkeys · Vanilla · Honeybees · NORTH AMERICA · Pumpkins · ATLANTIC OCEAN · Potatoes · Livestock - Cattle - Sheep - Pigs - Horses · Bananas · Turnips · Sugarcane · Peaches & Pears · Onions · Olives · Citrus Fruits

EUROPE, AFRICA, AND ASIA TO AMERICAS

Grains - Wheat - Rice - Barley - Oats · Grapes · Diseases · Coffee Beans · AFRICA

0 — 1,000 miles
0 — 1,000 kilometers
Mercator projection

90°W   60°W   30°W

N W E S

Using Geography Skills

Trade between the continents, known as the Columbian Exchange, changed life on both sides of the Atlantic.

1. **Movement** What, besides food, was part of the Columbian Exchange?
2. **Movement** Which continent do you think benefited the most from the Columbian Exchange? Explain.

Trade Grows The voyages of Columbus and other explorers brought together two parts of the world that previously had no contact: the continents of Europe, Asia, and Africa in one hemisphere and the Americas in the other.

Some American foods, such as chili peppers and peanuts, were taken to Europe, but they also made their way to Asia and Africa where they became popular. Both Europeans and Asians also began smoking tobacco, an American plant.

Foods, such as corn, spread to Asia and Africa, boosting population growth there. From Asia and Africa, Europeans brought to Europe and the Americas tropical products—bananas, coffee, tea, and sugarcane—as well as luxury goods, such as ivory, perfumes, silk, and gems.

Movement of Peoples and Cultures

New global trading links increased the movement of people and cultures from continent to continent. Europeans seeking wealth or fleeing economic distress and religious persecution moved to the Americas and other parts of the world. They exchanged food, ideas, and practices with the people living in these areas.

European influences profoundly affected local cultures. European traders spread European languages, and European missionaries taught Christianity and European values. Wealthy Europeans, in turn, developed an interest in the arts, styles, and foods of Asia, especially Chinese porcelain, Indian textiles, and Southeast Asian spices.

With their guns and powerful ships, the Europeans easily defeated Arab fleets and Indian princes. Across Asia, the Europeans forced local rulers to let them set up trading posts. Within a short time, England's East India Company had built an empire in India, and the Dutch East India Company had built an empire in Indonesia.

Not everything exchanged between Europe and America was good. When Europeans arrived in America, they were carrying germs that Native Americans had not previously been exposed to. Many diseases, including smallpox, measles, and malaria, swept across the Americas, killing millions of people.

Beginnings of Slave Trade A huge movement of people also took place after Europeans obtained sugarcane from Asia and began growing it in the Caribbean. To plant and harvest the sugarcane, they enslaved millions of Africans and moved them to the Americas.

Some Spanish settlers made large profits by exporting crops and raw materials back to Spain. In the West Indies, the main exports were tobacco and sugarcane. To raise these crops, the Spanish developed the plantation system. A plantation was a large estate.

The Spanish used Native Americans to work their plantations. The Spanish priest **Bartolomé de Las Casas** (bahr•TOH•loh•may day lahs KAHS•ahs) suggested replacing them with enslaved Africans—a suggestion he bitterly regretted later. He thought the Africans could endure the labor better than the Native Americans.

By the mid-1500s, the Spanish were bringing thousands from West Africa to the Americas. The Portuguese did the same in Brazil. For enslaved Africans, the voyage to America usually began with a march to a European fort on the West African coast. Tied together with ropes around their necks and hands, they were traded to Europeans, branded, and forced to board a ship. An estimated 10 to 12 million Africans were forcibly transported to the Americas between 1450 and 1870.

The Africans who survived the brutal ocean voyage were sold to plantation owners. By the late 1500s, plantation slave labor was an essential part of the economy of the Spanish colonies.

✓ **Reading Check** **Describe** How did the slave trade come into being?

History Online

Study Central Need help understanding the rise of modern capitalism? Visit tajww1.glencoe.com and click on Study Central.

Section 2 Review

Reading Summary

Review the Main Ideas

- The introduction of banking and capitalism allowed countries to increase their wealth by financing trading ventures abroad.

- The growth of mercantilism and trade led to the creation of colonies.

- Trade between Europe and Asia and the Americas led to exchanges of people, ideas, and products.

What Did You Learn?

1. What was the Commercial Revolution?

2. What were some of the things Europeans introduced to Native Americans?

Critical Thinking

3. **Explaining** Draw a chart like the one below and explain how each economic concept or action increased the wealth of European nations.

	Effect on European Wealth
Mercantilism	
Joint-stock company	
Slave trade	

4. **The Big Ideas** Explain how exploration brought about great change in Europe and the Americas.

5. **Creative Writing** Imagine you are a member of a trading company on an expedition to the Americas. Describe the people and things you see when you arrive in the Americas.

6. **ANALYSIS** **Analyzing Economics** Write a brief essay about joint-stock companies. Include a definition and an example from the chapter, as well as a modern-day company. Discuss the strengths and weaknesses of this business model.

Section 3

The Enlightenment

Guide to Reading

Looking Back, Looking Ahead
In Section 2, you learned how Europe gained wealth from overseas territories. In this section, you will learn how past civilizations contributed to our scientific, religious, and political thinking today.

Focusing on the Main Ideas
- Ancient cultures laid the foundation of many modern ideas. *(page 99)*
- Religious and philosophical thinkers changed the way people viewed Christianity and the government. *(page 102)*
- Science and the influence of reason led to new innovations in political thought. *(page 105)*

Meeting People
Thomas Aquinas (uh•KWY•nuhs)
Martin Luther
John Calvin
Thomas Hobbes (HAHBZ)
John Locke
Charles de Montesquieu
(MAHN•tuhs•KYOO)

Locating Places
Greece
Rome

Content Vocabulary
rule of law
covenant (KUH•vuh•nuhnt)
theology (thee•AH•luh•jee)
Renaissance (REH•nuh•SAHNTS)
scientific method
philosophe (FEE•luh•ZAWF)

Academic Vocabulary
pursue (puhr•SOO)
document (DAH•kyuh•muhnt)
contract
major

Reading Strategy
Organizing Information Re-create the diagram below. List changes in politics, religion, and science mentioned in this section.

	Changes
Politics	
Religion	
Science	

NATIONAL GEOGRAPHIC **Where & When?**

1200 — 1500 — 1800

1215
Magna Carta limits power of English king

1689
English Bill of Rights guarantees basic rights

1748
Montesquieu publishes *Spirit of Laws*

EUROPE CHINA INDIA AFRICA

Europe's Heritage of Ideas

Main Idea **Ancient cultures laid the foundation of many modern ideas.**

Reading Connection Do you chew gum, use an alarm clock to get up for school, or carry an umbrella when it rains? All of these things were originally created by ancient peoples. Read on to see which ideas and inventions originated in ancient cultures.

A European Story

Anton van Leeuwenhoek (LAY•vuhn•hook), a Dutch merchant in the late 1600s, had an unusual hobby that unlocked the door to an unknown world. By carefully grinding very small lenses out of clear glass, van Leeuwenhoek discovered that he could make things look much bigger than they appeared to the naked eye. His most remarkable find was a multitude of tiny microorganisms, which he described as "wretched beasties" with "incredibly thin feet" swimming through a tiny universe.

Leeuwenhoek's microscope captured the imagination of Europeans in the 1600s. His invention was part of the rich heritage of ideas that shaped the course of European history since ancient times. These ideas eventually spread to North America, where they helped shape the English colonies that were arising along the Atlantic seaboard.

The Greeks and Romans

The ancient Greeks developed philosophy, or "love of wisdom," because they believed the human mind could understand everything. Greek philosophy led to the study of history, mathematics, and political science. During the 400s B.C., the idea of democracy developed in Athens, one of **Greece's** powerful city-states. The Athenians had a direct democracy, in which people gathered at mass meetings to decide government matters. Every citizen could vote firsthand on laws and policies.

Rome was the next important ancient European civilization. Early Rome began as a republic, a form of government in which the citizens elect their leaders to office. In a republic, the citizens have power. The idea of a republic later shaped the founding of the U.S. government. Another of Rome's chief gifts was the idea of the **"rule of law."** This means that the law should apply to everyone equally and that all people should be treated the same. This understanding of justice is at the basis of the American legal system today.

Judaism and Christianity

The Jews were a unique group among the peoples who made up Rome's empire. Most religions of the ancient world worshipped many gods, but the Jews gave their allegiance to one God. The Hebrew Bible describes a **covenant** (KUH•vuh•nuhnt), or agreement between the Jews and their God. In the agreement, God promises to protect the Israelites if they follow his laws. The idea of a covenant, or binding agreement, later influenced the American colonists when they set up their societies in North America.

A major Jewish contribution to the West was the Ten Commandments. Jews believed that God revealed the Ten Commandments to a prophet called Moses. These moral principles found in the Hebrew Bible helped shape the moral laws of many nations.

◄ The Torah, the first five books of the Hebrew Bible

The Ten Commandments told people not to steal, murder, or tell lies about others. They told people to avoid jealousy and to honor their parents. Like the Roman laws, the Ten Commandments reflect the idea of the "rule of law," that laws should apply to everyone equally.

About the A.D. 30s, a Jewish teacher named Jesus of Nazareth preached to Jews living in the Roman provinces of Judaea and Galilee. His message of love and forgiveness helped shape the values many people hold today. Reports of Jesus' resurrection, or rising from the dead, led to a new religion called Christianity.

Christianity soon spread to the European part of the Roman Empire. By A.D. 400, Christianity had become Rome's official religion. After the Roman government fell apart, Christianity survived to shape the civilization of the Middle Ages, the period between Rome's fall and the 1500s.

Advance of Learning While Christianity expanded in Europe, the religion of Islam began in the Arabian Peninsula with the preaching of Muhammad. Islam spread throughout the Middle East, North Africa, and Central Asia. Like Jews and Christians, Muslims—the followers of Islam—believe in one God.

During the Middle Ages, Muslim and Jewish scholars in Islamic lands made significant contributions to the culture of Europe. They saved much of the learning of the ancient world. Europeans in the West had lost this knowledge after the western Roman Empire fell.

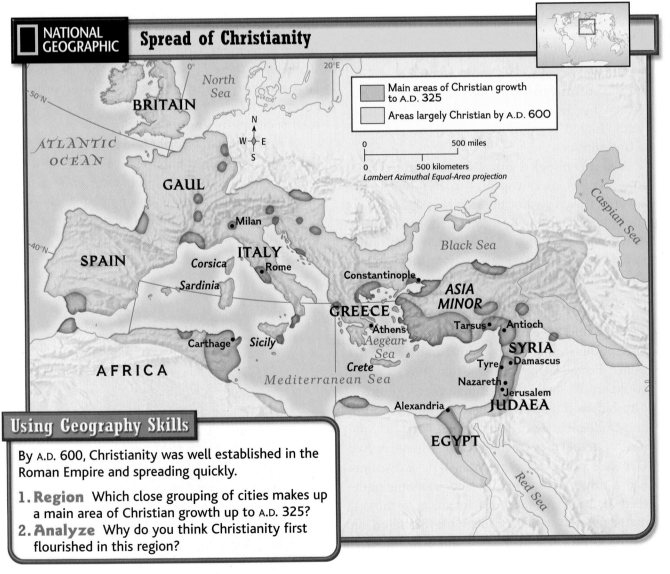

NATIONAL GEOGRAPHIC · **Spread of Christianity**

Main areas of Christian growth to A.D. 325
Areas largely Christian by A.D. 600

0 — 500 miles
0 — 500 kilometers
Lambert Azimuthal Equal-Area projection

Using Geography Skills

By A.D. 600, Christianity was well established in the Roman Empire and spreading quickly.

1. **Region** Which close grouping of cities makes up a main area of Christian growth up to A.D. 325?
2. **Analyze** Why do you think Christianity first flourished in this region?

اران واقی توانند سندو آنار اسیب شغافشرد وبانالخیر وساخن قرتنه آخریه ازعلت کناه اران
کنه شغافی دهدکه معاونت صرف بنند و ری حکیم این مقدمات ازعلم طب تیار نموم من یقی

Picturing **History**

Muslim doctors' discoveries helped develop European medicine. *How did Muslim scholars contribute to the culture of Europe?*

Islamic Influence The Muslims also made many advances in the study of mathematics and medicine, and they introduced the system of Arabic numerals that we use today.

Islamic influences were part of a new wave of learning that shaped Europe during the Middle Ages. Another influence came from universities, which first arose in Europe during the 1100s and 1200s. Universities were self-governing groups of scholars who, in turn, educated and trained new scholars. Because universities enjoyed independence from political and church officials, they could freely investigate knowledge in a wide range of fields, such as theology, law, and medicine.

The first European university appeared in Bologna (boh•LOH•nyah), Italy. A great teacher named Inerius, who taught Roman law, attracted students to Bologna from all over Europe. The first university in northern Europe was the University of Paris. In the late 1100s, a number of students and teachers left Paris and started a university at Oxford, England. Kings, popes, and princes thought it honorable to found new universities. By 1500, there were 80 universities in Europe.

Development of Scholasticism Beginning in the 1100s, a new way of thinking called scholasticism began to change **theology** (thee•AH•luh•jee), or the study of religion and God. Its followers used reason to explore questions of faith.

A Catholic priest named **Thomas Aquinas** (uh•KWY•nuhs) was scholasticism's best-known champion. In the 1200s, Aquinas wrote several works explaining that the Greek philosopher Aristotle would have agreed with many Christian teachings.

What Is Natural Law? Aquinas wrote about government as well as theology, with an emphasis on the idea of natural law. People who believe in natural law think there are some laws that are simply part of human nature. These laws do not have to be made by governments.

Aquinas claimed that natural law gave people certain rights that the government should not take away. These included the right to live, to learn, to worship, and to reproduce. Aquinas's writings on natural law have influenced governments to the present day. Our belief that people have rights can partly be traced to the ideas of Aquinas.

The Latin Language Roman writers influenced later writers in Europe and America, but the language of the Romans, Latin, had a great impact on future generations. Latin became Europe's language for government, trade, and learning until about 1500. Latin became the basis of many modern European languages, including Italian, French, and Spanish.

✓ **Reading Check** **Describe** What was the importance of the Ten Commandments?

New Ideas

Main Idea Religious and philosophical thinkers changed the way people viewed Christianity and the government.

Reading Connection Does your family or someone you know attend a church or other place of worship? Read on to find out how religious sects formed in Christianity.

From the 1400s to the 1700s, Europeans gained new knowledge, explored lands overseas, and spread Christianity. Meanwhile, cultural, religious, and political changes took place in their homeland that would have profound effects on the rest of the world.

The Renaissance
From about 1350 to 1550, a powerful new spirit emerged in the city-states of Italy and spread throughout Europe. The development of banking and the expansion of trade with Asia made Italian merchants wealthy. These citizens were able to **pursue** an interest in the region's past and learn more about the glorious civilizations of ancient Rome and Greece.

Because they wanted to improve their knowledge of people and the world, Italians studied the classical—ancient Greek and Roman—works with new interest. Scholars translated Greek manuscripts on philosophy, poetry, and science. Influenced by the classical texts, a great many authors began to write about the individual and the universe. Artists studied the sculpture and architecture of the classical world. They especially admired the harmony and balance in Greek art, with its realistic way of portraying people.

This period of intellectual and artistic creativity became known as the **Renaissance** (REH•nuh•SAHNTS). A French word meaning "rebirth," it refers to the renewed interest in classical Greek and Roman learning. Over the next two centuries, the Renaissance spread north, south, and west, reaching Spain and northern Europe in the 1400s.

The Rise of Protestantism
Protests against church abuses soon led to a split in western Christianity. In 1517 a German monk named **Martin Luther** criticized the authority of the pope, the leader of the Roman Catholic Church, and many Catholic teachings and practices. Within a few years, Luther had many followers. They broke away from Catholicism to begin their own Christian churches. Martin Luther's protests were the start of a new form of Christianity known as Protestantism.

During the next few years, Luther's religious movement grew. Luther was able to gain the support of many of the German rulers among the numerous states that made up the Holy Roman Empire.

From Germany, Luther's ideas spread rapidly. **John Calvin,** a French religious thinker, also broke away from the Catholic Church. Like Luther, Calvin rejected the idea that good works would ensure a person's salvation. He believed that God had already chosen those who would be saved.

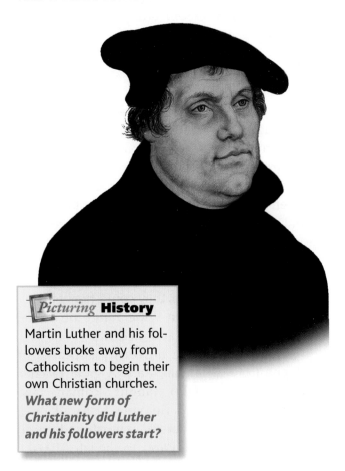

Picturing **History**

Martin Luther and his followers broke away from Catholicism to begin their own Christian churches. *What new form of Christianity did Luther and his followers start?*

To prove they were saved, Calvin's followers worked hard, behaved well, and obeyed the laws of their towns. In this way, Calvin's ideas, which became known as Calvinism, became a powerful tool in society. His ideas encouraged people to work hard at their business and to behave themselves.

Who Were the Puritans?

King Henry VIII replaced the pope as head of the Church in England in 1534. His daughter, Queen Elizabeth I, later made this English, or Anglican, Church Protestant with some Catholic features. Some English Protestants, however, were dissatisfied with Elizabeth's reforms. Known as Puritans, they wanted to "purify" the Anglican Church of its remaining Catholic beliefs and rituals.

Queen Elizabeth I tolerated the Puritans, but when James I became king in 1603, the Puritans faced harder times. James I and the king who came after him, Charles I, persecuted the Puritans. They shut down Puritan churches and jailed Puritan leaders. Many Puritans decided to move to America to practice their religion freely. There they founded colonies that eventually became the American states of Massachusetts, Connecticut, New Hampshire, and Rhode Island.

Royal Power and Citizens' Rights

During the 1600s and 1700s, powerful kings and queens ruled most of Europe. Under a system known as absolutism, monarchs held absolute, or total, power. They claimed to rule by divine right, or by the will of God. This meant that rulers did not answer to their people but to God alone.

During the late 1600s, however, political changes began that steadily limited the power of monarchs. In 1688 the English Parliament took action. It forced out King James and placed his daughter Mary and her husband William on the throne. This change, which showed the power of the elected representatives over the monarch, came to be known as the Glorious Revolution.

William and Mary signed an English Bill of Rights in 1689 guaranteeing certain basic rights to all citizens. This **document** became part of the heritage of English law that the American colonists would share. It later inspired the American political leaders who created the American Bill of Rights.

Hobbes and Locke

During the 1600s, these political changes sparked a great deal of thought and debate about the purpose of government. Two major English thinkers—**Thomas Hobbes** (HAHBZ) and **John Locke**—developed very different ideas about how England's government should work.

In his book, *Leviathan*, Hobbes argued that absolute monarchy was the best form of government. According to Hobbes, humans were naturally selfish and violent. They could not be trusted to make decisions on their own. Left to themselves, people would make life "nasty, brutish, and short." Therefore, Hobbes said, they needed to obey a government that had the power of a leviathan, or sea monster. To Hobbes, that meant the rule of a king, because only a strong ruler could give people direction.

Another English thinker, John Locke, thought differently. He affirmed citizens' rights and stated that government was answerable to the people. In 1690 he explained many of the ideas of the Glorious Revolution in a book called *Two Treatises of Civil Government*. Locke stated that government should be based on natural law. This law, said Locke, gave all people from their birth certain natural rights. Among them were the right to life, the right to liberty, and the right to own property.

Locke believed that the purpose of government was to protect these rights. All governments, he said, were based on a social **contract,** or an agreement between rulers and the people. If a ruler took away people's natural rights, the people had a right to revolt and set up a new government.

Reading Check **Explain** How did religious changes affect the governments of Europe?

Biography

JOHN LOCKE
1632–1704

Born in England, John Locke was a doctor, a philosopher, and a writer. Locke spelled out his political ideas in *Two Treatises of Civil Government,* first published in 1690.

Locke's writings were widely read and discussed in both Europe and America. His ideas deeply influenced the American colonists. Colonial leaders such as Benjamin Franklin, Thomas Jefferson, and James Madison read Locke's writings and discussed his ideas.

Locke and many Enlightenment thinkers believed that God had created an orderly universe governed by established laws. These laws were called natural laws and could be discovered by human reason. By using reason, for example, Sir Isaac Newton, the English physicist, discovered the law of gravity. Natural laws governed not only the physical universe, but also human relations.

The idea that human relations are governed by a set of established laws laid the foundation for the philosophy of natural rights. Locke believed that people in a "state of nature," or a time before the organization of government, had certain basic rights. These included rights to life, liberty, and property.

According to Locke, good government is based on a social contract between the people and the rulers. The people agree to give up some of their freedom and abide by the decisions of their government. In return, the government promises to protect the lives, property, and liberty of the people.

The American colonists accepted Locke's idea that government was legitimate only as long as people continued to consent to it. Both the Declaration of Independence and the Constitution, written nearly a century after Locke lived, reflect Locke's revolutionary ideas.

"All peaceful beginnings of government have been laid in the consent of the people."

—John Locke,
Second Treatise of Civil Government

Then and Now

Compare the political thought of John Locke to the American form of government. What would Locke support? What would he not support?

A New View of the World

Main Idea Science and the influence of reason led to new innovations in political thought.

Reading Connection Does your school have a student council? This is usually a group of students who lobby the administration on behalf of the student body. Read on to find out how citizens' rights played a role in governmental reform.

While religious and political changes came to Europe, many European thinkers began to take a more experimental approach to science. They tested new and old theories and evaluated the results. They also began applying reason and scientific ideas to government. They claimed that there was a natural law, or a law that applied to everyone and could be understood by reason. This law was the key to understanding government.

Triumph of Reason
During the 1500s, European thinkers began to break with old scientific ideas. They increasingly understood that advances in science could come only through mathematics and experimentation. Scientists, such as Nicolaus Copernicus and Galileo Galilei, disagreed with the ancient view that the earth was the center of the universe. Instead, they held to the idea that the sun was the center of the universe and that the planets moved in orbits around the sun.

Sir Isaac Newton further claimed that the physical universe followed natural laws. He believed that the force of gravity held the entire solar system together by keeping the sun and the planets in their orbits.

The Scientific Method
Scientific thought was also influenced by the English thinker Francis Bacon, who lived from 1561 to 1626. Bacon believed that ideas based on tradition should be put aside. He developed the **scientific method,** an orderly way of collecting and analyzing evidence. It is still the process used in scientific research today.

The scientific method is made up of several steps. First, a scientist begins with careful observation of facts and then tries to find a hypothesis, or explanation of the facts. Through experiments, the scientist tests the hypothesis under all possible conditions to see if it is true. Finally, after repeated experiments show that the hypothesis is true, then it is considered a scientific law.

Enlightenment Thinkers
As the Scientific Revolution advanced, many educated Europeans came to believe that reason was a much better guide than faith or tradition. To them, reason was a light that revealed error and showed the way to truth. As a result, the 1700s became known as the Age of Enlightenment.

France was the **major** center of the Enlightenment. As the Enlightenment spread, thinkers in France and elsewhere became known by the French word **philosophe** (FEE•luh•ZAWF), which means "philosopher." Most philosophes were writers, teachers, journalists, and observers of society.

The philosophes wanted to use reason to change society. They attacked superstition, or unreasoned beliefs. They also disagreed with Church leaders who opposed new scientific discoveries. The philosophes believed in the individual's right to liberty. They used their skills as writers to spread their ideas across Europe.

Who Were Voltaire and Diderot?
One of the greatest thinkers of the Enlightenment was François-Marie Arouet, known as Voltaire (vohl•TAR). Voltaire blamed Catholic Church leaders for keeping knowledge from people in order to maintain the Church's power. Voltaire also opposed the government supporting one religion while forbidding others. He thought people should be free to choose their own beliefs.

Denis Diderot was the French philosophe who did the most to spread Enlightenment ideas. He published a 28-volume encyclopedia. His project, which began in the 1750s, took about 20 years to complete.

Guarantees of Rights

The Magna Carta and the English Bill of Rights are two important documents that were integral in forming American political thought. Each contributed an essential building block for the American political principles found in the Declaration of Independence, the Bill of Rights, and the Constitution.

The rights of English citizens, referred to in the Magna Carta, is an important principle of American government. This excerpt from the Magna Carta describes the right to a trial by jury:

"No free man shall be taken, imprisoned, [seized], outlawed, banished, or in any way destroyed, . . . except by the lawful judgment of his peers and by the law of the land."

The English Bill of Rights assured the people of certain basic rights. Among these are:

"That the freedom of speech and debates or proceedings in Parliament ought not to be impeached or questioned in any court or place out of Parliament."

The founding documents of our nation express these freedoms and the principle of limited government—a government on which strict limits are placed, usually by a constitution.

King John signs the Magna Carta. ▶

 Document-Based Question

The idea of limited government is an important principle of American government. Why must government be limited?

The *Encyclopedia* included a wide range of topics, such as science, religion, government, and the arts. It became an important weapon in the philosophes' fight against traditional ways.

Who Was Montesquieu? In 1748 Baron **Charles de Montesquieu** (MAHN•tuhs•KYOO) published a book called *Spirit of Laws*. In this book, Montesquieu said that England's government was the best because it had a separation of powers. Separation of powers means that power should be divided equally among the branches of government: executive, legislative, and judicial.

The legislative branch would make the laws, and the executive branch would enforce them. The judicial branch would interpret the laws and judge when they were broken. By separating these powers, government could not become too powerful and threaten people's rights.

Who Was Rousseau? By the late 1700s, some European thinkers were starting to criticize Enlightenment ideas. One of these thinkers was Jean-Jacques Rousseau (zhahn zhak ru•SOH). Rousseau claimed that supporters of the Enlightenment relied too much on reason. Instead, people should pay more attention to their feelings.

What Is a Social Contract? According to Rousseau, human beings were naturally good, but civilized life corrupted them. He thought people could improve themselves by living simpler lives closer to nature. In 1762 Rousseau published a book called *The Social Contract*. In this work, Rousseau wrote that a workable government should be based on a social contract. This is an agreement in which everyone in a society agrees to be governed by the general will, or what the people as a whole want.

The Magna Carta In the 1600s and 1700s, ideas of political change spread back and forth across the Atlantic Ocean. The pattern started with the arrival of the first English colonists in North America. They carried with them ideas born of the political struggles in England. By the time the first colonists reached North America, the idea of limited government had become an acceptable part of the English system. The Magna Carta of 1215 had limited royal power and protected nobles from unlawful loss of life, liberty, and property. During the next few centuries, these rights were extended to more and more English people.

The English Bill of Rights In 1689 the English Bill of Rights stated that the monarch could not tax people without Parliament's consent. People had a right to a fair and speedy trial by a jury of their peers. People could also petition the king without fear of being punished. The English colonists in North America shared a belief in these rights with the people of England.

Representative Government From England the American colonists also brought the idea of representative government in which people elect delegates to make laws and conduct government affairs for them. Parliament was a representative assembly that had made laws for England since the mid-1200s. In America colonial legislatures grew directly out of this practice of having representatives pass laws.

For political ideas, the colonists also looked to thinkers of the Enlightenment. John Locke's ideas seemed to fit the colonial experience. Although most had probably never heard of Locke himself, the ideas of natural rights and government responsible to the people became the basis of protest and revolt in the colonies. Colonial leaders, such as Benjamin Franklin, Thomas Jefferson, and James Madison, regarded these ideas as political truths. Locke's ideas became so influential that they have been called the "textbook of the American Revolution."

Reading Check **Summarize** What were the ideas of Charles de Montesquieu?

Study Central Need help understanding the Enlightenment? Visit tajww1.glencoe.com and click on Study Central.

Section 3 Review

Reading Summary

Review the Main Ideas

- Rome and Greece became the basis for much political and scientific thought.

- The Renaissance brought about religious and political changes that sought to increase the rights of human beings.

- Political thinkers argued that citizens had religious, political, and social rights.

What Did You Learn?

1. What was the purpose of the English Parliament?

2. What is the Scientific Method?

Critical Thinking

3. **Contrast** How did the ideas of Hobbes and Locke differ?

4. **Identifying** Who were three of the Enlightenment thinkers?

Enlightenment Thinkers

5. **The Big Ideas** How did political, technological, and religious changes affect the formation of the American government? Write a paragraph describing your conclusions.

6. **Persuasive Writing** Imagine you are an English noble in favor of the Magna Carta. Write a letter to the king explaining why he should sign the document.

Analyzing Primary Sources

Cultures in Contact

Before the 1400s, Native Americans had little contact with people from other continents. Improved methods of sea travel and the desire for goods led to the growth of overseas trade in the 1400s and 1500s. During this time, people from Europe came into direct contact with people from the Americas.

Read the passages on pages 108 and 109 and answer the questions that follow.

Columbus lands on San Salvador in October 1492. ▶

Reader's Dictionary

reeds: tall grasses with slim stems that grow in wet areas

bear arms: carry or possess weapons

hawks' bells: small, lightweight bells attached to a trained hawk to help an owner find a lost bird

causeway: a raised road across wet ground or water

Mexico: Tenochtitlán

cues (KYOOS): temples

vein (VAYN): way of thinking

Columbus Crosses the Atlantic

Christopher Columbus left Spain in August 1492 with about 90 sailors on three ships. On October 11 he wrote this in his log:

The crew of the *Pinta* spotted some . . . **reeds** and some other plants; they also saw what looked like a small board or plank. A stick was recovered that looks manmade, perhaps carved with an iron tool . . . but even these few [things] made the crew breathe easier; in fact, the men have even become cheerful.

Other entries in Columbus's log describe the islanders that he met.

They are [a] friendly and well-dispositioned people who **[bear]** no **arms** except for small spears, and they have no iron. I showed one my sword, and through ignorance he grabbed it by the blade and cut himself. . . .

They traded and gave everything they had with good will, but it seems to me that they have very little. . . .

[They] came swimming to our ships and in boats made from one log. They brought us parrots, balls of cotton thread, spears, and many other things, . . . For these items we swapped them little glass beads and **hawks' bells.**

—from *The Log of Christopher Columbus*

Cortés Encounters the Aztec

The soldier and writer Bernal Díaz de Castillo was part of Hernán Cortés's army. These Spaniards fought their way across the Aztec empire to the capital at Tenochtitlán. Castillo wrote the following about what he saw:

And when we saw all those cities and villages built in the water, and other great towns on dry land, and that straight and level **causeway** leading to **Mexico,** we were astounded. These great towns and **cues** and buildings rising from the water, all made of stone, seemed like an enchanted vision. . . . Indeed, some of our soldiers asked whether it was not all a dream. It is not surprising therefore that I should write in this **vein.** It was all so wonderful that I do not know how to describe this first glimpse of things never heard of, seen or dreamed of before. . . .

[In the marketplace], we were astounded at the great number of people and the quantities of merchandise, and at the orderliness and good arrangements that prevailed, for we had never seen such a thing before. . . .

[In the market] they have a building there also in which three judges sit, and there are officials like constables who examine the merchandise. . . .

—from *The Conquest of New Spain*

▲ **Montezuma and Cortés meet after Cortés entered Tenochtitlán.**

DBQ Document-Based Questions

Columbus Crosses the Atlantic

1. What item did the crew take from the sea and examine?
2. How did Columbus's crew react when they saw the objects in the sea?
3. According to Columbus, why did the islander cut himself on the sword?
4. What items did Columbus and his crew exchange with the islanders?

Cortés Encounters the Aztec

5. What surprised Castillo and Cortés's army about the land of the Aztec?

6. Why did some soldiers compare what they saw with a dream?

Read to Write

7. Imagine you are one of the Native Americans who has just met Columbus or Cortés. What do you notice about him? What do you think of him? How do you feel about this meeting? Write a journal entry describing what you observed and how you reacted to this encounter.

Review Content Vocabulary

Write the vocabulary word that completes each sentence. Write a sentence for each word not used.

a. technology   d. entrepreneur

b. Renaissance   e. rule of law

c. Northwest Passage   f. mercantilism

1. The ___ states that all people are equal under the law and should be treated as such.

2. England, France, and the Netherlands hoped to find a ___ to Asia.

3. During the ___, many political and religious changes took place.

4. The theory of ___ stated that a country could become prosperous by mining silver and gold found in other countries.

Review the Main Ideas

Section 1 • Age of Exploration

5. What led to the European era of exploration?

6. What were English, French, and Dutch explorers searching for while charting the coast of North America?

Section 2 • Rise of Modern Capitalism

7. What made trading ventures in different countries so difficult?

8. What were the benefits of establishing overseas colonies?

Section 3 • The Enlightenment

9. What is the rule of law?

10. How did John Calvin contribute to religious changes in Europe?

11. What did Copernicus and Galileo believe about the universe?

Critical Thinking

12. **Describe** What was the Columbian Exchange? How did it change Europe and the Americas?

13. **Determining Cause and Effect** Re-create the diagram below. Identify three reasons for the voyages of exploration and three effects that resulted from the exploration.

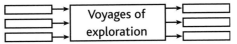

14. **Contrast** How did Judaism differ from most other religions during the Roman era?

Geography Skills

Study the map below and answer the questions that follow.

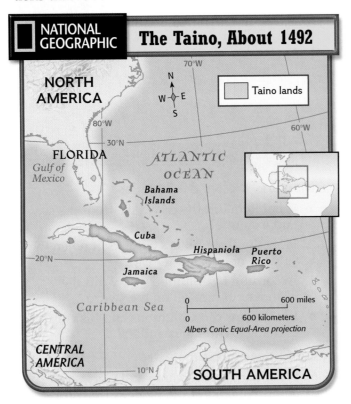

NATIONAL GEOGRAPHIC

The Taino, About 1492

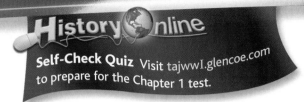

History Online

Self-Check Quiz Visit tajwwI.glencoe.com to prepare for the Chapter 1 test.

15. **Place** What are some of the islands on which the Taino lived?

16. **Location** Between which continents was the Taino homeland located?

17. **Movement** If you traveled from Cuba to Puerto Rico, in what direction would you be going?

Read to Write

18. **The Big Ideas** **Descriptive Writing** Choose an event mentioned in the chapter that had an impact on the Americas. Describe how that event influenced life in the Americas.

19. **Using Your FOLDABLES** Use the information from your completed chapter opener foldable to create a compare-contrast chart of the three countries that were exploring the Americas. Include in the chart their reasons for embarking on explorations, the areas they explored, and the goods and ideas they obtained from the regions.

Using Academic Vocabulary

Read the following sentences and in your own words, write the meaning of the underlined academic vocabulary word.

20. The Magna Carta is an important <u>document</u>.

21. Venice and Genoa became <u>major</u> trading cities.

22. Christopher Columbus hoped that the king and queen of Spain would <u>finance</u> his exploration.

23. Traders wanted to <u>export</u> goods to China and to other areas of the world.

Linking Past and Present

24. **Science Connection** Sir Francis Bacon was the first person to describe the Scientific Method. Describe this method in your own words. Then, describe a modern-day scenario in which scientists are using this method.

Reviewing Skills

25. **READING SKILL** **Previewing** Take a look at the Big Ideas on page 113. Select one and write a paragraph describing the relationship between that idea and something you learned in this chapter.

26. **ANALYSIS SKILL** **Summarize** Describe Montesquieu's theories on government. Contrast these with views held by Thomas Hobbes.

Standardized Test Practice

Read the passage below and answer the following questions.

> The *Legislative cannot transfer the Power of Making Laws* to any other hands. For it being but a delegated Power from the People, they who have it, cannot pass it over to others. The People alone can appoint the Form of the Commonwealth, which is by Constituting the Legislative, and appointing in whose hands that shall be.
>
> —*from* Second Treatise of Civil Government *by John Locke*

27 **According to Locke, what branch of government makes the laws?**

  A judicial

  B executive

  C legislative

  D state governments

28 **Who gives government its power?**

  A the legislature

  B the president

  C the Supreme Court

  D the people

Chapter 2

Road to Independence

◀ The Old North Bridge, Concord, Massachusetts

NATIONAL GEOGRAPHIC

Where&When?

Saratoga
Boston
New York
Philadelphia
Yorktown
Charles Town

1600	1700	1800

1620
Mayflower Compact is signed

1682
William Penn plans colony

1775
Boston Tea Party takes place

1781
Americans gain independence with victory at Yorktown

The Big Ideas

Section 1 — Founding the American Colonies

Geography shapes the physical, economic, and political challenges a region faces. Peoples of various cultures and religions settled the early North American colonies.

Section 2 — Life in Colonial America

Geography shapes the physical, economic, and political challenges a region faces. Although the regions of colonial America differed, an American identity was growing.

Section 3 — Trouble in the Colonies

Political ideas and major events shape how people form governments. British policies came into conflict with American ideas about self-government.

Section 4 — War of Independence

Political ideas and major events shape how people form governments. The United States declared independence in 1776, but it took several years of war and turmoil to earn recognition as a new nation.

 View the Chapter 2 video in the Glencoe Video Program.

FOLDABLES™
Study Organizer

Cause and Effect Make this foldable to show the causes and effects of the events that led the Americans to declare independence from Great Britain.

Step 1 Fold one sheet of paper in half from side to side.

Fold the sheet vertically.

Step 2 Fold again, 1 inch from the top. (Tip: The middle knuckle of your index finger is about 1 inch long.)

Step 3 Open and label as shown.

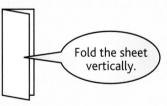
British Actions | Colonial Reactions

Draw lines along the fold lines.

Reading and Writing As you read this chapter, fill in the causes (British actions) and effects (Colonial reactions) in the correct columns of your foldable.

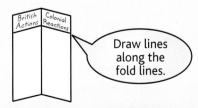

Chapter 2

Get Ready to Read

Identifying the Main Idea

READING SKILL

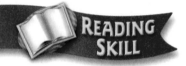

1 Learn It!

Main ideas are the most important ideas in a paragraph, section, or chapter. Supporting details are facts or examples that explain the main idea. Historical details, such as names, dates, and events, are easier to remember when they are connected to a main idea. Understanding the main idea allows you to grasp the whole picture or story. Read the excerpt below and notice how the author explains the main idea.

Main Idea

Supporting Details

The Spanish, however, did not ignore the lands north of Mexico and the Caribbean. During the 1600s, they built settlements and forts along the northern edge of their American empire. These settlements, such as St. Augustine in Florida and Santa Fe in New Mexico, were intended to keep other Europeans out of Spanish territory. Spanish missionary-priests, such as Junípero Serra (hoo • NEE • puh • ROH SEHR • UH) **and Eusebio Kino** (yoo • SEE • bee • oh), **also headed north. They set up missions, or religious communities, to teach Christianity and European ways to the Native Americans. Missions were set up in New Mexico, Texas, California, and other areas of North America.**

—from page 117

Reading Tip

The main idea is often the first sentence in a paragraph but not always.

2 Practice It!

Read the following paragraph. Draw a graphic organizer like the one below to show the main idea and supporting details.

Read to Write·······

Use the main idea that appears under one of the headings in Section 1 of this chapter as the first sentence in a paragraph. As you read, complete the paragraph with supporting details.

> The Great Awakening is the name for the powerful religious revival that swept through the colonies beginning in the 1730s. Christian ministers such as George Whitefield and Jonathan Edwards preached throughout the colonies, drawing huge crowds. The Great Awakening had a lasting effect on the way in which the colonists viewed themselves, their relationships with one another, and their faith.
>
> —*from page 128*

Main Idea

▲ Massachusetts preacher and philosopher Jonathan Edwards

3 Apply It!

Pick a paragraph from another section of this chapter and diagram the main idea as you did above.

Founding the American Colonies

Guide to Reading

Looking Back, Looking Ahead
You learned that Europeans explored and began to colonize the Americas in the 1400s and 1500s. In North America, early English colonies faced hardships, but in time they began to flourish.

Focusing on the Main Ideas
- Spain, France, and the Netherlands founded colonies in North America. **(page 117)**
- The first permanent English settlement in North America was at Jamestown. **(page 119)**
- The English established 13 colonies along the east coast of North America. **(page 120)**

Locating Places
New England Colonies
Middle Colonies
Southern Colonies

Meeting People
Samuel de Champlain (sham•PLAYN)
Roger Williams
William Penn

Content Vocabulary
charter
burgess (BUHR•juhs)
Mayflower Compact
constitution (KAHN•stuh•TOO•shuhn)
toleration (TAH•luh•RAY•shuhn)
dissenter (dih•SEHN•tuhr)
persecute (PUHR•sih•KYOOT)
diversity (duh•VUHR•suh•TEE)
debtor (DEH•tuhr)

Academic Vocabulary
survive (suhr•VYV)
grant
military (MIH•luh•TEHR•ee)

Reading Strategy
Classifying Information Create a diagram like the one below with a row for each colony studied in the section. Fill in the names of the colonies and details on why or how the colony was settled.

Colony	Reasons the colony was settled

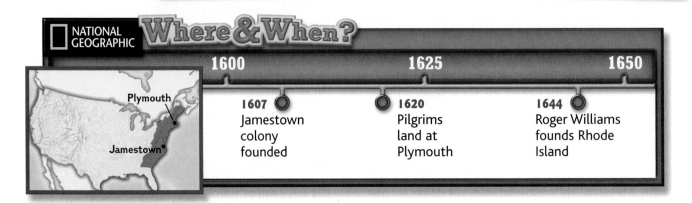

NATIONAL GEOGRAPHIC Where & When?

Plymouth
Jamestown

1600	1625	1650

1607 Jamestown colony founded

1620 Pilgrims land at Plymouth

1644 Roger Williams founds Rhode Island

Settlements in America

Main Idea Spain, France, and the Netherlands founded colonies in North America.

Reading Connection How far would you travel to create a new home? What would it be like if you did not know what to expect? How would you plan for it? Read to learn about Europeans who created settlements in North America.

In Chapter 1, you learned that Spain and Portugal built colonies in the Americas during the 1500s. Beginning in the 1600s, France, England, and other European countries began setting up their own colonies in the Americas. Most Spanish colonies were in the Caribbean, Mexico, and Central America, and most French and English colonies were in North America.

The Spanish, however, did not ignore the lands north of Mexico and the Caribbean. During the 1600s, they built settlements and forts along the northern edge of their American empire. These settlements, such as St. Augustine in Florida and Santa Fe in New Mexico, were intended to keep other Europeans out of Spanish territory. Spanish missionary-priests, such as Junípero Serra (hoo•NEE•puh•ROH SEHR•UH) and Eusebio Kino (yoo•SEE•bee•oh), also headed north. They set up missions, or religious communities, to teach Christianity and European ways to the Native Americans. Missions were set up in New Mexico, Texas, California, and other areas of North America.

France's Fur-Trading Empire The French came to North America to make money from fur trading. By the 1600s, beaver fur had become popular in Europe. In 1608 the French explorer **Samuel de Champlain** (sham•PLAYN) set up a trading post named Quebec (kih•BEHK) in what is now Canada. Quebec became the capital of the colony of New France.

From Quebec, French fur trappers, explorers, and missionaries moved into other parts of North America. In 1673 the explorers Louis Joliet and Jacques Marquette discovered the Mississippi River. Then, in 1682, a French explorer named René-Robert Cavalier, Sieur de La Salle followed the Mississippi all the way to the Gulf of Mexico. He named the region Louisiana in honor of France's King Louis XIV. The French settlers in southern Louisiana also began bringing in enslaved Africans to grow sugarcane, rice, and tobacco.

The Dutch in North America The Dutch also founded colonies in North America. Although their country, the Netherlands, was small, its large fleet of sailing ships sailed all over the world. In 1621 the Dutch set up a trading colony—New Netherland—centered in the area of the present-day state of New York. New Amsterdam, the capital, was located on the tip of Manhattan Island where the Hudson River enters New York Harbor. Today, it is known as New York City.

Reading Check **Identify** Name several early Spanish settlements in North America.

Picturing **History**

In the 1600s, French fur traders moved into parts of North America. *In what areas did the French settle?*

Biography

JUNÍPERO SERRA
1713–1784

The Spanish settlers who came to North America had two aims. They wanted to claim land and to convert the Native Americans to Catholicism. To achieve these goals, the Spaniards set up fortified religious settlements known as missions.

Born in 1713 on an island off the Spanish Coast, Junípero Serra became a Franciscan priest. Because he wanted to work as a missionary among Native Americans, he left Spain in 1749 to travel to Mexico.

At the age of 55, he was sent to take control of Upper California. He established a mission in San Diego in 1769 and later founded eight other missions. By 1820 there were 21 missions stretching up the California coast to San Francisco. Taking as his motto "Always to go forward and never to turn back," Junípero Serra traveled by foot from mission to mission. Despite his crippled leg, Father Serra visited each of his missions regularly.

Father Serra's missions usually were built a day's march from each other. Travelers always had a place to rest after a long day's journey. This also made it easier to trade and sell their food and crafts. The missionaries also built the missions near the coast so that ships could get fresh supplies before heading out to sea.

Each mission was unique in a few ways, but they all had the same basic plan: a large, four-sided building with a central courtyard. The mission was a bustling world of workshops, storage areas, gardens, and living quarters. Father Serra believed that the Native Americans should "have their own lands and crops so that poverty will not make them [leave the mission]." The location of the mission was often determined by the availability of wood, water, and fields for raising crops and grazing the livestock that the Spanish brought to the Americas.

"Always . . . go forward and never . . . turn back."
—Junípero Serra

Then and Now

Research the different groups of Native Americans with whom Father Serra came into contact during his explorations and missionary work. Do any of these groups still exist today?

The Virginia Colony

Main Idea The first permanent English settlement in North America was at Jamestown.

Reading Connection Would you be willing to stay in a community with few jobs and where many of the residents were starving? Read to find out what happened to the people of Jamestown and what discovery saved the town.

In 1587 a group of English colonists financed by Sir Walter Raleigh sailed for North America. There, they founded a colony on Roanoke (RO•uh•nohk) Island off the coast of present-day North Carolina. After six years, however, the colonists disappeared. No one knows for certain what happened to them. For this reason, Roanoke Island became known as the "Lost Colony."

Virginia For a time, the failure of the Roanoke colony discouraged further plans for English colonies in North America. However, in 1606 the idea emerged again. The Virginia Company, an English joint-stock company, received a **charter,** or the right to organize a settlement. With the backing of the company, more than 100 people braved an Atlantic crossing and set up the first permanent English settlement in North America in 1607. The settlers named it Jamestown after King James I. Jamestown was the first town of a new colony called Virginia.

Life in Virginia was very hard. The colonists had come hoping to find gold or silver. Instead, they could barely find enough to eat. Many settlers died from starvation and the cold winters, and others were killed in clashes with Native Americans. The colony **survived** under the leadership of Captain John Smith, a soldier and explorer. Smith forced the settlers to farm and managed to get corn from the Native Americans.

During those first years, the colony made no money for the merchants who had invested in it. It might have collapsed had not one of its settlers, John Rolfe, discovered that tobacco could grow in Virginia's soil. Tobacco became the first

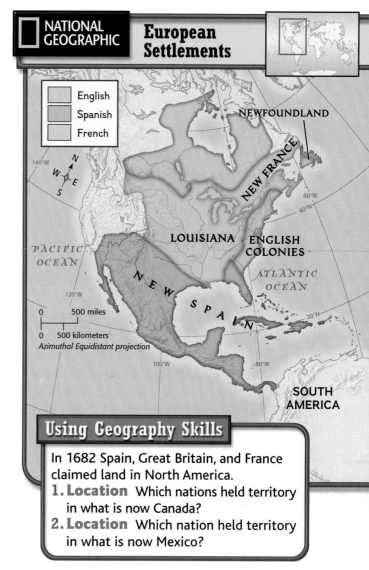

NATIONAL GEOGRAPHIC

European Settlements

English
Spanish
French

NEWFOUNDLAND

NEW FRANCE

PACIFIC OCEAN

LOUISIANA

ENGLISH COLONIES

ATLANTIC OCEAN

NEW SPAIN

0   500 miles
0   500 kilometers
Azimuthal Equidistant projection

SOUTH AMERICA

Using Geography Skills

In 1682 Spain, Great Britain, and France claimed land in North America.
1. **Location** Which nations held territory in what is now Canada?
2. **Location** Which nation held territory in what is now Mexico?

cash crop of the English colonies. A cash crop is grown in large quantities to sell for profit.

Self-Government in Virginia To attract more settlers, the Virginia Company gave the colonists in Virginia the right to elect **burgesses** (BUHR•juhs•ehs), or representatives, from among the men who owned land. The first House of Burgesses met in 1619. It was patterned after the English Parliament and voted on laws for the Virginia Colony. The House of Burgesses set an example for representative government. It was not long before other colonies set up their own legislatures as well.

Reading Check **Identify** Who was John Smith? How did he help the Virginia settlers?

The 13 English Colonies

Main Idea The English established 13 colonies along the east coast of North America.

Reading Connection Would you be willing to move across the ocean to unexplored, possibly dangerous territory to gain certain freedoms or perhaps just to get a new start on life? Read to find out why English settlers came to North America.

Not all English settlers came to North America in search of wealth. Some came to find religious freedom. In Chapter 1, you learned that many Protestants in England were dissatisfied with the Anglican Church. Some, called Puritans, wanted to stay in the Church but rid it of Catholic rituals and practices. Others, known as Separatists, wanted to leave the Church entirely and set up their own local congregations. King James I and his son King Charles I both believed that Puritans and Separatists were a threat to their authority and persecuted them.

The Pilgrims Arrive in New England

In 1620 a group of Separatists called Pilgrims decided to go to America so they could worship freely. They received grants of land from the Virginia Company and sailed for Virginia on the *Mayflower*. Strong winds blew the *Mayflower* off course, causing the Pilgrims to land in New England just north of Cape Cod in present-day Massachusetts. They went ashore on a cold, bleak day in December at a place called Plymouth.

The Mayflower Compact

Plymouth was outside the territory of the Virginia Company and its laws. To provide order, the Pilgrims signed a formal document called the **Mayflower Compact,** which set up a civil government. The signers also promised to obey the laws passed "for the general good of the colony." The Mayflower Compact was an important step in the development of democratic government in America. The people of Plymouth governed themselves for 70 years with almost no outside control. Then in 1691, Plymouth became part of a Puritan colony called Massachusetts.

TECHNOLOGY & History

The *Mayflower*

In September 1620, 102 passengers set off on the *Mayflower* on the journey across the Atlantic. The 2,750-mile trip took more than two months. In early November, the *Mayflower* reached the shores of America.

Massachusetts The success of the Pilgrims encouraged persecuted Puritans to begin leaving England for America. In 1629 a group of Puritans formed a company and received a royal charter to settle an area north of Plymouth. Led by John Winthrop, the Puritans landed in America and founded the colony of Massachusetts and its capital, Boston. John Winthrop made their intentions clear:

> 66 [W]e shall be as a city upon a hill. The eyes of all people are upon us. 99
>
> —from "A Model of Christian Charity"

Others soon followed. By 1643 more than 20,000 Puritans had moved to America.

An elected group ran the colony through a General Court owned by the founding company. When the settlers insisted on having a larger role in the government, the company created a colonial legislature. Every adult male who owned property and was a church member could vote for the governor and for representatives to the General Court.

The Puritans came to America to put their religious beliefs into practice. They made the Protestant Congregationalist faith the colony's official religion. However, they barred members of other faiths from practicing their beliefs. Groups of people who disagreed with the Puritan leaders of Massachusetts were expelled and had to form new colonies in neighboring areas.

Connecticut and Rhode Island In the colony of Connecticut, settlers led by Thomas Hooker in 1639 adopted a plan of government called the Fundamental Orders of Connecticut. This was the first written **constitution** (KAHN•stuh•TOO•shuhn), or formal plan of government, in America. It described the organization of representative government in detail.

Another colony, Rhode Island, was founded by the Puritan minister **Roger Williams.** Williams believed that people should be free to follow their consciences in religious matters. In his view, the church and the government should be completely separate. Williams also believed it was wrong for settlers to take land away from the Native Americans. These ideas caused Massachusetts leaders to banish Williams. In 1644 he set up the Rhode Island colony east of Connecticut. With its policy of religious **toleration** (TAH•luh•RAY•shuhn), the acceptance of different beliefs, Rhode Island became a safe place for **dissenters** (dih•SEHN•tuhrz), or people who disagreed with established views. It was the first place in America where people of all faiths could worship freely.

The Middle Colonies In 1660 England had two clusters of colonies in what is now the United States—**New England Colonies** such as Massachusetts in the north, and agricultural colonies such as Virginia in the south. Between the two groups of English colonies were lands that the Dutch controlled. During the 1660s, these lands came under English rule and were known as the **Middle Colonies.** They included New York, Pennsylvania, New Jersey, and Delaware.

Key

1 Most of the crew slept in the tiny cabins in the **forecastle,** which also served as the ship's kitchen.

2 The *Mayflower* was a supply ship. It was not built to carry passengers. **'Tween decks** are where the passengers of the *Mayflower* slept and kept their belongings.

3 The **main hold** is the main cargo area. It holds most of the ship's stores of food and supplies and tools.

4 The **helmsman** moves a long lever called the **whipstaff** that moves the rudder and steers the ship.

5 The **great cabin** is the quarters for the commander of the ship.

New York The desire for wealth drew the English to the area that was to become the colony of New York. Since the 1620s, this area had been ruled by the Dutch as New Netherland. In 1664 an English fleet took control of the prized port of New Amsterdam, and the Dutch quickly surrendered. England's King Charles II then gave New Netherland to his brother, the Duke of York, who renamed it New York. The port of New Amsterdam, later called New York City, became one of the fastest-growing commercial ports in England's American colonies.

A governor and council appointed by the Duke of York directed New York's affairs. The colonists demanded a representative government like the governments of the other English colonies. The duke resisted the ideas, but the people of New York would not give up. Finally, in 1691 the English government allowed New York to elect a legislature.

Pennsylvania The Quakers, a Protestant group that had been **persecuted** (PUHR•sih•KYOOT•ehd), or treated harshly because of their beliefs or differences, in England, founded the colony of Pennsylvania. In 1680 **William Penn,** a wealthy English Quaker, received the land in payment for a debt King Charles II owed Penn's father. Pennsylvania, or "Penn's Woods," extended inland from the Delaware River and was as large as England.

William Penn saw Pennsylvania as a "holy experiment," a chance to put in practice the Quaker ideals of toleration and equality. In 1682 he sailed to America to supervise the building of Philadelphia, the "city of brotherly love." Penn believed that

> ❝ Any government is free to the people under it . . . where the laws rule, and the people are a party to those laws. ❞
>
> —from the *Frame of Government of Pennsylvania*

Penn believed that the land belonged to the Native Americans and that settlers should pay for it. Penn advertised his new colony, and by 1683 more than 3,000 English, Welsh, Irish, Dutch, and German settlers had arrived. In 1701 in the Charter of Liberties, Penn **granted** the colonists the right to elect representatives to the legislative assembly.

NATIONAL GEOGRAPHIC

Thirteen Colonies

ME.
(Part of
MASS.)

N.H. • Portsmouth

Boston
MASS. • Plymouth
• Providence
N.Y.
Hartford • R.I.
CONN.
New Haven — 40°N

N.J. • New York City
70°W
PA.
• Philadelphia

Baltimore • — DEL.
MD.

VA. • Williamsburg
• Jamestown

ATLANTIC OCEAN

N.C.

Lake Ontario

Lake Erie

APPALACHIAN MOUNTAINS

S.C.
Charles
Town •
GA.
Savannah •

	New England Colonies
	Middle Colonies
	Southern Colonies

0 ——— 200 miles
0 ——— 200 kilometers
Albers Conic Equal-Area Projection
80°W ————— 30°N

N
W ⊕ E
S

Using Geography Skills

By 1732 English settlers had founded 12 colonies on the eastern coast of what is now the United States.

1. **Region** What five colonies made up the Southern Colonies?
2. **Analyze** What geographic feature made Philadelphia and New York centers for trade?

Virginia and the Southern Colonies After early hardships, Virginia prospered from growing tobacco. Wealthy planters held the best land near the coast, so new settlers pushed inland. They increasingly began to settle on land belonging to Native Americans. In 1622 a revolt by a Native American group called the Powhatan Confederation nearly destroyed the colony. Following this revolt, the Virginia Company was accused of mismanaging the colony and lost its charter. In 1624 Virginia became a royal colony, with a governor and council appointed by the king. The House of Burgesses was retained, but its laws now had to receive royal approval. In addition, the Anglican Church was made the official religion of the colony.

Maryland While Virginia struggled and grew, other English colonies were founded in the south. A Catholic noble, George Calvert, who held the title of Lord Baltimore, wanted to set up a safe place for fellow Catholics who faced persecution in England. His dream came true in 1632 when King Charles I gave him a colony north of Virginia. Calvert died before actually receiving the grant. His son Cecilius Calvert, the second Lord Baltimore, took charge of the colony. It was named Maryland after the English queen, Henrietta Maria.

Conflict, however, soon divided Maryland. Protestants as well as Catholics settled in the colony. Soon the Protestants outnumbered the Catholics. To protect Catholics from any attempt to make Maryland a Protestant colony, Lord Baltimore passed a law called the Act of Toleration in 1649. The act granted Protestants and Catholics the right to worship freely. Although the Act initially failed in its goal, it was an early step toward the later acceptance of religious **diversity** (duh•VUHR•suh•TEE), or variety, in the colonies.

The Carolinas In the 1660s, King Charles II issued charters creating a large colony south of Virginia called Carolina. The king gave the colony to a group of eight prominent members of his court. The Carolina proprietors carved out large estates for themselves and provided money to bring colonists over from England.

Picturing **History**

Plantation agriculture became an important part of the economy of the Southern colonies. *Why did Carolina separate and become two colonies?*

Carolina, however, did not develop according to plan. By the early 1700s, Carolina's settlers wanted a greater role in the colony's government. In 1719 the settlers in southern Carolina seized control from its proprietors. In 1729 Carolina became two royal colonies—North and South Carolina.

Georgia Georgia, the last of the English colonies in America to be established, was founded in 1733. A group led by General James Oglethorpe received a charter to create a colony where English **debtors** (DEH•tuhrs)—people who are unable to repay their debts—could make a fresh start. However, most of Georgia's settlers were poor people from the British Isles or religious refugees from Europe's mainland.

The British government had another reason for creating Georgia. This colony could protect the other British colonies from Spanish attack.

Great Britain and Spain had been at war in the early 1700s, and new conflicts over territory in North America were always breaking out. Located between Spanish Florida and South Carolina, Georgia could serve as a **military** barrier against Spain.

Many of the new settlers complained about the limits on the size of landholdings and the law banning slave labor. Oglethorpe reluctantly agreed to lift these bans. Frustrated by the colonists' demands and the colony's slow growth, Oglethorpe turned the colony back over to the king in 1751. By that time, British settlers had been in what is now the eastern United States for almost 150 years. They had lined the Atlantic coast with colonies.

✓ **Reading Check** **Explain** What was Maryland's Act of Toleration, and why was it important?

History Online

Study Central Need help understanding colonial settlements? Visit tajww1.glencoe.com and click on Study Central.

Section 1 Review

Reading Summary

Review the Main Ideas

- A number of European countries, including England, Spain, France, and the Netherlands, founded colonies in North America.

- The English settlers in Jamestown, Virginia, set up a representative government based on what they had known in England.

- The New England, Middle, and Southern Colonies were settled by the English and other Europeans for a variety of reasons, including religious freedom and financial gain.

What Did You Learn?

1. Why did the French originally come to North America?

2. What was the House of Burgesses?

Critical Thinking

3. **Organizing Information** Draw a table like the one below and fill in details about the New England, Middle, and Southern Colonies.

Region	Information
New England	
Middle Colonies	
Southern Colonies	

4. **Analyze** What was the Mayflower Compact and why was it important?

5. **The Big Ideas** What challenges did early English settlers in North America face? Write a short essay that summarizes your conclusions.

6. **Expository Writing** Write a short essay describing the importance of the search for religious freedom in the settling of America. Describe the founding of specific colonies in your essay.

7. **READING** **Identifying the Main Idea** Using the essay you wrote on the importance of religious freedom, summarize the main idea and supporting points from your essay.

Section 2

Life in Colonial America

Guide to Reading

Looking Back, Looking Ahead

You read how the 13 English colonies were founded. Those colonies continued to grow and develop their own culture and beliefs about government.

Focusing on the Main Ideas

- As the population of the colonies grew, agriculture and trade increased. *(page 126)*
- An American culture, influenced by religion and education, began to develop. *(page 128)*
- Although the American colonies developed some self-government, the British still set many laws, especially those concerning trade. *(page 130)*

Locating Places

New York City
Philadelphia

Meeting People

Benjamin Franklin

Content Vocabulary

subsistence farming
triangular trade
cash crop
indentured servant (ihn•DEHN•shuhrd)
overseer
charter colony
proprietary colony
   (pruh•PRY•uh•TERH•ee)
royal colony

Academic Vocabulary

adapt
principle (PRIHN•suh•puhl)

Reading Strategy

Organizing Information Use a chart like the one below to describe the differences in the economies of the New England, Middle, and Southern Colonies.

Economic Development		
New England	Middle Colonies	Southern Colonies

NATIONAL GEOGRAPHIC **Who & When?**

1700 — 1750 — 1800

African drum

1700s Thousands of Africans are brought to America

1730s Great Awakening takes root

c. 1760 New York City's population reaches 25,000

George Whitefield

The Colonies Grow

Main Idea As the population of the colonies grew, agriculture and trade increased.

Reading Connection Is your community or region known for any special product, either agricultural or manufactured? Read to find out how the economies of the New England, Middle, and Southern Colonies differed.

An American Story

In 1760 Englishman Andrew Burnaby traveled throughout the North American colonies, observing American life. He could not imagine that these colonies would ever join in union for they were as different from one another as "fire and water," and each colony was jealous of the other.

Commercial New England

Although Burnaby believed that the colonies would never unite, the colonies continued to grow. Economic success and religious and political freedoms drew a steady flow of new settlers.

Long winters and thin, rocky soil in New England made large-scale farming difficult. Farmers there practiced **subsistence farming,** which means that they generally produced just enough to meet the needs of their families, with little left over to sell or exchange.

Shipbuilding was an important New England industry. The lumber for building ships came from the forests of New England and was transported down rivers to the shipyards in coastal towns.

Colonial Trade

As the center of the shipping trade in America, New England linked the different English American colonies and linked America to other parts of the world. Some ships followed routes that came to be called the **triangular trade** because the routes formed a triangle. On one leg of such a route, ships brought sugar and molasses from the West Indies to the New England Colonies. In New England, the molasses was made into rum. Next, the rum and other manufactured goods were shipped to West Africa where they were traded for enslaved Africans. On the final leg of the route, the enslaved Africans were taken to the West Indies where they were sold to planters. The profit was used to buy more molasses—and the process started over.

Growth of the Middle Colonies

The Middle Colonies enjoyed fertile soil and a slightly milder climate than New England's. Farmers in this region cultivated larger areas of land and produced bigger harvests than did New Englanders. In New York and Pennsylvania, farmers grew large quantities of wheat and other **cash crops**—crops that could be sold easily in markets in the colonies and overseas.

Farmers sent cargoes of wheat and livestock to **New York City** and **Philadelphia** for shipment, and these cities became busy ports. By the 1760s, New York, with 25,000 people, and Philadelphia, with 30,000 people, were the largest cities in the American colonies.

Like the New England Colonies, the Middle Colonies also had industries. Some were home-based crafts such as carpentry and flour making. Others included larger businesses such as lumbering, mining, and small-scale manufacturing.

The Middle Colonies attracted many German, Dutch, Swedish, and other non-English settlers. They gave the Middle Colonies a cultural diversity, or variety, that was not found in New England. With the diversity came tolerance for religious and cultural differences.

Plantation Life in the South

With their rich soil and warm climate, the Southern Colonies were well suited to the growing of cash crops. These included tobacco, rice, and indigo, a blue flowering plant used to dye textiles. Most cash crops were grown on large farms called plantations. At first planters, or plantation owners, used **indentured servants** (ihn•DEHN•shurd) to work in the fields. Indentured servants were laborers who agreed to work without pay for a certain period of time to pay for their passage to America.

When indentured servants became scarce and expensive, Southern farmers used enslaved Africans instead. Independent small farmers grew corn and tobacco on small farms. They usually worked alone or with their families. Independent small farmers outnumbered the large plantation owners. The plantation owners, however, had greater wealth and more influence. They controlled the economic and political life of the region.

Slavery in the Southern Colonies The slave trade and slavery were major parts of colonial economies. The inhumane part of the triangular trade, shipping enslaved Africans to the Americas, was known as the Middle Passage. Olaudah Equiano, a young African forced onto a ship to the Americas, later described the horror of the voyage across the Atlantic:

> 66 We were all put under deck. . . .
> The stench . . . was so intolerably
> loathsome, that it was dangerous
> to remain there for any time. . . .
> The closeness of the place, and the
> heat of the climate, added to the
> number in the ship, which was so
> crowded that each had scarcely
> room to turn himself, almost
> suffocated us. . . . 99
>
> —from *The Interesting Narrative of
> the Life of Olaudah Equiano*

Most enslaved Africans in the southern colonies lived on plantations. Some of the Africans did housework, but most worked in the fields and often suffered great cruelty. The large plantation owners hired **overseers,** or bosses, to keep the slaves working hard. All the Southern Colonies had slave codes, which were strict rules governing the behavior and punishment of enslaved Africans. All white colonists were encouraged to enforce these laws against enslaved Africans.

African Traditions Although the enslaved Africans had strong family ties, their families were often torn apart. Slaveholders could split up families by selling a spouse, a parent, or a child to another slaveholder. Slaves who worked on plantations found a source of strength in their African roots. They developed a culture that drew on the languages, customs, and religions of their West African homelands.

Some enslaved Africans learned trades such as carpentry, blacksmithing, or weaving. Those lucky enough to be able to buy their freedom joined the small population of free African Americans.

Criticism of Slavery Slavery was one reason for the economic success of the Southern Colonies. That success, however, was built on the idea that one human being could own another. Some colonists did not believe in slavery. Many Puritans refused to hold enslaved people. In Pennsylvania, Quakers and Mennonites condemned slavery. Eventually, the debate over slavery would erupt in a bloody war, pitting North against South.

Reading Check Explain Why were the Southern Colonies especially well suited for growing cash crops?

Picturing **History**

Among the early immigrants to America were some who did not come willingly. Western and Central Africans were taken by force from their homes, shipped across the Atlantic Ocean, and sold as slaves in North and South America. *What does the term* Middle Passage *refer to?*

An Emerging Culture

(Main Idea) **An American culture, influenced by religion and education, began to develop.**

Reading Connection What are some things you consider truly American? Perhaps baseball or a summer picnic with hamburgers and hot dogs? Read to find out how the colonists began to form a culture that was different from those European cultures.

Throughout the colonies, people **adapted** their traditions to the new conditions of life in America. Religion, education, and the arts contributed to a new American culture.

The Great Awakening Religion had a strong influence in colonial life. In the 1730s and 1740s, a religious revival called the Great Awakening swept through the colonies. In New England and the Middle Colonies, ministers called for "a new birth," a return to the strong faith of earlier days.

The most important effect of the Great Awakening was greater religious and political freedom in the colonies. More colonists chose their own faith, and the strength of established official churches declined. As a Baptist preacher noted soon after the Great Awakening, "the common people now claim as good a right to judge and act in matters of religion as civil rulers or the learned clergy."

Why It Matters

The Great Awakening

The Great Awakening is the name for the powerful religious revival that swept over the colonies beginning in the 1720s. Christian ministers such as George Whitefield and Jonathan Edwards preached throughout the colonies, drawing huge crowds. The Great Awakening had a lasting effect on the way in which the colonists viewed themselves, their relationships with one another, and their faith.

Causes and Effects of the Great Awakening

Causes

- Jonathan Edwards, George Whitefield, and others preach of the need for a revival of religious belief.
- Awareness of the importance of religion in people's lives grows.
- A religious revival sweeps through America in the mid-1700s.

◄ Jonathan Edwards

The Great Awakening also for the first time united colonists from north to south in a common cause. This paved the way for the rapid spread of political ideas and revolutionary fervor during the struggle for independence.

Education in the Colonies Most colonists valued education. Children were often taught to read and write at home by their parents, even though the daily chores left little time for lessons. In 1647 the Massachusetts Puritans passed a public education law. Each community had to have a teacher whose wages would be paid through taxes. Although some communities did not set up schools, most did. In the Middle Colonies, schooling was not as universal as in New England, but it was widespread. In the Southern Colonies, formal education was generally limited to children of large landowners and professionals such as lawyers and doctors. Even where schools were desired, the widely separated plantations and farms of the South made them impractical. Young children were usually educated by their parents or by tutors.

By modern standards, schools in the American colonies were primitive. Schools had few books, and instruction was given only two or three months a year. Only a small percentage of children received education beyond the primary level. Most girls received little formal education. Despite these shortcomings, few regions of the world had such a high proportion of people who could read or write.

Education was closely related to religion. The first colleges—Harvard, William and Mary, and Yale—were established to train ministers. Six colleges were in operation by 1763; all but two were founded by religious groups primarily for the training of ministers.

By the middle of the 1700s, many educated colonists also were influenced by the Enlightenment. This movement, which began in Europe, spread the idea that knowledge, reason, and science could improve society. The best-known scientist in the colonies was **Benjamin Franklin.** Franklin's greatest services to his fellow Americans would come during the 1770s when he would help guide the colonies to freedom.

The Press in America Schools and colleges spread knowledge. So did books, newspapers, and almanacs. Because paper and type were expensive, most books came from Britain. Newspapers, printed weekly, were mostly four pages in length. Almanacs attracted as many readers as newspapers. In addition to a calendar, dates of holidays, times of sunset and sunrise, almanacs published advice on farming, poems, news of the year, and practical advice.

✓ **Reading Check** **Analyze** What was the Enlightenment, and what effect did it have in the colonies?

Effects

- New religious groups such as the Baptists, Methodists, and Presbyterians take root.
- Emphasis on education grows.
- Belief grows that all people are equal before God.
- Makes Americans more willing to challenge authority prior to the American Revolution.

◀ George Whitefield

Colonial Government

Main Idea **Although the American colonies developed some self-government, the British still set many laws, especially those concerning trade.**

Reading Connection How would you feel if your parents or teachers told you that you could only trade lunch snacks or baseball cards with certain people, even if someone else had a better card or dessert they were willing to trade? Read to find out how the British attempted to maintain control over colonial trade.

In Chapter 1, you learned that the English colonists brought with them ideas about government that had been developing in England for centuries. At the heart of the English system were two **principles**—limited government and representative government. As the colonies grew, they relied more and more on their own governments to make local laws.

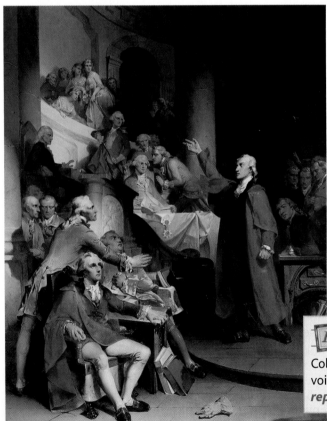

Self-Government in America The 13 colonies began either as charter or proprietary colonies. **Charter colonies,** such as Massachusetts, had a charter, or a grant of rights and privileges, granted by the English monarch to stockholders. **Proprietary colonies** (pruh•PRY•uh•TEHR•ee), such as Pennsylvania, were owned by an individual proprietor or by a small group of proprietors.

Over time, English monarchs began to change colonies into **royal colonies.** Such colonies were under direct English control. In each, Parliament appointed a governor and council, known as the upper house. The colonists selected an assembly, the lower house. The governor and council members usually did what English leaders told them to do. However, this often led to conflicts with the colonists in the assembly, especially when officials tried to enforce tax laws and trade restrictions.

Colonial legislatures gave only some people a voice in government. White men who owned property had the right to vote; however, women, indentured servants, landless poor, and African Americans could not vote. In spite of these limits, a higher proportion of people became involved in government in the colonies than anywhere in the European world. This strong participation gave Americans training that was valuable when the colonies became independent.

British Colonial Policies During the early 1700s, many changes occurred in England and its overseas colonies. In 1707 England united with Scotland and became the United Kingdom. The term *British* came to mean both the English and the Scots. By 1750 Great Britain had become the world's most powerful trading empire.

Picturing **History**

Colonial legislatures gave some Americans a voice in government. *What groups were not represented?*

For many years, Great Britain had allowed the American colonies the freedom to run their local affairs. However, the British government controlled the colonies' trade according to the ideas of mercantilism. The American colonies produced raw materials such as tobacco, rice, indigo, wheat, lumber, fur, deerskin leather, fish, and whale products. These were shipped to Great Britain and traded for manufactured goods such as clothing, furniture, and goods from Asia, including tea and spices.

To control this trade, Britain passed a series of laws called Navigation Acts in the 1650s. Under these laws, the colonists had to sell their raw materials to Britain even if they could get a better price elsewhere. Any goods bought by the colonies from other countries in Europe had to go to England first and be taxed before they could be sent to the Americas. The trade laws also said that all trade goods had to be carried on ships built in Britain or the colonies and that the crews had to be British as well.

Colonial Resistance The colonists at first accepted the trade laws because they were guaranteed a place to sell their raw materials. Later, the colonists came to resent British restrictions. With population in the colonies growing, the colonists wanted to make their own manufactured goods. They also wanted to sell their products elsewhere if they could get higher prices. Many colonial merchants began smuggling, or shipping goods in and out of the country without paying taxes or getting government permission. Controls on trade would later cause conflict between the American colonies and England.

✓ **Reading Check** **Compare** How did charter colonies and proprietary colonies differ?

History Online

Study Central Need help understanding American self-government? Visit tajwwI.glencoe.com and click on Study Central.

Section 2 Review

Reading Summary

Review the Main Ideas

• As the colonies grew, differing economies developed in the New England, Middle, and Southern Colonies.

• In the colonies, family life, education, and religion were important in the emerging American culture.

• Even with British restrictions, especially on trade, the principle of self-government took a strong hold in the colonies.

What Did You Learn?

1. What was the triangular trade?

2. What were some cash crops grown on southern plantations? What crops were grown on smaller independent farms?

Critical Thinking

3. **Compare and Contrast** Draw a chart like the one below. Fill in details comparing farming in the New England and Southern Colonies.

	Similarities	Differences
New England		
Southern Colonies		

4. **Determining Cause and Effect** What effects did the Great Awakening have on the American colonies?

5. **The Big Ideas** How did geography affect the economies of the three colonial regions?

6. **Descriptive Writing** Imagine you live in New England in the mid-1700s and are visiting cousins on a farm in the Carolinas. Write a letter to a friend at home describing your visit to the farm.

Connecting to the Constitution

The Road to Representative Government

Why It Matters Many of the rights that American citizens enjoy today can be traced back to the political and legal traditions of England. When English people began settling here in the 1600s, they brought with them a tradition of limited and representative government.

Limited Government By the time the first colonists reached North America, the idea that government was not all-powerful had become an accepted part of the English system. The concept first appeared in the Magna Carta, or Great Charter, that King John was forced to sign in 1215. The Magna Carta established the principle of limited government, in which the power of the **monarch,** or ruler, was limited, not absolute. This document protected the nobles' privileges and upheld their authority. It also granted certain rights to all landholders—rights that eventually came to apply to all English people.

English Parliamentary Traditions The English people had a firm belief in **representative government,** in which people elect delegates to make laws and conduct government. The English Parliament was a representative assembly with the power to make laws. It consisted of two houses, the House of Lords and the House of Commons. American legislatures grew from the English practice of representation.

In the mid-1600s, Parliament and King James II began a struggle for power. In 1688 Parliament removed King James II from the throne and crowned William and Mary to rule.

"Freedom of religion, freedom of the press, trial by jury, habeas corpus, and a representative legislature . . . I consider as the essentials constituting free government, ..."

—*Thomas Jefferson in a letter to Pierre Samuel Dupont de Nemours, 1815*

◀ **Thomas Jefferson**

▲ **By signing the Mayflower Compact, the Pilgrims established a set of rules under which they would govern themselves.**

appointed by the Virginia Company, a group of merchants from London. In 1619, however, the colonists chose two representatives from each community to meet with the governor and his council. These 22 men were called burgesses. They formed the House of Burgesses, which was the first representative assembly, or legislature, in the English colonies. The House of Burgesses had little power, but it marked the beginning of self-government in colonial America.

The Mayflower Compact In 1620, shortly after the House of Burgesses was formed, a new group of colonists, known as the Pilgrims, arrived in America. Even before their ship, the *Mayflower*, reached America, the Pilgrims realized they needed rules to govern themselves if they were to survive in a new land. They drew up a written plan for their government called the Mayflower Compact.

The Mayflower Compact stated that the government would make "just and equal laws . . . for the general good of the colony." The compact set up a direct democracy in which all men would vote and the majority would rule. (As was common at this time, only adult males were permitted to vote.)

The Mayflower Compact established a tradition of direct democracy. Throughout the colonial period—and in parts of New England today—citizens meet at town meetings to discuss and vote on important issues.

This peaceful transfer of power, known as the Glorious Revolution, changed the idea of government in England. From that time on, no ruler would have more power than the legislature.

The English Bill of Rights To set clear limits to what a ruler could and could not do, Parliament drew up the English Bill of Rights in 1689. The document stated that the monarch could not suspend Parliament's laws; the monarch also could not create special courts, impose taxes, or raise an army without Parliament's consent. The Bill of Rights also declared that members of Parliament would be freely elected and be guaranteed free speech during meetings, that every citizen would have the right to a fair trial by jury in court cases, and that cruel and unusual punishments would be banned.

The English Heritage in America

English settlers in the American colonies established traditions of representative government that they had learned in England. They believed that the ruler was not above the law. They also expected to have a voice in government and other basic rights. Many of the early state constitutions listed the rights of the citizens.

The Virginia House of Burgesses

The first permanent English settlement in North America was Jamestown. At first, the Jamestown colony was managed by a governor and council

Checking for Understanding

1. What is the system of representative government? Where did this system come from?

2. What is important about the Virginia House of Burgesses?

Critical Thinking

3. **Evaluate** The idea of limited government, first established in the Magna Carta, is an important principle of the U.S. Constitution. Do you believe governments should be limited? Why or why not?

Trouble in the Colonies

Guide to Reading

Looking Back, Looking Ahead

In the last section, you read about the beginnings of colonial resistance to British colonial policies. British attempts to tax the colonists brought the Americans and British to conflict.

Focusing on the Main Ideas

- Following Britain's victory in the French and Indian War, the British prohibited colonists from moving west of the Appalachian Mountains and taxed the colonists to pay for the war. *(page 135)*
- British actions, including sending more troops to Boston and passing new taxes, brought strong responses from the colonists. *(page 137)*
- After colonial leaders met to discuss their relations with Britain, the first shots of the American Revolution were fired. *(page 139)*

Meeting People

Crispus Attucks
Samuel Adams
John Adams
Patrick Henry

George Washington
King George III
Paul Revere

Content Vocabulary

import
smuggling
boycott
repeal (rih•PEEL)
resolution
militia (muh•LIH•shuh)
minutemen

Academic Vocabulary

convince
violate (VY•uh•LAYT)
correspond

Reading Strategy

Organizing Information Use a diagram like the one below to describe how the Intolerable Acts affected Massachusetts colonists.

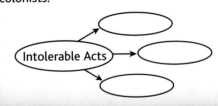

Intolerable Acts

NATIONAL GEOGRAPHIC

Where & When?

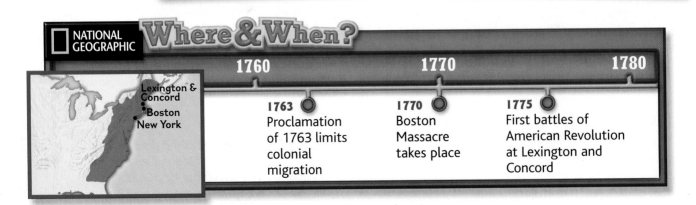

Lexington & Concord
Boston
New York

1760   1770   1780

1763 Proclamation of 1763 limits colonial migration

1770 Boston Massacre takes place

1775 First battles of American Revolution at Lexington and Concord

New British Policies

Main Idea Following Britain's victory in the French and Indian War, the British prohibited colonists from moving west of the Appalachian Mountains and taxed the colonists to pay for the war.

Reading Connection Have you ever stopped buying a product, perhaps because the manufacturer changed the product or raised its price? Read to find out how the American colonists protested British actions, in part by refusing to buy British products.

An American Story

During the colonial period, Britain and France struggled for control of eastern North America. As their settlements moved inland, both nations claimed the vast territory between the Appalachian Mountains and the Mississippi River. In 1758 writer Nathaniel Ames noted,

66 The parts of North America which may be claimed by Great Britain or France are of as much worth as either kingdom. That fertile country to the west of the Appalachian Mountains [is the] 'Garden of the World'! 99

—from the *Astronomical Diary and Almanack,* 1758

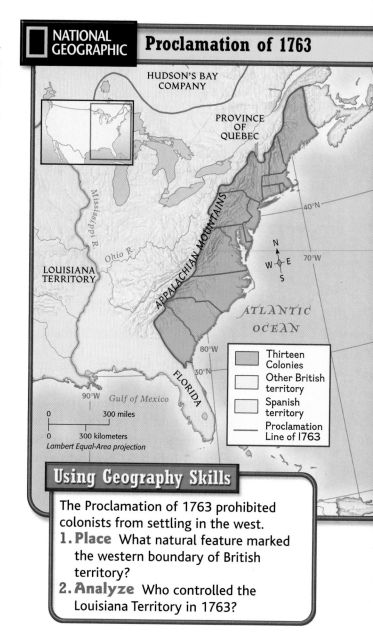

NATIONAL GEOGRAPHIC Proclamation of 1763

Using Geography Skills

The Proclamation of 1763 prohibited colonists from settling in the west.
1. **Place** What natural feature marked the western boundary of British territory?
2. **Analyze** Who controlled the Louisiana Territory in 1763?

The French and Indian War In 1754 British-French rivalry led to the outbreak of the French and Indian War. Colonial leaders met in Albany, New York, to find a way for the colonies to defend themselves against the French. The leaders adopted the Albany Plan of Union, calling for "one general government" for 11 of the American colonies. However, the plan was not approved. After Britain won the war in 1763, the colonies began to act together. Their united action, however, was directed against Britain itself. What developments brought about this unusual turn of events?

The Proclamation of 1763 Victory in 1763 gained for the British nearly all of France's North American empire. That same year, Britain issued a proclamation that prohibited colonists from moving west of the Appalachian Mountains. Stopping western settlement allowed British officials to control settler movement and avoid a conflict with Native Americans. It also prevented colonists from moving away from the coast—where Britain's important markets and investments were. To protect their interests, the British planned to keep 10,000 troops in America.

The Stamp Act required colonists to buy revenue stamps for newspapers, licenses, and documents. ▶

▼ The snake on the banner symbolized united American resistance to the British.

DONT TREAD ON ME

The British Tax the Colonies

Alarmed colonists, however, saw the proclamation as a limit on their freedom of movement. They also feared that the large number of British troops might be used to interfere with their liberties. As a result, feelings of distrust began to grow between Britain and its American colonies.

Britain faced financial problems. The French and Indian War was very costly and left the British government deep in debt. Desperate for money, the British made plans to tax the colonies and tighten trade rules.

In 1764 the British Parliament passed the Sugar Act, which lowered the tax on molasses that had been **imported,** or bought from foreign markets, by the colonists. The British government hoped the lower tax would **convince** the colonists to pay the tax instead of **smuggling.** Smuggling means to trade illegally with other nations. The colonists believed their rights as Englishmen were being **violated.** James Otis, a young lawyer in Boston, argued that:

❝ no parts of [England's colonies] can be taxed without their consent . . . every part has a right to be represented. ❞

—from *The Rights of the British Colonies*

What Was the Stamp Act?

In 1765 Parliament passed another law in an effort to raise money. This law, known as the Stamp Act, placed a tax on newspapers and other printed material. All of these items had to bear a stamp showing that the tax was paid. The colonists were outraged. In October, delegates from nine colonies met in New York at the Stamp Act Congress. They sent a letter to the British government stating that the colonies could not be taxed except by their own assemblies. Colonists refused to use the stamps. They also **boycotted,** or refused to buy, British goods.

In February 1766, Parliament gave in to the colonists' demands and **repealed** (rih•PEELD), or cancelled, the Stamp Act. On the same day, however, it passed the Declaratory Act. This law stated that Parliament had the right to tax and make decisions for the British colonies "in all cases." The colonists might have won one battle, but the war over making decisions for the colonies had just begun.

New Taxes

In 1767 Parliament passed another set of tax laws known as the Townshend Acts. In these acts, the British leaders tried to avoid some of the problems the Stamp Act caused. They understood that the colonists would not tolerate internal taxes—those levied or paid inside the colonies. As a result, the new taxes applied only to imported goods, with the tax being paid at the port of entry. The taxed goods, however, included basic items—such as glass, tea, paper, and lead—that the colonists had to import because they did not produce them.

The Colonists React

By this time, the colonists were outraged by *any* taxes Parliament passed. They believed that only their own representatives had the right to levy taxes on them. The colonists responded by bringing back the boycott that had worked so well against the Stamp Act. The boycott proved to be even more widespread this time.

✓ **Reading Check** **Explain** What was the Proclamation of 1763, and why did it anger American colonists?

Tax Protests Lead to Revolt

Main Idea British actions, including sending more troops to Boston and passing new taxes, brought strong responses from the colonists.

Reading Connection How might you protest a new community or school rule that you believed was unfair? Read to find out how American protests to British measures became forceful.

Colonial protests like those related to the Stamp Act made British colonial officials nervous. Worried customs officers sent word back to Britain that the colonies were close to rebellion. Parliament responded by sending two regiments of troops to Boston. As angry Bostonians jeered, the newly arrived "redcoats" set up camp right in the center of the city.

The Boston Massacre On March 5, 1770, tensions between the redcoats and Bostonians reached a peak. That day a crowd of colonists began insulting soldiers and throwing stones, snowballs, oyster shells, and pieces of wood at the soldiers. "Fire, you bloodybacks, you lobsters," the crowd screamed. "You dare not fire."

After one of the soldiers was knocked down, the nervous and confused soldiers did fire. Seven shots rang out, killing five colonists. Among the dead was **Crispus Attucks,** a dockworker who was part African, part Native American. The colonists called the tragic encounter the Boston Massacre.

The Boston Massacre led many colonists to call for stronger boycotts on British goods. Aware of the growing opposition to its policies, Parliament repealed all the Townshend Acts taxes except the one on tea. Many colonists believed they had won another victory. They started to trade with British merchants again.

Some colonial leaders, however, continued to call for resistance to British rule. In 1772 the Massachusetts radical leader **Samuel Adams** revived the Boston committee of **correspondence,** an organization used in earlier protests. The committee circulated writings about colonists' grievances against Britain.

Picturing **History**

The Bloody Massacre (below) is an engraving by Paul Revere. The site of the Boston Massacre in present-day Boston is pictured to the right. *How did the colonists react to the news of the Boston Massacre?*

Soon other committees of correspondence sprang up throughout the colonies, bringing together protesters opposed to British measures.

Crisis Over Tea By the early 1770s, some Americans considered British colonial policy a "conspiracy against liberty." The British government's actions seemed to confirm that view. In 1773 Parliament passed the Tea Act. It allowed the British East India Company to ship tea to the colonies without paying the taxes colonial tea merchants had to pay. This allowed the company to sell its tea very cheaply and threatened to drive the colonial tea merchants out of business.

In Massachusetts, angry colonists decided to take action. A group of protestors dressed as Native Americans boarded several British ships in Boston Harbor and dumped their cargoes of tea overboard, an event that became known as the Boston Tea Party. Word of this act of defiance spread throughout the colonies. Men and women gathered in the streets to celebrate.

To punish the colonists, Parliament in 1774 passed the Coercive Acts, which closed down Boston Harbor and put the government of Massachusetts under military rule. The laws also said that British troops should be quartered, or given a place to live in colonists' homes. The colonists called these the Intolerable Acts, or laws they could not bear. They maintained that the Coercive Acts violated their rights as English citizens.

✓ **Reading Check** **Analyze** Why were American colonists especially angry with the Tea Act?

MORE ABOUT...

The Boston Tea Party

The Boston Tea Party is one of the significant events that ultimately led to American independence.

By 1770, most of the Townshend Acts have been repealed. The tax on tea remains.

In November 1773, the citizens of Boston refuse to allow three British ships to unload 342 chests of tea.

On the evening of December 16, Boston citizens disguised as Native Americans board the ships and empty the tea into Boston Harbor.

King George III and Parliament respond by closing the city port.

"Fellow countrymen, we cannot afford to give a single inch! If we retreat now, everything we have done becomes useless!"

— *Samuel Adams, December 1773*

TEA THROWN INTO BOSTON HARBOR DEC 16 1773.

A Call to Arms

Main Idea After colonial leaders met to discuss their relations with Britain, the first shots of the American Revolution were fired.

Reading Connection Have you ever served on a student council or another youth group? If so, did that group work together for the benefit of all members? Read to find out how Americans from nearly every colony came together to discuss the colonies' disagreements with Britain.

Colonial leaders realized the colonies had to act together in their opposition to British policies. In September 1774, fifty-six men arrived in the city of Philadelphia. Sent as delegates from all the colonies except Georgia, these men had come to establish a political body to represent American interests and challenge British control. They called the new organization the Continental Congress.

Leaders from all the colonies attended the Continental Congress. Massachusetts sent Samuel Adams and his younger cousin **John Adams,** a successful lawyer. New York sent John Jay, another lawyer. From Virginia came Richard Henry Lee and **Patrick Henry,** two of the most outspoken defenders of colonial rights, as well as **George Washington.** Patrick Henry summarized the meaning of the gathering: "The distinctions between Virginians, Pennsylvanians, New Yorkers, and New Englanders are no more.... I am not a Virginian, but an American."

The delegates were hardly united in their views, but they realized they needed to work together. First they drafted a statement of grievances calling for the repeal of 13 acts of Parliament passed since 1763. They declared that these laws violated the colonists' rights.

The delegates also voted to boycott all British goods and trade. No British products could be brought into or consumed in the colonies, and no colonial goods could be shipped to Britain. The Continental Congress's most important **resolution,** or formal expression

of an opinion, concerned the armed forces. After much debate the delegates decided to form militias. A **militia** (muh•LIH•shuh) is a group of citizen soldiers. If fighting broke out, the colonies would be ready with their own armed forces.

Primary Sources

The Coming Conflict

▲ Teapot, c.1770

The American people hoped that the boycott called for by the Continental Congress against British goods and trade would win a quick victory without war. Some members of the Continental Congress believed that economic pressure would force Britain to back down. Richard Henry Lee of Virginia noted that the British "army and fleet will be recalled, and Britain will give up her foolish project."

Other members of the Continental Congress doubted that Great Britain would back down.

In a paper titled "Broken Hints," Joseph Hawley of Massachusetts wrote:

"We must fight, if we cannot otherwise rid ourselves of British taxation, all revenues, or the constitution or form of government enacted for us by the British Parliament....

Fight we must, finally, unless Britain retreats."

DBQ Document-Based Question

According to Lee, how will Great Britain react? Do Lee or Hawley believe that war is certain to come? Explain your reasoning.

Preparing for Battle People in the colonies and in Britain wondered whether this meant war. The answer came soon after the Continental Congress adjourned in October.

Colonists expected that if fighting against the British broke out, it would begin in New England. Militia companies in Massachusetts held frequent training sessions, made bullets, and stockpiled rifles and muskets. Some companies, known as **minutemen,** boasted that they would be ready to fight on a minute's notice.

The British also prepared for conflict. **King George III** announced to Parliament that the New England colonies were "in a state of rebellion." By April 1775, British general Sir Thomas Gage had 3,000 soldiers under his command in and around Boston. Gage had instructions to take away the weapons of the Massachusetts militia and arrest the leaders.

Gage learned that the militia was storing arms and ammunition at Concord, a town 20 miles northwest of Boston. He ordered 700 troops to Concord to seize artillery.

Alerting the Colonists On the night of April 18, 1775, the colonists **Paul Revere** and William Dawes rode to Lexington, a town east of Concord, to warn that the British were coming. Revere galloped off across the moonlit countryside, shouting, "The regulars are out!" to the people and houses he passed along the way. When he reached Lexington, he raced to tell Sam Adams and John Hancock his news. Adams could barely control his excitement. "What a glorious morning this is!" Adams was ready to fight for American independence.

Fighting at Lexington and Concord At dawn the redcoats approached Lexington. When they reached the center of the town they discovered a group of about 70 minutemen who had been alerted by Revere and Dawes.

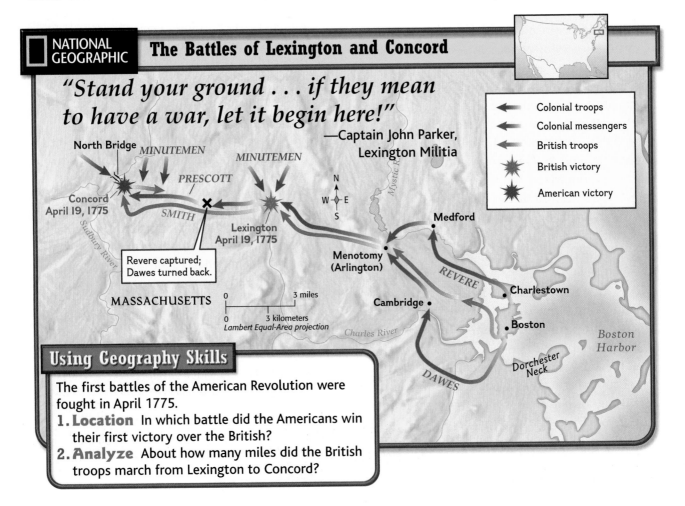

NATIONAL GEOGRAPHIC

The Battles of Lexington and Concord

"Stand your ground . . . if they mean to have a war, let it begin here!"
—Captain John Parker, Lexington Militia

North Bridge   MINUTEMEN   MINUTEMEN
PRESCOTT
Concord
April 19, 1775   SMITH
Revere captured;
Dawes turned back.   Lexington
April 19, 1775

MASSACHUSETTS

Sudbury River

0   3 miles
0   3 kilometers
Lambert Equal-Area projection

Charles River

Medford
Menotomy
(Arlington)   REVERE
Cambridge   Charlestown
Boston
DAWES   Dorchester
Neck
Mystic R.
Boston
Harbor

Legend:
- Colonial troops
- Colonial messengers
- British troops
- British victory
- American victory

Using Geography Skills

The first battles of the American Revolution were fought in April 1775.

1. **Location** In which battle did the Americans win their first victory over the British?
2. **Analyze** About how many miles did the British troops march from Lexington to Concord?

Led by Captain John Parker, the minutemen had positioned themselves on the town common with muskets in hand.

A shot was fired, and then both sides let loose with an exchange of bullets. When the fighting was over, eight minutemen lay dead. The first shots had been fired. But who had fired them? According to one of the minutemen at Lexington, British Major John Pitcairn had given the order to fire. British officers and soldiers told a different story. They claimed that the minutemen had fired first.

The British troops continued their march to Concord. When they arrived there, they discovered that most of the militia's gunpowder had already been removed. They destroyed the remaining supplies. At Concord's North Bridge, the minutemen were waiting for them.

Messengers on horseback had spread word of the British movements. All along the road from Concord to Boston, farmers, blacksmiths, saddle makers, and clerks hid behind trees, rocks, and stone fences. As the British marched down the road, the militia fired. By the time the redcoats reached Boston, more than 200 were wounded and 73 were dead. Making matters worse for the British, more than 20,000 militiamen now held Boston under siege.

The Coming Revolution After the bloodshed in Massachusettes, colonial leaders appealed for separation from Great Britain. Many colonists were not ready for independence. As you will see, events during the winter of 1775–1776, however, moved the colonists ever closer to the fight for independence.

Looking back, the poet Ralph Waldo Emerson wrote in "The Concord Hymn" that the Americans at Lexington and Concord had fired the "shot heard 'round the world." The battle for America's independence from Great Britain had begun.

✓ **Reading Check** **Identify** What is a militia?

Study Central Need help understanding the road to war? Visit tajwwI.glencoe.com and click on Study Central.

Section 3 Review

Reading Summary

Review the Main Ideas

- American colonists protested restrictive tax laws enacted by the British to help pay for the French and Indian War, such as the Sugar Act and the Stamp Act.

- Events such as the Boston Massacre and the Boston Tea Party demonstrated the growing level of conflict between the British and the Americans.

- Fighting broke out between colonial militia and British troops at Lexington and Concord in Massachusetts in 1775.

What Did You Learn?

1. Why did the British issue the Proclamation of 1763?

2. How did the British punish the colonists for the Boston Tea Party?

Critical Thinking

3. **Sequencing Information** Re-create the diagram below. Fill in important events with their dates beginning with the Boston Massacre and ending with the fighting at Lexington and Concord.

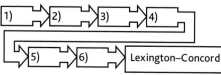

4. **Drawing Conclusions** Do you think the Boston Tea Party was a turning point in the relationship between the British and the colonists? Explain.

5. **The Big Ideas** What political ideas led to the formation of the Continental Congress?

6. **ANALYSIS** **Economics and History** How did laws passed by the British Parliament after 1763 affect American trade and industry? How did the British intend to help their economy through these laws?

PAUL REVERE'S RIDE

By Henry Wadsworth Longfellow

Before You Read

The Scene: A group of friends is gathered around a fire at the Wayside Inn near Boston. Each person in turn tells a story in verse.

The Characters: The landlord is the first storyteller. The patriot Paul Revere is the topic of the landlord's poem.

The Plot: Paul Revere is waiting for a signal. It will be one or two lanterns in the belfry, or bell tower, of the Old North Church in Boston. When Revere sees the signal, he sets off to warn the Patriots. The British troops are on the way to seize the Patriots' guns and gunpowder.

Vocabulary Preview

dread: fear because of evil that is about to occur

gilded: covered with a thin layer of gold

impetuous: acting suddenly without thought

somber: shaded as to be dark and gloomy

stealthy: slow and careful

tranquil: calm

Have you ever wondered what actually happened during an important historical event? In this poem, the landlord at the Wayside Inn is describing what he thinks Paul Revere's ride to Lexington and Concord was like.

◀ *Paul Revere* by John Singleton Copley

As You Read

Longfellow vividly describes the places in the poem—Boston Harbor, the Old North Church, and the towns—that Revere visits on his ride. These descriptions give the poem a special tone, or feeling. Think about what it might have been like to be a Patriot in Massachusetts at the time of Revere's ride. What do you think it may have been like to make that ride? What kind of person could do such a dangerous thing?

Listen, my children, and you shall hear
Of the midnight ride of Paul Revere,
On the eighteenth of April, in Seventy-five;
Hardly a man is now alive
Who remembers that famous day and year.

He said to his friend, "If the British march
By land or sea from the town to-night,
Hang a lantern aloft in the belfry arch
Of the North Church tower as a signal light,—
One, if by land, and two, if by sea;
And I on the opposite shore will be,
Ready to ride and spread the alarm
Through every Middlesex[1] village and farm,
For the country folk to be up and to arm."

Then he said, "Good night!" and with muffled[2] oar
Silently rowed to the Charlestown shore,
Just as the moon rose over the bay,
Where swinging wide at her moorings[3] lay
The Somerset, British man-of-war;[4]
A phantom ship, with each mast and spar[5]
Across the moon like a prison bar,
And a huge black hulk, that was magnified
By its own reflection in the tide.

---

[1] **Middlesex:** Massachusetts county
[2] **muffled:** wrapped with something to dull the sound
[3] **moorings:** lines or chains holding a ship in place
[4] **man-of-war:** warship
[5] **spar:** strong piece of wood used to support sails

Meanwhile, his friend, through alley and street,
Wanders and watches with eager ears,
Till in the silence around him he hears
The muster[6] of men at the barrack[7] door,
The sound of arms, and the tramp of feet,
And the measured tread of the grenadiers,[8]
Marching down to their boats on the shore.

Then he climbed the tower of the Old North Church,
By the wooden stairs, with stealthy tread,
To the belfry-chamber overhead,
And startled the pigeons from their perch
On the sombre rafters, that round him made
Masses and moving shapes of shade,—
By the trembling ladder, steep and tall,
To the highest window in the wall,
Where he paused to listen and look down
A moment on the roofs of the town,
And the moonlight flowing over all.

---

[6] **muster:** an assembling group (of soldiers)
[7] **barrack:** building in which soldiers live
[8] **grenadiers:** soldiers

Beneath, in the churchyard, lay the dead,
In their night-encampment[9] on the hill,
Wrapped in silence so deep and still
That he could hear, like a sentinel's[10] tread,
The watchful night-wind, as it went
Creeping along from tent to tent,
And seeming to whisper, "All is well!"
A moment only he feels the spell
Of the place and the hour, and the secret dread
Of the lonely belfry and the dead;
For suddenly all his thoughts are bent
On a shadowy something far away,
Where the river widens to meet the bay,—
A line of black that bends and floats
On the rising tide, like a bridge of boats.

---

[9] **encampment:** place where a group
is camped
[10] **sentinel:** guard

Meanwhile, impatient to mount and ride,
Booted and spurred, with a heavy stride
On the opposite shore walked Paul Revere.
Now he patted his horse's side,
Now gazed at the landscape far and near,
Then, impetuous, stamped the earth,
And turned and tightened his saddle-girth,[11]
But mostly he watched with eager search
The belfry-tower of the Old North Church,
As it rose above the graves on the hill,
Lonely and spectral[12] and sombre and still.
And lo! as he looks, on the belfry's height
A glimmer, and then a gleam of light!
He springs to the saddle, the bridle he turns,
But lingers and gazes, till full on his sight
A second lamp in the belfry burns!

A hurry of hoofs in a village street,
A shape in the moonlight, a bulk in the dark,
And beneath, from the pebbles, in passing, a spark
Struck out by a steed[13] flying fearless and fleet;
That was all! And yet, through the gloom and the light,
The fate of a nation was riding that night;
And the spark struck out by that steed, in his flight,
Kindled the land into flame with its heat.

He has left the village and mounted the steep,
And beneath him, tranquil and broad and deep,
Is the Mystic,[14] meeting the ocean tides;
And under the alders[15] that skirt its edge,
Now soft on the sand, now loud on the ledge,
Is heard the tramp of his steed as he rides.

---

[11] **girth:** strap that goes around the body
of an animal
[12] **spectral:** ghostly
[13] **steed:** horse
[14] **Mystic:** river that flows into Boston Harbor
[15] **alders:** type of tree

It was twelve by the village clock,
When he crossed the bridge into Medford town.
He heard the crowing of the cock,
And the barking of the farmer's dog,
And felt the damp of the river fog,
That rises after the sun goes down.

It was one by the village clock,
When he galloped into Lexington.
He saw the gilded weathercock[16]
Swim in the moonlight as he passed,
And the meeting-house windows, blank and bare,
Gaze at him with a spectral glare,
As if they already stood aghast[17]
At the bloody work they would look upon.

---

[16] **weathercock:** a movable device in the shape of
a rooster that shows the direction of the wind
[17] **aghast:** shocked

It was two by the village clock,
When he came to the bridge in Concord town.
He heard the bleating of the flock,
And the twitter of birds among the trees,
And felt the breath of the morning breeze
Blowing over the meadows brown.
And one was safe and asleep in his bed
Who at the bridge would be first to fall,
Who that day would be lying dead,
Pierced by a British musket-ball.[18]

---

[18] **musket-ball:** bullet from a gun

You know the rest. In the books you have read,
How the British Regulars fired and fled,—
How the farmers gave them ball for ball,
From behind each fence and farm-yard wall,
Chasing the red-coats down the lane,
Then crossing the fields to emerge again
Under the trees at the turn of the road,
And only pausing to fire and load.

So through the night rode Paul Revere;
And so through the night went his cry of alarm
To every Middlesex village and farm,—
A cry of defiance and not of fear,
A voice in the darkness, a knock at the door,
And a word that shall echo forevermore!
For, borne on the night-wind of the Past,
Through all our history, to the last,
In the hour of darkness and peril and need,
The people will waken and listen to hear
The hurrying hoof-beats of that steed,
And the midnight message of Paul Revere.

Responding to the Literature

1. According to the speaker in the first stanza, did Revere's ride happen recently or a long time ago? What shows when it took place?

2. What did it mean if Revere saw one lantern in the belfry? What did it mean if he saw two?

3. **Analyze** How did Longfellow use repetition in the poem? Why did he use it?

4. **Explain** What is the meaning of the following lines?

   That he could hear, like a sentinel's tread,
   The watchful night-wind, as it went
   Creeping along from tent to tent,
   And seeming to whisper, "All is well!"

5. **Read to Write** What kind of person do you think Paul Revere was? What actions in the poem show these characteristics?

Reading On Your Own...

Do you want to learn more about the Age of Exploration and life in the American colonies? You might be interested in the following books.

Nonfiction

From Coronado to Escalante: The Explorers of the Spanish Southwest by John M. Morris describes two kinds of searches. Coronado's is for gold and Escalante's is for converts to Catholicism. As readers follow these men, they see the land and Native Americans as the Spanish saw them.

Historical Fiction

I, Juan de Pareja by Elizabeth Barton de Treviño tells the tale of the African slave Juan and his famous master, the Spanish painter Velasquez. This story describes how Juan becomes an accomplished artist in spite of the laws against slaves learning how to paint.

Historical Fiction

Maggie's Choice by Norma Jean Lutz takes place during the Great Awakening. When a slave girl dies, Maggie must choose between her conscience, which is supported by the teachings of Jonathan Edwards, and her wealthy friends' way of life.

Biography

John Peter Zenger by Karen T. Westermann describes Zenger and what happened as the result of his dangerous decision to criticize the colonial government in his newspaper. Zenger's trial was one of the reasons freedom of the press was included in the Bill of Rights.

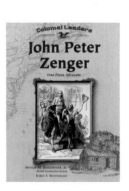

Section 4

War of Independence

Guide to Reading

Looking Back, Looking Ahead
You learned that American colonists and British troops fired the first shots of the Revolutionary War at Lexington and Concord. It took many battles, fought throughout the colonies, and many casualties before the Americans won their independence.

Focusing on the Main Ideas

- As colonial forces and British troops continued to fight, colonial leaders met again to plan their resistance to Britain. *(page 150)*
- The Declaration of Independence used traditional English political rights to call for independence for the colonies. *(page 152)*
- America's victory and independence led to revolutions in other parts of the world. *(page 153)*

Meeting People
Thomas Paine
Bernardo de Gálvez
Marquis de Lafayette (LAH•fee•EHT)
John Paul Jones

Content Vocabulary
petition (puh•TIH•shuhn)
preamble (PREE•AM•buhl)
Patriots
neutral (NOO•truhl)
Loyalists
guerrilla warfare (guh•RIH•luh)

Academic Vocabulary
challenge
secure (sih•KYUR)
technique (tehk•NEEK)
occupy (AH•kyuh•PY)

Reading Strategy
Organizing Information Draw a diagram like the one below. Use it to list the reasons why the Americans were able to defeat the British in the Revolutionary War.

Reasons for the British defeat

NATIONAL GEOGRAPHIC Where & When?

- Saratoga
- Philadelphia
- Yorktown

1776   1779   1782

1776 American colonies declare independence

1777 American armies victorious at Saratoga

1781 British surrender at Yorktown

Moving Toward Independence

Main Idea As colonial forces and British troops continued to fight, colonial leaders met again to plan their resistance to Britain.

Reading Connection Have you ever read a book that was so well written and so powerful that it changed your mind about a subject? Read to find out about a pamphlet that changed many Americans' minds about remaining united with Britain.

An American Story

On June 16, 1775, about 1,200 militiamen under Colonel William Prescott set up fortifications at Bunker Hill and nearby Breed's Hill, across the harbor from Boston. The next day, the British redcoats crossed the harbor and charged up Breed's Hill. With his forces low on ammunition, Colonel Prescott reportedly shouted the order:

❝ Don't fire until you see the whites of their eyes. ❞

The Americans opened fire, forcing the British to retreat. The redcoats charged two more times, receiving furious fire. In the end the Americans ran out of gunpowder and had to withdraw.

The British won the Battle of Bunker Hill but suffered heavy losses. As one British officer wrote in his diary, "A dear bought victory, another such would have ruined us." The British learned that defeating the Americans on the battlefield would not be easy.

The Second Continental Congress

As fighting raged in the Boston area, the Second Continental Congress met in Philadelphia. Among its delegates were distinguished colonial leaders such as John and Samuel Adams, Patrick Henry, George Washington, Benjamin Franklin, and Thomas Jefferson.

The Second Continental Congress began to govern the colonies. It immediately created the Continental Army to fight against Britain in a more organized way than the colonial militias could. The Congress unanimously chose George Washington to be the army's commander.

Congress Petitions King George

After Washington left to take charge of the colonial forces in Boston, the delegates offered Britain a chance to avoid war. In July, the Continental Congress sent a **petition** (puh•TIH•shuhn), or formal request, to King George III. Called the Olive Branch Petition, it assured the king of the colonists' desire for peace. It asked the king to protect the colonists' rights, which Parliament seemed determined to destroy. George III refused. Instead he prepared for war, hiring more than 30,000 German troops to send to America to fight beside British troops.

Who Was Thomas Paine?

By late 1775 and early 1776, more and more Americans began to think that independence was the only answer. In January 1776, a writer named **Thomas Paine** convinced many when he published a pamphlet called *Common Sense*. Paine used strong language to condemn the king and called for complete separation from Britain. He told the colonists that their cause was not just a squabble over taxes but a struggle for freedom:

❝ The cause of America is in a great measure the cause of all mankind. ❞
—*Common Sense*

Common Sense circulated widely and helped convince thousands of American colonists that it was "time to part." At the Second Continental Congress in Philadelphia, delegates appointed a committee to draft a declaration of independence. Thomas Jefferson of Virginia wrote the historic document. After making some changes, the Congress approved the Declaration of Independence on July 4, 1776.

✓**Reading Check** **Explain** How did the Battle of Bunker Hill change British expectations about the war?

Biography

BENJAMIN FRANKLIN
1706–1790

Benjamin Franklin, born in Boston in 1706, was the 15th of 17 children in the Franklin family. Although Franklin loved learning, he left school at the age of 10 to help his father in the candle-making profession. Unsatisfied with this life, Franklin began learning the printer's trade two years later. By the time he was 23, he owned his own newspaper in Philadelphia. Soon afterward, he began publishing *Poor Richard's Almanack,* a calendar filled with advice, philosophy, and wise sayings, such as "Early to bed, early to rise, makes a man healthy, wealthy, and wise." With sales in the thousands every year, it became, next to the Bible, the most widely read publication in the colonies.

> *"Be civil to all; sociable to many; familiar with few; friend to one; enemy to none."*
> **—Benjamin Franklin,**
> *Poor Richard's Almanack*

Franklin was also deeply interested in science. In 1748 he sold his printing business so that he would have time to work on his inventions. He invented the lightning rod, bifocal eyeglasses, and the Franklin stove for heating. Energetic and open-minded, Franklin served in the Pennsylvania Assembly for many years. He founded a hospital, a fire department, America's first lending library, and an academy of higher learning that later became the University of Pennsylvania.

Franklin's greatest services to his fellow Americans came during the 1770s. As a statesman and patriot, Franklin helped guide the colonies toward independence. In 1775, Franklin became a member of the Second Continental Congress and helped draft the Declaration of Independence. In 1776 he traveled to France, seeking the country's support in the fight for independence. Franklin remained an asset to the United States up until his death. After the American Revolution, he served in the Constitutional Convention and later headed an abolition society.

◀ **Poor Richard's Almanack**

Then and Now

Name a person living today who resembles Franklin in either scientific, political, or social endeavors.

The Colonies Declare Independence

Main Idea The Declaration of Independence used traditional English political rights to call for independence for the colonies.

Reading Connection Why do you think governments are formed? How does the government help you, and what could you do if the government stopped helping you? Read to find out how the writer of the Declaration of Independence addressed these questions.

In the Declaration of Independence, Jefferson explained why the colonies were founding a new nation. To do this, he drew from earlier English documents, such as the Magna Carta and the English Bill of Rights. Both documents established the idea that governments are not all powerful and that rulers had to obey the laws and treat citizens fairly.

Picturing **History**

Thomas Jefferson prepared the draft of the Declaration, and Benjamin Franklin and John Adams made suggestions. *Why is July 4, 1776, a historic day?*

Above all, Jefferson drew on the ideas of thinkers such as English philosopher John Locke to set out the colonies' reasons for proclaiming their freedom. Locke wrote that people were born with certain natural rights to life, liberty, and property; that people formed governments to protect these rights; and that a government that interferes with these rights might rightfully be overthrown.

The Declaration has four major sections. The **preamble** (PREE•AM•buhl), or introduction, states that people who wish to form a new country should explain their reasons for doing so. The next two sections list the rights the colonists believed they should have and their complaints against Britain. The final section proclaims the existence of the new nation.

The Declaration of Independence states what Jefferson and many Americans thought were universal principles. It begins with a description of traditional English political rights.

> **We hold these truths to be self-evident, that all men are created equal, that they are endowed by their Creator with certain unalienable Rights, that among these are Life, Liberty, and the pursuit of Happiness.**

The Declaration ends by announcing America's new status. Now pledging "to each other our Lives, our Fortunes, and our sacred Honor," the Americans declared themselves a new nation. The struggle for American independence—the American Revolution—had begun.

Reading Check **Identify** What does the preamble to the Declaration of Independence state?

History Online

Student Web Activity Visit tajww1.glencoe.com and click on *Chapter 2—Student Web Activities* for an activity on the Declaration of Independence.

The American Revolution

Main Idea America's victory and independence led to revolutions in other parts of the world.

Reading Connection Has someone else's success ever encouraged you to work harder toward a goal? Read to find out how the American victory over the British led to political revolutions in other colonies.

After the colonial leaders declared independence in July 1776, the war for freedom was unavoidable. The British planned to crush the rebellion by force. Most of the **Patriots**—Americans who supported independence—believed the British would give up after losing one or two major battles.

Not all Americans, however, supported the struggle for independence. Some people were **neutral** (NOO•truhl), taking neither side in the conflict. Still other Americans—known as **Loyalists**—remained loyal to Great Britain. At least one American in five was a Loyalist—perhaps as many as one in three.

Early Campaigns During the summer of 1776, Britain sent 32,000 troops across the Atlantic to New York. The British hoped the sheer size of their army would convince the Patriots to give up. In late August, British armies defeated George Washington's forces on New York's Long Island. By late November, the Patriots had retreated across New Jersey into Pennsylvania. Meanwhile, the British army settled in New York for the winter of 1776, leaving some troops in New Jersey at Trenton and Princeton.

Stationed across the Delaware River from the British camp in New Jersey, Washington saw a chance to catch the British off guard. On Christmas night 1776, Washington took 2,400 troops across the icy river and surprised the enemy at Trenton the next day. The British sent reinforcements, but Washington led his troops away from these soldiers. Washington then marched the army to Princeton, where they drove away the British. One discouraged British soldier wrote in his diary that the American victory made the Americans "all liberty mad again."

History *Through Art*

Washington Crossing the Delaware by Emanuel Leutze George Washington led his troops across the Delaware River on Christmas night in a surprise attack on British troops at Trenton. *What effect did the victory at Trenton have on the American cause?*

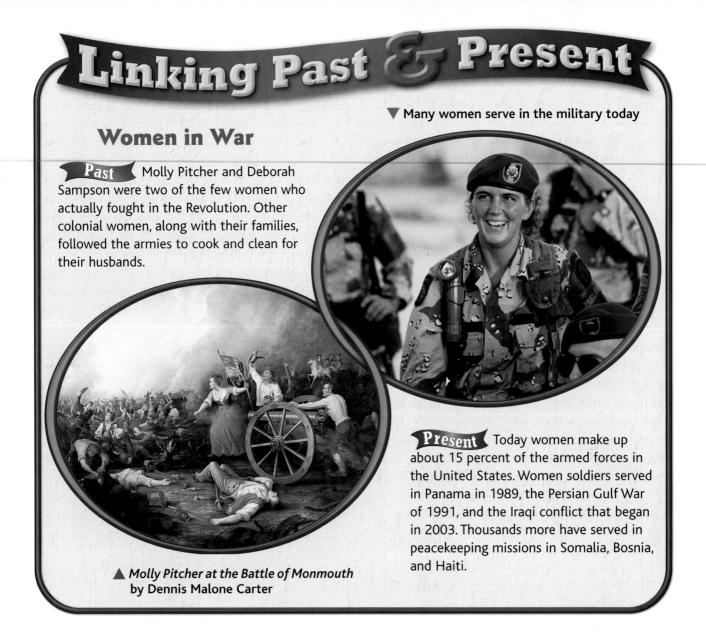

Linking Past & Present

Women in War

▼ Many women serve in the military today

Past Molly Pitcher and Deborah Sampson were two of the few women who actually fought in the Revolution. Other colonial women, along with their families, followed the armies to cook and clean for their husbands.

Present Today women make up about 15 percent of the armed forces in the United States. Women soldiers served in Panama in 1989, the Persian Gulf War of 1991, and the Iraqi conflict that began in 2003. Thousands more have served in peacekeeping missions in Somalia, Bosnia, and Haiti.

▲ *Molly Pitcher at the Battle of Monmouth* by Dennis Malone Carter

The Battle of Saratoga In 1777 the British decided to split New England from the Middle Colonies by taking control of New York's Hudson River valley. The plan called for three British forces to meet at Albany, New York, and destroy the Patriot troops.

A British force under General John Burgoyne advanced southward from Canada. When Burgoyne reached the town of Saratoga in New York, the other two British forces had not arrived. Soon, Burgoyne's forces found themselves surrounded by a larger American army under General Horatio Gates. After a desperate attack, the British realized they were trapped, and Burgoyne surrendered on October 17, 1777. The Battle of Saratoga was the first major American victory in the war.

Winter at Valley Forge As the winter of 1777 approached, other British forces settled in comfort in Philadelphia. Meanwhile, George Washington set up camp at Valley Forge, 20 miles to the west of the British.

Washington and his troops endured a winter of terrible suffering and difficult conditions, lacking decent food, clothing, and shelter. Washington's greatest **challenge** at Valley Forge was keeping the Continental Army together. Yet with strong determination, the Continental Army survived the winter, and conditions gradually improved.

Gaining Allies The victory at Saratoga boosted American spirits. Even more, Saratoga marked a turning point.

The European nations, especially France, realized that the United States might actually win its war against Britain. In 1778 the French declared war on Britain and provided aid to the Americans.

Other European nations also helped the Patriots. Spain declared war on Britain in 1779, and the Spanish governor of Louisiana, **Bernardo de Gálvez,** raised an army. Gálvez's army forced British troops from towns and forts along the Gulf of Mexico. His efforts **secured** the southern frontiers of the United States.

Individual foreigners also helped the Americans. One of the hardy soldiers at Valley Forge was a French nobleman, the **Marquis de Lafayette** (LAH•fee•EHT). Dedicated to the ideas of the Declaration of Independence, Lafayette was a trusted aide to Washington. Two Poles—Thaddeus Kosciusko (kawsh•CHUSH•koh), an engineer, and Casimir Pulaski, a cavalry officer—also helped the Americans. Friedrich von Steuben (STOO•buhn), a former army officer from Germany, turned the ragged Continental Army into a more effective fighting force.

Life on the Home Front
The war changed the lives of all Americans, even those who stayed at home. With thousands of men away in military service, women took over the duties that had once been the responsibility of their husbands or fathers. Other women ran their husband's or their own businesses.

The ideals of liberty and freedom that inspired the American Revolution caused some women to question their place in society. Abigail Adams was a dedicated champion of women's interests. She wrote to her husband, John Adams, who was a member of the Second Continental Congress:

> **❝I can not say that I think you very generous to the ladies, for whilst you are proclaiming peace and good will to men, emancipating all nations, you insist upon retaining an absolute power over wives. ❞**
> —Letter, May 7, 1776

The Revolutionary War ideals of freedom and liberty inspired some white Americans to question slavery. From the beginning of the war, African American soldiers fought for the American cause. To some who were fighting for freedom, both African American and white, the Revolution seemed to bring nearer the day when slavery would be abolished. Vermont, New Hampshire, Massachusetts, and Pennsylvania attempted to end slavery in their states. The issue of slavery would remain unsettled for many years, however.

War in the West and on Sea
Along the northwestern frontier, the British and their Native American allies were raiding American settlements. During 1778 and 1779, George Rogers Clark, an officer in the Virginia militia, seized British posts in present-day Illinois and Indiana. Clark's victories strengthened the American position in the West.

Other battles raged at sea. A daring American naval officer, **John Paul Jones,** raided British ports. In September 1779, Jones's ship *Bonhomme Richard* fought the British warship *Serapis.* At one point, Jones's ship was so badly damaged that the British captain asked whether Jones wished to surrender. Jones is said to have answered, "I have not yet begun to fight." In the end the *Serapis* surrendered, making John Paul Jones a naval hero to the American Patriots.

▲ Many soldiers from other countries and about 5,000 African American soldiers fought for American independence.

Struggles in the South By 1778 the British hoped to use sea power and Loyalist support to win victories in the South. By 1780, British forces had seized Savannah and Charles Town. The British, however, could not control their conquered areas. This was due to a new kind of warfare carried out by the Patriots.

As British troops moved through the countryside, small forces of Patriots attacked them. Bands of soldiers suddenly struck and then disappeared. This hit-and-run **technique** of **guerrilla warfare** (guh•RIH•luh) caught the British off guard.

The War Is Won In 1780 the war was at a critical point. Both armies needed a victory to win. This finally came in 1781 at the Battle of Yorktown on the coast of Virginia. The French navy blocked the British from escaping by sea, while American and French forces surrounded and trapped the British inside Yorktown. Realizing they could not win, the British laid down their weapons.

The Treaty of Paris Britain's defeat at Yorktown did not end the Revolutionary War. The fighting dragged on in some areas for two more years. Peace negotiations, however, began in Paris. Benjamin Franklin, John Adams, and John Jay represented the United States. The final settlement, known as the Treaty of Paris, was signed on September 3, 1783.

The Treaty of Paris was a triumph for the Americans. Great Britain recognized the United States as an independent nation. The territory claimed by the new nation extended from the Atlantic Ocean west to the Mississippi River and from Canada in the north to Spanish Florida in the south. The Revolutionary War was over. The creation of a new nation was about to begin.

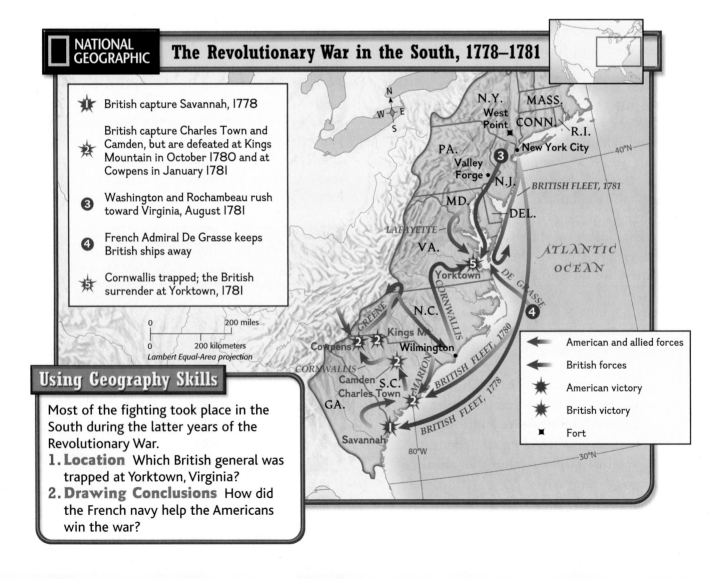

NATIONAL GEOGRAPHIC

The Revolutionary War in the South, 1778–1781

1 British capture Savannah, 1778

2 British capture Charles Town and Camden, but are defeated at Kings Mountain in October 1780 and at Cowpens in January 1781

3 Washington and Rochambeau rush toward Virginia, August 1781

4 French Admiral De Grasse keeps British ships away

5 Cornwallis trapped; the British surrender at Yorktown, 1781

0   200 miles
0   200 kilometers
Lambert Equal-Area projection

N.Y.
West Point
MASS.
CONN.
R.I.
PA.
New York City
40°N
Valley Forge
3
N.J.
MD.
BRITISH FLEET, 1781
LAFAYETTE
DEL.
VA.
ATLANTIC OCEAN
5
Yorktown
DE GRASSE
CORNWALLIS
GREENE
N.C.
4
Cowpens
2 **2**
Kings Mt.
Wilmington
BRITISH FLEET, 1780
CORNWALLIS
MARION
Camden
S.C.
Charles Town
2
GA.
BRITISH FLEET, 1778
Savannah
1
80°W
30°N

← American and allied forces
← British forces
✴ American victory
✴ British victory
■ Fort

Using Geography Skills

Most of the fighting took place in the South during the latter years of the Revolutionary War.

1. **Location** Which British general was trapped at Yorktown, Virginia?
2. **Drawing Conclusions** How did the French navy help the Americans win the war?

Why the Americans Won How were the Patriots able to win the Revolutionary War? The Americans had several advantages. They fought on their own land, while the British had to bring troops and supplies from far away. The British succeeded in **occupying** cities but had difficulty controlling the countryside. Help from other nations also contributed to the American victory.

Perhaps most important, the American Revolution was a people's movement. Its outcome depended not on any one battle or event but on the determination and spirit of all the Patriots.

A Model for Others In 1776 the American colonists began a revolution, making clear the principles of freedom and rights outlined in the Declaration of Independence. These ideas bounded back across the Atlantic to influence the French Revolution. French rebels in 1789 fought in defense of "Liberty, Equality, and Fraternity." French revolutionaries repeated the principles of the American Declaration of Independence: "Men are born and remain free and equal in rights."

In 1791 the ideals of the American and French revolutions traveled across the Caribbean and the Atlantic to the French-held island colony of Saint Domingue. Inspired by talk of freedom, enslaved Africans took up arms. Led by Toussaint-Louverture, they rejected French rule. In 1804 Saint Domingue—part of present-day Haiti—became the second nation in the Americas to achieve independence from colonial rule.

Reading Check **Summarize** Why was the Battle of Saratoga a turning point in the war?

History Online

Study Central Need help understanding the American Revolution? Visit tajwwI.glencoe.com and click on Study Central.

Section 4 Review

Reading Summary

Review the Main Ideas

• The Second Continental Congress met to discuss governing the colonies and to form the Continental Army to fight the British.

• The Declaration of Independence, written by Thomas Jefferson, declared the American colonies to be a new, independent nation.

• The American victory inspired other peoples to seek independence and rebel against their governments.

What Did You Learn?

1. For what did Thomas Paine argue in *Common Sense?*

2. What was guerrilla warfare, and why was it effective?

Critical Thinking

3. **Organizing Information** Draw a chart like the one below. Fill in the names and dates of major Revolutionary War battles and provide details about each battle.

Battle	What Occurred

4. **Predict** What might have happened if the French had not allied with the colonists during the Revolutionary War?

5. **The Big Ideas** On what laws and political ideas did Jefferson draw when writing the Declaration of Independence?

6. **Math Connection** Examine the list of representatives to the Second Continental Congress on page 167 who signed the Declaration of Independence. Draw a bar graph depicting the number of men representing each state. Use the X-axis for the states and the Y-axis for numbers of men.

You Decide . . .

Independence: Yes or No?

Many American colonists joined the movement for independence. Still, many Americans did not want to break away from Great Britain.

For Independence

Many colonists in the summer of 1775 were not prepared to break away from Great Britain. The colonists resented British taxes. Because they had no representation in Parliament, as people in Great Britain did, the colonists believed that Parliament had no right to tax them. They summarized their feelings with the slogan "No taxation without representation." Most members of the Second Continental Congress wanted the right to govern themselves, but they did not want to break with the British Empire.

By 1776, however, opinion had changed. Frustrated by Britain's refusal to compromise, many Patriot leaders began to call for independence. Influential in swaying the colonists toward the idea of separating from Great Britain was Thomas Paine's pamphlet *Common Sense*, which first appeared in January 1776. Paine made an impassioned appeal:

"I have heard it asserted by some, that as America hath flourished under her former connexion with Great Britain, the same connexion is necessary towards her future happiness. . . . I answer roundly, that America would have flourished as much, and probably much more, had no European power [taken notice of her]. . . . Everything that is right or natural pleads for separation. The blood of the slain, the weeping voice of nature cries, 'TIS TIME TO PART.'"

The Patriots believed that fighting for liberty set an example for others to follow. Ben Franklin wrote to a friend that "our cause is the cause of all mankind, and that we are fighting for their liberty in defending our own."

◀ **Thomas Paine**

Against Independence

The American Revolution was not only a war between the British and the Americans. It also divided Americans themselves. While American Patriots fought passionately for independence, other Americans fought just as fiercely for their British king. Americans who felt a strong sense of loyalty to the king and believed British law should be upheld came to be known as Loyalists.

Loyalists came from all parts of American society. Many Loyalists lived in Georgia, the Carolinas, and New England; the Patriots though were strong in New England and Virginia. Political differences divided communities and even split families. Benjamin Franklin's son, William, served as Royal Governor of New Jersey. When the Revolution began, William remained loyal to Britain and quarreled bitterly with his father.

Loyalists answered Paine's *Common Sense* with pamphlets of their own. One who did was Charles Inglis, a minister from New York. He wrote: "By a connection with Great Britain, our trade would still have the protection of the greatest naval power in the world." Inglis also said that if the American colonies did not give up their fight for independence, Britain would exert its great power and the result would be:

"Ruthless war, with all its aggravated horrors, will ravage our once happy land—our seacoasts and ports will be ruined, and our ships taken. Torrents of blood will be spilt, and thousands reduced to beggary and wretchedness."

You Be The Historian

DBQ **Document-Based Questions**

1. What economic argument does Paine use to support separation from Great Britain?

2. What does Inglis believe will result from war with Britain?

3. Were the reasons for or against American independence convincing? Write a short letter to Inglis in which you support the Patriot or Loyalist position. Use facts to support your position.

Analyzing Primary Sources

Life in the American Colonies

Throughout the 1600s and 1700s, more and more English people settled in the 13 colonies along the Atlantic coast of North America. How did these settlers adapt to their new homes? What was their everyday life like? You can get a glimpse of life in colonial America by analyzing letters and published writings from this era.

Read the passages on pages 160 and 161, and answer the questions that follow.

William Penn inspecting ▶ deeds during survey expedition of Philadelphia

Reader's Dictionary

tolerable (TAH • luh • ruh • buhl): satisfactory

Languedoc (lahng • DAWK): region in southern France

generation (JEH • nuh • RAY • shuhn): age group

descent (dih • SEHNT): line of ancestors; birth

poultry (POHL • tree): chickens

Penn's Colony

William Penn wrote of the new Pennsylvania colony with pride.

We have laid out a town a mile wide and two miles deep, with 150 very **tolerable** houses. . . . [It is] the largest town south of New York and already the envy of its neighbors.

The air is serene as in **Languedoc,** a most fragrant smell of cedar, pine and sassafras. . . . In short, I am fully satisfied with the country, . . . I must, without vanity, confess that I have led the greatest colony in America. . . .

—Letters to John Aubrey and Lord Halifax, 1683

The Germantown Protest

One of the earliest protests in North America against the enslavement of Africans was this statement written in 1688 by a religious group known as the Mennonites.

Now, though, they are black, we cannot conceive there is more liberty to have them slaves, . . . [than] to have other white ones. There is a saying, that we should do to all men like as we will be done ourselves; making no difference of what **generation, descent,** or color they are. . . .

Pray, what thing in the world can be done worse towards us, than if men should rob or steal us away, and sell us for slaves to strange countries; separating husbands from their wives and children. . . .

—*Germantown Protest*

Poor Richard's Almanack

Ben Franklin published Poor Richard's Almanack every year from 1733 to 1758. The almanack included weather forecasts, statistics, and other useful or interesting information. Franklin also included proverbs, or short witty sayings, like those that follow. See if you recognize any of them.

a. Early to bed and early to rise, makes a man healthy wealthy and wise.

b. Little strokes, fell great oaks.

c. Glass, china, and reputation, are easily crack'd, and never well mended.

d. An open foe may prove a curse; but a pretended friend is worse.

e. One today is worth two tomorrows.

f. Haste makes waste.

g. Beware of little expenses, a small leak will sink a great ship.

h. The sleeping fox catches no **poultry.**

i. A Slip of the Foot you may soon recover: But a Slip of the Tongue you may never get over.

—*Poor Richard's Almanack*

DBQ Document-Based Questions

Penn's Colony

1. How does Penn describe the houses in the colony?

2. Is Penn proud of the colony? How can you tell?

The Germantown Protest

3. What arguments do the writers use as evidence that slavery is evil?

4. What familiar saying is used to make the writers' point about slavery? Why is this saying used?

Poor Richard's Almanack

5. Which of the proverbs have you heard or read? Why do you think Franklin's proverbs are still popular today?

6. Write the meaning of three of the proverbs in your own words.

Read to Write

7. Write a proverb about something that is part of your everyday life. Compare your proverb about life today with one of Franklin's proverbs. What is the same and what is different about the two proverbs?

Review Content Vocabulary

Match the definitions in the second column to the terms in the first column.

1. burgess
2. militia
3. smuggling
4. boycott
5. tolerance

a. trading illegally with another country
b. representative
c. group of citizen soldiers
d. acceptance of different beliefs
e. refuse to buy

Review the Main Ideas

Section 1 • Founding the American Colonies

6. Why did the Virginia Company create the House of Burgesses?

7. Describe the role of religious freedom in the founding of two of the colonies.

Section 2 • Life in Colonial America

8. What was the Great Awakening, and how did it represent the unique American culture that was developing?

9. What was England's reason for the Navigation Acts?

Section 3 • Trouble in the Colonies

10. How did the British government use the colonies to raise revenue?

11. What incident caused the British Parliament to pass the Coercive Acts?

Section 4 • War of Independence

12. According to the Declaration of Independence, if a government does not protect the basic rights of the people it governs, what is the right of the people?

13. What fighting method did the Americans use to keep the British from controlling the Southern Colonies?

Critical Thinking

14. **Predict** What might have happened if Britain had allowed the American colonists more control in creating regulations dealing with colonial trade?

15. **Analyze** What did Patrick Henry mean when he said, "I am not a Virginian, but an American"?

16. **Conclude** Why do you think the British found it easier to capture American cities than to take over the American countryside?

Geography Skills

Study the map below and answer the following questions.

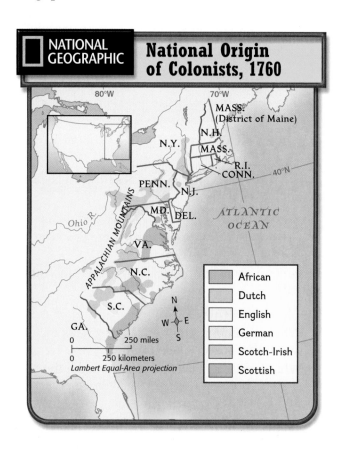

NATIONAL GEOGRAPHIC

National Origin of Colonists, 1760

African
Dutch
English
German
Scotch-Irish
Scottish

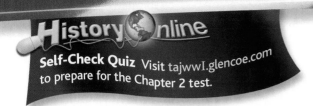
History Online

Self-Check Quiz Visit tajwwI.glencoe.com to prepare for the Chapter 2 test.

17. **Human-Environment Interaction** What geographical feature served as a boundary to westward settlement in 1760?

18. **Location** Which colony had the largest area of Scottish settlement?

19. **Human-Environment Interaction** Describe the location of the colonies' African population. Why was that population found in those colonies?

Read to Write

20. **The Big Ideas** **Evaluate** Write a short essay describing why the American colonists had strong views about self-government.

21. **Using Your FOLDABLES** Draw a graphic organizer that describes the events that led the Americans to declare independence from Great Britain. As you discuss the causes and effects, imagine other possible outcomes to the same situations. Could war have been avoided through diplomacy? Write an essay that summarizes your conclusions.

Using Academic Vocabulary

Choose an academic vocabulary word to complete each sentence. You may need to change the form of the word to provide the best answer.

   grant   adapt

   secure   violate

22. The Continental Army had to _____ its battle tactics to defeat the highly organized British forces.

23. Colonial leaders believed that British taxation policies _____ their natural rights to representative government.

Building Citizenship

24. **Researching** America's heritage of religious diversity and toleration began in the colonial period. Use the Internet and other sources to research modern laws that are meant to promote religious freedom and toleration. Prepare a report to share with the class.

Reviewing Skills

25. **READING SKILL** **Identifying the Main Idea** Read the "List of Grievances" in the Declaration of Independence. List the main idea and supporting points outlined in that section. Rewrite the grievances in your own words, using the main and supporting points you identified.

26. **ANALYSIS SKILL** **Infer** Why do you think Thomas Jefferson relied so heavily on earlier British documents and on the thoughts of British philosophers as he wrote the Declaration of Independence? Write a short essay explaining your conclusions.

Standardized Test Practice

Read the passage below and answer the following questions.

An English philosopher named John Locke wrote about his belief that people had natural rights. These included the right to life, liberty, and property. In *Two Treatises of Government*, Locke wrote that people created government to protect natural rights. If a government failed in its basic duty of protecting natural rights, people had the right to overthrow the government.

27 **Locke's ideas, as stated in the paragraph above, contributed to the**

   A Proclamation of 1763.

   B Intolerable Acts.

   C Declaration of Independence.

   D Articles of Confederation.

The Declaration of Independence

In Congress, July 4, 1776. The unanimous Declaration of the thirteen united States of America,

[Preamble]

When in the Course of human events, it becomes necessary for one people to dissolve the political bands which have connected them with another, and to assume among the Powers of the earth, the separate and equal station to which the Laws of Nature and of Nature's God entitle them, a decent respect to the opinions of mankind requires that they should declare the causes which **impel** them to the separation.

[Declaration of Natural Rights]

We hold these truths to be self-evident, that all men are created equal, that they are **endowed** by their Creator with certain unalienable Rights, that among these are Life, Liberty and the pursuit of Happiness.

That to secure these rights, Governments are instituted among Men, deriving their just powers from the consent of the governed,

That whenever any Form of Government becomes destructive of these ends, it is the Right of the People to alter or to abolish it, and to institute new Government, laying its foundation on such principles and organizing its powers in such form, as to them shall seem most likely to effect their Safety and Happiness. Prudence, indeed, will dictate that Governments long established should not be changed for light and transient causes; and accordingly all experience hath shown, that mankind are more disposed to suffer, while evils are sufferable, than to right themselves by abolishing the forms to which they are accustomed. But when a long train of abuses and usurpations, pursuing invariably the same Object evinces a design to reduce them under absolute **Despotism,** it is their right, it is their duty, to throw off such Government, and to provide new Guards for their future security.

[List of Grievances]

Such has been the patient sufferance of these Colonies; and such is now the necessity which constrains them to alter their former Systems of Government. The history of the present King of Great Britain is a history of repeated injuries and **usurpations,** all having in direct object the establishment of an absolute Tyranny over these States. To prove this, let Facts be submitted to a candid world.

He has refused his Assent to Laws, the most wholesome and necessary for the public good.

What It Means

The Preamble The Declaration of Independence has four parts. The Preamble explains why the Continental Congress drew up the Declaration.

impel *force*

What It Means

Natural Rights The second part, the Declaration of Natural Rights, lists the rights of the citizens. It goes on to explain that, in a republic, people form a government to protect their rights.

endowed *provided*

despotism *unlimited power*

What It Means

List of Grievances The third part of the Declaration lists the colonists' complaints against the British government. Notice that King George III is singled out for blame.

usurpations *unjust uses of power*

He has forbidden his Governors to pass Laws of immediate and pressing importance, unless suspended in their operation till his Assent should be obtained; and when so suspended, he has utterly neglected to attend to them.

He has refused to pass other Laws for the accommodation of large districts of people, unless those people would **relinquish** the right of Representation in the Legislature, a right **inestimable** to them and formidable to tyrants only.

> **relinquish** *give up*
> **inestimable** *priceless*

He has called together legislative bodies at places unusual, uncomfortable, and distant from the depository of their Public Records, for the sole purpose of fatiguing them into compliance with his measures.

He has dissolved Representative Houses repeatedly, for opposing with manly firmness his invasions on the rights of the people.

He has refused for a long time, after such dissolutions, to cause others to be elected; whereby the Legislative Powers, incapable of **Annihilation,** have returned to the People at large for their exercise; the State remaining in the mean time exposed to all the dangers of invasion from without, and **convulsions** within.

> **annihilation** *destruction*
>
> **convulsions** *violent disturbances*

He has endeavoured to prevent the population of these States; for that purpose obstructing the Laws for **Naturalization of Foreigners;** refusing to pass others to encourage their migrations hither, and raising the conditions of new Appropriations of Lands.

> **Naturalization of Foreigners**
> *process by which foreign-born persons become citizens*

He has obstructed the Administration of Justice, by refusing his Assent to Laws for establishing Judiciary Powers.

He has made Judges dependent on his Will alone, for the **tenure** of their offices, and the amount and payment of their salaries.

> **tenure** *term*

He has erected a multitude of New Offices, and sent hither swarms of Officers to harass our people, and eat out their substance.

He has kept among us, in times of peace, Standing Armies without the Consent of our legislature.

He has affected to render the Military independent of and superior to the Civil Power.

He has combined with others to subject us to a jurisdiction foreign to our constitution, and unacknowledged by our laws; giving his Assent to their acts of pretended legislation:

quartering *lodging*

For **quartering** large bodies of troops among us:

For protecting them, by a mock Trial, from Punishment for any Murders which they should commit on the Inhabitants of these States:

For cutting off our Trade with all parts of the world:

For imposing taxes on us without our Consent:

For depriving us in many cases, of the benefits of Trial by Jury:

For transporting us beyond Seas to be tried for pretended offences:

For abolishing the free System of English Laws in a neighbouring Province, establishing therein an Arbitrary government, and enlarging its Boundaries so as to **render** it at once an example and fit instrument for introducing the same absolute rule into these Colonies:

render *make*

For taking away our Charters, abolishing our most valuable Laws, and altering fundamentally the Forms of our Governments:

For suspending our own Legislature, and declaring themselves invested with Power to legislate for us in all cases whatsoever.

abdicated *given up*

He has **abdicated** Government here, by declaring us out of his Protection and waging War against us.

He has plundered our seas, ravaged our Coasts, burnt our towns, and destroyed the lives of our people.

He is at this time transporting large armies of foreign mercenaries to compleat the works of death, desolation and tyranny, already begun with circumstances of Cruelty & **perfidy** scarcely paralleled in the most barbarous ages, and totally unworthy the Head of a civilized nation.

perfidy *violation of trust*

He has constrained our fellow Citizens taken Captive on the high Seas to bear Arms against their Country, to become the executioners of their friends and Brethren, or to fall themselves by their Hands.

insurrections *rebellions*

He has excited domestic **insurrections** amongst us, and has endeavoured to bring on the inhabitants of our frontiers, the merciless Indian Savages, whose known rule of warfare, is an undistinguished destruction of all ages, sexes and conditions.

petitioned for redress *asked formally for a correction of wrongs*

In every stage of these Oppressions We have **Petitioned for Redress** in the most humble terms: Our repeated Petitions have been answered only by repeated injury. A Prince, whose character is thus marked by every act which may define a Tyrant, is unfit to be the ruler of a free People.

unwarrantable jurisdiction *unjustified authority*

Nor have We been wanting in attention to our British brethren. We have warned them from time to time of attempts by their legislature to extend an **unwarrantable jurisdiction** over us. We have reminded them of the circumstances of our emigration and settlement here. We have appealed to their native justice and magnanimity, and we have conjured them by the ties of our common kindred to disavow these usurpations, which, would inevitably interrupt our connections and correspondence. They too have been deaf to the voice of justice and of **consanguinity.** We must, therefore, acquiesce in the necessity, which denounces our Separation, and hold them, as we hold the rest of mankind, Enemies in War, in Peace Friends.

consanguinity *originating from the same ancestor*

[Resolution of Independence by the United States]

We, therefore, the Representatives of the united States of America, in General Congress, Assembled, appealing to the Supreme Judge of the world for the **rectitude** of our intentions, do, in the Name, and by Authority of the good People of these Colonies, solemnly publish and declare, That these United Colonies are, and of Right ought to be Free and Independent States; that they are Absolved from all Allegiance to the British Crown, and that all political connection between them and the State of Great Britain, is and ought to be totally dissolved; and that as Free and Independent States, they have full Power to levy War, conclude Peace, contract Alliances, establish Commerce, and to do all other Acts and Things which Independent States may of right do.

And for the support of this Declaration, with a firm reliance on the Protection of Divine Providence, we mutually pledge to each other our Lives, our Fortunes and our sacred Honor.

John Hancock
    President from
    Massachusetts

Georgia
Button Gwinnett
Lyman Hall
George Walton

North Carolina
William Hooper
Joseph Hewes
John Penn

South Carolina
Edward Rutledge
Thomas Heyward, Jr.
Thomas Lynch, Jr.
Arthur Middleton

Maryland
Samuel Chase
William Paca
Thomas Stone
Charles Carroll
    of Carrollton

Virginia
George Wythe
Richard Henry Lee
Thomas Jefferson
Benjamin Harrison
Thomas Nelson, Jr.
Francis Lightfoot Lee
Carter Braxton

Pennsylvania
Robert Morris
Benjamin Rush
Benjamin Franklin
John Morton
George Clymer
James Smith
George Taylor
James Wilson
George Ross

Delaware
Caesar Rodney
George Read
Thomas McKean

New York
William Floyd
Philip Livingston
Francis Lewis
Lewis Morris

New Jersey
Richard Stockton
John Witherspoon
Francis Hopkinson
John Hart
Abraham Clark

New Hampshire
Josiah Bartlett
William Whipple
Matthew Thornton

Massachusetts
Samuel Adams
John Adams
Robert Treat Paine
Elbridge Gerry

Rhode Island
Stephen Hopkins
William Ellery

Connecticut
Samuel Huntington
William Williams
Oliver Wolcott
Roger Sherman

What It Means
Resolution of Independence
The Final section declares that the colonies are "Free and Independent States" with the full power to make war, to form alliances, and to trade with other countries.

rectitude *rightness*

What It Means
Signers of the Declaration The signers, as representatives of the American people, declared the colonies independent from Great Britain. Most members signed the document on August 2, 1776.

A Changing World

Native Americans were the first people to live in the Americas. Europeans and enslaved Africans arrived next. In England new ideas about government evolved. English colonists used those ideas to form the United States of America.

	Chapter 1 Expanding Horizons	**Chapter 2** Road to Independence
When	• 1200s–1700s	• 1600s–1700s
Where	• Europe • Asia • Africa • Central America • South America • North America	• New England • West Africa • West Indies • Southern Colonies • Middle Colonies • Great Britain

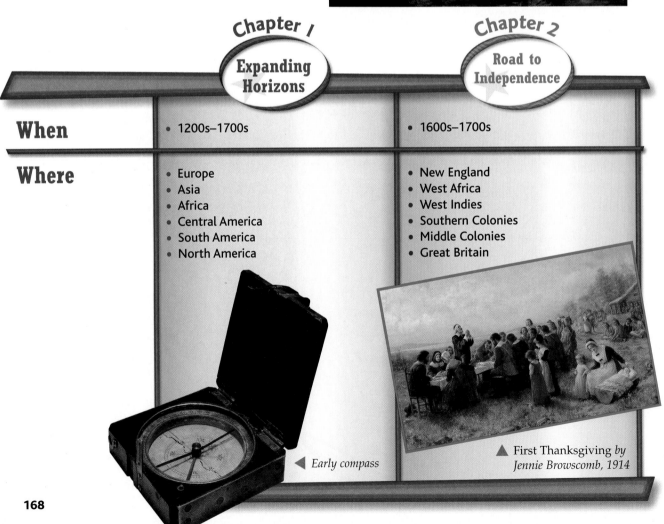

◀ *Early compass*

▲ First Thanksgiving *by Jennie Browscomb, 1914*

Chapter 1 — Expanding Horizons

Chapter 2 — Road to Independence

Major Events

Expanding Horizons
- **1215** King John signs Magna Carta
- **c. 1400s** Technological advances lead to Age of Exploration and growth of trade
- **1492** Columbus reaches the Americas
- **1517** Martin Luther's calls for change begin the Reformation
- **1521, 1532** Conquistadors conquer Aztec and Inca empires
- **1588** English defeat Spanish Armada
- **c. 1600s** Governments begin to charter banks
- **c. 1600s** Mercantilism becomes basis for national policies
- **1689** Bill of Rights guarantees all English people basic rights
- **1690** John Locke states that people have rights based on natural law

Road to Independence
- **1607** Jamestown is first permanent English colony
- **1619** Representatives to House of Burgesses meet
- **1620** Pilgrims sign Mayflower Compact
- **1730s–1740s** Great Awakening sweeps through English colonies
- **1763** Proclamation of 1763 forbids settlement west of Appalachians
- **1770** Boston Massacre leads to more boycotts of British goods
- **1773** Boston Tea Party protests tax on tea
- **1775** First battles of Revolution are fought at Lexington and Concord
- **1776** Declaration of Independence is signed
- **1781** British surrender at Yorktown

Some Important People

Expanding Horizons
- Christopher Columbus
- Queen Elizabeth I
- John Locke
- Isaac Newton

Christopher ▶ Columbus

Road to Independence
- Roger Williams
- Jonathan Edwards
- Benjamin Franklin
- George Washington

How do these events and ideas affect our lives today?

Expanding Horizons
- School subjects are rooted in Renaissance learning.
- Spanish heritage is an important part of North American culture.

Road to Independence
- American Patriots supported rights (free speech, religion, press) that we enjoy today.

Revolutionary ▲ War drum and fife

What was happening in the world at this time?

Expanding Horizons
- **1405** Chinese navigator Zheng He begins voyages of discovery
- **1493** Muhammad Ture expands Songhai empire in West Africa
- **1543** Copernicus believes sun is at center of universe

Road to Independence
- **1689** Peter the Great works to reform Russia
- **1770** Captain James Cook claims Australia for Great Britian

Peter the Great ▶

Unit 2

Creating a Nation

Why It's Important

After the American Revolution, the new nation struggled to draw up a plan of government. Created to meet the needs of a changing nation, the Constitution has been the fundamental law of the United States for more than 200 years. Many developments of this period shape our lives today.

- The Constitution is central to American life and ideals.

- The Constitution has served as a model for many constitutions all over the world.

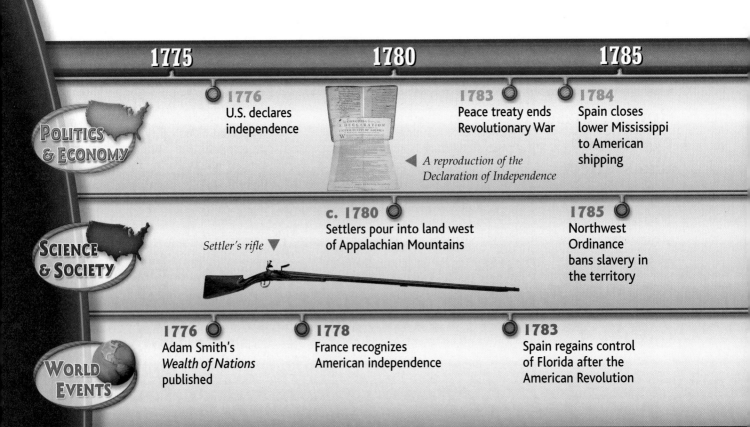

1775

1780

1785

POLITICS & ECONOMY

1776
U.S. declares independence

1783
Peace treaty ends Revolutionary War

A reproduction of the Declaration of Independence ◀

1784
Spain closes lower Mississippi to American shipping

SCIENCE & SOCIETY

Settler's rifle ▼

c. 1780
Settlers pour into land west of Appalachian Mountains

1785
Northwest Ordinance bans slavery in the territory

WORLD EVENTS

1776
Adam Smith's *Wealth of Nations* published

1778
France recognizes American independence

1783
Spain regains control of Florida after the American Revolution

Where in the United States?

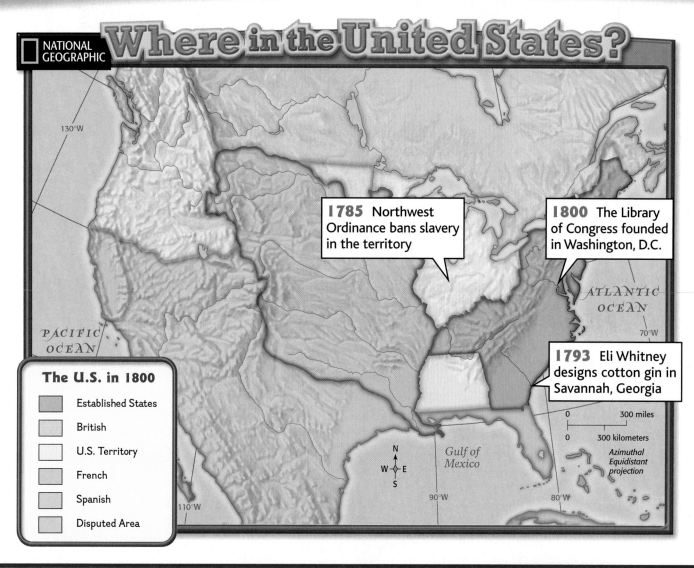

1785 Northwest Ordinance bans slavery in the territory

1800 The Library of Congress founded in Washington, D.C.

ATLANTIC OCEAN

1793 Eli Whitney designs cotton gin in Savannah, Georgia

PACIFIC OCEAN

The U.S. in 1800

- Established States
- British
- U.S. Territory
- French
- Spanish
- Disputed Area

130°W
110°W
70°W
90°W
80°W

N
W E
S

Gulf of Mexico

0   300 miles
0   300 kilometers

Azimuthal Equidistant projection

1790   **1795**   **1800**

1788
U.S. Constitution ratified

1791
Bill of Rights is added to Constitution

1795
George Washington uses first presidential veto

George Washington ▶

1786
Thomas Jefferson's Virginia Statute for Religious Freedom is adopted

1793
Eli Whitney designs cotton gin in Savannah, Georgia

Eli Whitney ▶

▼ *The Library of Congress*

1800
The Library of Congress founded in Washington, D.C.

1789
French Revolution begins

1796
English doctor Edward Jenner invents smallpox vaccine

1799
Rosetta Stone discovered

◀ Conquerors of the Bastille

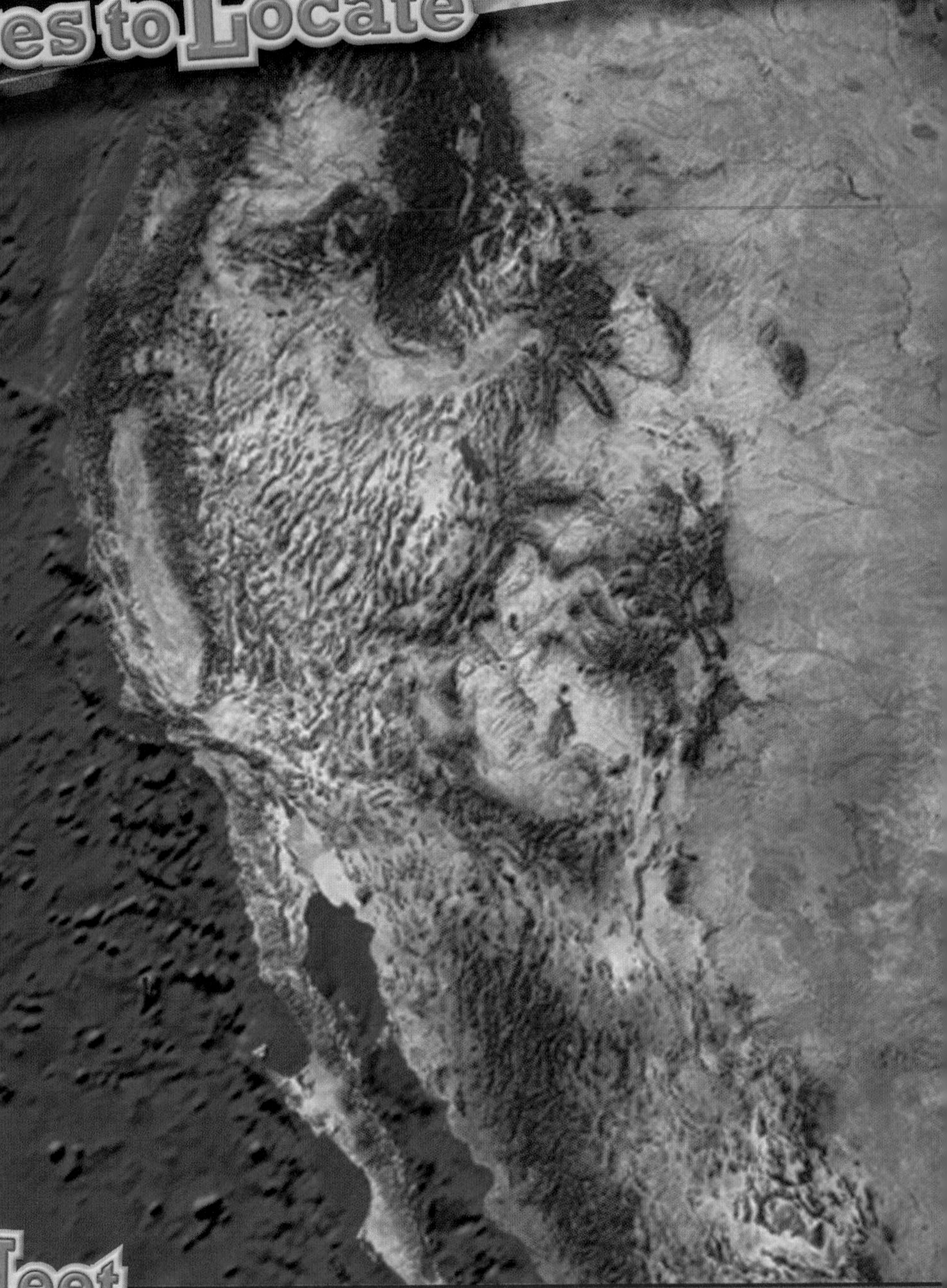

① THE NORTHWEST TERRITORY

See *A More Perfect Union*
Chapter 3

② SHAYS'S REBELLION

See *A More Perfect Union*
Chapter 3

People to Meet

Richard Allen
1760–1831
Philadelphia
preacher
Chapter 3, page 196

Absalom Jones
1746–1818
Philadelphia
preacher
Chapter 3, page 196

James Madison
1751–1836
Architect of the
Constitution
Chapter 3, page 198

Roger Sherman
1721–1793
Creator of the Great
Compromise
Chapter 3, page 199

③ INDEPENDENCE HALL

See *A More Perfect Union*
Chapter 3

④ THE CAPITOL

See *The Constitution*
Chapter 4

George Mason
1725–1792
Political leader
Chapter 3, page 201

Mercy Otis Warren
1728–1814
Political writer
Chapter 3, page 206

Gouverneur Morris
1752–1816
Writer and editor of
the Constitution
Chapter 4, page 220

John Marshall
1755–1835
Chief Justice of the
Supreme Court
Chapter 4, page 232

A More Perfect Union

◀ Philadelphia's
Independence Hall

Where & When?

NORTHWEST
TERRITORY

THE UNITED
STATES

1770	1780	1790
1777 Articles of Confederation written	1787 U.S. Constitution signed	1788 U.S. Constitution ratified

The Big Ideas

Section 1 — The Articles of Confederation

Political ideas and major events shape how people form governments. When the American colonies broke their political ties with Great Britain, they faced the task of forming independent governments at both the state and national levels.

Section 2 — Convention and Compromise

A constitution reflects the values and goals of a society that creates it. The new Constitution corrected the weaknesses of government under the Articles of Confederation.

Section 3 — A New Plan of Government

Political ideas and major events shape how people form governments. The United States system of government rests on the Constitution.

 View the Chapter 3 video in the Glencoe Video Program.

FOLDABLES™
Study Organizer

Compare and Contrast Make this foldable to help you compare the Articles of Confederation to the U.S. Constitution.

Step 1 Fold a sheet of paper from side to side, leaving a 2-inch tab uncovered along the side.

Fold it so the left edge lies 2 inches from the right edge.

Step 2 Turn the paper and fold it into thirds.

Reading and Writing As you read the chapter, write what you learn about these documents under the appropriate tabs.

Step 3 Unfold and cut along the two inside fold lines.

Cut along the two folds on the front flap to make 3 tabs.

Step 4 Label the foldable as shown.

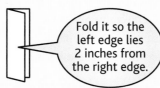
A More Perfect Union

Articles of Confederation · Both · U.S. Constitution

Get Ready to Read

Making Connections

1 Learn It!

Good readers make connections between what they are reading and what they know. Some connections are based on personal experiences (text-to-self). Readers also make connections to things they have read in other books (text-to-text). Finally, good readers make connections to things that happen in other places (text-to-world). Making these connections helps you understand words or ideas that are unfamiliar to you and gain knowledge about the world. As you read, ask yourself connecting questions. Are you reminded of something from your life, something you have read, or a person or event in another place or time? Read the paragraph below with these questions in mind.

Text-to-self:
What do you know about how people think and act? What do you think about government?

Framers of the Constitution got many ideas on the nature of people and government from European writers of the Enlightenment. The Enlightenment (ihn•LY•tuhn•muhnt) was a movement of the 1700s that promoted knowledge, reason, and science as the means to improve society.

—*from page 203*

Text-to-text:
What did you read about the Enlightenment in Chapter 1?

Reading Tip

Make connections with important ideas, times, and topics in your life. Connecting helps you remember new information.

Text-to-world:
What other countries have governments based on ideals of the Enlightenment? How do knowledge, reason, and science impact government today?

2 Practice It!

Read the following paragraphs. Then make a list of connections you made to the ideas in the reading. Compare your lists and discuss your answers with a partner.

Read to Write·······

Choose one of the connections you made that was different than your partner's or one that you think was more important. Write a paragraph to explain why you made such a connection. Use vivid details.

The Northwest Ordinance provided a democratic model for national expansion. When the population of a territory reached 60,000, its people could petition, or apply to Congress, for statehood. Each new state would come into the Union with the same rights and privileges as the original 13 states.

The Northwest Ordinance also guaranteed certain rights to people living in the territory. These rights included freedom of religion, property rights, and the right to trial by jury.
—*from page 181–182*

NATIONAL GEOGRAPHIC   **The Northwest Territory**

- Lake Superior
- SPANISH LOUISIANA
- Mississippi R.
- WISCONSIN
- Lake Huron
- MICHIGAN
- Lake Michigan
- Lake Erie
- ILLINOIS
- INDIANA
- OHIO
- Ohio R.

Northwest Territory
Present-day state boundaries

0   200 miles
0   200 kilometers
Albers Conic Equal-Area projection

3 Apply It!

As you read this chapter, choose five words or phrases that make a connection to something you already know.

Section 1

The Articles of Confederation

Guide to Reading

Looking Back, Looking Ahead

In Chapter 2, you learned about the American Revolution. The United States was now independent, but it remained to be seen whether the new nation could survive.

Focusing on the Main Ideas

- As soon as the Declaration of Independence was signed, the 13 states began writing their own constitutions. *(page 179)*
- Americans realized the necessity of establishing a central, or national, government for the 13 states. *(page 180)*
- The weaknesses of the Articles of Confederation created problems for the new country. *(page 183)*

Locating Places

Appalachian Mountains
(A•puh•LAY•chuhn)
Northwest Territory

Meeting People

Robert Morris

John Jay

Content Vocabulary

popular sovereignty
(PAH•pyuh•luhr SAH•vuhrn•tee)
bicameral (by•KAM•ruhl)
confederation
(kuhn•FEH•duh•RAY•shuhn)
sovereignty (SAH•vuhrn•tee)
ratify (RA•tuh•fy)
ordinance (AWR•duhn•uhnts)
right of deposit (di•PAH•zuht)

Academic Vocabulary

interpret (ihn•TUHR•pruht)
authority (uh•THAHR•uh•tee)

Reading Strategy

Organizing Information Draw a diagram like the one below. In each oval, list a power you think a national government should have.

Powers of government

Where & When?

NATIONAL GEOGRAPHIC

| 1775 | 1780 | 1785 | 1790 |

1777
Articles of Confederation written

1781
All states approve Confederation government

1787
Northwest Ordinance is passed

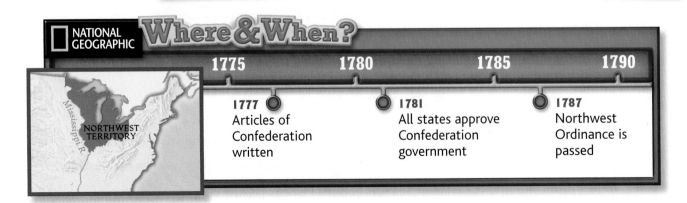

NORTHWEST TERRITORY

Mississippi R.

Thirteen Independent States

Main Idea As soon as the Declaration of Independence was signed, the 13 states began writing their own constitutions.

Reading Connection What makes people get along with one another? Do they need rules or a strong leader? Read to learn how the people of the new states answered these questions.

An American Story

In 1783 an enslaved Massachusetts man named Quock Walker made an important decision. He took legal action against a white man who had assaulted him. The case reached the state supreme court. Chief Justice William Cushing agreed with Walker:

> **66** Our constitution [of Massachusetts] sets out with declaring that all men are born free and equal—and that every subject is entitled to liberty. . . . This being the case, I think the idea of slavery is inconsistent with our own conduct and constitution. **99**
>
> —William Cushing,
> from his private notebook

The Quock Walker case demonstrated that the Massachusetts courts would not support slavery. Because of this ruling and other anti-slavery efforts, slavery ceased to exist in Massachusetts.

State Constitutions Even before the Declaration of Independence was signed, American colonists discussed the possibility of independence and American leaders began preparing new state constitutions to replace the old colonial charters. Many of the new state governments were based upon ideals expressed in the Declaration of Independence. American ideals of individual rights to "life, liberty, and the pursuit of happiness" are in the Declaration. So are such values as **popular sovereignty** (PAH•pyuh•luhr SAH•vuhrn•tee)—government by consent of the governed—and equal justice under law. These ideals were also an important part of the early state constitutions.

Systems of Government In January 1776, New Hampshire became the first colony to organize as a state and craft a constitution. By 1780, the other former colonies had followed suit.

The new state constitutions set up a similar system of government. Each state had a legislature to create laws, and most of these legislatures were **bicameral** (by•KAM•ruhl), like the English Parliament; that is, they were divided into two parts, or houses. Each state also had a chief executive called the governor, who was elected by the legislature or by the citizens. The governor's job was to carry out the laws. To prevent abuses by a single ruler most states' constitutions limited the power of the governor. Finally, each state had judges and courts to **interpret** the laws—to decide what the laws meant and how they applied to each new situation.

Preserving Rights To keep power in the hands of the people, state legislators were popularly elected, and elections were frequent. In most states, only white males who were at least 21 years old could vote. These citizens also had to own a certain amount of property or pay a certain amount of taxes. Some states allowed free African American males to vote.

Most state constitutions included a bill of rights, guaranteeing certain freedoms and legal protections to the state's citizens. Some of these rights, such as trial by jury and protection of personal property, can be traced back to the Magna Carta and the English Bill of Rights. As you learned earlier, these documents helped establish the idea that people have rights and that the power of the government should be limited.

✓ Reading Check **Explain** Describe the branches of the new state government.

Forming the New Government

Main Idea Americans realized the necessity of establishing a central, or national, government for the 13 states.

Reading Connection Would you be surprised to learn that the Constitution of the United States was not our nation's first plan of government? Read to find out about the nation's first constitution.

Although each state was well prepared and eager to govern itself when independence was declared, a state could not do some things on its own. It could not raise and maintain a large army, for example, and Americans knew that 13 small, separate forces would be no match for the mighty British army. Americans realized that if they wanted to win the war with Great Britain, they needed a single, strong army under central control. For this and other reasons, the Second Continental Congress made plans for a union of the states.

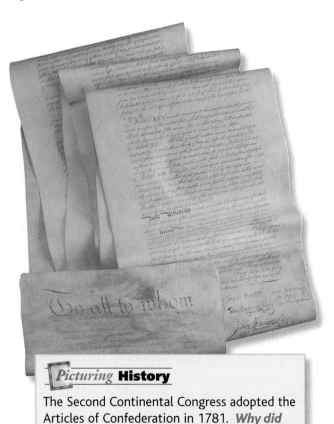

Picturing **History**

The Second Continental Congress adopted the Articles of Confederation in 1781. *Why did the Congress form a union of states?*

A Confederation of States At the same time that Jefferson was drafting the Declaration of Independence, members of the Continental Congress were developing a plan for the new government. In 1777 the Congress detailed these plans in a document called the Articles of Confederation, the first constitution of the United States of America.

A confederation is a voluntary association of independent states. In a **confederation** (kuhn•FEH•duh•RAY•shuhn), the member states agree to let the central government undertake a limited number of activities, such as forming an army.

The Articles set up a one-house legislature called the Congress. Although the states could send between two and seven delegates to the congress, each state, no matter what the size, had only one vote. The issue of **sovereignty** (SAH•vuhrn•tee), or supreme power, was an important part of the Articles of Confederation:

> **❝ Each state retains its sovereignty, freedom and independence, and every power, jurisdiction and right, which is not by this Confederation expressly delegated to the United States in Congress assembled. ❞**
>
> —Article II,
> Articles of Confederation

The Powers of Congress Congress had several powers under the Articles of Confederation. Congress had the **authority** to conduct foreign affairs, maintain armed forces, borrow money, and issue currency. These powers of Congress were quite limited, though.

As a result of their negative experiences with the British government, the 13 states refused to give the Congress two important powers. It had no power to enforce its laws and no power to tax. The Articles allowed the Congress to ask the states for money but not to demand it. The Congress could not, in fact, require the states to do anything. Without money or real power over the states, the Confederation Congress commanded so little respect that its members often did not bother to attend sessions.

Weaknesses of the Articles By 1781 all 13 states had **ratified** (RA•tuh•fyd), or approved, the Articles of Confederation. Within the next few years, however, it became clear that the Articles had some serious flaws.

To begin with, the Congress could not pass a law unless nine states voted in favor of it. Any attempt to amend, or change, the Articles required a unanimous vote of all 13 states. These strict voting requirements made it difficult for the Congress to accomplish much.

Even when the Congress managed to pass laws, it could not enforce them. Unlike the state constitutions, the Articles did not provide for a chief executive or for courts. If a state decided to ignore a law, the Congress could do nothing.

Despite the weaknesses of the Articles, the Confederation government accomplished some important tasks. Perhaps its greatest achievement was establishing a fair policy for the development of the lands west of the **Appalachian Mountains** (A•puh•LAY•chuhn).

Western Land Policies At the beginning of the Revolutionary War, only a few thousand non-Indian settlers lived west of the Appalachian Mountains. By the 1790s, the number was approaching 120,000. These settlers hoped to organize their lands as states and join the union, but the Articles contained no provision for adding states. Congress knew that it had to extend its authority over the territory.

Lacking the power to tax or regulate trade, the only way for the Confederation Congress to raise money to pay its debts and operate the government was to sell land. To get people to buy land and settle in the western region, the Congress had to establish a system for dividing and selling the land and governing the new settlements.

In 1785 Congress passed an **ordinance** (AWR•duhn•uhnts), or law, that established a procedure for surveying and selling the western lands. The new law divided the land into local government units called townships, which are perfectly squared blocks usually six miles wide and six miles long. These townships were to be further divided into 36 sections of 640 acres each that would be sold at public auction for at least a dollar an acre.

The Northwest Ordinance Two years later, Congress passed the Northwest Ordinance, which created a single **Northwest Territory** out of the lands north of the Ohio River and east of the Mississippi River. The lands were to be divided into not fewer than three nor more than five smaller territories.

The Northwest Ordinance provided a democratic model for national expansion. When the population of a territory reached 60,000, its people could petition, or apply to Congress, for statehood. Each new state would come into the Union with the same rights and privileges as the original 13 states.

Weaknesses in the Articles of Confederation

Weakness	Result
Congress has no power to tax.	It had to rely on the states to collect and forward taxes, which the states were reluctant to do. The central government was always short of money.
Congress has no power to enforce its laws.	Congress depended on the states to enforce its laws, which they rarely did.
There was no executive branch.	Coordinating the work of the national government was almost impossible.
Nine states had to approve any law before it could be passed.	Most laws were difficult, if not impossible, to enact.
Congress could not force the states to meet military quotas.	Congress could not draft soldiers to form a standing army.

Understanding Charts

The national government had limited powers. It depended on states for revenue, soldiers, and law enforcement.

Analyze Why did the states approve a government with many weaknesses?

The Northwest Ordinance also guaranteed certain rights to people living in the territory. These rights included freedom of religion, property rights, and the right to trial by jury. The ordinance also included a clause stating,

> **"There shall be neither slavery nor involuntary servitude in [the] territory."**
>
> —Article 6,
> The Northwest Ordinance

This clause is very important. It marked the United States's first attempt to stop the spread of slavery.

Which States Were Formed? The Confederation's western ordinances had an enormous effect on American expansion and development. The Ordinance of 1785 and the Northwest Ordinance described the steps by which new states would be formed. These policies opened the way for settlement of the Northwest Territory in a clear and orderly manner.

Ohio was the first state admitted (1803) to the Union from the Northwest Territory. Other states were admitted later. The present-day states of Indiana, Illinois, Michigan, and Wisconsin eventually were formed from the Northwest Territory.

Reading Check **Explain** What was the purpose of the Northwest Ordinance?

Why It Matters

Surveying the Land

When the Revolution began, only a few thousand white settlers lived west of the Appalachian Mountains. By the 1790s their numbers had increased to about 120,000. Through the Ordinance of 1785, Congress created a system for surveying—taking a detailed measurement of an area of land—and selling the western lands.

The Ordinance at first applied only to what was then called the Northwest Territory—present-day Ohio, Indiana, Michigan, Illinois, and Wisconsin. It established a system of land survey and settlement that we still use today.

The Land Ordinance led to the sale of large amounts of land and speeded settlement of the Northwest Territory.

Trouble on Two Fronts

Main Idea The weaknesses of the Articles of Confederation created problems for the new country.

Reading Connection Imagine paying 10 times the normal price for a gallon of milk or a loaf of bread. Read to find out why the price of goods soared during this era.

Although successful in establishing western land policies, the Confederation government had problems dealing with other important issues. Congress was powerless to regulate trade, so each state passed laws taxing goods from its neighbors. New York taxed firewood from Connecticut and cabbage from New Jersey. New Jersey retaliated by charging New York for a harbor lighthouse on the New Jersey side of the Hudson River. Congress had so little power that it could not deal effectively with the country's economic problems. It also failed to solve trade problems.

Economic Problems By 1781 the money printed during the Revolutionary War had depreciated, or fallen in value, so much that it was almost worthless. Unable to collect taxes, both the Congress and the states had printed their own paper money.

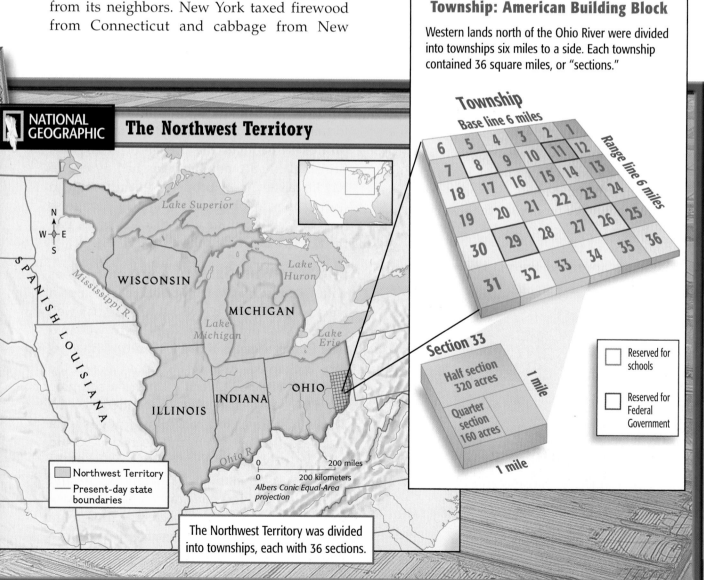

NATIONAL GEOGRAPHIC

The Northwest Territory

Lake Superior

SPANISH LOUISIANA

Mississippi R.

WISCONSIN

MICHIGAN

Lake Michigan

Lake Huron

Lake Erie

ILLINOIS

INDIANA

OHIO

Ohio R.

0   200 miles
0   200 kilometers
Albers Conic Equal-Area projection

Northwest Territory
Present-day state boundaries

The Northwest Territory was divided into townships, each with 36 sections.

Township: American Building Block

Western lands north of the Ohio River were divided into townships six miles to a side. Each township contained 36 square miles, or "sections."

Township
Base line 6 miles
Range line 6 miles

6	5	4	3	2	1
7	8	9	10	11	12
18	17	16	15	14	13
19	20	21	22	23	24
30	29	28	27	26	25
31	32	33	34	35	36

Section 33

Half section 320 acres

Quarter section 160 acres

1 mile

1 mile

Reserved for schools

Reserved for Federal Government

The money constantly declined in purchasing power because people feared that it could not be redeemed in gold or silver; if a $10 bill was worth $3 when it came into their hands, it might be worth only $2 or less when they spent it. The value of the money fell, while the price of food and other goods soared. Between 1779 and 1781, the number of Continental dollars required to buy one Spanish silver dollar rose from 40 to 146. In some towns, angry mobs seized overpriced sugar, tea, and bread from storekeepers.

Why Did the Debt Grow?

Fighting the war left the Continental Congress with a large debt. Congress had borrowed money from American citizens and foreign governments during the war. It still owed the Revolutionary soldiers their pay for military service. Lacking the power to tax, the Confederation could not pay its debts. It requested funds from the states, but the states contributed only a small portion of the money needed.

Faced with a total collapse of the country's finances, the Confederation created a department of finance under Philadelphia merchant **Robert Morris.** Morris personally pledged large amounts of money for the war effort.

Some members wanted to give Congress some power to tax to raise funds. Although 12 states approved the plan, Rhode Island's opposition killed the measure. A second effort five years later also failed to win unanimous approval. The financial crisis only worsened.

Problems With Britain

As the weaknesses of the new American government became clear, the United States had problems with other nations. In the Treaty of Paris of 1783, Britain had promised to withdraw from the lands east of the Mississippi River. Yet British troops continued to occupy several strategic forts in the Great Lakes region. These forts were the centers of a profitable fur trade that Great Britain was determined to keep. The weak Confederation government could do nothing about the presence of foreign troops on American soil.

British trade policy caused other problems. American merchants complained that the British were keeping Americans out of the West Indies and other profitable British markets.

In 1784 Congress sent John Adams to London to discuss these difficulties. The British, however, were not willing to talk. They pointed to the failure of the United States to honor its promises made in the Treaty of Paris. The British claimed that Americans had agreed to pay Loyalists for the property taken from them during the Revolutionary War. The Congress had, in fact, recommended that the states pay the Loyalists, but the states had refused.

Problems With Spain

If American relations with Great Britain were poor, affairs with Spain were worse. Spain, which held Florida as well as lands west of the Mississippi River, was anxious to halt American expansion into the territory it claimed. As a result, Spain closed the lower Mississippi River to American shipping in 1784. Western settlers depended on the Mississippi River for trade. Bulky goods from the West—lumber, grain, and deerskins—could not be carried easily over the mountains to the East, but had to float down the Ohio and Mississippi Rivers on rafts and flatboats. **John Jay,** the American secretary of foreign affairs, noted that Americans accepted the idea that it was their right to use the Mississippi River to transport goods.

▲ Continental currency

What Is the Right of Deposit? Westerners wanted the **right of deposit** (di•PAH•zuht) at New Orleans—that is, permission to put goods ashore for transfer to ocean-going ships. When Spain refused this request, westerners asked Congress for a treaty with Spain that would grant free navigation along the Mississippi River.

In 1786 American diplomats reached an agreement with Spain. The people living in the Southern states, however, blocked the agreement because it did not include the right to use the Mississippi River.

The Government Falters The weakness of the Confederation and its inability to deal with problems worried many leaders. Peace with the British may have been won, but peace within the new nation was hard to find. The states bickered among themselves and refused to support the new central government in almost every way. Each state was beginning to act as an independent country, threatening the unity of the new United States. Some Vermont leaders even considered becoming part of Great Britain again. Only 18 members representing 8 states voted on the Confederation's most important piece of legislation, the Northwest Ordinance.

In a letter to one of George Washington's personal aides during the American Revolution, Washington noted that:

> 66 We are one nation today and thirteen tomorrow—Who will treat with us on such terms? 99
>
> —George Washington,
> Letter to James McHenry,
> 22 August 1785

By the late 1780s, many national leaders had become dissatisfied with the weaknesses of the Confederation.

✓ **Reading Check** **Analyze** Why did Spain close the lower Mississippi River to American trade?

Study Central Need help understanding the Articles of Confederation? Visit tajww1.glencoe.com and click on Study Central.

Section 1 Review

Reading Summary

Review the Main Ideas

- The 13 states began writing their own constitutions.

- Americans knew the importance of establishing a national government for the 13 states.

- Problems arose for the nation because of the weaknesses of the Articles of Confederation.

What Did You Learn?

1. What did the Ordinance of 1785 accomplish?

2. Why was the right of deposit at New Orleans important for western farmers?

Critical Thinking

3. **Organizing** Draw a diagram to summarize the strengths and weaknesses of the Confederation government.

The Articles of Confederation	
Strengths	Weaknesses

4. **Expository Writing** Imagine you are on a committee to write a new state constitution. List three freedoms you want attached to your state's constitution. Explain why you believe it is important to guarantee these rights.

5. **READING** **Making Connections** Read the passage called "Problems With Britain." Make three connections with what you read: text-to-text, text-to-self, and text-to-world. Write a sentence describing each of these connections.

Second Daughter

By Mildred Pitts Walter

Before You Read

The Scene: The events in this part of the story take place in a courtroom in Great Barrington, which is in western Massachusetts. The year is 1781.

The Characters: Judge and Mistress Ashley own several slaves. They include Aissa, her older brother Brom, her older sister Bett, and her sister's daughter Little Bett. Lawyers Noble and Canfield represent the Ashleys. Lawyers Reeve and Sedgwick represent Bett and Brom.

The Plot: Aissa is telling the story. After Mistress Ashley accidentally strikes Bett with a red-hot shovel, Brom and Bett ask the court for their freedom. During the trial, Aissa and Little Bett are in the back of the courtroom.

Vocabulary Preview

bared: uncovered; showed
clammy: cold and damp
folly: lack of good sense or judgment
pity: feeling of sorrow for someone else's suffering
rational: able to think

squared: changed from a slumped over position to a straightened one
title: document that proves that something is lawful
valid: acceptable by law

Have you ever noticed how sporting events and trials are alike? In both, each side tries to score points. In baseball, for example, players make runs to score points. In a trial, each lawyer gives evidence. Someone's freedom often depends on a lawyer's success.

As You Read

Earlier in this story, a very emotional scene took place in the Ashleys' kitchen. Bett angrily told Mistress Ashley that she was leaving and not coming back. The mistress got very upset, cried, and apologized to Bett. Then she told Bett that she could not leave, but Bett did. The following scene is also about Bett's freedom, but it takes place in a courtroom. Think about how the setting affects what people say and do.

Master Noble called Master Ashley to the stand and questioned him: How had he come to own us? Had he seen to it that we were well fed, clothed, and housed? Had he seen to it that we were changed from heathens[1] to Christians? The master answered, "Yes, I have." When Master Reeve said he had no questions, Master Noble said, "I call Mistress Anna Ashley."

There was a stir in the crowd as she made her way to the stand. As always, when she was in public, she was confident and assured. She seemed not to notice anything around her, except once to raise her eyes to the ceiling. She mopped her brow, suffering from the heat. "Will you describe to the court your relationship with your servant, Bett?" her lawyer asked.

"Bett is like one in my family. She was born on my father's land and has been a servant of mine even before I married her master. We have never quarreled, and I have been nothing but kind to her."

I was afraid I was going to start laughing, so I closed my ears and mind to her and held on to keep from being tossed out of the place. How could she sit there pretending that she was a good mistress? I looked at my sister, who sat upright and calm, and I wondered, if asked to disagree with the mistress, would she have the will to do so?

---

[1] **heathens:** at this time and place, someone who does not believe in the Christian God

Master Reeve said he had no questions for the mistress and called Bett. I could tell that Bett was reluctant. He whispered something to her, and finally she came forward and sat in the seat where the mistress had sat. "Your honor," Master Reeve said, "I would like to prove that the mistress Ashley is not the kind mistress she claims." He then turned to the jury. "The issue here is not whether the Ashleys have been kind. The issue is, do they have the right to hold Bett and Brom as slaves for life?" He turned to Bett. "Has Mistress Ashley ever in any way abused you?"

My sister looked at the judge and then at Lawyer Reeve. She did not speak. The courtroom was hushed, waiting. Answer him! I wanted to say. Why didn't she tell them and show the ugly wound on her arm?

Bett looked at the mistress, who was staring Bett in the face. "Yes, Master Reeve, she is not the kind person she wants people to believe she is. I have been in her household many years and was never paid one pence.[2] We work six days a week and sometimes on the seventh. But whether she is kind or not, the constitution says we have rights to our freedom."

"No further questions," Mr. Reeve said.

Master Noble stood and said, "Bett, you sit here well dressed, in good health, with nothing to even hint at your being anything but blessed[3] to be a servant of the Ashleys." There was applause and sounds of "Hear, hear!"

The judge pounded on his desk. "There must be order in this court. Continue, Mr. Noble."

"You know your master and mistress have been good to you, haven't they, Bett?"

"I object," Lawyer Reeve said. "Whether they were good to her is not the question here."

"Objection sustained."

"Your honor, my worthy opponent asked if she had been abused. May I rephrase the question? What proof can you give to this court of Mistress Ashley's abuse?" Lawyer Noble asked.

My sister looked at the mistress, then at the judge. She did not answer. Was she afraid, thinking What if we lost? What would the master and mistress do to us? I felt cold sweat rolling down my sides. In that room that had been almost unbearably warm, I became chilled.

---

[2] **pence:** a unit of British money that has very little value

[3] **blessed:** bringing pleasure or good luck

Suddenly Bett squared her shoulders. Without saying a word, she rolled up her sleeve and bared the wound. It was still scarlet with the healing pulling the muscles tight, making the arm twist out of shape, limiting its range of movement.[4] She held her arm so that all could see. There was a gasp in the audience.

Lawyer Noble rushed to the mistress. Lawyer Canfield joined him, and they whispered in conversation with her. The mistress lowered her head when her lawyer said, almost in a whisper, "I have no further questions."

The judge asked if there were other witnesses and questions. Both sides said, "No, your honor." Then the judge gave final instructions to the jury: "You have heard the arguments in this case. You are bound[5] by the law, only by the law, that has been presented here, not by pity and sympathy for either side. It is your duty to determine if the idea of slavery is not in keeping with our own conduct and with our constitution, and that, therefore, there can be no such thing as life servitude[6] of a rational creature." Then he said, "We'll hear your closing statements now."

In his closing statement, Master Noble reminded the jury of Master Ashley's outstanding citizenship. "He is one who sits in judgment and knows the law. Would he break the laws that he so proudly administers? I say no, he would not." He went on and on.

"Gentlemen of the jury, Master and Mistress Ashley have every right to hold on to their servants, as all of our history declares. The Ashleys along with other great men, Thomas Jefferson, our great General Washington, and many others, hold slaves.

---

[4] **range of movement:** ability to move left and right and up and down
[5] **bound:** held to by law or duty
[6] **servitude:** a condition in which one lacks liberty

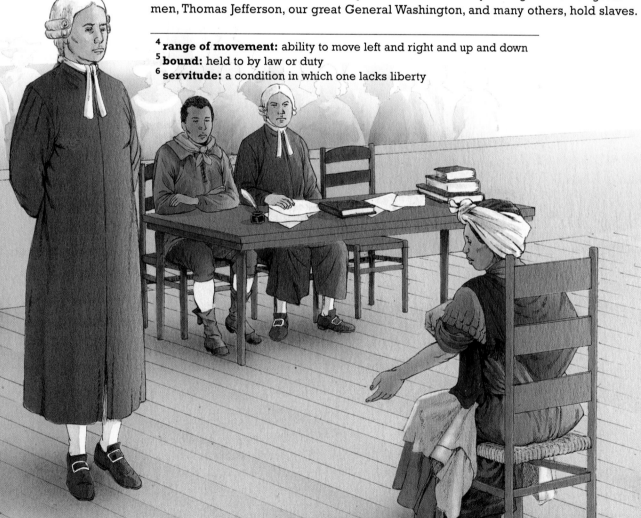

Are they not good law-abiding[7] citizens? They know that these people are not capable of caring for themselves. If freed, how will they live? Will their freedom make them wards[8] of the state, so that you and I will have to care for them? Let Master Ashley continue to keep his servants, for we all know he is a good kind master. I rest my case."

The applause from the crowd was hammered down by the gavel in the judge's hand. I was so angry and upset that I missed the beginning of Lawyer Reeve's closing.

". . . There are some things in our history that Mr. Noble did not dare talk about that have happened in this very state of Massachusetts and this Berkshire County. Many of you remember the meeting held in the town of Sheffield where even some of you approved without a single 'nay' these words: 'Resolved that Mankind in a State of Nature[9] are equal, free and independent of each other, and have a right to the undisturbed enjoyment of their lives, their liberty and their property.'

"One of those men who hold slaves, Thomas Jefferson, echoed *your* feelings in the Declaration of Independence when he wrote, 'We hold these truths to be self-evident, that all men are created equal, that they are endowed by their Creator with certain unalienable rights, that among these are life, liberty and the pursuit of happiness.' You continued that idea in your state constitution with a bill of rights."

I was so happy when he told them that Bett was a midwife[10] and Brom a herdsman,[11] who could certainly take care of themselves. There was some laughter when he mentioned how long Bett and Brom had worked and the folly of the idea that they couldn't look after themselves. But the place got real quiet when he came to the end.

"I say that the city of Sheffield and Berkshire County, the first to have a meeting and a petition on ending slavery and on declaring in favor of independence from the king, is no place where a citizen can be called law abiding if he claims ownership of another human being.

"Gentlemen of the jury, make the Declaration of Independence and your state constitution meaningful in our lives now. Declare that no title to a slave is valid, and grant Brom and Bett their liberty so that they may pursue happiness. I rest my case."

There was no applause, but the silence was complete. The judge waited; no one stirred. "The jury will now convene." He called the bailiff,[12] who escorted the jury to the room where they would decide the verdict.

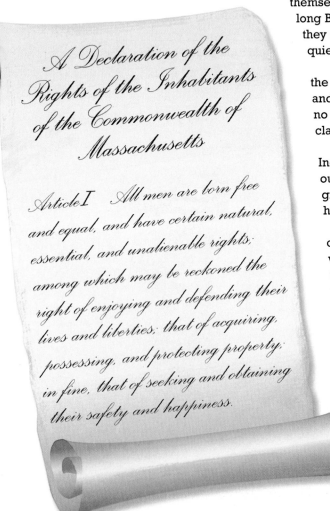

A Declaration of the Rights of the Inhabitants of the Commonwealth of Massachusetts

Article I   All men are born free and equal, and have certain natural, essential, and unalienable rights: among which may be reckoned the right of enjoying and defending their lives and liberties; that of acquiring, possessing, and protecting property; in fine, that of seeking and obtaining their safety and happiness.

---

[7] **law-abiding:** obedient to the law
[8] **wards:** people that the court has put under the control of someone other than their parents
[9] **State of Nature:** time before the establishment of government
[10] **midwife:** a woman who helps another woman who is giving birth
[11] **herdsman:** a person who takes care of livestock
[12] **bailiff:** an officer in some U.S. courts who acts as a messenger or usher

What would happen now? I thought of the applause when Lawyer Noble said that Bett looked anything but mistreated. What if they agree with the master that he has a right to us as his property? I can't go back to that house. But where will I go?

In spite of my worry and fears, time did not drag, and before two hours had passed the bailiff announced that the session would begin again. "All rise." The judge entered.

After we were all seated, the judge asked the jury foreman, "Have you reached a verdict?"

The foreman replied, "We have, Your Honor."

My heartbeat could be seen in my chest and my hands were clammy with sweat. Oh, God, let them. Please let them say we're free.

"We find for the plaintiffs.[13] The said Brom and Bett are not and were not legally Negro servants of him, the said John Ashley, during life. We further assess thirty shillings, lawful silver money damages."

Did I hear right? I looked at the mistress. Her face was red with anger. Then I looked at my sister, who was smiling and embracing her lawyers. I wanted to join her and Brom up front to share that moment, but the judge was banging his gavel. "Order, order! I adjudge[14] and determine in accordance with the jury's verdict that Brom and Bett are free. I accept the jury's recommendation that the Ashleys pay Brom and Bett thirty shillings damages. In addition, the court assesses the Ashleys the cost of this suit, five pounds, fourteen shillings, and four pence. This court is adjourned."

Finally, the four of us were together. "We are free!" Bett cried. "Can you believe it, *free*." We all four hugged each other and tears of joy flowed.

---

[13] **plaintiffs:** person who brings a legal action; opposite of *defendant*
[14] **adjudge:** decide or rule upon

Responding to the Literature

1. On what did Bett base her claim to freedom?

2. On what three ideas did Lawyer Noble base the Ashleys' right to keep Brom and Bett as slaves?

3. **Conclude** What is the general meaning of the word *pounds* in "the court assesses the Ashleys the cost of this suit, five pounds, fourteen shillings, and four pence"? Why, do you think, *pounds* means this?

4. **Evaluate** Think about the testimony and the lawyers' arguments during the trial. Choose one fact and one opinion from them. Explain why one is a fact and the other is an opinion.

5. **Read to Write** Use descriptions and details from the scene to show how setting affected its mood and tone. Was the mood mostly angry, funny, or something else? What was the writer's attitude toward the case?

Reading On Your Own...

Do you want to learn more about the writing of the Constitution, the Founding Fathers, and Shays's Rebellion? You might be interested in the following books.

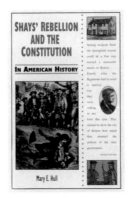

Nonfiction

Shays' Rebellion and the Constitution in American History by Mary E. Hull describes Shays's Rebellion and its effects on taxation in the United States. This book explains why people who had just experienced the hardships of one revolution were willing to go through another one.

Nonfiction

Shh! We're Writing the Constitution by Jean Fritz humorously introduces the people at the Constitutional Convention. She also clearly explains the kinds of choices that these men made as they tried to form a workable government.

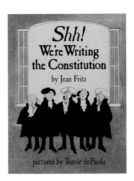

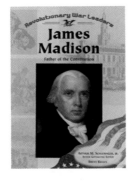

Biography

James Madison: Father of the Constitution by Brent P. Kelley describes Madison's life and his contributions to the United States. These include his work on the Constitution, the Federalist Papers, and the Bill of Rights.

Nonfiction

Blessings of Liberty: Safeguarding Civil Rights by William C. Lowe explains what civil rights are and why they are important. He also describes six of those rights—freedom of religion, expression, and the press; the right to due process; voting rights; and equality under the law. Interesting parts of this description include how these rights have gradually changed and people who helped win them.

Section 2

Convention and Compromise

Guide to Reading

Looking Back, Looking Ahead
You read about the weaknesses of the Articles of Confederation. Many Americans concluded that the United States needed a new constitution.

Focusing on the (Main Ideas)
- The government under the Articles of Confederation faced many problems. *(page 194)*
- National leaders worked to produce a new constitution for the United States. *(page 197)*
- The Constitutional Convention broke the deadlock over the form the new government would take. *(page 199)*

Meeting People
Daniel Shays
James Madison
Alexander Hamilton
Gouverneur Morris
Edmund Randolph
Roger Sherman

Content Vocabulary
depression
manumission (MAN•yuh•MIH•shuhn)
proportional (pruh•POHR•shuh•nuhl)
compromise

Academic Vocabulary
participate (pahr•TIH•suh•PAYT)
currency (KUHR•uhn•see)
levy (leh•VEE)
regulate (REH•gyuh•LAYT)
adequate (A•dih•kwuht)

Reading Strategy
Organizing Information Create a diagram like the one below to describe the role each individual played in creating the new plan of government.

Person	Roles
Edmund Randolph	
James Madison	
Roger Sherman	

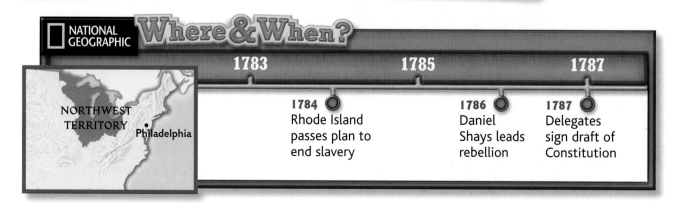

NATIONAL GEOGRAPHIC — Where & When?

NORTHWEST TERRITORY · Philadelphia

1783 — 1785 — 1787

1784 Rhode Island passes plan to end slavery

1786 Daniel Shays leads rebellion

1787 Delegates sign draft of Constitution

Troubles Under the Articles

Main Idea **The government under the Articles of Confederation faced many problems.**

Reading Connection You make a plan but the plan is not working—what do you do? Find out how American leaders decided to fix the problems of the Articles of Confederation.

An American Story

By 1786 many Americans observed that the Confederation was not working. George Washington himself agreed that the United States was really "thirteen Sovereignties pulling against each other." In the spring of 1787, Washington joined delegates from Virginia and 11 other states who gathered in Philadelphia to address this problem. Rhode Island decided not to **participate.** The delegates came "for the sole and express purpose of revising the Articles of Confederation."

Economic Depression The call to revise the Articles of Confederation came while the young nation faced difficult problems. Many Americans believed that the Confederation government was too weak to deal with these challenges. After the Revolutionary War ended, the United States went through a **depression,** a period when economic activity slowed and unemployment increased. Southern plantations had been damaged during the war, and rice exports dropped sharply. Trade also fell off when the British closed the profitable West Indies (Caribbean) market to American merchants. What little money there was went to pay foreign debts, and a serious **currency** shortage resulted. Each state printed its own money. The value of the money differed from state to state, and the money often was not accepted outside the states issuing it.

American farmers suffered because they could not sell their goods. They had problems paying the requests for money that the states **levied** to meet Revolutionary War debts. As a result, state officials seized farmers' lands to pay their debts and threw many farmers into jail. Murmurs of protest soon grew into revolt.

Shays's Rebellion Resentment grew especially strong in Massachusetts. Farmers viewed the new government as just another form of tyranny. They wanted the government to issue paper money and make new policies to relieve debtors. In a letter to state officials, some farmers said "many of our good inhabitants are now confined in [jail] for debt and taxes."

In August 1786, a convention of delegates from 50 Massachusetts towns met in Hatfield, Massachusetts. The delegates drew up a petition to the state government protesting the new taxes. State officials replied that the Hatfield convention was against the law and the delegates were rebels.

Picturing **History**

Only through donations was Massachusetts able to raise a militia to defeat Shays. *Why did Shays's Rebellion frighten many Americans?*

Angry farmers lashed out. Led by **Daniel Shays,** a former Continental Army captain, they forced courts in western Massachusetts to close so judges could not confiscate farmers' lands.

In January 1787, Shays led more than 1,000 farmers toward the federal arsenal in Springfield, Massachusetts, to seize arms and ammunition. The state militia ordered the advancing farmers to halt, then fired over their heads. The farmers did not stop, and the militia fired again, killing four rebels. Shays and his followers scattered, and the uprising was over.

Shays's Rebellion frightened many national leaders. They worried that the government could not control unrest and prevent violence. On hearing of the rebellion, George Washington wondered whether "mankind, when left to themselves, are unfit for their own government." Thomas Jefferson, minister to France at the time, had a different view. "A little rebellion, now and then," he wrote, "is a good thing."

The Issue of Slavery The Revolutionary War brought attention to the contradiction between the American battle for liberty and the practice of slavery. The Southern states accepted the institution of slavery. The plantation system of the South had been built on slavery, and many Southerners feared that their economy could not survive without it.

Although slavery was not a major source of labor in the North, it existed and was legal in all the Northern states. Many individuals and groups began to work to end the institution of slavery. In 1774 Quakers in Pennsylvania organized the first American antislavery society. Six years later, Pennsylvania passed a law that provided for the gradual freeing of enslaved people.

Between 1783 and 1804, Connecticut, Rhode Island, New York, and New Jersey passed laws that gradually ended slavery. Still, free African Americans faced discrimination. They were barred from many public places. Few states gave free African Americans the right to vote.

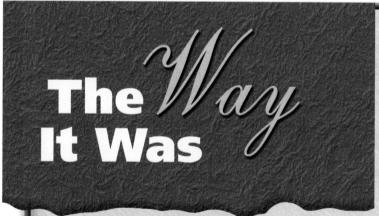

◄ The coneflower is a popular Native American plant. As medicine, it is commonly called Echinacea.

Home Remedies

In an age before germs and proper sanitation were understood, home remedies for illnesses became an everyday part of life in early America. While some folk remedies, such as herbal teas, might have had positive effects, other cures could make the patient worse.

For a venomous snakebite, a part of the snake was placed on top of the wound. This, it was thought, would draw out the poison.

Some remedies used by Native Americans were later adopted by Europeans. The Inca, for example, found that boiling a certain kind of tree bark in water eased the symptoms of malaria. But it was not until the 1900s that the ingredient in the tree bark—quinine—was finally isolated.

Richard Allen and Absalom Jones

Philadelphia preachers Richard Allen and Absalom Jones founded the Free American Society and later set up the first African American churches.

▲ Richard Allen

Born in slavery, Richard Allen was freed and became a Methodist minister. Allen and Absalom Jones founded an independent Methodist church for black members. In the early 1800s, some African American movements encouraged immigration to Africa. Allen and Jones opposed this idea, stating that since

▲ Absalom Jones

"our ancestors (not of choice) were the first successful cultivators of the wilds of America, we their descendants feel ourselves entitled to participate in the blessings of her luxurient soil...."

—Bethel Church Resolution

 Document-Based Question

Why did Allen and Jones believe African Americans should stay in America even though they had been brought there against their will?

The children of most free blacks had to attend separate schools. Free African Americans established their own institutions—churches, schools, and mutual-aid societies—to seek opportunity.

An increasing number of slaveholders began freeing the enslaved people that they held after the war. Virginia passed a law that encouraged **manumission** (MAN•yuh•MIH•shuhn), the freeing of individual enslaved persons, and the state's population of free African Americans grew.

The abolition of slavery in the North divided the new country on the issue of whether people should be allowed to hold other human beings in bondage. This division came at the time when many American leaders had decided that the Articles of Confederation needed to be strengthened. In the summer of 1787, when state representatives assembled to plan a new government, they compromised on this issue. It would take years of debate, bloodshed, and ultimately a war to settle the slavery question.

A Call for Change The American Revolution had led to a union of 13 states, but it had not yet created a nation. Some leaders believed that a strong national government was the solution to America's problems. They demanded a reform of the Articles of Confederation.

Two Americans who were active in the movement for change were **James Madison,** a Virginia planter, and **Alexander Hamilton,** a New York lawyer. In September 1786, Hamilton proposed calling a convention in Philadelphia to discuss trade issues. He also suggested that this convention consider what possible changes were needed to make the Articles work.

At first, George Washington was not enthusiastic about the movement to revise the Articles of Confederation. When he heard the news of Shays's Rebellion, Washington changed his mind. After Washington agreed to attend the Philadelphia convention, the meeting took on greater significance.

Reading Check **Evaluate** Why did Madison and Hamilton call for a convention in 1787?

The Constitutional Convention

Main Idea National leaders worked to produce a new constitution for the United States.

Reading Connection Why is it important for a nation to establish a set of laws? Read to find out the issues American leaders faced in organizing a new constitution.

The Philadelphia meeting began in May 1787 and continued through one of the hottest summers on record. The 55 delegates included planters, merchants, lawyers, physicians, generals, governors, and a college president. Three of the delegates were under 30 years of age, and one, Benjamin Franklin, was over 80. Many were well educated. At a time when only one white man in 1,000 went to college, 26 of the delegates had college degrees. Native Americans, African Americans, and women were not considered part of the political process, so none attended.

Several men stood out as leaders. The presence of George Washington and Benjamin Franklin ensured that many people would trust the Convention's work. Two Philadelphians also played key roles. James Wilson often read Franklin's speeches and did important work on the details of the Constitution. **Gouverneur Morris,** a powerful speaker and writer, wrote the final draft of the Constitution.

Two revolutionary leaders who had thought deeply about the best form of government were absent. John Adams of Massachusetts and Thomas Jefferson of Virginia were in Europe serving as ambassadors. From Virginia came **Edmund Randolph** and James Madison. Both were keen supporters of a strong national government. Randolph had served in the Continental Congress and was governor of Virginia. Madison's careful notes are the major source of information about the Convention's work. Madison is often called the Father of the Constitution because he was the author of the basic plan of government that the Convention adopted.

▲ Delegates to the Constitutional Convention met in this room at Independence Hall.

Working on the Constitution

The delegates to the Constitutional Convention worked for 116 days (of which they actually met on 89) in a room where the windows were usually shut. None of the delegates wanted anybody to hear what they were doing, because they did not want rumors spread about the form of government upon which they would ultimately decide. Besides, if they opened the windows, hordes of flies would descend upon them. The air became humid and hot by noon of each day.

Biography

JAMES MADISON
c. 1751–1836

Born in 1751, Madison was still a young man at the time of the American Revolution, but his brilliant, incisive mind made him one of the more valuable leaders of the Patriots. After the war, he played a major role at the Constitutional Convention.

As one of the delegates from Virginia, Madison participated in the lengthy, often heated discussions that created a foundation of government. He kept meticulous notes and tried to impress upon the other delegates the need for an effective central government. Power was to be distributed throughout the whole. Every right had to be balanced by a corresponding responsibility.

Madison became the chief architect of the Constitution, and his notes became the best record of what happened at the Convention. There were no official transcripts of the work of the delegates. If Madison had not kept a private diary of the events, historians might know little about what happened in Philadelphia. "Every word *[of the Constitution]*," he later wrote, "decides a question between power and liberty."

After the Constitution went into effect, Madison became a leader of the new national government. In developing the Bill of Rights, he once again was trying to achieve the difficult balance between the rights of the people and the power of government. In 1808 Madison became the fourth president of the United States. Throughout his career, he continued to defend the principle of balance that was built into the Constitution.

"In framing a government . . . you must first enable the government to control the governed; and in the next place, oblige it to control itself."

—James Madison
The Federalist, No. 51

Then and Now

What qualities did Madison possess that made him a leader and an important part of the constitutional process? Do you think these are important qualities for a political leader today? Explain.

Organization The Convention began by unanimously choosing George Washington to preside over the meetings. It was also decided that each state would have one vote on all questions. Decisions would be made by a majority vote of those states present. The delegates decided to keep the sessions secret. This decision made it possible for the delegates to talk freely.

The Virginia Plan After the rules were adopted, the Convention opened with a surprise. Edmund Randolph proposed that the delegates create a strong national government instead of revising the Articles of Confederation. He introduced the Virginia Plan, which was largely the work of James Madison.

The plan called for a two-house legislature, a chief executive chosen by the legislature, and a court system. The members of the lower house of the legislature would be elected by the people. The members of the upper house would be chosen by the lower house. In both houses, the number of representatives would be **proportional** (pruh•POHR•shuh•nuhl), or corresponding in size, to the population of each state. This would give Virginia many more delegates than Delaware, the smallest state.

Delegates from small states objected to the plan. They preferred the Confederation system in which all states were represented equally. On June 15 William Paterson of New Jersey presented an alternative plan that revised the Articles of Confederation, which was all the convention was empowered to do.

The New Jersey Plan The New Jersey Plan kept the Confederation's one-house legislature, with one vote for each state. Congress, however, could set taxes and **regulate** trade—powers it did not have under the Articles. Congress would elect a weak executive branch consisting of more than one person. Paterson argued that the Convention should not deprive the smaller states of the equality they had under the Articles.

Reading Check **Explain** Why did some delegates criticize the Virginia Plan?

Compromise Wins Out

Main Idea The Constitutional Convention broke the deadlock over the form the new government would take.

Reading Connection Have you and a rival ever set aside your differences to work for a common cause? This happened when American leaders resolved their differences to create a new constitution.

The convention delegates had to decide whether they were simply revising the Articles of Confederation or writing a constitution for a new national government. On June 19 the states voted to work toward a national government based on the Virginia Plan, but they still had to resolve the thorny issue of representation that divided the large and small states.

As the convention delegates struggled to deal with difficult questions, tempers and temperatures grew hotter. How were the members of Congress to be elected? How would state representation be determined in the upper and lower houses? Were enslaved people to be counted as part of the population on which representation was based?

Under Franklin's leadership, the convention appointed a "grand committee" to try to resolve their disagreements. **Roger Sherman** of Connecticut suggested what came to be known as the Great Compromise. A **compromise** is an agreement between two or more sides in which each side gives up some of what it wants.

Sherman proposed a two-house legislature. In the lower house—the House of Representatives—the number of seats for each state would vary according to the state's population. In the upper house—the Senate—each state would have two members.

Another compromise by the delegates dealt with counting enslaved people. Southern states wanted to include the enslaved in their population counts to gain delegates in the House of Representatives.

Linking Past & Present

Symbols of the Nation

Past For Americans, the flag has always had a special meaning. It is a symbol of our nation's freedom and democracy. On June 14, 1777, the Continental Congress designed the first Stars and Stripes. The first flag had 13 stars and 13 stripes. Each star represented a state. Each stripe represented one of the 13 colonies that formed the Union.

▼ **The Stars and Stripes today**

▲ **A legend says that Betsy Ross created the American flag.**

Present Many of the symbols through which we express our American identity—heroes, songs, legends, flags, monuments—developed in the early 1800s. Some of our holidays, such as the Fourth of July, and the ways we celebrate them with parades, speeches, and picnics, became established during that time. *What are other symbols of our nation?*

Objections Are Raised Northern states objected to this idea because enslaved people were legally considered property. Some delegates from Northern states argued that the enslaved, as property, should be counted for the purpose of taxation but not representation. However, neither side considered giving enslaved people the right to vote.

The committee's solution, known as the Three-Fifths Compromise, was to count each enslaved person as three-fifths of a free person for both taxation and representation. In other words, every five enslaved persons would equal three free persons. On July 12, the convention delegates voted to approve the Three-Fifths Compromise. Four days later, they agreed that each state should elect two senators.

Slave Trade The dispute over how to count enslaved people was not the only issue dividing the delegates. The convention needed to resolve another difficult issue that divided the Northern and Southern states. Some Northern delegates wanted to slow the spread of slavery and stop the importation of new slaves. Southern states considered slavery and the slave trade essential to their economies.

To keep the Southern states in the nation, Northerners agreed that the Congress could not interfere with the slave trade until 1808. Beginning that year, Congress could limit the slave trade if it chose to.

Approving the Constitution George Mason of Virginia proposed a bill of rights to be included in the Constitution. Some delegates worried that without the protection of a bill of rights, the new national government might abuse its power. However, most of the delegates believed that the Constitution, with its carefully defined listing of government powers, provided **adequate** protection of individual rights. Mason's proposal was defeated.

The committees finished their work on the Constitution in late summer. On September 17, 1787, the delegates assembled in the Philadelphia State House to sign the document. Franklin made a final plea for approval: "I consent to this Constitution because I expect no better, and because I am not sure, that it is not the best."

Student Web Activity Visit tajwwI.glencoe.com and click on *Chapter 3—Student Web Activities* for an activity on the Constitutional Convention.

Three delegates refused to sign—Elbridge Gerry of Massachusetts, and Edmund Randolph and George Mason of Virginia. Gerry and Mason would not sign without a bill of rights.

The Confederation Congress then sent the approved draft of the Constitution to the states for consideration. To amend the Articles of Confederation had required unanimous approval of the states. The delegates agreed to change the approval process for the Constitution. When 9 of the 13 states had approved, the new government of the United States would come into existence.

(See pages 248–269 for the entire text of the Constitution.)

Reading Check Analyze Who refused to sign the Constitution? Explain why.

Study Central Need help understanding the Constitutional Convention? Visit tajwwI.glencoe.com and click on Study Central.

Section 2 Review

Reading Summary

Review the Main Ideas

- The government under the Articles of Confederation faced many problems.

- National leaders worked to produce a new constitution for the United States.

- The Constitutional Convention broke the deadlock over the form the new government would take.

What Did You Learn?

1. Explain what caused Shays's Rebellion. What was one effect?

2. According to the Virginia Plan, who elected the members of the lower house?

Critical Thinking

3. **Analyzing Information** Recreate the diagram below and identify arguments for and against approving the Constitution.

Ratification	
Arguments for	Arguments against

4. **The Big Ideas** How did the new Constitution reflect the values of the men who wrote it?

5. **ANALYSIS** How did the Great Compromise satisfy both the small and the large states on the question of representation? Why was this compromise important? Write a paragraph summarizing your conclusions.

6. **Persuasive Writing** Write a short speech in favor of either the Virginia Plan or the New Jersey Plan.

Section 3

A New Plan of Government

Guide to Reading

Looking Back, Looking Ahead

You read about the compromises that the delegates made to create a new form of government. The Constitution was based on the political ideals of the people who wrote it.

Focusing on the Main Ideas

- Ideas and thinkers of the past influenced the creation of the United States Constitution. *(page 203)*
- The Constitution outlines the responsibilities and the limits of the three branches of government. *(page 204)*
- Americans reacted to the proposed Constitution in different ways. *(page 206)*

Meeting People

John Jay
Mercy Otis Warren

Content Vocabulary

Enlightenment (ihn•LY•tuhn•muhnt)
federalism
article
legislative branch (LEH•juhs•LAY•tihv)
executive branch (ihg•ZEH•kuh•tihv)
judicial branch (ju•DIH•shuhl)
checks and balances
ratify (RA•tuh•FY)
Federalist
Antifederalist

Academic Vocabulary

promote (pruh•MOHT)
conduct (kuhn•DUHKT)

Reading Strategy

Organizing Information Create a diagram to explain how the system of checks and balances works.

	Has check or balance over:	Example
President		
Congress		
Supreme Court		

NATIONAL GEOGRAPHIC Where & When?

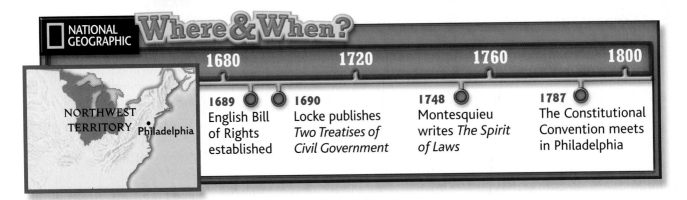

NORTHWEST TERRITORY Philadelphia

1680   1720   1760   1800

1689 English Bill of Rights established

1690 Locke publishes *Two Treatises of Civil Government*

1748 Montesquieu writes *The Spirit of Laws*

1787 The Constitutional Convention meets in Philadelphia

Roots of the Constitution

Main Idea Ideas and thinkers of the past influenced the creation of the United States Constitution.

Reading Connection Do you have a role model? Has a person you know influenced you to do better in school or take part in a helping activity? Read to learn about the thinkers who influenced the creation of the Constitution.

An American Story

As Benjamin Franklin was leaving the last session of the Constitutional Congress, a woman asked, "What kind of government have you given us, Dr. Franklin? A republic or a monarchy?" Franklin answered, "A republic, Madam, if you can keep it." Franklin's response indicated that a republic—a system of government in which the people elect representatives to exercise power for them—requires citizens to take an active role.

What Ideas Influenced the Framers?

After four long and difficult months, Franklin and the other delegates had produced a new constitution. The document provided the framework for a strong central government for the United States.

Although a uniquely American document, the Constitution has roots in many other civilizations. The delegates had studied and discussed the history of political development at length—starting with ancient Greece—so that their new government could avoid the mistakes of the past.

The Framers who shaped the document were familiar with the parliamentary system of Britain, and many had participated in the colonial assemblies or their state assemblies. They valued the individual rights guaranteed by the British judicial system. Although the Americans had broken away from Britain, they respected many British traditions.

The Magna Carta (1215) had placed limits on the power of the British monarch. England's lawmaking body, which is called Parliament, emerged as a force that the king had to depend on to pay for wars and to finance the royal government. Like Parliament, the assemblies that developed in the Thirteen Colonies controlled their colony's funds. For that reason, the assemblies had some control over colonial governors.

The English Bill of Rights of 1689 provided another important model for Americans. Many Americans believed that the Constitution also needed a bill of rights.

Enlightenment Thinkers Framers of the Constitution got many ideas on the nature of people and government from European writers of the Enlightenment. The **Enlightenment** (ihn•LY•tuhn•muhnt) was a movement of the 1700s that **promoted** knowledge, reason, and science as the means to improve society. James Madison and other architects of the Constitution were familiar with the work of John Locke and Baron de Montesquieu (mahn•tuhs•KYOO), two important philosophers.

Locke, an English philosopher, believed that all people have natural rights. These natural rights include the rights to life, liberty, and property. Many Americans interpreted natural rights to mean the rights of Englishmen defined in the Magna Carta and the English Bill of Rights.

▲ John Locke

In *The Spirit of Laws* (1748), the French writer Montesquieu declared that the powers of government should be separated and balanced against each other. This separation would keep any one person or group from gaining too much power. Following the ideas of Montesquieu, the Framers of the Constitution carefully specified and divided the powers of government.

Reading Check **Identify** What is a republic?

The Federal System

Main Idea **The Constitution outlines the responsibilities and limits of the three branches of government.**

Reading Connection Do you think it is important to identify what leaders can and cannot do? Read to find out why the Constitution limits the government and what those limits are.

The Constitution created a federal system of government that divided powers between the national, or federal, government and the

America's *Architecture*

The Old Senate Chamber The U.S. Senate met in the Old Senate Chamber from 1810 until 1859. The two-story chamber is semicircular in shape and measures 75 feet long and 50 feet wide. Two visitors' galleries overlook the chamber. After the Senate moved to its present location, the room was occupied by the Supreme Court from 1860 until 1935. *Which branches of government conducted business in the chamber?*

states. Under the Articles of Confederation, the states retained their sovereignty. Under the Constitution, the states gave up some of their powers to the federal government while keeping others.

Shared Powers **Federalism,** or sharing power between the federal and state governments, is one of the distinctive features of the United States government. Under the Constitution, the federal government gained broad powers to tax, regulate trade, control the currency, raise an army, and declare war. It could also pass laws that were "necessary and proper" for carrying out its responsibilities.

However, the Constitution left important powers in the hands of the states. The states had the power to pass and enforce laws and regulate trade within their borders. They could also establish local governments, schools, and other institutions affecting their citizens.

Supreme Law of the Land The Constitution and the laws that Congress passed were to be "the supreme law of the land." No state could make laws or take actions that went against the Constitution. Any dispute between the federal government and the states was to be settled by the federal courts on the basis of the Constitution. Under the new federal system, the Constitution became the final and supreme authority.

The Organization of Government Influenced by Montesquieu's idea of a division of powers, the Framers divided the federal government into three branches—legislative, executive, and judicial. The first three **articles,** or parts, of the Constitution describe the powers and responsibilities of each branch.

Article I of the Constitution establishes Congress, the **legislative branch** (LEH•juhs•LAY•tihv), or lawmaking branch, of the government. The Congress of the United States is comprised of the House of Representatives and the Senate.

The powers of Congress include collecting taxes, coining money, and regulating trade. Congress can also declare war and "raise and support armies." Finally, it makes all laws needed to fulfill the functions given to it as stated in the Constitution.

The Executive Branch Memories of King George III's rule made some delegates reluctant to establish a powerful executive, or ruler. Others believed that the Confederation had failed, in part, because it lacked an executive branch or president. They argued that a strong executive would serve as a check, or limit, on Congress.

Article II of the Constitution established the **executive branch** (ihg•ZEH•kuh•tihv), headed by the president, to carry out the nation's laws. The president serves as commander in chief of the armed forces and **conducts** relations with other countries.

The Judicial Branch Article III of the Constitution deals with the **judicial branch** (ju•DIH•shuhl), or court system, of the United States. The nation's judicial power resides in "one supreme Court" and any other lower federal courts that Congress might establish. The Supreme Court and the federal courts hear cases involving the Constitution, laws passed by Congress, and disputes between states.

System of Checks and Balances An important distinctive feature of our government is the separation of powers. The Constitution divides government power among the legislative, executive, and judicial branches. To keep any one branch from gaining too much power, the Framers built in a system of **checks and balances.** The three branches of government have roles that check, or limit, the others so that no single branch can dominate the government.

Both the House and the Senate must pass a bill for it to become law. The president can check Congress by vetoing, or rejecting, the bill. However, Congress can then check the president by overriding, or voting down, the veto. To override a veto, two-thirds of the members of both houses of Congress must vote for the bill.

The system of checks and balances also applies to the Supreme Court. The president appoints Supreme Court justices, and the Senate must approve the appointments.

Over time, the Court became a check on Congress and the president by ruling on the constitutionality of laws and presidential acts. The system has been successful in maintaining a balance of power among the branches of the federal government.

With these revolutionary changes, Americans showed the world that it was possible for a people to change its form of government through discussion and choice—rather than through chaos, force, or war. The rest of the world watched the new nation with interest to see whether its experiment in self-government would really work.

Reading Check **Explain** Why does the Constitution divide government power among the legislative, executive, and judicial branches?

The Debate Over Ratification

Main Idea Americans reacted to the proposed Constitution in different ways.

Reading Connection Have you taken sides on an important issue? What arguments have you used to support your position? Read to learn about the arguments that Americans used to support or oppose ratification of the Constitution.

The delegates at Philadelphia had produced the Constitution, but its acceptance depended upon the will of the people. Gaining approval of the Constitution, with its radical new plan of government, was not going to be easy.

Before the Constitution could go into effect, nine states needed to **ratify** (RA•tuh•FY), or approve, it. State legislatures set up special ratifying conventions to consider the document. By late 1787 these conventions started to meet. Rhode Island stood apart. Its leaders opposed the Constitution from the beginning and therefore did not call a convention to approve it.

Federalists Supporters of the new Constitution were called **Federalists.** Three of the nation's most gifted political thinkers—James Madison, Alexander Hamilton, and **John Jay**—also backed the Constitution.

Madison, Hamilton, and Jay worked together to write a series of essays explaining and defending the Constitution. These essays appeared in newspapers around the country and were widely read. Called the *Federalist Papers*, they were later published as a book and sent to delegates at the remaining ratifying conventions. Jefferson described the series of essays as "the best commentary on the principles of government which was ever written."

Antifederalists The Federalists called those who opposed ratification **Antifederalists.** Antifederalists criticized the Constitution because it lacked a bill of rights to protect individual freedoms. Antifederalists believed that no government could be trusted to protect the freedom of its citizens. Several state conventions took a stand and announced that they would not ratify the Constitution without the addition of a bill of rights.

Mercy Otis Warren, a Massachusetts opponent of the Constitution, expressed the problem faced by many Antifederalists. She admitted the need for a strong government but feared it.

Powers of the Federal Government

	Articles of Confederation	United States Constitution
Declare war; make peace	✔	✔
Coin money	✔	✔
Manage foreign affairs	✔	✔
Establish a postal system	✔	✔
Impose taxes		✔
Regulate trade		✔
Organize a court system		✔
Call state militias for service		✔
Protect copyrights		✔
Take other necessary actions to run the federal government		✔

Understanding Charts

The Articles of Confederation and the U.S. Constitution specified certain powers that would be given to the federal government.

1. **Identify** Which document allowed the government to organize state militias?
2. **Analyze** In what ways are the two documents similar?

> 66 We have struggled for liberty and made costly sacrifices . . . and there are still many among us who [value liberty] too much to relinquish . . . the rights of man for the dignity of government. 99
>
> —Mercy Otis Warren,
> September 29, 1787

In many ways the debate between Federalists and Antifederalists came down to their different fears. Federalists feared disorder without a strong central government. They believed that more uprisings like Shays's Rebellion would occur without a national government capable of maintaining order. The Antifederalists feared oppression more than disorder. They worried about the concentration of power that would result from a strong national government.

Adopting the Constitution With the promise of a bill of rights, many Americans began to favor the Constitution. Many small states ratified it quickly because they were pleased with equal representation in the new Senate. On June 21, 1788, the ninth state—New Hampshire—ratified it. However, without the support of two critical states—New York and Virginia—the future of the new government was not promising. Neither state had ratified yet, and both had strong Antifederalist groups.

In Virginia, George Washington, James Madison, and Edmund Randolph helped swing a close vote on June 25, 1788. In New York, Alexander Hamilton argued for ratification for six weeks. Finally, on July 26, the Federalists in New York won by only three votes. North Carolina ratified in November 1789, and Rhode Island ratified in May 1790.

After ratification came the celebrations. Boston, New York, and Philadelphia held big parades accompanied by cannon salutes and ringing church bells. Smaller celebrations took place in hundreds of American towns.

The task of creating the Constitution had ended. The Federalists promised to add a bill of rights after the new government took office. Now it was time for the nation to elect leaders and begin the work of government.

Reading Check **Explain** According to the Antifederalists, why was a bill of rights important?

Study Central Need help understanding the development of the Constitution? Visit tajww1.glencoe.com and click on Study Central.

Section 3 Review

Reading Summary

Review the Main Ideas

• Ideas and thinkers of the past influenced the creation of the United States Constitution.

• The Constitution outlines the responsibilities and the limits of the three branches of government.

• Americans reacted to the proposed Constitution in different ways.

What Did You Learn?

1. What influence did John Locke have on American government?

2. Why was the support of New York and Virginia vital to ratifying the Constitution?

Critical Thinking

3. **Comparing** Re-create the diagram below. Describe the differences between Federalist and Antifederalist views on the Constitution.

Views on the Constitution	
Federalist	Antifederalist

4. **The Big Ideas** Why did the Framers of the Constitution believe that a division of powers and a system of checks and balances were necessary in a government?

5. **Persuasive Writing** Search your local newspaper for articles that deal with constitutional issues. Select an issue from one of the articles and write a letter to your senator or representatives expressing your opinion about the issue.

You Decide . . .

Ratifying the Constitution

The delegates at Philadelphia had produced the Constitution, but its acceptance depended upon the will of the American people. In each of the 13 states, voters selected delegates to special conventions that would decide whether to accept or reject the new plan of government. Once 9 of the 13 conventions had ratified the Constitution, it could go into effect.

For Ratification

Those who favored the Constitution called themselves Federalists. Federalists wanted a strong government capable of handling the problems facing the United States both at home and abroad. They believed that the new Constitution protected the rights of the states, but gave the central government enough power to function effectively.

James Wilson of Philadelphia was a major force in drafting the Constitution. In a speech to the Pennsylvania Ratifying Convention, Wilson said:

"I am satisfied that anything nearer to perfection could not have been accomplished. If there are errors, it should be remembered, that the seeds of reformation are sown in the work itself, and the concurrence of two thirds of the Congress may at any time introduce alterations and amendments. Regarding it then, in every point of view, with a candid and disinterested mind, I am bold to assert, that it is the best form of government which has ever been offered to the world."

In a series of 85 essays known as *The Federalist Papers*, Alexander Hamilton, James Madison, and John Jay defended the Constitution. In *Federalist*, No. 70, Hamilton argued against the idea of a president with limited or few powers:

"A feeble executive implies a feeble execution of the government. A feeble execution is but another phrase for a bad execution; and a government ill executed, whatever it may be in theory, must be, in practice, a bad government."

Hamilton also believed that a bill of rights would be unnecessary and dangerous. Hamilton wrote that the Constitution gave the national government only limited power. It did not have the power to infringe on the rights of the citizens. Therefore, Hamilton noted, a bill of rights protecting the people's rights is not needed.

Alexander Hamilton ▶

Against Ratification

Ratification, however, was not a sure thing. Many people who remembered British tyranny were against a powerful national government. Opponents of the Constitution, called Antifederalists, felt that a strong central government was a threat to liberty.

In the Virginia ratification convention of 1788, Patrick Henry spoke out against the adoption of the Constitution:

"I look upon that paper [the Constitution] as the most fatal plan that could be possibly conceived to enslave a free people."

The Antifederalists' strongest argument, however, was that the Constitution lacked a bill of rights. They feared losing the liberties they had gained during the Revolution and wanted to include a guarantee of those liberties in the Constitution. Mercy Otis Warren wrote that "The rights of the individual should be the primary object of all governments."

George Mason of Virginia refused to sign the Constitution because it did not contain a bill of rights. In a letter explaining his objections to the Constitution, Mason stated that the Constitution has

"no declaration of rights: and the laws of the general government being paramount to the laws and constitutions of the several states, the declarations of rights, in the separate states, are no security. Nor are the people secured even in the enjoyment of the benefit of the common law."

◀ **George Mason**

You Be The Historian

DBQ **Document-Based Questions**

1. What group was opposed to ratification of the Constitution?

2. Who argued that the Constitution could be changed if problems arose?

3. What was Hamilton's major argument in *The Federalist*, No. 70?

Forming a New Nation

Americans fought for their independence from Great Britain between 1776 and 1783. After the Revolutionary War, a great deal of work needed to be done to establish a new nation. Where would they start? How would they form a new government that served the people better than the last government? To understand the people who called themselves Americans, you can look at letters and writings of the eighteenth century.

Read the passages on pages 210 and 211 and answer the questions that follow.

"Ship of State" float parading through New York during the 1788 ratification ▶

Reader's Dictionary

allies (A • LYS): people or groups joined in alliance or agreement

justice: fairness in the way people are treated or decisions are made

acquainted (uh • KWAYNT • ihd): having some knowledge of something

haughty (HAW • tee): behaving in a superior, arrogant way

appellation (A • puh • LAY • shuhn): the name or title of someone or something

perpetual: occurring over and over

contention (kuhn • TEHN • shuhn): disagreement or competition between rivals

The Oneida and the Use of Land

The Oneida Indian Nation fought on the side of the Patriots during the American Revolution. In March 1788, leaders of the Oneida people sent this message to the New York State legislature.

Brothers. We are your **allies,** we are a free people, our chiefs have directed us to speak to you, as such, therefore, open your ears and hear our words.

Brothers. In your late war with the people on the other side of the great water, . . . we fought by your side, our blood flowed together, and the bones of our warriors mingled with yours; . . .

[W]e received an invitation to meet some of your chiefs . . . ; those chiefs who then met us will doubtless remember how much we were disappointed, when they told us they were only sent to buy our lands. . . .

Brothers. We are determined then never to sell any more; the experience of all the Indian nations to the east and south of us has fully convinced us, that if we follow their example we shall soon share their fate. We wish that our children and grandchildren may derive a comfortable living from the lands which the Great Spirit has given us and our forefathers. . . .

Brothers. We wish you to consider this matter well, and to do us **justice**. . . .

—*Proceedings of the Commissioners of Indian Affairs*

What Is an American?

J. *Hector St. John Crèvecoeur of France traveled widely in the American colonies and farmed in New York. His* Letters From an American Farmer *was published in 1782.*

I wish I could be **acquainted** with the feelings and thoughts which must . . . present themselves to the mind of an enlightened Englishman, when he first lands on the continent. . . . If he travels through our rural districts he views not the hostile castle, and the **haughty** mansion, contrasted with the clay-built hut and miserable [cabin], where cattle and men help to keep each other warm, and dwell in meanness, smoke, and indigence. A pleasing uniformity of decent competence appears throughout our habitations. The meanest of our log-houses is dry and comfortable. . . . Lawyer or merchant are the fairest titles our towns afford; that of a farmer is the only **appellation** of the rural inhabitants of our country. It must take some time [before] he can reconcile himself to our dictionary, which is but short in words of dignity, and names of honour. . . .

What then is the American, this new man? He is either a European, or the descendant of a European, hence that strange mixture of blood, which you will find in no other country. I could point out to you a family whose

▲ *The Peale Family* **by Charles Willson Peale, c. 1770–1773** American artists favored informal scenes over the more formal European styles.

grandfather was an Englishman, whose wife was Dutch, and whose son married a French woman, and whose present four sons have now four wives of different nations. . . .

He does not find, as in Europe, a crowded society, where every place is over-stocked; he does not feel that **perpetual** collision of parties, that difficulty of beginning, that **contention** which oversets so many. There is room for everybody in America; has he particular talent, or industry? He exerts it in order to produce a livelihood, and it succeeds. . . .

—*Letters From an American Farmer*

DBQ Document-Based Questions

The Oneida and the Use of Land

1. Who are the "Brothers" that the Oneida leaders address? Why would the Oneida address legislators in this way?

2. What are the Oneida asking for?

3. What do the Oneida pledge to never do? Why did they make this decision and statement?

What Is an American?

4. How does de Crèvecoeur describe the typical home in the colonies?

5. Why might de Crèvecoeur refer to the American as a "new man"?

6. How are Americans described in comparison to Europeans?

7. What is meant by "there is room for everybody in America"? Is this still true today?

Read to Write

8. What does it mean to have justice in America? What would it look like? How would it work? How would the authors of these documents define justice in their time? How would you define justice in America today? Compare and contrast the ideas from different eras.

Review Content Vocabulary

Write the vocabulary word that completes each sentence. Write a sentence for each word that is not used.

- a. bicameral
- b. ratify
- c. compromise
- d. republic
- e. executive branch

1. To resolve their differences, the delegates used _____, with each side giving up something but gaining something else.

2. A legislature divided into two parts, or houses, is called _____.

3. On June 21, 1788, New Hampshire became the ninth state to _____ the Constitution.

4. A(n) _____ is a system of government in which the people elect representatives to exercise power for them.

Review the Main Ideas

Section 1 • The Articles of Confederation

5. What was the purpose of the Articles of Confederation?

6. How did the Northwest Ordinance provide for the country's expansion?

Section 2 • Convention and Compromise

7. According to the Virginia Plan, how was the legislature to be set up?

8. How did the Great Compromise address the issue of representation in Congress?

Section 3 • A New Plan of Government

9. Why did some Americans want a bill of rights added to the Constitution?

10. Why is it important that the powers of government are separated?

Critical Thinking

11. **Identify** What was the purpose of holding secret sessions at the Constitutional Convention? If you had been a delegate, would you have been in favor of secret sessions? Why or why not?

12. **Analyze** Why was a system of checks and balances built into the Constitution?

Geography Skills

Study the map below and answer the following questions.

NATIONAL GEOGRAPHIC

Land Claims in North America, 1783

140°W

PACIFIC OCEAN
120°W

ATLANTIC OCEAN

0   500 miles

0   500 kilometers   100°W   80°W
Azimuthal Equidistant projection

SOUTH AMERICA

- United States
- British
- Spanish
- Russian
- Disputed territory

13. **Place** Who controlled the area in which you live today?

14. **Region** What country held territory directly west of the United States?

Read to Write

15. **The Big Ideas Government and Democracy** Write a short essay discussing the many compromises that are reflected in the final version of the U.S. Constitution.

16. **Using Your FOLDABLES** Use the information you wrote in your foldable to create a fill-in-the blank quiz for a classmate. Write a paragraph about one of the sections, leaving blanks for your classmates to fill in. Also write an answer key.

Using Academic Vocabulary

17. Write two words that are related to the academic vocabulary word *currency*.

Building Citizenship

18. **Interviewing** Interview students from your school and adults from your community to find out what they know about the powers of government specified in the Constitution. Prepare a list of questions to use in your interviews. Compile the answers and present a report to your class.

Reviewing Skills

19. **READING SKILL Making Connections** Review the literature excerpt called "Second Daughter." Write a paragraph describing the connections you made while reading. Be sure to include text-to-self, text-to-text, and text-to-world connections.

20. **ANALYSIS SKILL Paraphrasing** Select a quotation or primary source from one of the sections in this chapter. Reread it and then paraphrase what you have read.

Standardized Test Practice

Read the passage below and answer the following questions.

> The Senate of the United States shall be composed of two Senators from each State, chosen by the Legislature thereof, for six Years; and each Senator shall have one vote.
>
> —U.S. Constitution, Article I, Section 3.1

21 **According to the above excerpt from the U.S. Constitution, by whom were Senators originally chosen?**

  A other Senators

  B members of the U.S. House of Representatives

  C the voters of the state

  D the state's legislature

22 **Each of the states enacted state constitutions in the late 1700s. All state constitutions**

  A established equal rights for all persons living in the state.

  B set up legislative and executive branches of state government.

  C granted women the right to vote.

  D agreed that states would be supervised by the federal government.

23 **The law that established a procedure for surveying and selling the western lands north of the Ohio River was the**

  A Ordinance of 1785.

  B Virginia Plan.

  C New Jersey Plan.

  D Bill of Rights.

The Constitution

▼ The National Archives, Washington, D.C.

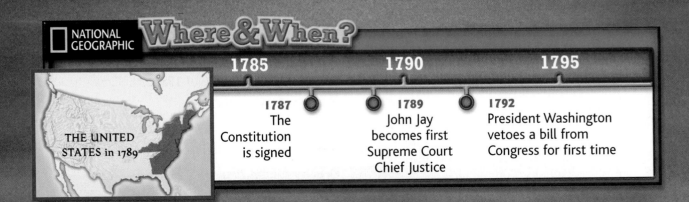

NATIONAL GEOGRAPHIC **Where & When?**

THE UNITED STATES in 1789

1785   1790   1795

1787
The Constitution is signed

1789
John Jay becomes first Supreme Court Chief Justice

1792
President Washington vetoes a bill from Congress for first time

The Big Ideas

Goals of the Constitution

A constitution reflects the values and goals of the society that creates it. For more than 200 years, the Constitution has provided the framework for the United States government and has helped preserve the basic rights of American citizens.

The Federal Government

Political ideas and major events shape how people form governments. The Constitution provided for a United States government that was set up as three equal branches with different responsibilities.

Citizens' Rights and Responsibilities

Citizen participation is essential to the foundation and preservation of the U.S. political system. Citizens of the United States have certain duties and responsibilities that help maintain our form of government.

 View the Chapter 4 video in the Glencoe Video Program.

Know-Want-Learn Make this foldable to determine what you already know, to identify what you want to know, and to record what you learn about the Constitution of the United States.

Step 1 Fold a sheet of paper into thirds from top to bottom.

Step 2 Turn the paper horizontally, unfold, and label the three columns as shown.

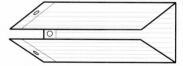

Reading and Writing Before you read the chapter, write what you already know about the Constitution in the "Know" column. Write what you want to know about the Constitution in the "Want to Know" column. Then, as you read the chapter, write what you learn in the "Learned" column. Check to see if you have learned what you wanted to know (from the second column).

Get Ready to Read

Summarizing Information

READING SKILL

1 Learn It!

Summarizing helps you clarify key points in your own words. You can summarize what you have read by pausing and restating the main ideas of the text. Then answer the key questions *Who? What? Where? When? Why?* and *How?* Read the information under "Major Principles" on page 221. Work with a partner to summarize the main points of what you read.

Did your summary include some of these details?

- The Constitution rests on seven major principles.

- Those principles are: popular sovereignty, republicanism, limited government, federalism, separation of powers, checks and balances, and individual rights.

Reading Tip

As you read, take note of the sections that you may want to go over again.

② Practice It!

With a partner, read the paragraph below. Then read the sections titled "Rights of American Citizens" on page 235 and "Citizen Participation" on page 236. Work together to make a list summarizing what you read. As you discuss your conclusions, see if you can answer the questions that follow.

Read to Write
Choose two editorials in your local newspaper. Read them carefully and then summarize each writer's main point.

It is the combination of rights, responsibilities, and duties that characterize what it means to be a citizen of a free democratic society. As citizens, we are free to exercise our rights. In return we are expected to fulfill certain duties and responsibilities.

- What is a citizen?
- What are the rights citizens hold?
- What is the difference between duty and responsibility?
- What is one of the most important responsibilities of citizens?

Citizens take part in ▶ a town hall meeting.

③ Apply It!

As you read this chapter, keep track of the main ideas of each section.

Goals of the Constitution

Guide to Reading

Looking Back, Looking Ahead

You read that the last of the 13 states ratified the Constitution in 1790. The ratifying states had closely examined the goals of and the principles behind the document creating the new government.

Focusing on the **Main Ideas**

- The Preamble to the Constitution describes six goals for the United States government. *(page 219)*
- The Constitution is based on seven major principles. *(page 221)*
- The Framers wrote the Constitution so that it could be altered or adapted to meet changing needs. *(page 224)*

Content Vocabulary

Preamble
popular sovereignty (SAH•vuhrn•tee)
republicanism
federalism
enumerated powers
  (ih•NYOO•muh•RAYT•ehd)
reserved powers
concurrent powers (kuhn•KUHR•uhnt)
amendment

implied powers (ihm•PLYD)
judicial review

Academic Vocabulary

function (FUHNG•shuhn)
cooperate (koh•AH•puh•RAYT)
anticipate (an•TIH•suh•PAYT)

Reading Strategy

Organizing Information Use a diagram like the one below to list the seven major principles on which the Constitution is based.

Major Principles Behind the Constitution

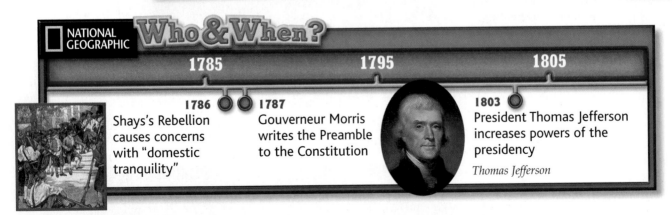

NATIONAL GEOGRAPHIC

Who & When?

1785   1795   1805

1786 Shays's Rebellion causes concerns with "domestic tranquility"

1787 Gouverneur Morris writes the Preamble to the Constitution

1803 President Thomas Jefferson increases powers of the presidency

Thomas Jefferson

Goals of the Constitution

Main Idea The Preamble to the Constitution describes six goals for the United States government.

Reading Connection Just as you often determine goals when working on a project, the creators of the Constitution thought about what they wanted the new government to do for the nation's people. Read to find out the goals set by the Constitution's Framers for the United States government.

An American Story

On September 17, 1787, the delegates to the Constitutional Convention signed the document. When it came Benjamin Franklin's turn to sign, the elderly leader had to be helped forward in order to write his name on the parchment. Tears streamed down his face as he signed. He looked at the carving of the sun on the back of George Washington's chair. "I have often looked at that sun behind the president of the convention without being able to tell whether it was rising or setting," he said, "but now, I have the happiness to know that it is a rising and not a setting sun."

The rising sun that Franklin spoke of was the new government of a very young country, the United States of America.

The Preamble The **Preamble,** or introduction, to the Constitution, written by Gouverneur Morris, begins "We the People." It reflects the basic principle of the new American government—the right of the people to govern themselves. The Preamble also lists six goals for the United States government:

“ . . . to form a more perfect Union, establish Justice, insure domestic Tranquility, provide for the common defence [defense], promote the general Welfare, and secure the Blessings of Liberty to ourselves and our Posterity. . . ”

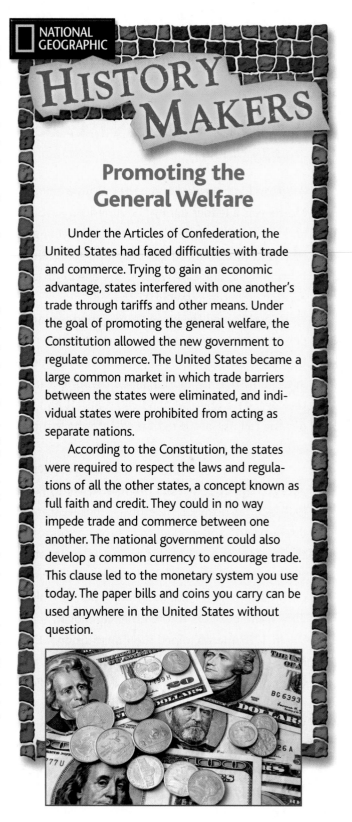

NATIONAL GEOGRAPHIC

HISTORY MAKERS

Promoting the General Welfare

Under the Articles of Confederation, the United States had faced difficulties with trade and commerce. Trying to gain an economic advantage, states interfered with one another's trade through tariffs and other means. Under the goal of promoting the general welfare, the Constitution allowed the new government to regulate commerce. The United States became a large common market in which trade barriers between the states were eliminated, and individual states were prohibited from acting as separate nations.

According to the Constitution, the states were required to respect the laws and regulations of all the other states, a concept known as full faith and credit. They could in no way impede trade and commerce between one another. The national government could also develop a common currency to encourage trade. This clause led to the monetary system you use today. The paper bills and coins you carry can be used anywhere in the United States without question.

These goals guided the Constitution's Framers as they created the new government. They remain as important today as they were when the Constitution was written.

Biography

GOUVERNEUR MORRIS
1752–1816

A brilliant speaker and writer, Gouverneur Morris was a leader during the American Revolution and the Constitutional Convention. As a young man, Morris devoted himself to education, graduating from King's College in 1768, at the age of 16, and earning a degree in law in 1771.

Morris joined the struggle for American independence although his family supported the Loyalist cause. While his brother served as an officer in the British army, Morris joined the American military despite a physical handicap that left him without the full use of his right arm. Later he lost his left leg in an accident.

In 1778 Morris became one of the youngest delegates to the Continental Congress. At Valley Forge, he had seen "an army of skeletons . . . naked, starved, sick, discouraged," and worked to improve conditions for the soldiers. In 1781 Morris served as an assistant to the Minister of Finance. He developed the system of decimal coinage, or the addition of pennies, nickels, dimes, and quarters to the American dollar.

In 1787 Morris joined the Constitutional Convention as a delegate from Pennsylvania. He was an opponent of slavery and tried to get the Constitutional Convention to ban it. He wrote the inspiring Preamble to the Constitution and helped write and edit much of the rest of the document. Because of his belief in nationalism, Morris changed the first line of the Constitution from "We the people of the states of New Hampshire, Massachusetts, . . ." with all 13 states listed, to "We the people of the United States." James Madison said of Morris: "A better choice [to rework the Constitution] could not have been made."

"We the people of the United States . . ."
—from the *Preamble to the U.S. Constitution*

Then and Now

Although physically impaired, Morris made a significant impact on American history. Can you identify other local or national leaders like him?

To Form a More Perfect Union Under the Articles of Confederation, the states **functioned** like independent nations, often disagreeing on defense and finances. To form "a more perfect Union," the Framers believed the states needed to agree to operate as a single country and **cooperate** on major issues.

To Establish Justice For the Framers, treating each citizen equally was a fundamental principle. The Constitution provides a national system of courts to protect the people's rights and to hear cases involving violations of federal law and disputes among the states.

To Insure Domestic Tranquility The violent protests of Shays's Rebellion in 1786 shocked Americans. The Constitution seeks to "insure domestic Tranquility"—that is, to keep peace among the people.

To Provide for the Common Defense Under the Articles of Confederation, the nation's defense depended on state militias. The Constitution gives the federal government the power to maintain armed forces to protect the country and its citizens from attack.

To Promote the General Welfare The Declaration of Independence states that the purpose of government is to promote "Life, Liberty, and the pursuit of Happiness" for the people of the nation. The Constitution includes ways to "promote the general Welfare"—or well-being—of the people by maintaining order, protecting individual liberties, regulating commerce and bankruptcies, and promoting science and technology by granting patents.

To Secure the Blessings of Liberty The Framers believed that preserving liberty should be a major goal of the Constitution. The Constitution guarantees that no American's basic rights will be taken away now or for posterity (generations not yet born).

Reading Check **Analyze** What is the purpose of the Preamble?

Major Principles

Main Idea The Constitution is based on seven major principles.

Reading Connection What are principles? What principles do you live by? Read to discover how the basic principles of the Constitution have remained the same for more than 200 years.

The principles outlined in the Constitution were the Framers' solution to the problems of a representative government. The Constitution rests on seven major principles: (1) popular sovereignty, (2) republicanism, (3) limited government, (4) federalism, (5) separation of powers, (6) checks and balances, and (7) individual rights.

Major Principles of the Constitution	
Popular Sovereignty	People are the source of the government's power.
Republicanism	People elect their political representatives.
Limited Government	The Constitution limits the actions of government by specifically listing powers it does and does not have.
Federalism	In this government system, power is divided between national and state governments.
Separation of Powers	Each of the three branches of government has its own responsibilities.
Checks and Balances	Each branch of government holds some control over the other two branches.
Individual Rights	Basic liberties and rights of all citizens are guaranteed in the Bill of Rights.

Understanding Charts

The principles outlined in the Constitution were the Framers' solution to the complex problems presented by a representative government.

Analyze What is the relationship between checks and balances and separation of powers?

Popular Sovereignty The Declaration of Independence states that governments derive their powers from "the consent of the governed." The opening words of the Constitution, "We the people," reinforce this idea of **popular sovereignty**—or authority of the people.

Republicanism Under **republicanism**, voters hold sovereign power. The people choose their representatives in government. Today, the terms *republic* and *representative democracy* mean the same thing: a system of limited government where the people are the ultimate source of governmental power.

Limited Government The Framers agreed that the nation needed strong central authority but feared misuse of power. By creating a limited government, they made certain the government would have only those powers granted by the people.

Article I of the Constitution states the powers that the government has as well as the powers that it does not have. Other limits on government appear in the Bill of Rights, which guarantees certain rights and liberties to the people. Limited government can be described as the "rule of law." No people or groups are above the law.

Federalism Under the Constitution, states gave up some independence. They could no longer print their own money or tax imports from other states. Nevertheless, each state governed itself much as it had in the past. This system, in which the power to govern is shared between the national government and the states, is called the federal system, or **federalism**. This system allows each state to deal with its needs in its own way. At the same time, it lets the states act together to deal with matters that affect all Americans.

The Constitution defines three types of government powers. **Enumerated powers** (ih•NYOO•muh•RAYT•ehd) belong only to the federal government. These include the power to coin money, regulate interstate and foreign trade, maintain the armed forces, and create federal courts. The powers retained by the states are known as **reserved powers**. They include such rights as the power to establish schools, pass marriage laws, and regulate trade within a state. Although reserved powers are not listed specifically in the Constitution, the Tenth Amendment says that all powers not specifically granted to the federal government "are reserved to the States."

The third set of powers defined by the Constitution are **concurrent powers** (kuhn•KUHR•uhnt)—powers shared by the state and federal governments. Among these powers are the right to raise taxes, borrow money, and provide for public welfare.

When conflicts arise between state law and federal law, the Constitution declares that the Constitution is "the supreme Law of the Land." Conflicts between state law and federal law must be settled in a federal court.

The Federal System

National Government

Enumerated Powers
- Regulate trade
- Coin money
- Provide an army and navy
- Conduct foreign affairs
- Set up federal courts

National & State Governments

Concurrent Powers
- Enforce the laws
- Establish courts
- Collect taxes
- Borrow money
- Provide for the general welfare

State Governments

Reserved Powers
- Regulate trade within the state
- Establish local government systems
- Conduct elections
- Establish public school systems

Separation of Powers To prevent any single group or institution in government from gaining too much authority, the Framers divided the federal government into three branches. The three branches are the legislative, the executive, and the judicial. Each branch has its own functions and powers. The legislative branch, Congress, makes the laws. The executive branch, headed by the president, carries out the laws. The judicial branch, consisting of the Supreme Court and other federal courts, interprets and applies the laws.

Checks and Balances As an additional safeguard, the Framers established a system of checks and balances. Under this system, each branch of government can check, or limit, the power of the other branches. For example, the legislative branch, Congress, can pass a law. Then the executive branch, headed by the president, can reject the law by vetoing it. However, Congress can override, or reverse, the president's veto if two-thirds of the members of both houses vote again to approve the law.

Over the years, the Supreme Court has acquired the power to determine the meaning of the Constitution. The Supreme Court can also declare that a law or a government policy goes against the Constitution. In doing so, the Court provides a check on the powers of Congress and the president. Judicial decisions—those made by the courts—can be overruled by amending the Constitution. The president and the Senate provide a check on the judicial branch through their power to appoint and approve federal judges. Congress can also change a law so that it no longer conflicts with the Constitution, or it can amend the Constitution.

Individual Rights The Bill of Rights became part of the Constitution in 1791. These first 10 **amendments,** or changes to the Constitution, protect basic liberties and rights that you may take for granted—including freedom of speech, freedom of the press, freedom of assembly, and freedom of religion.

The 17 amendments that follow the Bill of Rights expand the rights of Americans and adjust certain provisions of the Constitution. Included among them are amendments that abolish slavery, define citizenship, guarantee the right to vote to all citizens, authorize an income tax, and set a two-term limit on the presidency.

Reading Check **Explain** What is popular sovereignty?

The Bill of Rights

1	Guarantees freedom of religion, speech, assembly, and press, and the right of people to petition the government
2	Protects the rights of states to maintain a militia and of citizens to bear arms
3	Restricts quartering of troops in private homes
4	Protects against "unreasonable searches and seizures"
5	Assures the right not to be deprived of "life, liberty, or property, without due process of law"
6	Guarantees the right to a speedy and public trial by an impartial jury
7	Assures the right to a jury trial in cases involving the common law (the law established by previous court decisions)
8	Protects against excessive bail, or cruel and unusual punishment
9	Provides that people's rights are not restricted to those specified in the first eight amendments
10	Restates the Constitution's principle of federalism by providing that powers not granted to the national government nor prohibited to the states are reserved to the states and to the people

Understanding Charts

The Bill of Rights protects many of the basic liberties we expect as Americans today.

Analyze Which of these amendments appear to be responses to British abuses before the Revolution?

A Living Constitution

The Framers wrote the Constitution so that it could be altered or adapted to meet changing needs.

Reading Connection How do you think the Constitution and our government have changed in the 200 years since they were created? Read to find out how the Framers planned for changes to be possible.

Two years after the Constitutional Convention, Benjamin Franklin wrote, "Our Constitution is in actual operation; everything appears to promise that it will last; but in this world nothing is certain but death and taxes."

Despite Franklin's uncertainty about the future of the nation's Constitution, it is still very much alive today. The Constitution has survived because it allows the government to deal with matters the Framers never **anticipated**— such as regulating nuclear power plants. In addition the Constitution contains a provision for amending—changing or adding to—the document.

Amending the Constitution The Framers intentionally made the amendment process difficult to discourage minor or frequent changes being made. Although more than 9,000 amendments have been proposed since 1788, only 27 of them have become part of the Constitution.

An amendment may be proposed in two ways: by the vote of two-thirds of both houses of Congress or by two-thirds of the state legislatures asking for a special convention on the amendment. Ratification of an amendment requires approval by three-fourths of the states.

Interpreting the Constitution The Constitution includes two provisions that give Congress the power to act as needed to meet changing conditions. The first of these provisions is what is known as the "elastic clause" (Article I, Section 8). It directs Congress to "make all Laws which shall be necessary and proper" for executing all the powers of government. Congress has interpreted this clause to mean that it has certain **implied powers** (ihm•PLYD), meaning powers not specifically defined in the Constitution.

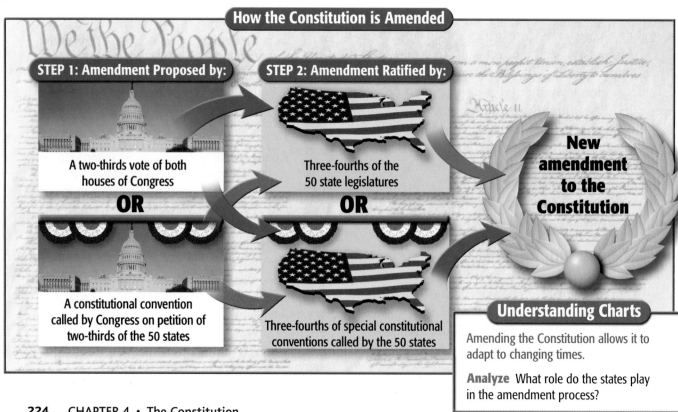

How the Constitution is Amended

STEP 1: Amendment Proposed by:

A two-thirds vote of both houses of Congress

OR

A constitutional convention called by Congress on petition of two-thirds of the 50 states

STEP 2: Amendment Ratified by:

Three-fourths of the 50 state legislatures

OR

Three-fourths of special constitutional conventions called by the 50 states

New amendment to the Constitution

Understanding Charts

Amending the Constitution allows it to adapt to changing times.

Analyze What role do the states play in the amendment process?

The second provision used to expand congressional authority, the "commerce clause" (Article I, Section 8), gives Congress the power to "regulate Commerce with foreign Nations, and among the several States." Congress has used this clause to expand its powers into a number of areas, including regulation of the airline industry, radio and television, and nuclear energy.

Powers of the Presidency The Constitution describes the role and the powers of the president in general terms. This has allowed the executive branch to extend its powers. In 1803, for example, President Thomas Jefferson approved a treaty with France that enabled the United States to buy an enormous tract of land.

The Courts The role of the judicial branch has also grown as powers implied in the Constitution have been put into practice. In 1803 Chief Justice John Marshall expanded the powers of the Supreme Court by striking down an act of Congress in the case of *Marbury* v. *Madison*.

In that decision, the Court defined its right to determine whether a law violates the Constitution. Although not mentioned in the Constitution, **judicial review** has become a major power of the judicial branch.

The process of amending the Constitution and applying its principles in new areas helps keep our government strong and functioning well. In 1974 Barbara Jordan, an African American member of Congress and a constitutional scholar, spoke in ringing tones of her faith in the Constitution:

> **❝ But through the process of amendment, interpretation, and court decision I have finally been included in 'We, the people.' ❞**
>
> —Barbara Jordan, *Opening Statement to the House Judiciary Committee*

Reading Check **Explain** What are implied powers?

History Online

Study Central Need help understanding the goals of the Constitution? Visit tajww1.glencoe.com and click on Study Central.

Section 1 Review

Reading Summary

Review the Main Ideas

- The six goals of the Constitution include providing for the common defense and promoting the general welfare of the people.

- The seven principles outlined in the Constitution were meant as solutions to the problems of a representative government.

- The amendment process allows for changes to the Constitution.

What Did You Learn?

1. What does *domestic tranquility* mean?

2. Explain the origin of judicial review.

Critical Thinking

3. **Comparing** Re-create the diagram below and describe how each branch of government has power over another branch.

Branch	Power
Legislative	
Executive	
Judicial	

4. **Evaluate** What is the importance of federalism in the Constitution?

5. **The Big Ideas** How does the ability to interpret and amend the Constitution represent a compromise?

6. **READING Summarizing** Write a short essay summarizing the major principles found in the Preamble.

The Federal Government

Guide to Reading

Looking Back, Looking Ahead

You learned that separation of powers and checks and balances are important principles behind the Constitution. These principles are apparent in the organization of the federal government.

Focusing on the Main Ideas

- The legislative branch is responsible for making the nation's laws. *(page 227)*
- The executive branch carries out the laws made by the legislative branch. *(page 229)*
- The Supreme Court and a number of lesser courts make up the judicial branch. *(page 230)*

Content Vocabulary

appropriate (uh•PROH•pree•AYT)
impeach (ihm•PEECH)
constituent (kuhn•STIHCH•wuhnt)

Academic Vocabulary

monitor (MAH•nuh•tuhr)
intervene (IHN•tuhr•VEEN)
assume (uh•SOOM)

Reading Strategy

Summarizing Information Draw a diagram like the one below and list some of the responsibilities and powers of Congress.

Congress

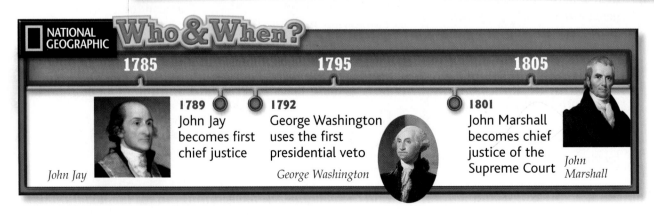

NATIONAL GEOGRAPHIC **Who & When?**

| 1785 | 1795 | 1805 |

1789 John Jay becomes first chief justice

John Jay

1792 George Washington uses the first presidential veto

George Washington

1801 John Marshall becomes chief justice of the Supreme Court

John Marshall

The Legislative Branch

Main Idea **The legislative branch is responsible for making the nation's laws.**

Reading Connection Have you ever considered how important our country's laws are to the success of our nation? Read to find out about the branch of government that creates the laws for the United States.

Congress, the legislative branch of the government, makes the nation's laws. It also has the power to "lay and collect taxes" and to declare war. Congress has two houses, the House of Representatives and the Senate.

The House and Senate Today
The House of Representatives has 435 voting members and five nonvoting delegates from the District of Columbia, Puerto Rico, Guam, American Samoa, and the Virgin Islands. The number of representatives from each state is determined by the state's population. Representatives, who must be at least 25 years old, serve 2-year terms.

The Senate consists of 100 senators, 2 from each state. Senators, who must be at least 30 years old, serve 6-year terms. The senators' terms are staggered, which means that one-third of the Senate seats come up for election every 2 years.

The Role of Congress
Congress has two primary functions: to make the nation's laws and to control government spending. The government cannot spend any money unless Congress **appropriates** (uh•PROH•pree•AYTS), or sets aside, funds. All tax and spending bills must originate in the House of Representatives and gain approval in both the House and the Senate before moving on to the president for signature.

Congress also serves as a watchdog over the executive branch, **monitoring** its actions and investigating possible abuses of power. The House of Representatives can **impeach** (ihm•PEECH), or bring formal charges against, any federal official it suspects of wrongdoing.

If an official is impeached, the Senate acts as a court and tries the accused official. Officials who are found guilty may be removed from office.

The Senate also holds certain special powers. Only the Senate can ratify treaties made by the president and confirm presidential appointments of federal officials, such as department heads, ambassadors, and federal judges.

All members of Congress have the responsibility of representing their **constituents** (kuhn•STIHCH•wuhntz), the people of their home states and districts. As a constituent, you can expect your senators and representatives to promote and protect your state's interests as well as those of the nation.

Congress at Work
Thousands of bills, or proposed laws, are introduced in Congress every year. Because individual members of Congress cannot possibly study all these bills carefully, both houses use committees of selected members to evaluate proposed legislation.

Standing committees are permanent committees in both the House and the Senate that specialize in a particular topic, such as agriculture, commerce, or veterans' affairs. These committees usually are broken down into subcommittees that focus on a particular aspect of a problem or issue. The House and the Senate sometimes form temporary select committees to deal with issues requiring special attention.

▲ Seal of the U.S. Congress

The Lawmaking Process Occasionally the House and the Senate form joint committees with members from both houses. These committees meet to consider specific issues, such as the system of federal taxation. One type of joint committee, a conference committee, has a special function. If the House and the Senate pass different versions of a bill, a conference committee tries to work out a compromise bill that is acceptable to both houses.

Committee Action When it receives a bill, a committee can reject it outright, "pigeonhole" it by setting it aside without reviewing it, or prepare it for consideration by the full House or Senate. While preparing bills, committees hold public hearings at which citizens can present arguments and documents supporting or opposing the bills.

Once a bill is approved by a committee in either house of Congress, it is sent to the full Senate or House for debate. After debate the bill may be passed, rejected, or returned to committee for further changes.

When both houses pass a bill, the bill goes to the president. If the president approves the bill and signs it, it becomes law. If the president vetoes the bill, it does not become law, unless Congress overrides (cancels) the presidential veto by a vote of two-thirds of the members in each house. The first congressional bill to be vetoed was in 1792 by President George Washington. It concerned the reassignment of districts for U.S. Representatives and was not overridden.

Reading Check **Sequence** List the basic steps of how a bill becomes a law.

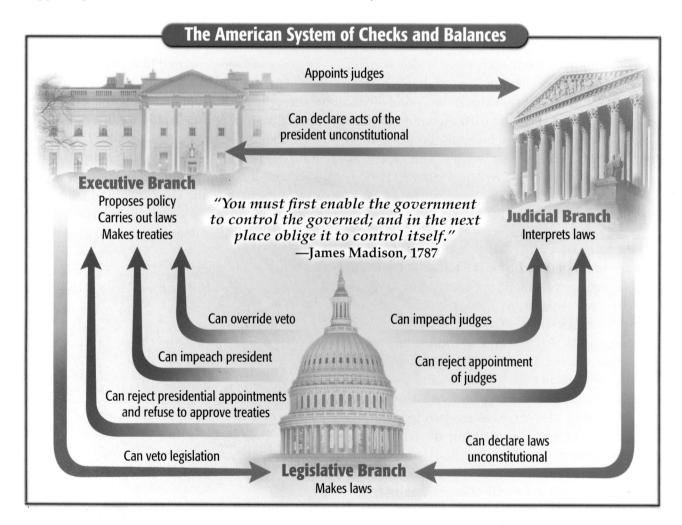

The American System of Checks and Balances

Appoints judges

Can declare acts of the president unconstitutional

Executive Branch
Proposes policy
Carries out laws
Makes treaties

"You must first enable the government to control the governed; and in the next place oblige it to control itself."
—James Madison, 1787

Judicial Branch
Interprets laws

Can override veto

Can impeach judges

Can impeach president

Can reject appointment of judges

Can reject presidential appointments and refuse to approve treaties

Can veto legislation

Can declare laws unconstitutional

Legislative Branch
Makes laws

The Executive Branch

Main Idea **The executive branch carries out the laws made by the legislative branch.**

Reading Connection How important is the leader of a club or the captain of a team? What duties does he or she carry out? Read to find out the many duties held by the president of the United States.

The executive branch of government includes the president; the vice president; and various executive offices, departments, and agencies. The executive branch carries out the laws that Congress passes.

Chief Executive The president plays a number of different roles in government, each of which has specific powers and responsibilities. These roles include the nation's chief executive, chief diplomat, commander in chief, chief of state, and legislative leader.

As chief executive, the president is responsible for carrying out the nation's laws. Many executive departments and agencies assist the president in this job.

Chief Diplomat As chief diplomat, the president directs foreign policy, appoints ambassadors, and negotiates treaties with other nations. Treaties must be approved by a two-thirds vote of the Senate before they go into effect.

Commander in Chief As commander in chief of the armed forces, the president can use the military to **intervene** or offer assistance in crisis situations at home and around the world. The president cannot declare war; only Congress holds this power. The president can send troops to other parts of the world for up to 60 days but must notify Congress when doing so. The troops may remain longer only if Congress gives approval or declares war. The president may also use the military to control serious disorders in the nation.

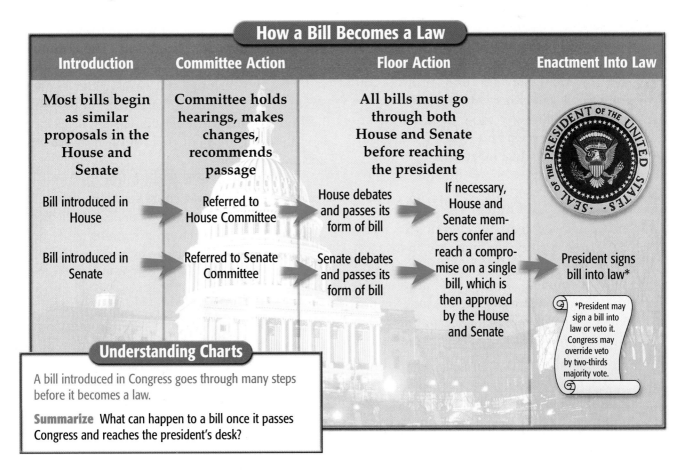

How a Bill Becomes a Law

Introduction	Committee Action	Floor Action	Enactment Into Law
Most bills begin as similar proposals in the House and Senate	**Committee holds hearings, makes changes, recommends passage**	**All bills must go through both House and Senate before reaching the president**	
Bill introduced in House	Referred to House Committee	House debates and passes its form of bill	If necessary, House and Senate members confer and reach a compromise on a single bill, which is then approved by the House and Senate
Bill introduced in Senate	Referred to Senate Committee	Senate debates and passes its form of bill	President signs bill into law*

*President may sign a bill into law or veto it. Congress may override veto by two-thirds majority vote.

Understanding Charts

A bill introduced in Congress goes through many steps before it becomes a law.

Summarize What can happen to a bill once it passes Congress and reaches the president's desk?

Chief of State As chief of state, the president serves a symbolic role as the representative of all Americans. The president fulfills this role when receiving foreign ambassadors or heads of state, visiting foreign nations, or bestowing honors on Americans.

Legislative Leader The president serves as a legislative leader by proposing laws to Congress and working for their passage. In the annual State of the Union address, the president presents goals for legislation.

The Executive Branch at Work Many executive offices, departments, and independent agencies help the president carry out and enforce the nation's laws. The Executive Office of the President (EOP) is made up of individuals and agencies that directly assist the president. Presidents rely heavily on the EOP for advice and for gathering information.

What Is the Cabinet? The executive branch also includes executive departments, each responsible for a different area of government. For example, the Department of State plans and carries out foreign policy, and the Department of the Interior manages and protects the nation's public lands and natural resources. The heads, or secretaries, of these departments are members of the president's cabinet, a group that helps the president make decisions and set government policy.

Independent Agencies The independent agencies manage federal programs in many fields. These include aeronautics and space, banking, communications, farm credit, and trade. Government corporations are government agencies that are run like privately owned businesses. One government corporation whose services you may often use is the United States Postal Service.

Reading Check **Describe** What is the president's cabinet?

The Judicial Branch

Main Idea **The Supreme Court and a number of lesser courts make up the judicial branch.**

Reading Connection Do you think a society could exist without a court system that determines in a fair manner if laws have been broken? Read to find out about the powers of the courts as established in the Constitution.

Article III of the Constitution called for the creation of a Supreme Court and "such inferior [lower] courts as Congress may from time to time ordain and establish." In 1789 Congress passed a Judiciary Act, which added a series of district courts to the federal court system. Congress added appeals courts, sometimes called circuit courts, in 1891 to ease the workload of the Supreme Court.

Lower Federal Courts At the lowest level of the federal court system are the United States district courts. These courts consider criminal and civil cases that come under federal, rather than state, authority. The criminal cases include such offenses as kidnapping and federal tax evasion. Civil cases cover claims against the federal government and cases involving constitutional rights, such as free speech. There are 94 district courts in the nation and the territories.

The next level of federal courts, the appeals courts, reviews district court decisions in which the losing side has asked for a review of the verdict. If an appeals court disagrees with the lower court's decision, it can either overturn the verdict or order a retrial. The United States has 14 appeals courts.

The Supreme Court The Supreme Court stands at the top of the American legal system. Article III of the Constitution created the Supreme Court as one of three coequal branches of the national government, along with Congress and the president.

The Supreme Court is led by a chief justice. John Jay became the first chief justice in 1789. Congress sets the number of associate justices and has the power to change that number. Over the years it has varied from four to nine, but it has been nine since 1869.

The Constitution does not describe the duties of the chief justice or the associate justices. Instead, the duties have developed from laws, through tradition, and as the needs and circumstances of the nation have developed. The main duty of the justices is to hear and rule on cases. This duty involves them in three decision-making tasks: deciding which cases to hear from among the thousands appealed to the Court each year; deciding the case itself; and determining an explanation for the decision, called the Court's opinion.

Judicial Review As you have read, the Supreme Court's power to examine the laws and actions of local, state, and national governments and to cancel them if they violate the Constitution is called judicial review. The Supreme Court, under Chief Justice John Marshall, first **assumed** the power of judicial review in the case of *Marbury* v. *Madison* (1803). Since then, the Court has invalidated, or canceled, nearly 200 provisions of federal law.

The Supreme Court may also review presidential policies. In the case of *Ex parte Milligan* (1866), the Court ruled that President Lincoln's suspension of certain civil rights during the Civil War was unconstitutional. In its decision, the Court noted that the "Constitution of the United States is a law for rulers and people, equally in war and in peace."

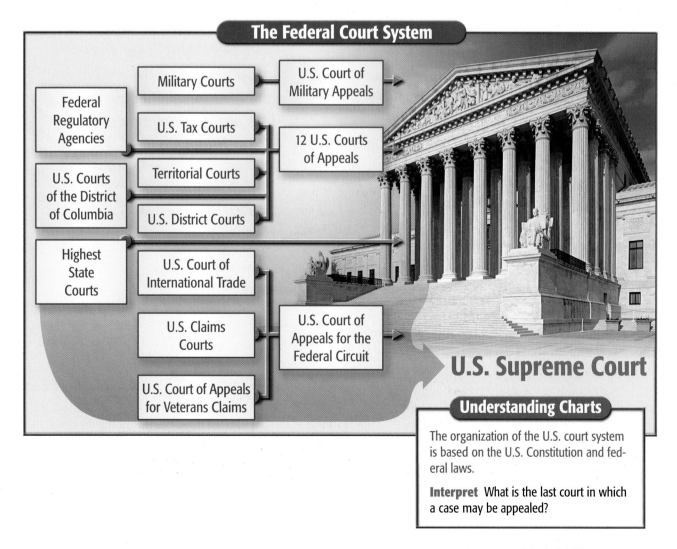

The Federal Court System

- Military Courts
- U.S. Tax Courts
- Territorial Courts
- U.S. District Courts
- U.S. Court of International Trade
- U.S. Claims Courts
- U.S. Court of Appeals for Veterans Claims

Federal Regulatory Agencies

U.S. Courts of the District of Columbia

Highest State Courts

U.S. Court of Military Appeals

12 U.S. Courts of Appeals

U.S. Court of Appeals for the Federal Circuit

U.S. Supreme Court

Understanding Charts

The organization of the U.S. court system is based on the U.S. Constitution and federal laws.

Interpret What is the last court in which a case may be appealed?

Biography

JOHN MARSHALL
1755–1835

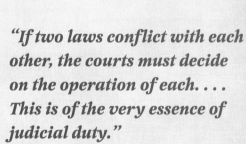

John Marshall is the only individual to serve in the House of Representatives, the Senate, the president's cabinet, as governor of a state, and as Supreme Court chief justice. John Adams once said that his greatest act as president was "the gift of John Marshall to the people." Marshall, the fourth chief justice of the United States, hardly looked like the head of the Supreme Court. He often wore mismatched clothes and an old floppy hat. He rejected the gold-braided robes worn by justices at the time in favor of the simple black robes worn by justices today.

Marshall, the oldest of 15 children, grew up on the Virginia frontier. At the outbreak of the Revolutionary War, Marshall joined a Virginia regiment. He never forgot the reasons for which he joined the American Revolution. As a soldier, he once sewed the words "Liberty or Death" onto his shirt. He brought those same principles to his tenure as chief justice and supported both the national government and the new Constitution.

Marshall served in the Virginia legislature and supported the Federalist party. In 1800 President John Adams appointed him secretary of state. In January 1801, Adams appointed Marshall chief justice of the United States. Marshall served in that position 34 years.

Marshall heard cases and made landmark rulings that continue to guide the Supreme Court and the nation's government today. In deciding the case of *Marbury* v. *Madison* in 1803, the Marshall court established the principle of judicial review of acts of Congress. Marshall reinforced the ideas that the Supreme Court is the final authority to interpret the Constitution and that the Constitution truly was the "supreme law of the land."

> *"If two laws conflict with each other, the courts must decide on the operation of each. . . . This is of the very essence of judicial duty."*
>
> **—John Marshall,**
> ***Marbury* v. *Madison* (1803)**

Then and Now

John Marshall had an important impact on the position of the Supreme Court in the country's government. Research a current Supreme Court justice and describe the impact he or she has had upon the court or upon the nation.

Reviewing State Laws Judicial review of state laws and actions may have as much significance as the Court's activities at the federal level. One important case involved segregation in schools. Many cities had segregated schools: white students attended one school and black students attended a different school. In 1896 the Supreme Court had ruled in *Plessy* v. *Ferguson* that segregation was constitutional as long as equal facilities were provided for both races.

One important case involved a young African American girl named Linda Brown, who was not allowed to attend her neighborhood school in Topeka, Kansas, because of her race. She was told to attend an all-black school across town. Her parents then sued the Topeka school board, arguing that black children were not getting the same quality of education as white children.

On May 17, 1954, the Supreme Court ruled unanimously in the case of *Brown* v. *Board of Education of Topeka, Kansas*, that segregation in public schools was unconstitutional. The *Brown* decision overturned the *Plessy* decision. The *Brown* decision also cleared the way for the end of segregated schools throughout the nation.

✓ **Reading Check**

Describe How was the court system set up?

▶ Linda Brown was at the center of the important Supreme Court case, *Brown* v. *Board of Education of Topeka, Kansas*.

Section 2 Review

Study Central Need help understanding the branches of federal government? Visit tajwwI.glencoe.com and click on Study Central.

Reading Summary

Review the Main Ideas

- Congress works to make the nation's laws and to control government spending.

- Many executive departments and agencies assist the president in carrying out the nation's laws.

- The judicial branch settles disputes and interprets the meaning of laws.

What Did You Learn?

1. List three responsibilities of the president.

2. Does the Constitution describe the duties of the Supreme Court? How have these duties developed?

Critical Thinking

3. **Organizing Information** Recreate the diagram below and provide five different kinds of congressional committees.

Committees

4. **The Big Ideas** How does politics affect Supreme Court decisions? Give one example from 1803 and one from modern history.

5. **Creative Writing** Write a help-wanted ad for the position of president of the United States. Describe the various responsibilities and what skills might be needed to fulfill those duties.

6. **ANALYSIS** **Evaluate** Describe the role of the legislative branch in government spending and how that role relates to legislators' constituencies.

Citizens' Rights and Responsibilities

Guide to Reading

Looking Back, Looking Ahead

You learned about the three branches of the federal government and the people who make up those branches. American citizens must also actively participate to make the government work.

Focusing on the Main Ideas

- Americans have certain rights that are protected in the Constitution. *(page 235)*
- American citizens are expected to carry out certain duties and responsibilities. *(page 236)*

Content Vocabulary

due process of law
citizen (SIH•tuh•zuhn)
naturalization
    (NA•chuh•ruh•luh•ZAY•shuhn)

Academic Vocabulary

involve (ihn•VAHLV)
diminish (duh•MIH•nihsh)
environment (ihn•VY•ruhn•muhnt)

Reading Strategy

Summarizing Information Draw a chart like the one below and fill in some of the rights, duties, and responsibilities of American citizens.

Rights	Duties	Responsibilities

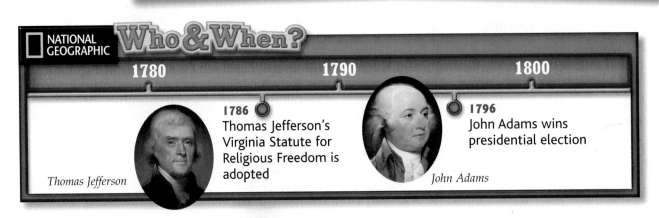

NATIONAL GEOGRAPHIC Who & When?

1780   1790   1800

Thomas Jefferson

1786 Thomas Jefferson's Virginia Statute for Religious Freedom is adopted

1796 John Adams wins presidential election

John Adams

Rights of American Citizens

Main Idea Americans have certain rights that are protected in the Constitution.

Reading Connection What do you consider to be some of your basic rights as an American? Freedom of speech? Freedom of religion? Read to find out where these rights are guaranteed in the Constitution.

An American Story

66 **We hold these truths to be self-evident, that all men are created equal, that they are endowed by their Creator with certain unalienable Rights, that among these are Life, Liberty and the pursuit of Happiness.** 99

These words from the Declaration of Independence continue to inspire Americans. They have encouraged Americans to pursue the ideals expressed in the Declaration and to create a Constitution and a Bill of Rights that protect these rights. The rights of Americans fall into three broad categories: the right to be protected from unfair actions of the government, to have equal treatment under the law, and to have basic freedoms.

Due Process The Fifth Amendment states that no person shall "be deprived of life, liberty, or property, without due process of law." **Due process of law** means that the government must follow certain procedures that have been established by law and are guaranteed in the Constitution. All people must be treated according to these principles.

Equal Protection All Americans, regardless of race, religious beliefs, or political beliefs, have the right to be treated the same under the law. The Fourteenth Amendment requires every state to grant its citizens "equal protection of the laws."

Primary Sources

Statute for Religious Freedom

▲ Thomas Jefferson

Many people came to America in search of religious freedom. In 1777 Thomas Jefferson wrote a resolution on religious freedom that was adopted by the Virginia state legislature in 1786. Commonly known as the Statute for Religious Freedom, the resolution said:

"No man shall be compelled to frequent or support any religious worship, place or ministry whatsoever, nor shall be enforced, restrained, molested, or [burdened] in his body or goods, nor shall otherwise suffer on account of his religious opinions or belief; but that all men shall be free to profess, and by argument to maintain, their opinion in matters of religion, and that the same shall in no wise diminish, enlarge or affect their civil capacities."

—Thomas Jefferson, "Virginia Statute of Religious Liberty"

A few years after this resolution was adopted, the United States became an independent country, and freedom of religion was one of the principles upon which the nation was founded.

DBQ Document-Based Question

Jefferson wrote that "no man shall be compelled to frequent or support any religious worship." Write a sentence in your own words that expresses this statement.

Basic Freedoms The basic freedoms **involve** the liberties outlined in the First Amendment—freedom of speech, freedom of religion, freedom of the press, freedom of assembly, and the right to petition. In a democratic society such as ours, power exists in the hands of the people. Therefore, its citizens must be able to exchange ideas freely.

The First Amendment, part of the Bill of Rights, which was added to the Constitution in 1791, allows citizens to criticize the government, in speech or in the press, without fear of punishment. It also states that the government cannot endorse a religion, nor can it prohibit citizens from practicing a religion if they choose to do so. In addition, the Ninth Amendment states that the rights of Americans are not limited to those mentioned in the Constitution. This has allowed our basic freedoms to continue to grow. The Twenty-sixth Amendment, for example, extends the right to vote to American citizens who are 18 years of age.

The ultimate responsibility to protect these rights lies with the American people. Voting and expressing our opinions to our elected representatives help uphold our rights. Judge Learned Hand expressed:

> 66 Liberty lies in the hearts of men and women; when it dies there, . . . no constitution, no law, no court can even do much to help it. 99
>
> —Learned Hand,
> *The Spirit of Liberty*

Limits on Rights Our rights are not unlimited. The government can establish laws or rules to restrict certain standards to protect the health, safety, security, and moral standards of a community. Moreover, rights may be limited to prevent one person's rights from interfering with the rights of others. The restrictions of rights, however, must be reasonable and must apply to everyone equally.

✓ **Reading Check** **Summarize** What is due process of law?

Citizen Participation

Main Idea **American citizens are expected to carry out certain duties and responsibilities.**

Reading Connection Would a democracy be effective if few of the citizens voted? Read to find out what it means to be a good citizen.

An American Story

On September 11, 2001, terrorist attacks killed thousands of Americans. President George W. Bush led the nation during the troubled times. He said:

> 66 [A]fter America was attacked, it was as if our entire country looked into a mirror, and saw our better selves. We were reminded that we are citizens, with obligations to each other, to our country, and to history. 99

What Is a Citizen? A **citizen** (SIH•tuh•zuhn) is a person who owes loyalty to and is entitled to the protection of a state or nation. How do you become an American citizen? Generally, citizenship is granted to anyone born within the borders of the United States. Citizenship is also granted to anyone born outside the United States if one parent is a United States citizen. A person of foreign birth can also become a citizen through the process of **naturalization** (NA•chuh•ruh•luh•ZAY•shuhn).

To qualify, applicants must be at least 18 years old. They must have been lawfully admitted for permanent residence and have lived in the United States for at least five years. They must possess good moral character and accept the principles of the Constitution. Applicants must also understand English and demonstrate an understanding of U.S. history and government. Before being granted citizenship, applicants must be willing to give up any foreign allegiance and must promise to obey the Constitution and the laws of the United States.

As citizens of the United States, we are expected to carry out certain duties and responsibilities. Duties are things we are required to do by law. Responsibilities are things we should do. Fulfilling both our duties and our responsibilities helps ensure that we have a good government and that we continue to enjoy the rights that the Framers set forth.

Duties One of the duties of all Americans is to obey the law. Laws serve three important functions. They help maintain order; they protect the health, safety, and property of all citizens; and they make it possible for people to live together peacefully. If you disobey laws, for example, you may endanger others and interfere with the smooth functioning of society. If you believe a law needs to be changed, you can work through your elected representatives to improve it.

Americans also have a duty to pay taxes. The government uses tax money to defend the nation, provide health insurance for people over age 65, and build roads and bridges. Americans benefit from services provided by the government.

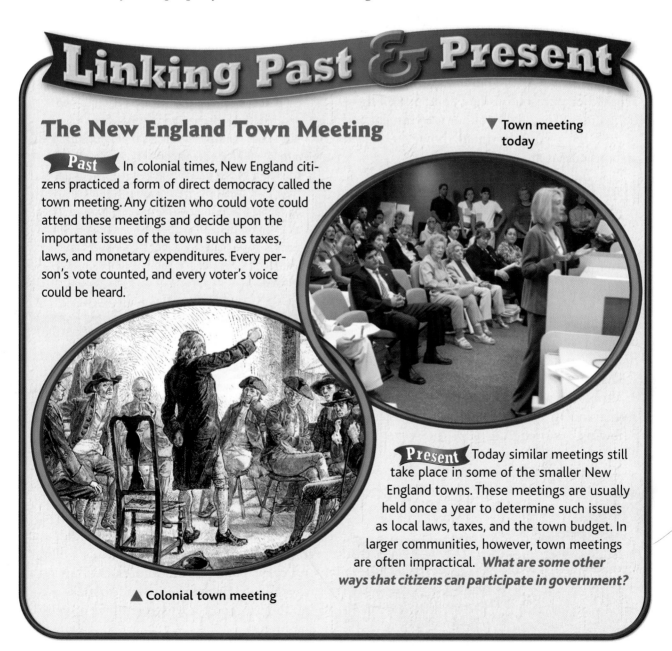

Linking Past & Present

The New England Town Meeting

▼ Town meeting today

Past In colonial times, New England citizens practiced a form of direct democracy called the town meeting. Any citizen who could vote could attend these meetings and decide upon the important issues of the town such as taxes, laws, and monetary expenditures. Every person's vote counted, and every voter's voice could be heard.

Present Today similar meetings still take place in some of the smaller New England towns. These meetings are usually held once a year to determine such issues as local laws, taxes, and the town budget. In larger communities, however, town meetings are often impractical. *What are some other ways that citizens can participate in government?*

▲ Colonial town meeting

Another duty of citizens is to defend the nation. All males aged 18 and older must register with the government in case they are needed for military service. The nation no longer has a draft, or required military service, but a war could make the draft necessary again.

The Constitution guarantees all Americans the right to a trial by a jury of their peers (equals). For this reason, you should be prepared to serve on a jury when you become eligible at the age of 18. Having a large group of jurors on hand is necessary to guarantee the right to a fair and speedy trial.

Responsibilities All citizens have responsibilities. However, the responsibilities of citizens are not as clear-cut as their duties. Because responsibilities are voluntary, people are not arrested or punished if they do not fulfill these obligations. The quality of our government and of our lives will **diminish,** however, if our responsibilities are not carried out.

Civic Republicanism Keep in mind that one of your reponsibilities as a citizen is to know what the government is doing and to voice your opinion when you feel strongly about something the government has done or has failed to do. You can let your representatives know how you feel about issues through letters, telephone calls, and petitions. When the government learns that most people favor or oppose an action, it usually follows their wishes.

You also need to be informed about your rights and to exercise them when necessary. Knowing your rights helps preserve them. Other responsibilities include respecting diversity, accepting responsibility for your actions, supporting your family, and volunteering within your community.

Student Web Activity Visit tajwwl.glencoe.com and click on Chapter 4—Student Web Activities for an activity on volunteering opportunities.

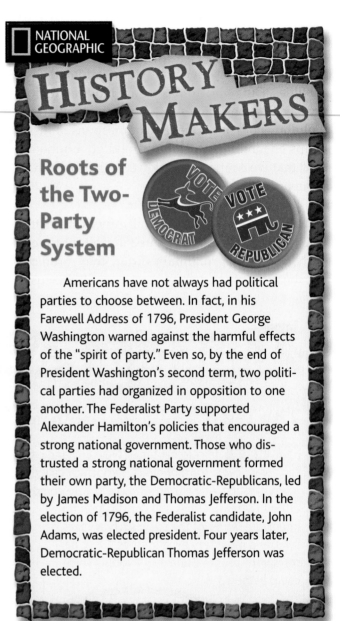

NATIONAL GEOGRAPHIC

HISTORY MAKERS

Roots of the Two-Party System

Americans have not always had political parties to choose between. In fact, in his Farewell Address of 1796, President George Washington warned against the harmful effects of the "spirit of party." Even so, by the end of President Washington's second term, two political parties had organized in opposition to one another. The Federalist Party supported Alexander Hamilton's policies that encouraged a strong national government. Those who distrusted a strong national government formed their own party, the Democratic-Republicans, led by James Madison and Thomas Jefferson. In the election of 1796, the Federalist candidate, John Adams, was elected president. Four years later, Democratic-Republican Thomas Jefferson was elected.

Other Ways to Participate Perhaps your most important responsibility as an American citizen will be to vote when you reach the age of 18. Voting allows you to participate in government and guide its direction. If you disapprove of the job your representatives are doing, it will be your responsibility to help elect others.

While not everyone holds public office, everyone can participate in government in other ways. Working on a political campaign, volunteering to help in a hospital or a library, and participating in a local park cleanup are all ways to take responsibility and to make a contribution to good government and a well-run community.

You read earlier that when a bill is in a House or Senate committee for discussion, citizens are sometimes allowed to present arguments supporting or opposing the bill. The people making the arguments often work for special interest groups. Belonging or contributing to a special interest group is another way citizens can participate in government and the making of laws. Through interest groups, citizens communicate their "wants," or policy goals, to government leaders—the president, Congress, state legislators, the mayor, or city council.

Interest groups represent a variety of causes. Many groups deal with economic interests, including groups like the National Association of Manufacturers and powerful labor organizations. Other interest groups deal with more specific causes. The Sierra Club supports issues to protect the **environment,** and MADD works to prevent drunken driving.

Another way for citizens to be involved in the political process is to join a political party. Political parties choose candidates to run for the various political offices. Political parties also present voters with views on a wide variety of issues. They consider conflicting issues and problems that affect all Americans, not just certain groups. Political parties keep citizens informed about these issues, as well as about how party members and members of the opposition are performing in office. Belonging to a party involves no obligations or duties besides voting, although party members can also volunteer during campaigns.

Respecting Others' Rights To enjoy your rights to the fullest, you must be prepared to respect the rights of others. Respecting the rights of others also means respecting the rights of people with whom you may disagree. Respecting and accepting others regardless of race, religion, beliefs, or other differences is essential to the success of a democracy. All Americans are entitled to the same respect and good treatment.

✓**Reading Check** **Identify** What is naturalization?

History Online

Study Central Need help understanding citizens' rights and responsibilities? Visit tajwwI.glencoe.com and click on Study Central.

Section 3 Review

Reading Summary

Review the Main Ideas

- Americans have the right to be protected from unfair actions of the government, to be treated equally under the law, and to have basic freedoms.

- Americans have certain duties, such as obeying the laws, and responsibilities, such as staying informed about one's rights, that they must carry out.

What Did You Learn?

1. Are the rights of American citizens unlimited? Explain.

2. Why are personal responsibilities important?

Critical Thinking

3. **Organizing Information** Recreate the diagram below and provide the three categories of American rights.

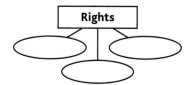

Rights

4. **The Big Ideas** How does citizen participation, as described in this section, help preserve the American political system?

5. **Creative Writing** One responsibility of being an American citizen is to become involved in the democratic system. Make a poster showing how students can get involved in their community's democracy. Display your poster in a prominent place in school.

Connecting to the Constitution

Freedom of the Press

Why It Matters Freedom of the press means the right to publish facts, ideas, and opinions without interference from the government or private groups. This right applies to printed materials, including books and newspapers, and to electronic communications, including radio, television, movies, and computer networks. Such a free flow of materials allows the people in a democracy to receive the information they need to make informed decisions.

The First Amendment In the United States, freedom of the press is guaranteed by the First Amendment to the Constitution, which says in part that "Congress shall make no law . . . abridging [limiting] the freedom . . . of the press." Because of this guarantee, writers, editors, and journalists have the freedom to decide what goes in or stays out of their publications. This independence has led many to call the press a "watchdog" over government. This means that the press watches government actions and helps keep the government responsible to the people.

The mass media—newspapers, magazines, television, radio, and the Internet—however, are not totally free of government regulation. Many reasonable restrictions can be placed on rights of the media. For example, no person has the right to libel, or use printed words to injure another person's character or reputation. Laws also prohibit the printing and distribution of obscene materials.

John Peter Zenger's *New York Weekly Journal* ▶

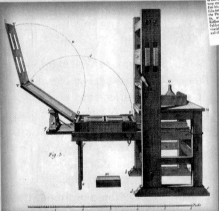

"[W]ere it left to me to decide whether we should have a government without newspapers or newspapers without a government, I should not hesitate a moment to prefer the latter."

—*Thomas Jefferson, Letter to Colonel Edward Carrington, January 16, 1787.*

◀ **Printing press**

▲ *Press coverage can be limited by order of the judge. Here, members of the press, barred from the courtroom, wait for a chance to interview participants.*

The Zenger Case

Freedom of the press was an important issue in colonial America. Newspapers in colonial cities, such as Boston and Philadelphia, carried political news and often faced government censorship. Censorship is the banning of printed materials because they contain unpopular or offensive ideas. In 1733 publisher John Peter Zenger, in his paper the *New-York Weekly Journal*, accused New York's royal governor of corruption. Zenger was arrested and put on trial. His lawyer argued that free speech was a basic right of the British people. The jury found Zenger not guilty.

The Government and the Press

After the American Revolution, several states provided for freedom of the press in their state constitutions. Later, the First Amendment of the U.S. Constitution provided for a free press in American society as a whole. At times, however, the government, in the name of public interest, has attempted to regulate the press.

Supreme Court rulings allowed the press to be limited when the printed materials might threaten national security. During World War I, publishing materials that were critical of the government was considered a crime. A 1931 Supreme Court ruling, however, struck down a Minnesota state law that banned publication of magazine or newspaper articles that were critical of public officials. Although censorship occurred during World War II, it was a voluntary system with which most newspapers and magazines cooperated. A Supreme Court ruling in the 1970s allowed the publication of a secret government report about the Vietnam War. The government could not prove that publishing it endangered national security.

Free Press and Trials

In some trials, reporters have refused to testify in order to protect confidential, or secret, sources. Although the Supreme Court has ruled that reporters must cooperate during trials, many states have enacted so-called shield laws. These laws provide reporters with some protection against having to reveal confidential information.

Another issue deals with gag orders. Such orders were given to prevent information about a criminal case from being published, especially if that information might violate a defendant's right to a fair trial. The Supreme Court ruled that gag orders are unconstitutional except in extraordinary circumstances.

Radio, Television, and the Internet

Today, First Amendment rights must be considered for the many new forms of media that have developed since the Framers first discussed freedom of the press. The Federal Communications Commission (FCC) is the government agency that regulates radio and television. The FCC cannot censor materials before they are broadcast, but it does prohibit the use of indecent language.

In the 1990s, Congress passed legislation to prevent children from accessing indecent materials on the Internet. The Supreme Court, however, struck down the law, ruling that speech on the Internet was entitled to First Amendment protection.

Checking for Understanding

1. Why is freedom of the press important in a democracy? What guarantees freedom of the press in the United States?

2. When can the United States government censor information before it is published?

Critical Thinking

3. **Conclude** What responsibilities should the press have toward the American people?

Analyzing Primary Sources

A New Constitution

Throughout the new nation, people discussed a Constitution for America. Many people supported ideas for a stronger central government, but many others did not. People worried about the protection of individual rights for all citizens. How would Americans settle their differences of opinion and reach an agreement on governing the nation?

Read the passages on pages 242 and 243, then answer the questions that follow.

The Federalist Papers supported ▶ ratification of the Constitution.

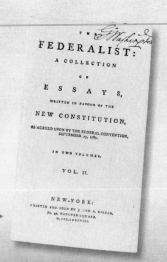

Reader's Dictionary

enumerated (ih • NOO • muh • RAYT • ehd): a number of named things on a list

monopolies (muh • NAH • puh • lees): situations in which a single company controls an industry

aristocracy (AR • uh • STAH • kruh • see): governing by a small group of people, particularly nobility

latent (LAY • tuhnt): underlying

faction (FAK • shuhn): a group that has specific interests or beliefs that are in conflict with the larger group

actuated (AK • chuh • WAYT • ehd): moved to action

annihilation (uh • NY • uh • LAY • shuhn): the complete destruction of something

fallible (FA • luh • buhl): liable to be wrong or make mistakes

The Federalist, No.10

In 1787 and 1788, James Madison, Alexander Hamilton, and John Jay wrote 85 anonymous articles for the New York Journal. *The purpose of these articles was to persuade the people of New York to ratify the proposed Constitution. These articles became known as* The Federalist Papers. *This article focused on divisions, or factions, among people:*

Among the numerous advantages promised by a well-constructed Union, none deserves to be more accurately developed than its tendency to break and control the violence of **faction**. . . .

By a faction, I understand a number of citizens, whether amounting to a majority or minority of the whole, who are united and **actuated** by some common impulse of passion, or of interest, adverse to the rights of other citizens, or to the permanent and aggregate [collected] interests of the community. . . .

There are . . . two methods of removing the causes of faction: the one, by destroying the liberty which is essential to its existence; the other, by giving to every citizen the same opinions, the same passions, and the same interests.

It could never be more truly said than of the first remedy that it was worse than the disease. Liberty is to faction what air is to fire, [a fuel] without which it instantly expires. But it could not be a less folly to abolish

▲ James Madison

liberty, which is essential to political life, because it nourishes faction than it would be to wish the **annihilation** of air, which is essential to animal life, because it imparts to fire its destructive agency.

The second [remedy] is as impracticable as the first would be unwise. As long as the reason of man continues **fallible**, and he is at liberty to exercise it, different opinions will be formed. . . .

The **latent** causes of faction are thus sown in the nature of man; and we see them everywhere brought into different degrees of activity, according to the different circumstances of civil society. . . . But the most common and durable source of factions has been the various and unequal distribution of property. Those who hold and those who are without property have ever formed distinct interests in society.

— James Madison

Objections to the Constitution

George Mason served as a state leader in Virginia in the 1780s. Mason opposed the Constitution and wrote pamphlets to express his concerns:

Under their own construction of the general clause at the end of the **enumerated** powers, the Congress may grant **monopolies** in trade and commerce, constitute new crimes, inflict unusual and severe punishments, and extend their power as far as they shall think proper; so that the state legislatures have no security for the powers now presumed to remain to them; or the people for their rights. There is no declaration of any kind for preserving the liberty of the press, the trial by jury in civil cases, nor against the danger of standing armies in time of peace. . . .

This government will commence in a moderate **aristocracy;** it is at present impossible to foresee whether it will, in its operation, produce a monarchy, or a corrupt oppressive aristocracy; it will most probably vibrate some years between the two, and then terminate in the one or the other.

▲ George Mason

DBQ Document-Based Questions

The Federalist, No. 10

1. How does Madison describe factions?

2. What is identified as a main source of factions?

3. What two ways are proposed to eliminate factions?

4. What would be lost if factions were eliminated in the Union?

Objections to the Constitution

5. What were Mason's concerns about the U.S. Constitution?

6. What did Mason suggest would happen to the government?

7. Was Mason correct in his predictions about America's government?

Read to Write

8. Imagine that you are a New York delegate trying to decide whether or not to ratify the U.S. Constitution. Write a response to the article and pamphlet that you just read. Explain your decision to ratify or not using information from the above texts. Try to persuade others to follow your decision.

Review Content Vocabulary

1. On a sheet of paper, use all of the following terms in a short paragraph related to the Constitution.

   a. popular sovereignty
   b. reserved powers
   c. amendment
   d. implied powers
   e. judicial review
   f. enumerated powers

Review the Main Ideas

Section 1 • Goals of the Constitution

2. List the six goals of government stated in the Preamble.

3. Explain why the amendment process is so difficult.

Section 2 • The Federal Government

4. Why does Congress use committees to evaluate proposed legislation?

5. Describe the main duty of the justices of the Supreme Court, along with the tasks involved.

Section 3 • Citizens' Rights and Responsibilities

6. Why is responsible citizenship important? Provide examples of responsible citizenship.

7. What are the basic freedoms outlined in the First Amendment?

Critical Thinking

8. **Analyze** Describe why limited government, republicanism, and popular sovereignty are important parts of the Constitution.

9. **Comparing** Some people argue that there should be a limit on the number of terms a senator or representative can serve. Compare the advantages and the disadvantages of the present system, which does not limit these terms.

10. **Predict** Predict what might have happened to the United States if the Framers had not provided for a system of checks and balances.

Geography Skills

Study the map below and answer the following questions.

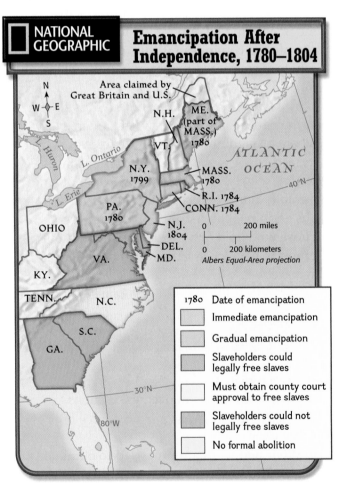

NATIONAL GEOGRAPHIC
Emancipation After Independence, 1780–1804

1780 Date of emancipation

Immediate emancipation

Gradual emancipation

Slaveholders could legally free slaves

Must obtain county court approval to free slaves

Slaveholders could not legally free slaves

No formal abolition

11. **Place** Which state freed enslaved people in 1780?

12. **Place** Which states required court approval to free enslaved people?

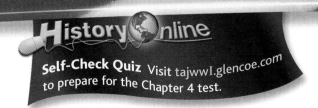

History Online

Self-Check Quiz Visit tajwwI.glencoe.com to prepare for the Chapter 4 test.

Read to Write

13. **Speech Writing** Part of your responsibility as an American citizen is to be informed about what the government is doing and to voice your opinion about its actions. Draft a speech you would give at a school-wide meeting outlining your views on issues your school or community is currently facing.

14. **The Big Ideas** **Citizen Participation** In an essay, discuss why citizen participation is essential to preserving the American political system and how the basic freedoms outlined in the Constitution allow for that participation.

15. **Using Your** **FOLDABLES** Write a short essay that describes what you have learned about the Constitution. Include a summary of what you already knew and what you wanted to learn.

Using Academic Vocabulary

16. Use each of the following academic vocabulary words in a separate sentence:

function   grant
intervene   diminish

Building Citizenship

17. **Researching Local Government** Contact a local government official to find out about the basic plan, or constitution, of your city or town. Share your findings with the class.

Reviewing Skills

18. **READING SKILL** **Summarizing** Read the summary of *Marbury* v. *Madison* on page 225. Summarize the important parts of the passage.

19. **ANALYSIS SKILL** **Evaluating** Reread the Bill of Rights, and identify one freedom that is protected there. Then review your local newspapers for an article relating to that freedom. Based on the article you read, is that freedom being protected or threatened?

Standardized Test Practice

Select the best answer for each of the following questions.

20 Under the Constitution, the president chooses judges to serve on the Supreme Court, but each choice must be approved by the Senate. This is an example of what principle of government?

A checks and balances

B federalism

C separation of powers

D judicial review

21 The highest level of the American judicial system is the

A appeals court.

B president's cabinet.

C Supreme Court.

D House of Representatives.

22 The government powers that are shared between the federal and state governments are known as

A enumerated powers.

B popular powers.

C reserved powers.

D concurrent powers.

Creating a Nation

Government under the Articles of Confederation was weak. When the Founders wrote a new constitution, they created a strong government. It was based on British traditions and the ideas of the Enlightenment.

	Chapter 3 A More Perfect Union	**Chapter 4** The Constitution
When	• 1777–1790	• 1787–present
Where	• The Northeast • The Northwest Territory • The South	• Philadelphia, Pennsylvania

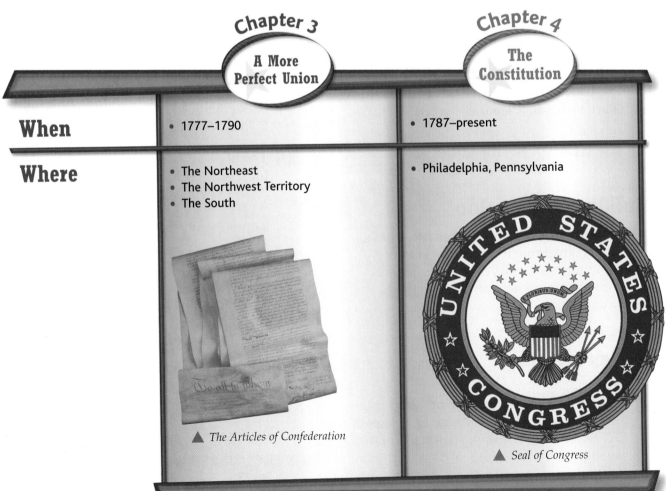

▲ *The Articles of Confederation*

▲ *Seal of Congress*

Chapter 3
A More Perfect Union

Chapter 4
The Constitution

Major Events

Chapter 3:
- **1776–1780** Colonies become states with written constitutions
- **1777** The Articles of Confederation are the first constitution of the United States of America
- **1785** Ordinance of 1785 provides way to survey and sell western lands
- **1786–1787** Shays's Rebellion challenges national government
- **1787** Northwest Ordinance sets up system under which western lands may become states
- **1787** Constitutional Convention meets
- **1787** Three-fifths Compromise is temporary solution to slavery issue
- **1787–1790** Federalists work for ratification of the Constitution and Antifederalists work for its defeat

Chapter 4:
- **1791** Bill of Rights added to Constitution
- **1803** *Marbury* v. *Madison* establishes Supreme Court's power of judicial review
- **1866** *Ex parte Milligan* demonstrates Supreme Court's power to review presidential policies
- **1954** *Brown* v. *Board of Education* demonstrates Supreme Court's right to review state laws

Linda Brown ▶

Some Important People

Chapter 3:
- Daniel Shays
- James Madison
- Edmund Randolph
- Roger Sherman
- Alexander Hamilton

James Madison ▶

Chapter 4:
- Gouverneur Morris
- John Marshall

Gouverneur Morris ▶

How do these events and ideas affect our lives today?

Chapter 3:
- Since the Articles of Confederation could not solve serious problems, the Founders developed a new constitution. We live under that constitution today.

Chapter 4:
- The Bill of Rights guarantees certain rights and freedoms to all U.S. citizens. The government may not make laws that take them away.

What was happening in the world at this time?

Chapter 3:
- **1785** Russians settle in the Aleutian Islands near Alaska
- **1787** Britain's Edmund Cartwright patents a power loom
- **1787** Japanese rioters break into rice warehouses and other shops throughout the nation

Chapter 4:
- **1795** France creates Republican constitution
- **1824** A new constitution establishes the Federal Republic of Mexico
- **1946** Japan adopts a democratic constitution

The Constitution of the United States

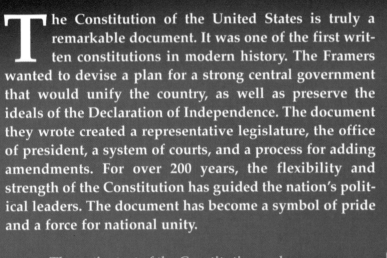

The Constitution of the United States is truly a remarkable document. It was one of the first written constitutions in modern history. The Framers wanted to devise a plan for a strong central government that would unify the country, as well as preserve the ideals of the Declaration of Independence. The document they wrote created a representative legislature, the office of president, a system of courts, and a process for adding amendments. For over 200 years, the flexibility and strength of the Constitution has guided the nation's political leaders. The document has become a symbol of pride and a force for national unity.

The entire text of the Constitution and its amendments follows. Those passages that have been set aside, outdated by the passage of time, or changed by the adoption of amendments are printed in blue. Also included are explanatory notes that will help clarify the meaning of each article and section.

*James Madison,
author of the
Constitution*

Preamble

We the People of the United States, in Order to form a more perfect Union, establish Justice, insure domestic Tranquility, provide for the common defence, promote the general Welfare, and secure the Blessings of Liberty to ourselves and our Posterity, do ordain and establish this Constitution for the United States of America.

Article I

Section 1

All legislative Powers herein granted shall be vested in a Congress of the United States, which shall consist of a Senate and House of Representatives.

Section 2

[1.] The House of Representatives shall be composed of Members chosen every second Year by the People of the several States, and the Electors in each State shall have the Qualifications requisite for Electors of the most numerous Branch of the State Legislature.

[2.] No person shall be a Representative who shall not have attained to the Age of twenty five Years, and been seven Years a Citizen of the United States, and who shall not, when elected, be an Inhabitant of that State in which he shall be chosen.

[3.] Representatives and direct Taxes shall be apportioned among the several States which may be included within this Union, according to their respective Numbers, which shall be determined by adding to the whole Number of free Persons, including those bound to Service for a Term of Years, and excluding Indians not taxed, three fifths of all other Persons. The actual Enumeration shall be made within three Years after the first Meeting of the Congress of the United States, and within every subsequent Term of ten Years, in such Manner as they shall by Law direct. The Number of Representatives shall not exceed one for every thirty Thousand, but each State shall have at Least one Representative; and until such enumeration shall be made, the State of New Hampshire shall be entitled to chuse three; Massachusetts eight, Rhode-Island and Providence Plantations one, Connecticut five, New-York six, New Jersey four, Pennsylvania eight, Delaware one, Maryland six, Virginia ten, North Carolina five, South Carolina five, and Georgia three.

[4.] When vacancies happen in the Representation from any State, the Executive Authority thereof shall issue Writs of Election to fill such Vacancies.

[5.] The House of Representatives shall chuse their Speaker and other Officers; and shall have the sole Power of Impeachment.

The Preamble introduces the Constitution and sets forth the general purposes for which the government was established. The Preamble also declares that the power of the government comes from the people.

The printed text of the document shows the spelling and punctuation of the parchment original.

Article I. The Legislative Branch

The Constitution contains seven divisions called articles. Each article covers a general topic. For example, Articles I, II, and III create the three branches of the national government—the legislative, executive, and judicial branches. Most of the articles are divided into sections.

Section 2. House of Representatives

Division of Representatives Among the States The number of representatives from each state is based on the size of the state's population. Each state is entitled to at least one representative. *What are the qualifications for members of the House of Representatives?*

Vocabulary

preamble: *introduction*
constitution: *principles and laws of a nation*
enumeration: *census or population count*
impeachment: *bringing charges against an official*

Section 3. The Senate

Number of Members, Terms of Office, and Voting Procedure Originally, senators were chosen by the state legislators of their own states. The Seventeenth Amendment changed this, so that senators are now elected by the people. There are 100 senators, 2 from each state. The vice president serves as president of the Senate.

John Adams, the first vice president

Section 3. The Senate

Trial of Impeachment One of Congress's powers is the power to impeach—to accuse government officials of wrongdoing, put them on trial, and if necessary remove them from office. *Which body has the power to decide the official's guilt or innocence?*

Vocabulary

president pro tempore: *presiding officer of Senate who serves when the vice president is absent*
indictment: *charging a person with an offense*
quorum: *minimum number of members that must be present to conduct sessions*
adjourn: *to suspend a session*
immunity privilege: *members cannot be sued or prosecuted for anything they say in Congress*
emoluments: *salaries*
bill: *draft of a proposed law*
revenue: *income raised by government*

Section 3

[1.] The Senate of the United States shall be composed of two Senators from each State, chosen by the Legislature thereof, for six Years; and each Senator shall have one Vote.

[2.] Immediately after they shall be assembled in Consequence of the first Election, they shall be divided as equally as may be into three Classes. The Seats of the Senators of the first Class shall be vacated at the Expiration of the second Year, of the second Class at the Expiration of the fourth Year, and of the third Class at the Expiration of the sixth Year, so that one third may be chosen every second Year; and if Vacancies happen by Resignation, or otherwise, during the Recess of the Legislature of any State, the Executive thereof may make temporary Appointments until the next Meeting of the Legislature, which shall then fill such Vacancies.

[3.] No Person shall be a Senator who shall not have attained to the Age of thirty Years, and been nine Years a Citizen of the United States, and who shall not, when elected, be an Inhabitant of that State for which he shall be chosen.

[4.] The Vice President of the United States shall be President of the Senate, but shall have no Vote, unless they be equally divided.

[5.] The Senate shall chuse their other Officers, and also a President pro tempore, in the Absence of the Vice President, or when he shall exercise the Office of the President of the United States.

[6.] The Senate shall have the sole Power to try all Impeachments. When sitting for that Purpose, they shall be on Oath or Affirmation. When the President of the United States is tried, the Chief Justice shall preside: And no Person shall be convicted without the Concurrence of two thirds of the Members present.

[7.] Judgment in Cases of Impeachment shall not extend further than to removal from Office, and disqualification to hold and enjoy any Office of honor, Trust or Profit under the United States: but the Party convicted shall nevertheless be liable and subject to Indictment, Trial, Judgment and Punishment, according to Law.

Section 4

[1.] The Times, Places and Manner of holding Elections for Senators and Representatives, shall be prescribed in each State by the Legislature thereof; but the Congress may at any time by Law make or alter such Regulations, except as to the Places of chusing Senators.

[2.] The Congress shall assemble at least once in every Year, and such Meeting shall be on the first Monday in December, unless they shall by Law appoint a different Day.

Section 5

[1.] Each House shall be the Judge of the Elections, Returns and Qualifications of its own Members, and a Majority of each shall constitute a Quorum to do Business; but a smaller Number may adjourn from day to day, and may be authorized to compel the Attendance of absent Members, in such Manner, and under such Penalties as each House may provide.

[2.] Each House may determine the Rules of its Proceedings, punish its Members for disorderly Behaviour, and, with the Concurrence of two thirds, expel a Member.

[3.] Each House shall keep a Journal of its Proceedings, and from time to time publish the same, excepting such Parts as may in their Judgment require Secrecy; and the Yeas and Nays of the Members of either House on any question shall, at the Desire of one fifth of those Present, be entered on the Journal.

[4.] Neither House, during the Session of Congress, shall, without the Consent of the other, adjourn for more than three days, nor to any other Place than that in which the two Houses shall be sitting.

Section 6

[1.] The Senators and Representatives shall receive a Compensation for their Services, to be ascertained by Law, and paid out of the Treasury of the United States. They shall in all Cases, except Treason, Felony and Breach of the Peace, be privileged from Arrest during their Attendance at the Session of their respective Houses, and in going to and returning from the same; and for any Speech or Debate in either House, they shall not be questioned in any other Place.

[2.] No Senator or Representative shall, during the Time for which he was elected, be appointed to any civil Office under the Authority of the United States, which shall have been created, or the Emoluments whereof shall have been encreased during such time; and no Person holding any Office under the United States, shall be a Member of either House during his Continuance in Office.

Section 7

[1.] All Bills for raising Revenue shall originate in the House of Representatives; but the Senate may propose or concur with Amendments as on other Bills.

[2.] Every Bill which shall have passed the House of Representatives and the Senate, shall, before it become a Law, be presented to the President of the United States; If he approve he shall sign it, but if not he shall return it, with his Objections to that House in which it shall have originated, who shall enter the Objections at large on their Journal, and proceed to reconsider it. If after such Reconsideration two thirds of that House shall agree to pass the Bill, it shall be sent, together with the Objections, to the other House, by which it shall likewise be reconsidered, and if approved by two thirds

Senate gavel

Section 6. Privileges and Restrictions

Pay and Privileges To strengthen the federal government, the Founders set congressional salaries to be paid by the United States Treasury rather than by members' respective states. Originally, members were paid $6 per day. In 2002, all members of Congress received a base salary of $150,000.

Section 7. Passing Laws

Revenue Bills All tax laws must originate in the House of Representatives. This ensures that the branch of Congress that is elected by the people every two years has the major role in determining taxes.

Section 7. Passing Laws

How Bills Become Laws A bill may become a law only by passing both houses of Congress and by being signed by the president. The president can check Congress by rejecting–vetoing–its legislation. *How can Congress override the president's veto?*

Civil War money

Section 8. Powers Granted to Congress

Expressed Powers Expressed powers are those powers directly stated in the Constitution. Most of the expressed powers of Congress are listed in Article I, Section 8. These powers are also called enumerated powers because they are numbered 1–18. *Which clause gives Congress the power to declare war?*

Section 8. Powers Granted to Congress

The Commerce Clause Congress has the power to make laws that control trade, or commerce. This trade may be with other countries, among the states, or with Native Americans. During the 1800s, the Supreme Court ruled that the tribes were independent nations. Congress may limit their independence, however, because they are inside the United States. The Constitution does not state how Congress may limit the tribes. As a result, the tribes have had changing amounts of independence over the years.

Vocabulary

resolution: *legislature's formal expression of opinion*

naturalization: *procedure by which a citizen of a foreign nation becomes a citizen of the United States*

tribunal: *a court*

letter of marque: *authority given to a citizen to outfit an armed ship and use it to attack enemy ships in time of war*

reprisal: *taking by force property or territory belonging to another country or to its citizens*

insurrection: *rebellion*

of that House, it shall become a Law. But in all such Cases the Votes of both Houses shall be determined by yeas and Nays, and the Names of the Persons voting for and against the Bill shall be entered on the Journal of each House respectively. If any Bill shall not be returned by the President within ten Days (Sundays excepted) after it shall have been presented to him, the Same shall be a Law, in like Manner as if he had signed it, unless the Congress by their Adjournment prevent its Return, in which Case it shall not be a Law.

[3.] Every Order, Resolution, or Vote to which the Concurrence of the Senate and House of Representatives may be necessary (except on a question of Adjournment) shall be presented to the President of the United States; and before the Same shall take Effect, shall be approved by him, or being disapproved by him, shall be repassed by two thirds of the Senate and House of Representatives, according to the Rules and Limitations prescribed in the Case of a Bill.

Section 8

[1.] The Congress shall have the Power To lay and collect Taxes, Duties, Imposts and Excises, to pay the Debts and provide for the common Defence and general Welfare of the United States; but all Duties, Imposts and Excises shall be uniform throughout the United States;

[2.] To borrow Money on the credit of the United States;

[3.] To regulate Commerce with foreign Nations, and among the several States, and with the Indian Tribes;

[4.] To establish an uniform Rule of Naturalization, and uniform Laws on the subject of Bankruptcies throughout the United States;

[5.] To coin Money, regulate the Value thereof, and of foreign Coin, and fix the Standard of Weights and Measures;

[6.] To provide for the Punishment of counterfeiting the Securities and current Coin of the United States;

[7.] To establish Post Offices and post Roads;

[8.] To promote the Progress of Science and useful Arts, by securing for limited Times to Authors and Inventors the exclusive Right to their respective Writings and Discoveries;

[9.] To constitute Tribunals inferior to the supreme Court;

[10.] To define and punish Piracies and Felonies committed on the high Seas, and Offences against the Law of Nations;

[11.] To declare War, grant Letters of Marque and Reprisal, and make Rules concerning Captures on Land and Water;

[12.] To raise and support Armies, but no Appropriation of Money to that Use shall be for a longer Term than two Years;

[13.] To provide and maintain a Navy;

[14.] To make Rules for the Government and Regulation of the land and naval Forces;

[15.] To provide for calling forth the Militia to execute the Laws of the Union, suppress Insurrections and repel Invasions;

[16.] To provide for organizing, arming, and disciplining, the Militia, and for governing such Part of them as may be employed in the Service of the United States, reserving to the States respectively, the Appointment of the Officers, and the Authority of training the Militia according to the discipline prescribed by Congress;

[17.] To exercise exclusive Legislation in all Cases whatsoever, over such District (not exceeding ten Miles square) as may, by Cession of particular States, and the Acceptance of Congress, become the Seat of Government of the United States, and to exercise like Authority over all Places purchased by the Consent of the Legislature of the State in which the Same shall be, for the Erection of Forts, Magazines, Arsenals, dock-Yards, and other needful Buildings;—And

[18.] To make all Laws which shall be necessary and proper for carrying into Execution the foregoing Powers, and all other Powers vested by this Constitution in the Government of the United States, or in any Department or Officer thereof.

Section 9

[1.] The Migration or Importation of such Persons as any of the States now existing shall think proper to admit, shall not be prohibited by the Congress prior to the Year one thousand eight hundred and eight, but a Tax or duty may be imposed on such Importation, not exceeding ten dollars for each Person.

[2.] The Privilege of the Writ of Habeas Corpus shall not be suspended, unless when in Cases of Rebellion or Invasion the public Safety may require it.

[3.] No Bill of Attainder or ex post facto Law shall be passed.

[4.] No Capitation, or other direct, Tax shall be laid, unless in Proportion to the Census or Enumeration herein before directed to be taken.

[5.] No Tax or Duty shall be laid on Articles exported from any State.

[6.] No Preference shall be given by any Regulation of Commerce or Revenue to the Ports of one State over those of another: nor shall Vessels bound to, or from, one State, be obliged to enter, clear, or pay Duties in another.

Seal of the U.S. Navy

Section 8. Powers Granted to Congress

Elastic Clause The final enumerated power is often called the "elastic clause." This clause gives Congress the right to make all laws "necessary and proper" to carry out the powers expressed in the other clauses of Article I. It is called the elastic clause because it lets Congress "stretch" its powers to meet situations the Founders could never have anticipated.

What does the phrase "necessary and proper" in the elastic clause mean? Almost from the beginning, this phrase was a subject of dispute. The issue was whether a strict or a broad interpretation of the Constitution should be applied. The dispute was first addressed in 1819, in the case of *McCulloch* v. *Maryland*, when the Supreme Court ruled in favor of a broad interpretation.

Section 9. Powers Denied to the Federal Government

Habeas Corpus A writ of habeas corpus issued by a judge requires a law official to bring a prisoner to court and show cause for holding the prisoner. A bill of attainder is a bill that punished a person without a jury trial. An "ex post facto" law is one that makes an act a crime after the act has been committed. *What does the Constitution say about bills of attainder?*

[7.] No Money shall be drawn from the Treasury, but in Consequence of Appropriations made by Law; and a regular Statement and Account of the Receipts and Expenditures of all public Money shall be published from time to time.

[8.] No Title of Nobility shall be granted by the United States: And no Person holding any Office of Profit or Trust under them, shall, without the Consent of the Congress, accept of any present, Emolument, Office, or Title, of any kind whatever, from any King, Prince, or foreign State.

Section 10

[1.] No State shall enter into any Treaty, Alliance, or Confederation; grant Letters of Marque and Reprisal; coin Money; emit Bills of Credit; make any Thing but gold and silver Coin a Tender in Payment of Debts; pass any Bill of Attainder, ex post facto Law, or Law impairing the Obligation of Contracts, or grant any Title of Nobility.

[2.] No State shall, without the Consent of the Congress, lay any Imposts or Duties on Imports or Exports, except what may be absolutely necessary for executing it's inspection Laws: and the net Produce of all Duties and Imposts, laid by any State on Imports and Exports, shall be for the Use of the Treasury of the United States; and all such Laws shall be subject to the Revision and Controul of the Congress.

[3.] No State shall, without the Consent of Congress, lay any Duty of Tonnage, keep Troops, or Ships of War in time of Peace, enter into any Agreement or Compact with another State, or with a foreign Power, or engage in War, unless actually invaded, or in such imminent Danger as will not admit of delay.

Article II

Section 1

[1.] The executive Power shall be vested in a President of the United States of America. He shall hold his Office during the Term of four Years, and, together with the Vice President, chosen for the same Term, be elected, as follows

[2.] Each State shall appoint, in such Manner as the Legislature thereof may direct, a Number of Electors, equal to the whole Number of Senators and Representatives to which the State may be entitled in the Congress: but no Senator or Representative, or Person holding an Office of Trust or Profit under the United States, shall be appointed an Elector.

[3.] The Electors shall meet in their respective States, and vote by Ballot for two Persons, of whom one at least shall not be an Inhabitant of the same State with

---

Section 10. Powers Denied to the States

Limitations on Power Section 10 lists limits on the states. These restrictions were designed, in part, to prevent an overlapping in functions and authority with the federal government.

United States coins

Article II. The Executive Branch

Article II creates an executive branch to carry out laws passed by Congress. Article II lists the powers and duties of the presidency, describes qualifications for office and procedures for electing the president, and provides for a vice president.

Vocabulary

appropriations: *funds set aside for a specific use*
emolument: *payment*
impost: *tax*
duty: *tax*

themselves. And they shall make a List of all the Persons voted for, and of the Number of Votes for each; which List they shall sign and certify, and transmit sealed to the Seat of the Government of the United States, directed to the President of the Senate. The President of the Senate shall, in the Presence of the Senate and House of Representatives, open all the Certificates, and the Votes shall then be counted. The Person having the greatest Number of Votes shall be the President, if such Number be a Majority of the whole Number of Electors appointed; and if there be more than one who have such Majority, and have an equal Number of Votes, then the House of Representatives shall immediately chuse by Ballot one of them for President; and if no person have a Majority, then from the five highest on the List the said House shall in like Manner chuse the President. But in chusing the President, the Votes shall be taken by States, the Representation from each State having one Vote; A quorum for this Purpose shall consist of a Member or Members from two thirds of the States, and a Majority of all the States shall be necessary to a Choice. In every Case, after the Choice of the President, the Person having the greatest Number of Votes of the Electors shall be the Vice President. But if there should remain two or more who have equal Votes, the Senate shall chuse from them by Ballot the Vice President.

[4.] The Congress may determine the Time of chusing the Electors, and the Day on which they shall give their Votes; which Day shall be the same throughout the United States.

[5.] No Person except a natural born Citizen, or a Citizen of the United States, at the time of the Adoption of this Constitution, shall be eligible to the Office of President; neither shall any Person be eligible to that Office who shall not have attained to the Age of thirty five Years, and been fourteen Years a Resident within the United States.

[6.] In Case of the Removal of the President from Office, or of his Death, Resignation, or Inability to discharge the Powers and Duties of the said Office, the Same shall devolve on the Vice President, and the Congress may by Law provide for the Case of Removal, Death, Resignation or Inability, both of the President and Vice President, declaring what Officer shall then act as President, and such Officer shall act accordingly, until the Disability be removed, or a President shall be elected.

[7.] The President shall, at stated Times, receive for his Services, a Compensation, which shall neither be encreased nor diminished during the Period for which he shall have been elected, and he shall not receive within that Period any other Emolument from the United States, or any of them.

[8.] Before he enter on the Execution of his Office, he shall take the following Oath or Affirmation:—"I do solemnly swear (or affirm) that I will faithfully execute the Office of President of the United States, and will to the best of my Ability, preserve, protect and defend the Constitution of the United States."

Section 1. President and Vice President

Former Method of Election The Twelfth Amendment, added in 1804, changed the method of electing the president stated in Article II, Section 1, paragraph 3. The Twelfth Amendment requires that the electors cast separate ballots for president and vice president.

George Washington, the first president

Section 1. President and Vice President

Qualifications The president must be a citizen of the United States by birth, at least 35 years of age, and a resident of the United States for 14 years.

Section 1. President and Vice President

Vacancies If the president dies, resigns, is removed from office by impeachment, or is unable to carry out the duties of the office, the vice president assumes the duties of the president. The Twenty-fifth Amendment sets procedures for presidential succession.

Section 1. President and Vice President

Salary Originally, the president's salary was $25,000 per year. The president's current salary is $400,000 plus a $50,000 nontaxable expense account per year. The president also receives living accommodations in two residences–the White House and Camp David.

Section 2. Powers of the President

Military, Cabinet, Pardons Mention of "the principal officer in each of the executive departments" is the only suggestion of the president's cabinet to be found in the Constitution. The cabinet is an advisory body, and its power depends on the president. Section 2, Clause 1 also makes the president—a civilian—the head of the armed services. This established the principle of civilian control of the military.

Section 2. Powers of the President

Treaties and Appointments An executive order is a command issued by a president to exercise a power which he has been given by the U.S. Constitution or by a federal statute. In times of emergency, presidents sometimes have used the executive order to override the Constitution of the United States and the Congress. During the Civil War, President Lincoln suspended many fundamental rights guaranteed in the Constitution and the Bill of Rights. He closed down newspapers that opposed his policies and imprisoned some who disagreed with him. Lincoln said that these actions were justified to preserve the Union.

Impeachment ticket

Article III. The Judicial Branch

The term *judicial* refers to courts. The Constitution set up only the Supreme Court but provided for the establishment of other federal courts. The judiciary of the United States has two different systems of courts. One system consists of the federal courts, whose powers derive from the Constitution and federal laws. The other includes the courts of each of the 50 states, whose powers derive from state constitutions and laws.

Section 2

[1.] The President shall be Commander in Chief of the Army and Navy of the United States, and of the Militia of the several States, when called into the actual Service of the United States; he may require the Opinion, in writing, of the principal Officer in each of the executive Departments, upon any Subject relating to the Duties of their respective Offices, and he shall have Power to grant Reprieves and Pardons for Offences against the United States, except in Cases of Impeachment.

[2.] He shall have Power, by and with the Advice and Consent of the Senate, to make Treaties, provided two thirds of the Senators present concur; and he shall nominate, and by and with the Advice and Consent of the Senate, shall appoint Ambassadors, other public Ministers and Consuls, Judges of the supreme Court, and all other Officers of the United States, whose Appointments are not herein otherwise provided for, and which shall be established by Law: but the Congress may by Law vest the Appointment of such inferior Officers, as they think proper, in the President alone, in the Courts of Law, or in the Heads of Departments.

[3.] The President shall have Power to fill up all Vacancies that may happen during the Recess of the Senate, by granting Commissions which shall expire at the End of their next Session.

Section 3

He shall from time to time give to the Congress Information of the State of the Union, and recommend to their Consideration such Measures as he shall judge necessary and expedient; he may, on extraordinary Occasions, convene both Houses, or either of them, and in Case of Disagreement between them, with Respect to the Time of Adjournment, he may adjourn them to such Time as he shall think proper; he shall receive Ambassadors and other public Ministers; he shall take Care that the Laws be faithfully executed, and shall Commission all the Officers of the United States.

Section 4

The President, Vice President and all civil Officers of the United States, shall be removed from Office on Impeachment for, and Conviction of, Treason, Bribery, or other high Crimes and Misdemeanors.

Article III

Section 1

The judicial Power of the United States, shall be vested in one supreme Court, and in such inferior Courts as the Congress may from time to time ordain and establish. The Judges, both of the supreme and inferior Courts, shall hold their Offices during good Behaviour, and shall, at stated Times, receive for their Services, a Compensation, which shall not be diminished during their Continuance in Office.

Section 2

[1.] The judicial Power shall extend to all Cases, in Law and Equity, arising under this Constitution, the Laws of the United States, and Treaties made, or which shall be made, under their Authority;—to all Cases affecting Ambassadors, other public Ministers and Consuls;—to all Cases of admiralty and maritime Jurisdiction;—to Controversies to which the United States shall be a Party;—to Controversies between two or more States;—between a State and Citizens of another State;—between Citizens of different States,—between Citizens of the same State claiming Lands under Grants of different States, and between a State, or the Citizens thereof, and foreign States, Citizens or Subjects.

[2.] In all Cases affecting Ambassadors, other public Ministers and Consuls, and those in which a State shall be Party, the supreme Court shall have original Jurisdiction. In all the other Cases before mentioned, the supreme Court shall have appellate Jurisdiction, both as to Law and Fact, with such Exceptions, and under such Regulations as the Congress shall make.

[3.] The Trial of all Crimes, except in Cases of Impeachment, shall be by Jury; and such Trial shall be held in the State where the said Crimes shall have been committed; but when not committed within any State, the Trial shall be at such Place or Places as the Congress may by Law have directed.

Section 3

[1.] Treason against the United States, shall consist only in levying War against them, or in adhering to their Enemies, giving them Aid and Comfort. No Person shall be convicted of Treason unless on the Testimony of two Witnesses to the same overt Act, or on Confession in open Court.

[2.] The Congress shall have Power to declare the Punishment of Treason, but no Attainder of Treason shall work Corruption of Blood, or Forfeiture except during the Life of the Person attainted.

Article IV

Section 1

Full Faith and Credit shall be given in each State to the public Acts, Records, and judicial Proceedings of every other State. And the Congress may by general Laws prescribe the Manner in which such Acts, Records and Proceedings shall be proved, and the Effect thereof.

Section 2. Jurisdiction
Statute Law Federal courts deal mostly with "statute law," or laws passed by Congress, treaties, and cases involving the Constitution itself.

Section 2. Jurisdiction
The Supreme Court A Court with "original jurisdiction" has the authority to be the first court to hear a case. The Supreme Court primarily has "appellate jurisdiction" and mostly hears cases appealed from lower courts.

Article IV. Relations Among the States

Article IV explains the relationship of the states to one another and to the national government. This article requires each state to give citizens of other states the same rights as its own citizens, addresses admitting new states, and guarantees that the national government will protect the states.

Vocabulary

original jurisdiction: *authority to be the first court to hear a case*

appellate jurisdiction: *authority to hear cases that have been appealed from lower courts*

treason: *violation of the allegiance owed by a person to his or her own country, for example, by aiding an enemy*

Section 3. New States and Territories

New States Congress has the power to admit new states. It also determines the basic guidelines for applying for statehood. Two states, Maine and West Virginia, were created within the boundaries of another state. In the case of West Virginia, President Lincoln recognized the West Virginia government as the legal government of Virginia during the Civil War. This allowed West Virginia to secede from Virginia without obtaining approval from the Virginia legislature.

Section 4. Federal Protection for States

Republic Government can be classified in many different ways. The ancient Greek philosopher Aristotle classified government based on the question: Who governs? According to Aristotle, all governments belong to one of three major groups: (1) autocracy—rule by one person; (2) oligarchy—rule by a few persons; or (3) democracy—rule by many persons. A republic is a form of democracy in which the people elect representatives to make laws and conduct government.

Article V. The Amendment Process

Article V spells out the ways that the Constitution can be amended, or changed. All of the 27 amendments were proposed by a two-thirds vote of both houses of Congress. Only the Twenty-first Amendment was ratified by constitutional conventions of the states. All other amendments have been ratified by state legislatures. *What is an amendment?*

Vocabulary

extradition: *surrender of a criminal to another authority*
amendment: *a change to the Constitution*
ratification: *process by which an amendment is approved*

Section 2

[1.] The Citizens of each State shall be entitled to all Privileges and Immunities of Citizens in the several States.

[2.] A Person charged in any State with Treason, Felony, or other Crime, who shall flee from Justice, and be found in another State, shall on Demand of the executive Authority of the State from which he fled, be delivered up, to be removed to the State having Jurisdiction of the Crime.

[3.] No Person held to Service of Labour in one State, under the Laws thereof, escaping into another, shall, in Consequence of any Law or Regulation therein, be discharged from such Service or Labour, but shall be delivered up on Claim of the Party to whom such Service or Labour may be due.

Section 3

[1.] New States may be admitted by the Congress into this Union; but no new State shall be formed or erected within the Jurisdiction of any other State; nor any State be formed by the Junction of two or more States, or Parts of States, without the Consent of the Legislatures of the States concerned as well as of the Congress.

[2.] The Congress shall have Power to dispose of and make all needful Rules and Regulations respecting the Territory or other Property belonging to the United States; and nothing in this Constitution shall be so construed as to Prejudice any Claims of the United States, or of any particular State.

Section 4

The United States shall guarantee to every State in this Union a Republican Form of Government, and shall protect each of them against Invasion; and on Application of the Legislature, or of the Executive (when the Legislature cannot be convened) against domestic Violence.

Article V

The Congress, whenever two thirds of both Houses shall deem it necessary, shall propose Amendments to this Constitution, or, on the Application of the Legislatures of two thirds of the several States, shall call a Convention for proposing Amendments, which, in either Case, shall be valid to all Intents and Purposes, as Part of this Constitution, when ratified by the Legislatures of three fourths of the several States, or by Conventions in three fourths thereof, as the one or the other Mode of Ratification may be proposed by the Congress; Provided that no Amendment which may be made prior to the Year One thousand eight hundred and eight shall in any Manner affect the first and fourth Clauses in the Ninth Section of the first Article; and that no State, without its Consent, shall be deprived of its equal Suffrage in the Senate.

Article VI

[1.] All Debts contracted and Engagements entered into, before the Adoption of this Constitution, shall be as valid against the United States under this Constitution, as under the Confederation.

[2.] This Constitution, and the Laws of the United States which shall be made in Pursuance thereof; and all Treaties made, or which shall be made, under the Authority of the United States, shall be the supreme Law of the Land; and the Judges in every State shall be bound thereby, any Thing in the Constitution or Laws of any State to the Contrary notwithstanding.

[3.] The Senators and Representatives before mentioned, and the Members of the several State Legislatures, and all executive and judicial Officers, both of the United States and of the several States, shall be bound by Oath or Affirmation, to support this Constitution; but no religious Test shall ever be required as a Qualification to any Office or public Trust under the United States.

Article VII

The Ratification of the Conventions of nine States, shall be sufficient for the Establishment of this Constitution between the States so ratifying the Same.

Done in Convention by the Unanimous Consent of the States present the Seventeenth Day of September in the Year of our Lord one thousand seven hundred and Eighty seven and of the Independence of the United States of America the Twelfth. In witness whereof We have hereunto subscribed our Names,

Article VI. National Supremacy

Article VI contains the "supremacy clause." This clause establishes that the Constitution, laws passed by Congress, and treaties of the United States "shall be the supreme Law of the Land." The "supremacy clause" recognized the Constitution and federal laws as supreme when in conflict with those of the states.

Article VII. Ratification

Article VII addresses ratification and declares that the Constitution would take effect after it was ratified by nine states.

Signers

*George Washington, **President and Deputy from Virginia***

New Hampshire
John Langdon
Nicholas Gilman

Massachusetts
Nathaniel Gorham
Rufus King

Connecticut
William Samuel Johnson
Roger Sherman

New York
Alexander Hamilton

New Jersey
William Livingston
David Brearley
William Paterson
Jonathan Dayton

Pennsylvania
Benjamin Franklin
Thomas Mifflin
Robert Morris
George Clymer
Thomas FitzSimons
Jared Ingersoll
James Wilson
Gouverneur Morris

Delaware
George Read
Gunning Bedford, Jr.
John Dickinson
Richard Bassett
Jacob Broom

Maryland
James McHenry
Daniel of St. Thomas Jenifer
Daniel Carroll

Virginia
John Blair
James Madison, Jr.

North Carolina
William Blount
Richard Dobbs Spaight
Hugh Williamson

South Carolina
John Rutledge
Charles Cotesworth Pinckney
Charles Pinckney
Pierce Butler

Georgia
William Few
Abraham Baldwin

Attest: William Jackson,
Secretary

Bill of Rights

The first 10 amendments are known as the Bill of Rights (1791). These amendments limit the powers of government. The First Amendment protects the civil liberties of individuals in the United States. The amendment freedoms are not absolute, however. They are limited by the rights of other individuals. *What freedoms does the First Amendment protect?*

Amendment 2

Right to Bear Arms This amendment is often debated. Originally, it was intended to prevent the national government from repeating the actions of the British, who tried to take weapons away from the colonial militia, or armed forces of citizens. This amendment seems to support the right of citizens to own firearms, but the Supreme Court has ruled that it does not prevent Congress from regulating the interstate sale of weapons. *Why is the Second Amendment's meaning debated?*

Amendment 5

Rights of Accused Persons This amendment contains important protections for people accused of crimes. One of the protections is that government may not deprive any person of life, liberty, or property without due process of law. This means that the government must follow proper constitutional procedures in trials and in other actions it takes against individuals. *According to Amendment V, what is the function of a grand jury?*

Vocabulary

quarter: *to provide living accommodations*
probable cause: *police must have a reasonable basis to believe a person is linked to a crime*
warrant: *document that gives police particular rights or powers*
common law: *law established by previous court decisions*
bail: *money that an accused person provides to the court as a guarantee that he or she will be present for a trial*

Amendment I

Congress shall make no law respecting an establishment of religion, or prohibiting the free exercise thereof; or abridging the freedom of speech, or of the press; or the right of the people peaceably to assemble, and to petition the Government for a redress of grievances.

Amendment II

A well regulated Militia, being necessary to the security of a free State, the right of the people to keep and bear Arms, shall not be infringed.

Amendment III

No Soldier shall, in time of peace be quartered in any house, without the consent of the Owner, nor in time of war, but in a manner to be prescribed by law.

Amendment IV

The right of the people to be secure in their persons, houses, papers, and effects, against unreasonable searches and seizures, shall not be violated, and no Warrants shall issue, but upon probable cause, supported by Oath or affirmation, and particularly describing the place to be searched, and the persons or things to be seized.

Amendment V

No person shall be held to answer for a capital, or otherwise infamous crime, unless on a presentment or indictment of a Grand Jury, except in cases arising in the land or naval forces, or in the Militia, when in actual service in time of War or public danger; nor shall any person be subject for the same offence to be twice put in jeopardy of life or limb; nor shall be compelled in any criminal case to be a witness against himself, nor be deprived of life, liberty, or property, without due process of law; nor shall private property be taken for public use without just compensation.

Amendment VI

In all criminal prosecutions, the accused shall enjoy the right to a speedy and public trial, by an impartial jury of the State and district wherein the crime shall have been committed, which district shall have been previously ascertained by law, and to be informed of the nature and cause of the accusation; to be confronted with the witnesses against him; to have compulsory process for obtaining Witnesses in his favor, and to have the assistance of counsel for his defence.

Amendment VII

In Suits at common law, where the value in controversy shall exceed twenty dollars, the right of trial by jury shall be preserved, and no fact tried by a jury, shall be otherwise reexamined in any Court of the United States, than according to the rules of common law.

Amendment VIII

Excessive bail shall not be required, nor excessive fines imposed, nor cruel and unusual punishments inflicted.

Amendment IX

The enumeration in the Constitution, of certain rights, shall not be construed to deny or disparage others retained by the people.

Amendment X

The powers not delegated to the United States by the Constitution, nor prohibited by it to the States, are reserved to the States respectively, or to the people.

Amendment XI

The Judicial power of the United States shall not be construed to extend to any suit in law or equity, commenced or prosecuted against one of the United States by Citizens of another State, or by Citizens or Subjects of any Foreign State.

Amendment 6

Right to a Speedy, Fair Trial A basic protection is the right to a speedy, public trial. The jury must hear witnesses and evidence on both sides before deciding the guilt or innocence of a person charged with a crime. This amendment also provides that legal counsel must be provided to a defendant. In 1963, the Supreme Court ruled, in *Gideon* v. *Wainwright*, that if a defendant cannot afford a lawyer, the government must provide one to defend him or her. *Why is the right to a "speedy" trial important?*

Amendment 9

Powers Reserved to the People This amendment prevents government from claiming that the only rights people have are those listed in the Bill of Rights.

Amendment 10

Powers Reserved to the States The final amendment of the Bill of Rights protects the states and the people from an all-powerful federal government. It establishes that powers not given to the national government—or denied to the states—by the Constitution belong to the states or to the people.

Amendment 11

Suits Against States The Eleventh Amendment (1795) limits the jurisdiction of the federal courts. The Supreme Court had ruled that a federal court could try a lawsuit brought by citizens of South Carolina against the state of Georgia. This case, *Chisholm* v. *Georgia*, decided in 1793, raised a storm of protest, leading to passage of the Eleventh Amendment.

Amendment 12

Election of President and Vice President The Twelfth Amendment (1804) corrects a problem that had arisen in the method of electing the president and vice president. This amendment provides for the Electoral College to use separate ballots in voting for president and vice president. *If no candidate receives a majority of the electoral votes, who elects the president?*

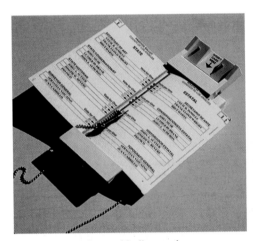

Ballot and ballot marker

Amendment 13

Abolition of Slavery Amendments Thirteen (1865), Fourteen (1868), and Fifteen (1870) often are called the Civil War amendments because they grew out of that great conflict. The Thirteenth Amendment outlaws slavery.

Vocabulary

majority: *more than half*
devolve: *to pass on*
abridge: *to reduce*
insurrection: *rebellion against the government*
emancipation: *freedom from slavery*

Amendment XII

The electors shall meet in their respective states and vote by ballot for President and Vice-President, one of whom, at least, shall not be an inhabitant of the same state with themselves; they shall name in their ballots the person voted for as President, and in distinct ballots the person voted for as Vice-President, and they shall make distinct lists of all persons voted for as President, and of all persons voted for as Vice-President, and of the number of votes for each, which lists they shall sign and certify, and transmit sealed to the seat of the government of the United States, directed to the President of the Senate;—The President of the Senate shall, in the presence of the Senate and House of Representatives, open all the certificates and the votes shall then be counted;—The person having the greatest number of votes for President, shall be the President, if such number be a majority of the whole number of Electors appointed; and if no person have such majority, then from the persons having the highest numbers not exceeding three on the list of those voted for as President, the House of Representatives shall choose immediately, by ballot, the President. But in choosing the President, the votes shall be taken by states, the representation from each state having one vote; a quorum for this purpose shall consist of a member or members from two-thirds of the states, and a majority of all the states shall be necessary to a choice. And if the House of Representatives shall not choose a President whenever the right of choice shall devolve upon them, before the fourth day of March next following, then the Vice-President shall act as President, as in the case of the death or other constitutional disability of the President. The person having the greatest number of votes as Vice-President, shall be the Vice-President, if such number be a majority of the whole number of Electors appointed, and if no person have a majority, then from the two highest numbers on the list, the Senate shall choose the Vice-President; a quorum for the purpose shall consist of two-thirds of the whole number of Senators, and a majority of the whole number shall be necessary to a choice. But no person constitutionally ineligible to the office of President shall be eligible to that of Vice-President of the United States.

Amendment XIII

Section 1

Neither slavery nor involuntary servitude, except as a punishment for crime whereof the party shall have been duly convicted, shall exist within the United States, or any place subject to their jurisdiction.

Section 2

Congress shall have power to enforce this article by appropriate legislation.

Amendment XIV

Section 1

All persons born or naturalized in the United States, and subject to the jurisdiction thereof, are citizens of the United States and of the State wherein they reside. No State shall make or enforce any law which shall abridge the privileges or immunities of citizens of the United States; nor shall any State deprive any person of life, liberty, or property, without due process of law; nor deny to any person within its jurisdiction the equal protection of the laws.

Section 2

Representatives shall be apportioned among the several States according to their respective numbers, counting the whole number of persons in each State, excluding Indians not taxed. But when the right to vote at any election for the choice of electors for President and Vice President of the United States, Representatives in Congress, the Executive and Judicial officers of a State, or the members of the Legislature thereof, is denied to any of the male inhabitants of such State, being twenty-one years of age, and citizens of the United States, or in any way abridged, except for participation in rebellion, or other crime, the basis of representation therein shall be reduced in the proportion which the number of such male citizens shall bear to the whole number of male citizens twenty-one years of age in such State.

Section 3

No person shall be a Senator or Representative in Congress, or elector of President and Vice President, or hold any office, civil or military, under the United States, or under any State, who, having previously taken an oath, as a member of Congress, or as an officer of the United States, or as a member of any State legislature, or as an executive or judicial officer of any State, to support the Constitution of the United States, shall have engaged in insurrection or rebellion against the same, or given aid or comfort to the enemies thereof. But Congress may by a vote of two-thirds of each House, remove such disability.

Section 4

The validity of the public debt of the United States, authorized by law, including debts incurred for payment of pensions and bounties for service in suppressing insurrection or rebellion, shall not be questioned. But neither the United States nor any State shall assume or pay any debt or obligation incurred in aid of insurrection or rebellion against the United States, or any claim for the loss or emancipation of any slave; but all such debts, obligations and claims shall be held illegal and void.

Amendment 14

Rights of Citizens The Fourteenth Amendment (1868) originally was intended to protect the legal rights of the freed slaves. Today it protects the rights of citizenship in general by prohibiting a state from depriving any person of life, liberty, or property without "due process of law." In addition, it states that all citizens have the right to equal protection of the law in all states.

Amendment 14. Section 2

Representation in Congress This section reduced the number of members a state had in the House of Representatives if it denied its citizens the right to vote. Later civil rights laws and the Twenty-fourth Amendment guaranteed the vote to African Americans.

Amendment 14. Section 3

Penalty for Engaging in Insurrection The leaders of the Confederacy were barred from state or federal offices unless Congress agreed to remove this ban. By the end of Reconstruction all but a few Confederate leaders were allowed to return to public life.

Amendment 14. Section 4

Public Debt The public debt acquired by the federal government during the Civil War was valid and could not be questioned by the South. However, the debts of the Confederacy were declared to be illegal. *Could former slaveholders collect payment for the loss of their slaves?*

Internal Revenue Service

Vocabulary

apportionment: *distribution of seats in House based on population*
vacancy: *an office or position that is unfilled or unoccupied*

Section 5

The Congress shall have power to enforce, by appropriate legislation, the provisions of this article.

Amendment XV

Section 1

The right of citizens of the United States to vote shall not be denied or abridged by the United States or by any State on account of race, color, or previous condition of servitude.

Section 2

The Congress shall have power to enforce this article by appropriate legislation.

Amendment XVI

The Congress shall have power to lay and collect taxes on incomes, from whatever source derived, without apportionment among the several States and without regard to any census or enumeration.

Amendment XVII

Section 1

The Senate of the United States shall be composed of two Senators from each State, elected by the people thereof, for six years; and each Senator shall have one vote. The electors in each State shall have the qualifications requisite for electors of the most numerous branch of the State legislatures.

Section 2

When vacancies happen in the representation of any State in the Senate, the executive authority of such State shall issue writs of election to fill such vacancies: *Provided*, That the legislature of any State may empower the executive thereof to make temporary appointments until the people fill the vacancies by election as the legislature may direct.

Section 3

This amendment shall not be so construed as to affect the election or term of any Senator chosen before it becomes valid as part of the Constitution.

Amendment XVIII

Section 1

After one year from ratification of this article, the manufacture, sale, or transportation of intoxicating liquors within, the importation thereof into, or the exportation thereof from the United States and all territory subject to the jurisdiction thereof for beverage purposes is hereby prohibited.

Section 2

The Congress and the several States shall have concurrent power to enforce this article by appropriate legislation.

Section 3

This article shall be inoperative unless it shall have been ratified as an amendment to the Constitution by the legislatures of the several States, as provided in the Constitution, within seven years from the date of the submission hereof to the States by the Congress.

Amendment XIX

Section 1

The right of citizens of the United States to vote shall not be denied or abridged by the United States or by any State on account of sex.

Section 2

Congress shall have power by appropriate legislation to enforce the provisions of this article.

Amendment XX

Section 1

The terms of the President and Vice President shall end at noon on the 20th day of January, and the terms of the Senators and Representatives at noon on the 3d day of January, of the years in which such terms would have ended if this article had not been ratified; and the terms of their successors shall then begin.

Section 2

The Congress shall assemble at least once in every year, and such meeting shall begin at noon on the 3d day of January, unless they shall by law appoint a different day.

Amendment 18
Prohibition of Alcoholic Beverages The Eighteenth Amendment (1919) prohibited the production, sale, or transportation of alcoholic beverages in the United States. Prohibition proved to be difficult to enforce. This amendment was later repealed by the Twenty-first Amendment.

Amendment 19
Woman Suffrage The Nineteenth Amendment (1920) guaranteed women the right to vote. By then women had already won the right to vote in many state elections, but the amendment put their right to vote in all state and national elections on a constitutional basis.

Amendment 20
"Lame-Duck" Amendment The Twentieth Amendment (1933) sets new dates for Congress to begin its term and for the inauguration of the president and vice president. Under the original Constitution, elected officials who retired or who had been defeated remained in office for several months. For the outgoing president, this period ran from November until March. Such outgoing officials had little influence and accomplished little, and they were called lame ducks because they were so inactive. *What date was fixed as Inauguration Day?*

Amendment 20. Section 3

Succession of President and Vice President This section provides that if the president-elect dies before taking office, the vice president-elect becomes president.

John Tyler was the first vice president to become president when a chief executive died.

Amendment 21

Repeal of Prohibition Amendment The Twenty-first Amendment (1933) repeals the Eighteenth Amendment. It is the only amendment ever passed to overturn an earlier amendment. It is also the only amendment ratified by special state conventions instead of state legislatures.

Vocabulary

president-elect: *individual who is elected president but has not yet begun serving his or her term*

District of Columbia: *site of nation's capital, occupying an area between Maryland and Virginia*

Section 3

If, at the time fixed for the beginning of the term of the President, the President elect shall have died, the Vice President elect shall become President. If a President shall not have been chosen before the time fixed for the beginning of his term, or if the President elect shall have failed to qualify, then the Vice President elect shall act as President until a President shall have qualified; and the Congress may by law provide for the case wherein neither a President elect nor a Vice President elect shall have qualified, declaring who shall then act as President, or the manner in which one who is to act shall be selected, and such person shall act accordingly until a President or Vice President shall have qualified.

Section 4

The Congress may by law provide for the case of the death of any of the persons from whom the House of Representatives may choose a President whenever the right of choice shall have devolved upon them, and for the case of the death of any of the persons from whom the Senate may choose a Vice President whenever the right of choice shall have devolved upon them.

Section 5

Sections 1 and 2 shall take effect on the 15th day of October following the ratification of this article.

Section 6

This article shall be inoperative unless it shall have been ratified as an amendment to the Constitution by the legislatures of three-fourths of the several States within seven years from the date of its submission.

Amendment XXI

Section 1

The eighteenth article of amendment to the Constitution of the United States is hereby repealed.

Section 2

The transportation or importation into any State, Territory, or possession of the United States for delivery or use therein of intoxicating liquors, in violation of the laws thereof, is hereby prohibited.

Section 3

This article shall be inoperative unless it shall have been ratified as an amendment to the Constitution by conventions in the several States, as provided in the Constitution, within seven years from the date of the submission hereof to the States by the Congress.

Amendment XXII

Section 1

No person shall be elected to the office of the President more than twice, and no person who had held the office of President, or acted as President, for more than two years of a term to which some other person was elected President shall be elected to the office of the President more than once. But this Article shall not apply to any person holding the office of President when this Article was proposed by the Congress, and shall not prevent any person who may be holding the office of President, or acting as President, during the term within which this Article becomes operative from holding the office of President or acting as President during the remainder of such term.

Section 2

This article shall be inoperative unless it shall have been ratified as an amendment to the Constitution by the legislatures of three-fourths of the several States within seven years from the date of its submission to the States by the Congress.

Amendment XXIII

Section 1

The District constituting the seat of Government of the United States shall appoint in such manner as the Congress may direct:

A number of electors of President and Vice President equal to the whole number of Senators and Representatives in Congress to which the District would be entitled if it were a State, but in no event more than the least populous State; they shall be in addition to those appointed by the States, but they shall be considered, for the purposes of the election of President and Vice President, to be electors appointed by a State; and they shall meet in the District and perform such duties as provided by the twelfth article of amendment.

Section 2

The Congress shall have power to enforce this article by appropriate legislation.

Amendment 22
Limit on Presidential Terms The Twenty-second Amendment (1951) limits presidents to a maximum of two elected terms. It was passed largely as a reaction to Franklin D. Roosevelt's election to four terms between 1933 and 1945.

Presidential campaign buttons

Amendment 23
Presidential Electors for the District of Columbia The Twenty-third Amendment (1961) allows citizens living in Washington, D.C., to vote for president and vice president, a right previously denied residents of the nation's capital. The District of Columbia now has three presidential electors, the number to which it would be entitled if it were a state.

Amendment XXIV

Section 1

The right of citizens of the United States to vote in any primary or other election for President or Vice-President, for electors for President or Vice President, or for Senator or Representative in Congress, shall not be denied or abridged by the United States or any State by reason of failure to pay any poll tax or other tax.

Section 2

The Congress shall have power to enforce this article by appropriate legislation.

Amendment XXV

Section 1

In case of the removal of the President from office or his death or resignation, the Vice President shall become President.

Section 2

Whenever there is a vacancy in the office of the Vice President, the President shall nominate a Vice President who shall take the office upon confirmation by a majority vote of both Houses of Congress.

Section 3

Whenever the President transmits to the President pro tempore of the Senate and the Speaker of the House of Representatives his written declaration that he is unable to discharge the powers and duties of his office, and until he transmits to them a written declaration to the contrary, such powers and duties shall be discharged by the Vice President as Acting President.

Section 4

Whenever the Vice President and a majority of either the principal officers of the executive departments or of such other body as Congress may by law provide, transmit to the President pro tempore of the Senate and the Speaker of the House of Representatives their written declaration that the President is unable to discharge the powers and duties of his office, the Vice President shall immediately assume the power and duties of the office of Acting President.

Thereafter, when the President transmits to the President pro tempore of the Senate and the Speaker of the House of Representatives his written declaration that no inability exists, he shall resume the powers and duties of his office unless the Vice President and a majority of either the principal officers of the executive department or of such other body as Congress may by law provide, transmit within four days to the President pro tempore of the Senate and the Speaker of the House of Representatives their written declaration that the President is unable to discharge the powers and duties of his office.

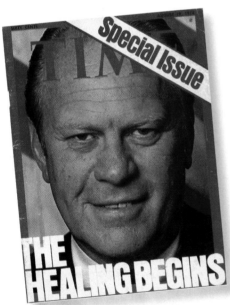

President Gerald Ford

Thereupon Congress shall decide the issue, assembling within forty-eight hours for that purpose if not in session. If the Congress, within twenty-one days after receipt of the latter written declaration, or, if Congress is not in session, within twenty-one days after Congress is required to assemble, determines by two-thirds vote of both Houses that the President is unable to discharge the powers and duties of his office, the Vice President shall continue to discharge the same as Acting President; otherwise, the President shall resume the power and duties of his office.

Amendment XXVI

Section 1
The right of citizens of the United States, who are eighteen years of age or older, to vote shall not be denied or abridged by the United States or by any State on account of age.

Section 2
The Congress shall have power to enforce this article by appropriate legislation.

Amendment XXVII
No law, varying the compensation for the services of Senators and Representatives, shall take effect, until an election of representatives shall have intervened.

Amendment 26
Eighteen-Year-Old Vote The Twenty-sixth Amendment (1971) guarantees the right to vote to all citizens 18 years of age and older.

Amendment 27
Restraint on Congressional Salaries The Twenty-seventh Amendment (1992) makes congressional pay raises effective during the term following their passage. James Madison offered the amendment in 1789, but it was never adopted. In 1982 Gregory Watson, then a student at the University of Texas, discovered the forgotten amendment while doing research for a school paper. Watson made the amendment's passage his crusade.

Joint meeting of Congress

Launching the Republic

Why It's Important

With the Constitution in place, the newly chosen government began to set procedures and customs for the country. The nation continued to gain new territory and grow, but faced challenges from other countries, including its old foe, Great Britain. The United States also set foreign policy that would guide its actions for many years.

- The American political process took shape during the country's early years.

- The United States began to establish its place in the world as it gained territory and fought wars with foreign powers.

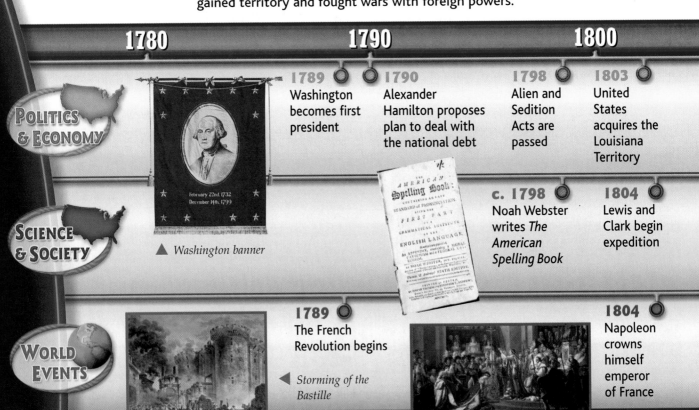

1780   **1790**   **1800**

POLITICS & ECONOMY

▲ *Washington banner*

1789
Washington becomes first president

1790
Alexander Hamilton proposes plan to deal with the national debt

1798
Alien and Sedition Acts are passed

1803
United States acquires the Louisiana Territory

SCIENCE & SOCIETY

c. 1798
Noah Webster writes *The American Spelling Book*

1804
Lewis and Clark begin expedition

WORLD EVENTS

1789
The French Revolution begins

◀ *Storming of the Bastille*

1804
Napoleon crowns himself emperor of France

Where in the United States?

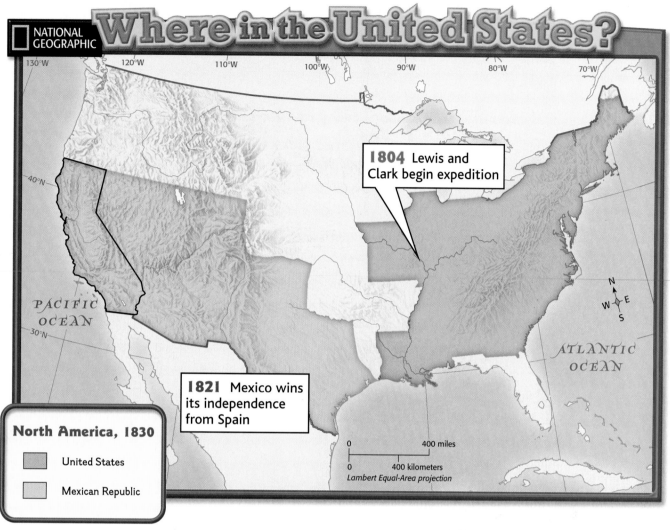

1804 Lewis and Clark begin expedition

1821 Mexico wins its independence from Spain

North America, 1830

United States

Mexican Republic

PACIFIC OCEAN

ATLANTIC OCEAN

40°N
30°N
130°W 120°W 110°W 100°W 90°W 80°W 70°W

0   400 miles
0   400 kilometers
Lambert Equal-Area projection

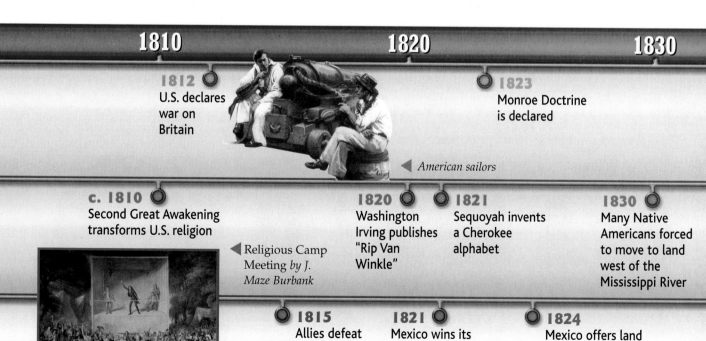

1810

1820

1830

1812
U.S. declares war on Britain

1823
Monroe Doctrine is declared

◄ *American sailors*

c. 1810
Second Great Awakening transforms U.S. religion

1820
Washington Irving publishes "Rip Van Winkle"

1821
Sequoyah invents a Cherokee alphabet

1830
Many Native Americans forced to move to land west of the Mississippi River

◄ *Religious Camp Meeting by J. Maze Burbank*

1815
Allies defeat Napoleon at Waterloo

1821
Mexico wins its independence from Spain

1824
Mexico offers land grants to Mexicans and immigrants

③

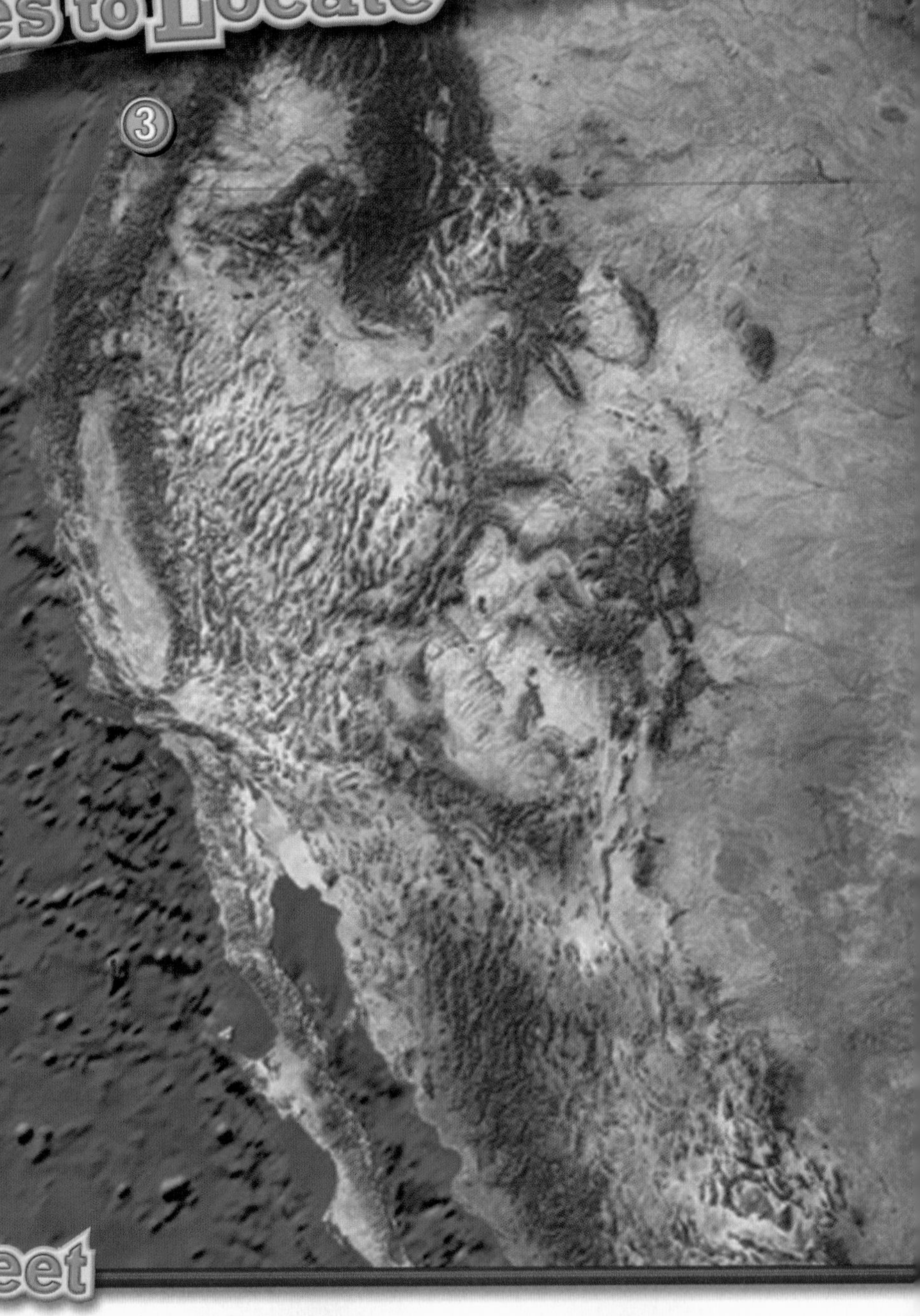

① TREATY OF GREENVILLE

See *The Federalist Era*
Chapter 5

② MONTICELLO

See *The Age of Jefferson*
Chapter 6

People to Meet

Alexander Hamilton
1755–1804
First Secretary of the
Treasury
Chapter 5, page 283

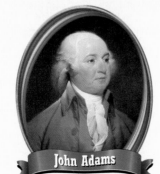

John Adams
1735–1826
First vice president
and second president
Chapter 5, page 294

Toussaint Louverture
c. 1743–1804
Haitian revolutionary
Chapter 6, page 313

Sacagawea
c. 1787–1812
Shoshone guide for
Lewis and Clark
Chapter 6, page 315

③ LEWIS AND CLARK

See *The Age of Jefferson*
Chapter 6

④ BATTLE OF NORTH POINT

See *Foreign Affairs in the Early Republic*
Chapter 7

① ② ④

James Fenimore Cooper
1789–1851
American writer
Chapter 6, page 324

Washington Irving
1783–1859
American writer
Chapter 6, page 324

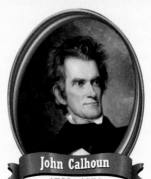

John Calhoun
1782–1850
Political leader
Chapter 7, page 344

Dolley Madison
1768–1849
First lady
Chapter 7, page 357

Chapter 5

The Federalist Era

The Capitol Building, Washington, D.C. ▶

Where & When?

Washington, D.C.

THE UNITED STATES in 1800

1788	1794	1800

1789
George Washington is nation's first president

1796
John Adams is elected president

1798
Congress passes Alien and Sedition Acts

The Big Ideas

The First President

Political ideas and major events shape how people form governments. President Washington and the first Congress built a new government.

Early Challenges

Political ideas and major events shape how people form governments. The new American government struggled to keep peace at home and avoid war abroad.

The First Political Parties

Citizen participation is essential to the foundation and preservation of the U.S. political system. By the election of 1796, two distinct political parties with different views had developed.

 View the Chapter 5 video in the Glencoe Video Program.

Summarizing Information Make this foldable and use it as a journal to help you record the major events that occurred as the new nation of the United States formed.

Step 1 Fold a sheet of paper from top to bottom.

Step 2 Then fold it in half from side to side.

Step 3 Label the foldable as shown.

Journal of American Firsts

Reading and Writing As you read the chapter, find the "firsts" experienced by the new nation, and record them in your foldable journal. For example, list the precedents set by President Washington and identify the first political parties.

Get Ready to Read

Recognizing Bias

1 Learn It!

Most people have feelings and ideas that affect their point of view. This viewpoint, or *bias,* influences the way they interpret events. For this reason, an idea that is stated as a fact may really be only an opinion. Recognizing bias will help you judge the accuracy of what you read. You can look for clues to help uncover bias in written form. Read the list below for hints you can use to identify bias.

- Identify the author of the statement, and examine his or her views and possible reasons for writing the material.

- Look for language that reflects an emotion or opinion—words such as *all, never, best, worst, might,* or *should.*

- Examine the writing for imbalances— focusing on one viewpoint and failing to discuss other perspectives.

Reading Tip

One way to identify bias is to find out more about the author. Can you find information about the author that will help you understand opinions he or she may express?

2 Practice It!

Look at the two quotes below. Each has a different opinion about "the people." On a separate sheet of paper, restate each opinion in your own words. Discuss your conclusions with a partner.

"The people are turbulent [disorderly] and changing. . . . They seldom judge or determine right."

—*Alexander Hamilton, Federalist, page 292*

▲ Alexander Hamilton

"I am not among those who fear the people. They, and not the rich, are our dependence [what we depend on] for continued freedom."

—*Thomas Jefferson, Republican, page 293*

▲ Thomas Jefferson

3 Apply It!

Look for examples of bias in comments made by key figures described in the text.

Section 1

The First President

Guide to Reading

Looking Back, Looking Ahead

American leaders faced a great challenge. Nobody knew if the political system laid out by the Constitution would work. Many people wondered: Could this new kind of government last?

Focusing on the Main Ideas

- President Washington and the new Congress established the departments in the executive branch, set up the nation's court system, and added the Bill of Rights to the Constitution. *(page 279)*
- Alexander Hamilton, the secretary of the treasury under Washington, worked to fix financial problems and strengthen the economy. *(page 281)*

Locating Places

Washington, D.C.

Meeting People

Thomas Jefferson
Alexander Hamilton
Henry Knox
Edmund Randolph
John Jay

Content Vocabulary

precedent (PREH•suh•duhnt)
cabinet
national debt (DEHT)
bond (BAHND)
speculator (SPEH•kyuh•LAY•tuhr)
unconstitutional
tariff (TAR•uhf)

Academic Vocabulary

ultimate (UHL•tuh•muht)
structure
confirm
revenue (REH•vuh•NOO)

Reading Strategy

Classifying Information Use a diagram like the one below to list the actions taken by Congress and Washington's first administration.

Actions	
Washington's First Administration	Congress

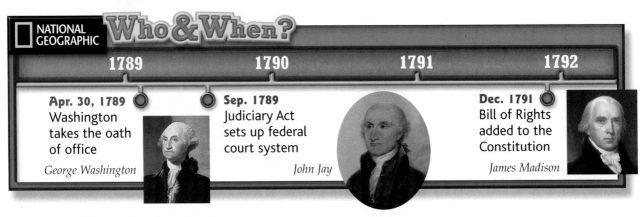

NATIONAL GEOGRAPHIC Who & When?

1789 — 1790 — 1791 — 1792

Apr. 30, 1789 Washington takes the oath of office
George Washington

Sep. 1789 Judiciary Act sets up federal court system
John Jay

Dec. 1791 Bill of Rights added to the Constitution
James Madison

President Washington

Main Idea President Washington and the new Congress established the departments in the executive branch, set up the nation's court system, and added the Bill of Rights to the Constitution.

Reading Connection If you were founding our nation's government, what do you think would be most important? As you read this section, think about the choices that Washington and the new Congress had to make.

An American Story

Celebrations erupted in the streets of Philadelphia, New York, Boston, and Charleston in 1789. News of the Constitution's ratification was greeted with relief and enthusiasm. All that was needed now was a leader to guide the new nation.

On April 6, the new Senate counted the presidential ballots. To no one's surprise, the votes were unanimous. Senator John Langdon wrote to General George Washington: "Sir, I have the honor to transmit to Your Excellency the information of your unanimous election to the office of President of the United States of America." Washington was ready to begin the difficult task of leading the country.

The Nation's First President The 57-year-old president-elect made his way slowly toward New York City, then the nation's capital. After the Constitutional Convention, George Washington had looked forward to a quiet retirement. Instead his fellow citizens elected him to the highest office in the land. On April 30, 1789, Washington took the oath of office as the first president of the United States under the federal Constitution. John Adams became vice president.

Perhaps no office in the new government created more suspicion among the people than the office of president. Many Americans feared that a president would try to become king, but Americans trusted Washington and they

believed that it was his leadership that brought them victory in the Revolutionary War. Equally important, he had willingly given up his military power as soon as the war was over to return to his civilian life tending his plantation.

Washington was aware of the difficulties he faced. He knew that the **precedents** (PREH• suh•duhnts), or traditions, he established as the nation's first president would shape the future of the United States. "No slip will pass unnoticed," he remarked. One precedent he established concerned the way people should address him. Vice President Adams supported "His Highness the President of the United States," but **ultimately** it was decided that "Mr. President" would be more appropriate.

Washington and the new Congress also had many decisions to make about the **structure** of government. For example, the Constitution gave Congress the power to establish executive departments, but it did not state whether the department heads would report to the president or to Congress.

The First Congress During the summer of 1789, Congress established three executive departments: a Department of State to take charge of foreign affairs, a Department of the Treasury to handle the nation's finances, and a Department of War to manage the military.

February 22nd, 1732
December 14th, 1799

▲ Banner celebrating George Washington

Congress also created the office of attorney general to handle the government's legal affairs and the office of postmaster general to direct the postal service. To head the departments, Washington chose prominent political figures of the day—**Thomas Jefferson** as secretary of state, **Alexander Hamilton** as secretary of the treasury, and **Henry Knox** as secretary of war. He appointed **Edmund Randolph** as attorney general. Washington met regularly with the three department heads and the attorney general, who together became known as the **cabinet.**

According to the Constitution, the Senate must approve presidential appointments to many important positions. However, other issues arose. For example, should the president be able to replace an official that he had appointed and the Senate had **confirmed?** Senators were evenly divided when they voted on the issue.

Vice President Adams broke the tie by voting to allow the president the authority to dismiss cabinet officers without the Senate's approval. This decision strengthened the president's position. It also helped establish the president's authority over the executive branch.

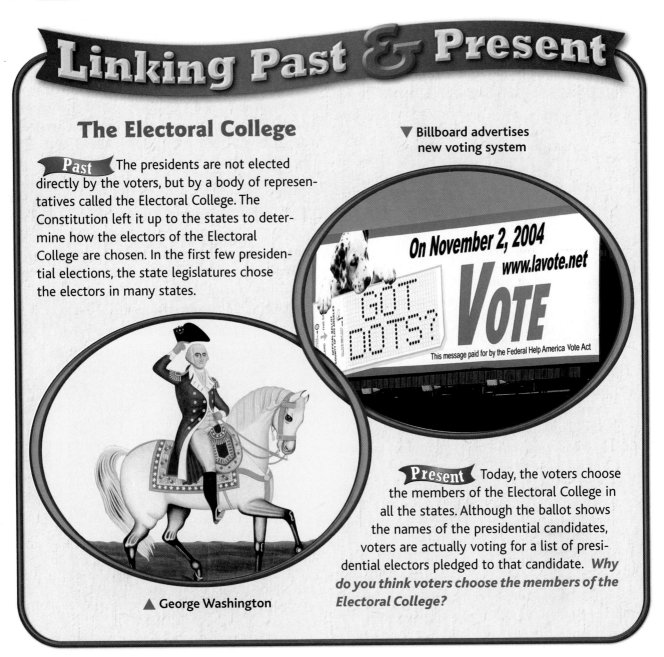

Linking Past & Present

The Electoral College

Past The presidents are not elected directly by the voters, but by a body of representatives called the Electoral College. The Constitution left it up to the states to determine how the electors of the Electoral College are chosen. In the first few presidential elections, the state legislatures chose the electors in many states.

▼ Billboard advertises new voting system

On November 2, 2004
www.lavote.net
GOT DOTS?
VOTE
This message paid for by the Federal Help America Vote Act

▲ George Washington

Present Today, the voters choose the members of the Electoral College in all the states. Although the ballot shows the names of the presidential candidates, voters are actually voting for a list of presidential electors pledged to that candidate. *Why do you think voters choose the members of the Electoral College?*

What Did the Judiciary Act Do? The first Congress also had to decide how to set up the nation's court system. The Constitution briefly mentioned a supreme court but did not provide details about the court system. This became a job for Congress.

In the Judiciary Act of 1789, Congress established the Supreme Court and the lower federal courts: district courts and courts of appeals. The Supreme Court would be the final authority on many issues. Washington nominated **John Jay** to lead the Supreme Court as chief justice, and the Senate approved Jay's nomination. With the Judiciary Act, Congress had taken the first steps toward creating a strong and independent national judiciary.

The Bill of Rights

Americans mistrusted strong central governments. They had fought a revolution to throw off one and did not want to replace it with another. Many people insisted that the Constitution needed to include guarantees of personal liberties. Some states had supported the Constitution on the condition that a bill of rights be added to protect individual rights.

James Madison introduced a set of amendments during the first session of Congress. Congress passed 12 amendments, and the states ratified 10 of them. In December 1791, these 10 amendments were added to the Constitution and became known as the Bill of Rights.

The Bill of Rights protects our individual liberties. Government may not interfere with freedom of speech, press, or religion and must provide a fair and speedy trial for those accused of crimes. The Tenth Amendment protects the rights of states and individuals by saying that powers not specifically given to the federal government "are reserved to the States respectively, or to the people." With the Tenth Amendment, Madison hoped to use the states as an important line of defense against a too-powerful national government. 📖 *(See pages 260–261 for the entire text of the Bill of Rights.)*

✓ Reading Check **Describe** Why was the Bill of Rights created?

Strengthening the Economy

Main Idea Alexander Hamilton, the secretary of the treasury under Washington, worked to fix financial problems and strengthen the economy.

Reading Connection Have you ever borrowed money from a family member or one of your friends? By doing so, you acquired a debt and had to figure out how and when to pay it back. Hamilton faced a similar challenge with the nation's debt.

Washington himself rarely proposed laws, and he almost always approved the bills that were passed by Congress. The first president concentrated on foreign affairs and military matters and left the government's economic policies to his secretary of the treasury, Alexander Hamilton.

The new nation faced serious financial problems. The **national debt** (DEHT)—the amount the nation's government owed—was growing. The United States owed millions of dollars to France and the Netherlands for loans made during and after the Revolutionary War. The Continental Congress also had borrowed millions of dollars from American citizens.

What Was Hamilton's Plan? In 1790 Hamilton proposed that the new government pay off the millions of dollars in debts owed by the Confederation government to other countries and to individual American citizens. The states had fought for the nation's independence, Hamilton argued, so the national government should pay for the cost of their help. Hamilton also believed that federal payment of state debts would give the states a strong interest in the success of the national government.

Opposition to the Plan Congress readily agreed to pay the money owed to other nations, but Hamilton's plan to pay off the debt to American citizens unleashed a storm of protest. When the government borrowed money during the American Revolution, it issued **bonds** (BAHNDZ)—paper notes promising to repay the money in a certain length of time.

While waiting for the payment, many original bond owners—shopkeepers, farmers, and soldiers—had sold the bonds for less than their value. They were purchased by **speculators** (SPEH•kyuh•LAY•tuhrz), people who take risks with their money in order to make a larger profit. Hamilton proposed that these bonds be paid off at their original value. Opponents believed that Hamilton's plan would make speculators rich.

The original bond owners felt betrayed by Hamilton's proposal. They had lost money on the bonds they had bought in support of the war effort while new bond owners would profit.

NATIONAL GEOGRAPHIC

HISTORY MAKERS

The Capitol

The Capitol is the seat of the United States Congress in Washington, D.C. Built on a hill popularly called Capitol Hill, the Capitol contains floor space equivalent to more than 16 acres. The dome of the United States Capitol, finished in

▲ The Capitol

1863, is one of the most famous landmarks in the United States. Other important parts of the Capitol include the Rotunda directly under the dome, the Senate Chamber in the north wing, the House chamber in the south wing, and the National Statuary Hall.

Opponents in Congress argued that the proposal was contrary to "national justice, gratitude, and humanity."

Even stronger opposition came from the Southern states, which had accumulated much less debt than the Northern states. Southern states complained that they would have to pay more than their share under Hamilton's plan.

Compromise Results in a Capital To win support for his plan, Hamilton worked out a compromise with Southern leaders. They voted for his plan to pay off the state debts, and in return he supported locating the permanent capital in the South. A special district was laid out between Virginia and Maryland along the banks of the Potomac River. This district became **Washington, D.C.** While workers prepared the new city for the federal government, the nation's capital was moved from New York to Philadelphia.

The Fight Over the Bank Hamilton made other proposals for building a strong national economy. He asked Congress to create a national bank, the Bank of the United States. The bank would be a place for the federal government to deposit money raised from taxes. The bank could also provide loans to government and to businesses.

Madison and Jefferson opposed the idea of a national bank. They believed it would give the wealthy too much power over national finances. They also charged that the Bank was **unconstitutional**—that it was inconsistent with the Constitution. Hamilton argued that although the Constitution did not specifically say that Congress could create a bank, Congress still had the power to do so. In the end, the president agreed with Hamilton and signed the bill creating the national bank.

What Is a Tariff? Although most Americans earned their living by farming, Hamilton thought the development of manufacturing would make America's economy stronger. He proposed a **tariff** (TAR•uhf)—a tax on imports—to encourage people to buy American products.

ALEXANDER HAMILTON
1755–1804

Alexander Hamilton was born on the West Indies island of Nevis, where he worked as a clerk as a young man. In 1773 he moved to New York and studied at King's College. Hamilton quickly became involved in the fight for American independence. He impressed General George Washington, who made him one of his aides-de-camp (secretaries). Hamilton and Washington established a strong friendship and Hamilton served his country on the battlefield and in government.

Hamilton was elected to the Continental Congress and was a driving force in the ratification of the Constitution. Hamilton, James Madison, and John Jay wrote a series of essays called *The Federalist Papers* that explained how the new Constitution worked and why it was needed. Hamilton became the nation's first Secretary of the Treasury. He believed that manufacturing and trade were the basis of national wealth and power. He favored policies that would support these areas of the economy.

During Washington's presidency, Hamilton and Secretary of State Thomas Jefferson had some major differences. They disagreed strongly about how the U.S. government should operate. Hamilton was the leader of the Federalist Party, and Jefferson led the Democratic-Republican Party. These two men became, in essence, the founders of today's political parties.

When Jefferson and Aaron Burr tied with 73 electoral votes in the presidential election of 1800, the Federalist-controlled House of Representatives had to choose a president. Hamilton urged his followers to support Jefferson, and Jefferson became the new president. After Burr failed in his bid to become president, he campaigned to become governor of New York in 1804. Hamilton worked actively against Burr. When Burr lost, he blamed his defeat on Hamilton and challenged him to a duel. Hamilton was fatally wounded and died on July 12, 1804, ending the life of one of the nation's most influential leaders.

"A feeble executive implies a feeble execution of the government."
—**Alexander Hamilton,** *The Federalist*, No. 70

Then and Now

Which of Hamilton's actions do you think most influenced the nation's government? Explain your reasoning.

Opposition to the Tariff This protective tariff would not only raise revenue for the new national government, but also protect American industry from foreign competition. However, many Americans were against the tariff.

The South, having little industry to protect, opposed protective tariffs. Congress rejected protective tariffs but did pass low tariffs to raise money. By the 1790s, the **revenue** from tariffs provided 90 percent of the national government's income.

Taxes The final part of Hamilton's economic program concerned the creation of national taxes. The government needed additional funds to operate and to make interest payments on the national debt. At Hamilton's request, Congress approved a variety of taxes, including one on whiskey distilled in the United States.

Hamilton and Jefferson Under Alexander Hamilton's economic program, the national government exercised new financial powers. Soon, however, well-organized opposition to Hamilton's political and economic beliefs grew.

The opposition to Hamilton was led by Thomas Jefferson and James Madison. Where Hamilton's policies favored merchants, bankers, and speculators, his opponents spoke for the interests of the farmers and laborers. When Hamilton favored increasing the power of the federal government, Jefferson wanted to limit it. They had a very different vision of what America should become.

✓ **Reading Check** **Compare** Summarize the arguments for and against protective tariffs.

Study Central Need help understanding Washington's presidency? Visit tajww1.glencoe.com and click on Study Central.

Section 1 Review

Reading Summary

Review the Main Ideas

- President Washington and the first Congress established the cabinet and a federal court system. The first 10 amendments to the Constitution, the Bill of Rights, were introduced during the first session of Congress.

- Under Secretary of the Treasury Alexander Hamilton, the national government agreed to pay off states' debts, created a national bank, and put in place a number of tariffs and taxes.

What Did You Learn?

1. What challenges did Washington face as the nation's first president?

2. Name one thing Hamilton wanted to do to create a stable economic system and strengthen the economy.

Critical Thinking

3. **Comparing** Re-create the diagram below. Compare the views of Hamilton and Jefferson. In the boxes, write "for" or "against" for each issue.

Issue	Hamilton	Jefferson
National bank		
Protective tariff		
National taxes		

4. **The Big Ideas** What compromise led to acceptance of Hamilton's plan for reducing the national debt?

5. **Expository Writing** Imagine you are choosing the first cabinet members. Write job descriptions for the secretaries of state, treasury, and war.

6. **READING** **Recognizing Bias** Read Hamilton's quote. Explain in writing why it does or does not contain bias.

"Can a democratic assembly . . . steadily pursue the public good? Nothing but a permanent body can check the imprudence [disregard of others] of democracy."

Early Challenges

Guide to Reading

Looking Back, Looking Ahead

The United States needed money to pay its war debts and to finance national growth. Although located an ocean away from Europe, the United States could not hope to exist in isolation. The nation had to respond to overseas pressures.

Focusing on the Main Ideas

- Hamilton's taxes led to rebellion in western Pennsylvania and changed the way the government handled protesters. *(page 286)*
- The new government faced difficult problems in the West. *(page 287)*
- President Washington wanted the nation to remain neutral in foreign conflicts. *(page 288)*

Locating Places

Fallen Timbers
New Orleans

Meeting People

Anthony Wayne
Edmond Genêt (zhuh•NAY)
Thomas Pinckney (PINGK•nee)

Content Vocabulary

neutrality (noo•TRA•luh•tee)
impressment (ihm•PREHS•muhnt)

Academic Vocabulary

transport
maintain

Reading Strategy

Classifying Information As you read the section, re-create the diagram below and list results of government actions during the early Republic.

Government action	Results
Treaty of Greenville	
Proclamation of Neutrality	
Jay's Treaty	
Pinckney's Treaty	

NATIONAL GEOGRAPHIC Where & When?

1791   1793   1795

Nov. 1791 Little Turtle defeats St. Clair's forces

July 1794 Whiskey Rebellion

Aug. 1794 Battle of Fallen Timbers

Oct. 1795 Spain opens Mississippi River to American shipping

Fallen Timbers

New Orleans

Mississippi R.

Appalachian Mts.

The Whiskey Rebellion

Main Idea Hamilton's taxes led to rebellion in western Pennsylvania and changed the way the government handled protesters.

Reading Connection Is there a recent government action that you have opposed? What actions did you take? Read to learn what actions the farmers took in regards to the whiskey tax.

An American Story

Far removed from the bustle of trade and shipping along the Atlantic coast, farmers on the western frontier lived quite differently. In fact, western ways seemed almost primitive to travelers from the East. Easterners seemed to notice only the poor roads and the plain diet of corn and salted pork. Living in scattered, isolated homesteads, frontier farmers were proud of their self-reliance. They wanted no "eastern" tax collectors heading their way.

Life in the West In the days before canals and railroads, the Western farmers did not ship their grain east of the Appalachian Mountains because **transporting** the grain was expensive.

Picturing **History**

In 1794 President Washington sent nearly 15,000 troops to crush the Whiskey Rebellion. *What did Washington's action say about the government use of force?*

A wagonload of whiskey was worth much more than a wagonload of grain, so Western farmers distilled their grain into whiskey before they shipped it to market.

The farmers rarely had cash. As a result, most lived on a system of bartering—exchanging whiskey and other items they produced for goods they needed.

The Tax Leads to Protests In 1791 both houses of Congress approved a bill that placed a special tax on whiskey and other alcoholic beverages. Secretary of the Treasury Alexander Hamilton wanted the tax to help prevent the national debt from growing.

The farmers' resistance was mostly peaceful—until July 1794, when federal officers stepped up efforts to collect the tax. Then a large mob of farmers armed with swords, guns, and pitchforks attacked tax collectors and burned down buildings.

The armed protest, called the Whiskey Rebellion, alarmed government leaders as had Shays's Rebellion in 1786. *(See Chapter 3, pages 194–195.)* Now, however, the national government had the taxing and military power that it lacked in 1786. The secretary of the treasury, Alexander Hamilton, urged President Washington to use the full power of the federal government to crush the challenge. The president sent an army of 15,000 across the Appalachian Mountains, only to find that the rebels had already disbanded.

By his action, Washington sent a clear message to those who opposed government actions. If citizens wished to change the law, they had to do so peacefully, through constitutional means such as proposing legislation or using the courts. Otherwise, government would use force when necessary to **maintain** order.

Reading Check **Explain** How did the Whiskey Rebellion affect the way government handled protesters?

Struggle Over the West

Main Idea The new government faced difficult problems in the West.

Reading Connection Imagine you are a member of George Washington's government in 1791. Could you balance the interests of settlers who are moving into the Northwest Territory with the interests of the Native American nations who live there? Read on to see how President Washington handled a similar challenge.

The Native Americans who lived between the Appalachian Mountains and the Mississippi River insisted that the United States had no authority over them.

Armed to defend their lands and encouraged by the British and the Spanish, Native Americans battled settlers over frontier land. Hundreds of people were killed.

Washington sent an army under the command of General Arthur St. Clair to restore order in the Northwest Territory. In November 1791, St. Clair's forces were defeated by Little Turtle, chief of the Miami people. More than 600 American soldiers died in a battle by the Wabash River.

Battle of Fallen Timbers The Native Americans demanded that all settlers north of the Ohio River leave the territory. Washington sent another army headed by **Anthony Wayne,** a former Revolutionary War general, to challenge their demands. In August 1794, his army defeated more than 1,000 Native Americans who fought under Shawnee chief Blue Jacket at the Battle of **Fallen Timbers** (near present-day Toledo, Ohio). The Battle of Fallen Timbers crushed the Native Americans' hopes of keeping their land. In the Treaty of Greenville (1795), the Native Americans agreed to surrender most of their land in present-day Ohio.

✓ Reading Check **Explain** Why did President Washington send troops to the Northwest Territory?

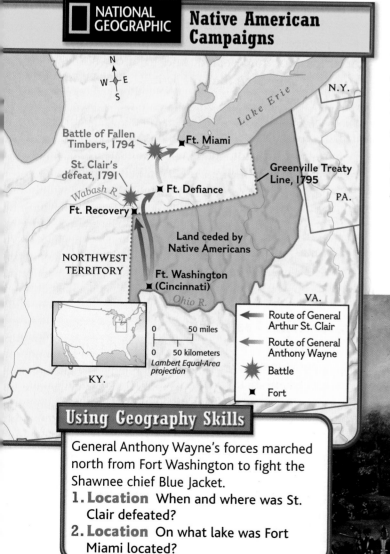

NATIONAL GEOGRAPHIC — Native American Campaigns

Battle of Fallen Timbers, 1794
Ft. Miami
St. Clair's defeat, 1791
Wabash R.
Ft. Defiance
Ft. Recovery
Lake Erie
N.Y.
Greenville Treaty Line, 1795
PA.
Land ceded by Native Americans
NORTHWEST TERRITORY
Ft. Washington (Cincinnati)
Ohio R.
VA.
KY.

0   50 miles
0   50 kilometers
Lambert Equal-Area projection

Route of General Arthur St. Clair
Route of General Anthony Wayne
Battle
Fort

Using Geography Skills

General Anthony Wayne's forces marched north from Fort Washington to fight the Shawnee chief Blue Jacket.

1. **Location** When and where was St. Clair defeated?
2. **Location** On what lake was Fort Miami located?

Picturing History

Upon signing the Treaty of Greenville, 12 Native American nations received $20,000 worth of goods to share. *How did the treaty affect white settlement?*

Problems With Europe

Main Idea President Washington wanted the nation to remain neutral in foreign conflicts.

Reading Connection Have you ever felt like you were in the middle of a disagreement between two other people? Read on to see how President Washington looked for middle ground in a war between Great Britain and France.

Shortly after Washington was inaugurated in 1789, the French Revolution began. At first most Americans cheered upon hearing the news. The French people had helped the Americans in their struggle for independence, and their revolution seemed to reflect many of the ideals of the American Revolution.

By 1793 the French Revolution had turned bloody. The leaders had executed the king and queen of France and thousands of French citizens. Public opinion in the United States started to divide. The violence of the French Revolution offended many Americans. Others hailed the new republic as a copy of the United States.

When Britain and France went to war in 1793, Washington hoped that the nation could maintain its **neutrality** (noo•TRA•luh•tee)—that is, that it would not take sides in the conflict between France and Britain. As time went on, however, remaining neutral became increasingly difficult.

Washington Proclaims Neutrality The French wanted the help of the United States. In April 1793, they sent diplomat **Edmond Genêt** (zhuh•NAY) to the United States. His mission was to recruit American volunteers to attack British ships.

President Washington took action to discourage American involvement. On April 22, he issued a Proclamation of Neutrality. It prohibited American citizens from fighting in the war and barred French and British warships from American ports. Genêt's plans eventually failed, but he did manage to sign up a few hundred Americans to serve on French ships. These ships seized British vessels and stole their cargoes.

Outraged by the French attacks at sea, the British began capturing American ships that traded with the French. The British also stopped American merchant ships and forced their crews into the British navy. This practice, known as **impressment** (ihm•PREHS•muhnt), infuriated the Americans. British attacks on American ships and sailors pushed the nation close to war with Great Britain.

A Controversial Treaty President Washington decided to make one last effort to come to a peaceful solution with Britain. He sent John Jay, chief justice of the Supreme Court, to negotiate.

The British were willing to listen to Jay's proposals. War with the United States would only make it harder to carry on the war with France. In addition, Britain did not want to lose its profitable trade with the United States.

In Jay's Treaty the British agreed to evacuate British forts on American soil, to pay damages for ships they had seized, and to allow some American ships to trade with British colonies in the Caribbean.

Despite these gains, few Americans approved of Jay's Treaty. They protested that the treaty did not deal with the issue of impressment and did not mention British interference with American trade. Although President Washington found fault with Jay's Treaty, he realized it would end an explosive crisis with Great Britain. He sent the treaty to the Senate, which approved it after a fierce debate.

Treaty With Spain When Jay's Treaty was made, Spanish leaders realized that the United States and Great Britain might now join forces to seize Spanish territory in North America. Spain wanted to establish a positive relationship with the United States and was willing to offer concessions. President Washington sent **Thomas Pinckney** (PINGK•nee) to Spain to try to settle the differences between the two nations. In 1795 Pinckney's Treaty gave the Americans free navigation of the Mississippi River and the right to trade at **New Orleans.**

Washington's Farewell In September 1796, after serving two four-year terms as president, Washington announced he would not seek a third term. By choosing to serve only two terms, Washington had set a precedent that later presidents would follow.

Plagued with a variety of ailments, the 64-year-old president looked forward to retirement. He also felt troubled over the divisions that had developed in American politics and with what he considered a grave danger to the new nation—the growth of political parties.

Washington's "Farewell Address" was published in a Philadelphia newspaper. In it he attacked the evils of political parties and entanglement in foreign affairs. He urged citizens to

> 66 Observe good faith and justice toward all nations. . . . It is our true policy to steer clear of permanent alliances. 99
>
> —George Washington

Washington's "Farewell Address" included his explanation for not seeking a third term as president. Even more important, he gave the young republic his best advice on the conduct of politics and foreign affairs.

Washington's parting words influenced the nation's foreign policy for more than 100 years. The text of his address is still read aloud in the United States Senate each year on Washington's birthday. *(See page 852 of the Appendix for an excerpt from Washington's Farewell Address.)*

Upon returning to Mount Vernon, Washington had every reason to feel proud of his administration's achievements. Most of the difficulties of the Confederation period had been overcome. In the difficult situation presented by war between France and Britain, Washington had steered a course that kept the United States prosperous and at peace.

Reading Check **Explain** What was the impact of Washington's Farewell Address?

Study Central Need help understanding the government's early challenges? Visit tajwwI.glencoe.com and click on Study Central.

Section 2 Review

Reading Summary

Review the Main Ideas

- On the western frontier, protests against new taxes led to the Whiskey Rebellion, which collapsed when President Washington sent troops to the area.

- Following their defeat at the Battle of Fallen Timbers, Native Americans gave up their claims to lands in Ohio.

- A number of treaties and a policy of neutrality helped the United States remain at peace with the European powers.

What Did You Learn?

1. What message was Washington sending to the American people when he used force to stop the Whiskey Rebellion?

2. What precedent did George Washington set for future presidents?

Critical Thinking

3. **Determining Cause and Effect** Re-create the diagram below. In the boxes, list the cause and effects of the Whiskey Rebellion.

4. **The Big Ideas** How did the Treaty of Greenville affect the land claims of Native Americans in the Northwest Territory?

5. **Creative Writing** Imagine you are a Shawnee following chief Blue Jacket. Write a speech you could give to the Shawnee about the implications of giving up your lands.

6. **ANALYSIS** **Evaluate** What did the United States have to gain by remaining neutral in foreign affairs? Write a short essay describing your conclusions.

Section 3 · The First Political Parties

Guide to Reading

Looking Back, Looking Ahead
Today the United States has two major political parties. The origins of the nation's two-party political system are found in the conflicts between the followers of Alexander Hamilton and Thomas Jefferson.

Focusing on the Main Ideas
- Americans began to take opposing sides on issues by 1796, and, as a result, two political parties emerged. *(page 291)*
- John Adams dealt with many things in office, including a dispute with France, which led to a group of measures called the Alien and Sedition Acts. *(page 293)*

Meeting People
Philip Freneau (frih•NOH)
Charles de Talleyrand (TA•lee•RAND)

Content Vocabulary
partisan (PAHR•tuh•zuhn)
implied powers
caucus (KAW•kuhs)
alien (AY•lee•uhn)
sedition (sih•DIH•shuhn)
nullify (NUH•luh•FY)
states' rights

Academic Vocabulary
distinct
contrast
accompany (uh•KUHM•puh•nee)
assign (uh•SYN)

Reading Strategy
Classifying Information As you read Section 3, create a diagram like the one below and list the differences between the Federalists and the Democratic-Republicans.

Issue	Federalists	Democratic-Republicans
Role of federal government		

NATIONAL GEOGRAPHIC Where & When?

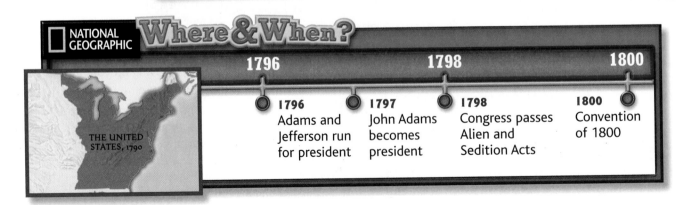

THE UNITED STATES, 1790

1796 — **1798** — **1800**

1796 Adams and Jefferson run for president

1797 John Adams becomes president

1798 Congress passes Alien and Sedition Acts

1800 Convention of 1800

Opposing Views

Main Idea Americans began to take opposing sides on issues by 1796, and, as a result, two political parties emerged.

Reading Connection Think about a time when you disagreed with something that one of your classmates said. Did you voice your opinion? Read to learn what happened when conflict occurred between the supporters of Hamilton and Jefferson.

Although hailed by Americans as the nation's greatest leader, George Washington did not escape criticism during his two terms as president. From time to time, harsh attacks on his policies and on his personality appeared in newspapers. One paper even called Washington "the misfortune of his country."

How Did Americans View the President?

Most attacks on Washington came from supporters of Thomas Jefferson. They were trying to discredit the policies of Washington and Hamilton by attacking the president. By 1796 Americans were beginning to divide into opposing groups and to form political parties.

In Washington's cabinet, Hamilton and Jefferson often took opposing sides. They disagreed on economic policy and foreign relations, on the power of the federal government, and on interpretations of the Constitution. Even Washington was sometimes **partisan** (PAHR•tuh•zuhn)—favoring one side of an issue. Although he believed he stood above politics, Washington usually supported Hamilton's positions.

Political Parties Emerge

Like Hamilton and Jefferson, Congress and the nation at large also had differences. By the mid-1790s, two **distinct** political parties had taken shape.

The name *Federalist* had first described someone who supported ratification of the Constitution. By the 1790s the word was applied to the group of people who supported the policies of the Washington administration.

Generally, Federalists stood for a strong federal government. They admired Britain because of its stability and distrusted France because of the violent changes following the French Revolution. Federalist policies tended to favor banking and business. Federalists received the strongest support in the Northeast and from wealthy plantation owners in the South.

Efforts to turn opinion against the Federalists began seriously in late 1791 when **Philip Freneau** (frih•NOH) began publishing the *National Gazette*. Jefferson, then secretary of state, helped the newspaper get started. Later he and Madison organized people who disagreed with Hamilton.

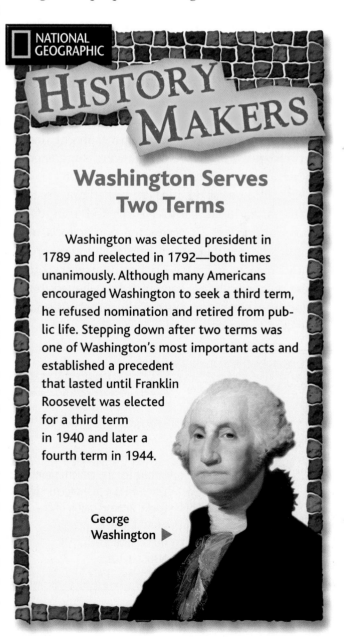

NATIONAL GEOGRAPHIC

HISTORY MAKERS

Washington Serves Two Terms

Washington was elected president in 1789 and reelected in 1792—both times unanimously. Although many Americans encouraged Washington to seek a third term, he refused nomination and retired from public life. Stepping down after two terms was one of Washington's most important acts and established a precedent that lasted until Franklin Roosevelt was elected for a third term in 1940 and later a fourth term in 1944.

George Washington ▶

The followers of Jefferson and Madison called their party the Republicans, or the Democratic-Republicans. The Republicans wanted to limit government. They feared that a strong government would endanger people's liberties. They supported the French and condemned what they regarded as the Washington administration's pro-British policies. Republican policies appealed to small farmers and urban workers, especially in the Middle Atlantic states and the South.

Views of the Constitution One difference between Federalists and Republicans concerned the basis of government power. In Hamilton's view, the federal government had **implied powers,** powers that were suggested but not directly stated in the Constitution.

Hamilton used the idea of implied powers to justify a national bank. He argued that the Constitution gave Congress the power to issue money and regulate trade, and a national bank would clearly help the government carry out these responsibilities. Therefore, he believed that creating a bank was within the constitutional power of Congress.

Jefferson and Madison, however, believed in a strict interpretation of the Constitution. They accepted the idea of implied powers, but in a much more limited sense than Hamilton did. They believed that implied powers are those powers that are "absolutely necessary" for Congress to exercise its stated powers.

The People's Role The differences between the parties, however, went even deeper. Federalists and Republicans had sharply opposing views on the role ordinary people should play in government.

Federalists supported representative government, in which elected officials ruled in the people's name. They did not believe that it was wise to let the public become too involved in politics. Hamilton said:

> ❝ The people are turbulent [disorderly] and changing; they seldom judge or determine right. ❞
>
> —Alexander Hamilton,
> Speech on the Constitutional
> Convention

Public office, Federalists thought, should be held by honest and educated men who own property and would protect everyone's rights. In **contrast,** the Republicans feared a strong central government controlled by a few people.

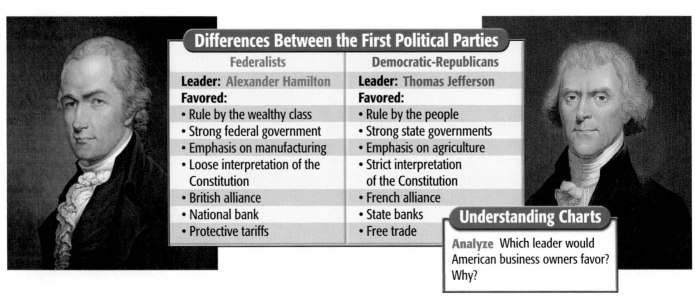

Differences Between the First Political Parties

Federalists	Democratic-Republicans
Leader: Alexander Hamilton	**Leader:** Thomas Jefferson
Favored:	**Favored:**
• Rule by the wealthy class	• Rule by the people
• Strong federal government	• Strong state governments
• Emphasis on manufacturing	• Emphasis on agriculture
• Loose interpretation of the Constitution	• Strict interpretation of the Constitution
• British alliance	• French alliance
• National bank	• State banks
• Protective tariffs	• Free trade

Understanding Charts

Analyze Which leader would American business owners favor? Why?

The Republicans believed that liberty would be safe only if ordinary people participated in government. As Jefferson explained:

> **❝** I am not among those who fear the people. They, and not the rich, are our dependence [what we depend on] for continued freedom. **❞**
>
> —Letter to Samuel Kercheval

Washington tried to get his two advisers to work out their differences. Nevertheless, by 1793 Jefferson was so unhappy that he resigned as secretary of state. In 1795 Hamilton resigned, too, as secretary of the treasury. The rival political parties moved further apart.

The Election of 1796 In the presidential election of 1796, candidates sought office for the first time as members of a party. To prepare for the election, the Federalists and the Republicans held meetings called **caucuses** (KAW•kuhs•ihz). At the caucuses, members of Congress and other leaders chose their party's candidates for office.

The Federalists nominated Vice President John Adams for president and Charles Pinckney for vice president. The Republicans nominated Jefferson for president and Aaron Burr for vice president. Adams and Jefferson, who had been good friends, became rivals. The Federalists expected to carry New England. The Republicans' strength lay in the South, which would give most of its votes to Jefferson.

In the end, Adams received 71 electoral votes, winning the election. Jefferson finished second with 68 votes. According to the Constitution at that time, the person with the second-highest number of electoral votes became vice president. Jefferson therefore became the new vice president. The administration that took office on March 4, 1797, had a Federalist president and a Republican vice president.

✓ Reading Check **Explain** Which political party would a Boston factory owner most likely support?

President John Adams

Main Idea John Adams dealt with many things in office, including a dispute with France, which led to a group of measures called the Alien and Sedition Acts.

Reading Connection Do you think you should be free to say or write anything you want about the government? Do you think the government has the right to send you to jail if you criticize its policies? The Federalists passed laws restricting freedom of speech. Read on to find out why.

John Adams had spent much of his life in government. One of Massachusetts's most active patriots, he later became ambassador to France and to Great Britain. He helped negotiate the Treaty of Paris that ended the Revolution. Under Washington, he served two terms as vice president.

John's wife, Abigail, actively supported the American cause and raised their sons and daughter while John was away on government business. Abigail also capably managed their family farm in Braintree, Massachusetts.

The XYZ Affair When Adams took office, the nation faced a crisis with France. The French regarded Jay's Treaty, signed in 1794, as an American attempt to help the British in their war with France. To punish the United States, the French seized American ships that carried cargo to Britain.

Adams wanted to avoid war with France. In the fall of 1797, he sent a delegation to Paris to try to resolve the dispute. French foreign minister **Charles de Talleyrand** (TA•lee•RAND), however, refused to meet with the Americans. Instead, Talleyrand sent three agents who demanded a bribe and a loan for France from the Americans. "Not a sixpence," the Americans replied and sent a report of the incident to the United States. Adams was furious. Referring to the three French agents as X, Y, and Z, the president urged Congress to prepare for war. The incident became known as the XYZ affair.

Biography

ABIGAIL ADAMS
1744–1818

JOHN ADAMS
1735–1826

John Adams, a young lawyer, and Abigail Smith were married in 1764. The young couple lived on a farm in Braintree, Massachusetts, and had five children. John was one of the leaders of the movement for independence. In late 1774 John Adams went to Philadelphia as a delegate to the Continental Congress, while Abigail Adams remained in Massachusetts to manage their business affairs and take care of the family. During most of the Confederation period, Abigail Adams lived in Europe with John, who was the first American minister to Great Britain. Eventually, when John was elected the second president of the United States, Abigail became the first First Lady to preside over the still unfinished White House.

▲ Abigail Adams

Although she lacked a formal education, Abigail Adams developed a notable talent as a letter writer. Letter writing, she said, was "a habit, the pleasure of which increases with practice, but becomes irksome by neglect." In one of her most well-known letters, she made the following plea to her husband and his associates in the Continental Congress.

"Remember the Ladies, and be more generous and favourable to them than your ancestors. Do not put such unlimited power into the hands of the Husbands. Remember all Men would be tyrants if they could. If [particular] care and attention is not paid to the Ladies we are determined to foment a Rebellion, and will not hold ourselves bound by any Laws in which we have no voice."

Despite the hopes of Abigail and many women, they still could not vote or hold office in the years after the American Revolution. Abigail Adams believed strongly in equal rights for women and African Americans at a time in history when such views were not well received.

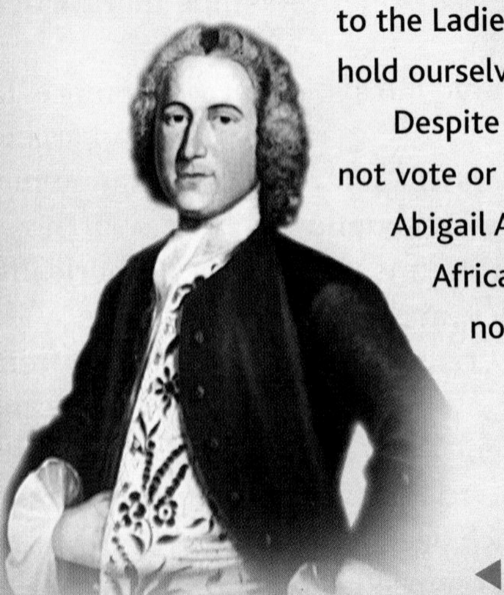

◄ John Adams

Then and Now

How does the role of women in government differ today from their role during Abigail Adams's time?

Undeclared War With France Congress responded with a program to strengthen the armed forces. It established the Navy Department in April 1798 and set aside money for building warships. Congress also increased the size of the army. George Washington was appointed commanding general.

Between 1798 and 1800, United States and French naval vessels clashed on a number of occasions, although war was not formally declared. Adams's representatives negotiated an agreement with France in September 1800 that ensured peace.

In the view of most Americans, France had become an enemy. The Republican Party, friendly toward France in the past, hesitated to turn around and condemn France. As a result, in the 1798 elections, Americans voted some Republicans out of office.

Alien and Sedition Acts The threat of war with France made Americans more suspicious of **aliens** (AY•lee•uhnz)—immigrants who were not citizens but were living in the nation. Many Europeans who came to the United States in the 1790s supported the ideals of the French Revolution. Some Americans questioned whether these aliens would remain loyal if the United States went to war with France. Because many of the newcomers to the nation were anti-British, many of them tended to support the Republican Party.

Federalists in Congress responded with strict laws to protect the nation's security. In 1798 they passed a group of measures known as the Alien and Sedition Acts. **Sedition** (sih•DIH•shuhn) refers to activities aimed at weakening established government. Many Federalists believed that the laws would weaken the Republican Party.

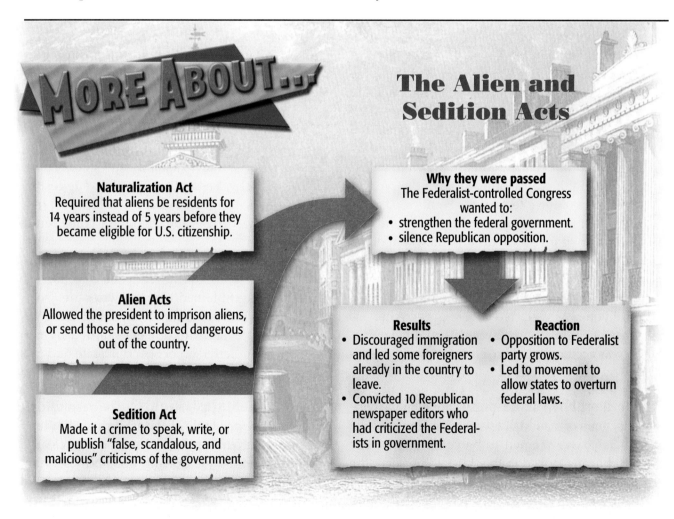

MORE ABOUT...

The Alien and Sedition Acts

Naturalization Act
Required that aliens be residents for 14 years instead of 5 years before they became eligible for U.S. citizenship.

Alien Acts
Allowed the president to imprison aliens, or send those he considered dangerous out of the country.

Sedition Act
Made it a crime to speak, write, or publish "false, scandalous, and malicious" criticisms of the government.

Why they were passed
The Federalist-controlled Congress wanted to:
• strengthen the federal government.
• silence Republican opposition.

Results
• Discouraged immigration and led some foreigners already in the country to leave.
• Convicted 10 Republican newspaper editors who had criticized the Federalists in government.

Reaction
• Opposition to Federalist party grows.
• Led to movement to allow states to overturn federal laws.

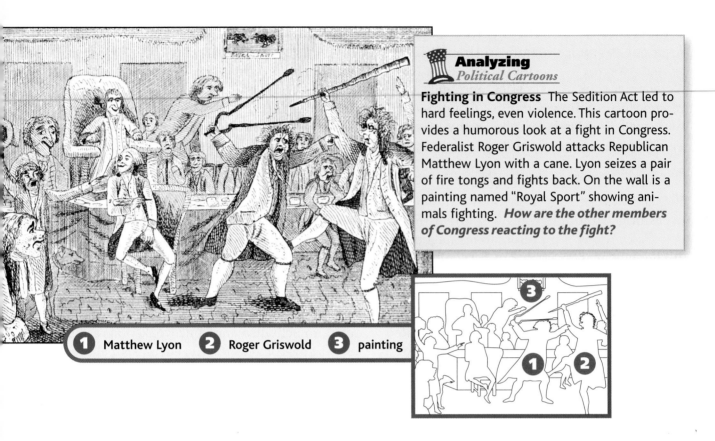

1 Matthew Lyon **2** Roger Griswold **3** painting

What Effects Did the Acts Have?

As it turned out, the anti-Republican laws hurt the Federalist Party more. The Alien Acts offended new immigrants and drove them more than ever to the support of the Republicans. Ten Republicans, mostly newspaper editors, who were jailed under the Sedition Act were hailed as heroes in the cause of freedom of the press.

Typical of the effects of the Sedition Act was the case of Matthew Lyon of Vermont, who was the editor of an Antifederalist newspaper. In 1798 he was convicted under the Sedition Act for the publication in the *Vermont Journal* of a letter criticizing President John Adams. While in jail, Lyon was reelected to Congress. After his release from prison he set off for Philadelphia. He was **accompanied** on the first day of his journey by a long parade of followers.

The Republicans Respond

For some Americans, fears of a strong central government abusing its power seemed to be coming true. The Republicans looked to the states to preserve the people's liberties and stand up to what they regarded as Federalist tyranny. Madison and Jefferson drafted documents of protest that were passed by the Virginia and Kentucky legislatures.

The Virginia and Kentucky Resolutions of 1798 and 1799 claimed that the Alien and Sedition Acts could not be put into action because they violated the Constitution. The Kentucky Resolutions further suggested that states might **nullify** (NUH•luh•FY)— legally overturn—federal laws considered unconstitutional.

What does nullification mean? Thomas Jefferson, who authored the Kentucky Resolutions, explained that the states are "sovereign and independent." If an act of the government exceeded the powers granted by the Constitution, Jefferson believed, a state had the right to refuse to obey.

What Are States' Rights?

The resolutions affirmed the principle of **states' rights**—limiting the federal government to those powers clearly **assigned** to it by the Constitution and reserving to the states all other powers not expressly forbidden to them.

To phrase it differently, the state had the right to assert its power to protect its citizens from the misuse of federal power. The issue of states' rights would arise again and again in the nation's early history.

Federalists criticized the Kentucky and Virginia Resolutions as a step toward the breakup of the Union. They argued that if any state could nullify any federal law it considered unconstitutional, the power of the federal government would cease.

Making Peace With France As the election of 1800 approached, the Federalists found themselves under attack. They urged Adams to step up the war with France. If war continued, the Federalists expected to win reelection. They believed Americans would be reluctant to elect a new president in wartime. Adams refused to rush to war, especially for his own political gain. Instead he appointed a new commission to seek peace with France.

In 1800 the French agreed to a treaty and stopped attacks on American ships. Although the agreement with France was in the best interest of the United States, it hurt Adams's chance for reelection. Rather than applauding the agreement, Hamilton and his supporters now opposed their own president. Federalist leaders were furious, but they could not long oppose an effort to make peace. By the end of Adams's presidency, peace with France had been restored.

Adams's action in making peace against the wishes of most of his party was a courageous act. Proud of his nonpartisan action, Adams wrote that on his gravestone he wanted written "Here lies John Adams who took upon himself the responsibility of the peace with France in the year 1800."

With the Federalists split, the Republican prospects for capturing the presidency improved. The way was prepared for Thomas Jefferson in the election of 1800.

✓ **Reading Check** **Summarize** How did the peace agreement with France affect the Federalists?

Study Central Need help understanding the origins of political parites? Visit tajww1.glencoe.com and click on Study Central.

Section 3 Review

Reading Summary

Review the Main Ideas

- By the election of 1796, the political parties known as the Federalists and the Republicans had developed.

- During President John Adams's term, the threat of war with France led to the passage of the Alien and Sedition Acts, which were greatly opposed by the Republicans.

What Did You Learn?

1. Who was elected president in 1796, and who became vice president?

2. What does "sedition" refer to in the Alien and Sedition Acts?

Critical Thinking

3. **Classifying Information** Re-create the diagram below. Provide information about the election of 1796 in the spaces provided.

Presidential Election of 1796		
Candidate		
Electoral votes		
Elected position		

4. **The Big Ideas** How were the Federalists different from the Republicans in how they viewed the Constitution?

5. **Drawing Conclusions** Do you think the development of political parties was necessary? Why or why not? Write a short essay justifying your conclusion.

6. **Persuasive Writing** Design a campaign poster or button for the presidential candidate you would have chosen in 1796. Write a short paragraph that summarizes your reasons for your choice.

Analyzing Primary Sources

Challenging Times

Even after the ratification of the U.S. Constitution, the leaders and citizens of this young nation faced many challenges. With an outline for how the government should work and the leadership of George Washington, people began to work together to launch this new republic.

Read the passages on pages 298 and 299 and answer the questions that follow.

Painter and President by J.L.G. Ferris ▶

Reader's Dictionary

embarking (ihm • BAHRK • ihng): setting out

integrity (ihn • TEH • gruh • tee): honesty

gallery: outdoor balcony

proclamation (PRAH • kluh • MAY • shuhn): announcement

agitated (A • juh • TAYT • ihd): upset and nervous

ungainly: awkward, clumsy

plainest manner: in a simple way

On Becoming President

Americans were happy that the hero of the American Revolution, George Washington, was elected the nation's first president. Washington expressed his feelings about becoming president in a letter.

I am **embarking** . . . on this voyage, but what returns will be made for them [Americans], Heaven alone can foretell. **Integrity** and firmness is all I can promise; these, be the voyage long or short, never shall forsake me although I may be deserted by all men.

—Letter to Henry Knox, April 1789

Washington's First Inaugural

Pennsylvania Senator William Maclay was one of the many witnesses to the nation's first presidential inauguration. He wrote about the event in his journal.

[T]he President was conducted out of the middle window into the **gallery** [overlooking Wall Street], and the oath was administered by the Chancellor [the highest judicial officer in the state of New York]. Notice that the business done was communicated to the crowd by **proclamation** . . . who gave three cheers, and repeated it on the President's bowing to them.

As the company returned into the Senate chamber, the President took the chair and the Senators and Representatives their seats. He rose, and all arose also and [he] addressed them. This great man was **agitated** and embarrassed more than ever he was by the leveled cannon or pointed musket. He trembled, and several times could scarce make out to read, though it must be supposed he had often read it before…. When he came to the words *all the world*, he made a flourish with his right hand, which left rather an **ungainly** impression. I sincerely, for my part, wished all set ceremony in the hands of the dancing-masters, and that this first of men had read off his address in the **plainest manner,** without ever taking his eyes from the paper, for I felt hurt that he was not first in everything.

—from the Journal of William Maclay

The Great Seal of the United States

The Great Seal of the United States is the official seal of the United States government. The seal appears on important government documents. First adopted in 1782, it remains in use today.

The Great Seal ▶

The face of the seal shows an American eagle with its wings spread. The seal also includes the motto *E pluribus unum* ("From many, one"). Most Americans may not know it, but they often carry around the seal. The one-dollar bill shows both sides of the Great Seal.

The seal's reverse side shows a 13-step pyramid with the year 1776 in Roman numerals at the base. Below the pyramid, a scroll reads, *Novus Ordo Seclorum*, meaning "New Order of the Ages." It refers to the year 1776 as the beginning of a new era.

The number 13 is featured prominently on the Great Seal. There are 13 stars in the crest above the eagle, 13 stripes on the eagle's shield, 13 arrows in the eagle's left claw, and 13 olives and leaves in the eagle's right claw. Why thirteen? The number represents the original 13 states of the nation.

 Document-Based Questions

On Becoming President

1. What promise did Washington make?
2. How would you describe Washington's feelings about becoming president? Explain your answer.

Washington's First Inaugural

3. What events at Washington's inaugural did Maclay seem to like?
4. What was it about Washington's public speaking manner that troubled Maclay?

The Great Seal of the United States

5. What image on the Great Seal is one of the nation's symbols?

Read to Write

6. Choose a U.S. president that has been in office during the last 50 years. Do research to find out how that president might have viewed his role. Playing the role of this president, write a letter similar to George Washington's letter. Then design a symbol that would have been appropriate for the nation under that president's leadership.

Review Content Vocabulary

1. Use the following terms to write a paragraph about the new U.S. government:

   cabinet   **implied powers**

   caucus   **states' rights**

Review the Main Ideas

Section 1 • The First President

2. Why did Hamilton want national taxes? Why did some oppose the taxes?

3. What was the importance of the Judiciary Act of 1789?

Section 2 • Early Challenges

4. What caused farmers in western Pennsylvania to revolt during the Whiskey Rebellion?

5. What was the significance of the Battle of Fallen Timbers?

Section 3 • The First Political Parties

6. According to Hamilton, what are implied powers?

7. What actions by France led to an undeclared war with the United States?

Critical Thinking

8. **Evaluate** Refer to the grievances listed in the Declaration of Independence. How were these grievances addressed in the Bill of Rights?

9. **Analyze** What did President Washington say in his Farewell Address about political parties and foreign policy?

10. **Compare and Contrast** In a brief essay, compare the positions of the Federalists and Democratic-Republicans on the national bank.

Geography Skills

Using this map, answer the following questions about the election of 1796.

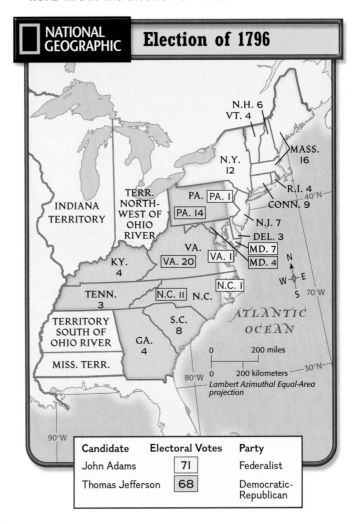

NATIONAL GEOGRAPHIC **Election of 1796**

Candidate	Electoral Votes	Party
John Adams	71	Federalist
Thomas Jefferson	68	Democratic-Republican

11. **Identify** How many states did John Adams win? How many did Thomas Jefferson win?

12. **Evaluate** What was the total electoral vote count for each man? What was the election result?

13. **Region** What was the distribution of votes by state? What pattern do you see?

History Online

Self-Check Quiz Visit tajwwI.glencoe.com to prepare for the Chapter 5 test.

Read to Write

14. **The Big Ideas** **Government and Democracy** Political ideas and major events shape how people form governments. Select an event from this chapter. Write an essay describing how people and ideas affected government through that event.

15. **Using Your** **FOLDABLES** Review the "American firsts" that you listed in your foldable. Using numbers, rank each first from the most important to the least important. Explain the reasons for your highest and lowest rankings.

Using Academic Vocabulary

16. Read the following sentence and then write the meaning of the underlined word.

The new federal government was interested in increasing <u>revenue</u> in order to pay off its debts.

Building Citizenship

17. **Researching** Work in groups of four to discuss and develop answers to these questions:

- How does the Bill of Rights reflect the principle of limited government?
- What are two individual rights protected in the Bill of Rights?
- Why would it be necessary to change the Constitution?

Reviewing Skills

18. **READING SKILL** **Recognizing Bias** Imagine that you were living in the United States in 1798. Write an editorial to your newspaper that demonstrates bias about your view as to whether the Alien and Sedition Acts violated the U.S. Constitution. Use details from the text and chart about the Alien and Sedition Acts on page 295.

19. **ANALYSIS SKILL** **Sequencing Information** Create a time line that lists key events in President Adams's dispute with France. Write a paragraph analyzing President Adams's handling of this dispute.

Standardized Test Practice

Select the best answer for each of the following questions.

20 **Thomas Jefferson and Alexander Hamilton served as members of Washington's**

A congress.

B judiciary.

C cabinet.

D military.

21 **Which amendment of the Bill of Rights protects the rights of the states?**

A First Amendment

B Fifth Amendment

C Sixth Amendment

D Tenth Amendment

22 **The XYZ Affair dealt with problems between the United States and**

A France.

B Spain.

C Great Britain.

D Canada.

23 **Hamilton proposed a national tax on imports, or a(n)**

A bond.

B impressment.

C caucus.

D tariff.

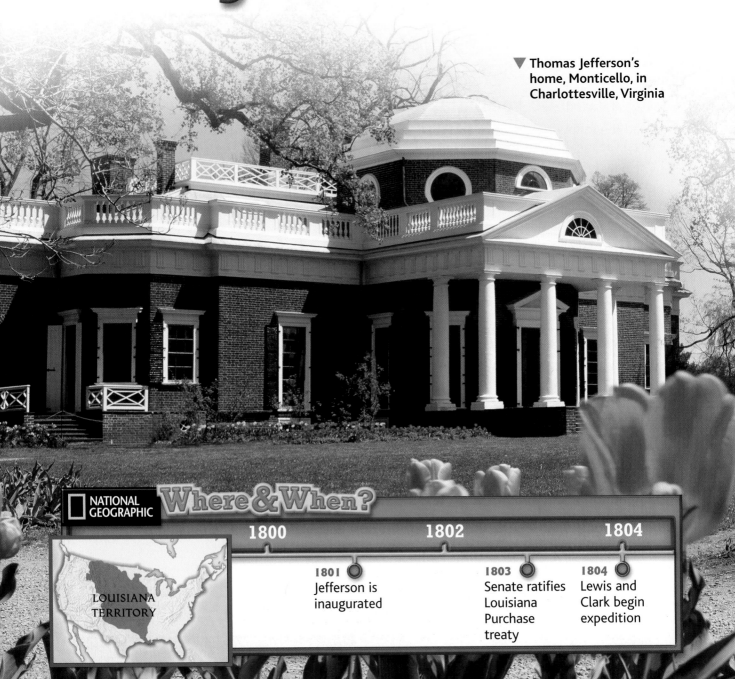

The Age of Jefferson

▼ Thomas Jefferson's home, Monticello, in Charlottesville, Virginia

NATIONAL GEOGRAPHIC Where&When?

LOUISIANA TERRITORY

1800	1802	1804
1801 Jefferson is inaugurated	**1803** Senate ratifies Louisiana Purchase treaty	**1804** Lewis and Clark begin expedition

The Big Ideas

The Republicans Take Power

Political ideas and major events shape how people form governments. The election of 1800 marked the transfer of power from one political party to another through a democratic election.

The Louisiana Purchase

Geography shapes the physical, economic, and political challenges a region faces. The Louisiana Purchase opened a vast area to exploration and settlement.

Daily Life in Early America

Political, social, religious, and economic changes influence the way Americans think and act. A powerful wave of nationalism swept through American life. Americans began to create a distinct culture.

 View the Chapter 6 video in the Glencoe Video Program.

FOLDABLES™
Study Organizer

Organizing Information Make this foldable to organize information and sequence events about the Jefferson era into a flowchart.

Step 1 Fold a sheet of paper in half from side to side.

Fold it so the left edge lies about $\frac{1}{2}$ inch from the right edge.

Step 2 Cut the top layer only to make five tabs.

This will make five tabs.

Step 3 Label your foldable as shown.

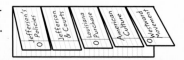

Reading and Writing
As you read, select key facts about the events of the Jefferson era and write them under the tabs of your foldable.

Get Ready to Read

Compare and Contrast

1 Learn It!

Good readers compare and contrast information as they read. This means they look for similarities and differences. They compare the ways in which people, places, or ideas are the same or different in order to understand how each is unique. Look for signal words in the text to let you know when the author is giving information for comparing or contrasting. Some comparison signal words are *similarly, at the same time,* and *likewise.* Contrast signal words include *however, rather, on the other hand, yet, but,* and *or.* Read the excerpt below and notice how the author uses contrast to discuss conflicting opinions.

> Federalists charged the Republican Jefferson, who believed in freedom of religion, with being "godless." Republicans warned that the Federalists would bring back monarchy. Federalists, they claimed, only represented the interests of wealthy people with property.
>
> — *from page 307*

Reading Tip

As you read, use other skills, such as summarizing and connecting, to help you understand comparisons and contrasts.

2 Practice It!

Read the section called "Conflict in the West" on page 329. Use the questions below to help you identify the different responses of Native American groups to white settlers who moved into their lands. Create a graphic organizer to record your answers.

- **What did the Native Americans have in common?**

- **How were their reactions to white settlement different?**

- **What results did Native Americans experience?**

Read to Write·······
Make a graphic organizer to record differences between living today and in 1803. Then, write a short paragraph summarizing your thoughts.

Sequoyah developed the alphabet for the Cherokee language. ▶

3 Apply It!

Compare and contrast political parties today and political parties at the time of Jefferson.

The Republicans Take Power

Guide to Reading

Looking Back, Looking Ahead
The presidency of Thomas Jefferson launched a new era, a time of many changes and rapid growth for the new nation.

Focusing on the Main Ideas
- The election of 1800 showed that power in the United States could be peacefully transferred even when political parties are in disagreement. *(page 307)*
- Jefferson worked to limit the scope of the federal government and shift control of the federal courts away from the Federalists. *(page 308)*

Locating Places
Washington, D.C.
Potomac River (puh • TOH • mihk)

Meeting People
Thomas Jefferson
Aaron Burr
Albert Gallatin
John Marshall

Content Vocabulary
laissez-faire (LEH • ZAY FEHR)
judicial review

Academic Vocabulary
require (rih • KWYR)
philosophy (fuh • LAH • suh • fee)
significant (sig • NIH • fih • kuhnt)
ensure (ihn • SHUR)

Reading Strategy
Organizing Information As you read the section, use a diagram like the one shown here to identify ways Republicans tried to reduce the role of government.

> **Reducing the role of government**

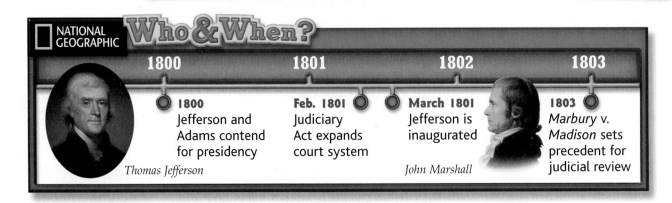

NATIONAL GEOGRAPHIC **Who & When?**

1800 — **1800** Jefferson and Adams contend for presidency

Thomas Jefferson

1801 — **Feb. 1801** Judiciary Act expands court system

1802 — **March 1801** Jefferson is inaugurated

John Marshall

1803 — **1803** *Marbury* v. *Madison* sets precedent for judicial review

Jefferson Becomes President

Main Idea The election of 1800 showed that power in the United States could be peacefully transferred even when political parties are in disagreement.

Reading Connection Do you think it is more important for the president to dress formally or casually? Why? Read to learn what changed when Jefferson became president.

An American Story

In 1801 **Washington, D.C.,** was slowly rising from a swampy site on the **Potomac River** (puh•TOH•mihk). The nation's new capital had only two prominent buildings—the president's mansion (later called the White House) and the still-unfinished Capitol. Between them stretched about two miles of muddy streets on which pigs and chickens roamed freely.

Very few people liked being in Washington. It was hot and humid in the summer, and the river and swamps were a breeding ground for mosquitoes. Abigail Adams, the wife of John Adams, called the new capital "the very dirtiest Hole."

The Election of 1800

In 1800 Federalists supported President Adams for a second term and Charles Pinckney of South Carolina for vice president. Republicans nominated **Thomas Jefferson** for president and **Aaron Burr** of New York for vice president.

The election campaign of 1800 differed greatly from campaigns of today. Neither Adams nor Jefferson traveled around the country making speeches. Instead the candidates and their followers wrote letters to leading citizens and newspapers to publicize their views. The letter-writing campaign, however, was not polite.

Federalists charged the Republican Jefferson, who believed in freedom of religion, with being "godless." Republicans warned that the Federalists would bring back monarchy. Federalists, they claimed, only represented the interests of wealthy people with property.

Election Deadlock

When members of the Electoral College voted, Jefferson and Burr each received 73 votes. Because of this tie, the House of Representatives had to decide the election. At the time, the electors voted for each presidential and vice-presidential candidate individually rather than voting for a party's candidates as a team.

In the House, Federalists saw a chance to prevent the election of Jefferson by supporting Burr. For 35 ballots, the election remained tied. Finally, at Alexander Hamilton's urging, one Federalist decided not to vote for Burr. Jefferson became president, and Burr became vice president.

To prevent another tie between a presidential and a vice-presidential candidate, Congress passed the Twelfth Amendment to the Constitution in 1803. This amendment, ratified in 1804, **requires** electors to vote for the president and vice president on separate ballots. (*See page 262 for the entire text of the Twelfth Amendment.*)

Jefferson's Inauguration

On March 4, 1801, the day of the presidential inauguration, Jefferson dressed in everyday clothes. He left his boardinghouse and walked to the Senate to be sworn in as president. President Adams had slipped out of the presidential mansion and left the city so he would not have to watch Jefferson become president.

In his Inaugural Address, Jefferson tried to reach out to Federalists: "We are all Republicans, we are all Federalists," he said. Then he outlined some of his goals, which included maintaining "a wise and frugal [economical] government" and "the support of state governments in all their rights." He believed that a large federal government threatened liberty and that the states could best protect freedom.

Jefferson believed in reducing the power and size of the federal government. These ideas were similar to the French **philosophy** of **laissez-faire** (LEH•ZAY FEHR), which means "let (people) do (as they choose)."

Reading Check **Describe** What does the Twelfth Amendment to the Constitution require?

Jefferson's Policies

(Main Idea) **Jefferson worked to limit the scope of the federal government and shift control of the federal courts away from the Federalists.**

Reading Connection How should the federal government balance individual liberty with national interests? Read on to learn of changes Jefferson made to deal with this question.

In 1801, when Jefferson became president, the entire federal government consisted of only a few hundred people. This was exactly how Jefferson thought it should be. (Today nearly 3 million civilians work for the federal government.) In Jefferson's view, the national government should conduct foreign affairs and limit its domestic actions to delivering the mail, collecting customs duties, and taking a census every 10 years.

Jefferson Takes Charge When Jefferson entered office, he surrounded himself with men who shared his Republican principles. His secretary of state was his friend and fellow Virginian, James Madison. For secretary of the treasury, he chose **Albert Gallatin,** a Pennsylvanian with a strong grasp of financial matters.

Jefferson and Gallatin aimed to reduce the national debt that the Federalists had left. They scaled down military expenses by cutting the army by one-third and reducing the navy from 25 to 7 ships. By slashing spending, Jefferson and Gallatin **significantly** lowered the national debt within a few years.

Between the election and Jefferson's inauguration, Federalists in Congress passed the Judiciary Act of 1801. This act increased the number of federal judges. Outgoing President John Adams then filled many positions with Federalists.

▲ Abigail Adams in the unfinished White House

The *Way* It Was

Washington in 1800

The United States government moved to the new capital city of Washington, D.C., in 1800. Being located along the Potomac River, Washington was expected to emerge as a great trading city, but the plans for a great city had not proceeded very far. The president's house, with laundry sometimes hanging in the unfinished East Room, stood in an open field with two boxlike buildings for executive offices nearby. More than a mile away, across a swamp, stood the partly built Capitol. Members of Congress lived in crowded boardinghouses. The streets were mostly muddy wagon tracks, bordered with the stumps of trees that had been recently cut. Some Americans criticized the choice of Washington as the capital. They believed that the government should move to a larger city.

The judges that President Adams appointed were known as "midnight judges" because Adams supposedly signed appointments for judges until midnight on his last day in office. Through these appointments Adams **ensured** that Federalists would control the courts.

Marbury v. Madison The appointments could not take effect, however, until the legal papers (commissions) for these last-minute "midnight judges" were delivered. When Jefferson became president on March 4, a few of the commissions had not yet been delivered. He told Secretary of State Madison not to deliver them. One commission was addressed to William Marbury.

To force the delivery of his commission, Marbury took his case directly to the Supreme Court. Chief Justice **John Marshall** turned down Marbury's claim. Marshall noted that the Constitution did not give the Court jurisdiction to decide Marbury's case.

In his opinion, Marshall set out three principles of **judicial review:** (a) The Constitution is the supreme law of the land. (b) When a conflict arises between the Constitution and any other

Student Web Activity Visit tajww1.glencoe.com and click on *Chapter 6—Student Web Activities* for an activity on the history of the Supreme Court.

law, the Constitution must be followed. (c) The judicial branch has a duty to uphold the Constitution. The courts must be able to determine when a federal law conflicts with the Constitution and to nullify, or cancel, unconstitutional laws.

Marshall not only extended the power of the Court, he also broadened federal power at the expense of the states. In *McCulloch* v. *Maryland* (1819), the Court held that the elastic clause allows Congress to do more than the Constitution expressly authorizes it to do. In *Gibbons* v. *Ogden* (1824) the Court held that federal law takes precedence over state law in interstate transportation. 📖 *(See the Supreme Court Case Summaries beginning on page 846 for more on these cases.)*

✓ **Reading Check** **Explain** How did the changes that Jefferson made reflect his views about government?

Study Central Need help understanding Jefferson's election and his policies? Visit tajww1.glencoe.com and click on Study Central.

Section 1 Review

Reading Summary

Review the Main Ideas

- In the presidential election of 1800, Republican Thomas Jefferson defeated Federalist John Adams.

- After taking office as the first Republican president, Jefferson began to implement his party's ideas on how the government should function.

What Did You Learn?

1. Explain how Jefferson cut government spending.

2. Name the court case that established judicial review.

Critical Thinking

3. **Determining Cause and Effect** Re-create the diagram below and list the effects caused by the appointment of the "midnight judges."

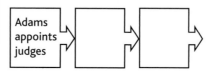

4. **The Big Ideas** How did Jefferson try to calm Federalist fears of Republican rule?

5. **READING** **Compare and Contrast** Election campaigns have changed since 1800. Write an essay that compares and contrasts current campaigns with those of Jefferson's time.

Connecting to the Constitution

The Supreme Court and the Economy

Why It Matters People in the United States are free to own property; to make a profit; and to make their own choices about what to produce, buy, and sell. The Framers of the U.S. Constitution believed that economic freedom is a basic right of citizens. As a result, the Constitution laid the basis for an economy based on capitalism, or free enterprise.

Although capitalism is the basis of the American economic system, ours is a mixed economy—a system in which the government both supports and regulates private enterprise. Over the years, the American judicial system—headed by the Supreme Court—has made decisions that have encouraged business competition and private property ownership. However, the Court also has expanded the power of the government to regulate, or lay down rules for, the economy as a whole.

The Commerce Power Article I, Section 8 of the Constitution gives Congress the authority to regulate commerce. It is known as the commerce clause. Under the Articles of Confederation, each state jealously guarded its own commerce. Trade barriers among the states restricted commerce and stood in the way of a strong national economy. The Framers of the U.S. Constitution sought to avoid state rivalries by giving Congress the power to regulate all forms of commerce among the states. It also affirmed Congress's right to regulate trade with foreign nations.

"An unlimited power to tax involves, necessarily, a power to destroy; because there is a limit beyond which no institution and no property can bear taxation."

—John Marshall, *McCulloch* v. *Maryland*, 1819

◀ **John Marshall**

▲ **The young nation's growing trade meant new laws were needed to regulate commerce.**

Over the years, the Supreme Court has expanded this commerce power to include a wide range of economic activities. The judiciary today consistently interprets *commerce* to mean nearly all activities concerned with the production, buying, selling, and transporting of goods. Appealing to the commerce clause, and with the Court's backing, Congress has passed many laws that prohibit, promote, and establish rules for many areas of business activity.

Judicial Review

In exercising its authority, the Supreme Court has a major tool: the power of **judicial review.** This is the right to examine government laws and actions and to cancel them if they violate the Constitution. Article III of the Constitution states that the

> *"judicial power shall extend to all cases . . . arising under this Constitution."*

The Founders, however, did not clearly give the power of judicial review to the Court. In fact, the Supreme Court in its early days had a minor role in the federal government compared with the Congress and the Presidency. You might ask: How did the Supreme Court acquire the power to influence the economy as well as other areas of American society?

The Marshall Court

The Court's role began to change when John Marshall was appointed Chief Justice of the Supreme Court in 1801. Marshall headed the Court until 1835 and helped increase its power. In the case *Marbury* v. *Madison* (1803), the Supreme Court first established the power of judicial review and ruled an act of Congress unconstitutional. By doing this, the Court defined its role as the final authority on what the Constitution means.

In other important decisions, Marshall used federal power to overturn state restrictions on the economy. In this way, the Marshall Court gave legal support to free enterprise ideas and practices. In *Fletcher* v. *Peck* (1810) the Court declared a Georgia law unconstitutional because it broke the **sanctity of contracts**—the idea that such written agreements are legally binding. The Supreme Court ruled that a land grant was a valid contract and could not be repealed even if corruption was involved. In *Dartmouth College* v. *Woodward* (1819), the Court again upheld the sanctity of contracts. In this case, the Court found it unconstitutional for New Hampshire's legislature to change the Dartmouth College charter and to change the college from a private school into a state university.

Finally, in *Gibbons* v. *Ogden* (1824), the Supreme Court struck down a New York law that gave a company the sole right to operate steamboats on New York waters. In taking this step, Marshall stated that federal power was superior to state power in all matters of **interstate commerce,** or trade among states. New York argued that the states had the right to control commerce involving only products. The Court, however, ruled that *all* forms of business across state lines came under the Constitution's commerce clause. This decision opened the way for Congress to involve itself in nearly all areas of the national economy.

Checking for Understanding

1. What is the commerce clause?
2. Why was *Gibbons* v. *Ogden* an important case?

Critical Thinking

3. **Conclude** Why is the idea of sanctity of contracts necessary to a capitalist economic system?
4. **Analyze** Why did the Supreme Court extend the commerce clause to include a wide range of economic activities?

The Louisiana Purchase

Guide to Reading

Looking Back, Looking Ahead
In the early 1800s, the United States experienced rapid growth. The Louisiana Purchase doubled the size of the nation and created remarkable opportunities.

Focusing on the Main Ideas
- As Americans moved west in the early 1800s, Spain and France made a secret agreement about land that affected American trade. *(page 313)*
- The Louisiana Purchase opened a vast area to exploration and settlement. *(page 314)*

Locating Places
Louisiana Territory
New Orleans
St. Louis
Missouri River

Meeting People
Meriwether Lewis
William Clark
Sacagawea (SA•kuh•juh•WEE•uh)
Zebulon Pike

Content Vocabulary
Conestoga wagon
   (KAH•nuh•STOH•guh)
secede (sih•SEED)

Academic Vocabulary
enormous (in•NAWR•muhs)
generation (JEH•nuh•RAY•shuhn)

Reading Strategy
Classifying Information As you read the section, re-create the diagram below and describe the areas that Lewis and Clark and Zebulon Pike explored.

Explorer	Region explored
Meriwether Lewis and William Clark	
Zebulon Pike	

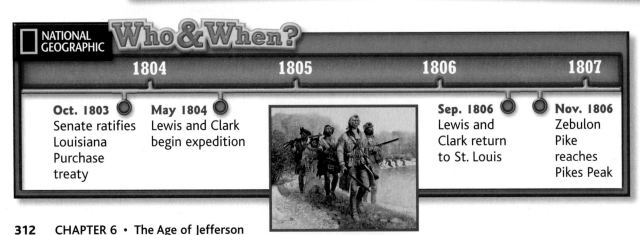

NATIONAL GEOGRAPHIC **Who & When?**

1804	1805	1806	1807

Oct. 1803
Senate ratifies Louisiana Purchase treaty

May 1804
Lewis and Clark begin expedition

Sep. 1806
Lewis and Clark return to St. Louis

Nov. 1806
Zebulon Pike reaches Pikes Peak

Western Territory

Main Idea As Americans moved west in the early 1800s, Spain and France made a secret agreement about land that affected American trade.

Reading Connection What challenges come with moving? Read to learn what the pioneers faced as they went west.

An American Story

Why did Americans risk everything they had to travel west? An English visitor, Harriet Martineau, observed:

> **❝**The pride and delight of Americans is in their quantity of land. . . . The possession of land is the aim of all action . . . and the cure for all social evils. . . . If a man is disappointed in politics or love, he goes and buys land.**❞**
>
> —from *Society in America*

Moving West During the early 1800s, more and more Americans moved west in search of land and adventure. These pioneers headed over the mountains into Kentucky and Tennessee and the less settled areas of the Northwest Territory. Most of these pioneers were farmers. They made a long and exhausting journey over the Appalachian Mountains.

Settlers loaded their household goods into **Conestoga wagons** (KAH•nuh•STOH•guh), sturdy vehicles topped with white canvas. For these westward-bound pioneers, two vital possessions were a rifle for protection and hunting and an ax to hack their way through the dense forests.

In 1800 the territory of the United States extended only as far west as the Mississippi River. The area to the west of the river—known as the **Louisiana Territory**—belonged to Spain. It was an **enormous** area of land, extending south to the city of **New Orleans** and west to the Rocky Mountains. Its northern boundaries remained undefined.

Many pioneers established farms along rivers that fed into the upper Mississippi River. The Spanish allowed Americans to sail on the lower Mississippi and trade in New Orleans. For the western farmers, this right was vital. The goods they sent downriver were unloaded in New Orleans and sent by ship to markets on the East Coast.

The French Threat In 1802 the Spanish suddenly changed their policy. They refused to allow American goods to move into or past New Orleans. That same year, President Jefferson learned that Spain and France had made a secret agreement that transferred the Louisiana Territory to France. Jefferson was alarmed. He thought French control would jeopardize American trade on the Mississippi River. He authorized Robert Livingston, the new minister to France, to negotiate for the purchase of New Orleans and other French territory.

Revolt in Santo Domingo The leader of France, Napoleon Bonaparte (nuh•POHL•yuhn BOH•nuh•PAHRT), hoped to use Santo Domingo as a Caribbean naval base from which he could control an American empire. However, a revolt in Santo Domingo ended Bonaparte's dream of a Western empire.

Inspired by the ideas of the French Revolution, enslaved Africans and other laborers in Santo Domingo rebelled against the island's plantation owners. After fierce and bitter fighting, the rebels, led by Toussaint-Louverture (TOO•SA LOO•vuhr•TYUR), declared the colony an independent republic. Toussaint set up an independent government.

In 1802 Napoleon sent troops to regain control. The French captured Toussaint but could not regain control of the island. By 1804 the French were driven out of Santo Domingo and the country regained its original name of Haiti.

✓ Reading Check **Explain** Why was the Mississippi River important to western farmers?

The Nation Expands

Main Idea **The Louisiana Purchase opened a vast area to exploration and settlement.**

Reading Connection Imagine you are preparing to lead an expedition to explore new lands. Who would you travel with? What research would you do? Read on to learn about Lewis and Clark's travels in the Louisiana Territory.

Without Santo Domingo, Napoleon had little use for Louisiana. The French believed they had something to sell that the United States might want to buy. French foreign minister Charles de Talleyrand informed American diplomats that the entire Louisiana Territory was for sale. Livingston and James Monroe, Jefferson's new special representative, were taken completely by surprise. Accepting the offer went far beyond what they were authorized to do, but the deal was too good to pass up. After a few days of negotiation, the parties agreed on a price of $15 million.

The Louisiana Purchase pleased Jefferson. The new territory would provide cheap and abundant land for farmers for **generations** to come. He worried, however, whether the purchase was legal. The Constitution said nothing about acquiring new territory. By what authority could he justify the purchase? Livingston wrote from Paris, urging Jefferson to accept the deal before Napoleon changed his mind. Jefferson decided the government's treaty-making powers allowed the purchase of the new territory. The Senate gave its approval in October 1803. With the ratification of the treaty, the size of the United States doubled.

TECHNOLOGY & History

The Conestoga Wagon

By the mid-1700s, sturdy Conestoga wagons transported settlers and their freight over the Appalachian Mountains. These wagons were first built in the Conestoga Creek region of Lancaster, Pennsylvania. As people pushed even farther westward, the Conestoga was seen rolling across the plains toward Oregon and California. **Why did Conestoga wagons have a high front and back?**

1 Six to eight draft horses or a dozen oxen pull the wagon. The driver rides or walks beside the animals.

2 The boat-shaped wagon's high front and back keep goods from falling out on steep mountain trails.

3 A **toolbox** attached to the side of the wagon holds spare parts for needed repairs.

4 A white canvas cloth stretches over the hoops, or **wagon bows.** This cover protects passengers and cargo from heat, rain, and snow.

5 Broad **wheels** help keep the heavy wagon from being mired in the mud.

The average Conestoga wagon was 21 feet long, 11 feet high, and 4 feet in width and depth. It could carry up to 12,000 pounds of cargo.

3 toolbox

2

wagon bows

4

1

5 wheels

The Expedition West Very little was known about the area west of the Mississippi, and it excited Jefferson's curiosity. Even before the Louisiana Purchase was complete, he persuaded Congress to sponsor an expedition to explore the new territory. Jefferson was particularly interested in the expedition as a scientific venture. Congress was interested in the natural resources in the territory and in sites for military forts.

Who Were Lewis and Clark? To head the expedition, Jefferson chose his private secretary, 28-year-old **Meriwether Lewis.** Lewis was well qualified to lead this journey of exploration. He had joined the militia during the Whiskey Rebellion and had been in the army since that time. The expedition's co-leader was **William Clark,** 32, a friend of Lewis's from military service. Both Lewis and Clark were knowledgeable amateur scientists. Together they assembled a crew that included expert gunsmiths, carpenters, scouts, and a cook. Two men of mixed Native American and French heritage served as interpreters. Clark's servant, an African American named York, rounded out the group. York's skills in hunting and fishing made him a valuable member of the expedition. He was particularly successful in making friends with the Native Americans they met along the way.

The expedition left **St. Louis** in the spring of 1804 and slowly worked its way up the **Missouri River.** Lewis and Clark kept a journal of their voyage and made notes on what they saw and did.

Along their journey they encountered Native American groups. One young Shoshone woman named **Sacagawea** (SA•kuh•juh•WEE•uh) joined their group as a guide. After 18 months and nearly 4,000 miles, Lewis and Clark reached the Pacific Ocean. After spending the winter there, both explorers headed back east along separate routes.

When the expedition returned in September 1806, they had collected and recorded valuable information on people, plants, animals, and the geography of the West. The expedition also helped the United States lay claim to the northern region between the Rocky Mountains and the Pacific Ocean known as Oregon. Within a few years, fur traders based in St. Louis were traveling to and settling in the Rockies. Perhaps most important, the journey provided inspiration to a nation of people eager to move westward.

Picturing **History**

Soldiers fire a salute during ceremonies in which Louisiana was officially transferred to the United States. *How did the Louisiana Purchase change the size of the United States?*

Pike's Expedition Even before Lewis and Clark returned, Jefferson sent others to explore the wilderness. Lieutenant **Zebulon Pike** led two expeditions between 1805 and 1807, traveling through the upper Mississippi River valley and into the region that is now the state of Colorado. In Colorado, Pike found a snow-capped mountain he called Grand Peak. Today this mountain is known as Pikes Peak. Pike's account of his expeditions gave Americans their first detailed description of the Great Plains and the Rocky Mountains.

Federalists Plan to Secede Many Federalists opposed the Louisiana Purchase. They feared that the states carved out of the new territory would become Republican, reducing the Federalists' power. A group of Federalists in Massachusetts plotted to **secede** (sih•SEED)—withdraw—from the United States. They wanted New England to form a separate "Northern Confederacy." The plotters realized that to have any chance of success, the Northern Confederacy would have to include New York as well as New England.

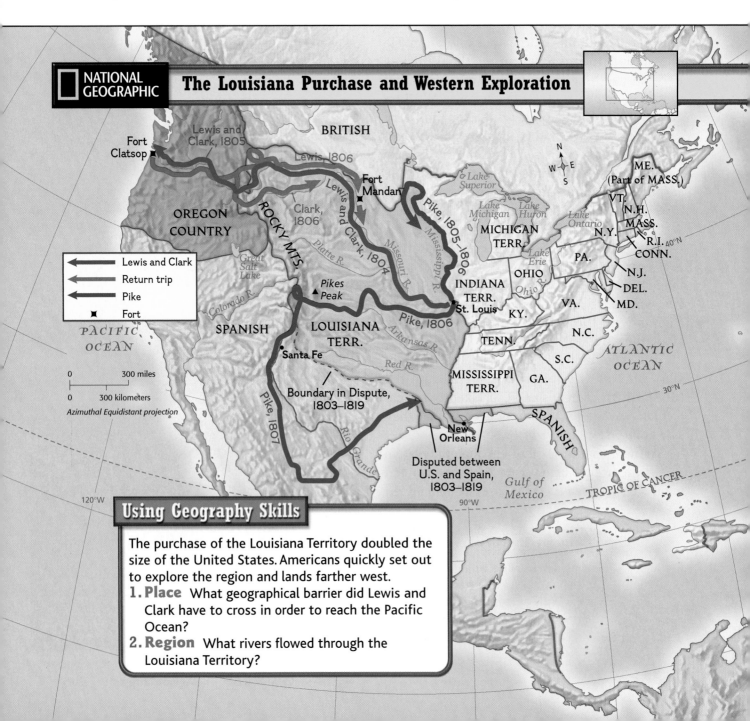

NATIONAL GEOGRAPHIC

The Louisiana Purchase and Western Exploration

Legend:
- Lewis and Clark
- Return trip
- Pike
- Fort

Using Geography Skills

The purchase of the Louisiana Territory doubled the size of the United States. Americans quickly set out to explore the region and lands farther west.

1. **Place** What geographical barrier did Lewis and Clark have to cross in order to reach the Pacific Ocean?
2. **Region** What rivers flowed through the Louisiana Territory?

Federalists Support Burr In 1804 the Republican caucus nominated Thomas Jefferson for a second term as president. Jefferson and the Republicans, in doubt about Burr's loyalty to the party, did not nominate Burr for another term as vice president. Instead, they chose George Clinton of New York. Burr then decided to run for governor of New York. Many Federalists supported Burr as they were searching for a powerful ally in New York who would support their plan for the Northern Confederacy. Alexander Hamilton, however, threw his weight against Burr's election.

Burr and Hamilton Alexander Hamilton had never trusted Aaron Burr. Now Hamilton was concerned about rumors that Burr had secretly agreed to lead New York out of the Union. Hamilton called Burr "a dangerous man." When Burr lost the election for governor, he blamed Hamilton and challenged him to a duel. In July 1804, the two men—armed with pistols—met in Weehawken, New Jersey. Hamilton hated dueling and pledged not to shoot at his rival. Burr, however, did fire and aimed to hit Hamilton. Seriously wounded, Hamilton died the next day. Burr fled to avoid arrest on the charge of murder.

The Northern Confederacy Fails With Burr on the run and with almost no support in the New England states, the plans for the Northern Confederacy failed. The results of the election of 1804 showed how thoroughly the Federalists had been discredited. Jefferson and Clinton captured 162 electoral votes to 14 for the Federalist candidates Charles Pinckney and Rufus King.

✓ **Reading Check** **Summarize** Why did France sell the Louisiana Territory to the United States?

History Online

Study Central Need help understanding the Louisiana Purchase and its exploration? Visit tajww1.glencoe.com and click on Study Central.

Section 2 Review

Reading Summary

Review the Main Ideas

- American settlers in the West depended on the use of the lower Mississippi River and the port of New Orleans to trade their farm products. That control was threatened when France gained control of the Louisiana Territory.

- After the purchase of Louisiana from the French, President Jefferson sent Lewis and Clark and others to explore the new territory.

What Did You Learn?

1. Which European countries controlled the Louisiana Territory until 1800?

2. Name the famous Native American woman who Lewis and Clark met along their journey.

Critical Thinking

3. **Organizing Information** Create a diagram like the one below that lists the benefits of acquiring the Louisiana Territory.

4. **The Big Ideas** Why was the French port of New Orleans important to the United States?

5. **Determining Cause and Effect** How could the Lewis and Clark expedition prepare people who wanted to move west? Write a paragraph describing your conclusions.

6. **ANALYSIS** **Assess** What was the relationship between the Louisiana Purchase and political power? How did Jefferson's political opponents react? Write an essay explaining your assessment.

GEOGRAPHY & HISTORY

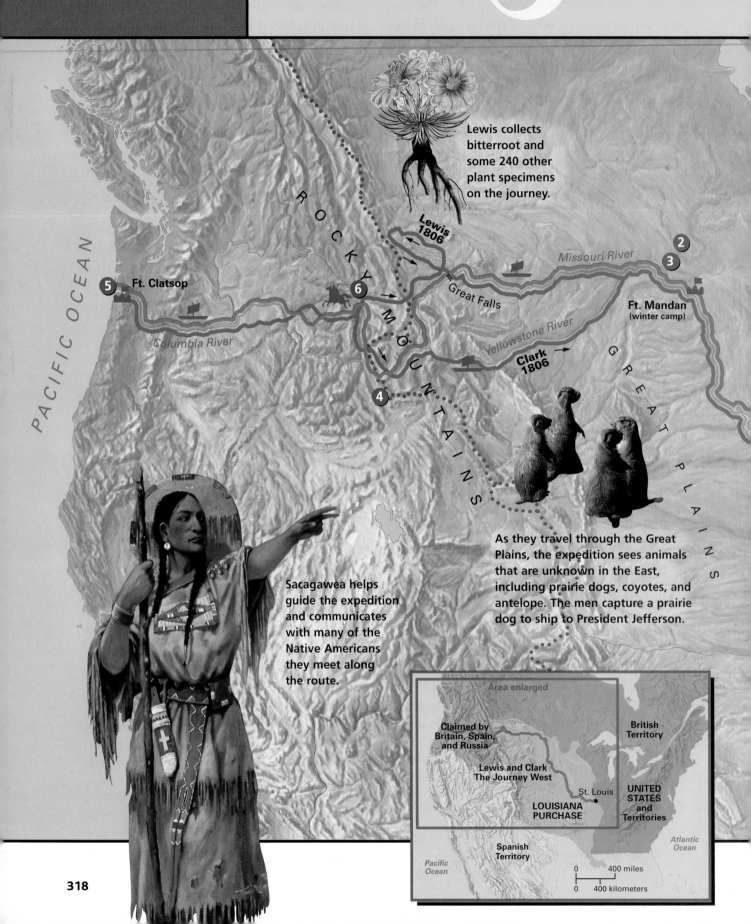

Lewis collects bitterroot and some 240 other plant specimens on the journey.

Lewis 1806

ROCKY MOUNTAINS

Missouri River

2

3

Great Falls

6

5 Ft. Clatsop

Columbia River

Ft. Mandan (winter camp)

Yellowstone River

Clark 1806

GREAT PLAINS

PACIFIC OCEAN

4

As they travel through the Great Plains, the expedition sees animals that are unknown in the East, including prairie dogs, coyotes, and antelope. The men capture a prairie dog to ship to President Jefferson.

Sacagawea helps guide the expedition and communicates with many of the Native Americans they meet along the route.

Area enlarged

Claimed by Britain, Spain, and Russia

British Territory

Lewis and Clark The Journey West

St. Louis

UNITED STATES and Territories

LOUISIANA PURCHASE

Atlantic Ocean

Spanish Territory

Pacific Ocean

| 0 | 400 miles |
| 0 | 400 kilometers |

The explorers travel up the Missouri River in a large keelboat and smaller boats called pirogues.

INTO THE UNKNOWN

LEWIS AND CLARK In 1803 President Jefferson set up the Corps of Discovery to find a water route to the Pacific and explore the recently acquired Louisiana Purchase. In the spring of 1804, William Clark and Meriwether Lewis, with a company of recruits, set off from St. Louis.

1804 THE JOURNEY WEST

1 MAY 14 The members of the Corps of Discovery, which number over 45, embark on the expedition, which would eventually cover more than 7,700 miles.

2 NOVEMBER The explorers set up a winter camp near the villages of the Mandans and Hidatsas. Sacagawea, a Shoshone woman who had been kidnapped by the Hidatsa, joins the expedition.

1805

3 APRIL 7 Lewis and Clark send a group back on the keelboat with reports and specimens of some of the plants and animals that were unknown in the East. The expedition continues in smaller boats.

4 AUGUST 12 Lewis realizes that there is no Northwest Passage—or river route—to the Pacific. The Corps continues on horseback.

5 DECEMBER 25 The expedition celebrates Christmas in its new winter quarters, Fort Clatsop.

1806 THE RETURN TRIP

6 JULY 3 The expedition splits into smaller units to explore more of the Louisiana Territory. They reunite on August 12.

7 SEPTEMBER 23 The Corps of Discovery finally arrives back in St. Louis. The explorers had established peaceful contact with many Native Americans and accumulated a wealth of geographic information. Fur traders and others, armed with the new knowledge, soon start heading west.

LEARNING from GEOGRAPHY

1. What obstacles do you think would have been the most difficult for the expedition?

2. Write a paragraph that describes the importance of teamwork in helping the Corps of Discovery reach its goals.

319

Section 3

Daily Life in Early America

Guide to Reading

Looking Back, Looking Ahead
The growth of nationalism and democracy led to the rise of a truly American culture.

Focusing on the (Main Ideas)
- A strong sense of national identity grew among Americans. *(page 321)*
- Americans began to create their own unique culture. *(page 322)*
- People living in different regions developed different ways to use and farm the land. *(page 326)*
- An increasing number of Americans chose to move west into new territory. *(page 328)*

Meeting People
Washington Irving
James Fenimore Cooper
George Caleb Bingham
Stephen C. Foster

Content Vocabulary
nationalism
planters

Academic Vocabulary
available (uh•VAY•luh•buhl)
unique (yu•NEEK)
occupy (AH•kyuh•PY)
contrary (KAHN•TREHR•ee)
conflict (KAHN•FLIHKT)
migrate (MY•GRAYT)

Reading Strategy
Organizing Information As you read this section, use a diagram like the one shown list achievements in these fields.

Achievements			
Literature	Art	Music	Architecture

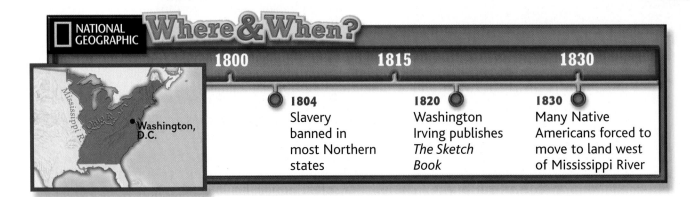

NATIONAL GEOGRAPHIC Where & When?

1800 — 1815 — 1830

1804 Slavery banned in most Northern states

1820 Washington Irving publishes *The Sketch Book*

1830 Many Native Americans forced to move to land west of Mississippi River

Creating a Democratic Society

(Main Idea) **A strong sense of national identity grew among Americans.**

Reading Connection What type of school do you attend? Do you think education should be available to everyone? In the early years of the Republic, only a few groups of people had access to schools. Read on to learn more.

An American Story

Lewis and Clark returned to Washington, D.C., in 1806. The maps that they drew made it easier for new settlers to follow the way west. The United States, President Jefferson said, was "a rising nation, spread over a wide and fruitful land."

Nationalism During the age of Jefferson, a spirit of nationalism spread throughout the United States. **Nationalism** is a feeling of pride in a nation and loyalty to its goals. At this time, the United States's territory and population grew, and national prosperity increased as well. Americans felt confident and united about their new nation and its future.

As the country expanded, American society became increasingly democratic. This meant that the ideas of equality and natural rights influenced every part of American life. People excluded from power and influence—poor white males, women, and both enslaved and free African Americans—began to demand the basic dignity promised in the Declaration of Independence.

Education During the early republic, many Americans came to believe that a strong democracy depended on well-educated citizens. Jefferson expressed this belief when he said,

> ❝If a nation expects to be ignorant and free, in a state of civilization, it expects what never was and never will be.❞
> —Letter to Charles Yancey, 1816

To advance education on the frontier, schools were provided for in the Northwest Ordinance of 1787.

Despite these intentions, many Americans did not have the opportunity to attend school in the early 1800s. Most schools were run by private groups and were open only to those who could afford to pay for them. Some students were educated at home or at dame schools. Dame schools were generally taught by women in their own homes. The teacher taught the children to read and write and other useful skills such as sewing.

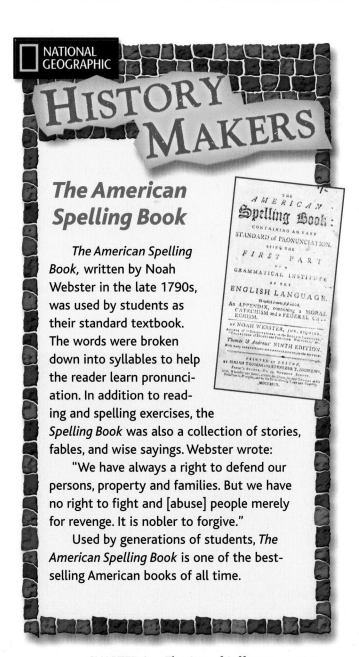

NATIONAL GEOGRAPHIC

HISTORY MAKERS

The American Spelling Book

The American Spelling Book, written by Noah Webster in the late 1790s, was used by students as their standard textbook. The words were broken down into syllables to help the reader learn pronunciation. In addition to reading and spelling exercises, the *Spelling Book* was also a collection of stories, fables, and wise sayings. Webster wrote:

"We have always a right to defend our persons, property and families. But we have no right to fight and [abuse] people merely for revenge. It is nobler to forgive."

Used by generations of students, *The American Spelling Book* is one of the best-selling American books of all time.

Massachusetts and Philadelphia, however, had public schools that provided free education. Their success increased demands for a nationwide system of public schools that would make education **available** to all citizens.

Religion A powerful influence on the growth of democracy was religion. During the early 1800s, a religious revival known as the Second Great Awakening swept the nation. At gatherings known as camp meetings, preachers offered a simple message that ordinary people could grasp. They stressed the equality of all believers before God and the promise of salvation for all who believed.

The Second Great Awakening had an important effect on the young republic. It gave people the determination to better their lives and improve society as a whole. Many Americans influenced by the Awakening joined movements to end slavery, curb drinking, and advance education.

Many African Americans were won to Christianity at this time. Inspired by the message of equality, they formed their own denominations and churches, including independent Baptist churches and the first African Methodist Episcopal Church.

✓ **Reading Check** **Explain** What message was stressed by preachers during the Second Great Awakening?

An American Culture

Main Idea Americans began to create their own unique culture.

Reading Connection What kinds of music do you like? What do you enjoy reading? Read on to learn more about the music and literature of the early Republic.

The growth of nationalism and democracy in the early republic led to the rise of a truly American culture. Since colonial times, cultural life in the United States had been strongly influenced by Europe, chiefly Great Britain. During the first decade of the 1800s, Americans began to create their own art forms, including literature, painting, music, and architecture.

Literature During the early 1800s, American writers started to turn away from European influences. They began using settings and characters that were typically American. In 1820 **Washington Irving** wrote *The Sketch Book,* a collection of short stories that were mostly set in rural New York. One story, "Rip Van Winkle," tells about a man who falls asleep in the woods for 20 years. Another story, "The Legend of Sleepy Hollow," describes the schoolteacher Ichabod Crane's encounter with a headless horseman.

History *Through Art*

Religious Camp Meeting by **J. Maze Burbank** A powerful influence on the growth of democracy was religion. At gatherings called camp meetings, preachers revived America's commitment to religion. *What was this religious revival called?*

Like other artists of the Hudson River School, Frederic Edwin Church showed scenes of nature untouched by settlement. *How was American art and literature changing during the early 1800s?*

In this passage, Irving describes the terror that Ichabod Crane felt as he came upon the headless horseman late at night:

> **Mounting a rising ground, which brought the figure of his fellow traveller in relief against the sky, gigantic in height, and muffled in a cloak, Ichabod was horror struck, on perceiving that [the rider] was headless! but his horror was still more increased, on observing, that the head, which should have rested on his shoulders, was carried before him on the pommel of the saddle! His terror rose to desperation; he rained a shower of kicks and blows upon [his horse] Gunpowder, hoping, by a sudden movement, to give his companion the slip—but the spectre started full jump with him. Away, then, they dashed, through thick and thin; stones flying, and sparks flashing, at every bound.**

—"The Legend of Sleepy Hollow"

Another New York author, **James Fenimore Cooper,** wrote novels such as *The Last of the Mohicans* and *The Deerslayer*. In these novels, a trapper folk hero of many names—Natty Bumppo, Leatherstocking, Deerslayer, and Pathfinder—is portrayed as strong, brave, resourceful, and honorable. When asked if he had ever shot an enemy that was capable of killing him, Deerslayer responded:

> **To own the truth, I never did," answered Deerslayer, "seeing that a fitting occasion never offered. The Delawares [a Native American group] have been peaceable since my sojourn with 'em, and I hold it to be [wrong] to take the life of a man, except in open and [generous] warfare.**

—from *The Deerslayer*

Biography

WASHINGTON IRVING
1783–1859
JAMES FENIMORE COOPER
1789–1851

James Fenimore Cooper ▶

In the 1800s, American literature became more "American." Writers, reflecting a sense of national pride, were turning away from European influences and writing about America. Authors such as James Fenimore Cooper and Washington Irving reveal the spirit of the expanding American frontier and of the possibilities for improvement and change.

Washington Irving was the first American writer to win international fame. *The Sketch Book* (1820), a collection of stories admired throughout Europe, included Irving's two most famous tales, "Rip Van Winkle" and "The Legend of Sleepy Hollow."

Irving was a born wanderer, even as a child. He later wrote, "I began my travels, and made many tours into foreign parts and unknown regions of my native city, to the frequent alarm of my parents."

Although he wrote many works, Cooper is best known for his novels about Natty Bumppo's frontier life. *The Leatherstocking Tales* is set in the huge expanse of the New York State frontier. Natty Bumppo is a trapper who is forced westward by the movement of settlers into his beloved frontier. Cooper is the first American writer to draw greatly from American history for his setting and characterization. As a result of reading Cooper's novels, generations of children—not only here but in France and Great Britain—gloried in the drama of Native Americans and pioneers on the frontier.

"Should we distrust the man, because his manners are not our manners, and that his skin is dark!"
—from *The Last of the Mohicans*

◀ Washington Irving

Then and Now

Why do you think works by Irving and Cooper are still popular today?

Other writers, such as William Cullen Bryant of Massachusetts, wrote poetry. Bryant expressed a love for natural beauty. His poem "Thanatopsis" appeared in 1817. In it, he suggested that by studying nature, people could better understand life and death.

Art During the early 1800s, American artists turned their attention to American people and landscapes. **George Caleb Bingham** painted fur traders, riverboat workers, and political speakers.

Another artist, George Catlin, was one of several artists who lived among the Native Americans and painted scenes of their daily life. Thomas Doughty was one of the first successful landscape painters and a leader of the Hudson River School of painting. This school was made up of artists who liked to paint views of the Catskill Mountains and the Hudson River in New York.

Music In the early 1800s, Americans developed their own forms of music. Instruments such as banjos and pianos were used to play American tunes. Musicals filled with American songs were performed in large cities and in barns, tents, or log cabins throughout the country.

One of the most successful American songwriters was **Stephen C. Foster.** Although born in Pennsylvania, Foster combined African and European music to create **uniquely** American melodies about life in the South, such as "My Old Kentucky Home" and "Swanee River."

Architecture American architects of the early 1800s developed their own forms of building based on the classical styles of ancient Greece and Rome. Classical designs became the model for public buildings all over the country, including the Capitol in Washington, D.C. Thomas Jefferson used classical styles when he planned his home, Monticello, and buildings for the University of Virginia. A style known as Greek Revival also was used for private homes, such as plantation houses in the South.

✓ **Reading Check** **Describe** What qualities did James Fenimore Cooper give his main character?

America's *Architecture*

University of Virginia Thomas Jefferson founded the University of Virginia to provide educational opportunity for all. Jefferson planned and supervised the construction, including a central domed round building called the Rotunda.

A Rural Nation

Main Idea People living in different regions developed different ways to use and farm the land.

Reading Connection Do you live in a neighborhood that works together? Read on to see how people in the early years of the Republic experienced work and community.

During the early 1800s, most Americans lived in rural areas and made their living on the land. People, however, **occupied** the land in very different ways in different regions of the country.

Farm Life in the North During the early years of the republic, people in the North tended to cluster in villages and towns made up of neat rows of wooden frame houses, churches, and stores. Beyond these settlements were farm communities located within a relatively short traveling distance of each other. Northern farmers cut down forests and created fields marked

Picturing **History**

Some people in the North lived in villages, but many lived and worked in rural areas. *What was the major economic activity in the North?*

by hedges or stone walls. They produced enough crops and livestock to sell or exchange in nearby marketplaces for teas, sugar, window glass, and tools.

Farming was the North's major economic activity, but not all rural people in the North worked on the land. Some labored in the small workshops, grain and saw mills, and iron forges that dotted the rural landscape. Others worked as craftspeople or day laborers in nearby towns.

The South's Plantation Culture While Northerners lived close together, Southerners lived on small farms or large plantations that were widely separated from each other. The South's economy depended on slavery and growing cash crops.

Beginning in the 1790s, the growth at home and in Great Britain of the textile industry turned cotton into a major cash crop throughout the South. Cotton production boomed, leading to an increase in demand for enslaved labor.

Because of their wealth from agriculture, **planters,** or large landowners, became the South's economic and social leaders. However, the planters were few in number. About three out of every four white Southerners was a small farmer who worked a small plot of land and had no enslaved workers.

Southern Slavery In time, slavery became "the peculiar institution" that set the South apart from the rest of the country. Most enslaved people in the South worked on farms and plantations. They labored together from dawn to dusk and were closely supervised. While enslaved men generally worked the fields, enslaved women cooked, cleaned, did laundry, sewed, and cared for the plantation's children.

Still, many enslaved people never saw a farm or plantation. They lived and worked in the South's towns and small cities. Enslaved people also carried out tasks other than farming. Some were coach drivers, household servants, and artisans. Others worked at ironworks or mined gold, coal, or salt.

Wherever they lived, enslaved people formed their own communities. During the evenings, they often shared in song, prayer, and dancing. As one slave recalled, "From sunup to sundown, we belonged to the master; but from sundown to sunup we were our own."

The Rise of Urban Life Most Americans were rural dwellers, but an increasing number of them were living in cities. In the North, cities such as Boston, New York City, and Philadelphia were thriving Atlantic seaports that exported American farm products and imported European manufactured goods. The South had fewer towns and cities than the North. From ports such as New Orleans, Charleston, and Savannah, Southern agricultural goods were shipped to Northern and European markets.

Life in Northern Cities During the early 1800s, America's cities had only a few small industries that made products, such as textiles, shoes, and metal goods. In the North, mills and factories grew and drew in workers from the farms or from overseas. Children also went to work in these industries.

With the rise of industries in the North, the gap between richer and poorer city residents widened. Prosperous merchants and businesspeople controlled urban economic and social life. A middle class of artisans, shopkeepers, and professionals shared modestly in the general prosperity. At the bottom was a growing working class, many of whose members had to struggle to survive. During the early 1800s, rising land values forced the lower classes into increasingly crowded tenements, or rented row houses. Meanwhile, more prosperous urban dwellers stayed in their own detached dwellings in fashionable neighborhoods.

Free African Americans Northern cities attracted many free African Americans during the early 1800s. After the American Revolution, slavery in the North declined. Why did this happen? Farming in the North came to depend on families and paid workers, not enslaved labor. Many northerners came to believe that slavery was **contrary** to the nation's ideals of equality and justice. By 1804 most northern states had passed laws ending slavery.

Still, free African Americans faced many obstacles to full equality. Only a few had voting rights. A small number owned their own homes or businesses. They were excluded from white churches and schools and increasingly from skilled jobs. African Americans responded by building their own churches, schools, newspapers, and charitable and social organizations. They used these institutions to develop their own culture and eventually to demand full freedom and equality.

✓ **Reading Check** **Identify** What group made up the South's political leaders?

Westward Movement

Main Idea An increasing number of Americans chose to move west into new territory.

Reading Connection If you could move somewhere new, where would you go? Would you drive, take a train, or fly to get there? Read to see how Americans in the early Republic realized their dreams on a new frontier.

While the North and South developed different ways of life, Americans in ever larger numbers pushed westward beyond the Appalachian Mountains. They were eager to claim new land and establish farms in the West. They also wanted to escape the growing population and restricting laws and taxes of the East.

How Did the Settlers Travel? Some settlers came to the West by horseback or wagon along difficult overland routes. Others traveled on boats that floated down waterways, such as the Ohio River and the Mississippi River. Upon arrival, settlers had to provide themselves with shelter, food, and clothing. They cut down trees, built log cabins, and cleared the land for farming. As expanding areas of land came under the farmers' plows, forests and wildlife increasingly gave way to human settlement.

What Was Life Like in the West? Living on the frontier was very rigorous. Pioneers wrestled with uncertain climate, limited supplies, and sometimes failing crops. Life could be lonesome. Settlements were far apart and often hard to reach. The few roads that existed were poor, and westerners found it difficult to transport goods and produce to eastern markets.

Despite hardships, pioneers still enjoyed themselves. Weddings, for example, were major events that drew people from the surrounding area. A short ceremony was followed by eating and dancing that lasted for days. The food was usually simple—bread and butter, fried pork, and wild fruits.

The Way It Was

Moving West

Rich soil and cheap land drew many farmers to the Northwest. Between 1800 and 1840, thousands of settlers poured into the region.

Once the pioneers arrived, their survival depended upon the long-handled axe and the rifle. With the axe, the farmer cleared trees from the land and fashioned the wood from those trees into cabins and crude furniture.

▲ Life in the West meant work for every member of a pioneer family.

A good rifle was also essential. It was used for defense from enemies—human and otherwise—and for shooting game for food. Until the 1840s, the weapon most settlers chose was the "Kentucky Rifle."

Conflict in the West As the settlers moved farther and farther west; they came into **conflict** with Native American groups that controlled the vast areas of land beyond the Appalachian Mountains. Native Americans were angry that land-hungry settlers began creating farms on tribal hunting grounds. As the pressures of settler expansion increased, Native Americans developed ways of resistance and survival.

Some Native American groups, like the Cherokee, tried to adjust peacefully to American settler ways. To defend their freedom and prevent further loss of land, the Cherokee adopted written laws and a constitution patterned after those of American states. Many Cherokee accepted Christianity and settled down as farmers, mill owners, and shopkeepers. Cherokee culture continued to flourish with the invention of a Cherokee alphabet by Sequoya in 1821. Sequoya developed symbols to represent all syllables in Cherokee speech. Many Cherokee learned how to read and write. Sequoya even published a Cherokee newspaper and translated parts of the Bible into Cherokee. As Cherokee self-confidence grew, so did the hostility of their settler neighbors.

Meanwhile, other Native American groups were opposed to accepting settler ways. Wanting to preserve their traditional culture, the Shawnee and the Creek prepared for armed resistance. In the end, neither peaceful adaptation nor armed resistance was successful. By 1830, Native Americans faced cultural loss, military defeat, or forced **migration** to lands west of the Mississippi River.

✓ Reading Check **Explain** Why were people eager to move west?

Section 3 Review

Study Central Need help understanding daily life in early America? Visit tajwwl.glencoe.com and click on Study Central.

Reading Summary

Review the (Main Ideas)

• During Jefferson's presidency, Americans developed a sense of pride, or nationalism.

• Literature, music, art, and architecture began to reflect distinctly American themes.

• Daily life in the young Republic was varied, based on regional differences and ethnicity.

• People were eager to take advantage of new land opportunities in the Louisiana Purchase.

What Did You Learn?

1. What was Jefferson's view of the relationship between education and democracy?

2. What institutions set the South apart from the rest of the country?

Critical Thinking

3. **Comparing** Create a table to describe economic activities and regional distinctions that developed in each area during this period.

	Urban	Rural
North		
South		

4. **The Big Ideas** Describe how a distinct American identity and culture grew during this period. Be sure to include references to literature, art, music, and architecture.

5. **Creative Writing** Imagine you can travel back in time. You are a newspaper reporter sent to write a story on either farming life in the South or the Native American experience after the Louisiana Purchase. Choose a topic and then identify people of the time to interview. Make a list of questions you would ask them and responses they might give you.

Analyzing Primary Sources

Looking Westward

The early 1800s was an important time in America. For the first time in modern history, the political power of a country transferred peacefully from one political party to another. It also marked a time of great expansion and change for the United States. The United States looked westward, and also began to look beyond its borders. As you read these primary source selections, think about why this was a time of such rapid growth for the nation.

Meriwether Lewis views the Rocky Mountains. ▶

Reader's Dictionary

maritime (MAR • uh • TYM): bordering on the ocean

garrison (GAR • uh • suhn): fort

pirogue (PEE • ROHG): dugout boat resembling canoes

trodden (TRAH • duhn): stepped

esteem (ihs • TEEM): value

benediction (BEH • nuh • dihk • shuhn): blessing

avarice (A • vuh • ruhs): greed

maxim (MAK • suhm): rule of conduct

California in 1804

Sea captain William Shaler visited the coast of California while engaged in trade with China and recorded his observations.

[The Spanish are] masters of the **maritime** part of the country only. Beyond that range of mountains [the Sierra Madre] the country is remarkably fine, well watered, and covered with forests: these they have not as yet been able to penetrate, on account of their being thickly inhabited by warlike tribes of Indians. I am informed that the government [aims] to establish lines of missions and **garrisons** from San Francisco to New Mexico, and by the country of the Colorado Indians to the same place, and by these means to complete the conquest of the country. But that is a project that does not seem likely to be very soon realized.

—*from Shaler's Journal*

The Explorations of Lewis and Clark

From 1804 to 1806, Meriwether Lewis and William Clark explored and mapped the Louisiana Territory.

Our vessels consisted of six small canoes, and two large [**pirogues**]. This little fleet, altho' not quite so respectable as those of Columbus or Capt. Cook, were still viewed by us with as much pleasure. . . .

We were now about to penetrate a country at least two thousand miles in width, on which the foot of civilized man had never **trodden.** The good or evil it had in store . . . was for experiment yet to determine. . . . [T]he picture which now presented itself to me was a most pleasing one. . . . I could but **esteem** this moment of my departure as among the most happy of my life.

—*from an April 1805 entry in the journal of Meriwether Lewis, as he prepares to leave Fort Mandan on the upper Missouri River*

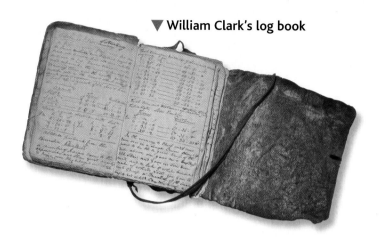

▼ **William Clark's log book**

Adams's Fourth of July Address

O*n July 4, 1821, Secretary of State John Quincy Adams took part in a ceremony held at the Capitol. Adams reads an original copy of the Declaration of Independence. He then gives a speech on American freedom and foreign policy.*

Wherever the standard of freedom and Independence has been or shall be unfurled, there will her [America's] heart, her **benedictions** and her prayers be. But she goes not abroad, in search of monsters to destroy. She is the well-wisher to the freedom and independence of all. . . . [But if the United States involves itself in the affairs of other nations, even those fighting for freedom, the nation would become involved] in all the wars of interest and intrigue, of individual **avarice,** envy, and ambition, which assume the colors and usurp the standard of freedom. The fundamental **maxims** of her policy would insensibly change from *liberty* to *force.* . . . She might become the dictatress [ruler] of the world. She would be no longer the ruler of her own spirit.

Document-Based Questions

California in 1804

1. What area of California do the Spanish control?
2. Does Shaler think it will take a long time for the Spanish to settle California? Why or why not?

The Explorations of Lewis and Clark

3. Is Lewis looking forward to the exploration? How can you tell?
4. At the start of their expedition, how many boats did Lewis and Clark have?

Adams's Fourth of July Address

5. Was Adams calling for a stronger U.S. role in other countries' affairs? Explain.

Read to Write

6. Imagine the land that was soon to be settled by American pioneers. What would people need in the 1800s to settle and develop the land? What tools would be required? What skills? How would settlers deal with Native Americans who were already living there? Write a list of things that early settlers would need to bring with them, as well as recommendations for what to do once they arrived.

Review Content Vocabulary

Define each of the terms below. Use them in a paragraph that discusses government in the early Republic.

1. laissez-faire
2. judicial review

Review the Main Ideas

Section 1 • The Republicans Take Power

3. What was the outcome of the election of 1800?
4. What Federalist measures were ended under Jefferson soon after he took office?

Section 2 • The Louisiana Purchase

5. How far west did U.S. territory extend in 1800?
6. Who sold the Louisiana Territory to the United States? How much did the United States pay for it?
7. How long did Lewis and Clark explore the Louisiana Territory?

Section 3 • Daily Life in Early America

8. What caused the surge of nationalism in the early Republic?
9. What effects did the Second Great Awakening have on American culture?
10. What land-use strategies were practiced by people in the North region?

Critical Thinking

11. **Analyze** Explain the significance of the *Marbury* v. *Madison* decision. Discuss why judicial review is important.
12. **Explore** What was the relationship between the revolt in Santo Domingo and France's interests in North America? How did these events affect U.S. territorial expansion?

13. **Explaining** What was the Federalist response to the Louisiana Purchase? What outcomes resulted from this political disagreement? How do you think this might affect future disagreements in the Republic?

Geography Skills

Study the map and answer the questions that follow.

NATIONAL GEOGRAPHIC **Washington, D.C.**

14. **Location** Along what two state borders is Washington, D.C., located?
15. **Location** What city on the map is located approximately 40 miles northeast of Washington, D.C.?

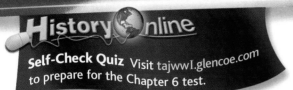

History Online

Self-Check Quiz Visit tajwwI.glencoe.com
to prepare for the Chapter 6 test.

Read to Write

16. **The Big Ideas** **Evaluate** Write an essay highlighting the impact of Jefferson's decision to buy the Louisiana Territory. Be sure to include references to politics, geography, trade, and migration.

17. **Narrative Writing** Imagine you were selected to travel with Lewis and Clark. Use the information in this chapter as well as other sources to write letters to your family to describe what you are seeing.

18. **Using Your** **FOLDABLES** You have been asked to give a speech to a large audience in Washington, D.C. Use the information from your completed chapter opener foldable to write a speech reviewing Jefferson's presidency.

Using Academic Vocabulary

Synonyms are words that have the same or nearly the same meaning. Choose the synonym that best matches each term's precise meaning.

19. **ensure**
   a. open   b. deliver   c. guarantee

20. **unique**
   a. ordinary   b. huge   c. rare

21. **migrate**
   a. travel   b. inhabit   c. distribute

Reviewing Skills

22. **READING SKILL** **Compare and Contrast** Review the descriptions of rural life in Section 3. Write an essay describing how people lived off the land in the North, South, and West. Note similarities and differences among the regions.

23. **ANALYSIS SKILL** **Predict** How would the Louisiana Purchase affect U.S. relationships with Native American cultures? Make three predictions based on what you have learned about their interactions from colonization through 1803.

Standardized Test Practice

Use the map below to answer the following questions.

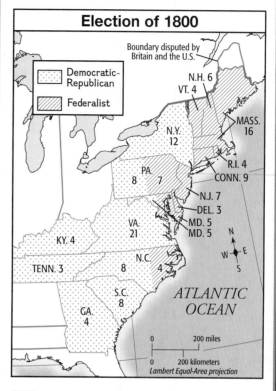

Election of 1800

Boundary disputed by Britain and the U.S.

Democratic-Republican

Federalist

N.H. 6
VT. 4
MASS. 16
N.Y. 12
R.I. 4
CONN. 9
PA. 8   7
N.J. 7
DEL. 3
VA. 21
MD. 5
MD. 5
KY. 4
N.C. 8   4
TENN. 3
S.C. 8
GA. 4

ATLANTIC OCEAN

0   200 miles
0   200 kilometers
Lambert Equal-Area projection

24 Which of the following statements about the election of 1800 is true?

A Federalists won Georgia's electoral votes.

B New Hampshire supported the Democratic-Republican ticket.

C Connecticut had seven electoral votes.

D Pennsylvania was one of the states that split its votes.

25 Which states split their electoral votes between Jefferson and Adams?

A Pennsylvania and Georgia

B Tennessee and New Hampshire

C North Carolina, New York, and Delaware

D Pennsylvania, Maryland, and North Carolina

Chapter 7

Foreign Affairs in the Early Republic

Fort Niagara in New York ▶

OREGON COUNTRY

FLORIDA

Spanish Treaty Line

1810   1820   1830

1812
War with Great Britain begins

1814
The British burn Washington, D.C.

1823
Monroe Doctrine is issued

The Big Ideas

A Time of Conflict

Political ideas and major events shape how people form governments. As the United States expanded its trade around the world, it faced a number of foreign challenges.

The War of 1812

Political ideas and major events shape how people form governments. Although the United States gained no territory from its victory in the War of 1812, American self-confidence increased greatly.

Foreign Relations

Political ideas and major events shape how people form governments. The wave of nationalism in Congress and among the American people influenced the nation's foreign affairs.

View the Chapter 7 video in the Glencoe Video Program.

FOLDABLES™
Study Organizer

Identifying Make this foldable to help you identify and learn key terms.

Step 1 Stack four sheets of paper, one on top of the other. On the top sheet of paper, draw a large circle.

Step 2 With the papers still stacked, cut out all four circles at the same time.

Reading and Writing As you read the chapter, write the Content Vocabulary terms for each section in your foldable. Write a definition for each term. Then turn your foldable over (upside down) and write a short sentence using each term on the other side of the pages.

Step 3 Staple the paper circles together at one point around the edge.

Staple here.

This makes a circular booklet.

Step 4 Label the front circle as shown and take notes on the pages that open to the right.

Chapter 7 Key Terms

Get Ready to Read

Identifying Cause and Effect

READING SKILL

1 Learn It!

Learning to identify causes and effects helps you understand how and why things happen in history. A *cause* is any person, event, or condition that makes something happen. What happens as a result is the *effect*. Use graphic organizers to help you sort and understand causes and effects in your reading. Read the following passage, and see how the information can be sorted.

CAUSE

> The warring nations enforced a new strategy.

> For two years, American shipping continued to prosper. By 1805, however, the warring nations enforced a new strategy. Britain blockaded the French coast and threatened to search all ships trading with France. France later announced that it would search and seize ships caught trading with Britain.
> —*from page 339*

EFFECTS

> Britain blockaded the French coast, threatening to search all ships.

> France announced it will search and seize all ships trading with Britain.

Reading Tip

To help you make sense of what you read, create different types of graphic organizers that suit your own learning style.

2 Practice It!

History is often a chain of causes and effects. The result, or effect, of one event can also be the cause of another effect. Read the passage called "Frontier Conflicts" from Section 1 on page 341. Then use the graphic organizer below, or create your own to show the chain of causes and effects explained in the passage.

CAUSE ☐

↓

EFFECT ☐

CAUSE

↓

EFFECT

CAUSE ☐

↓

EFFECT ☐

CAUSE

↓

EFFECT

☐

Read to Write
Choose a major event from the chapter. Then write a brief paragraph explaining what caused this event.

▼ American merchant ships

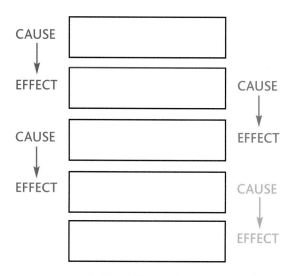

3 Apply It!

Identify causes and effects in the War of 1812 as you read the chapter. Find at least five causes and their effects, and create a graphic organizer to record them.

Section 1

A Time of Conflict

Guide to Reading

Looking Back, Looking Ahead
As the United States began to take a stronger role in world affairs, the new nation faced challenges.

Focusing on the Main Ideas
- In the early 1800s, the livelihoods of many Americans depended on foreign trade, but a war between Great Britain and France threatened U.S. shipping and trade. *(page 339)*
- President James Madison struggled with trade issues with France and Britain, as well as with tensions between Native Americans and white settlers. *(page 341)*

Meeting People
Stephen Decatur (dih•KAY•tuhr)
Tecumseh (tuh•KUHM•suh)
The Prophet
William Henry Harrison
Henry Clay
John Calhoun (kahl•HOON)

Locating Places
Barbary Coast states
Virginia
Ohio

Content Vocabulary
tribute (TRIH•byoot)
neutral rights
impressment
embargo (ihm•BAHR•goh)
War Hawks
nationalism

Academic Vocabulary
resolve
guarantee (GAR•uhn•TEE)
strategy
conclude

Reading Strategy
Classifying Information As you read the section, re-create the diagram below and describe in the box the actions the United States took in each of these situations.

U.S. actions
— Demand for tribute
— Attack on *Chesapeake*
— Tecumseh's confederation

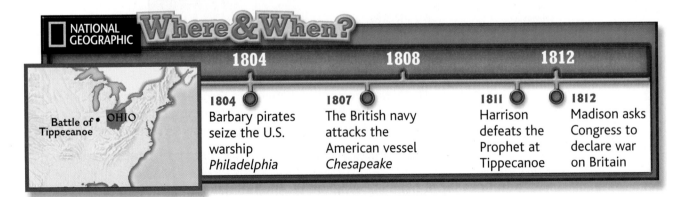

NATIONAL GEOGRAPHIC **Where & When?**

1804   1808   1812

Battle of Tippecanoe • OHIO

1804 Barbary pirates seize the U.S. warship *Philadelphia*

1807 The British navy attacks the American vessel *Chesapeake*

1811 Harrison defeats the Prophet at Tippecanoe

1812 Madison asks Congress to declare war on Britain

Freedom of the Seas

Main Idea In the early 1800s, the livelihoods of many Americans depended on foreign trade, but a war between Great Britain and France threatened U.S. shipping and trade.

Reading Connection Have you ever traveled by boat? If so, describe the experience. Read to learn what sailors on American merchant ships experienced in foreign seas.

An American Story

By the late 1700s, America faced challenges to its growing trade. In an address to Congress, President Thomas Jefferson described a problem with a country that was raiding American ships, as well as his response to that country.

> **66** Tripoli, the least considerable of the Barbary States, had come forward with demands unfounded. . . . The . . . demand admitted but one answer. I sent a small squadron of frigates [warships] into the Mediterranean. **99**
>
> —Thomas Jefferson,
> "First Annual Message to
> Congress, 1801"

Barbary Pirates Sailing in foreign seas was dangerous. In the Mediterranean, for example, ships had to be on guard for pirates from Tripoli and the other **Barbary Coast states** of North Africa. For years these Barbary pirates had raided ships in the area. They demanded **tribute** (TRIH•byoot), or protection money, from European governments to let their ships pass safely.

In 1804 the pirates seized the U.S. warship *Philadelphia* and towed it into Tripoli Harbor. They threw the captain and crew into jail. **Stephen Decatur** (dih•KAY•tuhr), a 25-year-old U.S. Navy captain, took action. Slipping into the heavily guarded harbor with a small raiding party, Decatur burned the captured ship to prevent the pirates from using it. A British admiral

praised the deed as the "most bold and daring act of the age." Negotiations finally ended the conflict with Tripoli in June 1805. Tripoli agreed to stop demanding tribute, but the United States had to pay a ransom of $60,000 for the release of the American prisoners.

Although the United States had resolved the threat from the Barbary pirates, Americans faced other challenges on the seas. U.S. foreign trade depended on being able to sail the seas freely. By the time Jefferson won reelection in 1804, two powerful European nations were already involved in a war that threatened to interfere with American trade.

Neutral Rights Violated When Britain and France went to war in 1803, America enjoyed a profitable trade with both countries. As long as the United States remained neutral during the war, shippers could continue doing business. A nation not involved in a conflict had **neutral rights**—the right to sail the seas and not take sides.

For two years, American shipping continued to prosper. By 1805 however, the warring nations enforced a new strategy. Britain blockaded the French coast and threatened to search all ships trading with France. France later announced that it would search and seize ships caught trading with Britain.

American Sailors Kidnapped The British needed sailors for their naval war against France. Conditions in the British Royal Navy were terrible. British sailors were poorly paid and fed, and badly treated. Many of them deserted, or ran away. Desperately in need of sailors, the British often used force to get them. British naval patrols claimed the right to stop American ships at sea and search for any sailors on board suspected of being deserters from the British navy.

The British would force sailors on these ships to serve in the British navy. This practice was called **impressment.** Although some of those taken were deserters from the British navy, thousands of native-born and naturalized American citizens were also impressed.

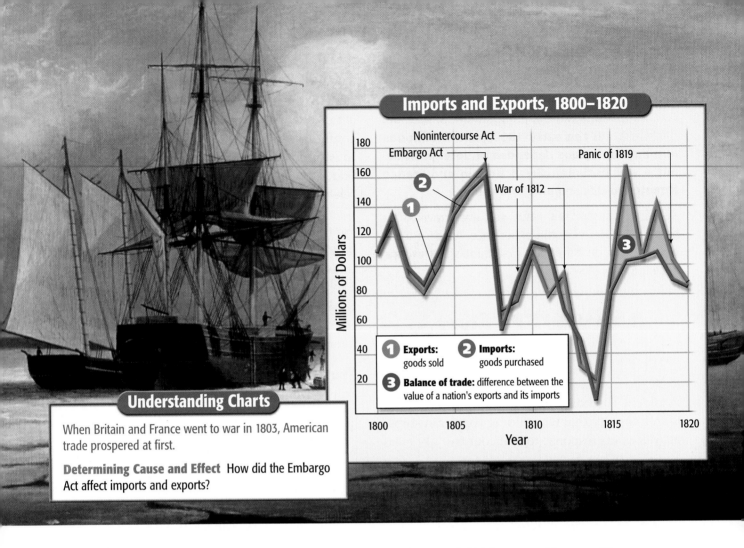

Imports and Exports, 1800–1820

Millions of Dollars / Year

- Nonintercourse Act
- Embargo Act
- War of 1812
- Panic of 1819

1 Exports: goods sold
2 Imports: goods purchased
3 Balance of trade: difference between the value of a nation's exports and its imports

Understanding Charts

When Britain and France went to war in 1803, American trade prospered at first.

Determining Cause and Effect How did the Embargo Act affect imports and exports?

Often the British would wait for American ships outside an American harbor. This happened in June 1807 off the coast of **Virginia.** A British warship, the *Leopard,* intercepted the American vessel *Chesapeake,* and the British demanded to search the ship for British deserters. When the *Chesapeake's* captain refused, the British opened fire, killing 3 and wounding 18.

A Disastrous Trade Ban Britain's practice of impressment and its violation of America's neutral rights led Jefferson to stop some trade with Britain. The attack on the *Chesapeake* triggered even stronger measures. In December 1807, the Republican Congress passed the Embargo Act. An **embargo** (ihm•BAHR•goh) prohibits trade with another country. The embargo banned imports from and exports to all foreign countries.

With the embargo, Jefferson and Madison hoped to hurt Britain but avoid war. They believed the British depended on American agricultural products. As it turned out, the embargo of 1807 was a disaster. The measure wiped out American trade with other nations. Worse, it proved ineffective against Britain. The British simply traded with Latin America for its agricultural goods.

Jefferson Leaves Office Following Washington's precedent, Jefferson made it clear in mid-1808 that he would not be a candidate for a third term. With Jefferson's approval, the Republicans chose James Madison as their candidate for president.

The Federalists again nominated Charles Pinckney and hoped that anger over the embargo would help their party. Pinckney won most of New England, but the Federalist party had little support in other regions. Madison won with 122 electoral votes to Pinckney's 47 votes.

Reading Check Evaluate How effective was the Embargo Act? Would such an act work today?

War Fever

Main Idea President James Madison struggled with trade issues with France and Britain, as well as with tensions between Native Americans and white settlers.

Reading Connection Why does tension between different groups occur? Think about this as you read about the conflicts among the various groups in this section.

James Madison became president during a difficult time. At home and abroad, the nation was involved in the embargo crisis. Meanwhile, Britain continued to claim the right to halt American ships, and cries for war with Britain grew stronger.

Closer to War

In 1810 Congress passed a law permitting direct trade with either France or Britain, depending on which country first lifted its trade restrictions against America. France's leader Napoleon Bonaparte seized the opportunity and promised to end France's trade restrictions.

Unfortunately for Madison, Napoleon had tricked the American administration. The French continued to seize American ships.

Americans were deeply divided. To some it seemed as if the nation was on the verge of war—but it was hard to decide if the enemy should be Britain or France. Madison knew that France had tricked him, but he continued to see Britain as the bigger threat to the United States.

Frontier Conflicts

While Madison was trying to decide how to **resolve** the difficulties with European powers, news arrived about problems in the West. **Ohio** had become a state in 1803. Between 1801 and 1810, white settlers continued to press for more land in the Ohio Valley. Now the settlers were moving onto lands that had been **guaranteed** to Native Americans by treaty.

As tensions increased, some Native Americans began renewing their contacts with British agents and fur traders in Canada. Others pursued a new **strategy**. A powerful Shawnee chief named **Tecumseh** (tuh•KUHM•suh) built a confederacy, or union, among Native American nations in the Northwest. Tecumseh believed that a strong confederacy—with the backing of the British in Canada—could put a halt to white movement onto Native American lands. Many Native Americans were ready to follow Tecumseh.

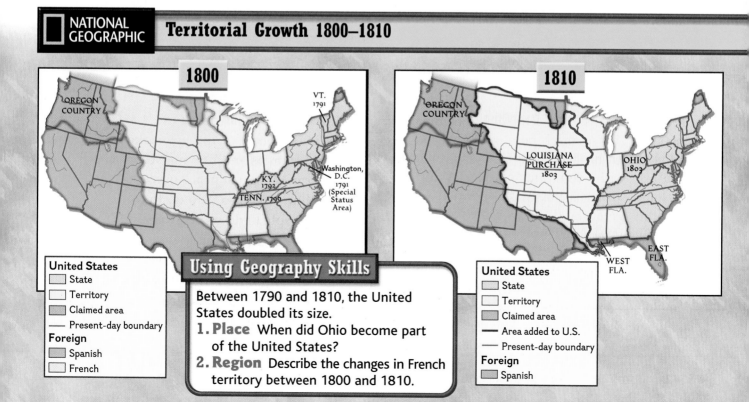

NATIONAL GEOGRAPHIC

Territorial Growth 1800–1810

1800

OREGON COUNTRY

VT. 1791

KY. 1792

TENN. 1796

Washington, D.C. 1791 (Special Status Area)

United States
- State
- Territory
- Claimed area
- — Present-day boundary

Foreign
- Spanish
- French

1810

OREGON COUNTRY

LOUISIANA PURCHASE 1803

OHIO 1803

WEST FLA.

EAST FLA.

United States
- State
- Territory
- Claimed area
- — Area added to U.S.
- — Present-day boundary

Foreign
- Spanish

Using Geography Skills

Between 1790 and 1810, the United States doubled its size.
1. **Place** When did Ohio become part of the United States?
2. **Region** Describe the changes in French territory between 1800 and 1810.

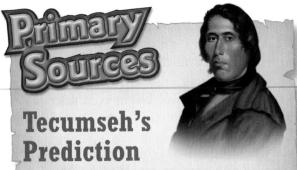

Primary Sources

Tecumseh's Prediction

When William Henry Harrison was serving as governor of Indiana, he told Tecumseh that only the president had the authority to return disputed lands to the Native Americans. Tecumseh replied:

"As the great chief [President Madison] is to determine the matter, . . . I hope the Great Spirit will put sense enough into his head to induce [make] him to direct you to give up this land. It is true he is so far off he will not be injured by the war . . . while you and I will have to fight it out."

—quoted in *The Old Northwest: A Chronicle of the Ohio Valley and Beyond*

Tecumseh's prediction came true.

 **Document-Based Question**

Do Tecumseh's words show respect for President Madison? For Harrison? Explain.

Tecumseh and the Prophet A commanding speaker, Tecumseh possessed great political skills. In his view, the U.S. government's treaties with separate Native American nations were worthless. "The Great Spirit gave this great [land] to his red children," he said. Tecumseh felt no one nation had the right to give it away.

Tecumseh had a powerful ally—his brother, Tenskwatawa, known as **the Prophet.** The Prophet urged Native Americans everywhere to return to the customs of their ancestors. They should, he said, give up practices learned from the white invaders—wearing western dress, using plows and firearms, and especially drinking alcohol. The Prophet attracted a huge following among Native Americans. He founded a village at a site in northern Indiana, near present-day Lafayette, where the Tippecanoe and Wabash Rivers meet. It was called Prophetstown.

A Meeting With Harrison The American governor of the Indiana Territory, General **William Henry Harrison,** became alarmed by the growing power of the two Shawnee brothers. He feared they would form an alliance with the British.

In a letter to Tecumseh, Harrison warned that the United States had many more warriors than all the Indian nations could put together.

❝ Do not think that the redcoats can protect you, they are not able to protect themselves. ❞

—*Messages and Letters of William Henry Harrison*

Tecumseh sent word that he would reply in person.

A few weeks later, Tecumseh came to Harrison and spoke to the white people assembled there:

❝ Brother, . . . Since the peace was made, you have killed some Shawnees, Delawares and Winnebagoes . . . You have taken land from us and I do not see how we can remain at peace if you continue to do so. You try to force red people to do some injury. It is you that are pushing them on to some mischief. You endeavor to make distinctions. You try to prevent the Indians from doing as they wish—to unite. ❞

—from *Tecumseh, an Indian Moses*

The Battle of Tippecanoe In 1811 while Tecumseh was in the South trying to expand his confederacy, Harrison decided to attack Prophetstown on the Tippecanoe River. After more than two hours of battle, the Prophet's forces fled the area in defeat. The Battle of Tippecanoe was proclaimed a glorious victory for the Americans. Harrison acquired the nickname "Tippecanoe" and his supporters used it as a patriotic rallying cry when he ran for president in 1840.

The Battle of Tippecanoe left about one fourth of Harrison's troops dead or wounded, but the impact on the Native Americans was far greater. Prophetstown was destroyed. The clash also shattered Native American confidence in the Prophet's leadership. Many, including Tecumseh, fled to Canada.

Tecumseh's flight to British-held Canada seemed to prove that the British were supporting and arming the Native Americans. To Harrison and to many white people who settled in the West, there seemed only one way to make the region secure from attack—to drive the British out of Canada and take over the province.

Who Were the War Hawks? Back in the nation's capital, President Madison faced demands for a more aggressive policy toward the British. The most insistent voices came from a group of young Republicans elected to Congress in 1810. Known as the **War Hawks,** they came from the South and the West. The War Hawks pressured the president to declare war against Britain.

Primary Sources

Blue Jacket ▶

Treaties with Native Americans

Many treaties between Native Americans and the U.S. government were signed during the early years of the new nation. These agreements included treaties with the Creeks (1790 and 1814); the Cherokee (1791 and 1794); the Oneida, Tuscarora, and Stockbridge (1794); and the Chickasaw (1805, 1816, and 1818).

Some treaties, like the Treaty of Greenville (1795), were signed to end conflicts. Other treaties ceded Indian land to the United States. White leaders and Indian leaders rarely trusted one another. Shawnee leader Blue Jacket is quoted as saying:

"From all quarters, we receive speeches from the Americans, and not one is alike. We suppose that they intend to deceive us."

—*American State Papers, Indian Affairs*

The treaties often proved impossible to enforce. Often, white settlers and soldiers crossed into territory and took land that was reserved for Native Americans. Some Native American chiefs were forced to sign a treaty under threat of military force, but they had no intention of abiding by the terms of the treaty. Some chiefs signed only to obtain badly needed items such as food, ammunition, and clothing. In addition, even if a Native American chief signed a treaty, that did not mean that the action was binding on anyone else in the tribe. Other members of the tribe could choose to ignore it.

 **Document-Based Question**

How would you describe Blue Jacket's view of the white leaders?

Biography

HENRY CLAY
1777–1852

JOHN C. CALHOUN
1782–1850

▲ Henry Clay

During their early years in Congress, Henry Clay and John C. Calhoun often joined in support of the young federal government. They were known as War Hawks because of the position they took on the War of 1812. Each argued in stirring speeches the need for a strong army and navy and for the establishment of a national bank.

Both Clay and Calhoun had long, distinguished careers in government. The careers of these two men reflected the conflict between nationalism and sectionalism in the early 1800s.

Born in Virginia, Clay moved to Kentucky, a state that kept him in Congress—and in the center of the political scene—for nearly 50 years. Clay was known as the Great Compromiser for his role in working out various agreements between leaders of the North and South. He served as a Kentucky state legislator, speaker of the U.S. House of Representatives, U.S. senator, and secretary of state.

Clay was a consistent champion of nationalism and devoted his career to strengthening the Union. Although nominated for president three times, the popularity of his opponents and weakness of his political party, the Whigs, kept him from achieving his lifelong goal of winning the presidency.

Calhoun represented South Carolina. He was an influential member of Congress and, at least for a time, a close friend of Henry Clay. Calhoun supported states' rights and the interests of the South. Fearing that the North intended to dominate the South, Calhoun spent the rest of his career trying to prevent the federal government from weakening states' rights and from interfering with the Southern way of life.

◀ John C. Calhoun

Then and Now

What political leaders represent the region in which you live? Do you think leaders should represent the views of the citizens who elected them?

The Push for War The War Hawks wanted revenge for British actions against Americans, and they were also eager to expand the nation's power. Their **nationalism,** or loyalty to their country, appealed to a renewed sense of American patriotism.

The leading War Hawks were **Henry Clay** from Kentucky and **John Calhoun** (kahl•HOON) from South Carolina, both in their 30s. Hunger for land heightened war fever. Westerners wanted to move north into the fertile forests of southern Canada. A war with Britain might make Canadian land available. Southerners wanted Spanish Florida.

The War Hawks urged major military spending. Through their efforts Congress quadrupled the army's size. The Federalists in the Northeast, however, remained strongly opposed to the war.

Declaring War By the spring of 1812, Madison **concluded** that war with Britain was inevitable. In a message to Congress in early June of 1812,

Madison asked for a declaration of war. His message emphasized national honor and the abuses suffered at the hands of the British.

> 66 [T]housands of American citizens . . . have been torn from their country and from everything dear to them [and] have been dragged on board ships of war of a foreign nation. 99
>
> —from Madison's "War Message to Congress"

In the meantime, the British had decided to end their policy of search and seizure of American ships. Unfortunately, because of the amount of time it took for news to travel across the Atlantic, this change in policy was not known in Washington. Word of the breakthrough arrived too late. Once set in motion, the war machine could not be stopped.

✓ **Reading Check** **Explain** Why did the War Hawks call for war with Britain?

History Online

Study Central Need help understanding U.S. foreign conflicts in the early 1800s? Visit tajww1.glencoe.com and click on Study Central.

Section 1 Review

Reading Summary

Review the Main Ideas

- In the early 1800s, American merchant ships were threatened by pirates and the British navy. Great Britain's violation of America's neutral rights led to the passage of the Embargo Act, which greatly hurt American trade.

- The War Hawks in Congress pressured President Madison to go to war as conflicts with Native Americans in the West arose and the conflict with Britain at sea continued.

What Did You Learn?

1. Describe the negotiations that ended the conflict between the United States and Tripoli.

2. Who were the leading War Hawks?

Critical Thinking

3. **Sequencing Information** Re-create the time line below and list key events in the nation's effort to remain neutral in the war between France and Britain.

```
                June     Dec.
   1805        1807     1807     1810
    |———————————|————————|————————|
```

4. **The Big Ideas** How did the conflict in Europe help the American shipping industry prosper?

5. **Analyze** How did frontier battles with Native Americans intensify Americans' anti-British feelings?

6. **READING** **Determining Cause and Effect** Write a short essay that identifies causes and effects in foreign affairs and the road to war during this period.

America's Literature

Crossing the Panther's Path

By Elizabeth Alder

Before You Read

The Scene: This part of the book is set at Grouseland, Governor Harrison's home in Vincennes, Indiana.

The Characters: Tecumseh is a leader of the Shawnee. His translator is Billy Caldwell, a teenager whose parents are Native American and white. William Henry Harrison is governor of the Indiana Territory. Shabonee is Native American and a follower of Tecumseh.

The Plot: Billy wants to help Native Americans regain the Ohio River valley. He believes Tecumseh can unite the tribes and accomplish this goal. In this part of the story, Tecumseh meets with Harrison. He wants to try to change Harrison's plans to help whites take over more Native American lands.

Vocabulary Preview

adversary: person who supports a different side of an opinion or disagreement; enemy

disdain: a feeling that someone or something is below one's notice; contempt

dismay: confusion about how to deal with a situation

emphatically: in a forceful way

haughty: blatantly proud and scornful

wrath: great anger that is caused by something unjust

Have you ever wanted someone to listen to your side of a disagreement? In this excerpt, Tecumseh explains Native American views about the ownership of land. In return, Tecumseh learns firsthand what Harrison thinks of Native Americans.

◀ **William Henry Harrison**

346

As You Read

Sometimes many people witness an event. Some of them record what they saw and heard. In such cases, the authors of historical novels may use that information in their stories. At other times, there are few or no records of what happened. Then authors imagine what people said and did. As you read, think about how the author may have used facts and imagination in this story.

Tecumseh halted a stone's throw from the porch steps, pausing in a small grove of trees. William Henry Harrison came out and waited for Tecumseh. It was clear that he wanted the Shawnee to come to him. But Tecumseh was satisfied where he was. Harrison paced. Finally, he sent an emissary[1] to invite the Indian forward.

"I do not care to talk with a roof above us," Tecumseh answered the man. "Tell your chief I prefer the council to be held here where I stand."

When he received the message, Harrison uncrossed his arms and angrily pointed his finger in his emissary's face. Then he pointed to Tecumseh emphatically. It was clear that the governor of the Indiana Territory was not pleased. Other advisers intervened,[2] perhaps suggesting a conciliatory[3] approach, and finally Harrison instructed men to carry out a table and chairs from the porch and set them at the edge of the grove.

Harrison strode forward then, followed by his advisers. The armed guard was close behind. Flipping his coattails out behind him, Harrison sat in one of the chairs provided. Tecumseh remained standing but signaled for his men to be seated in a semicircle behind him.

"Listen to me well," Tecumseh explained in English. His voice carried to the edge of the crowd that had gathered. He stood tall, his shoulders squared. A pair of eagle feathers adorned his hair and bands of silver encircled his wrists. It was a hot day, and his light brown skin glistened with sweat.

"I am a Shawnee. My forefathers were warriors. Their son is a warrior."

He spoke in measured[4] tones. He would not rush through what he had come to say.

"From them I take my only existence. From my tribe I take nothing. I have made myself what I am. And I would that I could make the red people as great as the conceptions of my own mind, when I think of the Great Spirit[5] that rules over us all," he said, shaking his head slowly. "I would not then come to Governor Harrison to ask him to tear up the treaty. But I would say to him, 'Brother, you have the liberty to return to your own country.'"

Harrison bristled[6] when Tecumseh addressed him as "Brother."

---

[1] **emissary:** agent, representative
[2] **intervened:** came between as a way of changing something
[3] **conciliatory:** way of gaining goodwill or calm
[4] **measured:** slow, unhurried, and careful
[5] **Great Spirit:** God
[6] **bristled:** swelled up and took on an angry appearance

Tecumseh ▶

Tecumseh paced across the open ground, sometimes facing Harrison, sometimes facing his own men. "You wish," he said in a richly modulated[7] voice, "to prevent the Indians from doing as we wish, to unite and let them consider their lands as the common property of the whole. You take the tribes aside and advise them not to come into this measure. You want by your distinctions of tribes, in allotting to each a particular tract of land, to make them war with each other. You never see an Indian endeavor to make the white people do this. You are continually driving the red people; at last you will drive them into the Great Lake,[8] where they can neither stand nor walk."

The governor's long face had reddened. He clasped the arms of his chair. Close by, his soldiers stood at attention, ready and menacing.

"Since my residence at Tippecanoe," Tecumseh continued, "we have endeavored to level all distinctions, to remove village chiefs, by whom all mischiefs are done. It is they who sell the land to the Americans.

"Brother," Tecumseh said accusingly, "these lands that were sold, and the goods that were given for them, were done by only a few. In the future, we are prepared to punish those who propose to sell land to the Americans. If you continue to purchase from them, it will make war among the different tribes, and I do not know what will be the consequences among the white people. Brother, I wish you would take pity on the red people and do as I have requested. If you will not give up the land and do cross the boundary of our present settlement, it will be very hard, and produce great trouble between us."

Tecumseh listed all the grievances the Indians held against the Americans. He protested the many treaties gained by guile[9] and the use of alcohol. He spoke of treaties broken by settlers and soldiers alike and of outrageous massacres against peaceful Indians. He spoke of Chief Cornstalk and the betrayal that had embittered[10] Indians throughout the Ohio Valley.

"The way," he said, nearly overcome with emotion, "the only way, to stop this evil is for the red men to unite in claiming a common and equal right in the land, as it was at first, and should be now—for it was never divided but belongs to all. No tribe has the right to sell, even to each other, much less to strangers."

Here Tecumseh chuckled bitterly, for the notion was preposterous to him. "Sell a country! Why not sell the air, the great sea, as well as the earth? Did not the Great Spirit make them all for the use of his children?"

The Americans murmured among themselves. Many were impressed by his eloquence.

"Everything I have told you is the truth," Tecumseh said. "The Great Spirit has inspired me.

---

[7] **modulated:** varied speed and loudness
[8] **Great Lake:** Lake Michigan
[9] **guile:** deceit; trickery
[10] **embittered:** badly disappointed

"Brother, I hope you will confess that you ought not to have listened to those bad birds who bring you ill news," he admonished,[11] referring to the spies Harrison had sent to Tippecanoe.

Satisfied then that he had said what he had come to say, he concluded with the words many Indian statesmen used to close their arguments: "I have spoken."

He sat down between Billy and Shabonee.

Harrison unfolded his long legs and rose to his full height. His father had been one of the signers of the Declaration of Independence, and the son's demeanor[12] was haughty. Blue steel flashed from his eyes. "It is ridiculous," he began contemptuously,[13] "for you to declare that the Indians are all one people. Why then do you speak in different tongues? The land along the Wabash[14] belongs to the Miami tribe. They decided to sell it, and they have been well paid. Tecumseh, you and your Shawnee have no business on that land—"

Before Harrison could finish, Tecumseh sprang to his feet shouting, *"You are a liar! Everything you have said is false! The Indians have been cheated and imposed upon by you and the Seventeen Fires.[15] Nothing you have said—before, or now at this council—can be trusted. You lie and you cheat!"*

In his wrath, Tecumseh had spoken in the Shawnee language. Billy froze with horror. He felt the blood drain from his face. He had, after all, been introduced as the translator should the need arise, and in the first rush of Tecumseh's words, Harrison had glanced toward him, silently demanding an answer. Did he dare translate this into English—before the governor of the territory, before his armed soldiers? A second wave of dismay washed over him as he saw Harrison turn back to Tecumseh. The American had stiffened, his nostrils flared, and Billy saw that there was no need for a translator. It was clear to everyone present what Tecumseh thought of his adversary.

One of the officers shouted, "Bring up the guard!"

Shabonee and the other chiefs leaped to their feet and drew their weapons. They encircled Tecumseh, shielding him with their bodies. As Harrison drew his sword from its scabbard,[16] Tecumseh shouted orders to his men hidden in the woods. They burst forward, many with their knives and tomahawks in their hands. Others were already taking up positions at the edge of the trees, aiming their rifles.

American soldiers were raising their rifles, too. Billy's heart hammered in his chest. His breathing was ragged—swift and shallow. He watched the two leaders glare at each other. It would take only the order "Fire!" on the American side, or for Tecumseh to shout the war cry, for Grouseland's lawn to explode in a violent bloodletting. Tecumseh had not come for this. He had come to speak to this man, to change his heart as he had so many others. He had not expected to be treated with such disdain. It was true, Billy imagined, that Tecumseh hated Harrison and all that he represented. But he had not come here today to make war.

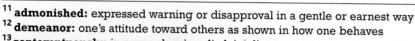

[11] **admonished:** expressed warning or disapproval in a gentle or earnest way
[12] **demeanor:** one's attitude toward others as shown in how one behaves
[13] **contemptuously:** in a way showing disdain, disrespect, or scorn
[14] **Wabash:** river that begins in western Ohio and flows west across Indiana
[15] **Seventeen Fires:** the United States
[16] **scabbard:** a case in which to carry a knife, sword, or bayonet

Billy felt certain that Harrison also regretted what had happened. A council must never be allowed to degenerate[17] into a skirmish. It would be a terrible blot on his career.

With a few curt words, Harrison asked Tecumseh to leave. "We shall speak tomorrow when our tempers have cooled," he said.

That evening, in the camp the Indians had made on the far side of the river, Tecumseh drew his inner circle together. "I should not have allowed my anger to drive me to speak as I did," he admitted. "The time for war has not yet come."

Billy slept little that night. He tossed and turned restlessly in his blanket. During the lonely hours of the night, he heard an owl call, and now and then the splash of a fish in the river. He had come to this council only because Tecumseh wouldn't listen to his protests. The youth had suspected from the beginning that Harrison would scoff at their entreaties[18] and speak to them with contempt. Billy was now very certain that the American would be satisfied with nothing less than driving the Indians from their land. There would be no compromises. War would come.

"Shabonee...are you awake?" Billy whispered to the gigantic figure stretched out next to him.

Light from the dying fire glinted in Shabonee's eyes as he woke. "Mmmm," he answered.

"Will Tecumseh go to war soon?"

Shabonee moaned. He raised himself up and leaned on one elbow. "What?"

Billy repeated his question.

Shabonee rubbed his eyes. "He will pick up the tomahawk when he is ready."

"Do you think he'll include me among his men?" Billy asked.

"I think he likes you. You stood like a straight tree before the Long Knives today."

Billy chuckled. He had told Shabonee his Mohawk name. "Inside, I was quivering like the leaves of the cottonwood tree," he admitted. "There were so many rifles pointed at us." He rolled over on his back and stared up at the stars. "I *do* want to be a warrior for my people."

"Which people?" Shabonee asked. He knew the British wanted the fur trade.

"The Indians."

"Stay among us, then," Shabonee said in way of invitation, "and learn our ways."

Billy nodded thoughtfully. It was true. He still had so much to learn. Eight moons ago, when he had argued with his father, he had thought himself very wise. Since then, he had slowly come to know how little wisdom he truly possessed.

The next afternoon, Tecumseh met with Harrison again. Billy was not surprised to see that the American soldiers were heavily armed and tense, their numbers doubled. This time Tecumseh went forward alone with only Billy to help interpret. He had said he was sometimes unsure of his English, and there must be no misunderstanding today.

The Shawnee leader was most anxious to speak of the borders between his people and the Americans.

"This new boundary you have drawn will cause trouble between our peoples," Tecumseh said as soon as Billy concluded translating the formal opening statements. "The old line must remain," he insisted.

Billy had heard the talk in Detroit. He had read the newspaper articles. He knew that Harrison was determined to enlarge American territory by crossing into Indian lands. Now it became clear from the governor's speech that as long as the Americans felt themselves to be numerically superior and better armed, they would not hesitate to take what they wanted.

"The tribes will lose their annuities if they follow you," Harrison threatened.

Tecumseh scowled as Billy finished translating it into Shawnee. He asked that the term *annuities* be explained further. These were gifts of goods or money, Billy explained.

---

[17] **degenerate:** break or sink down   [18] **entreaties:** requests

Part of the annuities were paid in the form of alcohol. "It disgusts me to see the Americans use their cheap tricks against the Indian nations," Tecumseh said when Billy finished. "You have no right to ply[19] the chiefs with whiskey until they are befuddled. It is forbidden by the Greenville Treaty. You must blame yourself as the cause of trouble between us and the tribes who sold the land to you." Tecumseh argued fiercely, "I want the present boundary line to continue. Should you cross it, I assure you it will be productive of bad consequences."

Tecumseh nodded for Billy to begin translating his words, while he watched Harrison's face to read any signs that might cross his features. He was answered only by Harrison's stony expression. Billy ended the talks as Tecumseh instructed him. "Governor Harrison," he said, "Chief Tecumseh desires that this disagreement be placed before the Great Chief of the Long Knives."

Harrison coolly agreed. "Yes, I will send word of your position to President Madison; however, I can assure you that the President will protect with the sword what he considers fairly bought."

"I do not wish to make war upon the United States," Tecumseh said emphatically. "I wish only that illegal purchases of Indian lands cease. Your stance forces us to ally ourselves with the British. Tell your President what is in my heart that he may know my intentions."

"I will tell the President what you have said," Harrison answered. "But I say there is not the least probability that he will accede[20] to your terms."

"As your Great Chief is to determine the matter, I hope the Great Spirit will put enough sense in his head to induce him to direct you to give up this land."

Tecumseh put his hand on the stone head of the tomahawk that jutted from his belt. The muscles in his jaw tightened. He seemed resigned to the knowledge that none of his arguments would turn the hearts of the Americans. He looked to the east. He knew that the American President lived many days' travel toward the rising sun. He had heard that Madison was a small man, undistinguished as a public speaker, who had never commanded soldiers in a battle. This seemed puzzling, for it was strength and eloquence and prowess[21] in combat that marked a man for greatness among the Indian nations.

---

[19] **ply:** to keep supplying something to
[20] **accede:** to give in to a request
[21] **prowess:** skill and courage

Responding to the Literature

1. What did Tecumseh compare selling land to? Why?

2. What kept a war from starting at this meeting?

3. **Analyze** In the first three paragraphs, how do Tecumseh and Harrison each try to show that he is more powerful?

4. **Explain** What are the literal and figurative meanings of this phrase: "The President will protect with the sword what he considers fairly bought"?

5. **Read to Write** Compare the information on pages 341–342 with this selection. How did the author use both fact and imagination to write this story? Include examples to support your conclusions. List other people or events in the story that you could verify as being real or imaginary.

Reading On Your Own...

Do you want to learn more about George Washington, Sacajawea, and the early years of the United States? You might be interested in the following books.

Biography

Founding Father: Rediscovering George Washington by Richard Brookhiser explores Washington as a person, a soldier, and a political leader. He explains why Washington was so important in forming the future of the United States.

Nonfiction

Old Ironsides: Americans Build a Fighting Ship by David Weitzman invites readers to see how this great warship was built. As readers follow John Aylwin, a young worker on the ship, they learn what it took to make "Old Ironsides."

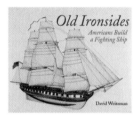

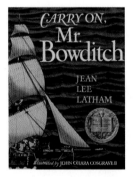

Historical Fiction

Carry On, Mr. Bowditch by Jean L. Latham tells the amazing tale of Nathaniel Bowditch. Although he had very little education, he mastered sea navigation during his voyages around the world. His book *American Practical Navigator* was used with few changes into the 1900s.

Historical Fiction

Sacajawea: The Story of Bird Woman and the Lewis and Clark Expedition by Joseph Bruchac has Sacajawea and Clark taking turns describing events. The story also includes parts of the explorers' journals and Shoshone tales.

The War of 1812

Guide to Reading

Looking Back, Looking Ahead

Beginning in 1812, the United States went to war with Britain. Fighting took place in the United States, in Canada, and at sea.

Focusing on the Main Ideas

• In 1812 the United States was at war with Britain and was unprepared from the onset. *(page 354)*

• Even though the last battle of the war, the Battle of New Orleans, took place two weeks after the war had officially ended, the American victory there instilled a strong sense of national pride. *(page 356)*

Locating Places

Detroit
Lake Erie

Meeting People

William Hull
Oliver Hazard Perry
Andrew Jackson
Francis Scott Key

Content Vocabulary

frigate (FRIH • guht)
privateer (PRY • vuh • TIHR)

Academic Vocabulary

consist (kuhn • SIHST)
assemble (uh • SEHM • buhl)
economy (ih • KAH • nuh • mee)

Reading Strategy

Taking Notes As you read this section, re-create the diagram below and describe each battle's outcome.

Battle	Outcome
Lake Erie	
Washington, D.C.	
New Orleans	

NATIONAL GEOGRAPHIC Where & When?

1812

June 1812 United States declares war on Britain

1813

Sep. 1813 Perry defeats the British navy on Lake Erie

1814

Aug. 1814 The British burn Washington, D.C.

1815

Jan. 1815 American forces win the Battle of New Orleans

Lake Erie • Baltimore • Washington, D.C. • New Orleans

War Begins

Main Idea In 1812 the United States was at war with Britain and was unprepared from the onset.

Reading Connection Have you ever been unprepared for a quiz or test? Read to learn what happened when the United States was unprepared in the beginning of the War of 1812.

At the beginning of the war, the U.S. army **consisted** of fewer than 7,000 troops. The states had between 50,000 and 100,000 militia, but the units were poorly trained. Additionally, many states opposed "Mr. Madison's war." The Americans also underestimated the strength of the British and their Native American allies.

Fighting began in July 1812, when General **William Hull** led the American army from **Detroit** into Canada. Hull was met by Tecumseh and his warriors. Fearing a massacre by the Native Americans, Hull surrendered Detroit to a small British force in August.

Another attempt by General William Henry Harrison was unsuccessful as well. Harrison realized that British control of Lake Erie prevented an American victory.

Naval Battles **Oliver Hazard Perry**, commander of the **Lake Erie** naval forces, had his orders. He was to **assemble** a fleet and seize the lake from the British. From his headquarters in Put-in-Bay, Ohio, Perry could watch the movements of the enemy ships. The showdown came on September 10, 1813, when the British ships sailed out to face the Americans. In the bloody battle that followed, Perry and his ships defeated the British naval force. After the battle, Perry sent General William Henry Harrison the message, "We have met the enemy and they are ours."

With Lake Erie in American hands, the British and their Native American allies tried to pull back from the Detroit area. Harrison and his troops cut them off. In the fierce Battle of the Thames on October 5, the great leader Tecumseh was killed.

Analyzing Political Cartoons

The cartoon shows Brother Jonathan forcing John Bull to drink a tankard of American medicine. Brother Jonathan was used to represent Americans in many cartoons, beginning with the American Revolution. *Why is the name "Perry" on the tankard?*

Ⓐ John Bull represents Britain.   Ⓑ Brother Jonathan represents the United States.

The Americans also attacked the town of York (present-day Toronto, Canada), burning the parliament buildings. Canada remained unconquered, but by the end of 1813 the Americans had won some victories on land and at sea.

Republicans had reduced the size of the navy to help lower the national debt. However, the navy still boasted three of the fastest **frigates** (FRIH•guhts), or warships, afloat. Americans exulted when the *Constitution,* one of these frigates, destroyed two British vessels—the *Guerrière* in August 1812 and the *Java* four months later. After seeing a shot bounce off the *Constitution's* hull during battle, a sailor nicknamed the ship "Old Ironsides."

American **privateers** (PRY•vuh•TIHRZ), armed private ships, also staged spectacular attacks on British ships and captured numerous vessels. These victories were important for American morale.

Setback for Native Americans In March 1814, a lanky Tennessee planter named **Andrew Jackson** led an attack against the Creeks in present-day Alabama. Jackson's forces slaughtered more than 550 of the Creek people. Known as the Battle of Horseshoe Bend, the defeat broke the Creeks' resistance and forced them to give up most of their lands to the United States.

✓ **Reading Check** **Evaluate** Do you think the United States was prepared to wage war? Explain.

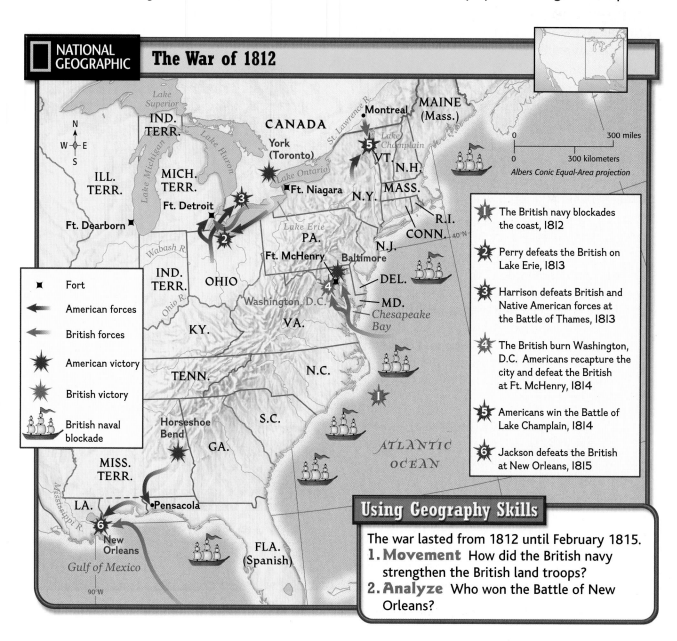

NATIONAL GEOGRAPHIC — The War of 1812

Legend:

- ✖ Fort
- ← American forces
- ← British forces
- ✦ American victory
- ✦ British victory
- 🛥 British naval blockade

1 The British navy blockades the coast, 1812

2 Perry defeats the British on Lake Erie, 1813

3 Harrison defeats British and Native American forces at the Battle of Thames, 1813

4 The British burn Washington, D.C. Americans recapture the city and defeat the British at Ft. McHenry, 1814

5 Americans win the Battle of Lake Champlain, 1814

6 Jackson defeats the British at New Orleans, 1815

0 — 300 miles
0 — 300 kilometers
Albers Conic Equal-Area projection

Using Geography Skills

The war lasted from 1812 until February 1815.
1. **Movement** How did the British navy strengthen the British land troops?
2. **Analyze** Who won the Battle of New Orleans?

The British Offensive

(Main Idea) **Even though the last battle of the war, the Battle of New Orleans, took place two weeks after the war had officially ended, the American victory there instilled a strong sense of national pride.**

Reading Connection When was the last time you were moved by patriotic feelings? What did you feel? Read to learn how the national anthem was inspired by the War of 1812.

British fortunes improved in the spring of 1814. They had been fighting a war with Napoleon and had won. With the war against France over, the British were able to send much of their navy and many more troops to deal with the United States.

Attack on Washington, D.C. In August 1814, the British sailed into Chesapeake Bay. Their destination was Washington, D.C. On the outskirts of Washington, D.C., the British troops quickly overpowered the American militia and then marched into the city. "They proceeded, without a moment's delay, to burn and destroy everything in the most distant degree connected with government," reported a British officer.

The Capitol and the president's mansion were among the buildings burned. Watching from outside the city, President Madison, his wife Dolley Madison, and the cabinet saw the night sky turn orange. Fortunately, a violent thunderstorm put out the fires before they could do more damage. August 24, 1814, was a low point for the Americans.

Primary Sources

"The Star-Spangled Banner"

On the night of September 13, 1814, Francis Scott Key, a young Maryland lawyer, watched from Baltimore Harbor as the British bombarded Fort McHenry. The shelling continued into the morning hours. A huge American flag waved over the fort. As the sun rose, Key strained to see if the flag still waved. To his great joy, it did. He took a letter from his pocket and began scribbling these words for a poem on the back:

"O! say can you see by the dawn's
early light,
What so proudly we hail'd at the
twilight's last gleaming;
Whose broad stripes and bright stars,
through the perilous fight,
O'er the ramparts we watch'd
were so gallantly streaming;

▲ The first Star-Spangled Banner, 1779–1818

And the rocket's red glare, the bombs
bursting in air,
Gave proof through the night that our
flag was still there;
O! say does that star spangled banner
yet wave,
O'er the land of the free, and the home
of the brave."

 Document-Based Question

Why was it important to Key that the flag still waved over the fort?

Biography

DOLLEY MADISON
1768–1849

Born in North Carolina, Dolley Payne grew up in Virginia under the strict influence of her Quaker family and neighborhood. While still heeding the requirements of the Quaker lifestyle, Dolley's jubilant and warm personality greeted everyone she met. At age 15, her family moved to Philadelphia, and there she married John Todd, Jr. As Dolley Todd, she gave birth to two children. Later, Dolley lost her husband and one child during a yellow fever epidemic in 1793.

The following year she married James Madison. While her husband was secretary of state, Dolley Madison served as unofficial first lady for the widower president, Thomas Jefferson. She became the nation's official first lady when James Madison was elected president in 1808.

Dolley's tenure as first lady was punctuated by social gatherings and Wednesday evening "drawing rooms" attended by the time's most important citizens and politicians. Her character made even the most ill-at-ease feel at home in the White House, and her insight into political matters was well regarded and well used by her husband.

During the War of 1812 she showed remarkable bravery. In 1814 as the British approached the capital, she refused to leave the executive mansion until she had packed up many valuable government documents, a painting of George Washington, and other priceless valuables.

> *"I must leave [the White House] or the retreating army will make me a prisoner in it, by filling up the road I am directed to take. When I shall again write you, or where I shall be tomorrow, I cannot tell!!"*
> **—Dolley Madison,**
> **letter to her sister Anna Cutts,**
> **August 23, 1814**

Then and Now

Compare Dolley Madison to the present first lady. How are they similar? How are they different?

357

Battle of North Point **by Don Troiani** At North Point, Americans soldiers battled British forces advancing on Baltimore. The clash slowed the British advance, giving the Americans time to reinforce their defenses around the city. *What happened when the British tried to enter Baltimore?*

Baltimore Holds Firm Much to everyone's surprise, the British did not try to hold Washington. They left the city and sailed north to Baltimore. Baltimore, however, was ready and waiting—with barricaded roads, a blocked harbor, and some 13,000 militiamen. The British attacked in mid-September. They were kept from entering the town by a determined defense and ferocious bombardment from Fort McHenry in the harbor.

During the night of September 13–14, a young attorney named **Francis Scott Key** watched as the bombs burst over Fort McHenry. Finally, "by the dawn's early light," Key was able to see that the American flag still flew over the fort. Deeply moved by patriotic feeling, Key wrote a poem called "The Star-Spangled Banner." In 1931 Congress designated "The Star-Spangled Banner" as the national anthem.

Defeat at Plattsburgh Meanwhile, in the north, General Sir George Prevost led more than 10,000 British troops into New York State from Canada. The first British goal was to capture Plattsburgh, a key city on the shore of Lake Champlain. The invasion was stopped when an American naval force on Lake Champlain defeated the British fleet in September 1814. Knowing the American ships could use their control of the lake to bombard them and land troops behind them, the British retreated to Canada.

After the Battle of Lake Champlain, the British decided the war in North America was too costly and unnecessary. Napoleon had been defeated in Europe. To keep fighting the United States would gain little and was not worth the effort.

The War Ends American and British representatives signed a peace agreement on December 24, 1814, in Ghent, Belgium. The Treaty of Ghent did not change any existing borders. Nothing was mentioned about the impressment of sailors, but with Napoleon's defeat, neutral rights was no longer an issue.

Before word of the treaty had reached the United States, one final—and ferocious—battle occurred at New Orleans. In December 1814, British army troops moved toward New Orleans. Awaiting them behind earthen fortifications was an American army led by Andrew Jackson.

On January 8, 1815, the British troops advanced. The redcoats were no match for Jackson's soldiers, who shot from behind bales of cotton. In a short but gruesome battle, hundreds of British soldiers were killed. At the Battle of New Orleans, Americans achieved a decisive victory. Andrew Jackson became a hero, and his fame helped him win the presidency in 1828.

American Nationalism Most New England Federalists had opposed "Mr. Madison's war" from the start. In December 1814, unhappy New England Federalists gathered in Connecticut at the Hartford Convention. A few favored secession. Most wanted to remain within the Union, however. To protect their interests, they drew up a list of proposed amendments to the Constitution.

After the convention broke up, word came of Jackson's spectacular victory at New Orleans, followed by news of the peace treaty. In this moment of triumph, the Federalist grievances seemed unpatriotic. The party lost respect in the eyes of the public. Most Americans felt proud and self-confident at the end of the War of 1812. The young nation had gained new respect from other nations in the world. Americans felt a renewed sense of patriotism and a strong national identity.

Although the Federalist Party weakened, its philosophy of strong national government was carried on by the War Hawks, who were part of the Republican Party. They favored trade, western expansion, the energetic development of the **economy,** and a strong army and navy.

✔ **Reading Check** **Analyze** Did the Treaty of Ghent resolve any major issues? Explain.

Study Central Need help understanding the War of 1812? Visit tajww1.glencoe.com and click on Study Central.

What Did You Learn?

1. Who won the Battle of Lake Champlain? Why was it an important victory?

2. What were the effects of the Battle of New Orleans?

Critical Thinking

3. **Determining Cause and Effect** Re-create the diagram below. In the ovals, list four effects that the War of 1812 had on the United States.

Effects of the War of 1812

4. **The Big Ideas** Why did the Federalist Party lose support after the War of 1812?

5. **Creative Writing** Imagine if Francis Scott Key had been at the Battle of New Orleans instead of in Baltimore. Rewrite "The Star-Spangled Banner" based on what occurred in that battle.

6. **ANALYSIS** **Making Connections** Explain the relationship between Britain's war with France and the War of 1812 and the Treaty of Ghent.

Reading Summary

Review the Main Ideas

• While at first unprepared and experiencing setbacks on the battlefield, American forces soon began to gain victories on land and at sea in the War of 1812.

• In 1814 the British succeeded in capturing Washington, D.C., but they lost a number of other important battles, including the one at New Orleans.

TIME NOTEBOOK

What were people's lives like in the past?

What—and who—were people talking about? What did they eat? What did they do for fun? These two pages will give you some clues to everyday life in the U.S. as you step back in time with TIME Notebook.

Profile

SAGOYEWATHA *is the great Iroquois leader some call Red Jacket. Why? Because he fought with the British in the Revolutionary War. Sagoyewatha means "He Causes Them to Be Awake." Below is part of a speech Sagoyewatha delivered in 1805 to a group of religious leaders from Boston:*

"BROTHERS, OUR (NATIVE AMERICAN) SEATS were once large and yours (colonists) were small. You have now become a great people, and we have scarcely a place left to spread our blankets. You have got our country but are not satisfied; you want to force your religion upon us....

Brothers, continue to listen. You say there is but one way to worship and serve the Great Spirit. If there is but one religion, why do you white people differ so much about it?...

Brothers, we...also have a religion which was given to our forefathers and has been handed down to us, their children...."

Sagoyewatha

1790s WORD PLAY

Ahoy There!

The U.S.S. *Constitution,* a powerful frigate, or warship, was launched in 1797 with a crew of 450 and 54 cannons. Want to join the crew? First, you must prove you can understand a sailor's vocabulary.
Match each word or phrase in the first column with its original meaning.

1. Keel over
2. Try a new tack
3. Let the cat out of the bag
4. Mind your p's and q's
5. Shipshape

a. Sailors who do wrong are disciplined with a cat-o'-nine-tails whip that's kept in a red sack

b. Putting a ship in for repair

c. Bartenders keep track of what sailors drink and owe by marking numbers under "pints" and "quarts"

d. The course or direction boats take into the wind

e. Good condition

answers: 1. b; 2. d; 3. a; 4. c; 5. e

VERBATIM

WHAT PEOPLE ARE SAYING

❝We are one.❞
❝Mind your business.❞
FIRST OFFICIAL U.S. COIN,
sayings are on the front and back of the coin minted in 1787

❝I die hard, but I am not afraid to go.❞
GEORGE WASHINGTON,
on his deathbed in 1799

❝My mother and myself begged Mr. Carter not to sell this child out of Fredg [plantation], he gave us his word and honor that he would not, but as soon as we left him, he sold the child.❞
JAMES CARTER,
African American slave of Landon Carter, writing around 1790 about his sister, whom he never saw again

❝May the Lord bless King George, convert him, and take him to heaven, as we want no more of him.❞
REVEREND JOHN GRUBER,
to his Baltimore congregation during the War of 1812

NATIVE AMERICAN LIFE

Sports Story

GEORGE CATLIN *is a white man with a strong interest in Native American life. This lawyer has made a name for himself as an artist, painting portraits of Native American leaders, families, and everyday Western life. Here he paints with words, telling us about a game (one the French call lacrosse) played by Choctaw men:*

"EACH PARTY (TEAM) HAD THEIR GOAL MADE WITH TWO UPRIGHT POSTS, about 25 feet high and six feet apart, set firm in the ground, with a pole across at the top. These goals were about 40 to 50 rods (660–825 feet) apart. At a point just halfway between was another small stake, driven down, where the ball was to be thrown up at the firing of a gun, to be struggled for by the players … who were some 600 or 700 in numbers, and were (trying) to catch the ball in their sticks, and throw it home and between their respective stakes.…For each time that the ball was passed between the stakes of either party, one was counted for their game…until the successful party arrived to 100, which was the limit of the game, and accomplished at an hour's sun."

NATIONAL GALLERY OF ART

RIGHT: George Catlin *painted this picture of a 15-year-old Native American girl. Her name, Ka-te-qua, means "female eagle."*

BELOW: *Painting by* **George Catlin** *of* **Choctaw athletes** *playing their version of lacrosse.*

NUMBERS

U.S. AT THE TIME

30 Number of treaties that took away Native American land or moved their borders. The treaties were between the U.S. and the Creeks, Choctaws, and Chickasaws between 1789 and 1825

$158 million
The price the U.S. spent to fight the War of 1812

First Elizabeth Seton founds the Sisters of Charity, a Roman Catholic order, in 1809

First Mary Kies becomes the first woman to receive a U.S. patent in 1809 for a method of weaving straw with silk

$3,820.33 Amount paid to Paul Revere for providing the U.S.S. *Constitution* with copper parts and a ship's bell in 1797

45 feet Length of the dinosaur dug up by Lewis and Clark on their 1804 expedition

Foreign Relations

Guide to Reading

Looking Back, Looking Ahead
In Section 2, you learned about the War of 1812. In this section you will read about the United States's relations with foreign countries in the postwar period.

Focusing on the Main Ideas
- After the War of 1812, a new spirit of nationalism took hold in American society. *(page 363)*
- In 1823 the United States proclaimed its dominant role in the Americas with the Monroe Doctrine. *(page 366)*

Locating Places
Louisiana Territory
Oregon Country
Spanish East Florida
Mexico

Meeting People
James Monroe
John Quincy Adams
Andrew Jackson
Miguel Hidalgo (ee•DAHL•goh)
Simón Bolívar (see•MOHN buh•LEE•VAHR)
José de San Martín
  (hoh•ZAY day SAHN mahr•TEEN)

Content Vocabulary
disarmament (dih•SAHR•muh•muhnt)
demilitarize (dee•MIH•luh•tuh•RYZ)
court-martial

Academic Vocabulary
establish (ihs•TA•blihsh)
demonstrate (DEH•muhn•STRAYT)
policy (PAH•luh•see)

Reading Strategy
Organizing Information Create a diagram like the one below to list three disputed territories in North America.

Disputed Territories

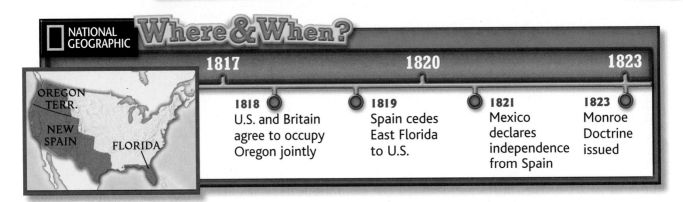

NATIONAL GEOGRAPHIC Where & When?

1817   1820   1823

OREGON TERR.
NEW SPAIN
FLORIDA

1818 U.S. and Britain agree to occupy Oregon jointly

1819 Spain cedes East Florida to U.S.

1821 Mexico declares independence from Spain

1823 Monroe Doctrine issued

Relations With European Powers

Main Idea After the War of 1812, a new spirit of nationalism took hold in American society.

Reading Connection Think about your favorite sports team. Do you feel they are better than or superior to any other team? Read on to find out about the feeling of national pride many Americans felt.

An American Story

Following the War of 1812, Americans felt buoyed by a new sense of pride and faith in the United States. In his Inaugural Address on March 4, 1817, President **James Monroe** expressed feelings of hope and optimism for the country.

> ❝ Never did a government commence under auspices so favorable. . . . If we look to the history of other nations, ancient or modern, we find no example of a growth so rapid, so gigantic, of a people so prosperous and happy. . . . If we persevere . . . we can not fail . . . to attain the high destiny which seems to await us. ❞

—from James Monroe's Inaugural Address, 1817

Era of Good Feelings The absence of major political divisions after the War of 1812 helped forge this sense of national unity. As political differences seemed to fade away, a Boston newspaper called these years the Era of Good Feelings. The president himself symbolized these good feelings. Monroe had been involved in national politics since the American Revolution. He wore breeches and powdered wigs—a style no longer in fashion. With his sense of dignity, Monroe represented a united America free of political strife.

Early in his presidency, Monroe toured the nation. No president since George Washington had done this. He paid his own expenses and tried to travel without an official escort. Everywhere Monroe went, local officials greeted him, and local people celebrated his visit. However, Monroe did not think this outpouring of support was meant for him personally. He wrote former President Madison that they revealed "a desire in the body of the people to show their attachment to the union." During this time, Americans began to think of themselves as equal, or even superior, to Europeans. Abigail Adams, wife of the second president John Adams, wrote from England to her sister back in Massachusetts: "Do you know that European birds have not half the melody of ours? Nor is their fruit half so sweet, nor their flowers half so fragrant, nor their manners half so pure, nor their people half so virtuous."

Despite such boasting, many Americans realized that the United States needed peaceful relations with the European powers to grow and develop. The young American republic had to put differences aside and **establish** a new relationship with the "Old World."

Relations With Britain In the years after the War of 1812, President Monroe and his secretary of state, **John Quincy Adams,** moved to resolve long-standing disputes with Great Britain. In 1817, in the Rush-Bagot Treaty, the United States and Britain agreed to set limits on the number of naval vessels each could have on the Great Lakes. The treaty provided for the **disarmament** (dih•SAHR•muh•muhnt)—the removal of weapons—along an important part of the border between the United States and British Canada.

Setting a Northern Boundary The United States also worked with Britain to establish the American-Canadian boundary farther west. A second agreement with Britain, the Convention of 1818, set the boundary of the **Louisiana Territory** between the United States and Canada at the 49th parallel. The convention created a secure and **demilitarized** (dee•MIH•luh•tuh•RYZD) border—a border without armed forces.

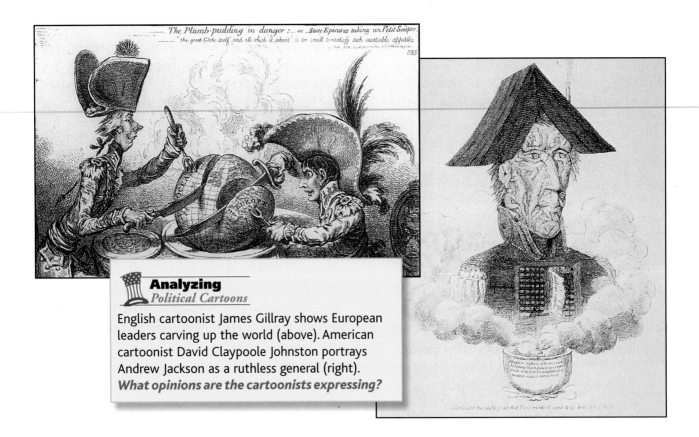

The Plumb-pudding in danger:— or State Epicures taking un Petit Souper.
"the great Globe itself, and all which it inherit," is too small to satisfy such insatiable appetites.

Analyzing
Political Cartoons

English cartoonist James Gillray shows European leaders carving up the world (above). American cartoonist David Claypoole Johnston portrays Andrew Jackson as a ruthless general (right).
What opinions are the cartoonists expressing?

Decades later, after lingering tensions had settled, the American-Canadian boundary became known as the longest unguarded border in the world. Through Adams's efforts, Americans also gained the right to settle in the **Oregon Country,** a vast area extending from California to Alaska.

Oregon Many Americans wanted control of the Oregon Country so they could gain access to the Pacific Ocean. In the early 1800s, four countries—Britain, Spain, Russia, and the United States—claimed this vast, rugged land. Spain and Russia eventually gave up their claims, leaving control of Oregon to Britain and the United States.

Both countries based their claims to the Oregon on the explorations of American and British fur trappers and traders. To prevent a war over Oregon, British and American diplomats worked to settle the dispute peacefully. In the Convention of 1818, Britain and the United States agreed to jointly occupy Oregon. This meant that people from both the nations could settle there.

In the following years, thousands of Americans streamed into the Oregon Country. The number of British settlers remained small, however. As the American presence grew, the question of who should own Oregon arose again. In the Treaty of 1846, Britain and the United States compromised by dividing Oregon into American and British portions at latitude 49°N.

Relations With Spain The United States also worked to settle border disputes with Spain. In the early 1800s, Spain owned East Florida and also claimed West Florida. The United States contended that West Florida was part of the Louisiana Purchase. In 1810 and 1812, Americans simply added parts of West Florida to Louisiana and Mississippi. Spain objected but took no action.

In April 1818, General **Andrew Jackson** invaded **Spanish East Florida,** seizing control of two Spanish forts. Jackson had been ordered to stop Seminole raids on American territory from Florida. In capturing the Spanish forts, however, Jackson went beyond his instructions.

Adams-Onís Treaty Luis de Onís, the Spanish minister to the United States, protested forcefully and demanded the punishment of Jackson and his officers. Secretary of War John Calhoun said that Jackson should be **court-martialed**—tried by a military court—for overstepping instructions. Secretary of State John Quincy Adams disagreed.

Although Secretary of State Adams had not authorized Jackson's raid, he did nothing to stop it. Adams guessed that the Spanish did not want war and that they might be ready to settle the Florida dispute. He was right. For the Spanish, the raid had **demonstrated** the military strength of the United States. Already troubled by rebellions in Mexico and South America, Spain signed the Adams-Onís Treaty in 1819. Spain gave East Florida to the United States and abandoned all claims to West Florida.

The two countries also agreed on a border between the United States and Spanish possessions in the West. These lands had been in dispute since 1803, when the United States received the Louisiana Territory. In the Adams-Onís Treaty, the United States gave up its claims to Spanish Texas and took over responsibility for paying the $5 million that American citizens claimed Spain owed them for damages. The treaty also extended the border northwest from the Gulf of Mexico to the 42nd parallel and then west to the Pacific, recognizing the United States's claim to the Oregon Country. America had become a transcontinental power.

The Struggle for Frontier Lands

In the early 1800s, Spain held most of the land west of the Mississippi River, with the exception of Oregon and the Louisiana Territory. Spanish officials tried to keep Americans and other foreigners out of this frontier area. However, they found it increasingly difficult to enforce this policy. When Mexico won its freedom from Spain in 1821, it gained control of this vast area of 75,000 Spanish-speaking inhabitants and 150,000 Native Americans. The Mexicans also faced the American push for expansion that Spain had tried to block.

Why Did Mexico Change Its Policy?

Economics finally won out over politics. In 1823 the Mexican government decided to welcome American traders and settlers into its frontier lands. It hoped that increased trade and population would boost the region's economy. Shortly, Americans began arriving in the region to settle.

Mexican officials soon questioned the wisdom of their invitation. Most of the new settlers remained American, and many disliked and even resisted Mexican laws and customs. At the same time, in the United States, an increasing number of Americans were accepting the idea that the United States had a right to expand its territory from the Atlantic Ocean to the Pacific Ocean. This expansion, it was believed, would make the young country rich and more powerful. It would also provide security, because an enlarged United States would be bordered by the sea instead of by foreign powers. As a result, many Americans saw the advantage of obtaining Mexico's frontier lands and extending United States territory to the Pacific.

Conflict With Mexico The United States tried to buy territory from **Mexico,** but the Mexicans refused. Relations between the two countries worsened when American settlers in Texas revolted against Mexican rule. Texas gained its independence in 1836 and U.S. statehood in 1845. These events greatly angered Mexico, which broke diplomatic ties with the United States. A dispute over the Texas-Mexico border caused more trouble. By the following year, Mexico and the United States were at war. Mexico was defeated and lost almost half of its territory to the United States. In 1848 the peace treaty ending the war gave the United States the area that today includes California, New Mexico, Arizona, and a number of other western states.

✓ **Reading Check** **Explain** Why was Andrew Jackson's action considered by some to be unlawful?

The United States and Latin America

Main Idea In 1823 the United States proclaimed its dominant role in the Americas with the Monroe Doctrine.

Reading Connection You recall how the American colonies felt about throwing off British rule. Read on to find out how many Latin American countries gained independence from Spain.

While working out its relations with Europe after the War of 1812, the United States pursued new policies with Latin America. These policies would guide the nation's relations in the Western Hemisphere for years to come.

During the early 1800s, Spain controlled a vast colonial empire that included what is now the southwestern United States, Mexico, Central America, and all of South America except Portuguese-ruled Brazil. At this time, the Spanish and Portuguese faced a series of challenges within their empires. Although the United States had given little thought to Europe's Latin American colonies before 1800, it voiced support when those colonies began their struggles for independence from Spain and Portugal.

Mexico In the fall of 1810, a priest, **Miguel Hidalgo** (ee•DAHL•goh), led a rebellion against the Spanish government of Mexico. Hidalgo called for racial equality and the redistribution of land. The Spanish defeated the revolutionary forces and executed Hidalgo. Mexico finally gained its independence in 1821. Along with independence, Mexico also gained control of the northern frontier lands that included present-day Texas, Arizona, New Mexico, Nevada, Utah, western Colorado, California, and small parts of Wyoming, Kansas, and Oklahoma.

Bolívar and San Martín In South America, independence came largely as a result of the efforts of two men. **Simón Bolívar** (see•MOHN buh•LEE•VAHR), also known as "the Liberator," led the movement that won freedom for the present-day countries of Venezuela, Colombia, Panama, Bolivia, and Ecuador. **José de San Martín** (hoh•ZAY day SAHN mahr•TEEN) successfully achieved independence for Chile and Peru. By 1824 the revolutionaries' military victory was complete, and most of South America had liberated itself from Spain. Portugal's large colony of Brazil gained its independence peacefully in 1822.

In working for independence, Simón Bolívar and other Latin American leaders were inspired by the example of the United States. Americans, in turn, were glad to see European empires further weakened. They looked forward to increased trade between the United States and Latin America and to the spread of American ideals within the region.

▲ Miguel Hidalgo

History Online

Student Web Activity Visit tajwwI.glencoe.com and click on *Chapter 7—Student Web Activities* for an activity on democratic movements in the Americas.

On July 4, 1821, Secretary of State John Quincy Adams gave a speech to Congress. He said: "Wherever the standard of freedom and Independence has been or shall be unfurled, there will her heart, her benedictions, her prayers be." Adams meant that the United States should support colonies that wanted to gain their freedom. To demonstrate this support, President Monroe quickly recognized the independence of the Latin American republics.

The Monroe Doctrine In 1822 the Quadruple Alliance—France, Austria, Russia, and Prussia—discussed a plan to help Spain regain its American holdings. The possibility of increased European involvement in North America led President Monroe to consider action.

President Monroe declared in 1823 that the American continents were "not to be considered as subjects for future colonization by any European powers." Any foreign military expeditions sent to the Western Hemisphere would be seen as a threat to the United States, Monroe warned. No European country should interfere in United States affairs, at home or abroad.

The president's proclamation, later called the Monroe Doctrine, was a bold act. The United States might not have been able to back up its new **policy** if challenged. The Monroe Doctrine marked the beginning of a long-term American policy of preventing other great powers from interfering in Latin American political affairs. By keeping the European powers out of the Americas, the Monroe Doctrine upheld George Washington's policy of avoiding entangling alliances in European power struggles.

✓ Reading Check **Identify** What event led to the creation of the Monroe Doctrine?

History Online

Study Central Need help understanding independence movements in the Americas? Visit tajww1.glencoe.com and click on Study Central.

Section 3 Review

Reading Summary

Review the Main Ideas

• Following the War of 1812, Americans entered into a period known as the Era of Good Feelings in which they felt politically and economically secure.

• Latin American countries, inspired by the American Revolution, fought for independence from Spain.

What Did You Learn?

1. Why did America support the Latin American countries in their fight for independence?

2. What were the provisions of the Monroe Doctrine?

Critical Thinking

3. **Summarizing** Draw a table like the one below and summarize what happened in each territorial dispute.

Territory	Action
Oregon Country	
Louisiana Territory	
Spanish East Florida	
Texas	

4. **The Big Ideas** Why do you think the United States wanted dominance over most of the territories in North America?

5. **Persuasive Writing** Reread the section on the seizure of Spanish forts in Florida by Andrew Jackson. Choose a side either for or against Andrew Jackson's actions, and write a letter to the president stating why you feel Jackson either should or should not be court-martialed.

Analyzing Primary Sources

Nationalism in the United States

In the early 1800s, the idea of being an American and part of a country called the "United States" was still new. If the United States was going to succeed as a country, people would need to think of themselves as being Americans. Feelings of nationalism—loyalty to a nation and the promotion of its interests above all others—began to grow. Some Americans expressed pride in their new nation in songs and poems. The War of 1812 helped bring about even stronger feelings of nationalism.

Read the passages on pages 368 and 369 and answer the questions that follow.

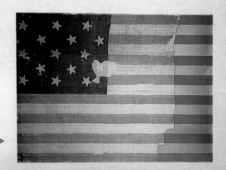

Flag flown at Fort McHenry during the War of 1812 ▶

Reader's Dictionary

Ramilies, Nimrod: British ships

valor (VA • luhr): courage, bravery

maritime (MAR • uh • TYM): relating to ships and the sea

submission (suhb • MIH • shuhn): giving in to the will or power of another

intriguing (ihn • TREE • gihng): making secret plans

diminished (duh • MIH • nihshd): made less

strife (STRYF): conflict, struggle

prosecute (PRAH • sih • KYOOT): carry out

The Battle of Stonington

This excerpt is from a song by Philip Freneau that describes the British attack on Stonington, Connecticut, in 1814.

Three gallant ships from England came,
Freighted deep with fire and flame,
And other things we need not name,
To have a dash at Stonington. . . .

The **Ramilies** first began the attack,
And **Nimrod** made a mighty crack,
And none can tell what kept them back
From setting fire to Stonington. . . .

To have a turn we thought but fair.
We Yankees brought two guns to bear,
And, sir, it would have made you stare
To have seen the smoke at Stonington. . . .

The Ramilies then gave up the fray [fight],
And with her comrades sneaked away;
Such was the **valor** on that day
Of British [sailors] at Stonington. . . .

—Philip Freneau

War and Expansion

A number of young War Hawks were elected to Congress in 1810. In this speech, War Hawk Felix Grundy explains why the United States should go to war with Great Britain.

What, Mr. Speaker, are we now called on to decide? It is whether we will resist by force the attempt made by that government to subject our **maritime** rights to . . . her will; . . . Sir, I prefer war to **submission**. . . .

This war, if carried on successfully, will have its advantages. We shall drive the British from our continent—they will no longer have an opportunity of **intriguing** with our Indian neighbors. . . . That nation will lose her Canadian trade, and, by having no resting place in this country, her means of annoying us will be **diminished**. . . . I am willing to receive the Canadians as adopted brethren; . . . [I] therefore feel anxious not only to add the Floridas to the South, but the Canadas to the North of this empire.

—from a speech in the
House of Representatives,
December 1811

Against the Draft

In 1813 President Madison proposed a bill that would draft, or force, men into the army. Representative Daniel Webster of New Hampshire spoke against this bill. At the same time, he criticized the war.

Is this, sir, consistent with the character of a free government? Is this civil liberty? Is this the real character of our Constitution? No, sir, indeed it is not. . . .

If, sir, in this **strife** he [the draftee] fall; if, while ready to obey every rightful command of government, he is forced from his home

against right, not to contend for the defense of his country but to **prosecute** a miserable and detestable project of invasion, and in that strife he fall, 'tis murder.

—from a speech in the
House of Representatives,
December 9, 1814

▲ Daniel Webster

DBQ Document-Based Questions

The Battle of Stonington

1. How was the Battle of Stonington fought?
2. Who won the battle? How?

War and Expansion

3. What government is Grundy referring to in the first paragraph?
4. Whose empire does Grundy want the Floridas and the Canadas to belong to?

Against the Draft

5. What is a military draft?
6. How does Webster object to the draft?

Read to Write

7. Evaluate Grundy's and Webster's arguments about the War of 1812. What arguments does each man use to support his beliefs about the war? What do you think of each argument? Write a short essay on the topic.

Chapter 7 Assessment

Review Content Vocabulary

Match each word with the correct definition below.

1. tribute
2. frigate
3. disarmament
4. demilitarized
5. nationalism
6. privateer
7. embargo
8. neutral rights

a. armed private ship
b. the removal of weapons
c. money paid to gain protection from someone or something
d. an order that prohibits trade with other countries
e. without military occupation
f. the ability to sail the seas and not take sides in a conflict
g. a warship
h. loyalty to one's country

Review the Main Ideas

Section 1 • A Time of Conflict

9. How did the Embargo Act of 1807 hurt the United States?
10. Who were the War Hawks?

Section 2 • The War of 1812

11. What were the important naval victories early in the War of 1812?
12. What battle occurred after the Treaty of Ghent was signed? What was its significance?

Section 3 • Foreign Relations

13. Which nations signed the Rush-Bagot Treaty?
14. What line of latitude did the United States and Great Britain agree upon as the border of the Oregon Territory?

Critical Thinking

15. **Evaluate** Why was the Florida territory so important to Spain and the United States?
16. **Analyze** When was the Battle of Horseshoe Bend? Why was it important?
17. **Comparing** Describe the differences between the War Hawks and the Federalists in their views of the War of 1812.

Geography Skills

In 1819 Spain ceded Florida to the United States in the Adams-Onís Treaty. Study the map and answer the questions that follow.

NATIONAL GEOGRAPHIC
Acquisition of Florida, 1819

18. **Region** When was the largest portion of Florida acquired from Spain?
19. **Location** What body of water blocked further expansion of Florida to the west?
20. **Movement** In what direction did the United States acquire the various parts of Florida?

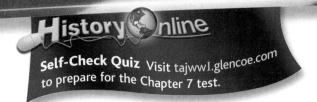

History Online

Self-Check Quiz Visit tajwwI.glencoe.com to prepare for the Chapter 7 test.

Read to Write

21. **The Big Ideas Expository Writing** Using library or Internet resources, research the American Revolution and one of the Latin American wars for independence mentioned in Section 3. Compare and contrast the two wars for independence in a brief essay.

22. **Creative Writing** Imagine you are a soldier during the War of 1812. Write a letter home to your family describing the things you see and how you feel about your place in the war.

23. **Using Your FOLDABLES** Use the information from your completed chapter foldable to create a brief study guide for the chapter. Your study guide should include at least five questions for each section. Questions should focus on the main ideas. Exchange your study guide with a partner and answer each of the questions.

Using Academic Vocabulary

24. Use each of the following academic vocabulary words in a sentence.

   strategy   establish
   conclude   policy

Building Citizenship

25. **Analyzing Current Events** With a partner, choose a recent event for which you will be able to locate primary and secondary sources of information. Compare the primary source with one secondary source. Prepare a report for the class in which you describe the event and compare the information in the primary and secondary sources.

Reviewing Skills

26. **READING SKILL** **Determining Cause and Effect** What were the effects of Jackson's invasion of Spanish East Florida in 1818? Write a paragraph discussing the impact on U.S. territorial expansion.

27. **ANALYSIS SKILL** **Compare and Contrast** Reread the sections in this chapter on Tecumseh. Summarize his point of view on American settlement of Native American lands and contrast that with what Harrison's view would have been.

Standardized Test Practice

Read the passage below and answer the following questions.

> The American continents, by the free and independent condition which they have assumed and maintain, are henceforth not to be considered as subjects for future colonization by any European powers.
>
> We . . . should consider any attempt on their part to extend their system to any portion of this hemisphere as dangerous to our peace and safety.
>
> —The Monroe Doctrine

28 To what nations did Monroe direct his statements?

   A Russia

   B Central America

   C South America

   D European nations

29 The Monroe Doctrine sent a clear message from the United States. The doctrine was designed to

   A preserve the United States's trade routes with Europe.

   B prevent Central American countries from declaring war against the United States.

   C prohibit European nations from colonizing any lands in the Western Hemisphere.

   D protect the United States from invasion by European nations.

Launching the Republic

The early years of the United States saw the nation struggling to survive and expanding westward. A unique American culture continued to develop. Even in these early days, the issue of slavery divided the country.

	Chapter 5 The Federalist Era	Chapter 6 The Age of Jefferson	Chapter 7 Foreign Affairs in the Early Republic
When	• 1789–1800	• 1800–1812	• 1812–1830
Where	• New York • Northwest Territory • Great Britain • Spain • France	• Washington, D.C. • Louisiana Territory • Mississippi River • France • Santo Domingo • Colorado • the North • the South	• Mediterranean Sea • Ohio • Washington, D.C. • Baltimore, Maryland • Oregon • Florida • Mexico • Texas • Latin America

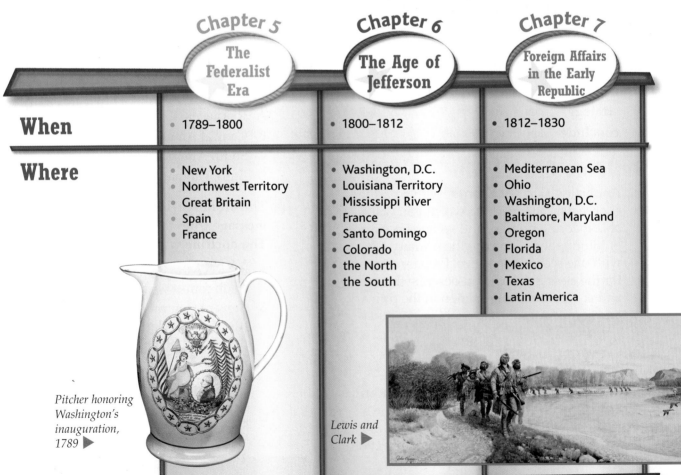

Pitcher honoring Washington's inauguration, 1789 ▶

Lewis and Clark ▶

	Chapter 5 The Federalist Era	**Chapter 6** The Age of Jefferson	**Chapter 7** Foreign Affairs in the Early Republic
Major Events	• **1789** Judiciary Act • **1790s** Emergence of political parties • **1791** Bill of Rights • **1791** National Bank • **1793** Proclamation of Neutrality • **1794** Whiskey Rebellion • **1794** Battle of Fallen Timbers • **1794** Jay's Treaty • **1796** Washington's Farewell Address • **1796** XYZ Affair • **1798** Alien and Sedition Acts • **1798–1799** Virginia and Kentucky Resolutions	• **1801** Judiciary Act • **1801** Jefferson's Inaugural Address • **1803** *Marbury* v. *Madison* • **1803** Louisiana Purchase ratified • **1804–1806** Lewis and Clark expedition • **early 1800s** Second Great Awakening *William Clark's journal* ▼	• **1807** Embargo Act • **1809** Nonintercourse Act • **1811** Battle of Tippecanoe • **1812–1814** War of 1812 • **1814** British burn government buildings in Washington, D.C. • **1815** Battle of New Orleans • **1817** Rush-Bagot Treaty • **1819** Adams-Onís Treaty • **1821** Mexican independence • **1823** Monroe Doctrine • **1824** Most South American countries independent
Some Important People	• George Washington • Thomas Jefferson • Alexander Hamilton • John Jay • Edmond Genêt • John Adams • Charles de Talleyrand	• Thomas Jefferson • Albert Gallatin • John Marshall • Napoleon Bonaparte • Toussaint-Louverture • Meriwether Lewis • William Clark • Sacagawea • Zebulon Pike	• Thomas Jefferson • James Madison • Tecumseh • William Henry Harrison • Henry Clay • John Calhoun • Andrew Jackson • James Monroe *Tecumseh* ▲
How do these events and ideas affect our lives today?	• Most candidates for office today belong to a political party. They run on the policies supported by their party.	• Lands that were part of the Louisiana Purchase are now part of the United States.	• The Monroe Doctrine set the tone for future relations between the United States and Latin America.
What was happening in the world at this time?	• **1792** Denmark is the first country to abolish slave trade • **1794** Polish uprising put down by Russians	• **1801** Ireland becomes part of Great Britain • **1803** Czar Alexander I establishes free, universal education in Russia	• **1819** Britain sets a 12-hour working day for children • **1829** Greece gains independence from the Ottoman Empire

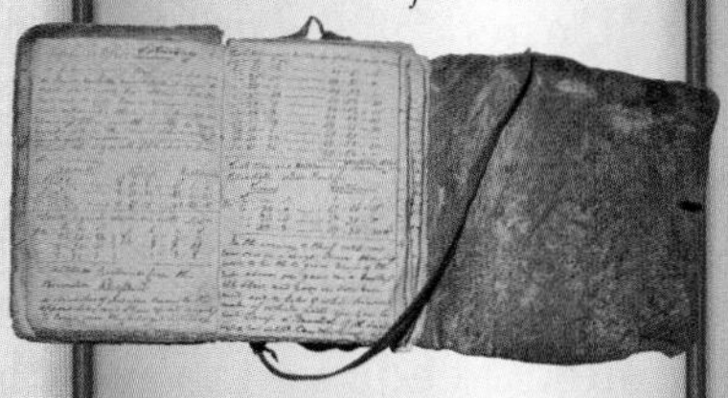

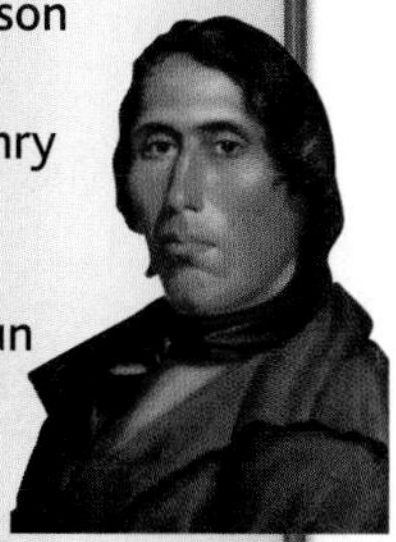

The Young Republic

Why It's Important

The United States continued to grow, both geographically and economically. Industry boomed in the North, and cotton became a major crop in the South. At the same time, settlers streamed to newly opened territories in the West. Certain groups of Americans, such as women and African Americans, pursued freedoms that would take many years to achieve.

- The United States grew greatly in size and wealth.

- More Americans gained the right to vote, and reform movements took root.

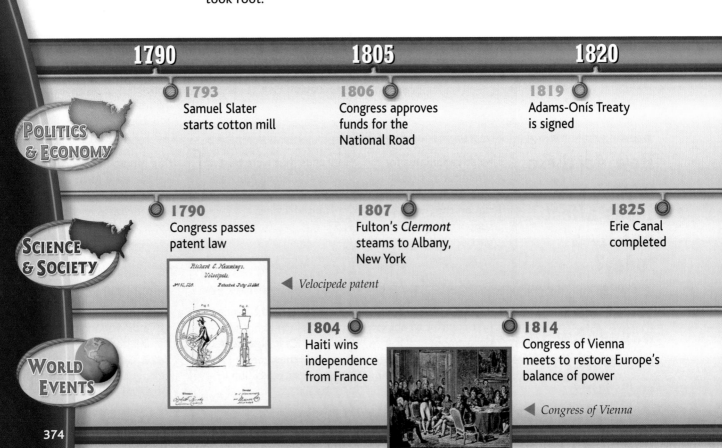

1790   **1805**   **1820**

POLITICS & ECONOMY

1793
Samuel Slater starts cotton mill

1806
Congress approves funds for the National Road

1819
Adams-Onís Treaty is signed

SCIENCE & SOCIETY

1790
Congress passes patent law

1807
Fulton's *Clermont* steams to Albany, New York

1825
Erie Canal completed

◀ *Velocipede patent*

WORLD EVENTS

1804
Haiti wins independence from France

1814
Congress of Vienna meets to restore Europe's balance of power

◀ *Congress of Vienna*

Where in the United States?

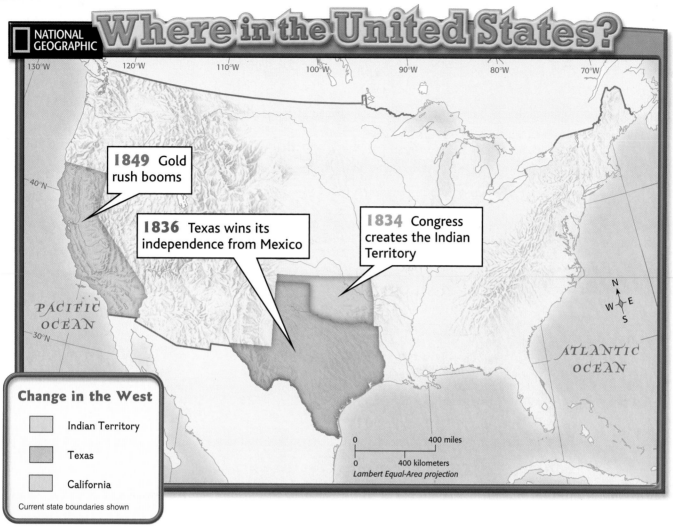

1849 Gold rush booms

1836 Texas wins its independence from Mexico

1834 Congress creates the Indian Territory

PACIFIC OCEAN

ATLANTIC OCEAN

Change in the West

- Indian Territory
- Texas
- California

Current state boundaries shown

0   400 miles

0   400 kilometers

Lambert Equal-Area projection

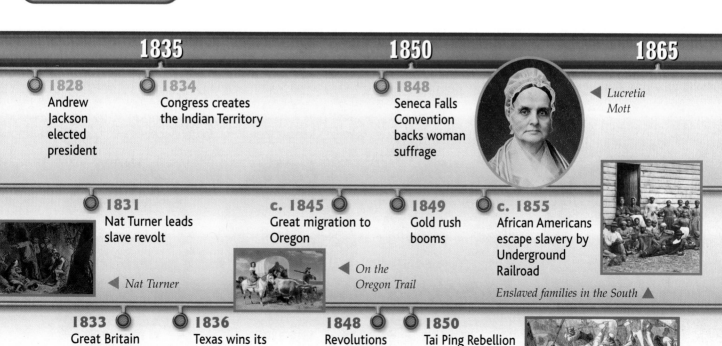

1835   **1850**   **1865**

1828 Andrew Jackson elected president

1834 Congress creates the Indian Territory

1848 Seneca Falls Convention backs woman suffrage

◄ Lucretia Mott

1831 Nat Turner leads slave revolt

c. 1845 Great migration to Oregon

1849 Gold rush booms

c. 1855 African Americans escape slavery by Underground Railroad

◄ Nat Turner

◄ On the Oregon Trail

Enslaved families in the South ▲

1833 Great Britain abolishes slavery in its colonies

1836 Texas wins its independence from Mexico

1848 Revolutions sweep through Europe

1850 Tai Ping Rebellion begins in China

Tai Ping Rebellion ►

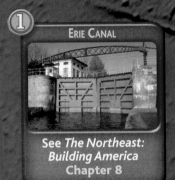

① ERIE CANAL

See *The Northeast: Building America* **Chapter 8**

② TRAIL OF TEARS

See *The Age of Jackson* **Chapter 10**

④

③

People to Meet

Eli Whitney
1765–1825
American inventor
Chapter 8, page 384

Dorothea Dix
1802–1887
Prison reformer
Chapter 8, page 405

Elizabeth Cady Stanton
1815–1902
Women's rights
activist
Chapter 8, page 409

Harriet Tubman
c. 1820–1913
African American
leader
Chapter 9, page 436

③ **THE ALAMO**

See *Manifest Destiny*
Chapter 11

④ **THE GOLD RUSH**

See *Manifest Destiny*
Chapter 11

① ②

Andrew Jackson
1767–1845
Seventh president of
the United States
Chapter 10, page 447

Sequoya
c. 1760–1845
Inventor of Cherokee
alphabet
Chapter 10, page 453

Osceola
c. 1804–1838
Seminole leader
Chapter 10, page 456

John C. Frémont
1813–1890
American explorer of
California
Chapter 11, page 494

The Northeast: Building Industry

◀ Mill in Plymouth, Massachusetts

NATIONAL GEOGRAPHIC Where & When?

1805	1820	1835	1850
1806 Congress approves funds for the National Road	**1825** Erie Canal is completed	**1833** Oberlin College admits women and African Americans	**1848** First women's rights convention held

Buffalo Boston
Detroit
Cincinnati New York

History Online
Chapter Overview Visit tajww1.glencoe.com for a preview of Chapter 8.

The Big Ideas

Economic Growth
Geography shapes the physical, economic, and political challenges a region faces. New technology produced the Industrial Revolution.

A System of Transportation
Geography shapes the physical, economic, and political challenges a region faces. Improvements in transportation led to Western settlement.

The North's People
Differences in economic, political, and social beliefs and practices can lead to division within a nation and have lasting consequences. The North saw an increase in industrialism and the growth of cities.

Reforms and Reformers
Reactions to social injustice can lead to reform movements. Many Americans worked for reform in education and other areas.

The Women's Movement
Reactions to social injustice can lead to reform movements. Women lobbied for increased rights and an equal status with men in America.

 View the Chapter 8 video in the Glencoe Video Program.

Organizing Make this foldable to organize information from the chapter to help you learn more about the changes in the North.

Step 1 Collect three sheets of paper and place them on top of one another about 1 inch apart.

Keep the edges straight.

Step 2 Fold up the bottom edges of the paper to form 6 tabs.

This makes all tabs the same size.

Step 3 When all the tabs are the same size, fold the paper to hold the tabs in place and staple the sheets together. Turn the paper and label each tab as shown.

Staple together along the fold.

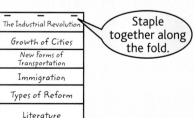

The Industrial Revolution
Growth of Cities
New Forms of Transportation
Immigration
Types of Reform
Literature

Reading and Writing As you read, use your foldable to write under each appropriate tab what you learned about the people, the economy, and the culture of the North.

Chapter 8

Get Ready to Read

Problems and Solutions

READING SKILL

1 Learn It!

To explain how and why a person, society, or government made a particular decision in history, authors sometimes use a problem/solution approach in their writing. You can recognize a problem/solution structure by asking three questions. What was the problem? What was the solution? What were the results of that solution? As you read the text below, notice how the author used a problem/solution approach to explain how reformers developed methods to teach people with disabilities.

> Some reformers focused on teaching people with disabilities. Thomas Gallaudet (GA • luh • DEHT), who developed a method to educate people who were hearing impaired, opened the Hartford School for the Deaf in Connecticut in 1817.
>
> At about the same time, Dr. Samuel Gridley Howe advanced the cause of those who were visually impaired. He developed books with large raised letters that people with sight impairments could "read" with their fingers. Howe headed the Perkins Institute, a school for the blind, in Boston.
>
> —*from page 405*

Reading Tip

As you read, make a chart listing problems and solutions that are described in the text.

2 Practice It!

As you read this chapter, complete a chart like the one below to show how Americans solved problems by inventing new machines.

Problem	Solution
Need more thread to make cloth →	Spinning jenny
Cotton bolls difficult to clean →	
Machine parts are hard to find →	

Read to Write ········

Understanding problems and creating solutions is part of everyday life. Can you think of a challenge you have had this week? How have you found solutions? Write a short paragraph describing one of your own problem/solution situations.

▲ Eli Whitney

Cotton gin ▶

3 Apply It!

As you read this chapter, watch for ways that everyday people met the challenges they faced.

Section 1

Economic Growth

Guide to Reading

Looking Back, Looking Ahead
Beginning in the early 1800s, revolutions in industry brought great changes to the North.

Focusing on the Main Ideas
- New technology led to changes in the way things are made. *(page 383)*
- The growth of factories and trade led to the growth of cities. *(page 386)*

Meeting People
Eli Whitney
Samuel Slater
Francis Cabot Lowell

Content Vocabulary
Industrial Revolution (ihn•DUHS• tree•uhl REH•vuh•LOO•shuhn)
capitalism
capital (KA•puh•tuhl)
free enterprise (EHN•tuhr•PRYZ)
technology (tehk•NAH•luh•jee)
cotton gin
patent (PA•tuhnt)
factory system
interchangeable parts
(IHN•tuhr•CHAYN•juh•buhl)

Academic Vocabulary
percent
expand
concentrate (KAHN•suhn•TRAYT)

Reading Strategy
Organizing Information As you read the section, re-create the diagram below and describe in the ovals changes brought about by the Industrial Revolution.

Industrial Revolution

NATIONAL GEOGRAPHIC **Who & When?**

1780   1800   1820

Velocipede patent

1790 Congress passes patent law

1793 Samuel Slater starts cotton mill

1814 Textile plant opens in Waltham, Massachusetts

Samuel Slater

The Growth of Industry

Main Idea **New technology led to changes in the way things are made.**

Reading Connection Do you know someone who works in a factory? What is his or her job like? Read to learn how new technology spurred the Industrial Revolution in New England and what working in mills or factories was like.

From colonial times, most of the people of New England had lived and worked on farms. Work on a new farm was difficult. Eager to plant crops, the farmers first cleared the land. The trees were felled for building materials, fences, and firewood. People believed that trees grew on the most fertile land. As a result, they often cut down all the trees in an area. This created problems. Often the soil eroded without the protection of trees and tree roots.

A New Way of Working
During the colonial era, workers were in short supply. Americans learned to develop tools that made work easier and more efficient.

People working in their homes or in workshops made cloth and most other goods. Using hand tools, they produced furniture, farm equipment, household items, and clothing.

In the mid-1700s, however, the way goods were made began to change. These changes appeared first in Great Britain. British inventors created machinery to perform some of the work involved in cloth making, such as spinning. The machines ran on waterpower, so British cloth makers built mills along rivers and installed the machines in these mills. People left their homes and farms to work in the mills and earn wages. The changes this system brought about were so great that this historic development is known as the **Industrial Revolution** (ihn•DUHS•tree•uhl REH•vuh•LOO•shuhn).

The Industrial Revolution
The Industrial Revolution began to take root in the United States around 1800, appearing first in New England—Massachusetts, Rhode Island, Connecticut, Vermont, and New Hampshire. New England's soil was poor, and farming was difficult. As a result, some people were willing to leave their farms to find work elsewhere. Also, New England had many rushing rivers and streams. These provided the waterpower necessary to run the machinery in the new factories.

New England's Geography
New England's geographic location also proved to be an advantage. It was close to other resources, including coal and iron from nearby Pennsylvania. New England also had many ports. Through these ports passed the cotton shipped from Southern states to New England factories, as well as the finished cloth produced in the North and bound for markets throughout the nation.

A Changing Economy
The economic system of the United States is called **capitalism.** Under capitalism, individuals put their **capital** (KA•puh•tuhl), or money, into a business in hopes of making a profit.

Free enterprise (EHN•tuhr•PRYZ) is another term used to describe the American economy. In a system of free enterprise, people are free to buy, sell, and produce whatever they want. They can also work wherever they wish. The major elements of free enterprise are competition, profit, private property, and economic freedom. Business owners have the freedom to produce the products that they think will be the most profitable. Buyers also compete to find the best products at the lowest prices.

▲ **American blacksmith, early 1800s woodcut**

New Technology Workers, waterpower, location, and capital were key factors in New England's Industrial Revolution. Yet without the invention of new machines and **technology** (tehk•NAH•luh•jee)—scientific discoveries that simplify work—the Industrial Revolution could not have taken place.

Inventions such as the spinning jenny and the water frame, which spun thread, and the power loom, which wove the thread into cloth, made it possible to perform many steps in making cloth by machine, saving time and money. Because these new machines ran on waterpower, most mills were built near rivers.

Another invention greatly increased the production of cotton. In 1793 **Eli Whitney** of Massachusetts invented the **cotton gin,** a simple machine that quickly and efficiently removed seeds from cotton fiber. The cotton gin enabled one worker, usually a slave, to clean cotton as fast as 50 people working by hand.

In 1790 Congress passed a patent law to protect the rights of those who developed "useful and important inventions." A **patent** (PA•tuhnt) gives an inventor the sole legal right to the invention and its profits for a certain period of time. One of the first patents went to Jacob Perkins for a machine to make nails.

TECHNOLOGY & History

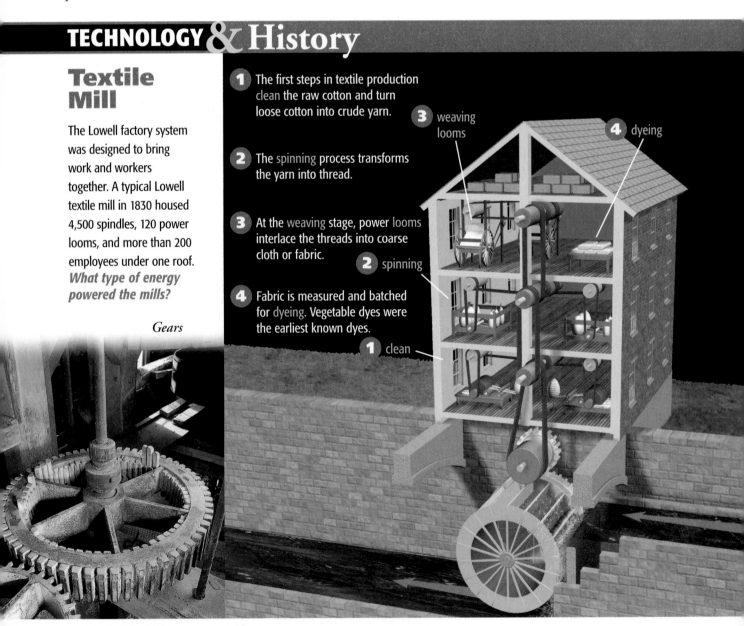

Textile Mill

The Lowell factory system was designed to bring work and workers together. A typical Lowell textile mill in 1830 housed 4,500 spindles, 120 power looms, and more than 200 employees under one roof. *What type of energy powered the mills?*

Gears

1 The first steps in textile production clean the raw cotton and turn loose cotton into crude yarn.

2 The spinning process transforms the yarn into thread.

3 At the weaving stage, power looms interlace the threads into coarse cloth or fabric.

4 Fabric is measured and batched for dyeing. Vegetable dyes were the earliest known dyes.

3 weaving looms

4 dyeing

2 spinning

1 clean

New England Factories The British tried to keep their new industrial technology a secret. Great Britain even passed laws prohibiting their machinery as well as their skilled mechanics from leaving the country. However, a few enterprising workers managed to slip away to the United States.

In Britain **Samuel Slater** had worked in a factory that used machines invented by Richard Arkwright for spinning cotton thread. Slater memorized the design of Arkwright's machines and slipped out of Britain. Once in the United States, Slater operated a cotton mill in Pawtucket, Rhode Island, in 1793. There he duplicated all of Arkwright's machines. Using these machines, the mill produced cotton thread. Slater's mill marked an important step in the Industrial Revolution in America.

In 1814 **Francis Cabot Lowell** opened a textile plant in Waltham, Massachusetts. The plan he implemented went several steps beyond Slater's mill. For the first time, all the stages of cloth making were performed under one roof. Lowell's mill launched the **factory system,** a system that brought manufacturing steps together in one place to increase efficiency. The factory system was a significant development in the way goods were made and another important part of the Industrial Revolution. By 1840 many textile mills were operating in the Northeast. Industrialists soon applied factory techniques to the production of lumber, shoes, leather, and other products.

Interchangeable Parts The inventor Eli Whitney started the use of **interchangeable parts** (IHN•tuhr•CHAYN•juh•buhl). These were identical machine parts that could be put together quickly to make a complete product. Because all the parts were alike, they could be manufactured with less-skilled labor and they made machine repair easier. Interchangeable parts opened the way for producing many different kinds of goods on a mass scale and for reducing the price of the goods.

✓ **Reading Check** **Analyze** Why were the first mills in Great Britain built near rivers?

Primary Sources

Lowell Girls

Many of the workers in the mills in Lowell, Massachusetts, were young girls. Lucy Larcom started working in the mills when she was 11 years old. She later recalled her life at the factory:

"At this time I had learned to do a spinner's work, and I obtained permission to tend some frames that stood directly in front of the river-windows, with only them and the wall behind me, extending half the length of the mill, and one young woman beside me, at the farther end of the row. She was a sober, mature person, who scarcely thought it worth her while to speak often to a child like me; and I was, when with strangers, rather a reserved girl; so I kept myself occupied with the river, my work, and my thoughts. . . .

Still, we did not call ourselves ladies. We did not forget that we were working-girls, wearing coarse aprons suitable to our work, and that there was some danger of our becoming drudges."

—Lucy Larcom,
A New England Girlhood

DBQ **Document-Based Question**

What "danger" does Lucy foresee?

A Changing Economy

Main Ideas The growth of factories and trade led to the growth of cities.

Reading Connection Do you think you would rather work on a farm or in a factory? Read to learn what caused agriculture to expand at the same time that factories and towns were growing.

Although many New Englanders went to work in factories, most Americans still lived and worked on farms. In the 1820s, more than 65 **percent** of Americans were farmers.

In the Northeast, farms tended to be small, and the produce was usually marketed locally. In the South, cotton production increased dramatically. The demand for cotton had grown steadily with the development of the textile industries of New England and Europe. Southern plantation owners used enslaved workers to plant, tend, and pick the cotton. The cotton gin—which made it possible to clean the cotton faster and less expensively than by hand—encouraged the planters to raise larger crops. Between 1790 and 1820, cotton production soared from 3,000 to more than 300,000 bales a year.

There were also changes in the West. Agriculture in that region **expanded.** Southern farmers seeking new land moved west to plant cotton. Western farmers north of the Ohio River **concentrated** on raising pork and cash crops such as corn and wheat.

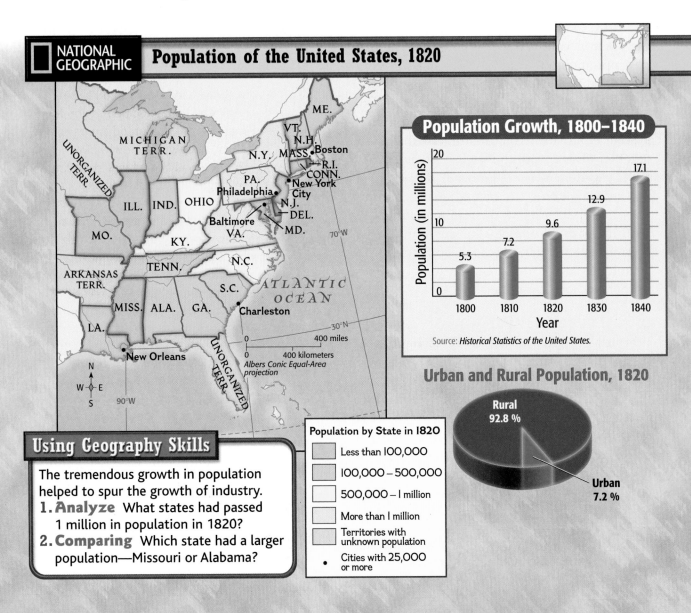

NATIONAL GEOGRAPHIC **Population of the United States, 1820**

Population Growth, 1800–1840

Population (in millions)

Year	Population
1800	5.3
1810	7.2
1820	9.6
1830	12.9
1840	17.1

Source: *Historical Statistics of the United States.*

Urban and Rural Population, 1820

Rural 92.8 %

Urban 7.2 %

Population by State in 1820
- Less than 100,000
- 100,000 – 500,000
- 500,000 – 1 million
- More than 1 million
- Territories with unknown population
- Cities with 25,000 or more

Using Geography Skills

The tremendous growth in population helped to spur the growth of industry.
1. **Analyze** What states had passed 1 million in population in 1820?
2. **Comparing** Which state had a larger population—Missouri or Alabama?

Economic Independence Most new industries were financed by small investors—merchants, shopkeepers, and farmers. These people invested some of their money in the hope of earning profits if the new businesses succeeded. Low taxes, few government regulations, and competition encouraged people to invest in new industries.

Cities Come of Age The growth of factories and trade spurred the growth of towns and cities. The new industrial towns grew quickest. Many developed along rivers and streams to take advantage of the waterpower. Older cities such as New York, Boston, and Baltimore also grew as centers of commerce and trade. To the west, towns like Pittsburgh, Cincinnati, and Louisville profited from their locations on major rivers. As nearby farmers shipped more and more of their products by water, these towns grew rapidly.

Cities and towns looked different from modern urban areas. Buildings were made of wood or brick. Streets and sidewalks were unpaved, and barnyard animals often roamed freely. No sewers existed to carry waste and dirty water away, so the danger of diseases such as cholera and yellow fever was very real. In 1793, for example, a yellow fever epidemic in Philadelphia killed thousands of people.

Fire posed another threat to cities. Sparks from a fireplace or chimney could easily ignite a wooden building and spread to others. Few towns or cities had organized fire companies, so fires could be disastrous.

Cities and towns of the period also had advantages, however. Some people left farming because cities and towns offered a variety of jobs and steady wages. As cities grew, they added libraries, museums, and shops that were unavailable in the countryside. For many, the jobs and attractions of city life outweighed any of the dangers.

✓ Reading Check **Analyze** Why did cities such as Pittsburgh and Louisville grow?

History Online
Study Central Need help understanding the growth of industry in cities? Visit tajww1.glencoe.com and click on Study Central.

Section 1 Review

Reading Summary

Review the Main Ideas

- The Industrial Revolution first began in the United States in New England, thanks to new technology, local resources, and the capitalist economic system.

- As large businesses continued to grow in the East, so did towns and cities. Further west, agriculture expanded, along with towns such as Cincinnati and Louisville.

What Did You Learn?

1. Describe the reasons New England was ideal for the development of factories.

2. How did farming in the Northeast differ from that in the South?

Critical Thinking

3. **Classifying Information** Re-create the diagram below and describe the major elements of the free enterprise system.

Free enterprise system

4. **The Big Ideas** Was new technology necessary for the Industrial Revolution? Explain.

5. **Economic Factors** How did the cotton gin affect cotton production?

6. **READING** **Problems and Solutions** Write a paragraph describing the relationship between the quality of farmland and the growth of new industry in New England using a problem/solution structure.

Section 2

A System of Transportation

Guide to Reading

Looking Back, Looking Ahead
In the last section, you learned how the Industrial Revolution changed the American economy. In this section, you will learn how changes in transportation helped the nation expand.

Focusing on the Main Ideas
- Transportation routes such as roads improved as settlers moved west, and steamboats greatly improved the transport of goods along rivers. *(page 389)*
- Business and government officials came up with a plan to build a canal to link the eastern and western parts of the country. *(page 392)*
- Americans continued to move westward, settling near rivers so they could ship their crops to market. *(page 393)*

Locating Places
Hudson River
Albany
Lake Erie
Erie Canal

Meeting People
Robert Fulton

Content Vocabulary
census (SEHN•suhs)
turnpike
canal (kuh•NAL)
lock

Academic Vocabulary
undertake (UHN•duhr•TAYK)
equip (ih•KWIHP)

Reading Strategy
Taking Notes As you read the section, re-create the diagram below and describe why each was important to the nation's growth.

	Significance
National Road	
John Fitch	
Erie Canal	

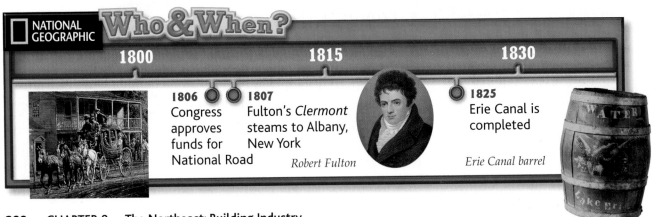

NATIONAL GEOGRAPHIC **Who & When?**

1800 — 1815 — 1830

1806 Congress approves funds for National Road

1807 Fulton's *Clermont* steams to Albany, New York

Robert Fulton

1825 Erie Canal is completed

Erie Canal barrel

Moving West

Main Idea Transportation routes such as roads improved as settlers moved west, and steamboats greatly improved the transport of goods along rivers.

Reading Connection Have you ever gone on a trip to another state? Read to learn how transportation was different in the 1800s and how the new network of roads connected the country.

An American Story

In the 1820s Congressman Henry Clay of Kentucky prepared an ambitious program to improve transportation and strengthen the nation's economy called the American System. The American System included building canals and roads to link the South, Northeast, and West together. The American System, Clay believed, would bring the United States "to that height to which God and nature had destined it." Even before Clay's plans, Americans were working to improve transportation.

Growth and Movement The first **census** (SEHN•suhs)—the official count of a population—of the nation in 1790 revealed a population of nearly 4 million. Most Americans counted lived east of the Appalachian Mountains and within a few hundred miles of the Atlantic coast.

Within a few decades this changed. The number of settlers heading west increased greatly. In 1811 a Pennsylvania resident reported seeing 236 wagons filled with people and their possessions on the road to Pittsburgh. In 1820, just 30 years after the first census, the population of the United States had more than doubled to about 10 million people, with nearly 2 million living west of the Appalachians.

Traveling west was not easy in the late 1790s and early 1800s. The 363-mile trip from New York City to Buffalo could take as long as three weeks. A pioneer family heading west with a wagonload of household goods faced hardship and danger along the way.

Roads and Turnpikes The nation needed good inland roads for travel and for the shipment of goods. Private companies built many **turnpikes,** or toll roads. The fees travelers paid to use those roads helped pay for construction. Many of the roads had a base of crushed stone. In areas where the land was often muddy, companies built "corduroy roads," which consisted of logs laid side by side like the ridges of corduroy cloth.

When Ohio joined the Union in 1803, the new state asked the federal government to build a road to connect it with the East. In 1806 Congress approved funds for a National Road to the West and five years later agreed on the route. Because work on the road stopped during the War of 1812, the first section, from Maryland to western Virginia, did not open until 1818. In later years, the National Road reached Ohio and continued on to Vandalia, Illinois. Congress viewed the National Road as a military necessity, but it did not **undertake** other road-building projects.

River Travel River travel had definite advantages over wagon and horse travel. It was far more comfortable than travel over the bumpy roads, and pioneers could load all their goods on river barges—if they were heading downstream in the direction of the current.

River travel had two problems, however. The first related to the geography of the eastern United States. Most major rivers in the region flowed in a north-south direction, not east to west, where most people and goods were headed. Second, traveling upstream by barge against the current was an extremely difficult and slow way to travel.

History Online

Student Web Activity Visit tajwwI.glencoe.com and click on *Chapter 8—Student Web Activities* for an activity on the National Road.

The Era of the Steamboat Steam engines were already being used in the 1780s and 1790s to power boats in quiet waters. Inventor James Rumsey **equipped** a small boat on the Potomac River with a steam engine. John Fitch, another inventor, built a steamboat that navigated the Delaware River. Neither boat, however, had enough power to withstand the strong currents and winds found in large rivers or open bodies of water.

In 1802 Robert Livingston, a political and business leader, hired **Robert Fulton** to develop a steamboat with a powerful engine. Livingston wanted the steamboat to carry cargo and passengers up the **Hudson River** from New York City to **Albany.**

In 1807 Fulton had his steamboat, the *Clermont*, ready for a trial. Powered by a newly designed engine, the *Clermont* made the 150-mile trip from New York to Albany in the unheard-of time of 32 hours. Using only sails, the trip would have taken four days. About 140 feet long and 14 feet wide, the *Clermont* offered great comforts to its passengers. They could sit or stroll about on deck, and at night they could relax in the sleeping compartments below deck. The engine was noisy, but its power provided a fairly smooth ride.

Steamboats ushered in a new age in river travel. They greatly improved the transport of goods and passengers along major inland rivers. Shipping goods became cheaper and faster. Steamboats also played an important role in the growth of river cities such as Cincinnati and St. Louis. By 1850 more than 700 steamboats traveled along the nation's waterways.

✓ Reading Check **Compare** What advantages did steamboat travel have over wagon and horse travel?

TECHNOLOGY & History

The *Clermont*

On August 17, 1807, the *Clermont* steamed up the Hudson River from New York City on its way to Albany, New York. The trip took only 32 hours—a commercial success. **What type of energy was used to power this ship?**

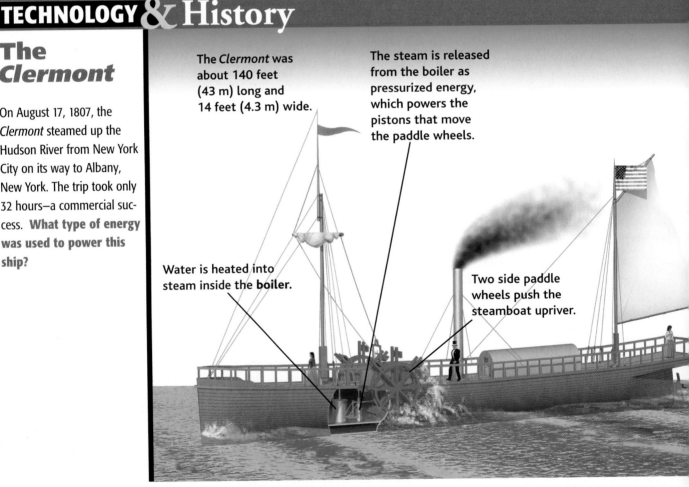

The *Clermont* was about 140 feet (43 m) long and 14 feet (4.3 m) wide.

The steam is released from the boiler as pressurized energy, which powers the pistons that move the paddle wheels.

Water is heated into steam inside the **boiler.**

Two side paddle wheels push the steamboat upriver.

Biography

ROBERT FULTON
1765–1815

Robert Fulton grew up in Lancaster, Pennsylvania. At an early age he created his own lead pencils and rockets. While living in Europe in the late 1790s, Fulton designed and built a submarine called the *Nautilus* to be used in France's war against Britain. Submarine warfare became common later.

Fulton returned to the United States and developed a steamboat engine that was more powerful and provided a smoother ride than previous engines. On August 18, 1807, Fulton's *Clermont* made its first successful run. The *Clermont* made its first voyages on the Hudson River, chugging the 150 miles from New York City to Albany at about five miles per hour.

By demonstrating the usefulness of two-way river travel, Fulton launched the steamboat era. In the years between 1830 and 1850, the steamboat became the most important means of transportation on major rivers.

Steamboats cruised in and out of the Great Lakes, as well as up and down the Mississippi River and its tributaries. By 1850 more than 700 steamboats, also called riverboats, traveled along the nation's waterways.

Fulton designed many other devices such as submarines and steam warships. He also engineered canal systems. Thomas Jefferson and James Madison considered him a mechanical genius with many talents. When the United States went to war with Great Britain in the War of 1812, President Madison said, "I have been asked, on a number of occasions, how the United States could conceivably defeat England, with the resources of its vast empire. I invariably reply, 'The United States has Robert Fulton, and he is all the empire we need.'"

> *"I have no time to listen to such nonsense."*
> **—Napoleon Bonaparte about Fulton's plans for a steam-powered engine**

Then and Now

What modern inventions have changed the way we travel?

Canals

Main Idea Business and government officials came up with a plan to build a canal to link the eastern and western parts of the country.

Reading Connection Have you ever worked long and hard to build something? Did you feel a sense of accomplishment when you finished? Read to learn the accomplishment of thousands of laborers who worked on the construction of the 363-mile Erie Canal.

Although steamboats represented a great improvement in transportation, their routes depended on the existing river system. Steamboats could not effectively tie the eastern and western parts of the country together.

In New York, business and government officials led by De Witt Clinton came up with a plan to link New York City with the Great Lakes region. They would build a **canal** (kuh•NAL)—an artificial waterway—across New York State, connecting Albany on the Hudson River with Buffalo on **Lake Erie.**

Building the Erie Canal Thousands of laborers, many of them Irish immigrants, worked on the construction of the 363-mile **Erie Canal.** Along the canal, they built a series of **locks**—separate compartments where water levels were raised or lowered. Locks provided a way to raise and lower boats at places where canal levels changed.

After more than two years of digging, the Erie Canal opened on October 26, 1825. Clinton boarded a barge in Buffalo and journeyed on the canal to New York City. As crowds cheered in New York, the officials poured water from Lake Erie into the Atlantic. The East and Midwest were joined.

TECHNOLOGY & History

How a Canal Works

A ship traveling downstream enters a lock and remains there while a gate is closed behind it, creating a watertight chamber. Water is slowly released through the downstream gate to lower the water level in the lock. The downstream gate is then opened, and the ship continues on its way at a lower elevation. To raise a ship, water is added to the lock through the upstream gate. **What happens as a boat travels through each lock of the canal?**

"Get up there mule, here comes a lock
We'll make Rome 'fore 6 'clock
And back we'll go to our home dock
Right back home to Buffalo"

The "lock" in the song verse refers to the Erie Canal. Locks are chambers, with gates at each end, that raise and lower ships to compensate for elevation changes along a waterway.

In its early years, the canal did not allow steamboats because their powerful engines could damage the earthen embankments along the canal. Instead, teams of mules or horses hauled the boats and barges. In the 1840s, the canal banks were reinforced to accommodate steam tugboats pulling barges.

The success of the Erie Canal led to an explosion in canal building. By 1850 the United States had more than 3,600 miles of canals. Canals lowered the cost of shipping goods and brought prosperity to the towns along their routes. Canals also created opportunities for new businesses to supply food, shelter, and other necessities to workers—and later to travelers on the canals. Perhaps most important, they helped unite the growing country.

Reading Check **Identify** What two cities did the Erie Canal connect?

Western Settlement

Main Idea **Americans continued to move westward, settling near rivers so they could ship their crops to market.**

Reading Connection What do you do when you get together with your friends? Do you watch a movie or play soccer? Read to learn what kinds of social events western families had in the early 1800s.

Americans moved westward in waves. The first wave began before the 1790s and led to the admission of four new states between 1791 and 1803—Vermont, Kentucky, Tennessee, and Ohio. A second wave of westward growth began between 1816 and 1821. Five new western states were created—Indiana, Illinois, Mississippi, Alabama, and Missouri.

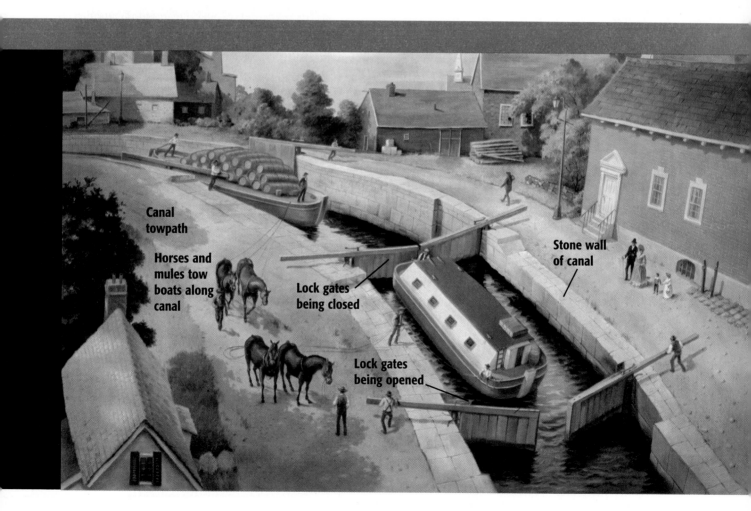

Canal towpath

Horses and mules tow boats along canal

Lock gates being closed

Lock gates being opened

Stone wall of canal

The new states reflected the dramatic growth of the region west of the Appalachians. Ohio, for example, had only 45,000 settlers in 1800. By 1820 it had 581,000.

Pioneer families tended to settle in communities along the great rivers, such as the Ohio and the Mississippi, so that they could ship their crops to market. The expansion of canals, which crisscrossed the land in the 1820s and 1830s, allowed people to live farther away from the rivers.

Pioneer families often gathered together for social events. Men took part in sports such as wrestling. Women met for quilting and sewing parties. Both men and women participated in cornhuskings—gatherings where farm families shared the work of stripping the husks from ears of corn.

Their lives did not include the conveniences of Eastern town life, but the pioneers had not moved to be pampered. They wanted to make a new life for themselves and their families.

Transportation and Daily Life Improved transportation meant that people could now buy goods produced in distant places. Rural Americans could hang curtains sewn from cloth manufactured in the mills of New England. Citizens of Illinois could enjoy the same foods, fashions, and household furnishings as residents of Vermont.

The new transportation changed America in other ways as well. In 1825 Congress established home delivery of letters by mail, and in 1847 the first national postage stamps were created. With the mail came newspapers, which brought national issues to the attention of remote rural communities.

✓ **Reading Check** **Identify** Which states were formed between 1791 and 1803?

Study Central Need help understanding the effects of changes in transportation? Visit tajwwI.glencoe.com and click on Study Central.

Section 2 Review

Reading Summary

Review the Main Ideas

- Settlers used new roads and turnpikes to move west of the Appalachians, and steamboats opened a new era of river travel.

- The success of the Erie Canal led to the building of other canals to link the East and Midwest.

- Although life west of the Appalachian Mountains was often difficult, the population there grew tremendously in the early 1800s.

What Did You Learn?

1. Describe the improvements in transportation during the westward expansion in the early 1800s.

2. What were the benefits of canals in the mid-1800s?

Critical Thinking

3. **Comparing** What forms of communication and transportation linked East to West in the early 1800s? What links exist today? Re-create the diagram below and compare the links.

Links	
Early 1800s	Today

4. **The Big Ideas** How did better transportation affect westward expansion?

5. **Descriptive Writing** Write a newspaper headline along with a brief article describing one of the events discussed in this section, such as a trip on an early steamboat or the opening of the Erie Canal.

6. **ANALYSIS** **Sequencing** Draw a time line identifying major developments in transportation during this period.

Section 3

The North's People

Guide to Reading

Looking Back, Looking Ahead
In Section 2, you learned how advances in transportation changed the geography of America. In Section 3, you will learn about the people and the economy of the North.

Focusing on the Main Ideas
- As industrialism grew in the North, many saw the need for reforms in working conditions. *(page 396)*
- Immigrants entered northern cities from many parts of Europe. They often faced hardships and discrimination upon arriving in America. *(page 398)*

Meeting People
Henry Boyd
Samuel Cornish
John B. Russwurm
Sarah G. Bagley

Content Vocabulary
trade union
strike
prejudice (PREH•juh•duhs)
discrimination
    (dis•KRIH•muh•NAY•shuhn)
famine (FA•muhn)
nativist (NAY•tih•VIHST)

Academic Vocabulary
shift
manual

Reading Strategy
Determining Cause and Effect As you read the section, re-create the diagram below and list two reasons for the growth of cities.

Growth of Cities

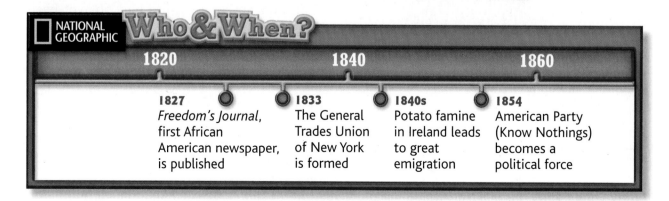

NATIONAL GEOGRAPHIC Who & When?

1820 — 1840 — 1860

1827
Freedom's Journal, first African American newspaper, is published

1833
The General Trades Union of New York is formed

1840s
Potato famine in Ireland leads to great emigration

1854
American Party (Know Nothings) becomes a political force

Northern Factories

Main Idea As industrialism grew in the North, many saw the need for reforms in working conditions.

Reading Connection Do you baby-sit or mow lawns to earn money? Do you think the money you earn is fair for the job you perform? Read on to learn about how workers organized to receive better pay and improve working conditions.

An American Story

"At first the hours seemed very long, but I was so interested in learning that I endured it very well; when I went out at night the sound of the mill was in my ears," a Northern mill worker wrote in 1844.

The worker compared the noise of the cotton mill to the deafening roar of Niagara Falls.

Picturing **History**

Girls as young as this one often worked in the textile factories that were built in the northeastern United States. *Why was factory work dangerous?*

The roar of machinery was only one of the features of factory life that these workers had to adjust to. Industrialization created new challenges for the men, women, and children who worked in the nation's factories.

What Were Working Conditions Like?

Between 1820 and 1860, more and more of America's manufacturing **shifted** to mills and factories. Machines took over many of the production tasks.

In the early 1800s, in the mills established in Lowell, Massachusetts, the entire production process was brought together under one roof, setting up the factory system. In addition to textiles and clothing, factories now produced such items as shoes, watches, guns, sewing machines, and agricultural machinery.

As the factory system developed, working conditions worsened. Factory owners wanted their employees to work longer hours to produce more goods. By 1840 factory employees worked an average of 11.4 hours per day. As the workday grew longer, on-the-job accidents became more common.

Factory work was often dangerous. For example, the long leather belts that connected the machines to the factory's water-powered driveshaft had no protective shields. Workers often suffered injuries such as lost fingers and broken bones from the rapidly spinning belts. Young children working on machines with powerful moving parts were especially at risk.

Workers often labored under unpleasant conditions. In the summer, factories were miserably hot and stifling. The machines gave off heat, and air-conditioning had not yet been invented. In the winter, workers suffered because most factories had no heating.

Factory owners often showed more concern for profits than for the comfort and safety of their employees. Employers knew they could easily replace an unhappy worker with someone else who was eager for a job. No laws existed to regulate working conditions or to protect workers.

Attempts to Organize By the 1830s, workers began organizing to improve working conditions. Skilled workers formed **trade unions**—organizations of workers with the same trade, or skill. Steadily deteriorating working conditions led unskilled workers to organize as well.

In the mid-1830s, skilled workers in New York City staged a series of **strikes,** refusing to work in order to put pressure on employers. Workers wanted higher wages and to limit their workday to 10 hours. Groups of skilled workers formed the General Trades Union of New York.

In the early 1800s, going on strike was illegal. Striking workers could be punished by the law, or they could be fired from their jobs. In 1842 a Massachusetts court ruled that workers did have the right to strike. In other cities and states, workers won some protections. However, it would be many years before workers received federal protection of their right to strike.

African American Workers Slavery had largely disappeared from the North by 1820. However, racial **prejudice** (PREH•juh•duhs)—an unfair opinion that is not based on facts—and **discrimination** (dis•KRIH•muh•NAY•shuhn)—unfair treatment of a group—remained in Northern states. For example, both Rhode Island and Pennsylvania passed laws prohibiting free African Americans from voting.

Most communities would not allow free African Americans to attend public schools and barred them from public facilities, as well. Often African Americans were forced into segregated, or separate, schools and hospitals.

Some African Americans found success in business. **Henry Boyd** owned a furniture manufacturing company in Cincinnati, Ohio. In 1827 **Samuel Cornish** and **John B. Russwurm** founded *Freedom's Journal,* the nation's first African American newspaper. In 1845 Macon B. Allen became the first African American licensed to practice law in the United States.

Women Workers Women took jobs in the developing mills and factories. However, employers discriminated against women,

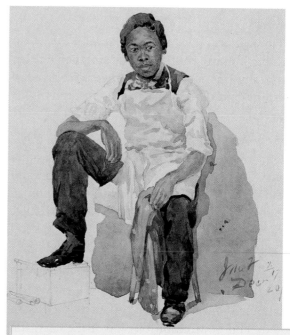

History *Through Art*

Young Man in White Apron **by John Mackie Falconer** The artist of this painting was known for his watercolors depicting New York City workers such as this African American clerk. ***How did prejudice affect the lives of African Americans in the North?***

paying them less than male workers. When men began to form unions, they excluded women. Male workers wanted women kept out of the workplace so that more jobs would be available for men.

Some female workers attempted to organize in the 1830s and 1840s. In Massachusetts the Lowell Female Labor Reform Organization, founded by a weaver named **Sarah G. Bagley,** petitioned the state legislature for a 10-hour day in 1845. Because most of the petition's signers were women, the legislature did not discuss the petition.

Most of the early efforts by women to achieve equality and justice in the workplace failed. They led, however, to later movements to correct the injustices against female workers.

Reading Check **Describe** How did conditions for workers change as the factory system developed?

The Rise of Cities

Main Idea Immigrants entered northern cities from many parts of Europe. They often faced hardships and discrimination upon arriving in America.

Reading Connection Did you know that the tradition of decorating a tree at Christmas comes from a German tradition? Many of our foods, words, and traditions originated in other countries. Read on to find out how immigrants influenced Northern cities.

....

The growth of factories helped Northern cities grow. People looking for work moved to the cities, where most of the factories were located. The population of New York City, the nation's largest city, reached 800,000, and Philadelphia's population was more than 500,000 in 1860.

Between 1820 and 1840, communities that had been small villages became major cities, including St. Louis, Pittsburgh, Cincinnati, and Louisville. All of them profited from their location on the Mississippi River or one of the river's branches. These cities became centers of the growing trade that connected the farmers of the Midwest with the cities of the Northeast. After 1830 the Great Lakes became a center for shipping, creating major new urban centers. These centers included Buffalo, Detroit, Milwaukee, and Chicago.

Immigration Immigration, which is the movement of people into a country, increased dramatically between 1840 and 1860. American manufacturers welcomed immigrants, many of whom were willing to work for low pay.

The largest group of immigrants to the United States at this time traveled across the Atlantic from Ireland. Between 1846 and 1860, more than 1.5 million Irish immigrants arrived in the United States, settling mostly in the Northeast. Today, more people of Irish descent live in the United States than in Ireland.

The Irish migration to the United States was brought on by the Great Irish Famine. A **famine**

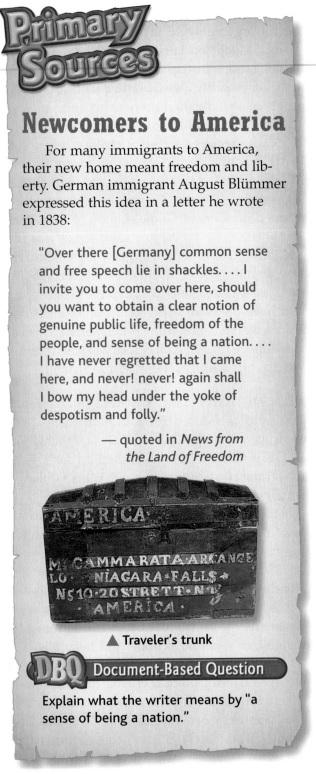

Primary Sources

Newcomers to America

For many immigrants to America, their new home meant freedom and liberty. German immigrant August Blümmer expressed this idea in a letter he wrote in 1838:

"Over there [Germany] common sense and free speech lie in shackles. . . . I invite you to come over here, should you want to obtain a clear notion of genuine public life, freedom of the people, and sense of being a nation. . . . I have never regretted that I came here, and never! never! again shall I bow my head under the yoke of despotism and folly."

— quoted in *News from the Land of Freedom*

▲ Traveler's trunk

DBQ **Document-Based Question**

Explain what the writer means by "a sense of being a nation."

(FA•muhn) is an extreme shortage of food. Potatoes were the main staple of the Irish diet. When a devastating blight, or disease, destroyed Irish potato crops in the 1840s, starvation struck the country. More than 1 million people died from the lack of food and from diseases.

Although most of the immigrants had been farmers in Ireland, they were too poor to buy land in the United States. For this reason, many Irish immigrants took low-paying factory jobs in Northern cities. The men who came from Ireland worked in factories or performed **manual** labor, such as working on the railroads. The women became servants and factory workers.

The second-largest group of immigrants in the United States between 1820 and 1860 came from Germany. Some sought work and opportunity. Others had left their homes because of the failure of a democratic revolution in Germany in 1848. During this time, many German Jews came to the United States seeking religious freedom.

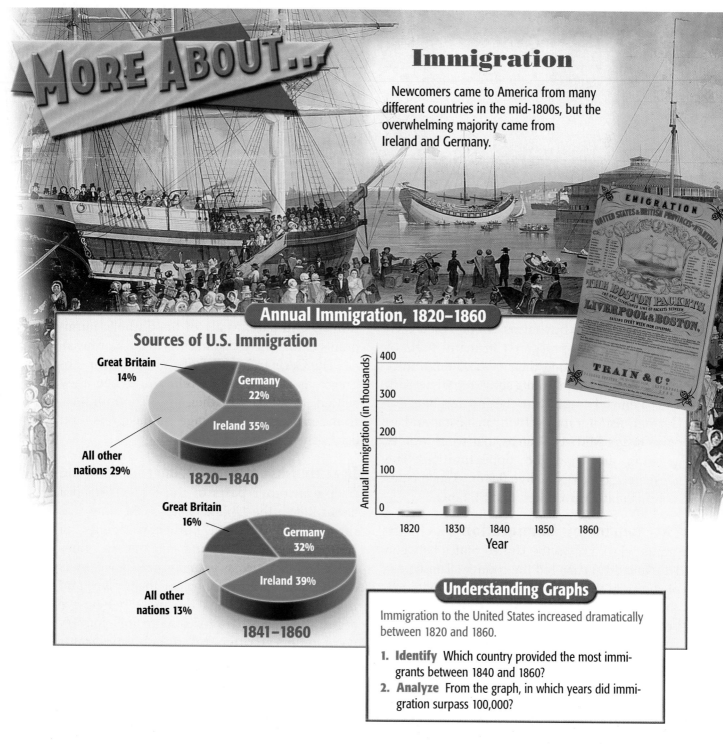

MORE ABOUT...

Immigration

Newcomers came to America from many different countries in the mid-1800s, but the overwhelming majority came from Ireland and Germany.

EMIGRATION
UNITED STATES & BRITISH PROVINCES OF N. AMERICA
THE BOSTON PACKETS,
1st ONLY ESTABLISHED LINE OF PACKETS BETWEEN
LIVERPOOL & BOSTON,
SAILING EVERY WEEK FROM LIVERPOOL.
TRAIN & Cº

Annual Immigration, 1820–1860

Sources of U.S. Immigration

1820–1840
- Great Britain 14%
- Germany 22%
- Ireland 35%
- All other nations 29%

1841–1860
- Great Britain 16%
- Germany 32%
- Ireland 39%
- All other nations 13%

Annual Immigration (in thousands)

Year	
1820	
1830	
1840	
1850	
1860	

Understanding Graphs

Immigration to the United States increased dramatically between 1820 and 1860.

1. **Identify** Which country provided the most immigrants between 1840 and 1860?
2. **Analyze** From the graph, in which years did immigration surpass 100,000?

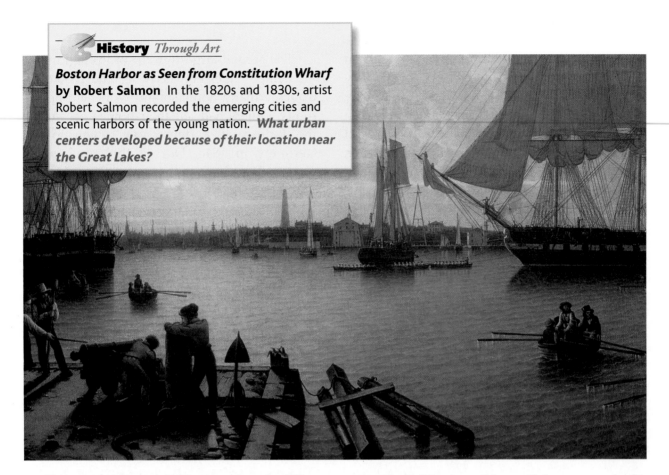

Between 1848 and 1860, more than 1 million
German immigrants settled in the United
States. Many German immigrants arrived with
enough money to buy farms or open their own
businesses. They prospered in many parts of
the country, founding their own communities.
Some German immigrants settled in New York
and Pennsylvania, but large numbers of
German immigrants settled on farms and in
cities in the Midwest—areas that were rapidly
growing and had job opportunities. The
Germans gave a distinctive flavor to such cities
as Cincinnati, Milwaukee, and St. Louis.

The Impact of Immigration

The immi-
grants who came to the United States between
1820 and 1860 changed the country. These people brought their languages, customs, religions,
and ways of life with them, some of which
became part of American culture.

Before the early 1800s, the majority of immigrants to America had been either Protestants
from Great Britain or Africans brought forcibly to
America as slaves. At the time, the country had
relatively few Catholics, and most of them lived

around Baltimore, New Orleans, and St.
Augustine. Most of the Irish immigrants and
about half of the German immigrants were
Roman Catholics. Many of the Catholic immigrants of this era settled in cities in the Northeast.

The German immigrants brought their language as well as their religion. When they
settled, they lived in their own communities,
founded German-language publications, and
established musical societies.

Learning About Life in America

How did
people in other parts of the world find out
about life in the United States? One way was
through advertising. European agents of
railroad companies and steamship lines
described America as a land where newcomers
could make a better living for themselves and
their families. Perhaps the most persuasive
arguments for others to come to this country
were letters written by recent immigrants
to their family and friends. "If you wish to
be happy and independent, then come
here," wrote a German farmer from his new
home in Missouri.

Immigrants Face Prejudice During the colonial period, workers were badly needed in all the colonies and immigrants had been readily accepted in many communities. In the 1830s and 1840s, however, some native-born Americans began to resent the newcomers, especially the Irish immigrants. Some Americans resented them because they dressed and sounded "different" and because they were Catholics.

People who were opposed to immigration were known as **nativists** (NAY•tih•VIHSTS) because they believed that immigration threatened the future of "native"—American-born—citizens. Some nativists accused immigrants of taking jobs from "real" Americans and were angry that immigrants would work for lower wages. Others accused the newcomers of bringing crime and disease to American cities. Immigrants who lived in crowded slums were often targets of this kind of prejudice.

The Know-Nothing Party The nativists formed secret anti-Catholic societies, and in the 1850s they joined to form a new political party: the American Party. By 1854 the party had become a force in American politics. Because members of nativist groups often answered questions about their organization with the statement "I know nothing," their party came to be known as the Know-Nothing Party. They did this to protect the secrecy of their organization.

The Know-Nothings called for stricter citizenship laws—extending the immigrants' waiting period for citizenship from 5 to 14 years—and wanted to ban foreign-born citizens from holding office.

In the mid-1850s, the Know-Nothing movement split into a Northern branch and a Southern branch over the question of slavery. At this time, the slavery issue was also dividing the Northern and Southern states of the nation.

Reading Check **Identify** Which two nations provided the largest number of immigrants to the United States during this era?

History Online

Study Central Need help understanding the people and economy of the North? Visit tajwwI.glencoe.com and click on Study Central.

Section 3 Review

Reading Summary

Review the Main Ideas

- Northern factories grew in the mid-1800s and many workers faced discrimination and unsafe working conditions.

- Immigrants flooded into the North seeking better opportunities than existed in their own countries.

What Did You Learn?

1. What was the nation's largest city in 1860?

2. How did German and Irish immigrants differ in where they settled?

Critical Thinking

3. **Determining Cause and Effect** Re-create the diagram below and list reasons workers formed labor unions.

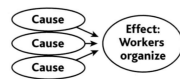

4. **The Big Ideas** Study the graphs on page 399. Did immigration from Ireland increase or decrease after 1840? How did immigration from Germany change?

5. **Expository Writing** Write two paragraphs on being an American: one to defend the nativist point of view and the other to appreciate the value of diversity in immigration. Look through your local newspaper for examples of each point of view.

Reforms and Reformers

Guide to Reading

Looking Back, Looking Ahead

In the last section, you learned about what life was like in the Northern cities. In Section 4, you will learn about how reformers worked to make life better for many Americans.

Focusing on the Main Ideas

- Religious and philosophical ideas inspired various reform movements. *(page 403)*
- Reformers wanted to make education accessible to all citizens. *(page 405)*
- A new wave of literature that was distinctly American swept the United States. *(page 406)*

Meeting People

Henry David Thoreau (thuh•ROH)
Ralph Waldo Emerson
Horace Mann
Thomas Gallaudet (GA•luh•DEHT)
Dr. Samuel Gridley Howe
Dorothea Dix
Margaret Fuller
Emily Dickinson

Content Vocabulary

utopia (yu•TOH•pee•uh)
revival
temperance (TEHM•puh•ruhns)
normal school
transcendentalist
    (TRAN•sehn•DEHN•tuhl•ihst)

Academic Vocabulary

founded
focus
publish

Reading Strategy

Taking Notes Re-create the diagram below and identify these reformers' contributions as you read Section 4.

	Contributions
Horace Mann	
Thomas Gallaudet	
Dorothea Dix	

NATIONAL GEOGRAPHIC Who & When?

1820 — 1835 — 1850

1825 Robert Owen establishes New Harmony, Indiana

1837 Horace Mann initiates education reform

Horace Mann

1843 Dorothea Dix reveals abuses of mentally ill

Dorothea Dix

The Reforming Spirit

Main Idea Religious and philosophical ideas inspired various reform movements.

Reading Connection Do your parents set limits on how much junk food you can consume? Read on to find out how reformers sought to place limits on the consumption of alcohol.

An American Story

Because he had refused to pay a one-dollar tax to vote, **Henry David Thoreau** (thuh•ROH) sat on a hard, wooden bench in a jail cell. He did not want his money to support the Mexican War. As he looked through the cell bars, he heard a voice. "Why are you here?" asked his friend **Ralph Waldo Emerson.** Thoreau replied, "Why are you *not* here?" Thoreau would later write:

> 66 Under a government which imprisons any unjustly, the true place for a just man is also a prison. 99
>
> —from "Civil Disobedience"

Utopias Thoreau represented a new spirit of reform in America. The men and women who led the reform movement wanted to extend the nation's ideals of liberty and equality to all Americans. They believed the nation should live up to the noble goals stated in the Declaration of Independence and the Constitution.

The spirit of reform brought changes to American religion, politics, education, art, and literature. Some reformers sought to improve society by forming **utopias** (yu•TOH•pee•uhs), communities based on a vision of a perfect society. In 1825 Robert Owen established New Harmony, Indiana, a village dedicated to cooperation rather than competition among its members. **Founded** on high hopes and sometimes impractical ideas, few of the utopian communities lasted more than a few years.

The Second Great Awakening

In the early 1800s, a wave of religious fervor—known as the Second Great Awakening—stirred the nation. The movement began with frontier camp meetings called **revivals.** People came from miles around to hear eloquent preachers such as Charles Finney. The experience often made men and women eager to reform both their own lives and the world. The Second Great Awakening increased church membership and inspired many to do missionary work and take part in reform movements.

What Was the Temperance Movement?

Religious leaders led a war against alcohol. Alcohol abuse was common in the early 1800s, especially in the West and among urban workers. Reformers blamed alcohol for poverty, the breakup of families, and crime. They called for **temperance** (TEHM•puh•ruhns), drinking little or no alcohol.

Temperance crusaders used lectures, pamphlets, and revival-style rallies to warn people of the dangers of liquor. The temperance movement gained a major victory in 1851, when Maine passed a law banning the manufacture and sale of alcoholic beverages. Other states passed similar laws, but most were repealed within several years.

Reading Check Analyze What were the effects of the Second Great Awakening?

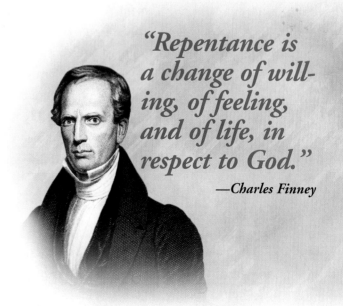

"Repentance is a change of willing, of feeling, and of life, in respect to God."
—*Charles Finney*

Biography

HENRY DAVID THOREAU
1817–1862

MARTIN LUTHER KING, JR.
1929–1968

Henry David Thoreau believed strongly in personal freedom. He thought that if a government or society interfered with a person's life, that person had the right to protest. When Thoreau saw something in society that he thought was unjust, he spoke out.

In his 1849 essay "Civil Disobedience," Thoreau supported the peaceful protest of unfair laws. "Unjust laws exist," he wrote, "shall we be content to obey them, or shall we endeavor to amend them . . . ?"

Many of Thoreau's ideas had a far-reaching impact. In India during the mid-twentieth century, the leader Mohandas Gandhi used Thoreau's ideas of civil disobedience through nonviolence to win eventual freedom for his nation. The nonviolent protests of Dr. Martin Luther King, Jr., in the civil rights movement of the 1950s and 1960s were also based, in part, on ideas expressed by Thoreau and Gandhi.

▲ Henry David Thoreau

Dr. King grew up in Atlanta, Georgia. Both his father and his mother's father were Baptist ministers. When King became a minister, he used his position to fight racial inequality.

In the 1950s, Dr. Martin Luther King, Jr., became one of the main leaders of the civil rights movement. A Baptist minister and stirring speaker, King believed in nonviolent resistance—the peaceful protest of unfair laws. He told people to disobey unjust laws, but asked them to love their oppressors and never fight with them even if provoked. King organized marches, boycotts, and demonstrations that opened many people's eyes to the need for change.

King is probably most famous for the march he led on Washington to support a civil rights bill. On August 28, 1963, Dr. King delivered a powerful speech outlining his dream of freedom and equality.

▲ Martin Luther King, Jr.

Then and Now

Give examples of how civil disobedience could be used today to help remedy society's ills.

Reforming Education

Main Idea **Reformers wanted to make education accessible to all citizens.**

Reading Connection Do you know of any students with visual or hearing impairments who attend your school? Most likely your school has resources to help these students learn. Read on to find out how reformers opened education to those it had previously been unable to reach.

In the early 1800s, only New England provided free elementary education. In other areas, parents had to pay fees or send their children to schools for the poor—a choice some parents refused out of pride. Some communities had no schools at all.

In the early 1800s, many reformers began to push for a system of public education—government-funded schools that were open to all citizens. The leader of educational reform was **Horace Mann,** a lawyer who became the head of the Massachusetts Board of Education in 1837. Mann lengthened the school year to six months, made improvements in the school curriculum, doubled teachers' salaries, and developed better ways of training teachers.

Partly due to Mann's effort, Massachusetts in 1839 founded the nation's first state-supported **normal school,** a school for training high school graduates as teachers. Other states soon adopted Mann's reforms.

How Did Education Change?

By the 1850s, most states had accepted three basic principles of public education: that schools should be free and supported by taxes, that teachers should be trained, and that children should be required to attend school. These principles did not go into effect immediately though. Schools were poorly funded, and many teachers lacked training. In addition, some people opposed compulsory, or required, education.

Most females received a limited education. Parents often kept their daughters from school because of the belief that a woman's role was to become a wife and mother and that this role did not require an education. When girls did go to school, they often studied music or needlework rather than science, mathematics, and history, which were considered "men's" subjects.

Higher Education

Dozens of new colleges were created during the age of reform. Most admitted only men. Religious groups founded many colleges between 1820 and 1850, including Trinity and Wesleyan in Connecticut.

Slowly, higher education became available to groups that were previously denied the opportunity. Oberlin College of Ohio, founded in 1833, admitted both women and African Americans. In 1837 a teacher named Mary Lyon in Massachusetts opened Mount Holyoke, the nation's first permanent women's college. The first college for African Americans, Ashmun Institute, opened in Pennsylvania in 1854.

People With Special Needs

Some reformers focused on teaching people with disabilities. **Thomas Gallaudet** (GA•luh•DEHT), who developed a method to educate people who were hearing impaired, opened the Hartford School for the Deaf in Connecticut in 1817.

At about the same time, **Dr. Samuel Gridley Howe** advanced the cause of those who were visually impaired. He developed books with large raised letters that people with sight impairments could "read" with their fingers. Howe headed the Perkins Institute, a school for the blind, in Boston.

When schoolteacher **Dorothea Dix** began visiting prisons in 1841, she found that the prisoners were often living in inhumane conditions—chained to the walls with little or no clothing, often in unheated cells. To her further horror, she learned that some of the inmates were guilty of no crime—they were mentally ill persons. Dix made it her life's work to educate the public about the poor conditions for both the mentally ill and for prisoners.

Reading Check **Identify** How did Dr. Samuel Howe help the visually impaired?

Cultural Trends

(Main Idea) A new wave of literature that was distinctly American swept the United States.

Reading Connection Have you read Henry David Thoreau, Ralph Waldo Emerson, or Emily Dickinson for any of your English classes? Read on to find out how these writers changed literature in America in the 1800s.

The changes in American society influenced art and literature. Earlier generations of American painters and writers looked to Europe for their inspiration and models. Beginning in the 1820s, American writers and artists developed their own style and explored uniquely American themes.

Who Were the Transcendentalists? The American spirit of reform influenced **transcendentalists** (TRAN•sehn•DEHN•tuhl•ihsts). Transcendentalists stressed the relationship between humans and nature, as well as the importance of the individual conscience. Writers such as **Margaret Fuller,** Ralph Waldo Emerson, and Henry David Thoreau were leading transcendentalists. Through her writings, Fuller supported rights for women. In his poems and essays, Emerson urged people to listen to the inner voice of conscience and to break the bonds of prejudice.

Thoreau put his beliefs into practice through civil disobedience—refusing to obey laws he thought were unjust. In 1846 Thoreau went to jail rather than pay a tax to support the Mexican War.

The Way It Was

One-Room Schoolhouse

The Country School by Winslow Homer

Until education became widespread, many children learned to read and write in one-room schoolhouses. Students of all ages learned mostly by rote—one group recited while the rest studied their lessons. Two popular schoolbooks of the 1800s were the *McGuffey Readers* and the *Columbian Orator.* Both of these schoolbooks provided moral lessons as well as lessons in reading and grammar. Excerpts in these readers came from well-known speeches and works of literature, as well as passages from the Bible and other religious texts.

Hornbook, left
Lunch pail, center,
Page from *McGuffey's Readers*, right

American Writers Emerge The transcendentalists were not the only important writers of this time. Many poets created impressive works about American subjects during this period. Henry Wadsworth Longfellow wrote narrative, or story, poems, such as the "Song of Hiawatha." John Greenleaf Whittier in "Snow-Bound" described winter on a New England farm. Edgar Allan Poe, a poet and short-story writer, told tales involving the terrors that lurk in the world of imagination and dreams.

Perhaps the most important poet of the era was Walt Whitman, who **published** a volume of poetry in 1855 called *Leaves of Grass.* Whitman loved nature, the common people, and American democracy, and his famous work reflects these passions. The best-remembered woman poet of the era was **Emily Dickinson,** who wrote simple, personal, deeply emotional poetry.

In a poem called "Hope," Dickinson compares hope with a bird:

> 66 'Hope' is the thing with feathers—
> That perches in the soul—
> And sings the tune without the words—
> And never stops—at all— 99
> —Emily Dickinson, "Hope"

Women writers of the period were generally not taken seriously, yet they were the authors of the most popular fiction. Harriet Beecher Stowe wrote the most successful best-seller of the mid-1800s, *Uncle Tom's Cabin.* Stowe's novel explores the injustice of slavery—an issue that took on new urgency during the age of reform.

Reading Check **Describe** What was one of the subjects that Margaret Fuller wrote about?

Section 4 Review

History Online

Study Central Need help understanding American literature? Visit tajww1.glencoe.com and click on Study Central.

Reading Summary

Review the Main Ideas

- Reformers attempted to make the United States a better place for its citizens.

- Reforms in secondary and higher education allowed more Americans to become educated.

- American literature gained a new voice through the writings of Thoreau, Emerson, Dickinson, and others.

What Did You Learn?

1. What did Horace Mann accomplish?

2. How did Thoreau act on his beliefs? What impact might such acts have had on the government?

Critical Thinking

3. **Determining Cause and Effect** Re-create the diagram below and describe two ways the religious movement influenced reform.

```
┌──────────┐     ┌──────┐
│ Religious│─────┤      │
│ movement │     ├──────┤
└──────────┘     │      │
                 └──────┘
```

4. **The Big Ideas** Who was Horace Mann, and what was his contribution to public education? How were women and African Americans able to have access to education? Summarize your conclusions in a short essay.

5. **Biography** Using your textbook, the library, and the Internet, learn more about Thomas Gallaudet, Dorothea Dix, or Samuel Gridley Howe. Write a short biography of the person you chose. Include key events in his or her life and the person's impact on the world.

The Women's Movement

Guide to Reading

Looking Back, Looking Ahead
In Section 4, you learned about the reform movement that swept America in the 1800s. In Section 5, you will learn about how that movement influenced women to lobby for increased rights.

Focusing on the Main Ideas
- Many women believed they should have the same opportunities as men, and they organized to gain these rights. *(page 409)*
- Women made progress in gaining equality in education, marriage laws, and the professional sector. *(page 411)*

Meeting People
Lucretia Mott
Elizabeth Cady Stanton
Susan B. Anthony
Mary Lyon
Elizabeth Blackwell

Content Vocabulary
suffrage (SUH•frihj)
coeducation

Academic Vocabulary
ministry (MIH•nuh•stree)
goal

Reading Strategy
Taking Notes As you read the section, use a chart like the one below to identify the contributions these individuals made to women's rights.

	Contributions
Lucretia Mott	
Elizabeth Cady Stanton	
Susan B. Anthony	

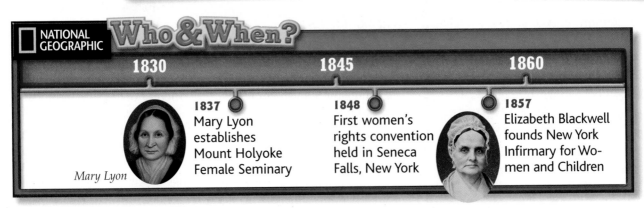

NATIONAL GEOGRAPHIC **Who & When?**

1830   1845   1860

1837 Mary Lyon establishes Mount Holyoke Female Seminary

Mary Lyon

1848 First women's rights convention held in Seneca Falls, New York

1857 Elizabeth Blackwell founds New York Infirmary for Women and Children

Lucretia Mott

Women and Reform

Main Idea **Many women believed they should have the same opportunities as men, and they organized to gain these rights.**

Reading Connection Can you imagine a time when women were not allowed to vote and had limited access to education and jobs? Read on to see how women worked to change their status in America.

An American Story

Women who fought to end slavery began to recognize their own bondage. On April 19, 1850, about 400 women met at a Quaker meeting-house in the small town of Salem, Ohio. They came together "to assert their rights as independent human beings." One speaker stated: "[W]e should demand our recognition as equal members of the human family."

The Seneca Falls Convention Many women abolitionists also worked for women's rights. Like many of the women reformers, **Lucretia Mott** was a Quaker. Quaker women enjoyed a certain amount of equality in their own communities. Mott gave lectures in Philadelphia calling for temperance, peace, workers' rights, and abolition. Mott also helped fugitive slaves and organized the Philadelphia Female Anti-Slavery Society. At the world antislavery convention in London, Mott met **Elizabeth Cady Stanton.** There the two female abolitionists joined forces to work for women's rights.

In July 1848, Elizabeth Cady Stanton, Lucretia Mott, and a few other women organized the first women's rights convention in Seneca Falls, New York. About 200 women and 40 men attended.

The convention issued a Declaration of Sentiments and Resolutions modeled on the Declaration of Independence. The women's document declared: "We hold these truths to be self-evident: that all men and women are created equal."

The women's declaration called for an end to all laws that discriminated against women. It demanded that women be allowed to enter the all-male world of trades, professions, and businesses. The most controversial issue at the Seneca Falls Convention concerned **suffrage** (SUH•frihj), or the right to vote.

Elizabeth Stanton insisted that the declaration include a demand for woman suffrage, but delegates thought the idea of women voting was too radical. After much debate, the demand for woman suffrage in the United States was included. 📖 *(See page 854 of the Appendix for excerpts of the Seneca Falls Declaration.)*

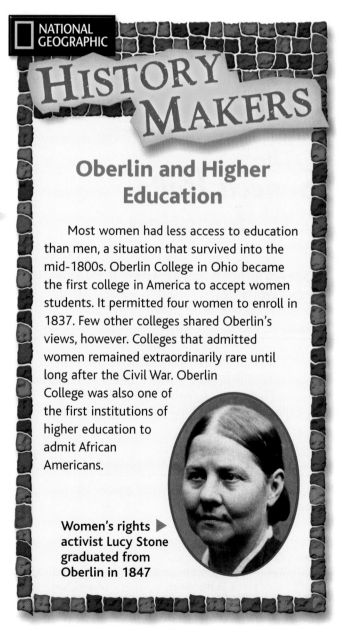

NATIONAL GEOGRAPHIC

HISTORY MAKERS

Oberlin and Higher Education

Most women had less access to education than men, a situation that survived into the mid-1800s. Oberlin College in Ohio became the first college in America to accept women students. It permitted four women to enroll in 1837. Few other colleges shared Oberlin's views, however. Colleges that admitted women remained extraordinarily rare until long after the Civil War. Oberlin College was also one of the first institutions of higher education to admit African Americans.

Women's rights ▶ activist Lucy Stone graduated from Oberlin in 1847

The Women's Rights Movement The Seneca Falls Convention paved the way for the growth of the women's rights movement. During the 1800s, women held several national conventions. Many reformers—male and female—joined the movement.

Susan B. Anthony, the daughter of a Quaker abolitionist in rural New York, worked for women's rights and temperance. She called for equal pay for women, college training for girls, and **coeducation**—the teaching of boys and girls together.

Susan B. Anthony met Elizabeth Cady Stanton at a temperance meeting in 1851. They became lifelong friends and partners in the struggle for women's rights. For the rest of the century, Anthony and Stanton led the women's movement. They worked with other women to win the right to vote, which was granted by several states. It was not until 1920, however, that woman suffrage became a reality everywhere in the United States.

✓ **Reading Check** **Explain** What is suffrage?

Why It Matters

Raising the Status of Women

The Seneca Falls Convention

Throughout the nation's history, women had fought side by side with the men to build a new nation and to ensure freedom. Even though the Declaration of Independence promised equality for all, the promise rang hollow for women.

Female reformers began a campaign for their own rights. In 1848 Lucretia Mott and Elizabeth Cady Stanton organized the Seneca Falls Convention. One of the resolutions demanded suffrage, or the right to vote, for women. This marked the beginning of a long, hard road to gain equal rights.

Lucretia Mott (below) and Susan B. Anthony were leaders in the effort to allow women a greater role in American society.

"We hold these truths to be self-evident: that all men and women are created equal."
—Declaration of the
Seneca Falls Convention, 1848

Gaining the Right to Vote, 1848–1920

The Seneca Falls Convention led to the growth of the woman suffrage movement.

1848 →	**1850** →	**1866** →	**1869** →	**1878** →	**1884** →
Seneca Falls Convention	First national women's rights convention held in Worcester, Massachusetts	Susan B. Anthony forms Equal Rights Association	Women granted voting rights in Wyoming Territory	Woman suffrage amendment first introduced in U.S. Congress	Belva Lockwood runs for president

Progress by American Women

Main Idea Women made progress in gaining equality in education, marriage laws, and the professional sector.

Reading Connection Laws are often put in place to protect individuals and society—for example, laws against speeding or stealing. How would you feel about laws that barred women from the same privileges as men? Is that fair or discriminatory? Read on to find out how women worked for change.

In the early 1800s, the Industrial Revolution began to change the economic roles of men and women. In the 1700s, most economic activity took place in or near the home because a great many Americans lived and worked in a rural farm setting. Although husbands and wives had separate chores, their main effort was maintaining the farm. By the mid-1800s, these circumstances had started to change, especially in the north-eastern states.

Maria Mitchell gained world renown when she discovered a comet in 1847. She became a professor of astronomy and the first woman elected to the American Academy of Arts and Sciences.

Mary Ann Shadd Cary was the first African American woman in the nation to earn a law degree.

Elizabeth Blackwell was the first woman to receive a medical degree in the United States.

Helen Keller overcame the challenges of an illness that left her deaf, blind, and mute to help others with similar disabilities.

Susette La Flesche was a member of the Omaha tribe and campaigned for Native American rights.

1893 → Colorado adopts woman suffrage

1896 → Utah joins the Union, granting women full suffrage

1910–1918 → States including Washington, Kansas, and Michigan adopt woman suffrage

1919 → House and Senate pass the federal woman suffrage amendment

1920 → Tennessee ratifies the Nineteenth Amendment, called the Susan B. Anthony Amendment. It becomes law on August 26, 1920.

On Equality for Women

Sarah Grimké ▶

Sarah and Angeline Grimké were daughters of a wealthy South Carolina judge and plantation owner. The sisters fought against the institution of slavery. They also spoke out for women's rights. In this passage, Sarah Grimké writes about the differences in pay for men and women.

"There is another way in which the general opinion, that women are inferior to men, is manifested [shown], that bears with tremendous effect on the laboring class, and indeed on almost all who are [obliged] to earn a subsistence [living], whether it be by mental or physical exertion. I allude [refer] to the [unequal] value set on the time and labor of men and of women. A man who is engaged in teaching, can always, I believe, command a higher price . . . than a woman—even when he teaches the same branches [subjects], and is not in any respect superior to the woman. . . . In tailoring, a man [earns] twice or three times as much for making a waistcoat or pantaloons as a woman, although the work done by each may be equally good. In those employments [jobs] which are peculiar to women, their time is estimated at only half the value of that of men. A woman who goes out to wash, works as hard in proportion as a wood sawyer, or a coal heaver, but she is not generally able to make more than half as much by a day's work."

—*Letters on the Equality of the Sexes*

DBQ Document-Based Question

What point is Sarah Grimké making about women and men workers in the same occupation?

The development of factories separated the home from the workplace. Men now often left home to go to work, while women tended the house and children.

As the nature of work changed, many Americans began to divide life into two areas of activities—the home and the workplace. Many believed the home to be the proper area for women, partly because of popular ideas about the family. Some also believed that women belonged in the home because the outside world was seen as dangerous and corrupt.

The Great Awakening greatly influenced the American family. For many parents, raising children was a serious responsibility because it prepared young people for a disciplined Christian life. Women often were viewed as kinder and more moral than men, and they were expected to be models of goodness for their children and husbands.

The idea grew that women should be homemakers and should take the main responsibility for raising the sons and daughters. Magazine articles and novels aimed at women supported the value of their role at home.

Opportunities for Education Pioneers in women's education began to call for more opportunity. Early pioneers such as Catherine Beecher and Emma Hart Willard believed that women should be educated for their traditional roles in life. They also thought that women could be capable teachers. Beecher, the daughter of a minister and reformer, wrote a book called *A Treatise on Domestic Economy*. It gave instructions on children, cooking, and health matters. The Milwaukee College for Women set up courses based on Beecher's ideas "to train women to be healthful, intelligent, and successful wives, mothers, and housekeepers."

After her marriage, Emma Willard educated herself in subjects considered suitable only for boys, such as science and mathematics. In 1821 Willard established the Troy Female Seminary in New York. The school taught mathematics, history, geography, and physics, as well as the usual homemaking subjects.

Mary Lyon established Mount Holyoke Female Seminary in Massachusetts in 1837. It was the first institution of higher education for women only. Lyon modeled its curriculum on that of nearby Amherst College.

Marriage and Family Laws

During the 1800s, women made some gains in the area of marriage and property laws. New York, Pennsylvania, Indiana, Wisconsin, Mississippi, and the new state of California recognized the right of women to own property after their marriage.

Some states passed laws permitting women to share the guardianship of their children jointly with their husbands. Indiana was the first of several states that allowed women to seek divorce if their husbands were chronic abusers of alcohol.

Breaking Barriers

In the 1800s, women had few career choices. They could become elementary school teachers—although school boards often paid lower salaries to women than to men. Breaking into fields such as medicine and the **ministry** was more difficult. Some determined women, however, succeeded in entering these all-male professions.

Hoping to study medicine, **Elizabeth Blackwell** was turned down by more than 20 schools. Finally accepted by Geneva College in New York, Blackwell graduated at the head of her class. She went on to win acceptance and fame as a doctor.

Despite the accomplishments of notable women, gains in education, and changes in state laws, women in the 1800s remained limited by social customs and expectations. The early feminists—like the abolitionists, temperance workers, and other activists of the age of reform—had just begun the long struggle to achieve their **goals.**

Reading Check **Identify** Who established the Troy Female Seminary?

Section 5 Review

Study Central Need help understanding the women's movement? Visit tajww1.glencoe.com and click on Study Central.

Reading Summary

Review the Main Ideas

- The abolitionist movement helped women see the discrimination they encountered in their own lives, and they organized to end this discrimination.

- Women created their own schools and colleges, increased their legal standing in their families, and gained more professional choices.

What Did You Learn?

1. How did the fight to end slavery help spark the women's movement?

2. Discuss three goals of the women's rights movement.

Critical Thinking

3. **Organizing Information** Recreate the diagram below and list the areas where women gained rights.

4. **The Big Ideas** What qualities do you think women such as Susan B. Anthony, Elizabeth Cady Stanton, and Elizabeth Blackwell shared?

5. **Sequencing Information** Study the information on the feature on the Seneca Falls Convention on pages 410–411. When did Wyoming women gain the right to vote? What "first" did Elizabeth Blackwell accomplish?

Analyzing Primary Sources

Life in the North

In the early 1800s, the northeast United States underwent rapid change. The Industrial Revolution led to new jobs, and new forms of transportation, such as canals and railroads, developed. A Second Great Awakening led to a renewed interest in religion and reform.

Read the passages on pages 414 and 415 and answer the questions that follow.

This scene shows Lockport on the Erie Canal near Buffalo, New York. ▶

Reader's Dictionary

exempted (ihg • ZEHMPT • ihd): excused from something that others must do

pervading (puhr • VAYD • ihng): spreading throughout all parts

melodious (muh • LOH • dee • uhs): having a pleasant sound

tumultuously (tu • MUHL • chuh • wuhs • lee): violently and in confusion

quivered: shook, shivered, trembled

occupation (AH • kyuh • PAY • shuhn): job

station: position in society

packet: passenger boat that usually carries mail and cargo

salons (suh • LAHNZ): sitting rooms

ventilators (VEHN • tuhl • AY • tuhrz): air vents

Religious Camp Meeting

By the 1830s, the Second Great Awakening was in full swing. One revivalist, James Finley, described a revival meeting:

The noise was like the roar of Niagara [Falls]. . . . I counted seven ministers, all preaching at one time, some on stumps, others on wagons . . . no sex nor color, class nor description, were **exempted** from the **pervading** influence of the spirit; even from the age of 8 months to 60 years . . . some of the people were singing, others praying, some crying for mercy . . . some struck with terror . . . others surrounding them with **melodious** song. A peculiar sensation came over me. My heart beat **tumultuously,** my knees trembled, my lips **quivered,** and I felt as though I must fall to the ground.

—James Finley

◀ **Camp meetings could attract thousands of people for days of prayer, song, and expressions of faith.**

American Notes

British writer Charles Dickens traveled to America in 1842. After returning to England, he published American Notes, a book about what he had seen in America. In this excerpt, Dickens describes his visit to a factory in Lowell, Massachusetts.

The rooms in which they worked were as well ordered as themselves. In the windows of some there were green plants, which were trained to shade the glass; in all, there was as much fresh air, cleanliness, and comfort as the nature of the **occupation** would possibly admit of. . . .

They have got up among themselves a periodical called THE LOWELL OFFERING, "a repository of original articles, written exclusively by females actively employed in the mills,"—which is duly printed, published, and sold; and whereof I brought away from Lowell four hundred good solid pages, which I have read from beginning to end. . . .

It is their **station** to work. And they *do* work. They labour in these mills, upon an average, twelve hours a day, which is unquestionably work, and pretty tight work too.

—from *American Notes* by Charles Dickens

Travel on the Erie Canal

This is an 1843 advertisement for traveling on the canal.

—from *Canal Days in America: The History and Romance of Old Towpaths and Waterways*

DBQ Document-Based Questions

Religious Camp Meeting

1. Finley says that the camp meeting is like the roar of Niagara. What is he comparing?

2. Who does the preaching affect?

American Notes

3. According to Dickens, what are conditions in the factory like?

4. How long is the workday?

Travel on the Erie Canal

5. According to the poster, how long does it take to travel from Niagara Falls to Albany if people take a packet boat?

6. What new conveniences do these packet boats have?

Read to Write

7. Review the readings looking for three sentences that are complicated or confusing. Work through each sentence to clarify the meaning for yourself, and then restate that meaning on your paper.

Chapter 8 Assessment

Review Content Vocabulary

1. Use the following words in a paragraph about the Industrial Revolution.

   capital   free enterprise

   technology   factory system

Review the Main Ideas

Section 1 • Economic Growth

2. How did the landscape of New England affect how and where people lived in the late 1700s and early 1800s?

3. How did new technology contribute to the growth of the Industrial Revolution?

Section 2 • A System of Transportation

4. How did canals boost the economy of the Great Lakes region?

5. What was the purpose of canal locks?

Section 3 • The North's People

6. Give three reasons why cities grew in the early 1800s.

7. In what ways were women in the work-force discriminated against?

8. Why did immigration from Germany increase after 1848?

Section 4 • Reforms and Reformers

9. What were the founders of utopias hoping to achieve?

10. What problems in society did reformers in the temperance movement blame on alcohol?

11. What were the basic principles of public education?

Section 5 • The Women's Movement

12. What role did Catherine Beecher play in education for women?

13. What was the significance of the Seneca Falls convention?

Critical Thinking

14. **Compare** Discuss an advantage and a disadvantage of city life in the North.

15. **Explain** How did the Industrial Revolution make the United States more economically independent in the early 1800s?

Geography Skills

Study the map below and answer the following questions.

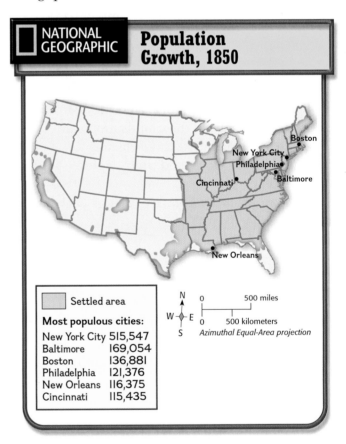

NATIONAL GEOGRAPHIC Population Growth, 1850

Settled area

Most populous cities:

New York City	515,547
Baltimore	169,054
Boston	136,881
Philadelphia	121,376
New Orleans	116,375
Cincinnati	115,435

500 miles

500 kilometers

Azimuthal Equal-Area projection

16. **Location** Which city had the largest population in 1850?

17. **Region** Which area of the country was most heavily settled?

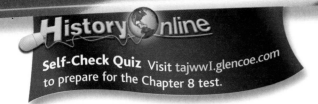
Read to Write

18. The Big Ideas Descriptive Writing
Review Section 2 of the chapter for information about what it was like to live in the Midwest in the early 1800s. Using the information you find, write a postcard to a friend describing your social life.

19. Using Your FOLDABLES Use the information you collected in your foldable to create a compare-contrast chart. In your chart, you will assess the roots, goals, and achievements of social reform, educational reform, and the women's rights movement. How are these movements similar? How do they differ?

Using Academic Vocabulary

20. Use two of the following academic vocabulary words to complete the sentence.

focus   expand

manual   goal

As the U.S. economy continued to ___, immigrants provided much of the ___ labor.

Building Citizenship Skills

21. Explore Working with two other students, contact a local historical society to learn about your community's history. Prepare a list of questions to ask your historical society. Then interview people in your neighborhood to learn about their roots in the community. Find out when their families first settled there. Write a history of the community and give a copy of it to the historical society.

Reviewing Skills

22. READING SKILL Problems and Solutions
This chapter highlighted various problems, or challenges, that groups of people faced. Choose one group and describe their unique challenges and the ways in which people attempted to face those challenges.

23. ANALYSIS SKILL Describe Identify and describe the economic impact of canals on the Northeast.

Standardized Test Practice

Answer the following questions.

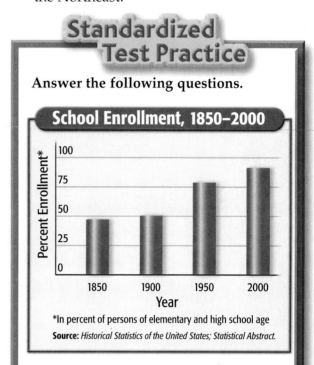

School Enrollment, 1850–2000

*In percent of persons of elementary and high school age
Source: *Historical Statistics of the United States; Statistical Abstract.*

24 According to the graph above, the greatest increase in the percentage of school enrollment occurred between

  A 1850 and 1880.

  B 1850 and 1900.

  C 1900 and 1950.

  D 1950 and 2000.

25 Labor unions were formed for all of the following reasons EXCEPT

  A to improve workers' wages.

  B to protect factory owners from being sued.

  C to make factories safer.

  D to prevent children from working long hours.

The South

▼ Drayton Hall Plantation, near Charleston, South Carolina

NATIONAL GEOGRAPHIC **Where & When?**

Cotton-producing area

•Richmond

•Charleston

New Orleans•

1790	1825	1860
1793 The cotton gin is invented	**1831** Nat Turner's slave revolt strikes fear in Southerners	**1860** Baltimore's population is over 200,000

The Big Ideas

Section 1

Southern Cotton Kingdom

Geography shapes the physical, economic, and political challenges a region faces. Cotton was vital to the economy of the South.

Section 2

Life in the South

Geography shapes the physical, economic, and political challenges a region faces. Most of the people in the South worked in agriculture in the first half of the 1800s.

Section 3

The Peculiar Institution

Differences in economic, political, and social beliefs and practices can lead to division within a nation and have lasting consequences. Enslaved African Americans developed a unique culture and fought against slavery.

 View the Chapter 9 video in the Glencoe Video Program.

FOLDABLES™
Study Organizer

Summarizing Make this foldable and use it as a journal to help you take notes about the South during the period from 1800 to 1850.

Step 1 Stack four sheets of paper, one on top of the other. On the top sheet of paper, trace a large circle.

Step 2 With the papers still stacked, cut out all four circles at the same time.

Reading and Writing As you read the chapter, write what you learn about the South in your foldable.

Step 3 Staple the paper circles together at one point around the edge.

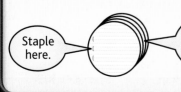

Staple here.

This makes a circular booklet.

Step 4 Label the front cover as shown and take notes on the pages that open to the right.

Living and Working in the South

Get Ready to Read

Questioning

1 Learn It!

One way to understand what you are reading is to interact with the text by asking questions. What questions would you like answered? What are you curious about? As you read, you may be able to locate the answer in the next paragraph or section. Practice asking questions by turning headings into questions. For instance, a heading that reads "Life Under Slavery" can be turned into the question "What was life like under slavery?" Read this selection from Chapter 9. What questions do you have?

Reading Tip

Good questions start with key words such as *who, what, when, where, why,* and *how.*

> Enslaved people faced constant uncertainty and danger. American law in the early 1800s did not protect enslaved families. At any time, a husband or wife could be sold to a different owner, or a slaveholder's death could lead to the breakup of an enslaved family. Although marriage between enslaved people was not recognized by law, many couples did marry. Their marriage ceremonies included the phrase "until death or separation do us part"—recognizing the possibility that their life together might end with the sale of one spouse.
>
> — *from page 433*

2 Practice It!

Read the following paragraph, and answer this question with a partner: What were the economic goals of a plantation owner?

The main economic goal for large plantation owners was to earn profits. Such plantations had fixed costs—regular expenses such as housing and feeding workers and maintaining cotton gins and other equipment. Fixed costs remained about the same year after year.

Cotton prices, however, varied from season to season, depending on the market. To receive the best prices, planters sold their cotton to agents in cities such as New Orleans, Charleston, Mobile, and Savannah. The cotton exchanges, or trade centers, in Southern cities were of vital importance to those involved in the cotton economy. The agents of the exchanges extended credit—a form of loan—to the planters and held the cotton for several months until the price rose. Then the agents sold the cotton. This system kept the planters always in debt because they did not receive payment for their cotton until the agents sold it.

—*from page 429*

Read to Write

Write a *What If* paragraph based on what you read in this chapter. For example, *what if* the South had become industrialized like the North? Your paragraph should answer your *What If* question.

▲ Plantation in the South

3 Apply It!

As you read the chapter, look for answers to section headings that are in the form of questions. For the other sections, turn the headings into questions that you can answer as you read.

Southern Cotton Kingdom

Guide to Reading

Looking Back, Looking Ahead

In the last chapter, you learned about life in and the economy of the Northeastern states. In this section, you will learn about the economy of the South.

Focusing on the Main Ideas

- Unlike the North, the Southern economy remained mainly agrarian. *(page 423)*
- For many reasons, industry developed slowly in the South. *(page 424)*

Locating Places

Upper South
Deep South

Meeting People

Eli Whitney
William Gregg
Joseph Reid Anderson

Content Vocabulary

cotton gin
capital (KA•puh•tuhl)

Academic Vocabulary

predominant (prih•DAH•muh•nuhnt)
sum

Reading Strategy

Comparing As you read the section, re-create the diagram below. In the ovals, give reasons why cotton production grew but industrial growth was slower.

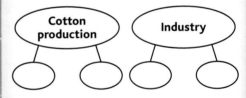

Cotton production   Industry

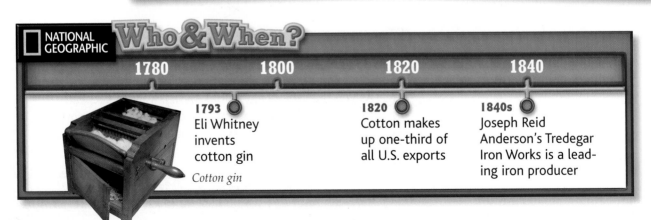

NATIONAL GEOGRAPHIC **Who & When?**

1780	1800	1820	1840

1793
Eli Whitney invents cotton gin
Cotton gin

1820
Cotton makes up one-third of all U.S. exports

1840s
Joseph Reid Anderson's Tredegar Iron Works is a leading iron producer

Rise of the Cotton Kingdom

Main Idea Unlike the North, the Southern economy remained mainly agrarian.

Reading Connection Check the label on your pants or shirt. What materials are found in the fabric? Chances are you wear something at least partly made of cotton. Read on to find out how cotton was a major economic asset to the Deep South.

An American Story

Cotton was not the only crop grown in the South, but it was the crop that fueled the Southern economy. Southerners began saying, rightly, "Cotton is king." "Look which way you will, you see it; and see [cotton] moving," wrote a visitor to Mobile, Alabama. "Keel boats, ships, brigs, schooners, wharves, stores, and press-houses, all appeared to be full."

Cotton Rules the Deep South Most Southerners lived along the Atlantic coast in Maryland, Virginia, Tennessee, and North Carolina in what came to be known as the **Upper South.** By 1850 the South had changed. Its population had spread inland to the states of the **Deep South**—Georgia, South Carolina, Alabama, Mississippi, Louisiana, Florida, Arkansas, and Texas.

In colonial times, rice, indigo (a plant used to make blue dye), and tobacco made up the South's main crops. After the American Revolution, demand for these crops decreased. European mills, however, wanted Southern cotton to make into cloth. But cotton was difficult to produce. After cotton was harvested, workers had to painstakingly separate the plant's sticky seeds from the cotton fibers.

In 1793 **Eli Whitney** invented the cotton gin. The **cotton gin** was a compact machine that removed seeds from cotton fibers much more quickly than could be done by hand. Because cotton could be processed more easily, Southern planters wanted to grow more. As a result, they depended on slave labor to plant and pick cotton.

By 1860 the economies of the Deep South and the Upper South had developed in different ways. Both parts of the South were agricultural, but the Upper South still produced tobacco, hemp, wheat, and vegetables. The Deep South was committed to cotton and, in some areas, to rice and sugarcane.

The value of enslaved people increased because of their key role in producing cotton and sugar. In time, the Upper South became a center for the sale of enslaved people.

Reading Check **Describe** What effect did the cotton gin have on the South's economy?

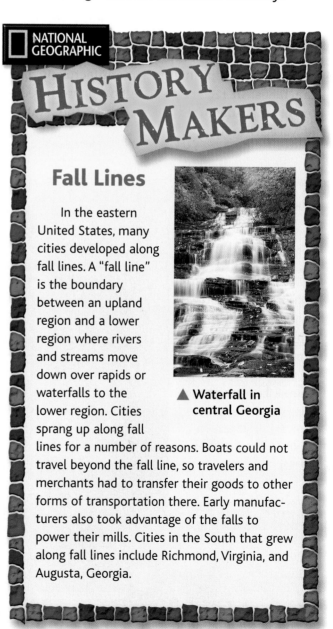

NATIONAL GEOGRAPHIC

HISTORY MAKERS

Fall Lines

In the eastern United States, many cities developed along fall lines. A "fall line" is the boundary between an upland region and a lower region where rivers and streams move down over rapids or waterfalls to the lower region. Cities sprang up along fall lines for a number of reasons. Boats could not travel beyond the fall line, so travelers and merchants had to transfer their goods to other forms of transportation there. Early manufacturers also took advantage of the falls to power their mills. Cities in the South that grew along fall lines include Richmond, Virginia, and Augusta, Georgia.

▲ **Waterfall in central Georgia**

Industry in the South

Main Idea For many reasons, industry developed slowly in the South.

Reading Connection How do you get to school each morning? Do you take the bus or ride in a car, or do you walk to school? Read on to find out what modes of transportation transported people and goods in the South.

The economy of the South prospered between 1820 and 1860. Unlike the industrial North, however, the South remained **predominantly** rural, and its economy became increasingly different from the Northern economy. The South accounted for only a small percentage of the nation's manufacturing in the 1850s. In fact, the entire South produced fewer manufactured goods than the state of Massachusetts.

Barriers to Industry Why was there little industry in the South? One reason was the boom in cotton sales. Because agriculture was so profitable, Southerners remained committed to farming rather than starting new businesses.

Another reason was the lack of **capital** (KA•puh•tuhl)—money to invest in businesses—in the South. To develop industries required money, but many Southerners had their wealth invested in land and slaves. Planters would have had to sell slaves to raise the money to build factories. Most wealthy Southerners were unwilling to do this. They believed that an economy based on cotton and slavery would continue to prosper.

In addition, the market for manufactured goods in the South was smaller than it was in the North. A large portion of the Southern population consisted of enslaved people with no money to buy merchandise. So the limited local market discouraged industries from developing.

TECHNOLOGY & History

The Cotton Gin

In 1793 Eli Whitney visited Catherine Greene, a Georgia plantation owner. She asked him to build a device that removed the seeds from cotton pods. Whitney called the machine the cotton gin—*gin* being short for "engine". **How did the invention of the cotton gin affect slavery?**

Eli Whitney

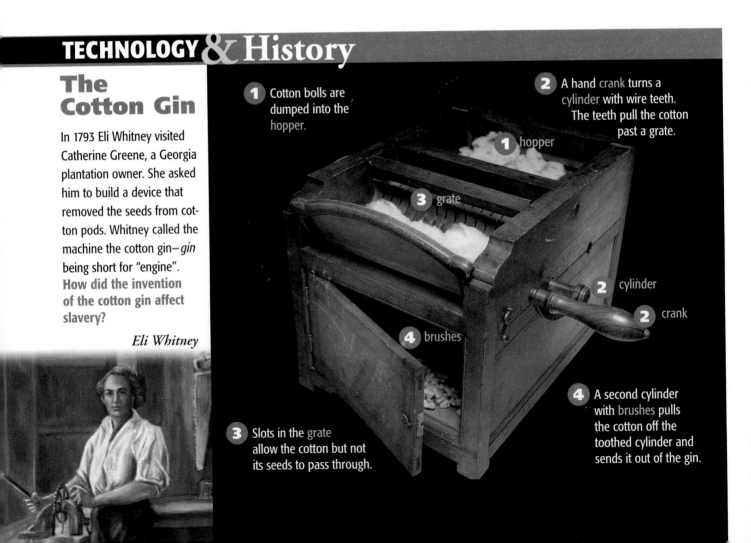

1 Cotton bolls are dumped into the hopper.

2 A hand crank turns a cylinder with wire teeth. The teeth pull the cotton past a grate.

1 hopper

3 grate

3 Slots in the grate allow the cotton but not its seeds to pass through.

2 cylinder

2 crank

4 brushes

4 A second cylinder with brushes pulls the cotton off the toothed cylinder and sends it out of the gin.

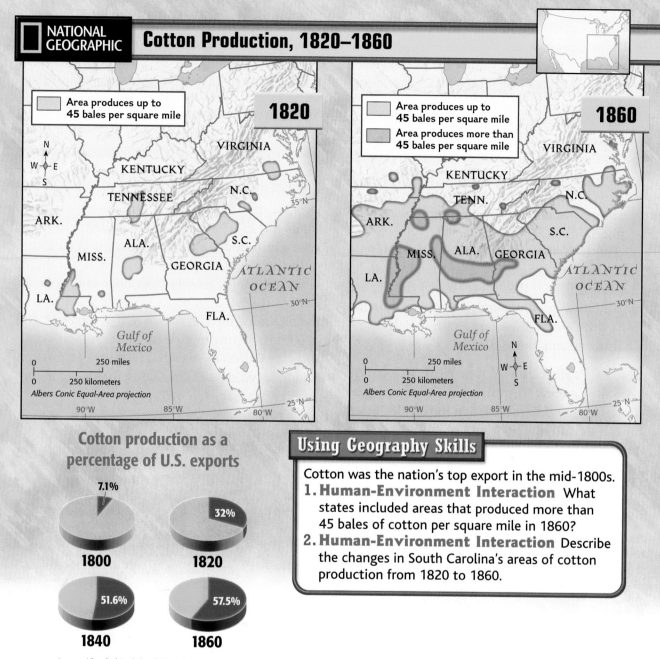

NATIONAL GEOGRAPHIC

Cotton Production, 1820–1860

1820

Area produces up to 45 bales per square mile

VIRGINIA
KENTUCKY
TENNESSEE
N.C.
ARK.
ALA.
S.C.
MISS.
GEORGIA
ATLANTIC OCEAN
LA.
FLA.
Gulf of Mexico

0 — 250 miles
0 — 250 kilometers
Albers Conic Equal-Area projection

1860

Area produces up to 45 bales per square mile

Area produces more than 45 bales per square mile

VIRGINIA
KENTUCKY
TENN.
N.C.
ARK.
S.C.
MISS.
ALA.
GEORGIA
LA.
ATLANTIC OCEAN
FLA.
Gulf of Mexico

0 — 250 miles
0 — 250 kilometers
Albers Conic Equal-Area projection

Cotton production as a percentage of U.S. exports

7.1%
1800

32%
1820

51.6%
1840

57.5%
1860

Source: *Historical Statistics of the United States.*

Using Geography Skills

Cotton was the nation's top export in the mid-1800s.
1. **Human-Environment Interaction** What states included areas that produced more than 45 bales of cotton per square mile in 1860?
2. **Human-Environment Interaction** Describe the changes in South Carolina's areas of cotton production from 1820 to 1860.

Another reason for the lack of industry is that some Southerners did not want industry to flourish there. One political leader **summed** up the Southerners' point of view this way:

> ❝ As long as we have our rice, our sugar, our tobacco, and our cotton, we can command wealth to purchase all we want. ❞
>
> —quoted in *Louis T. Wigfall, Southern Fire-Eater*

Southern Factories While most Southerners felt confident about the future of the cotton economy, some leaders wanted to develop industry in the region. These leaders argued that by remaining committed to cotton production, the South was becoming dependent on the North for manufactured goods. These Southerners also argued that factories and workshops would revive the economy of the Upper South, which was less prosperous than the cotton states.

One Southerner who shared this view was **William Gregg,** a merchant from Charleston, South Carolina. After touring New England's textile mills in 1844, Gregg opened his own textile factory in South Carolina.

In Richmond, Virginia, **Joseph Reid Anderson** took over the Tredegar Iron Works in the 1840s and made it one of the nation's leading producers of iron. Years later, during the Civil War, Tredegar provided artillery (weapons) and other iron products for the Southern forces.

The industries that Gregg and Anderson built were the exception rather than the rule in the South. For the most part, the South remained a region of rural villages and plantations with only three large cities: Baltimore, Charleston, and New Orleans.

Cotton Production Moves West To keep up with the demand for raw cotton, cotton plantations sprang up to the west, in the fertile "black belt" (so called for its rich, black soil) of Mississippi and Alabama, and in the rich bottomlands along the Mississippi River and its tributaries. The growing population in these areas led to statehood for Mississippi in 1817, for Alabama in 1819, and for Arkansas in 1836.

Southern Transportation Natural waterways provided the chief means for transporting goods in the South. Most towns were located on the seacoast or along rivers. There were few canals, and roads were poor.

Like the North, the South also built railroads but to a lesser extent. Southern rail lines were short, local, and did not connect all parts of the region in a network. As a result, Southern cities grew more slowly than cities in the North and Midwest, where railways provided the major routes for commerce and settlement. By 1860 only about one-third of the nation's rail lines lay within the South. The railway shortage would have devastating consequences for the South during the Civil War.

Reading Check **Explain** What is capital? Why is it important for economic growth?

History Online

Study Central Need help understanding the economy of the South? Visit tajww1.glencoe.com and click on Study Central.

Section 1 Review

What Did You Learn?

1. What were the major crops in the Deep South?

2. Why did the invention of the cotton gin increase the demand for enslaved people?

Critical Thinking

3. **Comparing** How did agriculture in the Upper South differ from agriculture in the Deep South? Re-create the diagram below and describe the differences.

Agriculture	
Upper South	Deep South

4. **The Big Ideas** How might the banning of slavery have affected the South's economy?

5. **Determining Cause and Effect** Describe transportation in the South during this period. How did transportation affect or limit other areas of Southern life?

6. **READING** **Asking Questions** Turn the two Main Ideas listed in the Reading Summary into questions and then answer them.

Reading Summary

Review the Main Ideas

• The success of cotton production in the South kept it an agrarian region.

• Lack of capital, a small market for manufactured goods, and a desire to remain agrarian hindered the growth of industry in the South.

Section 2

Life in the South

Guide to Reading

Looking Back, Looking Ahead
In the last section, you learned about the economy of the South. In this section, you will read about the way of life of the Southern people.

Focusing on the Main Ideas
- Most farmers in the South did not own slaves and lived in poor rural areas. *(page 428)*
- Plantations varied in size and wealth and contained varying numbers of enslaved people. *(page 429)*
- The South was home to several large cities, and education began to grow in the mid-1800s. *(page 430)*

Locating Places
New Orleans
Charleston
Mobile
Savannah
Columbia
Chattanooga
Montgomery
Atlanta

Content Vocabulary
yeoman (YOH•muhn)
tenant farmer (TEH•nuhnt)
fixed cost
credit
overseer (OH•vuhr•SEE•uhr)

Academic Vocabulary
purchase
exceed (ihk•SEED)

Reading Strategy
Organizing Information As you read the section, re-create the diagram below and describe the work that was done on Southern plantations.

Working on a plantation

NATIONAL GEOGRAPHIC Where & When?

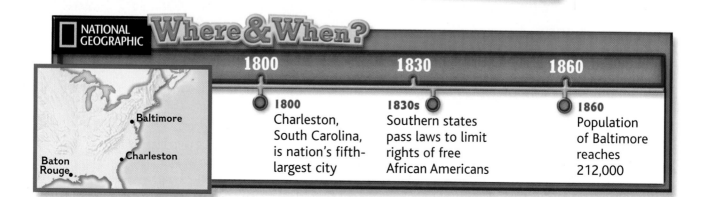

1800

1830

1860

1800
Charleston, South Carolina, is nation's fifth-largest city

1830s
Southern states pass laws to limit rights of free African Americans

1860
Population of Baltimore reaches 212,000

Life on the Small Farms

Main Idea Most farmers in the South did not own slaves and lived in poor rural areas.

Reading Connection When you think about the South during the height of slavery, what images come to mind? Read on to find out what the South was really like during the 1800s.

Popular novels and films often portray the South before 1860 as a land of stately plantations owned by rich white slaveholders. In reality, most white Southerners were either small farmers without slaves or planters with a handful of slaves. Only a few planters could afford the many enslaved people and the lavish mansions shown in fictional accounts of the Old South. Most white Southerners fit into one of four categories: yeomen, tenant farmers, the rural poor, or plantation owners.

Small Farmers and the Rural Poor The farmers who did not have slaves—**yeomen** (YOH•muhn)—made up the largest group of whites in the South. Most yeomen owned land. Although they lived throughout the region, they were most numerous in the Upper South and in the hilly rural areas of the Deep South, where the land was unsuited to large plantations.

A yeoman's farm usually ranged from 50 to 200 acres. Yeomen grew crops both for their own use and to sell, and they often traded their produce to local merchants and workers for goods and services.

Most Southern whites did not live in elegant mansions or on large plantations. They lived in far simpler homes, though the structure of their homes changed over time. In the early 1800s, many lived in cottages built of wood and plaster with thatched roofs. Later many lived in one-story frame houses or log cabins.

Not all Southern whites owned land. Some rented land or worked as **tenant farmers** (TEH•nuhnt) on landlords' estates. Others—the rural poor—lived in crude cabins in wooded areas where they could clear a few trees, plant some corn, and keep a hog or a cow. They also fished and hunted for food.

The poor people of the rural South were fiercely independent. They refused to take any job that resembled the work of enslaved people. Although looked down on by other whites, the rural poor were proud of being self-sufficient.

Reading Check **Identify** What group made up the largest number of whites in the South?

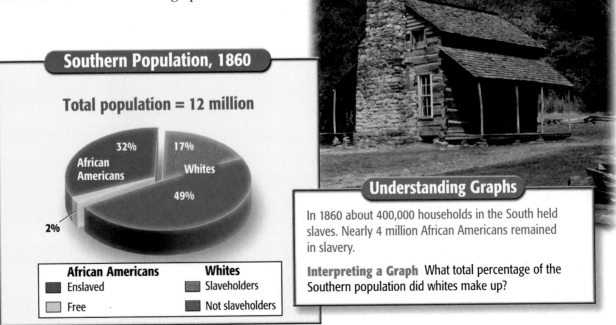

Southern Population, 1860

Total population = 12 million

32% African Americans

17% Whites

49%

2%

African Americans
- Enslaved
- Free

Whites
- Slaveholders
- Not slaveholders

Understanding Graphs

In 1860 about 400,000 households in the South held slaves. Nearly 4 million African Americans remained in slavery.

Interpreting a Graph What total percentage of the Southern population did whites make up?

Plantations

Main Idea Plantations varied in size and wealth and contained varying numbers of enslaved people.

Reading Connection Imagine that you want to open your own business. What things do you need to get your business started? Read on to find out what plantation owners needed to keep their plantations running.

A large plantation might cover several thousand acres. Well-to-do plantation owners usually lived in comfortable but not luxurious farmhouses. They measured their wealth partly by the number of enslaved people they controlled and partly by such possessions as homes, furnishings, and clothing. A small group of plantation owners in the South—about 12 percent of the population—held more than half of the slaves. About half of the planters held fewer than five enslaved workers.

A few free African Americans possessed slaves. The Metoyer family of Louisiana owned thousands of acres of land and more than 400 slaves. Most often, these slaveholders were free African Americans who **purchased** their own family members in order to free them.

Plantation Owners The main economic goal for large plantation owners was to earn profits. Such plantations had **fixed costs**—regular expenses such as housing and feeding workers and maintaining cotton gins and other equipment. Fixed costs remained about the same year after year.

Cotton prices, however, varied from season to season, depending on the market. To receive the best prices, planters sold their cotton to

Picturing **History**

Although wealthy planters were not numerous, they dominated the economy and political system of the South. *What were the duties of the wife of a plantation owner?*

agents in cities such as **New Orleans, Charleston, Mobile,** and **Savannah.** The cotton exchanges, or trade centers, in Southern cities were of vital importance to those involved in the cotton economy. The agents of the exchanges extended **credit**—a form of loan—to the planters and held the cotton for several months until the price rose. Then the agents sold the cotton. This system kept the planters always in debt because they did not receive payment for their cotton until the agents sold it.

Plantation Wives The wife of a plantation owner generally was in charge of watching over the enslaved workers who toiled in her home and tending to them when they became ill. Her responsibilities also included supervising the plantation's buildings and the fruit and vegetable gardens. Some wives served as accountants, keeping the plantation's financial records.

Women often led a difficult and lonely life on the plantation. When plantation agriculture spread westward into Alabama and Mississippi, many planters' wives felt they were moving into a hostile, uncivilized region. Planters traveled frequently to look at new land or to deal with agents in New Orleans or Memphis, so their wives spent long periods alone at the plantation.

History Online

Student Web Activity Visit tajwwI.glencoe.com and click on *Chapter 9—Student Web Activities* for an activity on family life in the South.

Work on the Plantation Large plantations needed many different kinds of workers. Some enslaved people worked in the house, cleaning, cooking, doing laundry, sewing, and serving meals. They were called domestic slaves. Other enslaved people were trained as blacksmiths, carpenters, shoemakers, or weavers. Still others worked in the pastures, tending the horses, cows, sheep, and pigs. Most of the enslaved African Americans, however, were field hands. They worked from sunrise to sunset planting, cultivating, and picking cotton and other crops. They were supervised by an **overseer** (OH•vuhr•SEE•uhr)—a plantation manager.

✓ **Reading Check** **Explain** Why were so many slaves needed on a plantation?

Picturing **History**

This photo shows businesses along a street in Atlanta, Georgia, around 1860. *Why did cities such as Atlanta and Columbia, South Carolina, grow as centers of trade?*

City Life and Education

Main Idea The South was home to several large cities, and education began to grow in the mid-1800s.

Reading Connection Imagine living in a town of only a few hundred people. The closest school is miles away—too far to walk—and transportation is not readily accessible. Read on to find out why it was hard for many families to send their children to school in the South.

Although the South was primarily an agricultural region, it was the site of several large cities by the mid-1800s. By 1860 the population of Baltimore had reached 212,000 and the population of New Orleans **exceeded** 165,000. The ten largest cities in the South were either seaports or river ports.

With the coming of the railroad, many other cities began to grow as centers of trade. Among the cities located at the crossroads of the railways were **Columbia**, South Carolina; **Chattanooga**, Tennessee; **Montgomery**, Alabama; Jackson, Mississippi; and **Atlanta**, Georgia. The population of Southern cities included white city dwellers, some enslaved workers, and many of the South's free African Americans.

The cities provided free African Americans with opportunities to form their own communities. African American barbers, carpenters, and small traders offered their services throughout their communities. Free African Americans also founded their own churches and institutions. In New Orleans, many of them were well-educated and prosperous. They used their resources to form an opera company.

Although some free African Americans prospered in the cities, their lives were far from secure. Between 1830 and 1860, Southern states passed laws that limited the rights of free African Americans. Most states would not allow them to migrate from other states. Although spared the horrors of slavery, free African Americans were denied an equal share in economic and political life.

Education Plantation owners and those who could afford to do so often sent their children to private schools. One of the best known was the academy operated by Moses Waddel in Willington, South Carolina. Students attended six days a week. The Bible and classical literature were stressed, but the courses also included mathematics, religion, Greek, Latin, and public speaking.

In many smaller rural areas, classes met in small schoolhouses or in church buildings. School terms lasted only three to four months. Due to poverty, few books were available for study.

During this era, no statewide public school system existed. However, cities such as Charleston, Louisville, and Mobile did establish excellent public schools.

By the mid-1800s, education was growing. Hundreds of public schools were operating in North Carolina by 1860. Even before that, the Kentucky legislature set up a funding system for public schools. Many states in the South also had charity schools. There are schools for students whose parents could not afford to pay.

Although the number of schools and teachers in the South grew, the South lagged behind other areas of the country in literacy, the number of people who can read or write. One reason for this was the geography of the South. Even in the more heavily populated Southern states there were few people per square mile. Virginia and North Carolina had fewer than 15 white inhabitants per square mile. In contrast, Massachusetts had 127 inhabitants per square mile.

It was too great a hardship for many Southern families to send their children great distances to attend school. In addition, many Southerners believed education was a private matter, not a state function; therefore, the state should not spend money on education.

Reading Check **Identify** What Southern city had surpassed 200,000 in population by the year 1860?

History Online

Study Central Need help understanding Southern life in the mid-1800s? Visit tajww1.glencoe.com and click on Study Central.

Section 2 Review

Reading Summary

Review the Main Ideas

- Many farmers in the South were yeomen who lived on small farms.

- Many plantations were small and had relatively few slaves.

- By the mid-1800s, the number of cities in the South was increasing, and education was growing.

What Did You Learn?

1. List two differences between yeoman and plantation owners.

2. Explain why some free African Americans might own slaves.

Critical Thinking

3. **Comparing** Create a chart like the one below and compare the life of a plantation owner to that of a small farmer.

Plantation Owner	Small Farmer

4. **The Big Ideas** Describe the life of free African Americans in Southern cities.

5. **Descriptive Writing** Study the pictures on pages 429 and 430. Write a paragraph explaining what you think the pictures portray about life in the South.

6. **ANALYSIS** **Explain** Write a short paragraph explaining the relationship between the plantation owner and the cotton exchange. Then, discuss which job you would choose.

Section 3

The Peculiar Institution

Guide to Reading

Looking Back, Looking Ahead

In Section 2, you learned about the life of Southern whites in the country, as well as about life in Southern cities. In this section, you will learn about slavery and the lives of African Americans in the South.

Focusing on the Main Ideas

- Enslaved African Americans faced many hardships but were able to create family lives, religious beliefs, and a distinct culture. *(page 433)*
- Many enslaved people fought against slavery. *(page 434)*

Meeting People

Nat Turner

Harriet Tubman

Frederick Douglass

Content Vocabulary

spiritual (SPIHR•ih•chuh•wuhl)

slave codes

Academic Vocabulary

constant

communicate

Reading Strategy

Organizing Information Create a chart like the one below to list aspects of African American life in the South.

Way of Life	Aspects
Family Life	
Culture	
Religion	

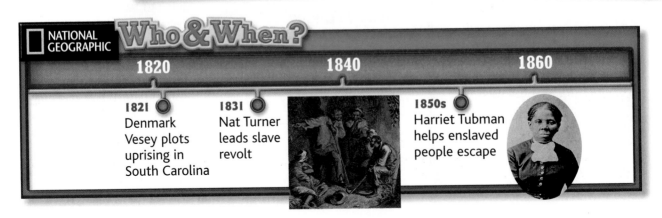

NATIONAL GEOGRAPHIC

Who & When?

1820   1840   1860

1821 Denmark Vesey plots uprising in South Carolina

1831 Nat Turner leads slave revolt

1850s Harriet Tubman helps enslaved people escape

Life Under Slavery

Main Idea Enslaved African Americans faced many hardships but were able to create family lives, religious beliefs, and a distinct culture.

Reading Connection Imagine being taken to a foreign land where you do not speak the language and do not understand the customs. How would you adapt to such a situation? Read on to find out how enslaved Southerners developed family and social ties to cope with their situation.

An American Story

Planters gathered in the bright Savannah sunshine. They were there to bid on a strong slave who could plow their fields. Fear and grief clouded the enslaved man's face because he had been forced to leave his wife and children. Later, he wrote this letter:

> 66 My Dear wife I [write] . . . with much regret to inform you that I am Sold to a man by the name of Peterson. . . . Give my love to my father and mother and tell them good Bye for me. And if we Shall not meet in this world, I hope to meet in heaven. My Dear wife for you and my Children my pen cannot Express the [grief] I feel to be parted from you all. 99

—as quoted in *The Black Family in Slavery and Freedom, 1750–1925*

Family Life Enslaved people faced **constant** uncertainty and danger. American law in the early 1800s did not protect enslaved families. At any time, a husband or wife could be sold to a different owner, or a slaveholder's death could lead to the breakup of an enslaved family. Although marriage between enslaved people was not recognized by law, many couples did marry. Their marriage ceremonies included the phrase "until death or separation do us part"—recognizing the possibility that their life together might end with the sale of one spouse.

To provide some measure of stability in their lives, enslaved African Americans established a network of relatives and friends, who made up their extended family. If a father or mother were sold away, an aunt, uncle, or close friend could raise the children left behind. Large, close-knit extended families became a vital feature of African American culture.

African American Culture Enslaved African Americans endured their hardships by extending their own culture, fellowship, and community. They fused African and American elements into a new culture.

The growth of the African American population came mainly from children born in the United States. In 1808 Congress had outlawed the slave trade. Although slavery remained legal in the Southern States, no new slaves could enter the United States. By 1860 almost all the enslaved people in the South had been born there.

These native-born African Americans practiced their African customs. They continued to enjoy African music and dance. They passed traditional African folk stories to their children. Some wrapped colored cloths around their heads in the African style. Although a large number of enslaved African Americans accepted Christianity, they often followed the religious beliefs and practices of their African ancestors as well.

African American Christianity For many enslaved African Americans, Christianity became a religion of hope and resistance. They prayed fervently for the day when they would be free from bondage.

The passionate beliefs of the Southern slaves found expression in the **spiritual** (SPIHR•ih•chuh•wuhl), an African American religious folk song. The song "Didn't My Lord Deliver Daniel," for example, refers to the biblical story of Daniel, who was saved from the lions' den.

> **"** Didn't my Lord deliver Daniel, deliver Daniel, deliver Daniel? Didn't my Lord deliver Daniel, And why [not] every man? **"**
>
> — from *Wade in the Water*

Spirituals provided a way for the enslaved African Americans to **communicate** secretly with one another. The spirituals often reflected the connection African American enslaved people felt to enslaved people who were depicted in the Bible. Passed down through the oral tradition, spirituals helped form an African American culture. They also became one of the best-known forms of American music.

✓ **Reading Check** **Explain** How did the African American spiritual develop?

Resisting Slavery

Main Idea Many enslaved people fought against slavery.

Reading Connection How do you react when someone treats you unfairly? Read on to find out how enslaved people resisted.

Enslaved people had few legal rights. Between 1830 and 1860, life under slavery became even more difficult because the **slave codes**—the laws in the Southern states that controlled enslaved people—became more severe. In existence since the 1700s, slave codes were written to prevent the event white Southerners dreaded most—the slave rebellion. For this reason slave codes prohibited slaves from assembling in large groups and from leaving their master's property without a written pass.

Primary Sources

Working the Cotton Fields

Solomon Northup was a free black who was kidnapped and sold into slavery. He picked cotton on a Louisiana plantation for 12 years before winning his freedom. His description of picking cotton follows.

When a new hand, one unaccustomed to the business, is sent for the first time into the field, he is whipped up smartly, and made for that day to pick as fast as he can possibly. At night it is weighed, so that his capability in cotton picking is known. He must bring in the same weight each night following. If it falls short, it is considered evidence that he has been laggard, and a greater or less number of lashes is the penalty. . . . The hands are required to be in the cotton field as soon as it is light in the morning, and, with the exception of ten or fifteen minutes, which is given them at noon to swallow their allowance of cold bacon, they are not permitted to be a moment idle until it is too dark to see, and when the moon is full, they often times labor till the middle of the night. They do not dare to stop even at dinner time, nor return to the quarters, however late it be, until the order to halt is given by the driver. . . .

—from *Twelve Years a Slave* by Solomon Northup

▲ **Solomon Northup**

 **Document-Based Question**

Why do you think it seems like Northup's perspective is that of an outsider?

More About...

Living Under Slavery

Enslaved workers reached the fields before the sun came up, and they stayed there until sundown. Planters wanted to keep the slaves busy all the time, which meant long and grueling days in the fields. Enslaved women as well as men were required to do heavy fieldwork. Young children carried buckets of water. By the age of 10, they were considered ready for fieldwork.

Cabins were usually made of small logs, about 10 to 20 feet square. Often, two or three families shared a cabin.

Heavy iron leg shackles were used to punish workers, especially those who tried to run away.

Enslaved people had few personal possessions.

When rented to other masters, enslaved people wore identification tags.

Slave codes also made it a crime to teach enslaved people to read or write. White Southerners believed a slave who did not know how to read and write was less likely to rebel.

Rebellions Some enslaved African Americans did rebel openly against their masters. One was **Nat Turner,** a popular religious leader among his fellow slaves. Turner had taught himself to read and write. In 1831 Turner led a group of followers on a brief, violent rampage in Southhampton County, Virginia, that resulted in the death of at least 55 whites. Nat Turner was hanged, but his rebellion frightened whites and led to more severe slave codes.

Even before the rebellion led by Nat Turner, other enslaved persons had plotted uprisings in the South. In 1800 Gabriel Prosser planned a rebellion to capture Richmond, Virginia, and massacre whites. An informer gave the plot away, and Prosser and 35 others were convicted and executed.

Denmark Vesey, a Charleston, South Carolina, carpenter, who had earlier purchased his freedom, was outraged by the existence of slavery. His reading of the Bible and the Declaration of Independence fueled his hatred of slavery. His 1821 plan for a slave revolt failed when it was betrayed at the last moment by some of his followers.

Biography

HARRIET TUBMAN
1820–1913

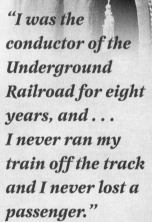

Born a slave in Maryland, Harriet Tubman worked in plantation fields until she was nearly 30 years old. Then she made her break for freedom, escaping to the North with the help of the Underground Railroad. While jubilant over the success of her escape when she crossed the line from Delaware into Pennsylvania, Tubman's happiness was short-lived. She explained, "I was *free*, but there was no one to welcome me to the land of freedom. . . . [M]y home, after all, was down in Maryland, because my father, my mother, my brothers, my sisters, and friends were there. But I was free and *they should be free!*"

Settling in Philadelphia, Tubman met many abolitionists who shared her desire to bring Southern slaves to the North. Realizing the risks of being captured, Tubman courageously made 19 trips back into the South during the 1850s to help other enslaved people escape. Altogether she assisted about 70 individuals—including her parents—to escape from slavery.

Tubman did not establish the Underground Railroad, but she certainly became its most famous and successful conductor. Tubman was known as the "Moses of her people" for leading slaves to freedom in the North. Despite huge rewards offered in the South for her capture and arrest, Tubman always managed to elude her enemies.

During the Civil War, Tubman assisted the Union army as a nurse and a spy, caring for the sick and wounded and making trips behind enemy lines to scout out Confederate troops. Tubman continued to experience discrimination at the end of the war and was never paid for her services in the army. Despite financial difficulties, Tubman opened her home in New York to African Americans journeying North after the war. Many were sick or near starvation, and she fed them, clothed them, and cared for them. In 1896 Tubman opened a center for the sick and needy on land across from her home. Until her death in 1913, Tubman continued to help those in need and continued to support civil and women's rights.

"I was the conductor of the Underground Railroad for eight years, and . . . I never ran my train off the track and I never lost a passenger."

**—Harriet Tubman,
from *Women's Voices: Quotations by Women***

Then and Now

Many African Americans relied on Tubman and other abolitionists to survive in the North. If a present-day family moved to a new city, what resources could they use to help them find work, shelter, and other necessities?

Other Forms of Resistance Armed rebellions were rare, however. African Americans in the South knew that they would only lose in an armed uprising. For the most part enslaved people resisted slavery by working slowly or by pretending to be ill. Occasionally resistance took more active forms, such as setting fire to a plantation building or breaking tools. Resistance helped enslaved African Americans endure their lives by striking back at white masters—and perhaps establishing boundaries that white people would respect.

Escaping Slavery Some enslaved African Americans tried to run away to the free states in the North. A few succeeded. **Harriet Tubman** and **Frederick Douglass,** two African American leaders who were born into slavery, gained their freedom when they fled to the North.

Yet for most enslaved people, getting to the North was almost impossible, especially from the Deep South. Most slaves who succeeded in running away escaped from the Upper South. The Underground Railroad—a network of "safe houses" owned by free blacks and whites who opposed slavery—offered assistance to runaway slaves. Some slaves ran away to find relatives on nearby plantations or to escape punishment.

Most runaways were captured and returned to their owners. Discipline was usually severe. The most common punishment for captured runaways was whipping.

Even if an enslaved man or woman escaped to the free states in the North, they were not always safe there. In some Northern communities, fugitive slaves were captured and returned to the South. This prevented many slaves from settling in free states and forced them to escape to Canada, where slavery was banned in 1834.

Reading Check **Summarize** Besides rebellions, what other forms did resistance to slavery take?

History Online
Study Central Need help understanding how African Americans in the South lived? Visit tajww1.glencoe.com and click on Study Central.

Section 3 Review

Reading Summary

Review the Main Ideas

- Enslaved Southerners developed a culture and religion that had both African and American elements.

- While some enslaved people attempted to rebel openly against slavery, others resisted by running away, refusing to work, or destroying farm tools.

What Did You Learn?

1. Why were extended families vital to African American culture?

2. What was the Underground Railroad?

Critical Thinking

3. **Classify** Re-create the diagram below. In the boxes, briefly explain how the slave codes operated.

Slave Codes	
Education	Assembly

4. **The Big Ideas** Trace the development of the unique elements of African American slave culture in the South.

5. **Summarize** Who were Denmark Vesey and Nat Turner? Write a short paragraph about their efforts against slavery.

6. **Creative Writing** Imagine you are enslaved on a Southern plantation. Write a description of a typical day that you might experience.

Cotton and Slavery in the South

Industry boomed in the North, but agriculture reigned in the South. Cotton was the South's most important crop. The production of cotton depended on a large supply of cheap labor. In the South, enslaved African Americans supplied that labor.

Read the passages on pages 438 and 439 and answer the questions that follow.

Many people copied Eli Whitney's ▶ cotton gin and ignored his patent because the gin was so easy to make.

Reader's Dictionary

patent: a document that gives the inventor the sole legal right to an invention for a period of time

miry (MYR • ee): muddy

pigsty: enclosed area where pigs live

speculator (SPEH • kyuh • LAY • tuhr): an individual who buys or sells land in hopes of making a profit

A New Invention

E*li Whitney had invented a workable cotton gin by 1793. One of his next steps was to apply for a patent for the machine. In the following letter, Whitney tells his family, who live in Westboro, Massachusetts, about the progress he is making and his plans.*

March 30, 1794

It is with no small satisfaction that I have in my power to inform you I am in good health. I have just returned from Philadelphia. My business there was to lodge a Model of my machine and receive a **Patent** for it. I accomplished everything agreeable to my wishes. I had the satisfaction to hear it declared by a number of the first men in America that my machine is the most perfect & the most valuable invention that has ever appeared in this Country. I have received my Patent. . . .

I wish very much to see you before I go. But should I come to Westboro' now I must neglect my business so much as to lose several Hundred Dollars. If you come [here] I shall be able to show you my machine. I have six of them nearly complete which I expect to carry to the Southward with me. I shall leave this place for Georgia in about twelve or fourteen days at the farthest. . . . Though I have as yet expended much more money than profits of the machine have been heretofore, and am at present a little pressed for money, I am by no means in the least discouraged. And I shall probably gain some honour as well as some profit by the Invention. . . .

—from *The World of Eli Whitney*

The Living Conditions of Enslaved Persons

Josiah Henson was an enslaved person. He escaped and later wrote about his life. In this excerpt, he describes the area where the slaves lived.

We lodged in log huts, and on the bare ground. Wooden floors were an unknown luxury. In a single room were huddled, like cattle, ten or a dozen persons, men, women, and children. . . . Our beds were collections of straw and old rags, thrown down in the corners and boxed in with boards; a single blanket the only covering. . . . The wind whistled and the rain and snow blew in through the cracks, and the damp earth soaked in the moisture till the floor was **miry** as a **pigsty.**

—from *Uncle Tom's Story of His Life. An Autobiography of the Rev. Josiah Henson*

▲ Slave quarters were usually gathered together in one area of a plantation.

News From the South

The American Anti-Slavery Society published American Slavery As It Is *by Sarah and Angelina Grimké and Angelina's husband Theodore Weld in 1839. For this book, Weld gathered newspaper ads from Southern papers to show the effects of slavery.*

From the "Richmond (Va.) Compiler," Sept. 8, 1837. Ranaway from the subscriber, Ben. He ran off without any known cause, and *I suppose he is aiming to go to his wife, who was carried from the neighborhood last winter.*

JOHN HUNT.

From the "Jackson (Tenn.) Telegraph," Sept. 14, 1838. Committed to the jail of Madison county, a negro woman, who calls her name Fanny, and says she belongs to William Miller, of Mobile. She formerly belonged to John Givins, of this county, who now owns *several of her children.*

DAVID SHROPSHIRE, Jailor.

From the "Richmond (Va.) Enquirer," Feb. 20, 1838. Stop the Runaway!!!—$25 Reward. Ranaway from the Eagle Tavern, a negro fellow, named Nat. He is no doubt attempting to *follow his wife, who was lately sold to a* **speculator** named Redmond. The above reward will be paid by Mrs. Lucy M. Downman, of Sussex county, Va.

 DBQ Document-Based Questions

A New Invention

1. What has Whitney recently obtained?
2. How successful has Whitney been in making money from the cotton gin?

The Living Conditions of Enslaved Persons

3. How weatherproof are the cabins? Why do you think that?

News From the South

4. According to the ads, why do slaves run away?

Read to Write

5. Imagine that you are living in the early 1800s. You know nothing about slavery. Then you read "The Living Conditions of Enslaved Persons" and "News from the South." Write an editorial to your local newspaper about slavery. What do you think about the fact that there is slavery in the United States?

Review Content Vocabulary

Write the vocabulary word that best completes each sentence. Write a sentence for each word not used.

- a. yeomen
- b. capital
- c. cotton gin
- d. slave codes
- e. tenant farmers
- f. spiritual

1. The South lacked the ___ needed to develop industries.
2. ___ farmers owned land and lived mostly in the Upper South.
3. A(n) ___ is an African religious folk song.
4. The South's ___ made it difficult for enslaved African Americans to gain an education.

Review the Main Ideas

Section 1 • Southern Cotton Kingdom

5. How did the cotton gin affect cotton production?
6. Why was there little industry in the South?

Section 2 • Life in the South

7. What were the main duties of plantation wives?
8. What obstacles existed to gaining an education in the South?

Section 3 • The Peculiar Institution

9. Why were escaped slaves not always safe in the North?
10. What was the purpose of the slave codes?

Critical Thinking

11. **Analyze** How did enslaved African Americans hold on to their African customs?
12. **Conclude** Why was the production of cotton so lucrative in the South?

13. **Explain** How did African Christianity help slaves cope with their situation?
14. **Summarize** What was life like for most whites in the South?

Geography Skills

The map shows Southern cities with more than 10,000 people in 1850. Study the map and answer the following questions.

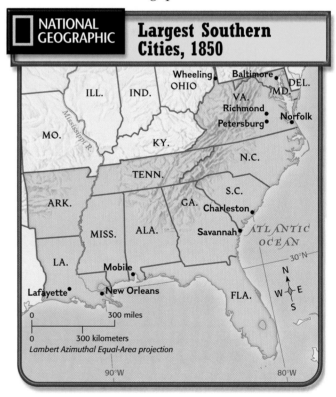

Largest Southern Cities, 1850

15. **Location** Which state had four of the South's major cities?
16. **Region** Which of the major cities shown were in the Deep South?
17. **Human-Environment Interaction** What do the locations of many of the Southern cities have in common? Why is that significant?

History Online

Self-Check Quiz Visit tajwwI.glencoe.com to prepare for the Chapter 9 test.

Read to Write

18. **The Big Ideas** **Expository Writing** Use the Internet or library resources to identify arguments Southerners used to defend slavery. Write a short paper in which you explain why these arguments may have found support in the South.

19. **Narrative Writing** Imagine that you are a slave who has been sold away from your family to another plantation. Write a letter to your family telling them how you feel about your separation.

20. **Using Your FOLDABLES** Use the information you created in your foldable to create a summary of the chapter. In your summary, be sure to cover the main ideas and events that were discussed.

Using Academic Vocabulary

Read the following sentences. Then, in your own words, write the meaning of the underlined academic vocabulary word.

21. The doctor's patients were <u>predominantly</u> elderly.

22. The estimate noted that the cost was not to <u>exceed</u> $75.

Building Citizenship

23. **Explain** Choose an issue you think is important to your community or the nation today. Explain why you think it is important and how you would take steps to resolve that issue. Compare your solutions with steps government officials are taking to address the issue.

Reviewing Skills

24. **READING SKILL** **Asking Questions** Using your local newspaper or an Internet news site, find an article about human rights. Write questions about any elements of the story you do not understand. Then describe how you could get your questions answered.

25. **ANALYSIS SKILL** **Inferring** Read the following quote, then identify the region you think the speaker might be from and explain your answer:

"We are an agricultural people. . . . We have no cities—we don't want them. . . . We want no manufactures: we desire no trading, no mechanical or manufacturing classes. As long as we have our rice, our sugar, our tobacco, and our cotton, we can command wealth to purchase all we want."

Standardized Test Practice

Select the best answer for each of the following questions.

26 The economy of the Deep South was based on

  A growing cotton.

  B growing tobacco.

  C manufacturing.

  D growing vegetables.

27 The white supervisor of enslaved workers on a plantation was known as a(n)

  A blacksmith.

  B yeoman.

  C overseer.

  D tenant.

28 The Southern laws that controlled enslaved people were called

  A spirituals.

  B overseers.

  C credits.

  D slave codes.

The Age of Jackson

▼ The White House, Washington, D.C.

NATIONAL GEOGRAPHIC **Who & When?**

1825	1835	1845

1828
Andrew Jackson elected president

1838
Cherokee begin Trail of Tears

1841
President William Henry Harrison dies in office

The Big Ideas

Section 1 — Jacksonian Democracy

Political ideas and major events shape how people form governments. President Andrew Jackson brought many changes to the American political system.

Section 2 — The Removal of Native Americans

Differences in economic, political, and social beliefs and practices can lead to division within a nation and have lasting consequences. Many Native Americans were forced off their lands in the Southeast.

Section 3 — Jackson and the Bank

Differences in economic, political, and social beliefs and practices can lead to division within a nation and have lasting consequences. Economic issues had a strong effect on politics and government in the mid-1800s.

 View the Chapter 10 video in the Glencoe Video Program.

 **FOLDABLES™ Study Organizer**

Evaluating Information Make this foldable to help you ask and answer questions about the Jackson era.

Step 1 Fold a sheet of paper in half from side to side, leaving a $\frac{1}{2}$-inch tab along the side.

Leave $\frac{1}{2}$-inch tab here.

Step 2 Turn the paper and fold it into fourths.

Fold in half, then fold in half again.

Step 3 Unfold and cut up along the three fold lines.

 Make four tabs.

Step 4 Label your foldable as shown.

 Who? What? When? Why?

Reading and Writing As you read, ask yourself "who" Andrew Jackson was, "what" he did, "when" he did it, and "why" it happened. Write your thoughts and facts under each appropriate tab.

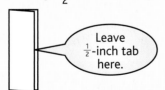

Get Ready to Read

Question-and-Answer Relationships

1 Learn It!

Knowing how to find answers to questions will help you on reviews and tests. Some answers can be found in the textbook, while other answers require you to go beyond the text. These answers might be based on knowledge you already have or things you have personally experienced.

How were the Seminole able to resist removal?

They joined forces with a group of African Americans and used guerrilla tactics.

This answer comes directly from the text.

The Seminole people of Florida were the only Native Americans who successfully resisted their removal. . . . The Seminole decided to go to war against the United States instead.

In 1835 the Seminole **joined forces with a group of African Americans** who had run away to escape slavery. . . . They used **guerrilla tactics** (guh • RIH • luh), making surprise attacks and then retreating back into the forests and swamps.

—from page 455

Reading Tip

As you read, keep track of questions you answer in the chapter. This will help you remember what you have read.

What are guerrilla tactics? This answer is not directly stated. You need to rely on information you already know or draw conclusions based on how this term is used in the text.

2 Practice It!

Read the excerpt below. Answer the following questions and discuss them with a partner.

> Two months after Van Buren took office, the country entered a severe economic depression, a period in which business and employment fall to a very low level. The depression began with the Panic of 1837, a time when land values dropped sharply, investments declined suddenly, and banks failed.
>
> Within a few weeks, thousands of businesses had closed and hundreds of thousands of people had lost their jobs. Many Americans could not afford food or rent.
>
> *—from page 460*

Read to Write

Pick three Content Vocabulary terms from Section 1 and write a question about each one. As you read the section, write a sentence or two answering each question based on what you learned.

- What is a depression?
- What started the depression of 1837?
- Do you think people who lived on farms or people who lived in cities were more deeply affected by the depression of 1837?

▲ Martin Van Buren

3 Apply It!

Look closely at the Reading Check questions throughout the chapter. Which questions can be answered with information directly from the text? Which require you to go beyond the text?

Jacksonian Democracy

Guide to Reading

Looking Back, Looking Ahead
In the last chapter, you learned about the people and economy of the South. In this section, you will learn about the Jackson presidency.

Focusing on the Main Ideas
- Adams and Jackson introduced new ways of campaigning in the elections of 1824 and 1828. *(page 447)*
- The United States's political system changed under Andrew Jackson, becoming more democratic. *(page 448)*
- The fight over tariffs divided the nation and raised the question of states' rights versus the rights of the federal government. *(page 450)*

Meeting People
Henry Clay
Andrew Jackson
John Quincy Adams
John C. Calhoun (kal•HOON)
Daniel Webster
Robert Hayne (HAYN)

Content Vocabulary
favorite son
plurality (plu•RA•luh•tee)
mudslinging
landslide
suffrage
bureaucracy (byu•RAH•kruh•see)
spoils system
caucus (KAW•kuhs)
tariff (TAR•uhf)
nullify
secede (sih•SEED)

Academic Vocabulary
role (ROHL)
issue (IH•SHOO)

Reading Strategy
Organizing Information As you read Section 1, create a chart to describe the political parties in 1828.

	Candidate	Views
Democratic-Republicans		
National Republicans		

NATIONAL GEOGRAPHIC **Who & When?**

1824 — 1828 — 1832

1825 John Quincy Adams wins presidency in House election

1828 Andrew Jackson elected president

1830 Webster and Hayne debate

The Elections of 1824 and 1828

Main Idea Adams and Jackson introduced new ways of campaigning in the elections of 1824 and 1828.

Reading Connection Think of the ways that presidential candidates campaign in current times. What methods do they use? Read on to find out how Adams and Jackson brought about new ways of campaigning.

The Election of 1824 In 1824 several candidates competed for the presidency. Three of them were **favorite sons,** meaning their home states supported them rather than the national party. They were **Henry Clay** of Kentucky, **Andrew Jackson** of Tennessee, and **John Quincy Adams** of Massachusetts, son of the former president.

In the election Jackson won the most popular votes. However, no candidate received a majority, or more than half, of the electoral votes. Jackson won 99 electoral votes, giving him a **plurality** (plu•RA•luh•tee), or largest single share. Under the Twelfth Amendment, when no candidate gets a majority of electoral votes, the House of Representatives selects the president.

While the House prepared to vote, Clay and Adams made an agreement. Clay would use his influence as Speaker of the House to defeat Jackson. In return, Clay may have hoped to become secretary of state. With Clay's help,

Adams was elected president. Adams then named Clay as secretary of state. Jackson's followers accused the two men of making a "corrupt bargain" and stealing the election.

The "corrupt bargain," as well as unpopular policies, cast a shadow over Adams's presidency. Adams favored a stronger navy and federal government direction of the economy. Such ideas horrified people who wanted a more limited federal **role.** Congress turned down many of Adams's proposals.

The Election of 1828 By 1828 there were two political parties: the Democratic-Republicans, who supported Jackson, and the National Republicans, who backed Adams. The Democratic-Republicans favored states' rights and mistrusted strong central government. Many Democrats were frontier people, immigrants, or city workers. The National Republicans wanted a strong central government. They supported federal measures, such as road building and a national bank, that would help the economy. Many were merchants or farmers.

During the campaign, both parties resorted to **mudslinging,** attempts to ruin their opponent's reputation with insults. Supporters of John Quincy Adams passed out a pamphlet attacking Jackson. One of the illustrations showed Jackson plunging his sword through the body of a helpless civilian. Meanwhile, Jackson's supporters accused Adams of kidnapping a young American girl and selling her to the ruler of Russia.

Jackson Forever!
The Hero of Two Wars and of Or'eans!
The Man of the People!
HE WHO COULD NOT BARTER NOR BARGAIN FOR THE
PRESIDENCY!
Who, although a *A Military Chieftain,"* valued the purity of Elections and of the Electors, MORE than the Office of PRESIDENT itself! Although the greatest in the gift of his countrymen, and the highest in point of dignity of any in the world,
BECAUSE
It should be derived from the
PEOPLE!
No Gag Laws! No Black Cockades! No Reign of Terror! No Standing Army or Navy Officers, when under the pay of Government, to browbeat, or
KNOCK DOWN
Old Revolutionary Characters, or our Representatives while in the discharge of their duty. To the Polls then, and vote for those who will support
OLD HICKORY
AND THE ELECTORAL LAW.

Election of 1824			
Candidate	Electoral Vote	Popular Vote	House Vote
Jackson	99	153,544	7
Adams	84	108,740	13
Crawford	41	46,618	4
Clay	37	47,136	–

Understanding Charts

The presidential election of 1824 was decided in the House of Representatives.

Analyze Which candidate received the most electoral votes?

The parties also aroused enthusiasm with slogans, rallies, and buttons. These new strategies became a permanent part of American political life. In the election, Jackson won the votes of frontier people. He also did well in the South, which liked his call for states' rights. South Carolina's **John C. Calhoun** (kal•HOON) of South Carolina, who had served as Adams's vice president, switched parties to run with Jackson. Jackson won in a **landslide,** an overwhelming victory, with 56 percent of the popular vote and 178 electoral votes.

Reading Check **Describe** Why were Adams and Clay accused of making a "corrupt bargain"?

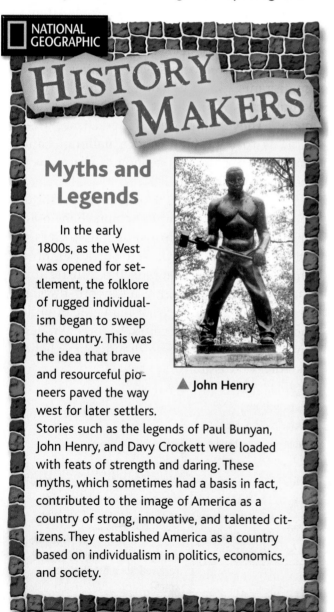

HISTORY MAKERS

Myths and Legends

In the early 1800s, as the West was opened for settlement, the folklore of rugged individualism began to sweep the country. This was the idea that brave and resourceful pioneers paved the way west for later settlers.

▲ John Henry

Stories such as the legends of Paul Bunyan, John Henry, and Davy Crockett were loaded with feats of strength and daring. These myths, which sometimes had a basis in fact, contributed to the image of America as a country of strong, innovative, and talented citizens. They established America as a country based on individualism in politics, economics, and society.

Jackson as President

Main Idea The United States's political system changed under Andrew Jackson, becoming more democratic.

Reading Connection What are the requirements for today's citizens to be eligible to vote? Read on to find out how President Jackson expanded suffrage to include a larger number of people.

Andrew Jackson was a man most Americans admired—a patriot, a self-made man, and a war hero. On March 4, 1829, thousands of farmers, craft workers, and other ordinary Americans crowded into the nation's capital to hear Jackson's Inaugural Address. After Jackson's speech, a crowd joined him at a White House reception. They filled the elegant rooms of the mansion, trampling on the carpets with muddy shoes, spilling food on sofas and chairs. They were there to shake the hand of the new president who seemed just like them.

Why Was Jackson Popular? Jackson gained fame during the War of 1812. He led the troops that defeated the Creek Nation in the Battle of Horseshoe Bend and defeated the British at the Battle of New Orleans. His troops called him "Old Hickory" because he was as tough as a hickory—a hardwood tree.

Small farmers, craft workers, and others who felt left out of the expanding American economy admired Jackson. They felt that his rise from poverty to the White House demonstrated the American success story. His popularity with the common man changed politics in Washington, D.C.

How Did Voting Rights Change? President Andrew Jackson promised "equal protection and equal benefits" for all Americans—at least for all white American men. During his first term, a spirit of equality spread through American politics. In the nation's early years, most states had limited **suffrage,** or the right to vote, for men who owned property or paid taxes.

Analyzing
Political Cartoons

A Political Card Game Andrew Jackson plays a card game with his political enemies. *Why did Jackson's opponents criticize the spoils system?*

A Andrew Jackson **B** Nicholas Biddle **C** Henry Clay **D** John C. Calhoun

Starting in 1815 Western and Eastern states alike relaxed the property requirements for voting. In the 1820s, people who had not been allowed to vote—white male sharecroppers, factory workers, and many others—voted for the first time. However, women still could not vote, and African Americans and Native Americans had few rights of any kind.

Another change was in the selection of presidential electors. By 1828, 22 of the 24 states changed their constitutions to allow the people, rather than the state legislatures, to choose presidential electors.

What Is the Spoils System? Democrats carried the spirit of democracy into government. Their goal was to shake up the federal **bureaucracy** (byu•RAH•kruh•see), a system in which nonelected officials carry out laws. Democrats argued that ordinary citizens could handle any government job. President Jackson replaced many federal workers with his supporters. The fired employees charged that Jackson was acting like a tyrant. Jackson responded that a new set of federal employees would be good for democracy.

One Jackson supporter explained it another way: "To the victors belong the spoils." In other words, because the Jacksonians had won the

presidential election, they had the right to the spoils—benefits of victory—such as handing out government jobs to supporters. The practice of replacing government employees with the winning candidate's supporters became known as the **spoils system.**

What Electoral Changes Occurred? Jackson's supporters worked to make the political system more democratic as well. They abandoned the unpopular **caucus** (KAW•kuhs) system. In this system, major political candidates were chosen by committees made up of members of Congress. The caucuses were replaced by nominating conventions in which delegates from the states selected the party's presidential candidate.

The Democrats held their first national party convention in 1832 in Baltimore, Maryland. The convention drew delegates from each state in the Union. The delegates decided to nominate the candidate who could gather two-thirds of the vote, and Jackson won the nomination. This system allowed many people to participate in the selection of political candidates.

Reading Check **Compare** Compare the caucus system and nominating conventions. Why was the new system more popular with the people?

The Tariff Debate

Main Idea The fight over tariffs divided the nation and raised the question of states' rights versus the rights of the federal government.

Reading Connection What items do you own that were made in the United States? What items of yours were manufactured overseas? Read on to learn how foreign imports led to protests in the South.

Americans from different parts of the country disagreed strongly on some **issues.** One such issue was the **tariff** (TAR•uhf), a fee paid by merchants who imported goods. While president, Jackson faced a tariff crisis that tested the national government's powers.

In 1828 Congress passed a law that placed a very high tariff on manufactured goods from Europe. Manufacturers in the United States—mostly in the Northeast—welcomed the tariff. Because tariffs made European goods more expensive, American consumers were more likely to buy American-made goods.

Analyzing *Political Cartoons*

King Andrew Some people called Andrew Jackson "a man of the people." Others called him a power-hungry ruler. *What symbols does the cartoonist use to suggest items of royalty?*

Southerners, however, despised the new tariff. There were fewer manufacturers in the South so they did not benefit from increased sales. They called it the Tariff of Abominations—something hateful. These critics argued that although tariffs forced consumers to buy American goods, tariffs also meant higher prices.

How Did the South Protest the Tariff?

Southern politicians were ready to act. Vice President John C. Calhoun argued that a state or group of states had the right to **nullify,** or cancel, a federal law it considered against state interests. Some Southerners called for the Southern states to **secede** (sih•SEED), or break away, from the United States and form their own government. When Calhoun explored this idea, troubling questions arose. The United States had been a nation for nearly 50 years. What if a state disagreed with the federal government? Did a state have the right to go its own way? This debate would continue for decades and eventually lead to civil war.

Calhoun drew from ideas in the Virginia and Kentucky Resolutions of 1798–1799. Calhoun argued that since the federal government was a creation of the states, the states have the power to decide whether federal laws are constitutional. The alternative to state sovereignty, Calhoun pointed out, is to allow the Supreme Court or Congress to tell the people what our Constitution means and what laws we must obey.

The Webster-Hayne Debate In January 1830, Senator **Daniel Webster** of Massachusetts delivered a stinging attack on nullification.

Webster stood on the floor of the Senate to challenge a speech given by **Robert Hayne** (HAYN), a young senator from South Carolina. Hayne had defended the idea that the states had a right to nullify acts of the federal government and even to secede.

In his response, Webster defended the Constitution and the Union. He argued that nullification could only mean the end of the Union. Webster closed with the ringing statement, "Liberty and Union, now and forever, one and inseparable!"

Jackson Takes a Stand Nobody knew Jackson's thoughts about nullification. In 1830 Jackson made his position clear at a dinner given by supporters of states' rights. In a toast, Jackson said: "Our federal union . . . must be preserved!" The audience was stunned, but Calhoun quickly responded, "The Union—next to our liberty, most dear." He meant that the Union's fate must take second place to a state's liberty to overrule the Constitution if its interests were threatened.

Calhoun realized that Jackson would not change his views. Wanting to speak for the South in Congress, Calhoun won election to the Senate in December 1832. Two weeks later, he resigned the vice presidency.

What Was the Nullification Crisis? Anger over the tariff continued to build in the South. The Union seemed on the verge of splitting apart. In 1832 Congress passed a new, lower tariff, hoping that the protest in the South would die down. Southern leaders continued their protests, however. The South Carolina legislature passed the Nullification Act, refusing to pay the "illegal" tariffs of 1828 and 1832. It threatened secession if the federal government interfered.

To ease the crisis, President Jackson supported a compromise bill by Henry Clay to lower the tariff. To make sure that the South would accept the compromise, he had Congress pass a Force Bill, allowing military action to enforce acts of Congress. In response, South Carolina nullified the Force Act. Calhoun and his supporters claimed victory because they believed they had forced a revision of the tariff. However, they also had to recognize that a state could not leave the Union without a fight.

✓ **Reading Check** **Summarize** Why did South Carolina pass the Nullification Act?

Study Central Need help understanding Jackson's presidency? Visit tajwwI.glencoe.com and click on Study Central.

Reading Summary

Review the **Main Ideas**

- The election of 1824 was widely seen as corrupt, and the election of 1828 ushered a president to power who identified with much of the American public.

- Elections became more democratic as caucuses were eradicated and suffrage was extended to more voters.

- The introduction of a tariff on imported goods caused many Southerners to turn against the government and lobby for state rights.

What Did You Learn?

1. Why did the House of Representatives select the president in the 1824 presidential election?

2. What election practices used in the 1828 presidential campaign are still used today?

Critical Thinking

3. **Organizing Information** Recreate the diagram below and describe the changes that took place in the political system under Andrew Jackson.

4. **The Big Ideas** What was the main reason President Adams was not popular with the Democratic-Republicans?

5. **Expository Writing** Prepare a list of five questions that you might have asked President Jackson if you had interviewed him.

6. **READING** Question and Answer Relationships Look at questions 1 and 2 above. Will the answers come directly from the text or do they require you to draw on other information as well? Explain.

Section 2

The Removal of Native Americans

Guide to Reading

Looking Back, Looking Ahead

In Section 1, you learned about some of the actions Andrew Jackson took as president. In Section 2, you will learn about his policies toward Native Americans.

Focusing on the Main Ideas

- As settlements spread westward, many Native Americans were forced off their lands. *(page 453)*
- Some groups of Native Americans attempted to resist relocation. Most were eventually taken from their lands by force. *(page 455)*

Meeting People

Black Hawk
Osceola (AH•see•OH•luh)

Content Vocabulary

relocate
guerrilla tactics (guh•RIH•luh)

Academic Vocabulary

federal (FEH•duh•ruhl)
remove (rih•MOOV)

Reading Strategy

Taking Notes As you read Section 2, create a chart like the one below that describes what happened to each group of Native Americans as the United States expanded.

	Description
Cherokee	
Sauk/Fox	
Seminole	

NATIONAL GEOGRAPHIC Who & When?

1830 — 1835 — 1840

1830 Congress passes the Indian Removal Act

1835 Seminole refuse to leave Florida
Osceola

1838 Cherokee driven from their home-lands on the Trail of Tears

Moving Native Americans

Main Idea **As settlements spread westward, many Native Americans were forced off their lands.**

Reading Connection How long have you lived in your community? Can you imagine being forced to leave and settle elsewhere? Read on to find out how many Native Americans were forced onto reservations in the West.

The Cherokee held their land long before European settlers arrived. Through treaties with the United States government, the Cherokee became a separate nation within Georgia. By the early 1800s, the Cherokee had their own schools, their own newspaper, and their own written constitution. Sequoya's invention of a Cherokee alphabet enabled many of the Cherokee to read and write in their own language. The Cherokee farmed some of Georgia's richest land, and in 1829 gold was discovered there. White Americans began trespassing on Cherokee territory in pursuit of riches.

What Is Relocation?

While the United States had expanded westward by the 1830s, large numbers of Native Americans still lived in the eastern part of the country. In Georgia, Alabama, Mississippi, and Florida lived the "Five Civilized Tribes"—the Cherokee, Creek, Seminole, Chickasaw, and Choctaw. These tribes had established successful farming societies.

Because the area west of the Mississippi River was dry and seemed unsuitable for farming, few white Americans lived there. Many settlers wanted the **federal** government to **relocate** Native Americans living in the Southeast. They wanted to force the Native Americans to leave their land and move west of the Mississippi River. President Andrew Jackson, a man of the frontier himself, supported the settlers' demand for Native American land.

What Was the Indian Removal Act?

In 1830 Congress passed the Indian Removal Act. It allowed the federal government to pay

Picturing **History**

Sequoya holds a sample of the Cherokee alphabet. *What happened to the Cherokee people in the 1830s?*

Native Americans to move west. Jackson then sent officials to negotiate treaties with Native Americans of the Southeast. In 1834 Congress created the Indian Territory, an area in present-day Oklahoma, for these Native Americans.

The Cherokee Nation

The Cherokee Nation, however, refused to give up its land. In treaties of the 1790s, the federal government had recognized the Cherokee people as a separate nation with their own laws. Georgia, however, refused to recognize Cherokee laws.

The Cherokee sued the state and eventually took their case to the Supreme Court. In *Worcester* v. *Georgia* (1832), Chief Justice John Marshall ruled that Georgia had no right to interfere with the Cherokee. The Native Americans, he said, were protected by the federal government and the Constitution. 📖 *(See page 849 of the Appendix for a summary of* Worcester v. Georgia.*)*

President Jackson had supported Georgia's efforts to **remove** the Cherokee. He vowed to ignore the Supreme Court's ruling. "John Marshall has made his decision," Jackson reportedly said. "Now let him enforce it."

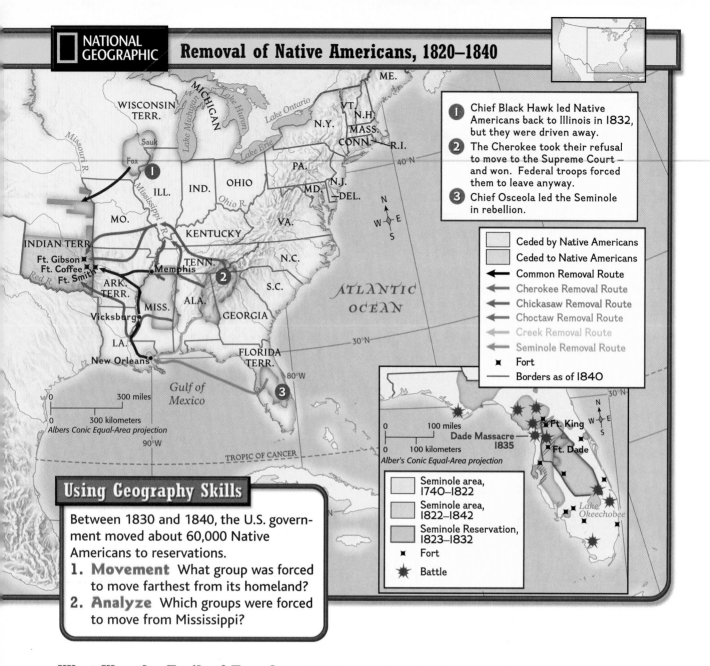

NATIONAL GEOGRAPHIC

Removal of Native Americans, 1820–1840

1. Chief Black Hawk led Native Americans back to Illinois in 1832, but they were driven away.
2. The Cherokee took their refusal to move to the Supreme Court — and won. Federal troops forced them to leave anyway.
3. Chief Osceola led the Seminole in rebellion.

Ceded by Native Americans
Ceded to Native Americans
Common Removal Route
Cherokee Removal Route
Chickasaw Removal Route
Choctaw Removal Route
Creek Removal Route
Seminole Removal Route
Fort
Borders as of 1840

Seminole area, 1740–1822
Seminole area, 1822–1842
Seminole Reservation, 1823–1832
Fort
Battle

Dade Massacre 1835
Ft. King
Ft. Dade
Lake Okeechobee

Using Geography Skills

Between 1830 and 1840, the U.S. government moved about 60,000 Native Americans to reservations.

1. **Movement** What group was forced to move farthest from its homeland?
2. **Analyze** Which groups were forced to move from Mississippi?

What Was the Trail of Tears? In 1835 the federal government persuaded a few Cherokee to sign a treaty giving up their people's land. Yet most of the Cherokee refused to honor the treaty. They wrote a protest letter to the government and people of the United States pleading for understanding. It did not soften the resolve of President Jackson or the area's white settlers. In 1838 federal troops under General Winfield Scott came to remove the Cherokee from their homes and lead them west. 📖 *(See page 853 of the Appendix for the text of the Cherokee protest.)*

Scott threatened force if the Cherokee did not leave. The Cherokee knew that fighting would only lead to their doom. Filled with sadness and anger, their leaders yielded, and then the long march to the West began. One man in Kentucky wrote of seeing hundreds of Cherokee marching by:

> 66 Even [the] aged . . . were traveling with heavy burdens attached to the back. . . . 99
>
> —from *The Trail of Tears*

Brutal weather along the way claimed thousands of Cherokee lives. Their forced journey west became known to Cherokee people as the Trail Where They Cried. Historians call it the Trail of Tears.

✓ **Reading Check** **Explain** What was the purpose of the Indian Removal Act?

Native American Resistance

(Main Idea) **Some groups of Native Americans attempted to resist relocation. Most were eventually taken from their lands by force.**

Reading Connection Have you ever been told to do something you thought was wrong? Did you attempt to resist? Read on to find out how some Native Americans resisted relocation.

An American Story

In 1832 the Sauk chieftain, **Black Hawk,** led a force of Sauk and Fox people back to Illinois, their homeland. They wanted to recapture this area, which had been given up in a treaty. The state militia and federal troops responded with force, killing hundreds of Sauk and Fox and chasing the survivors into present-day Iowa. The troops pursued the people and slaughtered most of them.

The Seminole The Seminole people of Florida were the only Native Americans who successfully resisted their removal. Although they were pressured in the early 1830s to sign treaties giving up their land, the Seminole chief, **Osceola** (AH•see•OH•luh), and some of

History Online

Student Web Activity Visit tajwwI.glencoe.com and click on *Chapter 10—Student Web Activities* for an activity on the Trail of Tears.

his people refused to leave Florida. The Seminole decided to go to war against the United States instead.

In 1835 the Seminole joined forces with a group of African Americans who had run away to escape slavery. Together they attacked white settlements along the Florida coast. They used **guerrilla tactics** (guh•RIH•luh), making surprise attacks and then retreating back into the forests and swamps. In December 1835, Seminole ambushed soldiers under the command of Major Francis Dade. Only a few of the 110 soldiers survived the attack. The Dade Massacre led to sending more troops and equipment to fight the Seminole.

By 1842 more than 1,500 American soldiers had died in the Seminole wars. The government gave up and allowed the Seminole to remain in Florida. Many Seminole, however, had died in the long war, and many more were captured and forced to move westward. After 1842 only a few scattered groups of Native Americans lived east of the Mississippi. Most had been removed to the West.

Native Americans had given up more than 100 million acres of eastern land to the federal government. They had received in return about $68 million and 32 million acres in lands west of the Mississippi River.

History *Through Art*

***Trail of Tears* by Robert Lindneux** Native Americans who were forced from their land traveled west in the 1830s. *Why was the forced march called the Trail of Tears?*

Biography

OSCEOLA
c. 1804–1838

Osceola was born in 1804. His ancestors were Creek, African American, British, Irish, and Scottish. After President Jackson signed the Indian Removal Act in 1830, Osceola became the leader of the Seminoles and led successful attacks on United States forts. He was much revered among the Seminole for his ability as a warrior and his refusal to yield to the government's demands.

The Seminoles hid in the swampy lands of the Everglades throughout 1836 and continued to carry out attacks on U.S. soldiers, as well as on local farms and businesses. However, as food became scarce, the Seminoles grew tired, sick, and hungry. A group of Seminole chiefs negotiated peace with the soldiers and offered to move to a reservation in Arkansas. In exchange, they requested that the many runaway slaves who had found refuge with them be allowed to remain with the Seminoles and not be returned to slavery. The army agreed but later broke the promise and declared that those slaves who had joined the Seminoles after the start of the war would be taken back to their owners. Angered over this violation of the new treaty, the Seminoles again moved into the swamps and the war resumed.

The U.S. Army captured one of the Seminole leaders. It offered to release him if Osceola agreed to talks. Osceola tried to surrender but was captured. He and his family were imprisoned, and he died of a throat infection in 1838. Most of the Seminoles were removed from Florida to the Oklahoma Territory. Some Seminoles remained in Florida and settled in reservations there. Although Osceola had fought against the United States, he was respected as a hero and given a funeral with full military honors.

"You have guns, and so do we; . . . You have men and so have we; Your men will fight, and so will ours until the last drop of the Seminoles' blood has moistened the dust of his hunting grounds."
—Osceola in a letter to General Clinch

Then and Now

Osceola and his men had many advantages during the Seminole wars. His men knew the terrain and had superior fighting skills. Research to find information about a recent or current war. Describe the advantages and disadvantages each side possessed.

"We told them to let us alone, and keep away from us; but they followed on."

—Black Hawk, Sauk leader (left), pictured here with his son, Whirling Thunder

The Five Civilized Tribes The Five Civilized Tribes were relocated in present-day Oklahoma on lands claimed by several Plains groups, including the Osage, Comanche, and Kiowa. The Plains groups agreed to let the Five Civilized Tribes live in peace. Settled in their new homes,

the Five Tribes developed their governments, improved their farms, and built schools.

✓ **Reading Check** **Compare** How was the response of the Seminoles different from that of the Cherokee when they were removed from their lands?

History Online

Study Central Need help understanding the removal of Native Americans? Visit tajww1.glencoe.com and click on Study Central.

Section 2 Review

Reading Summary

Review the Main Ideas

• Native Americans' requests to remain on their lands were refused, and they were often forcibly removed.

• Native Americans often resisted, waging war against the United States in an attempt to keep their land.

What Did You Learn?

1. Describe how President Jackson reacted to the Supreme Court decision supporting the Cherokees' rights.

2. How were the Seminole able to resist relocation?

Critical Thinking

3. **Organizing Information** Recreate the diagram below to show how the Cherokee were eventually removed from their land.

1835 treaty with Cherokee

⬇

⬇

⬇

4. **The Big Ideas** How was Georgia's policy toward the Cherokee different from previous federal policy?

5. **Persuasive Writing** Write a letter to Andrew Jackson telling him why the Native Americans should or should not be allowed to stay in their homelands.

6. **ANALYSIS** **Time Line** Create a time line of John Marshall's career as a Supreme Court Justice. Use the index of your book to find other references to him. On your time line, note which decisions brought him into conflict with the president of the time.

Guide to Reading

Looking Back, Looking Ahead

In Section 2, you learned about the removal of Native Americans to Western lands. In this section, you will learn about Jackson's fight with the National Bank and the election of the Whigs to power.

Focusing on the Main Ideas

- President Jackson forced the National Bank to close, and the Panic of 1837 caused economic problems that split the Democratic Party. *(page 459)*
- After Harrison's death, Tyler took the presidency in a direction opposed to the Whigs' goals, and the Whigs lost power after 1844. *(page 461)*

Meeting People

Nicholas Biddle

Martin Van Buren

William Henry Harrison

John Tyler

Content Vocabulary

veto

depression

laissez-faire (LEH • SAY • FEHR)

Academic Vocabulary

contribute (kuhn • TRIH • byuht)

symbol (SIHM • buhl)

Reading Strategy

Sequencing Information As you read the section, re-create the diagram below. In the spaces provided, describe the steps Andrew Jackson took that put the Bank of the United States out of business.

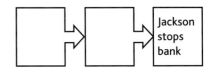

Jackson stops bank

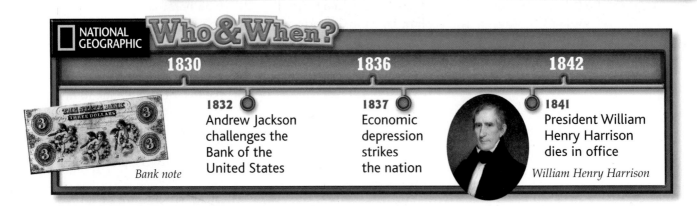

NATIONAL GEOGRAPHIC — Who & When?

1830 — 1836 — 1842

1832 Andrew Jackson challenges the Bank of the United States

Bank note

1837 Economic depression strikes the nation

1841 President William Henry Harrison dies in office

William Henry Harrison

War Against the Bank

Main Idea President Jackson forced the National Bank to close, and the Panic of 1837 caused economic problems that split the Democratic Party.

Reading Connection Do you have a bank account? Do you know what would happen to your money if an economic crisis occurred? Read on to find out what happened to banks during the Panic of 1837.

Jackson had another great struggle during his presidency. For years, he had criticized the Bank of the United States as being an organization of wealthy Easterners over which ordinary citizens had no control. The Bank of the United States was a powerful institution. It held the federal government's money and controlled much of the country's money supply. Although the Bank had been chartered by Congress, it was run by private bankers rather than elected officials.

The Bank's president, **Nicholas Biddle,** represented everything Jackson disliked. Jackson prided himself on being a self-made man who started with nothing. Biddle, on the other hand, came from a wealthy family.

In 1832 Jackson's opponents gave him the chance to take action against the Bank. Senators Henry Clay and Daniel Webster, friends of Biddle, planned to use the Bank to defeat Jackson in the 1832 presidential election. They persuaded Biddle to apply early for a new charter—a government permit to operate the Bank—even though the Bank's current charter did not expire until 1836.

Clay and Webster believed the Bank had popular support. They thought that an attempt by Jackson to take away its charter would lead to his defeat and allow Henry Clay to be elected president. When the bill to renew the Bank's charter came to Jackson for signature, he was sick in bed. Jackson told his friend **Martin Van Buren,** "The bank, Mr. Van Buren, is trying to kill me. But I will kill it!" Jackson **vetoed,** or rejected, the bill.

▼ Paper money issued in mid-1800s

Jackson, like many others, believed the Bank was unconstitutional despite the Supreme Court's decision to the contrary in *McCulloch* v. *Maryland* (1819). In a message to Congress, Jackson denounced the Bank arguing that:

❝ when the laws... make the rich richer and the potent more powerful, the humble members of society—the farmers, mechanics, and laborers—who have neither the time nor the means of securing like favors to themselves, have a right to complain of the injustice of their Government. ❞

—Andrew Jackson, as quoted in *The Annals of America*

Once again, Jackson was publicly opposing a ruling by the Supreme Court, as he had in *Worcester* v. *Georgia.*

The Election of 1832

Webster and Clay were right about one thing. The Bank of the United States did play a large part in the campaign of 1832. Their strategy for gaining support for Clay as president, however, backfired. Most people supported Jackson's veto of the bank charter bill. Jackson was reelected, receiving 55 percent of the popular vote and collecting 219 electoral votes to Clay's 49. Martin Van Buren was elected vice president.

Once reelected, Jackson decided on a plan to "kill" the Bank. He ordered the withdrawal of all government deposits from the Bank and placed the funds in smaller state banks.

Many cartoons from the period depicted Jackson's battle against the Second Bank of the United States. **Does this cartoon support the president or the Bank? Explain.**

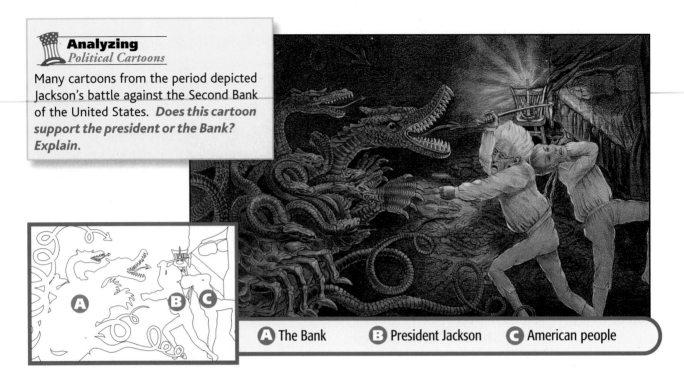

Ⓐ The Bank　　　Ⓑ President Jackson　　　Ⓒ American people

Without those government deposits, the National Bank could not do business. By putting an end to the Bank, Jackson had won a political victory. Later, however, critics charged that the end of the National Bank **contributed** to the economic problems that the nation faced in the years ahead.

What Caused Economic Problems? When Jackson decided not to run for a third term in 1836, the Democrats selected Martin Van Buren of New York, Jackson's vice president, as their candidate. Van Buren faced bitter opposition from the Whigs, a new political party that included former National Republicans and other anti-Jackson forces. Jackson's great popularity and his personal support helped Van Buren easily defeat several Whig opponents. Van Buren was inaugurated in 1837.

Two months after Van Buren took office, the country entered a severe economic **depression,** a period in which business and employment fall to a very low level. The depression began with the Panic of 1837, a time when land values dropped sharply, investments declined suddenly, and banks failed.

Within a few weeks, thousands of businesses had closed and hundreds of thousands of people had lost their jobs. Many Americans could not afford food or rent. In February 1837, people in New York put up signs voicing their anger: "Bread, Meat, Rent, and Fuel! Their prices must come down!"

President Van Buren believed in the principle of **laissez-faire** (LEH•SAY•FEHR)—that government should interfere as little as possible in the nation's economy. However, Van Buren believed that some actions were necessary. Van Buren persuaded Congress to establish an independent federal treasury in 1840. The government would no longer deposit its money with private individual banks as it had started to do during President Jackson's war with the Bank of the United States. Instead, the government would store its money in the federal treasury. The new system, Van Buren believed, would guard against bank crises.

Van Buren called the new law a "second declaration of independence" because it separated government finances from those of the nation's banks. However, criticism of the act came from members of Van Buren's own Democratic Party as well as from Whigs. The split in the Democratic Party meant the Whigs had a chance to win the presidency in 1840.

✓ **Reading Check** **Explain** What was the new treasury system supposed to prevent?

The Whigs Come to Power

Main Idea After Harrison's death, Tyler took the presidency in a direction opposed to the Whigs' goals, and the Whigs lost power after 1844.

Reading Connection What kind of political disagreements take place in your community? Read on to find out how the Whig Party lost the election of 1844 due to internal disputes.

With the country still in a depression, the Whigs hoped to beat Van Buren in the election of 1840. Their candidates were the military hero **William Henry Harrison** and his running mate **John Tyler.** Because Harrison had won fame in the Battle of Tippecanoe, the Whigs' campaign slogan was "Tippecanoe and Tyler Too."

Harrison sought the votes of laborers and farmers. Harrison was portrayed as a "man of the people." Whig cartoons showed him in front of a log cabin, the Whigs' campaign **symbol.** The log cabin campaign worked, and Harrison won easily. Four weeks after his inauguration in 1841, Harrison died of pneumonia. John Tyler became the first vice president to gain the presidency because the elected president died in office.

Although Tyler had been elected as a Whig, he had once been a Democrat. As president, Tyler backed states' rights and vetoed several Whig-sponsored bills. This lack of party loyalty angered Whigs. Most of the cabinet resigned, and Whig leaders in Congress expelled Tyler from the party.

Whig leaders, however, could not agree on policies. This division partly explains why the Whig candidate, Henry Clay, lost the election of 1844 to Democratic candidate Polk. After only four years, the Whigs were out of power again.

✓ **Reading Check** **Describe** How did John Tyler become president?

History Online

Study Central Need help understanding Jackson and the Bank? Visit tajww1.glencoe.com and click on Study Central.

Section 3 Review

Reading Summary

Review the Main Ideas

- Jackson waged a war against the bank and won not only his side of the war but the election of 1832 as well.

- Criticism over Van Buren's response to the Panic of 1837 brought the Whigs to power, but dissension among members of the party helped a Democrat to win the next election.

What Did You Learn?

1. List Jackson's reasons for wanting to "kill" the Bank of the United States.

2. What tactics did the Whigs borrow from Jackson's campaign to win the election of 1840?

Critical Thinking

3. **Organizing Information** Re-create the diagram below to show how the Panic of 1837 affected the presidency of Martin Van Buren.

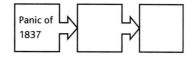

4. **The Big Ideas** Why did President Van Buren do little to solve the nation's economic problems during the depression?

5. **Creative Writing** Write a campaign slogan for Van Buren or Harrison in the election of 1840. Then design a campaign button that incorporates your slogan.

Analyzing Primary Sources

Jacksonian Democracy

The spirit of Jacksonian democracy was seen in the 1829 inauguration of America's new president, Andrew Jackson. Unlike previous presidents, Jackson invited "common people" to his inauguration and presented himself as one of them. Called "the people's choice," Jackson responded to the wishes of ordinary Americans who wanted changes in their government's leadership.

Jackson is sworn in as president. ▶

Reader's Dictionary

tranquil (TRAN • kwuhl): free of disturbance or commotion

edifice (EH • duh • fuhs): a building, especially one that is large or impressive

portico (POHR • tih • KOH): a covered entrance or walkway

rotunda (roh • TUHN • duh): a large round room or hall

rends: disturbs the silence or pierces the air with a loud sound

reverberate: to echo repeatedly

sublime (suh • BLYM): awe-inspiringly beautiful

pecuniary (pih • KYOO • nee • EHR • ee): relating to or involving money

incalculably (ihn • KAL • kyuh • luh • buh • lee): too great or numerous to be measured

solicitude (suh • LIH • suh • TOOD): concern and consideration

The Inauguration of Andrew Jackson

In 1829 Andrew Jackson became president. A Washington resident, Mrs. Samuel Harrison Smith, wrote about Jackson's inauguration in a letter:

Thousands and thousands of people, without distinction of rank, collected in an immense mass round the Capitol, silent, orderly and **tranquil,** with their eyes fixed on the front of that **edifice,** waiting the appearance of the President in the **portico.** The door from the **Rotunda** opens, preceded by the marshals, surrounded by the Judges of the Supreme Court, the old man with his gray locks, that crown of glory, advances, bows to the people, who greet him with a shout that **rends** the air, the Cannons from the heights around, . . . proclaim the oath he has taken and all the hills **reverberate** the sound. It was grand,—it was **sublime!** An almost breathless silence, succeeded and the multitude was still,—listening to catch the sound of his voice, [though] it was so low, as to be heard only by those nearest to him. After reading his speech, the oath was administered to him by the Chief Justice. The Marshal presented the Bible. The President took it from his hands, pressed his lips to it, laid it reverently down, then bowed again to the people—Yes, to the people in all their majesty.

—from *The First Forty Years of Washington Society*

Indian Removal

In 1830 President Andrew Jackson delivered a message to Congress describing his plans for removing Native Americans from their lands by forcing them west to an area beyond the Mississippi River.

The consequences of a speedy removal will be important to the United States, to individual states, and to the Indians themselves. The **pecuniary** advantages which it promises to the government are the least of its recommendations. It puts an end to all possible danger of collision between the authorities of the general and state governments on account of the Indians. It will place a dense and civilized population in large tracts of country now occupied by a few savage hunters. By opening the whole territory between Tennessee on the north and Louisiana on the south to the settlement of the whites it will **incalculably** strengthen the southwestern frontier and render the adjacent states strong enough to repel future invasions without remote aid. It will relieve the whole state of Mississippi and the western part of Alabama of Indian occupancy, and enable those states to advance rapidly in population, wealth, and power.

It will separate the Indians from immediate contact with settlements of whites; free them from the power of the states; enable them to pursue happiness in their own way and under their own rude institutions; will retard the progress of decay, which is lessening their numbers, and perhaps cause them gradually, under the protection of the government and through the influence of good counsels, to cast off their savage habits and become an interesting, civilized, and Christian community. These consequences, some of them so certain and the rest so probable, make the complete execution of the plan sanctioned by Congress at their last session an object of much **solicitude.**

—Message to Congress, December 6, 1830

▲ John Ross (left), the principal chief of the Cherokee, opposed the removal of his people. Rebecca Neugin (right) was one of the Cherokee forced to march west to Oklahoma. In this 1931 photograph, Neugin is 96 years old.

 Document-Based Questions

The Inauguration of Andrew Jackson

1. How do you think Mrs. Smith's account of this event might be different from a news reporter's account?

Indian Removal

2. What does President Jackson state is the best reason for the removal of Native Americans?

3. How will the Native Americans benefit from this plan, according to President Jackson?

Read to Write

4. President Jackson was known as a "man of the people." Is this perception apparent in these documents? Do you see any inconsistencies? Summarize your conclusions. Next, identify a political leader that has an image in popular culture and contrast that with policy decisions made by that leader. Compare the contemporary leader you chose with Andrew Jackson.

Reviewing Content Vocabulary

Match each word below to the correct definition.

a. plurality   e. landslide

b. suffrage   f. secede

c. majority   g. depression

d. nullify

___ 1. a period in which business and employment fall to very low levels

___ 2. a portion that is more than half

___ 3. to cancel

___ 4. the largest single share of something

___ 5. an overwhelming victory

___ 6. the right to vote

___ 7. to break away

Review the (Main Ideas)

Section 1 • Jacksonian Democracy

8. How did the supporters of Jackson and Adams differ in their beliefs?

9. What were some of the political tactics used by Democratic-Republicans and the National Republicans in the election of 1828?

10. Which Americans were prohibited from voting in most states before the 1800s?

Section 2 • The Removal of Native Americans

11. Who did the Seminoles join forces with as they fought against forced removal from their land?

12. What was the outcome of *Worcester* v. *Georgia*?

Section 3 • Jackson and the Bank

13. How did the Panic of 1837 affect the nation's economy?

14. Why was Harrison's log cabin campaign successful?

Critical Thinking

15. **Conclude** President Andrew Jackson promised "equal protection and equal benefits" for all Americans. Do you think he included Native Americans in his promise? Why or why not?

16. **Organizing Information** Re-create the chart below. List the issues that Jackson dealt with during his presidency. Then describe how he responded to each issue.

Issues	Jackson's response

Geography Skills

The issue of states' rights was debated in the election of 1828. Study the map below and answer the questions that follow.

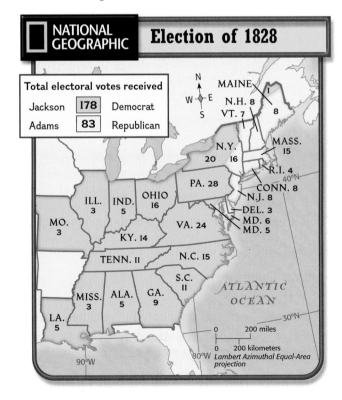

NATIONAL GEOGRAPHIC   **Election of 1828**

Total electoral votes received

Jackson **178** Democrat

Adams **83** Republican

History Online

Self-Check Quiz Visit tajwwI.glencoe.com
to prepare for the Chapter 10 test.

17. Region Which general areas of the United States voted for Andrew Jackson in the election of 1828?

18. Location Which candidate won more votes in Adams's home state of Massachusetts?

Read to Write

19. The Big Ideas Persuasive Writing Choose one of the events in this chapter over which Americans were divided in opinion. Choose one side or the other and write a short essay arguing why you think your view is correct.

20. Using Your FOLDABLES Use the information you gathered in your foldable to create a time line of Andrew Jackson's presidency. Illustrate your time line with drawings or pictures.

Using Academic Vocabulary

Some words like *issue* have multiple meanings. Find definitions of the word *issue*. It can be a noun or a verb. Write T for True or F for False to indicate whether the following statements use the correct meaning of the word *issue*.

21. An important <u>issue</u> during Andrew Jackson's presidency was the National Bank.

22. The Five Civilized Tribes <u>issued</u> farming societies with successful economies.

Building Citizenship

23. Become an Informed Voter With a partner, choose an election in your community. Outline how you would become informed on the candidates and/or the issues. Share your outline and your findings with the class.

Economics Connection

24. Predict How would an economic recession or depression affect your life today? Write a few paragraphs describing your ideas.

Reviewing Skills

25. READING SKILL **Question and Answer Relationships** Write your own review questions and answers. Write two that are directly from the text and two that require other information.

26. ANALYSIS SKILL **Compare and Contrast** Read the primary source document on the Cherokee removal on page 853. Then reread the passage on page 454 that deals with this event. Write a summary paragraph comparing the primary and secondary sources.

Standardized Test Practice

Select the best answer to each of the following questions.

27 In *Worcester* v. *Georgia*, Chief Justice John Marshall ruled that the state of Georgia

  A must adopt the spoils system.

  B had no right to interfere with the Cherokee.

  C could limit suffrage.

  D must support the National Bank.

28 Which of the following statements expresses an opinion about Andrew Jackson?

  A Jackson served two terms as president.

  B He spoke out against South Carolina's Nullification Act.

  C Jackson created the best system of filling government positions.

  D Jackson supported the Indian Removal Act.

Manifest Destiny

▼ The Alamo,
San Antonio, Texas

NATIONAL GEOGRAPHIC **Where & When?**

Areas of Settlement, 1850

| 1820 | 1835 | 1850 |

1821
California becomes a state of Mexico

1836
Whitmans build mission in Oregon country

1845
The United States annexes Texas

1850
California becomes a state

The Big Ideas

Westward to the Pacific

Geography influences the divergent paths of people resulting in physical, economic, and political challenges and rewards. Manifest Destiny is the idea that it was inevitable that the United States would extend its borders from the Atlantic Ocean to the Pacific Ocean.

Independence for Texas

Immigration influences a nation's or region's economy and society. American settlers began moving into the part of Mexico called Texas in the 1820s. Conflict forced Mexico to grant Texas its independence.

War With Mexico

Conflict often brings about great change. Through war with Mexico and diplomatic negotiations with Great Britain, the United States acquired Texas, Oregon, California, Utah, and the remainder of the Southwest.

New Settlers in California and Utah

Immigration influences a nation's or region's economy and society. By 1850, thousands of American settlers had crossed the Great Plains for new homes.

 View the Chapter 11 video in the Glencoe Video Program.

Organizing Information Make this foldable to organize information from the chapter to help you learn more about how Manifest Destiny led to western expansion.

Step 1 Collect three sheets of paper and place them on top of one another about 1 inch apart.

Keep the edges straight.

Step 2 Fold up the bottom edges of the paper to form 6 tabs.

This makes all tabs the same size.

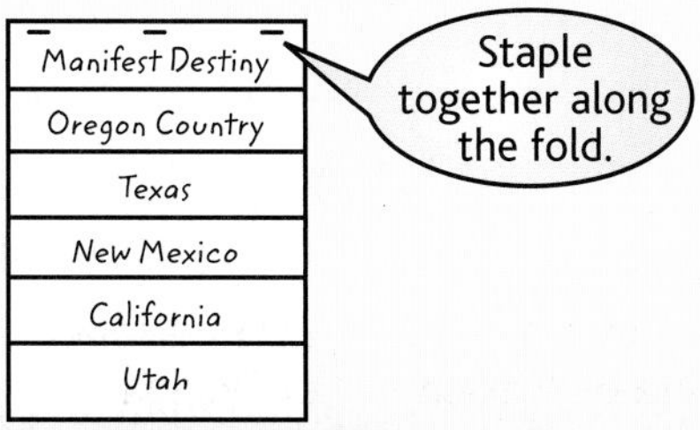

Reading and Writing As you read, use your foldable to write under each appropriate tab what you learn about Manifest Destiny and how it affected the borders of the United States.

Step 3 When all the tabs are the same size, fold the paper to hold the tabs in place and staple the sheets together along the fold. Turn the paper and label each tab as shown.

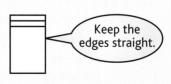

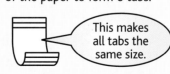
Staple together along the fold.

Manifest Destiny
Oregon Country
Texas
New Mexico
California
Utah

Get Ready to Read

New Vocabulary

READING SKILL

1 Learn It!

What should you do if you find a word you do not know or understand? Here are some suggested strategies:

1. Use context clues (from the sentence or paragraph) to help you define it.
2. Look for prefixes, suffixes, or root words that you already know.
3. Write it down and ask for help with the meaning.
4. Guess at its meaning.
5. Look it up in the glossary or a dictionary.

Look at the word boomtowns in the following passage. See how context clues can help you understand its meaning:

Context Clue

Boomtowns were new communities.

Context Clue

They were built almost overnight.

As people rushed to a new area to look for gold, they built new communities, called boomtowns, almost overnight. At one site on the Yuba River where only two houses stood in September 1849, a miner arrived the next year to find a town of 1,000 people "with a large number of hotels, stores, groceries, bakeries and . . . gambling houses." The miners gave some of the boomtowns colorful names such as Shinbone Peak and You Bet.

—*from page 503*

Reading Tip

To use context to help you define a word, read the sentences before and after the word.

Context Clue

They had characteristics similar to other towns.

② Practice It!

List three things in these paragraphs that help you understand the term *rendezvous* (RAHN•dih•voo). Write a sentence defining the word.

Read to Write⋯⋯⋯
Write a paragraph about a *rendezvous* you could have with your friends.

Some mountain men worked for fur-trading companies, but others sold their furs to the highest bidder. Throughout the spring and early summer, they traveled across the mountains, setting traps and then collecting the beaver pelts. In late summer, they gathered for a rendezvous (RAHN • dih • voo), or meeting.

For the mountain men, the annual rendezvous was the high point of the year. They met with trading companies to exchange their beaver skins for traps, guns, coffee, and other goods. They met old friends and exchanged news. They swapped stories about who had been on the most exciting adventures.

—*from page 472*

◄ Mountain man

③ Apply It!

Make a vocabulary bookmark with a 2-inch-wide strip of paper. As you read the chapter, keep track of the words you do not know or want to learn more about.

Westward to the Pacific

Guide to Reading

Looking Back, Looking Ahead

Americans had begun moving to Texas in the 1820s. By the 1830s and 1840s, they were making their way to Oregon.

Focusing on the Main Ideas

- Many Americans wanted control of the Oregon country to gain access to the Pacific Ocean. *(page 471)*
- Increased American settlement led the United States and Britain to divide Oregon. *(page 473)*

Locating Places

Oregon Country
Columbia River
Oregon Trail

Meeting People

John Jacob Astor
Jim Beckwourth
Jedediah Smith
Marcus Whitman
Narcissa Whitman
James K. Polk

Content Vocabulary

joint occupation
mountain man
rendezvous (RAHN•dih•VOO)
emigrant (EH•mih•gruhnt)
Manifest Destiny

Academic Vocabulary

access (AK•SEHS)
annual (AN•yuh•wuhl)
route (ROWT)
sole (SOHL)

Reading Strategy

Sequencing Information As you read Section 1, re-create the diagram below and in the boxes list key events that occurred.

1819	1825	1836	1846

NATIONAL GEOGRAPHIC Who & When?

1810 — 1830 — 1850

1819 Adams-Onís Treaty is signed

1840s Great migration to Oregon

1844 James K. Polk elected president

James K. Polk

Rivalry in the Northwest

Main Idea Many Americans wanted control of the Oregon Country to gain access to the Pacific Ocean.

Reading Connection Have you ever moved to a new city or town? Saying good-bye can be difficult, but the possibilities are exciting. Read to find out about people who moved to new lands.

An American Story

On an April morning in 1851, 13-year-old Martha Gay said good-bye to her friends, her home, and the familiar world of Springfield, Missouri. She and her family were beginning a long, hazardous journey. The townsfolk watched as the family left in four big wagons pulled by teams of oxen. "Farewell sermons were preached and prayers offered for our safety," Martha wrote years later. "All places of business and the school were closed . . . and everybody came to say good-bye to us." This same scene occurred many times in the 1840s and 1850s as thousands of families set out for the Oregon Country.

What Was Oregon Country?

The **Oregon Country** was the huge area that lay between the Pacific Ocean and the Rocky Mountains north of California. It included all of what is now Oregon, Washington, and Idaho plus parts of Montana and Wyoming. The region also contained about half of what is now the Canadian province of British Columbia.

In the early 1800s, four nations claimed the vast, rugged land known as the Oregon Country. The United States based its claim on Robert Gray's exploration of the **Columbia River** in 1792 and on the Lewis and Clark expedition. Great Britain based

its claim on British explorations of the Columbia River. Spain, which controlled California to the south, claimed a share of Oregon. Russia had settlements that stretched south from Alaska into California. Fort Ross in California was the Russians' southernmost settlement.

Adams-Onís Treaty Many Americans wanted control of the Oregon country and its **access** to the Pacific Ocean to build trade. Secretary of State John Quincy Adams played a key role in promoting this goal. In 1819 he negotiated a treaty with Spanish foreign minister Louis de Onís. In the Adams-Onís Treaty, the Spanish agreed to set the limits of their territory at what is now California's northern border and gave up any claim to Oregon. In 1824 Russia also surrendered its claim. Only Britain remained to challenge American control of Oregon.

In 1818 Adams had worked out an agreement with Britain for **joint occupation** of the area. This meant that people from both the United States and Great Britain could settle in Oregon. When Adams became president in 1825, he proposed that the two nations divide Oregon along the 49°N line of latitude.

"To explore unknown regions . . . was his chief delight."

—Clerk in a fur trade company describing Joseph Walker, an early explorer of Yosemite

Britain refused Adams's proposal, insisting on a larger share of the territory. Unable to resolve their dispute, the two countries agreed to allow both British and Americans to settle there.

Who Were the Mountain Men? The first Americans to reach the Oregon Country were not farmers but fur traders. They had come to trap beaver, whose skins were in great demand in the eastern United States and in Europe. The beaver skins were used to make hats, which were very popular at that time. The British established several trading posts in the region, as did American merchant **John Jacob Astor** of New York. In 1808 Astor organized the American Fur Company. It soon became the largest of the fur companies in America, allowing Astor to build up trade with the East Coast, the Pacific Northwest, and China. Astor and his family later became one of the wealthiest families in America.

Fur companies hired trappers, who over time became known as **mountain men.** Many mountain men had Native American wives and adopted Native American ways. They lived in lodges and dressed in fringed buckskin pants, moccasins, and beads.

Some mountain men worked for fur-trading companies, but others sold their furs to the highest bidder. Throughout the spring and early summer, they traveled across the mountains, setting traps and then collecting the beaver pelts. In late summer, they gathered for a **rendezvous** (RAHN•dih•voo), or meeting.

For the mountain men, the **annual** rendezvous was the high point of the year. They met with the trading companies to exchange their beaver skins for traps, guns, coffee, and other goods. They met old friends and exchanged news. They swapped stories about who had been on the most exciting adventures.

As they roamed the region searching for beaver, the mountain men explored the mountains, valleys, and trails of the West. **Jim Beckwourth,** an African American mountain man from Virginia, explored Wyoming's Green River. Robert Stuart and **Jedediah Smith** both found the South Pass, a broad break through the Rockies. South Pass later became the main **route** that settlers took to Oregon.

To survive in the wilderness, a mountain man had to be skillful and resourceful. Trapper Joe Meek told how, when faced with starvation, he once held his hands "in an anthill until they were covered with ants, then greedily licked them off." The mountain men took pride in joking about the dangers they faced.

In time, the mountain men killed off most of the beaver and could no longer trap the once plentiful animals. Some went to settle on farms in Oregon. With their knowledge of the western lands, though, some mountain men found new work. Jim Bridger, Kit Carson, and others acted as guides to lead the parties of settlers now streaming west.

✓ **Reading Check** **Explain** Why did trading posts develop in the Oregon Country?

Picturing **History**

Jim Beckwourth (right) explored many parts of the West, including the Green River area of Wyoming (left). *How did mountain men make their living?*

Settling Oregon

(Main Idea) **Increased American settlement led the United States and Britain to divide Oregon.**

Reading Connection If you could travel across the United States, where would you go? Read on to learn more about the settlement of the Oregon Country.

Americans began settling the Oregon Country in the 1830s. Reports of the fertile land and economic troubles in the East made the West look attractive.

The Whitman Mission Among the first settlers of the Oregon Country were missionaries who wanted to bring Christianity to the Native Americans. **Dr. Marcus Whitman** and his wife **Narcissa** went to Oregon in 1836 and built a mission among the Cayuse people near the present site of Walla Walla, Washington.

New settlers unknowingly brought measles to the mission. An epidemic killed many of the Native American children. Blaming the Whitmans for the sickness, the Cayuse attacked the mission in November 1847.

The Oregon Trail

The Importance of the Trail The Oregon Trail was much more than just a trail to Oregon. It served as the most practical route to the western United States. The pioneers traveled in large groups, often of related families. Some went all the way to Oregon in search of farmland. Many others split off for California in search of gold.

The Journey The trip west lasted five or six months. The pioneers had to start in the spring and complete the trip before winter snows blocked the mountain passes. The trail crossed difficult terrain. The pioneers walked across seemingly endless plains, forded swift rivers, and labored up high mountains.

Problems Along the Way Although the pioneers feared attacks by Native Americans, such attacks did not often occur. More often Native Americans assisted the pioneers, serving as guides and trading necessary food and supplies. About 1 in 10 of the pioneers died on the trail, perishing from disease, overwork, hunger, or accidents.

When did use of the trail stop? With the building of a transcontinental railroad in 1869, the days of using the Oregon Trail as a corridor to the West were over.

"We are creeping along slowly, one wagon after another, the same old gait, and the same thing over, out of one mud hole into another all day."

—*Amelia Stewart Knight, 1853*

"After Laramie we entered the great American desert, which was hard on the teams. Sickness became common. . . ."

—*Catherine Sager Pringle, 1844*

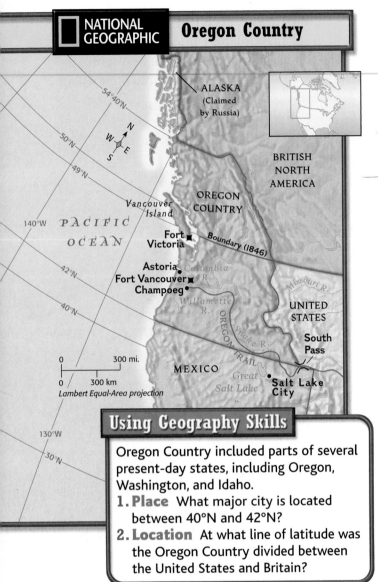

NATIONAL GEOGRAPHIC **Oregon Country**

ALASKA
(Claimed by Russia)

BRITISH NORTH AMERICA

OREGON COUNTRY

Vancouver Island

PACIFIC OCEAN

Fort Victoria

Boundary (1846)

Astoria
Fort Vancouver
Champoeg
Columbia R.

Willamette R.

UNITED STATES

Missouri R.

Snake R.

OREGON TRAIL

South Pass

MEXICO

Great Salt Lake

Salt Lake City

0   300 mi.
0   300 km
Lambert Equal-Area projection

Using Geography Skills

Oregon Country included parts of several present-day states, including Oregon, Washington, and Idaho.
1. **Place** What major city is located between 40°N and 42°N?
2. **Location** At what line of latitude was the Oregon Country divided between the United States and Britain?

The Cayuse killed the Whitmans and 11 others. Despite this tragedy, the flood of new settlers into Oregon continued.

The Oregon Trail In the early 1840s, "Oregon fever"—a desire to follow others to Oregon—began to sweep through the towns of the Mississippi Valley. People formed societies to gather information about Oregon and to plan and make the long journey. The "great migration" had begun. Tens of thousands of Americans made the trip. These pioneers were called **emigrants** (EH•mih•gruhnts) because they left the United States to go to Oregon, which was not yet a state.

Before the difficult 2,000-mile journey, these pioneers stuffed their canvas-covered wagons, called prairie schooners, with supplies. From a distance, these wagons looked like schooners (ships) at sea. Gathering in Independence or other towns in Missouri, they followed the **Oregon Trail** across the Great Plains, along the Platte River, and through the South Pass of the Rocky Mountains. On the other side, they took the trail north and west along the Snake and Columbia Rivers into Oregon Country.

Most American pioneers headed for the fertile Willamette Valley south of the Columbia River. Between 1840 and 1845, the number of American settlers in the area increased from 500 to 5,000, while the British population remained at about 700. The question of ownership of Oregon arose again.

What Is Manifest Destiny? Many Americans thought their nation had a special role to fulfill. In the 1800s, many believed that the United States's mission was to occupy the entire continent. In 1819 John Quincy Adams expressed what many Americans were thinking when he said expansion to the Pacific was as inevitable "as that the Mississippi should flow to the sea."

In the 1840s, newspaper editor John O'Sullivan put the idea of a national mission in more specific words. O'Sullivan declared it was America's "**Manifest Destiny** to overspread and to possess the whole of the continent which Providence has given us." O'Sullivan meant that the United States was clearly destined—set apart for a special purpose—to extend its boundaries all the way to the Pacific.

"Fifty-four Forty or Fight" The settlers in Oregon insisted that the United States should have **sole** ownership of the area. More and more Americans agreed. In Congress, Tennessee representative Davy Crockett compared joint occupancy—shared ownership—to the time he shared a tree with a panther. "The place [was] big enough for us both," said Crockett, "but we couldn't agree to stay there together." As pressure mounted, Oregon became a major issue in the 1844 presidential election.

In 1844 the Democrats were expected to nominate former president Martin Van Buren for president. Then the unexpected happened. The Democratic Party nominated **James K. Polk,** a former Congressman and governor of Tennessee for president. Polk supported American claims for sole ownership of Oregon. Democrats campaigned using the slogan "Fifty-four Forty or Fight." The slogan referred to the line of latitude that Democrats believed should be the nation's northern border in Oregon. Polk's campaign slogan captured the imagination of the voters.

Henry Clay of the Whig Party, Polk's principal opponent, did not take a strong position on the Oregon issue. Polk won 50 percent of the popular vote and 170 electoral votes to Clay's 48 percent and 105 electoral votes.

Reaching a Settlement Filled with the spirit of Manifest Destiny, President Polk was determined to make Oregon part of the United States. Britain would not accept a border at "Fifty-four Forty," however, because this would have meant giving up its claim entirely. Instead, in June 1846, the two countries compromised, setting the boundary between the American and British portions of Oregon at latitude 49°N. The two nations had finally resolved the Oregon issue.

During the 1830s, Americans sought to fulfill their Manifest Destiny by looking at other regions as well as Oregon. At that time, much attention was also focused on Texas.

✓ **Reading Check** **Explain** What did some Americans see as the purpose of Manifest Destiny?

Study Central Need help understanding Manifest Destiny? Visit tajwwl.glencoe.com and click on Study Central.

Section 1 Review

Reading Summary

Review the Main Ideas

• Oregon Country was the key element to the United States gaining access to the Pacific Ocean, and the government negotiated agreements with other nations toward accomplishing that goal.

• Many Americans made plans to settle in Oregon Territory, while ownership of the land drove political decisions.

What Did You Learn?

1. Which four countries claimed parts of the Oregon Country?

2. What mission does Manifest Destiny express?

Critical Thinking

3. **Determining Cause and Effect** Re-create the diagram below. In the box, describe how the fur trade led to interest in Oregon.

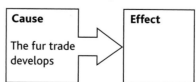

Cause	Effect
The fur trade develops	

4. **The Big Ideas** How did the idea of Manifest Destiny help Americans justify their desire to extend the United States to the Pacific Ocean?

5. **Picturing History** Study the painting on page 473. Do you think it provides a realistic portrayal of the journey west? Why or why not?

6. **READING** New Vocabulary Write a paragraph using the following vocabulary terms: mountain man, rendezvous, and Manifest Destiny. Provide context clues, assuming that your readers will not know the meaning of these words.

You Decide . . .

Manifest Destiny: Justified or Not?

Did Manifest Destiny contradict the spirit of equality important to so many Americans?

▲ Albert Gallatin

Not Justified

Albert Gallatin was one of many Americans who opposed Manifest Destiny. At the age of 86, after a distinguished career in public service, Gallatin became president of the New York Historical Society. The war against Mexico revived his interest in politics:

"It is said that the people of the United States have a hereditary superiority of race over the Mexicans, which gives them the right to subjugate and keep in bondage the inferior nation. . . . Is it compatible with the principle of democracy, which rejects every hereditary claim of individuals, to admit a hereditary superiority of races? . . . Can you for a moment suppose that a very doubtful descent from men who lived 1,000 years ago has transmitted to you a superiority over your fellow men?

. . . At this time the claim is but a pretext for covering and justifying unjust usurpation and unbounded ambition.

. . . Among ourselves the most ignorant, the most inferior, either in physical or mental faculties, is recognized as having equal rights, and he has an equal vote with anyone, however superior to him in all those respects. This is founded on the immutable principle that no one man is born with the right of governing another man."

—quoted in *The Annals of America*

Justified

John L. O'Sullivan first used the phrase Manifest Destiny in a July 1845 edition of the *United States Magazine and Democratic Review.* In the following article, he promotes the spread of democracy: O'Sullivan supported Manifest Destiny.

"Texas is now ours. Already, before these words are written, her Convention has undoubtedly ratified the acceptance by her Congress, of our proffered invitation into the Union. . . . Her star and her stripe may already be said to have taken their place in the glorious blazon of our common nationality. . . .

. . . The next session of Congress will see the representatives of the new young state in their places in both our halls of national legislation, side by side with those of the old Thirteen.

Why . . . [have] other nations . . . undertaken to intrude themselves into [the question of Texas?] between us and the proper parties to the case, in a spirit of hostile interference against us, for the avowed object of thwarting our policy and hampering our power, limiting our greatness and checking the fulfillment of our manifest destiny to overspread the continent allotted by Providence for the free development of our yearly multiplying millions."

—quoted in *Annexation*

▲ *Spirit of the Frontier* by John Gast

You Be The Historian

DBQ Document-Based Questions

1. What does Albert Gallatin think is the real motivation underlying the idea of Manifest Destiny?

2. Imagine you could interview Gallatin and O'Sullivan. Write a list of three questions you could ask each man about his views on Manifest Destiny.

What were people's lives like in the past?

What—and who—were people talking about? What did they eat? What did they do for fun? These two pages will give you some clues to everyday life in the U.S. as you step back in time with TIME Notebook.

Profile

*It's 1853, and **AMELIA STEWART** is heading west to Oregon with her husband and seven children in a covered wagon. How hard can the five-month trip be? Here are two entries from her diary:*

MONDAY, AUGUST 8 We have to make a drive of 22 miles without water today. Have our cans filled to drink. Here we left, unknowingly, our [daughter] Lucy behind, not a soul had missed her until we had gone some miles, when we stopped a while to rest the cattle; just then another train drove up behind us, with Lucy. She was terribly frightened and said she was sitting under the bank of the river when we started, busy watching some wagons cross, and did not know that we were ready....It was a lesson for all of us.

FRIDAY, AUGUST 12 Lost one of our oxen. We were traveling slowly along, when he dropped dead in the yoke....I could hardly help shedding tears, when we drove round this poor ox who had helped us along thus far, and had given us his very last step.

BROWN BROTHERS

MILESTONES

EVENTS OF THE TIME

CLOTHED. Hundreds of miners in 1850 by **LEVI STRAUSS**. Using canvas he originally intended to make into tents, Levi made sturdy, tough pants with lots of pockets—perfect clothing for the rough work of mining. Can you imagine anyone in the city ever wearing them?

BETTMANN/CORBIS

MARCHED. Just under 100 camels in 1857, from San Antonio to Los Angeles, led by hired Turkish, Greek, and Armenian camel drivers. It is hoped the desert beasts will help the U.S. Army open the West.

MAILED. Thousands of letters carried by **PONY EXPRESS** in 1860 from Missouri to California in an extremely short time—only 10 days! Riders switch to fresh horses every 10 or 15 miles and continue through the night, blizzards, and attacks by outlaws.

FRONTIER FOOD

Trail Mix

Hard Tack for a Hard Trip

INGREDIENTS: 3 cups flour • 3 tsp. salt • 1 cup water

Mix all ingredients and stir until it becomes too difficult. Knead the dough; add more flour until mixture is very dry. Roll to 1/2-inch thickness and cut into 3" squares, poke with a skewer [pin] to make several holes in each piece (for easy breaking). Bake 30 minutes in a hot oven until hard. Store for up to 10 years.

WESTERN WORD PLAY

Word Watch

Can you talk "Western"? Match the words below to their meaning.

1. maverick
2. Hangtown fry
3. grubstake
4. bonanza
5. palo alto
6. pard or rawwheel

a. gold rush favorite, made of eggs, bacon, and oysters

b. inexperienced '49er; eastern type not used to wearing boots

c. a lucky discovery of gold; a source of sudden wealth

d. a style of hat worn by gold rush miners

e. an individual who takes an independent stand, from the name of a Texas cattleman who left his herd unbranded

f. food provided by an investor to a gold prospector in exchange for a share of whatever gold the prospector finds

answers: 1. e; 2. a; 3. f; 4. c; 5. d; 6. b

The Price of a Life

This notice appeared in 1852.

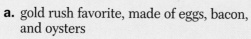

CREDIT SALE OF A CHOICE GANG OF 41

SLAVES!

COMPRISING MECHANICS, LABORERS, ETC.

FOR THE SETTLEMENT OF A CO-PARTNERSHIP OF RAILROAD CONTRACTORS

BY J. A. BEARD & MAY, J. A. BEARD, AUCT'R.

WILL BE SOLD AT AUCTION, AT BANKS' ARCADE, MAGAZINE STREET.

SALE OF SLAVES AND STOCK

The Negroes and Stock listed below are a Prime Lot, and belong to the ESTATE OF THE LATE LUTHER McGOWAN, and will be sold on Monday, Sept. 22nd, 1852, at the Fair Grounds, in Savannah, Georgia, at 1:00 P.M. The Negroes will be taken to the grounds two days previous to the Sale, so that they may be inspected by prospective buyers.

On account of the low prices listed below, they will be sold for cash only, and must be taken into custody within two hours after sale.

No.	Name	Age	Remarks	Price
1	Lunesta	27	Prime Rice Planter	
2	Violet	16	Housework and Nursemaid	$1,275.00
3	Lizzie	30	Rice, Unsound	900.00
4	Minda	27	Cotton, Prime Woman	300.00
5	Adam	28	Cotton, Prime Young Man	1,200.00
6	Abel	41	Rice Hand, Eyesight Poor	1,100.00
7	Tanney	22	Prime Cotton Hand	675.00
8	Flementina	39		

CHICAGO HISTORICAL SOCIETY/PHOTO RESEARCHERS INC.

NUMBERS

U.S. AT THE TIME

$81,249,700
Estimated value of gold mined in 1852

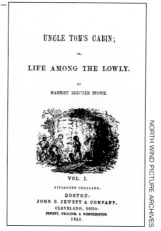

89 Days it takes the American clipper ship, the *Flying Cloud,* to go from Boston around Cape Horn to San Francisco in 1851—a trip that normally takes eight or nine months

BROWN BROTHERS

12 Poems included in Walt Whitman's new collection, called *Leaves of Grass* (1855)

33 Number of states in 1859 after Oregon enters the union

100 Seats in Congress won by the Republicans in 1854, the year the party was created

300,000 Copies of Harriet Beecher Stowe's novel, *Uncle Tom's Cabin,* sold in 1852

UNCLE TOM'S CABIN;
or,
LIFE AMONG THE LOWLY.
BY
HARRIET BEECHER STOWE.

VOL. I.

FIFTEENTH THOUSAND.

BOSTON:
JOHN P. JEWETT & COMPANY.
CLEVELAND, OHIO:
JEWETT, PROCTOR & WORTHINGTON.
1852.

NORTH WIND PICTURE ARCHIVES

Section 2

Independence for Texas

Guide to Reading

Looking Back, Looking Ahead
In the last section, you read about new settlements in Oregon country and the annexation of that land to the United States. In this section, you will learn about settlement in Texas.

Focusing on the Main Ideas
- Texas was settled by people from Mexico and the United States, creating cultural tension. *(page 481)*
- Texans wanted to be a nation separate from Mexico. *(page 483)*

Locating Places
Texas
Mexico
Alamo

Meeting People
Davy Crockett
Stephen F. Austin
General Antonio López de Santa Anna

Content Vocabulary
Tejano (teh•HAH•noh)
empresario (ehm•pray•SAR•ih•oh)
decree (dih•KREE)
annex (A•nehks)

Academic Vocabulary
status
similar

Reading Strategy
Sequencing Information As you read Section 2, re-create the diagram below. In the boxes, list key events that occurred in Texas.

1835   **1836**

| Oct. | Dec. | Mar. | May |
| Feb. | Apr. | Sept. |

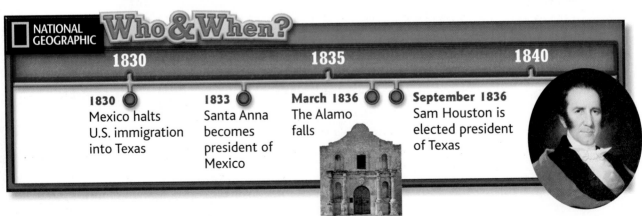

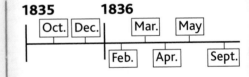

NATIONAL GEOGRAPHIC Who & When?

1830   **1835**   **1840**

1830 Mexico halts U.S. immigration into Texas

1833 Santa Anna becomes president of Mexico

March 1836 The Alamo falls

September 1836 Sam Houston is elected president of Texas

A Clash of Cultures

Main Idea Texas was settled by people from Mexico and the United States, creating cultural tension.

Reading Connection Did you know that Texas was not always part of the United States? Read to find out how this important region was the scene of international conflict.

An American Story

Davy Crockett's skill as a hunter and story-teller helped get him elected to three terms in Congress representing Tennessee. But when he started his first political campaign, Crockett was doubtful about his chances of winning. "The thought of having to make a speech made my knees feel mighty weak and set my heart to fluttering." Fortunately for Crockett, the other candidates spoke all day and tired out the audience. "When they were all done," Crockett boasted, "I got up and told some laughable story, and quit. . . . I went home, and didn't go back again till after the election was over." In the end, Crockett won the election by a wide margin.

Conflict Over Texas In 1835 **Davy Crockett** lost his seat in Congress. He then left Tennessee and headed southwest to **Texas.** Crockett thought he could make a new start there. Little did he know his deeds in Texas would bring him greater fame than his adventures on the frontier or his years in Congress.

In 1803 the United States laid claim to Texas as part of the Louisiana Purchase. Spain protested, and in 1819 the United States agreed to drop its claim. At that time, most of Texas's 3,000 residents were *Tejanos* (teh•HAH•nohs), or Mexicans who claimed Texas as their home.

Native Americans, such as the Comanches, Apaches, and Kiowas, also lived in the area.

Wanting to promote Texas's growth, the Spanish offered vast tracts of land to people who agreed to bring families to settle on the land. The people who obtained these grants and recruited settlers were called *empresarios* (ehm•pray•SAR•ih•ohs). Moses Austin of Missouri received the first land grant in 1821. Before Austin set up his colony, **Mexico** declared its independence from Spain. Austin died soon afterward, and the land passed to his son, **Stephen F. Austin.** The younger Austin recruited 300 American families to settle the fertile land along the Brazos and Colorado Rivers of Texas. Austin's success made him a leader among the American settlers in Texas.

Picturing **History**

This April 1836 poster from New Orleans asked for volunteers during the Texas War for Independence. Tennessee frontiersman Davy Crockett was one of the many who came to Texas. *Why did Crockett go to Texas?*

Why Did Tension Grow? By 1830 Americans in Texas far outnumbered Mexicans and the American settlers had not adopted Mexican ways. In 1830 Mexico issued a **decree** (dih•KREE), or official order, that stopped all immigration from the United States. A tax was also placed on American goods entering Texas. These new policies angered the Texans. Many depended on trade with the United States and hoped for more Americans to settle in Texas. Those colonists who held slaves also feared that Mexico would try to end slavery in the territory.

Why Did Hopes for Reconciliation Fade? Some of the American settlers called for independence. Others hoped to stay within Mexico, but on better terms. In 1833 the Mexican president, **General Antonio López de Santa Anna,** agreed to remove the ban on American settlers. However, he refused to change Texas's political **status.** When Austin began making plans for independence, the Mexican government arrested him. Meanwhile, Santa Anna became a dictator and overthrew Mexico's constitution. Without a constitution to protect their rights, Texans felt betrayed. Austin believed the time had come to act. He urged the people to unite:

> ❝ War is our only recourse. There is no other remedy. We must defend our rights . . . by the force of arms. ❞
>
> —quoted in *Southwestern Historical Quarterly*

Reading Check **Explain** Why was colonization of Americans into Texas failing?

What If...

The Defenders Had Not Stayed at the Alamo?

William Travis and almost 200 other defenders were determined to hold the Alamo. Travis wrote several messages to the people of Texas and the United States asking them for assistance. Travis's appeal was unsuccessful. Texas military forces were not yet well organized and were badly scattered. Travis's letter of February 24, 1836, is one of the finest statements of courage in American history.

The defenders—mostly volunteers—were free to leave whenever they chose. But they decided to defend the Alamo for a cause in which they believed.

Santa Anna hoped the fall of the Alamo would convince other Texans that it was useless to resist his armies. Instead, the heroism of those in the Alamo inspired other Texans to carry on the struggle. "Remember the Alamo!" became the battle cry of Texas's army.

Travis's Appeal for Aid at the Alamo, February 24, 1836

To the People of Texas and All Americans in the World—

Fellow Citizens and Compatriots:

I am besieged by a thousand or more of the Mexicans under Santa Anna. I have sustained a continual Bombardment & cannonade for 24 hours & have not lost a man. The enemy has demanded a surrender at discretion, otherwise the garrison are to be put to the sword if the fort is taken. I have answered the demand with a cannon shot, and our flag still waves proudly from the walls. I shall never surrender or retreat.

Then, I call on you in the name of Liberty, of patriotism, & of everything dear to the American character, to come to our aid with all dispatch. The enemy is receiving reinforcements daily & will no doubt increase to three or four thousand in four or five days. If this call is neglected I am determined to sustain myself as long as possible & die like a soldier who never forgets what is due to his honor & that of his country.

Victory or Death
William Barret Travis
Lt. Col. Comdt.

The Struggle for Independence

Main Idea Texans wanted to be a nation separate from Mexico.

Reading Connection Would you have the courage to stand up to a huge army for something you believed in? Read on to see how the soldiers at the Alamo defended their beliefs.

During 1835 unrest grew among Texans and occasionally resulted in open conflict. Santa Anna sent an army into Texas late that year to punish the rebels. In October some Mexican troops tried to seize a cannon held by Texans at the town of Gonzales. During the battle, the Texans taunted the Mexican troops, decorating the front of the cannon with a white flag that bore the words "Come and Take It." After a brief struggle, the Texans drove back the Mexican troops. Texans considered this to be the first fight of the Texan Revolution.

The Texans called on volunteers to join their fight. They offered free land to anyone who would help. Davy Crockett and many others—including a number of African Americans and Tejanos—answered that call.

In December 1835, the Texans scored an important victory. They liberated the city of San Antonio from the control of a larger Mexican force. The Texas army at San Antonio included more than 100 Tejanos. Many of them served in a scouting company commanded by Captain Juan Seguín. Born in San Antonio, Seguín was an outspoken champion of the Texans' demand for independence.

Despite these victories, the Texans encountered problems. With the Mexican withdrawal, some Texans left San Antonio, thinking the war was won. Various groups argued over what course of action to follow. In early 1836, when Texas should have been making preparations to face Santa Anna, little was being done.

What Happened at the Alamo? Santa Anna marched north, furious about the loss of San Antonio. When his army reached San Antonio in late February 1836, it found a small Texan force barricaded inside a nearby mission called the **Alamo.**

Although the Texans had cannons, they lacked gunpowder. Worse, they had only about 160 soldiers to face Santa Anna's army of several thousand. The Texans did have brave leaders, though, including Davy Crockett, who had arrived with a band of sharpshooters from Tennessee, and a tough Texan named Jim Bowie. The American commander, William B. Travis, was only 26 years old, but he was determined to hold the mission. Travis managed to send messengers through the Mexican lines. He wrote several messages asking others to come to the aid of his soldiers. In his last message, Travis described the fighting that had already taken place and repeated his request for assistance.

W hat might have happened?

1. Do you think the stand at the Alamo helped the cause of Texas independence even though it was a defeat for the Texans? Explain.

2. Did history take a different course because of the decision to defend the Alamo? Explain.

Travis warned that "the power of Santa Anna is to be met here, or in the colonies; we had better meet them here than to suffer a war of devastation to rage in our settlements."

Travis concluded with the statement that he and his troops were determined to hold the Alamo. For 13 long days, the defenders of the Alamo kept Santa Anna's army at bay with rifle fire. During the siege, 32 volunteers from Gonzales slipped through the Mexican lines to join the Alamo's defenders.

On March 6, 1836, Mexican cannon fire smashed the Alamo's walls, and the Mexicans launched an all-out attack. The Alamo defenders killed many Mexican soldiers, but the Mexicans were too numerous to hold back. They finally entered the fortress, killing William Travis, Davy Crockett, Jim Bowie, and all the other defenders. Only a few women and children and some servants survived to tell of the battle.

In the words of Santa Anna's aide, "The Texans fought more like devils than like men." The defenders of the Alamo had killed hundreds of Mexican soldiers. But more important, they had bought Texans some much needed time.

History Online

Student Web Activity Visit tajwwI.glencoe.com and click on *Chapter 11—Student Web Activities* for an activity on the fight for Texas independence.

Texas Declares Its Independence During the siege of the Alamo, Texan leaders were meeting at Washington-on-the-Brazos, where they were drawing up a new constitution. There, on March 2, 1836—four days before the fall of the Alamo—American settlers and Tejanos firmly declared independence from Mexico and established the Republic of Texas. Thus, Texas became a country and a neighbor to the United States.

The Texas Declaration of Independence was in some ways **similar** to the Declaration of the United States, which had been written 60 years earlier. The Texas Declaration stated that the government of Santa Anna had violated the liberties guaranteed under the Mexican Constitution. The Texas Declaration also charged that Texans had been deprived of freedom of religion, the right to trial by jury, the right to bear arms, and the right to petition.

The Declaration stated that the Texans' protests against these policies were met with force. The Mexican government had sent a large army to drive Texans from their homes. Because of these grievances, the declaration proclaimed the following:

> ❝ The people of Texas. . . . do now constitute a free, sovereign, and independent republic. . . . ❞
> —from the Texas Declaration of Independence

With Mexican troops in Texas, it was not possible to hold elections to ratify the constitution and vote for leaders of the new republic. Texas leaders set up a temporary government. They selected officers to serve until regular elections could be held.

David G. Burnet, an early pioneer in Texas, was chosen president and Lorenzo de Zavala, vice president. De Zavala had worked to establish a democratic government in Mexico. He moved to Texas when it became clear that Santa Anna would not make reforms.

The government named Sam Houston as commander in chief of the Texas forces. Houston had come to Texas in 1833. Raised among the Cherokee people, he became a soldier, fighting with Andrew Jackson against the Creek people in the Creek Wars (1813–1814). A politician as well, Houston had served in Congress and as governor of Tennessee.

Houston wanted to prevent areas from being overrun by the Mexican troops. He ordered the troops at the city of Goliad to abandon their position. As they retreated, however, they came face to face with Mexican troops. After a fierce fight, several hundred Texans surrendered. On Santa Anna's orders, the Texans were executed a few days later.

The Battle of San Jacinto Houston moved his small army eastward about 100 miles, watching the movements of Santa Anna and waiting for a chance to strike. Six weeks after the Alamo, he found the opportunity.

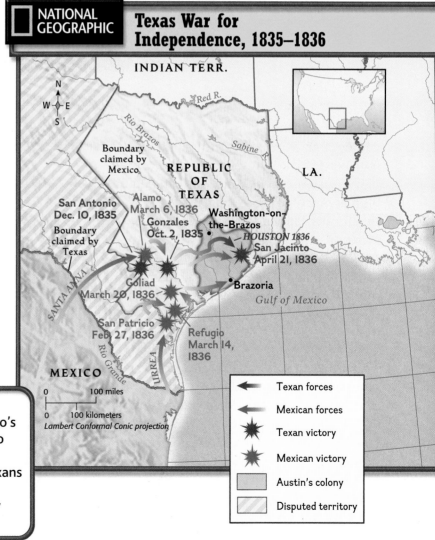

NATIONAL GEOGRAPHIC

Texas War for Independence, 1835–1836

INDIAN TERR.

Red R.

Rio Brazos

Sabine R.

Boundary claimed by Mexico

REPUBLIC OF TEXAS

LA.

San Antonio Dec. 10, 1835

Boundary claimed by Texas

Alamo March 6, 1836

Gonzales Oct. 2, 1835

Washington-on-the-Brazos

HOUSTON 1836

San Jacinto April 21, 1836

Goliad March 20, 1836

Brazoria

Gulf of Mexico

San Patricio Feb. 27, 1836

Refugio March 14, 1836

URREA

Rio Grande

SANTA ANNA

MEXICO

0   100 miles

0   100 kilometers
Lambert Conformal Conic projection

← Texan forces
← Mexican forces
✹ Texan victory
✹ Mexican victory
▨ Austin's colony
▨ Disputed territory

After adding some new troops, Houston gathered an army of about 900 at San Jacinto (SAN huh•SIHN•toh), near the site of present-day Houston. Santa Anna was camped nearby with an army of more than 1,300. On April 21, the Texans launched a surprise attack on the Mexican camp, shouting, "Remember the Alamo! Remember Goliad!"

They killed more than 600 soldiers and captured about 700 more—including Santa Anna. On May 14, 1836, Santa Anna signed a treaty that recognized the independence of Texas.

The Lone Star Republic Texans elected Sam Houston as their president, in September 1836. Houston sent a delegation to Washington, D.C., asking the United States to **annex** (A•nehks)— take control of—Texas. However, the nation's president, Andrew Jackson, refused because the addition of another slave state would upset the balance of slave and free states in Congress. For the moment, Texas would remain an independent country.

The Question of Annexation Despite rapid population growth, the new republic faced political and financial difficulties. The Mexican government refused to honor Santa Anna's recognition of independence, and fighting continued between Texas and Mexico.

Many Texans still hoped to join the United States. Southerners favored the annexation of Texas, but Northerners objected that Texas would add another slave state to the Union. President Martin Van Buren, like Jackson, did not want to inflame the slavery issue. He put off the question of annexing Texas.

John Tyler, who became the nation's president in 1841, was the first vice president to become president upon the death of a chief executive. He succeeded William Henry Harrison, who died in April, just one month after taking office. He became ill after spending his inauguration day outdoors in bad weather.

Once he became president, Tyler supported adding Texas to the Union and persuaded Texas to reapply for annexation. However, the U.S. Senate was divided over slavery and failed to ratify the annexation treaty.

Texas Becomes a State The situation changed with the 1844 presidential campaign. The feeling of Manifest Destiny was growing throughout the country. The South favored annexation of Texas. The North demanded that the United States gain control of the Oregon country from Britain. The Democratic candidate, James K. Polk, supported both actions. The Whig candidate, Henry Clay, initially opposed adding Texas to the Union. When he finally supported annexation, it lost him votes in the North—and the election.

After Polk's victory, supporters of annexation pressed the issue in Congress. They proposed and passed a resolution to annex Texas. On December 29, 1845, Texas officially became a state of the United States.

✓ **Reading Check** **Analyze** How has early Texas history influenced its reputation as a land of rugged individualists?

"We must now act or abandon all hope!"

—*Sam Houston, before the Battle of San Jacinto*

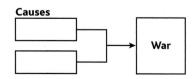

Section 2 Review

History Online

Study Central Need help understanding Texas's battle for independence? Visit tajwwI.glencoe.com and click on Study Central.

Reading Summary

Review the Main Ideas

• The majority of settlers in Texas were from the United States. American influence in the territory caused concern among Mexicans in Texas and Mexico.

• Texans struggled to create a state independent from Mexico, eventually achieving that goal in May 1836.

What Did You Learn?

1. What did the Spanish do to promote the growth of Texas?

2. Which leader of Mexico fought against the Texans?

Critical Thinking

3. **Categorizing Information** Re-create the diagram below. In the boxes, describe two causes of the war between Mexico and Americans in Texas.

Causes

```
┌─────────┐
│         │
└─────────┘       ┌───────┐
             ───▶ │  War  │
┌─────────┐       └───────┘
│         │
└─────────┘
```

4. **The Big Ideas** Why did Northerners and Southerners disagree on the annexation of Texas? Explain.

5. **Analyze** How did the fall of the Alamo help the cause of Texas independence, even though it was a defeat for the Texans?

6. **ANALYSIS** **Sequencing Information** Study the map on page 485. Place these battles in order on a time line, starting with the earliest: Gonzalez, San Jacinto, the Alamo, Goliad.

0 ——————————— 300 miles

0 ——————————— 300 kilometers

Albers Conic Equal-Area projection

WASHINGTON

Columbia R.

OREGON

What do rivers provide?
Rivers provide energy, food, transportation, and water for drinking and for irrigation.

What is a river? A river is freshwater flowing across the surface of the land, usually to the sea. Rivers are formed when one stream meets another and they come together. These smaller streams are called tributaries.

NEVADA

UTAH

COLORADO

CALIFORNIA

Colorado R.

NEW MEXICO

ARIZONA

PACIFIC OCEAN

TEXAS

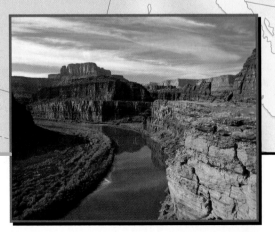

What is the Colorado River Basin? The Colorado River and its tributaries are called the Colorado River Basin. A basin is an area of land drained by a river and its tributaries. The Colorado River and its tributaries drain more than 240,000 square miles in the United States.

CANADA

Gulf of Mexico

VITAL RESOURCES

Water—or rather the scarcity of it—defines the western
states where precipitation averages just half that of the
eastern states. In 1879 explorer John Wesley Powell correctly predicted that the ability to determine water rights
and manage rivers was the key to settling this arid land.

COLORADO RIVER The Colorado River plunges 1,450 miles
from the Rocky Mountains to the Gulf of California, through
several states and two countries. Early settlers complained that
its silt-laden waters were "too thick to drink, and too thin to
plow." Today, a complex system of dams and canals controls
and disperses the water to thirsty fields and
cities from Colorado to Mexico. In the 1920s,
the "Law of the River" apportioned the water
between the seven Colorado River Basin states.

COLUMBIA RIVER This clear water once
flowed unimpeded 1,243 miles from Canada
to the Pacific Northwest. Today, 14 dams block
the main course but provide cheap electricity,
irrigation, drinking water, and flood control
for millions of people. The human-caused
changes reduced both salmon runs and the
traditional jobs tied to them, prompting a new
look at how humans use this vital waterway.

SACRAMENTO/SAN JOAQUIN RIVERS Fed
by winter snows in the lofty Sierra Nevada and
Cascade Mountains, these rivers and a dozen
tributaries drain California's vast interior. Complicated laws and a scheme of
dams, reservoirs, and aqueducts channel this precious water to immense
farmlands and densely populated cities
throughout California.

▲ John Wesley Powell
(right) and Paiute
Chief Tau-gu during
an expedition to
the Grand Canyon

LEARNING from GEOGRAPHY

1. **What changes helped bring water to many
   regions? What problems did these changes cause?**

2. **What regulations did "The Law of the River"
   establish?**

War With Mexico

Guide to Reading

Looking Back, Looking Ahead

You read about the Texans' brave struggle for independence. This section will focus on the war with Mexico over the California and New Mexico provinces.

Focusing on the Main Ideas

- The Santa Fe Trail was a busy trade route through New Mexico, a large region governed by Mexico. *(page 491)*
- California was settled and populated by diverse cultures. *(page 492)*
- Strained relations between the United States and Mexico resulted in war. *(page 495)*

Locating Places

Santa Fe (SAN•tuh FAY)

El Camino Real
  (kah•MEE•noh RAY•ahl)

Nueces River (nu•AY•suhs)

Bear Flag Republic

Meeting People

William Becknell

Jedediah Smith

María Amparo Ruiz de Burton

John C. Frémont

Content Vocabulary

ranchero (ran•CHEHR•oh)

rancho (RAN•choh)

Californio (ka•luh•FAWR•nee•OH)

cede (SEED)

Academic Vocabulary

concept

devote

Reading Strategy

Taking Notes As you read the section, describe the actions and achievements of each of the individuals in the table.

	Actions taken
William Becknell	
Jedediah Smith	
John C. Frémont	

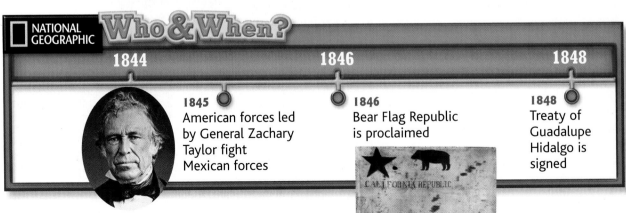

NATIONAL GEOGRAPHIC Who & When?

1844   **1846**   **1848**

1845 American forces led by General Zachary Taylor fight Mexican forces

1846 Bear Flag Republic is proclaimed

1848 Treaty of Guadalupe Hidalgo is signed

CALIFORNIA REPUBLIC

The New Mexico Territory

Main Idea The Santa Fe Trail was a busy trade route through New Mexico, a large region governed by Mexico.

Reading Connection Can you imagine walking from Missouri to Arizona, or beyond? Read on to see how traders did just that.

An American Story

Long lines of covered wagons stretched as far as the eye could see. "All's set!" a driver called out. "All's set!" everyone shouted in reply.

"Then the 'Heps!' of drivers—the cracking of whips—the trampling of feet—the occasional creak of wheels—the rumbling of wagons—form a new scene of [intense] confusion," reported Josiah Gregg. Gregg was one of the traders who traveled west on the Santa Fe Trail in the 1830s to sell cloth, knives, and other goods in New Mexico.

What Areas Did New Mexico Include?

In the early 1800s, New Mexico was the name of a vast region sandwiched between the Texas and California territories. It included all of present-day New Mexico, Arizona, and Nevada, and parts of Colorado and Utah.

Native American peoples had lived in the area for thousands of years. Spanish conquistadors began exploring the region in the late 1500s and made it part of Spain's colony of Mexico. In 1610 the Spanish founded the settlement of **Santa Fe** (SAN•tuh FAY). When Mexico won its independence from Spain in 1821, it inherited the New Mexico province.

The Spanish had tried to keep Americans away from Santa Fe, fearing that Americans would want to take over the area. The Mexican government changed this policy, welcoming American traders into New Mexico. It hoped that trade would boost the economy of the province.

How Was the Santa Fe Trail Used?

William Becknell, the first American trader to reach Santa Fe, arrived in 1821 with a pack of mules loaded with manufactured goods to exchange for furs.

Becknell's route into New Mexico came to be known as the Santa Fe Trail. The trail left the Missouri River near Independence, Missouri, and crossed the prairies to the Arkansas River. It followed the river west toward the Rocky Mountains before turning south into New Mexico. Because the trail was mostly flat, on later trips Becknell used wagons to carry his merchandise.

Other traders followed Becknell, and the Santa Fe Trail became a busy trade route for hundreds of wagons. Americans brought cloth and firearms, which they exchanged in Santa Fe for silver, furs, and mules. The trail remained in use until the arrival of the railroad in 1880.

As trade with New Mexico increased, Americans began settling in the region. In the United States, the **concept** of Manifest Destiny became popular, and many people saw New Mexico as territory worth acquiring. At the same time, they eyed another prize—the Mexican territory of California, which would provide access to the Pacific.

Reading Check **Identify** Where did the Santa Fe Trail end? What was it used for?

▲ Santa Fe Trail marker

California's Spanish Culture

Main Idea **California was settled and populated by diverse cultures.**

Reading Connection Imagine you lived in California in the mid-1800s. Would you like to have been a Native American, a rancher, or a settler from the East?

Spanish explorers and missionaries from Mexico had been the first Europeans to settle in California. Explorer Juan Bautista de Anza opened the overland route from Mexico to California and established the first settlement at San Francisco in 1776. Seven years earlier, Captain Gaspar de Portolá and Father Junípero Serra began building a string of missions that eventually extended from San Diego to Sonoma. These missions were connected along a route known as *El Camino Real* (kah•MEE•noh RAY•ahl), "the King's Highway," named for the king of Spain who ordered the missions built.

The mission system was a key part of Spain's plan to colonize California. The Spanish used the missions to convert Native Americans to Christianity. By 1820 California had 21 missions, with about 20,000 Native Americans living in them. In 1820 American mountain man **Jedediah Smith** visited the San Gabriel Mission east of present-day Los Angeles. Smith reported that the Native Americans farmed thousands of acres and worked at weaving and other crafts. He described the missions as "large farming and grazing establishments." Another American in Smith's party called the Native Americans "slaves in every sense of the word."

California After 1821 After Mexico gained its independence from Spain in 1821, California became a state of Mexico. At the time only a few hundred Spanish settlers lived in California, but emigrants began arriving from Mexico. The wealthier settlers lived on ranches **devoted** to raising cattle and horses.

In 1833 the Mexican government passed a law abolishing the Spanish missions. The government gave some of the lands to Native Americans and sold the remainder. Mexican settlers called **rancheros** (ran•CHEHR•ohs)—ranch owners—bought these lands and built huge properties called **ranchos** (RAN•chohs).

History *Through Art*

***Vaqueros in a Horse Corral* by James Walker**
Mexican American cowhands, or vaqueros, work on a ranch in the Southwest. *Why did the number of ranchos grow in the 1820s and 1830s?*

Biography

MARÍA AMPARO RUIZ DE BURTON
1832–1895

María Amparo Ruiz de Burton was the first Mexican American to publish a novel in English in the United States. Born into a wealthy family in Baja California in 1832, she stood to inherit the vast landholdings of her grandfather. She would eventually learn, however, that though the treaty of Guadalupe Hidalgo ensured the land rights of Mexican American citizens, these rights would not be enforced.

After the war with Mexico, María married Colonel Henry Burton, an officer in the U.S. army. In 1859 the Burton family moved to Rhode Island, and María did not return to California until 1869 after the death of her husband. When she returned, she found that much of the land she and her husband owned had been sold and that the rest was inhabited by American squatters. In 1851 the California Land Act made all land owned by Mexicans public domain and available for settlement until the land titles of the original owners could be verified. Burton began a lengthy and expensive legal battle that would continue until her death in 1895. She died destitute and landless.

"I think but few Americans know or believe to what extent we have been wronged by Congressional action."
—from *The Squatter and the Don*

Burton wrote two novels during her battles with the government over her land. Her first novel, *Who Would Have Thought It?*, challenges the idea of American supremacy by claiming that Mexicans are as white by blood as Americans. Although this argument maintains a social hierarchy of certain races over others, her statements on the treatment of Mexicans and on U.S. political corruption were important to the time period. Her second novel, *The Squatter and the Don,* again deals with the problems of corruption and racism by focusing on land battles in California. Burton's legacy impacted both literature and Mexican American history. Her fight for her land, though unsuccessful, exposed the discriminatory actions by many Americans against Mexican citizens.

Then and Now

Burton fought for most of her life for her land. Find someone today who similarly has fought for his or her rights.

Picturing History

Established in 1826, Monterey was the capital of California until 1847. *When did California become a state of Mexico?*

Manifest Destiny and California

Americans had been visiting California for years. Most arrived on trading or whaling ships, although a few hardy travelers like Jedediah Smith came overland from the East. Soon more began to arrive by land and sea.

At first, the Mexican authorities welcomed Americans in California. In 1839 they granted land in the Sacramento Valley to John Sutter, a German immigrant. There Sutter built a trading post that became one of the first stopping points for Americans reaching California.

The newcomers included agents for American shipping companies, fur traders from Oregon, and merchants from New Mexico. In the 1840s, families began to arrive in California to settle. They made the long journey from Missouri on the Oregon Trail and then turned south after crossing the Rocky Mountains. Still, by 1845 the American population of California numbered only about 700. Most Americans lived in the Sacramento River valley.

Some American travelers wrote glowing reports of California. **John C. Frémont,** an army officer who made several trips through California in the 1840s, wrote of the region's mild climate, scenic beauty, and abundance of natural resources.

Americans began to talk about adding California to the nation. Shippers and manufacturers hoped to build ports on the Pacific coast for trade with China and Japan. Many Americans saw the advantage of extending United States territory to the Pacific. That way, the nation would be safely bordered by the sea instead of by a foreign power, namely Mexico. William Marcy, U.S. Secretary of War, wrote:

> 66 It is the wish . . . of the United States to provide for [California] a free government with the least possible delay, similar to that which exists in our territories. 99
> —letter to Colonel Stevenson

President James Polk twice offered to buy California and New Mexico from Mexico, but Mexico refused. Soon, the United States would take over both regions by force.

Reading Check **Examine** What made California attractive for U.S. expansion?

War With Mexico

....

Main Idea Strained relations between the United States and Mexico resulted in war.

Reading Connection How much would you pay for California and New Mexico? Read to learn what President Polk offered and how his offer was received.

....

President James K. Polk was determined to get the California and New Mexico territories from Mexico. Their possession would guarantee that the United States had clear passage to the Pacific Ocean—an important consideration because the British still occupied part of Oregon. Polk's main reason, though, involved fulfilling the nation's Manifest Destiny. Like many Americans, Polk believed California and New Mexico belonged to the United States.

After Mexico refused to sell California and New Mexico, President Polk plotted to pull the Mexican provinces into the Union through war. He wanted, however, to provoke Mexico into taking military action first. This way Polk could justify the war to Congress and the American people.

Relations between Mexico and the United States had been strained for some years. When the United States annexed Texas in 1845, the situation worsened. Mexico, which had never recognized the independence of Texas, charged that the annexation was illegal.

Another dispute concerned the Texas-Mexico border. The United States insisted that the Rio Grande formed the border.

Mexico claimed that the border lay along the **Nueces River** (nu•AY•suhs), 150 miles farther north. Because of this dispute, Mexico had stopped payments to American citizens for losses suffered during Mexico's war for independence.

Polk sent an agent, John Slidell, to Mexico City to propose a deal. Slidell was authorized to offer $30 million for California and New Mexico in return for Mexico's acceptance of the Rio Grande as the Texas boundary. In addition, the United States would take over payment of Mexico's debts to American citizens.

How Did Conflict Begin? Mexican officials refused to meet with Slidell and stated their plan to reclaim Texas. Polk then ordered General Zachary Taylor to march his soldiers across the Nueces River into the disputed border area.

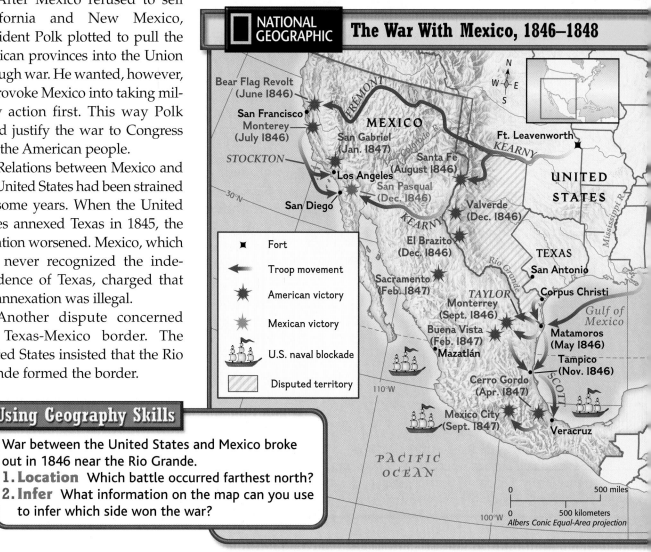

NATIONAL GEOGRAPHIC — **The War With Mexico, 1846–1848**

Using Geography Skills

War between the United States and Mexico broke out in 1846 near the Rio Grande.
1. **Location** Which battle occurred farthest north?
2. **Infer** What information on the map can you use to infer which side won the war?

Taylor followed the order and built a fort there. In April 1846, Mexican soldiers attacked a small force of Taylor's soldiers. Taylor quickly notified Polk. On May 9, Polk told Congress that "Mexico has . . . shed blood on American soil." Congress passed a declaration of war against Mexico.

How Was News of the War Received?
The war with Mexico divided Americans. Polk's party, the Democrats, generally backed it. Many Whigs believed the war was aggressive and unjust. Northerners accused the Democrats of waging war to spread slavery.

Illinois congressman Abraham Lincoln demanded to know the exact spot where the first attack on American troops had occurred. He claimed that the spot was clearly in Mexico and that Polk had no reason for blaming Mexico.

Frederick Douglass, an African American leader, called the war "disgraceful." He believed that the Southern states would bring slavery to any new territories won in the war. Newspapers mostly backed the war, and volunteers rushed to join the military.

Picturing History
In June 1846, settlers in northern California declared California independent of Mexico and renamed the region the Bear Flag Republic. *What was John C. Frémont's role in the uprising?*

Polk's War Plan
President Polk planned for American forces to drive Mexico out of the disputed border region in Texas. Then, the forces would move into New Mexico and California. Finally, Mexico City, the capital of Mexico, would be taken.

In September 1846, General Taylor's forces crossed the Rio Grande and captured the town of Monterrey. About five months later, he defeated the Mexicans again at Buena Vista. The Texas border was secure.

While Taylor advanced in northern Mexico, General Stephen Watts Kearney led his troops to California and New Mexico. In the summer of 1846, Kearny led about 1,500 cavalry soldiers along the Santa Fe Trail from Missouri to New Mexico. The Americans captured New Mexico's capital, Sante Fe, without firing a shot. Kearny and his forces then moved westward across the deserts to California.

What Was the Bear Flag Republic?
In June 1846, a small group of Americans had seized the town of Sonoma north of San Francisco and proclaimed the independent Republic of California. They called the new country the **Bear Flag Republic** because their flag showed a bear and star on a white background. John C. Frémont and mountain man Kit Carson joined the Americans in Sonoma.

Though unaware of the outbreak of war with Mexico, Frémont declared he would seize California. Frémont's actions outraged many **Californios** (ka•luh•FAWR•nee•OHS), the Mexicans who lived in California. They might have supported a revolt for local control of government, but they opposed what looked like an attempt by a band of Americans to seize land.

Naval Intervention
In July 1846, U.S. naval forces under Commodore John Sloat captured the ports of Monterey and San Francisco. Sloat declared California annexed to the United States. Sloat's fleet then sailed for San Diego, carrying Frémont and Carson. The Americans captured San Diego and moved north toward Los Angeles.

Carson headed east with the news of California's annexation. On the way, he joined Kearny's force, marching west from Santa Fe.

After Sloat's ships left, many Californios in San Diego rose up against the Americans controlling the city. General Kearny's troops arrived in the midst of the uprising. They faced a stiff fight but finally won. By January 1847, California was under American control.

The Capture of Mexico City After these victories, American forces set out to take Mexico City. In March 1847, troops under General Winfield Scott landed on the coast of Mexico, near the port of Veracruz. Scott captured the city and then began a 300-mile march to Mexico City. On the way, the Americans battled Mexican soldiers and armed citizens. By mid-September, Mexico City had been taken, and the Mexican government surrendered.

What Were the Terms of the Peace Treaty?

Peace talks began in January 1848. A month later, the Treaty of Guadalupe Hidalgo (GWAH•duhl•OOP hih•DAL•goh) was signed. In the treaty, Mexico gave up all claims to Texas and agreed to the Rio Grande as the border between Texas and Mexico. Also, in what was called the Mexican Cession, Mexico **ceded** (SEED•uhd)— gave—California and New Mexico to the United States. In return, the United States gave Mexico $15 million.

In 1853 the United States paid Mexico another $10 million for the Gadsden Purchase, a strip of land along the southern edge of present-day Arizona and New Mexico. With this purchase, the United States mainland reached its present size. All that remained was to settle the newly won territories.

✓ **Reading Check** **Describe** What lands did Mexico cede to the United States?

Study Central Need help understanding the war with Mexico? Visit taj.www1.glencoe.com and click on Study Central.

Section 3 Review

Study Central Need help understanding the war with Mexico? Visit taj.www1.glencoe.com and click on Study Central.

Reading Summary

Review the Main Ideas

- Americans established a busy trade route called the Santa Fe Trail through a large region governed by Mexico, called New Mexico.

- The cultures of Mexicans, Native Americans, and white Americans intermingled in California.

- The United States continued to pursue annexing California and the rest of the New Mexico region, which eventually resulted in war between the United States and Mexico.

What Did You Learn?

1. According to the Mexican government, where was the border between Texas and Mexico?

2. How much did the United States pay for New Mexico and California?

Critical Thinking

3. **Categorizing Information** Re-create the diagram below and describe the three parts of Polk's strategy to extend U.S. territory.

Polk's Strategy

4. **The Big Ideas** Why did the Spanish establish missions? What happened to the mission land after Mexico gained its independence?

5. **Analyzing Literature** Explain the meaning of this statement from page 493: "I think but few Americans know or believe to what extent we have been wronged by Congressional action."

6. **Geography Skills** List the battles that appear on the map on page 495 in order from first to last. Identify each as a Mexican victory or a U.S. victory.

Connecting to the Constitution

Admission of New States

Why It Matters In 1783 the United States was made up of 13 states. It also included lands that stretched west to the Mississippi River. In the years that followed, the United States added more territory by buying lands, fighting wars, and signing treaties. In these ways, the territory of the United States has gradually spread to form the 50 states that we know today.

Joining the Union The U.S. Constitution gives Congress the power to admit new states to the Union. Once admitted to the Union, each state is equal to every other state and has the right to control its internal affairs. No state has more privileges or fewer responsibilities than any other. All states in the Union are bound to support the Constitution.

Thirty-seven states have been admitted to the Union since the Constitution was ratified. Of these 37 states, 30 were admitted after often lengthy periods as United States territories. However, some states—Vermont, Kentucky, Tennessee, and Maine—were formed from existing states with the approval of those states and Congress.

To become a state, a territory usually **petitions,** or asks, Congress to be admitted into the Union. If the petition is approved, Congress passes an enabling act. When signed by the president, an enabling act allows the people of the territory to prepare a constitution setting up a representative, republican government. Next, the territory elects delegates to draft a constitution. If approved by the residents of the territory, the document is sent to Congress for approval. Once approved, Congress then passes an act of admission—a law that makes the territory a state.

▲ California state seal

◄ California's State Capitol in Sacramento

"The powers not delegated [given] to the United States by the Constitution, nor prohibited by it to the States, are reserved to the States respectively, or to the people."

—10th Amendment, U.S. Constitution

Alaska state flag ▼

The Northwest Ordinance of 1787

The Northwest Ordinance of 1787 set up the Northwest Territory, the first territorial government in the United States. At the same time, the ordinance laid down a plan for eventually dividing the territory into states to be admitted into the Union. By 1850 six states—Ohio, Indiana, Illinois, Michigan, Wisconsin, and Minnesota—had been formed from the old Northwest Territory. From the early 1800s, to the present day, this plan with only minor changes has served as the model for admitting new states into the Union.

Westward Expansion

During the 1840s, many Americans believed in **Manifest Destiny,** the idea that the United States should stretch from the Atlantic Ocean to the Pacific Ocean. Conflict soon arose between the United States and Mexico over Mexican-ruled lands in the West. In 1836 Texas had broken away from Mexico and became a republic. Its largely American-born leaders sought **annexation,** or admission, to the United States. In 1845 Congress passed a joint resolution to annex Texas. Bypassing becoming a territory, Texas was immediately admitted into the Union as a state.

Texas's annexation and border disputes led to war between the United States and Mexico in 1846. After Mexico's defeat, the Treaty of Guadalupe Hidalgo in 1848 gave the United States the area that today includes California, Nevada, Arizona, New Mexico, Utah, and western Colorado. In 1854 the United States bought the remaining portions of present-day Arizona and New Mexico from Mexico. With this land purchase, the general boundaries of the mainland United States reached their final form.

Slavery and New States

After the Mexican War, Northerners wanted to ban slavery in the new territories gained from Mexico. Southerners claimed that the territories belonged to the entire nation. Therefore, all Americans had equal rights in them, including the right to bring in slavery. A crisis erupted in 1849 when California sought admission to the Union as a free state. Again, the balance between North and South was threatened, this time in the North's favor. In the Compromise of 1850, Congress finally decided that California would be admitted as a free state. In the other lands gained from Mexico, however, territorial governments would allow slavery.

Toward 50 States

In the late 1800s, the country entered a period of industrial growth. Railroads finally spanned the continent, and waves of settlers moved to the West. One by one, the western territories became states of the United States. In 1912 New Mexico and Arizona became the 47th and 48th—and final—states on the U.S. mainland.

The most recent states to be admitted are Alaska and Hawaii. Both lie outside the mainland United States. The United States bought Alaska from Russia in 1867 for $7.2 million in gold. Hawaii, once an independent kingdom, was annexed to the United States in 1898. In joining the Union, both territories shortened the statehood admissions process. They each adopted a proposed constitution without waiting for an enabling act. Both were admitted as states in 1959.

Checking for Understanding

1. How are states usually admitted to the Union?

2. What issue caused difficulties concerning the admission of states during much of the 1800s?

Critical Thinking

3. **Connect** How was the creation of new territories and states related to westward expansion?

New Settlers in California and Utah

Guide to Reading

Looking Back, Looking Ahead

California and the New Mexico provinces became part of the United States in 1846. Many American settlers were eager to move there for a variety of reasons.

Focusing on the Main Ideas

- The discovery of gold in California had a significant impact on the settlement and economy of the region. *(page 501)*
- Utah was settled by Mormons, a religious group looking for safe haven. *(page 505)*

Meeting People

James Marshall
Joseph Smith
Brigham Young

Content Vocabulary

forty-niner
boomtown
vigilante (VIH•juh•LAN•tee)

Academic Vocabulary

range
community
item
pose
vision (VIH•zhuhn)

Reading Strategy

Organizing Information As you read this section, re-create the diagram below. In the boxes, describe who these groups and individuals were and what their role was in the settlement of California and Utah.

	What was their role?
Forty-niners	
Mormons	
Brigham Young	

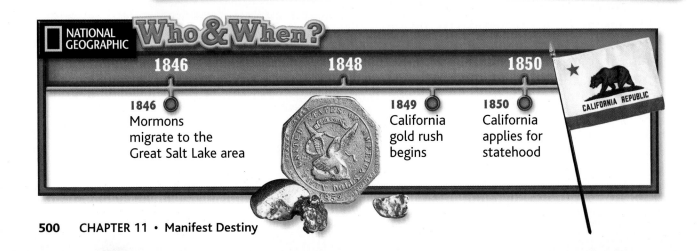

NATIONAL GEOGRAPHIC **Who & When?**

1846   1848   1850

1846 Mormons migrate to the Great Salt Lake area

1849 California gold rush begins

1850 California applies for statehood

CALIFORNIA REPUBLIC

The California Gold Rush

Main Idea **The discovery of gold in California had a significant impact on the settlement and economy of the region.**

Reading Connection Have you ever found money on the street? Imagine how exciting it would be to find a place where you could pick up money off the ground. Read to find out how dreams of easy gold brought many people to California.

An American Story

James Marshall was building a sawmill on the South Fork of the American River in California. He worked for John Sutter, who owned a vast tract of land about 40 miles from present-day Sacramento. On January 24, 1848, Marshall saw something shining in a ditch. "I reached my hand down and picked it up," he wrote later. "It made my heart thump, for I was certain it was gold." Looking around, he found other shiny pieces. Marshall rushed to show the glittering pieces to Sutter, who determined that they were gold. Sutter tried to keep the discovery a secret, but word soon leaked out. The great California Gold Rush was under way!

Who Were the Forty-Niners? People from all over the world flocked to California in search of quick riches. Nearly 100,000 people came to California looking for gold in 1848 and 1849. Those who arrived in 1849 were called **forty-niners.** An official in Monterey reported that "the farmers have thrown aside their plows, the lawyers their briefs [statement of a client's case], the doctors their pills, the priests their prayer books, and all are now digging gold." By the end of 1848, they had taken $6 million in gold from the American River. In modern-day value, the gold would be worth more than $100 million.

Many of the gold seekers came to California by sea. Thousands of forty-niners sailed to San Francisco from New York, Boston, and Galveston. Most traveled around the southern tip of South America. By far the greatest number of gold seekers came overland, traveling on the Oregon Trail or Santa Fe Trail and then pushing westward through California's Sierra Nevada mountain **range.**

Americans made up more than half of the forty-niners. Others came from Mexico, South America, Europe, and Australia. About 300 men arrived from China, the first large group of Asian immigrants to come to America. Although some eventually returned to China, many remained, establishing California's Chinese American **community.**

Land Rights The Treaty of Guadalupe Hidalgo ending the war with Mexico made Californios (Hispanic Californians) citizens of the United States. The treaty also guaranteed them the rights to their lands. But these rights would soon be weakened.

The Land Law of 1851 set up a group of people to review the Californios' land rights. The Californios had to prove what land they owned. When a new settler claimed the rights to a Californio's land, the two parties would go to court. Some Californios were able to prove their claims by providing official documents. Many, however, lost their land.

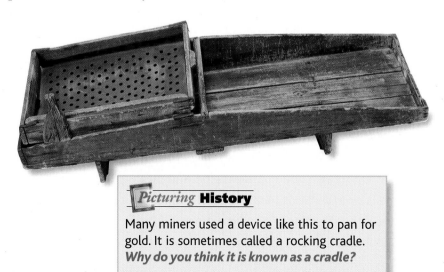

Picturing **History**

Many miners used a device like this to pan for gold. It is sometimes called a rocking cradle. *Why do you think it is known as a cradle?*

Biography

JOHN BIDWELL
1819–1900

ANNIE BIDWELL
1839–1918

The Bidwell mansion in Chico, California, stands as a monument to two pioneers who dedicated their lives to agricultural and social reform. John Bidwell set out from Missouri in 1841 on an overland journey to California. The expedition set out with not much more than the vague knowledge that California lay somewhere to the west.

Upon arriving in California, John Bidwell befriended John Sutter and was able to make a large fortune mining gold. Bidwell soon turned to agricultural endeavors, introducing Bermuda grass and the casaba melon to California. In 1868 John married Annie Ellicott Kennedy, a young woman from Washington, D.C. The construction of the Bidwell mansion had begun three years before. Upon its completion, Annie used its various rooms to educate the Mechoopda, a tribe of Native Americans who lived on the land surrounding the mansion.

Both John and Annie joined the Temperance movement. John ran unsuccessfully for president on the prohibition ticket in 1892, and Annie joined the Woman's Christian Temperance Union. Annie also championed women's rights and joined the woman suffrage movement, at which time she met and befriended Susan B. Anthony.

As the Gold Rush boomed in California, John noticed the effects hydraulic mining had on the California environment. This process of mining caused silt to sift down upon farms and streams and eroded the Sierra hillsides. John testified in *Woodruff* v. *North Bloomfield,* an environmental case that ended hydraulic mining in the United States. The Bidwells left an unforgettable impact on the Chico region of California. They aided the development of agriculture in the region, and their mansion still stands today as a historic park under the direction of the Department of Parks and Recreation of California.

> *"Our ignorance of the route was complete. We knew that California lay west, and that was the extent of our knowledge. . . ."*
> —**John Bidwell**

Then and Now

The Bidwells were dedicated to environmental causes. Research a current environmentalist and explain how his or her actions are similar to the Bidwells'.

Life in California As people rushed to a new area to look for gold, they built new communities, called **boomtowns,** almost overnight. At one site on the Yuba River where only two houses stood in September 1849, a miner arrived the next year to find a town of 1,000 people "with a large number of hotels, stores, groceries, bakeries, and . . . gambling houses." The miners gave some of the boomtowns colorful names such as Shinbone Peak and You Bet. Cities also flourished during the Gold Rush. As ships arrived daily with gold seekers and adventurers, San Francisco quickly grew from a tiny village to a city of about 20,000 people. By 1860 the city had 57,000 residents, making it the fifteenth largest American city and the largest city west of the Mississippi River.

Most of the hopeful forty-niners had no experience in mining. Rushing furiously from place to place, they attacked hillsides with pickaxes and shovels and spent hours bent over streambeds, "washing" or "panning" the water to seek gold dust and nuggets.

Linking Past & Present

Blue Jeans

▼ Jeans are popular everyday wear.

Past In 1873 Levi Strauss, a dry goods merchant living in San Francisco, and Jacob Davis, a Nevada tailor, developed and began to market denim pants reinforced with small copper tacks called rivets.

Present At one time, jeans were associated exclusively with hard work. Now they're worn everywhere. Levi's popular denims—called blue jeans today—are known for their durability and quality. *Why do you think miners and farmers were among the first to wear Levi's denims?*

▲ Early Levi ads were aimed at miners and farmers.

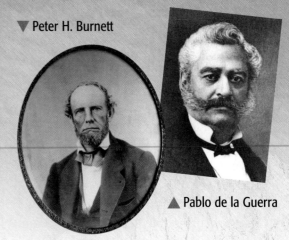

▼ Peter H. Burnett

▲ Pablo de la Guerra

The Way It Was

The California Constitution

Forty-eight delegates met in Monterey to draw up a constitution in September of 1849. Eight delegates were Californios. A declaration of rights guaranteed freedom of assembly, religion, and speech. The first section of the California Declaration of Rights begins:

66All men are by nature free and independent, and have certain inalienable rights, among which are those of enjoying and defending life and liberty, acquiring, possessing, and protecting property: and pursuing and obtaining safety and happiness.99

The right to vote was extended to all white males over the age of 21 who had been residents of California for 30 days. Pablo de la Guerra of Santa Barbara led other Hispanic delegates to the convention in arguing for the right to vote for Native Americans, African Americans, and mestizos. The delegates agreed to recognize any man who had been a Mexican citizen, regardless of race, as a citizen of California. However, African Americans and Native Americans who were not of Mexican descent would not be included.

Californians approved the constitution in November 1849 by a vote of more than 12,000 to 811. Voters elected Peter H. Burnett governor and chose members of the state legislature and a representative to the United States Congress.

The California Gold Rush more than doubled the world's supply of gold. For all their effort, however, very few of the forty-niners achieved lasting wealth. Most of the miners found little or no gold. Many of those who did find gold lost their riches through gambling or wild spending.

Merchants, however, made huge profits. They could charge whatever they liked because the miners had no place else to go to buy food and other essential **items.** Eggs sold for $10 a dozen. Mining tools were expensive too, and the price of a burro went from $15 to $40.

Gold Rush Society Very few women lived in the mining camps, which were filled with men of all backgrounds. Lonely and suffering from the hardships of mining, many men spent their free hours drinking, gambling, and fighting.

Mining towns had no police or prisons, so lawbreakers **posed** a real threat to business owners and miners. One miner wrote:

66Robberies and murders were almost of daily occurrence. Threats had been made to burn down the town. 99

—from *California Men and Events*

Concerned citizens formed vigilance committees to protect themselves. The **vigilantes** (VIH•juh•LAN•tees) took the law into their own hands, acting as police, judge, jury, and sometimes executioner.

Economic and Political Progress The Gold Rush ended within a few years but had lasting effects on California's economy. Agriculture, shipping, and trade expanded to meet the miners' needs for food and other goods. Many people who had come looking for gold stayed to farm or run a business. California's population soared, rising from about 20,000 in 1848 to more than 220,000 only four years later.

Such rapid growth brought the need for more effective government. In March 1850, California applied for statehood. Because California's new constitution banned slavery, however, the request caused a crisis in Congress. The South opposed making California a state because it would upset the balance of free and slave states. California did not become a state until Congress worked out a compromise six months later.

✓ **Reading Check** **Explain** Why did the forty-niners come to California?

A Religious Refuge in Utah

Main Idea Utah was settled by Mormons, a religious group looking for safe haven.

Reading Connection If you were building a new home what would you do first? Read on to see how the Mormons made the most of the harsh terrain they settled.

In 1855, a visitor to the Utah Territory wrote admiringly of:

> ❝ [The] indomitable energy . . . which seems to possess the entire Mormon community. ❞
> —Howard Stansbury

This account described the Mormons, or members of the Church of Jesus Christ of Latter-day Saints. Mormons had come to Utah to fulfill their **vision** of the godly life.

Picturing **History**

Several thousand Mormons forged their way west along a path that became known as the Mormon Trail. *Where did the Mormons settle?*

How Was the Mormon Religion Founded?

In 1830 **Joseph Smith** of New York State had visions that led him to found the Mormon church. The visions also inspired him to build an ideal society.

Smith believed that property should be held in common. He also favored polygamy, the idea that a man could have more than one wife. This angered many people, so the Mormons eventually gave up this practice.

Smith formed a community in New York, but neighbors disapproved of the Mormons' religion. They forced the Mormons to move on. From New York, the Mormons went to Ohio, then to Missouri, and then to Illinois.

In 1844 a mob in Illinois killed Smith, and **Brigham Young** took over as the Mormon leader. Young decided that the Mormons should move again, this time near the Great Salt Lake in present-day Utah. Although part of Mexico at that time, no Mexicans had settled in the area because of its harsh terrain.

A Haven in the Desert

About 12,000 Mormons made the trek to the Great Salt Lake area. It was the largest single migration in American history. The hard-working Mormons made their new home, Deseret, flourish. They planned their towns carefully and built irrigation canals to water their farms. They also set up industries so they could be self-sufficient. Mormon merchants sold supplies to forty-niners who were headed westward.

In 1848 the United States acquired the Great Salt Lake area from Mexico. Two years later Congress set up the Utah Territory, and Brigham Young became its governor. Utah did not easily become part of the United States, however. The Mormons wanted to be left alone and resisted federal authority. In the late 1850s, war almost broke out between the Mormons and the United States Army. Utah did not become a state until 1896.

Reading Check **Explain** Why was Deseret able to grow economically?

Section 4 Review

Study Central Need help understanding the settlement of California and Utah? Visit tajww1.glencoe.com and click on Study Central.

Reading Summary

Review the Main Ideas

• Settlement of California was significantly impacted by the discovery of gold in 1849.

• Joseph Smith and Brigham Young led the Mormons on a cross-country journey to find a safe haven for settlement. Eventually, they chose present-day Utah to establish their community.

What Did You Learn?

1. Why was California's entry into the Union delayed?

2. What is another name for the Mormons?

Critical Thinking

3. **Organizing Information** Re-create the diagram below. In the boxes, describe how the Gold Rush helped California's economy grow.

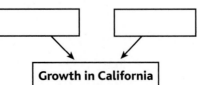

Growth in California

4. **The Big Ideas** What steps did Californians take to apply for statehood? When was California admitted?

5. **Predicting Consequences** How might the history of California be different if the Gold Rush had not happened?

6. **Creative Writing** You are living in a boomtown in California in the mid-1800s. Write a week's worth of journal entries, recording what your life is like.

Thunder on the Sierra

By Kathy Balmes

Before You Read

The Scene: This part of the story takes place at Señor Sosa's gold claim in the Sierra in 1852.

The Characters: Mateo is a 13-year-old boy who trades with miners in the California gold camps. His pack animals are mules with names, such as Fabio and Cisco. Señor Sosa has a gold claim in the mountains somewhere between the mining camps of Indian Gulch and Poverty Hill.

The Plot: While restocking supplies that he will sell to the gold miners, Mateo agrees to deliver a letter to a Señor Sosa if he can find the man.

Vocabulary Preview

decaying: rotting
ghastly: scary like a ghost or corpse
glossy: shiny on the surface
hue (HYOO): color or shade of color
moan: long, low sound of pain, sorrow, or grief

nauseating (NAW • zhee • AYT • ihng): causing a strong sick feeling in the stomach
stench: strong, bad smell

Has a promise ever led you into an unexpected situation? That's what happened to Mateo.

America's Literature

As You Read

A novel has a main plot that relates to the action in all or almost all of the book. The main plot in Thunder on the Sierra *concerns Mateo's desire to get back his stolen horse. This novel also has subplots, or shorter plots, that occur in part of the story. As you read, think about the subplot that takes place in this excerpt. What is the problem or conflict? How is it resolved? Or is it solved?*

When I first came across Señor Sosa's camp, I thought it was deserted. I had crossed between Indian Gulch and Poverty Hill twice, looking for the man. I was ready to give up when a downpour started, and I saw a broken down shack. As I hobbled[1] and unloaded the mules a short distance away, I heard a low moan. I pushed the door of the shack open. Inside was dark. A nauseating stench, like a decaying corpse, almost knocked me backwards.

"Hello? Who are you?" a weak voice asked in Spanish.

"My name is Mateo."

"You must be an angel. Good. I'm finally dying."

"No. I'm not an angel. I'm an arriero,"[2] I replied.

"My name is Sebástiano Sosa."

I had found my man.

"Are you sick or hurt?" I asked, knowing it must be one or the other.

"Sick."

Even though it was pouring rain, I hesitated to enter the shack.

"Do you have cholera[3] or dysentery[4] or malaria?[5] I have quinine. It can ease malaria."

"I don't have malaria."

---

[1] **hobbled:** tied a rope or strap around two legs
[2] **arriero:** a person who drives mules
[3] **cholera:** very severe diarrhea that can kill the patient
[4] **dysentery:** severe diarrhea
[5] **malaria:** severe chills and fever

I pushed down my fear of the deadly cholera and entered the shack. He had not been able to get up from his bed. His shack smelled of vomit, urine, and diarrhea. I breathed through my mouth to avoid the overwhelming odors.

I had never seen anyone in such awful condition. His bleeding gums made his attempt to smile ghastly. His skin had a purple hue. His arms were swollen to double their normal size. They were black where his blood vessels had broken. He was hideous. But as I moved closer, I could see what was wrong with him.

"What have you been eating?" I asked.

"Nothing lately. Before that only spoiled salt pork and flour fried in grease," he said weakly.

"For how long?" I asked.

"Months," he said.

"Were you always alone?" I said.

"No. I had a partner. We had studied law together before the gold rush. We met again in the diggings.[6] But he gave up this summer. We hadn't found any gold, and our food was running out. He left for San Francisco to start a law firm. I planned to follow him back in a few weeks to become his law partner."

"Why didn't you?" I asked.

"I found gold. Not much. But enough to keep me here panning. After a few months I got sick. My arms and legs swelled. Now it hurts me to move," he said.

"You have scurvy. I've seen it in other camps where the miners don't have good food. You're the worst case I've ever seen."

The watery brown eyes pleaded, "Can you help me?"

"Yes. You need fruits and vegetables. I have some in my packs. I'll stay until you are strong enough to take care of yourself."

The sick man lay back and closed his eyes. "God bless you. You are an angel," he murmured.

I brought him raisins and dried apples from Fabio's pack. I filled his cup with water and fed him. His breath stunk like an animal that had been dead for a month. He could barely chew and swallow. Was I too late?

---

[6] **diggings:** area where people are looking for gold

"I can't make a fire to cook potatoes and onions for you until the rain stops. I'm going to hike around and see if I can find some wild greens. An old Indian showed me which plants cure scurvy."

I looked around for the plants. But I found nothing.

The rain had stopped by the time I returned. I took dry wood from inside the shack and built a fire outside. I fried a pan full of onions and potatoes. The wonderful aroma floated into the shack.

I brought a plate of vegetables to his bed.

"Smells good," said the grateful man.

"Eat as much as you can. It will make you better."

I fed him. But he wasn't able to chew much.

I noticed a copy of *Robinson Crusoe*[7] and three law books on a crude wooden shelf. The law books reminded me of the letter. *I'll wait until he's stronger,* I thought. *It might be bad news.*

I slept outside the door. I couldn't stand the smell in the shack.

The sick man seemed a little better in the morning and ate more of the onions and potatoes. I heated the dried fruit in water until it became plump and easier for him to swallow.

After breakfast I moved the mules to a new place to graze and informed them that they had the rest of the week off. I returned to the shack.

"Can you walk outside so I can clean your cabin? You can lean on me."

"I'll try," Señor Sosa replied weakly.

After I settled him in the sunshine, I cleaned his shack. Señor Sosa looked spent[8] when I helped him back inside and settled him in his clean bed. He slept all afternoon.

The next morning I helped him peel off his dirty clothes, wash, and put on clean ones. After I fed him lunch I asked, "Would you like me to read you *Robinson Crusoe?*"

"That would ease my suffering, Mateo, my angel."

---

[7] *Robinson Crusoe:* story about a man who is marooned on a desert island for many years
[8] **spent:** exhausted

After I had read for about an hour, a movement in a shadowy corner of the cabin caught my eye. I saw a small, sleek[9] animal slink out of a hole under the crude boards and bound gracefully onto Señor Sosa's bed.

"Is that supposed to be in here?" I asked, pointing to the small animal with round, bright eyes. It looked like a tiny raccoon, only cuter, and its coat was softer.

Señor Sosa smiled. "She's my pet," he said as he stroked her velvet fur. "Madalena was my only companion before you came. She's a ringtail. They're so good at catching rats and mice that they're often called miner's cats. This cabin would be overrun with rodents if she didn't eat them."

"She's pretty," I said.

"Madalena has been a great comfort. I figured she'd keep the rodents off my corpse. I'd been warned that one in five miners died in the first year of the gold rush. I didn't believe it. Now I wonder how so many survived."

I reached out a hand to pet the glossy fur. But Madalena darted off the bed and down the hole.

The next morning the lawyer was noticeably healthier. *He's a young man,* I realized with amazement. *It's time,* I decided.

"I have a letter for you," I announced after he fed himself breakfast.

Señor Sosa stared at me in surprise.

"It's from your partner in San Francisco. He said it's important. I kept it until you were strong, in case it's bad news."

"Read it to me, Mateo. I am still weak."

"Yes, señor. The letter is dated September 15, 1852."

"What month is it now, Mateo?"

"December, señor."

"Continue."

I read: " *'My Friend, I hope this letter finds you in good health.'* "

The lawyer snorted. "Go on," he urged.

---

[9] **sleek:** smooth and glossy

Please join me in San Francisco immediately. Because we are Spanish-speaking lawyers, who also speak English, we are needed to help rancheros to prove in court that they own the land they live on.

Disappointed Yankee miners often want land in California. They have pressured the American government to issue the Land Act of 1851. It requires all rancheros to submit proof, within two years, that their land was given to them by the Spanish or Mexican governments. Often the land grants are not well documented so lawyers and courts find it easy to detect some flaw in the titles. Many Californios have already lost part or all of their ranchos. Others don't realize that their ranchos are in danger.

The court's deadline is approaching. I have too much business to handle by myself. It cannot wait. I need your help. Please join me in San Francisco. I anxiously await you.

Sincerely,
Your Partner,
Manuel Torres Vargas

After I finished reading him the letter, we sat in stunned silence. . . .

"I'm leaving here as soon as I'm able. Will you sell me a mule? I have gold. I'll pay you twice what it is worth. That should satisfy its owner. Please?"

"Yes, señor. And I'll sell you the food you will need. Tomorrow I must be on my way. There are miners waiting for supplies."

Responding to the Literature

1. How did Mateo find Señor Sosa?

2. Why did Mateo wait to read the letter to Señor Sosa?

3. **Synthesize** Use the word *scurvy* in a sentence that shows its meaning. You may define scurvy, use it as an example, or compare or contrast it.

4. **Infer** What country were Mateo and Señor Sosa originally citizens of? Give examples from the selection of how the author established this fact.

5. **Read to Write** This excerpt contains one of the subplots in *Thunder on the Sierra*. Describe the subplot. What is the conflict? Is the conflict resolved? Explain. What new conflict does the letter raise?

Reading On Your Own...

Do you want to learn more about Andrew Jackson and the new groups of people who became part of the United States? You might be interested in the following books.

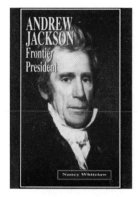

Biography

Andrew Jackson: Frontier President by Nancy Whitelaw describes the life of this colorful frontiersman who became president. She includes his two terms as president and his many firsts in that position.

Nonfiction

Black Potatoes: The Story of the Great Irish Famine, 1845–1850 by Susan Campbell Bartoletti leads readers through five years of failed potato crops in Ireland. The story of millions of Irish dying and emigrating is told in first-person accounts, news reports, and sketches.

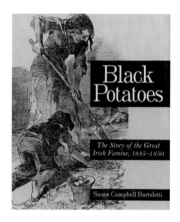

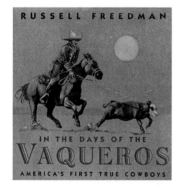

Nonfiction

In the Days of the Vaqueros: America's First True Cowboys by Russell Freedman tracks the origins of the cowboy back to Spanish Mexico in the 1500s. Freedman describes the equipment and techniques that they developed, their migration to California, and the debt that American settlers owed the vaqueros.

Historical Fiction

The Journal of Wong Ming-Chung by Laurence Yep recounts the experiences of a Chinese immigrant, nicknamed "Runt," and his uncle during the California Gold Rush. When it becomes clear that there is no Golden Mountain, they develop other ingenious ways to find opportunity in the United States.

Analyzing Primary Sources

Going to War With Mexico

The war with Mexico (1846–1848) was supported by President James K. Polk and those who believed in Manifest Destiny. This war was fought to settle the border dispute between the United States and Mexico after Texas declared independence from Mexico. When the Mexican War was over, the United States had gained the vast California and New Mexico territories.

Read the passages on pages 514 and 515 and answer the questions that follow.

Mormons heading west in Conestoga wagon trains ▶

Reader's Dictionary

forbearance (fawr • BAR • uhns): patience, tolerance, or self control

vindicate (VIHN • duh • KAYT): to free from blame or guilt

declivity (dih • KLIHV • uht • ee): a descending slope

lauded (LAWD • ihd): celebrated

extolled (ihk • STOHLD): praised highly

Declaration of War With Mexico

On May 9, 1846, after several Americans were killed by Mexican troops in the borderlands between Texas and Mexico, President James Polk declared to Congress that the United States and Mexico were at war.

The cup of **forbearance** had been exhausted even before the recent information from the frontier of the Del Norte. But now, after reiterated menaces, Mexico has passed the boundary of the United States, has invaded our territory and shed American blood upon the American soil. She has proclaimed that hostilities have commenced, and that the two nations are now at war.

As war exists, and, notwithstanding, all our efforts to avoid it, exists by the act of Mexico herself, we are called upon by every consideration of duty and patriotism to **vindicate** with decision the honor, the rights, and the interests of our country. . . .

The Oregon Trail

In The Oregon Trail, *historian Francis Parkman tells of his encounters during an 1845 journey through the West.*

When we came to the descent of the broad shallow valley . . . an unlooked for sight awaited us. The stream glistened at the bottom, and along its banks were pitched a multitude of tents, while hundreds of cattle were feeding over the meadows. Bodies of troops, both horse and foot, and long trains of wagons, with men, women, and children, were moving over the opposite ridge and descending the broad **declivity** before us. These were the

Mormon battalion in the service of government, together with a considerable number of Missouri Volunteers. The Mormons were to be paid off in California, and they were allowed to bring with them their families and property. . . . to found, it might be, a Mormon empire in California.

Petition for Justice

The Chinese immigrants who came to California during the Gold Rush suffered much prejudice and violence. Chinese merchant Pun Chi describes the discrimination in a petition for justice from Congress.

When your honorable government threw open the territory of California, the people of other lands were welcomed here to search for gold and to engage in trade. The shipmasters of your respected nation came over to our country, **lauded** the equality of your laws, **extolled** the beauty of your manners and customs, and made it known that your officers and people were extremely cordial toward the Chinese. . . . we trusted in your sincerity. Not deterred by the long voyage, we came here presuming that our arrival would be hailed with cordiality and favor. But, alas! what times are these! —when former kind relations are forgotten, when we Chinese are viewed like thieves and enemies, when in the administration of justice our testimony is not received, when in the legal collection of the licenses we are injured and plundered, and villains of other nations are encouraged to rob and do violence to us! Our numberless wrongs it is most painful even to recite.

▲ **Engraving of Chinese miners in California**

DBQ Document-Based Questions

Declaration of War With Mexico

1. Who does Polk blame for causing the war?
2. Why does Polk believe the United States should go to war with Mexico?

The Oregon Trail

3. What does Parkman see in the valley that is so surprising?
4. Who was working for the government?

Petition for Justice

5. According to Pun Chi, how did Chinese immigrants expect to be treated in America?

6. What injustices were being committed against the Chinese in California?

Read to Write

7. Suppose the United States still had much unsettled western land, with no claims on it and little government or population. Imagine that you are preparing to move to this new territory. Write a letter to your family explaining your reasons and your plans. Use references to the primary sources you just read.

Review Content Vocabulary

Use the following vocabulary terms to create a newspaper article in which you describe events in the Southwest during this era.

1. emigrant
2. *Tejano*
3. *empresario*
4. ranchero
5. forty-niner

Review the Main Ideas

Section 1 • Westward to the Pacific

6. What agreement did the United States and Great Britain reach about the Oregon Territory?

7. What was Manifest Destiny?

Section 2 • Independence for Texas

8. Who was Stephen Austin? What was his role in early Texas history?

9. What was the outcome of the Battle of San Jacinto?

Section 3 • War With Mexico

10. Some Americans believed that annexing California would benefit national security. Why?

11. Identify the two main causes of the United States's war with Mexico.

Section 4 • New Settlers in California and Utah

12. What started the California Gold Rush?

13. Why did Mormons emigrate to Utah?

Critical Thinking

14. **Determining Cause and Effect** How did economic troubles in the East affect settlement in the Oregon area?

15. **Conclude** How did the war with Mexico change the U.S. border and its land holdings?

16. **Drawing Conclusions** How do you think the government of Mexico reacted to the American idea of Manifest Destiny?

17. **Compare** How did the negotiations between the United States and Britain over the Oregon Territory differ from those between the United States and Mexico over the Southwest?

Geography Skills

Study the routes of the western trails shown on the map. Then answer the questions that follow.

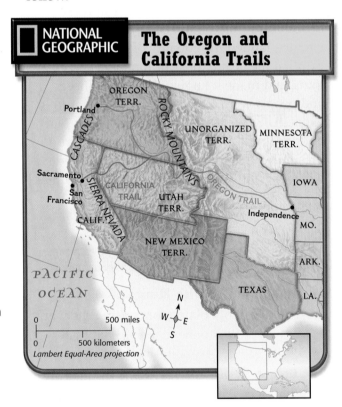

NATIONAL GEOGRAPHIC The Oregon and California Trails

18. **Region** Which mountains did settlers have to cross to reach Oregon's Pacific coast? California's Pacific coast?

19. **Location** In what city did the Oregon Trail begin? In what city did it end?

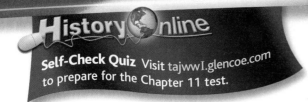
History Online

Self-Check Quiz Visit tajwwl.glencoe.com to prepare for the Chapter 11 test.

Read to Write

20. **The Big Ideas** **Evaluate** How did immigration impact the economy and society of Texas, California, and Utah? Write an essay summarizing your conclusions.

21. **Using Your FOLDABLES** Manifest Destiny was a term first used by a reporter in 1845. Was he introducing a new concept for Americans or describing something that settlers had believed since colonial times? Does Manifest Destiny have any modern forms? Explain your conclusions in a short essay.

Academic Vocabulary

Choose an academic vocabulary word to complete each sentence.

   a. range
   b. access
   c. route
   d. vision

22. The United States government was eager to have ___ to the Pacific Ocean.

23. Political leaders had a clear ___ of Manifest Destiny and pursued acquiring new territory for Americans to settle.

Building Citizenship

24. **Analyze** According to the Constitution of the United States, what steps need to be taken in order for new states to enter the Union? Why was Texas admitted by a joint resolution of the Senate rather than by treaty? Explain.

Reviewing Skills

25. **READING SKILL** **New Vocabulary** Write definitions for the words *emigrant* and *immigrant.* Clearly explain what each term means. Then use each of these words in a sentence.

26. **ANALYSIS SKILL** **Predicting** Write a paragraph predicting how Manifest Destiny will affect relationships with Native Americans.

Standardized Test Practice

Select the best answer for the following questions.

27 The discovery of gold in California led to which of the following?

   A discovery of gold in the Black Hills of the Dakotas

   B increased western expansion and foreign immigration

   C annexation of California as a slave state

   D war with Mexico over the independence of California

28 The Mormons immigrated to the West to

   A mine for gold.

   B settle Texas.

   C escape further religious persecution.

   D purchase California from Mexico.

29 Some Northern leaders opposed admitting Texas to the United States because

   A Texas was part of Mexico.

   B they feared Texas would become a slave state.

   C Texans did not want to join the Union.

   D they feared Texas would become a free state.

Unit 4 REVIEW

The Young Republic

Between 1800 and 1860, the United States grew stronger as it expanded to the Pacific Ocean. At the same time, the North, the South, and the West developed sectional differences that would affect the country's future.

	Chapter 8	Chapter 9	Chapter 10	Chapter 11
	The Northeast: Building Industry	The South	The Age of Jackson	Manifest Destiny
When	• 1790–1850	• 1820–1860	• 1815–1848	• 1819–1858
Where	• New England • the South • the West • New York • the North	• the South • Upper South • Deep South	• the South • the Northeast • Georgia • Alabama • Mississippi • Florida • Indian Territory	• Oregon Country • Texas • Mexico • New Mexico Territory • California • Utah

▲ The textile mills in Lowell, Massachusetts, employed many young women.

◄ Goblet showing Andrew Jackson's log cabin

	Chapter 8 The Northeast: Building Industry	**Chapter 9** The South	**Chapter 10** The Age of Jackson	**Chapter 11** Manifest Destiny
Major Events	• c.1800 Industrial Revolution • 1807 Steamboat *Clermont* • c. 1820s on Changes in art and literature • 1825 Erie Canal • 1840s–1860s Millions of new immigrants • 1848 Seneca Falls Convention	• 1793 Cotton gin • 1808 End of importing slaves • 1830–1860 More severe slave codes • 1831 Nat Turner's rebellion • 1840s Tredegar Iron Works is a leading iron producer • 1860 South has only one-third of nation's rail lines • 1860 New Orleans has 168,000 people	• 1820s Expansion of voting rights • 1830 Webster-Hayne Debate • 1830 Indian Removal Act • 1832 Nullification Act • 1832 Veto of National Bank • 1835–1842 Seminole wars • 1837 Panic of 1837 • 1838 Trail of Tears	• 1830–1840s American settlers in Oregon • 1835–1836 Texas War for Independence • 1845 Texas statehood • 1846–1847 Mexican War • 1846 Bear Flag Republic • 1846 Mormons migrate to Utah • 1848 California gold rush • 1853 Gadsden Purchase
	Erie Canal barrel			
Some Important People	• Samuel Slater • Francis Cabot Lowell • Robert Fulton • Horace Mann • Henry David Thoreau • Henry Wadsworth Longfellow • Elizabeth Cady Stanton • Susan B. Anthony	• Eli Whitney • William Gregg • Joseph Reid Anderson • Nat Turner • Harriet Tubman • Frederick Douglass	• Andrew Jackson • Henry Clay • John Q. Adams • John C. Calhoun • Daniel Webster • Black Hawk • Osceola • Martin Van Buren	• William Henry Harrison • John Q. Adams • James Polk • Henry Clay • Stephen Austin • Santa Anna • Sam Houston • John Frémont • Zachary Taylor • Joseph Smith • Brigham Young
		Harriet Tubman		
How do these events and ideas affect our lives today?	• The United States began to emerge as an industrial giant during this period.	• The heritage of discrimination and unequal rights created by slavery still poses problems today.	• Many Native Americans still live on reservations. *Queen Victoria*	• The United States grew from coast to coast during this period.
What was happening in the world at this time?	• 1830 Canned foods are sold in England for the first time • 1840 Steamships begin to cross the Atlantic	• 1831 A slave revolt in Jamaica fails and hundreds of rebels are put to death • 1847 Liberia becomes Africa's first free republic	• 1837 Victoria becomes Britain's Queen • 1841 New Zealand becomes a British colony	• 1842 China cedes Hong Kong to the British • 1854 The Crimean War begins

Civil War and Reconstruction

Why It's Important

Because of the issue of slavery, relations between the North and the South grew more hostile. Soon the two sides met in the most horrible war the country had ever seen. With the North's victory slavery was ended, but the reunited nation faced key issues that would take many decades to reconcile.

- While the North and South had made several compromises on slavery over the years, the issue eventually split the country.

- The Civil War and Reconstruction freed the slaves, but issues related to civil rights and equal opportunity still exist today.

1820   1840

POLITICS & ECONOMY

1820
Congress passes Missouri Compromise

1833
Tariff is lowered as a result of North-South compromise

Dred Scott ▶

1857
Supreme Court announces *Dred Scott* decision

SCIENCE & SOCIETY

1821
Benjamin Lundy founds newspaper that spreads the abolitionist message

1833
William Lloyd Garrison founds the American Antislavery Society

c. 1843
Sojourner Truth dedicates her life to the causes of abolition and women's rights

Sojourner Truth ▶

WORLD EVENTS

1848
The Communist Manifesto is published

1853
Commodore Perry arrives in Japan

Commodore Perry ▶

Where in the United States?

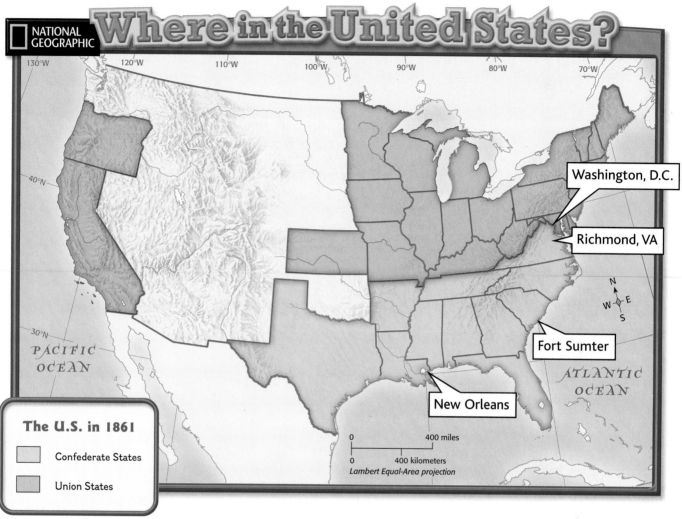

Washington, D.C.

Richmond, VA

Fort Sumter

New Orleans

PACIFIC OCEAN

ATLANTIC OCEAN

The U.S. in 1861

Confederate States

Union States

0   400 miles

0   400 kilometers

Lambert Equal-Area projection

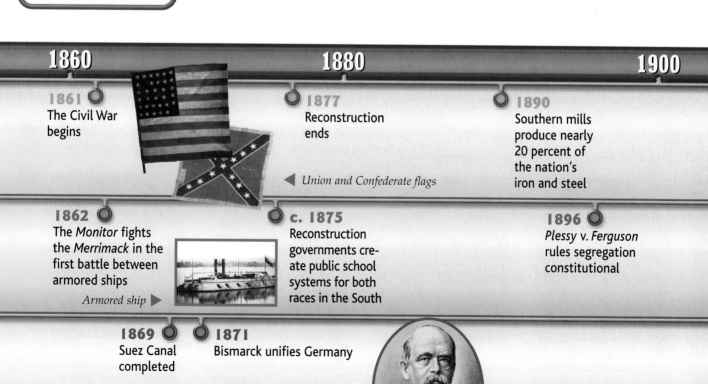

1860

1880

1900

1861
The Civil War begins

1877
Reconstruction ends

1890
Southern mills produce nearly 20 percent of the nation's iron and steel

◄ *Union and Confederate flags*

1862
The *Monitor* fights the *Merrimack* in the first battle between armored ships

Armored ship ▶

c. 1875
Reconstruction governments create public school systems for both races in the South

1896
Plessy v. *Ferguson* rules segregation constitutional

1869
Suez Canal completed

1871
Bismarck unifies Germany

◄ *Otto von Bismarck*

① **FORT SUMTER**

See *Road to Civil War*
Chapter 12

② **GETTYSBURG**

See *The Civil War*
Chapter 13

People to Meet

Frederick Douglass
c. 1817–1895
African American
leader
Chapter 12, page 532

Sojourner Truth
c. 1797–1883
African American
leader
Chapter 12, page 532

Dred Scott
c. 1800–1857
Subject of Supreme
Court case on slavery
Chapter 12, page 549

Abraham Lincoln
1809–1865
Sixteenth president
of the United States
Chapter 12, page 552

③ APPOMATTOX COURT HOUSE

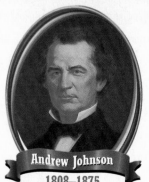

See *The Civil War*
Chapter 13

④ FORD'S THEATER

See *Reconstruction*
Chapter 14

Ulysses S. Grant
1822–1885
Union general
Chapter 13, page 611

Robert E. Lee
1807–1870
Confederate general
Chapter 13, page 611

Clara Barton
1821–1912
Civil War nurse
Chapter 13, page 601

Andrew Johnson
1808–1875
Seventeenth president
of the United States
Chapter 14, page 628

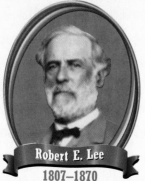

Chapter 12

Road to Civil War

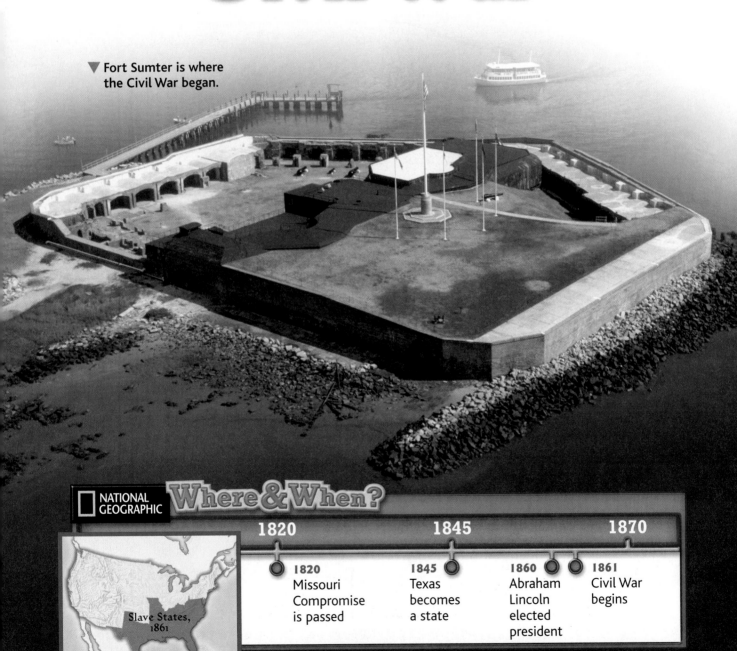

▼ Fort Sumter is where the Civil War began.

NATIONAL GEOGRAPHIC **Where & When?**

Slave States, 1861

1820	1845	1870

1820
Missouri Compromise is passed

1845
Texas becomes a state

1860
Abraham Lincoln elected president

1861
Civil War begins

History Online
Chapter Overview Visit tajww1.glencoe.com for a preview of Chapter 12.

The Big Ideas

Abolitionists

Reactions to social injustice can lead to reform movements. Many reformers turned their attention to eliminating slavery.

Slavery and the West

Differences in economic, political, and social beliefs and practices can lead to division within a nation and have lasting consequences. The question of whether to admit new states as free states or slave states arose.

A Nation Dividing

Differences in economic, political, and social beliefs and practices can lead to division within a nation and have lasting consequences. Growing tensions over slavery eventually led to violence in the new territories.

Challenges to Slavery

Conflict often brings about great change. A new antislavery party and a Supreme Court decision divided the nation further on slavery.

Secession and War

Conflict often brings about great change. In response to Lincoln's election as president, most Southern states left the Union.

 View the Chapter 12 video in the Glencoe Video Program.

Study Organizer

Sequencing Events Make and use this foldable to sequence some of the key events that led to the Civil War.

Step 1 Fold a sheet of paper in half from side to side, leaving a $\frac{1}{2}$-inch tab along the side.

Leave $\frac{1}{2}$-inch tab here.

Step 2 Cut the top flap to make 5 tabs.

Make five tabs.

Step 3 Label your foldable as shown.

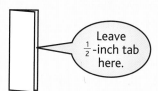

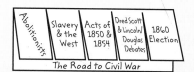
Abolitionists | Slavery & the West | Acts of 1850 & 1854 | Dred Scott & Lincoln/Douglas Debates | 1860 Election

The Road to Civil War

Reading and Writing
As you read, write facts about the events under each appropriate tab of your foldable. How did these events lead to the Civil War?

Chapter 12

Get Ready to Read

Making Inferences

READING SKILL

1 Learn It!

Good readers make inferences to help them understand text. Another way to describe this skill is "reading between the lines." Use this skill to look for clues that might explain what is occurring in the passage even though it may not be explicitly stated. Think about what you already know and draw conclusions based on this knowledge. Because it is impossible to include every detail, the author relies on a reader's ability to infer. Making inferences will draw on many of the other reading strategies you have been using in this book, including recognizing bias and questioning. When you read the paragraph below, answer the question "What did the people in Boston think of slavery?"

> On May 24, 1854, the people of Boston erupted in outrage. Federal officers had seized Anthony Burns, a runaway slave who lived in Boston, to send him back to slavery. Abolitionists tried to rescue Burns from the federal courthouse, and city leaders attempted to buy his freedom. All efforts failed. . . . In a gesture of bitter protest, Bostonians draped buildings in black and hung the American flag upside down.
>
> —*from page 533*

Reading Tip

As you read, ask yourself "What facts or information does the author expect me to already know about this topic?"

② Practice It!

With a partner, discuss these questions to make more inferences from the passage about Anthony Burns. Be sure to discuss why this account may have been included by the author.

- **What was the opinion of the Boston public? The city leaders?**

- **What message did they want to send to the federal government?**

- **A flag flown upside down is a naval distress signal. Why did they choose this signal?**

- **The issue of slavery divided Americans in the 1850s. What are some issues today that divide Americans? What distinguishes a divisive issue from one that can be solved through compromise?**

Read to Write········

Can you rewrite the passage about Anthony Burns from his perspective? Use the same facts but convey a different impression.

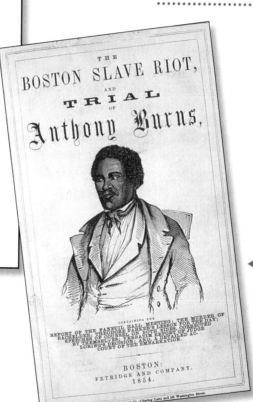

◀ Pamphlet, 1854

③ Apply It!

As you read this chapter, practice your skill at making inferences by making connections and asking questions. Try to think about the information "between the lines."

Abolitionists

Guide to Reading

Looking Back, Looking Ahead

You learned earlier that slave labor was important to the South. You will now read about how groups and individuals worked to end slavery and to free individual enslaved people.

Focusing on the Main Ideas

- By the early 1800s, a growing number of Americans had begun to demand an immediate end to slavery in the South. *(page 529)*
- The issue of slavery became the most pressing social issue for reformers, beginning in the 1830s. *(page 530)*
- Abolitionists established a network of routes and risked their lives to help African Americans escape slavery. *(page 533)*

Meeting People

William Lloyd Garrison
Sarah and Angelina Grimké
David Walker
Frederick Douglass
Sojourner Truth

Content Vocabulary

abolitionist (A•buh•LIH•shuhn•ihst)
Underground Railroad
  (UHN•duhr•GROWND RAYUHL•ROHD)

Academic Vocabulary

notion (NOH•shuhn)
publication (PUH•bluh•KAY•shuhn)

Reading Strategy

Organizing Information Create a diagram like the one below. As you read the section, identify five abolitionists. Below each name, write a sentence describing his or her role in the movement.

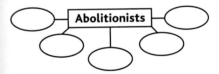

Abolitionists

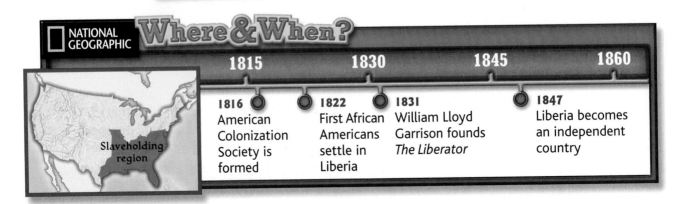

NATIONAL GEOGRAPHIC Where & When?

| 1815 | 1830 | 1845 | 1860 |

1816 American Colonization Society is formed

1822 First African Americans settle in Liberia

1831 William Lloyd Garrison founds *The Liberator*

1847 Liberia becomes an independent country

Slaveholding region

Early Efforts to End Slavery

Main Idea By the early 1800s, a growing number of Americans had begun to demand an immediate end to slavery in the South.

Reading Connection Can you think of an issue that caused disagreement in your family or group of friends? Read to learn how divisive the issue of slavery was to the nation.

An American Story

William Lloyd Garrison, a dramatic and spirited man, fought strongly for the right of African Americans to be free. On one occasion, Garrison was present when Frederick Douglass, an African American who had escaped from slavery, spoke to a white audience about life as a slave. Douglass electrified his listeners with a powerful speech. Suddenly, Garrison leaped to his feet. "Is this a man," he demanded of the audience, "or a thing?" Garrison shared Douglass's outrage at the **notion** that people could be bought and sold like objects.

The spirit of reform that swept the United States in the early 1800s was not limited to improving education and expanding the arts. It also included the efforts of **abolitionists** (A•buh•LIH•shuhn•ihsts) like Garrison and Douglass—members of the growing band of reformers who worked to abolish, or end, slavery.

Even before the American Revolution, some Americans had tried to limit or end slavery. At the Constitutional Convention in 1787, the delegates had reached a compromise on the difficult issue, agreeing to let each state decide whether to allow slavery. By the early 1800s, Northern states had ended slavery, but it continued in the South.

The religious revival and the reform movement of the early and mid-1800s gave new life to the antislavery movement. Many Americans came to believe that slavery was wrong. Yet not all Northerners shared this view. The conflict over slavery continued to build.

Many of the men and women who led the antislavery movement came from the Quaker faith. One Quaker, Benjamin Lundy, wrote:

> ❝I heard the wail of the captive; I felt his pang of distress, and the iron entered my soul.❞
>
> —from *Historical Collections of Ohio*

Lundy founded a newspaper in 1821 to spread the abolitionist message.

American Colonization Society The first large-scale antislavery effort was aimed at resettling African Americans in Africa or the Caribbean. The American Colonization Society, formed in 1816 by a group of white Virginians, attempted to free enslaved workers gradually by buying them from slaveholders and sending them abroad to start new lives.

The society raised enough money from private donors, Congress, and a few state legislatures to send several groups of African Americans out of the country. Some went to the west coast of Africa, where the society had acquired land for a colony. In 1822 the first African American settlers arrived in this colony, called Liberia, Latin for "place of freedom."

In 1847 Liberia became an independent country. American emigration to Liberia continued until the Civil War. Some 12,000 to 20,000 African Americans settled in the new country between 1822 and 1865.

The American Colonization Society did not halt the growth of slavery. The number of enslaved people continued to increase at a steady pace, and the society could only resettle a small number of African Americans. Furthermore, most African Americans regarded the United States as their home and were not prepared to migrate to another continent. Many were from families that had lived in America for several generations. They simply wanted to be free in American society.

Reading Check **Explain** How did the American Colonization Society fight slavery?

The New Abolitionists

Main Idea The issue of slavery became the most pressing social issue for reformers, beginning in the 1830s.

Reading Connection Think of a person or a leader whom you admire. Does he or she stand up for others? Read to learn how abolitionists worked to end slavery.

The Movement Changes Reformers realized that the gradual approach to ending slavery had failed. Moreover, the numbers of enslaved persons had sharply increased because the cotton boom in the Deep South made planters increasingly dependent on slave labor. Beginning in about 1830, the American antislavery movement took on new life. Soon it became the most pressing social issue for reformers.

Picturing History

In 1831 William Lloyd Garrison began publishing a newspaper called *The Liberator*. *What was Garrison's position regarding slavery?*

William Lloyd Garrison An abolitionist named **William Lloyd Garrison** stimulated the growth of the antislavery movement. In 1829 Garrison left Massachusetts to work for the country's leading antislavery newspaper in Baltimore. Impatient with the paper's moderate position, Garrison returned to Boston in 1831 to found his own newspaper, *The Liberator.*

Garrison was one of the first white abolitionists to call for the "immediate and complete emancipation [freeing]" of enslaved people. In the first issue of his paper, he wrote: "I will not retreat a single inch—AND I WILL BE HEARD."

Garrison *was* heard. He attracted enough followers to start the New England Anti-Slavery Society in 1832 and the American Anti-Slavery Society the next year. The abolitionist movement grew rapidly. By 1838 the antislavery societies Garrison started had more than 1,000 chapters, or local branches.

The Grimké Sisters Among the first women who spoke out publicly against slavery were **Sarah and Angelina Grimké.** Born in South Carolina to a wealthy slaveholding family, the sisters moved to Philadelphia in 1832.

In the North, the Grimké sisters lectured and wrote against slavery. At one antislavery meeting, Angelina Grimké exclaimed:

> **❝** As a Southerner, I feel that it is my duty to stand up . . . against slavery. I have seen it—I have seen it. **❞**
>
> —Angelina Grimké, lecture, 1838

The Grimkés persuaded their mother to give them their share of the family inheritance. Instead of money or land, the sisters asked for several of the enslaved workers, whom they immediately freed.

The Grimkés and Angelina's husband, abolitionist Theodore Weld, wrote *American Slavery As It Is* in 1839. This collection of firsthand accounts of life under slavery was an influential abolitionist **publication,** selling more than 100,000 copies in its first year.

African American Abolitionists White abolitionists drew public attention to the cause, but African Americans played a major role in the abolitionist movement from the start. The abolition of slavery was an especially important goal to the free African Americans of the North.

Many African Americans in the North lived in poverty in cities. Although they were excluded from most jobs and were often attacked by white mobs, a great many of these African Americans were intensely proud of their freedom and wanted to help those who were still enslaved.

African Americans took an active part in organizing and directing the American Anti-Slavery Society, and they subscribed in large numbers to William Lloyd Garrison's *The Liberator.* In 1827 Samuel Cornish and John Russwurm started the country's first African American newspaper, *Freedom's Journal.* Most of the other newspapers that African Americans founded before the Civil War also promoted abolition.

Born a free man in North Carolina, writer **David Walker** of Boston published an impassioned argument against slavery, challenging African Americans to rebel and overthrow slavery by force. "America is more our country than it is the whites'—we have enriched it with our blood and tears," he wrote.

In 1830 free African American leaders held their first convention in Philadelphia. Delegates met "to devise ways and means for the bettering of our condition." They discussed starting an African American college and encouraging free African Americans to emigrate to Canada.

Primary Sources

Abolishing Slavery

While serving in the House of Representatives, former President John Quincy Adams battled slavery. In 1839 he proposed a constitutional amendment that provided for the abolition of slavery. Its three provisions follow.

◄ John Quincy Adams

1st From and after the 4th of July, 1842, there shall be, throughout the United States, no hereditary slavery; but on and after that day every child born within the United States, their Territories or jurisdiction, shall be born free.

2d. With the exception of the Territory of Florida, there shall henceforth never be admitted into this Union any State, the constitution of which shall tolerate within the same the existence of slavery.

3d. From and after the 4th of July, 1845, there shall be neither slavery nor slave trade at the seat of Government of the United States.

DBQ Document-Based Questions

1. How would each part of the amendment bring about the end of slavery?
2. Was Adams providing for its immediate or gradual end? Why do you think he chose this method?

Frederick Douglass **Frederick Douglass,** the most widely known African American abolitionist, was born enslaved in Maryland. After teaching himself to read and write, he escaped from slavery in Maryland in 1838 and settled first in Massachusetts and then in New York.

As a runaway, Douglass could have been captured and returned to slavery. Still, he joined the Massachusetts Anti-Slavery Society and traveled widely to address abolitionist meetings. A powerful speaker, Douglass often moved listeners to tears with his message. At an Independence Day gathering, he told the audience:

> 66 What, to the American slave, is your [Fourth] of July? I answer; a day that reveals to him, more than all other days in the year, the gross injustice and cruelty to which he is the constant victim. To him, your celebration is a sham . . . your national greatness, swelling vanity; your sounds of rejoicing are empty and heartless . . . your shouts of liberty and equality, hollow mockery. 99
>
> —from *Frederick Douglass: Selected Speeches and Writings*

For 16 years, Douglass edited an antislavery newspaper called the *North Star.* Douglass won admiration as a powerful and influential speaker and writer. He traveled abroad, speaking to huge antislavery audiences in London and the West Indies.

Douglass returned to the United States because he believed abolitionists must fight slavery at its source. He insisted that African Americans receive not only their freedom but full equality with whites as well. In 1847 friends helped Douglass purchase his freedom from the slaveholder in Maryland from whom he had fled.

Sojourner Truth "I was born a slave in Ulster County, New York," Isabella Baumfree began when she told her story to audiences. Called "Belle," she lived in the cellar of a slaveholder's house. She escaped in 1826 and gained official freedom in 1827 when New York banned slavery. Quaker friends then helped her recover one son who had been sold as a slave. She eventually settled in New York City with her two youngest children. She supported her family by doing domestic work. During this time, she began preaching in the streets.

In 1843 Belle chose a new name. "**Sojourner Truth** is my name," she said, "because from this day I will walk in the light of [God's] truth." She dedicated her life to the movements for abolition and for women's rights.

Reading Check **Explain** Why did Frederick Douglass return to the United States?

The Underground Railroad

Main Idea **Abolitionists established a network of routes and risked their lives to help African Americans escape slavery.**

Reading Connection Can you think of an example in recent times when people fled to avoid oppression? Read and find out about the Underground Railroad.

An American Story

On May 24, 1854, the people of Boston erupted in outrage. Federal officers had seized Anthony Burns, a runaway slave who lived in Boston, to send him back to slavery. Abolitionists tried to rescue Burns from the federal courthouse, and city leaders attempted to buy his freedom.

All efforts failed. Local militia units joined the marines and cavalry in Boston to keep order. Federal troops escorted Burns to a ship that would carry him back to Virginia and slavery. In a gesture of bitter protest, Bostonians draped buildings in black and hung the American flag upside down.

The Fugitive Slave Act The Fugitive Slave Act of 1850 required all citizens to help catch runaways. Anyone who aided a fugitive could be fined or imprisoned. People in the South believed the law would force Northerners to recognize the rights of Southerners. Instead, enforcement of the law led to mounting anger in the North, convincing more people of the evils of slavery. After passage of the Fugitive Slave Act, slaveholders stepped up efforts to catch runaway slaves.

NATIONAL GEOGRAPHIC

The Underground Railroad

→ Underground Railroad routes
▭ Slaveholding regions
▭ Non-slaveholding regions

CANADA

Albany • Portland
Buffalo • Boston • Providence
London • New York City
Windsor • Toledo • Cleveland • Pittsburgh • Philadelphia
Des Moines • Chicago • Columbus • Baltimore
Indianapolis • Marietta • ⊕ Washington, D.C.
Springfield • Cincinnati • Ironton
Chester • Evansville • Richmond
Cairo • Nashville • New Bern
Little Rock • ATLANTIC OCEAN
Atlanta • Charleston
Jackson • Montgomery
Tallahassee
New Orleans

40°N

N
W — E
S

0 ___ 300 miles
0 ___ 300 kilometers
Albers Conic Equal-Area projection

"I sometimes dream that I am pursued, and when I wake, I am scared almost to death."
—Nancy Howard, 1855

80°W   70°W
20°N

Using Geography Skills

Many enslaved African Americans escaped to freedom with the help of the Underground Railroad.

1. **Movement** Which river did enslaved persons cross before reaching Indiana and Ohio?
2. **Analyze** About how many miles did an enslaved person travel from Montgomery, Alabama, to Windsor, Canada?

Slaveholders even tried to capture runaways who had lived in freedom in the North for years. Sometimes they seized African Americans who were not escaped slaves and forced them into slavery.

Resistance to the Law In spite of the penalties, many Northerners refused to cooperate with the law's enforcement. The **Underground Railroad,** a network of free African Americans and whites, helped runaways make their way to freedom. Antislavery groups tried to rescue African Americans who were being pursued or to free those who were captured. In Boston, members of one such group followed federal agents shouting, "Slave hunters—there go the slave hunters." People contributed funds to buy the freedom of African Americans. Northern juries refused to convict those accused of breaking the Fugitive Slave Law.

Harriet Tubman Born as a slave in Maryland, Harriet Tubman worked in plantation fields until she was nearly 30 years old. Then she made her break for freedom, escaping to the North with the help of the Underground Railroad. Settling in Philadelphia, Tubman met many abolitionists who shared her desire to bring Southern slaves to the North. Realizing the risks of being captured, Tubman courageously made 19 trips back into the South during the 1850s to help other enslaved people escape. Altogether she assisted about 70 individuals—including her parents—to escape from slavery. Tubman became the most successful conductor on the Underground Railroad. She was known as the "Moses of her people" for leading slaves to freedom in the North.

✓ **Reading Check** **Identify** What was the Underground Railroad?

History Online

Study Central Need help understanding abolitionism? Visit tajww1.glencoe.com and click on Study Central.

Section 1 Review

Reading Summary

Review the Main Ideas

• In the early 1800s, one major antislavery movement worked to resettle freed slaves in the country of Liberia in Africa.

• The antislavery movement became stronger in the 1830s, spurred on by a number of abolitionists, both white, such as William Lloyd Garrison and the Grimké sisters, and African American, such as Frederick Douglass and Sojourner Truth.

• Abolitionists helped runaway slaves escape, but many others in both the North and the South opposed abolition.

What Did You Learn?

1. Describe the American Colonization Society's solution to slavery.

2. How did William Lloyd Garrison help the abolitionist movement?

Critical Thinking

3. **Organizing Information** Use a diagram like the one below to identify actions that abolitionists took to free enslaved people.

Freeing of Enslaved People

4. **The Big Ideas** What role did Harriet Tubman play in the antislavery movement?

5. **Comparing** How did the goals and strategies of the American Colonization Society differ from those of the abolitionist movement?

6. **READING** **Making Inferences** Reread the primary source quotes from this section. Write a paragraph that makes inferences to describe each person's views of slavery.

Section 2

Slavery and the West

Guide to Reading

Looking Back, Looking Ahead

As you know, abolitionists tried to end slavery. At the same time, the possible spread of slavery into the West was an issue that repeatedly divided the nation.

Focusing on the Main Ideas

- The Missouri Compromise helped resolve the issue of whether new states would be slave states or free states. *(page 536)*
- The Kentucky Resolution first advanced the doctrine of nullification. *(page 537)*
- In the 1840s, the issue of slavery in new territories was once again at the forefront. *(page 539)*
- Henry Clay presented a plan to settle the slavery debate that resulted in the Compromise of 1850. *(page 541)*

Meeting People

James K. Polk
Millard Fillmore
Stephen A. Douglas

Content Vocabulary

sectionalism (SEHK•shnuh•LIH•zuhm)
nullify (NUH•luh•FY)
protective tariff
  (pruh•TEHK•tihv TAR•uhf)
fugitive (FYOO•juh•tihv)
secede (sih•SEED)
abstain (uhb•STAYN)

Academic Vocabulary

debate
controversy (KAHN•truh•VUHR•see)
collapse

Reading Strategy

Organizing Information As you read the section, describe how these compromises dealt with the admission of new states.

Admission of New States	
The Missouri Compromise	The Compromise of 1850

NATIONAL GEOGRAPHIC **Where & When?**

Free states and territories, 1850
Washington, D.C.
California admitted 1850

1820 — 1840 — 1860

1820 Missouri Compromise is passed

1845 Texas becomes a state

1848 Free-Soil Party nominates Van Buren

1850 Compromise of 1850 diverts war

The Missouri Compromise

Main Idea The Missouri Compromise helped resolve the issue of whether new states would be slave states or free states.

Reading Connection Do you compete with a nearby school in sports or another activity? If so, you probably feel loyalty to the school you attend. Read to learn how in the early 1800s, differences between the North and South led to sectionalism, which is loyalty to a particular region.

An American Story

"The deed is done. The . . . chains of slavery are forged for [many] yet unborn. Humble yourselves in the dust, ye high-minded citizens of Connecticut. Let your cheeks be red as crimson. On *your* representatives rests the stigma of this foul disgrace." These biting, fiery words were published in a Connecticut newspaper in 1820. They were in response to members of Congress who had helped pave the way for the admission of Missouri as a slaveholding state.

What Is Sectionalism? The request by slaveholding Missouri to join the Union in 1819 caused an angry debate that worried former president Thomas Jefferson and Secretary of State John Quincy Adams. Jefferson called the dispute "a fire-bell in the night" that "awakened

and filled me with terror." Adams accurately predicted that the bitter **debate** was "a mere preamble—a title-page to a great tragic volume."

Many Missouri settlers had brought enslaved African Americans into the territory with them. By 1819 the Missouri Territory included about 50,000 whites and 10,000 slaves. When Missouri applied to Congress for admission as a state, its constitution allowed slavery.

In 1819 eleven states permitted slavery and eleven did not. The Senate—with two members from each state—was therefore evenly balanced between slave and free states. The admission of a new state would upset that balance.

In addition the North and the South, with their different economic systems, were competing for new lands in the western territories. At the same time, a growing number of Northerners wanted to restrict or ban slavery. Southerners, even those who disliked slavery, opposed these antislavery efforts. They resented the interference by outsiders in Southerners' affairs. These differences between the North and the South grew into **sectionalism** (SEHK•shnuh•LIH•zuhm)—an exaggerated loyalty to a particular region of the country.

Clay's Proposal The Senate suggested a way to resolve the crisis by allowing Missouri's admittance as a slave state while simultaneously admitting Maine as a free state. Maine, formerly part of Massachusetts, had also applied for admission to the Union. The Senate also sought to settle the issue of slavery in the territories for good. It proposed prohibiting slavery in the remainder of the Louisiana Purchase north of 36°30'N latitude.

Speaker of the House Henry Clay of Kentucky skillfully maneuvered the Senate bill to passage in 1820 by dividing it into three proposals. The Missouri Compromise preserved the balance between slave and free states in the Senate and quieted the bitter debate in Congress over slavery. However, this would not last.

✓ Reading Check **Explain** How did sectionalism contribute to the ongoing debate about the admission of states?

"I know no South, no North, no East, no West, to which I owe any allegiance."
—Henry Clay

Nullification

Main Idea The Kentucky Resolution first advanced the doctrine of nullification.

Reading Connection Have you ever wanted to overturn a decision that you thought was unfair? Read to learn how nullification legally permitted states to overturn unconstitutional laws.

Southerners argued that states could **nullify** (NUH•luh•FY), or legally overturn, federal laws that they considered unconstitutional. The issue of nullification arose again and again in the nation's early history.

Virginia and Kentucky Resolutions

Nullification was first expressed in the Virginia and Kentucky Resolutions of 1798–1799. These resolutions, written by Thomas Jefferson and James Madison, declared that the Federalists' Alien and Sedition laws were unconstitutional. *(See pages 295-96.)* Jefferson and Madison used the ideas of John Locke and the Tenth Amendment to the Constitution to argue that the federal government had been formed by a contract among the states. The federal government possessed only certain powers. Whenever a state decided that the federal government passed a law that went beyond these powers, the state had the right to nullify the law.

What Was the Hartford Convention? The

issue of nullification reappeared during the War of 1812, this time among Federalists in New England. Many New Englanders opposed the war. One reason was that many people there made their living by trade, which was greatly hurt when the war began. Many Federalists also believed that Republicans in the South and West brought about the war. Delegates from the New England states revived the idea of nullification and proposed amendments to the Constitution at a meeting called the Hartford Convention. *(See page 359.)* The Federalists made no progress with their demands, and with the end of the war, the power of the Federalist party declined.

Picturing **History**

Calhoun was a nationalist in his early career, but he changed to a champion of states' rights. *How were the Ordinance of Nullification and the Virginia and Kentucky Resolutions alike?*

The Tariff Controversy The nullification **controversy** arose again in the 1820s and 1830s, this time over the issue of protective tariffs. **Protective tariffs** (pruh•TEHK•tihv TAR•uhfs) are taxes that are placed on goods that come from another country. Protective tariffs raise the price of goods from other countries. A tax on imported shoes, for example, makes American-made shoes more attractive to consumers.

By the 1820s, most Southerners had become convinced that protective tariffs were harmful to the South. Although such tariffs helped the young industries of the North, they also raised the prices of manufactured goods purchased in the South. People in the South felt that it was unjust for them to bear the expense for the development of another region of the country.

Ordinance of Nullification When Congress passed the tariff of 1828, John C. Calhoun of South Carolina argued that the tariff was "unconstitutional, oppressive, and unjust." Calhoun based his argument on the ideas that Jefferson and Madison had used in defending the Virginia and Kentucky Resolutions. In 1832 Congress passed a new tariff law. Although the tax rates were lower than those of 1828, they were still high. South Carolina called a special convention that voted for an Ordinance of Nullification against the new tariff.

Calhoun had raised an important issue— the supremacy of the national government versus state sovereignty. The states' rights doctrine, first found in the Virginia and Kentucky Resolutions, had taken a giant step toward secession. If states were sovereign, they had a right to secede from the Union.

Can a State Nullify a Law? Early in 1830, Calhoun's doctrine of nullification came before the United States Senate during a debate over land policy. People in the West were angry because of a bill that would limit the sale of western lands. Robert Y. Hayne of South Carolina argued that the western states could nullify the bill if it became law.

Daniel Webster of Massachusetts replied to Hayne. Webster denied that the Constitution was just a compact between the states, to be interpreted as each state chose. On the contrary, he said, only the Supreme Court could decide whether a law was constitutional. Webster argued that the federal government was sovereign, that the Union was perpetual, and that any attempt to dismember it was nothing less than treason. Webster closed with this ringing statement: "Liberty and Union, now and forever, one and inseparable."

In 1833 the nullification crisis was settled by a compromise. The tariff was lowered and, in response, South Carolina withdrew its Ordinance of Nullification. Both sides claimed victory, and the issue was laid to rest—at least temporarily.

✓ **Reading Check** **Analyze** Why did the South and the Northeast try to use nullification?

▼ Early railroads helped industry grow.

The Way It Was

Agrarians and Industrialists

Sectionalism, the rivalry between one region and another, was based on economic and political interests. One rivalry that developed was between agrarians and industrialists.

Agrarianism

Thomas Jefferson believed that the strength of the United States was its independent farmers. His ideas are sometimes referred to as agrarianism. Jefferson argued that owning land enabled people to be independent. As long as most people owned their own land, they would fight to preserve the Republic.

Jefferson believed that too much of an emphasis on industry and trade would lead to a society that was divided between the rich who owned everything and the poor who worked for wages. He also believed that the wealthy would corrupt the government and threaten the rights and liberties of ordinary people.

New Western Lands

Main Idea In the 1840s, the issue of slavery in new territories was once again at the forefront.

Reading Connection Can you think of a debate you have been a part of that turned out to be difficult to resolve? Read to learn how Congress continued to struggle with a solution concerning slavery.

For the next 25 years, Congress avoided the issue of slavery's expansion. In the 1840s, however, this heated debate moved back into Congress. Again, the dispute was over slavery in new territories. The territories involved were Texas, which had won its independence from Mexico in 1836, and New Mexico and California, which were still part of Mexico.

Many Southerners hoped to see Texas, where slavery already existed, join the Union. As a result, the annexation of Texas became the main issue in the presidential election of 1844. Democrat **James K. Polk** of Tennessee won the election and pressed forward on acquiring Texas. Texas became a state in 1845. At the same time, support for taking over New Mexico and California also grew in the South. The federal government's actions on these lands led to war with Mexico.

Conflicting Views Just months after the war with Mexico began, Representative David Wilmot of Pennsylvania introduced a proposal in Congress. Called the Wilmot Proviso, it specified that slavery should be prohibited in any lands that might be acquired from Mexico.

During the 1800s, many Americans kept Jefferson's ideal of small, independent farming communities as the model society. Agrarians, particularly in the South, were alarmed at the changes that industrialization was producing in the nation's cities. They viewed independent farming as a way to escape degrading factory work and the unhealthy and overcrowded large cities.

Industrialism

The Industrial Revolution changed the Northeast from a region where families lived and worked together at farming, crafts, and home-based businesses to one in which people earned their livings by working for others in industry. Many Americans believed that manufacturing and trade were the basis of national wealth and power. They favored policies that would support these areas of the economy.

Although industrial growth caused problems, economic progress also made life easier in many ways. Improved transportation and mass production meant that more goods were available to more people. American living standards were surpassing those of European countries.

In the cities, people were beginning to enjoy new comforts and conveniences such as gas streetlights and better sewer systems. Some Americans came to believe that they were living in an age of progress. They expected that new inventions, along with America's abundant resources, would improve life for Americans and set an example for other countries of the world.

▼ Many Americans made their living by farming.

Picturing **History**

By 1848 the population of San Francisco was about 1,000 residents. The population of the city and the California territory would grow greatly during the gold rush. *What issue during the presidential election campaign of 1848 involved California?*

Southerners protested furiously. They wanted to keep open the possibility of introducing slavery to California and New Mexico. Senator John C. Calhoun of South Carolina countered Wilmot's proposal with another. It stated that neither Congress nor any territorial government had the authority to ban slavery from a territory or regulate it in any way.

Neither Wilmot's nor Calhoun's proposal passed, but both caused bitter debate. By the time of the 1848 presidential election, the United States had acquired the territories of California and New Mexico from Mexico but had taken no action on the issue of slavery in those areas.

The Free-Soil Party The debate over slavery led to the formation of a new political party. In 1848 the Whigs chose Zachary Taylor, a Southerner and a hero of the war with Mexico, as their presidential candidate. The Democrats selected Senator Lewis Cass of Michigan. Neither candidate took a stand on slavery in the territories. They were both afraid of losing votes.

This failure to take a position angered voters. Many antislavery Democrats and Whigs left their parties and joined with members of the old Liberty Party to form the Free-Soil Party. The new party proclaimed "Free Soil, Free Speech, Free Labor, and Free Men," and endorsed the Wilmot Proviso. The party nominated former president Martin Van Buren as its presidential candidate.

Whig candidate Zachary Taylor won the election, receiving 163 electoral votes to 127 for Cass. The Whig's strategy of maintaining neutrality helped them win the election. Van Buren failed to receive a single electoral vote, and captured only 14 percent of the popular vote in the North. However, several candidates of the Free-Soil Party won seats in Congress.

Reading Check **Explain** How was John C. Calhoun's proposal different from the Wilmot Proviso?

The Search for Compromise

Main Idea Henry Clay presented a plan to settle the slavery debate that resulted in the Compromise of 1850.

Reading Connection Do you remember an argument you have had recently? How did you resolve the argument? Read to learn how Congress settled its dividing issues in 1850.

Once in office, President Zachary Taylor urged leaders in the two territories of California and New Mexico to apply for statehood immediately. After these lands had become states, he reasoned, their citizens could decide whether to allow slavery. New Mexico did not apply for statehood, but California did in 1850.

Taylor's plan ran into trouble when California's statehood became tangled up with other issues before Congress. Antislavery forces wanted to abolish slavery in the District of Columbia, the nation's capital. Southerners wanted a strong national law requiring states to return **fugitive** (FYOO•juh•tihv), or runaway, slaves to their masters. Another dispute involved the New Mexico–Texas border.

The greatest obstacle to Taylor's plan was concern over the balance of power in the Senate. In 1849 the nation included 15 slave states and 15 free states. If California entered as a free state—and New Mexico, Oregon, and Utah followed as free states—which seemed likely—the South would be hopelessly outvoted in the Senate. As tension grew, some Southerners began talking about having their states **secede** (sih•SEED) from, or leave, the United States.

The Debate Begins In January 1850, Henry Clay, now a senator, presented a plan to settle all the issues dividing Congress. First, California would be admitted as a free state. Second, the New Mexico Territory would have no restrictions on slavery. Third, the New Mexico–Texas border dispute would be settled in favor of New Mexico. Fourth, the slave trade, but not slavery itself, would be abolished in the District of Columbia. Finally, Clay pushed for a stronger fugitive slave law.

Clay's proposal launched an emotional debate in Congress that raged for seven months. Senator Calhoun opposed Clay's plan. He believed that the only way to save the Union was to protect slavery. If Congress admitted California as a free state, Calhoun warned, the Southern states would have to leave the Union.

Senator Daniel Webster supported Clay's plan. He argued that antislavery forces lost little in agreeing to the compromise.

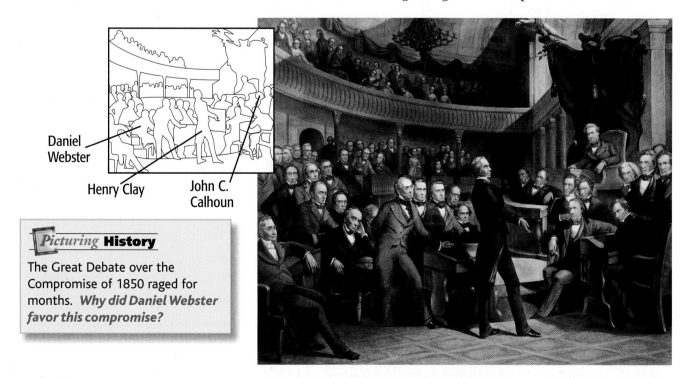

Daniel Webster

Henry Clay

John C. Calhoun

Picturing **History**

The Great Debate over the Compromise of 1850 raged for months. *Why did Daniel Webster favor this compromise?*

Webster reasoned that geography would prevent slavery from taking root in the new territories, because most of the land was not suited for plantations. What was most important was to preserve the Union.

The Compromise of 1850 Clay's plan could not pass as a complete package. Too many members of Congress objected to one part of it or another. On July 4, 1850, before the issue could be decided, President Taylor **collapsed** with a severe stomach illness. He died five days later, having served just 16 months as president. The new president, **Millard Fillmore,** supported some form of compromise. At the same time, **Stephen A. Douglas,** a young senator from Illinois, took charge of efforts to resolve the crisis. Douglas divided Clay's plan into a series of measures that Congress could vote on separately. In this way, members of Congress would not have to support proposals they opposed.

President Fillmore persuaded several Whig representatives to **abstain** (uhb•STAYN)—not to cast votes—on measures they opposed. Congress finally passed a series of five separate bills in August and September of 1850. Taken together these laws, known as the Compromise of 1850, contained the five main points of Clay's original plan. Fillmore believed they settled the conflict between North and South. The president would soon be proved wrong.

Reading Check **Explain** How did the Compromise of 1850 affect the New Mexico Territory? What role did California play in this?

Study Central Need help understanding the issue of slavery in the West? Visit tajww1.glencoe.com and click on Study Central.

Section 2 Review

Reading Summary

Review the Main Ideas

- The Missouri Compromise allowed both Missouri and Maine to enter the Union in order to maintain the balance between slave and free states.

- In the 1820s and 1830s, South Carolina threatened to nullify federal tariff laws.

- The acquisition of new territories in the West—Texas, New Mexico, and California—created more conflicts over slavery.

- The Compromise of 1850, developed by Henry Clay, included a number of provisions dealing with slavery that temporarily resolved the debate between the North and South.

What Did You Learn?

1. List the provisions of the Missouri Compromise.

2. Why did it matter if California entered as a slave state or a free state?

Critical Thinking

3. **Comparing** Re-create the table below and describe what the North and South each gained from the Compromise of 1850.

Compromise of 1850	
Northern gains	Southern gains

4. **The Big Ideas** Why was the Free-Soil Party created?

5. **Analyze** What was the Wilmot Proviso? Why was it controversial?

6. **Persuasive Writing** Create a poster for the Free-Soil Party presidential candidate. Include slogans and symbols to gain popular support.

7. **ANALYSIS** **Making Connections** Make a time line highlighting key issues of federal sovereignty versus states' rights. Include the Virginia-Kentucky Resolutions of 1798–99 and the Compromise of 1850.

Section 3

A Nation Dividing

Guide to Reading

Looking Back, Looking Ahead

The Compromise of 1850 seemed to have settled the problem of slavery in new states. When statehood for Kansas and Nebraska drew near, however, slavery again divided the nation.

Focusing on the (Main Ideas)

• The Kansas-Nebraska Act resulted from another dispute over slavery in Congress. *(page 544)*

• Violence erupted as proslavery and antislavery forces came to arms when the new proslavery Kansas legislature was elected. *(page 546)*

Locating Places

Kansas
Nebraska

Meeting People

Harriet Beecher Stowe
John Brown
Charles Sumner
Preston Brooks

Content Vocabulary

popular sovereignty (SAH•vruhn•tee)
border ruffians (RUH•fee•uhns)
civil war

Academic Vocabulary

reveal
inevitable (ih•NEH•vuh•tuh•buhl)

Reading Strategy

Taking Notes As you read the section, re-create the table below and describe how Southerners and Northerners reacted to the Kansas-Nebraska Act.

Kansas-Nebraska Act	
Southern reaction	Northern reaction

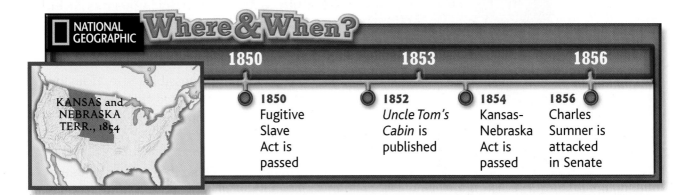

NATIONAL GEOGRAPHIC **Where & When?**

KANSAS and NEBRASKA TERR., 1854

1850	1853	1856

1850 Fugitive Slave Act is passed

1852 *Uncle Tom's Cabin* is published

1854 Kansas-Nebraska Act is passed

1856 Charles Sumner is attacked in Senate

The Kansas-Nebraska Act

The Kansas-Nebraska Act resulted from another dispute over slavery in Congress.

Reading Connection Do you know where the present-day states of Kansas and Nebraska are located? Find them on the Reference Atlas maps in the front of your book. Read to learn what happened in this part of the country in the mid-1850s.

Franklin Pierce, a New Hampshire Democrat who supported the Fugitive Slave Act, became president in 1853. Pierce intended to enforce the Fugitive Slave Act, and his actions hardened the opposition to slavery. **Harriet Beecher Stowe's** popular book *Uncle Tom's Cabin* added fuel to antislavery feelings with its description of slavery as a cruel and inhuman system.

In 1854 the dispute over slavery erupted in Congress again. The cause was a bill introduced by Stephen A. Douglas, the Illinois senator who had forged the Compromise of 1850. Hoping to encourage settlement of the West and open the way for a transcontinental railroad, Douglas

Picturing **History**

Stephen Douglas enthusiastically supported national expansion. *Why did the Kansas-Nebraska Act reopen the question of whether slavery should be allowed in the territories?*

proposed organizing the region west of Missouri and Iowa as the territories of **Kansas** and **Nebraska.** Douglas was developing a plan for the nation to expand that both the North and the South would accept. Instead his bill reopened the conflict about slavery in the territories.

Geography of Slavery Because of their location, Kansas and Nebraska seemed likely to become free states. Both lay north of 36°30'N latitude, the line established in the Missouri Compromise as the boundary of slavery. Douglas knew that Southerners would object to having Kansas and Nebraska become free states because it would give the North more members in the Senate. As a result, Douglas proposed abandoning the Missouri Compromise and letting the settlers in each territory vote on whether to allow slavery. He called this **popular sovereignty** (SAH•vruhn•tee)—allowing the people to decide.

Passage of the Act Many Northerners protested strongly. Douglas's plan to repeal the Missouri Compromise would allow slavery into areas that had been free for more than 30 years. Opponents of the bill demanded that Congress vote down the bill.

Southerners in Congress, however, provided solid support for the bill. They expected that Kansas would be settled in large part by slaveholders from Missouri who would vote to keep slavery legal. With some support from Northern Democrats and the backing of President Pierce, Congress passed the Kansas-Nebraska Act in May 1854.

Division Grows Northern Democrats in the House split almost evenly on the vote, **revealing** deep divisions in the party. Many Northerners became convinced that compromise with the South was no longer possible. Sam Houston, senator from Texas, predicted that the bill "will convulse [upset] the country from Maine to the Rio Grande."

✓ **Reading Check** **Describe** Write a definition of *popular sovereignty* in your own words.

Biography

HARRIET BEECHER STOWE
1811–1896

Writer Harriet Beecher Stowe called the Fugitive Slave Act a "nightmare abomination." Stowe, born Harriet Elizabeth Beecher to a New England minister, moved to Cincinnati with her family when she was 21. There, on the banks of the Ohio River, she saw enslaved people being loaded onto ships to be taken to slave markets. Stowe was introduced to many abolitionists, some of whom owned safe houses along the Underground Railroad. Stowe strongly opposed slavery, but for some time, she did not know how she could help end it. With the help of her children and husband, Stowe developed an antislavery story called *Uncle Tom's Cabin*. Packed with dramatic incidents and vivid characters, the novel shows slavery as a cruel and brutal system.

Published in 1852, *Uncle Tom's Cabin* quickly became a sensation, selling more than 300,000 copies in the first year. Some people, however, strongly opposed the book. Its sales were banned in the South, and many slaveholders said the book unfairly and inaccurately represented their way of life. To counter these accusations, Stowe published *A Key to Uncle Tom's Cabin; Presenting the Original Facts and Documents Upon Which It Is Based*. This book detailed Stowe's extensive research into slavery in the South. The book had such an impact on public feelings about slavery that when Abraham Lincoln was introduced to Stowe during the Civil War, he said, "so you're the little woman who wrote the book that started this great war."

After the Civil War, Stowe continued to write. She began to speak publicly and gave readings of *Uncle Tom's Cabin* to many large audiences. In 1896, at the age of 85, Stowe died. Her famous book has since been adapted into plays and songs, and remains a much-read novel from the Civil War era.

> *"[I hope these writings] awaken sympathy and feeling for the African race, as they exist among us; to show their wrongs and sorrows . . ."*
>
> **—Harriet Beecher Stowe**

Then and Now

Write a short story similar to *Uncle Tom's Cabin* about a group of people who are unfairly treated in today's world. Be sure to research the topic so that your story remains as factual as possible.

Conflict in Kansas

Main Idea Violence erupted as proslavery and antislavery forces came to arms when the new proslavery Kansas legislature was elected.

Reading Connection Think of an issue that is important to you. What would you be willing to do to stand up for that issue? Read to learn how the rival groups in Kansas clashed in the mid-1800s over slavery.

Right after passage of the Kansas-Nebraska Act, proslavery and antislavery groups rushed supporters into Kansas. In the spring of 1855, when elections took place in Kansas, a proslavery legislature was elected.

Although only about 1,500 voters lived in Kansas at the time, more than 6,000 people cast ballots in the elections. Thousands of proslavery supporters from Missouri had crossed the border just to vote in the election. These Missourians traveled in armed groups and became known as **border ruffians** (RUH•fee•uhns). Soon after the election, the new Kansas legislature passed laws supporting slavery. One law even restricted political office to only those candidates who supported slavery.

The antislavery people refused to accept these laws. Instead they armed themselves, held their own elections, and adopted a constitution that banned slavery. By January 1856, rival governments existed in Kansas, one for and one against slavery. Each asked Congress for recognition. To confuse matters further, President Pierce and the U.S. Senate favored the proslavery government, and the U.S. House of Representatives backed the forces that were opposed to slavery.

With proslavery and antislavery forces in Kansas arming themselves, the outbreak of violence became **inevitable.** In May 1856, about 800 slavery supporters attacked the town of Lawrence, the antislavery capital.

 **Slavery and Sectionalism**

The Compromise of 1850

- Free states
- Slave states
- Territory closed to slaveholding
- Territory open to slaveholding
- Indian Territory

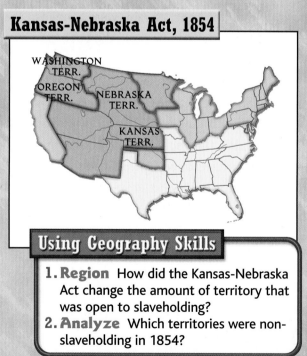

Kansas-Nebraska Act, 1854

Using Geography Skills

1. **Region** How did the Kansas-Nebraska Act change the amount of territory that was open to slaveholding?
2. **Analyze** Which territories were non-slaveholding in 1854?

The slavery supporters destroyed the town, burned the hotel and the home of the governor, and tore down two newspaper offices. Soon after, forces opposed to slavery retaliated.

"Bleeding Kansas" **John Brown,** a fervent abolitionist, believed God had chosen him to end slavery. When he heard of the attack on Lawrence, Brown went into a rage. He vowed to "strike terror in the hearts of the proslavery people." One night, Brown led four of his sons and two other men along Pottawatomie Creek, where they seized and killed five supporters of slavery.

More violence followed as armed bands roamed the territory. Newspapers began referring to "Bleeding Kansas" and "the Civil War in Kansas." A **civil war** is a conflict between citizens of the same country. Not until October of 1856 did John Geary, the newly appointed territorial governor, stop the bloodshed in Kansas. Geary ordered 1,300 federal troops to suppress the guerrilla forces.

Violence in Congress The violence that erupted in Kansas spilled over to the halls of the U.S. Congress as well. Abolitionist senator **Charles Sumner** of Massachusetts delivered a speech entitled "The Crime Against Kansas." Sumner lashed out against proslavery forces in Kansas. He also criticized proslavery senators, repeatedly attacking Andrew P. Butler of South Carolina.

Two days after the speech, Butler's distant cousin, Representative **Preston Brooks,** walked into the Senate chamber. He hit Sumner again and again over the head and shoulders with a cane. Sumner fell to the floor, unconscious and bleeding. He suffered injuries so severe that he did not return to the Senate for several years. The Brooks-Sumner incident and the fighting in "Bleeding Kansas" revealed the rising level of hostility between North and South.

Reading Check **Predict** Who do you predict will be the combatants if the United States is torn apart by Civil War?

Study Central Need help understanding the Kansas-Nebraska Act and its effects? Visit tajww1.glencoe.com and click on Study Central.

Section 3 Review

Reading Summary

Review the Main Ideas

- The Kansas-Nebraska Act abandoned the provisions of the Missouri Compromise and put in place the doctrine of popular sovereignty to decide the issue of slavery in new territories.

- In Kansas antislavery and proslavery forces came into violent conflict.

What Did You Learn?

1. Who were the border ruffians?

2. How many cast votes in the Kansas elections? How did that compare with the population at the time?

Critical Thinking

3. **Organizing Information** Re-create the diagram below and list the steps that led to bloodshed in Kansas.

Step → Bloodshed in Kansas
Step
Step

4. **The Big Ideas** How did popular sovereignty lead to violence in Kansas?

5. **Predicting Consequences** Could the violence in Kansas have been prevented if Congress had not abandoned the Missouri Compromise? Explain.

6. **Persuasive Writing** Decide whether you would have been for or against the Kansas-Nebraska Act and the concept of popular sovereignty. Then write a newspaper editorial arguing your position.

Challenges to Slavery

Guide to Reading

Looking Back, Looking Ahead
You learned that the issue of slavery led to civil war in Kansas. You will next read about how slavery led to the founding of a new political party and additional bloodshed.

Focusing on the Main Ideas
- The Supreme Court's decision in the *Dred Scott* case resulted in even more division in the country. *(page 549)*
- The Lincoln-Douglas debates helped Lincoln emerge as a leader. *(page 552)*

Meeting People
John C. Frémont
James Buchanan
Dred Scott
Roger B. Taney (TAW•nee)
Abraham Lincoln

Content Vocabulary
arsenal (AHR•suhn•uhl)
martyr (MAHR•tuhr)

Academic Vocabulary
restrict
topic

Reading Strategy
Classifying Information As you read the section, re-create the diagram below and list major events that occurred in each year.

1846	1854	1856	1858

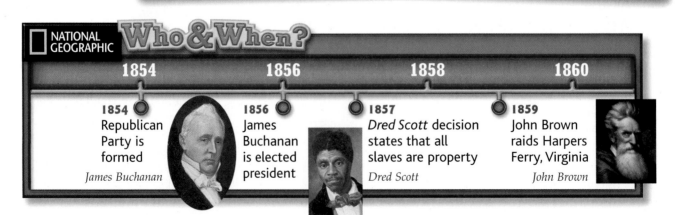

NATIONAL GEOGRAPHIC Who & When?

| 1854 | 1856 | 1858 | 1860 |

1854 Republican Party is formed

James Buchanan

1856 James Buchanan is elected president

1857 *Dred Scott* decision states that all slaves are property

Dred Scott

1859 John Brown raids Harpers Ferry, Virginia

John Brown

The *Dred Scott* Decision

Main Idea The Supreme Court's decision in the *Dred Scott* case resulted in even more division in the country.

Reading Connection How would you feel if the Supreme Court decided that you were "property"? Read to find out how the decision in the *Dred Scott* case shocked the nation.

An American Story

Many people considered John Brown to be a radical murderer, but others viewed him as a fighter for the cause of freedom. When he was executed in 1859, a magazine published this imaginative account of Brown's exit from the jail,

> **❝ a black woman, with her little child in arms, stood near his way.... He stopped . . . , and with the tenderness of one whose love is as broad as the brotherhood of man, kissed the child. . . . ❞**

—from *The Anglo-African Magazine*

Why Was the Republican Party Founded?

Even before Brown's raid, other events had driven the North and South further apart. After the Kansas-Nebraska Act, the Democratic Party began to divide along sectional lines, with Northern Democrats leaving the party. Differing views over the slavery issue destroyed the Whig Party.

In 1854 antislavery Whigs and Democrats joined forces with Free-Soilers to form the Republican Party. The Republicans challenged the proslavery Whigs and Democrats, choosing candidates to run in the state and congressional elections of 1854. Their main message was that the government should ban slavery from new territories.

The Republican Party quickly showed its strength in the North. In the election, the Republicans won control of the House of Representatives and of several state governments. In the South, the Republicans had almost no support.

Almost three-fourths of the Democratic candidates from free states lost in 1854. The party was increasingly becoming a Southern party.

The Election of 1856 Democrats and Republicans met again in the presidential election of 1856. The Whig Party, disintegrating over the slavery issue, did not offer a candidate of its own.

The Republicans chose **John C. Frémont** of California as their candidate for president. Frémont had gained fame as an explorer in the West. The party platform called for free territories, and its campaign slogan became "Free soil, free speech, and Frémont."

The Democratic Party nominated **James Buchanan** of Pennsylvania, an experienced diplomat and former member of Congress. The party endorsed the idea of popular sovereignty.

The American Party, or Know-Nothings, had grown quickly between 1853 and 1856 by attacking immigrants. The Know-Nothings nominated former president Millard Fillmore.

The presidential vote divided along sectional lines. Buchanan won the election, winning all of the Southern states except Maryland, and received 174 electoral votes compared to 114 for Frémont and 8 for Fillmore. Frémont did not receive a single electoral vote south of the Mason-Dixon line, but he carried 11 of the 16 free states.

The *Dred Scott* Decision Until 1857 some slaves who had lived in free states or territories were successful when they sued for their freedom. Biddy Mason had done this in California. The case of another slave, Dred Scott, however, went all the way to the Supreme Court. On March 6, 1857, the Court announced a decision about slavery and the territories that shook the nation.

Dred Scott was an enslaved African American who was bought by an army doctor in Missouri, a slave state. In the 1830s, the doctor moved his household to Illinois, a free state, and then to the Wisconsin Territory, where slavery was banned by the Northwest Ordinance of 1787. Later the family returned to Missouri, where the doctor died.

In 1846 with the help of antislavery lawyers, Scott sued for his freedom. He claimed he should be free because he had once lived on free soil. Eleven years later, in the midst of growing anger over the slavery issue, the case reached the Supreme Court.

The Court's Decision The case attracted enormous attention. Although the immediate issue was Dred Scott's status, the Court also had the opportunity to rule on the question of slavery in territories. Many Americans hoped that the Court would resolve the issue for good.

The Court's decision electrified the nation. Chief Justice **Roger B. Taney** (TAW•nee) said

that Dred Scott was still a slave. As a slave, Scott was not a citizen and had no right to bring a lawsuit. Taney could have stopped there, but he decided to address the broader issues.

Taney wrote that Scott's residence on free soil did not make him free. An enslaved person was property, and the Fifth Amendment prohibits Congress from taking away property without "due process of law."

Finally, Taney wrote that Congress had no power to prohibit slavery in any territory. The Missouri Compromise—which had banned slavery north of 36°30′N latitude—was unconstitutional. For that matter, so was popular sovereignty. Not even the voters in a territory could prohibit slavery because that would amount to taking away a person's property. In effect, the decision meant that the Constitution protected slavery. 📖 *(See page 846 of the Appendix for a summary of the Dred Scott decision.)*

Reaction to the Decision Rather than settling the issue, the Supreme Court's decision divided the country even more. Many Southerners were elated. The Court had reaffirmed what many in the South had always maintained: Nothing could legally prevent the spread of slavery. Northern Democrats were pleased that the Republicans' main issue—**restricting** the spread of slavery—had been ruled unconstitutional.

Republicans and other antislavery groups were outraged, calling the *Dred Scott* decision "the greatest crime" ever committed in the nation's courts.

✓ **Reading Check** **Explain** How did the *Dred Scott* decision regulate the spread of slavery?

Picturing **History**

Chief Justice Roger B. Taney (above right) delivered the Supreme Court's ruling in the *Dred Scott* case. The decision made Scott a topic for the nation's press. *What impression of Scott's family do you get from the engravings shown here?*

Biography

BRIDGET MASON
1818–1891

Born a slave in 1818, Bridget Mason had worked on plantations in Georgia and Mississippi. In 1851 slave-holder Robert Smith moved his family and their 12 slaves to California. Among the slaves were Bridget —or Biddy as she was usually called—and her three children. Smith's plan to start a ranch and mine for gold did not work. In the autumn of 1855, Smith made plans to move to Texas.

Before Smith could leave, charges were filed against him for planning to move enslaved people from California, a free state, to Texas, a slave state. In court, Smith's attorney argued that Biddy and the other slaves had agreed to come to California and were willing to go to Texas.

Before Judge Benjamin Hayes issued his verdict, he wanted to hear how Biddy felt about moving to Texas. Biddy told the judge, "Mr. Smith told me I would be just as free in Texas as here." But she admitted she "always feared this trip to Texas since I first heard of it." In his decision, Hayes said that Biddy and the others were "entitled to their freedom and cannot be held in slavery or involuntary servitude . . . [they] are free forever."

In 1856 when Biddy was declared free, she and her family decided to settle in Los Angeles. Biddy first worked as a servant, then was hired by Dr. John Strother Griffin to help care for his patients. Saving her money, she purchased her first home in 1866. Biddy soon bought and sold more property, making money during the mid-1870s when property in Los Angeles was in demand.

Biddy devoted her life to helping others. She helped form the First African Methodist Episcopal Church in 1872, visited jail inmates, and provided food and shelter for the poor. When floods struck the Los Angeles area in the 1880s, Biddy paid to feed the flood victims.

"If you hold your hand closed, nothing good can come in. The open hand is blessed, for it gives in abundance, even as it receives."
—Bridget Mason

Then and Now

Read the quote above. Can you think of anyone today who lives by that motto? Explain.

551

Lincoln and Douglas

Main Idea The Lincoln-Douglas debates helped Lincoln emerge as a leader.

Reading Connection If you really wanted something, what risks would you be willing to take? Read to learn how Lincoln, who was nearly unknown, challenged Douglas to a series of debates and emerged as a leader.

In the congressional election of 1858, the Senate race in Illinois was the center of national attention. The current senator, Democrat Stephen A. Douglas, ran against Republican challenger **Abraham Lincoln.** People considered Douglas a likely candidate for president in 1860. Lincoln was nearly an unknown.

Short and powerful, Douglas was called "the Little Giant." He disliked slavery but thought that the controversy over it would interfere with the nation's growth. He believed the issue could be resolved through popular sovereignty.

Born in the poor backcountry of Kentucky, Abraham Lincoln moved to Indiana as a child, and later to Illinois. Like Douglas, Lincoln was intelligent, ambitious, and a successful lawyer. Lincoln started his campaign with a memorable speech, in which he declared:

❝ A house divided against itself cannot stand. I believe this government cannot endure permanently half slave and half free. I do not expect the Union to be dissolved—I do not expect the house to fall—but I do expect it will cease to be divided. It will become all one thing or all the other. ❞

The Lincoln-Douglas Debates Not as well known as Douglas, Lincoln challenged the senator to a series of debates. Douglas reluctantly agreed. The two met seven times in August, September, and October of 1858 in towns throughout Illinois. Thousands came to these debates. The main **topic,** of course, was slavery.

During the debate at Freeport, Lincoln questioned Douglas about his views on popular sovereignty. Could the people of a territory legally exclude slavery before achieving statehood? Douglas replied that the people could exclude slavery by refusing to pass laws protecting slaveholders' rights. Douglas's response, which satisfied antislavery followers but lost him support in the South, became known as the Freeport Doctrine.

"This republic can exist forever divided into free and slave states, as our fathers made it."
—Stephen Douglas

"I believe this government cannot endure permanently half slave and half free."
—Abraham Lincoln

Douglas claimed that Lincoln wanted African Americans to be fully equal to whites. Lincoln denied this. Still, Lincoln said, "in the right to eat the bread . . . which his own hand earns, [an African American] is my equal and the equal of [Senator] Douglas, and the equal of every living man." The real issue, Lincoln said, is "between the men who think slavery a wrong and those who do not think it wrong. The Republican Party thinks it wrong."

Following the debates, Douglas won a narrow victory in the election. Lincoln lost the election, but the debates had earned him a national reputation.

The Raid on Harpers Ferry After the 1858 elections, Southerners began to feel threatened by growing Republican power. In late 1859, an act of violence greatly increased their fears. On October 16, the abolitionist John Brown led 18 men, both whites and African Americans, on a raid on Harpers Ferry, Virginia. His target was an **arsenal** (AHR•suhn•uhl), a storage place for weapons and ammunition. Brown—who had killed five proslavery Kansans in 1856—hoped to start a rebellion against slaveholders by arming enslaved African Americans. His raid was financed by a group of abolitionists.

Brown and his men were quickly defeated by local citizens and federal troops. Brown was convicted of treason and murder and was sentenced to hang. His execution caused an uproar in the North. Some antislavery Northerners, including Republican leaders, denounced Brown's use of violence. Others viewed Brown as a hero. Writer Ralph Waldo Emerson called Brown a **martyr** (MAHR•tuhr)—a person who dies for a cause he believes in.

John Brown's death became a rallying point for abolitionists. When Southerners learned of Brown's connection to abolitionists, their fears of a great Northern conspiracy against them seemed to be confirmed. The nation was nearing disaster.

Reading Check **Identify** What was John Brown's target when he led a raid on Harpers Ferry?

Study Central Need help understanding the nation's division on slavery? Visit tajww1.glencoe.com and click on Study Central.

Section 4 Review

Reading Summary

Review the Main Ideas

- The Republican Party became a major political force, while the Supreme Court ruled in the *Dred Scott* case that the spread of slavery could not be restricted.

- Debates between Abraham Lincoln and Stephen Douglas helped put Lincoln in the national spotlight.

What Did You Learn?

1. Discuss the stages in the development of the Republican Party.

2. Who financed John Brown's raid on Harpers Ferry?

Critical Thinking

3. **Organizing Information** Re-create the table shown here, and describe the positions taken by Lincoln and Douglas in their debates.

Lincoln-Douglas Debates	
Lincoln's position	Douglas's position

4. **The Big Ideas** How did the *Dred Scott* decision reverse an earlier ruling made by Congress?

5. **Making Inferences** Why did Lincoln emerge as a leader after the Lincoln-Douglas debates?

6. **Descriptive Writing** Write a short biographical essay on either John Brown, Dred Scott, or Stephen Douglas. Include key events from the person's life that relate to events leading up to the Civil War.

Section 5

Secession and War

Guide to Reading

Looking Back, Looking Ahead
As you know, the *Dred Scott* decision and John Brown's raid further divided the nation. Read to learn how the election of 1860 affected the possible disaster that faced the country.

Focusing on the Main Ideas
- A split occurred in the Democratic Party, which allowed Lincoln to win the election of 1860. *(page 555)*
- South Carolina led other Southern states in seceding from the Union. *(page 556)*
- The Civil War began when Confederate forces attacked Fort Sumter in South Carolina. *(page 558)*

Locating Places
South Carolina
Fort Sumter

Meeting People
John Crittenden
Jefferson Davis

Content Vocabulary
border states
secession (sih•SEH•shuhn)
states' rights

Academic Vocabulary
eventual (ih•VEHNT•shuh•wuhl)
justify
theory

Reading Strategy
Classifying Information As you read the section, re-create the time line below and list the major events at each time.

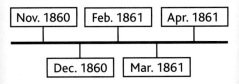

Nov. 1860	Feb. 1861	Apr. 1861

Dec. 1860	Mar. 1861

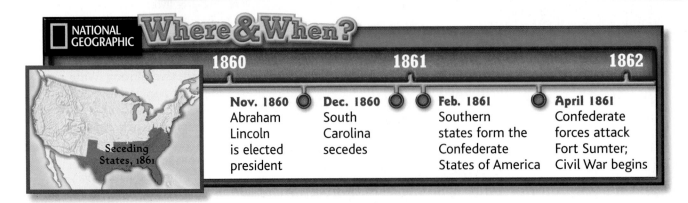

NATIONAL GEOGRAPHIC **Where & When?**

1860   1861   1862

Nov. 1860 Abraham Lincoln is elected president

Dec. 1860 South Carolina secedes

Feb. 1861 Southern states form the Confederate States of America

April 1861 Confederate forces attack Fort Sumter; Civil War begins

Seceding States, 1861

The Election of 1860

Main Idea A split occurred in the Democratic Party, which allowed Lincoln to win the election of 1860.

Reading Connection Think of an issue that you feel strongly about. Do you think your views would affect your choice for president? Read to learn how the slavery issue affected the election of 1860.

An American Story

After John Brown's raid on Harpers Ferry, calls for secession grew. South Carolina's *Charleston Mercury* declared "The day of compromise is passed . . . [T]here is no peace for the South in the Union." The *Nashville Union and American* said, "The South will hold the whole party of Republicans responsible for the bloodshed at Harpers Ferry."

Republicans argued that secession was only a scare tactic, aimed at frightening voters from casting their ballot for Abraham Lincoln. To many Southerners, however, Lincoln's election would be a signal that their position in the Union was hopeless.

Many Parties Would the Union break up? That was the burning question in the months before the presidential election of 1860. The issue of slavery **eventually** caused a break in the Democratic Party. Northern Democrats nominated Stephen Douglas for the presidency and supported popular sovereignty. Southern Democrats—vowing to uphold slavery—nominated John C. Breckinridge of Kentucky and supported the *Dred Scott* decision. Southern Democrats denounced John Brown's raid as "among the gravest of crimes." Northern and Southern moderates formed the Constitutional Union Party and nominated John Bell of Tennessee. This party took no position on slavery. However, voters in the North and South would no longer tolerate neutrality on this important issue.

Lincoln Nominated The Republicans nominated Abraham Lincoln. Their platform, designed to attract voters from many quarters, was that slavery should be left undisturbed where it existed, but that it should be excluded from the territories. Many Southerners feared, however, that a Republican victory would encourage slave revolts.

Lincoln Elected Lincoln won a clear majority of the electoral votes—180 out of 303. He received 40 percent of the popular vote. Douglas was second with 30 percent of the vote.

The vote was along purely sectional lines. Lincoln's name did not even appear on the ballot in most Southern states, but he won every Northern state. Breckinridge swept the South, and Bell took most **border states.** These states were located between the North and the South. They were divided over whether to stay in the Union or join the Confederacy. Douglas won only the state of Missouri and three of New Jersey's seven electoral votes.

Reading Check **Examine** What caused the split in the Democratic Party in 1860?

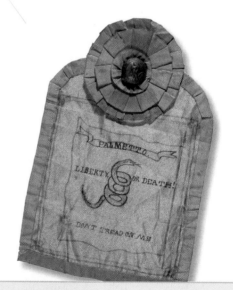

Picturing History

Patriots used the mottos on this secessionist ribbon during the American Revolution. *What did they mean during the Revolution? Why do you think secessionists used these mottos?*

The South Secedes

Main Idea South Carolina led other Southern states in seceding from the Union.

Reading Connection Have you ever been so angry that you needed to leave a room? Read to find out about the South's decision to leave the Union.

In the election of 1860, the more populous North had outvoted the South. The victory for Lincoln was a short-lived one, however, for the nation Lincoln was to lead would soon disintegrate.

Lincoln and the Republicans had promised not to disturb slavery where it already existed. Many people in the South, however, did not trust the party, fearing that the Republican administration would not protect Southern rights. On December 20, 1860, the South's long-standing threat to leave the Union became a reality when **South Carolina** held a special convention and voted to secede.

Attempt at Compromise Even after South Carolina's action, many people still wished to preserve the Union. The question was *how.* As other Southern states debated **secession** (sih•SEH•shuhn)—withdrawal from the Union—leaders in Washington, D.C., worked frantically to fashion a last-minute compromise. On December 18, 1860, Senator **John Crittenden** of Kentucky proposed a series of amendments to the Constitution. Central to Crittenden's plan was a provision to protect slavery south of 36°30′N latitude—the line set by the Missouri Compromise—in all territories "now held or hereafter acquired."

Republicans considered this unacceptable. They had just won an election on the principle that slavery would not be extended in any territories. "Now we are told . . .," Lincoln wrote,

❝the government shall be broken up, unless we surrender to those we have beaten.❞

—*letter to James T. Hale, January 11, 1861*

Leaders in the South also rejected the plan. "We spit upon every plan to compromise," exclaimed one Southern leader. "No human power can save the Union," wrote another.

The Confederacy By February 1861, Texas, Louisiana, Mississippi, Alabama, Florida, and Georgia had joined South Carolina and also seceded. Delegates from these states and South Carolina met in Montgomery, Alabama, on February 4 to form a new nation and government. Calling themselves the Confederate States of America, or the Confederacy, they chose **Jefferson Davis,** a senator from Mississippi, as their president.

Southerners **justified** secession with the **theory** of **states' rights.** The states, they argued, had voluntarily chosen to enter the Union. They defined the Constitution as a contract among the independent states. Now because the national government had violated that contract—by refusing to enforce the Fugitive Slave Act and by denying the Southern states equal rights in the territories—the states felt justified in leaving the Union.

Reactions to Secession Many Southerners welcomed secession. Senator Albert Brown of Mississippi said in a speech to a Southern audience "disunion is a fearful thing, but emancipation is worse." In Charleston, South Carolina, people rang church bells, fired cannons, and celebrated in the streets. A newspaper in Atlanta, Georgia, said the South "will never submit" and would defend its liberties no matter what the cost.

Other Southerners, however, were alarmed. A South Carolinian wrote, "My heart has been rent [torn] by . . . the destruction of my country— the dismemberment of that great and glorious Union."

Student Web Activity Visit tajww1.glencoe.com and click on *Chapter 12—Student Web Activities* for an activity on the period leading up to the Civil War.

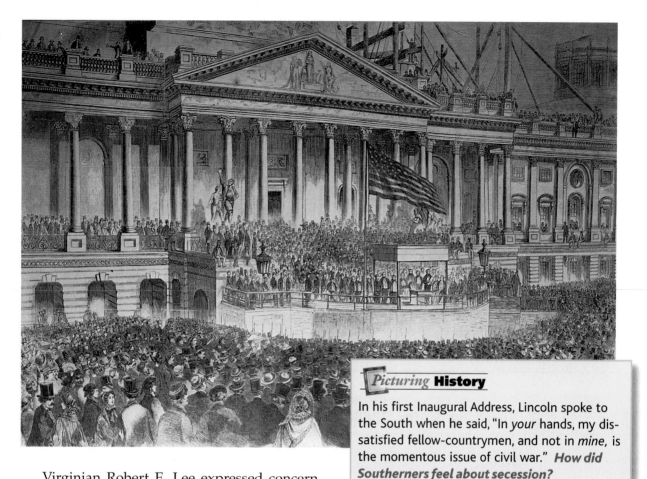

Virginian Robert E. Lee expressed concern about the future. "I see only that a fearful calamity is upon us," he wrote.

In the North, some abolitionists preferred to allow the Southern states to leave. If the Union could be kept together only by compromising on slavery, they declared, then let the Union be destroyed. Most Northerners, however, believed that the Union must be preserved. For Lincoln the issue was "whether in a free government the minority have the right to break up the government whenever they choose."

Presidential Responses Lincoln had won the election, but he was not yet president. James Buchanan's term ran until March 4, 1861. In December 1860, Buchanan sent a message to Congress saying that the Southern states had no right to secede. Then he added that he had no power to stop them from doing so.

As Lincoln prepared for his inauguration on March 4, 1861, people in both the North and the South wondered what he would say and do. They wondered, too, what would happen in Virginia, Maryland, North Carolina, Kentucky,

Tennessee, Missouri, and Arkansas. These slave states had chosen to remain in the Union, but the decision was not final. If the United States used force against the Confederate States of America, the remaining slave states also might secede. In his Inaugural Address, the new president mixed toughness and words of peace. He said that secession would not be permitted, vowing to hold federal property in the South and to enforce the laws of the United States. At the same time, Lincoln pleaded with the people of the South for reconciliation:

66 We are not enemies, but friends. We must not be enemies. Though passion may have strained, it must not break our bonds of affection. 99

—from *Inaugural Addresses of the Presidents*

✔ **Reading Check** **Explain** How did the seceding states justify their right to leave the Union?

Fort Sumter

Main Idea The Civil War began when Confederate forces attacked Fort Sumter in South Carolina.

Reading Connection Have you ever been startled by a loud noise? Read to learn how Fort Sumter was attacked on April 12, 1861, and what it was like from inside the fort.

The South soon tested President Lincoln's vow to hold federal property. Confederate forces had already seized some United States forts within their states. Although Lincoln did not want to start a war by trying to take the forts back, allowing the Confederates to keep them would amount to admitting their right to secede.

On the day after his inauguration, Lincoln received a dispatch from Major Robert Anderson, the commander of **Fort Sumter**, a United States fort on an island guarding Charleston Harbor. The message warned that the fort was low on supplies and that the Confederates demanded its surrender.

The War Begins Lincoln responded by sending a message to Governor Francis Pickens of South Carolina. He informed Pickens that he was sending an unarmed expedition with supplies to Fort Sumter.

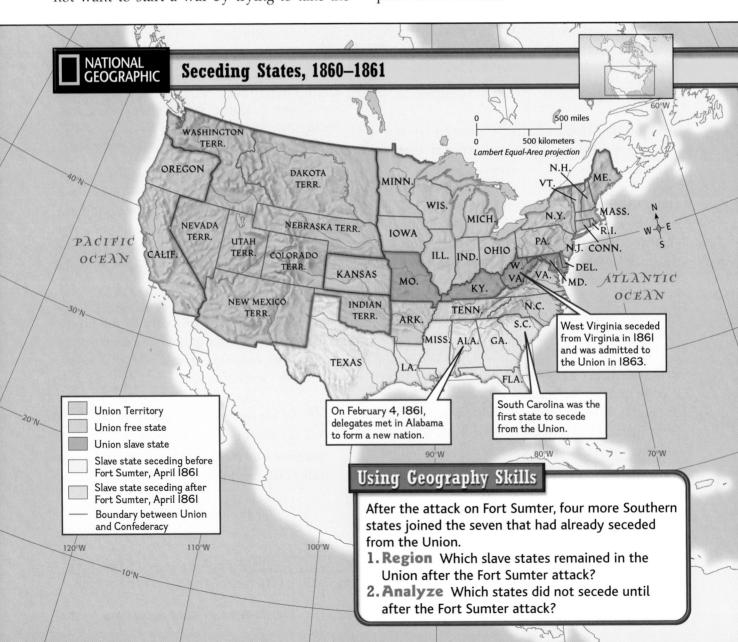

NATIONAL GEOGRAPHIC
Seceding States, 1860–1861

West Virginia seceded from Virginia in 1861 and was admitted to the Union in 1863.

On February 4, 1861, delegates met in Alabama to form a new nation.

South Carolina was the first state to secede from the Union.

Legend:
- Union Territory
- Union free state
- Union slave state
- Slave state seceding before Fort Sumter, April 1861
- Slave state seceding after Fort Sumter, April 1861
- Boundary between Union and Confederacy

Using Geography Skills

After the attack on Fort Sumter, four more Southern states joined the seven that had already seceded from the Union.

1. **Region** Which slave states remained in the Union after the Fort Sumter attack?
2. **Analyze** Which states did not secede until after the Fort Sumter attack?

Lincoln promised that Union forces would not "throw in men, arms, or ammunition" unless they were fired upon. The president thus left the decision to start shooting up to the Confederates.

Confederate president Jefferson Davis and his advisers made a fateful choice. They ordered their forces to attack Fort Sumter before the Union supplies could arrive. Confederate guns opened fire on the fort early on April 12, 1861. Union captain Abner Doubleday witnessed the attack from inside the fort:

> **❝Showers of balls . . . and shells . . . poured into the fort in one incessant stream, causing great flakes of masonry to fall in all directions. ❞**
>
> —as quoted in *Voices of the Civil War*

High seas had prevented Union relief ships from reaching the fort. The Union garrison held out for 33 hours before surrendering on April 14. Thousands of shots were exchanged during the siege, but no lives were lost on either side. The Confederates hoisted their flag over the fort, and all the guns in the harbor sounded a triumphant salute.

Once Fort Sumter was attacked, both the North and South took action. President Lincoln issued a call for 75,000 troops to fight to save the Union, and volunteers quickly signed up. Meanwhile, volunteers signed up to fight for the South, and Virginia, North Carolina, Tennessee, and Arkansas voted to join the Confederacy. The Civil War had begun.

✓Reading Check **Explain** What action did Lincoln take after the attack on Fort Sumter?

Study Central Need help understanding the election of 1860, secession, and war? Visit tajwwI.glencoe.com and click on Study Central.

Section 5 Review

Reading Summary

Review the Main Ideas

- In a contest in which votes were split between four candidates, Abraham Lincoln came out the winner of the 1860 presidential election.

- Following Lincoln's election, a number of Southern states seceded from the Union and formed the Confederate States of America.

- The Confederate attack on Fort Sumter in the harbor of Charleston, South Carolina, marked the beginning of the Civil War.

What Did You Learn?

1. What was Senator John Crittenden's last-minute proposal to save the Union?

2. Who served as the president of the Confederate States of America?

Critical Thinking

3. **Sequencing Events** Re-create the diagram below. Fill in the events leading up to the surrender of Fort Sumter and the start of the Civil War.

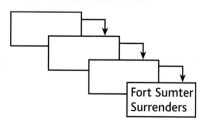

4. **The Big Ideas** What role did sectionalism play in Lincoln's victory in the 1860 election?

5. **Drawing Conclusions** Based on what you read, how would you describe President Lincoln's priorities as he took office in March 1861?

6. **Expository Writing** Write a paragraph describing what you consider to be key reasons for the Civil War.

You Decide . . .

Union or Confederacy?

President Abraham Lincoln and Jefferson Davis, president of the Confederacy, were inaugurated just several weeks apart. These excerpts from their Inaugural Addresses will help you understand differing points of view about secession from the United States in 1861.

Abraham Lincoln—Union

I hold, that . . . the Union of these States is perpetual [forever]. Perpetuity is implied, if not expressed, in the fundamental law of all national governments.

One section of our country believes slavery is right, and ought to be extended, while the other believes it is wrong, and ought not to be extended. This is the only substantial dispute. . . .

Physically speaking, we cannot separate. We cannot remove our respective sections from each other, nor build an impassable wall between them. A husband and wife may be divorced, and go out of the presence, and beyond the reach of each other; but the different parts of our country cannot do this. . . .

In your hands, my dissatisfied fellow country-men, and not in mine, is the momentous issue of civil war.

—from Abraham Lincoln's
First Inaugural Address,
March 4, 1861

Abraham Lincoln ▶

Jefferson Davis—Confederacy

Our present condition [as a new confederacy] . . . illustrates the American idea that governments rest upon the consent of the governed, and that it is the right of the people to alter or abolish governments whenever they become destructive of the ends for which they were established. . . . In this they [the people of the Confederacy] merely asserted a right which the Declaration of Independence of 1776 had defined to be inalienable. . . . [I]t is by abuse of language that their act has been denominated [called] a revolution. They formed a new alliance, but within each State its government has remained, the rights of person and property have not been disturbed. . . .

As a necessity, not a choice, we have resorted to the remedy of separation; and henceforth our energies must be directed to the conduct of our own affairs, and the [continuation] of the Confederacy which we have formed. If a just perception of mutual interest shall permit us peaceably to pursue our separate political career, my most earnest desire will have been fulfilled. But if this be denied to us . . . [we will be forced] to appeal to arms. . . .

—from Jefferson Davis's
Inaugural Address,
February 18, 1861

◀ **Jefferson Davis**

You Be The Historian

DBQ Document-Based Questions

1. According to Lincoln, what was the major disagreement between the North and South?

2. What did Lincoln compare the United States to?

3. Did Lincoln and Davis say anything in their addresses that was similar? Explain.

Analyzing Primary Sources

Challenging Slavery

In the days leading up to the Civil War, people throughout the United States debated about economics, states' rights, and the institution of slavery. Antislavery society and religious group members were vocal, as were politicians, business people, and plantation owners. In some cases, the voices of both free and enslaved African Americans could be heard.

Read the passages on pages 562 and 563 and answer the questions that follow.

Banner celebrating Garrison's abolitionist ▶ newspaper, *The Liberator*

Reader's Dictionary

severity (suh • VEHR • uh • tee): being strict, stern, or harsh

moderation (MAH • duh • RAY • shuhn): limiting or controlling something so as not to be extreme or excessive

ravisher: one who carries somebody or something off by violent force

extricate (EHK • struh • KAYT): to release somebody or something with difficulty from being constrained

equivocate (ih • KWIH • vuh • KAYT): to speak vaguely, especially in order to mislead

dissolution (DIH • suh • LOO • shun): the act or process of dissolving

atone (uh • TOHN): to make amends

The Liberator

Through *his newspaper,* The Liberator, *abolitionist William Lloyd Garrison demanded the immediate emancipation of all slaves. Founded in 1831 in Boston,* The Liberator *continued publishing antislavery messages under Garrison's leadership for 35 years. In one edition, he wrote:*

[I support] the "self-evident truth" . . . that all men are created equal, and endowed by their Creator with certain inalienable rights. . . .

I am aware that many object to the **severity** of my language; but is there not cause for severity? I *will be* as harsh as truth and as uncompromising as justice. On this subject I do not wish to think or speak, or write with **moderation.** No! No! Tell a man whose house is on fire to give a moderate alarm; tell him to moderately rescue his wife from the hands of a **ravisher;** tell the mother to gradually **extricate** her babe from the fire into which it has fallen—but urge me not to use moderation in a cause like the present. I am in earnest; I will not **equivocate;** I will not excuse; I will not retreat a single inch—AND I WILL BE HEARD. . . .

On the Eve of War

Mrs. *Eugene McLean kept a diary of her experiences as an Army officer's wife during the Civil War. This passage describes her thoughts after the fall of Fort Sumter. Her husband joined the Confederate Army.*

Strange, strange, strange, how we have accustomed ourselves to the thought, and accept the **dissolution** of the Union as a natural consequence! Whom have we to blame for bringing us to this state . . . ? Wherever the fault lies, I do not envy them their feelings in this hour, and fear both sections will **atone** in mourning and ashes for the crime.

Swing Low, Sweet Chariot

S*pirituals—songs of salvation—provided the enslaved African Americans who wrote and sang them with not only a measure of comfort in bleak times but with a means for communicating secretly among themselves. Here is an example of a popular song that was sung by enslaved African Americans at work:*

Swing low, sweet chariot,
Coming for to carry me home,
Swing low, sweet chariot,
Coming for to carry me home.
I looked over Jordan, and what did I see,

▲ **The spiritual is a unique and important part of African American history.**

Coming for to carry me home;
A band of angels coming after me,
Coming for to carry me home.
If you get there before I do,
Coming for to carry me home;
Tell all my friends I'm coming too,
Coming for to carry me home.
Swing low, sweet chariot,
Coming for to carry me home,
Swing low, sweet chariot,
Coming for to carry me home.
—*Selected Famous Negro Spirituals*

 Document-Based Questions

The Liberator

1. Who do you think Garrison is referring to when he states that he is aware that many object to the severity of his language?

2. What analogies does Garrison use to make his point about the need for severity over moderation?

On the Eve of War

3. How does the author feel about secession?

4. Does she blame either the Union or the Confederacy for the war? Explain.

Swing Low, Sweet Chariot

5. What does the phrase "swing low, sweet chariot" mean? What is meant by the lines "If you get there before I do . . . Tell all my friends I'm coming too"?

6. Why do you think enslaved African Americans sang this song?

Read to Write

7. Review each of the readings. Do you think these were written to inform, to entertain, to tell a story, or to persuade the reader? Write a one-page paper and give reasons for your answer.

Review Content Vocabulary

1. Use the following terms to write a brief paragraph describing events in the United States just prior to 1860.

   secede

   fugitive

   civil war

   abolitionist

Review the Main Ideas

Section 1 • Abolitionists

2. How was William Lloyd Garrison effective in the antislavery movement?

3. What was the purpose of the American Colonization Society?

Section 2 • Slavery and the West

4. What was the purpose of the Missouri Compromise?

5. List the five parts of the Compromise of 1850.

Section 3 • A Nation Dividing

6. What was Stephen Douglas's solution to the slavery issue in the Kansas and Nebraska territories?

7. How did abolitionists and African Americans resist the Fugitive Slave Act?

Section 4 • Challenges to Slavery

8. How did Abraham Lincoln become a national figure in politics?

9. What was the *Dred Scott* decision? What did it mean for those opposed to slavery?

Section 5 • Secession and War

10. Why were there four parties and candidates in the presidential election of 1860?

11. How did Lincoln plan to prevent secession?

Critical Thinking

12. **Evaluate** Why was the balance of free and slave states in the Senate such an important issue?

13. **Analyze** What contributions did Frederick Douglass make to the abolitionist movement? Was he successful? Describe your conclusions in a paragraph.

Geography Skills

Study the map below and answer the following questions.

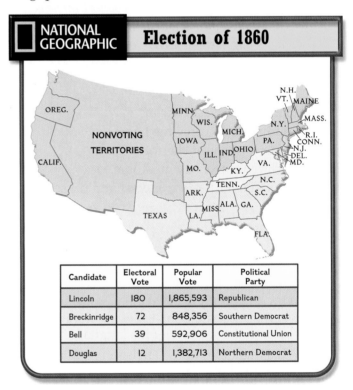

NATIONAL GEOGRAPHIC — **Election of 1860**

Candidate	Electoral Vote	Popular Vote	Political Party
Lincoln	180	1,865,593	Republican
Breckinridge	72	848,356	Southern Democrat
Bell	39	592,906	Constitutional Union
Douglas	12	1,382,713	Northern Democrat

14. **Location** Which states supported Douglas?

15. **Region** In what region(s) was the Republican Party strongest?

16. **Region** In what region did Breckinridge find support?

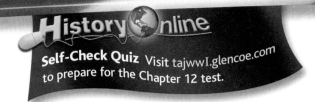
History Online
Self-Check Quiz Visit tajwwI.glencoe.com
to prepare for the Chapter 12 test.

Read to Write

17. **The Big Ideas** **Conflict and War**
Make a list of 10 important events that you read about in this chapter. Select the two events that you think did the most to create conflict between the North and South. Write a one-page essay in which you explain how these events led to war.

18. **Using Your FOLDABLES** Use the information you listed in your foldable to create a brief study guide for the chapter. For each section, your study guide should include at least five questions that focus on the main ideas.

Using Academic Vocabulary

19. Write two words that are related to each of the following academic vocabulary words.
publication **controversy** **inevitable**

Building Citizenship

20. **Making Compromises** With a partner, think of a controversial issue that is a source of disagreement today. Take opposite sides on the issue; then work together to come up with a list of three compromises that would make the solution to this problem acceptable to both sides.

Linking Past and Present

21. **Political Parties** Search the Internet for a list of political parties in existence today. Research to find the date that the party was founded and its current goals. Create a table that briefly summarizes this information. Then compare your table to the political parties discussed in Chapter 12.

Reviewing Skills

22. **READING SKILL** **Making Inferences**
Reread Jefferson Davis's Inaugural Address on page 561. How do you think Davis feels about his new role? How does he feel about the prospect of war? Write a paragraph explaining your conclusions.

23. **ANALYSIS SKILL** **Sequencing Information**
Draw two time lines highlighting key figures, dates, and milestones in the abolitionist movement and the political battle over slavery.

Standardized Test Practice

Use the map below to answer the following question.

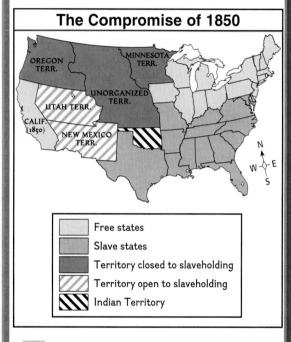

The Compromise of 1850

- Free states
- Slave states
- Territory closed to slaveholding
- Territory open to slaveholding
- Indian Territory

24 **Which of the following statements is true?**

A The Compromise of 1850 allowed the Oregon Territory to be open to slaveholding.

B The Compromise of 1850 did not make any land on the Pacific Ocean open to slaveholding.

C The Compromise of 1850 made every state touching the southern border of the United States open to slaveholding.

D The Compromise of 1850 gave the Minnesota Territory the authority to choose whether it would allow slaveholding.

The Civil War

Gettysburg Battlefield ▶

NATIONAL GEOGRAPHIC

Who & When?

1861	1863	1865
1861 Civil War begins with battle at Fort Sumter	**1863** Emancipation Proclamation issued	**1865** War ends; Lincoln assassinated

1862 Robert E. Lee commands Confederate army

The Big Ideas

History Online
Chapter Overview Visit tajwwI.glencoe.com for a preview of Chapter 13.

Section 1 — The Two Sides

Differences in economic, political, and social beliefs and practices can lead to division within a nation and have lasting consequences. The Union and the Confederacy prepared for war.

Section 2 — Early Years of the War

Conflict often brings about great change. Neither the Union nor the Confederate forces gained a strong early advantage.

Section 3 — A Call to Freedom

Reactions to social injustice can lead to reform movements. African Americans struggled for their civil rights.

Section 4 — Life During the Civil War

Citizen participation is essential to the foundation and preservation of the U.S. political system. Civilians as well as soldiers had an impact on the war effort.

Section 5 — The Way to Victory

Conflict often brings about great change. Aggressive offensives resulted in a victory for the Union.

 View the Chapter 13 video in the Glencoe Video Program.

FOLDABLES™ Study Organizer

Organizing Information Make this foldable to help you organize what you learn about the Civil War.

Step 1 Fold a sheet of paper in half from side to side.

Fold it so the left edge lies about $\frac{1}{2}$ inch from the right edge.

Step 2 Turn the paper and fold it into thirds.

Step 3 Unfold and cut the top layer only along both folds.

This will make three tabs.

Step 4 Label your foldable as shown.

Before the War | During the War | After the War

The Civil War

Reading and Writing As you read the chapter, list events that occurred before, during, and after the Civil War under the appropriate tabs of your foldable.

Chapter 13

Get Ready to Read

Evaluation

READING SKILL

1 Learn It!

Good readers evaluate information as they read. That means they draw conclusions and determine the significance of events, ideas, and people that they read about. As you read history, ask yourself such questions as:

- What caused this person or group of people to react that way? In the same situation, how did other people in history react?
- What words has the author chosen to describe this event or person? How do these words help me form an opinion?
- Is the information that I'm reading based on fact or opinion?

Keep these questions in mind as you read the excerpt below.

> Gone were the parades and masses of volunteers, the fancy uniforms, and the optimism of the first years of the war. From 1862 until 1865, the soldiers and civilians faced a grim conflict marked by death, destruction, and wrenching change. What endured on each side was a fierce dedication to its own cause.
>
> —*from page 605*

Reading Tip

As you read, write down some of your conclusions or opinions in your notebook. When you finish the chapter, go back and review them. Did your conclusions and opinions change?

568

② Practice It!

Turn to page 600 and read the passage called "Treating the Sick and Wounded." Then, use the questions below to evaluate what you read.

- Were women well received as nurses in Civil War hospitals?

- What did doctors and other men initially think about women assisting in hospitals?

- How do you feel about this? Do you agree?

- How did some women respond to being discouraged from nursing?

- What word did the author use to describe women who disregarded the objections of men? Does that word give you a clue to the author's opinions?

- Do you think that you would be able to work in a battlefield hospital? Why or why not?

Read to Write

You can also use your evaluation skills when you observe images. Select a painting or photograph in this chapter depicting a war scene and describe what you see and how you would evaluate it.

Image of nurse with soldier ▶

③ Apply It!

Choose one paragraph in Section 1 to evaluate. Write a list of five questions that you would ask as a part of that evaluation.

The Two Sides

Guide to Reading

Looking Back, Looking Ahead
After the firing on Fort Sumter, the Union and the Confederacy called for volunteers to fight.

Focusing on the Main Ideas
- Both the North and the South had strengths and weaknesses that helped determine their military strategies. *(page 571)*
- Soldiers in the Civil War came from every region, and each side expected an early victory. *(page 574)*

Locating Places
Richmond, Virginia

Meeting People
Jefferson Davis
Mary Todd Lincoln
Robert E. Lee
William Tecumseh Sherman

Content Vocabulary
border state
blockade (blah•KAYD)
offensive (uh•FEHN•sihv)
Rebel (REH•buhl)
Yankee (YANG•kee)

Academic Vocabulary
obvious (AHB•vee•uhs)
sufficient (suh•FIH•shuhnt)
primary (PRY•MEHR•ee)

Reading Strategy
Classifying Information As you read the section, complete a chart like the one shown here by listing the strengths and weaknesses of the Union and the Confederacy.

	Union	Confederacy
Strengths		
Weaknesses		

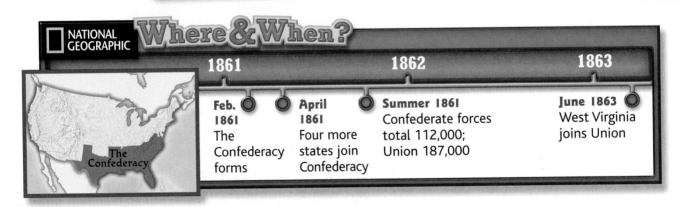

NATIONAL GEOGRAPHIC Where & When?

1861	1862	1863

The Confederacy

Feb. 1861 The Confederacy forms

April 1861 Four more states join Confederacy

Summer 1861 Confederate forces total 112,000; Union 187,000

June 1863 West Virginia joins Union

Comparing North and South

Main Idea Both the North and the South had strengths and weaknesses that helped determine their military strategies.

Reading Connection Which do you think would be more important to a country at war: an army with experienced leaders or a large number of factories? Read to find out the advantages held by both the North and the South at the beginning of the war.

An American Story

Union sergeant Driscoll directed his troops at Malvern Hill on July 1, 1862. The enemy fought fiercely, especially one young Confederate soldier. Driscoll raised his rifle, took aim, and shot the boy. As he passed the spot where the boy had fallen, Driscoll turned the daring soldier over to see what he looked like. The boy opened his eyes and faintly murmured "Father," then his eyes fluttered shut, never to open again. A Union captain, D.P. Conyngham, later wrote,

❝I will forever recollect the frantic grief of Driscoll; it was harrowing to witness. He [had killed] his son, who had gone South before the war.❞

—as quoted in *A Civil War Treasury of Tales, Legends and Folklore*

Like the Driscolls, many families were divided by the war. Neither side imagined, however, that the war would cost such a terrible price in human life. During the four years of fighting, hundreds of thousands of Americans were killed in battle.

The Border States By February 1861, seven states had left the Union and formed the Confederacy. After the Confederate bombardment of Fort Sumter, President Abraham Lincoln issued a call for troops to save the Union. His action caused Virginia, North Carolina, Tennessee, and Arkansas to join the Confederacy. These four states brought needed soldiers and supplies to the Confederacy. For its capital, the Confederacy chose **Richmond, Virginia,** a city located only about 100 miles from the Union capital of Washington, D.C.

Four states that allowed slavery—Missouri, Kentucky, Maryland, and Delaware—remained in the Union. The people of these **border states** were divided over which side to support. Missouri, Kentucky, and Maryland had such strong support for the South that the three states teetered on the brink of secession. Losing the border states would seriously damage the North. Each of the four states had strategic locations.

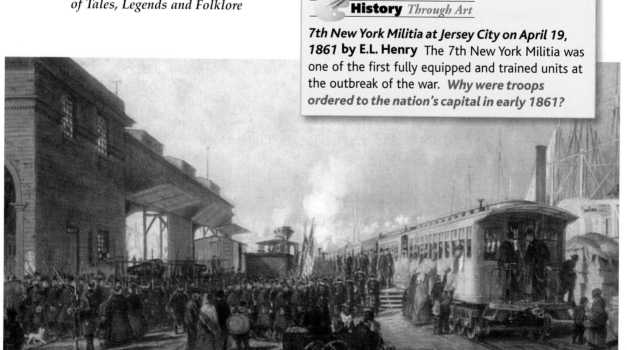

History *Through Art*

7th New York Militia at Jersey City on April 19, 1861 by E.L. Henry The 7th New York Militia was one of the first fully equipped and trained units at the outbreak of the war. *Why were troops ordered to the nation's capital in early 1861?*

Missouri could control parts of the Mississippi River and major routes to the West. Kentucky controlled the Ohio River. Delaware was close to the important Northern city of Philadelphia.

Maryland, perhaps the most important of the border states, was close to Richmond. Vital railroad lines passed through Maryland. Most importantly, Washington, D.C., lay within the state. If Maryland seceded, the North's government would be surrounded.

Maryland's key role became clear in April 1861. A mob in Baltimore attacked Northern troops; Confederate sympathizers burned railroad bridges and cut the telegraph line to Washington, isolating the capital from the rest of the North. Northern troops soon arrived and restored order, but the nation's capital had suffered some anxious days.

Remaining With the Union

Lincoln had to move cautiously to avoid upsetting people in the border states. If he announced that he aimed to end slavery, groups supporting the Confederacy might take their states out of the Union. If he ordered Northern troops into Kentucky, its citizens could decide to support the South.

In some ways, Lincoln acted boldly. He suspended some constitutional rights and used his power to arrest people who supported secession.

In the end, Lincoln's approach worked. The border states stayed in the Union, but many of their citizens joined armies of the South.

Strengths and Weaknesses

When the war began, both sides had advantages and disadvantages. How they would use those strengths and weaknesses would determine the war's outcome.

The North enjoyed the advantages of a larger population, more industry, and more abundant resources than the South. It had a better banking system, which helped raise money for the war. The North also possessed more ships and had a larger and more efficient railway network.

The North also faced disadvantages. Bringing the Southern states back into the Union would be difficult. The North would have to invade the South—a large area filled with a hostile population. To win the war, the North had to occupy the Confederacy's territory and subdue a population of millions. In addition, the Southern people's support for the war remained strong. Recalling the example of the American Revolution, when the smaller, weaker colonies had won independence from wealthy Great Britain, many believed the South had a good chance of winning.

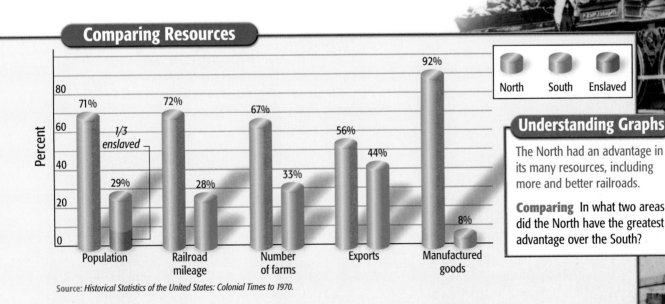

Comparing Resources

Percent

Population	71%	29%	1/3 enslaved
Railroad mileage	72%	28%	
Number of farms	67%	33%	
Exports	56%	44%	
Manufactured goods	92%	8%	

North South Enslaved

Source: *Historical Statistics of the United States: Colonial Times to 1970.*

Understanding Graphs

The North had an advantage in its many resources, including more and better railroads.

Comparing In what two areas did the North have the greatest advantage over the South?

One Northern advantage was not **obvious** until later. Both sides greatly underestimated Abraham Lincoln. His dedication and intelligence would lead the North to victory.

One of the main advantages for Southerners was fighting in familiar territory—defending their land, their homes, and their way of life.

The military leadership of the South, at least at first, was superior to the North's. Southern families had a strong tradition of military training and service, and military college graduates provided the South with a large pool of officers. Overseeing the Southern effort was Confederate president **Jefferson Davis,** a West Point graduate and an experienced soldier.

The South also faced some disadvantages. It had a smaller population of free men to draw upon in building an army. It also possessed very few factories to manufacture weapons and other supplies, and it produced less than half as much food as the North. With less than half the miles of railroad tracks and vastly fewer trains than the North, the Confederate government had difficulty delivering food, weapons, and other supplies to its troops.

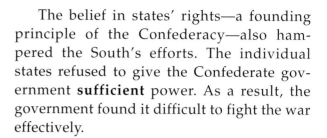

The belief in states' rights—a founding principle of the Confederacy—also hampered the South's efforts. The individual states refused to give the Confederate government **sufficient** power. As a result, the government found it difficult to fight the war effectively.

War Aims and Strategy The North and the South entered the Civil War with different goals. The main goal of the North was to bring the Southern states back into the Union. Ending slavery was not a major Northern goal at first, but this changed as the war continued.

The Union's plan for winning the war included three main strategies. First, the North would **blockade** (blah•KAYD), or close, Southern ports to prevent supplies from reaching the South—and to prevent the South from earning money by exporting cotton. Second, the Union intended to gain control of the Mississippi River to cut Southern supply lines and to divide the Confederacy. Third, the North planned to take control of Richmond, Virginia, the Confederate capital.

For the South, the **primary** aim of the war was to win recognition as an independent nation. Independence would allow Southerners to preserve their traditional way of life—a way of life that included slavery.

To achieve this goal, the South worked out a defensive strategy. It planned to defend its homeland, holding on to as much territory as possible until the North tired of fighting. The South expected that Britain and France, which imported large quantities of Southern cotton, would pressure the North to end the war to restore their cotton supplies.

During the war, Southern leaders sometimes changed strategy and took the **offensive** (uh•FEHN•sihv)—went on the attack. They moved their armies northward to threaten Washington, D.C., and other Northern cities, hoping to persuade the North that it could not win the war.

✓ Reading Check **Compare** What advantages and disadvantages did each side possess?

American People at War

Main Idea Soldiers in the Civil War came from every region, and each side expected an early victory.

Reading Connection What motivates men and women to join the armed forces today? Read to find out about the backgrounds of the soldiers in the Union and Confederate armies.

The Civil War was more than a war between the states. It often pitted brother against brother, parents against their children, and neighbor against neighbor.

American Against American

The leaders from both North and South—and their families—felt these divisions. President Lincoln's wife, **Mary Todd Lincoln,** had several relatives who fought in the Confederate army. John Crittenden, a senator from Kentucky, had two sons who became generals in the war—one for the Confederacy and one for the Union. Officers on both sides—including Confederate general **Robert E. Lee,** and Union generals George McClellan and **William Tecumseh Sherman**—had attended the United States Military Academy at West Point, never dreaming that they would one day command forces fighting against each other.

Who Were the Soldiers?

Most of the soldiers were young. The average recruit was 25 years old, but about 40 percent were 21 or younger. Ted Upson of Indiana was only 16 when he begged his father to let him join the Union army. His father replied, "This Union your ancestors and mine helped to make must be saved from destruction."

William Stone from Louisiana rushed to join the Confederate army after the attack on Fort Sumter. His sister Kate wrote that he was "wild to be off to Virginia. He so fears that the fighting will be over before he can get there."

Soldiers came from every region and all walks of life. Most, though, came from farms. Almost half of the North's troops and more than 60 percent of the South's had owned or worked on farms. The Union army did not permit African Americans to join at first, but they did serve later. Lincoln's early terms of enlistment asked governors to supply soldiers for 90 days. When the conflict did not end quickly, soldiers' terms became longer.

By the summer of 1861, the Confederate army had about 112,000 soldiers, who were sometimes called **Rebels** (REH•buhlz). The Union had about 187,000 soldiers, or **Yankees** (YANG•keez), as they were also known. By the end of the war, about 850,000 men fought for the Confederacy and about 2.1 million men fought for the Union.

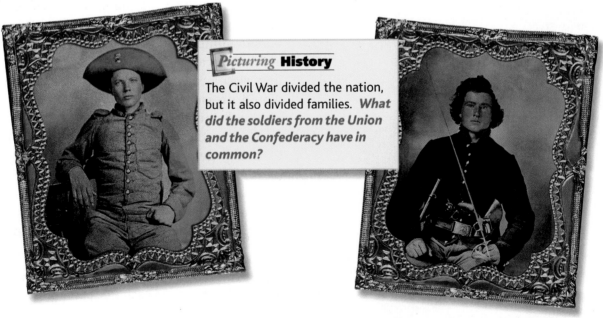

Picturing **History**

The Civil War divided the nation, but it also divided families. *What did the soldiers from the Union and the Confederacy have in common?*

The Union number included just under 200,000 African Americans. About 10,000 Hispanic soldiers fought in the conflict.

False Hopes When the war began, each side expected an early victory. A Confederate soldier from a town in Alabama expected the war to be over well within a year because "we are going to kill the last Yankee before that time if there is any fight in them still." Northerners were just as confident that they would beat the South quickly.

Some leaders saw the situation more clearly. Northern general William Tecumseh Sherman wrote, "I think it is to be a long war—very long—much longer than any politician thinks." The first spring of the war proved that Sherman's prediction was accurate. From the first battle, both sides learned there would be no quick victory.

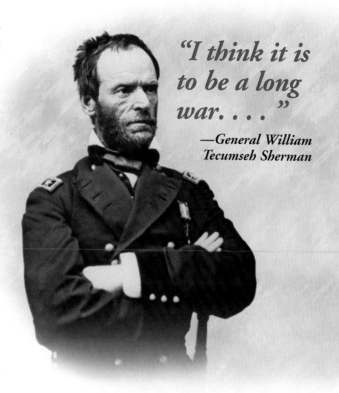

"I think it is to be a long war. . . ."

—*General William Tecumseh Sherman*

✓ **Reading Check** **Compare** Which side had the larger fighting force?

History Online

Study Central Need help understanding the start of the Civil War? Visit tajww1.glencoe.com and click on Study Central.

Section 1 Review

Reading Summary

Review the Main Ideas

- The North hoped to use its large number of soldiers and industry to cut off supplies to the South, and the South planned to fight defensively and win foreign recognition.

- Many of the soldiers from both North and South were young, had come from farms, and mistakenly expected a short war.

What Did You Learn?

1. Why were the border states important to the North and the South?

2. Why was the Civil War especially difficult for families?

Critical Thinking

3. **Comparing** Create a diagram to compare Northern and Southern aims and strategies.

	North	**South**
Aims		
Strategies		

4. **Analyze** How did a strong belief in states' rights affect the South during the war?

5. **The Big Ideas** How did the South's economy differ from that of the North, and how did it place the South at a disadvantage during the war?

6. **READING** **Evaluating Text** Reread the passage at the beginning of Section 1 about Union sergeant Driscoll. Using your evaluation skills, write a short paragraph that explains why the author chose to include this account. How does it relate to what you read in that section?

Early Years of the War

Guide to Reading

Looking Back, Looking Ahead
In 1861, the Union and Confederacy expected a brief war and early victory.

Focusing on the (Main Ideas)
- The North realized with the first major battle that the war would be a long, difficult struggle. *(page 577)*
- The North set up a blockade along the South's coastline, which caused serious problems for the South. *(page 578)*
- The action shifted to the West after the First Battle of Bull Run as each side reorganized its forces. *(page 579)*
- Battles continued, and after several Southern victories, Lincoln removed General McClellan for his failure to act in these battles. *(page 580)*

Locating Places
Norfolk, Virginia

Meeting People
"Stonewall" Jackson
George B. McClellan
Ulysses S. Grant
David Farragut (FAR•uh•guht)

Content Vocabulary
ironclad
casualty (KAZH•wuhl•tee)

Academic Vocabulary
reinforce (REE•uhn•FOHRS)
abandon (uh•BAN•duhn)
prospect (PRAH•spehkt)
evaluate (ih•VAL•yuh•WAYT)
encounter (ihn•KOWN•tuhr)

Reading Strategy
Classifying Information As you read, describe the outcome of each of these battles on a chart like the one shown.

Battle	Outcome
First Battle of Bull Run (Manassas)	
Monitor v. *Merrimack*	
Antietam	

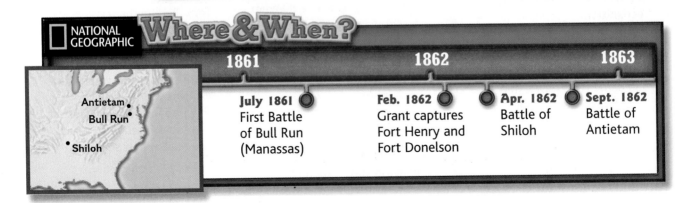

NATIONAL GEOGRAPHIC **Where & When?**

1861   1862   1863

July 1861 First Battle of Bull Run (Manassas)

Feb. 1862 Grant captures Fort Henry and Fort Donelson

Apr. 1862 Battle of Shiloh

Sept. 1862 Battle of Antietam

Antietam
Bull Run
Shiloh

The First Battle

Main Idea The North realized with the first major battle that the war would be a long, difficult struggle.

Reading Connection What goes through the mind of a soldier in battle for the first time? Read to learn about the Battle of Bull Run and the soldiers involved.

An American Story

Sunday, July 21, 1861, was a pleasant, sunny day in Washington, D.C. Hundreds of cheerful residents left the city and planned to picnic while watching the first battle between the Union and the Confederate armies. Expecting to see Union troops crush the Rebels, they looked forward to a quick victory. The Confederate soldiers also expected a quick victory.

> 66 [The soldiers] carried dress suits with them, and any quantity of fine linen. . . . Every soldier, nearly, had a servant with him, and a whole lot of spoons and forks, so as to live comfortably and elegantly in camp. . . . 99
>
> —Mary A. Ward,
> *Voices of the Civil War*

First Battle of Bull Run This first major battle of the Civil War was fought in northern Virginia, about five miles from a town called Manassas Junction near Bull Run—a small river in the area. Usually called the First Battle of Bull Run, it began when about 30,000 inexperienced Union troops attacked a smaller, equally inexperienced Confederate force.

The Yankees drove the Confederates back at first. Then the Rebels rallied, inspired by **reinforcements** under General Thomas Jackson. Jackson, who fought the enemy heroically "like a stone wall," became known thereafter as **"Stonewall" Jackson.**

The Confederates surged forward with a strange, unearthly scream that came to be known as the Rebel yell. Terrified, the Northern soldiers began to drop their guns and packs and run. One Union soldier wrote:

> 66 As we gained the cover of the woods the stampede became even more frightful, for the baggage wagons and ambulances became entangled with the artillery and rendered the scene even more dreadful than the battle. . . . 99
>
> —Corporal Samuel J. English,
> letter to his mother, July 1861

The Union army began an orderly retreat that quickly became a mad stampede when the retreating Union troops collided with the civilians, fleeing in panic back to Washington, D.C.

A Shock for the North The outcome of the battle shocked the North, but President Abraham Lincoln was ready to act. He issued a call for more volunteers for the army. He signed two bills requesting a total of 1 million soldiers, who would serve for three years. Volunteers soon crowded into recruiting offices. Lincoln also appointed a new general, **George B. McClellan,** to head the Union army of the East—called the Army of the Potomac—and to organize the troops.

✓ Reading Check **Explain** How did the First Battle of Bull Run change expectations about the war?

◀ Civil War cannon

War at Sea

Main Idea) The North set up a blockade along the South's coastline, which caused serious problems for the South.

Reading Connection Have you ever toured an old warship? Read to learn about the first battle between metal-covered ships.

Even before Bull Run, Lincoln had ordered a naval blockade of Southern ports. An effective blockade would prevent the South from exporting its cotton and from importing the supplies necessary to continue the war.

The blockade caused serious problems for the South. Goods such as coffee, shoes, nails, and salt—as well as guns and ammunition—were in short supply in the South throughout the war.

The *Monitor* Versus the *Merrimack*

The South did not intend to let the blockade go unchallenged. Southerners salvaged the *Merrimack*, a Union warship that Northern forces had **abandoned** when Confederate forces seized the naval shipyard in **Norfolk, Virginia.** The Confederates rebuilt the wooden ship, covered it with thick iron plates, and renamed it the *Virginia*.

On March 8, 1862, this **ironclad,** or warship, attacked a group of Union ships off the coast of Virginia. The North's wooden warships could not damage the Confederate ship—shells simply bounced off its sides.

The North sent an iron-clad ship of its own, the *Monitor,* to engage the Confederate ship in battle. On March 9, the two ironclads exchanged fire, but neither ship could sink the other. The Union succeeded in keeping the *Merrimack* in the harbor, so it never again threatened Northern ships. The battle marked a new age in naval warfare—the first battle between two metal-covered ships. Both the North and the South used these ships as models to build more iron-clad ships.

✓ Reading Check) **Explain** What was the significance of the battle of the ironclads?

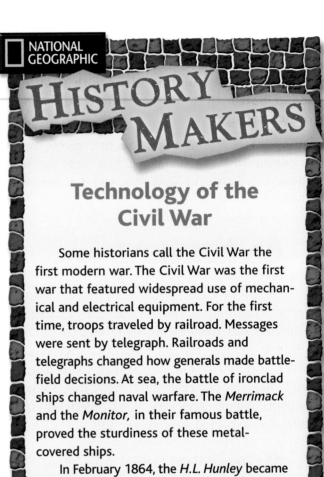

NATIONAL GEOGRAPHIC
HISTORY MAKERS

Technology of the Civil War

Some historians call the Civil War the first modern war. The Civil War was the first war that featured widespread use of mechanical and electrical equipment. For the first time, troops traveled by railroad. Messages were sent by telegraph. Railroads and telegraphs changed how generals made battlefield decisions. At sea, the battle of ironclad ships changed naval warfare. The *Merrimack* and the *Monitor,* in their famous battle, proved the sturdiness of these metal-covered ships.

In February 1864, the *H.L. Hunley* became the first submarine to sink an enemy warship in combat. *The Hunley,* however, never returned to port. For more than 130 years, the disappearance of the submarine remained a mystery. In August 2000, a team of divers located the long-lost ship, and the *H.L. Hunley* was raised from the waters of Charleston Harbor in South Carolina.

▲ Ironclads marked the beginning of the modern, armored, self-propelled warship.

War in the West

Main Idea The action shifted to the West after the First Battle of Bull Run as each side reorganized its forces.

Reading Connection Do you have a nickname, or know someone who does? Read to find out how General Ulysses S. Grant earned his unusual nickname.

After the First Battle of Bull Run in July 1861, the war in the East settled into a stalemate as each side built its strength. Generals focused on training raw recruits, turning civilians into soldiers. For a while, the action shifted to the West.

Early Victories for the North

One of the North's primary goals in the West was to gain control of the Mississippi and Tennessee Rivers. This would split the Confederacy and hinder Southern efforts to transport goods.

The Union launched its operations in the West from Cairo, Illinois. The Union commander at Cairo was **Ulysses S. Grant.** Early in 1862, Grant was ordered to move against Confederate forces in Kentucky and Tennessee. On February 6, with the aid of a fleet of newly made ironclads, Grant captured Fort Henry on the Tennessee River. Ten days later, Grant captured Fort Donelson on the Cumberland. When the Confederate commander at Fort Donelson realized he was trapped, he asked Grant for his terms. Grant's reply was:

> **❝ No terms except an unconditional and immediate surrender can be accepted. ❞**
>
> —Ulysses S. Grant,
> note to General Simon Buckner

"Unconditional Surrender" Grant became the North's new hero. Ulysses S. Grant had earned a new nickname. Grant's victories helped secure the lower Tennessee River. They also opened a path for Union troops to march into Tennessee, Mississippi, and Alabama.

The Battle of Shiloh

General Grant and about 40,000 troops then headed south along the Tennessee River toward Corinth, Mississippi, an important railroad junction. In early April 1862, the Union army camped at Pittsburg Landing, 20 miles from Corinth. Nearby was a church named Shiloh. Additional Union forces came from Nashville to join Grant.

Early on the morning of April 6, Confederate forces launched a surprise attack on the Union troops. The Battle of Shiloh lasted two days, with some of the most bitter, bloody fighting of the war. The first day, the Confederates drove Grant and his troops back to the Tennessee River. The second day, the Union forces recovered. Aided by the 25,000 troops from Nashville and shelling by gunboats on the river, they defeated the Confederates, who withdrew to Corinth.

The losses in the Battle of Shiloh were enormous. Together the two armies suffered more than 20,000 **casualties** (KAZH•wuhl•teez)—people who are killed or wounded. Confederate general Johnston also died in the bloodbath.

After their narrow victory at Shiloh, Union forces gained control of Corinth on May 30. Memphis, Tennessee, fell to Union armies on June 6. The North seemed well on its way to controlling the Mississippi River.

New Orleans Falls

A few weeks after Shiloh, the North won another important victory. On April 25, 1862, Union naval forces under **David Farragut** (FAR•uh•guht) captured New Orleans, Louisiana, the South's largest city. Farragut, who was of Spanish descent, had grown up in the South but remained loyal to the Union. His capture of New Orleans, near the mouth of the Mississippi River, meant that the Confederacy could no longer use the river to carry its goods to sea. Together with Grant's victories to the north, Farragut's capture of New Orleans gave the Union control of almost the entire Mississippi River.

✓ Reading Check Analyze Why was control of the Mississippi River important to the North and to the South?

War in the East

Main Idea Battles continued, and after several Southern victories, Lincoln removed General McClellan for his failure to act in these battles.

Reading Connection Have you heard the expression "he who hesitates is lost"? Read and find out about a Union general whose hesitancy cost many lives.

While Union and Confederate troops were struggling for control of Tennessee and the Mississippi River, another major military campaign was being waged in the east. General George B. McClellan led the Union army in the east.

McClellan Hesitates In the East, General McClellan was training the Army of the Potomac to be an effective fighting force. An expert at training soldiers, McClellan reorganized and drilled the Army of the Potomac.

However, when faced with the **prospect** of battle, McClellan was cautious and worried

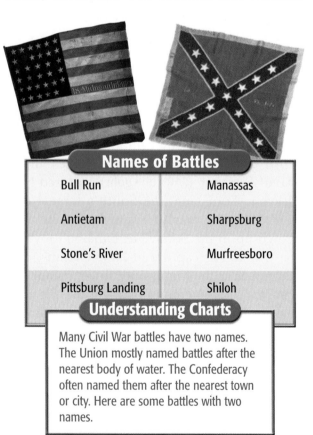

Names of Battles	
Bull Run	Manassas
Antietam	Sharpsburg
Stone's River	Murfreesboro
Pittsburg Landing	Shiloh

Understanding Charts

Many Civil War battles have two names. The Union mostly named battles after the nearest body of water. The Confederacy often named them after the nearest town or city. Here are some battles with two names.

that his troops were not ready. He hesitated to fight because of reports that overestimated the size of the Rebel forces. Finally, in March 1862, the Army of the Potomac was ready for action. Its goal was to capture Richmond, the Confederate capital.

Instead of advancing directly overland to Richmond as Lincoln wished, McClellan moved his huge army by ship to a peninsula between the York and the James Rivers southeast of the city. From there he began a major offensive known as the Peninsular Campaign. The operation took many weeks.

Time passed and opportunities to attack slipped away as General McClellan readied his troops and tried to **evaluate** the enemy's strength. Lincoln, constantly prodding McClellan to fight, ended one message with an urgent plea: "You must act." McClellan did not act. His delays allowed the Confederates to prepare their defense of Richmond. At the end of June, the Union forces finally met the Confederates in a series of **encounters** known as the Seven Days' Battles.

In these battles, Confederate general Robert E. Lee took command of the army opposing McClellan. Before the battles began, Lee's cavalry leader, James E.B. (J.E.B.) Stuart, performed a daring tactic. He led his 1,200 troops in a circle around the Union army, gathering vital information about Union positions and boosting Southern morale. Lee's forces eventually drove the Yankees back. The Union troops had failed to capture Richmond.

Gloom in the North Reports from Richmond disheartened the North. Another call was made for volunteers—300,000 this time—but the response was slow. The Southern strategy of making the North weary of war seemed to be working. The defeat had not been complete, however. McClellan's army had been pushed back, but it was larger than Lee's and still only 25 miles from Richmond. President Lincoln ordered him to move his army back to northern Virginia and join the troops led by Major General John Pope.

Stonewall Jackson's forces moved north to attack Pope's supply base at Manassas. Jackson's troops marched 50 miles in two days and were then joined by the rest of Lee's army. On August 29, 1862, Pope attacked the approaching Confederates and started the Second Battle of Bull Run. The battle ended in a Confederate victory. Richmond was no longer threatened. Instead, the situation of the two sides was completely reversed. Lee and the Confederates now stood only 20 miles from Washington, D.C.

History Online

Student Web Activity Visit tajww1.glencoe.com and click on *Chapter 13—Student Web Activities* for an activity on the Second Battle of Bull Run.

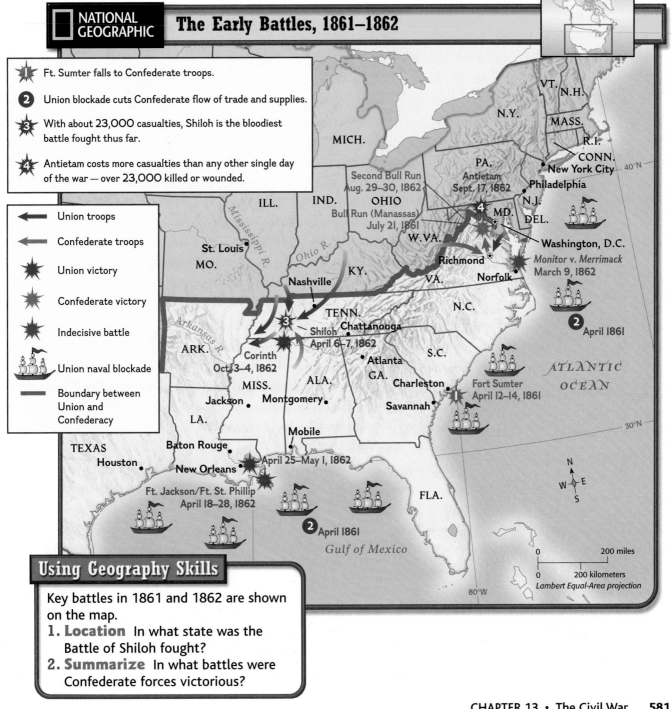

NATIONAL GEOGRAPHIC · The Early Battles, 1861–1862

1 Ft. Sumter falls to Confederate troops.

2 Union blockade cuts Confederate flow of trade and supplies.

3 With about 23,000 casualties, Shiloh is the bloodiest battle fought thus far.

4 Antietam costs more casualties than any other single day of the war — over 23,000 killed or wounded.

← Union troops
← Confederate troops
✳ Union victory
✳ Confederate victory
✳ Indecisive battle
⛵ Union naval blockade
— Boundary between Union and Confederacy

Second Bull Run Aug. 29–30, 1862
Antietam Sept. 17, 1862
Bull Run (Manassas) July 21, 1861
Monitor v. Merrimack March 9, 1862
Shiloh April 6–7, 1862
Corinth Oct. 3–4, 1862
Fort Sumter April 12–14, 1861
Ft. Jackson/Ft. St. Phillip April 18–28, 1862
April 25–May 1, 1862
2 April 1861
2 April 1861

Using Geography Skills

Key battles in 1861 and 1862 are shown on the map.
1. **Location** In what state was the Battle of Shiloh fought?
2. **Summarize** In what battles were Confederate forces victorious?

Lee Enters Maryland Following these Southern victories, Confederate president Jefferson Davis ordered Lee to launch an offensive into Maryland, northwest of Washington. He hoped another victory would win aid from Great Britain and France. Lee also issued a proclamation urging the people of Maryland to join the Confederacy.

As Lee's army marched into Maryland in September 1862, McClellan and 80,000 Union troops moved slowly after them. On September 13, the North had an extraordinary piece of good luck. In a field near Frederick, Maryland, two Union soldiers found a copy of Lee's orders for his army wrapped around three cigars. The bundle had probably been dropped by a Southern officer.

Now McClellan knew exactly what Lee planned to do. He also learned that Lee's army was divided into four parts. This provided McClellan with an opportunity to overwhelm Lee's army one piece at a time.

The Battle of Antietam Once again, McClellan was overly cautious. He waited four days before he decided to attack the Confederates. This enabled Lee to gather most of his forces together near Sharpsburg, Maryland, along the Antietam Creek.

The Union and the Confederate armies clashed on September 17 in the Battle of Antietam. It was the single bloodiest day of the entire war. A Union officer wrote that

> 66 In the time that I am writing every stalk of corn in [cornfields to the north] was cut as closely as could have been done with a knife, and the slain lay in rows precisely as they had stood in their ranks a few moments before. 99
>
> —**Major General Joseph Hooker,** *Eyewitness Accounts*

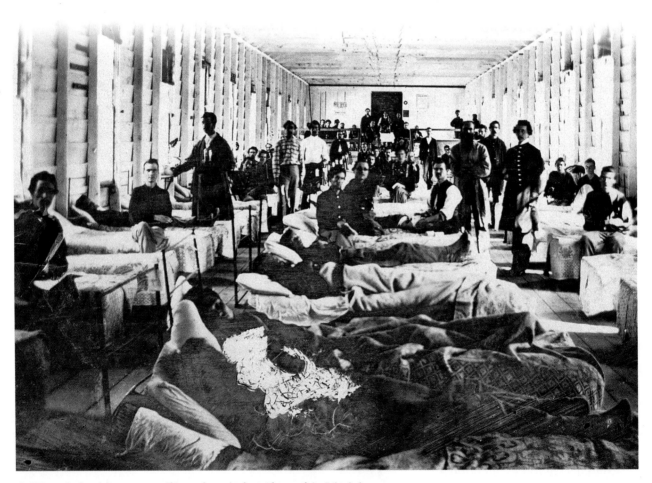

▲ Wounded soldiers at a military hospital at Alexandria, Virginia

By the time the fighting ended, close to 6,000 Union and Confederate soldiers lay dead or dying, and another 17,000 were seriously wounded. Although both armies suffered heavy losses, neither was destroyed.

The day after the battle, Lee withdrew to Virginia. The Confederate retreat allowed the Union troops to claim victory. However, McClellan, who had been ordered by President Lincoln to "destroy the rebel army," did not pursue the Confederate troops. The president, disgusted with McClellan's failure to follow up his victory, removed McClellan from his command in November. Lincoln placed General Ambrose Burnside in command.

The Battle of Antietam was a crucial victory for the Union. The British government had been ready to intervene in the war as a mediator if Lee's invasion had succeeded. It had also begun making plans to recognize the Confederacy in the event the North rejected mediation. With Lee's defeat, the British decided to withhold its support, and the South lost its best chance at gaining international recognition and support.

Antietam had a profound impact on the war. The Army of the Potomac finally gained some confidence, having forced Lee and his soldiers back south. More important, the battle marked a major change in Northern war aims. President Lincoln used the battle to take action against slavery.

Reading Check Summarize What was the outcome of the Seven Days' Battles?

Study Central Need help understanding early battles of the Civil War? Visit tajwwI.glencoe.com and click on Study Central.

Section 2 Review

Reading Summary

Review the Main Ideas

- Following the first major battle of the war, the Battle of Bull Run, which ended in a Confederate victory, the Union called for more troops and planned for a long war.

- A new era in naval warfare emerged as ironclad ships, belonging to the Union and Confederacy, fought for the first time.

- The Union gained a number of victories in the West as the North and South fought for control of the Mississippi River.

- In the East, the Union faced defeat, although a Confederate invasion of Maryland was turned back at the Battle of Antietam.

What Did You Learn?

1. Explain why the North wanted to blockade the South.

2. Which general won victories for the Union at Fort Henry and Fort Donelson? What nickname did he earn at the second battle?

Critical Thinking

3. **Drawing Conclusions** Why was control of the Mississippi River important? Use a diagram like the one shown here.

4. **Analyze** Why was Union general McClellan not effective as a military commander?

5. **The Big Ideas** What was the importance of the Union victory at the Battle of Antietam?

6. **ANALYSIS** Analyze You read about General Lee's battle orders that were dropped and found by a Union soldier. Write a short paragraph explaining the role of chance and error in this discovery and McClellan's use of the information.

Rifles for Watie

By Harold Keith

Before You Read

The Scene: This selection takes place at the Battle of Prairie Grove in northwest Arkansas. The date is December 7, 1862.

The Characters: Jeff Bussey is a private in the First Kansas Regiment of Infantry. His best friends, Noah Babbitt, Bill Earie, and Big Jake Lonegan are all in the same company, and Captain Clardy commands it. Mary and Bess are his sisters, and Ring is his dog. The Union army is under General Blunt.

The Plot: Jeff joined the army to defend his home from Confederate raiders. They were destroying the homes and farms of Union supporters in Kansas. Jeff has wanted to be in a battle since he joined the army.

Vocabulary Preview

acrid: smelling or tasting bitter

din: loud or confused sound

doleful: expressing grief; sad

gaunt: very thin and bony

ominously: in a way that is a sign of future trouble or evil

perplexed: puzzled

ricocheting: hitting a hard surface lightly and bouncing back

sheepishly: acting in an embarrassed way after becoming aware of a mistake

Have you ever wanted to do something because it seemed exciting? Was it as you imagined it would be, or was it different? Jeff is about to have his wish to be in a battle fulfilled. What will it be like?

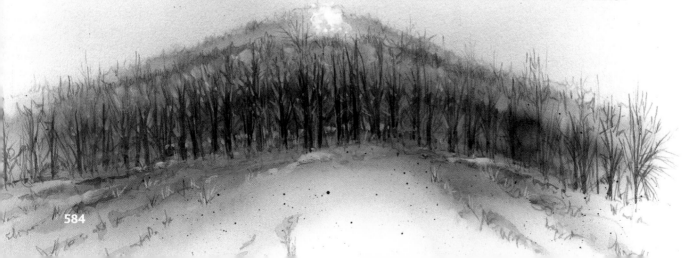

As You Read

Writers may choose words and events to state an opinion. For example, Jeff lives with Confederates in another part of Rifles for Watie. *During this experience, he discovers that they are no different than any other people. As you read this selection, notice the kinds of words and events the author used. Think about what the writer may be saying concerning war.*

Jeff saw a tiny, circular puff of white smoke blossom above the trees. Then suddenly on the prairie some fifty yards in front of their line, a dash of dust, and something whizzed noisily over their heads, buzzing like a monster bee.

"Blam!"

Jeff dove flat on his stomach. He felt a painful jar as several of his comrades jumped in on top of him to escape the glancing rebel cannon ball.

"Boys, if I ain't flat enough, won't some o' you please jump on me and mash me flatter?" Bill Earie said weakly from the bottom of the pile.

"Git back into line!" Clardy roared sternly. "Eyes front! Stop your cowardly dodging! Any man leaving his station again will be shot!" With the flat[1] of his sword, Clardy spanked a timid recruit in the seat of his pants and pushed another roughly into position.

Sheepishly they re-formed their line. Jeff felt his breathing quicken. He saw another tiny spiral of smoke appear above the tops of the trees. This time a charge of grape[2] came flying overhead, screeching like forty locomotives. Again the men ducked instinctively, but this time only a few left the line.

"It's all right, boys," Jeff heard Bill giggle in his nervous tenor.[3] "Just dodge the biggest of 'em."

---

[1] **flat:** side
[2] **grape:** short for grape shot, which is a group of small iron balls shot from a cannon
[3] **tenor:** a man's singing voice with the highest natural range

Jeff felt a hysterical urge to laugh but discovered that he couldn't. For some strange reason, his throat had gone dry as a bone. The insides of his palms itched, and he could hear his pulse pounding. Again he checked the load in his rifle and was angry at himself. He knew there was nothing wrong with the rifle load.

Furious because he couldn't control his odd behavior, he clenched his jaws and shook his head vigorously. He had looked forward so long to his first battle. And now that the long-awaited moment had finally come, he discovered that some queer species of paralysis[4] had gripped his legs. His chest felt heavy, as if a blacksmith's anvil[5] was weighing it down. It was hard for him to breathe.

Noah looked at him anxiously. "What's the matter, youngster?"

Jeff licked his lips and swallowed once. Perplexed, he shook his brown head. "I don't know. My stomach feels bashful." Embarrassed, he looked around, hoping nobody would get the wrong idea and impute[6] this accursed nervousness to cowardice. He was fiercely determined not to disgrace his family or his county.

Suddenly the Union drums began to roll, loudly and ominously. . . . "Fall in!"

Obediently Jeff backed into line, dressing up[7] on Noah's tall form next to him. A spiteful[8] crackle of rifle fire, punctuated by the deeper roar of cannon, broke suddenly from the woods. Now the stinking, acrid odor of gunpowder was on the air. A rebel bombshell screeched over their heads, hunting for them. Jeff imagined he could hear it say, "Where-is-yuh, where-is-yuh, where-is-yuh—booooom!"

He began to hear tiny thuds here and there in the ground. They reminded him of the first, isolated dropping of hailstones during a spring storm on the Kansas prairies. Tardily he realized they were rebel rifle bullets.

"Fix bayonets!" Mechanically Jeff groped for the scabbard at his belt. Fingers shaking, he managed to clamp the long knife over the muzzle of his rifle. He shot a quick look at Noah. It was good to have Noah next to him.

"Be ready, youngster! We're goin' in after 'em!" Noah yelled. Jeff pulled a couple of long breaths and felt the goose bumps rising on his arms.

He heard Clardy cursing. Big Jake Lonegan had thrown down his musket and run in terror to the rear. Jeff felt a powerful urge to follow him. He could hear the officers shouting threats, too, but they failed to stop the big sergeant or even to slow him down.

---

[4] **paralysis:** loss of ability to feel or move a body part or parts

[5] **anvil:** heavy metal block that has a flat top on which heated metal objects are hammered into shape

[6] **impute:** to falsely put the responsibility on

[7] **dressing up:** standing in a straight line and at the correct distance

[8] **spiteful:** annoying

"Eyes front!" bellowed Clardy. "Any man leaving his position will be shot!"

Swallowing nervously, Jeff found he could not keep his thoughts on the coming battle. Oddly, they kept wandering back to Linn County. It was a Sunday afternoon, and his family had probably just returned from church in the rock mission at Sugar Mound. He could see his mother, busy over her fireplace ovens, cooking the Sunday dinner, with Bess and Mary both helping, each careful not to soil the Sunday dresses they had not yet taken off. He could see his father unhitching Jack and Beck from the buckboard and Ring crouching mischievously by the gooseberry bushes, waiting to give the mules a run when they were liberated through the corral gate.

Tears stung Jeff's eyes. Angry at himself for showing emotion, he winked them off. What in the world was the matter with him? The rebel fire grew hotter. What funny music the rebel Minie balls[9] made. Some of them mewed like kittens. Others hummed like angry hornets or whined like ricocheting nails.

A soldier on Jeff's right went down with a strangled moan, clutching and raking at his stomach. Jeff began to pray hard, straight from the heart. He hadn't dreamed that war was anything like this. He vowed[10] that if by some miracle he came out alive, he would always go to church thereafter.

"Forward march!" Jeff barely heard the command above the battle's din. But every man obeyed. Bayoneted muskets carried at the ready, they strode blindly forward to whatever fate awaited them. . . .

Bullets zipped all about them. Jeff wondered how it felt to be hit by a musket ball; whether it stung or whether it burned. He wondered why their own artillery hadn't begun shooting.

---

[9] **Minie balls:** rifle bullets with cone-shaped heads that were used in muzzle-loading guns
[10] **vowed:** promised seriously; pledged

Looking to both right and left, he found himself part of a long blue line of soldiers moving at a quick walk toward the woods ahead. Men all around him were taking off their coats and dropping them on the prairie. Jeff peeled off his, flung it to the ground and felt a little better. He wouldn't need it anyhow because he expected to be killed.

"Flam-a-dee! Flam-a-dee! Flam-a-dee-dee!" rattled the drums, sounding their doleful call to death. They entered the woods. A wounded horse screamed in agony.[11] Stifling an impulse to turn and run, he clenched his teeth and kept advancing, dreading what lay ahead because he couldn't see it, nor imagine what it was like.

Although it was December, sweat ran down the tip of his nose. The winter sun gleamed brightly off his steel bayonet.

Noah, tall, gaunt, looking grim as death, was walking in a low crouch, his bayonet-tipped musket held in front of him. Jeff felt a little better. Just being close to Noah helped. The presence of the other men helped, too.

He stumbled over a fallen log but kept going. His mind was sharp now. He began to recall all the mean things he had ever done and how he might never have time to atone[12] for them. Life was running out on him. He wasn't ready to die. He didn't want to be rushed into it. He needed more time to think about it. After all, a person died just once. Anybody who let himself get killed was just plain stupid. The world was a wonderful place to live. No matter how revered he was in life, a dead person was so completely out of things. Even his own relatives soon forgot him and quickly reshaped their lives without him.

"Ba-loom! Ba-loom!"

A sudden rush of air passed overhead, and Jeff's heart leaped thankfully. Casting a startled look back over his shoulder, he saw streaks of orange-gold flame burst from Blunt's forward guns as the Union batteries,[13] elevating their cannon, fired over the heads of their infantry, using two-second fuses. For the first time he appreciated how dependent the infantry and artillery were upon each other.

"Charge bayonets!"

With a wild yell the long blue line leaped forward. Sprinting at breakneck speed, Jeff yelled at the top of his lungs, too. Their little red and white striped flag with the blue patch in the comer was going along with them at a jerky motion. There was a steady rattle of musket fire ahead. Gaps were torn in the line by the rebel volleys.[14] They began to run through clouds of sulphurous[15] smoke. It stank and made his eyes smart. . . .

---

[11] **agony:** extreme pain for a long time
[12] **atone:** make up for
[13] **batteries:** groupings of similar things so that they can be used together
[14] **volleys:** firings of many guns or other weapons at the same time
[15] **sulphurous:** made from sulphur, one of the chemicals in gunpowder and matches

A rebel bullet sheared off a branch a yard away. Jeff dove to his knees, furious at the stupidity of both armies standing in line and shooting at one another like duelists at ten paces. On his right, he saw Noah firing carefully off one knee. That still wasn't low enough for Jeff.

Flat on his belly, he began firing as fast as he could. Loading a single-shot musket was an intricate operation. Rolling over on his back, he bit off the end of the paper cartridge, thrust it in the gun, poured powder into the muzzle, withdrew his iron ramrod from the groove beneath the barrel, and rammed the charge and the bullet down the barrel. Then he pulled the hammer back with his thumb and stuck [on] a percussion cap.[16] . . . After that, all he had to do was draw a bead on the enemy and press the trigger. With the firing of the shot, smoke and fire from the black gunpowder belched into his face, and then he had the whole thing to do over.

Each time he fired, Jeff scrambled to his feet, ran forward a few steps, then dropped again to reload. He bit the cartridges off so fast that he swallowed some of the spilled powder. It tasted bitter. He wanted to rinse his mouth. But he couldn't. His canteen had been full of good, cold Arkansas spring water but he had foolishly thrown it away with his coat. Hot with battle now, he felt only that he wanted to encounter the worst and get it over as quickly as possible.

---

[16] **percussion cap:** a thin container that holds material that will explode when hit

Responding to the Literature

1. Onomatopoeia is the use of a word or words to imitate the sound that something makes. Write two examples of onomatopoeia in this selection.

2. What would happen to a soldier if he left his unit before the battle?

3. **Analyze** What are the literal and figurative meanings of this phrase: "a charge of grape came flying overhead, screeching like forty locomotives"?

4. **Compare and Contrast** Describe Jeff's opinion of what being in a battle is like. Include examples to show how his opinion changed during the story.

5. **Read to Write** Write a report of 500 to 700 words on one of these battles: Chickamauga, Chancellorsville, or Shiloh. Include the reason for the battle, what happened, and its casualties. Include a map of the area and at least one quotation. Explain how the battle is or is not similar to the one in the story.

Reading On Your Own...

Do you want to learn more about people who experienced the Civil War?
If so, check out the following books:

Historical Fiction

Across Five Aprils by Irene Hunt recounts what happens to Jethro Creighton during the Civil War. When his older brothers and teacher join the Union and Confederate armies, Jethro must run the family farm. He experiences the hopes and fears of a land at war and struggles to understand what is happening.

Historical Fiction

The Bravest Girl in Sharpsburg by Kathleen Ernst tells the story of two girls whose friendship is ended by their differing loyalties to the North and the South. When Confederate troops march into their hometown, the girls are thrown into the middle of a battle. After many hardships, their friendship is restored.

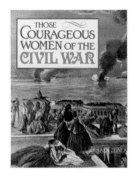

Nonfiction

Those Courageous Women of the Civil War by Karen Zeinert describes the many roles that women played during the war. In addition to keeping farms, businesses, and homes functioning, they were doctors, nurses, spies, and soldiers.

Biography

Lincoln: A Photobiography by Russell Freedman describes the private and public life of Abraham Lincoln. In this description, the author traces how Lincoln reached the decision to emancipate the slaves. There is also a generous presentation of pictures of Lincoln, his family, and his associates throughout the book.

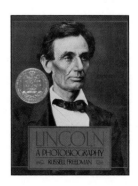

Section 3

A Call to Freedom

Guide to Reading

Looking Back, Looking Ahead

As the war continued, African Americans gained opportunities to contribute to the war effort. The Emancipation Proclamation officially permitted African Americans to enlist in the Union army and navy.

Focusing on the Main Ideas

- Lincoln signed the Emancipation Proclamation, which led to the passing of the Thirteenth Amendment freeing enslaved Americans. *(page 592)*
- The Civil War provided opportunities for African Americans to contribute to the war effort. *(page 595)*

Meeting People

Harriet Tubman

Content Vocabulary

emancipate (ih•MAN•suh•PAYT)
ratify (RA•tuh•FY)

Academic Vocabulary

reluctance (rih•LUHK•tuhns)
area

Reading Strategy

Taking Notes As you read the section, complete a table like the one shown describing what the Emancipation Proclamation and the Thirteenth Amendment to the Constitution were meant to accomplish.

	Accomplishments
Emancipation Proclamation	
Thirteenth Amendment	

NATIONAL GEOGRAPHIC **Who & When?**

1862   **1863**   **1864**   **1865**

1862 African Americans begin to serve in Union army

Jan. 1863 Lincoln signs the Emancipation Proclamation

July 1863 Nearly half of the 54th Massachusetts Regiment is wiped out

1865 Thirteenth Amendment is ratified

Emancipation

Main Idea Lincoln signed the Emancipation Proclamation, which led to the passing of the Thirteenth Amendment, freeing enslaved Americans.

Reading Connection Do you recall a time when an announcement had everyone talking? Read and find out about an announcement by Lincoln that changed lives forever.

President Lincoln shook many hands on New Year's Day of 1863, as a reception was held to commemorate the official signing of the Emancipation Proclamation. Diplomats, cabinet members, and army officers filed past the president, and when he finally left the reception, he noted that his arm was very stiff. As the document was presented, Lincoln remarked:

❝Now, this signature is one that will be closely examined and if they find my hand trembled, they will say 'he had some compunctions [second thoughts].' But, any way, it is going to be done!❞

—from *Lincoln*

Why It Matters

The Emancipation Proclamation

On January 1, 1863, President Lincoln issued the Emancipation Proclamation to a nation divided by war. The proclamation stated that all enslaved people in the states controlled by the Confederacy were free.

"If my name ever goes into history, it will be for this act."
—*Abraham Lincoln, 1863*

"The Emancipation Proclamation is the greatest event of our nation's history."
—*Frederick Douglass, 1864*

The Legacy of Freedom

Where America stands today on the issues of human freedom was fueled by the Emancipation Proclamation.

1863 ➡ Emancipation Proclamation issued

1865 ➡ Thirteenth Amendment abolishes slavery

1868 ➡ Fourteenth Amendment guarantees citizens equal protection

1870 ➡ Fifteenth Amendment strengthens voting rights

1954 ➡ *Brown* v. *Board of Education of Topeka, Kansas* ruling outlaws school segregation

From the start of the war through the brutal Battle of Antietam, the Northerners' main goal was to preserve the Union rather than to destroy slavery. Abolitionists did not control the North, or even the Republican Party. Abraham Lincoln and other Republican leaders insisted on many occasions that they would act only to prevent the expansion of slavery.

Although Lincoln considered slavery immoral, he showed **reluctance** to move against slavery because of the border states. Lincoln knew that making an issue of slavery would divide the people and make the war less popular. In August 1862, Abraham Lincoln responded to pressure to declare an end to slavery.

> **"If I could save the Union without freeing any slave, I would do it; if I could save it by freeing all the slaves, I would do it; and if I could save it by freeing some and leaving others alone, I would also do that. What I do about slavery, . . . I do because I believe it helps to save the Union."**
>
> —Letter to Horace Greeley, August 22, 1862

That was his official position. His personal wish was "that all men everywhere could be free."

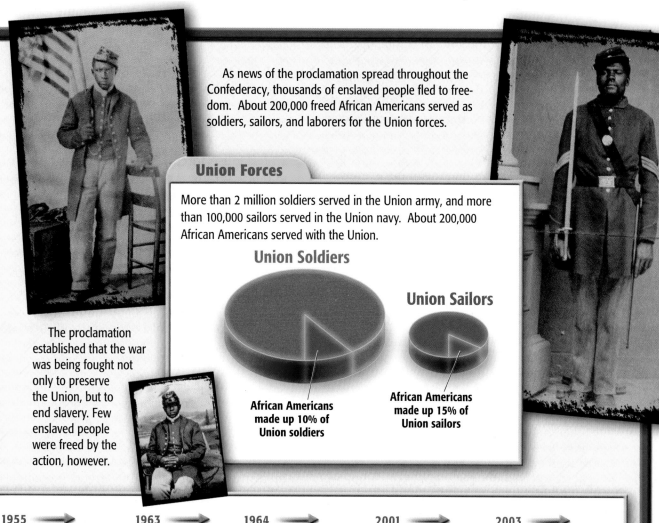

As news of the proclamation spread throughout the Confederacy, thousands of enslaved people fled to freedom. About 200,000 freed African Americans served as soldiers, sailors, and laborers for the Union forces.

The proclamation established that the war was being fought not only to preserve the Union, but to end slavery. Few enslaved people were freed by the action, however.

Union Forces

More than 2 million soldiers served in the Union army, and more than 100,000 sailors served in the Union navy. About 200,000 African Americans served with the Union.

Union Soldiers

Union Sailors

African Americans made up 10% of Union soldiers

African Americans made up 15% of Union sailors

1955	1963	1964	2001	2003
Rosa Parks refuses to give up her bus seat; Montgomery, Alabama	March on Washington	Twenty-fourth Amendment ends use of poll tax; Civil Rights Act passed	Colin Powell named secretary of state	Scheduled work on national monument to Martin Luther King, Jr., begins

Changing Attitudes As the war went on, attitudes toward slavery began to change. More Northerners believed that slavery was helping the war effort in the South. Enslaved people in the Confederacy raised crops used to feed the armies and did the heavy work in the trenches at the army camps. In the North's view, anything that weakened slavery struck a blow against the Confederacy.

As early as May 1861, some African Americans in the South escaped slavery by going into territory held by the Union army. In 1861 and 1862, Congress passed laws that freed enslaved people who were held by those active in the rebellion against the Union.

Antietam and the Proclamation Lincoln was keenly aware of the shift in public opinion. He also knew that striking a blow against slavery would make Britain and France less likely to aid the South. Moreover, Lincoln became convinced that slavery helped the South continue fighting. Every enslaved person who worked enabled a white Southerner to fight in the Confederate army.

Lincoln also had political reasons for taking action on slavery. He believed it was important that the president rather than the antislavery Republicans in Congress make the decision on ending slavery. Lincoln told the members of his cabinet:

> **❝I must do the best I can, and bear the responsibility. ❞**

By the summer of 1862, Lincoln had decided to **emancipate** (ih•MAN•suh•PAYT)—or free—all enslaved African Americans in the South. He waited for the right moment so that he would not appear to be acting in desperation when the North seemed to be losing the war.

On September 22, 1862, five days after the Union forces turned back the Confederate troops at the Battle of Antietam, Lincoln announced his plan to issue an order freeing all enslaved people in the Confederacy. On January 1, 1863, Lincoln signed the Emancipation Proclamation, which said:

> **❝. . . all persons held as slaves within any state . . . in rebellion against the United States, shall be then, thenceforward, and forever free. ❞**
>
> —The Emancipation Proclamation

Effects of the Proclamation The Emancipation Proclamation applied only to **areas** that the Confederacy controlled. Lincoln knew, however, that many enslaved people would hear about the proclamation. He hoped that knowledge of it would encourage them to run away from their slaveholders. Even before the Emancipation Proclamation, some 100,000 African Americans had left slavery for the safety of the Union. 📖 *(See page 855 of the Appendix for the text of the Emancipation Proclamation.)*

Despite the limitations of the Emancipation Proclamation, African Americans in the North greeted it joyfully. On the day it was signed, a crowd of African Americans gathered at the White House to cheer the president. Frederick Douglass wrote, "We shout for joy that we live to record this righteous decree."

The proclamation had the desired effect in Europe as well. The Confederacy had been seeking support from its trading partners, Britain and France. However, the British took a strong position against slavery. Once Lincoln proclaimed emancipation, Britain and France decided to withhold recognition of the Confederacy.

In 1864 Republican leaders in Congress prepared a constitutional amendment to abolish slavery in the United States. In 1865 Congress passed the Thirteenth Amendment, which was **ratified** (RA•tuh•FYD), or approved, the same year by states loyal to the Union. It was this amendment that truly freed enslaved Americans. 📖 *(See page 262 for the complete text of the Thirteenth Amendment.)*

☑ **Reading Check** **Explain** What did the Thirteenth Amendment do that the Emancipation Proclamation did not do?

African Americans in the War

Main Idea The Civil War provided opportunities for African Americans to contribute to the war effort.

Reading Connection How do you think freed African Americans affected the Union war effort? Read to find out how many formerly enslaved people fought against the South during the Civil War.

The Emancipation Proclamation announced Lincoln's decision to permit African Americans to join the Union army. In the South, as well as in the North, the Civil War was changing the lives of all African Americans.

In the South

When the war began, more than 3.5 million enslaved people lived in the Confederacy. Making up more than 30 percent of the region's population and the bulk of its workforce, enslaved workers labored on plantations and in vital iron, salt, and lead mines. Some worked as nurses in military hospitals and cooks in the army. By the end of the war, about one-sixth of the enslaved population had fled to areas controlled by Union armies.

The possibility of a slave rebellion terrified white Southerners. For this reason, most Southerners refused to use African Americans as soldiers—for then they would be given weapons.

Near the end of the war, however, the Confederate military became desperate. Robert E. Lee and some others supported using African Americans as soldiers and believed that those who fought should be freed. The Confederate Congress passed a law in 1865 to enlist enslaved people. The war ended before any regiments could be organized.

Helping the North

The story was different in the North. At the start of the war, African Americans were not permitted to serve as soldiers in the Union army. This disappointed many free African Americans who had volunteered to fight for the Union.

Yet African Americans who wished to help the war effort found ways to do so. Although the army would not accept them, the Union navy did. African Americans who had escaped slavery often proved to be useful as guides and spies because of their knowledge of the South. Some women, such as **Harriet Tubman,** who had helped dozens escape slavery by way of the Underground Railroad, repeatedly spied behind Confederate lines.

▲ Nearly 200,000 African Americans joined Union forces.

African American Soldiers In 1862 Congress passed a law allowing African Americans to serve in the Union army. By the end of the war, African American volunteers made up nearly 10 percent of the Union army and about 15 percent of the navy. In all, nearly 200,000 African Americans served. About 37,000 lost their lives defending the Union. By becoming soldiers, African Americans were taking an important step toward securing civil rights.

African American soldiers were organized into regiments separate from the rest of the Union army. Most commanding officers of these regiments were white. African Americans received lower pay than white soldiers at first, but protests led to equal pay in 1864.

One of the most famous African American regiments was the 54th Massachusetts, led by white abolitionists. On July 18, 1863, the 54th spearheaded an attack on a Confederate fortification near Charleston, South Carolina.

Under heavy fire, the troops battled their way to the top of the fort. The Confederates drove them back with heavy fire. Nearly half of the 54th were wounded, captured, or killed. Their bravery won respect for African American troops.

Many white Southerners, outraged that African American soldiers were fighting for the Union, threatened to execute any they captured. In a few instances, this threat was carried out. However, enslaved workers were overjoyed when they saw that the Union army included African American soldiers. As one African American regiment entered Wilmington, North Carolina, young and old ran through the streets, shouting and praising God. One of the soldiers said, "We could then truly see what we have been fighting for."

✔ **Reading Check** **Compare** How were African American soldiers treated differently than white soldiers?

History Online

Study Central Need help understanding life for African Americans during the war? Visit tajww1.glencoe.com and click on Study Central.

Section 3 Review

Reading Summary

Review the Main Ideas

- The Emancipation Proclamation freed all enslaved African Americans who were living in Confederate states.

- Many free African Americans and African Americans who had escaped from slavery enlisted with the Union army and fought in the war.

What Did You Learn?

1. Summarize President Lincoln's reasons for issuing the Emancipation Proclamation.

2. How did Harriet Tubman help the North?

Critical Thinking

3. **Determining Cause and Effect** Re-create the diagram below and list the factors that caused Lincoln to change his war goals to include freeing enslaved persons.

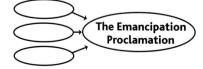

The Emancipation Proclamation

4. **Comparing** How did President Lincoln's political stand on slavery differ from his personal stand?

5. **The Big Ideas** Describe the role of African Americans in the Union army. How were they treated, and how did President Lincoln justify their role?

6. **Creative Writing** Write the dialogue for a short play in which enslaved African Americans on a Southern plantation learn of the Emancipation Proclamation and discuss what it means to them.

Section 4

Life During the Civil War

Guide to Reading

Looking Back, Looking Ahead
The Civil War affected civilians as well as soldiers. Civilians had an important impact on the war effort.

Focusing on the Main Ideas

- In both the North and the South, civilians and soldiers suffered terrible hardships and faced new challenges. *(page 598)*
- Many Northern and Southern women took on new responsibilities during the war. *(page 599)*
- The war efforts of the Union and the Confederate governments faced opposition. *(page 600)*
- The war created economic problems in the North and in the South. *(page 603)*

Meeting People
Mary Chesnut
Rose O'Neal Greenhow
Belle Boyd
Loretta Janeta Velázquez
  (vuh • LAS • kwihz)
Dorothea Dix
Clara Barton
Sally Tompkins

Content Vocabulary
habeas corpus
  (HAY • bee • uhs KAWR • puhs)
draft
bounty
inflation (ihn • FLAY • shuhn)

Academic Vocabulary
distribute (dih • STRIH • byuht)
substitute
occur (uh • KUHR)

Reading Strategy
Classifying Information As you read the section, complete a table like the one shown by describing the roles of these individuals during the war.

Person	Role
Loretta Janeta Velázquez	
Dorothea Dix	
Clara Barton	

NATIONAL GEOGRAPHIC **Who & When?**

1861 — **1862** — **1863** — **1864**

1861
Union Congress passes income tax
Union soldier

Apr. 1862
Confederate Congress passes draft
Confederate soldier

Mar. 1863
Union passes draft law

July 1863
Angry mobs oppose the draft in New York City

The Lives of Soldiers

Main Idea In both the North and the South, civilians and soldiers suffered terrible hardships and faced new challenges.

Reading Connection How do most movies portray the life of a soldier? Do they make the military life seem exciting and filled with action? Read to find out what life was really like for a Civil War soldier.

A soldier's life was not easy. In touching letters to their families and friends at home, soldiers described what they saw and how they felt—their boredom, discomfort, sickness, fear, and horror.

At the start of the war, men in both the North and the South rushed to volunteer for the armies. Their enthusiasm did not last.

Most of the time, the soldiers lived in camps. Camp life had its pleasant moments of songs, stories, letters from home, and baseball games. Often, however, a soldier's life was dull, a routine of drills, bad food, marches, and rain.

The Reality of War In spite of some moments of calm, the reality of war was never far away. Both sides suffered terrible losses. The new rifles used during the Civil War fired with greater accuracy than the muskets of earlier wars.

Medical facilities were overwhelmed by the thousands of casualties in each battle. After the Battle of Shiloh, many wounded soldiers lay in the rain for more than 24 hours waiting for medical treatment. A Union soldier recalled, "Many had died there, and others were in the last agonies as we passed. Their groans and cries were heart-rending."

Faced with such horrors, many men deserted. About 1 of every 11 Union soldiers and 1 of every 8 Confederates ran away because of fear, hunger, or sickness.

Rebel soldiers suffered from a lack of food and supplies. One reason for Lee's invasion of Maryland in 1862 was to allow his army to feed off Maryland crops. A woman who saw the Confederates march to Antietam recalled the "gaunt starvation that looked from their cavernous eyes."

✓ Reading Check **Explain** Why did many soldiers desert from the armies?

Picturing **History**

Some paintings offered an idealized picture of the Civil War. Photographs provided a chilling account of life—and death—at the front lines. *In what ways might photographs have affected Americans' view of the war in a way that paintings did not?*

Women and the War

Main Idea Many Northern and Southern women took on new responsibilities during the war.

Reading Connection Think of ways the women in your family would be affected by a war in their own backyards. Read to learn the many ways women were affected by the Civil War.

In times of war, people often fill new roles. Women in the North and the South became teachers and office workers, and they managed farms. They also suffered the loss of husbands, fathers, sons, and brothers. As **Mary Chesnut** of South Carolina wrote:

❝Does anyone wonder [why] so many women die? Grief and constant anxiety kill nearly as many women at home as men are killed on the battle-field.❞

—from *Mary Chesnut's Civil War*

Women performed many jobs that helped the soldiers and the armies. They rolled bandages, wove blankets, and made ammunition. Many women collected food, clothing, and medicine to **distribute** to the troops. They also raised money for supplies.

Life at Home For the most part, Northerners saw the war from a distance, since most of the battles took place in the South. News from the battlefront and letters home from the soldiers kept the war in people's minds.

Almost every woman who stayed at home was touched in some way by the war. But while everyday life in the North suffered little disruption, life in the South was dramatically changed.

Those who lived in the paths of marching armies lost crops and homes. As one Southerner noted: the South had depended upon the outside world "for everything from a hairpin to a toothpick, and from a cradle to a coffin." As the war dragged on, shortages became more commonplace.

Picturing **History**

This 1862 photo shows a Union soldier with his family at the front near Washington, D.C. Most soldiers on both sides, however, faced long separations from their families. *What other hardships did Civil War soldiers face?*

The South ran out of almost everything. Shortages in feed for animals and salt for curing meant that little meat was available. Shortages of meat were matched by shortages of clothing, medicine, and even shelter.

Women as Spies Some women served as spies. Harriet Tubman spied for the North. **Rose O'Neal Greenhow** entertained Union leaders in Washington, D.C., picking up information about Union plans that she passed to the South. Greenhow was caught and exiled to the South.

Belle Boyd, of Virginia, informed Confederate generals of Union army movements in the Shenandoah Valley. Some women disguised themselves as men and became soldiers. A Cuban native, **Loretta Janeta Velázquez** (vuh•LAS•kwihz), of New Orleans, reportedly fought for the South at the First Battle of Bull Run and at Shiloh.

Treating the Sick and Wounded In the Civil War, thousands of women served as nurses. At first many doctors did not want women nurses because they felt that women were too delicate for such work. Men disapproved of women doing what was considered men's work. Also, it was thought improper for women to tend the bodies of unknown men.

Strong-minded women disregarded these objections. In the North, **Dorothea Dix,** the reformer for conditions of prisoners and people with disabilities, organized large numbers of women to serve as military nurses. Another Northerner, **Clara Barton,** became famous for her work with wounded soldiers. In the South, **Sally Tompkins** established a hospital for soldiers in Richmond, Virginia.

Nursing was hard work. Kate Cummings of Alabama, who nursed the wounded in Corinth after the Battle of Shiloh, wrote, "Nothing that I had ever heard or read had given me the faintest idea of the horrors witnessed here."

✔ **Reading Check** **Describe** What role did Sally Tompkins play in the war effort? Which other women played a similar role in the North?

Opposition to the War

Main Idea **The war efforts of the Union and the Confederate governments faced opposition.**

Reading Connection Can you think of a time when you disagreed or opposed something? Did you take action? Read to learn how various people opposed the Civil War and why.

Both the Union and the Confederate governments faced opposition. Politicians objected to war policies, and ordinary citizens protested the way the war affected their lives.

When the war began, Northern Democrats split into two groups. One group supported most of Lincoln's wartime policies. The other, the "Peace Democrats," favored negotiating with the Confederacy. The Peace Democrats warned that continuing the war would lead to "terrible social change and revolution."

Conflict With the Copperheads Republicans called the Peace Democrats "Copperheads" after a poisonous snake that strikes without warning. When Union armies lost battles, support for the Copperheads rose.

Some Republicans suspected Copperheads of aiding the Confederates. The president ordered the arrest of anyone interfering with the war effort, such as discouraging men from enlisting in the army. Several times Lincoln suspended the right of **habeas corpus** (HAY•bee•uhs KAWR•puhs), which guarantees accused individuals the right to a hearing before being jailed. Lincoln defended his actions, asking:

❝ Must I shoot a simple-minded soldier boy who deserts, while I must not touch a hair of a wily agitator who induces him to desert? ❞
—Letter to Erastus Corning, June 12, 1863

Enlistments Decline As the war dragged on, fewer men volunteered to serve. Enlisting enough soldiers became a problem, so the Confederacy and the Union tried new measures.

Biography

CLARA BARTON
1821–1912

When the Civil War began, Clara Barton, a U.S. Patent Office clerk, began collecting provisions for the Union army. In 1862 she began to deliver supplies directly to the front and to tend to the wounded and dying during battle.

The youngest of five children, Barton often felt out of place among her successful older brothers and sisters. When her brother, David, suffered a work-related accident, Barton found her place in the family as David's nurse and caregiver. Her talent for nursing led her into a life in which she was satisfied only when helping and caring for others.

Arriving at the Battle of Antietam to deliver supplies, Barton watched as surgeons dressed the soldiers' wounds with corn husks because they did not have bandages. As the battle raged around her, Barton comforted the wounded and helped the doctors with their work. For her courage, Barton became known as "the angel of the battlefield."

As the Civil War drew to a close, Barton set up an office to assist families and friends looking for missing soldiers and prisoners of war. Thousands of letters came flooding in written by mothers looking for sons and wives looking for husbands. Barton began to publish advertisements in newspapers asking readers to send information on the whereabouts of any soldier listed in the ad. By 1868 she had identified 22,000 missing men.

" . . . I shall remain here while anyone remains, and do whatever comes to my hand. I may be compelled to face danger, but never fear it, and while our soldiers can stand and fight, I can stand and feed and nurse them."
—Letter to her father, 1861

Then and Now

Look online or in the phone book to find your local chapter of the Red Cross. Call or e-mail your local office and find out the following information: What kind of work has the chapter recently done? How can volunteers aid the organization?

Draft Laws In April 1862, the Confederate Congress passed a **draft** law that required men between ages 18 and 35 to serve in the army for three years. A person could avoid the draft by hiring a **substitute** to serve in his place.

Union states encouraged enlistment by offering **bounties**—payments to encourage volunteers. In March 1863, when this system failed, the North turned to a draft. All men from age 20 to 45 had to register, and the army drew the soldiers it needed from this pool of names. A person could avoid the draft by hiring a substitute or by paying the government $300.

Protests against the draft erupted in several Northern cities. The worst disturbance took place in New York City in July 1863. Angry mobs, opposed to the draft and to fighting to free African Americans, went on a rampage of burning, looting, and killing. After four days of terror, more than 100 people were dead.

No disturbance as severe took place in the South, but many opposed the draft. The strong opposition led Jefferson Davis, the president of the Confederacy, to proclaim military law and suspend habeas corpus as Lincoln had done early in the war. Davis's action outraged Southerners, who feared that they would lose the liberties for which they had gone to war.

✓ **Reading Check** **Examine** Why did the governments institute a draft? Why did protests occur in some places?

TECHNOLOGY & History

Civil War Camera

Photographer Mathew Brady and his many assistants recorded the camps, lives, and deaths of soldiers in more than 10,000 photos. **What is the biggest difference between this camera and a more modern one?**

Photographer Mathew Brady

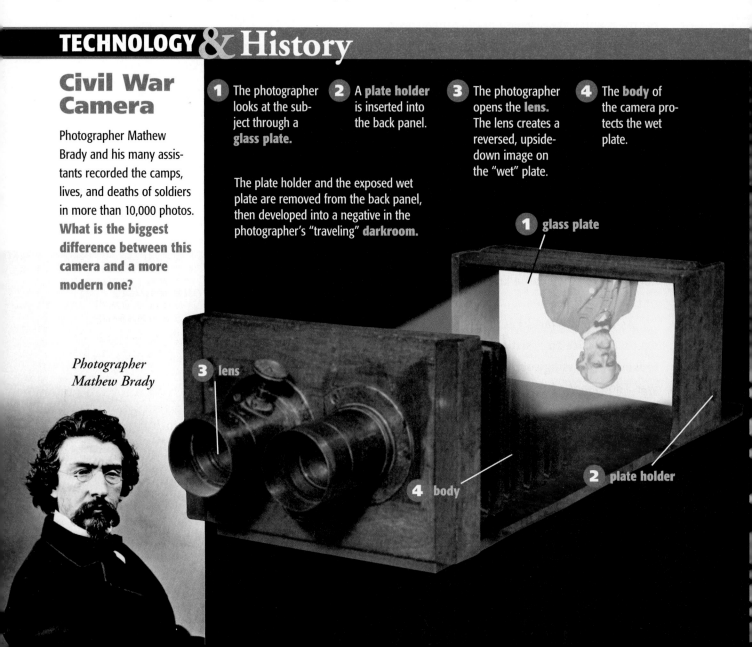

1 The photographer looks at the subject through a **glass plate.**

The plate holder and the exposed wet plate are removed from the back panel, then developed into a negative in the photographer's "traveling" **darkroom.**

2 A **plate holder** is inserted into the back panel.

3 The photographer opens the **lens.** The lens creates a reversed, upside-down image on the "wet" plate.

4 The **body** of the camera protects the wet plate.

1 glass plate

3 lens

4 body

2 plate holder

War and the Economy

Main Idea The war created economic problems in the North and in the South.

Reading Connection If you had to choose a side to fight for in the Civil War, which side would you choose? Read to learn the effects the war economy had on both the North and South.

The Civil War is often called the first "modern" war because it required the total commitment of resources. Such a war has an impact on every part of life. However, the impact was more devastating on the South than on the North.

The South struggled to carry out its war effort. Its government encouraged factories to supply arms and ammunition, but the South lacked the industry to provide necessities for civilians and for the military.

The economy of the South suffered far more than that of the North. Because most fighting **occurred** in the South, Southern farmland was overrun and rail lines were torn up.

The North's blockade of Southern ports caused severe shortages of essential goods. A scarcity of food led to riots in Atlanta, Richmond, and other cities. **Inflation** (ihn•FLAY•shuhn)—a general increase in the level of prices—was much worse in the South.

These conditions affected soldiers. Worries about their families caused many men to desert. A Mississippi soldier who overstayed his leave to help his family wrote the governor: "We are poor men and are willing to defend our country but our families [come] first."

✓ Reading Check **Explain** What is inflation? What hardships did inflation cause in the South?

Study Central Need help understanding how the war affected daily life? Visit tajww1.glencoe.com and click on Study Central.

Section 4 Review

Reading Summary

Review the Main Ideas

- Civil War soldiers faced boredom in camp and terrible horrors on the battlefield.

- During the Civil War, women took over men's jobs on farms and in factories. They also served as nurses and spies.

- Opposition to the war was especially strong in the North, and as the war dragged on, both the North and the South faced declining enlistments.

- During the war, the North's economy suffered some, but the South's economy faced ruin as the fighting devastated farmland and rail lines.

What Did You Learn?

1. Why was life on the home front more difficult for Southerners?

2. What do Rose O'Neal Greenhow, Belle Boyd, and Loretta Janeta Velázquez have in common with Harriet Tubman?

Critical Thinking

3. **Analyze** Describe three ways that women in the North and South contributed to the war effort.

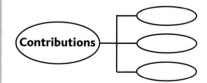

4. **Evaluate** Why do you think President Lincoln believed the Copperheads were a threat to the Union war effort?

5. **The Big Ideas** Describe the methods used by both the North and the South to enlist men into the army in the later years of the war.

6. **Economics** List three sectors of the economy that welcomed women during the Civil War. Describe the jobs women held and contributions they made.

Section 5

The Way to Victory

Guide to Reading

Looking Back, Looking Ahead

The Civil War continued with the Confederacy gaining the upper hand by 1863. However, victories at Gettysburg and Vicksburg turned the tide in favor of the Union.

Focusing on the Main Ideas

- After Confederate victories in Fredericksburg and Chancellorsville, a turning point occurred when Union forces won in Gettysburg and Vicksburg. *(page 605)*
- The end of the war was in sight with Sherman's capture of Atlanta and Grant's pursuit of the Confederates in Virginia. *(page 607)*
- After four years of war that claimed the lives of more than 600,000 Americans, the Northern forces defeated the Southern forces. *(page 610)*

Locating Places

Chancellorsville, Virginia
Vicksburg, Mississippi
Petersburg, Virginia
Mobile Bay

Savannah, Georgia
Appomattox Court House

Meeting People

Ambrose Burnside
Joseph Hooker
George Meade
William Tecumseh Sherman

Content Vocabulary

entrench (ihn•TREHNCH)
total war

Academic Vocabulary

outcome
nevertheless (NEH•vuhr•thuh•LEHS)

Reading Strategy

Organizing Information Use a web like the one shown to describe the strategy Grant adopted to defeat the Confederacy.

Grant's Strategy

NATIONAL GEOGRAPHIC | **Where & When?**

1862	1863	1864	1865
Dec. 1862 Lee wins the Battle of Fredericksburg	**July 1863** Battle of Gettysburg	**Mar. 1864** Grant takes over Union command	**Apr. 1865** Lee surrenders to Grant

Gettysburg
Fredericksburg
Appomattox Court House

The Tide of War Turns

Main Idea After Confederate victories in Fredericksburg and Chancellorsville, a turning point occurred when Union forces won in Gettysburg and Vicksburg.

Reading Connection Why was the small Pennsylvania town of Gettysburg so important that Lincoln gave one of his most famous speeches there? Read to find out how Gettysburg came to be at the center of the Civil War's greatest battle.

An American Story

"My shoes are gone; my clothes are almost gone. I'm weary, I'm sick, I'm hungry. My family have been killed or scattered, and may be now wandering helpless and unprotected in a strange country. And I have suffered all this for my country. I love my country. I would die—yes, I would die willingly because I love my country. But if this war is ever over, I'll . . . [n]ever love another country!" A Confederate soldier expressed these thoughts during difficult times in 1863.

The Reality of War
Gone were the parades and masses of volunteers, the fancy uniforms, and the optimism of the first years of the war. From 1862 until 1865, the soldiers and civilians faced a grim conflict marked by death, destruction, and wrenching change. What endured on each side was a fierce dedication to its own cause.

The winter of 1862–1863 saw gloom in the North and hope in the South. Robert E. Lee's Army of Northern Virginia seemed unbeatable. Lee's grasp of strategy made him more than a match for weak Union generals.

Fredericksburg and Chancellorsville
Lee needed little skill to win the Battle of Fredericksburg. On December 13, 1862, Union general **Ambrose Burnside** clashed with Lee near the Virginia town. Burnside had the larger army, but the Confederates were **entrenched,** or set up in a strong position, on a number of hills south of the town. Repeated attacks failed to overcome Lee's troops as thousands of Union soldiers fell on the hillside. Devastated by his failure, Burnside resigned his command and was replaced by General **Joseph Hooker.**

Hooker rebuilt the army and in early May 1863, launched a campaign against Lee. Before Hooker could mount a major attack, Lee struck at **Chancellorsville, Virginia,** a few miles west of Fredericksburg. Boldly dividing his troops for an assault on the Union forces, Lee won another victory—but the **outcome** proved costly. The battle's heavy casualties included General Stonewall Jackson.

On May 2, Jackson and his troops attacked Union troops at dusk. One of the Confederate companies fired on Jackson's party by mistake, wounding the general in the left arm. Jackson's arm had to be amputated, and he died a week later.

The Battle of Gettysburg
Despite heavy losses, Lee began moving north in June with an army of 75,000. Another victory—one on Northern soil—might persuade Britain and France to aid the Confederacy. Union general Hooker wanted to advance against Richmond, but Lincoln told him to attack Lee's army. When Hooker failed to do this, Lincoln replaced him with General **George Meade.** Meade's mission was to find and fight Lee's forces and to protect Washington and Baltimore from Confederate attack.

The two armies met on July 1, 1863, near the small town of Gettysburg, Pennsylvania. The three-day Battle of Gettysburg began when Union cavalry surprised Rebel infantry, who were looking for shoes. Outnumbered, the Northerners fought desperately to hold the town before retreating to Cemetery Ridge, a line of hills south of Gettysburg. The next day, the Rebels launched another assault, but a counterattack saved the Union position.

On the third and final day of battle, Lee decided to launch an attack, determined to "create a panic and virtually destroy the [Union] army."

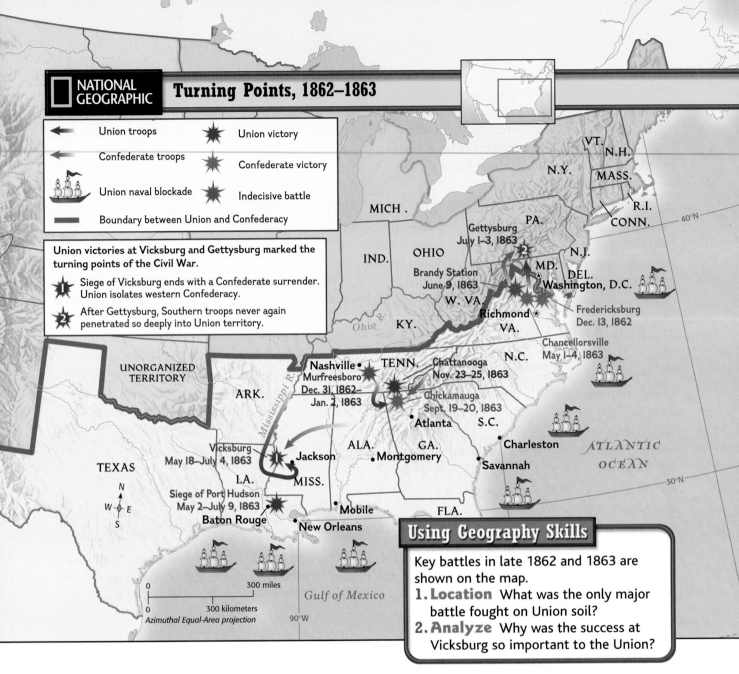

Turning Points, 1862–1863

Union troops

Confederate troops

Union naval blockade

Boundary between Union and Confederacy

Union victory

Confederate victory

Indecisive battle

Union victories at Vicksburg and Gettysburg marked the turning points of the Civil War.

1. Siege of Vicksburg ends with a Confederate surrender. Union isolates western Confederacy.

2. After Gettysburg, Southern troops never again penetrated so deeply into Union territory.

Gettysburg
July 1–3, 1863

Brandy Station
June 9, 1863

Washington, D.C.

Fredericksburg
Dec. 13, 1862

Richmond

Chancellorsville
May 1–4, 1863

Nashville
Murfreesboro
Dec. 31, 1862–
Jan. 2, 1863

Chattanooga
Nov. 23–25, 1863

Chickamauga
Sept. 19–20, 1863

Atlanta

Charleston

Savannah

Vicksburg
May 18–July 4, 1863

Jackson

Siege of Port Hudson
May 2–July 9, 1863

Baton Rouge

Mobile

New Orleans

UNORGANIZED TERRITORY

ARK.

TEXAS

LA.

MISS.

ALA.

GA.

S.C.

N.C.

TENN.

KY.

W. VA.

VA.

MD.

DEL.

N.J.

PA.

OHIO

IND.

MICH.

N.Y.

VT.

N.H.

MASS.

R.I.

CONN.

FLA.

ATLANTIC OCEAN

Gulf of Mexico

Mississippi R.

Ohio R.

0   300 miles
0   300 kilometers
Azimuthal Equal-Area projection

40°N

30°N

90°W

Using Geography Skills

Key battles in late 1862 and 1863 are shown on the map.

1. **Location** What was the only major battle fought on Union soil?

2. **Analyze** Why was the success at Vicksburg so important to the Union?

This last attack, led by General George Pickett, is remembered as Pickett's Charge. About 14,000 Confederate soldiers advanced across about one-half mile of open ground toward the Union lines. They made easy targets for Union fire as they marched. Barely half of the Rebels returned from the charge. Lee knew the battle was lost. "It's all my fault," he told his troops as they retreated to Virginia.

Victory at Vicksburg Meanwhile, a great Union victory took place at **Vicksburg, Mississippi.** Vicksburg stood on a high bluff above the Mississippi River. To gain control of the river, one of the North's major war goals, the Union needed to seize Vicksburg. For several

weeks, Union forces under Ulysses S. Grant had laid siege to the town. Finally, on July 4, 1863, Vicksburg surrendered.

With the surrender of Vicksburg and then Port Hudson in Louisiana, the Union now held the entire Mississippi River. Texas, Louisiana, and Arkansas were sealed off from the rest of the Confederacy.

The Union victories at Gettysburg and Vicksburg marked a turning point in the war. They drove Lee's army out of Pennsylvania, secured the Mississippi as a Union highway, and cut the South in two. **Nevertheless,** the South still had troops and a will to fight. The war would continue for two more terrible years.

Lincoln at Gettysburg On November 19, 1863, at a ceremony dedicating a cemetery at Gettysburg, President Lincoln beautifully expressed what the war had come to mean: "It is for us the living . . . to be here dedicated to the great task remaining before us . . . that these dead shall not have died in vain—that this nation shall have a new birth of freedom; and that this government, of the people, by the people, for the people, shall not perish from the earth."

The speech went beyond the immediacy of the battlefield horrors and instead emphasized Americans' shared ideals. 📖 *(See page 856 of the Appendix for the entire text of the Gettysburg Address.)*

✓ **Reading Check** **Identify** What battle victories gave the Union control of the Mississippi River?

Final Phases of the War

Main Idea **The end of the war was in sight with Sherman's capture of Atlanta and Grant's pursuit of the Confederates in Virginia.**

Reading Connection Do you think an army should attack an enemy's civilian population? Read to find out why General Sherman waged "total war" as his army marched through Georgia.

In November 1863, Grant, General **William Tecumseh Sherman,** and another general won an important victory at Chattanooga, Tennessee. Following the Northern triumphs at Vicksburg and Gettysburg, Chattanooga further weakened the Confederates. The following March, President Lincoln turned to Grant for help.

Primary Sources

What Was the Reaction to the Gettysburg Address?

President Abraham Lincoln delivered the Gettysburg Address on November 19, 1863, during the dedication of the Gettysburg National Cemetery. The dedication was in honor of the more than 7,000 Union and Confederate soldiers who died in the Battle of Gettysburg earlier that year. Lincoln's brief speech is often recognized as one of the finest speeches in the English language. It is also one of the most moving speeches in the nation's history.

On the day following the Gettysburg dedication, many of the nation's newspapers reprinted the speech. Some newspapers praised the speech. The *Chicago Tribune* noted that:

"The dedicatory remarks by President Lincoln will live among the annals of man."

▲ **Gettysburg Cemetery**

Other newspapers did not think it was a worthy address by a president. *The Harrisburg* (Pennsylvania) *Patriot* criticized the speech, noting:

"We pass over the silly remarks of the President; for the credit of the Nation we are willing that the veil of oblivion shall be dropped over them and that they shall no more be repeated or thought of."

 Document-Based Question

The Gettysburg Address is considered one of the great speeches. Why do you think some Americans were critical of the address?

Ulysses S. Grant was average and unimpressive in appearance. His early army career was not impressive either, and in 1854 he had been forced to resign because of a drinking problem. When the war began, he rejoined the army. His victories in the West and his willingness to attack hard impressed President Lincoln. "I can't spare this man," the president said. "He fights." After the victory at Chattanooga, Lincoln named Grant commander of all the Union armies.

Grant devised a plan to attack the Confederacy on all fronts. The Army of the Potomac would try to crush Lee's army in Virginia. The western army, under Sherman, would advance to Atlanta, Georgia, and crush the Confederate forces in the Deep South. If the plan succeeded, they would destroy the Confederacy.

Grant soon put his strategy into effect. In May and June of 1864, Grant's army of 115,000 men smashed into Lee's 64,000 troops in a series of three battles near Richmond, Virginia—the Battles of the Wilderness, Spotsylvania Courthouse, and Cold Harbor. Each time, Confederate lines held, but each time Grant quickly resumed the attack.

The battles cost the North thousands of men. Critics called Grant a butcher, but he said, "I propose to fight it out on this line if it takes all summer." Lincoln supported Grant.

After Cold Harbor, Grant swung south of Richmond to attack **Petersburg, Virginia,** an important railroad center. If it fell, Richmond would be cut off from the rest of the Confederacy. Grant's assault turned into a nine-month siege.

NATIONAL GEOGRAPHIC — The Civil War: Battles and Strategies

☐ Confederate Control
▨ Union Control
⛴ Union naval blockade

The Anaconda Plan From the beginning, the Northern war strategy was to invade the South and divide it. As the plan—called the Anaconda Plan—progressed, the North blocked Southern supply lines and isolated Confederate troops.

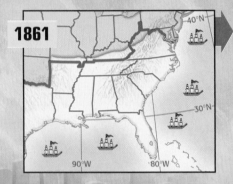

1861

1863

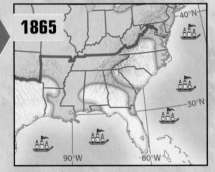

1865

Early Stages Confederate troops won most of the battles in the first year of the Civil War.

Union Gains Union control of the Mississippi River cut off Texas and Arkansas, the South's leading food producers, from the Confederacy.

Final Stages By 1865 the Union controlled large parts of the Confederacy.

Lives Lost
More lives were lost in the Civil War than in any other major American conflict. Deadly weapons, poor medical practices, infection, and disease contributed to this.

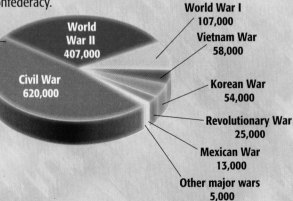

World War II
407,000

Civil War
620,000

World War I
107,000

Vietnam War
58,000

Korean War
54,000

Revolutionary War
25,000

Mexican War
13,000

Other major wars
5,000

The Election of 1864 To the war-weary North, the events of the first half of 1864 were discouraging. Grant was stuck outside Richmond and Petersburg, and Sherman was stuck outside Atlanta. In the summer of 1864, Lincoln's chances for reelection did not look good. "I am going to be beaten and unless some great change takes place, badly beaten," he said.

Great changes did take place. In August, David Farragut led a Union fleet into **Mobile Bay.** The Union now controlled the Gulf of Mexico. In September, news arrived that Sherman had captured Atlanta. With these victories, the end of the war was in sight. Lincoln easily won reelection, taking 55 percent of the popular vote.

Total War Leaving Atlanta in ruins, Sherman convinced Grant to let him try a bold plan. Sherman's army began a "march to the sea" to **Savannah, Georgia.** As the army advanced, it lived off the land. Union troops took what food they needed and tore up railroad lines and fields in an effort to destroy anything useful to the South. They cut a path of destruction sometimes 50 miles wide. This method of waging war was known as **total war.**

After capturing Savannah in December, Sherman turned north. The army marched through South Carolina, devastating the state. Sherman planned to join Grant's forces in Virginia.

Reading Check **Describe** What was the "march to the sea"?

NATIONAL GEOGRAPHIC

The Final Battles, 1864–1865

The Wilderness
May 5–6, 1864

Cold Harbor
June 3, 1864

Petersburg siege
June 5, 1864–April 3, 1865

Appomattox Court House
April 9, 1865

Nashville
Dec. 15–16, 1864

Bentonville
March 19–21, 1865

Franklin
Nov. 30, 1864

Wilmington
February 12–22, 1865

Kennesaw Mountain
June 27, 1864

Atlanta
July 20–Sept. 2, 1864

SHERMAN'S MARCH TO THE SEA 1864

Mobile Bay
August 2–23, 1864

Azimuthal Equal-Area projection

0 ___ 300 miles
0 ___ 300 kilometers

Legend
← Union troops
← Confederate troops
▬ Boundary between Union and Confederacy
✴ Union victory
✴ Confederate victory
✴ Indecisive battle

Victory for the North

Main Idea After four years of war that claimed the lives of more than 600,000 Americans, the Northern forces defeated the Southern forces.

Reading Connection After several years of terrible fighting and death, do you think a victorious general might want to punish the soldiers of the defeated army? Read to find out how General Grant treated the defeated Confederate soldiers after General Lee's surrender.

In his second Inaugural Address on March 4, 1865, Lincoln spoke of the coming peace:

> **66** With malice toward none, with charity for all . . . let us strive on to finish the work we are in, to bind up the nation's wounds . . . to do all which may achieve and cherish a just and lasting peace among ourselves and with all nations. **99**

Throughout the fall and winter of 1864, Grant continued the siege of Petersburg. Lee and his troops defended the town, but sickness, hunger, casualties, and desertion weakened them. Finally, on April 2, 1865, the Confederate lines broke and Lee withdrew his troops.

Richmond fell the same day. Rebel troops, government officials, and many residents fled the Confederate capital.

As they left, they set fire to much of the city to keep it from falling into Union hands.

On April 4, Lincoln visited Richmond and walked its streets. One elderly African American man approached the president, took off his hat, and bowed. Tearfully, he said, "May God bless you." Lincoln removed his own hat and bowed in return.

Surrender at Appomattox Lee moved his army west of Richmond, hoping to link up with the small Confederate force that was trying to stop Sherman's advance. But the Union army blocked his escape route. Realizing the situation was hopeless, Lee said:

> **66** There is nothing left [for] me but to go and see General Grant, and I [would] rather die a thousand deaths. **99**
>
> —as quoted in *Voices of the Civil War*

On April 9, 1865, Lee and his troops surrendered to Grant in a small Virginia village called **Appomattox Court House.**

Picturing **History**

After Robert E. Lee surrendered to Ulysses S. Grant, Grant ordered Union troops not to celebrate. "The war is over," he said, "the rebels are our countrymen again." *Where did Lee surrender?*

Biography

ROBERT E. LEE
1807–1870

ULYSSES S. GRANT
1822–1885

The two outstanding generals of the Civil War, Robert E. Lee and Ulysses S. Grant, were both excellent leaders. But only one could emerge the victor. At the beginning of the war, most people would have guessed that Lee would be the winner.

Lee was born to a prominent Virginia family. In 1828 he graduated from West Point at the top of his class. During the war with Mexico, he proved his skill and daring as a soldier.

When the Civil War broke out, Lincoln asked Lee to take command of the Union forces. Lee was torn, because he did not believe in slavery or secession. But when Virginia seceded, he felt that his loyalty had to lie with his home state. Instead of fighting for the Union, he became the South's most brilliant strategist.

When Lee surrendered at Appomattox, he surrendered to a general who was almost his complete opposite. Grant was the son of a farmer and a tanner. Although he went to West Point, he was only an average student. He distinguished himself in the war with Mexico but later resigned from the army. During the next few years, he failed repeatedly in farming and in business.

When the Civil War started, Grant volunteered his services. At first he had trouble being accepted into the Union army. Once accepted, however, he impressed Lincoln with his ability. In 1864 Grant was given command of the Union armies. His abilities to plan and make decisions, backed by the North's superior resources, changed the strategy—and the outcome—of the Civil War.

▲ Robert E. Lee

◄ Ulysses S. Grant

Then and Now

Can you think of any military leaders today who have the qualities that made Grant and Lee great generals?

Terms of Surrender Grant's terms were generous. The Confederate soldiers had to lay down their arms but then were free to go home. Grant allowed them to keep their horses so that they could, as he said, "put in a crop to carry themselves and their families through the next winter." Grant also ordered three days' worth of food sent to Lee's hungry troops.

Several days after Lee's surrender, the Confederate forces in North Carolina surrendered. Jefferson Davis, the president of the Confederacy, was captured in Georgia on May 10. The Civil War was over at last.

A New President President Lincoln did not live to see the end of the war, however. On April 14, 1865, just five days after Lee's surrender, Lincoln was assassinated by John Wilkes Booth, a fanatical Confederate sympathizer. Booth's deed was a tragedy for both North and South, for it removed the one person who could best "bind up the nation's wounds."

A Richmond, Virginia, newspaper called Lincoln's death "the heaviest blow which has ever fallen upon the people of the South." A young Southern woman wrote in her diary, "The most terrible part of the war is now to come."

Picturing **History**

By April 1865, many major cities of the Confederacy, including Atlanta, had felt the full force of war. *What is total war?*

Lincoln's vice president, Andrew Johnson, became president. Johnson had been a Democrat living in Tennessee before the Civil War. He had served as a mayor and state legislator before being elected to the United States Senate. When Tennessee seceded from the Union, Johnson remained loyal and stayed in the U.S. Senate, making him a hero in the North.

Results of the War The Civil War was the most devastating conflict in American history. More than 600,000 soldiers died, and the war caused billions of dollars of damage, most of it in the South. The devastation had left the South's economy in a state of collapse. Roughly two thirds of the transportation system lay in ruins, with many bridges destroyed and miles of railroad twisted and rendered useless. The war also created bitter feelings among defeated Southerners that lasted for generations.

The war had other consequences as well. The North's victory saved the Union. The federal government was strengthened and was now clearly more powerful than the states. Finally, the war freed millions of African Americans. The end of slavery, however, did not solve the problems that the newly freed African Americans were to face.

Following the war, many questions remained. No one yet knew how to bring the Southern states back into the Union, nor what the status of African Americans would be in Southern society. Americans from the North and the South tried to answer these questions in the years following the Civil War—an era known as Reconstruction.

✓ Reading Check **Identify** Where did General Lee surrender?

Study Central Need help understanding the conclusion of the war? Visit tajwwI.glencoe.com and click on Study Central.

Section 5 Review

Reading Summary

Review the Main Ideas

- The Confederate army seemed unbeatable after the Battles of Fredericksburg and Chancellorsville, but Northern victories at Gettysburg and Vicksburg turned the tide of the war for the Union.

- In the West, Sherman's army captured Atlanta and marched to the Atlantic coast. In the East, Grant's army maintained a strong offensive against the Confederate army under General Lee.

- In early April 1865, Grant's forces captured Richmond, and Lee's Confederate army surrendered soon after.

What Did You Learn?

1. Identify the reasons that Gettysburg and Vicksburg were important battles.

2. At what Virginia town did Lee defeat Burnside's forces?

Critical Thinking

3. **Analyze** Use a chart like the one shown to explain the significance of each battle listed.

Battle	Importance
Gettysburg	
Vicksburg	
Mobile Bay	
Richmond	

4. **Math Connection** Using the chart on page 608, create two new charts or graphs that communicate the same information in different ways.

5. **The Big Ideas** How did battlefield events affect Lincoln's reelection?

6. **Expository Writing** Refer to Lincoln's Gettysburg Address on page 856. Write an essay discussing Lincoln's ideas on freedom and the importance of saving the Union.

West Woods

Hagerstown Pike

Dunker Church

This is the area that is shown above.

Potomac River

Hagerstown Pike

Dunker Church

Bloody Lane

Union Headquarters

SHARPSBURG

Confederate Headquarters

Antietam Creek

0   1/2 mile
0   1/2 kilometer

ANTIETAM: THE BLOODIEST DAY

FOUGHT ON SEPTEMBER 17, 1862, the Battle of Antietam, or Sharpsburg, was the bloodiest day in American history, with more than 23,000 soldiers killed or wounded. Antietam changed the course of the Civil War. McClellan's Union forces stopped Lee's invasion of the North and forced him on the defensive. This strategic victory encouraged Lincoln to issue the Emancipation Proclamation.

MORNING

The battle began at dawn when Union artillery fired on Stonewall Jackson's forces in Miller Cornfield north of town. Union troops attacked the Confederates north of Dunker Church. For three hours, the battle lines swept back and forth along the West and East Woods, the Cornfield, and along Hagerstown Pike.

MIDDAY

Union soldiers emerged from the East Woods and were turned back by the Confederates in the West Woods. Later, the Yankees advanced toward "Bloody Lane," a sunken farm road held by the Confederates just south of Dunker Church. The Confederates held their line until midday, when the fighting stopped briefly.

AFTERNOON

After much fighting, the Union troops crossed Antietam Creek and slowly drove the Confederate forces back toward Sharpsburg. Just when all hope seemed lost, Confederate forces arrived from Harpers Ferry and stopped the Union advance. The day ended in a standoff that halted Lee's march northward. The next day, Lee began his retreat along the Potomac River.

LEARNING from GEOGRAPHY

1. **How do you think Bloody Lane got its name?**

2. **Why do you think Lee retreated after the Battle of Antietam?**

Analyzing Primary Sources

A Nation Divided By War

Between 1861 and 1865, a Civil War divided the people of the United States. The South wanted to become an independent nation, upholding its rights to enslave African Americans, protect its economy, and retain states' rights. The North refused to allow the South to break away from the Union.

Read the passages on pages 616 and 617 and answer the questions that follow.

General Sherman led Union troops through Georgia in 1864. ▶

Reader's Dictionary

enlist: join the armed forces

apparel (uh • PAR • uhl): clothing

deprived (dih • PRYVD): taken away from

spires (SPYRZ): church steeples

horde: a large group or crowd

crimson (KRIHM • zuhn): red

fourscore: 80

Early Days of the War

Theodore Upson, a 17 year-old Indiana boy, writes about his feelings during the first days of the Civil War.

We had another meeting at the school house last night; we are raising money to take care of the families of those who **enlist**. . . . I said I would go but they laughed at me and said they wanted men not boys for this job; that it would all be over soon; that those fellows down South are big bluffers and would rather talk than fight. I am not so sure about that. . . . Mother had a letter from the Hales. Charlie and his Father are in their army and Dayton wanted to go but was too young. I wonder if I were in our army and they should meet me would they shoot me. I suppose they would.

—*With Sherman to the Sea*

Destruction Caused by Troops

In 1864 Union troops march through Georgia, destroying everything in their path. One Southerner, Dolly Sumner Lunt, describes the situation in her diary.

July 29, 1864—Sleepless nights. . . . They robbed every house on the road of its provisions, sometimes taking every piece of meat, blankets and wearing **apparel,** silver and arms of every description. . . . Is this the way to make us love them and their Union? Let the poor people answer [those] whom they have **deprived** of every mouthful of meat and of their livestock to make any!

—*A Woman's Wartime Journal*

Barbara Frietchie

John Greenleaf Whittier stated that this poem is based on a real incident in Frederick, Maryland. Barbara Frietchie was intensely loyal to the Union.

Up from the meadows rich with corn,
Clear in the cool September morn,

The cluster **spires** of Frederick stand
Green-walled by the hills of Maryland.

Round about them orchards sweep,
Apple and peach tree fruited deep,

Fair as the garden of the Lord
To the eyes of the famished rebel **horde,**

On that pleasant morn of the early fall
When Lee marched over the mountain wall;

Over the mountains winding down,
Horse and foot, into Frederick town.

Forty flags with their silver stars,
Forty flags with their **crimson** bars,

Flapped in the morning wind: the sun
Of noon looked down, and saw not one.

Up rose old Barbara Frietchie then,
Bowed with her **fourscore** years and ten;

Bravest of all in Frederick town,
She took up the flag the men hauled down;

In her attic window the staff she set,
To show that one heart was loyal yet.

Up the street came the rebel tread,
Stonewall Jackson riding ahead.

Under his slouched hat left and right
He glanced; the old flag met his sight.

"Halt!"—the dust-brown ranks stood fast.
"Fire!"—out blazed the rifle-blast.

It shivered the window, pane and sash;
It rent the banner with seam and gash,

Quick, as it fell, from the broken staff
Dame Barbara snatched the silken scarf.

She leaned far out on the window-sill,
And shook it forth with a royal will.

"Shoot, if you must, this old gray head,
But spare your country's flag," she said.

—excerpted from "Barbara Frietchie"
by John Greenleaf Whittier
in *The Annals of America,* vol. 9

◀ **Confederate battle flag**

 Document-Based Questions

Early Days of the War

1. Why was money being raised?
2. What does Theodore think might happen if he were in the Union army and ran into the Hales?

Destruction Caused by Troops

3. According to Lunt, what did the Yankees do?
4. What is the situation of poor people because of these Yankee actions?

Barbara Frietchie

5. Who came marching into Frederick?
6. What did Barbara Frietchie do that was so unusual?

Read to Write

7. The lives of the people in these readings changed because of the experience of war. Write about an experience that completely changed your attitude toward something. Explain how your outlook changed.

Review Content Vocabulary

1. Write a one page essay about the Civil War using the following words.

   a. border state

   b. casualty

   c. emancipate

   d. draft

   e. entrenched

   f. total war

Review the Main Ideas

Section 1 • The Two Sides

2. Why did the Union blockade Southern ports?

3. What three advantages did the Confederate states have in the war?

Section 2 • Early Years of the War

4. Who were the presidents of the United States and of the Confederate States of America?

5. Which battle is known as the bloodiest of the Civil War and why?

Section 3 • A Call to Freedom

6. In what ways did African Americans contribute to the war effort?

7. What did the Emancipation Proclamation state?

Section 4 • Life During the Civil War

8. What role did Clara Barton play in the Civil War?

9. How did the Civil War hurt the South's economy?

Section 5 • The Way to Victory

10. What was the outcome of the Battle of Gettysburg?

11. What terms of surrender did Grant offer to Lee?

Critical Thinking

12. **Determining Cause and Effect** Why was controlling the Mississippi River vital to the North and the South?

13. **Infer** Why do you think General Lee was such an effective military leader?

Geography Skills

Study the map below and answer the following questions.

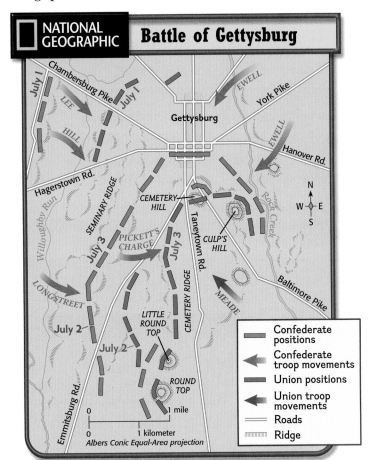

NATIONAL GEOGRAPHIC **Battle of Gettysburg**

14. **Location** Along what ridge were the Union troops positioned?

15. **Movement** Who led forces across Rock Creek?

Read to Write

16. **The Big Ideas** **Evaluate** Write a short essay that describes the impact that civilians had on the war effort. Include references to both the North and the South.

17. **Paraphrase** To explain his reelection, Lincoln stated, "it was not best to swap horses while crossing the river." Write a paragraph that explains Lincoln's quotation and how it applied to his career.

18. **Using Your FOLDABLES** Use your foldable to write three sentences that summarize the main ideas of this chapter. Share your sentences with the class, and listen to their sentences. Then vote for the one you think best summarizes the chapter.

Using Academic Vocabulary

19. Write a paragraph that uses these academic vocabulary words to describe an event from this chapter:
    a. sufficient
    b. reinforce
    c. encounter

Linking Past and Present

20. **Making Connections** A writ of habeas corpus is a court order that guarantees a person who is arrested the right to appear before a judge in a court of law. During the Civil War, President Lincoln suspended habeas corpus. What recent crisis led to similar actions? Write a short essay describing these actions and why they were taken.

Economics Connection

21. **Comparing** Economic differences had always existed between the North and the South. From your reading of Chapter 13, would you say that the North or the South was better equipped economically for war? Explain your reasoning.

Reviewing Skills

22. **READING SKILL** **Evaluate** Review the section called "Total War" on page 609. Write a paragraph that evaluates the effectiveness of this strategy in accomplishing the Union's goals. Take into account the impact of this on the Confederacy and its civilians.

23. **ANALYSIS SKILL** **Sequencing Information** Draw a time line that includes the major battles you read about in this chapter. Include battle dates, locations, and outcomes.

Standardized Test Practice

Select the best answer for each of the following questions.

24 **By gaining control of the Mississippi and Tennessee rivers, the Union was able to**

   A capture Fort Sumter.

   B force the Confederacy to surrender.

   C split the Confederacy.

   D defeat the Confederate forces at Gettysburg.

25 **The Thirteenth Amendment was important because**

   A it gave women the right to vote.

   B it outlawed secession.

   C it abolished slavery in the United States.

   D limited the President to two terms in office.

Reconstruction

◀ Ruins of a railroad depot, Charleston, South Carolina

NATIONAL GEOGRAPHIC

Who & When?

1860	1870	1880

1865 President Lincoln is assassinated

1870 Fifteenth Amendment extends voting rights

Members of Congress

1877 Reconstruction ends

History **Online**
Chapter Overview Visit tajww1.glencoe.com
for a preview of Chapter 14.

The Big Ideas

Reconstruction Plans

Political ideas and major events shape how people form governments.
Northern politicians disagreed on how to bring the southern states
back into the Union.

Radicals in Control

A constitution reflects the values and goals of the society that creates it.
The Radical Republicans in Congress worked to ensure the rights of
the newly freed African Americans in the South.

The South During Reconstruction

Political ideas and major events shape how people form governments.
African Americans in the South made some gains in government and
education, but many white Southerners attempted to limit their rights.

Change in the South

**Economic, social, and political changes create new traditions, values, and
beliefs.** As Reconstruction ended, white Southerners attempted to
make economic changes in the South, while restricting the rights of
African Americans.

 View the Chapter 14 video in the Glencoe Video Program.

Study Organizer

Comparison Make this foldable to help you compare and contrast Reconstruction
in the Northen and Southern states.

Step 1 Mark the midpoint
of the side edge of a sheet
of paper.

Draw a mark
at the midpoint.

Step 2 Turn the paper
and fold the edges in to
touch at the midpoint.

Step 3 Turn and label
your foldable as shown.

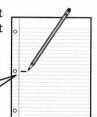

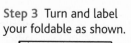
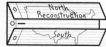

Reading and Writing
As you read the chapter,
write facts that show
how Reconstruction
differed and was the
same in the Northern
states and Southern
states. Write the facts in
the appropriate places
inside your foldable.

Get Ready to Read

Monitoring and Clarifying

READING SKILL

1 Learn It!

Good readers monitor their understanding of text. When a portion of the reading is confusing, good readers use strategies to understand, such as looking up new words, rereading, and reading a bit farther to locate more information. This is called clarifying. As you read, stop and determine which parts were unclear. Identify unfamiliar words, and look on the page for supporting diagrams, maps, or pictures that might help you. Read the following paragraph using these techniques.

What is a reconstruction government? Was it explained earlier in the chapter?

> In the 1870s, Reconstruction governments began creating public school systems for both races, which had not existed in the South before the war. Within a few years, more than 50 percent of the white children and about 40 percent of African American children in the South were enrolled in public schools. Northern missionary societies also established academies offering advanced education for African Americans.
> —*from page 638*

Reading Tip

As you read, make a list of words you don't know. Look them up in the dictionary. Practice using them and your vocabulary words in sentences.

What were the children doing who were not enrolled in public schools?

What is a missionary society? Is it defined in the glossary?

Practice It!

Read the passage on the Freedmen's Bureau from Section 1.
With a partner, see if you can answer the questions below:

> More progress was made in helping freed African Americans. In March 1865, Congress and the president set up a new government agency to help former enslaved persons, or freedmen. It was known as the Freedmen's Bureau.
>
> After the war, the Freedmen's Bureau helped African Americans adjust to freedom. The agency distributed food and clothing, and provided medical services that lowered the death rate among freed African Americans. It also set up schools staffed by Northern teachers such as Charlotte Forten and gave aid to new African American schools of high learning, such as Atlanta University, Howard University, and Fisk University. The bureau helped freed people acquire land or work with fair wages. Although the main goal of the bureau was to aid African Americans, it also helped pro-Union Southerners.
>
> —*from page 626*

Read to Write

Look in your local newspaper or a magazine for an interview with a famous person. Based on what you read, what additional questions would you ask?

▼ Mother and daughter reading

Monitor	Clarify
Were there any unfamiliar words?	Look in a glossary or dictionary
Do you know what the Freedmen's Bureau was?	
Who created the new agency?	Reread selection

Apply It!

As you read this chapter, identify one topic or event that you would like explained more fully. Then, do research to find answers to the questions you have. Use your answers to write a paragraph of explanation.

Section 1

Reconstruction Plans

Guide to Reading

Looking Back, Looking Ahead

You learned that the Civil War ended in a Northern victory but at terrible costs to both sides. Northern politicians needed to figure out how to return the Southern states to the Union and what rights to allow the newly freed African Americans.

Focusing on the Main Ideas

- Differences over how Reconstruction after the Civil War should be carried out divided the government. *(page 625)*
- After Lincoln was assassinated, Johnson became president and announced his plan of "Restoration." *(page 626)*

Meeting People

Thaddeus Stevens
Charlotte Forten
John Wilkes Booth
Andrew Johnson

Content Vocabulary

Reconstruction
  (REE•kuhn•STRUHK•shuhn)
amnesty (AM•nuh•stee)
radical (RA•dih•kuhl)
freedmen

Academic Vocabulary

period
approach (uh•PROHCH)
deny (dih•NY)
aid

Reading Strategy

Taking Notes As you read the section, re-create the diagram below and describe each of the Reconstruction plans.

Plan	Description
Ten Percent Plan	
Wade-Davis Plan	
Restoration	

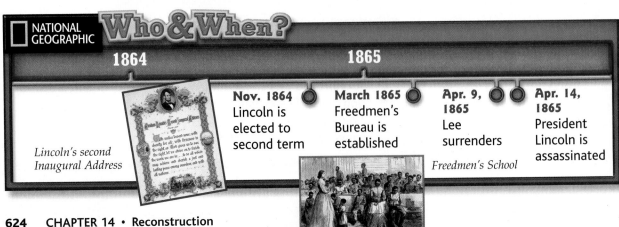

NATIONAL GEOGRAPHIC

Who & When?

1864

1865

Lincoln's second Inaugural Address

Nov. 1864 Lincoln is elected to second term

March 1865 Freedmen's Bureau is established

Freedmen's School

Apr. 9, 1865 Lee surrenders

Apr. 14, 1865 President Lincoln is assassinated

Reconstruction Debate

(Main Idea) **Differences over how Reconstruction after the Civil War should be carried out divided the government.**

Reading Connection How would you have established terms of peace and rebuilding following the Civil War? Read to find out how President Lincoln and the Republicans in Congress disagreed about the treatment of the Southern states as they returned to the Union.

An American Story

When Confederate soldiers—tired, ragged, and hungry—went home at the end of the war, they often returned to a ruined land. Mary Chesnut of South Carolina wrote about what she saw and felt when she traveled:

❝CAMDEN, S. C., *May 2, 1865.* Since we left Chester nothing but solitude, nothing but tall blackened chimneys, to show that any man has ever trod this road before. This is Sherman's track. It is hard not to curse him. I wept incessantly at first. The roses of the gardens are already hiding the ruins.❞

—Mary Chesnut,
A Diary From Dixie

Destruction in the South The war saved the Union but left the South devastated. Cities and plantations were in ruin, and roads, bridges and railroads were destroyed. More than 258,000 Confederate soldiers had died in the war, and illness and injuries weakened thousands more. Americans everywhere agreed that the South needed to be rebuilt, but they disagreed bitterly over how to accomplish it. This **period** of rebuilding is called **Reconstruction** (REE•kuhn•STRUHK•shuhn). This term also refers to the various plans for carrying out the rebuilding.

"*We have turned. . . loose four million slaves without a hut to shelter them or a cent in their pockets.*"

—*Thaddeus Stevens in a speech to Congress, December 1865*

Lincoln's Plan President Lincoln offered the first plan for accepting the South back into the Union. In December 1863, during the Civil War, the president announced the Ten Percent Plan. When 10 percent of the voters of a state took an oath of loyalty to the Union, the State could form a government and adopt a new constitution that banned slavery.

Lincoln wanted to encourage pro-Union Southerners to run the state governments. He believed that punishing the South would only delay healing the torn nation. The president offered **amnesty** (AM•nuh•stee)—immunity from prosecution—to all white Southerners, except Confederate leaders, who gave loyalty to the Union. In 1864 three states under Union occupation—Louisiana, Arkansas, and Tennessee—set up governments under Lincoln's plan. Some Republicans considered Lincoln's plan too mild. Favoring a more **radical,** or extreme, **approach,** they were called Radical Republicans.

The Radicals' Plan A leading Radical Republican, **Thaddeus Stevens,** declared that the foundations of the South "must be broken up and relaid, or all our blood and treasure have been spent in vain." Controlled by Radical Republicans, Congress voted to **deny** seats to representatives from any state reconstructed under Lincoln's plan. Then it began to create its own more radical plan.

In July 1864, Congress passed the Wade-Davis Bill. First, most white males in a state had to swear loyalty to the Union. Second, only white males who swore they had not fought the Union could vote for delegates to a constitutional convention. Former Confederates were barred from public office. Finally, any new state constitution had to end slavery. Only then could a state rejoin the Union.

Lincoln refused to sign the bill into law. He did, however, want new state governments that would restore order quickly. He realized that he would have to compromise with the Radical Republicans.

The Freedmen's Bureau More progress was made in helping freed African Americans. In March 1865, Congress and the president set up a new government agency to help former enslaved persons, or **freedmen.** It was known as the Freedmen's Bureau.

After the war, the Freedmen's Bureau helped African Americans adjust to freedom. The agency distributed food and clothing, and provided medical services that lowered the death rate among freed African Americans. It also set up schools staffed by Northern teachers such as **Charlotte Forten** and gave **aid** to new African American schools of higher learning, such as Atlanta University, Howard University, and Fisk University. The bureau helped freed people acquire land or work with fair wages. Although the main goal of the bureau was to aid African Americans, it also helped pro-Union Southerners.

✔**Reading Check** **Explain** What was Lincoln's Ten Percent Plan?

Lincoln Is Assassinated

Main Idea After Lincoln was assassinated, Johnson became president and announced his plan of "Restoration."

Reading Connection How do you think the loss of a strong leader might impact a nation during a difficult time? Read to find out how the death of Lincoln affected the course of Reconstruction.

A terrible event soon threw the debates over Reconstruction into confusion. On the evening of April 14, 1865, President and Mrs. Lincoln attended a play at Ford's Theater in Washington, D.C. As the Lincolns watched the play from a private box in the balcony, **John Wilkes Booth,** a pro-Confederate actor, entered the box and shot the president in the head. He then leaped to the stage and escaped from the theater. The wounded president died a few hours later.

After fleeing Ford's Theater, Booth rode on horseback to Virginia. There, Union troops tracked him down and cornered him in a barn. When Booth refused to give up, he was shot to death. Booth was part of a small group that had plotted to kill several government officials.

A Nation Mourns News of Lincoln's death shocked the nation. African Americans mourned the death of the man who had helped them win their freedom. Northern whites grieved for the leader who had saved the Union.

A funeral train carried Lincoln's body on a 1,700-mile journey from Washington, D.C., to his home town of Springfield, Illinois. Thousands of people lined the route. At night, bonfires and torches lit the way. By day, bells tolled and cannons fired.

Lincoln's second Inaugural Address, read at the cemetery, reminded Americans of his plan "to do all which may achieve and cherish a just, and a lasting peace, among ourselves, and with all nations." The future, however, was in the hands of those who favored harsher measures against the former Confederacy.

Biography

CHARLOTTE FORTEN
1837–1914

Charlotte Forten was the first northern African American schoolteacher to go south to teach former slaves. In late 1861, Union army forces captured a group of islands off the coast of South Carolina and Georgia. Thousands of enslaved people had been left there as their owners fled from the northern soldiers. Many government leaders and abolitionists saw this as a chance to show that former slaves could live successfully as free citizens. The Port Royal Experiment gave educational and medical aid to the freed slaves on the islands. Charlotte Forten was one of the teachers who volunteered to help. She taught there from 1862 to 1864.

Forten was born in Philadelphia. She studied in Salem, Massachusetts, from 1854 to 1856. For two years, she taught elementary school there. However, she wanted to be part of a larger cause. The Port Royal Experiment gave her the opportunity to help others.

Forten kept a journal of her years on the Sea Islands. In it she expressed her commitment to help the former slaves. She also revealed her own feelings as a young African American woman growing up in a mostly white country.

"This morning a large number—superintendents, teachers, and freed people, assembled in the little Baptist church. It was a sight that I shall not soon forget—that crowd of eager, happy black faces from which the shadow of slavery had forever passed. 'Forever free!' 'Forever free!' Those magical words were all the time singing themselves in my soul. . . ."

Later, she lived in Washington, D.C., and continued to support equal rights for African Americans.

A FREE BLACK GIRL BEFORE THE CIVIL WAR

The Diary of Charlotte Forten, 1854

"[T]he eyes of these freed children see no clouds in it."
—from *Life on the Sea Islands* by **Charlotte Forten**

Then and Now

Through her work in education, Charlotte Forten influenced many people. What teachers have influenced you and helped you learn?

A New President When Lincoln died, Vice President **Andrew Johnson** became president. Johnson was Southern born but pro Union. When Johnson's state (Tennessee) seceded in 1861, Johnson rejected its action and remained in his Senate seat.

In 1864 the Republicans nominated him for vice president. As Lincoln's running mate, Johnson had sharply attacked southern leaders. He once said:

> 66 Treason, must be made odious [hateful] and Traitors punished. 99
>
> —as Tennessee war governor, 1862

The Radical Republicans were pleased with Johnson's statements and expected him to be harsher than Lincoln toward the South. Johnson announced his own Reconstruction plan, which he called "Restoration," in May 1865. Under his plan, most Southerners would be granted amnesty once they swore loyalty to the Union. High-ranking or wealthy Confederates could be

pardoned by appealing to the president. This provision revealed Johnson's desire to humiliate the wealthy leaders who he believed had tricked the South's people into seceding.

Johnson also allowed only loyal, pardoned whites to vote for delegates to the state constitutional conventions. Stating that "white men alone must manage the South," Johnson opposed African Africans having equal rights or the vote.

The Thirteenth Amendment Before entering the Union, a state had to denounce secession and end slavery. States also had to ratify the Thirteenth Amendment to the Constitution, which Congress had passed in January 1865. The amendment abolished slavery in all of the United States. By the end of 1865, all the former Confederate states except Texas had new governments and were ready to rejoin the Union.

✓ **Reading Check** **Compare** How did President Johnson's plan for Reconstruction differ from that of the Radical Republicans?

Study Central Need help understanding Reconstruction? Visit tajwwI.glencoe.com and click on Study Central.

Section 1 Review

Reading Summary

Review the Main Ideas

- The plan for Reconstruction developed by the Radical Republicans was much harsher than that proposed by President Lincoln.

- Following the assassination of President Lincoln, President Andrew Johnson took office and announced his plan for the "Restoration" of the South.

What Did You Learn?

1. What did the Thirteenth Amendment provide?

2. What was the Freedmen's Bureau, and what was its goal?

Critical Thinking

3. **Comparing** Re-create the diagram below and compare Lincoln's Ten Percent Plan to the Radical Republicans' Wade-Davis Bill.

Reconstruction Plans	
Ten Percent Plan	Wade-Davis Bill

4. **Drawing Conclusions** Do you think President Johnson's early ties to the South influenced his Reconstruction plans? Explain your answer.

5. **The Big Ideas** How did Lincoln's and the Radical Republicans' ideas about Reconstruction differ?

6. **READING Monitoring and Clarifying** Reread the passage called "Lincoln's Plan" on page 625. What words were new to you? List words you did not know and define them.

Guide to Reading

Looking Back, Looking Ahead

You learned that after Lincoln was assassinated, Andrew Johnson became president and proposed his own plan for restoring the Southern states into the Union. The Radical Republicans in Congress, however, had very different ideas about how the Southern states should be allowed to rejoin the North.

Focusing on the Main Ideas

- When Northerners realized that African Americans in the South were still being mistreated, Congress worked to find a solution. *(page 630)*
- Radical Republicans were able to put their version of Reconstruction into action. *(page 631)*

Meeting People

Edwin Stanton

Ulysses S. Grant

Content Vocabulary

black codes

override

impeach (ihm•PEECH)

Academic Vocabulary

prohibit (proh•HIH•buht)

enable (ih•NAY•buhl)

Reading Strategy

Organizing Information As you read the section, re-create the diagram below and provide information about impeachment.

Impeachment	
What is it?	
Who was impeached?	
Outcome of the trial?	

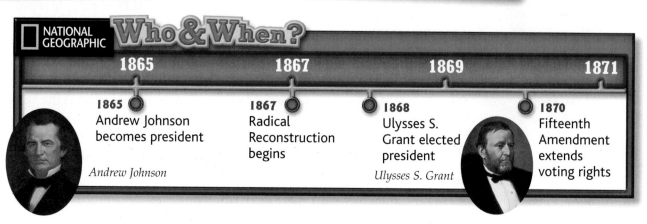

NATIONAL GEOGRAPHIC **Who & When?**

1865   1867   1869   1871

1865 Andrew Johnson becomes president

Andrew Johnson

1867 Radical Reconstruction begins

1868 Ulysses S. Grant elected president

Ulysses S. Grant

1870 Fifteenth Amendment extends voting rights

African Americans' Rights

Main Idea When Northerners realized that African Americans in the South were still being mistreated, Congress worked to find a solution.

Reading Connection Do you know the requirements for being a United States citizen? Is being born in this country enough to make a person a citizen? Read to find out how Congress made sure that the African Americans freed after the Civil War became citizens.

An American Story

In May 1866, white mobs in Memphis, Tennessee, burned African American churches, schools, and homes. Close to 50 people, nearly all of them African American, died. Many Northerners saw the violence as an attempt by whites to keep African Americans from exercising their rights. This and similar riots in the South made Radical Republicans realize that the Johnson Reconstruction plan was not strong enough.

Southern Representatives During the fall of 1865, Southerners created new state governments based on the Johnson plan. They also elected to Congress new representatives, some of whom had been leading Confederate officials. When the Southern representatives arrived in Washington, D.C., Congress refused to seat them. Many Republicans opposed readmitting the South on such easy terms.

▲ As early as 1865, groups were forming to commit violence against African Americans. This flag is the symbol for one such group, the Ku Klux Klan.

To many Northerners, Johnson's plan was robbing the Union of its hard-won victory. Northerners also realized that the treatment of African Americans in the South was not improving.

Black Codes By the spring of 1866, Southern states had passed **black codes,** or laws that aimed to control freed men and women. The black codes trampled the rights of African Americans. They permitted plantation owners to exploit African American workers and allowed officials to arrest and fine jobless African Americans. The black codes also banned African Americans from owning or renting farms. To freed men and women and many Northerners, the black codes brought back slavery in disguise.

Challenging the Codes In early 1866, Congress gave the Freedmen's Bureau new powers. The agency now was able to set up special courts to try individuals charged with violating the rights of African Americans. African Americans could serve on juries in these courts. This gave them the opportunity to play a new role in pursuing justice.

Congress also passed a civil rights bill that overturned the black codes. This measure made African Americans full citizens and gave the federal government power to intervene in state affairs to protect African American rights.

President Johnson vetoed both bills, arguing that the federal government was going beyond its proper authority. He also said that the measures were unconstitutional because they were passed by a Congress that did not include representation from all the states. By raising the issue of representation, Johnson indirectly threatened to veto any bill passed by this Congress.

Republicans in Congress had enough votes to **override,** or defeat, both vetoes, and the bills became law. As the split between the president and Congress grew, the chances of them working together faded. The Radical Republicans rejected any compromise and drafted a new Reconstruction plan—one led by Congress.

The Fourteenth Amendment Although the Thirteenth Amendment ensured the freedom of African Americans, it did not guarantee them full rights. After the Civil War, many Southern states passed laws that kept African Americans from holding certain jobs, limited their property rights, and restricted them in other ways.

To remedy this situation, Congress passed the Fourteenth Amendment to the Constitution in 1866. The Fourteenth Amendment was enacted in 1868. This new amendment gave full citizenship to all people born in the United States. Because most African Americans were American born, they became full citizens. The amendment also required every state to grant its citizens "equal protection of the laws."

This clause has been extremely important. In recent years, it has been used to benefit women, people with disabilities, and other groups whose rights have not always been protected fairly. The amendment also stated that no state could take away a citizen's life, liberty, and property "without due process of law." States that kept any adult male citizen from voting could lose part of their representation in Congress. Finally, the amendment barred leading former Confederates from holding national or state office unless pardoned by Congress. 📖 *(See pages 263–264 for the entire text of the Fourteenth Amendment.)*

Congress declared that Southern states had to ratify the amendment to rejoin the Union. Of the 11 Southern states, the only state to ratify was Tennessee. The refusal of the other Southern states delayed the adoption of the amendment until 1868.

Republican Victory In the congressional elections of 1866, President Johnson campaigned vigorously against the Fourteenth Amendment and its supporters. Many Northerners objected to the nasty tone of Johnson's campaign. The Republicans won a solid victory, giving Congress the signal to take Reconstruction into its own hands.

✔️ **Reading Check** **Describe** What does the Fourteenth Amendment provide?

Radical Reconstruction

Main Idea Radical Republicans were able to put their version of Reconstruction into action.

Reading Connection If you were a member of Congress during this time, what do you think would be most important to include in Reconstruction plans? Read to learn some of the plans that Congress passed.

The Republicans in Congress quickly took charge of Reconstruction. President Johnson could do little to stop them because Congress could easily override his vetoes. Thus began a period known as Radical Reconstruction.

🎨 **History** *Through Art*

His First Vote **by Thomas Waterman Wood**
Wood's oil painting emphasized the importance of the ballot to African American voters. *How did African American males gain the right to vote?*

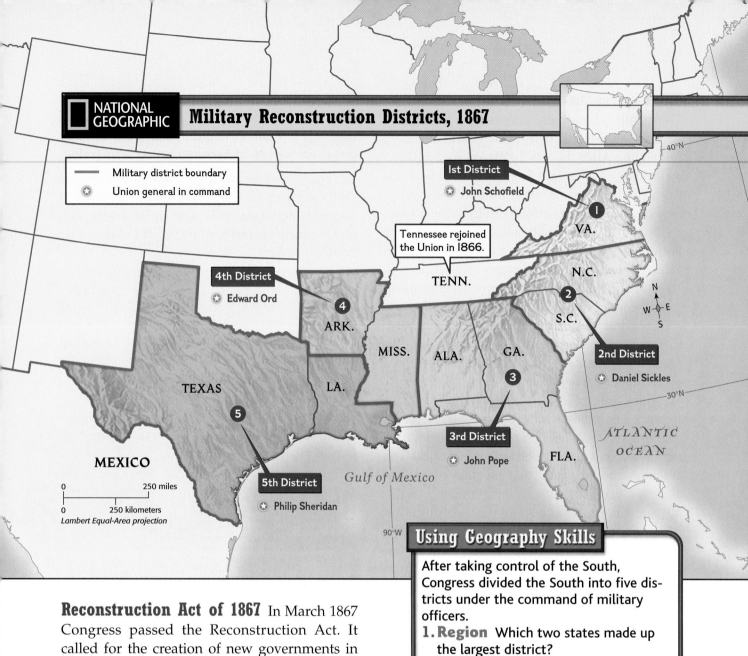

Military Reconstruction Districts, 1867

— Military district boundary

⊛ Union general in command

1st District
⊛ John Schofield

VA.

Tennessee rejoined the Union in 1866.

TENN.

N.C.

4th District
⊛ Edward Ord

4
ARK.

S.C.

2

2nd District
⊛ Daniel Sickles

MISS. ALA. GA.

TEXAS

5

3

LA.

3rd District
⊛ John Pope

FLA.

MEXICO

0 ___ 250 miles
0 ___ 250 kilometers
Lambert Equal-Area projection

ATLANTIC OCEAN

5th District
⊛ Philip Sheridan

Gulf of Mexico

90°W

40°N

30°N

N W E S

Using Geography Skills

After taking control of the South, Congress divided the South into five districts under the command of military officers.

1. **Region** Which two states made up the largest district?
2. **Analyze** Why did no Union troops occupy Tennessee?

Reconstruction Act of 1867 In March 1867 Congress passed the Reconstruction Act. It called for the creation of new governments in the 10 Southern states that had not ratified the Fourteenth Amendment. Tennessee, which had ratified the amendment, kept its government, and the state rejoined the Union.

The act divided the 10 Southern states into five military districts and placed each under the authority of a military commander until new governments were formed. The act also guaranteed African American males the right to vote in state elections, and it prevented former Confederate leaders from holding political office.

To rejoin the Union, the states had to ratify the Fourteenth Amendment and submit new state constitutions to Congress for approval. A Second Reconstruction Act required the military commanders to register voters and prepare for state constitutional conventions.

The Readmission of States Many white Southerners refused to take part in the elections for constitutional conventions and state governments. Thousands of newly registered African American voters did use their right to vote. In the elections, Republicans gained control of Southern state governments. By 1868 seven Southern states—Alabama, Arkansas, Florida, Georgia, Louisiana, North Carolina, and South Carolina—had established new governments and met the conditions for readmission to the Union. By 1870 Mississippi, Virginia, and Texas were restored to the Union.

Challenge to Johnson Strongly opposed to Radical Reconstruction, President Johnson had the power as commander in chief of the army to direct the actions of the military governors. For this reason, Congress passed several laws to limit the president's power.

One of these laws, the Tenure of Office Act of March 1867, was a deliberate challenge. It **prohibited** the president from removing government officials, including members of his own cabinet, without the Senate's approval. The act violated the tradition that presidents controlled their cabinets, and it threatened presidential power.

Impeaching the President The conflict between Johnson and the Radicals grew more intense. In August 1867—when Congress was not in session—Johnson suspended Secretary of War **Edwin Stanton** without the Senate's approval.

When the Senate met again and refused to approve the suspension, Johnson removed Stanton from office—a deliberate violation of the Tenure of Office Act. Johnson angered the Republicans further by appointing some generals the Radicals opposed as commanders of Southern military districts.

Outraged by Johnson's actions, the House of Representatives voted to **impeach** (ihm • PEECH) —formally charge with wrongdoing—the president. The House accused Johnson of misconduct and sent the case to the Senate for trial.

The Constitution allows Congress to remove from office any federal official who has committed serious wrongdoing. If a majority of the House votes to impeach a public official, the Senate acts as jury and decides by a two-thirds vote whether to convict and remove the person from office.

The Impeachment Trial The trial began in March 1868 and lasted almost three months. Johnson's defenders claimed that the president was exercising his right to challenge laws he considered unconstitutional. The impeachment, they argued, was politically motivated and thus contrary to the spirit of the Constitution.

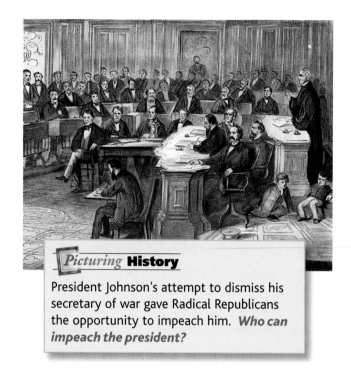

Picturing **History**

President Johnson's attempt to dismiss his secretary of war gave Radical Republicans the opportunity to impeach him. *Who can impeach the president?*

Samuel J. Tilden, a Democrat from New York, claimed that Congress was trying to remove the president from office without accusing him of a crime "or anything more than a mere difference of opinion."

Johnson's accusers argued that Congress should retain the supreme power to make the laws. Senator Charles Sumner of Massachusetts declared that Johnson had turned

❝ the veto power conferred by the Constitution as a remedy for ill-considered legislation . . . into a weapon of offense against Congress. ❞

> —Charles Sumner, at Johnson's impeachment trial

In May the senators cast two votes. In both instances, the result was 35 to 19 votes to convict the president—one vote short of the two-thirds majority required by the Constitution for conviction. Several moderate Republicans voted for a verdict of not guilty because they did not believe a president should be removed from office for political differences. As a result, Johnson stayed in office until the end of his term in March 1869.

Only two presidents have been impeached: Johnson in 1868 and Bill Clinton in 1998. Both presidents were tried by the Senate and acquitted (they were not removed from office).

Election of 1868 By the presidential election of 1868, most Southern states had rejoined the Union. Many Americans hoped that conflicts over Reconstruction and sectional divisions were behind them.

Abandoning Johnson, the Republicans chose General **Ulysses S. Grant**, the Civil War hero, as their presidential candidate. The Democrats nominated Horatio Seymour, a former governor of New York.

Grant won the election, gaining 214 of 294 electoral votes. He also received most of the votes of African Americans in the South. The 1868 election was a vote on Reconstruction, and the voters supported the Republican approach to the issue.

The Fifteenth Amendment The election of 1868 made some Republicans realize that if African Americans could vote throughout the country, they could help Republicans win elections. After the election, Republicans developed their last major piece of Reconstruction legislation. In February 1869, Congress passed the Fifteenth Amendment. It prohibited the state and federal governments from denying the right to vote to any male citizen because of "race, color, or previous condition of servitude."

African American men won the right to vote when the Fifteenth Amendment was ratified and became law in February 1870. Republicans thought that the power of the ballot would **enable** African Americans to protect themselves. That belief, it turned out, was too optimistic.

📖 (See page 264 for the entire text of the Fifteenth Amendment.)

✔ **Reading Check** **Explain** What two presidents have been impeached by Congress?

Study Central Need help understanding Radical Reconstruction? Visit tajww1.glencoe.com and click on Study Central.

What Did You Learn?

1. Discuss two ways Southerners violated Lincoln's plan for Reconstruction.

2. What is impeachment? Was President Johnson impeached?

Critical Thinking

3. **Summarizing** Re-create the diagram below and answer the questions about these amendments.

	Date ratified	Impact on life
Fourteenth Amendment		
Fifteenth Amendment		

4. **The Big Ideas** Why did the Radical Republicans in Congress turn to constitutional amendments to guarantee the rights of African Americans?

5. **ANALYSIS** **Analyze** How did disagreement over states' rights and federal sovereignty affect Reconstruction plans? What examples of the "balance of power" and the system of checks and balances established by the Constitution can you find in this section? Write an essay summarizing your conclusion.

Reading Summary

Review the Main Ideas

- To challenge the South's black codes, which limited the rights of newly freed African Americans, the Republicans in Congress passed legislation addressing civil rights and creating the Freedmen's Bureau.

- President Johnson's opposition to the Reconstruction plans of the Radical Republicans led to his impeachment trial.

Section 3

The South During Reconstruction

Guide to Reading

Looking Back, Looking Ahead

You learned that Congress passed the Fourteenth and Fifteenth Amendments to help African Americans gain equal rights. Although African Americans made some gains, most white Southerners refused to recognize their rights.

Focusing on the Main Ideas

- Violence against African Americans and their white supporters took place during Reconstruction. *(page 636)*
- After the Civil War, the South had to rebuild not only its farms and roads, but its social and political structures as well. *(page 638)*

Meeting People

Hiram Revels

Frederick Douglass

Blanche K. Bruce

Content Vocabulary

scalawag (SKA•lih•WAG)

carpetbagger (KAHR•puht•BA•guhr)

corruption (kuh•RUHP•shuhn)

integrate (IN•tuh•GRAYT)

sharecropping (SHEHR•KRAHP•ihng)

Academic Vocabulary

dominate (DAH•muh•NAYT)

brief (BREEF)

region (REE•juhn)

create (kree•AYT)

Reading Strategy

Organizing Information As you read the section, re-create the diagram below and describe improvements in the South in education.

Improvements in education

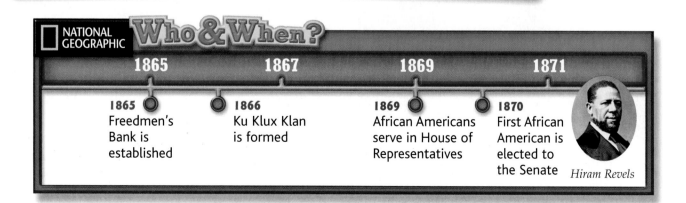

NATIONAL GEOGRAPHIC **Who & When?**

1865 — **1867** — **1869** — **1871**

1865 Freedmen's Bank is established

1866 Ku Klux Klan is formed

1869 African Americans serve in House of Representatives

1870 First African American is elected to the Senate

Hiram Revels

New Groups Take Charge

Main Idea Violence against African Americans and their white supporters took place during Reconstruction.

Reading Connection How might you feel if someone tried to take away your rights through threats and violence? Read to find out how some white Southerners attempted to intimidate African Americans and keep them from voting and exercising their rights.

An American Story

"The dust of our fathers mingles with yours in the same graveyards. . . . This is your country, but it is ours too." So spoke an emancipated African American after the Civil War. Most formerly enslaved people did not seek revenge or power over whites, only respect and equality. The petition of an African American convention in 1865 stated:

Picturing **History**

In 1870 Hiram Revels was elected to the Senate. *What state did he represent?*

66 We simply desire that we shall be recognized as men; . . . that the same laws which govern *white men* shall direct colored men; . . . that we be dealt with as others, in equity [fairness] and justice. 99

—**Address of the Colored State Convention to the People of the State of South Carolina**

Republicans Take Charge During Reconstruction, the Republicans came to **dominate** Southern politics. Support for the Republican party came from African Americans, white Southerners who backed Republican goals, and white settlers from the North. These groups ran state governments.

African Americans in Government African Americans played an important role both as voters and as officials. In some states, they contributed heavily to Republican victories. African Americans did not control the government of any state, although they **briefly** had a majority in the lower house of the South Carolina legislature. In other Southern states, they held major positions but never in proportion to their numbers.

At the national level, 16 African Americans served in the House of Representatives and 2 in the Senate between 1869 and 1880. **Hiram Revels,** one of the African American senators, was an ordained minister who had recruited African Americans for the Union army. He also started a school for freed African Americans in Missouri and served as a chaplain of an African American regiment in Mississippi. Revels remained in Mississippi after the war and was elected to the Senate in 1870. **Frederick Douglass** was also an important leader who insisted on full equality for African Americans.

Blanche K. Bruce, the other African American senator, also came from Mississippi. A former runaway slave, Bruce taught in an African American school in Missouri when the war began. In 1869 he went to Mississippi and entered politics. He was elected to the Senate in 1874.

Biography

FREDERICK DOUGLASS
1817–1895

Frederick Douglass lived as a slave for 21 years before he escaped to the North in 1838. He was born on a Maryland plantation in 1817, and his early years were characterized by beatings, poor living conditions, and constant shuffling from one plantation to another. The wife of one of his masters, Sophia Auld, took a liking to Douglass and began to teach him to read and write. Her efforts stopped after her husband learned of her teachings, and Douglass took it upon himself to continue where she had left off.

The more Douglass read, the more he felt the injustice of slavery. In 1838 Douglass made his way north by disguising himself as a free African American sailor. In Massachusetts, he quickly emerged as a leader of the movement for liberty for African Americans. In 1841 Douglass became a well-known speaker for the American Anti-Slavery Society. Douglass traveled through the Northern states speaking against slavery and for the equality of African Americans. When the Civil War began, Douglass urged President Lincoln to free the enslaved people, and he helped organize African American troops to fight for freedom.

After Lincoln was assassinated, Douglass opposed President Johnson's Reconstruction program. Instead he supported the Radical Republican plan. A skilled and powerful speaker, Douglass traveled throughout the nation insisting on full equality for African Americans. He was particularly outspoken in support of the Fifteenth Amendment, guaranteeing African American men the right to vote.

"Whenever my condition was improved, instead of its increasing my contentment, it only increased my desire to be free."

—from *Narrative of the Life of Frederick Douglass, an American Slave*

Douglass continued to support civil rights causes late into his life. He also wrote, started his own newspaper, and gave lectures. On January 20, 1895, he gave a speech at a meeting of women's rights advocates in Washington, D.C. Later that night, he died of a heart attack.

Then and Now

Frederick Douglass overcame many obstacles to be a leader in the fight for freedom. Can you think of any present-day individuals who overcame obstacles to excel at something? Explain.

Scalawags and Carpetbaggers Some Southern whites—for example, non-slaveholding farmers and pro-Union business leaders— backed the Republicans. Former Confederates called them **scalawags** (SKA•lih•WAGZ), a term meaning "worthless rascals." Also, many Northern whites living in the South, such as Union army veterans and Freedmen's Bureau members, were Republican supporters. Critics called them **carpetbaggers** (KAHR•puht•BA• guhrz) because some arrived with their belongings in cheap suitcases made of carpet fabric.

Many Southerners accused Reconstruction governments of **corruption** (kuh•RUHP•shuhn), or dishonest or illegal actions. Although some officials made money illegally, probably less corruption occurred in the South than in the North.

Resistance to Reconstruction
Most Southern whites opposed efforts to expand African Americans' rights. Life soon became difficult for African Americans. Most white landowners refused to rent land to freedmen. Store owners refused African Americans credit, and employers would not hire them.

Secret societies, such as the Ku Klux Klan, used fear and violence to deny rights to freed men and women. Wearing white sheets and hoods, Klan members killed many African Americans and their white friends. They beat and wounded many more and burned African American homes, schools, and churches. Many Southerners, especially planters and Democrats, backed the Klan and other violent groups. These Southerners, who had the most to gain from the return of white supremacy, saw violence as a defense against Republican rule.

✓ Reading Check **Explain** Why did laws to control the Ku Klux Klan have little effect?

History Online

Student Web Activity Visit tajwwI.glencoe.com and click on *Chapter 14—Student Web Activities* for an activity on the first African American members of Congress.

Some Improvements

Main Idea **After the Civil War, the South had to rebuild not only its farms and roads, but its social and political structures as well.**

Reading Connection How important is education to a person's ability to function as a citizen and to protect his or her rights? Read to find out about the improvements Reconstruction brought to education for African Americans in the South.

Despite the violence, Reconstruction brought important changes throughout the South. This was especially true in education.

Education improved for both African Americans and whites. African Americans saw education as an important step to a better life. In many **regions,** they created their own schools, contributing both labor and money to build the schools.

The Freedmen's Bureau and private charities played a major role in spreading education. Northern women and free African Americans came South to teach in these schools. By 1870 about 4,000 schools had been established, with 200,000 students. More than half the teachers in these schools were African American.

Public Schools In the 1870s, Reconstruction governments began **creating** public school systems for both races, which had not existed in the South before the war. Within a few years, more than 50 percent of the white children and about 40 percent of African American children in the South were enrolled in public schools. Northern missionary societies also established academies offering advanced education for African Americans. Some academies developed into colleges and universities, such as Morehouse College and Atlanta University.

Generally, African American and white students attended different schools. Only Louisiana, South Carolina, and Florida required that schools be **integrated** (IN•tuh•GRAYT•ihd)—include both whites and African Americans—but the laws were not enforced.

Farming the Land Along with education, most freed people wanted land. Some African Americans were able to buy land with the assistance of the Freedmen's Bank, established in 1865. Most, however, failed to get their own land.

The most common form of farmwork for freed individuals was **sharecropping** (SHEHR•KRAHP•ihng). In this system, a landowner rented a plot of land to a sharecropper, or farmer, along with a crude shack, some seeds and tools, and perhaps a mule. Sharecroppers did not pay their rent in cash. Instead, they paid a share of their crops—often as much as one-half to two-thirds—to cover their rent as well as the cost of the seed, fertilizer, tools, and animals they needed.

After paying the landowners, sharecroppers often had little left to sell. Sometimes they had barely enough to feed their families. For many, sharecropping was little better than slavery.

Reading Check **Explain** How did sharecroppers get land to farm?

▲ Mother and daughter reading

Study Central Need help understanding life in the South during Reconstruction? Visit tajwwI.glencoe.com and click on Study Central.

Section 3 Review

Reading Summary

Review the Main Ideas

- Some African Americans, along with white Northerners and white Southerners who had opposed the Confederacy, served in government; other Southerners used violence to prevent African Americans from exercising their rights.

- New schools in the South helped African Americans gain an education, but most African Americans were denied the opportunity to own land.

What Did You Learn?

1. How did some Southerners try to maintain control over freed people?

2. What role did scalawags and carpetbaggers play in Reconstruction?

Critical Thinking

3. **Organizing Information** Re-create the diagram below and identify the three groups that made up the Southern Republican Party.

4. **The Big Ideas** Why were the political ideas of the Radical Republicans difficult to carry out in the South?

5. **Persuasive Writing** Imagine you are a newspaper journalist in 1869 and have set up interviews with an African American senator from Mississippi, a carpetbagger living in Georgia, and a white plantation owner from South Carolina. List questions you could ask about Reconstruction. Imagine how each would respond, and write a newspaper article detailing your interview.

Section 4

Change in the South

Guide to Reading

Looking Back, Looking Ahead

You read earlier that Reconstruction met resistance in the South, and African Americans made few real economic gains there. By the mid-1870s, Reconstruction was coming to an end, and the South was undergoing even more changes.

Focusing on the Main Ideas

- Democrats steadily regained control of Southern governments as support for Radical Reconstruction policies decreased. *(page 641)*
- When Reconstruction ended, many changes took place in the South including a political shift and growth in industry. *(page 645)*
- As Reconstruction ended, true freedom for African Americans became a distant dream. *(page 647)*

Meeting People

Horace Greeley
Rutherford B. Hayes
Samuel Tilden
Henry Grady
James Duke
W.E.B. Du Bois (doo BAWIHS)

Content Vocabulary

reconciliation
(REH • kuhn • SIH • lee • AY • shuhn)
commission
cash crop
poll tax
literacy test (LIH • tuh • ruh • see)
grandfather clause
segregation (SEH • grih • GAY • shuhn)
lynching (LIHNCH • ihng)

Academic Vocabulary

exploit (EHK • SPLOYT)
enforce (ihn • FOHRS)
eliminate (ih • LIH • muh • NAYT)
commit

Reading Strategy

Comparing As you read the section, re-create the diagram below and list the advantages and disadvantages of an agricultural economy.

Agricultural Economy

Advantages	Disadvantages

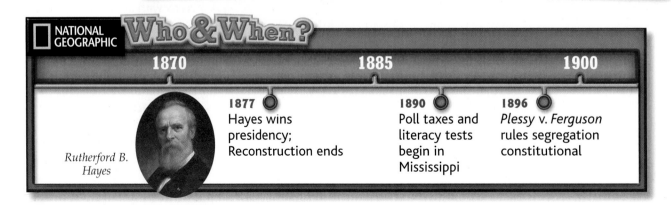

NATIONAL GEOGRAPHIC **Who & When?**

1870 — 1885 — 1900

Rutherford B. Hayes

1877
Hayes wins presidency; Reconstruction ends

1890
Poll taxes and literacy tests begin in Mississippi

1896
Plessy v. *Ferguson* rules segregation constitutional

Reconstruction Ends

Main Idea Democrats steadily regained control of Southern governments as support for Radical Reconstruction policies decreased.

Reading Connection How does politics affect your local community? Do you think issues like equality and fair treatment for African Americans should be influenced by politics? Read on to see how the changing political landscape dramatically affected Reconstruction in the 1870s.

An American Story

Before and during Reconstruction, freed African Americans began moving to Northern cities and to the West in hopes of a better life. Often they faced hostility. One example is the Cox family. Freed by slaveholder John Randolph in Virginia, the Cox family purchased a tract of land in Mercer County, Ohio. When they arrived in their new home, white settlers "came out in force, with their muskets patrolled the banks of the canal and refused to let them settle on their own purchased land." Yet many freed families continued to try to find a new life for themselves.

These reasons for leaving one area and going to another are called push-pull factors. Push factors (racial segregation, Jim Crow laws) drive people away from an area. Pull factors (the opportunity to own land) attract people towards an area.

Loss of Support

During the Grant administration, Northerners began losing interest in Reconstruction. Many believed it was time for the South to solve its own problems.

Reconstruction declined for other reasons. The old Radical leaders began to disappear from the political scene. Thaddeus Stevens died in 1868, and others retired or lost elections.

Another factor that weakened enthusiasm for Reconstruction was racial prejudice in the North. This prejudice was **exploited** by opponents of Reconstruction. They argued that only Southerners really knew how to deal with

African Americans and that the fate of the freed people should be left to the South. Southerners protested what they called "bayonet rule"—the use of federal troops to support Reconstruction governments. President Grant had sent federal troops to the South to stop violence or to **enforce** the law only when absolutely necessary. Generally, though, he tried to avoid any clashes with the South.

Republican Revolt

In the early 1870s, reports of corruption in Grant's administration and in Reconstruction governments spread throughout the nation. Some Republicans split with the party over the issue of corruption. Another group of Republicans broke with the party over Reconstruction, proposing peaceful **reconciliation** (REH•kuhn•SIH•lee•AY•shuhn)—coming together again—with Southern whites. Calling themselves Liberal Republicans, these two groups nominated **Horace Greeley**, a newspaper editor from New York, to run against Grant in the 1872 presidential election.

Analyzing Political Cartoons

Problems in the Grant administration hurt the Republican Party. *Who does the woman at the far right represent? Why is she turning away?*

The Democrats also supported Greeley for president because he offered a chance to defeat the Republicans. Despite the division in the Republican ranks, however, Grant was reelected.

The Amnesty Act
During the 1872 election campaign, Liberal Republicans called for expanded amnesty for white Southerners. In May 1872, Congress passed the Amnesty Act, which pardoned most former Confederates. Nearly all white Southerners could vote and hold office again. The amnesty changed the political balance in the South by restoring full rights to people who supported the Democratic Party.

Democrats Regain Power
In Southern states such as Virginia and North Carolina, where a majority of voters were white, Democrats soon regained control of state governments. In states where African Americans held a majority or where white and African American populations were nearly equal, the Ku Klux Klan and other violent groups helped the Democrats take power by terrorizing Republican voters.

By the election of 1875, Republican political power in Mississippi was quickly eroding. African American leaders urged voters to go to the polls on election day in spite of threats of violence by Democrats. In a Mississippi newspaper, fourteen African American leaders claimed:

> 66 The success of the Democratic Party will, to all intents and purposes, sound the death knell of all the hopes that the colored man has indulged of educating, elevating and improving his race in this State . . . 99
>
> —from the *Jackson Pilot*, October 4, 1875

What If...

Lincoln Had Survived?

Lincoln's main goal had been to preserve the Union. In his second Inaugural Address, he indicated that he would deal compassionately with the South after the war ended:

> 66 With malice toward none; with charity for all, with firmness in the right as God gives us to see the right, let us strive on to finish the work we are in, to bind up the nation's wounds, to care for him who shall have borne the battle and for his widow and his orphan. . . . 99
>
> —Abraham Lincoln, Second Inaugural Address, March 1865

President Lincoln did not live to carry out his plan. On April 14, 1865, just five days after Lee's surrender, he was assassinated.

Andrew Johnson, who succeeded to the presidency, attempted to carry out Lincoln's Reconstruction policies. He was hampered in this effort because as an unelected president he had little popular following. In addition, as a former Democrat, he could not command the support of the Republican majority in Congress. As a Tennessean and former slaveholder, he offended the Radicals. If these handicaps were not enough, his critics viewed Johnson as self-righteous, hot-tempered, stubborn, and crude.

In March 1868, the House adopted 11 articles of impeachment against Johnson. Although Johnson was acquitted and served out his term, any influence he might have had on Reconstruction was lost.

Ticket to Johnson's ▶
impeachment trial

By 1876 Republicans held a majority in Congress in only three Southern states—Florida, South Carolina, and Louisiana. During these years, the Republicans had other problems they could not blame on the Democrats. In 1873 a series of political scandals came to light. Investigations uncovered top government officials making unfair business deals, scheming to withhold public tax money, and accepting bribes. One scandal involved the vice president, and another the secretary of war. These scandals further damaged the Grant administration and the Republicans. At the same time, the nation suffered an economic depression. Blame for the hard times fell on the Republicans.

By the time of the congressional elections in 1874, charges of corruption and economic mismanagement had badly weakened the Republican Party. Democrats gained seats in the Senate and won control of the House. For the first time since the Civil War, the Democratic Party controlled a part of the federal government. This situation further weakened Congress's commitment to Reconstruction and protecting the rights of newly freed African Americans.

The Election of 1876 President Grant considered running for a third term in 1876. Most Republican leaders preferred a new candidate—one who could win back the Liberal Republicans and unite the party.

The Republicans nominated **Rutherford B. Hayes,** governor of Ohio, for president. A champion of political reform, Hayes had a reputation for honesty, and he held moderate views on Reconstruction. The Democrats nominated New York governor **Samuel Tilden.** Tilden had gained national fame for fighting political corruption in New York City.

After the election, Tilden appeared to be the winner, receiving almost 250,000 more votes than Hayes. However, disputed returns from Florida, Louisiana, South Carolina, and Oregon—representing 20 electoral votes—kept the outcome in doubt. Tilden had 184 electoral votes, only one short of what he needed to win. Yet if Hayes received all 20 of the disputed votes, he would have the 185 electoral votes required for victory.

In January Congress created a special **commission,** or group, of seven Republicans, seven Democrats, and one independent to review the election results. But the independent resigned, and a Republican took his place. After examining the reports of state review boards, the commission voted 8 to 7 to award all 20 disputed votes, and the election, to Hayes. The vote followed party lines.

Democrats in Congress threatened to fight the decision to award the presidency to Hayes. Inauguration Day approached, yet the country still had no new president. Finally, Republican and Southern Democratic leaders met secretly to work out an agreement.

▼ *Lincoln's funeral carriage*

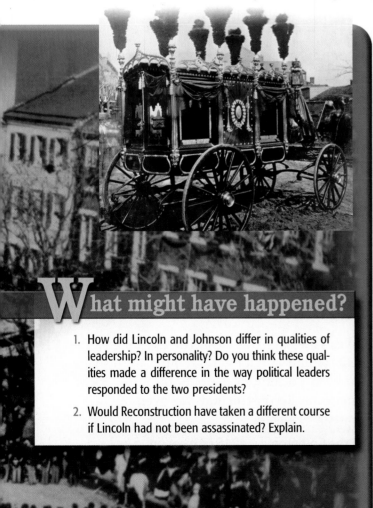

What might have happened?

1. How did Lincoln and Johnson differ in qualities of leadership? In personality? Do you think these qualities made a difference in the way political leaders responded to the two presidents?

2. Would Reconstruction have taken a different course if Lincoln had not been assassinated? Explain.

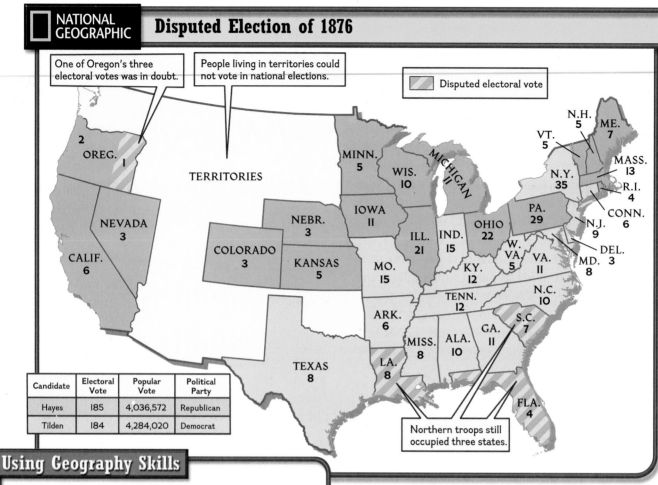

NATIONAL GEOGRAPHIC **Disputed Election of 1876**

One of Oregon's three electoral votes was in doubt.

People living in territories could not vote in national elections.

Disputed electoral vote

Northern troops still occupied three states.

Candidate	Electoral Vote	Popular Vote	Political Party
Hayes	185	4,036,572	Republican
Tilden	184	4,284,020	Democrat

Using Geography Skills

Because of some conflicting results, a committee of 15 members from Congress and the Supreme Court decided the final count in the 1876 election.

1. **Location** Which Southern states sent in election returns that were disputed?
2. **Analyze** By how many electoral votes did Hayes finally win?

Compromise of 1877 Southern Democratic leaders agreed to accept Hayes as president. On March 2, 1877—almost four months after the election—Congress confirmed the verdict of the commission and declared Hayes the winner. He was inaugurated president two days later.

The deal congressional leaders made to settle the election dispute, the Compromise of 1877, included various favors to the South. The new government would give more aid to the region and withdraw all remaining troops from Southern states. The Democrats, in turn, promised to maintain African Americans' rights.

In his Inaugural Address, Hayes declared that what the South needed most was the restoration of "wise, honest, and peaceful local self-government." During a goodwill trip to the South, Hayes announced his intention of letting Southerners handle racial issues. In Atlanta he told an African American audience:

66 . . . [your] rights and interests would be safer if this great mass of intelligent white men were let alone by the general Government. **99**

Hayes's message was clear. The federal government would no longer attempt to reshape Southern society or help Southern African Americans. Reconstruction was over.

Reading Check **Summarize** What effect did the Compromise of 1877 have on Reconstruction?

The South After Reconstruction

Main Idea When Reconstruction ended, many changes took place in the South including a political shift and growth in industry.

Reading Connection How difficult do you think it would be for an area to change its economy from agricultural to industrial? Read to find out how Southern leaders attempted to create a "New South" with strong industries that could compete with those in the North.

An American Story

John Lynch, a member of Congress who had once been enslaved, spoke these words:

❝ I am treated, not as an American citizen, but as a brute. . . . [A]nd for what? Not that I am unable to or unwilling to pay my way; not that I am obnoxious in my personal appearance or disrespectful in my conduct; but simply because I happen to be of a darker complexion. ❞

—quoted in "John Roy Lynch"

At the end of Reconstruction, many African Americans faced lives of poverty, indignity, and despair.

A New Ruling Party

Many Southern whites hated Republicans because of their role in the Civil War and during Reconstruction. When Reconstruction ended, political power in the South shifted from the Republicans to the Democrats.

In some regions, the ruling Democrats were the large landowners and other groups that had held power before the Civil War. In most areas, however, a new ruling class took charge. Among their ranks were merchants, bankers, industrialists, and other business leaders who supported economic development and opposed Northern interference. These Democrats called themselves "Redeemers" because they had "redeemed," or saved, the South from Republican rule.

The Redeemers adopted conservative policies such as lower taxes, less public spending, and reduced government services. They drastically cut, or even **eliminated,** many social services started during Reconstruction, including public education. Their one-party rule and conservative policies dominated Southern politics well into the 1900s.

Rise of the "New South"

By the 1880s, forward-looking Southerners were convinced that their region must develop a strong industrial economy. They argued that the South had lost the Civil War because its industry and manufacturing did not match the North's.

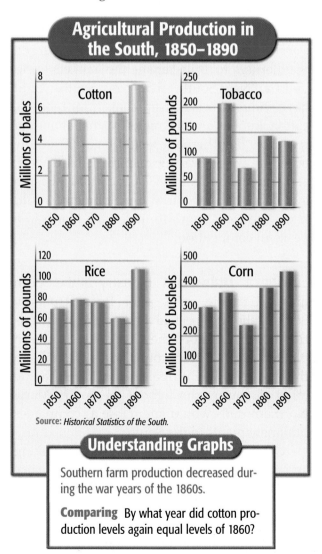

Agricultural Production in the South, 1850–1890

Source: *Historical Statistics of the South.*

Understanding Graphs

Southern farm production decreased during the war years of the 1860s.

Comparing By what year did cotton production levels again equal levels of 1860?

Picturing **History**

During this era, iron and steel industries developed in the South. *How did the Bessemer process help these industries grow?*

Henry Grady, editor of the *Atlanta Constitution,* headed a group that urged Southerners to "out-Yankee the Yankees" and build a "New South." This New South would have industries based on coal, iron, tobacco, cotton, lumber, and the region's other abundant resources. Southerners would create this new economy by embracing a spirit of hard work and regional pride. In 1886 Grady told a Boston audience that industrial development would allow the New South to match the North in a peaceful competition.

Southern Industries Industry in the South made dramatic gains after Reconstruction. Some of the strongest advances were in the textile industry. Before the Civil War, Southern planters had shipped cotton to textile mills in the North or in Europe. In the 1880s, textile mills sprang up throughout the South. Many Northern mills would later close as companies built new plants in the South.

Other important industries were lumbering and tobacco processing. The tobacco industry was developed largely through the efforts of **James Duke** of North Carolina. Duke's American Tobacco Company eventually controlled almost all tobacco manufacturing.

The iron and steel industry also grew rapidly. In the mid-1800s, William Kelly, an American ironworker, and Henry Bessemer, a British engineer, had developed methods —called the Bessemer process—to inexpensively produce steel from iron. Steel answered industry's need for a sturdy, workable metal. By 1890 Southern mills produced nearly 20 percent of the nation's iron and steel. Much of the industry was in Alabama near deposits of iron ore.

A cheap and reliable workforce helped the South's industry grow. Most factory workers put in long hours for low wages. Sometimes whole families, including children, worked in factories. African Americans worked in the lowest-paying jobs.

More railroads aided the rise of industry. By 1870 the South's war-damaged railroads were largely rebuilt and expanded. Still, the South was not as industrialized as the North. It remained primarily agricultural.

Rural Economy Supporters of the New South also hoped to change Southern agriculture. Their goal was small, profitable farms raising many crops rather than plantations devoted to cotton. A different economy emerged, however. Some plantations were broken up, but large landowners held on to their land. When estates were divided, much of the land went to sharecropping and tenant farming, neither of which was profitable.

Debt also caused problems. Poor farmers used credit to get food and supplies. Merchants who sold on credit charged high prices, and farmers' debts rose. To repay debts, farmers grew **cash crops**—crops that could be sold for money.

Too much cotton, a major cash crop, forced prices down, however. Farmers then had to grow even more cotton to recover their losses. Sharecropping and reliance on one cash crop kept Southern agriculture from advancing. The rural South sank deeper into poverty and debt.

Reading Check **Describe** What happened to prices when too much cotton was produced?

A Divided Society

Main Idea As Reconstruction ended, true freedom for African Americans became a distant dream.

Reading Connection What might it be like to be forced to pass an impossibly difficult test in order to earn a basic right, when others do not have to take the test at all? Read to find out how white Southerners attempted to prevent African Americans from voting.

As Reconstruction ended, African Americans' dreams for justice faded. In the last 20 years of the 1800s, racism became firmly entrenched, and individuals took steps to keep African Americans separated from whites and to deny them basic rights.

Voting Restrictions The Fifteenth Amendment prohibited any state from denying an individual the right to vote because of race. Southern leaders, however, found ways to get around the amendment and prevent African Americans from voting.

Many Southern states required a **poll tax,** a fee that people had to pay before voting. Because many African Americans could not afford the tax, they could not vote. The tax also prevented many poor whites from voting.

What Is a Literacy Test? Another approach was to make prospective voters take a **literacy test** (LIH•tuh•ruh•see) in which they had to read and explain difficult parts of state constitutions or the federal Constitution. Because most African Americans had little education, literacy tests prevented many from voting.

Jim Crow Laws

Southern communities and states passed laws that enforced segregation between the black and white races.

Railroads The conductor of each passenger train is authorized and required to assign each passenger to the car or the division of the car, when it is divided by a partition, designated for the race to which such passenger belongs. (Alabama)

Restaurants All persons licensed to conduct a restaurant, shall serve either white people exclusively or colored people exclusively and shall not sell to the two races within the same room or serve the two races anywhere under the same license. (Georgia)

Education The schools for white children and the schools for Negro children shall be conducted separately. (Florida)

▲ Business sign of the era

Libraries The state librarian is directed to fit up and maintain a separate place for the use of the colored people who may come to the library for the purpose of reading books or periodicals. (North Carolina)

—*Race, Racism, and the Law*

DBQ Document-Based Question

What do these laws have in common?

Analyzing Political Cartoons

African Americans were often barred from voting. **What do the people in the cartoon represent?**

Literacy tests could also keep some whites from voting. For this reason, some states passed **grandfather clauses.** These laws allowed individuals who did not pass the literacy test to vote if their fathers or grandfathers had voted before Reconstruction. Because African Americans could not vote until 1867, they were excluded. Georgia enacted a poll tax and other limits as early as 1870. Such laws, however, did not become widespread until after 1889. African Americans continued to vote in some states until the end of the 1800s. Then, voting laws and the constant threat of violence caused African American voting to decline drastically.

Jim Crow Laws Another set of laws hurt African Americans. By the 1890s, **segregation** (SEH•grih•GAY•shuhn), or the separation of the races, was a prominent feature of life in the South.

The Southern states formed a segregated society by passing so-called Jim Crow laws. Taking their name from a character in a song, Jim Crow laws required African Americans and whites to be separated in almost every public place where they might come in contact with each other.

In 1896 the Supreme Court upheld Jim Crow laws and segregation in *Plessy* v. *Ferguson.* The case involved a Louisiana law requiring separate sections on trains for African Americans. The Court ruled that segregation was legal as long as African Americans had access to public facilities or accommodations equal to those of whites. 📖 *(See page 849 of the Appendix for a summary of* Plessy v. Ferguson.*)*

One problem, however, was that the facilities were separate but in no way equal. Southern states spent much more money on schools and other facilities for whites than on those for African Americans. This "separate but equal" doctrine provided a legal foundation for segregation in the South that lasted more than 50 years.

Along with restrictions on voting rights and laws passed to segregate society, white violence against African Americans increased. This violence took many terrible forms, including **lynching** (LIHNCH•ihng), in which an angry mob killed a person by hanging. African Americans were lynched because they were suspected of **committing** crimes—or because they did not behave as whites thought they should behave.

Reconstruction's Impact Reconstruction was both a success and a failure. It helped the South recover from the Civil War and begin rebuilding its battered economy. Yet economic recovery was far from complete. Although Southern agriculture took a new form, the South was still a rural economy, and that economy was still very poor.

Under Reconstruction, African Americans gained greater equality and began creating their own institutions. They joined with whites in new governments, fairer and more democratic than the South had ever seen. This improvement for African Americans did not last long, however.

In the words of African American writer and civil rights leader **W.E.B. Du Bois** (doo BAWIHS),

> ❝ The slave went free; stood a brief moment in the sun; then moved back again toward slavery. ❞
>
> —from *Black Reconstruction*

The biggest disappointment of Reconstruction was that it did not make good on the promise of true freedom for freed African Americans. With troop withdrawals and the end of Reconstruction, African Americans lost most of the gains they had made. The South soon created a segregated society.

The Civil War had ended slavery, but the failure of Reconstruction left many African Americans trapped in economic, political, and social circumstances whereby they lost most of their newly gained freedom.

▲ W.E.B. Du Bois demanded full political rights for African Americans.

✓ Reading Check **Describe** What is segregation? How was segregation carried out?

Study Central Need help understanding the end of Reconstruction? Visit tajww1.glencoe.com and click on Study Central.

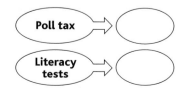

Section 4 Review

Reading Summary

Review the Main Ideas

• As support for Reconstruction weakened, Democrats regained power in the South. Reconstruction ended because of a political compromise that allowed Rutherford B. Hayes to become president.

• A number of industries, such as textiles and steel, developed in the South, but agriculture also remained important.

• Following the end of Reconstruction, African Americans in the South lost many of the rights they had briefly gained.

What Did You Learn?

1. Why was the presidential election of 1876 controversial?

2. Who was reelected president in 1872?

Critical Thinking

3. **Organizing Information** Re-create the diagram below and describe how the poll tax and literacy tests restricted voting rights.

```
( Poll tax ) ⟶ (   )

( Literacy tests ) ⟶ (   )
```

4. **Determining Cause and Effect** Explain how the Amnesty Act helped the Democratic Party regain its strength.

5. **The Big Ideas** What ideas led to political changes in the South beginning in the early 1870s?

6. **Analyze** Find two secondary sources that discuss Reconstruction—one from the 1800s and one written in the past 20 years. Identify how the views expressed in the later source are based on new historical information or research.

Connecting to the Constitution

Citizenship

Why It Matters Today, most people are citizens of the country in which they live. They are community members who owe loyalty to that country. They also expect to be protected by it. Citizens may share a common history, common customs, or common values. They agree to follow the laws and to accept the government's authority.

Who Are U.S. Citizens? Every country has rules about how people gain citizenship. In the United States, a citizen is a person who by birth or by choice owes loyalty to this nation. In the Fourteenth Amendment, the U.S. Constitution states that anyone "born or naturalized in the United States" is a citizen. If you were born in the United States and its territories, you automatically are an American citizen by birth. Foreigners who choose to become U.S. citizens do so through naturalization. **Naturalization** is the legal process by which a person becomes a citizen. Naturalized citizens have all the rights and duties of citizens by birth except the right to be president or vice president.

National and State Citizenship Over the years, the basis of citizenship has changed greatly in the United States. Today, citizenship relates both to the nation as a whole and to the states. This was not always so, however.

The Articles of the Constitution mention citizenship only as a qualification for holding office in the federal government. The Constitution's writers assumed that the states would decide who was or was not a citizen. Their citizens were also citizens of the United States. The exceptions were African Americans and immigrants who became citizens through naturalization.

"Our Constitution is color-blind, and neither knows nor tolerates classes among citizens. In respect of civil rights, all citizens are equal before the law."

—Justice John Marshall Harlan, 1896

◀ **New American citizens pledging allegiance**

The basis of state citizenship became an issue in the *Dred Scott* v. *Sandford* case in 1857. The Supreme Court, led by Chief Justice Roger Taney, ruled that Dred Scott, an enslaved African American, could not bring a legal suit in a federal court. Taney reasoned that African Americans, whether enslaved or free, were not United States citizens at the time the Constitution was adopted. Therefore, they could not claim citizenship. Only descendants of people who were state citizens at that time, or immigrants who became citizens through naturalization, were U.S. citizens.

The Fourteenth Amendment

The *Dred Scott* decision caused great outrage and protest in the North. It added to the tensions that led to the Civil War. After the war ended, many Southern states passed laws that kept African Americans from holding certain jobs, limited their property rights, and restricted them in other ways. To remedy this situation, the Fourteenth Amendment was enacted in 1868.

The new amendment clearly stated what citizenship is at both the national and state levels of government. Overruling the *Dred Scott* decision, the Fourteenth Amendment stated that a United States citizen is anyone "born or naturalized in the United States." This definition included most African Americans. It guaranteed that people of all races born in the United States are citizens, making state citizenship an automatic result of national citizenship.

Denial of Citizens' Rights

The Fourteenth Amendment granted citizenship to former enslaved African Americans and their descendants. It also guaranteed their rights as citizens. The amendment did this by requiring every state to grant citizens equal protection under the laws.

Despite this guarantee, African Americans routinely faced **discrimination,** or unfair treatment based on prejudice against a certain group. In the late 1800s, Southern states, for example, passed so-called Jim Crow laws requiring African Americans and whites to be separated in most public places, such as schools. Later, African Americans had to ride in the back of buses and sit in separate sections of restaurants and theaters.

The Supreme Court supported Jim Crow laws in *Plessy* v. *Ferguson* (1896). The Court said the Fourteenth Amendment allowed separate facilities for different races as long as those facilities were equal. For the next 50 years, this decision was used to justify segregation in the United States.

Extension of Citizens' Rights

By the 1950s, society's views on racial segregation were beginning to change. In 1954 in the case of *Brown* v. *Board of Education of Topeka*, the Court overturned the ruling of "separate but equal." The justices ruled that racially separate schools are unequal simply because they are separate. The unanimous opinion of the Court found that segregation was a violation of the Fourteenth Amendment's principle of equal protection under the law.

Linda Brown was able to attend the school of her choice after the *Brown* decision. ▶

Checking for Understanding

1. How do people become citizens in the United States?
2. Why did the Supreme Court overturn the "separate but equal" idea in *Brown* v. *Board of Education of Topeka*?

Critical Thinking

3. Why do you think the writers of the Constitution assumed that the states would decide who was or who was not a citizen?
4. How was the promise of the Fourteenth Amendment fulfilled in the mid-twentieth century?

Analyzing Primary Sources

Reconstruction

Most of the Civil War was waged in the South. After the war, the South faced the huge task of rebuilding. In addition, freed African Americans had to make a new life for themselves. There was also the difficult problem of how to make the former Confederacy and the Union into one nation again.

Read the passages on pages 652 and 653 and answer the questions that follow.

The head of the Freedmen's Bureau (seated at the far right) is pictured with students in a Freedmen's school. ▶

Reader's Dictionary

charge: blame

exterminating (ihk • STUHR • muh • NAYT • ihng)**:** getting rid of completely

emerged: have risen from a low condition

bondage (BAHN • dihj)**:** slavery

plea (PLEE)**:** serious or sincere call for help

quarters: places

The South in Ruins

Newspaper reporter Sidney Andrews toured major Southern cities in the fall of 1865. He wrote the following account about Columbia, South Carolina.

Columbia was doubtless once the gem of the state. . . . What with its broad streets, beautiful shade trees, handsome lawns . . . I can easily see that it must have been a delightful place of residence. No South Carolinian with whom I have spoken hesitates an instant in declaring that [Columbia] was the most beautiful city on the continent; and, as already mentioned, they **charge** its destruction directly to General Sherman.

[Columbia] is now a wilderness of ruins. Its heart is but a mass of blackened chimneys and crumbling walls. Two thirds of the buildings in the place were burned, including, without exception, everything in the business portion. Not a store, office, or shop escaped; and for a distance of three fourths of a mile on each of twelve streets there was not a building left. . . .

The work of clearing away the ruins is going on, not rapidly or extensively, to be sure, but something is doing, and many small houses of the cheaper sort are going up. Yet, at the best, this generation will not ever again see the beautiful city of a year ago.

—from *The South Since the War*

On the Plight of African Americans

In 1867 Frederick Douglass appealed to Congress on behalf of African Americans.

Yet the negroes have marvelously survived all the **exterminating** forces of slavery, and have **emerged** at the end of two hundred and fifty years of **bondage,** not [sad and hateful], but cheerful, hopeful, and forgiving. They now stand before Congress and the country, not complaining of the past, but simply asking for a better future. . . .

It is true that a strong **plea** for equal suffrage might be addressed to the national sense of honor. Something, too, might be said of national gratitude. A nation might well hesitate before the temptation to betray its allies. There is something . . . mean, to say nothing of the cruelty, in placing the loyal negroes of the South under the political power of their Rebel masters. . . . We asked the negroes to [support] our cause, to be our friends, to fight for us, and against their masters; and now, after they have done all that we asked them to do, . . . it is proposed in some **quarters** to turn them over to the political control of the common enemy of the government and of the negro. . . .

What, then, is the work before Congress? . . . In a word, it must [allow African Americans to vote], and by means of the loyal negroes and the loyal white men of the South build up a national party there, and in time bridge the [gap] between North and South, so that our country may have a common liberty and a common civilization.

—*An Appeal to Congress for Impartial Suffrage*

 Document-Based Questions

The South in Ruins

1. To what does Andrews compare Columbia? Why?

2. What does Andrews mean when he writes that "Not a store, office, or shop escaped"?

On the Plight of African Americans

3. According to Douglass, why does the United States owe a debt of gratitude to African Americans?

4. How did Douglass think that Congress could ensure the nation a common liberty and civilization for whites and African Americans?

Read to Write

5. During Reconstruction, some people worked to get African Americans the same rights as whites. List the rights that these primary sources include and others that you know about. Then research the civil rights movement of the 1960s. What right or rights were African Americans seeking at that time? Compare and contrast the rights and the methods used to gain them in the two time periods.

Review Content Vocabulary

Each of the following statements is false. Replace each word in italics with a content vocabulary word that makes the statement true. Write the correct words on a separate sheet of paper.

___ 1. The reorganization of the Southern states after the war was called *integration*.

___ 2. *Carpetbaggers* were Southern whites who sided with Republicans.

___ 3. To *grant amnesty* is to formally charge with a crime.

___ 4. Fees called *grandfather clauses* were often required before voters could cast their ballots in the south.

Review the Main Ideas

Section 1 • Reconstruction Plans

5. What services did the Freedmen's Bureau provide?

6. Who succeeded Lincoln as president?

Section 2 • Radicals in Control

7. How was the Fourteenth Amendment supposed to help African Americans?

8. What verdict did the Senate reach in the trial of President Johnson?

Section 3 • The South During Reconstruction

9. What role did African Americans play in early Reconstruction politics in the South?

10. What tactic did the Ku Klux Klan use to influence elections in the South?

Section 4 • Change in the South

11. Why was a special commission needed to decide the presidential election of 1876?

12. What Supreme Court decision upheld the legality of segregation so long as "separate but equal" facilities were provided?

Critical Thinking

13. **Analyze** How did the black codes deny rights?

14. **Evaluate** Explain the following quote as it applies to Reconstruction: "The slave went free; stood a brief moment in the sun; then moved back again toward slavery."

Geography Skills

Study the map below and answer the question that follows.

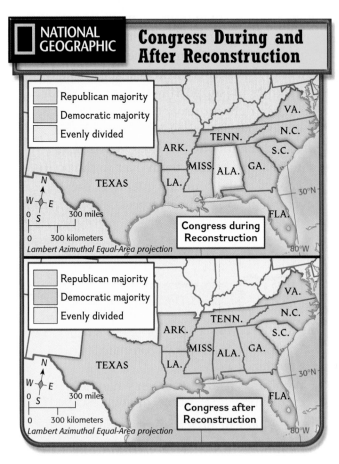

NATIONAL GEOGRAPHIC
Congress During and After Reconstruction

Republican majority
Democratic majority
Evenly divided

Congress during Reconstruction

Lambert Azimuthal Equal-Area projection

Republican majority
Democratic majority
Evenly divided

Congress after Reconstruction

Lambert Azimuthal Equal-Area projection

15. **Summarize** Write a paragraph summarizing the changes in congressional representation during and after Reconstruction.

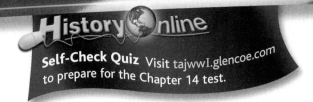
Read to Write

16. **The Big Ideas** **Expository Writing**
Review the chapter to make a list of specific ways that Southern states tried to deny equal rights to African Americans after the war. Then decide which amendment(s)—Thirteenth, Fourteenth, or Fifteenth—should have prevented each action. Include this information in an essay.

17. **Using Your** **FOLDABLES** Use the information you wrote in your foldable to create a fill-in-the-blank quiz for a classmate. Write a paragraph about one of the sections, leaving blanks for your classmate to fill in. Leave blanks for vocabulary words or significant places and people.

Using Academic Vocabulary

Choose the academic vocabulary word that best completes each sentence. You may need to change the form of the word to provide the best answer (for example, "create" becomes "creating").

create   enable   dominate

exploit   eliminate

18. Many Americans thought the poll tax was unfair and sought to _____ it.

19. Republicans in the South thought that the power of the ballot would _____ African Americans to protect themselves.

20. In the 1870s, Reconstruction governments began _____ public school systems.

21. The Radical Republicans began to _____ the Reconstruction process.

Building Citizenship

22. **Registering to Vote** Laws about voter registration vary from place to place. Working with a partner, contact your local election board to find out what the requirements for voter registration are in your community. Then design a brochure that encourages citizens to register to vote.

Reviewing Skills

23. **READING SKILL** **Monitoring and Clarifying** Turn to pages 263–264 and read the Fourteenth and Fifteenth Amendments to the U.S. Constitution. Write down concepts that are unfamiliar to you and what you will do to understand them. Then, write a paragraph summarizing the amendments in your own words.

24. **ANALYSIS SKILL** **Sequencing Events** Review this chapter and draw a time line of key events during Reconstruction. Identify the event that you believe had the most impact and write a short essay justifying your conclusions.

Standardized Test Practice

Read the passage below and answer the following question.

> The right of citizens of the United States to vote shall not be denied or abridged by the United States or any State on account of race, color, or previous condition of servitude.
> —*excerpt from the Fifteenth Amendment to the Constitution*

25 **The main idea of the Fifteenth Amendment is that**

    A enslaved people convicted of crimes had the right to a fair trial.

    B slavery was made illegal in every state of the Union.

    C the government was not allowed to deny a person's right to vote on the basis of race.

    D Congress had the right to set voting restrictions in whatever state it chose.

Civil War and Reconstruction

In Unit 5 you learned how social, economic, and political differences between the North and South grew. As compromises failed, the country plunged into civil war. Following the North's victory, bringing the country back together also proved challenging.

Chapter 12	**Chapter 13**	**Chapter 14**
Road to Civil War	**Civil War**	**Reconstruction**
When		
• 1820–1861	• 1861–1865	• 1865–1896
Where		
• New Western lands: Texas, New Mexico, California • Kansas and Nebraska Territories	• Bull Run • Shiloh • Antietam • Vicksburg • Gettysburg • Atlanta • Savannah • Appomattox Court House	• Military Reconstruction Districts in the South

Confederate soldier ▶

CAUTION!!!
COLORED PEOPLE
OF BOSTON, ONE & ALL,
You are hereby respectfully CAUTIONED and advised, to avoid conversing with the
Watchmen and Police Officers
of Boston,
For since the recent ORDER OF THE MAYOR & ALDERMEN, they are empowered to act as
KIDNAPPERS
AND
Slave Catchers,
And they have already been actually employed in
KIDNAPPING, CATCHING, AND KEEPING
SLAVES. Therefore, if you value your LIBERTY,
and the Welfare of the Fugitives among you, Shun
them in every possible manner, as so many HOUNDS
on the track of the most unfortunate of your race.
Keep a Sharp Look Out for
KIDNAPPERS, and have
TOP EYE open.
APRIL 24, 1851.

◀ *Poster warning African Americans*

	Chapter 12 Road to Civil War	**Chapter 13** Civil War	**Chapter 14** Reconstruction
Major Events	• **1820** Missouri Compromise • **1857** *Dred Scott* decision • **1860** Lincoln elected • **1861** Confederate States of America formed • **1861** Fort Sumter attacked	• **1861** First Battle of Bull Run • **1862** *Monitor* versus *Merrimack* • **1863** Emancipation Proclamation • **1863** Battles of Gettysburg and Vicksburg • **1864** Grant leads the Union army • **1865** Lee surrenders	• **1864** Wade-Davis Bill • **1865** Thirteenth Amendment passes • **1865** Lincoln assassinated • **1866–1870** Southern states readmitted to Union • **1866** Ku Klux Klan formed • **1868** President Andrew Johnson impeached • **1877** Reconstruction ends • **1896** *Plessy v. Ferguson*
Some Important People	• Henry Clay • Stephen Douglas • Harriet Beecher Stowe • Abraham Lincoln • John Brown • Dred Scott	• Jefferson Davis • Abraham Lincoln • "Stonewall" Jackson • Ulysses S. Grant • Robert E. Lee	• John Wilkes Booth • Andrew Johnson • Frederick Douglass • Rutherford B. Hayes *John Wilkes* ▲ *Booth pistol and poster*
How do these events and ideas affect our lives today?	• The events discussed in this chapter led up to the Civil War, which forever changed relations within our country. *Secessionist ribbon* ▶	• The Union victory established the power of the federal government over the states.	• The passage of the Fourteenth and Fifteenth Amendments established rights for all citizens.
What was happening in the world at this time?	• **1820** British settlers arrive in South Africa • **1857** Native troops rebel against the British in India • **1859** British scientist Charles Darwin publishes *On the Origin of Species*	• **1861** Kingdom of Italy is proclaimed • **1861** Russia's Czar Alexander II frees the serfs • **1863** The French occupy Mexico City *Czar Alexander II* ▶	• **1868** Meiji reforms begin in Japan • **1879** Britain gains control of Afghanistan • **1896** Ethiopia defeats Italian forces

Reshaping the Nation

Why It's Important

Following the Civil War, the United States grew at an even greater rate. Settlers flocked to the West and immigrants came to the great eastern cities to work in new factories. While the nation's economy grew strong, not everyone shared equally in the wealth, and reformers worked for equal rights and equal opportunity for all citizens.

- The settling of the Plains and the growth of industry helped the United States become an agricultural and industrial leader.

- America's tremendous growth also led to problems within society, which a number of reformers attempted to resolve.

1860   **1870**   **1880**

POLITICS & ECONOMY

1867
U.S. buys Alaska territory

1870
Rockefeller organizes Standard Oil Company

John Rockefeller ▶

1882
Chinese Exclusion Act is passed

Chinese Americans ▶

SCIENCE & SOCIETY

1862
Homestead Act gives free land to settlers

1869
Transcontinental railroad links the East and West

◀ *Golden railroad spike*

1879
Edison invents the electric lightbulb

WORLD EVENTS

1861
Giuseppe Garibaldi helps unite Italy

◀ *Giuseppe Garibaldi*

1876
Queen Victoria becomes "Empress of India"

Queen Victoria ▶

1884
European powers partition Africa

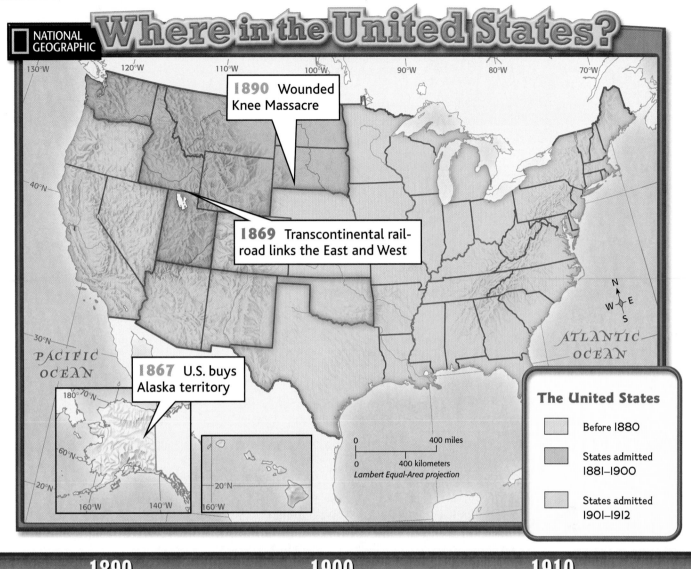

Where in the United States?

NATIONAL GEOGRAPHIC

1890 Wounded Knee Massacre

1869 Transcontinental railroad links the East and West

1867 U.S. buys Alaska territory

PACIFIC OCEAN

ATLANTIC OCEAN

400 miles
400 kilometers
Lambert Equal-Area projection

The United States

- Before 1880
- States admitted 1881–1900
- States admitted 1901–1912

1890

1886 American Federation of Labor forms

1890 Wounded Knee Massacre

1900

1901 Theodore Roosevelt becomes president

▲ Theodore Roosevelt

1910

1913 Congress passes the Seventeenth Amendment

1889 First skyscraper built in Chicago

1900 Nation's population passes 75 million

1908 Henry Ford introduces the Model T

Model T ▶

1895 Lumière brothers show first projected motion picture films

Emiliano Zapata ▶

1911 Zapata leads demand for land reform in Mexico

1914 World War I begins

① PROMONTORY SUMMIT

See *The Western Frontier* Chapter 15

② THE BROOKLYN BRIDGE

See *America Enters a New Century* Chapter 17

ALASKA

HAWAII

People to Meet

Chief Joseph

1840–1904

Nez Perce leader
Chapter 15, page 690

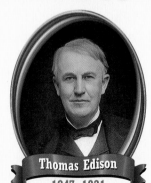

Thomas Edison

1847–1931

Inventor
Chapter 16, page 714

Mother Jones

1830–1930

Worker's rights leader
Chapter 16, page 728

Jane Addams

1860–1935

Founder of Chicago's Hull House
Chapter 17, page 753

③

②

③ CHICAGO SKYSCRAPER

See *America Enters a New Century* **Chapter 17**

④ YOSEMITE NATIONAL PARK

See *America Enters a New Century* **Chapter 17**

Booker T. Washington
1856–1915
Equal rights advocate
Chapter 17, page 781

Jacob Riis
1849–1914
Journalist
Chapter 17, page 768

Ida Wells
1862–1931
Journalist
Chapter 17, page 780

W.E.B. Du Bois
1868–1963
Equal rights advocate
Chapter 17, page 781

The Western Frontier

◀ Mother and child in a Wyoming wheat field

NATIONAL GEOGRAPHIC **Who & When?**

1860	1875	1890
1862 Homestead Act gives free land to settlers	**1869** Transcontinental railroad links East and West	**1890** Battle at Wounded Knee; Populist Party forms

Populist Party banner

Chapter Overview Visit tajww1.glencoe.com for a preview of Chapter 15.

The Big Ideas

The Mining Booms

Geography shapes the physical, economic, and political challenges a region faces. Rail lines and mining speeded the flow of settlers to the West.

Ranchers and Farmers

Geography shapes the physical, economic, and political challenges a region faces. Following the Civil War, settlers began to move west in great numbers.

Native American Struggles

Differences in economic, political, and social beliefs and practices can lead to division within a nation and have lasting consequences. The settlement of white people in the West forced change on the Native Americans of the Plains.

Farmers in Protest

Reactions to social injustice can lead to reform movements. In the late 1800s, farmers began to band together in groups and associations to fight their problems.

 View the Chapter 15 video in the Glencoe Video Program.

Evaluating Information Make this foldable to organize information and ask yourself questions as you read about the western frontier of the United States.

Step 1 Fold a sheet of paper in half from side to side, leaving a $\frac{1}{2}$-inch tab along the side.

Leave $\frac{1}{2}$-inch tab here.

Step 2 Turn the paper and fold it into fourths.

Fold in half, then fold in half again.

Reading and Writing As you read the chapter, ask yourself and write down questions (under each appropriate tab) about the tragedies and triumphs these four groups of people experienced during the expansion of the western frontier.

Step 3 Unfold and cut along the three fold lines.

Make four tabs.

Step 4 Label your foldable as shown.

Miners | Ranchers | Farmers | Native Americans

on the Western Frontier

Get Ready to Read

Visualizing

1 Learn It!

Creating pictures in your mind as you read—called visualizing—is a powerful aid to understanding. If you can visualize what you read, selections will be more vivid, and you will recall them better later. Authors use descriptive language to create a picture of a person, location, time, or event. These words appeal to the senses and may evoke sights, sounds, or smells. Authors also use words to describe feelings and emotions to make the text come alive to the reader. Good readers take the time to visualize people, places, and events. As you read the following paragraphs, make a picture in your mind of life in a boomtown.

> Boomtowns were largely men's towns in the early days. Men outnumbered women by two to one in Virginia City, and children made up less than 10 percent of the population.
>
> Eager to share in the riches of the boomtowns, some women opened businesses. Others worked as laundresses, cooks, or dance-hall entertainers. Women often added stability to the boomtowns, founding schools and churches and working to make the communities safer.
>
> —*from page 668*

Reading Tip

Look for descriptive words or images in the text to help you form a visual image of what you read.

② Practice It!

Now read the section below about cowhands. Discuss your impressions with a partner and then reread the selection. Did your visual image change at all?

Read to Write········

Think about your favorite place. In writing, describe the picture you have in your mind. Use vivid language and descriptive details.

Many cowhands were veterans of the Confederate army. Some were African Americans who moved west in search of a better life after the Civil War. Others were Hispanics. In fact, the traditions of cattle herding began with Hispanic ranch hands in the Spanish Southwest. These vaqueros (vah • KEHR • ohs) developed many of the skills—riding, roping, and branding—that cowhands used on the drives. Much of the language of the rancher today is derived from Spanish words used by vaqueros for centuries. Even the word *ranch* comes from the Spanish word *rancho*.

The cowhand's equipment was based on the vaquero's equipment too. Cowhands wore wide-brimmed hats to protect themselves from the sun and leather leggings, called chaps, to shield their legs from brush and mishaps with cattle. They used ropes called lariats to lasso cattle that strayed from the herd.

—*from page 674*

Cowhand Nat Love ▶

③ Apply It!

Before you begin reading this chapter, look at all the photographs, maps, and illustrations to help you visualize what you are about to read.

The Mining Booms

Guide to Reading

Looking Back, Looking Ahead

You read earlier about how the California Gold Rush brought thousands of people to California to try to make their fortunes. In the late 1850s, many more miners headed west as more precious metals were discovered.

Focusing on the Main Ideas

- In the late 1850s, discoveries of gold and silver sent miners flocking to the American West. *(page 667)*
- A number of boomtowns grew quickly in the mining areas of the West. *(page 668)*
- Railroads grew rapidly in the period following the Civil War. *(page 669)*

Locating Places

Pikes Peak
Virginia City, Nevada
Promontory Summit

Meeting People

Leland Stanford

Content Vocabulary

lode (LOHD)
ore
boomtown
vigilante (VIH•juh•LAN•tee)
subsidy (SUHB•suh•dee)
transcontinental
   (TRANS•kahn•tuhn•EHN•tuhl)

Academic Vocabulary

extract (ihk•STRAKT)
obtain (uhb•TAYN)

Reading Strategy

Analyzing Information As you read the section, re-create the diagram below and explain why these places were significant to the mining boom.

	Significance
Pikes Peak	
Comstock Lode	
Promontory Summit	

NATIONAL GEOGRAPHIC Where & When?

Central Pacific R.R.
Promontory Summit
Pikes Peak   Union Pacific R.R.

1855   1865   1875

1858 Gold is discovered at Pikes Peak

1869 Transcontinental railroad links East and West

1876 Colorado joins the Union

Mining Is Big Business

Main Idea In the late 1850s, discoveries of gold and silver sent miners flocking to the American West.

Reading Connection Have you ever wanted to take part in a great adventure? Read to find out about the gold and silver rushes that lured thousands of Americans into the West.

An American Story

❝ We'll need no pick or spade, no shovel, pan, or hoe, the largest chunks are 'top of ground. . . . We'll see hard times no more, and want [we'll] never know, when once we've filled our sacks with gold, Way out in Idaho. **❞**

—from *Way Out in Idaho*

Miners sang this hopeful song as they headed for new places where gold had been discovered.

Searching for Gold and Silver By the mid-1850s, the California Gold Rush had ended. Miners, still hoping to strike it rich, began prospecting in other parts of the West.

In 1858 a mining expedition found gold on the slopes of **Pikes Peak** in the Colorado Rockies. Newspapers claimed that miners were making $20 a day panning for gold—a large sum at a time when servants made less than a dollar a day. By the spring of 1859, about 50,000 prospectors had flocked to Colorado. Their slogan was "Pikes Peak or Bust."

Prospectors skimmed gold dust from streams or scratched particles of gold from the surface of the land. Most of the gold, however, was deep in underground **lodes** (LOHDZ), rich streaks of ore sandwiched between layers of rock. Mining this rock, or **ore,** and then **extracting** the gold required expensive machinery, many workers, and an organized business.

Picturing **History**
A miner works the Comstock Lode.
Where was the Comstock Lode located?

Companies made up of several investors had a better chance of getting rich in the goldfields than individual miners did. Mining companies soon replaced the lone miner.

The Comstock Lode In 1859 several prospectors found a rich lode of silver-bearing ore on the banks of the Carson River in Nevada. The discovery was called the Comstock Lode after Henry Comstock, who owned a share of the claim.

Thousands of mines opened near the site, but only a few were profitable. Mining companies reaped the largest share of the profits. When Comstock sold his share of the claim, he received $11,000 and two mules—a huge sum at the time. It was, however, just a tiny fraction of the hundreds of millions of dollars worth of gold and silver pulled from the Comstock Lode strike.

Reading Check **Describe** What was the Comstock Lode?

The Mining Frontier

Main Idea A number of boomtowns grew quickly in the mining areas of the West.

Reading Connection Have you ever seen a deserted section of a city where a factory has closed? Read to find out what happened to many mining towns in the West after the gold or silver in nearby mines was gone.

The gold strikes created **boomtowns**—towns that grew up almost overnight around mining sites. The Comstock boomtown was **Virginia City, Nevada.** In 1859 the town was a mining camp. Two years later, it had a stock exchange, hotels, banks, an opera company, and five newspapers.

Boomtowns were lively, and often lawless, places. Money came quickly—and was often spent just as quickly through extravagant living and gambling. A fortunate miner could earn as much as $2,000 a year, about four times the annual salary of a teacher at that time. Still food, lodging, clothing, and other goods were expensive in the boomtowns, draining miners' earnings.

Violence was part of everyday life in boomtowns. Few boomtowns had police or prisons, so citizens sometimes took the law into their own hands. These **vigilantes** (VIH•juh•LAN•tees) dealt out their own brand of justice without benefit of judge or jury, often hanging the accused person from the nearest tree.

Women in the Boomtowns Boomtowns were largely men's towns in the early days. Men outnumbered women by two to one in Virginia City, and children made up less than 10 percent of the population.

Eager to share in the riches of the boomtowns, some women opened businesses. Others worked as laundresses, cooks, or dance-hall entertainers. Women often added stability to the boomtowns, founding schools and churches and working to make the communities safer.

Changing Industry Many mining "booms" were followed by "busts." When the mines no longer yielded ore, people left the towns, and the deserted mine towns became known as ghost towns. At its peak in the 1870s, Virginia City had about 30,000 inhabitants. By 1900 its population had dropped to fewer than 4,000. Toward the end of the rush, gold and silver mining in some places gave way to the mining of other metals. Copper became the key metal found in Montana, New Mexico, and Arizona in the 1870s.

Mining helped the economy, but it hurt the environment. Wildlife was hunted to provide meat for the miners. Mining led to high levels of arsenic and mercury in the ground that contaminated land, lakes, and rivers.

What Were the New States? Frontier areas around the boomtowns eventually became states. Colorado joined the United States in 1876. North Dakota, South Dakota, Washington, and Montana became states in 1889. Wyoming and Idaho were admitted to the Union in 1890.

✓ Reading Check **Explain** Why did the population drop in many boomtowns?

Picturing **History**

The boomtown of Leadville, Colorado, surrounds a settler's cabin that sits in the middle of the main street. *What happened to many boomtowns when the mines closed?*

Railroads Connect East to West

Main Idea Railroads grew rapidly in the period following the Civil War.

Reading Connection Would you like to travel across the country by train? Read to find out how the first railroad to connect the east and west coasts was completed in 1869.

The western mines operated far from the industrial centers of the East and Midwest. For this reason, transportation played a vital role in the survival of mining communities. Gold and silver had little value unless they could reach factories, ports, and markets. At the same time, the miners and others in the boomtowns needed shipments of food and other supplies.

Wagon trains and stagecoach lines could not move people and goods fast enough to meet these demands. Railroads could—and did. The nation's railroad network expanded rapidly between 1865 and 1890. During that period, the number of miles of track in the United States grew from about 35,000 to more than 150,000.

Railroad construction was often supported by large government **subsidies** (SUHB•suh•dees)—financial aid and land grants from the government. Railroad executives pushed for free public land on which to lay track because a rail network would benefit the entire nation. The national government and states agreed. In all, the federal government granted more than 130 million acres of land to the railroad companies. Much of the land was purchased or **obtained** by treaties from Native Americans. The government grants included the land for the tracks plus strips of land along the railway, 20 to 80 miles wide. Railroad companies sold those strips of land to raise additional money for construction costs.

TECHNOLOGY & History

Steam Locomotive

Since 1825, when the first steam locomotive was built in the United States, trains have crisscrossed the country. As America's transportation needs increased, so did the miles of railroad track linking its people. **Why do you think steam power was the first power source for locomotives?**

1 The **firebox** burns coal, wood, or sometimes oil.

2 Water in the **boiler,** heated by gases from the firebox, creates steam.

3 The **smokebox** draws hot gases from the firebox and keeps an even fire.

4 In the **steam header tank,** the heated steam expands and creates great pressure.

5 Hot steam is piped to the **pistons.** The pistons power the **drive rods,** which in turn push the **drive wheels.**

States and local communities also helped the railroads. Towns offered cash subsidies to make sure that railroads came to their communities. For example, Los Angeles gave the Southern Pacific Railroad money and paid for a passenger terminal to ensure that the railroad would pass through its town.

Spanning the Continent The search for a route for a **transcontinental** (TRANS•kahn•tuhn•EHN•tuhl) rail line—one that would span the continent and connect the Atlantic and Pacific coasts—began in the 1850s. During the Civil War, the Union government chose a northerly route for the line. The government offered land grants to railroad companies that were willing to build the transcontinental railroad.

The challenge was enormous—laying track for more than 1,700 miles across hot plains and through rugged mountains. Two companies accepted the challenge. The Union Pacific Company began laying track westward from Omaha, Nebraska, while the Central Pacific Company worked eastward from Sacramento, California. The two companies competed fiercely. Each wanted to cover a greater distance in order to receive more of the government subsidies.

The Central Pacific hired about 10,000 Chinese laborers to work on its tracks. The first Chinese were hired in 1865 at about $28 per month. The Union Pacific relied on Irish and African American workers. All workers toiled for low wages in harsh conditions. In the choking heat of summer and the icy winds of winter, they cleared forests, blasted tunnels through mountains, and laid hundreds of miles of track. In the end, the Union Pacific workers laid 1,038 miles of track; Central Pacific workers laid 742 miles over a much harsher terrain.

The Transcontinental Railway On May 10, 1869, construction was completed. A Chinese crew was chosen to lay the final 10 miles of track, which was completed in only 12 hours. The two sets of track met at **Promontory Summit** in Utah Territory.

Leland Stanford, governor of California, drove a final golden spike into a tie to join the two railroads. According to Grenville Dodge, chief engineer for the Union Pacific:

❝Prayer was offered; a number of spikes were driven in the two adjoining rails. . . . The engineers ran up their locomotives until they touched . . . and thus the two roads were welded into one great trunk line from the Atlantic to the Pacific.❞

—from *Mine Eyes Have Seen*

What Effects Did Railroads Have? By 1883 two more transcontinental lines and dozens of shorter lines connected cities in the West with the rest of the nation. The railroads brought thousands of workers to the West. Trains carried metals and produce east and manufactured goods west. As more tracks were laid, more steel was needed, and the demand boosted the nation's steel industry. Coal producers, railroad car manufacturers, and construction companies also thrived as the railroads spread across the West.

Towns sprang up along the rail lines that carried farm goods to market. Some of these towns eventually grew into large cities such as Denver, Colorado. The railroads also brought the next wave of new settlers to the West—cattle ranchers and farmers.

Railroads even changed how people measured time. Before railroads, each community kept its own time. Clocks in Boston, for example, were 11 minutes ahead of clocks in New York. The demand for sensible train schedules, however, changed that. In 1883 the railroad companies divided the country into four time zones. All communities in each zone would share the same time, and each zone was exactly one hour apart from the zones on either side of it. Congress passed a law making this practice official in 1918.

✓ **Reading Check** **Identify** To what California city did the transcontinental railroad extend?

History Online

Study Central Need help understanding how mining affected railroad growth? Visit tajww1.glencoe.com and click on Study Central.

Section 1 Review

Reading Summary

Review the Main Ideas

- New discoveries of gold and silver, such as those at the Comstock Lode, brought thousands of miners to the West.

- Many of the boomtowns that developed as miners rushed to the West became ghost towns as the mines became depleted.

- The transcontinental railway connecting the East and West coasts was completed in 1869.

What Did You Learn?

1. Describe life in a boomtown.

2. What are subsidies, and why did the railroads receive them?

Critical Thinking

3. **Determining Cause and Effect** Re-create the diagram below and explain how railroads helped open the West to settlement.

```
     ( Coming of the railroad )
        /              \
   ( Effect )      ( Effect )
```

4.  **The Big Ideas** What were the economic effects of building railroads?

5. **Drawing Conclusions** Some boomtowns thrived after the mining boom, but others became ghost towns. Why do you think some towns survived and others did not?

6. **READING** **Visualizing** Imagine you are a prospector. Write a short paragraph describing what it was like to arrive at Pikes Peak in early summer 1859. Use strong, descriptive language so that your reader can visualize the scene.

Ranchers and Farmers

Guide to Reading

Looking Back, Looking Ahead
You learned that the transcontinental railroad linked the East and the West in 1869. The new railroads promoted ranching and farming in the Great Plains and the West.

Focusing on the Main Ideas

- Cattle ranching in Texas became a profitable business once the new railroad reached the Great Plains. *(page 673)*
- The work of the cowhands who drove the cattle north from Texas to the railroads was both difficult and dangerous. *(page 674)*
- Free land and new farming methods brought many settlers to the Great Plains. *(page 676)*

Locating Places
Sedalia, Missouri
Abilene, Kansas
Dodge City, Kansas
Cheyenne, Wyoming

Content Vocabulary
open range
brand
vaquero (vah • KEHR • oh)
homestead (HOHM • STEHD)
sodbuster (SAHD • BUHS • tuhr)
dry farming

Academic Vocabulary
derive (dih • RYV)
acquire (uh • KWYR)

Reading Strategy
Taking Notes As you read the section, re-create the diagram below and list the challenges settlers faced on the Great Plains.

Challenges

NATIONAL GEOGRAPHIC Where & When?

1860	1875	1890
1862 Homestead Act gives free land to settlers	**1867** Town of Abilene founded	**1889** Oklahoma land rush takes place

Omaha
Santa Fe
Abilene
—OKLAHOMA TERR.

Cattle on the Plains

Main Idea Cattle ranching in Texas became a profitable business once the new railroad reached the Great Plains.

Reading Connection Have you seen large trucks on highways carrying food and supplies to stores? Read to find out about the long, difficult journey that cowhands had to make in order for America's eastern cities to get beef in the mid-1800s.

An American Story

An old Texas cowhand, E.C. Abbott, recalled the early days of riding the trail:

> **" Here [were] all these cheap long-horned steers overrunning Texas; here was the rest of the country crying for beef—and no railroads to get them out. So they trailed them out, across hundreds of miles of wild country that was thick with Indians. . . . In 1867 the town of Abilene was founded at the end of the Kansas Pacific Railroad and that was when the trail really started. "**
>
> —from *We Pointed Them North*

The Texas Open Range When the Spanish settled Mexico and Texas, they brought a tough breed of cattle with them. Called longhorns because of their prominent horns, these cattle gradually spread across Texas.

At this time, much of Texas was **open range**—not fenced or divided into lots. Huge ranches covered other areas of the state. Ranchers added to their own herds by rounding up wild cattle. The ranchers burned a **brand,** or symbol, into the animals' hides to show who owned the cattle.

Railroads and Cow Towns Although Texas ranchers had plenty of cattle, the markets for beef were in the North and the East. In 1866 the Missouri Pacific Railroad reached Missouri, and Texas cattle suddenly increased in value. The cattle could be loaded onto trains in Missouri for shipment north and east. Some Texans drove their combined herds— sometimes 260,000 head of cattle—north to **Sedalia, Missouri,** the nearest rail point. Longhorns that had formerly been worth $3 each quickly rose in value to $40.

Cattle drives to cow towns—towns located near railroads to market and ship cattle— turned into a yearly event. Over the next decade, cow towns such as **Abilene, Kansas, Dodge City, Kansas,** and **Cheyenne, Wyoming,** became important rail stations.

What was the Long Drive? The sudden increase in the longhorns' value began what became known as the Long Drive—the herding of cattle 1,000 miles or more to meet the railroads. The drives left Texas in the spring, when there was enough grass along the way to feed the cattle. During the heyday of the "Cattle Kingdom," from the late 1860s to the mid-1880s, the trails carried more than 5 million cattle north.

Reading Check **Explain** Why did the value of cattle increase in the mid-1860s?

Nat Love was one ▶ of many African Americans who rode the cattle trails.

Life on the Trail

Main Idea The work of the cowhands who drive the cattle north from Texas to the railroads was both difficult and dangerous.

Reading Connection What do you know about cowhands in the old West based on the movies you have seen? Read to find out about the hazards faced by cowhands on the trail and what life in the "Wild West" was really like.

The cattle drives and the cowhands who worked on them captured the imagination of the nation. Cattle driving, however, was hard work. Cowhands rode in the saddle for up to 15 hours every day, in driving rain, dust storms, and blazing sun. Life on the trail was lonely too. Cowhands saw few outsiders.

Spanish Influence Many cowhands were veterans of the Confederate army. Some were African Americans who moved west in search of a better life after the Civil War. Others were Hispanics. In fact, the traditions of cattle herding began with Hispanic ranch hands in the Spanish Southwest. These **vaqueros** (vah•KEHR•ohs) developed many of the skills—riding, roping, and branding—that cowhands used on the drives. Much of the language of the rancher today is **derived** from Spanish words used by vaqueros for centuries. Even the word *ranch* comes from the Spanish word *rancho*.

The cowhand's equipment was based on the vaquero's equipment too. Cowhands wore wide-brimmed hats to protect themselves from the sun and leather leggings, called chaps, to shield their legs from brush and mishaps with cattle. They used ropes called lariats to lasso cattle that strayed from the herd.

Hazards on the Trail During the months on the trail, the cowhands faced violent storms, rustlers who tried to steal cattle, and many other dangers. They had to drive the herds across swift-flowing rivers, where cattle could be lost. One of the greatest dangers on the trail was the stampede, when thousands of cattle ran in panic.

History *Through Art*

Jerked Down **by Charles Russell** Celebrated for his detailed and dramatic scenes of Western life, Charles Russell depicts cowhands on their horses lassoing cattle. *Where did the traditions of cattle herding begin?*

Any sudden sound—a roar of thunder or the crack of a gunshot—could set off the cattle. Then the cowhands had to race on horseback with the stampeding cattle and bring them under control.

African American, Native American, Hispanic, and Anglo cowhands met and worked together. Yet discrimination existed in the West just as it did elsewhere in the nation. Non-Anglo cowhands rarely became trail bosses and often received less pay for their work. Some towns discriminated against Hispanics, segregated African Americans, and excluded Chinese cowhands altogether.

After many tiring weeks on the trail, the cowhands delivered their cattle and enjoyed some time off in cow towns. Cowhands drank and gambled, and got involved in fistfights and gunplay. Some towns, such as Dodge City and Abilene, were rowdy, lawless, and often violent. Eventually, though, they grew into settled, businesslike communities.

Ranching Becomes Big Business Ranchers were building herds in Wyoming, Montana, and other territories. At the same time, sheep ranchers were moving their flocks across the range, and farmers were trying to cultivate crops. Competition over land use and access resulted in range wars. After much loss of life, the range was fenced off with a new invention—barbed wire—which enabled hundreds of square miles to be fenced off cheaply and easily.

At first, ranchers saw barbed wire as more of a threat than an opportunity. They did not want to abandon open grazing and complained when farmers put up barriers that prevented livestock from roaming freely. Soon, however, ranchers used barbed wire to shut out those competing with them for land and to keep their animals closer to sources of food and water. For cowhands, barbed wire ended the excitement of long cattle drives. Ranch hands replaced cowboys.

The Cattle Kingdom Ends As profits from cattle increased, cattle ranching spread north from Texas. On the northern Plains, ranchers crossbred the longhorns with fatter Hereford and Angus cattle to produce hardy, plumper new breeds.

The sturdy crossbred cattle multiplied on open-range ranches. When cattle prices boomed in the early 1880s, ranchers became rich. The boom, however, was soon followed by a bust. Overgrazing depleted the grasslands. In addition, too many cattle glutted the beef market and prices fell. The bitterly cold winters of 1885 and 1886 killed large numbers of cattle.

The price collapse of the mid-1880s marked the end of the "Cattle Kingdom." The cattle industry survived, but was changed forever. Another type of life would rise on the Plains—farming.

✓ **Reading Check** **Describe** How did the Hispanics influence life in the West?

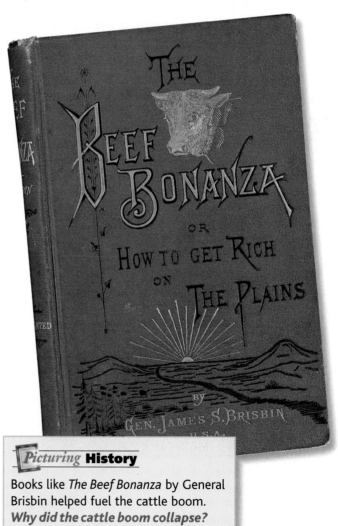

Picturing **History**

Books like *The Beef Bonanza* by General Brisbin helped fuel the cattle boom. *Why did the cattle boom collapse?*

Farmers Settle the Plains

Main Idea Free land and new farming methods brought many settlers to the Great Plains.

Reading Connection Have you ever experienced a drought or flood? Read on to learn about what farmers faced on the Great Plains, including droughts, flooding, plagues of insects, and harsh winters.

The early pioneers who reached the Great Plains did not believe they could farm the dry, treeless area. In the late 1860s, however, farmers began settling there and planting crops. Before long, much of the Plains became farmland. In 1872 a Nebraska settler wrote,

❝One year ago this was a vast houseless, uninhabited prairie. . . . Today I can see more than thirty dwellings from my door.❞

—from *Settling the West*

Several factors brought settlers to the Plains. The railroads made the journey west easier and cheaper. Above-average rainfall in the late 1870s made the Plains better suited to farming. Finally, new laws offered free land.

In 1862 Congress passed the Homestead Act, which gave 160 free acres of land to a settler who paid a filing fee and lived on the land for five years. This federal land policy brought farmers to the Plains to **homestead** (HOHM•STEHD)—earn ownership of land by settling on it.

Homesteading lured thousands of new settlers. Some were immigrants who had begun the process of becoming American citizens and were eligible to file for land. Others were women. Although married women could not claim land, single women and widows had the same rights as men—and they used the Homestead Act to **acquire** property.

Steamship companies went to great lengths to advertise the American Plains in Scandinavia. By 1880 more than 100,000 Swedes and Norwegians had settled in the northern Plains—Minnesota and the Dakotas. The Scandinavian influence remains strong in this region today.

Soon after the Civil War ended, many African American soldiers, called "Buffalo Soldiers," served in the West. Thousands of African Americans also migrated from the Southern states into Kansas in the late 1870s. They called themselves "Exodusters," from the biblical book of Exodus, which describes the Jews' escape from slavery in Egypt.

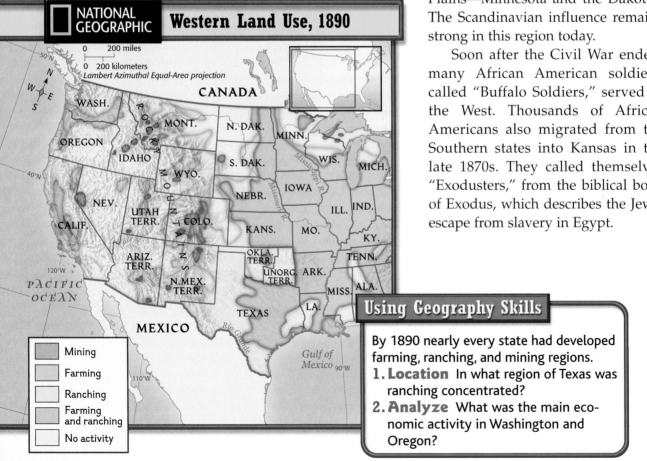

NATIONAL GEOGRAPHIC

Western Land Use, 1890

0   200 miles
0   200 kilometers
Lambert Azimuthal Equal-Area projection

Mining
Farming
Ranching
Farming and ranching
No activity

Using Geography Skills

By 1890 nearly every state had developed farming, ranching, and mining regions.
1. **Location** In what region of Texas was ranching concentrated?
2. **Analyze** What was the main economic activity in Washington and Oregon?

Biography

THE BUFFALO SOLDIERS

African Americans had fought in military conflicts since colonial times. Many had served and died during the Civil War.

When Congress set up the peacetime army after the Civil War, it also organized four segregated regiments of African American soldiers and cavalry, the 9th Cavalry, 10th Cavalry, 24th Infantry, and 25th Infantry. Many African Americans joined because of the opportunity for steady pay and a pension. These soldiers first served on the western frontier.

These segregated units answered the nation's call to arms not only in the West, but also in Cuba, the Philippines, Hawaii, and Mexico. They fought in the Indian Wars and served in the western United States from 1867 until 1896. According to legend, the men were called "Buffalo Soldiers" by the Apache and Cheyenne. The name was adopted by the African American soldiers as a sign of honor and respect.

The Buffalo Soldiers did not, however, receive equal treatment from the Anglo American settlers or soldiers. The Buffalo Soldiers were sometimes harassed and abused. Despite being mistreated, these regiments overcame hardships to become among the most decorated military units in the United States Army.

The army, recognizing the courage of the Buffalo Soldiers, presented the Medal of Honor to at least 20 Buffalo Soldiers for service during the wars in the American West. The Buffalo Soldiers also received commendations for their bravery in other wars and conflicts, including the Spanish-American War, World War I, and World War II.

In 1992 Colin Powell, who then served as chairman of the Joint Chiefs of Staff, dedicated a memorial to the Buffalo Soldiers in Fort Leavenworth, Kansas. In recognition, Powell noted that "since 1641 there has never been a time in this country when Blacks were unwilling to serve and sacrifice for America."

▲ Charles M. Young

"Colonel Charles Young . . . stands out as a shining example of the dedication, service, and commitment of the Buffalo Soldiers."

—quoted in Senate Resolution 97, 2001

Then and Now

Research the careers of some of the high-ranking African American officers in today's armed forces.

The Farmers' Frontier The climate of the Plains presented farmers with a great challenge. Generally there was little rainfall, but in some years rain came down in torrents, destroying crops and flooding homesteads. The other extreme—drought—also threatened crops and lives. Fire was another enemy. In times of drought, brushfires swept rapidly through a region, destroying crops, livestock, and homes.

Several times during the 1870s, swarms of grasshoppers swept over the Plains. Thousands of the insects would land on a field of corn. When they left, not a stalk remained.

In winters winds howled across the open Plains, and deep snow could bury animals and trap families in their homes. Families had to plan ahead and store food for the winter.

Farm Families Farming on the Great Plains was a family affair. Men labored hard in the fields. Women often did the same work, but they also cared for the children. A farm wife sewed clothing, made candles, and cooked and preserved food. She often also tended to the children's health and education. When her husband was away—taking the harvest to town or buying supplies—she was responsible for keeping the farm running.

When children grew old enough, they helped in the fields, tended animals, and did chores around the house. Farmwork often kept children from attending school.

Although separated by great distances, people took much pleasure in getting together for weddings, church services, picnics, and other occasions. As communities grew, schools and churches began to dot the rural landscape.

New Farming Methods The Plains could not be farmed by the usual methods of the 1860s. Most parts of the region had little rainfall and too few streams for irrigation. The Plains farmers, known as **sodbusters** (SAHD•BUHS•tuhrs), needed new methods and tools.

One approach, called **dry farming,** was to plant seeds deep in the ground where there was some moisture. Wooden plows could not penetrate the tough layer of sod, but in the late 1870s farmers could use the newly invented, lightweight steel plows to do the job.

The sodbusters had other tools to help them cultivate the Plains—windmills to pump water from deep in the ground and barbed wire fencing. With no wood to build fences, farmers used these wire fences to protect their land.

Dry farming, however, did not produce large crop yields, and the 160-acre grants were too small to make a living. Most farmers needed at least 300 acres, as well as advanced machinery, to make a farm profitable. Many farmers went into debt. Others lost ownership of their farms and then had to rent the land.

What Was the Oklahoma Land Rush? The last part of the Plains to be settled was the Oklahoma Territory, designated by Congress as Indian Territory in the 1830s. After years of pressure from land dealers and settlers' groups, the federal government opened Oklahoma to homesteaders in 1889. Settlers were eager to receive title to 160 acres of land. Their only condition was to remain on, improve, and develop the property for five years.

On the morning of April 22, 1889—the official opening day—more than 10,000 people lined up on the edge of this land. At the sound of a bugle, the homesteaders charged across the border to stake their claims. The eager settlers discovered that some people had already slipped into Oklahoma. These so-called "sooners" had claimed most of the best land. Within a few years, all of Oklahoma was opened to settlement.

Closing the Frontier Not long after the Oklahoma land rush, the government announced in the 1890 census that the frontier no longer existed. Settlement had changed the Plains dramatically. No one felt these changes more keenly than the Native Americans who had lived on the Plains for centuries.

✓ **Reading Check** **Explain** Why was the Homestead Act important to settlers?

History Online

Study Central Need help understanding ranching and farming on the Great Plains? Visit tajww1.glencoe.com and click on Study Central.

Section 2 Review

Reading Summary

Review the Main Ideas

- Cattle raised on the open range in Texas were driven north to railroad lines and shipped to eastern markets.

- Cowhands in the American West, who included African Americans, Native Americans, Hispanics, and whites, faced many dangers during cattle drives.

- The Homestead Act helped bring many settlers to the Great Plains.

What Did You Learn?

1. Explain why cow towns developed.

2. What new methods and tools helped settlers successfully farm the Great Plains?

Critical Thinking

3. **Determining Cause and Effect** Re-create the diagram below and explain how the Homestead Act encouraged settlement of the Great Plains.

Homestead Act

4. **Analyze** What opportunities did settlement on the Plains provide for women and African Americans?

5. **The Big Ideas** How did geography influence the settlement and economic growth of the Great Plains and American West?

6. **ANALYSIS** **Descriptive Writing** In an essay, discuss the growth, life, and decline of the Wild West in American history. Be sure to mention the geographical, economic, and social factors involved in that period in history.

A Lantern in Her Hand

By Bess Streeter Aldrich

Before You Read

The Scene: The homestead in this story is in eastern Nebraska. It is 1874.

The Characters: Will and Abbie Deal set up their homestead in 1868. Mack is their seven-year-old son. The Lutzes are their closest neighbors. The Reinmuellers live a little farther away.

The Plot: Will and his family went to Nebraska because they could own land there. Until this year, they have not had good crops because there has not been enough rain. They have also lived through a prairie fire and blizzards. Will and Abbie still believe, however, that the land is their fortune.

Vocabulary Preview

billowing: bulging or swelling out in the wind

colossal: huge, enormous

diabolical: like a devil; very evil

hazy: unclear because of smoke, dust, or clouds

incredulously: in a way that is unbelieving

perforations: holes

raw: not prepared for use; natural

uncanny: beyond ordinary human means or ability

Have you ever worked hard to make a wish come true? Were you able to reach your goal? Farming is an uncertain business, but it seems that Will and Abbie's hopes may soon be realized.

As You Read

Contrast and vivid description are two tools that writers use to emphasize the importance of an event. As you begin reading this selection, imagine what the homestead looks like. As you continue, pay close attention to the pictures the writer is painting with words. What changes do you see?

The crop of 1874 was the sixth crop and it seemed to give a little more promise than the previous ones. By the twentieth of July, Will had laid by all his corn. Most of his small grain[1] was in the shocks,[2] but one oat field of a few acres was still uncut. Standing there under the July sun, its ripened surface seemed to reflect back the yellow rays. In the afternoon Abbie went out to pick a mess[3] of beans. The garden had come to be Abbie's care. Aside from the potato crop, to which Will attended, she looked after the entire garden. It was quite generally so,—the men bending all their energies to bigger things, the corn and wheat and the stock, with the chickens and the gardens falling to the lot of the wives. Some of the women went into the fields. Christine Reinmueller was out beside Gus many days. Will drew the line at that. "When you have to do that, we'll quit," he said.

Abbie, in her starched[4] sunbonnet, began picking beans for supper. She could see Will and Henry Lutz working together, shocking the last of Henry's oats. To-morrow the two would work together on Will's last stand. It was nice for the men to be so neighborly.

It seemed hazy in the west. By the time she had finished the long rows, a big panful of the yellow pods in her arms, Will had come home from the Lutzes'. In the welcome shade of the house Abbie took off her bonnet, wiped her flushed perspiring face and waited for Will to come up.

"My...it's a scorcher." She looked hot and tired.

In a moment of tenderness, more to be desired because of its rarity, Will picked up Abbie's hands. The slender nails were stubbed and broken,—the grime of the garden was on her tapering fingers. He lifted her hand suddenly and kissed the hollow of it. As his lips touched the calloused palms, his eyes filled with rare tears. He uttered a short swift oath, "I wish you didn't have to, Abbie-girl. It's tough for you. Some day...in a few years...we'll pull out. Weather conditions may change... the land will be high....You can have better things...and your organ. That singing and painting of yours...maybe we can get to a teacher then...."

---

[1] **small grain:** grains, such as oat, rye, wheat; any grain that is not corn
[2] **in the shocks:** grain stacked in a standing position in a field to dry
[3] **mess:** enough food of one kind to serve as a meal or a dish
[4] **starched:** clothing that has been made stiff

It affected Abbie as it always did. In a moment like that it seemed the end and aim of everything... the family. All her dreams for herself were as nothing. In her own moment of emotion she returned, "We'll make it, Will... don't worry!"

For a moment they stood together looking out over the raw rolling acreage. Even as they looked, the sun darkened and the day took on a grayness. They looked for the storm, and heard it as soon as they saw it,—a great black cloud roar out of the west, with a million little hissing vibrations.[5] Their eyes on the sky, neither moved. Then there was a cessation[6] of the roaring, a soft thud of dropping things, and the cloud of a billion wings lay on the fields.

"Grasshoppers," they said simultaneously, incredulously.

The grasshoppers swarmed over the young waist-high corn and the pasture and the garden. By evening the long rows of sweet corn had been eaten to the plowed ground. The tender vines of the tomatoes were stripped down to the stalk. The buds of the fruit trees were gone. Part of the garden was a memory. The chickens had feasted themselves to the bursting point. Gus Reinmueller, driving up to the door, could hardly control his raring horses, so irritated were they by the bouncing, thumping pests. The farm was a squirming, greenish-gray mass of them.

All evening Will sat by the stove with his head in his hands. It was the first time he had visibly lost his grit. Abbie went over to him and ran her hand through his hair. She tried to think of something to console him. "Don't, Will. . . There's one thing we can do. There's the string of pearls. We can always fall back on it. There must be jewelry stores in Omaha that would take it and pay well. You can take the team and make the drive. . . You can do it in three days,. . . and I'll look after things here. When Mother gave the pearls to me, she said 'You'll ne'er starve with them'. . . and we won't, Will. We'll sell them for the children's sake."

Will threw her hands away from his hair roughly and stood up. "Hell. . . no!" He yelled it at her. "I've taken your music away from you and your painting and your teaching and some of your health. But, *by God*,. . . I won't take your mother's present to you."

He slammed the rough soddie door and went out to the barn.

By the next night the stalks of field corn were skeletons, a few delicate veins of leaves left, like so many white bones bleaching on the desert of the fields. At the end of three days the oat field was stripped almost as bare as the day the plow had finished its work. The young orchard was a graveyard of hopes. Some of the small grain previously harvested had been saved, and luckily, one digging of early potatoes was in the hole in the ground in which Will always kept them. But everything else went through the crunching incisors[7] of the horde. It was as though the little grayish-green fiends[8] became a composite whole,—one colossal insect into whose grinding maw[9] went all the green of the fields and the gardens, all the leaves and tender twigs of the young fruit trees, all the dreams and the hopes of the settlers.

The pests were everywhere. With nightmarish persistence, they appeared in everything. As tightly as Will kept the well covered, he drew them up in the bucket, so that he began going back to the old spring for water. Abbie caught them eating the curtains of the little half-windows and sent them to a fiery death. She was forced to dry the weekly wash around the cook stove, her one attempt to hang it in the sun ending speedily with a dozen perforations in the first billowing garment.

---

[5] **vibrations:** quick movements back and forth
[6] **cessation:** ending
[7] **incisors:** front teeth that are particularly good for cutting
[8] **fiends:** evil spirits
[9] **maw:** the jaws of an animal that has a huge appetite

The garden was a total loss. They had tried to save some of the beans by putting gunny-sacks[10] over them and weighting them down with stones from the creek bed. The grasshoppers, after eating the beans, had begun on the gunny-sacks.

"Will they eat the stones, too, Mother?" Mack wanted to know. And they could not laugh at him.

Abbie wrote a letter to her sister Mary, telling of this last hard piece of luck. Even letters were expensive luxuries so that one was made to do for the entire group of relatives back in eastern Iowa. She gave the letter to Will, who said that he would ride over to the little post office in the Lutz store as soon as he had finished caring for the stock. In an hour Will came in holding the letter by a corner. The edges of the envelope had been eaten all the way around with little neat flutings so that the two sides fell apart and the letter fluttered to the floor. The pocket of his old denim coat, where the letter had lain, was flapping down, cut on two sides by the same diabolical jaws.

What could you do? You could not fight them. You could not kill them. They were an army with an uncanny and unnatural power. Abbie looked out upon the devastation[11] of the fields and the garden upon which they both had worked so hard. The hot wind blew over the ruins with Mephistophelean[12] laughter. She looked up at the cloudless blue,—huge cruel, sardonic.[13]

---

[10] **gunny-sacks:** a bag made from coarse heavy material, such as burlap

[11] **devastation:** destruction

[12] **Mephistophelean:** like the proud fallen angel Mephistopheles who is cold-hearted, funny, and sardonic

[13] **sardonic:** making fun in a way that shows someone or something is not important

Responding to the Literature

1. What was Abbie doing when the selection started? What was Will doing?

2. How did Abbie and Will try to save the beans? What happened next?

3. **Analyze** In **foreshadowing** a writer gives clues to prepare readers for what will happen. What did the author foreshadow in this selection? How did she do it?

4. **Explain** What are the literal and figurative meanings of the following sentence? "The young orchard was a graveyard of hopes."

5. **Read to Write** In 500 to 700 words, write a story or describe an incident in your life. Base the narrative on an event related to your local weather, such as a hurricane or blizzard. As an alternative, you may use an environmental issue, such as water pollution or an endangered species. What was life like before and during this incident? Why was the event important? What was your attitude about it? Be sure to include dialogue in the narrative.

Reading On Your Own...

Do you want to learn more about life and inventions in the years between the Civil War and 1914? You might be interested in the following books.

Nonfiction

Native Americans and the Reservation in American History by Anita Louise McCormick recounts the history of relations between whites and Native Americans, beginning in the 1600s. McCormick also explains the historical and cultural beliefs that led members of each ethnic group to act as they did.

Biography

The Wright Brothers: How They Invented the Airplane by Russell Freedman does more than simply describe the brothers' experiments. Freedman has included portions of their journals and letters, plus photos that the brothers took as they documented their experiments.

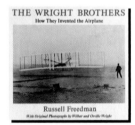

Historical Fiction

Dreams in the Golden Country: The Diary of Zipporah Feldman, a Jewish Immigrant Girl by Kathryn Lasky begins by describing the Feldmans' experience on Ellis Island. As the diary continues, Zipporah tells about their life in New York City in the early 1900s and her hopes for the future.

Nonfiction

McGuffey's Fourth Eclectic Reader by William McGuffey starts with directions to the teacher, followed by poetry and prose reading selections for students. This book gives the reader an interesting insight into what students read in the 1800s and why particular pieces were chosen.

Native American Struggles

Guide to Reading

Looking Back, Looking Ahead
You learned that following the Civil War, many whites moved to the Great Plains and the American West to mine, ranch, and farm. Many Native American groups, however, already lived in those areas, and the two peoples came into conflict.

Focusing on the Main Ideas
- The Native Americans of the Great Plains lived a nomadic lifestyle while following the great herds of buffalo. *(page 686)*
- During the late 1800s, whites and Native Americans fought while Native Americans tried to preserve their civilizations. *(page 687)*

Locating Places
Oklahoma
Dakota Territory
Black Hills
Little Bighorn River
Wounded Knee

Meeting People
Red Cloud
William Cody
Crazy Horse
Black Kettle
Sitting Bull
George Custer
Geronimo (juh•RAH•nuh•MOH)
Helen Hunt Jackson

Content Vocabulary
nomadic (noh•MA•dihk)
reservation

Academic Vocabulary
despite (di•SPYT)
achieve

Reading Strategy
Determining Cause and Effect As you read the section, re-create the diagram below and describe how Western settlement affected Native Americans.

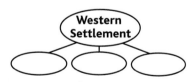

Western Settlement

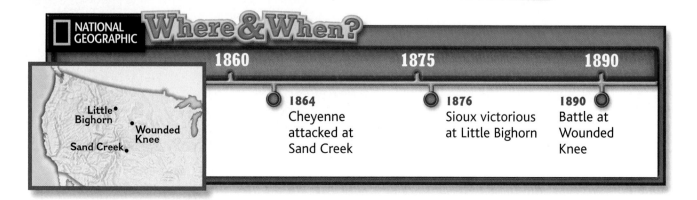

NATIONAL GEOGRAPHIC **Where & When?**

1860 1875 1890

1864 Cheyenne attacked at Sand Creek

1876 Sioux victorious at Little Bighorn

1890 Battle at Wounded Knee

Little Bighorn
Wounded Knee
Sand Creek

Following the Buffalo

Main Idea The Native Americans of the Great Plains lived a nomadic lifestyle while following the great herds of buffalo.

Reading Connection What might it be like to move from place to place throughout the year, following a large herd of animals so that your people could hunt and eat? Read to find out about the lifestyle of the Native Americans of the Great Plains.

In the mid-1850s, miners, railroads, cattle drivers, and farmers came to the Plains. Each new group threatened Native American culture. The Sioux chief **Red Cloud** lamented, "The white children [settlers] have surrounded me and left me nothing but an island."

For centuries the Great Plains was home to many Native American nations. The Omaha and the Osage nations lived in communities as farmers and hunters. The Sioux, the Comanche, and the Blackfeet lived a **nomadic** (noh•MA•dihk) life. They traveled vast distances following their main source of food—the great herds of buffalo that roamed the Great Plains.

Despite their differences, the people of the Plains were similar in many ways. Plains Indian nations, sometimes numbering several thousand people, were divided into bands consisting of up to 500 people each. A governing council headed each band, but most members participated in making decisions.

The women reared the children, cooked, and prepared hides. The men hunted, traded, and supervised the military life of the band. Most Plains Indians practiced a religion based on a belief in the spiritual power of the natural world.

Threats to the Buffalo At one time, the Plains Indians had millions of buffalo to supply their needs. After the Civil War, though, American hunters hired by the railroads began slaughtering the animals to feed the crews building the railroad. The railroad companies also wanted to prevent huge herds of buffalo from blocking the trains. **William Cody,** hired by the Kansas Pacific Railroad, once claimed that he had killed more than 4,000 buffalo in less than 18 months. He became known as Buffalo Bill. Starting in 1872, hunters targeted buffalo to sell the hides to the East, where tanneries made them into leather goods.

Reading Check **Describe** What is a nomadic way of life?

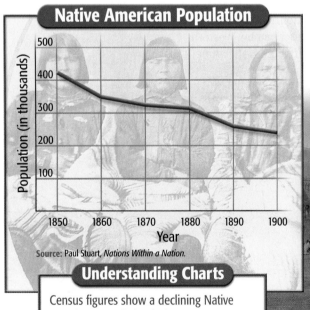

Native American Population

Source: Paul Stuart, Nations Within a Nation.

Understanding Charts

Census figures show a declining Native American population before 1900.

Analyze During what 10-year period did the Native American population decline the least?

▲ Native Americans of the Great Plains settled in one place for only part of the year.

Conflict

Main Idea During the late 1800s, whites and Native Americans fought while Native Americans tried to preserve their civilizations.

Reading Connection How would you react if the government suddenly forced you to move from your home? Read to find out how Native Americans reacted when settlers moved into their lands and attempted to change the way they lived.

As ranchers, miners, and farmers moved onto the Plains, they deprived Native Americans of their hunting grounds, broke treaties guaranteeing certain lands to the Plains Indians, and often forced them to relocate to new territory. Native Americans resisted by attacking wagon trains, stagecoaches, and ranches. Occasionally, an entire group would go to war against nearby settlers and troops. In the late 1860s, the government pursued a new Indian policy to deal with these challenges.

Reservation Policy In 1867 the federal government appointed the Indian Peace Commission to set policies for Native Americans. The commission recommended moving the Native Americans to a few large reservations—tracts of land set aside for them.

One large reservation was in **Oklahoma,** the "Indian Territory" that Congress had created in the 1830s for Native Americans who were relocated from the Southeast. Another one, meant for the Sioux people, was in the **Dakota Territory.** Managing the reservations would be the job of the federal Bureau of Indian Affairs.

Government agents often used trickery to persuade Native American nations to move to the reservations. Many reservations were located on poor land. In addition the government often failed to deliver promised food and supplies, and the goods that were delivered were of poor quality.

A great many Native Americans accepted the reservation policy at first. Many southern Kiowa, Comanche, Cheyenne, and Arapaho agreed to stay on the Oklahoma reservation. Thousands of Sioux agreed to move onto the Dakota reservation in the North.

Pockets of resistance remained, however. Some Native Americans refused to make the move, and some who tried reservation life abandoned it. The stage was set for trouble.

Conflict on the Plains During the 1860s, many armed clashes between Native Americans and whites took place. Minnesota Territory was the site of one especially bloody confrontation. Resentful of the settlers, Sioux warriors, led by Red Cloud, burned and looted white settlers' homes in the summer of 1862. Hundreds died before troops arrived from St. Paul and ended the uprising.

Following the Minnesota uprising, the army sent patrols far out onto the northern Great Plains. This action brought troops into contact with another branch of the Sioux—the nomadic Lakota. The Lakota fought hard to keep control of their hunting grounds, which extended from the Black Hills and the surrounding Badlands—rocky and barren terrain in the western parts of the Dakotas and northwestern Nebraska—westward to the Bighorn Mountains.

▲ **Native American buffalo shield**

"If we must die, we die defending our rights."
—*Sitting Bull*

The Sioux, along with Cheyenne and Arapaho warriors, staged a series of attacks from 1865 to 1867. The bloodiest incident occurred on December 21, 1866. Army troops, led by Captain William J. Fetterman, were manning a fort on the Bozeman Trail, used by prospectors to reach gold mines in Montana. A Sioux military leader, **Crazy Horse,** acted as a decoy and lured the troops into a deadly trap. He tricked the fort's commander into sending a detachment of about 80 soldiers in pursuit. Hundreds of warriors were waiting in ambush and wiped out the entire detachment. This incident came to be known as the Fetterman Massacre.

Colorado was another site of conflict. The number of miners who had flocked to Colorado in search of gold and silver grew. Bands of Cheyenne and Arapaho began raiding wagon trains and stealing cattle and horses from ranches. By the summer of 1864, travelers heading to Denver or the mining camps were no longer safe. Dozens of ranches had been burned, and an estimated 200 settlers had been killed. The territorial governor of Colorado ordered the Native Americans to surrender at Fort Lyon, where he said they would be given food and protection.

Although several hundred Native Americans surrendered at the fort, many others did not. In November 1864, Chief **Black Kettle** brought several hundred Cheyenne to negotiate a peace deal. They camped at Sand Creek. Shortly after, Colonel John Chivington led the Colorado Volunteers on an attack on the unsuspecting Cheyenne. Fourteen volunteers and hundreds of Cheyenne died. Retaliation by the Cheyenne was swift, causing widespread uprisings before some of the Cheyenne and Arapaho leaders agreed to stop the fighting in October 1865.

What Occurred at Little Bighorn? Treaties were supposed to bring peace, but tensions remained and erupted in more fighting a few years later. This time the conflict arose over the **Black Hills** of the Dakotas. The government had promised that "No white person or persons shall be permitted to settle upon or occupy" or even "to pass through" these hills. However, the hills were rumored to contain gold. Prospectors swarmed into the area.

The Sioux protested against the trespassers. Instead of protecting the Sioux's rights, the government tried to buy the hills. **Sitting Bull,** an important leader of the Lakota Sioux, refused. "I do not want to sell any land. Not even this much," he said, holding a pinch of dust.

Sitting Bull gathered Sioux and Cheyenne warriors along the **Little Bighorn River** in present-day Montana. They were joined by Crazy Horse, another Sioux chief, and his forces. The United States Army was ordered to round up the warriors and move them to reservations. The Seventh Cavalry, led by Lieutenant Colonel **George Custer,** was ordered to scout the Native American encampment.

Custer wanted the glory of leading a major victory. He divided his regiment and attacked the Native Americans on June 25, 1876. He had seriously underestimated their strength, however. With about 250 soldiers, Custer faced a Sioux and Cheyenne force of thousands. Custer and his entire command lost their lives. News of the army's defeat shocked the nation.

The Native American triumph at Little Bighorn was short-lived. The army soon crushed the uprising, sending most of the Native Americans to reservations. Sitting Bull and his followers fled north to Canada. By 1881, exhausted and starving, the Lakota and Cheyenne agreed to live on a reservation.

Who Were the Nez Perce?

Farther west, members of the Nez Perce, led by Chief Joseph, refused to be moved to a smaller reservation in Idaho in 1877. When the army came to relocate them, they fled their homes and traveled more than 1,000 miles. After a remarkable flight to Canada, Chief Joseph realized that resistance was hopeless. Finally, in October 1877, Chief Joseph surrendered, and his followers were moved to reservations.

The Apache Wars

Trouble also broke out in the Southwest. The Chiracahua Apache had been moved from their homeland in present-day New Mexico and Arizona to the San Carlos reservation in Arizona in the mid-1870s. Many Apache resented confinement to this reservation. The Apache leader, **Geronimo** (juh•RAH•nuh•MOH), escaped from San Carlos and fled to Mexico with a small band of followers. During the 1880s, he led raids against settlers and the army in Arizona. Army troops pursued Geronimo and his warriors. Several times Geronimo went back to the reservation only to leave again. Geronimo said, "Once I moved about like the wind. Now I surrender to you." In 1886 the Apache leader finally gave up—the last Native American to surrender formally to the United States.

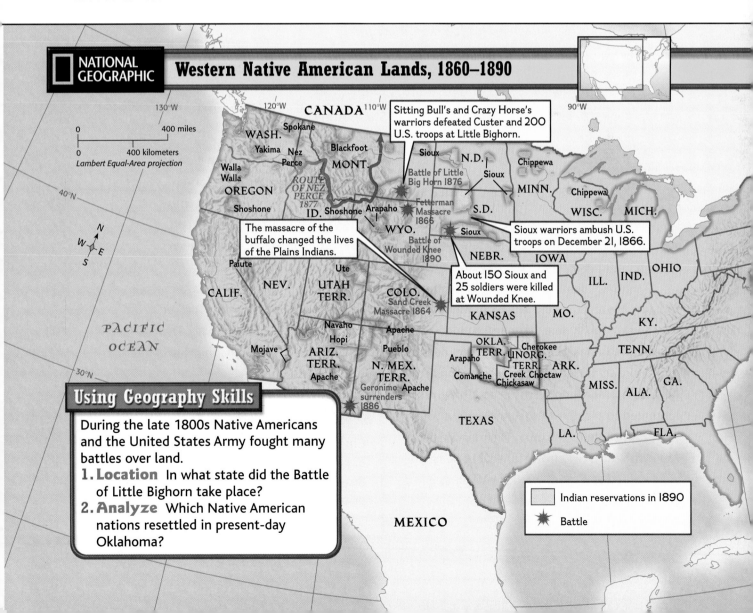

NATIONAL GEOGRAPHIC

Western Native American Lands, 1860–1890

Sitting Bull's and Crazy Horse's warriors defeated Custer and 200 U.S. troops at Little Bighorn.

The massacre of the buffalo changed the lives of the Plains Indians.

Sioux warriors ambush U.S. troops on December 21, 1866.

About 150 Sioux and 25 soldiers were killed at Wounded Knee.

Indian reservations in 1890

Battle

Using Geography Skills

During the late 1800s Native Americans and the United States Army fought many battles over land.

1. **Location** In what state did the Battle of Little Bighorn take place?
2. **Analyze** Which Native American nations resettled in present-day Oklahoma?

Biography

CHIEF JOSEPH
1840–1904

Chief Joseph was born in 1840 as Hin ma to yah lat k'it, which means Thunder Emerging from the Mountains. He grew up in the Wallowa Valley, located in present-day Oregon. In 1860, when gold was found on Nez Perce land, white settlers flooded into the region. In 1877 the United States government demanded that the Nez Perce give up their lands and move onto a reservation in Idaho. Chief Joseph, hoping to avoid violence, prepared his people for the move. He learned, however, that several young braves had attacked a group of white settlers. Fearing revenge, Chief Joseph led his followers more than 1,000 miles across Oregon, Washington, Idaho, and Montana.

For more than three months he managed to evade a U.S. force 10 times larger than his group. He made his way north toward Canada, hoping to escape the reach of the United States Army. Along the way, he won the admiration of many whites for his humane treatment of prisoners and for his concern for women, children, and the elderly.

"I will fight no more forever."

—Chief Joseph, from *A Patriot's Handbook*

In September 1877, the Nez Perce had reached the Bear Paw Mountains in Montana, just 40 miles from the Canadian border. As the Nez Perce rested before their move into Canada, a band of 400 soldiers surrounded the camp. After a fierce battle, Chief Joseph offered to surrender in return for safe passage to the reservation in Idaho. Chief Joseph's words of surrender reflect the tragedy of his people:

"The little children are freezing to death. My people . . . have no blankets, no food. . . . I am tired; my heart is sick and sad. From where the sun now stands I will fight no more forever."

The Nez Perce were taken not to Idaho, but to a swampy tract of land in Kansas. There, unused to the weather and the environment, many fell ill and died. Eventually, the Nez Perce were scattered among reservations in Oklahoma, Idaho, and Washington. Chief Joseph continued to plead with the government to allow his people to return to their land in the Wallowa Valley. His efforts failed, but he is remembered as a great warrior, as well as a man of peace.

Then and Now

Chief Joseph's reputation as a great leader arose in part from his ability and dignity in battle. Research to find at least three U.S. presidents or other government officials who built their reputations in the military.

A Changing Culture Many things contributed to changing the traditional way of life of Native Americans—the movement of whites onto their lands, the slaughter of the buffalo, United States Army attacks, and the reservation policy. More change came from well-meaning reformers who wanted to abolish reservations and absorb the Native Americans into white American culture.

American reformers such as **Helen Hunt Jackson** were horrified by the massacres of Native Americans and by the cruelty of the reservation system. Describing the whites' treatment of Native Americans in her 1881 book, *A Century of Dishonor*, Jackson wrote:

> ❝ It makes little difference . . . where one opens the record of the history of the Indians; every page and every year has its dark stain. The story of one tribe is the story of all, varied only by differences of time and place. ❞
>
> —Helen Hunt Jackson,
> *A Century of Dishonor*

Congress changed government policy with the Dawes Act in 1887. The law aimed to eliminate what white Americans regarded as the two weaknesses of Native American life: the lack of private property and the nomadic tradition.

The Dawes Act proposed to break up the reservations and to end identification with a tribal group. Each Native American would receive a plot of reservation land. The goal was to encourage native peoples to become farmers and, eventually, American citizens. Native American children would be sent to white-run boarding schools. Some of the reservation lands would be sold to support this schooling.

Over the next 50 years, the government divided up the reservations. Speculators acquired most of the valuable land. Native Americans often received dry, gravelly plots that were not suited to farming.

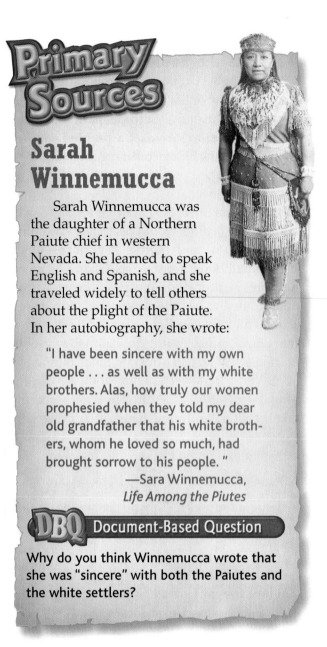

Primary Sources

Sarah Winnemucca

Sarah Winnemucca was the daughter of a Northern Paiute chief in western Nevada. She learned to speak English and Spanish, and she traveled widely to tell others about the plight of the Paiute. In her autobiography, she wrote:

"I have been sincere with my own people . . . as well as with my white brothers. Alas, how truly our women prophesied when they told my dear old grandfather that his white brothers, whom he loved so much, had brought sorrow to his people."
—Sara Winnemucca,
Life Among the Piutes

DBQ Document-Based Question

Why do you think Winnemucca wrote that she was "sincere" with both the Paiutes and the white settlers?

Cultural Impact This plan failed to **achieve** its goals. Some Native Americans succeeded as farmers or ranchers, but many had little training or enthusiasm for either pursuit. Their land allotments were too small to be profitable. Some Native Americans had adapted to life on reservations and did not want to see it transformed into homesteads. In the end, the Dawes Act did not benefit Native American nations. The culture of the Plains Indians was doomed because it was dependent on buffalo. Once the buffalo were wiped out, Native Americans on the Plains had no means to sustain their way of life and little interest in adopting white American culture in place of their own.

What Was the Battle at Wounded Knee?

The Dawes Act changed forever the Native American way of life and undermined their cultural traditions. In their despair, the Sioux turned in 1890 to Wovoka, a prophet. Wovoka claimed that the Sioux could regain their former greatness if they performed a ritual known as the Ghost Dance.

This ritual celebrated a hoped-for day of reckoning when settlers would disappear, the buffalo would return, and Native Americans would reunite with their deceased ancestors. As the ritual spread, reservation officials became alarmed and decided to ban the dance. Believing that the Sioux chief, Sitting Bull, was the leader of the movement, police went to his camp to arrest him. During a scuffle, they shot and killed Sitting Bull.

Several hundred Lakota Sioux fled in fear after Sitting Bull's death. They gathered at a creek called **Wounded Knee** in southwestern South Dakota. On December 29, 1890, the army went there to collect the Sioux's weapons. No one knows how the fighting started, but when a pistol shot rang out, the army responded with fire. More than 200 Sioux and 25 soldiers were killed.

Wounded Knee marked the end of armed conflict between whites and Native Americans. The Native Americans of the Plains had fought hundreds of battles from 1860 to 1890, but they could fight no more. They depended on the buffalo for food, clothing, fuel, and shelter. When the herds were wiped out, resistance became impossible. The Native Americans had lost their long struggle.

✓ **Reading Check** **Describe** What was the purpose of the Dawes Act?

History Online

Study Central Need help understanding Native American struggles? Visit tajwwI.glencoe.com and click on Study Central.

Section 3 Review

Reading Summary

Review the Main Ideas

- For centuries, Native Americans lived on the Great Plains. Some were farmers and others were nomadic. The buffalo supplied most of their needs.

- As white settlers continued to migrate and settle the West, Native American civilization was continually threatened. Conflict between the whites and the Native Americans persisted through the late 1800s.

What Did You Learn?

1. Who were Geronimo and Chief Joseph?

2. What was the Ghost Dance?

Critical Thinking

3. **Identifying Central Issues** Re-create the diagram below and identify ways the government reservation policy ignored the needs of Native Americans.

```
      Government
        Policy
   ◯    ◯    ◯
```

4. **The Big Ideas** How did differences in social beliefs between the white settlers and the Native Americans lead to the conflict that occurred in the West?

5. **Analyze** What two aspects of Native American life was the Dawes Act supposed to eliminate?

6. **Sequencing Information** Draw a time line that lists key developments between the U.S. government and Native American nations from 1860 to 1890.

7. **Creative Writing** From the point of view of a Native American, write a poem describing the Plains Indians' lifestyle or a battle or event that occurred on the Plains.

Section 4

Farmers in Protest

Guide to Reading

Looking Back, Looking Ahead
You learned that new farming methods and the defeat of the Native Americans allowed settlers to farm the Great Plains. In time, farmers began to organize to solve problems, such as falling crop prices.

Focusing on the Main Ideas
- When crop prices fell in the late 1800s, farmers began to organize politically. *(page 694)*
- In the 1890s, a political party developed supporting the views of farmers and the common people. *(page 695)*

Locating Places
Omaha, Nebraska

Meeting People
James B. Weaver
Grover Cleveland
William Jennings Bryan
William McKinley

Content Vocabulary
National Grange
cooperative (koh•AH•puh•ruh•tiv)
Populist Party (PAH•pyuh•lihst)
free silver

Academic Vocabulary
decline
dynamic (dy•NA•mihk)

Reading Strategy
Identifying Central Issues As you read the section, re-create the diagram below and identify the problems farmers faced in the late 1800s.

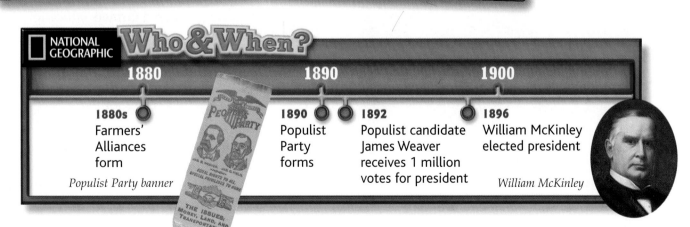

NATIONAL GEOGRAPHIC **Who & When?**

| 1880 | 1890 | 1900 |

1880s
Farmers' Alliances form

Populist Party banner

1890
Populist Party forms

1892
Populist candidate James Weaver receives 1 million votes for president

1896
William McKinley elected president

William McKinley

The Farmers Organize

Main Idea When crop prices fell in the late 1800s, farmers began to organize politically.

Reading Connection Have you heard the expression "strength in numbers"? Read to find out how farmers organized in groups in the late 1800s to help solve the challenges they faced.

An American Story

In the last decades of the 1800s, farmers suffered from falling prices and rising costs. They expressed their frustration in a popular song:

> ❝When the banker says he's broke,
> And the merchant's up in smoke,
> They forget that it's the farmer
>   feeds them all. . . .
> The farmer is the man,
> Lives on credit till the fall;
> With the interest rates so high,
> It's a wonder he don't die,
> For the mortgage man's the one
>   who gets it all. ❞
>
> —from "The Farmer Is the Man"

▲ Honoring the Farmer, 1870s poster

Crop Prices Fall After the Civil War, farming expanded in the West and the South, and more land came under cultivation. The supply of crops grew faster than the demand for them, however, and prices fell steadily. In 1866 a bushel of wheat sold for $1.45. By the mid-1880s, the price had dropped to 80 cents, and by the mid-1890s to 49 cents. At the same time, farmers' expenses—for transporting their goods to market, for seed, and for equipment and other manufactured goods—remained high.

Farmers blamed their troubles on three groups in particular. They resented the railroad companies, which charged farmers high rates to ship their crops. They were angry at the Eastern manufacturers, who charged high prices for their products. They also had problems with bankers.

Farmers needed to borrow money to buy seed, equipment, and other goods. After they sold their crops, they had to pay the high interest rates set by bankers. If crops failed and farmers could not repay the loans, they were in danger of losing their farms.

Farmers with small and middle-sized holdings struggled to survive. Senator William A. Peffer of Kansas summed up the farmers' plight when he noted that the railroad companies "took possession of the land" and the bankers "took possession of the farmer."

What Did the Grange Do? Farmers began to organize in an effort to solve their problems. Within a short time, they created a mass political movement. The first farmers' organization of this period was a network of local organizations that came to be called the **National Grange.** The Grange offered farmers education, fellowship, and support.

Above all, the Grange tried to encourage economic self-sufficiency. It set up "cash-only" **cooperatives** (koh•AH•puh•ruh•tivz), stores where farmers bought products from each other. The cooperatives charged lower prices than regular stores and provided an outlet for farmers' crops. The purpose of the "cash-only" policy was to remove the burden of credit buying that threatened farmers.

In the 1870s, the Grange tried to cut farmers' costs by asking state legislatures to place a limit on railroad shipping rates. Many Midwestern states did pass such laws. By 1878 however, the railroads had put so much pressure on state legislatures that these states repealed the rate regulations.

Adding to the problems of the Grange, the cooperatives also began to fail. Farmers were often short of cash and had to borrow money until their next crop was sold. The cash-only cooperative could not work if borrowing was necessary. By the late 1870s, the Grange had **declined.** Rural reformers then tried to help farmers through the Farmers' Alliances.

What Were Farmers' Alliances? The Farmers' Alliances were networks of organizations that sprang up in the West and the South in the 1880s. Alliance leaders extended the movement to other states. By 1890 the Southern Alliance had more than 3 million members, and the Colored Farmers' National Alliance, a separate organization of African American farmers, had 1 million members.

Like the Grange, the Farmers' Alliances sponsored education and cooperative buying and selling. The Alliances also proposed a plan in which the federal government would store farmers' crops in warehouses and lend money to the farmers. When the stored crops were sold, the farmers would pay back the loans. Such a plan would reduce the power that railroads, banks, and merchants had over farmers and would offer farmers some federal protection. Regional differences and personality clashes impacted the effectiveness of the Alliances, even as they moved into politics.

Reading Check **Describe** What is the purpose of a cooperative?

History Online

Student Web Activity Visit tajww1.glencoe.com and click on Chapter 15—Student Web Activities for an activity on the life of a farmer in the late 1800s.

A Party of the People

Main Idea In the 1890s, a political party developed supporting the views of farmers and the common people.

Reading Connection What beliefs and ideas do you think a political party today would have to support in order to be considered a party of the common people? Read to find out about the beginnings of the People's, or Populist, Party in the late 1800s.

In 1890 members of the Farmers' Alliance identified candidates who supported the cause of the farmer. That year, four governors in the South were elected after promising to support the Alliance program. Several Southern legislatures now had pro-Alliance majorities, and more than 40 Democrats who supported the Alliance program were elected to Congress. Alliance candidates in the West did equally well.

The Populist Party Pleased with such successes, Alliance leaders worked to turn the movement into a national political party. In February 1890, Alliance members formed the People's Party of the U.S.A., also known as the **Populist Party** (PAH•pyuh•lihst). The goals of this new party were rooted in populism, or appeal to the common people.

▲ Populist farmers gather in Dickinson County, Kansas.

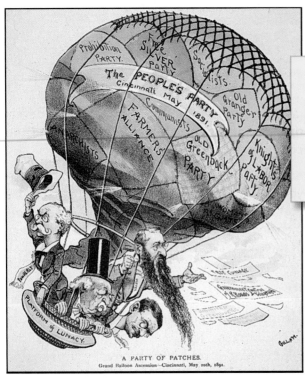

A PARTY OF PATCHES.
Grand Balloon Ascension—Cincinnati, May 20th, 1891.

Analyzing
Political Cartoons

Party of Patches The cartoonist shows the Populist Party as a collection of special interest groups and minor political parties. *Does the cartoon support or ridicule the Populist Party? Explain.*

The new party claimed that the government, not private companies, should own the railroads and telegraph lines. The Populists also wanted to replace the country's gold-based currency system with a flexible currency system that was based on **free silver**—the unlimited production of silver coins. They believed that putting more silver coins into the economy would give farmers more money to pay their debts.

The Populist Party supported a number of political and labor reforms. The party wanted election reforms such as limiting the president and vice president to a single term, electing senators directly, and introducing the use of secret ballots. The Populist Party also called for shorter hours for workers and the creation of a national income tax.

Populist Gains and Problems

At a convention in **Omaha, Nebraska,** in July 1892, the Populist Party nominated **James B. Weaver** of Iowa to run for president. In the election, Weaver received more than 1 million votes—8.5 percent of the total—and 22 electoral votes. **Grover Cleveland,** the Democratic candidate, won the election, but the Populists had done well for a third party.

The Populists made a strong showing in the state and local elections of 1894 and had hopes for building even stronger support in the presidential election of 1896. The party nominated a number of energetic candidates, but lacked money and organization.

Another blow against populism was struck by the Democratic Party in the South. In the 1890s, Democrat-controlled Southern state legislatures placed strict limits on the rights of African Americans to vote. Many freedmen—who might have supported the Populists—were unable to vote.

The Populist crusade for free silver and against the "money power" continued, however. Banking and business interests warned that coining unlimited amounts of new currency would lead to inflation and ruin the economy.

Farmers were joined by debtors in supporting free silver, hoping that loans could be repaid more cheaply. Silver-mining companies in the West also supported the cause. If the government coined large quantities of silver, they had a place to sell their metal.

In the mid-1890s, Democrats from farm and silver-producing states took up the free silver issue. This created a problem for Populists. Should they ally themselves with these Democrats? Or should they remain a separate party and risk dividing the free-silver vote?

The Election of 1896

President Grover Cleveland, a Democrat, opposed free silver. At their 1896 convention, however, the Democrats chose a candidate for president who supported free silver and other Populist goals.

The Democratic Party's candidate was 36-year-old **William Jennings Bryan,** known as the Great Commoner because of his appeal to average Americans. Bryan passionately believed in the farmers' causes.

The Populists decided to endorse Bryan as their candidate for president and to nominate their own candidate, Tom Watson of Georgia, for vice president. The Republicans nominated **William McKinley** of Ohio for president. A former representative and governor of Ohio, McKinley was a shrewd politician who opposed free silver.

A fiery and popular speaker, Bryan proved to be an outstanding campaigner. He crossed the nation giving one **dynamic** speech after another, attacking bankers and other money interests.

Bryan's strenuous campaigning did not produce an election victory. By the time of the election, an economic depression was nearly over, and voters believed that good times were returning. They put their trust in the Republican candidate McKinley, who represented stability. Even the economic situation of the farmers was improving. The Populists' message no longer seemed urgent. McKinley won 271 electoral votes to Bryan's 176. McKinley received 7.1 million popular votes to 6.5 million for Bryan.

The Populist ticket did poorly, receiving only 222,600 popular votes and no electoral votes.

The Populist Legacy The Populist Party had an impact on politics and government far beyond its showing in national elections. Minor parties have often promoted reform by taking clear-cut stands on controversial issues and proposing bold and original solutions. Reformers adopted many Populist ideas and succeeded in getting many new laws passed. Among the Populist proposals that were adopted and are still in place today are the federal income tax (Sixteenth Amendment, 1913), direct election of U.S. senators (Seventeenth Amendment, 1913), the secret ballot (late 1890s), and primary elections (Wisconsin, 1903). In the 1900s, the United States adopted an eight-hour workday.

✓ **Reading Check** Examine Why did the Republican candidate win the presidential election of 1896?

Study Central Need help understanding why farmers organized to protest? Visit tajww1.glencoe.com and click on Study Central.

Section 4 Review

Reading Summary

Review the Main Ideas

- To help solve their economic problems, farmers formed organizations such as the National Grange and Farmers' Alliances.

- In time the farm organizations developed into a national political party, the Populist Party.

What Did You Learn?

1. Which three groups did farmers blame for their problems? Why?

2. Who were the presidential candidates in the election of 1896?

Critical Thinking

3. **Analyze** Re-create the diagram below and explain what actions farmers took to address their problems.

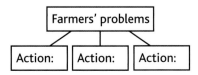

4. **Analyze** Why were granges and alliances formed?

5. **Infer** Why do you think the Populists considered themselves to be a party of the people?

6. **The Big Ideas** What reforms eventually resulted from the Populist campaign?

7. **Persuasive Writing** Write a campaign slogan for a Populist candidate who is running for office, and design a bumper sticker displaying your slogan.

Analyzing Primary Sources

On the Western Frontier

Following the Civil War, many settlers headed West to build new lives. Some of them raised cattle, others farmed the land. These settlers affected the people who had lived there for generations—the Native Americans. The government's plans for accommodating this expansion included moving Native Americans to reservations and schooling their children.

Read the passages on pages 698 and 699 and answer the questions that follow.

This painting by Charles M. Russell shows cowboys breaking camp while on a long drive. ▶

Reader's Dictionary

loaf: to spend time in idleness

afoot: on foot

blueing (BLOO • ing): a preparation used in laundering to counteract yellowing of white fabrics

abide (uh • BYD): to endure or withstand something

dumb (DUHM): not able to speak

detected: discovered, found out

On the Cattle Trail

Cowboy Andy Adams describes the start of his first cattle drive and the instructions given by the trail boss.

Flood seldom gave orders; but, as a number of us had never worked on the trail before, at breakfast on the morning of our start he gave in substance these general directions:

"Boys, the secret of trailing cattle is never to let your herd know that they are under restraint. Let everything that is done be done voluntarily by the cattle. From the moment you let them off the bed ground in the morning until they are bedded at night, never let a cow take a step, except in the direction of its destination.

In this manner you can **loaf** away the day, and cover from fifteen to twenty miles, and the herd in the meantime will enjoy all the freedom of an open range. Of course, it's long, tiresome hours to the men; but the condition of the herd and saddle stock demands sacrifices on our part, if any have to be made. And I want to caution you younger boys about your horses. . . . Accidents will happen to horses, but don't let it be your fault; keep your saddle blankets dry and clean, for no better word can be spoken of a man than that he is careful with his horses . . . we have not a horse to spare, and a man **afoot** is useless."

—from *Trail Drive: A True Narrative of Cowboy Life from Andy Adams' Log of a Cowboy*

Winter in Dakota Territory

Settlers endured challenging living conditions. Laura Ingalls Wilder wrote of her family's experiences during the bitter winter of 1880–81.

Ma said " . . . We must get out the washing while the weather's clear so we can."

All that day Laura and Carrie and Mary looked forward to the [magazine] *Youth's Companions* and often they spoke of them. But the bright day was short. They stirred and punched the clothes boiling on the stove; they lifted them on the broom handle into the tub where Ma soaped them and rubbed them. Laura rinsed them, Carrie stirred the **blueing** bag in the second rinse-water until it was blue enough. Laura made the boiled starch. And when for the last time Ma went out into the cold to hang the freezing wash on the line, Pa had come for dinner.

Then they washed the dishes, they scrubbed the floor and blacked the stove, and washed the inside of the windowpanes. Ma brought in the frozen-dry clothes and they sorted them and sprinkled them and rolled them tightly, ready for ironing. Twilight had come. It was too late to read that day and after supper there was no lamplight because they must save the last of the kerosene.

—from *The Long Winter*

◀ This shirt was part of the Ghost Dance in which the Sioux tried to preserve their way of life.

Indian School

In attempts to "civilize" Native American children, Indian schools were created in several parts of the country. In this passage, Ah-nen-la-de-ni of the Mohawk people describes his first experience in such a school.

After the almost complete freedom of reservation life the cramped quarters and the dull routine of the school were maddening to all us strangers. There were endless rules for us to study and **abide** by, and hardest of all was the rule against speaking to each other in our own language. We must speak English or remain silent, and those who knew no English were forced to be **dumb** or else break the rules in secret. This last we did quite frequently, and were punished, when **detected,** by being made to stand in the "public hall" for a long time or to march about the yard while the other boys were at play.

—from *Witnessing America*

DBQ Document-Based Questions

On the Cattle Trail

1. What seems to be the cowhand's biggest secret?
2. According to the foreman, what is worth the sacrifice of the cowboys' comfort?

Winter in Dakota Territory

3. How many steps were involved in washing the clothes for Laura's family?
4. What activity did Laura and her sisters look forward to doing once their chores were done?

Indian School

5. How does Ah-nen-la-de-ni describe school?
6. What is the hardest rule for the children to follow?

Read to Write

7. Reread the documents to find evidence that shows how each author needed to adapt to a new environment or circumstance. What adjustments did they make? Do they explain why? Write an essay explaining your conclusions.

Chapter 15 Assessment

Review Content Vocabulary

On a sheet of paper, create a crossword puzzle using the following terms. Use the terms' definitions as your crossword clues.

1. reservations
2. cooperatives
3. vigilantes
4. vaqueros
5. lodes
6. stampedes

Review the Main Ideas

Section 1 • The Mining Booms

7. What was the Comstock Lode?

8. In what ways did the railroads boost the American economy?

Section 2 • Ranchers and Farmers

9. What is a vaquero?

10. What attracted farmers to the Great Plains?

Section 3 • Native American Struggles

11. What actions by whites destroyed the buffalo population?

12. In what present-day state was the Indian Territory located?

Section 4 • Farmers in Protest

13. How did the Grange help farmers?

14. What political reforms did the Populists support?

Critical Thinking

15. **Analyze** How did the rush to find gold and silver spark the creation of new communities in the West?

16. **Economics Link** Why was the Cattle Kingdom dependent on the railroads?

17. **Determining Cause and Effect** Describe the problems that led farmers to organize granges and alliances.

Geography Skills

Study the map below and answer the following questions.

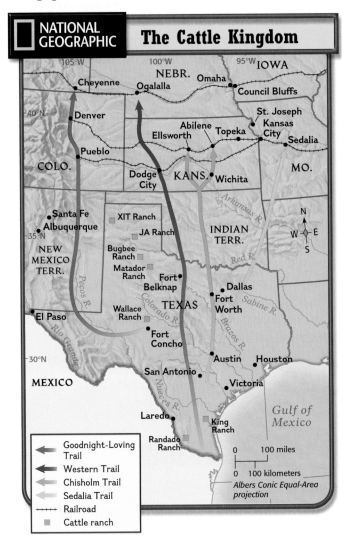

18. **Location** In what part of Texas were most of the large cattle ranches located?

19. **Movement** To which railroad towns did the Goodnight-Loving Trail run?

20. **Movement** Which cattle trails ran through Indian Territory?

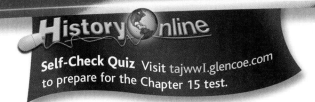

History Online

Self-Check Quiz Visit tajwwl.glencoe.com to prepare for the Chapter 15 test.

Read to Write

21. **The Big Ideas** **Analyze** Briefly discuss the geographic challenges faced by settlers and Native Americans in the American West and Great Plains. How did they overcome the challenges?

22. **Expository Writing** Reread and take notes on the section of the chapter that discusses the chores of a farm woman. Use your notes to create an hour-by-hour schedule to show one day's typical activities for a farm wife living on the Great Plains.

23. **Using Your FOLDABLES** Choose one of the four groups of people you learned about in this chapter. Describe that groups' triumphs and tragedies in a newspaper article you could have written in the late 1800s.

Using Academic Vocabulary

24. Read the following sentences and write the meaning of the underlined academic vocabulary word.

Power in a republic is <u>derived</u> from the people.

New machinery was developed to <u>extract</u> ore from the earth's crust.

Economics Connection

25. **Researching** Research to find information about a Native American reservation in the United States today. Write a report describing one of the major businesses on that reservation.

Reviewing Skills

26. **READING SKILL** **Visualizing** If you lived on the frontier in the late 1800s, would you have been a miner, a rancher, a Native American, or a farmer? Select one and write an essay describing a day in your life. Use clear descriptive language so that your readers have a good visual sense of what your life was like.

27. **ANALYSIS SKILL** **Composing** Reread the quote from the farmer's song on page 694. Write a song or poem that a banker or merchant might write.

Standardized Test Practice

Read the passage below and answer the following question.

> Having behind us the producing masses of this nation and the world, supported by the commercial interests, the laboring interests and the toilers everywhere, we will answer their demand for a gold standard by saying to them: You shall not press down upon the brow of labor this crown of thorns, you shall not crucify mankind upon a cross of gold.
> —William Jennings Bryan, "Cross of Gold" Speech, 1896

28 **By speaking against the gold standard, Bryan was showing his support for the Populist goal of**

A an eight-hour workday.

B a currency system based on free silver.

C farmers' cooperatives.

D an income tax.

29 **When Bryan refers to "the producing masses of this nation," he most likely is including**

A farmers.

B political leaders.

C manufacturers.

D Republicans.

The Growth of Industry

▼ Railroads sped industrialization in the late 1800s.

NATIONAL GEOGRAPHIC

Who & When?

1870   **1890**   **1910**

1870 Rockefeller organizes Standard Oil Company

1876 Bell patents the telephone

1886 Trade unions form AFL

1903 Wright brothers fly first motorized airplane

The Big Ideas

Railroads Lead the Way

Geography shapes the physical, economic, and political challenges a region faces. The spread of railroads across the country encouraged America's expanding economy.

Inventions

Innovations in technology and business help build a nation's industrial power. Inventions improved the transportation and communication networks that were vital to the nation's industrial growth.

The Age of Big Business

Innovations in technology and business help build a nation's industrial power. Corporations changed the American economy of the late 1800s.

Industrial Workers

Reactions to social injustice can lead to reform movements. Workers organized to demand better pay and working conditions.

 View the Chapter 16 video in the Glencoe Video Program.

Identifying Main Ideas Make this foldable to describe the growth of industry in the United States in the late 1800s.

Step 1 Fold two sheets of paper in half from top to bottom. Cut the papers in half along the folds.

Cut along the fold lines.

Step 2 Fold each of the four papers in half from top to bottom.

Step 4 Place the folded papers one on top of the other. Staple the four sections together and label each of the tabs **Railroads, Inventions, Big Business,** and **Industrial Workers.**

Step 3 On each folded paper, make a cut 1 inch from the side on the top flap.

1"

Cut 1 inch from the edge through the top flap only.

Staple here.  Railroads

Reading and Writing
As you read, write what you learn about the developments of industry under each appropriate tab.

Chapter 16

Get Ready to Read

Predicting Consequences

READING SKILL

1 Learn It!

Did you ever wish you could see into the future? Although it is impossible to predict future events, you can develop skills to help you identify the consequences of decisions or actions. Follow these steps to help you thoughtfully predict consequences:

- Review what you already know about a situation by listing facts, events, and people's responses. The list will help you recall events and how they affected people.

- Use your knowledge and observations of similar situations. In other words, ask yourself, "What were the consequences of a similar decision or action that occurred in the past?"

- Look for patterns. Try to determine what the patterns show. Are some consequences more likely to occur than others?

- Make a prediction.

Reading Tip

Read the first two pages of a chapter to get an overview of its contents. Next, reflect on what you have already studied. Last, make some educated guesses about what you might learn in the chapter.

2 Practice It!

You have already learned about some of the changes in transportation, trade, and settlement between 1800 and 1869. You learned that inland roads, along with the steamboat and the canal system, stimulated trade and settlement. Railroads spanning the continent took settlers and entrepreneurs into new regions of the United States. In this chapter, you will read more about how the railroad impacted life and industry, setting the stage for a new Industrial Revolution. Practice making some predictions about what you might learn. Complete the chart below, then discuss your predictions with a partner.

Event	Predicted results
Railroads made new regions accessible	New areas were settled by farmers, miners, and ranchers
Transcontinental railroad completed	Thousands of workers brought West
Several railroads connected East and West	
Railroads offered employment opportunities	
Railroad companies consolidated	

Read to Write

Based on what you read about labor conditions during the building of the transcontinental railroad, write a short paragraph predicting what labor conditions might have been like in other industries at that time.

European immigrants on a railroad flatcar view land open for settlement on the Great Plains.

3 Apply It!

Read the main ideas for this chapter. Take notes predicting what you'll discover. Monitor your progress to see if your expectations were accurate.

Railroads Lead the Way

Guide to Reading

Looking Back, Looking Ahead

In the last chapter, you read about the expansion of the nation into the West. In this chapter, you will read about America's economic expansion and the shift from an agricultural economy to an industrial nation.

Focusing on the Main Ideas

• Railroad barons used consolidation to expand their companies and create a growing system of railroads throughout the United States. *(page 707)*

• Railroad growth stimulated the economy, and innovations made railroad travel more efficient and profitable. *(page 709)*

Meeting People

Cornelius Vanderbilt

James J. Hill

Collis P. Huntington

Leland Stanford

George Westinghouse

Eli H. Janney

Gustavus Swift (guh • STAHV • uhs)

George M. Pullman

Content Vocabulary

consolidation
    (kuhn • SAH • luh • DAY • shuhn)

standard gauge (GAYJ)

rebate

pool

Academic Vocabulary

technology (tehk • NAH • luh • jee)

convert (kuhn • VUHRT)

network

Reading Strategy

Analyzing Information As you read the section, complete a diagram like the one shown by describing the contributions of the railroad to the growth of industry.

The role of the railroad

Where & When?

NATIONAL GEOGRAPHIC

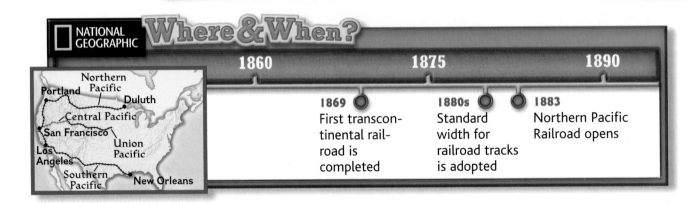

1860	1875	1890

1869 First transcontinental railroad is completed

1880s Standard width for railroad tracks is adopted

1883 Northern Pacific Railroad opens

Portland — Northern Pacific — Duluth
Central Pacific
San Francisco
Los Angeles — Union Pacific
Southern Pacific — New Orleans

Railroad Expansion

Main Idea Railroad barons used consolidation to expand their companies and create a growing system of railroads throughout the United States.

Reading Connection What methods do companies today use to expand their businesses? Read on to find out how railroads grew after the Civil War.

An American Story

Rugged construction gangs labored on the Union Pacific and other railways during the transportation boom of the late 1800s. The chorus of a favorite song told of the hard work of the tarriers, or drillers:

❝ *And drill, ye tarriers, drill!*
Drill, ye tarriers, drill!
For its work all day for sugar in
your tay,
Down behind of the railway and,
Drill, ye tarriers, drill!
And blast!
And fire! ❞

—Thomas Casey, 1888

Growth of the Rail System In the decades after the Civil War, railroads became a driving force behind America's economic growth. The first transcontinental railroad, completed in 1869, was soon followed by others. By the 1890s, five railway lines crossed the country, and hundreds of smaller lines branched off from them.

The expansion of the railroad system was accompanied by **consolidation** (kuhn•SAH•luh•DAY•shuhn)—the practice of combining separate companies—in the industry. Large railroad companies expanded by buying smaller companies or by driving them out of business. Consolidation made the large companies more efficient. After consolidation, a few powerful individuals known as railroad barons controlled the nation's rail traffic.

Railroad Barons New Yorker **Cornelius Vanderbilt,** one of the first railroad barons, gained control of the New York Central line and then other lines. His railroad empire stretched from New York City to the Great Lakes.

James J. Hill built the Great Northern line between Minnesota and Washington State. Until his death in 1916, Hill continued building and directing his ever-growing business empire. **Collis P. Huntington, Leland Stanford,** and two other partners founded the Central Pacific, which connected California and Utah.

The railroad barons were aggressive and competitive. They lived in an age when few laws had been passed to regulate business, and some of their methods were highly questionable. Nevertheless, the railroad barons played an important part in building the nation's transportation system.

✓ **Reading Check** **Analyze** What did consolidation mean for many small companies?

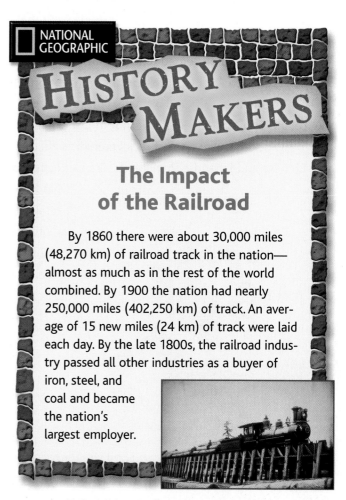

NATIONAL GEOGRAPHIC

HISTORY MAKERS

The Impact of the Railroad

By 1860 there were about 30,000 miles (48,270 km) of railroad track in the nation—almost as much as in the rest of the world combined. By 1900 the nation had nearly 250,000 miles (402,250 km) of track. An average of 15 new miles (24 km) of track were laid each day. By the late 1800s, the railroad industry passed all other industries as a buyer of iron, steel, and coal and became the nation's largest employer.

Biography

LELAND STANFORD
1824–1893

CHARLES CROCKER
1822–1888

▲ **Leland Stanford**

The Central Pacific Railroad began as the dream of engineer Theodore Judah. He sold stock in the new company to four Sacramento merchants: grocer Leland Stanford, shop owner Charles Crocker, and hardware store owners Mark Hopkins and Collis P. Huntington. The four men became known as "The Big Four" for their role in California's economic development.

In the early 1860s, these men managed the construction of the Central Pacific railroad. Eventually, they controlled a large railroad network that gave them great wealth and political power. Although some of their methods were questioned, the four business partners and their families donated land and money for the building of parks, churches, and libraries. Their donations either founded or helped fund art museums, including the Crocker Art Museum in Sacramento, the San Francisco Art Institute, and the Huntington Library and Art Gallery in San Marino.

Leland Stanford and his wife, Jane, donated land and money to create Stanford University. Leland Stanford became governor of California and later served as a United States senator.

Crocker fought against racial prejudice. He criticized unfair treatment of Native Americans and of Chinese and Japanese immigrants. Crocker believed that if "we deny to the individual, no matter what his creed, his color, or his nationality, the right to justice, which every man possesses . . . there will be no enduring prosperity and [the nation's] decline will surely follow."

Crocker gave money to support African American churches in California. He also supported African American schools and colleges in the southern United States.

▲ **Charles Crocker**

Then and Now

Is it important for people to donate to the arts and education? Why or why not?

Railroads Spur the Economy

Main Idea Railroad growth stimulated the economy, and innovations made railroad travel more efficient and profitable.

Reading Connection Can you think of a recent invention that has significantly changed the way in which you live? Read on to find out how railroads changed America in economic and social ways.

The fast-growing national rail system created new economic links in the country. The railroads carried raw materials such as iron ore, coal, and timber to factories. They also carried manufactured goods from factories to markets and transported produce from farming areas to the cities.

The national railroad system encouraged the expanding economy in many other ways. At first the demand for iron tracks and locomotives helped the iron mining and processing industries grow. Around 1880 railroad companies began using steel tracks. Steel is a metal made stronger by adding carbon and other elements to refined iron. The use of steel in railroad tracks stimulated America's steel industry.

The railroads also helped other industries thrive. The lumber industry, which supplied wood for railway ties, and the coal industry, which provided fuel for locomotives, saw extraordinary growth. In addition, railroad companies provided work for thousands of people who laid tracks and built stations and for those who manufactured railway cars and equipment.

Improving the Railroads Increased use made it necessary for railroads to expand and unify their systems. Railroads were being built across the country, but different lines used rails of different gauges, or widths. As a result, trains of one line could not use another line's tracks. Many early local lines carried goods for short distances and did not even connect with other lines. The gaps in service between the various lines made long-distance railroad travel slow and inefficient.

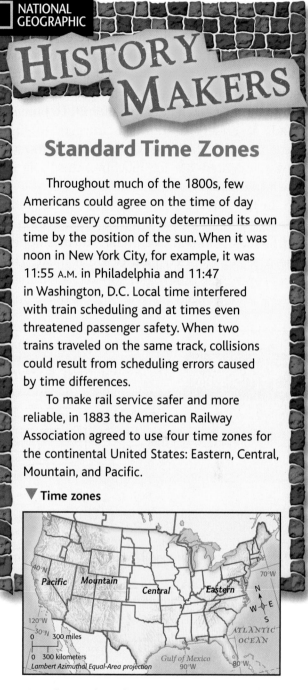

NATIONAL GEOGRAPHIC
HISTORY MAKERS

Standard Time Zones

Throughout much of the 1800s, few Americans could agree on the time of day because every community determined its own time by the position of the sun. When it was noon in New York City, for example, it was 11:55 A.M. in Philadelphia and 11:47 in Washington, D.C. Local time interfered with train scheduling and at times even threatened passenger safety. When two trains traveled on the same track, collisions could result from scheduling errors caused by time differences.

To make rail service safer and more reliable, in 1883 the American Railway Association agreed to use four time zones for the continental United States: Eastern, Central, Mountain, and Pacific.

▼ **Time zones**

As the railroad companies consolidated, railroad barons saw the advantages of being part of a national railroad network. During the late 1880s, almost all companies adopted a **standard gauge** (GAYJ) of 4 feet, 8.5 inches as the width of the railroad track. A standard gauge allowed faster shipment of goods at a reduced cost. It was no longer necessary to load and unload goods from one train to another. One train could make the entire journey.

Railroad Technology Railway transportation also improved with the introduction of new **technology.** Four developments were particularly important. Inventor **George Westinghouse** devised air brakes that improved the system for stopping trains, making train travel safer. Janney car couplers, named after inventor **Eli H. Janney,** made it easier for railroad workers to link cars. Shortly after the Civil War, Thaddeus Lowe invented the ice machine, the basis of the refrigerator.

In the early 1870s, **Gustavus Swift** (guh•STAHV•uhs) hired an engineer to develop a refrigerated railroad car. In 1877 Swift shipped the first refrigerated load of fresh meat. The widespread use of refrigeration kept food fresh longer and reduced the risk of food poisoning.

Finally, **George M. Pullman** developed the Pullman sleeping car—a luxury railway car with seats that **converted** into beds for overnight journeys. Pullman also introduced improved dining cars, raising train travel to a new level of comfort.

Competing for Customers As the railroad network continued to grow, the railroad companies competed fiercely with one another to keep old customers and to win new ones. Large railroads offered secret discounts called **rebates** to their biggest customers. Smaller railroads that could not match these rebates were sometimes forced out of business. Giving discounts to big customers raised freight rates for farmers and other customers who shipped small amounts of goods.

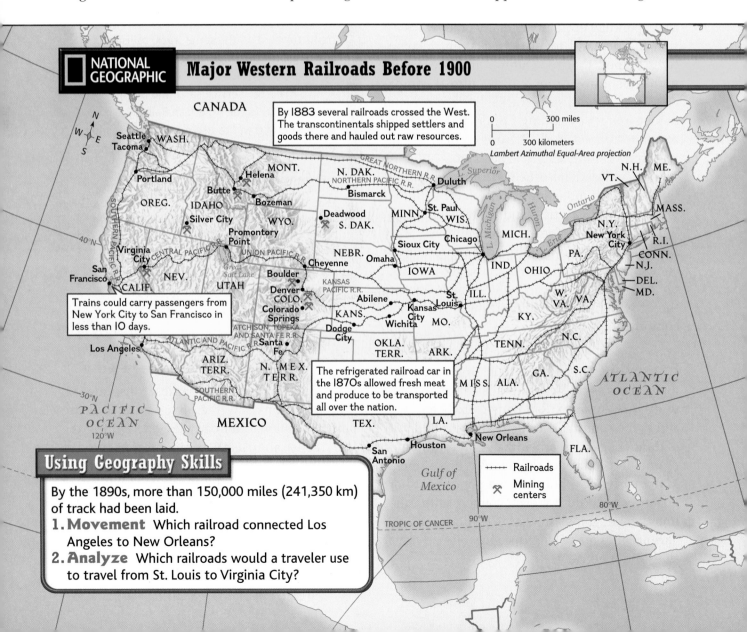

NATIONAL GEOGRAPHIC

Major Western Railroads Before 1900

By 1883 several railroads crossed the West. The transcontinentals shipped settlers and goods there and hauled out raw resources.

300 miles
300 kilometers
Lambert Azimuthal Equal-Area projection

Trains could carry passengers from New York City to San Francisco in less than 10 days.

The refrigerated railroad car in the 1870s allowed fresh meat and produce to be transported all over the nation.

Railroads
Mining centers

Using Geography Skills

By the 1890s, more than 150,000 miles (241,350 km) of track had been laid.

1. **Movement** Which railroad connected Los Angeles to New Orleans?
2. **Analyze** Which railroads would a traveler use to travel from St. Louis to Virginia City?

The railroad barons also made secret agreements among themselves, known as **pools.** They divided the railway business among their companies and set rates for a region. With no other competition in its region, a railroad could charge higher rates and earn greater profits. Although Congress and some states passed laws to regulate the railroads, these laws did little to curb the railroad barons.

How Did Railroads Change America? The growing railroad network paved the way for American industry to expand into the West. The center of the flour milling industry, for example, shifted westward in the 1800s, moving from the East Coast to Ohio, to Minneapolis, and finally to Kansas City.

Other industries followed the same pattern. As farmers settled the Great Plains, the manufacturing center for agricultural equipment moved from central New York State to Illinois and Wisconsin.

Railroads also touched the lives of thousands of Americans. Trains redistributed the population. They carried homesteaders into the Great Plains and the West. Trains also made it easy for people to move from rural areas to the cities.

As you have learned, railroads affected the way Americans thought about time as well. As train travel became more common, people began measuring distances by how many hours the trip would take rather than by the number of miles traveled. The spread of the railroad system led to a national system of time with four time zones.

The railroads opened the entire United States to settlement and economic growth and united the different regions of the country into a single **network.** At the same time, inventions that revolutionized transportation and communication brought Americans together in new ways.

✓**Reading Check** **Explain** Why was adopting standard-gauge tracks important for the railroad industry?

History Online

Study Central Need help understanding how railroad growth stimulated the economy? Visit tajww1.glencoe.com and click on Study Central.

Section 1 Review

Reading Summary

Review the Main Ideas

- After the Civil War, railroads continued to grow, allowing the faster transportation of goods and people.

- Railroads stimulated the American economy and resulted in many changes to the way Americans lived and traveled.

What Did You Learn?

1. How did railroad barons drive smaller companies out of business?

2. How did the railroads pave the way for the expansion of industry in the West?

Critical Thinking

3. **Organizing Information** Recreate the diagram below and identify the developments in technology that improved railroad transportation.

Railroad technology

4. **The Big Ideas** Explain how railroads changed the American economy.

5. **Expository Writing** Should the U.S. government have intervened to regulate unfair practices of the railroad barons? Explain your position in a short essay.

6. **READING** **Predict** Many innovations were made to improve railroad transportation. Write a short paragraph predicting the impact on the development of cities and regions.

Inventions

Guide to Reading

Looking Back, Looking Ahead

In the last section, you read about how the expansion of railroads stimulated various sectors of the economy. In this section, you will learn how inventions changed the lives of the American people.

Focusing on the (Main Ideas)

- New inventions improved communication and allowed Americans to contact one another over long distances. *(page 713)*
- The harnessing of electricity gave America a new source of power. *(page 714)*
- Improvements in transportation made travel easier and helped industries make their goods available to a wider audience. *(page 716)*

Meeting People

Samuel Morse

Alexander Graham Bell

Thomas Edison

Lewis Howard Latimer

Granville Woods

Henry Ford

Locating Places

Menlo Park, New Jersey

Detroit, Michigan

Content Vocabulary

assembly line

mass production

Academic Vocabulary

unify (YOO•nuh•FY)

transmit

device (dih•VYS)

Reading Strategy

Organizing Information As you read the section, re-create the diagram below to list each person's invention and to explain the significance of each invention to industrial growth.

	Invention	Significance
Samuel Morse		
Alexander Bell		
Thomas Edison		

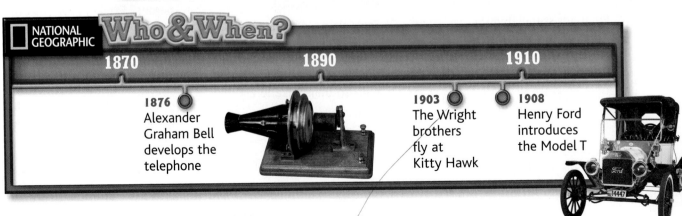

NATIONAL GEOGRAPHIC Who & When?

1870 — 1890 — 1910

1876 Alexander Graham Bell develops the telephone

1903 The Wright brothers fly at Kitty Hawk

1908 Henry Ford introduces the Model T

Communication Changes

Main Idea New inventions improved communication and allowed Americans to contact one another over long distances.

Reading Connection Do you use a cell phone or a computer to communicate with your friends? These are relatively new methods of communication. Read on to find out about the new methods of communication developed in the mid-1800s.

An American Story

In the early 1900s, American songwriters were caught up in the public fascination with new inventions. One of the most popular songs of 1905, "In My Merry Oldsmobile," celebrated the automobile:

> **Come away with me Lucile,**
> **In my merry Oldsmobile.**
> **Down the road of life we'll fly,**
> **Automobubbling you and I.**
> **To the church we'll swiftly steal,**
> **Then our wedding bells will peal;**
> **You can go as far as you like . . . ,**
> **In my merry Oldsmobile.**

—by Vincent Bryan and
Gus Edwards

How Did Life Change After 1870?

By 1910 Americans in cities drove cars through streets lit with electric lights. They went to department stores where they bought everything from kitchen sinks to shoes. Americans could also do their shopping by mail—or pick up the telephone and order groceries from the local store. The automobile, the electric light, and the telephone were all invented after 1870. Within a generation, they had become part of everyday life for millions of people. New inventions helped people communicate more quickly over long distances. Improvements in communication helped **unify** the regions of the country and promoted economic growth.

The Telegraph

Samuel Morse had introduced the telegraph in 1844. By 1860 the United States had thousands of miles of telegraph lines, which were controlled for the most part by the Western Union Telegraph Company. At telegraph offices, trained operators transmitted messages called telegrams in Morse code. Telegrams offered almost instant communication. Shopkeepers relied on telegrams to order goods, and reporters used them to **transmit** stories to their newspapers. Americans also began sending personal messages by telegram.

The telegraph soon linked the United States and Europe. In the 1860s news from Europe traveled to this country by ship and took several weeks. Cyrus Field wanted to speed up the process. After several unsuccessful attempts, in 1866 Field managed to lay a telegraph cable across the Atlantic Ocean. The new transatlantic telegraph carried messages in a matter of seconds, bringing the United States and Europe closer together.

The Telephone Rings

Alexander Graham Bell invented a **device** that revolutionized communications even more than Morse's telegraph. Born and educated in Scotland, Bell moved to the United States, where he studied ways of teaching people with hearing loss to speak. At the same time, he experimented with sending voices through electrical wires.

By 1876 Bell developed a device that transmitted speech—the telephone. While Bell was preparing to test the device, he accidentally spilled some battery acid on his clothes. In panic, Bell called out to his assistant in another room: "Mr. Watson, come here. I want you!" Watson heard Bell's voice coming through the telephone. The invention was a success.

Bell formed the Bell Telephone Company in 1877. By the 1890s, he had sold hundreds of thousands of phones. Most early telephone customers were businesses. Before long, though, telephones became common in homes.

Reading Check Explain How did the telegraph affect communication?

The Genius of Invention

Main Idea The harnessing of electricity gave America a new source of power.

Reading Connection As you get ready for school in the morning, think about all the ways that you use electricity. Do you need lights to shower and dress? Do you blow-dry your hair or make your breakfast in the microwave? Read on to find out how electricity improved the lives of people living in the late 1800s.

The late 1800s saw a burst of inventiveness in the United States. Between 1860 and 1890, the United States government granted more than 400,000 patents for new inventions.

Many of the inventions helped businesses operate more efficiently. Among these were Christopher Sholes's typewriter (1868) and William Burroughs's adding machine (1888).

Other inventions affected everyday life. In 1888 George Eastman invented a small box camera—the Kodak—that made it easier and less costly to take photographs. John Thurman developed a vacuum cleaner in 1899 that simplified housework.

The Wizard of Menlo Park Thomas Edison was called "dull" by his teachers. Because of poor hearing, he had trouble in school and often did not attend. His mother finally removed him from school and taught him at home.

The First Flight at Kitty Hawk

A small crowd of people assembled on the sand dunes at Kitty Hawk, North Carolina, to test the Wrights' Flyer. Covering a few hundred feet in 12 seconds, the flight came to a halt when the Flyer's wing caught on one of the dunes. It was enough to encourage the Wrights to try further flights though. They would soon have a practical aircraft, and the world would have a new form of transportation.

The Beginning of Controlled, Powered Flight
Inventors experimented with engine-powered aircraft in the 1800s, but the age of air travel did not begin until 1903 at Kitty Hawk, North Carolina. Orville and Wilbur Wright, brothers and bicycle mechanics, built a wood-and-canvas plane with a 12-horsepower engine. On the morning of December 17, Orville Wright took off in their plane and flew a distance of 120 feet.

Firsts in Aviation History

In less than 100 years, aviators advanced from making the first flight in a glider to breaking the speed of sound.

1853 → Human-carrying flight in a glider built by Sir George Cayley takes place

1874 → Steam-powered monoplane is briefly airborne

1903 → Wright brothers take flight at Kitty Hawk

1914 → Scheduled airline service opens between St. Petersburg and Tampa, Florida

1919 → First nonstop flight across the Atlantic Ocean

Edison loved anything related to science. His mother allowed him to set up a chemistry lab in the family's basement. When he was 12, he got a job working for the railroad, where he set up a new lab in an empty freight car. One day, Edison saved the life of a child who had fallen onto the tracks of an oncoming train. The child's father took an interest in Edison and taught him to use the telegraph. Edison's first invention was a gadget that sent automatic telegraph signals—which he invented so he could sleep on the job.

While still in his 20s, Thomas Edison decided to go into the "invention business." In 1876 Edison set up a workshop in **Menlo Park, New Jersey.** Out of this famous laboratory

History Online

Student Web Activity Visit tajww1.glencoe.com and click on *Chapter 16—Student Web Activities* for an activity on inventions.

came the phonograph, the motion picture projector, the telephone transmitter, and the storage battery. But Edison's most important invention was the electric lightbulb.

Edison developed the first workable lightbulb in 1879. He then designed power plants that could produce electric power and distribute it to lightbulbs. For Christmas in 1880, Edison used 40 bulbs to light up Menlo Park. Visitors came to see the "light of the future." He built the first central electric power plant in 1882 in New York City—illuminating 85 buildings!

Inventor George Westinghouse took Edison's work with electricity even further. In 1885 Westinghouse developed and built transformers that could send electric power more cheaply over longer distances. Soon electricity powered factories, trolleys, streetlights, and lamps all over America. Westinghouse also developed a system for transporting natural gas and invented many safety devices.

African American Inventors A number of African Americans contributed to the era of invention. **Lewis Howard Latimer,** an engineer, developed an improved filament for the lightbulb and joined Thomas Edison's company. **Granville Woods,** an electrical and mechanical engineer from Ohio, patented dozens of inventions. Among them were an electric incubator and railroad improvements such as an electromagnetic brake and an automatic circuit breaker. Elijah McCoy invented a mechanism for oiling machinery.

Jan E. Matzeliger, another African American inventor, developed a shoe-making machine that performed many steps that were previously done by hand. His device, which revolutionized the shoe industry, was adopted in shoe factories in the United States and overseas.

Reading Check **Evaluate** Which of Edison's inventions do you think is the most valuable to our world? Explain your reasoning.

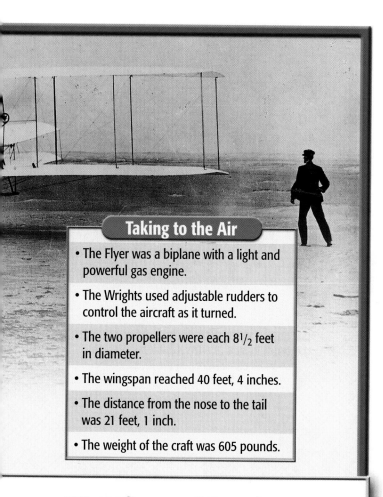

Taking to the Air

- The Flyer was a biplane with a light and powerful gas engine.
- The Wrights used adjustable rudders to control the aircraft as it turned.
- The two propellers were each 8½ feet in diameter.
- The wingspan reached 40 feet, 4 inches.
- The distance from the nose to the tail was 21 feet, 1 inch.
- The weight of the craft was 605 pounds.

1927 → Lindbergh completes first nonstop solo transatlantic flight

1947 → Chuck Yeager is first to fly faster than the speed of sound

A Changing Society

Main Idea Improvements in transportation made travel easier and helped industries make their goods available to a wider audience.

Reading Connection When your family takes a trip, how do you travel? Read on to find out how the automobile changed transportation.

In the 1900s, improvements ushered in a new era of transportation. After a period of experimentation, the automobile became a practical method of getting from place to place.

Henry Ford's Automobiles Henry Ford wanted to build an inexpensive car that would last a lifetime. While working as an engineer in **Detroit, Michigan,** in the 1890s, Ford had experimented with an automobile engine powered by gasoline. In 1903 he began designing cars at his automaking company.

In 1906 Ford told Charles Sorenson, later Ford's general superintendent, "We're going to get a car now that we can make in great volume and get the prices way down." For the next year, Ford and Sorenson worked on the Model T, building the car and testing it on rough roads. In 1908 Ford introduced the Model T to the public.

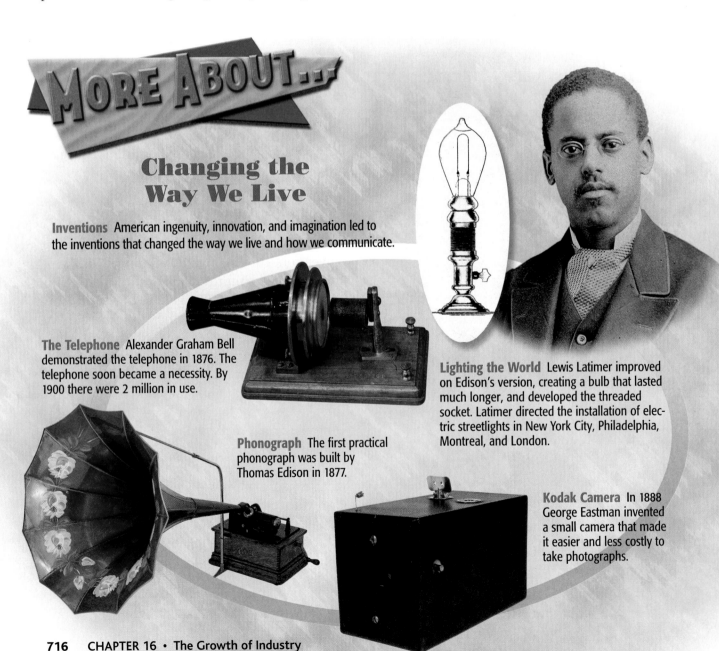

MORE ABOUT...

Changing the Way We Live

Inventions American ingenuity, innovation, and imagination led to the inventions that changed the way we live and how we communicate.

The Telephone Alexander Graham Bell demonstrated the telephone in 1876. The telephone soon became a necessity. By 1900 there were 2 million in use.

Phonograph The first practical phonograph was built by Thomas Edison in 1877.

Lighting the World Lewis Latimer improved on Edison's version, creating a bulb that lasted much longer, and developed the threaded socket. Latimer directed the installation of electric streetlights in New York City, Philadelphia, Montreal, and London.

Kodak Camera In 1888 George Eastman invented a small camera that made it easier and less costly to take photographs.

Sorenson described the sturdy black vehicle as ". . . a car which anyone could afford to buy, which anyone could drive anywhere, and which almost anyone could keep in repair."

The Model T became immensely popular. During the next 18 years, Ford's company sold 15 million Model T's. Henry Ford also pioneered a less expensive way to manufacture cars—the moving **assembly line.** On the line, each worker performed an assigned task again and again at a certain stage in the production of the automobile. The assembly line revolutionized industry, enabling manufacturers to produce large quantities of goods more quickly. This **mass production** of goods decreased manufacturing costs, so products could be sold more cheaply.

In 1908 the Model T's first year, it sold for $850. In 1914 mass production reduced the price to $490. By 1924 Model Ts were selling for $295. Ford's business philosophy was simple. "Every time I reduce the charge for our car by one dollar," he said, "I get a thousand new buyers. In this way, Ford made the automobile affordable for millions of Americans.

Selling Goods With factories churning out more and more products, merchants looked for better ways to sell their goods. One way was through the mail. In 1863 mail delivery to homes began—up to then, service was only to post offices. By the 1890s, the U.S. Post Office had expanded its delivery service in rural areas.

Some firms developed mail order businesses, receiving and shipping orders by mail. Companies such as Montgomery Ward and Sears Roebuck published catalogs that offered a wide range of goods from shoes to farm equipment. Catalogs introduced rural families to a wide assortment of goods not found in country stores.

Chain stores—stores with identical branches in many places—grew rapidly. F.W. Woolworth's chain of "five-and-ten-cent stores" specialized in everyday household and personal items at bargain prices. By 1911, more than a thousand Woolworth stores were in operation.

Reading Check **Describe** What qualities made the Model T popular?

History Online

Study Central Need help understanding how inventions changed peoples lives? Visit tajwwI.glencoe.com and click on Study Central.

Section 2 Review

Reading Summary

Review the Main Ideas

- The telegraph and the telephone changed the way Americans communicated.

- Electricity and other inventions lit up the world in a new way.

- The introduction of the automobile made it easier for people to travel and helped businesses bring their goods to new areas.

What Did You Learn?

1. Name and describe two inventions that changed the way Americans communicated.

2. How was transportation improved during the 1800s?

Critical Thinking

3. **Organizing Information** Re-create the diagram below, and classify each invention described in this section in one of the categories.

Mostly rural use	Mostly urban use	Both urban and rural	Mostly used by business and industry

4. **The Big Ideas** Which of the inventions discussed do you think had the greatest impact on the economy of the United States? Why?

5. **ANALYSIS** **Compare and Contrast** Study the photographs of the inventions and products that appear in this section. Which have undergone the greatest change? Why do you think this is so?

Section 3

The Age of Big Business

Guide to Reading

Looking Back, Looking Ahead

You have learned how inventions helped the American economy grow. In Section 3, you will learn how entrepreneurs gained control of various industries and turned them into successful businesses.

Focusing on the Main Ideas

- The American economy grew because the country contained abundant land, labor, and capital. *(page 719)*
- The development of the oil industry created one of the first monopolies. *(page 720)*
- Monopolies in the steel business and other industries created the need for government regulation. *(page 721)*

Locating Places

Pittsburgh, Pennsylvania (PIHTS•BUHRG)
Cleveland, Ohio
Chicago, Illinois
Birmingham, Alabama

Meeting People

John D. Rockefeller
Andrew Carnegie (KAHR•nuh•gee)
J. Pierpont Morgan

Content Vocabulary

corporation (KAWR•puh•RAY•shuhn)
stock
shareholder
dividend (DIH•vuh•DEHND)
horizontal integration (HAWR•uh• ZAHN•tuhl IHN•tuh•GRAY•shuhn)
trust
monopoly
vertical integration (VUHR•tih•kuhl)
philanthropy (fuh•LAN•thruh•pee)
merger (MUHR•juhr)

Academic Vocabulary

resource
invest

Reading Strategy

Analyzing Information Re-create the diagram below and explain the significance of each term in business in the late 1800s.

	Significance
Shareholders	
Stock exchanges	
Mergers	

NATIONAL GEOGRAPHIC **Who & When?**

1870   1885   1900

1870 Rockefeller organizes the Standard Oil Company

John D. Rockefeller

1882 Rockefeller organizes trust

1890 Andrew Carnegie dominates the steel industry

Andrew Carnegie

Foundations for Growth

Main Idea The American economy grew because the country contained abundant land, labor, and capital.

Reading Connection Imagine you want to start your own business. What is needed to get that business up and running? Read on to find out how industries in America gained the resources they needed to succeed.

The period from the end of the Civil War to 1900 was an era of unmatched economic growth in the United States. New methods in technology and business allowed the country to tap its rich supply of natural **resources,** increase its production, and raise the money needed for growth. The growing transportation system made it easier for merchants to reach distant markets.

What Are the Factors of Production?

The change from an agricultural economy to an industrial one was possible because the United States had the resources needed for a growing economy. Among these resources were what economists call the factors of production: land, labor, and capital.

The first factor of production, land, means not just the land itself but all natural resources. The United States held a variety of natural resources that had industrial uses.

The second production factor is labor. Large numbers of workers were needed to turn raw materials into goods. This need was met by the rapid growth of population. Between 1860 and 1900, the population of the country more than doubled.

The third production factor, capital, is the equipment—buildings, machinery, and tools—used in production. Land and labor are needed to produce capital goods. These goods, in turn, are essential for the production of consumer goods. The term *capital* is also used to mean money for investment. Huge amounts of money were needed to finance industrial growth. One source of money was the selling of stock by corporations. Another was corporate savings, or businesses investing a portion of their earnings in better equipment.

Raising Capital

With the economy growing after the Civil War, many businesses looked for ways to expand. To do so, they had to raise capital. They needed capital to buy raw materials and equipment, to pay workers, and to cover shipping and advertising costs.

One way a company could raise capital was by becoming a **corporation** (KAWR•puh•RAY•shuhn). A corporation is a company that sells **stock,** or shares, of its business to the public. The people who **invest** in the corporation by buying stock are its **shareholders,** or partial owners.

In good times, shareholders earn **dividends** (DIH•vuh•DEHNDZ)—cash payments from the corporation's profits—on the stock they own. If the company prospers, its stock rises in value, and the shareholders can sell it for a profit. If the company fails, however, the shareholders lose their investment. In the late 1800s, hundreds of thousands of people shared in corporate profits by buying and selling stocks in special markets known as stock exchanges.

Growth of Corporations

The nation's early corporations were created only for specific public benefits, such as the building of a highway. Soon many manufacturing and business firms were incorporating. Big corporations had several advantages over small manufacturing companies. Big corporations could produce goods more cheaply and efficiently. They could continue to operate in poor economic times by cutting prices to increase sales. Many were also able to negotiate refunds from the railroads, which lowered their operating costs further.

Banks played a major role in this period of economic growth. Businesses borrowed money from banks to start or expand their operations. The banks, in turn, made profits on the loans.

Reading Check **Explain** What happens to dividends when a company does well?

The Oil Business

Main Idea The development of the oil industry created one of the first monopolies.

Reading Connection Is there someone in your town who has started a successful business? What type of business is it? Read on to find out how John D. Rockefeller created an empire in the oil industry.

In 1870 **John D. Rockefeller** organized the Standard Oil Company of Ohio and set out to dominate the oil industry. One method Rockefeller used to build his empire was **horizontal integration** (HAWR•uh•ZAHN•tuhl IHN•tuh•GRAY•shuhn)—combining two or more firms producing the same kind of product. The corporation produced and used its own tank cars, pipelines, and even its own wooden barrels—made from forests owned by Standard Oil. Standard Oil grew in wealth and power, becoming the most famous corporate empire of the day.

To strengthen Standard Oil's position in the oil industry, Rockefeller lowered his prices to drive his competitors out of business. In addition, he pressured customers not to deal with rival oil companies, and he persuaded the railroads to grant him rebates in exchange for his business.

Rockefeller increased his control of the oil industry in 1882 by forming a **trust,** a group of companies managed by the same board of directors. First he acquired stock in many different oil companies. Then the shareholders of these companies traded their stock for Standard Oil stock, which paid higher dividends. This gave Standard Oil's board of directors ownership of the other companies' stock and the right to manage those companies. Rockefeller had created a **monopoly**—almost total control by a single producer—of the oil industry.

Reading Check **Explain** What method did Rockefeller use to build his oil empire?

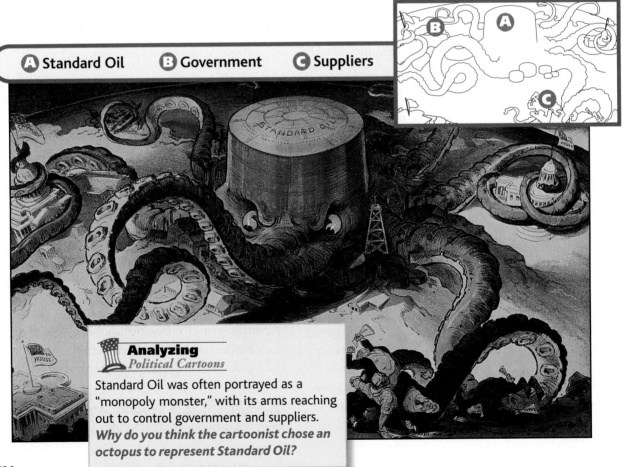

A Standard Oil   **B** Government   **C** Suppliers

Analyzing Political Cartoons

Standard Oil was often portrayed as a "monopoly monster," with its arms reaching out to control government and suppliers. *Why do you think the cartoonist chose an octopus to represent Standard Oil?*

The Steel Business

Main Idea **Monopolies in the steel business and other industries created the need for government regulation.**

Reading Connection What kinds of cars do people drive in your neighborhood? Chances are they do not all drive the same type of car. That is because car companies compete with each other to get people to buy their products. Read on to find out how monopolies came to dominate certain industries.

Steel also became a huge business in the late 1800s. Steel is a strong and long-lasting form of iron treated with carbon—the ideal material for railroad tracks, bridges, and many other products. Before the 1860s, however, steel was not widely used because it was expensive to manufacture. The development of new manufacturing techniques helped overcome this problem.

Steel Industry Growth

Two new methods of making steel—the Bessemer process, which was developed by Henry Bessemer of England, and the open-hearth process—changed the industry. With these new methods, mills could produce steel at affordable prices and in large quantities. In the 1870s, large steel mills were built close to sources of iron ore in western Pennsylvania and eastern Ohio. **Pittsburgh, Pennsylvania** (PIHTS•BUHRG), became the steel capital of the United States. Cities located near the mines and close to waterways like **Cleveland, Ohio; Chicago, Illinois; Birmingham, Alabama;** and Detroit, Michigan, also became centers of steel production.

Andrew Carnegie The leading figure in the early years of the American steel industry was **Andrew Carnegie** (KAHR•nuh•gee), son of a Scottish immigrant. Starting as a telegraph operator, Carnegie worked his way up to become manager of the Pennsylvania Railroad. While in that job, he introduced the first successful sleeping car. In 1865 he left the railroad to invest in the growing iron industry.

Carnegie soon realized that steel would have an enormous market. After learning about the Bessemer process, he built a steel plant near Pittsburgh that used the new process. Carnegie named the plant the J. Edgar Thompson Steel Works, after the president of the Pennsylvania Railroad—his biggest customer.

Vertical Integration By 1890 Andrew Carnegie dominated the steel industry. His company became powerful through **vertical integration** (VUHR•tih•kuhl), combining firms involved in different steps of manufacturing. Carnegie bought iron and coal mines, warehouses, ore ships, and railroads to gain control of all parts of the business of making and selling steel.

Analyzing Political Cartoons

Andrew Carnegie is shown (right) as a mason. The blocks are the libraries to which he has donated money. *What point do you think the cartoonist is making?*

Vol XLV No 2310

10 Cents a Copy
$4.00 a Year

HARPER'S WEEKLY

A JOURNAL OF CIVILIZATION

NEW YORK

MARCH 30, 1901

Harper's Weekly, March 30, 1901 BUILDING A VERY SOLID TEMPLE OF FAME

▲ John D. Rockefeller

When Carnegie combined all his holdings into the Carnegie Steel Company in 1900, he was producing one-third of the nation's steel. In 1901 Carnegie sold his steel company to banker **J. Pierpont Morgan.** Morgan combined the Carnegie company with other businesses to form the United States Steel Corporation, the world's first billion-dollar corporation.

Philanthropists Andrew Carnegie, John D. Rockefeller, and other industrial millionaires of the time grew interested in **philanthropy** (fuh•LAN•thruh•pee)—the use of money to benefit the community. The philanthropists founded schools, universities, and other civic institutions across the United States.

Carnegie donated $350 million to various organizations. He built Carnegie Hall in New York City, one of the world's most famous concert halls; the Carnegie Foundation for the

Advancement of Teaching; and more than 2,000 libraries worldwide. Carnegie often wrote about social and political issues. He felt that a person who has great wealth also has a duty to use the surplus to help humankind. He stated that a "man who dies rich dies disgraced." Rockefeller used his fortune to establish the University of Chicago in 1890 and New York's Rockefeller Institute for Medical Research.

Corporations Grow Larger In 1889 New Jersey encouraged the trend toward business monopolies by allowing holding companies to obtain charters, a practice that some states prohibited. A holding company would buy controlling interests in the stock of other companies instead of purchasing the companies outright. Rockefeller formed Standard Oil of New Jersey so that the corporation could expand its holdings. Other states also passed laws that made corporate **mergers** (MUHR•juhrz)—the combining of companies—easier.

Mergers concentrated economic power in a few giant corporations and a few powerful individuals, such as Rockefeller and banker J. Pierpont Morgan. By 1900 one-third of all American manufacturing was controlled by just 1 percent of the country's corporations. These giant corporations were the driving force behind the great economic growth of the period, but they also posed problems. On the one hand, many Americans admired the efficiencies that large businesses provided. On the other hand, some argued that a lack of competition hurt consumers. Without competition, corporations had no reason to keep their prices low or to improve their goods and services.

Big Business and Social Science Some business practices in the late 1800s were based on a scientific idea known as social Darwinism. Charles Darwin, a British scientist, had published a theory in 1859 that all plants and animals evolved over long periods of time by a process known as natural selection. According to the theory, organisms competed for survival, and those animals best adapted to the environment survived, while the others did not.

Later thinkers applied Darwin's biological theory to human society and business. Some industrial leaders, such as John D. Rockefeller, argued that "survival of the fittest" helped explain the growth of huge companies. As one supporter of social Darwinism put it,

> **❝We have unmistakable proof that throughout all past time, there has been a ceaseless devouring of the weak by the strong.❞**

—from *First Principles*
by Herbert Spencer

Carnegie argued that big companies like his own were beneficial to society. The revolution in productivity enabled "the poor to enjoy what the rich could not before afford." Companies that grew and thrived raised their workers' standard of living.

Government Regulation Due to increasing pressure from the public, government stepped in to regulate business. During the 1880s, several states passed laws restricting business mergers. Corporations, however, avoided these laws by doing business in states that had no such laws.

Public pressure for a federal law to prohibit trusts and monopolies led Congress to pass the Sherman Antitrust Act in 1890. The law sought "to protect trade and commerce against unlawful restraint and monopoly." The act did not clearly define either "trusts" or "monopolies," however.

In its early years, the Sherman Antitrust Act did little to curb the power of big business. By contrast, in the 1890s the government did use the act to stop a strike by railroad workers that threatened to slow the nation's mail delivery.

✓ **Reading Check** **Compare** How does vertical integration differ from horizontal integration?

Study Central Need help understanding how industries grew and became monopolies? Visit tajwwI.glencoe.com and click on Study Central.

Section 3 Review

Reading Summary

Review the Main Ideas

- The American economy shifted from agriculture to industry as the nation realized it had the necessary materials for industrial growth.

- As oil was discovered, boomtowns sprang up around centers of oil and Rockefeller created his oil monopoly.

- Carnegie dominated the steel industry and as competing companies were driven out of business, the government attempted to regulate industrial growth.

What Did You Learn?

1. Which cities became centers of steel production in the late 1800s?

2. How did state and federal governments respond to the growth of trusts and monopolies?

Critical Thinking

3. **Determining Cause and Effect** Re-create the diagram below and list the benefits of competition to consumers.

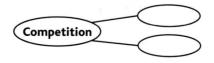

4. **The Big Ideas** Compare methods used by Rockefeller and Carnegie to build their industrial empires. Describe any differences between the two.

5. **Analyze** Study the cartoon on page 720. Whom do the figures represent? What is the cartoon saying about the Standard Oil Company?

6. **Expository Writing** Research to find a philanthropist who has supported the community in which you live. Write a short essay describing his or her contributions.

Section 4

Industrial Workers

Guide to Reading

Looking Back, Looking Ahead
In the last section, you read about how industries were able to grow and expand. In this section, you will read about the workers in these industries and the conditions in which they worked.

Focusing on the **Main Ideas**
- Industrialization created many jobs, but it also created hazardous working conditions. *(page 725)*
- Workers created labor unions to combat unsafe working conditions in many of the nation's industries. *(page 726)*
- Strikes often ended in violence, causing many people to turn against labor unions. *(page 727)*

Meeting People
Terence V. Powderly
Samuel Gompers
Mary Harris Jones
Eugene V. Debs (yoo • JEEN DEHBZ)
Grover Cleveland

Locating Places
Philadelphia, Pennsylvania
  (FIH • luh • DEHL • fee • uh)
New York City, New York
Homestead, Pennsylvania

Content Vocabulary
sweatshop
trade union
collective bargaining
strikebreaker
injunction (ihn • JUHNK • shuhn)

Academic Vocabulary
job
labor

Reading Strategy
Organizing Information As you read the section, re-create the diagram below and list actions labor unions took to improve working conditions.

Labor Unions

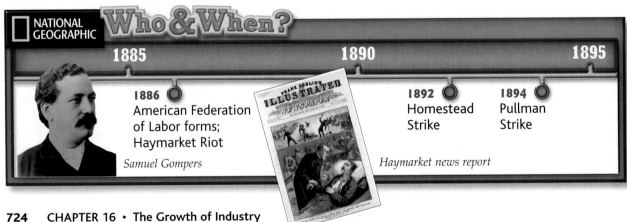

NATIONAL GEOGRAPHIC **Who & When?**

1885   1890   1895

1886
American Federation of Labor forms; Haymarket Riot

Samuel Gompers

1892
Homestead Strike

1894
Pullman Strike

Haymarket news report

Working Conditions

Main Idea Industrialization created many jobs, but it also created hazardous working conditions.

Reading Connection What do your parents or guardians do for a living? What safeguards are in place to protect them from getting hurt at their jobs or to help them if they do? Read on to find out about the working conditions in the late 1800s.

The industrial growth of the late 1800s created new **jobs.** Growth also raised the standard of living for many American workers. That is, necessities and luxuries were more available and affordable. Yet workers paid a price for economic progress. Factories had once been small workplaces where employers and employees knew one another and often worked side by side. As mass production spread, however, factories became larger and less personal.

Industrial laborers worked for 10 or 12 hours a day, six days a week. They could be fired at any time for any reason. Many lost their jobs during business downturns or were replaced by immigrants who were willing to work for lower pay.

Factories and mines were noisy, unhealthy, and unsafe. Accidents were common. Steel workers suffered burns from spills of hot steel. Coal miners died in cave-ins and from the effects of gas and coal dust. Textile workers' lungs were damaged by airborne lint. Garment workers toiled in crowded urban factories called **sweatshops,** where their eyesight was ruined by sewing for hours in poor light. Filled with flammable materials, the sweatshops were also terrible firetraps.

Women Workers

Although the majority of working women in the late 1800s had jobs as domestic servants, women also joined the industrial workforce, especially the textile industry. By 1900 more than one million women worked in industry. However, because no laws regulated workers' salaries, women generally received about half of what men earned for the same work. In addition, it was assumed that a woman had a man to support her—either her father or her husband. A man, therefore, needed higher wages because he was supporting a family.

Child Labor

Industries also hired children. In 1900 hundreds of thousands of children under 16 years of age worked in factories. Concerned groups brought child **labor** to the attention of their state legislatures. As a result, many states passed child labor laws. These laws stated that children working in factories had to be at least 12 years old and should not work more than 10 hours a day. Employers widely ignored child labor laws, however. Also, the laws did not apply to agriculture, which employed about one million children.

Reading Check **Examine** How did mass production change the size of factories?

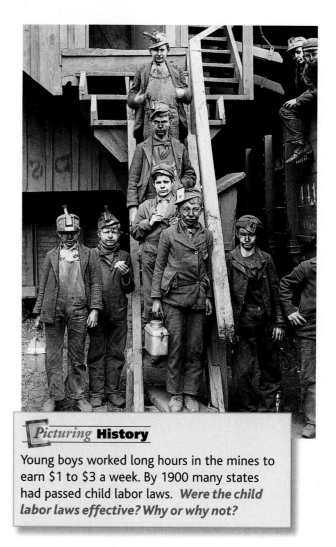

Picturing **History**

Young boys worked long hours in the mines to earn $1 to $3 a week. By 1900 many states had passed child labor laws. *Were the child labor laws effective? Why or why not?*

Labor Unions Form

Main Idea Workers created labor unions to combat unsafe working conditions in many of the nation's industries.

Reading Connection What do you think should be done about unsafe conditions at businesses and factories? Read on to learn about how employees attempted to change the conditions in which they worked.

Dissatisfied workers organized into groups—labor unions—to demand better pay and working conditions from their employers. Earlier in the 1800s, skilled workers had formed unions to represent workers in certain crafts or trades, such as carpentry. These **trade unions** had little influence because each represented only one trade. By the mid-1800s, labor leaders looked to expand their unions.

Noble and Holy Order Knights of Labor

In 1869 garment cutters in **Philadelphia, Pennsylvania** (FIH•luh•DEHL•fee•uh), founded the Noble and Holy Order of the Knights of Labor. Employers fired workers who joined labor organizations, so the Knights met secretly and used special handshakes to identify each other. Under the leadership of **Terence V. Powderly,** the Knights of Labor became a national labor organization in the 1880s.

Thos. Anshutz

Unlike most unions, the Knights recruited people who had been kept out of trade unions, including women, African Americans, immigrants, and unskilled laborers. The Knights of Labor grew rapidly to more than 700,000 members by 1886. However, setbacks in many strikes weakened the unions and resulted in the loss of members and power in the 1890s.

American Federation of Labor

In 1881 a group of national trade unions formed a federation that five years later became known as the American Federation of Labor (AFL). The AFL represented skilled workers in various crafts.

The AFL was led by **Samuel Gompers,** the tough, practical-minded president of the Cigar Makers' Union. The organization pressed for higher wages, shorter working hours, better working conditions, and the right to bargain collectively with employers. In the process of **collective bargaining,** unions represent workers in bargaining with management.

Although violent strikes turned some people against workers and unions in the late 1880s, the AFL survived and grew. By 1904 the AFL was able to claim more than 1.6 million members.

Women and the Unions

Many unions would not admit women workers, so some women formed their own unions. **Mary Harris Jones,** better known as Mother Jones, spent 50 years fighting for workers' rights.

In 1911 a fire broke out at the Triangle Shirtwaist Company factory, a crowded sweatshop in **New York City, New York.** The workers, mostly young immigrant women, could not escape from the building because the company had locked the doors to prevent employees from leaving early. Nearly 150 workers died in the fire. The disaster led the International Ladies' Garment Workers Union (ILGWU) to push for a safer working environment.

✓ **Reading Check** **Compare** Who was eligible for membership in the AFL? In the Knights of Labor?

The Unions Act

Main Idea Strikes often ended in violence, causing some people to turn against labor unions.

Reading Connection Do you know anyone who was laid off from a job or whose wages were lowered due to economic downturns? How did these people cope with their loss of wages? Read on to find out about the conflict between employers and labor unions as an economic depression set in during the late 1800s.

An American Story

On a spring day in 1886, about 12,000 workers in Chicago's Haymarket Square manufacturing district were on strike. At 2 o'clock, a man climbed up on an empty freight car near the crowd. He moved to the edge of the roof and waved frantically at the crowd below. "Stand firm," he yelled. "Let every man stand shoulder to shoulder and we will win this fight. We must have our rights. Strike while the iron is hot." The events at Haymarket Square soon turned violent, as did many other strikes.

Strikes and Strikebreakers Economic depressions in the 1870s and the 1890s led companies to fire workers and lower wages. Unions responded with large strikes that sometimes sparked violence.

Economic depression hit the nation following a financial panic in 1873. To cut costs, companies forced their workers to take pay cuts. In July 1877, as the depression continued, several railroads announced another round of wage cuts. This triggered the first nationwide labor protest. Angry strikers smashed equipment; tore up tracks; and blocked rail service in New York, Baltimore, Pittsburgh, Chicago, and other cities. The companies hired **strikebreakers** to replace the striking workers. State militia or federal troops restored order in different places. By the time the strike ended, however, more than 100 people lay dead, and millions of dollars of property had been destroyed.

Biography

MARY HARRIS JONES
1830–1930

▲ **Mary Harris Jones**

Mary Harris "Mother" Jones was born in Ireland and moved to the United States with her family. In 1867 her husband George and their four children died from yellow fever. Widowed and childless, Jones moved to Chicago and opened a dressmaker's shop.

By the 1880s, Jones was fully involved in the union movement and became one of its most important leaders. For the next 50 years, she traveled around the country speaking to workers and promoting unions. She said, "My address is like my shoes: it travels with me. I abide where there is a fight against wrong."

She told her listeners to "look on yourselves, and upon each other. Let us consider this together for I am one of you, and I know what it is to suffer."

CÉSAR ESTRADA CHÁVEZ
1927–1993

▲ **César Estrada Chávez**

César Chávez knew the suffering of farmworkers. He had labored in the fields since age 10, when his family lost their Arizona farm during the Great Depression. Like thousands of other farmers, the Chávez family became migrant workers. Chávez attended some 65 schools before dropping out at the end of eighth grade.

After serving in World War II, Chávez took a paid job to win greater rights for Mexican Americans. In 1962 with the support of his wife Helen Fabela Chávez, he returned to the fields and his dream of organizing farmworkers into a union.

In 1965 Chávez launched La Huelga—"the strike." He asked Americans to boycott grapes until growers in the San Joaquin Valley signed union contracts. Some 17 million Americans responded. "For the first time," Chávez said, "the farmworker got some power." The power came from the United Farm Workers, the first successful farmworkers union in the nation's history.

Then and Now

Mary Harris Jones and César Chávez both worked to better the lives of workers. Who might they choose to represent today? Why?

Major Strikes Antilabor feeling grew stronger after events in Chicago's Haymarket Square in May 1886. Striking workers from the McCormick Harvester Company gathered to protest the killings of four strikers the previous day. When police ordered the crowd to break up, an unidentified person threw a bomb that killed a police officer. Several more were killed in a riot that followed. Following the Haymarket Riot, some Americans associated the labor movement with violence and disorder.

In 1892 workers went on strike at Andrew Carnegie's steel plant in **Homestead, Pennsylvania.** Homestead managers hired nonunion workers and brought in 300 armed guards to protect them. A fierce battle left at least 10 people dead. The plant reopened with nonunion workers, protected by the troops. After the failure of the Homestead Strike, the steelworkers' union dwindled.

After employees of George Pullman's railway-car plant near Chicago went on strike in May 1894, Pullman closed the plant. One month later, workers in the American Railway Union supported the strikers by refusing to handle Pullman cars, paralyzing rail traffic.

Pullman and the railroad owners fought back. They persuaded U.S. Attorney General Richard Olney to obtain an **injunction** (ihn•JUHNK•shuhn), or court order, to stop the union from "obstructing the railways and holding up the mails." The workers and their leader, **Eugene V. Debs** (yoo•JEEN DEHBZ), refused to end the strike. Debs was arrested for interfering with the mail.

President **Grover Cleveland** sent federal troops to Chicago, and soon the strike was over. The failure of the Pullman Strike dealt another blow to the union movement. Despite these setbacks, workers continued to organize to work for better wages and working conditions.

Reading Check **Describe** Why did many railroad workers go on strike in 1877?

Study Central Need help understanding the labor movement? Visit tajwwl.glencoe.com and click on Study Central.

Section 4 Review

Reading Summary

Review the Main Ideas

- Industrial workers labored long hours for low pay, often in unsafe conditions.

- Labor unions helped workers gain economic and political power.

- Strikes ending in violence and deaths caused labor unions to lose much of their power.

What Did You Learn?

1. What role did Samuel Gompers play in union growth?

2. What were the goals of the American Federation of Labor when it was founded?

Critical Thinking

3. **Organizing Information** Recreate the diagram below and describe the roles each person played in labor-management issues.

Individual	Role
Terence Powderly	
Mary Harris Jones	
George Pullman	

4. **Analyze** Explain how the separate words in the term *sweatshop* can help you determine its meaning.

5. **The Big Ideas** Why do you think many Americans did or did not support the labor unions?

6. **Analyze** Find two sources that discuss unions—one from the early 20th century and one modern source. Identify how the authors view unions. How has new historical information impacted the views of the modern author?

Connecting to the Constitution

Government and Labor

Why It Matters Labor unions are an important part of the American society. They present the concerns of many workers to businesses and to the U.S. government at all levels. Through unions, workers try to improve their wages and working conditions. They also can gain a voice in almost all matters relating to their jobs. Unions have helped unite workers and provide a source of pride and a sense of dignity to workers.

In the past, unions were formed mainly by workers in heavy industries that produce goods such as machines, mining equipment, and steel. Today, however, people in jobs as different as airline workers, teachers, and professional athletes also belong to unions. Although only a small number of American workers are union members, the influence of unions is powerfully felt, especially on issues such as job safety, working conditions, and workers' grievances. In national, state, and local government, labor unions are active in backing candidates and laws favorable to their interests.

Government, Business, and Labor

During the late 1800s, some unions won recognition from employers and influenced local and state laws. However, the federal government and many state governments favored big business over labor unions. Many states passed laws to restrict union activities. On the national level, the Sherman Antitrust Act of 1890—passed to break up large companies that hindered trade—was used mostly against labor. The courts found union leaders guilty of breaking the law, stating that unions interfered with commerce. Judges often issued **injunctions**, or court orders, banning strikes.

During the early 1900s, the political climate changed. An increasing number of Americans began to call for limits on big business and more rights for workers. As a result, government attitudes toward labor began to change. Most of the larger cities and more than half the states placed limits on working hours for employees on public works.

"The fight is never about grapes or lettuce. It is always about people."

—César Chávez, quoted in *Great Labor Quotations*

◀ **César Chávez**

▲ *Union strikes, such as the Pullman strike of 1894, sometimes turned violent.*

The courts, however, supported employers who challenged state laws that tried to regulate wages and working conditions. In 1905, for example, the Supreme Court ruled in the case *Lochner* v. *New York* that states could not set limits on the working hours of bakery workers. The Court reasoned that the New York law was unconstitutional because it interfered with the right of employers and employees to make contracts, or agreements, about working hours. The Court's reasoning was based on the principle that individuals have "liberty of contract" based on the Fourteenth Amendment.

Protecting Unions and Workers

The Great Depression of the 1930s left many American workers without jobs. President Franklin D. Roosevelt's effort to end the Depression included helping labor. One of the most important laws passed by Congress during Roosevelt's administration was the Wagner Act in 1935. This law sought to protect the right of workers to organize and to bargain collectively, or hold contract talks with employers. Under the Wagner Act, companies could not punish a worker because of union activities. Another measure was the Fair Labor Standards Act of 1938. It set the first minimum wage for workers and banned child labor.

Many employers believed that the Wagner Act was unconstitutional, but the Supreme Court upheld the act. In the case *National Labor Relations Board* v. *Jones & Laughlin Steel Corporation* (1937), the Court ruled that local activities of trade unions may affect commerce.

Because Congress had the constitutional power to regulate commerce, it could also regulate relations between business and labor. This meant that the National Labor Relations Board created by Congress had the authority to punish businesses involved in interstate commerce that discriminated against union members.

Unions Today During the 1960s and 1970s, several groups, such as government workers and farmworkers, formed new unions. For example, César E. Chávez, a Mexican American labor leader, began to organize farmworkers in California. Chávez founded what is now the United Farm Workers of America (UFW), a union of migrant workers and other farm laborers. Union membership among other Hispanic Americans, African Americans, and women also increased during this period.

Over the years, labor unions—as well as economic prosperity—have raised workers' standards of living. However, as a result of political and economic changes, the number of workers belonging to unions has declined sharply in recent years. Unions face other challenges too. One is defending workers' interests in declining industries that have fewer jobs. Another is protecting the jobs and wages of workers affected by **automation,** or the use of machines to do tasks once performed by people. Despite these difficulties, labor unions remain a powerful force in American life.

Checking for Understanding

1. What reason did the courts of the late 1800s give for finding union leaders guilty of breaking the law?

2. How did the federal government help labor during the Great Depression?

Critical Thinking

3. **Evaluate** Why did the Supreme Court adjust its view on labor in *NLRB* v. *Jones & Laughlin Steel Company*?

4. **Analyze** Restate the Court's reasoning in *Lochner* v. *New York* and predict the ruling's impact on other industries.

Analyzing Primary Sources

The Growth of Industry in America

Following the Civil War, the railroads expanded throughout the country. The railroads and inventions created the chance for other industries to grow. Many companies in these industries had long working hours, paid minimal salaries, and provided unsafe working conditions.

Read the passages on pages 732 and 733 and answer the questions that follow.

These women are working on the cloth after ▶ it has been woven.

Reader's Dictionary

shaker: person who shook and turned the drill after each blow to keep the drill from getting caught in the rock or the rock dust

haste (HAYST): hurrying too fast

garments (GAHR • muhnts): pieces of clothing

inclined plane: slanted surface

slate: type of rock that is used for chalkboards and roof tiles

John Henry

"John Henry" is a song that railroad men sang as they worked. John Henry hand drilled holes into stone to place dynamite.

When John Henry was a little baby,
Sitting on his pappy's knee,
He grabbed a hammer and a little piece of steel,
Said, "This hammer'll be the death of me,
Lord, Lord,
This hammer'll be the death of me. . . ."

John Henry told his captain,
"A man ain't nothing but a man,
But before I'll let that steam drill beat me down
I'll die with my hammer in my hand,
Lord, Lord,
I'll die with my hammer in my hand."

John Henry said to his **shaker**,
"Now shaker, why don't you sing?
'Cause I'm throwing twelve pounds from my hips on down,
Just listen to that cold steel ring,
Lord, Lord,
Just listen to that cold steel ring."

The man that invented the steam drill,
He thought he was mighty fine,
But John Henry he made fourteen feet
While the steam drill only made nine,
Lord, Lord,
The steam drill only made nine.

John Henry hammered on the mountain
Till his hammer was striking fire,
He drove so hard he broke his poor heart,
Then he laid down his hammer and he died, Lord, Lord,
He laid down his hammer and he died.

They took John Henry to the graveyard,
And they buried him in the sand,
And every locomotive comes rolling by
Says, "There lies a steel-driving man,
Lord, Lord,
There lies a steel-driving man."
—Anonymous in *Annals of America*

The Sweatshop

In factories, people had to work very quickly. In this passage, a young woman described her day in a factory where clothing was made.

At seven o'clock we all sit down to our machines and the boss brings to each one the pile of work that he or she is to finish during the day. . . . This pile is put down beside the machine and as soon as a skirt is done it is laid on the other side of the machine. . . .

The machines go like mad all day, because the faster you work, the more money you get. Sometimes in my **haste** I get my finger caught and the needle goes right through it. . . . We all have accidents like that. . . . Sometimes a finger has to come off. . . .

All the time we are working the boss walks about examining the finished **garments** and making us do them over again if they are not just right. So we have to be careful as well as swift.

—Sadie Frowne, "The Story of a Sweatshop Girl"

Child Labor

Laws forbidding children to work did not exist or were not enforced at this time.

In a little room in this big, black shed—a room not twenty feet square—forty boys are picking their lives away. The floor of this room is an **inclined plane**, and a stream of coal pours constantly in. They work here, in this little black hole, all day and every day, . . . picking their way among the black coals, bending over till their little spines are curved. . . .

Not three boys in this roomful could read or write. Shut out from everything that is pleasant, with no chance to learn, with no knowledge of what is going on about them. . . .

They know nothing but the difference between **slate** and coal.

—from a local Labor Standard Newspaper, St. Clair, Pennsylvania

▲ **Young coal miners**

DBQ Document-Based Questions

John Henry

1. What does John Henry predict in the first stanza?
2. Who won the contest? How do you know?

The Sweatshop

3. Why do people work quickly at the factory?
4. Why do people have to work carefully?

Child Labor

5. Where do the boys work?
6. What is their job?

Read to Write

7. Make two lists—one labeled Working Conditions and the other Effects of Working Conditions. Use the information in "The Sweatshop," "Child Labor," and what you already know about working conditions at this time to complete the lists. Write a paragraph explaining how you feel about these conditions. Include ideas for how they could be improved.

Review Content Vocabulary

Write the key term that completes each sentence.

a. standard gauge
b. assembly line
c. horizontal integration
d. trade union
e. rebates

1. Railroads offered ___, or discounts, to their largest customers.

2. Railroad companies adopted 4 feet, 8.5 inches as the width of the railroad track, also known as the ___.

3. The Knights of Labor was a ___ of garment workers.

Review the Main Ideas

Section 1 • Railroads Lead the Way

4. What improvements in railway transportation were brought about by new technology?

5. Why did the American Railway Association divide the country into four time zones?

Section 2 • Inventions

6. What inventions improved communications in the late 1800s?

7. What manufacturing methods did Henry Ford use to make his new automobile affordable?

Section 3 • The Age of Big Business

8. What is vertical integration?

9. What action did Congress take to control trusts and monopolies in response to pressure from the American people?

Section 4 • Industrial Workers

10. What is collective bargaining?

11. How did the Haymarket Riot of 1886 affect public opinion about the labor movement?

Critical Thinking

12. **Conclude** Why did workers think that forming organized labor unions would help them get what they wanted from employers?

13. **Analyze** How did American industry benefit from the growing railroad network in the late 1800s?

Geography Skills

A cartogram is a kind of map used to present statistical information. On a population cartogram the sizes of the states appear in proportion to their populations. Study the population cartogram below and answer the following questions.

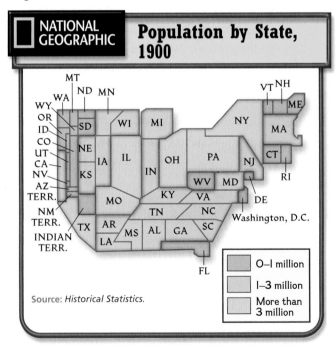

NATIONAL GEOGRAPHIC
Population by State, 1900

Source: *Historical Statistics.*

0–1 million
1–3 million
More than 3 million

14. **Location** Did Florida or Illinois have a larger population 1900?

15. **Location** Did North Dakota have more or fewer people than South Dakota?

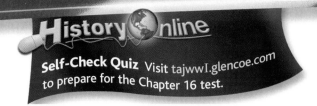

History Online

Self-Check Quiz Visit tajwwI.glencoe.com to prepare for the Chapter 16 test.

Read to Write

16. **The Big Ideas** Evaluate In a short essay, describe how the increasing size of corporations was both beneficial and harmful to American business.

17. **Summarize** Review the chapter for information about the four major union strikes between 1877 and 1894. Write a headline for each that might have appeared in newspapers following the strike.

18. **Using Your** FOLDABLES Write a poem, series of journal entries, or short story using the main ideas and supporting details from your completed foldable.

Using Academic Vocabulary

Identify the correct form of the academic vocabulary word to complete each sentence.

technology   technological   technologically

19. The computer is an example of a ___ advance.

transmit   transmits   transmitted

20. The reporter used the telegraph to ___ the story to the newspaper.

Building Citizenship

21. **Evaluate** With another student, write a short essay in which you support or criticize labor unions from the point of view of a young person who has just entered the workforce. Note how you think a union could or could not improve your life. Share your essay with the class.

Reviewing Skills

22. **READING SKILL** **Predicting Consequences** How would the growth of industry and new innovations in technology impact preparations for a war? Write a short essay predicting the potential effect.

23. **ANALYSIS SKILL** **Organizing Information** Do research to find the dates when the inventions described in this chapter were first created. Also find other inventions created by the inventors mentioned in the chapter, along with their dates of creation. Draw an annotated time line with the information you have found. Be sure to include the importance of each invention.

Standardized Test Practice

Select the best answer for each of the following questions.

24 The development of the transformers that Westinghouse built led to an increase in

   A the price of electricity.
   B the use of gas to heat homes.
   C the use of electricity to power factories.
   D imported goods.

25 John D. Rockefeller was the founder of the

   A Pennsylvania Railroad.
   B United States Steel Corporation.
   C Titusville oil well.
   D Standard Oil Company of Ohio.

26 The process in which a union represents its workers when negotiating with management is known as

   A collective bargaining.
   B strikebreaking.
   C vertical integration.
   D philanthropy.

Chapter 17

America Enters a New Century

▼ The growth of American cities continued throughout the twentieth century.

NATIONAL GEOGRAPHIC Who & When?

1880	1895	1910

1882 Chinese Exclusion Act passed

1884 First sky-scraper constructed in Chicago

1892 Ellis Island admits immigrants

1909 The NAACP is formed

W.E.B. Du Bois

The Big Ideas

History Online
Chapter Overview Visit tajww1.glencoe.com for a preview of Chapter 17.

The New Immigrants

Immigration influences a nation's or region's economy and society. In the late 1800s and early 1900s, the pattern of immigration was changing.

Moving to the City

Immigration influences a nation's or region's economy and society. Cities in the United States expanded rapidly in the late 1800s.

A Changing Culture

As a society matures, a distinctive culture can develop. A unique American culture was developing that affected many parts of American life.

The Progressive Movement

Reactions to social injustice can lead to reform movements. Many men and women became part of a widespread movement to bring about reform.

A Changing Nation

Political ideas and major events shape how people form governments. In the new century, the United States began to expand outwardly while still facing problems at home.

 View the Chapter 17 video in the Glencoe Video Program.

FOLDABLES™ Study Organizer

Analyzing Information Make this foldable to help you analyze information about the United States's people and policies as the country entered a new century.

Step 1 Fold a sheet of paper in half from side to side, leaving a $\frac{1}{2}$-inch tab along the side.

Leave $\frac{1}{2}$-inch tab here.

Step 2 Turn the paper and fold into fourths.

Fold in half, then fold in half again.

Reading and Writing As you read the chapter, write information about each topic under the appropriate tab.

Step 3 Unfold and cut up along the three fold lines.

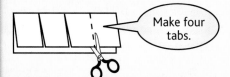
Make four tabs.

Step 4 Label your foldable as shown.

| New Immigrants and the City | American Culture | Reform and Battling Discrimination | The U.S. Expands |

Get Ready to Read

Visual Literacy

1 Learn It!

As you read and evaluate text, you are evaluating images as well. Painters and photographers use their craft to intentionally communicate ideas to the observer, in much the same way as authors use text.

Carefully study the image below. Then try to answer the following questions. What can you learn about the subject and the photographer?

- Why is this image here? What is it telling me?
- Is the image communicating facts or opinions?
- How does the image compare with what I already know?

Students at Tuskegee ▶
Institute

Reading Tip

When taking notes, be sure to include references to images. These will help you understand and remember important points in the text.

Practice It!

Political cartoons are another kind of image you will see. Political cartoons often appear on the editorial page of the newspaper. These cartoons express opinions on political issues. Political cartoons are good sources of historical information because they reflect opinions on current events.

Review this political cartoon. Its topic is immigration. Write three questions you could ask about this visual information. Then answer your questions with a short paragraph describing what you see. Check your conclusions as you read through the chapter.

Read to Write

Select two Internet news sites, one American and one from another country. Identify an image from each and describe the assumptions that went into placing the image on the Web site. Write an essay describing what you saw and interpreted.

FEBRUARY 7, 1885   COLUMBIA'S UNWELCOME GUESTS.

Apply It!

Review the images on page 736. Why were these images selected for the chapter opener? What do you think the author is trying to communicate with them?

The New Immigrants

Guide to Reading

Looking Back, Looking Ahead

You read about the tremendous growth in industry in the United States in the late 1800s. Large numbers of immigrants came to America in search of jobs.

Focusing on the Main Ideas

- The immigrants who arrived in America in the late 1800s came from many different countries. *(page 741)*
- After a difficult journey to America, many immigrants faced harsh working conditions. *(page 742)*
- Many native-born Americans resented the immigrants and pushed for laws to control their numbers. *(page 746)*

Locating Places

New York City
Ellis Island
Angel Island

Meeting People

Emma Lazarus
Grace Abbott
Julia Clifford Lathrop

Content Vocabulary

emigrate (EH•muh•GRAYT)
ethnic group
steerage (STIHR•ihj)
sweatshop
assimilate (uh•SIH•muh•LAYT)
nativist (NAY•tuh•vihst)

Academic Vocabulary

register (REH•juh•stuhr)
process
aspect (AS•PEHKT)

Reading Strategy

Analyzing Information As you study Section 1, re-create the diagram below and write the reasons immigrants came to America.

Reasons for immigrating

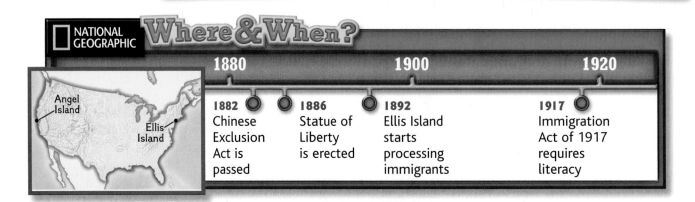

NATIONAL GEOGRAPHIC Where & When?

1880	1900	1920

1882 Chinese Exclusion Act is passed

1886 Statue of Liberty is erected

1892 Ellis Island starts processing immigrants

1917 Immigration Act of 1917 requires literacy

Angel Island

Ellis Island

A Flood of Immigrants

(Main Idea) **The immigrants who arrived in America in the late 1800s came from many different countries.**

Reading Connection Have you known anyone who has moved away because a parent or family member found a better job in another part of the country? Read to find out why immigrants to America in the late 1800s left Europe.

An American Story

In the 1870s, two young brothers left Italy for America.

66 We were so long on the water that we began to think we should never get to America. . . . We were all landed on an island and the bosses there said that Francisco and I must go back because we had not enough money, but a man named Bartolo came up and told them that . . . he was our uncle and would take care of us. . . . We came to Brooklyn to a wooden house on Adams Street that was full of Italians from Naples. Bartolo had a room on the third floor and there were fifteen men in the room, all boarding with Bartolo. . . . It was very hot in the room, but we were soon asleep, for we were very tired. 99

—from "Biography of a Bootblack"

Who Were the "New" Immigrants? Before 1865 most immigrants to the United States—except for the enslaved—came from northern and western Europe. The greater part of these "old" immigrants were Protestant, spoke English, and blended easily into American society. After the Civil War, even greater numbers of immigrants made the journey to the United States. The tide of newcomers reached a peak in 1907 when nearly 1.3 million people came to America.

Picturing **History**

Immigrants arrive in New York Harbor from Hamburg, Germany, in 1906. *Where did most immigrants to America come from after 1880?*

In the mid-1880s, the pattern of immigration started to change. Large groups of "new" immigrants arrived from eastern and southern Europe. Greeks, Russians, Hungarians, Italians, Turks, and Poles were among the newcomers. At the same time, the number of "old" immigrants started to decrease. By 1907 only about 20 percent of the immigrants came from northern and western Europe, while 80 percent came from southern and eastern Europe.

Many of the newcomers from eastern and southern Europe were Catholics or Jews. Few spoke English. Because of this, they did not blend into American society as easily as the "old" immigrants had. Many newcomers felt like outsiders, and they clustered together in urban neighborhoods made up of people of the same nationality.

Reasons for Emigrating

Why did so many people leave their homelands for the United States in the late 1800s and early 1900s? They were "pushed" away by difficult conditions at home and "pulled" to the United States by new opportunities.

Many people **emigrated** (EH•muh•GRAY•tuhd), or left their homelands, because of economic troubles. In Italy and Hungary, overcrowding and poverty made jobs scarce. Farmers in Croatia and Serbia could not own enough land to support their families. New machines such as looms put many craft workers out of work.

Persecution also drove people from their homelands. In some countries, the government passed laws or followed policies against certain **ethnic groups**—minorities that spoke different languages or followed different customs from those of most people in a country. Members of these ethnic groups often emigrated to escape discrimination or unfair laws. Many Jews fled persecution in Russia in the 1880s and came to the United States.

Immigrants saw the United States as a land of jobs, plentiful and affordable land, and opportunities for a better life. Although some immigrants returned to their homelands, ultimately, most decided to stay.

The Journey to America

Main Idea After a difficult journey to America, many immigrants faced harsh working conditions.

Reading Connection What would it be like to move to a place across an ocean, thousands of miles from home, where most people did not speak your language? Read to find out how immigrants to America in the late 1800s adjusted to their new lives.

Immigrants often had a difficult journey to America. Many had to first travel to a seaport to board a ship. Often they traveled for hundreds of miles to get to the port cities.

Then came the long ocean voyage to America—12 days across the Atlantic or several weeks across the Pacific. Immigrants usually could afford only the cheapest tickets, and they traveled in **steerage** (STIHR•ihj)—cramped, noisy quarters on the lower decks. One writer noted, "Crowds everywhere, ill smelling bunks, uninviting washrooms—this is steerage."

The Statue of Liberty Most European immigrants landed at **New York City.** After 1886 the magnificent sight of the Statue of Liberty, standing 300 feet above the ground, greeted the immigrants as they sailed into New York Harbor. The statue, a gift from France, seemed to promise hope for a better life in the new country. On the base of the statue, the stirring words of **Emma Lazarus,** an American poet, welcomed immigrants from Europe:

❝Give me your tired, your poor, Your huddled masses yearning to breathe free, The wretched refuse of your teeming shore. Send these, the homeless, tempest-tossed to me, I lift my lamp beside the golden door!❞
—from "The New Colossus"

Reading Check Describe Who were the "new" immigrants?

An American Story

Sailing from Ireland, a 15-year-old girl, Annie Moore, arrived in America on January 1, 1892. Accompanying her were her two brothers. Their parents had come to America two years earlier, leaving Annie and her brothers under the care of their aunt. The parents had finally made enough money to bring the children to America.

When Annie stepped off the gangplank, to her surprise, city and state leaders and immigration officials greeted her. Annie was the first of about 12 million people to enter the United States through Ellis Island, the new immigration processing center. Today, a statue of Annie Moore stands in the Ellis Island Museum in New York.

Entering America Before the new arrivals could actually pass through the "golden door" to America, they had to **register** at government reception centers. In the East, immigrants were **processed** at Castle Garden, a former fort on Manhattan Island, and after 1892 at **Ellis Island** in New York Harbor. Most Asian immigrants arrived in America on the West Coast and went through the processing center on **Angel Island** in San Francisco Bay. Examiners at the centers recorded the immigrants' names—sometimes shortening or simplifying a name they found too difficult to write. The examiners asked the immigrants where they came from, their occupation, and whether they had relatives in the United States. The examiners also gave health examinations. Immigrants with contagious illnesses could be refused permission to enter the United States.

Where Did Immigrants Find Work? After passing through the reception centers, most immigrants entered the United States. Where would they go? How would they live? Some had relatives or friends to stay with and to help them find jobs. Others knew no one and would have to strike out on their own.

An immigrant's greatest challenge was finding work. Sometimes organizations in his or her homeland recruited workers for jobs in the United States. The organization supplied American employers with unskilled workers who unloaded cargo or dug ditches.

Some of America's fastest-growing industries hired immigrant workers. In the steel mills of Pittsburgh, for example, most of the common laborers in the early 1900s were immigrant men. They might work 12 hours a day, seven days a week.

Picturing **History**

Immigrant children learned the English language and American customs in neighborhood schools. *How did language highlight the differences between generations of immigrants?*

Many immigrants, including women and children, worked in **sweatshops** in the garment industry. These were dark, crowded workshops where workers made clothing. The work was repetitious and hazardous, the pay low, and the hours long.

Pauline Newman, who later became an official in the International Ladies' Garment Workers Union, worked in a New York sweatshop as a child. She recalled:

> 66 During most of the year we youngsters worked overtime until 9 p.m. every night except Fridays and Saturdays. No, we did not get additional pay for overtime. At this point it is worth recording the [generosity] of the Triangle Waist Co. by giving us a piece of apple pie for supper instead of additional pay! 99

> —Pauline Newman,
> Letter to Michael and
> Hugh Owens

How Did Immigrants Adjust? Once they had moved to the United States, immigrants had to adjust to life in a new land. In their new homes, immigrants tried to preserve some **aspects** of their own cultures. At the same time, most wanted to **assimilate** (uh•SIH•muh•LAYT), or become part of the American culture. These two desires sometimes came into conflict.

NATIONAL GEOGRAPHIC

HISTORY MAKERS

Immigration Stations

The first stop for millions of immigrants was Ellis Island. About 12 million people passed through the Ellis Island immigration center between 1892 and 1954. The main building was reopened in 1990 as the Ellis Island Museum of Immigration. Located a short distance north of the Statue of Liberty in New York Harbor, Ellis Island stands as a memorial to the traditions of freedom and opportunity in America.

Hundreds of thousands of immigrants from Japan and China arrived on the West Coast during the late 1800s and early 1900s. In 1910 an immigration station was opened on Angel Island near San Francisco, California, to accommodate Asian immigrants.

▼ Immigrants arriving at Ellis Island

Immigrants at Angel Island ▶

Picturing **History**

In the cities, immigrants lived in neighborhoods that were often separated into ethnic groups. *How did immigrants try to adjust to their lives in the United States?*

Many immigrant parents continued to speak their native languages. Their children spoke English at school and with friends, but they also spoke their native language at home. On the other hand, the grandchildren of many immigrants spoke only English.

The role of immigrant women also changed in the United States, where women generally had more freedom than women in European and Asian countries. New lifestyles conflicted with traditional ways and sometimes caused family friction.

Where Did Immigrants Settle? Most of the new immigrants were from rural areas. Because they lacked the money to buy farmland in America, however, they often settled in industrial cities. With little or no education, they usually worked as unskilled laborers.

History Online

Student Web Activity Visit tajwwl.glencoe.com and click on *Chapter 17—Student Web Activities* for an activity on immigration.

Relatives who had already immigrated to the United States helped new arrivals get settled, and people of the same ethnic group naturally tended to form communities. As a result neighborhoods of Jewish, Italian, Polish, Chinese, and other groups quickly developed in New York, Chicago, San Francisco, and other large cities. The immigrants sought to re-create some of the life they had left behind. The communities they established revolved around a number of traditional institutions. Most important were the houses of worship—the churches and synagogues—where worship was conducted and holidays were celebrated as they had been in their homelands. Priests and rabbis often acted as community leaders.

The immigrants published newspapers in their native languages, opened stores and theaters, and organized social clubs. Ethnic communities and institutions helped the immigrants preserve their cultural heritage.

✔ **Reading Check** **Identify** What is assimilation?

Nativist Movement

(Main Idea) **Many native-born Americans resented the immigrants and pushed for laws to control their numbers.**

Reading Connection Have you ever been forced to share something you wanted to keep to yourself? How did that make you feel? Read to find out how some Americans felt about all the new immigrants who were pouring into the United States.

Assimilation was also slowed by the attitudes of many native-born Americans. Although employers were happy to hire immigrant workers at low wages, some American-born workers resented the immigrants. These Americans feared that the immigrants would take away their jobs or drive down everyone's wages by accepting lower pay.

Ethnic, religious, and racial differences contributed to tensions between Americans and the new immigrants. Some Americans argued that the new immigrants—with their foreign languages, unfamiliar religions, and distinctive customs—did not fit into American society.

People found it easy to blame immigrants for increasing crime, unemployment, and other problems. **Nativists** (NAY•tuh•vihsts) had opposed immigration earlier in the 1800s. Nativism gained strength in the late 1800s. Calls for restrictions on immigration mounted.

What Laws Limited Immigration? Lawmakers responded quickly to the tide of anti-immigrant feeling. In 1882 Congress passed the first law to limit immigration—the Chinese Exclusion Act. This law prohibited Chinese workers from entering the United States for 10 years. Congress extended the law in 1892 and again in 1902.

In 1907 the federal government and Japan came to a "gentleman's agreement." The Japanese agreed to limit the number of immigrants to the United States, and the Americans pledged fair treatment for Japanese Americans who were already in the United States.

Analyzing
Political Cartoons

In this cartoon, the female figure Columbia, representing the United States, turns away unwanted immigrants, such as criminals and those with radical political beliefs.
Why did some American-born workers resent the immigrants?

Other legislation affected immigrants from all nations. An 1882 law made each immigrant pay a tax and also barred criminals from entering the country. In 1897 Congress passed a bill requiring immigrants to be able to read and write in some language. Although President Cleveland vetoed the bill as unfair, Congress later passed the Immigration Act of 1917, which included a similar literacy requirement.

Support for Immigrants Despite some anti-immigrant sentiment, many Americans—including **Grace Abbott** and **Julia Clifford Lathrop,** who helped found the Immigrants' Protective League—spoke out in support of immigration. These Americans recognized that the United States was a nation of immigrants and that the newcomers made lasting contributions to their new society.

Immigrants' Contributions The new immigrants supplied the country's growing industries with the workers that were necessary for economic growth. At the same time, the new immigrants and their children—like the old immigrants before them—helped shape American life. They gave the nation its major religious groups—Protestants, Catholics, and Jews. As they became part of the society around them, they enriched that society with the customs, cultures, language, and literature of their homelands.

The effects of immigration were most visible in the cities, with their fast-growing ethnic neighborhoods. The flow of immigrants was one of the factors that transformed America's cities in the late 1800s and the early 1900s.

Reading Check **Explain** What was the nativist movement?

History Online

Study Central Need help understanding the immigrant experience? Visit tajwwI.glencoe.com and click on Study Central.

Section 1 Review

Reading Summary

Review the Main Ideas

- In the late 1800s, many of the immigrants who arrived in America came from southern and eastern Europe, rather than western and northern Europe.

- Many new immigrants to America settled in ethnic neighborhoods and found work in low-paying and sometimes dangerous workshops known as sweatshops.

- Americans who were members of the nativist movement called for laws to limit immigration.

What Did You Learn?

1. What was the difference between "old" and "new" immigration?

2. Which two cities were the points of entry into America for most immigrants?

Critical Thinking

3. **Analyze** Re-create the diagram below. List reasons people left their home countries (pushed) and came to the United States (pulled).

Pushed to Emigrate	Pulled to Immigrate

4. **Conclude** Why do you think some Americans blamed the "new" immigrants for many of society's problems?

5. **The Big Ideas** What were some of the cultural differences that immigrants had to adjust to in the United States? Explain the concept of assimilation and its effect on families and American culture.

6. **READING** **Visual Literacy** Select one of the photographs that appear in Section 1 and write a paragraph in which you describe the scene, as well as why the author included the image with the text. Include a title for the paragraph.

You Decide . . .

Should Immigration Be Limited?

Immigrants struggled to find their place in American society. They changed American society with customs from their cultures. Many Americans resisted these changes and warned against further immigration. Read to find out how Americans viewed new immigrants.

Yes

The Chinese come for a season only; and, while they give their labor, they do not [spend the money they earn] in the country. They do not come to settle or make homes. . . . To compare the Chinese with even the lowest white laborers is, therefore, absurd.

Our best interests are suffering of these Asiatic slaves; we are trying to make them live decently while here, and to discourage their arrival in such numbers as to drive white laborers out of the country. . . .

—San Francisco Real Estate Circular, September 1874

The Chinese Exclusion Act of 1882 reflected the widespread hostility against immigrant workers. The law halted immigration of Chinese workers and gained wide support from American labor unions.

Preamble. Whereas, in the opinion of the Government of the United States the coming of Chinese laborers to this country endangers the good order of certain localities within the territory thereof: Therefore,

Be it enacted by the Senate and House of Representatives of the United States of America in Congress assembled, That . . . until the expiration of 10 years next after the passage of this act, the coming of Chinese laborers to the United States be, and the same is hereby, suspended; and during such suspension it shall not be lawful for any Chinese laborer to come, or, . . . to remain within the United States.

—1882 Chinese Exclusion Act
47th Congress, 1st Session, 1882

◀ **Immigrants from China**

No

Author, traveler, and artist Constance Gordon-Cumming wrote about discrimination against Chinese immigrants.

[It is unbelievable that legislation against Chinese immigrants could have arisen] among a people whose national existence is based on the Declaration of Independence, and the assumption of liberty and equality of all men, without distinction of race or colour....

That [laws] so utterly un-American could have been suffered to pass, appears so extraordinary. . . .

—from *California As I Saw It, 1849–1900*

Attorney Louis Marshall was a consistent champion of the rights of immigrants to the United States.

In common with all other immigrants, those who have come from the countries sought to be tabooed [forbidden] have been industrious, and law-abiding and have made valuable contributions to our industrial, commercial and social development. . . .

To say that they are not assimilable argues ignorance. The facts show that they adopt American standards of living and that they are permeated [filled] with the spirit of our institutions. It is said that they speak foreign languages, but in those foreign languages they are taught to love our Government. . . .

—Attorney Louis Marshall
Speaks Out
Against Limiting
Immigration, 1924

▲ **Louis Marshall**

You Be The Historian

DBQ Document-Based Questions

1. What did the writer from San Francisco fear?

2. What did Louis Marshall claim about the immigrants' contributions?

3. What facts does Marshall use to support his view that the newcomers are "assimilable"?

Section 2

Moving to the City

Guide to Reading

Looking Back, Looking Ahead

You learned that millions of new immigrants arrived in the United States in the late 1800s and early 1900s. All of these new people led to tremendous growth and change in America's cities.

Focusing on the (Main Ideas)

- As Americans crowded into cities, strong contrasts emerged between the lives of the rich and the poor. *(page 751)*
- America's rapidly growing cities faced many problems. *(page 753)*
- As cities grew, Americans created new styles of buildings and improved forms of transportation. *(page 754)*

Locating Places

Central Park

Meeting People

Jane Addams

Elisha Otis

William LeBaron Jenney

Louis Sullivan

Frederick Law Olmsted (OHM•stehd)

Content Vocabulary

tenement (TEH•nuh•muhnt)

slum

suburb

Gilded Age (GIHL•duhd)

settlement house (SEH•tuhl•muhnt)

Academic Vocabulary

accommodate (uh•KAH•muh•DAYT)

professional (pruh•FEH•shuh•nuhl)

Reading Strategy

Analyzing Information As you study Section 2, re-create the diagram below and list three serious problems facing American cities in the late 1800s.

```
      Urban problems
     /      |       \
   ( )     ( )      ( )
```

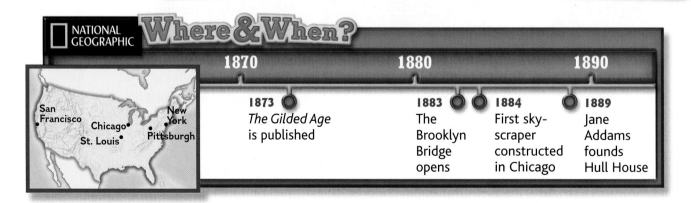

NATIONAL GEOGRAPHIC **Where & When?**

1870	1880	1890

1873 *The Gilded Age* is published

1883 The Brooklyn Bridge opens

1884 First sky-scraper constructed in Chicago

1889 Jane Addams founds Hull House

San Francisco • Chicago • St. Louis • Pittsburgh • New York

Growth of Cities

Main Idea As Americans crowded into cities, strong contrasts emerged between the lives of the rich and the poor.

Reading Connection Do you live in a city, in a suburb, or in a rural area? Read to find out the changes that all three places underwent in the late 1800s and early 1900s.

An American Story

A train pulling into Chicago in 1884 carried a young passenger named Hamlin Garland. For Garland, who had grown up on a farm, the big city was a bewildering sight. Garland later became famous for his stories about the Midwest. In one novel, he described his feeling of dismay when he first saw Chicago. "The mere thought of a million people stunned my imagination." Garland wondered, "How can so many people find a living in one place?"

Why Did Urban Areas Grow? American cities grew rapidly after the Civil War. In 1870 one American in four lived in cities with 2,500 or more people. By 1910 nearly half of the American population were city dwellers. The United States was changing from a rural to an urban nation.

Immigrants played an enormous part in the growth of cities. In major urban centers such as New York, Detroit, and Chicago, immigrants and their children made up 80 percent or more of the population by 1900. Native-born Americans also contributed to urban growth. Americans moved in huge numbers from farming areas to cities, looking for jobs.

Industrialization had also changed work on farms. New machinery produced crops, using fewer farmworkers. In addition, women in rural areas no longer had to make clothing and household goods. These items, made by machine, could now be bought in stores or from catalogs. Freed from such chores, many women left farms to look for jobs in the cities.

African Americans also migrated to cities in large numbers. Most African Americans lived in the rural South. Many began moving to Southern cities in search of jobs and to escape debt, injustice, or discrimination. After 1914 a large number of African Americans moved to Northern cities, which offered more jobs in industry and manufacturing than Southern cities did. Many African Americans also hoped to find less discrimination and violence in the North.

Transportation and Resources America's expanding railroad network fed the growth of the cities. Railroads helped people move to the cities, and they transported the raw materials for industry. Trains carried cattle to Chicago and Kansas City, making these cities great meatpacking centers.

Some cities flourished because of nearby resources. Pittsburgh developed rapidly as a center for iron and steel manufacturing because both iron ore and coal—to fuel the industry's huge furnaces—were found in the area.

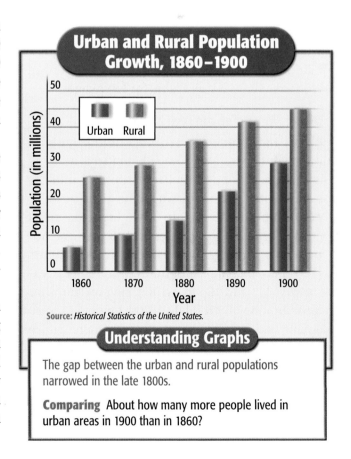

Urban and Rural Population Growth, 1860–1900

Urban   Rural

Population (in millions)

1860   1870   1880   1890   1900

Year

Source: *Historical Statistics of the United States.*

Understanding Graphs

The gap between the urban and rural populations narrowed in the late 1800s.

Comparing About how many more people lived in urban areas in 1900 than in 1860?

Picturing History

In 1900 New York City's East Side was crowded with new immigrants. *What were some other major urban centers in 1900?*

Seaports such as New York and San Francisco developed as American trade with the rest of the world increased. In addition, the immigrant population of these cities provided a large pool of workers who were available for low wages.

What Were Tenements?
Cities were exciting places that offered jobs, stores, and entertainment. But there was also substandard housing and desperate poverty. People poured into the cities faster than housing could be built to **accommodate** them. In the biggest, most crowded cities, the poorest residents—including most immigrants—lived in **tenements** (TEH•nuh•muhnts). Originally a tenement was simply a building in which several families rented rooms. By the late 1800s, however, a tenement had come to mean an apartment building in the **slums**—poor, run-down urban neighborhoods.

Tenements had many small, dark rooms. Three, four, or more people lived in each room. Usually several families had to share a cold-water tap and a toilet. Few tenement houses had hot water or bathtubs. A government inspector wrote of the "filthy and rotten tenements" of the Chicago slums in 1896, where children filled "every nook, eating and sleeping in every windowsill, pouring in and out of every door."

How Did the Middle Class Live?
The cities also had a growing middle class. The middle class included the families of **professional** people such as doctors, lawyers, and ministers. Some managers and salaried office clerks also became part of the middle class.

The middle class enjoyed a comfortable life. Many families moved from cities to the **suburbs,** residential areas that sprang up outside of city centers as a result of improvements in transportation. There they lived in houses with hot water, indoor toilets, and—by 1900—electricity. Middle-class families might have one or two servants and the leisure time to enjoy music, art, and literature.

What Was the Gilded Age?
At the top of the economic and social ladder stood the very rich. The wealthy lived very different lives from most Americans. They built enormous mansions in the cities and huge estates in the country. Some homes, such as those of J.P. Morgan and Henry Clay Frick in New York City, are now museums.

In these mansions, the rich lived lives of extreme luxury, throwing enormous parties and dinners. One party at a New York mansion had more than 1,000 guests and was estimated to have cost $75,000 for food and entertainment, which is equal to about $1.3 million today.

Mark Twain and Charles Dudley Warner published a novel in 1873 called *The Gilded Age.* The name—which refers to something covered with a thin layer of gold—became associated with America in the late 1800s. The **Gilded Age** (GIHL•duhd) suggested both the extravagant wealth of the time and the terrible poverty that lay underneath.

Reading Check **Describe** Why was tenement living difficult?

Cities in Crisis

Main Idea America's rapidly growing cities faced many problems.

Reading Connection What sort of problems do cities face today? Read to find out about the problems that arose as America's cities grew.

The rapid growth of the cities produced serious problems. The terrible overcrowding in tenement districts created sanitation and health problems. Garbage and horse manure accumulated in city streets, and the sewers could not handle the flow of human waste. Filth created a breeding ground for diseases, which spread rapidly through the crowded districts.

Fires were an ever-present threat. About 18,000 buildings were destroyed and 100,000 Chicagoans lost their homes in the Chicago fire of 1871. Two years later, Boston experienced a devastating fire.

Health and Crime Problems

In a poor Chicago neighborhood in 1900, babies often died of whooping cough, diphtheria, or measles before their first birthday. A section of New York was called the "lung block" because so many residents had tuberculosis.

In an effort to control disease, New York City began to screen schoolchildren for contagious diseases and to provide visiting nurses to mothers with young children. The city also established public health clinics for those who could not pay for medical care.

The poverty in the cities often led to increased crime. Orphaned and homeless children sometimes resorted to picking pockets and other minor crimes to survive. Gangs roaming the poor neighborhoods committed more serious crimes. Writer Jacob Riis reported:

❝The gang is the ripe fruit of tenement-house growth. It was born there.❞

—Jacob Riis,
How the Other Half Lives

Seeking Solutions

The problems of the cities did not go unnoticed. Many dedicated people worked to improve urban life and help the poor. Religious groups aided the poor. Some religious orders helped the poor in orphanages, prisons, and hospitals. Organizations such as the YMCA (Young Men's Christian Association) and YWCA (Young Women's Christian Association) offered recreation centers where city youngsters could meet and play.

The poor also received assistance from establishments called **settlement houses** (SEH•tuhl•muhnt). The settlement house movement had spread to the United States from Britain. Located in poor neighborhoods, settlement houses provided medical care, playgrounds, nurseries, and libraries as well as classes in English, music, and arts and crafts. Settlement workers—mostly women—also tried to get better police protection, garbage removal, and public parks for poor districts.

One of the most famous settlement houses was Chicago's Hull House, founded by **Jane Addams** in 1889. Addams paid all the expenses from her own income, until the activities at Hull House grew beyond her means. She then turned to the public to raise funds. Addams explained the purpose of Hull House:

❝We were ready to perform the humblest neighborhood services. We were asked to wash the new-born babies, and to prepare the dead for burial, to nurse the sick, and to 'mind the children.'❞

—Jane Addams,
Twenty Years at Hull House

Reading Check **Explain** What purpose did settlement houses serve?

The Changing City

Main Idea **As cities grew, Americans created new styles of buildings and improved forms of transportation.**

Reading Connection Have you ever admired the towering skyscrapers in a large city and wondered when the first tall buildings were made? Read to find out about the first skyscrapers and other advances that occurred in American cities.

Urban growth led to important new developments. In the late 1800s, cities saw the introduction of a new type of building, new kinds of public transportation, and public parks.

Building Up—Not Out Because of the limited space in cities, imaginative architects began building upward rather than outward. In the 1860s architects started to use iron frames to strengthen the walls of buildings. Iron supports—together with the safety elevator that **Elisha Otis** invented in 1852—made taller buildings possible.

In 1884 **William LeBaron Jenney** constructed a 10-story office building in Chicago. Supported by an iron-and-steel frame, it was the world's first skyscraper. Architect **Louis Sullivan** gave style to the skyscraper. "It must be every inch a proud and soaring thing, rising in sheer exultation," he said. Sullivan and his colleagues changed the face of America's cities.

Picturing **History**

The Woolworth Building was designed and built to be the tallest building in the world. *Where was the first skyscraper built, and how tall was it?*

Picturing **History**

Pedestrians stroll across a walkway on the Brooklyn Bridge in New York City. *How did the new bridges in New York City and St. Louis improve transportation?*

Soon architects were designing even taller structures. New York's Woolworth Building, completed in 1913, soared an incredible 55 stories—792 feet (241 m) high. People called the building the Cathedral of Commerce.

What New Designs Appeared in Cities?

Some people looked to reshape the urban landscape. A group known as the "City Beautiful" movement believed city dwellers should be able to enjoy the beauties of nature. **Frederick Law Olmsted** (OHM•stehd), a leader in this movement, designed New York's **Central Park** as well as several parks in Boston.

In 1892 and 1893, Chicago hosted a World's Fair on fairgrounds designed by Olmsted. The World's Fair revealed that American architecture was dynamic and original. The best architects thoroughly understood European styles and adapted them for modern use. The firm of McKim, Mead, and White used the Italian Renaissance style in its design for the Boston Public Library. Another architect, Henry Richardson, adapted styles from ancient Rome in his designs for churches, libraries, and even department stores.

New Forms of Transportation

As cities grew, people needed new means of transportation. Author Mark Twain complained in 1867 that

> ❝ [New York] is too large. You cannot accomplish anything . . . without devoting a whole day to it. . . . The distances are too great. ❞
>
> —Mark Twain, San Francisco *Alta California*

Streetcars, which horses pulled on tracks, provided public transportation at the time. Horses were slow, however, and left piles of manure. In 1873 San Francisco began construction of cable-car lines. A large underground cable powered by a motor at one end of the rail line moved passengers along.

In 1888 Richmond, Virginia, pioneered the use of the trolley car, a motorized train that was powered by electricity supplied through overhead cables. By the turn of the century, the trolley was everywhere. In 1897 Boston opened the nation's first subway, or underground railway. In 1904 New York City opened the first section of what was to become the largest subway system in the world.

Another improvement in transportation was street paving. During most of the 1800s, city streets remained poorly paved. Many streets were nothing more than sand and gravel. Other cities used wood blocks, brick, or cobblestone, all of which were bumpy, noisy, and hard to repair. The growing use of asphalt—a byproduct of petroleum refining—beginning in the 1890s made city streets smoother and quieter.

Building Bridges Bridge construction also improved urban transportation. Many American cities were divided or bounded by rivers. Using new construction technology, architects and engineers designed huge steel bridges to link sections of cities. The 520-foot (156-m) Eads Bridge across the Mississippi River in St. Louis opened in 1873. Ten years later New York's majestic Brooklyn Bridge, 1,600 feet (488 m) long, connected Manhattan and Brooklyn. Both bridges remain in use today.

The new forms of transportation not only helped people travel within the cities, but they also helped the cities grow. Middle-class suburbs developed along train or trolley lines stretching away from city centers. People who moved out of the city centers could easily travel downtown to work or shop.

The increase in immigration and the growth of the cities went hand in hand with other changes in American life. Education, culture, and recreation were changing too.

✓ **Reading Check** **Summarize** What new forms of urban transportation were developed?

History Online
Study Central Need help understanding the growth of American cities? Visit tajww1.glencoe.com and click on Study Central.

Section 2 Review

Reading Summary

Review the Main Ideas

- Both native-born Americans and immigrants flocked to the cities looking for jobs.

- Disease, fire, and crime were major problems faced by America's cities.

- Skyscrapers and parks, along with streetcars, paved roads, and bridges, became part of America's cityscapes.

What Did You Learn?

1. Who founded Hull House?

2. Who invented the safety elevator?

Critical Thinking

3. **Summarizing Information** Re-create the diagram below and describe three efforts made to improve living conditions in the cities.

Improving city life

4. **Analyze** How did the efforts of religious groups help those living in poverty?

5. **Summarize** Describe the differences in everyday life for the poor, middle-class, and wealthy in America's cities.

6. **The Big Ideas** Describe the relationship between improvements in transportation and the growth of cities and suburbs.

7. **ANALYSIS** **Linking Past to Present** Write an essay that describes efforts to enhance urban life during this period. How do those initiatives continue to affect city life today?

Guide to Reading

Looking Back, Looking Ahead

You learned that America's population boomed and its cities grew rapidly in the late 1800s and early 1900s. Elements of American culture—including education, the arts, and leisure activities—also changed during this period.

Focusing on the Main Ideas

- The expanding education system provided opportunities for Americans and new immigrants. *(page 758)*
- Reading for learning and pleasure grew more popular as education and leisure time increased for Americans. *(page 761)*
- American art, music, and leisure time activities continued to develop their own distinct style. *(page 762)*

Meeting People

John Dewey

Booker T. Washington

George Washington Carver

Joseph Pulitzer (PU•luht•suhr)

William Randolph Hearst (HUHRST)

Thomas Edison

Locating Places

Tuskegee Institute

Content Vocabulary

land-grant college

yellow journalism

realism (REE•uh•LIH•zuhm)

regionalism (REE•juh•nuhl•IZUHM)

ragtime

vaudeville (VAHD•vihl)

Academic Vocabulary

benefit (BEH•nuh•FIHT)

isolate (EYE•suh•LAYT)

ethnic

Reading Strategy

Classifying Information As you study Section 3, re-create the diagram below and describe the achievements of the persons listed.

	Achievements
John Dewey	
George Washington Carver	
Mary Cassatt	
Scott Joplin	

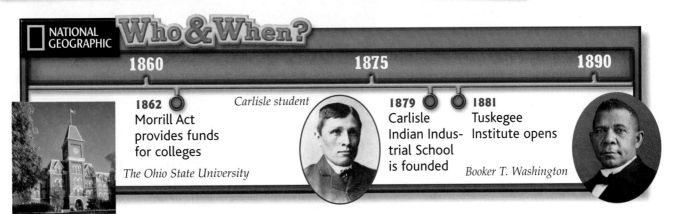

NATIONAL GEOGRAPHIC **Who & When?**

1860   1875   1890

1862 Morrill Act provides funds for colleges

The Ohio State University

Carlisle student

1879 Carlisle Indian Industrial School is founded

1881 Tuskegee Institute opens

Booker T. Washington

Expanding Education

Main Idea The expanding education system provided opportunities for Americans and new immigrants.

Reading Connection Today, laws require that all children attend school. Did you know that it was not always that way? Read to find out about the changes that occurred in education in the late 1800s and early 1900s.

An American Story

Mary Antin, a young girl who came to the United States from Russia in 1894, never forgot her first day of school.

> 66 Father himself conducted us to school. He would not have delegated that mission to the President of the United States. . . . [Education was] the essence of American opportunity, the treasure that no thief could touch, not even misfortune or poverty. . . . The doors stood open for every one of us. 99
>
> —Mary Antin, *The Promised Land*

How Did Enrollment Change?

Most Americans in 1865 had attended school for an average of only four years. Government and business leaders and reformers believed that for the nation to progress, the people needed more schooling. Toward the end of the 1800s, the "treasure" of education became more widely available to Americans.

By 1914 most states required children to have at least some schooling. More than 80 percent of all children between the ages of 5 and 17 were enrolled in elementary and secondary schools.

Public Schools The expansion of public education was particularly notable in high schools. The number of public high schools increased from 100 in 1860 to 6,000 in 1900, and to 12,000 in 1914. Despite this huge increase, however, many teenagers did not attend high school. Boys often went to work to help their families instead of attending school. The majority of high school students were girls.

The Way It Was

School Days

On the Bus

Students line up for a ride to school in Fresno, California. Few schools were lucky enough to have their own buses in the early 1900s. Not until 1939 were national standards for school buses adopted, including the color "school-bus yellow" to promote visibility and safety.

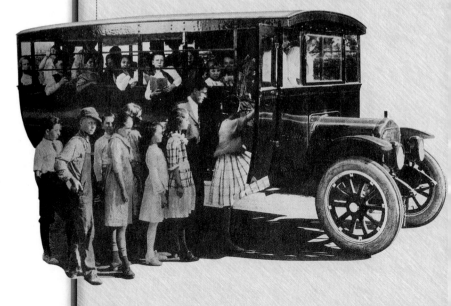

The **benefits** of a public school education were not shared equally by everyone. In the South, many African Americans received little or no education. In many parts of the country, African American children had no choice but to attend segregated elementary and secondary schools.

What Was Progressive Education? Around 1900 a new philosophy of education emerged in the United States. Supporters of this "progressive education" wanted to shape students' characters and teach them good citizenship as well as facts. They also believed children should learn through the use of hands-on activities. These ideas had the greatest effect in elementary schools.

John Dewey, the leading spokesperson for progressive education, criticized schools for overemphasizing memorization of information. Instead, Dewey argued, schools should relate learning to the interests, problems, and concerns of students.

Crossing Guard
A New York City police officer guides students on their way to school in 1899. By the early 1900s, the police provided this service in many communities.

Writing
By 1900, the Palmer method of penmanship was taught everywhere. In the Palmer method, some capital letters were no longer written separately, and entire words could be completed before the pen was lifted to cross a "t" or dot an "i." Writing sets included ink bottles like this one. Its double covers prevented evaporation and protected against leakage.

Bookmobile
Librarians attempted to provide reading material to rural communities. Here, a traveling library makes book deliveries in Washington County, Maryland.

The Classroom
Students observe an experiment and take notes during science class in 1900.

Elementary Students
The classroom was the primary place where immigrant children learned American ways.

How Did Higher Education Change?

Colleges and universities also changed and expanded. An 1862 law called the Morrill Act gave the states large amounts of federal land that could be sold to raise money for education. The states used these funds to start dozens of schools called **land-grant colleges.** Wealthy individuals also established and supported colleges and universities. Some schools were named for the donors—for example, Cornell University for Ezra Cornell and Stanford University for Leland Stanford.

In 1865 only a handful of American colleges admitted women. The new land-grant schools admitted women students, as did new women's colleges—Vassar, Smith, Wellesley, and Bryn Mawr—founded in the late 1800s. By 1890 women could attend a wide range of schools, and by 1910 almost 40 percent of all American college students were women.

Some new colleges, such as Hampton Institute in Virginia, provided higher education for African Americans and Native Americans. Howard University in Washington, D.C., founded shortly after the Civil War, had a largely African American student body. By the early 1870s, Howard offered degrees in theology, medicine, law, and agriculture. Prominent graduates of Howard include Thurgood

▲ Students in classroom at Tuskegee Institute

Marshall, who later became a justice of the Supreme Court, writer Toni Morrison, and political scientist Ralph Bunche, the first African American to win the Nobel Peace Prize.

One Hampton Institute student, **Booker T. Washington,** became an educator. In 1881 Washington founded the **Tuskegee Institute** in Alabama to train teachers and to provide practical education for African Americans. As a result of his work, Washington became influential in business and politics.

In 1896 scientist **George Washington Carver** joined the Tuskegee faculty. His research transformed agricultural development in the South. From the peanut, which was formerly of little use, Carver developed hundreds of products, including plastics and synthetic rubber.

Schools for Native Americans Reservation schools and boarding schools also opened to train Native Americans for jobs. The Carlisle Indian Industrial School in Pennsylvania was founded in 1879, and similar schools opened in the West. Although these schools provided Native Americans with training for jobs in industry, they also **isolated** Native Americans from their tribal traditions. Sometimes, boarding schools were located hundreds of miles away from a student's family.

▲ These two photographs of a young Navajo, Tom Torlino, show how his appearance changed a short time after he entered the Carlisle Indian School.

Reading Check **Compare** What did the colleges Bryn Mawr, Vassar, and Smith have in common?

A Nation of Readers

Main Idea Reading for learning and pleasure grew more popular as education and leisure time increased for Americans.

Reading Connection Do you read a newspaper every day? Read to find out about the growth of daily newspapers in America's large cities.

As opportunities for education grew, a growing number of Americans became interested in reading. Public libraries opened across the nation, mainly through the efforts of Andrew Carnegie. In 1881 the wealthy steel industrialist had made an extraordinary announcement. He pledged to build a public library in any city that would agree to pay its operating costs. In the next 30 years, Carnegie donated more than $30 million to found more than 2,000 libraries throughout the world.

Spreading the News Technological advances in printing, paper making, and communications made it possible to publish daily papers for large numbers of readers. The growing cities provided readers for the newspapers.

In 1883 **Joseph Pulitzer** (PU•luht•suhr) purchased the New York *World* and created a new kind of newspaper. The paper grabbed attention with illustrations, cartoons, and sensational stories with huge, shocking headlines, such as "ANOTHER MURDERER TO HANG." The *World* soon built up its circulation to more than one million readers every day.

William Randolph Hearst's (HUHRST) New York *Morning Journal* became even more successful than the *World*, attracting readers by exaggerating the dramatic or gruesome aspects of stories. This style of sensational writing became known as **yellow journalism**—a name that came from the paper's popular comic strip, "The Yellow Kid."

Newspapers published by **ethnic** groups and people of color thrived as well. By 1900 six daily Jewish-language newspapers were printed in New York City. African Americans started more than 1,000 newspapers between 1865 and 1900.

More magazines took advantage of printing improvements and mass circulation techniques to reach a national market. Between 1865 and 1900, the number of magazines in the United States rose from about 700 to 5,000. Some magazines of that era, such as *Ladies' Home Journal*, are still published today.

How Did Literature Change? Many writers of the era explored new themes and subjects. Their approach to literature was called **realism** (REE•uh•LIH•zuhm) because it dealt with the lives of people. Related to realism was **regionalism** (REE•juh•nuhl•IZUHM), writing that focused on a particular region of the country.

Mark Twain was a realist and a regionalist. Many of his books, including *The Adventures of Huckleberry Finn* and *The Adventures of Tom Sawyer*, are set along the Mississippi River, where Twain grew up.

Stephen Crane wrote about city slums in *Maggie* and about the Civil War in *The Red Badge of Courage*. In books such as *The Call of the Wild* and *The Sea Wolf*, Jack London portrayed the lives of miners and hunters in the far Northwest. Edith Wharton described the joys and sorrows of upper-class Easterners in *The House of Mirth* and *The Age of Innocence*.

Paul Laurence Dunbar, the son of former slaves, wrote poetry and novels that used the dialects and folktales of Southern African Americans. Dunbar was one of the first African American writers to gain fame worldwide.

Inexpensive paperback books appeared for the first time in the late 1800s. Many paperbacks featured lively adventure tales or stories of athletic boys and girls.

Horatio Alger wrote a successful series of young adult books with such titles as *Work and Win* and *Luck and Pluck*. Based on the idea that hard work and honesty brought success, Alger's books sold millions of copies.

Reading Check Explain What is regionalism?

Art, Music, and Leisure

Main Idea American art, music, and leisure time activities continued to develop their own distinct style.

Reading Connection Can you imagine the United States without baseball or football? What about without jazz music? Read to find out about the activities and art forms that took hold in America in the late 1800s.

For most of the 1800s, the work of American artists and musicians reflected a European influence. After the Civil War, Americans began to develop a distinctively American style.

What Did American Artists Paint? Some American painters pursued realist themes. Thomas Eakins painted the human anatomy and surgical operations. One of Eakins's students, Henry Tanner, depicted warm family scenes of African Americans in the South. Frederic Remington portrayed the American West, focusing on subjects such as cowhands and Native Americans. Winslow Homer was one of America's greatest artists. Homer painted Southern farmers, Adirondack campers, and stormy sea scenes. Although Homer died in 1910, his work remains popular with collectors and museum visitors. James Whistler's *Arrangement in Grey and Black,* commonly known as *Whistler's Mother,* is one of the best-known American paintings. Mary Cassatt was influential in the French Impressionist school of painting. Impressionists tried to capture the play of light, color, and patterns as they made immediate impressions on the senses.

Music in America More distinctively American kinds of music were also becoming popular. Bandleader John Philip Sousa composed many rousing marches, including "The Stars and Stripes Forever." African American musicians in New Orleans in the late 1800s developed an entirely new kind of music—jazz. Jazz combined elements of work songs, gospel music, spirituals, and African rhythms. Related to jazz was ragtime music. For about 20 years, beginning around the turn of the century, **ragtime**—with its complex rhythms—was the dominant force in popular music. One of the best-known ragtime composers is Scott Joplin. He wrote "Maple Leaf Rag" and many other well-known works.

The symphony orchestras of New York, Boston, and Philadelphia—all founded before 1900—were among the world's finest. Great singers and conductors came from all over the world to perform at New York's Metropolitan Opera House.

Leisure Time Although sweatshop workers labored long hours for six or even seven days a week, middle-class people and even some factory workers enjoyed increasing amounts of leisure time.

Unlike round-the-clock farmwork, professional and industrial jobs gave people hours and even days of free time. Americans developed new forms of recreation.

History *Through Art*

Girls with Lobster by **Winslow Homer**
Homer painted scenes of people enjoying the New Jersey and New England seashores.
What themes did many American painters represent in their works?

A favorite leisure-time activity for many people was watching and following sports. Baseball became the most popular spectator sport in America. By the turn of the century, both the National and American Leagues had been founded—each made up of teams from major cities. Another popular spectator sport was football, which developed from the English game of rugby. By the 1890s, college games were drawing huge crowds.

Basketball, invented by Dr. James Naismith of Springfield, Massachusetts, also became popular. Naismith developed the game in the 1890s as an indoor winter sport for his YMCA physical education classes. Considered the only major sport that is completely American in origin, basketball soon spread to other countries.

Americans not only watched but also participated in sports. Tennis and golf were enjoyed by the wealthy, usually in exclusive private clubs. Bicycling grew in popularity after

the "safety" bicycle was developed. These new bicycles used air-filled rubber tires instead of metal-rimmed wheels.

Large cities had many theaters. Plays performed ranged from serious dramas by Shakespeare to **vaudeville** (VAHD•vihl) shows, which were variety shows with dancing, singing, comedy, and magic acts. Tickets to vaudeville shows were inexpensive, making them very popular. The circus also attracted large crowds. In 1910 the United States had about 80 traveling circuses.

Thomas Edison invented "moving pictures" in the 1880s. The "movies" soon became enormously popular. Some theaters, called nickelodeons, charged five cents to see short films. The nickelodeons were the beginning of today's film industry.

Reading Check **Describe** What elements made up jazz music?

Study Central Need help understanding changes in American culture? Visit tajww1.glencoe.com and click on Study Central.

Reading Summary
Review the Main Ideas
- In the late 1800s and early 1900s, the number of public schools in the United States increased greatly, and the number of colleges for women and African Americans also grew.

- Newspaper and magazine readership increased greatly, and a number of American writers explored new themes.

- Distinctive styles of American art and music developed, and watching professional sports became a favorite leisure time activity.

What Did You Learn?

1. Describe the new philosophy of education that emerged around 1900.

2. What was yellow journalism?

Critical Thinking

3. **Summarizing Information** Re-create the diagram below and describe the work of each of these writers.

Writer	Description of work
Horatio Alger	
Stephen Crane	
Edith Wharton	

4. **The Big Ideas** Explain the correlation between leisure time and the development of the arts.

5. **Analyze** What did supporters of progressive education emphasize? What did they criticize in existing models of education?

6. **Creative Writing** Write a letter to Andrew Carnegie persuading him to establish a public library in your community. Describe the advantages of locating the library in your area and the benefits citizens would receive from his grant.

Section 4

The Progressive Movement

Guide to Reading

Looking Back, Looking Ahead

You learned that America's businesses and cities grew rapidly in the late 1800s. Such rapid growth allowed corruption in business and government to spread.

Focusing on the Main Ideas

- Americans took action against corruption in business and government. *(page 765)*
- New calls for reform were aided by writers who exposed government and business corruption. *(page 767)*
- In the early 1900s, more people received the right to vote, and the government began to regulate industry. *(page 769)*

Meeting People

William M. Tweed
Jacob Riis (REES)
Eugene V. Debs
Lincoln Steffens
Ida Tarbell
Upton Sinclair (sihn•KLEHR)
Robert La Follette (luh FAH•luht)
Theodore Roosevelt

Content Vocabulary

political machine
trust
oligopoly (AH•lih•GAH•puh•lee)
muckraker (MUHK•RAYK•uhr)
primary
initiative (ih•NIH•shuh•tiv)
referendum (REH•fuh•REHN•duhm)
recall
laissez-faire (LEH•ZAY•FEHR)
conservation

Academic Vocabulary

underlie
inspect

Reading Strategy

Organizing Information As you read Section 4, re-create the diagram below and list reforms for each category.

Reforms		
Government	Business	Voting

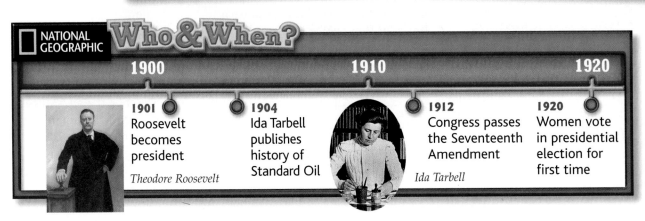

NATIONAL GEOGRAPHIC

Who & When?

1900 — 1910 — 1920

1901 Roosevelt becomes president

Theodore Roosevelt

1904 Ida Tarbell publishes history of Standard Oil

Ida Tarbell

1912 Congress passes the Seventeenth Amendment

1920 Women vote in presidential election for first time

Call for Reform

Main Idea **Americans took action against corruption in business and government.**

Reading Connection What would you think if the members of a school sports team who paid the coach the most money got to be the starting players? Read to find out how reformers worked to prevent unqualified and dishonest people from receiving important government jobs.

Many Americans called for reform in the late 1800s. The reformers, called progressives, had many different goals. These progressive reformers focused on urban problems, government, and business. They claimed that government and big business were taking advantage of the American people rather than serving them.

Fighting Corruption Political machines—powerful organizations linked to political parties—controlled local government in many cities. In each ward, or political district within a city, a machine representative controlled jobs and services. This representative was the political boss. A political boss was often a citizen's closest link to local government. Although they did help people, many bosses were dishonest.

Corrupt politicians found numerous ways to make money. They accepted bribes from tenement landlords in return for overlooking violations of city housing codes. They received campaign contributions from contractors hoping to do business with the city. They also accepted kickbacks. A kickback is an arrangement in which contractors padded the amount of their bill for city work and paid, or "kicked back," a percentage of that amount to the bosses.

Some politicians used their knowledge of city business for personal profit. One of the most corrupt city bosses, **William M. Tweed,** known as Boss Tweed, headed New York City's Democratic political machine in the 1860s and 1870s. Boss Tweed led a network of city officials called the Tweed ring.

Analyzing Political Cartoons

The Tweed Ring Boss Tweed and New York City officials are shown pointing to one another in response to the question "Who stole the people's money?" On Tweed's right, a man holds a hat labeled "Chairs," a reference to the $179,000 New York City paid for 40 chairs and 3 tables. Other contractors and cheats—their names on their coats—complete the "ring." *How did political bosses gain votes for their parties?*

"WHO STOLE THE PEOPLE'S MONEY?" — DO TELL .N.Y.TIMES   'TWAS HIM.

Ⓐ Boss Tweed   Ⓑ Peter Sweeny   Ⓒ Richard Connelly   Ⓓ Mayor A. Oakley Hall

The Tweed Ring controlled the police, courts, and some newspapers. Political cartoonist Thomas Nast exposed the Tweed ring's operations in his cartoons for *Harper's Weekly.* Tweed was convicted and sentenced to prison.

To break the power of political bosses, reformers founded organizations such as the National Municipal League in Philadelphia. These groups worked to make city governments more honest and efficient.

What Was the Spoils System?

The spoils system—rewarding political supporters with jobs and favors—had been common practice since the time of Andrew Jackson. Also called patronage, the system existed at all levels of government and led to numerous abuses. Many who received government jobs were not qualified. Some were dishonest.

A number of presidents, including Rutherford B. Hayes (1877–1881) and James Garfield (1881), wanted to change the spoils system. Hayes's efforts received little support, and Garfield was assassinated by an unsuccessful office seeker before he could launch his reforms.

When Vice President Chester A. Arthur succeeded Garfield, he tried to end the spoils system. In 1883 Congress passed the Pendleton Act, which established the Civil Service Commission to set up competitive examinations for federal jobs.

Controlling Business

During the late 1800s, many Americans came to believe that **trusts,** or combinations of companies, were becoming too large. They believed these trusts had too much control over the economy and the government. This public concern led to new laws.

In 1890 Congress passed the Sherman Antitrust Act, the first federal law to control trusts and monopolies. Supporters of the law hoped it would keep trusts from limiting competition. During the 1890s, however, the government rarely used the Sherman Act to curb business. Instead, it applied the act against labor unions, claiming that union strikes interfered with trade. Not until the early 1900s did the government win cases against trusts by using the Sherman Act.

Reining in the Railroads

The railroads functioned as an **oligopoly** (AH•lih•GAH•puh•lee)—a market structure in which a few large companies control the prices of the industry. In 1887 Congress passed the Interstate Commerce Act, which required railroads to charge "reasonable and just" rates and to publish those rates. The act also created the Interstate Commerce Commission (ICC) to supervise the railroad industry.

Lowering Tariffs

Reformers also wanted to lower tariffs. Many people believed that high tariffs led to higher prices for goods. In 1890 the Republicans raised tariffs sharply to protect American businesses from international competition. Voters showed their opposition to high tariffs by sending many Democrats to Congress. Grover Cleveland, who became president in 1893, also supported lower tariffs.

Reading Check **Explain** Why did many people want lower tariffs?

The New Reformers

Main Idea New calls for reform were aided by writers who exposed government and business corruption.

Reading Connection Have you ever watched the investigative reporters on your local television news shows? What sorts of problems do they report on? Read to find out about the investigative reporters who wrote about problems in government and business in the early 1900s.

An American Story

Newspaper reporter **Jacob Riis** (REES) shocked Americans with exposés of living conditions in large cities. With words and powerful photographs, Riis vividly portrayed immigrant life in New York City's crowded tenements.

> ❝ We used to go in the small hours of the morning into the worst tenements to count noses and see if the law against overcrowding was violated, and the sights I saw there gripped my heart until I felt that I must tell of them, or burst. ❞

—Jacob Riis,
The Making of an American

Socialists and Progressives

In the early 1900s, new ideas for correcting injustice and solving social problems emerged among American reformers. Socialism and progressivism were two such ideas.

Socialists believed a nation's resources and major industries should be owned and operated by the government on behalf of all the people—not by individuals and private companies for their own profit. **Eugene V. Debs** helped found the American Socialist Party in 1898. Under Debs's leadership, the party won some support in the early 1900s. Debs ran for president five times but never received more than 6 percent of the popular vote.

During the same period, progressives brought new energy to the reform movement. Like the socialists, many progressives were alarmed by the concentration of wealth and power in the hands of a few. Progressives rejected the socialist idea of government ownership of industries. Instead, they supported government efforts to regulate industry.

They also sought to reform government, to make it more efficient and better able to resist the influence of powerful business interests. Progressives also believed that society had an obligation to protect and help all its members. Many progressive reforms were meant to help those who lacked wealth and influence.

Who Were the Muckrakers? Journalists aided the reformers by exposing injustices and corruption. Investigative reporters wrote stories that brought problems to the attention of the public—and gained readers. These journalists were called **muckrakers** (MUHK•RAYK•uhrz) because they "raked" (exposed) the "muck" (dirt and corruption) **underlying** society.

One of the most effective muckrakers, **Lincoln Steffens,** reported for *McClure's Magazine.* Steffens's articles exposed corrupt machine politics in New York, Chicago, and other cities. **Ida Tarbell,** also writing for *McClure's,* described the unfair practices of the oil trust. Her articles led to public pressure for more government control over big business. In her 1904 book *The History of the Standard Oil Company,* she warned of the giant corporation's power.

In his novel *The Jungle,* published in 1906, **Upton Sinclair** (sihn•KLEHR) described the horrors of the meatpacking industry in Chicago. His vivid descriptions shocked Americans and helped persuade Congress to pass the Meat Inspection Act in 1906. That same year, Congress also passed the Pure Food and Drug Act, requiring accurate labeling of food and medicine and banning the sale of harmful food.

✓ **Reading Check** **Identify** Who wrote about unfair practices in the oil industry?

Biography

JACOB RIIS
1849–1914

Jacob Riis came to the United States from Denmark when he was 21. Riis lived in poverty for many years and often made police lodging houses his temporary home. In 1873 Riis began to work as a reporter and photographer for New York City newspapers. In addition to his own experience with poverty, Riis's job allowed him to further witness the poverty in which many lived in New York City.

Riis strongly believed that the poor were not to blame for their situation and felt that something should be done to help them. He realized he could use his newspaper stories to focus attention on the needs of the poor. Riis published many articles about the living conditions in the poorer sections of the city. These articles were accompanied by his photographs or illustrations, which brought to life the circumstances in which the city's inhabitants lived and worked. In 1890 Riis wrote *How the Other Half Lives*. By taking pictures of the tenements, Riis was able to bring the terrible conditions of the slums to the attention of readers. His book helped establish housing codes to prevent the worst abuses.

> *"The poor we shall always have with us, but the slum we need not have."*
>
> **—Jacob Riis, *Battle with the Slum***

When Theodore Roosevelt became the city's police commissioner, he asked Riis to present a reform program. Through Riis's efforts, many playgrounds and parks were established in the city. Riis helped make others aware of the problems many urban Americans faced in their daily lives. He was later known as one of the first muckraking journalists, a group of people whose articles and photographs exposed corruption and social problems in American life. Riis served as an example of what individuals could do to lessen these problems.

Then and Now

Are photographs still a powerful means of exposing corruption and injustice? Explain.

Expanding Democracy

Main Idea **In the early 1900s, more people received the right to vote, and the government began to regulate industry.**

Reading Connection Do you consider protecting public parks and the environment to be an important issue? Read to find out about one of the first American presidents to be concerned with the environment.

In the early 1900s, progressives backed a number of reforms designed to increase the people's direct control of the government. **Robert La Follette** (luh FAH•luht), known as "Fighting Bob," led Wisconsin's reform-minded Republicans. La Follette's greatest achievement was reforming the state electoral system. Candidates for general elections in Wisconsin had been chosen at state conventions run by party bosses. La Follette introduced a direct **primary** election, allowing the state's voters to choose their party's candidates. Reformers in other states copied this "Wisconsin idea."

What Was the Oregon System?

The state of Oregon also made important changes in the political process to give voters more power. The reforms in Oregon included a direct primary election and the initiative, the referendum, and the recall.

The **initiative** (ih•NIH•shuh•tiv) allowed citizens to place a measure or issue on the ballot in a state election. The **referendum** (REH•fuh•REHN•duhm) gave voters the opportunity to accept or reject measures that the state legislature enacted. The **recall** enabled voters to remove unsatisfactory elected officials from their jobs. These reforms were called the Oregon System. Other western states soon adopted the reforms.

Picturing **History**

Before the passage of the Nineteenth Amendment, many women campaigned for the right to vote. *Which was the first state to allow women to vote?*

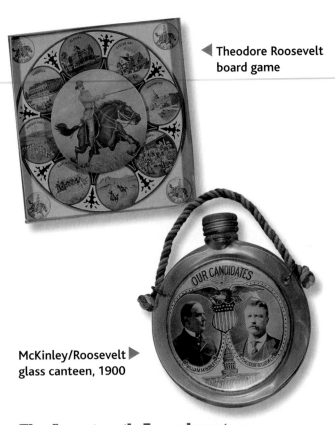

◀ Theodore Roosevelt
board game

McKinley/Roosevelt ▶
glass canteen, 1900

The Seventeenth Amendment Progressives also changed the way U.S. senators are elected. The Constitution had given state legislatures the responsibility for choosing senators, but party bosses and business interests often controlled the selection process. Progressives wanted to give the people an opportunity to vote for their senators directly. Support for this idea grew. In 1912 Congress passed the Seventeenth Amendment to the Constitution to provide for the direct election of senators. Ratified in 1913, the amendment gave the people a voice in selecting their representatives.

📖 *(See page 264 for the text of the Seventeenth Amendment.)*

The Fight for Suffrage At the Seneca Falls Convention in 1848, women had called for the right to vote. After the Civil War, Congress passed the Fifteenth Amendment, giving voting rights to freed men—but not to women. Some leading abolitionists became suffragists, men and women who fought for woman suffrage, or women's right to vote. The suffragists won their early victories in the West. First as a territory in

1869 and then as a state in 1890, Wyoming led the nation in giving women the vote. Between 1910 and 1913, six other states adopted woman suffrage. By 1919 women could vote in at least some elections in most of the 48 states.

In 1919 Congress voted in favor of the Nineteenth Amendment, which allowed woman suffrage. The amendment was ratified in 1920, in time for women to vote in that year's presidential election. For the first time, American women were able to participate in the election of their national leaders.

"Trustbuster" in the White House

President William McKinley, elected in 1900, was assassinated less than a year later. Suddenly, 42-year-old **Theodore Roosevelt**, the Republican vice president, took over the top office and became the youngest president in the nation's history. When Roosevelt moved into the White House in 1901, he brought progressivism with him.

President McKinley had favored big business, but President Roosevelt was known to support business regulation and other progressive reforms. In 1902 Roosevelt ordered the Justice Department to take legal action against certain trusts that had violated the Sherman Antitrust Act. His first target was the Northern Securities Company, a railroad monopoly formed by financiers J.P. Morgan and James J. Hill to control transportation in the Northwest. The Supreme Court finally decided that Northern Securities had illegally limited trade and ordered the trust to be taken apart.

During the rest of Roosevelt's term as president, he obtained a total of 25 indictments (legal charges) against trusts in the beef, oil, and tobacco industries. Although hailed as a trustbuster, Roosevelt did not want to break up all trusts. As he saw it, trusts should be regulated, not destroyed.

Roosevelt ran for the presidency in 1904, promising the people a Square Deal—fair and equal treatment for all. He was elected with more than 57 percent of the popular vote.

Roosevelt's Policies Roosevelt's "Square Deal" called for a considerable amount of government regulation of business. This contrasted with an attitude toward business that dated back to the presidency of Thomas Jefferson, which was summed up in the phrase **laissez-faire** (LEH•ZAY FEHR). This French term generally means "let people do as they choose."

Roosevelt introduced a new era of government regulation. He supported the Meat Inspection and Pure Food and Drug Acts; these acts gave the Department of Agriculture and the Food and Drug Administration the power to visit businesses and **inspect** their products.

Why Was Conservation Important?

Roosevelt held a lifelong enthusiasm for the great outdoors and the wilderness. He believed in the need for **conservation,** the protection and preservation of natural resources. As president,

Roosevelt took steps to conserve the country's forests, mineral deposits, and water resources. In 1905 he proposed the creation of the U.S. Forest Service. He pressured Congress to set aside millions of acres of national forests and created the nation's first wildlife sanctuaries. Roosevelt also formed the National Conservation Commission, which produced the first survey of the country's natural resources.

Roosevelt has been called America's first environmental president. While he made conservation an important public issue, Roosevelt also recognized the need for economic growth and development. He tried to strike a balance between business interests and protection of the environment and conservation.

✓ **Reading Check** **Identify** What reform allowed voters to place a measure on the ballot?

Study Central Need help understanding the Progressive Movement? Visit tajwwI.glencoe.com and click on Study Central.

Reading Summary

Review the Main Ideas

- Americans became angered by corrupt politicians who made money illegally and by large trusts, which began to control the economy and the government.

- Socialists and progressives wanted the government to more tightly control business practices, and reforming journalists exposed injustices and corruption in business.

- Changes led to more political control for common citizens, and the government began to regulate industry and conserve the environment.

What Did You Learn?

1. Explain how the Civil Service Commission helped eliminate the spoils system.

2. What industry did Upton Sinclair describe in his book *The Jungle*?

Critical Thinking

3. **Organizing Information** Recreate the diagram below and show how the Seventeenth Amendment reformed the political process.

Seventeenth Amendment	
Policy before	Policy after

4. **Compare and Contrast** Write a paragraph comparing socialist and progressive views on industry.

5. **Analyze** Examine the political cartoon on page 765. Why are the individuals pointing to someone else? What statement is cartoonist Thomas Nast making about the extent of political corruption in New York City?

6. **The Big Ideas** Write an essay summarizing the role of muckrakers in the reform movement. How would the reform movement have been different if the press were controlled by the government instead of being free?

WILD WONDERS

GRIZZLY BEARS, WOLVES, MOOSE, CARIBOU, DALL'S SHEEP and many other animals roam Alaska's Denali National Park and Preserve. Larger than Massachusetts, the six-million-acre park includes the highest mountain in North America.

The Alaskan wilderness area set aside as Mount McKinley National Park in 1917 was renamed Denali in 1980 when Congress tripled the size of the park. Denali was the peak's Native American name, meaning "the High One."

The idea of setting aside areas of natural beauty and historic importance for the benefit of the people dates back to the mid-1800s. Before then, Americans had viewed wild places either as obstacles or as a source of natural resources for people to use.

The conservation movement gained popularity in the early 1900s when President Theodore Roosevelt and other conservationists urged Americans to protect natural resources.

Today conservation continues to be an important issue. Although many of us enjoy visiting national parks such as Denali, the parks also serve as refuges for wildlife. Scientists study the plants and animals so that they can protect them. With 430 species of flowering plants, 37 species of mammals, and 156 species of birds, Denali is one of America's great areas of unspoiled wilderness.

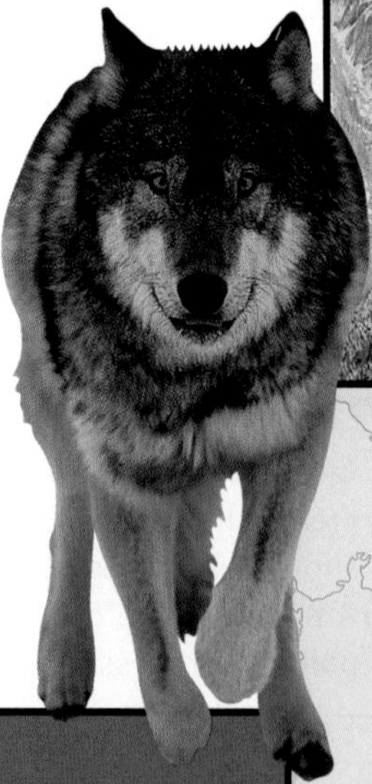

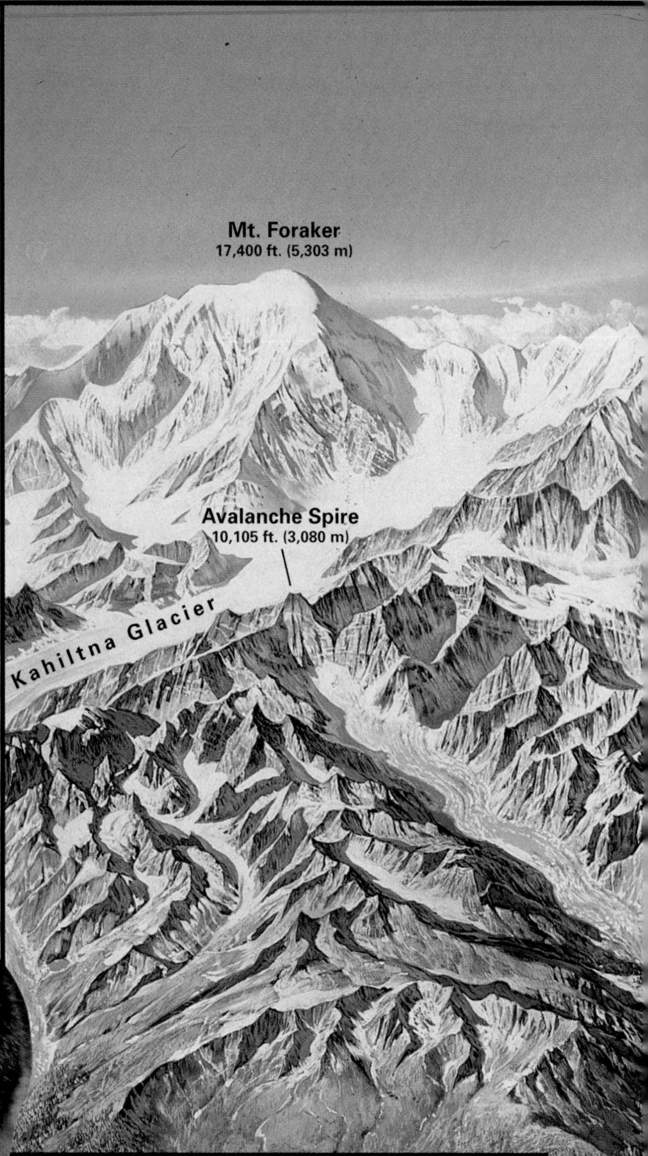

Mt. Foraker
17,400 ft. (5,303 m)

Avalanche Spire
10,105 ft. (3,080 m)

Kahiltna Glacier

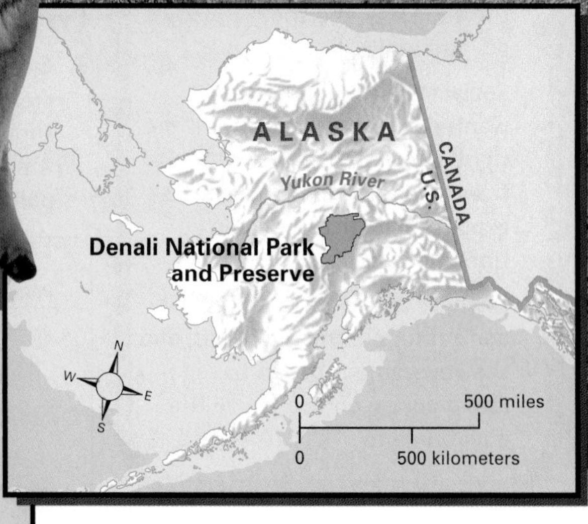

ALASKA
Yukon River
CANADA
U.S.

Denali National Park and Preserve

N
W   E
S

0   500 miles

0   500 kilometers

LEARNING from GEOGRAPHY

1. Which peaks are higher than 15,000 feet?

2. Do you think it is necessary for the government to aid environmental programs? Explain.

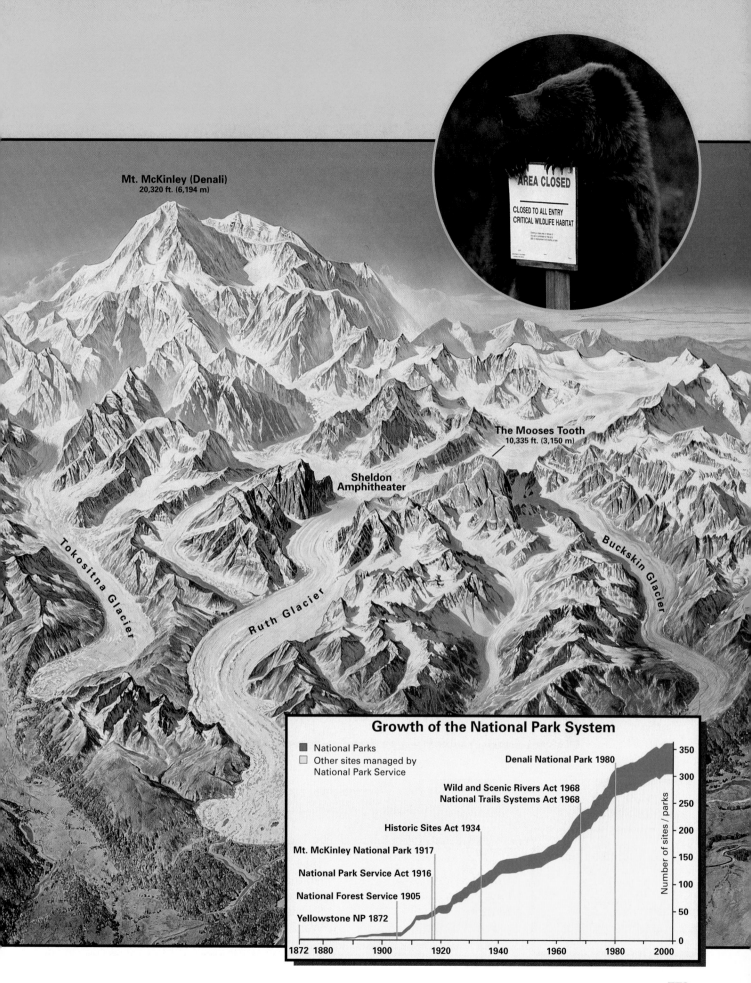

Mt. McKinley (Denali)
20,320 ft. (6,194 m)

AREA CLOSED

CLOSED TO ALL ENTRY
CRITICAL WILDLIFE HABITAT

The Mooses Tooth
10,335 ft. (3,150 m)

Sheldon
Amphitheater

Tokositna Glacier

Ruth Glacier

Buckskin Glacier

Growth of the National Park System

■ National Parks
□ Other sites managed by
National Park Service

Denali National Park 1980

Wild and Scenic Rivers Act 1968
National Trails Systems Act 1968

Historic Sites Act 1934

Mt. McKinley National Park 1917

National Park Service Act 1916

National Forest Service 1905

Yellowstone NP 1872

Number of sites / parks

350
300
250
200
150
100
50
0

1872 1880   1900   1920   1940   1960   1980   2000

A Changing Nation

Guide to Reading

Looking Back, Looking Ahead

You learned that American reformers attempted to reduce corruption in business and government. At the same time, Americans wanted to expand their power and trade around the world.

Focusing on the Main Ideas

- The United States demonstrated its power in areas such as Latin America and the Pacific. *(page 775)*
- Many ethnic and religious minorities in America faced discrimination and even violence. *(page 778)*
- Minority groups in the United States sought to end discrimination and gain equal rights. *(page 780)*

Locating Places

Alaska
Hawaiian Islands
Cuba
Guam
Philippines
Panama

Content Vocabulary

isthmus (IHS•muhs)
discrimination
  (dihs•KRIH•muh•NAY•shuhn)
ward
barrio (BAHR•ee•OH)

Academic Vocabulary

reject
modify (MAH•duh•FY)
bias (BY•uhs)

Reading Strategy

Analyzing Information As you study Section 5, re-create the diagram below and describe the policies listed.

	Description
Roosevelt Corollary	
Dollar Diplomacy	
Moral Diplomacy	

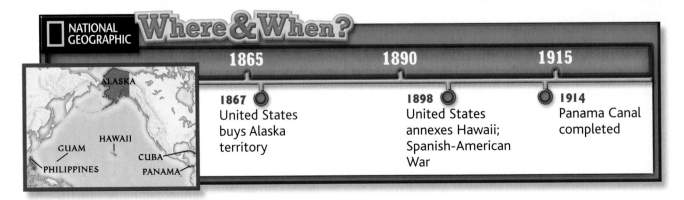

NATIONAL GEOGRAPHIC **Where & When?**

ALASKA
HAWAII
GUAM
PHILIPPINES
CUBA
PANAMA

1865   1890   1915

1867
United States buys Alaska territory

1898
United States annexes Hawaii; Spanish-American War

1914
Panama Canal completed

American Foreign Policy

The United States demonstrated its power in areas such as Latin America and the Pacific.

Reading Connection Have you ever wondered how the United States came to include places such as Alaska and Hawaii which are so far from the continental states? Read to find out how the United States expanded its power around the world.

An American Story

In the late 1800s and early 1900s, Americans looked beyond their borders and yearned for an empire. Merchants desired overseas markets, and adventurers wanted another frontier to conquer. Senator Albert Beveridge voiced the feelings of many when he proclaimed in 1900:

> ❝ The Philippines are ours forever.
> . . . And just beyond the Philippines
> are China's illimitable markets. We
> will not retreat from either. . . . The
> Pacific is our ocean. ❞
>
> —Albert Beveridge,
> "In Support of an American
> Empire"

Goals of Foreign Policy

When President George Washington published his Farewell Address in 1796, he advised Americans to increase trade with other countries but to have "as little political connection as possible." Above all else, he warned Americans to "steer clear of permanent alliances with any portion of the foreign world." These principles guided American foreign policy for about 100 years. However, various people interpreted Washington's words in different ways. Some believed he meant that the United States should follow a policy of isolationism, or noninvolvement, in world affairs. Others believed that Washington supported trade with other countries and was not calling for complete isolation from the world.

How Did the United States Expand?

Soon after the Civil War, some American leaders began to push for the United States to expand beyond its borders. They believed that acquiring new territories would increase trade and allow the United States to become a world power. In 1867 Secretary of State William Seward negotiated the purchase of **Alaska,** which was Russian territory at the time. At first, many people ridiculed Alaska as "Seward's Ice Box." The discovery of gold there later proved the value of the region's natural resources.

In 1898, during the presidency of William McKinley, the United States annexed—took control of—the **Hawaiian Islands.** The islands provided a base for the American navy. From Hawaii the United States could oversee its trade in Japan and China.

That same year, the United States went to war with Spain. The American press had aroused intense anger by reporting the brutal way that Spain crushed a rebellion in **Cuba.** Almost immediately, fighting extended to Spanish colonies in the Pacific Ocean as well as in Cuba. When the Spanish-American War ended, not only did Cuba gain its independence, but the United States also gained **Guam** and the **Philippines.**

Although about 400 American soldiers died fighting in the war, more than 2,000 died of diseases such as yellow fever, malaria, and other diseases contracted in the tropical climate. The African Americans who served faced the additional burden of discrimination. Serving in segregated units, African Americans battled alongside the Cuban rebel army, in which black and white troops fought as equals.

American Interest in Latin America

Since colonial times, the United States had carried on a flourishing trade with Latin America, including the Caribbean region. Fear of European influence in the region was a factor that led to the Monroe Doctrine in 1823, when President James Monroe warned European nations not to attempt to establish new colonies in North or South America.

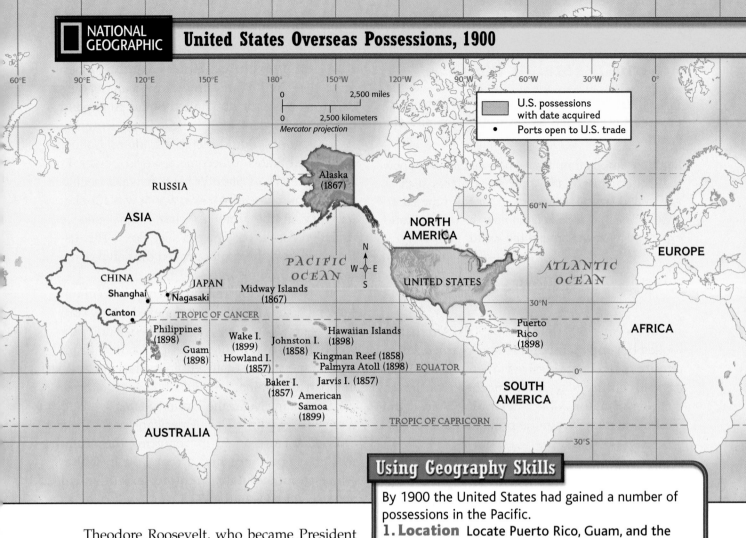

United States Overseas Possessions, 1900

NATIONAL GEOGRAPHIC

Legend:
- U.S. possessions with date acquired
- Ports open to U.S. trade

Alaska (1867)

RUSSIA

ASIA

NORTH AMERICA

EUROPE

CHINA

JAPAN

Shanghai · Nagasaki

Canton

PACIFIC OCEAN

UNITED STATES

ATLANTIC OCEAN

AFRICA

Midway Islands (1867)

TROPIC OF CANCER

Philippines (1898)

Wake I. (1899)

Guam (1898)

Howland I. (1857)

Johnston I. (1858)

Hawaiian Islands (1898)

Kingman Reef (1858)

Palmyra Atoll (1898)

EQUATOR

Baker I. (1857)

Jarvis I. (1857)

American Samoa (1899)

Puerto Rico (1898)

SOUTH AMERICA

AUSTRALIA

TROPIC OF CAPRICORN

2,500 miles / 2,500 kilometers — Mercator projection

Using Geography Skills

By 1900 the United States had gained a number of possessions in the Pacific.
1. **Location** Locate Puerto Rico, Guam, and the Philippines. Which of these is farthest from the continental United States?
2. **Analyze** When were the Hawaiian Islands acquired?

Theodore Roosevelt, who became President after McKinley's assassination in 1901, worried that instability in the Caribbean region would lead European powers to intervene. In 1902 Venezuela and the Dominican Republic were deeply in debt to European nations. Roosevelt was concerned that European powers would step in to protect their financial interests there.

The president responded to these incidents in 1904 by asserting America's right to act as a "policeman" in Latin America, intervening "however reluctantly . . . in cases of wrong-doing." This policy, known as the Roosevelt Corollary, was an addition to the Monroe Doctrine. Up to that time, the United States had used the Monroe Doctrine only to prevent European intervention in Latin America. Under the Roosevelt Corollary, the United States now claimed the right to intervene in the affairs of Latin American nations whenever those nations seemed unstable. Roosevelt liked to proclaim "Speak softly, but carry a big stick." He meant

that he preferred peace, but that he would use force when necessary. Roosevelt put his "big stick" to use to advance U.S. interests in Panama.

The Panama Canal For years the United States and other countries had wanted to build a canal across Central America to connect the Atlantic and Pacific Oceans. An ideal location for such a canal was across the **isthmus** (IHS•muhs) of **Panama.** An isthmus is a narrow strip of land that connects two larger landmasses—in this case, North and South America. Colombia, however, controlled Panama, and the Colombian legislature **rejected** the United States's offer to buy a strip of land across the isthmus.

To obtain the canal site, Roosevelt helped organize a revolt in Panama in 1903. With the help of American marines, the Panamanian rebels overthrew their Colombian rulers and set up their own government. The United States and the new government of Panama quickly signed a canal treaty. For $10 million plus an annual fee, Panama granted Americans control of a strip across the isthmus. Finished in 1914, the Panama Canal ranks as one of the great engineering works of all time.

Taft and Wilson Theodore Roosevelt thought of American power mostly in military terms. His successor in the White House, William Howard Taft, took a different view. Taft hoped to **modify** American foreign policy. He believed that American investments would bring stability to troubled areas of the world, as well as profit and power to the United States, without the need for force. Taft's approach was known as dollar diplomacy.

Elected in 1912, the new president, Woodrow Wilson said he wanted to promote democracy and further the cause of world peace. This new policy was called "moral diplomacy" because its purpose was to help other countries.

The Mexican Revolution From 1884 to 1911, a dictator named Porfirio Díaz, ruled Mexico. A few wealthy landowners dominated Mexican society. Most of the Mexican people were poor and owned no land. In 1911 Francisco Madero, a reformer who called for constitutional government and land reform, forced Díaz from power. Reform came slowly, however, and rebel groups fought against Madero's forces. Madero was captured and murdered and Venustiano Carranza, whose forces had acquired arms from the United States, became Mexico's president.

When the U.S. government came out openly in support of Carranza, rebel leader Pancho Villa retaliated by raiding U.S. border towns, most notably Columbus, New Mexico. American troops under General John J. Pershing crossed the border into Mexico and pursued Villa but were unsuccessful.

The Mexican Revolution had been the first major effort in Latin America to overturn the system of large estates in the hands of the few and raise the living standards for the Mexican people. Out of the revolution emerged historic social and economic reform. The revolution also was responsible for the first big wave of immigration from Mexico to the United States. More than 1 million refugees entered the United States. They influenced the culture and contributed to the economic and political development of the Southwest in particular and the nation as a whole.

✓ **Reading Check** Explain On what principles did Wilson base his foreign policy?

History *Through Art*

***Work Trains, Miraflores* by Alson Skinner Clark**
This painting shows the building of the Panama Canal. The stamp commemorates the canal's 25th anniversary. *What role did the United States play in the independence of Panama?*

Facing Prejudice at Home

Main Idea **Many ethnic and religious minorities in America faced discrimination and even violence.**

Reading Connection What might it have been like to travel thousands of miles to a new land, hoping to start a new, successful life, only to be told that you could go only to certain schools or hold certain low-paying jobs? Read to learn about the discrimination faced by some new immigrants to the United States around the turn of the century.

During the 1800s the overwhelming majority of Americans were white and Protestant and had been born in the United States. Many Americans believed that the United States should remain a white, Protestant nation. Nonwhite, non-Protestant, and nonnative residents often faced **discrimination** (dihs•KRIH•muh•NAY•shuhn) —unequal treatment because of their race, religion, ethnic background, or place of birth. The government rarely interfered with this discrimination.

Anti-Semitism Many Jewish immigrants came to the United States to escape prejudice in their homelands. Some of them found the same anti-Semitic attitudes in America. Landlords, employers, and schools discriminated against Jewish immigrants. Eastern European Jews faced prejudice both as Jews and as eastern Europeans, whom many Americans regarded as more foreign than western Europeans.

Anti-Catholicism Catholics also faced discrimination because of their religion. America's largely Protestant population feared that Catholic immigrants threatened the "American" way of life. Anti-Catholic Iowans formed the American Protective Association (APA) in 1887.

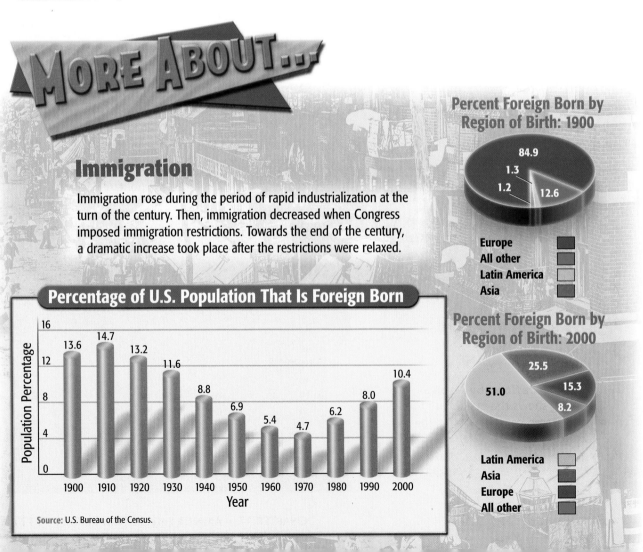

MORE ABOUT...

Immigration

Immigration rose during the period of rapid industrialization at the turn of the century. Then, immigration decreased when Congress imposed immigration restrictions. Towards the end of the century, a dramatic increase took place after the restrictions were relaxed.

Percent Foreign Born by Region of Birth: 1900

- 84.9
- 1.3
- 1.2
- 12.6

Europe
All other
Latin America
Asia

Percent Foreign Born by Region of Birth: 2000

- 25.5
- 51.0
- 15.3
- 8.2

Latin America
Asia
Europe
All other

Percentage of U.S. Population That Is Foreign Born

Year	Population Percentage
1900	13.6
1910	14.7
1920	13.2
1930	11.6
1940	8.8
1950	6.9
1960	5.4
1970	4.7
1980	6.2
1990	8.0
2000	10.4

Source: U.S. Bureau of the Census.

A Ku Klux Klan pamphlet (right) promotes the Klan's hate campaign. Meanwhile, opponents of lynching called for an end to racial murders. *What two groups experienced the terror of lynching?*

By the mid-1890s, the APA claimed a membership of two million, mostly in the West. Among other activities, the APA spread rumors that Catholics were preparing to take over the country.

What Were Anti-Asian Policies?

Discrimination was also based on race. In California and other Western states, Asians struggled against prejudice and resentment. White Americans claimed that Chinese immigrants, who worked for lower wages, took away jobs. Congress passed the Chinese Exclusion Act in 1882 to prevent Chinese immigrants from entering the United States.

America's westward expansion created opportunities for thousands of Japanese immigrants who came to the United States to work as railroad or farm laborers. Like the Chinese who had come before them, Japanese immigrants encountered prejudice. California would not allow them to become citizens. In 1906 in San Francisco, the school board tried to make Japanese children attend a separate school for Asians until President Roosevelt stepped in to prevent such segregation.

Roosevelt yielded to a rising tide of anti-Japanese feeling, however, and authorized the Gentlemen's Agreement with Japan in 1907. This agreement restricted Japanese immigration to the United States, but it did not bring an end to anti-Japanese feeling. In 1913 California made it illegal for Japanese immigrants to buy land. Other Western states passed similar laws.

Discrimination Against African Americans

Four-fifths of the nation's African Americans lived in the South. Most worked as rural sharecroppers or in low-paying jobs in the cities. They were separated from white society in their own neighborhoods, schools, parks, restaurants, theaters, and even cemeteries. In 1896 the Supreme Court legalized segregation in the case of *Plessy v. Ferguson,* which recognized "separate but equal" facilities.

The Ku Klux Klan, which had terrorized African Americans during Reconstruction, was reborn in Georgia in 1915. The new Klan wanted to restore white, Protestant America. The Klan lashed out against minorities—Catholics, Jews, and immigrants, as well as African Americans.

Racial Violence People who lost their jobs during the economic depressions of 1893 and 1907 sometimes unleashed their anger against African Americans and other minorities. More than 2,600 African Americans were lynched between 1886 and 1916, mostly in the South. Lynchings were also used to terrorize Chinese immigrants in the West.

Racial violence also occurred in the North, however. A 1908 riot in Springfield, Illinois, Abraham Lincoln's hometown, shocked the nation. A false accusation by a white woman led to the lynching of two African Americans, and dozens more were injured. No one was ever punished for these violent crimes.

Ida B. Wells, the editor of an African American newspaper in Memphis, Tennessee, was forced to leave town after publishing the names of people involved in a lynching. The incident started Wells on a national crusade to stop lynching. Although Congress rejected an anti-lynching bill, the number of lynchings decreased significantly in the 1900s due in great part to activists such as Wells.

Progressivism and Prejudice In the late 1800s and the early 1900s, many Americans held **biased** views. They believed that white, male, native-born Americans had the right to make decisions for all of society.

Most of the progressive reformers came from the middle and upper classes. They saw themselves as moral leaders working to improve the lives of people less fortunate than themselves. Nevertheless, the reforms they supported often discriminated against one group as they tried to help another group.

Trade unions often prohibited African Americans, women, and immigrants from joining. Skilled laborers, these unions argued, could obtain better working conditions for themselves if they did not demand improved conditions for all workers. In spite of these problems, progressive reforms did succeed in improving conditions for many Americans.

Reading Check **Identify** What Supreme Court decision legalized segregation?

Struggle for Equal Opportunity

Main Idea Minority groups in the United States sought to end discrimination and gain equal rights.

Reading Connection Have you ever joined a group that worked toward a common cause? Read to find out how some people formed groups to work to end discrimination.

Booker T. Washington, who founded the Tuskegee Institute, believed that if African Americans gained economic power, they would be in a better position to demand equality. Washington founded the National Negro Business League to promote business development among African Americans. In Washington's autobiography, *Up from Slavery*, he counseled African Americans to work patiently toward equality. Washington argued that equality would be achieved when African Americans gained the education and skills to become valuable members of their community.

Other African Americans had different ideas about attaining equality. W.E.B. Du Bois (doo•BAWIHS), an educator and activist, believed that gaining and using the right to vote would best help African Americans succeed. He helped found the National Association for the Advancement of Colored People (NAACP) in 1909. Some African Americans thought that they would be better off in separate societies, either in the United States or in Africa. They founded organizations to establish African American towns and promoted a back-to-Africa movement. These movements were not popular, however.

During the early 1900s, African Americans achieved success in a variety of professions. Chemist George Washington Carver, director of agricultural research at Tuskegee Institute, helped improve the economy of the South through his discoveries of plant products. Maggie Lena founded the St. Luke Penny Savings Bank in Richmond, Virginia. She was the first American woman to serve as a bank president.

Biography

BOOKER T. WASHINGTON
1856–1915

W.E.B. DU BOIS
1868–1963

In the late 1800s and early 1900s, two of the most important African American leaders were Booker T. Washington and W.E.B. Du Bois. Both men had the same goals, but they took different approaches to reaching those goals.

Washington was born into slavery. Later, he attended an industrial school and went on to become a teacher. As a teacher, he developed his own theories about education, which led him to found the Tuskegee Institute.

Washington became an influential leader who advised presidents and governors. He gained support because he was willing—temporarily—to compromise on political rights for African Americans. In return, Washington wanted support for African American schools, economic gains, and an end to violence against African Americans.

▲ **Booker T. Washington**

W.E.B. Du Bois, the first African American to receive a doctorate degree from Harvard, refused to accept racial inequality. Du Bois helped start the Niagara Movement in 1905 to fight against racial discrimination and demand full political rights and responsibilities for African Americans. Later, Du Bois joined others to form the National Association for the Advancement of Colored People (NAACP). This group today remains a force in the efforts to gain legal and economic equality for African Americans. Du Bois rejected Washington's emphasis on job skills and argued that the right to vote was the way to end racial inequality, stop lynching, and gain better schools. "The power of the ballot we need in sheer self-defense," he said, "else what shall save us from a second slavery?"

◄ **W.E.B. Du Bois**

Then and Now

Why did Washington and Du Bois take the stands they did? Which leaders today have taken stands for equal rights for all?

Native Americans Seek Justice The federal government's efforts to assimilate Native Americans into white society threatened to break down traditional native cultures. In 1910–1911 Native American leaders from around the country formed the Society of American Indians to seek justice for Native Americans, to improve their living conditions, and to educate white Americans about different Native American cultures. Some leaders believed that Native Americans should leave the reservations and make their own way in white society.

George Washington Carver

In his studies in botany and agriculture at the Tuskegee Institute, George Washington Carver made a number of amazing discoveries. He found dozens of new uses for plants such as the peanut and sweet potato. A teacher for nearly 50 years, Carver taught his students, often the children of formerly enslaved people, to conserve land and resources.

The primary idea in all of my work was to help the farmer and fill the poor man's empty dinner pail. . . . My idea is to help the "man farthest down," this is why I have made every process just as simply as I could to put it within his reach.
—George Washington Carver

DBQ Document-Based Question

What was Carver's purpose in much of his work? How did he do this?

Surprisingly, at the time the Fourteenth Amendment was passed, Native Americans, who were considered **wards,** or persons under the legal guardianship of the U.S. government, were not granted citizenship under the amendment. In 1924 Congress reversed this ruling by granting citizenship to all Native Americans who did not possess it.

Mexican Americans Work Together

Immigrants from Mexico had long come to the United States as laborers, especially in the West and Southwest. Like the Japanese and other immigrant groups, Mexican Americans encountered discrimination and violence. Relying on themselves to solve their problems, they formed *mutualistas*—self-defense associations—to raise money for insurance and legal help. One of the first *mutualistas* was the Alianza Hispano Americo (Hispanic American Alliance), formed in Tucson, Arizona, in 1894. In labor camps and Mexican neighborhoods called **barrios** (BAHR•ee•OHS), *mutualistas* worked to end overcrowding, poor sanitation, and inadequate public services.

César Chávez Organizes Mexican Workers

From the early 1900s on, some efforts were made to organize farmworkers but with little success. In the 1960s, however, César Chávez (CHAH•vehz), born in 1927, finally began making real headway in organizing the workers in the California vineyards and lettuce fields. In 1962 he organized farmworkers into the organization called the United Farm Workers (UFW) and started a five-year strike against California grape growers to force them to recognize the union. The UFW organized a nationwide boycott of table grapes. Sympathetic priests, civic groups, and students aided Chávez in his efforts. In 1965 he launched a strike that led to a nationwide boycott of produce not bearing the label of the United Farm Workers. In 1970, the strikers finally won, and the strike ended in a pact with the growers. By 1975 Chávez and the strikers had convinced the California legislature to pass a bill that gave farmworkers the same rights held by union members elsewhere.

Changes and Challenges By 1914 the United States had changed tremendously. Its population had grown and become more urban than rural. The nation had become industrialized, and people traveled by train, automobile, and even airplane.

While the United States had used its power to establish a limited empire in far-off lands, it had steered clear of Europe's arguments and wars. However, the conflict that was growing in Europe by 1914 would develop into a war that would entangle much of the world. Once the United States became involved, its position in the world would change forever.

Looking to the Future Then, as now, Americans approached the future as a free nation committed to the truths expressed in the Declaration of Independence. The Declaration protects the rights of the American people and states that the purpose of government is to protect these rights:

> 66 We hold these truths to be self-evident, that all men are created equal, that they are endowed by their Creator with certain unalienable Rights, that among these are Life, Liberty and the pursuit of Happiness. That to secure these rights, Governments are instituted among Men, deriving their just powers from the consent of the governed. . . . 99

✓ **Reading Check** **Describe** What were *mutualistas*?

Section 5 Review

Study Central Need help understanding the struggle for equal opportunity? Visit tajwwI.glencoe.com and click on Study Central.

Reading Summary
Review the Main Ideas

• The United States pursued an increasingly international role, especially in Latin America and the Pacific.

• Discrimination and violence were painful, pressing issues for many groups and often went unaddressed by the federal government.

• Minority groups developed strategies for working together to end racial and social discrimination.

What Did You Learn?

1. What was the significance of the Panama Canal?

2. How did the Supreme Court legalize segregation?

Critical Thinking

3. **Summarizing Information** Re-create the diagram below to describe how different minority groups worked toward equality and change.

	Describe
African Americans	
Native Americans	
Mexican Americans	

4. **The Big Ideas** Explain the United States's interest in Latin America.

5. **Describe** What was the impact of African Americans who pioneered new means for achieving equality? Write a paragraph that includes references to Booker T. Washington, George Washington Carver, and Maggie Lena.

6. **Linking Past to Present** Summarize the plight of Mexican farmworkers during this period and the impact of César Chávez later in the century. What was the lasting legacy of his work?

TIME NOTEBOOK

STEP BACK IN TIME

What—and who—were people talking about? What did they eat? What did they do for fun? These two pages will give you some clues to everyday life in the U.S. as you step back in time with TIME Notebook.

Profile

BOOKER T. WASHINGTON *Teaching industrial training as a means to success, in 1881 Washington founded the Tuskegee Institute in Alabama. Here is an excerpt from his autobiography,* Up From Slavery.

FROM THE VERY BEGINNING, AT TUSKEGEE, I was determined to have the students do not only the agricultural and domestic work, but to have them erect their own buildings. My plan was to have them, while performing this service, taught the latest and best methods of labour, so that the school would not only get the benefit of their efforts, but the students themselves would be taught to see not only utility in labour, but beauty and dignity. . . . My plan was not to teach them to work in the old way, but to show them how to make the forces of nature—air, water, steam, electricity, horse-power—assist them in their labour.

Booker T. Washington

VERBATIM

WHAT PEOPLE ARE SAYING

❝ If you pick up a starving dog and make him prosperous, he will not bite you. This is the principal difference between a dog and a man. ❞

MARK TWAIN,
author of
The Adventures of Tom Sawyer

❝ Speak softly and carry a big stick; you will go far. ❞
PRESIDENT TEDDY ROOSEVELT,
proposing action when asked how the United States will deal with its new far-flung colonies in 1901

❝ Give me your tired, your poor, your huddled masses yearning to breathe free. ❞
WORDS BY EMMA LAZARUS,
engraved on the Statue of Liberty in 1903

❝ Mountains! Look at them! ❞
EDWARD CORSI,
10-year-old Italian immigrant on spotting the high-rise buildings in New York City for the first time in 1907

It's The Law

Two laws were passed in 1902 to deal with the automobile.

❶ Tennessee demands all drivers give the public a week's notice before they start any trip.

❷ Vermont states an adult waving a red flag has to walk in front of any moving automobile.

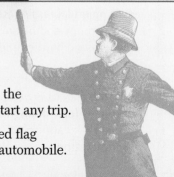

MILESTONES
EVENTS AND PEOPLE OF THE TIME

SIGNED UP. Sharpshooter **ANNIE OAKLEY** to Buffalo Bill's Wild West Show in 1885.

FLEW. 19-year-old Cromwell Dixon over the Continental Divide in 1911 in a biplane. At age 14, Dixon was building **DIRIGIBLES** (sausage-shaped balloons), including a model that could be pedaled through the air like a bicycle. Dixon later traveled around the country, flying at state fairs.

Annie Oakley

AMERICAN SCENE
Average Life Spans in 1900

Average life expectancy: **47.3 years**

Male life expectancy: **46.3 years**

Female life expectancy: **48.3 years**

White life expectancy: **47.6 years**

Nonwhite life expectancy: **33.0 years**

| 0 | 10 | 20 | 30 | 40 | 50 years |

TRANSPORTATION
Take a Ride in My Car!

Here's what one magazine from the early 1900s recommends you carry in your car at all times:

1 Efficient tire pump

1 Strong two-gallon can extra gasoline

1 Sheet fine sandpaper

1 Small, short-handled axe

1 Ball asbestos cord

4 Half-pound cans of meat or fish

2 Pounds sweet chocolate

BETTMANN/CORBIS

NUMBERS
U.S. AT THE TIME

12¢ Price of a dozen eggs in 1910

$12 Price of a sewing machine in 1900

SCHENECTADY MUSEUM/HALL OF ELECTRICAL HISTORY FOUNDATION/CORBIS

$12 Lowest price for a steamship ticket from Italy to America in 1905

$12 Average weekly salary (seven-day weeks/12-hour days) for arriving immigrants in 1907

Wright brothers

BETTMANN/CORBIS

12 seconds Air time of Wright brothers' first flight in 1903

1.2 million Approximate number of immigrants who entered the U.S. in 1907

395,000 Approximate number of immigrants in 1908 who gave up on America and returned home

50¢ Price of cheapest seat at baseball's first World Series in 1903

Analyzing Primary Sources

A Time of Change

The United States changed in the late 1800s and early 1900s. Cities grew as people poured into them, looking for work. In addition, reformers investigated the practices of big business. Read the passages on pages 786 and 787 and answer the questions that follow.

Jane Addams with immigrant
children at Hull House in Chicago ▶

Reader's Dictionary

initiative (ih • NIH • shuh • tiv): the first action in a process

ward: an area of a city

sanitary (SA • nuh • TEHR • ee): having to do with cleanliness

foul (FAUL): very dirty

bewildered (bih • WIHL • duhrd): confused

clutches: strong hold of claws

interpretation (ihn • TUHR • pruh • TAY • shuhn): explanation done in an understandable way

asylums (uh • SY • luhms): places for the care of the poor, sick, and insane

gash: long, deep cut

contagion (kuhn • TAY • juhn): spreading of disease

vats: large containers

refuse (REH • FYOOS): garbage

Hull House

In her book, Twenty Years at Hull-House, Jane Addams describes the area of the city where Hull House is located.

The policy of the public authorities of never taking an **initiative,** and always waiting to be urged to do their duty, is obviously fatal in a neighborhood where there is little initiative among the citizens. The idea underlying our self-government breaks down in such a **ward.** The streets are inexpressibly dirty, the number of schools inadequate, **sanitary** legislation unenforced, the street lighting bad, the paving miserable and altogether lacking in the alleys and smaller streets, and the stables **foul** beyond description. Hundreds of houses are unconnected with the street sewer.

Addams also explains how settlement houses help disadvantaged people.

We early found ourselves spending many hours in efforts to secure support for deserted women, insurance for **bewildered** widows, damages for injured operators, furniture from the **clutches** of the installment store. The Settlement is valuable as an information and **interpretation** bureau.

It constantly acts between the various institutions of the city and the people for whose benefit these institutions were erected. The hospitals, the county agencies, and State **asylums** are often but vague rumors to the people who need them most. Another function of the Settlement to its neighborhood resembles that of the big brother whose mere presence on the playground protects the little one from bullies.

—from *Twenty Years at Hull-House with Autobiographical Notes*

The Jungle

Upton Sinclair *writes about the meatpacking industry in his novel* The Jungle.

[Mikolas] is a beef-boner, and that is a dangerous trade, especially when you are on piecework and trying to earn a bride. Your hands are slippery, and your knife is slippery, and you are toiling like mad, when somebody happens to speak to you, or you strike a bone. Then your hand slips up on the blade, and there is a fearful **gash**. And that would not be so bad, only for the deadly **contagion.** The cut may heal, but you never can tell. Twice now; within the last three years, Mikolas has been lying at home with blood poisoning—once for three months and once for nearly seven. The last time, too, he lost his job, and that meant six weeks more of standing at the doors of the packing houses, at six o'clock on bitter winter mornings.

One character, Antanas, has a new job. He must mop up the chemicals used on the meat.

[T]he beef had lain in **vats** full of chemicals, and men with great forks speared it out and dumped it into trucks, to be taken to the cooking room. When they had speared out all they could reach, they emptied the vat on the floor, and then with shovels scraped up the balance and dumped it into the truck. This floor was filthy, yet they set Antanas with his mop slopping the "pickle" into a hole that connected with a sink, where it was caught and used over again forever; and if that were not enough, there was a trap [bend] in the pipe, where all the scraps of meat and odds and ends of **refuse** were caught, and every few days it was the old man's task to clean these out, and shovel their contents into one of the trucks with the rest of the meat!

—from *The Jungle*

◀ A famous muckraking book

 Document-Based Questions

Hull House

1. Why was the area around Hull House in such bad condition?
2. What did Addams mean by comparing the settlement house to a "big brother"?

The Jungle

3. Write three adjectives that describe the working conditions of Mikolas and Antanas.
4. How would you feel about eating meat that comes from a company like the one where Antanas is working? Why?

Read to Write

5. In these writings, Addams reports on social conditions and Sinclair reports on working conditions. Do you think these works were intended to inform or spark reform, or both? How do you think readers responded to these writings? How do you think government officials responded?

Review Content Vocabulary

For each of the pairs of terms below, write a sentence or short paragraph showing how the two are related.

1. emigrate, ethnic groups
2. slum, settlement house
3. trust, oligopoly

Review the Main Ideas

Section 1 • The New Immigrants

4. What was an immigrant's greatest challenge upon arriving in the United States?
5. What was the goal of the nativist movement?

Section 2 • Moving to the City

6. What were some important advances in transportation?
7. What were tenements and slums?

Section 3 • A Changing Culture

8. What was a land-grant college?
9. Who invented moving pictures?

Section 4 • The Progressive Movement

10. What was the spoils system?
11. What did President Roosevelt do to protect the environment?

Section 5 • A Changing Nation

12. How did the United States expand its territorial interests in the Pacific?
13. What was the Springfield riot of 1908?

Critical Thinking

14. **Explain** Why were minority groups discriminated against during this period? How did these groups respond?
15. **Compare and Contrast** How did Presidents Taft and Wilson differ in their views on international relations?

16. **Cause and Effect** Re-create the diagram below. Describe three ways newcomers to America tried to preserve their culture.

17. **Analyze** Why did leisure time develop for some Americans? How did that affect American culture?

Geography Skills

Study the map below and answer the following questions.

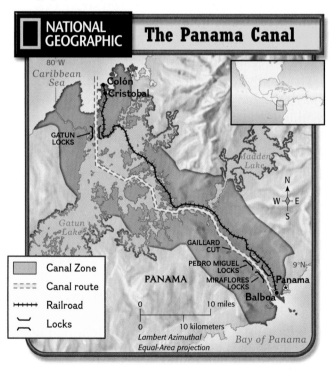

The Panama Canal

18. **Location** What bodies of water are shown on the map of the Panama Canal?
19. **Movement** Besides the canal, what other form of transportation is shown here?

Self-Check Quiz Visit tajwwI.glencoe.com to prepare for the Chapter 17 test.

Read to Write

20. **The Big Ideas** **Describe** Write an essay that describes the challenges that urban life posed around the turn of the century. Identify and describe efforts made by reformers to improve the quality of life of poor city dwellers.

21. **Using Your FOLDABLES** Use the information you listed in your foldable to create a brief study guide for the chapter. For each section, your study guide should include at least five questions that focus on the main ideas.

Using Academic Vocabulary

A suffix is a syllable placed after a base word to form a new word. For example, -less means "without." *Hopeless* means "without hope." Other suffixes are -al, -able, -ary, -ion, and -ism. For each of the academic vocabulary words, add a suffix to create a new word.

22. inspect

23. isolate

24. process

Linking Past and Present

25. **Organizing Information** Search the Internet to find three groups that work to protect the environment or our national parks. Write an essay that describes each group's efforts and connects their work to President Roosevelt's passion for the outdoors.

Building Citizenship

26. **Working for Equality** With a partner, check your local newspaper and magazines to identify instances of discrimination in your community. Together, generate a list of ideas that you think would help eliminate the prejudice and inequality that you read about.

Reviewing Skills

27. **READING SKILL** **Visual Literacy** Choose two photographs from this chapter and write an essay describing the significance of those images in illustrating the content of the chapter.

28. **ANALYSIS SKILL** **Economic Performance** Contrast Roosevelt's "Square Deal" with laissez-faire policy. Identify the economic benefits and weaknesses in both approaches to government regulation of business.

Standardized Test Practice

Read the passage below and answer the following question.

Between 1860 and 1900, American urban areas grew twice as fast as the total population. Chicago, which in the 1830s had been a frontier town with a few hundred residents, became a vast metropolis. New York became the second-largest city in the world. During the same span of years, the populations of Boston, Baltimore, and Philadelphia also grew rapidly.

29 The main idea of the passage is best expressed as:

A New York City grew rapidly.

B Only cities in the northeastern United States grew rapidly.

C The population of urban America grew at a very fast rate during this era.

D Rural growth continued, but not as quickly as urban growth.

Reshaping the Nation

After the Civil War, the United States experienced many changes. The frontier ceased to exist. The United States became an industrial nation with overseas possessions. Immigrants poured into the country. Progressives worked to reform government and control big business.

Chapter 15 The Western Frontier	Chapter 16 The Growth of Industry	Chapter 17 America Enters a New Century
When • 1858–1896	• 1865–1914	• 1865–1920
Where • Abilene and Dodge City, Kansas • Cheyenne, Wyoming • Pikes Peak • Virginia City, Nevada • Promontory Summit, Utah • Great Plains • Oklahoma • Dakota Territory • Arizona	• Menlo Park, New Jersey • Detroit, Michigan • Titusville, Pennsylvania • Cleveland, Ohio • Pittsburgh, Pennsylvania • Chicago, Illinois • Homestead, Pennsylvania	• New York City (Ellis Island) • San Francisco (Angel Island) • Chicago, Illinois • Kansas City, Kansas • Pittsburgh, Pennsylvania • Hawaii • Latin America • Philippine Islands

◄ *Cattle branding iron*

Panama Canal brochure ►

	Chapter 15 The Western Frontier	**Chapter 16** The Growth of Industry	**Chapter 17** America Enters a New Century
Major Events	• **1859** Silver discovered in Nevada • **1860s–mid-1880s** Cattle Kingdom • **1862** Homestead Act • **1867** Reservation policy • **1869** Transcontinental railroad completed • **1876** Battle of the Little Bighorn • **1889** Oklahoma Land Rush • **1890** Populist Party • **1890** Frontier no longer exists • **1890** Wounded Knee *Sioux Buffalo Shield ▶*	• **1869** Knights of Labor • **1870s** Steel mills open in Ohio and Pennsylvania • **1870** Standard Oil Company • **1876** Telephone • **1879** Electric lightbulb • **1880s** Railroads adopt standard gauge track • **1881** AFL forms • **1890** Sherman Antitrust Act • **1892** Homestead Strike • **1908** Model T Ford	• **Late 1800s** Realist themes in art and literature • **1882** Chinese Exclusion Act • **1884** First skyscraper • **1887** Interstate Commerce Act • **1896** *Plessy* v. *Ferguson* • **1898** Spanish-American War • **1907** 1.3 million immigrants arrive in America • **1910** Half of Americans live in cities • **1914** Panama Canal completed • **1920** Women gain right to vote
Some Important People	• Henry Comstock • Crazy Horse • Sitting Bull • George Custer • Geronimo • Helen Hunt Jackson • Grover Cleveland • William Jennings Bryan • William McKinley	• Cornelius Vanderbilt • Leland Stanford • Alexander Graham Bell • Thomas Edison • Henry Ford • John D. Rockefeller • Andrew Carnegie • Samuel Gompers *Andrew Carnegie ▶*	• Jane Addams • Booker T. Washington • Joseph Pulitzer • Jacob Riis • Eugene V. Debs • Ida Tarbell • Upton Sinclair • Robert La Follette • Theodore Roosevelt • César Chávez
How do these events and ideas affect our lives today?	• The settling of the Plains led to America's position as a major agricultural producer. *◀ Book on ranching*	• America's inventors and industrialists helped make the country the economic power that it is today.	• The muckrakers began a long tradition of investigative journalism in America.
What was happening in the world at this time?	• **1867** Dominion of Canada is formed • **1885** Berlin Conference divides Africa among European nations	• **1869** Suez Canal is completed • **1885** Transcontinental railway opens in Canada	• **1893** New Zealand is first country to allow women to vote in national elections • **1911** Norwegian explorer Roald Amundsen is first person to reach the South Pole

Connections to Today

Why It's Important

As you studied this text, you learned about how our nation's government, economy, and society first developed and began to change. In **Connections to Today,** *you will read about how those past changes affect your life today. By learning how things were, you will better understand how things are.*

As you read **Connections to Today,** *think about:*

- How have things changed over time?
- Why did these changes occur?
- As a citizen in a democracy, how can I influence events?
- How can I participate in public life?

Major Events: 1900 to the Present

	1900	1915	1930	1945
POLITICAL & ECONOMIC		**1917** U.S. enters World War I / **1920** Women win right to vote	**1929** Stock market crash triggers Great Depression	**1941** U.S. enters World War II
SCIENCE & SOCIETY	**1908** The Ford Model T automobile is introduced	**1919** Race riots in U.S. cities leave many dead and injured	**1928** Television broadcasts begin in the U.S.	**1945** U.S. develops the first atomic bomb
WORLD EVENTS	**1910** Mexican Revolution	**1914** World War I begins	**1939** World War II begins in Europe	**1948** Berlin Airlift

The Big Ideas

A Changing Nation in a Changing World Page 794

The nation's history has been shaped by significant individuals, groups, ideas, events, eras, and developments. Throughout the twentieth century and into the twenty-first century, one theme remained constant—change. Breakthroughs in science and technology have been as much a part of life as conflict and political and social change.

A Changing Society Page 798

Reactions to social injustice can lead to reform movements. In the past, discrimination caused most ethnic and racial groups to lag behind the white majority in jobs, income, and education. Read to find out what advances were made in the twentieth and twenty-first centuries.

New Roles, New Faces Page 806

The free-enterprise economy of the United States is consistent with the nation's history of rights and freedoms. Economic changes have eliminated certain kinds of jobs and created others. As jobs in all fields become more high tech and demanding, workers need to be better prepared and better educated.

Rights and Responsibilities Page 812

Citizen participation is essential to the foundation and preservation of the U.S. political system. When the founders, in the Declaration of Independence, stated that all people are created equal and all have the right to life, liberty, and the pursuit of happiness, they were stating the ideals of the American dream.

1960	1975	1990	2005

1965 U.S. combat troops arrive in Vietnam

1974 President Nixon resigns

1998 President Clinton impeached

2001 Terrorist attacks destroy World Trade Center and damage Pentagon

1954 Segregated schools ruled unconstitutional by Supreme Court

1969 American astronauts are first humans to walk on the moon

1990 Americans with Disabilities Act becomes law

1961 Berlin Wall built

1991 Soviet Union collapses

1993 European Union launched

2003 Saddam Hussein overthrown in Iraq

A Changing Nation in a Changing World

▲ The automobile became a vital part of American lives in the 1920s.

Turning Points, 1914–1950

From 1914 to 1950, the United States played a major role in shaping world affairs. The world plunged into two world wars in which the United States took part. After World War II, the democratic United States and the communist Soviet Union competed for influence in the world.

"The War to End All Wars"

In 1914 tensions in Europe sparked a world war. It was known as the Great War, the "war to end all wars," and later World War I. The conflict involved more nations, used more technological weapons, and resulted in more deaths than any previous war. The United States entered the war in 1917 and helped Britain and France defeat Germany and its allies. The war led to the collapse of empires and the rise of new nations.

From Boom to Bust

After World War I, Americans were tired of war and world responsibilities. They turned inward to look after their own affairs. People called the 1920s the Jazz Age—partly because of jazz, but also because of the restlessness and carefree mood of the time. The U.S. economy grew, and many Americans prospered. However, the strong economy faltered. By the end of the 1920s, thousands of Americans were jobless, and many farmers had lost their land. The Great Depression, triggered by the Stock Market Crash of 1929, endangered the nation's economic system. It soon spread throughout the rest of the industrialized world.

Around the World and at Home, 1900–1950

1900	1910	1920
1904 Russo-Japanese War	**1910** Mexican Revolution begins	**1920** Women win right to vote
	1914 World War I begins	

A Global Struggle

The worldwide depression aided the rise of dictatorships in Europe and Japan. These governments aggressively sought to expand their territories. World War II began when Germany invaded Poland. Britain and France responded by declaring war on Germany. In 1941 the Soviet Union joined the conflict when Germany invaded its territory. The United States entered the war later that year after Japan bombed the U.S. naval base at Pearl Harbor, Hawaii.

World War II, the most destructive war in history, resulted in the deaths of more than 40 million people. More than half of them were civilians, including about 6 million Jews and many others in the Holocaust.

At the end of the war, the United States emerged as one of the strongest nations in the world and the sole possessor of a powerful weapon—the atomic bomb.

Democracy Versus Communism

The democratic United States and the communist Soviet Union emerged from World War II as the two most powerful nations, struggling for world leadership. This rivalry became known as the Cold War because, although great tensions divided them, the two countries did not actually go to war with each other. Each side tried to gain allies and prove that its system of government—democracy or communism—was better than the other.

The Cold War turned "hot," however, when Communist North Korean soldiers invaded South Korea. United Nations troops led by the United States became involved in the conflict. The Communist Chinese came to the aid of their North Korean ally. The two sides finally agreed to stop fighting. They accepted an armistice line that divided Korea along the existing battlefront.

▲ The attack on Pearl Harbor drew the United States into World War II.

Review

1. What factors made World Wars I and II different from earlier wars?

2. Why were the 1920s called the Jazz Age? What happened to the U.S. economy at the end of this period?

3. Who was at odds during the Cold War?

1930	1940	1950
1929 Stock market crashes, triggering Great Depression	**1939** World War II begins in Europe	**1945** Germany and Japan surrender; World War II ends	**1950** North Korea invades South Korea

Modern America, 1950 to the Present

From the 1950s to the 1980s, the United States struggled with communism abroad and advanced civil rights at home. Americans prospered, and American culture spread around the globe. In the early 1990s, the Soviet Union collapsed, bringing the Cold War to an end. Meanwhile, new technologies and a changing population transformed America in new ways. Entering the new century, Americans responded to the global spread of terrorism by looking for fresh ways to preserve and protect their ideals in a changing world.

America in the 1950s

After years of "going without" during the Great Depression and World War II, Americans hungered for new cars, electronics, appliances, and gadgets. During the 1950s, the American economy began to grow rapidly and steadily. Between 1945 and 1960, the total value of goods and services produced in the United States increased about 250 percent. During the 1950s, 85 percent of new home construction took place in the suburbs—neighborhoods that were developed just outside of a city.

The Struggle for Civil Rights

In the 1950s, a tide of protest began to rise in America against deeply rooted attitudes of racism and discrimination. This campaign for equality gained momentum in the 1960s. African Americans, women, Hispanic Americans, and Native Americans became more active in seeking equal rights. Leaders such as Martin Luther King, Jr., and César Chávez developed peaceful methods of protest to realize this goal. Although the civil rights movement could not overcome all the obstacles that stood in the way of full equality, it achieved some stunning successes.

▼ After World War II, more Americans owned cars and homes than ever before.

▲ More than 200,000 people joined the March on Washington in August 1963 to call for civil rights legislation.

Around the World and at Home, 1950–Present

1950	1960	1970
1954 Polio vaccine given to school children	**1963** March on Washington rallies support for civil rights	**1973** U.S. ends involvement in Vietnam

Search for Stability

The Vietnam conflict—an effort to defeat communism in Southeast Asia—left scars on America. More than 58,000 U.S. troops died in Vietnam, and thousands more were wounded. The people of Southeast Asia also paid a price for war in Vietnam. Two million Vietnamese and uncounted Cambodians and Laotians were killed. Their villages and towns lay in ruins.

Dramatic change marked the period of the 1960s and 1970s. Faith in government was shaken by presidential scandal. Yet the American system of constitutional government worked and survived. The nation had responsibilities as a world power, faced conflict with the communist world, and carried out ventures in outer space. All of these tasks demanded that the nation learn new ways of carrying out its role in the world. Still, Americans tried to adjust to changes in ways that would assure the future of their democracy.

Toward a New Century

The 1980s and 1990s saw the dawn of a new era. With the collapse of communism in Europe, the Cold War came to an end. Relations between East and West changed dramatically. Meanwhile, after centuries of conflict, European nations began to unite economically and politically in the European Union. Worldwide pressure led to the end of apartheid—government-sponsored segregation—and the rise of a multiracial democratic government in South Africa. At home, new advances in technology, medicine, and industry transformed the American economy.

As the United States entered a new century, new challenges emerged. The terrorist attacks on New York City and Washington, D.C. began a new war against global terrorism, as well as renewed commitment to supporting freedom, equality, and democracy in America and abroad.

The attacks of September 11, 2001, shocked Americans, but also united them.

Review

1. Why did the United States fight a war in Vietnam?

2. What event changed East-West relations beginning in the late 1980s?

3. What new challenge did the United States and the world face at the beginning of the new century?

1980		1990		2000	

1989 Communism crumbles in Eastern Europe

1990 Allies launch Operation Desert Storm in Iraq

2001 Terrorists attack New York City and Washington, D.C.

2003 U.S. invades Iraq

A Changing Society

▲ Young boys working in a
Georgia mill, early 1900s

The Beginnings of Reform

The spirit of reform gained strength in the late 1800s and thrived during the early 1900s. The reformers were confident in their ability to improve government and the quality of life.

Problems in American Society

At the beginning of the 1900s, the United States was a different country than it is today. The vision described in the Declaration of Independence—that all are created equal and possess certain unalienable rights—remained a dream for many Americans. Women could not vote. Laws in many parts of the country enforced racial segregation. People with disabilities were often unable to enjoy the same range of opportunities as other people. Government did little to protect citizens from dangerous medicines, contaminated food, and unfair business practices. There was little concern that our country's air, water, and natural areas were at risk of being polluted or destroyed.

Equal Rights and Reform, 1900–1950

1900	1910	1920

1906 Pure Food and Drug Act passed

1916 Keating-Owen Child Labor Act passed

1919 Eighteenth Amendment prohibits alcohol

1920 Women vote in national election for the first time

▲ Women march for suffrage in New York City in 1920.

Progressive Reforms

Early in the century, reformers known as Progressives gained influence in local, state, and national government. Progressives believed that government should take a more active role in improving people's lives and solving society's problems.

Some Progressives took aim at political corruption, urban poverty, child labor, or questionable business practices. Others wanted to reform government itself to make it more able to deal with the nation's challenges. Still others wanted to ban the sale and consumption of alcohol. A quarter-century of Progressive reforms left their mark on the nation. As a result, Americans began to look to the government to protect their interests.

Review

1. What impact did Progressive policies have on how Americans perceived their government?

2. Explain the effect of Progressive reforms on the lives of Americans.

3. What reforms would you like to see enacted today? What could you do to make that possible?

1930		1940		1950
1929 Great Depression begins	**1935** Social Security Act adopted	**1938** Fair Labor Standards Act passed	**1944** GI Bill enacted	

The Struggle for Equal Rights

Reformers addressed a number of issues in the 1900s, and some of the most difficult struggles were those faced by African Americans and other ethnic groups. Their battles for equal rights led to major changes in American society.

African Americans Face Discrimination

Although amendments to the Constitution guaranteed rights to all Americans, African Americans and other groups still did not enjoy civil rights, or the rights of full citizenship and equality under the law. In the early 1900s, African Americans routinely faced discrimination. Laws in the South limited their right to vote. Laws in many parts of the nation barred African Americans from attending the same schools as white students. African Americans had to ride in the back of buses, sit in separate sections of restaurants and theaters, and stay in separate hotels. The social separation of races was known as segregation.

African Americans began to campaign actively for civil rights in the 1900s. In 1909 a group of African Americans and whites founded the National Association for the Advancement of Colored People (NAACP). That group sought to end discrimination through legal means. After African Americans fought with American forces in both world wars, the call for equal rights grew even stronger. A major victory in the struggle for civil rights occurred in 1948 when President Harry S. Truman issued an executive order that ended racial segregation in the armed forces.

▲ Separate drinking facilities for African Americans and whites

The Equal Rights Movement, 1900–1970

1900	1910	1920	1930
	1909 NAACP formed	**1917** African Americans serve as officers during World War I	**1930s** President Roosevelt appoints 45 African Americans to serve in New Deal agencies

The Civil Rights Era

The landmark 1954 Supreme Court decision *Brown v. Board of Education* ruled that segregated schools were unconstitutional. Schools began to desegregate, but the move faced great opposition in some parts of the country. A year later, a young minister led a successful boycott of the segregated Montgomery, Alabama, bus system. His name was Martin Luther King, Jr., and he would become the nation's most important civil rights leader. African Americans and whites protested against segregated facilities in restaurants, at bus and train stations, and in other areas. In many parts of the country, especially the South, the protesters were met with anger and violence.

Voter Registration Before and After the Voting Rights Act

- 7% of African American adults registered to vote in Mississippi in 1964 before passage of the Voting Rights Act of 1965

- 67% of African American adults in Mississippi registered to vote in 1969

- 70% of white adults registered to vote nationwide in 1964

- 90% of white adults registered to vote nationwide in 1969

Source: TIME.

◀ Forcing civil rights protesters to stop their marches, 1963

The Federal Government Takes a Role

Over time, more and more Americans grew sympathetic to the demands for equal rights. The federal government became an ally, passing and enforcing important new laws. These included the Civil Rights Act of 1964 and the Voting Rights Act of 1965. Presidents John F. Kennedy and Lyndon Johnson expressed sympathy for expanding and safeguarding civil rights.

Review

1. How did President Truman demonstrate important leadership for the movement for equality for all people?

2. Who would become the nation's most important civil rights leader?

1940	1950	1960	1970

1948 President Truman orders desegregation of U.S. military

1954 *Brown v. Board of Education*

1964 Civil Rights Act passed

1965 Voting Rights Act passed

Other Civil Rights Challenges

African Americans were not the only group in American society to face discrimination and inequality. Hispanics, Native Americans, and others also had to struggle to gain equal rights in the 1900s.

Hispanic Americans Seek Equal Rights

Other groups soon followed African Americans in demanding equal rights. The nation's Hispanic population grew rapidly during the 1960s. Including people of Mexican, Puerto Rican, Cuban, and other backgrounds, Hispanics often faced discrimination and had to cope with limited access to housing, education, and employment.

Many Mexican Americans, the largest Hispanic group, worked on large farms in western states. These farmworkers earned little pay and received few benefits. In the mid-1960s, César Chávez and Dolores Huerta successfully organized the United Farm Workers union in California to fight for better working conditions. Another group, La Raza Unida, organized voters in the Southwest and West.

Native Americans Struggle

Like other groups in the 1950s and 1960s, Native Americans suffered from discrimination in housing, employment, and health care. They, too, began to organize to combat racism and rebuild cultural identity. The American Indian Movement (AIM) led protests, which sometimes turned violent. Working through the federal courts, Native Americans won decisions that helped them establish their economic independence.

▲ The American Indian Movement protested civil rights violations.

Ethnic Groups and Equal Rights

1960

1970

1963 March on Washington for Equal Rights

1966 United Farm Workers formed by César Chávez and Dolores Huerta

1970 La Raza Unida formed by Jose Angel Gutierrez

A More Aggressive Approach

Most civil rights protesters followed the nonviolent teachings of Martin Luther King, Jr., and other leaders. Others, however, felt that violent opposition should be met with more aggressive methods. Leaders like Malcolm X and Stokely Carmichael endorsed an idea called Black Power, through which African Americans would build economic, political, and cultural strength. Frustration with the slow pace of improvement led to deadly riots in black neighborhoods of some large cities.

Entering a New Century

By the year 2000, America's ethnic and racial groups had achieved some remarkable successes. African Americans, Hispanics, and Asian Americans held thousands of elected offices throughout the nation. Business and educational leadership grew more diverse as well.

As the 2000s began, the United States had an increasingly diverse population. Hispanic Americans became the fastest growing ethnic group in the country, growing from 22.4 million in 1990 to 35.3 million in 2000. Increased immigration from Latin America, Asia, and Africa also had an impact on the country's population. For the first time since the early 1930s, one out of every ten Americans was foreign-born.

America has become increasingly appreciative of its multicultural heritage and respectful of diversity. Yet economic, social, and political challenges remain, and much still needs to be done.

Population of the United States by Race and Hispanic/Latino Origin

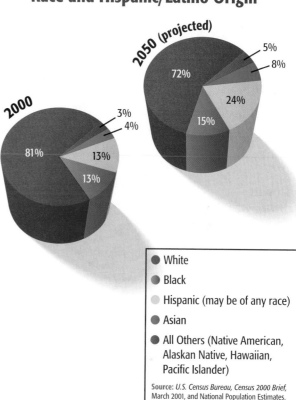

2050 (projected)
72%
5%
8%
24%
15%

2000
81%
3%
4%
13%
13%

- White
- Black
- Hispanic (may be of any race)
- Asian
- All Others (Native American, Alaskan Native, Hawaiian, Pacific Islander)

Source: U.S. Census Bureau, Census 2000 Brief, March 2001, and National Population Estimates.

Review

1. What did Chávez and Huerta do to aid Hispanic farmworkers?

2. How did the methods of Malcolm X and Stokely Carmichael differ from those of Martin Luther King, Jr.?

3. What challenges to civil rights still exist today? What could you do to make a difference?

1980   1990   2000

1974 Congressional act makes bilingual education available to Hispanic youth

1990 Antonia C. Novello becomes the first female and first Hispanic Surgeon General of the United States

2004 National Museum of the American Indian opens in Washington, D.C.

Into the Mainstream

The 1900s saw important advances in the status of women and people with disabilities. Another significant movement, with roots in the Progressive era, was environmentalism. As multiculturalism became more valued, religious distinctions were increasingly respected as well.

Women: Second-Class Citizens No More

Women pursued equal rights long before the 1900s. Early pioneers like Susan B. Anthony, Elizabeth Cady Stanton, and Lucretia Mott demanded suffrage, or voting rights. Women finally gained the right to vote in 1920, when the Nineteenth Amendment to the U.S. Constitution was approved. During the world wars, many women went to work outside the home. They began to demand the same rights and treatment as men. In the 1960s, women pressed for better educational opportunities, workplace equality, and easier access to health care under the leadership of groups like the National Organization for Women (NOW). An Equal Rights Amendment (ERA) passed in both houses of Congress in 1972 but was never ratified by enough states to become law.

Gaining Access for All Americans

Like women, people with disabilities often could not fully participate in American life. In 1990 the Americans with Disabilities Act (ADA) outlawed discrimination against people with physical or mental disabilities. Access ramps were added to buildings, and closed-caption TV programs became common.

Jeannette Rankin (above) was the first woman elected to the U.S. Congress (1917). In 2004 Kathleen Blanco (right) became the first woman governor of Louisiana.

▲ Demonstrators urging equal access for people with disabilities

Protecting All Americans, 1890–Present

1890	1905	1920	1935
1890 Women have right to vote in Wyoming	**1905** U.S. Forest Service created	**1916** Mosque established in Detroit, Michigan **1920** Women gain right to vote nationally	

Rise of Environmentalism

Activists in the 1960s and 1970s turned their attention to another challenge: protecting the earth's resources. Environmentalism was not new. Leaders such as Theodore Roosevelt and John Muir had warned Americans of the need to protect natural places. Groups like the Sierra Club (founded in 1892) and the U.S. Forest Service (created in 1905) worked to protect natural areas. A landmark 1962 book by Rachel Carson, *Silent Spring*, sounded an alarm about pesticides that grew into the environmental movement. Soon, the federal government, through its new Environmental Protection Agency (EPA) and laws like the Wilderness, Clean Air, and Endangered Species acts, took on the responsibility of safeguarding the environment.

Religious Diversity

One of the founding ideals of the United States was religious tolerance. As more people immigrated to the United States, the variety of religious beliefs also grew. Today, almost every religion has followers in the United States. In the period following the terrorist attacks on New York and Washington, D.C., in 2001, Americans wanted to show their respect for all religious faiths. This marked a time of great national unity and mutual tolerance. Annually, the president recognizes January 16 as Religious Freedom Day to commemorate the passage of the 1786 Virginia Statute for Religious Freedom, written by Thomas Jefferson.

Religious Membership in the United States*

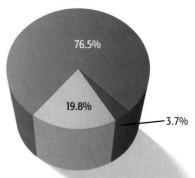

76.5%

19.8%

3.7%

● Christian Religious Groups–
   more than 159 million, including:

Catholic	50.9 million
Baptist	33.8 million
Methodist/Wesleyan	14.2 million
Lutheran	9.6 million
Presbyterian	5.6 million
Pentecostal/Charismatic	4.4 million
Episcopalian/Anglican	3.5 million

● Other Religious Groups–
   more than 7.7 million, including:

Jewish	2.8 million
Muslim/Islamic	1.1 million
Buddhist	1.0 million

○ Other/No religion specified

* Based on adult population

Source: *American Religious Identification Survey*, 2001; The Graduate Center of the City University of New York.

Review

1. What did the Americans With Disabilities Act accomplish?

2. What government agency was created to protect the environment?

3. What can you do to safeguard religious liberty?

1950   **1965**   **1980**   **1995**

1962
Silent Spring published by Rachel Carson

1970 Environmental Protection Agency formed

1981 Sandra Day O'Connor is first woman appointed to U.S. Supreme Court

New Roles, New Faces

Poverty in the United States: Total Number and Rate

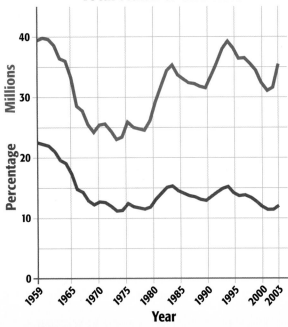

Source: U.S. Bureau of the Census.

Economic Growth

Manufacturing in the United States increased greatly in the late 1800s. During this period, the American economy changed from one that was primarily agricultural to one based on industry. The country's economy continued to grow tremendously in the 1900s.

An Industrial Powerhouse

Around the beginning of the 1900s, the United States surpassed Great Britain and Germany to become the world's leading industrial nation. By the end of the century, the U.S. economy had expanded so much that it was almost twice as large as the world's second largest, China's.

Mass production was the key to the growth of America's industrial might. This form of large-scale manufacturing increased supply and lowered costs to consumers. Thanks to Henry Ford's assembly line, automobiles became affordable for millions of consumers. His ideas were quickly put into place in other industries.

Depression and War

The production of consumer goods; heavy manufacturing; and processing of natural resources such as coal, iron, and oil grew at a rapid pace in the early 1900s. However, the Great Depression of the 1930s handcuffed the U.S. economy for a decade. Industrial production and agriculture fell steeply. Then in the early 1940s, manufacturing rebounded to supply the military during World War II.

An Expanding and Changing Economy, 1900–Present

1900	1915	1930	1945

1908 Ford's Model T is sold to the public

1912 Department of Labor created

1929 Stock market crash triggers Great Depression

1938 Fair Labor Standards Act passed

1941 U.S. enters World War II; economic growth surges

High-Tech Revolution

The 1950s and 1960s saw continued growth in the U.S. economy. In the 1970s, the nation faced economic roadblocks, such as high inflation, unemployment, and increased energy costs. By the 1980s, a new element had emerged to recharge America's economy—technology. The technology revolution transformed the infrastructure of business. Advances in computers, communications, and other high-tech fields led the U.S. economy—and society—into the next century.

The Income Gap Remains

Not all Americans have benefited from the expanding economy. Although the middle class has grown over the century, millions of people remain in poverty. The federal poverty level in 2003 was set at an income of $18,810 for a family of four. One in eight Americans, or 12.5 percent, lived at or below the poverty level. (See graph on page 806.) African Americans and children were more likely than others to be living in poverty.

One way the federal government has chosen to deal with poverty is the minimum wage. Since 1938, the government has required employers to pay a minimum hourly wage. (See graph above.) Today, younger workers may be paid less than minimum wage for their first 90 days on the job.

Federal Minimum Wage

Year	Hourly Wage
1997	$5.15
1991	$4.25
1981	$3.10
1974	$2.00
1968	$1.60
1956	$1.00
1950	$0.75
1945	$0.40
1938	$0.25

Source: http://usgovinfo.about.com/library/blminwage.htm

During the Great Depression, many Americans could not find work.

Review

1. What was the technology revolution?

2. About how many Americans live at or below the federal poverty level?

3. Why has American industry changed so much over the past century?

1960   1975   1990   2005

1970s Oil embargo and inflation hurt U.S. economy

1975 First personal computers are sold

1994 NAFTA creates huge free trade zone

Changing Nature of Work

As the American economy changed, so did the way the people of the United States worked. In the 1900s, the types of jobs held by most workers shifted from jobs that created goods to positions that offered services.

Moving to the Cities

At the beginning of the 1900s, many people were still moving from farms to the rapidly growing cities. Improved farm machinery made it possible to grow more crops using fewer workers. The higher wages paid in the cities also attracted workers. Many of those moving to the cities found work in newly opened factories. These workers became known as blue collar workers. Others found jobs in offices, schools, stores, and other nonfactory settings and were called white collar workers. By 1920 more than half of all Americans lived in towns or cities.

The Service Economy

Another significant change that took place during the twentieth century was the shift from manufacturing jobs to service industry jobs. Service jobs are those that provide services to people and businesses. They include banking and insurance, communications, retail sales, health care, education, and government. Today, much of the United States's total economic activity is made up of this type of business.

▼ America's workforce is diverse with jobs in many different fields.

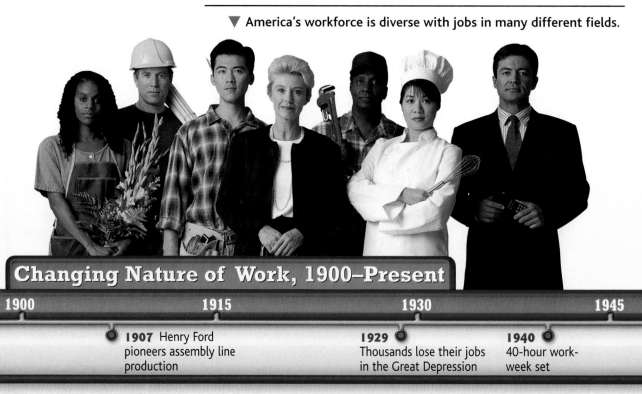

Changing Nature of Work, 1900–Present

1900	1915	1930	1945

1907 Henry Ford pioneers assembly line production

1929 Thousands lose their jobs in the Great Depression

1940 40-hour workweek set

Number of Employees in Selected Professions, 1910 and 2002

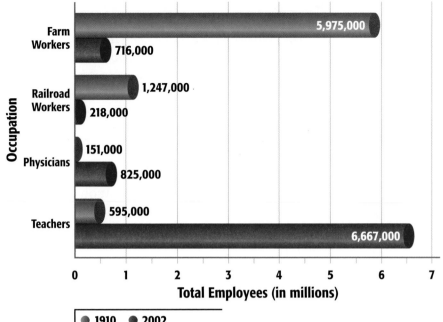

Occupation

Farm Workers — 5,975,000 / 716,000

Railroad Workers — 1,247,000 / 218,000

Physicians — 151,000 / 825,000

Teachers — 595,000 / 6,667,000

Total Employees (in millions)
0   1   2   3   4   5   6   7

● 1910   ● 2002

Sources: *Historical Statistics of the United States; Statistical Abstract of the United States,* 2003.

▼ World War II created opportunities for women.

Women in the war

WE CAN'T WIN WITHOUT THEM

Women Enter the Work Force

During the last century, many women entered the full-time workforce during economic boom times and especially during the two world wars. Often, these women would have to give up their jobs in order to make room for men needing work. Beginning in the 1960s, the women's liberation movement created a broader understanding of women's roles in the workplace. Many more women entered the working world, and they began to rise into positions that had not been possible before. Still, women generally earn less than men in the same profession. Today women are free to pursue their dreams in education, career, and family in ways that would have been hard to imagine in the past.

Review

1. Why did so many people leave farming as a way of life?

2. What is the difference between jobs in manufacturing and in the service industry?

1960	1975	1990	2005
1956 White-collar workers outnumber blue-collar workers for the first time	**1970** About 86 million people are in the U.S. workforce	**1999** About 140 million people are in the U.S. workforce	**2003** Women make up about 47% of the workforce

Changes in Education

The changes in American society and the economy also led to changes in education in the United States. Americans realized that success in an increasingly industrial and technological society required a higher level of education for all citizens.

Increases in School Enrollment

By 1900, the United States achieved the goal of providing public elementary education to all children. At that time, however, only a small number of teenagers went on to high school or college. One major development in education was the dramatic rise in high school and college enrollment. Today, about 53 million students are enrolled in the nation's public and private schools. Another 15.3 million attend colleges and universities.

Changes in the Classroom

The early 1900s brought far-reaching changes to public school education in the United States. Most students studied only reading, writing, and arithmetic. In the 1900s, schools became less formal and emphasized a well-rounded education that was able to meet the needs of individual children. Subjects were broadened to include geography, history, and science.

By 2000, technological advances promised more breakthroughs in education. Computers were increasingly common in schools. Technology made it possible for students to have access to more information than ever before. Students became empowered to learn on their own as well as in the classroom.

High School Enrollment

2000
94.0% enrolled

1950
76.1% enrolled

1900
10.2% enrolled

● 14 to 17 year olds not in high school

● 14 to 17 year olds enrolled in grades 9–12

Source: *Digest of Education Statistics*, 2003.

Changing Nature of Education, 1900–Present

1900	1915	1930	1945

1900 16.9 million children in U.S. public and private schools

1917 Smith-Hughes Act passed, providing federal funds for high school vocational education

Education and Government

Public education in the United States has historically been the responsibility of state and local governments. The federal government has expanded its role in education since the mid-1900s. It worked to ensure that every state provides equal educational opportunities for all citizens. In the mid-1950s, the U.S. Supreme Court ruled that public schools segregated by race were "inherently unequal" and ordered desegregation of schools. This ruling led to other measures to ensure equal educational opportunities for women, people with disabilities, and people who do not speak English.

Government has provided large amounts of money for education. This trend started after World War II, when Congress began granting funds to armed forces veterans to attend colleges and other schools. In the 1960s, Congress began passing laws to aid local schools and to improve the education of children from low-income families.

Since the 1980s, government leaders have worked to raise educational standards. In 2001 the No Child Left Behind Act introduced new federal requirements for student testing and measures for holding schools accountable for student progress.

Education and Income

As more Americans enrolled in schools during the twentieth century, education became a powerful social and economic force. Most Americans now expect schools to provide children with skills, values, and behaviors that will help them become responsible and productive citizens. Statistics show that people with a higher level of education make more money than those with less education.

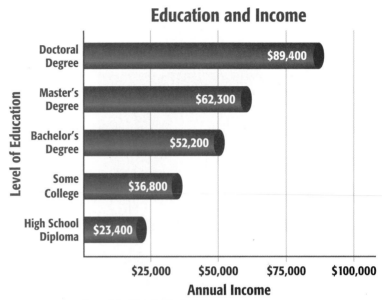

Education and Income

(Level of Education)

- Doctoral Degree — $89,400
- Master's Degree — $62,300
- Bachelor's Degree — $52,200
- Some College — $36,800
- High School Diploma — $23,400

Annual Income: $25,000 | $50,000 | $75,000 | $100,000

Source: National Center for Education Statistics.

Review

1. How did the classes taught in schools change in the 1900s?

2. How has the federal government increased its role in education?

3. Do you think the educational system prepares a person well for a role in society today? Explain.

1960   **1975**   **1990**   **2005**

1954 U.S. Supreme Court declares segregated schools unconstitutional

1979 Congress establishes the U.S. Department of Education

2001 No Child Left Behind Act passes

Rights and Responsibilities

Our System of Taxation

It is the combination of rights and responsibilities that characterizes what it means to be a citizen of a free and democratic society. As citizens, we are free to exercise our rights. In return, we are expected to fulfill certain responsibilities. One of a citizen's responsibilities is paying his or her fair share of taxes.

Paying Taxes

Taxes have been with us since the founding of our nation. British taxes that the colonists considered unfair were major causes of the American Revolution. Until the beginning of the 1900s, taxes were relatively low, as was government spending. Then, in 1913 the Sixteenth Amendment to the Constitution was passed. It allowed the federal government to tax the incomes of individuals and businesses. Since that time, income tax rates have gone up and down. This kind of tax, however, has been the government's primary way to get money to pay for its programs.

How Do Governments Pay for Their Programs?

Governments collect other kinds of taxes and fees as well. Social Security and Medicare taxes pay for retirement and medical benefits for older people. Most states use a sales tax to earn money. Real estate property taxes usually help pay for local schools. Excise taxes are special taxes that are attached to specific items. Tariffs are a kind of tax paid by foreign companies on goods they export to the United States. Poll taxes are taxes people pay to vote. These were made illegal in 1964 by the passage of the Twenty-fourth Amendment.

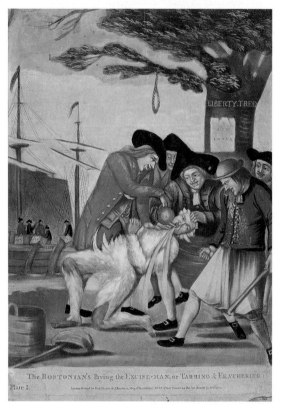

▲ American colonists protested against British taxes.

Taxation, 1900–Present

1900	1915	1930	1945

1913 Sixteenth Amendment gives U.S. government the power to tax incomes

1935 Tax levied on employers and workers to fund Social Security

Principles of Taxation

Taxes are usually justified according to one of two major principles. Under the *benefits-received principle*, those who use a particular government service should support it with taxes in proportion to the benefit they receive. Those who do not use a service do not pay taxes for it. A gasoline tax to pay for highway construction and repair is based on the benefits-received principle. Frequent users of the highways often buy more gasoline and, therefore, pay more in gasoline taxes.

Under the *ability-to-pay principle*, those with higher incomes pay more taxes than those with lower incomes, regardless of the number of government services they use. For example, in most cities all property owners, even those without school-aged children, must pay property taxes to support the local school system. Property taxes are calculated as a percentage of the value of a person's home. Thus, wealthier people pay more property taxes.

The "Tax Revolt"

By the 1970s, many Americans had come to resent the taxes they had to pay for expensive government programs. Led by California, voters rebelled against high taxes. In 1978 voters in the state approved Proposition 13. The referendum greatly reduced property taxes. As a result, state government programs were also reduced. Antitax movements quickly sprang up in other states. Conservatives argued that government had become too big, and tax cuts were instituted by the states and the federal government.

Review

1. What are poll taxes? Are they still part of voting today?

2. What was Proposition 13? What effect did it have on California and the nation?

3. What is the relationship between paying taxes and effective citizenship?

| 1960 | 1975 | 1990 | 2005 |

1978 California approves Proposition 13

1986 Tax Reform Act of 1986 reduced the number and level of tax rates

2004 President Bush signs $136 billion Corporate Tax Cut Bill

Obeying Our Laws

Another responsibility of citizens is to obey the law. City, state, and federal laws are made by legislators who are elected by the voters. These laws are designed for special purposes—to help people get along, to prevent accidents, to see that resources are used fairly, and so on. In a democracy like ours, people have an ethical obligation to obey laws made by the people they choose to govern them. If we do not obey the law, then governments cannot maintain order or protect our health, safety, and property.

Supporting Our Legal System

The Declaration of Independence states that "all men are created equal." This democratic ideal of equality means that all people are entitled to equal rights and treatment before the law. As citizens of a democracy, Americans also have a number of legal responsibilities. By fulfilling them, we ensure that our legal system works as it should and that our legal rights are protected.

A government's ability to enforce laws depends on people's willingness to obey the laws and to cooperate with law-enforcement authorities. The effectiveness of law-enforcement officials often depends on people's willingness to become involved and tell what they know about a crime. Serving on a jury and testifying in court are important responsibilities. The legal right to a jury trial can be effective only if people are willing to serve on juries and appear in court.

Americans must work peacefully to change unfair, outdated laws. This might involve gathering voters' signatures on petitions to place an issue on the ballot for a vote or asking legislatures to change the law.

▲ The United States Congress, made up of the Senate (above) and the House of Representatives, makes our nation's laws.

Laws and Policies, 1900 to the Present

1900	1915	1930	1945

1909 NAACP founded to advance African American rights

1934 Indian Reorganization Act restores traditional tribal government

1948 President Truman orders end to segregation in the armed forces

Respect Others' Rights

To enjoy your rights to the fullest, you must be prepared to respect other people's rights as well. For example, if you own a dog, you have an obligation to keep it from becoming a nuisance to your neighbors. If you are in the library, you should not interfere with anyone's right to work quietly.

Citizens also have a responsibility to show respect for public property and for the property of others. Some people might claim that "no one gets hurt" when they litter in a park or paint graffiti on a school wall, yet such public property belongs to all of us, and we all pay if it is damaged.

Vandalism and littering are actually more than disrespectful acts; they are crimes. Indeed, many of our laws have been enacted to encourage people to respect others' rights. If you have a party that gets out of hand, for example, you could be arrested for disturbing the peace.

Equal Rights for All

During the 1950s and 1960s, laws helped expand rights for many more Americans. One of the most important was the Supreme Court's 1954 ruling that "separate but equal" segregated schools were unconstitutional. In the decade that followed, the Court also made rulings that gave people accused of crimes certain rights, made the drawing of electoral districts more fair, and clarified a person's right to free speech. Two of the most influential laws of the 1960s were the Civil Rights Act of 1964 and the Voting Act of 1965. The first gave the federal government the power to fight racial discrimination. The second made it illegal to prevent any voter from voting.

The table on this page lists these and other landmark laws of recent decades.

Landmark Acts of the Civil Rights Movement

- **_Brown v. Board of Education of Topeka, Kansas,_ 1954**
  Supreme Court rules segregated schools unconstitutional

- **Civil Rights Act of 1957**
  Congress sets up commission on civil rights and creates a division of civil rights in Justice Department

- **Equal Pay Act of 1963**
  Bans wage discrimination based on race, gender, religion, or national origin

- **Civil Rights Act of 1964**
  Strenghtens Fourteenth Amendment protections; bans discrimination in employment, voting, and public accommodations

- **Voting Rights Act of 1965**
  Empowers federal government to intervene in voter registration discrimination

- **Open Housing Act of 1968**
  Prevents people who are selling or renting homes from using certain forms of discrimination

- **Equal Employment Opportunity Act of 1972**
  Provides that businesses receiving federal funds must have affirmative action programs to increase number of female and minority employees

- **Americans With Disabilities Act of 1990**
  Bans discrimination in employment, transportation, public accommodations, and telecommunications against persons with physical or mental disabilities

---

Review

1. How can citizens show support for our legal system?

2. What did the Civil Rights Act of 1964 give to the federal government?

3. Why it is important for citizens in a democracy to obey its laws?

1960	1975	1990	2005

1962 César Chávez founds NFWA in Fresno, California

1968 Congress passes Indian Civil Rights Act

1990 Americans With Disabilities Act becomes law

Voting

Voting is an important right of American citizenship. Without it, citizens would not be able to choose the people who will run their government. Voting is also a major responsibility. Those who do not vote are failing to carry out a civic responsibility. They are also handing over their share of political power to voters whose views they may oppose. President Franklin Roosevelt reminded Americans of the importance of voting when he said, "Let us never forget that government is ourselves. The ultimate rulers of our democracy . . . are the voters of this country."

▲ The efforts of suffragists like Alice Paul (above, center) ensured the right to vote for all Americans.

A Precious Right

The U.S. Constitution states that no state may deny the right to vote because of race, color, gender, or age—if the person is at least 18 years old. People who have been convicted of serious crimes are the most common exception to the general rules. To be eligible to vote, a person must be at least 18 years old, a resident of the state for a specific period of time, and a citizen of the United States. In most states, you must also be registered to vote.

Why People Don't Vote

Despite the fact that voting gives Americans a chance to participate in their government, not every person who is eligible to vote actually votes. Some citizens do not vote because they do not meet state voting requirements, or they have not reregistered after changing residences. Other Americans do not think that any of the candidates represent their feelings on issues, or they think that their vote will not make a difference. Another reason is apathy, or lack of interest. Ironically, changes in the twentieth century have made it possible for more Americans to cast ballots than ever before.

Voter and Citizen Participation, 1900–Present

1900	1915	1930	1945

1914 Women have right to vote in 11 states

1920 Nineteenth Amendment grants women right to vote

A Century of Progress

Beginning with the Nineteenth Amendment, which gave women the right to vote in 1920, new laws and court decisions have increased the number of voters. In 1964 the Twenty-fourth Amendment made poll taxes illegal. The next year, the landmark Voting Rights Act took registration out of the hands of local authorities, who often discriminated against African Americans. Within a year, more than 250,000 new black voters had registered. Helped by these new voters, the number of African American office-holders in the South increased from about 100 in 1965 to more than 500,000 in 1990.

Another large group of Americans received the vote in 1971. The Twenty-sixth Amendment lowered the voting age to 18 from 21. Typically, young voters, ages 18 to 24, have the lowest rates of participation of any age group. However, in the 2004 presidential election, 10.5 million under-25 voters voted, compared to 8.7 million in 2000, raising the turnout rate to 42.3 percent from 36.5 percent.

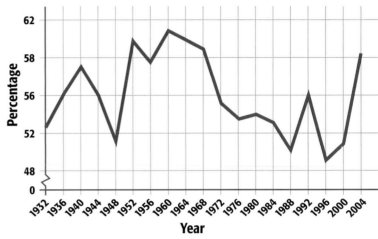

Percentage of Voting Age Who Voted*

Percentage vs *Year*

* Presidential elections

Source: Federal Election Commission; *Congressional Research Service reports.*

Why Your Vote Counts

The best way to prepare to vote is to stay informed about candidates and public issues. Newspapers, TV, radio, news magazines, and the Internet carry useful information. Other good sources include the *Voter's Information Bulletin;* the League of Women Voters; literature distributed by each political party; and information distributed by interest groups such as the American Conservative Union or the AFL-CIO Committee on Political Education. As you read about candidates and the issues they support, though, read carefully to separate facts from opinions. Everyone has different reasons for supporting particular candidates.

Review

1. What did the Twenty-sixth Amendment do?

2. How have laws protecting the right to vote changed in the past century?

3. Why is voting a vital civic responsibility?

1960	1975	1990	2005
1964 Civil Rights Act passes	**1971** Twenty-sixth Amendment lowers voting age to 18	**2004** 120 million Americans— 60 percent of all eligible voters— vote in the presidential election	

Shared Beliefs

The United States is a diverse country. Many different racial, ethnic, and religious groups live together peacefully. People with such varied backgrounds can succeed as a nation only when they share core values and respect the rights and beliefs of others.

Our Beliefs Unite Americans

What are the core beliefs that Americans share? Any list would include:

- a respect for the rights of each individual to equal treatment under the law, as described in the Constitution

- an appreciation of the cultural contributions of all the nation's people

- A respect for self-determination and an appreciation for community

- an awareness that it is each citizen's responsibility to participate thoughtfully in civic life

What beliefs would you add to this list?

Service Learning Facts

- 73% of America's 60 million young people believe they can make a difference in their communities

- 50% of U.S. high schools include organized service learning in their curriculum

- Teenagers volunteer 2.4 billion hours annually

- Teenage service is worth $34.4 billion to the U.S. economy

Sources: *Youth Services California*, www.yscal.org / U.S. Department of Education

What Is Effective Citizenship?

A key part of being an effective citizen is taking an active role in your community. You make a difference by engaging in community service where your efforts are needed, valued, and respected. Service learning is one way you can help your community. As you read, think about these questions: What exactly is service learning? Why should I participate? How do I get involved?

What Is Service Learning?

Performing important tasks that meet real community needs forms the basis of service learning. Service learning projects can be organized as a partnership between your school and your community. Examples of these projects are refurbishing parks, teaching younger children to read, and sharing your time with nursing home residents. Service learning requires an investment of your time as well as your talents. You and your team play an active role in planning the project and deciding how to use your skills and talents to complete your tasks.

Why Should I Participate?

You can make a difference. Share your knowledge and skills to help others in your school and community. You will cultivate new knowledge and develop new skills. A well-planned project gives you opportunities to practice your rights and responsibilities as a citizen. You take part in setting the goals of the project. You decide what you will do and how you will do it. An effective service learning project also provides time to share your thoughts about the service experience with others.

When you take part in your community and civic life, you not only help others, you also protect your rights. Supreme Court Justice Learned Hand expressed this view during an "I Am An American Day" celebration in 1944. His words are just as true today:

"Liberty lies in the hearts of men and women; when it dies there, no Constitution, no court, can even do much to help it."

Volunteer Opportunities
- ✔ Read to an elderly person
- ✔ Collect litter in your school yard
- ✔ Recycle at home
- ✔ Circulate a petition
- ✔ Put up a poster announcing Earth Day
- ✔ Bring groceries to a shut in

How Do I Get Involved?

Many students are already taking part in service learning. National organizations such as AmeriCorps and Learn and Serve America are always looking for volunteers. Forty-eight states are administering service learning programs through their state education agencies, and at least 64 percent of all public schools have students participating in community service activities recognized by the schools. By exploring the needs of your community, you can plan and organize your own service learning project.

Review

1. What is service learning?

2. Why should you get involved in your community?

3. How could your community be positively impacted by increased participation by its citizens?

Appendix

Contents

What Is an Appendix?

An appendix is the additional material you often find at the end of books. The following information will help you learn how to use the Appendix in **The American Journey to World War I.**

SkillBuilder Handbook

The **SkillBuilder Handbook** offers you information and practice using critical thinking and social studies skills. Mastering these skills will help you in all your courses.

Presidents of the United States

In this resource you will find information of interest on each of the nation's **presidents.**

Supreme Court Case Summaries

The **Supreme Court Case Summaries** discuss important Supreme Court cases. The summaries are listed in alphabetical order and include a summary of the facts of the case and its impact.

Documents of American History

This collection contains some of the most important writings in American history. Each **document** begins with an introduction that describes the author and places the selection within its historical context.

Glossary

A **glossary** is a list of important or difficult terms found in a textbook. Since words sometimes have other meanings, you may wish to consult a dictionary to find other uses for the term. The glossary gives a definition of each term as it is used in the book. The glossary also includes page numbers telling you where in the textbook the term is used.

Spanish Glossary

A **Spanish glossary** contains everything that an English glossary does, but it is in Spanish.

Gazetteer

A **gazetteer** (GA • zuh • TIHR) is a geographical dictionary. It lists some of the largest countries, cities, and several important geographic features. Each entry also includes a page number telling where this place is mentioned in this book.

Index

An **index** is an alphabetical listing that includes the subjects of the book and the page numbers where those subjects can be found. The index in this book also lets you know that certain pages contain maps, graphs, photos, or paintings about the subject.

Acknowledgements and Photo Credits

This section lists literary credits and/or photo credits for the book. You can look at this section to find out where the publisher of this textbook obtained the permission to use excerpts from other books or a photograph.

Test Yourself

Use the Appendix to answer these questions.

1. Who was the sixth president of the United States?
2. What was the Supreme Court's decision in *Marbury v. Madison?*
3. What was the purpose of issuing the Seneca Falls Declaration?
4. Through what parts of North America does the Columbia River flow?
5. What does the expression "favorite son" mean?

SkillBuilder Handbook

Contents

Taking Notes and Outlining

Why Learn This Skill?

One of the best ways to remember something is to write it down. Taking notes—writing down information in a brief and orderly form—not only helps you remember, but it also makes your studying easier.

1 Learning the Skill

There are several styles of note taking, but all explain and put information in a logical order. As you read, identify and summarize the main ideas and details that support them and write them in your notes. Paraphrase, or state in your own words, the information rather than copying it directly from the text. Using note cards or developing a personal "shorthand"—using symbols to represent words—can help.

You may also find it helpful to create an outline when taking notes. When outlining written material, first read the material to identify the main ideas. In textbooks, section headings provide clues to main topics. Then identify the subheadings. Place supporting details under the appropriate heading. The basic pattern for outlines is as follows:

Main Topic
  I. First idea or item
    A. First detail
      1. Subdetail
      2. Subdetail
    B. Second detail
  II. Second idea or item
    A. First detail
    B. Second detail
      1. Subdetail
      2. Subdetail
  III. Third idea or item, and so forth

2 Practicing the Skill

Look back at Chapter 6, Section 2. Take notes about the section and use these notes to create an outline of the main ideas, as shown at the bottom of the left column.

3 Applying the Skill

Scan a local newspaper for a short editorial or article about your local government. Take notes by using shorthand or by creating an outline. Summarize the article, using only your notes.

Reading a Time Line

Why Learn this Skill?

Knowing the relationship of time to events is important in studying history. A time line is a visual way to show the flow of dates and events. On most time lines, years are evenly spaced. For example, a time line showing 1,000 years might be divided into ten 100-year sections. Each event on a time line appears beside the date when the event took place.

1 Learning the Skill

To read a time line, follow these steps:

- Find the dates on the opposite ends of the time line to know the time span. Also note the intervals between dates on the time line.

- Study the order of events.

- Analyze relationships among events or look for trends.

2 Practicing the Skill

Analyze the time line about Magellan, which is at the bottom of the page. Use the time line to answer the questions below.

1. What time span is represented?

2. How many years does each of the sections represent?

3. Did Magellan's voyage to the Spice Islands occur before or after his voyage to the Philippines?

4. How long did it take for Magellan's men to go around the world?

3 Applying the Skill

List 10 key events that have occurred in your life and the dates on which these events occurred. Write the events in chronological order on a time line.

◀ Magellan

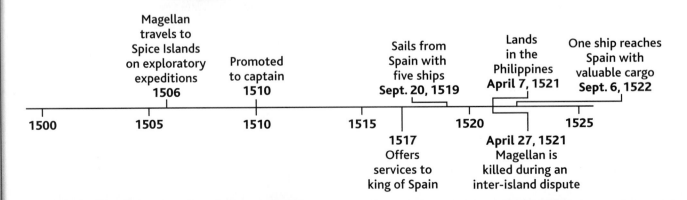

Magellan travels to Spice Islands on exploratory expeditions
1506

Promoted to captain
1510

Sails from Spain with five ships
Sept. 20, 1519

Lands in the Philippines
April 7, 1521

One ship reaches Spain with valuable cargo
Sept. 6, 1522

1500   **1505**   **1510**   **1515**   **1520**   **1525**

1517 Offers services to king of Spain

April 27, 1521 Magellan is killed during an inter-island dispute

Understanding the Parts of a Map

Why Learn This Skill?

Maps can direct you down the street or around the world. There are as many different kinds of maps as there are uses for them. Being able to read a map begins with learning about its parts.

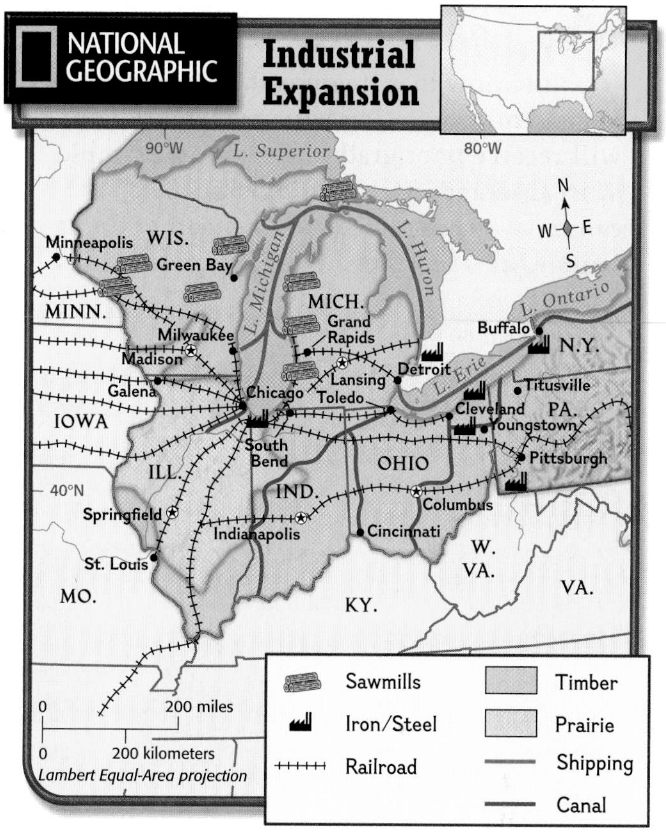

1 Learning the Skill

Maps usually include a key, a compass rose, and a scale bar. The map key explains the meaning of special colors, symbols, and lines used on the map.

After reading the map key, look for the compass rose. It is the direction marker that shows the cardinal directions of north, south, east, and west.

A measuring line, often called a scale bar, helps you estimate distance on a map. The map's scale tells you what distance on the earth is represented by the measurement on the scale bar. For example, 1 inch (2.54 cm) on the map may represent 100 miles (160.9 km) on the earth.

NATIONAL GEOGRAPHIC

Industrial Expansion

Map shows: Sawmills, Iron/Steel, Railroad, Timber, Prairie, Shipping, Canal

0 — 200 miles
0 — 200 kilometers
Lambert Equal-Area projection

2 Practicing the Skill

The map on this page shows industrial expansion in the late 1800s. Look at the parts of this map, and then answer the questions that follow.

1. What information is given in the key?

2. Which states have the most sawmills?

3. What direction would you travel from Springfield, Illinois, to Columbus, Ohio?

4. About how many miles is the route from Pittsburgh to Chicago?

3 Applying the Skill

Picture a mental image of your house or room. Draw a map showing the location of various areas. Include a map key explaining any symbols or colors you use. Also include a scale bar explaining the size of your map compared to the real area. Finally, add a compass rose and title to your map.

Understanding Cause and Effect

Why Learn This Skill?

You know that if you watch television instead of completing your homework you will receive poor grades. This is an example of a cause-and-effect relationship. The cause—watching television instead of doing homework—leads to an effect—poor grades.

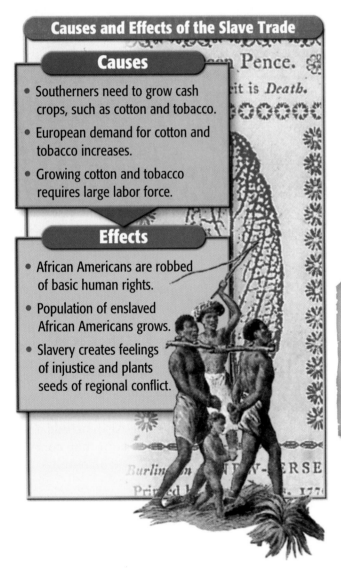

Causes and Effects of the Slave Trade

Causes

- Southerners need to grow cash crops, such as cotton and tobacco.
- European demand for cotton and tobacco increases.
- Growing cotton and tobacco requires large labor force.

Effects

- African Americans are robbed of basic human rights.
- Population of enslaved African Americans grows.
- Slavery creates feelings of injustice and plants seeds of regional conflict.

1 Learning the Skill

A *cause* is any person, event, or condition that makes something happen. What happens as a result is known as an *effect*.

These guidelines will help you identify cause and effect.

- Identify two or more events.
- Ask questions about why events occur.
- Look for "clue words" that alert you to cause and effect, such as *because, led to, brought about, produced,* and *therefore.*
- Identify the outcome of events.

2 Practicing the Skill

Study the cause-and-effect chart about the slave trade on this page. Think about the guidelines listed. Then answer the questions below.

1. What were some causes of the development of slavery in the South?
2. What were some of the short-term, or immediate, effects of enslaving Africans?
3. Read the second cause and second effect on the chart. How might these events be related?

3 Applying the Skill

Read an account of a recent event or chain of events in your community newspaper. Determine at least one cause and one effect of that event. Show the cause-and-effect relationship in a chart.

Making Comparisons

Why Learn This Skill?

Suppose you want to buy a portable compact disc (CD) player, and you must choose among three models. You would probably compare characteristics of the three models, such as price, sound quality, and size to figure out which model is best for you. When you study American history, you often compare people or events from one time period with those from a different time period.

1 Learning the Skill

When making comparisons, you examine two or more groups, situations, events, or documents. Then you identify similarities and differences. For example, the chart on this page compares two documents, specifically the powers each gave the federal government.

When making comparisons, you first decide what items will be compared and determine which characteristics you will use to compare them. Then you identify similarities and differences in these characteristics.

2 Practicing the Skill

Analyze the information on the chart on this page. Then answer the following questions.

1. What items are being compared?
2. Which document allowed the government to use state militias?
3. Which document allowed the government to regulate trade?
4. In what ways are the two documents different?
5. In what ways are the two documents similar?

Powers of the Federal Government

	Articles of Confederation	United States Constitution
Declare war; make peace	✔	✔
Coin money	✔	✔
Manage foreign affairs	✔	✔
Establish a postal system	✔	✔
Impose taxes		✔
Regulate trade		✔
Organize a court system		✔
Call state militias for service		✔
Protect copyrights		✔
Take other necessary actions to run the federal government		✔

3 Applying the Skill

On the editorial page of your local newspaper, find two letters to the editor that express different viewpoints on the same issue. Read the letters and identify the similarities and differences between the two points of view.

Drawing Inferences and Conclusions

Why Learn This Skill?

Have you ever heard someone say, "You can't judge him on face value"? It means that people, things you see, or things you read might not be as they appear to be. There might be a double or hidden meaning to what you see or hear.

1 Learning the Skill

To infer means to evaluate information and arrive at a conclusion. Inferences are ideas that are not directly stated. Making inferences involves reading between the lines to interpret what you are reading. You must then use your own knowledge and common sense to draw a conclusion.

Use the following steps to help you draw inferences and make conclusions:

- Read carefully for stated facts and ideas.

- Apply related information that you may already know to make inferences.

- Use your knowledge and insight to develop conclusions about these facts.

◀ James Madison

2 Practicing the Skill

Read the passage below and answer the questions that follow.

Quite often the British would lie in wait for American ships outside an American harbor. This happened in June 1807 off the coast of Virginia. A British warship, the *Leopard,* intercepted the American vessel *Chesapeake* and demanded to search it for British deserters. When the captain of the *Chesapeake* refused, the British opened fire, killing 3, wounding 18, and crippling the American ship.

As news of the attack spread, Americans reacted with an anti-British fury not seen since the Revolutionary War. Secretary of State James Madison called the attack an outrage.

1. What facts are given in the passage?

2. What can you infer about James Madison's political policy regarding Britain?

3. Knowing what you know about this period in America's past, what conclusions can you draw about how this incident relates to British and U.S. relations?

3 Applying the Skill

Choose a poem, or a quote found in a newspaper, that you think has more than one meaning. Share your selection with a classmate. Ask your classmate to infer the hidden meaning.

Predicting Consequences

Why Learn This Skill?

Did you ever wish you could see into the future? Predicting future events is very difficult. You can, however, develop skills that will help you identify the logical consequences of decisions or actions.

1 Learning the Skill

As you read in your book, think about what might come next. What you think will happen is your prediction. What happens as a result of an event is called a consequence.

Follow these steps to help you accurately predict consequences.

- Review what you already know by listing facts, events, and people's responses. The list will help you recall events and how they affected people.

- Ask yourself what prior knowledge you have about the events that are described.

- Use your knowledge and observations of similar situations. In other words, ask yourself, "What were the consequences of a similar decision or action that occurred in the past?"

- Map out all possible consequences or outcomes. Analyze each of the potential consequences by asking, "How likely is it that this will occur?"

2 Practicing the Skill

Read the paragraphs at the top of the next column. They are about the first presidency under the new Constitution. Then answer the questions that follow.

The new United States government faced many challenges during Washington's presidency. To limit the growing debt, Alexander Hamilton proposed the repayment of bonds issued during the American Revolution, the creation of a national bank, and the imposition of taxes on whiskey and other merchandise.

Each of these proposals encountered opposition. Southern states had amassed less debt during the war than Northern states. The Southern states felt that they would be paying more than their share to help end the debt. Many Americans feared that the creation of a national bank would take power away from state governments and make the rich wealthier. The tax on whiskey caused problems for farmers who lived by bartering and could not pay a monetary tax. While Washington and Hamilton were able to compromise with the opposition on most of these proposals, discontent still existed among many in the new United States.

1. Predict what you think is most likely to occur between discontented Americans and the government.

2. Explain why you made the prediction that you did.

3 Applying the Skill

Read newspapers for articles about an event that affects your community. Make an educated prediction about what will happen. Explain your reasoning.

Sequencing and Categorizing Information

Why Learn This Skill?

Sequencing is placing facts in the order in which they happened. Categorizing means grouping information by related facts and ideas. Both help you organize large quantities of information.

1 Learning the Skill

Follow these steps to learn sequencing and categorizing skills.

- When sequencing look for dates or clue words that describe chronological order: *in 2004, the late 1900s, first, then, finally, after,* and so on.

- Sequencing can be seen in time lines or graphs where information covers several years.

- To put information in categories, look for topics and facts that can be grouped together with similar characteristics. If the information is about farming, one category might be *tools of farming.*

- List these categories, or characteristics, as the headings on a chart.

- As you read, look for details and fill them in under the proper categories on the chart.

2 Practicing the Skill

Read the passages below and then answer the questions that follow.

- Before 1865 most immigrants to the United States—except for the enslaved—came from northern and western Europe.

- In the mid-1880s the pattern of immigration started to change. Large groups of "new" immigrants arrived from eastern and southern Europe.

- By 1907 only about 20 percent of immigrants came from northern and western Europe, while 80 percent came from southern and eastern Europe.

- After 1900 immigration from Mexico also increased. In addition many people came to the United States from China and Japan.

1. What information can be organized by sequencing?

2. What categories could you use to organize the information in the above list? What facts could be placed under each category?

3 Applying the Skill

Look at the Geographic Dictionary on pages 46–47. Record terms that would fit into the category "bodies of water." Also, find two newspaper articles about a local issue. Sequence or categorize the information in a chart.

◀ **Immigrants from China and Japan arrived in the late 1800s.**

Writing a Paragraph

Why Learn This Skill?

Paragraphs are the building blocks of an essay or other composition. Each paragraph is a unit—a group of sentences about a single topic or idea.

1 Learning the Skill

Most well-written paragraphs share four characteristics.

1. First, a paragraph expresses one main idea or is about one subject. A topic sentence states that main idea. The topic sentence may be located at the beginning, the middle, or the end of a paragraph.

2. Second, the rest of the sentences in a paragraph support the main idea. The main idea may be developed by facts, examples, and reasons.

3. Third, the sentences are arranged in a logical order.

4. Fourth, transitional words link sentences within the paragraph. These words can also link one paragraph with the next. Examples include *next, then, finally, also, because, however,* and *as a result.*

2 Practicing the Skill

Use the following sentences to build a paragraph containing a topic sentence and other sentences that give supporting details. Put the sentences in a logical order and add transitional words if you need to. Underline your topic sentence.

- Many such women became role models.

- Women also gained more free time as technology made housework easier.

- Their responsibilities at home lessened as families became smaller, more children spent the day at school, and men worked away from home.

- The situation of middle-class women changed during the late 1800s.

- Many more middle-class women were gaining higher education.

- These changes created the "new women"— a popular term for educated, up-to-date women who pursued interests outside of their homes.

- Many leaders of the urban reform movement were middle-class women.

3 Applying the Skill

Choose a topic concerning the Progressive Movement and write a paragraph about it. Then rewrite the paragraph with its sentences out of order. Exchange papers with a classmate. Have him or her find the topic sentence.

A suffragist ▶ asking for the right to vote

Analyzing Information

Why Learn This Skill?

Have you ever heard someone say, "Don't believe everything you read"? To be an informed citizen, you have to analyze information carefully as you read to make sure you understand the meaning and the intent of the writer.

1 Learning the Skill

Follow these steps to learn how to analyze.

- Identify the subject or topic of the information.

- How is the information organized? What are the main points?

- Think about how reliable the source of the information is.

- Summarize the information in your own words. Does the information agree with or contradict something you already know?

◀ Kit Carson

2 Practicing the Skill

Read the paragraph below that is from a Public Broadcasting System biography of Kit Carson. Then answer the questions that follow.

As was the case with many white trappers, Carson became somewhat integrated into the Indian world; he traveled and lived extensively among Indians, and his first two wives were Arapahoe and Cheyenne women. Carson was evidently unusual among trappers, however, for his self-restraint and temperate lifestyle. "Clean as a hound's tooth," according to one acquaintance, and a man whose "word was as sure as the sun comin' up." He was noted for an unassuming manner and implacable [firm] courage.

1. Was the information easy to understand? Explain.

2. Consider the source of the information. Does that make it seem more valid or less valid? Why?

3. Summarize the paragraph in a sentence of your own.

4. What is the main point of the paragraph?

3 Applying the Skill

Choose an article from a news magazine. Read it and analyze the information. Answer questions 1–4 as they apply to the article.

Distinguishing Fact From Opinion

Why Learn This Skill?

Suppose a friend says, "Our school's basketball team is awesome. That's a fact." Actually, it is not a fact; it is an opinion. Knowing how to tell the difference between a fact and an opinion can help you analyze the accuracy of political claims, advertisements, and many other kinds of statements.

1 Learning the Skill

A fact answers a specific question such as: What happened? Who did it? When and where did it happen? Why did it happen? Statements of fact can be checked for accuracy and proven.

An opinion, on the other hand, expresses beliefs, feelings, and judgments. Although it may reflect someone's thoughts, it is not possible to prove or disprove it.

An opinion often begins with phrases such as *I believe, I think, probably, it seems to me,* or *in my opinion.* It often contains words such as *might, could, should,* and *ought* and superlatives such as *best, worst,* and *greatest.* Judgment words that express approval or disapproval—such as *good, bad, poor,* and *satisfactory*—also usually indicate an opinion.

To distinguish between a fact and an opinion, ask yourself these questions:

- Does this statement give specific information about an event?

- Can I check the accuracy of this statement?

- Does this statement express someone's feelings, beliefs, or judgment?

- Does the statement include phrases such as *I believe,* superlatives, or judgment words?

2 Practicing the Skill

Read each numbered statement below. Tell whether each is a fact or an opinion, and explain how you arrived at your answer.

1. Paul Revere rode to Lexington with the news that the British soldiers were coming.
2. The British were the most feared soldiers in the world at that time.
3. The Daughters of Liberty opposed the Tea Act of 1773.
4. The Boston Tea Party raiders should have sunk the tea ships.
5. George III was a foolish king.

▲ Paul Revere's Ride

3 Applying the Skill

Analyze 10 advertisements. List the topics of each and at least three facts and three opinions presented in the ads.

Recognizing Bias

Why Learn This Skill?

Cats make better pets than dogs. If you say this, then you are stating a bias. A bias is a prejudice. It can prevent you from looking at a situation in a reasonable or truthful way. Recognizing bias will help you judge the accuracy of what you read.

1 Learning the Skill

Each of us has feelings and ideas that affect our point of view. Our opinions, or biases influence how we interpret events. Therefore, an idea that is stated as a fact may really be only an opinion. There are several clues to look for in order to recognize an author's bias.

- Identify the author and examine his or her views and possible reasons for writing the material.

- Look for language that reflects an emotion or opinion—words such as *all, never, best, worst, might,* or *should.*

- Examine the writing for imbalances—discussing only one viewpoint and failing to provide equal coverage for other possible viewpoints.

◀ William McKinley

2 Practicing the Skill

In the excerpt below, President William McKinley explains his decision to annex—add to U.S. territories—the Philippines. Read the excerpt. Answer the questions that follow.

I walked the floor of the White House night after night until midnight; and I am not ashamed to tell you gentlemen, that I went down on my knees and prayed [to] Almighty God for light and guidance more than one night. And one night late it came to me this way—I don't know how it was, but it came. . . . [T]hat there was nothing left for us to do but to take them all, and to educate the Filipinos, and uplift and civilize and Christianize them, and by God's grace do the very best we could by them, as our fellow-men for whom Christ also died. . . , and the next morning I sent for the chief engineer of the War Department (our map-maker), and I told him to put the Philippines on the map of the United States. . . , and there they will stay while I am President!

1. Imperialism consists of the actions one nation takes to control a weaker nation. Is McKinley stating a pro- or anti-imperialist bias? Which statements indicate bias?

2. What is the main reason McKinley wants to annex the Philippines?

3. What might people today think of this speech?

3 Applying the Skill

Look through the letters to the editor in your local newspaper. Write a short report analyzing one of the letters for evidence of bias.

Analyzing Library and Research Resources

Why Learn This Skill?

Imagine that your teacher has sent you to the library to write a report on the history of the Civil War. Knowing how to choose good sources for your research will help you save time in the library and write a better report.

1 Learning the Skill

Not all sources will be useful for your report on the Civil War. Even some sources that involve topics about the Civil War will not always provide the information you want. In analyzing sources for your research project, choose items that are nonfiction and that contain the most information about your topic.

When choosing research resources ask yourself these questions:

- Is the information up-to-date?

- Does the index have several pages listed for the topic?

- Is the resource written in a way that is easy to understand?

- Are there helpful illustrations and photos?

2 Practicing the Skill

Look at the following list of sources. Which would be most helpful in writing a report on the Civil War? Explain your choices.

1. A biographical dictionary of U.S. presidents
2. A history of America's Civil Rights Struggle
3. A photographic essay of the Civil War
4. A history of the United States from 1492–1900
5. The "C" volume of an encyclopedia
6. A history of the Republican Party in America
7. A historical atlas of the United States
8. A children's storybook about America in the 1800s
9. A book on the rise and fall of the South
10. A history of United States economic policy

3 Applying the Skill

Go to your local library or use the Internet to create a bibliography of sources you might use to write a report on the Civil War. List at least five sources.

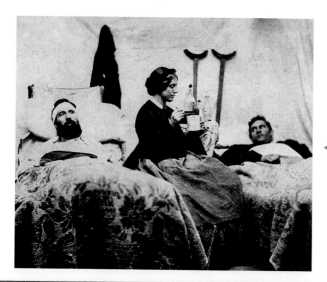

◄ Women made dramatic contributions to the Civil War by acting as nurses to the wounded.

Analyzing Primary Source Documents

Why Learn This Skill?

Historians determine what happened in the past by combing through bits of evidence to reconstruct events. These pieces of evidence are called primary sources. They are often first-person accounts from someone who saw or lived through what is being described. Examining primary sources can help you understand history.

1 Learning the Skill

Primary sources are records of events made by the people who witnessed them. They include letters, diaries, photographs and pictures, news articles, and legal documents.

To analyze primary sources, follow these steps:

- Identify when and where the document was written.

- Read the document for its content and try to answer the five "W" questions:

  <u>W</u>ho is it about?
  <u>W</u>hat is it about?
  <u>W</u>hen did it happen?
  <u>W</u>here did it happen?
  <u>W</u>hy did it happen?

- Identify the author's opinions.

2 Practicing the Skill

The primary source that follows comes from Speckled Snake, an elder of the Creek Nation, in 1829. He was more than 100 years old at the time he said these words. Read the quote, then answer the questions that follow.

> Brothers! I have listened to many talks from our Great Father. When he first came over the wide waters, he was but a little man.... But when the white man had warmed himself before the Indians' fire and filled himself with their hominy, he became very large. With a step he bestrode the mountains and his feet covered the plains and the valleys. His hand grasped the eastern and the western sea, and his head rested on the moon. Then he became our Great Father. Brothers, I have listened to a great many talks from our Great Father. But they always began and ended in this—"Get a little further; you are too near me."

1. What events is Speckled Snake describing?

2. Who was affected by these events?

3. What is Speckled Snake's general feeling toward the white man?

3 Applying the Skill

Find a primary source from your past—a photograph, a report card, an old newspaper clipping, or your first baseball card. Bring this source to class and explain what it shows about that time in your life.

▲ Choctaw forced from their land

Interpreting a Political Cartoon

Why Learn This Skill?

You have probably heard the saying, "A picture is worth a thousand words." For more than 200 years, political cartoonists have drawn pictures to present their opinions about a person or event. Learning to interpret political cartoons can help you understand issues of both the past and present.

1 Learning the Skill

Political cartoons state opinions about particular subjects. To illustrate those opinions, cartoonists provide clues, using several different techniques. They often exaggerate a person's physical features or appearance in a special effect called caricature. A caricature can be positive or negative, depending on the artist's point of view.

Cartoonists often use symbols to represent something else. The bald eagle is often shown in political cartoons as a symbol of the United States. Sometimes cartoonists help readers interpret their message by adding labels or captions.

To interpret a political cartoon, follow these steps:

- Read the caption and any other words printed in the cartoon.

- Analyze each element in the cartoon.

- Identify the clues: What is happening in the cartoon? Who or what is represented by each part of the drawing? Are there any symbols? To whom or what do they refer?

- Study all these elements to decide the point the cartoonist is making.

2 Practicing the Skill

Study the cartoon below and read the information about Jim Crow laws on pages 647–648. Then answer the following questions.

1. Are the white people in the cartoon friendly or unfriendly toward the African American? Explain.

2. What does the sign "POLLS" tell you about where the people are?

3. Who are the people represented in the cartoon?

4. What message do you think the cartoonist is trying to send?

3 Applying the Skill

Bring to class a copy of a political cartoon from a recent newspaper or magazine. Explain the cartoonist's point and the tools used to express it.

Analyzing News Media

Why Learn This Skill?

Every citizen needs to be aware of current issues and events to make good decisions when exercising citizenship rights.

1 Learning the Skill

To get an accurate profile of current events, you must learn to think critically about the news. The steps below will help you think critically.

- First, think about the source of the news story. Reports that reveal sources are more reliable than those that do not. If you know the sources, you can evaluate them. Can all facts be verified?

- Many news stories also interpret events. Such analyses may reflect a reporter's biases. Look for biases as you read or listen to news stories.

- Ask yourself whether the news is even-handed and thorough. Is it reported on the scene or secondhand? Does it represent both sides of an issue? The more sources cited for a fact, the more reliable it usually is.

◀ **Alexander Graham Bell makes the first phone call.**

2 Practicing the Skill

Below is an excerpt from an 1891 *New York Times* newspaper article. The article states that the Bell Company did not renew a patent on their telephone.

Read the excerpt below and answer the questions that follow.

> **THE TELEPHONE MONOPOLY**
>
> It is incredible that the Fifty-second Congress will pass an act to authorize the Bell Company to bleed for another seventeen years the public that has enriched the proprietors of that monopoly for nearly that period. ... But behind the company and the Congress there is the long-suffering public, ... [it] will unquestionably take a lively interest in killing off members who dare to support the pretensions of this arrogant and rapacious [greedy] monopoly."

1. What point is the article trying to make?
2. Does the article reflect bias or strong opinion? Explain.

3 Applying the Skill

Think of an issue in your community on which public opinion is divided. Read newspaper features and editorials about the issue and listen to television reports. What biases can you identify? Which reports are the most reliable?

Recognizing Economic Indicators

Why Learn This Skill?

Every day, business and government leaders are faced with the challenge of trying to predict what will happen to the economy in the coming months and years. To help these leaders in making decisions, economists have developed ways to measure an economy's performance. These are called economic indicators.

1 Learning the Skill

Economic indicators are statistics, or numbers, that tell how well the economy is doing and how well the economy is going to do in the future. They include the number of jobless, the rate at which prices rise over a period of time, and the amount of goods and services that are produced and sold. Each month, the U.S. Department of Commerce gathers data for 78 economic indicators. They cover all aspects of the state of the United States economy. The chart at the right lists some common terms for economic indicators that you may have read about or heard mentioned.

▲ Stock prices often rise and fall based on the news from economic indicators.

2 Practicing the Skill

Start an Economics Handbook. Using a dictionary, look up each economic term listed on this chart. Write a definition for each term in your Economics Handbook.

Economic Indicators

Term	Definition
Federal Reserve Bank	
Gross National Product (GNP)	
Depression	
Recession	
Inflation	
Import	
Export	
Interest Rates	
Consumer Index	
Federal Deficit	
Capital	
Stock Market	

3 Applying the Skill

At the library or on the Internet, find information about the current economic state of the United States. Using the terms that you have defined, write a few brief paragraphs describing the current economy.

Presidents of the United States

In this resource you will find portraits of the individuals who served as presidents of the United States, along with their occupations, political party affiliations, and other interesting facts.

**The Republican Party during this period developed into today's Democratic Party. Today's Republican Party originated in 1854.*

1 George Washington

1789–1797
Lived: 1732–1799
Born in: Virginia
Elected from: Virginia
Occupations: Soldier, Planter
Party: None
Vice President: John Adams

2 John Adams

1797–1801
Lived: 1735–1826
Born in: Massachusetts
Elected from: Massachusetts
Occupations: Teacher, Lawyer
Party: Federalist
Vice President: Thomas Jefferson

3 Thomas Jefferson

1801–1809
Lived: 1743–1826
Born in: Virginia
Elected from: Virginia
Occupations: Planter, Lawyer
Party: Republican**
Vice Presidents: Aaron Burr, George Clinton

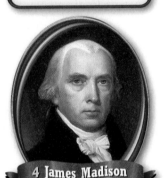

4 James Madison

1809–1817
Lived: 1751–1836
Born in: Virginia
Elected from: Virginia
Occupation: Planter
Party: Republican**
Vice Presidents: George Clinton, Elbridge Gerry

5 James Monroe

1817–1825
Lived: 1758–1831
Born in: Virginia
Elected from: Virginia
Occupation: Lawyer
Party: Republican**
Vice President: Daniel D. Tompkins

6 John Quincy Adams

1825–1829
Lived: 1767–1848
Born in: Massachusetts
Elected from: Massachusetts
Occupation: Lawyer
Party: Republican**
Vice President: John C. Calhoun

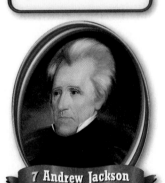

7 Andrew Jackson

1829–1837
Lived: 1767–1845
Born in: South Carolina
Elected from: Tennessee
Occupations: Lawyer, Soldier
Party: Democratic
Vice Presidents: John C. Calhoun, Martin Van Buren

8 Martin Van Buren

1837–1841
Lived: 1782–1862
Born in: New York
Elected from: New York
Occupation: Lawyer
Party: Democratic
Vice President: Richard M.
Johnson

9 William H. Harrsion

1841
Lived: 1773–1841
Born in: Virginia
Elected from: Ohio
Occupations: Soldier, Planter
Party: Whig
Vice President: John Tyler

10 John Tyler

1841–1845
Lived: 1790–1862
Born in: Virginia
Elected as V.P. from: Virginia;
Succeeded Harrison
Occupation: Lawyer
Party: Whig
Vice President: None

11 James K. Polk

1845–1849
Lived: 1795–1849
Born in: North Carolina
Elected from: Tennessee
Occupation: Lawyer
Party: Democratic
Vice President: George M.
Dallas

12 Zachary Taylor

1849–1850
Lived: 1784–1850
Born in: Virginia
Elected from: Louisiana
Occupation: Soldier
Party: Whig
Vice President: Millard
Fillmore

13 Millard Fillmore

1850–1853
Lived: 1800–1874
Born in: New York
Elected as V.P. from: New York;
Succeeded Taylor
Occupation: Lawyer
Party: Whig
Vice President: None

14 Franklin Pierce

1853–1857
Lived: 1804–1869
Born in: New Hampshire
Elected from: New Hampshire
Occupation: Lawyer
Party: Democratic
Vice President: William R. King

15 James Buchanan

1857–1861
Lived: 1791–1868
Born in: Pennsylvania
Elected from: Pennsylvania
Occupation: Lawyer
Party: Democratic
Vice President: John C.
Breckinridge

16 Abraham Lincoln

1861–1865
Lived: 1809–1865
Born in: Kentucky
Elected from: Illinois
Occupation: Lawyer
Party: Republican
Vice Presidents: Hannibal
Hamlin, Andrew Johnson

17 Andrew Johnson

1865–1869
Lived: 1808–1875
Born in: North Carolina
Elected as V.P. from:
Tennessee; Succeeded
Lincoln
Occupation: Tailor
Party: Republican
Vice President: None

18 Ulysses S. Grant

1869–1877
Lived: 1822–1885
Born in: Ohio
Elected from: Illinois
Occupations: Farmer, Soldier
Party: Republican
Vice Presidents: Schuyler
Colfax, Henry Wilson

19 Rutherford B. Hayes

1877–1881
Lived: 1822–1893
Born in: Ohio
Elected from: Ohio
Occupation: Lawyer
Party: Republican
Vice President: William A.
Wheeler

20 James A. Garfield

1881
Lived: 1831–1881
Born in: Ohio
Elected from: Ohio
Occupations: Laborer, Professor
Party: Republican
Vice President: Chester A.
Arthur

21 Chester A. Arthur

1881–1885
Lived: 1830–1886
Born in: Vermont
Elected as V.P. from: New York;
Succeeded Garfield
Occupations: Teacher, Lawyer
Party: Republican
Vice President: None

22 Grover Cleveland

1885–1889
Lived: 1837–1908
Born in: New Jersey
Elected from: New York
Occupation: Lawyer
Party: Democratic
Vice President: Thomas A.
Hendricks

23 Benjamin Harrison

1889–1893
Lived: 1833–1901
Born in: Ohio
Elected from: Indiana
Occupation: Lawyer
Party: Republican
Vice President: Levi P. Morton

24 Grover Cleveland

1893–1897
Lived: 1837–1908
Born in: New Jersey
Elected from: New York
Occupation: Lawyer
Party: Democratic
Vice President: Adlai E.
Stevenson

25 William McKinley

1897–1901
Lived: 1843–1901
Born in: Ohio
Elected from: Ohio
Occupations: Teacher, Lawyer
Party: Republican
Vice Presidents: Garret Hobart,
Theodore Roosevelt

U.S. Presidents

26 Theodore Roosevelt

1901–1909
Lived: 1858–1919
Born in: New York
Elected as V.P. from: New York; Succeeded McKinley
Occupations: Historian, Rancher
Party: Republican
Vice President: Charles W. Fairbanks

27 William H. Taft

1909–1913
Lived: 1857–1930
Born in: Ohio
Elected from: Ohio
Occupation: Lawyer
Party: Republican
Vice President: James S. Sherman

28 Woodrow Wilson

1913–1921
Lived: 1856–1924
Born in: Virginia
Elected from: New Jersey
Occupation: College Professor
Party: Democratic
Vice President: Thomas R. Marshall

29 Warren G. Harding

1921–1923
Lived: 1865–1923
Born in: Ohio
Elected from: Ohio
Occupations: Newspaper Editor, Publisher
Party: Republican
Vice President: Calvin Coolidge

30 Calvin Coolidge

1923–1929
Lived: 1872–1933
Born in: Vermont
Elected as V.P. from: Massachusetts; Succeeded Harding
Occupation: Lawyer
Party: Republican
Vice President: Charles G. Dawes

31 Herbert C. Hoover

1929–1933
Lived: 1874–1964
Born in: Iowa
Elected from: California
Occupation: Engineer
Party: Republican
Vice President: Charles Curtis

32 Franklin D. Roosevelt

1933–1945
Lived: 1882–1945
Born in: New York
Elected from: New York
Occupation: Lawyer
Party: Democratic
Vice Presidents: John N. Garner, Henry A. Wallace, Harry S. Truman

33 Harry S. Truman

1945–1953
Lived: 1884–1972
Born in: Missouri
Elected as V.P. from: Missouri; Succeeded Roosevelt
Occupations: Clerk, Farmer
Party: Democratic
Vice President: Alben W. Barkley

34 Dwight D. Eisenhower

1953–1961
Lived: 1890–1969
Born in: Texas
Elected from: New York
Occupation: Soldier
Party: Republican
Vice President: Richard M. Nixon

35 John F. Kennedy

1961–1963
Lived: 1917–1963
Born in: Massachusetts
Elected from: Massachusetts
Occupations: Author, Reporter
Party: Democratic
Vice President: Lyndon B. Johnson

36 Lyndon B. Johnson

1963–1969
Lived: 1908–1973
Born in: Texas
Elected as V.P. from: Texas; Succeeded Kennedy
Occupation: Teacher
Party: Democratic
Vice President: Hubert H. Humphrey

37 Richard M. Nixon

1969–1974
Lived: 1913–1994
Born in: California
Elected from: New York
Occupation: Lawyer
Party: Republican
Vice Presidents: Spiro T. Agnew, Gerald R. Ford

38 Gerald R. Ford

1974–1977
Lived: 1913–
Born in: Nebraska; Appointed as V.P. upon Agnew's resignation; Succeeded Nixon
Occupation: Lawyer
Party: Republican
Vice President: Nelson A. Rockefeller

39 James E. Carter, Jr.

1977–1981
Lived: 1924–
Born in: Georgia
Elected from: Georgia
Occupations: Business, Farmer
Party: Democratic
Vice President: Walter F. Mondale

40 Ronald W. Reagan

1981–1989
Lived: 1911–2004
Born in: Illinois
Elected from: California
Occupations: Actor, Lecturer
Party: Republican
Vice President: George H.W. Bush

41 George H. W. Bush

1989–1993
Lived: 1924–
Born in: Massachusetts
Elected from: Texas
Occupation: Business
Party: Republican
Vice President: J. Danforth Quayle

42 William J. Clinton

1993–2001
Lived: 1946–
Born in: Arkansas
Elected from: Arkansas
Occupation: Lawyer
Party: Democratic
Vice President: Albert Gore, Jr.

43 George W. Bush

2001–
Lived: 1946–
Born in: Connecticut
Elected from: Texas
Occupation: Business
Party: Republican
Vice President: Richard B. Cheney

U.S. Presidents

Honoring America

For Americans, the flag has always had a special meaning. It is a symbol of our nation's freedom and democracy.

Flag Etiquette

Over the years, Americans have developed rules and customs concerning the use and display of the flag. One of the most important things every American should remember is to treat the flag with respect.

- The flag should be raised and lowered by hand and displayed only from sunrise to sunset. On special occasions, the flag may be displayed at night, but it should be illuminated.

- The flag may be displayed on all days, weather permitting, particularly on national and state holidays and on historic and special occasions.

- No flag may be flown above the American flag or to the right of it at the same height.

- The flag should never touch the ground or floor beneath it.

- The flag may be flown at half-staff by order of the president, usually to mourn the death of a public official.

- The flag may be flown upside down only to signal distress.

- The flag should never be carried flat or horizontally, but always carried aloft and free.

- When the flag becomes old and tattered, it should be destroyed by burning. According to an approved custom, the Union (stars on blue field) is first cut from the flag; then the two pieces, which no longer form a flag, are burned.

The American's Creed

I believe in the United States of America as a Government of the people, by the people, for the people, whose just powers are derived from the consent of the governed; a democracy in a republic; a sovereign Nation of many sovereign States; a perfect union, one and inseparable; established upon those principles of freedom, equality, justice, and humanity for which American patriots sacrificed their lives and fortunes.

I therefore believe it is my duty to my Country to love it; to support its Constitution; to obey its laws; to respect its flag, and to defend it against all enemies.

The Pledge of Allegiance

I pledge allegiance to the Flag of the United States of America and to the Republic for which it stands, one Nation under God, indivisible, with liberty and justice for all.

Supreme Court Case Summaries

The following summaries give details about important Supreme Court cases.

BROWN v. BOARD OF EDUCATION (1954)

In *Brown* v. *Board of Education of Topeka, Kansas*, the Supreme Court overruled *Plessy* v. *Ferguson* (1896) making the separate-but-equal doctrine in public schools unconstitutional. The Supreme Court rejected the idea that truly equal but separate schools for African American and white students would be constitutional. The Court explained that the Fourteenth Amendment's requirement that all persons be guaranteed equal protection of the law is not met simply by ensuring that African American and white schools "have been equalized…with respect to buildings, curricula, qualifications and salaries, and other tangible factors."

The Court then ruled that racial segregation in public schools violates the Equal Protection Clause of the Constitution because it is inherently unequal. In other words, nothing can make racially segregated public schools equal under the Constitution because the very fact of separation marks the separated race as inferior. In practical terms, the Court's decision in this case has been extended beyond public education to virtually all public accommodations and activities.

DRED SCOTT v. SANDFORD (1857)

Dred Scott was taken by slaveholder John Sandford to the free state of Illinois and to the Wisconsin Territory, which had also banned slavery. Later they returned to a slave state, Missouri. Several years later, Scott sued for his freedom under the Missouri legal principle of "once free, always free." In other words, under state law enslaved people were entitled to freedom if they had lived in a free state at any time.

Dred Scott

Missouri courts ruled against Scott, but he appealed the case all the way to the United States Supreme Court.

The Supreme Court decided this case before the Fourteenth Amendment was added to the Constitution. (The Fourteenth Amendment provides that anyone born or naturalized in the United States is a citizen of the nation and of his or her state of residence.) The court held that enslaved African Americans were property, not citizens, and thus had no rights under the Constitution. The decision also declared that it was unconstitutional to prohibit slavery in the territories. Many people in the North were outraged by the decision, which moved the nation closer to civil war.

GIBBONS v. OGDEN (1824)

Thomas Gibbons had a federal license to operate a steamboat along the coast, but he did not have a license from the state of New York to travel on New York waters. He wanted to run a steamboat line between Manhattan and New Jersey that would compete with Aaron Ogden's company. Ogden had a New York license. Gibbons sued for the freedom to use his federal license to compete against Ogden on New York waters.

Gibbons won the case. The Supreme Court made it clear that the authority of Congress to regulate interstate commerce (among states) includes the authority to regulate intrastate commerce (within a single state) that bears on, or relates to, interstate commerce.

Before this decision, it was thought that the Constitution would permit a state to close its borders to interstate commercial activity—which, in effect, would stop such activity in its tracks. This case says that a state can regulate purely internal commercial activity, but only Congress can regulate commercial activity that has both intrastate and interstate dimensions.

GIDEON v. WAINWRIGHT (1963)

After being accused of robbery, Clarence Gideon defended himself in a Florida court because the judge in the case refused to appoint a free lawyer. The jury found Gideon guilty. Eventually, Gideon appealed his conviction to the United States Supreme Court, claiming that by failing to appoint a lawyer the lower court had violated his rights under the Sixth and Fourteenth Amendments.

The Supreme Court agreed with Gideon. In *Gideon v. Wainwright* the Supreme Court held for the first time that poor defendants in criminal cases have the right to a state-paid attorney under the Sixth Amendment. The rule announced in this case has been refined to apply whenever the defendant, if convicted, can be sentenced to more than six months in jail or prison.

KOREMATSU v. UNITED STATES (1944)

After the Japanese bombing of Pearl Harbor in 1941, thousands of Japanese Americans on the West Coast were forced to abandon their homes and businesses, and they were moved to internment camps in California, Idaho, Utah, Arizona, Wyoming, Colorado, and Arkansas. The prison-like camps offered poor food and cramped quarters.

In 1983 Fred Korematsu (center) won a reversal of his conviction.

The Supreme Court's decision in *Korematsu v. United States* supported the authority of the federal government to move Japanese Americans, many of whom were citizens, from designated military areas that included almost the entire West Coast. The government defended the so-called exclusion orders as a necessary response to Japan's attack on Pearl Harbor. Only after his reelection in 1944 did President Franklin Roosevelt rescind the evacuation orders, and by the end of 1945 the camps were closed.

MARBURY v. MADISON (1803)

During his last days in office, President John Adams, a Federalist, appointed William Marbury and several other men as judges. This action angered the incoming Democratic-Republican president Thomas Jefferson. Jefferson then ordered James Madison, his secretary of state, not to deliver the commissions, thus blocking the appointments. William Marbury sued. He asked the Supreme Court to order Madison to deliver the commission that would make him a judge.

The Court ruled against Marbury, but more importantly, the decision in this case established one of the most significant principles of American constitutional law. The Supreme Court held that it is the Court itself that has the final say on what the Constitution means. This right is known as judicial review. It is also the Supreme Court that has the final say in whether or not an act of government—legislative or executive at the federal, state, or local level—violates the Constitution.

McCULLOCH v. MARYLAND (1819)

Following the War of 1812, the United States experienced years of high inflation and general economic turmoil. In an attempt to stabilize the economy, the United States Congress chartered a Second Bank of the United States in 1816. Maryland and several other states, however, opposed the competition that the new national bank created and passed state laws taxing its branches.

In 1818, James McCulloch, head of the Baltimore branch of the Second Bank of the United States, refused to pay the tax to the state of Maryland. The case worked its way through the Maryland state courts all the way to the United States Supreme Court.

The Supreme Court declared the Maryland tax unconstitutional and void. More importantly, the decision established the foundation for expanded Congressional authority. The Court held that the necessary and proper clause of the Constitution allows Congress to do more than the Constitution expressly states it may do. The decision allows Congress to enact nearly any law that will help it achieve any of its constitutional duties. For example, Congress has the express authority to regulate interstate commerce. The necessary and proper clause permits Congress to do so in ways not actually specified in the Constitution.

MIRANDA v. ARIZONA (1966)

In 1963, police in Arizona arrested Ernesto Miranda for kidnapping. The court found Miranda guilty on the basis of a signed confession. The police admitted that neither before nor during the questioning had Miranda been advised of his right to consult with an attorney before answering any questions or of his right to have an attorney present during the interrogation.

In 1963 the arrest of Ernesto Miranda (right) led to a landmark decision.

Miranda appealed his conviction, claiming that police had violated his right against self-incrimination under the Fifth Amendment by not informing him of his legal rights during the questioning.

Miranda won the case. The Supreme Court held that a person in police custody cannot be questioned unless told that he or she has: 1) the right to remain silent, 2) the right to an attorney (at government expense if the accused is unable to pay), and 3) that anything the person says after stating that he or she understands these rights can be used as evidence of guilt at trial. These rights have come to be called the Miranda warning. They are intended to ensure that an accused person in custody will not unknowingly give up the Fifth Amendment's protection against self-incrimination.

NEW YORK TIMES COMPANY v. UNITED STATES (1971)

In June 1971, the New York Times published its first installment of the "Pentagon Papers," a classified document about government actions in the Vietnam War era. The secret document had been leaked to the Times by antiwar activist Daniel Ellsberg, who had previously worked in national security for the government. President Richard Nixon went to court to block further publication of the Pentagon Papers. The New York Times appealed to the Supreme Court to allow it to continue publishing without government interference.

The Supreme Court's ruling in this case upheld earlier decisions that established the doctrine of prior restraint. This doctrine protects the press (broadly defined as radio and television, newspapers, filmmakers and distributors, etc.) from government attempts to block publication. Except in extraordinary circumstances, the press must be allowed to publish.

PLESSY V. FERGUSON (1896)

In the late 1800s, railroad companies in Louisiana were required by state law to provide "separate-but-equal" cars for white and African American passengers. In 1890 a group of citizens in New Orleans selected Homer Plessy to challenge that law. In 1892, Plessy boarded a whites-only car and refused to move. He was arrested. Plessy appealed to the Supreme Court, arguing that the Louisiana separate-but-equal law violated his right to equal protection under the Fourteenth Amendment.

Homer Plessy lost the case. The Plessy decision upheld the separate-but-equal doctrine used by Southern states to perpetuate segregation following the Civil War. The court ruled that the Fourteenth Amendment's equal protection clause required only equal public facilities for the two races, not equal access to the same facilities. This decision was overruled in 1954 by *Brown* v. *Board of Education of Topeka, Kansas* (discussed previously).

ROE V. WADE (1973)

Roe v. *Wade* challenged restrictive abortion laws in both Texas and Georgia. The suit was brought in the name of Jane Roe, an alias used to protect the privacy of the plaintiff.

In this decision, the Supreme Court ruled that females have a constitutional right under various provisions of the Constitution—most notably, the due process clause—to decide whether or not to terminate a pregnancy. The Supreme Court's decision in this case was the most significant in a long line of decisions over a period of 50 years that recognized a constitutional right of privacy, even though the word *privacy* is not found in the Constitution.

UNITED STATES V. NIXON (1974)

In the early 1970s, President Nixon was named an unindicted coconspirator in the criminal investigation that arose in the aftermath of a break-in at the offices of the Democratic Party in Washington, D.C. A federal judge had ordered President Nixon to turn over tapes of conversations he had with his advisers about the break-in. Nixon resisted the order, claiming that the conversations were entitled to absolute confidentiality by Article II of the Constitution.

The decision in this case made it clear that the president is not above the law. The Supreme Court held that only those presidential conversations and communications that relate to performing the duties of the office of president are confidential and protected from a judicial order of disclosure. The Court ordered Nixon to give up the tapes, which revealed evidence linking the president to the conspiracy to obstruct justice. He resigned from office shortly thereafter.

WORCESTER V. GEORGIA (1832)

State officials in Georgia wanted to remove the Cherokees from land that had been guaranteed to them in treaties. Samuel Worcester was a Congregational missionary who worked with the Cherokee people. He was arrested for failure to have a license that the state required to live in Cherokee country and for refusing to obey an order from the Georgia militia to leave Cherokee lands. Worcester then sued the state of Georgia. He claimed that Georgia had no legal authority on Cherokee land because the United States government recognized the Cherokee in Georgia as a separate nation.

The Supreme Court agreed with Worcester by a vote of 5 to 1. Chief Justice John Marshall wrote the majority opinion which said that Native American nations were a distinct people with the right to have independent political communities and that only the federal government had authority over matters that involved the Cherokee.

President Andrew Jackson supported Georgia's efforts to remove the Cherokee to Indian Territory and refused to enforce the court's ruling. After the ruling Jackson remarked, "John Marshall has made his decision. Now let him enforce it."

The Magna Carta

The Magna Carta, signed by King John in 1215, marked a decisive step forward in the development of constitutional government in England. Later, it became a model for colonists who carried the Magna Carta's guarantees of legal and political rights to America.

1. . . . [T]hat the English Church shall be free, and shall have its rights undiminished, and its liberties unimpaired. . . . we have also granted, for us and our heirs for ever, all the liberties written out below, to have and to keep for them and their heirs, of us and our heirs:

39. No free man shall be seized or imprisoned, or stripped of his rights or possessions, or outlawed or exiled, or deprived of his standing in any other way, nor will we proceed with force against him, or send others to do so, except by the lawful judgement of his equals or by the law of the land.

40. To no one will we sell, to no one deny or delay right or justice.

41. All merchants may enter or leave England unharmed and without fear, and may stay or travel within it, by land or water, for purposes of trade, free from all illegal exactions, in accordance with ancient and lawful customs. This, however, does not apply in time of war to merchants from a country that is at war with us.

42. In future it shall be lawful for any man to leave and return to our kingdom unharmed and without fear, by land or water, preserving his allegiance to us, except in time of war, for some short period, for the common benefit of the realm.

60. All these customs and liberties that we have granted shall be observed in our kingdom in so far as concerns our own relations with our subjects. Let all men of our kingdom, whether clergy or laymen, observe them similarly in their relations with their own men.

63. . . . Both we and the barons have sworn that all this shall be observed in good faith and without deceit. Witness the abovementioned people and many others. Given by our hand in the meadow that is called Runnymede, between Windsor and Staines, on the fifteenth day of June in the seventeenth year of our reign.

◀ **Illuminated manuscript, Middle Ages**

The Mayflower Compact

On November 21, 1620, 41 colonists aboard the Mayflower drafted this agreement. The Mayflower Compact was the first plan of self-government enacted in the English colonies.

IN The Name of God, Amen. We, whose names are underwritten, the Loyal Subjects of our dread Sovereign Lord King James, by the Grace of God, of Great Britain, France, and Ireland, King, Defender of the Faith, &c. Having undertaken for the Glory of God, and Advancement of the Christian Faith, and the Honour of our King and Country, a Voyage to plant the first colony in the northern Parts of Virginia; Do by these Presents, solemnly and mutually in the Presence of God and one another, covenant and combine ourselves together into a civil Body Politick, for our better Ordering and Preservation, and Furtherance of the Ends aforesaid: And by Virtue hereof do enact, constitute, and frame, such just and equal Laws, Ordinances, Acts, Constitutions, and Offices, from time to time, as shall be thought most meet and convenient for the general Good of the Colony; unto which we promise all due Submission and Obedience. In Witness whereof we have hereunto subscribed our names at Cape Cod the eleventh of November, in the Reign of our Sovereign Lord King James of England, France, and Ireland, the eighteenth and of Scotland, the fifty-fourth. Anno Domini, 1620

The Federalist, No. 10

James Madison wrote several articles supporting ratification of the Constitution. Below, Madison argues for the idea of a federal republic.

By a faction, I understand a number of citizens . . . who are united and actuated by some common impulse . . . adversed to the rights of other citizens. . . .

The inference to which we are brought is, that the CAUSES of faction cannot be removed, and that relief is only to be sought in the means of controlling its EFFECTS. . . .

A republic, by which I mean a government in which the scheme of representation takes place, . . . promises the cure for which we are seeking. . . .

The two great points of difference between a democracy and a republic are: first, the delegation of the government, in the latter, to a small number of citizens elected by the rest; secondly, the greater number of citizens, and greater sphere of country, over which the latter may be extended.

▲ James Madison

The effect of the first difference is . . . to refine and enlarge the public views, by passing them through the medium of a chosen body of citizens, whose wisdom may best discern the true interest of their country, and whose patriotism and love of justice will be least likely to sacrifice it to temporary or partial considerations.

Washington's Farewell Address

At the end of his second term as president, George Washington spoke of the dangers facing the young nation. He warned against the dangers of political parties and sectionalism, and he advised the nation against permanent alliances with other nations.

Citizens by birth or choice of a common country, that country has a right to concentrate your affections. The name of American, which belongs to you, in your national capacity, must always exalt the just pride of patriotism more than any appellation derived from local discriminations. With slight shades of difference, you have the same religion, manners, habits, and political principles. You have in a common cause fought and triumphed together. . . .

In contemplating the causes which may disturb our Union, it occurs as matter of serious concern that any ground should have been furnished for characterizing parties by *geographical* discriminations. . . .

▲ George Washington

No alliances, however strict between the parts, can be an adequate substitute. They must inevitably experience the infractions and interruptions which all alliances in all times have experienced. . . .

The great rule of conduct for us, in regard to foreign nations, is in extending our commercial relations to have with them as little *political* connection as possible. . . .

. . . I anticipate with pleasing expectations that retreat in which I promise myself to realize . . . the sweet enjoyment of partaking, in the midst of my fellow citizens, the benign influence of good laws under a free government, the ever favorite object of my heart, and the happy reward, as I trust, of our mutual cares, labors, and dangers.

The Star-Spangled Banner

During the British bombardment of Fort McHenry during the War of 1812, a young Baltimore lawyer named Francis Scott Key was inspired by the sight to write the words to "The Star-Spangled Banner." Although it became popular immediately, it was not until 1931 that Congress officially declared this song our national anthem.

O! say can you see by the dawn's early light,
What so proudly we hail'd at the twilight's last gleaming;

Whose broad stripes and bright stars, through the perilous fight,
O'er the ramparts we watch'd were so gallantly streaming;
And the rockets' red glare, the bombs bursting in air,
Gave proof through the night that our flag was still there;
O! say does that star-spangled banner yet wave,
O'er the land of the free, and the home of the brave.

The Monroe Doctrine

▲ James Monroe

In an 1823 address to Congress, President James Monroe proclaimed the Monroe Doctrine. Designed to end European influence in the Western Hemisphere, it became a cornerstone of United States foreign policy.

With the existing colonies or dependencies of any European power we have not interfered and shall not interfere. But with the governments who have declared their independence and maintained it, and whose independence we have, on great consideration and on just principles, acknowledged, we could not view any interposition for the purpose of oppressing them, or controlling in any other manner their destiny, by any European power in any other light than as the manifestation of an unfriendly disposition toward the United States. . . .

Our policy in regard to Europe, which was adopted at an early stage of the wars which have so long agitated that quarter of the globe, nevertheless remains the same, which is not to interfere in the internal concerns of any of its powers; to consider the government de facto as the legitimate government for us; to cultivate friendly relations with it, and to preserve those relations by a frank, firm, and manly policy, meeting in all instances the just claims of every power, submitting to injuries from none.

The Memorial of the Cherokee Nation

The Indian Removal Act of 1830 called for moving Native Americans west of the Mississippi River. Cherokee leaders protested the policy.

We are aware, that some persons suppose it will be for our advantage to remove beyond the Mississippi. We think otherwise. Our people universally think otherwise. . . .

We wish to remain on the land of our fathers. We have a perfect and original right to remain without interruption or molestation. The treaties with us, and laws of the United States made in pursuance of treaties, guaranty our residence and our privileges, and secure us against intruders. Our only request is, that these treaties may be fulfilled, and these laws executed. . . .

. . . We have been called a poor, ignorant, and degraded people. We certainly are not rich; nor have we ever boasted of our knowledge, or our moral or intellectual elevation. But there is not a man within our limits so ignorant as not to know that he has a right to live on the land of his fathers, in the possession of his immemorial privileges, and that this right has been acknowledged and guaranteed by the United States; nor is there a man so degraded as not to feel a keen sense of injury, on being deprived of this right and driven into exile.

▲ Beaded shoulder bag, Cherokee people

The Seneca Falls Declaration

One of the first documents to express the desire for equal rights for women is the Declaration of Sentiments and Resolutions, issued in 1848 at the Seneca Falls Convention in Seneca Falls, New York. Led by Lucretia Mott and Elizabeth Cady Stanton, the delegates adopted a set of resolutions that called for woman suffrage and opportunities for women in employment and education. Excerpts from the Declaration follow.

When, in the course of human events, it becomes necessary for one portion of the family of man to assume among the people of the earth a position different from that which they have hitherto occupied, but one to which the laws of nature and of nature's God entitle them, a decent respect to the opinions of mankind requires that they should declare the causes that impel them to such a course.

We hold these truths to be self-evident: that all men and women are created equal; that they are endowed by their Creator with certain inalienable rights; that among these are life, liberty, and the pursuit of happiness; that to secure these rights governments are instituted, deriving their just powers from the consent of the governed. Whenever any form of government becomes destructive of these ends, it is the right of those who suffer from it to refuse allegiance to it, and to insist upon the institution of a new government, laying its foundation on such principles, and organizing its powers in such form as to them shall seem most likely to effect their safety and happiness. Prudence, indeed, will dictate that governments long established should not be changed for light and transient causes; . . . But when a long train of abuses and usurpations, pursuing invariably the same object, evinces a design to reduce them under absolute despotism, it is their duty to throw off such government, and to provide new guards for their future security. . . .

The history of mankind is a history of repeated injuries and usurpations on the part of man toward woman, having in direct object the establishment of an absolute tyranny over her. To prove this, let facts be submitted to a candid world. . . .

Now, in view of this entire disfranchisement of one-half the people of this country, their social and religious degradation,—in view of the unjust laws above mentioned, and because women do feel themselves aggrieved, oppressed, and fraudulently deprived of their most sacred rights, we insist that they have immediate admission to all the rights and privileges which belong to them as citizens of these United States.

▲ **Elizabeth Cady Stanton**

The Emancipation Proclamation

On January 1, 1863, President Abraham Lincoln issued the Emancipation Proclamation, which freed all enslaved people in states under Confederate control. The Proclamation was a step toward the Thirteenth Amendment (1865), which ended slavery in all of the United States.

That on the 1st day of January, in the year of our Lord [1863], all persons held as slaves within any state or designated part of a state, the people whereof shall then be in rebellion against the United States, shall be then, thenceforward, and forever free; and the Executive Government of the United States, including the military and naval authority thereof, will recognize and maintain the freedom of such persons, and will do no act or acts to repress such persons, or any of them, in any efforts they may make for their actual freedom.

That the Executive will, on the 1st day of January aforesaid, by proclamation, designate the states and parts of states, if any, in which the people thereof, respectively, shall then be in rebellion against the United States; and the fact that any state, or the people thereof, shall on that day be, in good faith, represented in the Congress of the United States by members chosen thereto at elections wherein a majority of the qualified voters of such state shall have participated, shall, in the absence of strong countervailing testimony, be deemed conclusive evidence that such state, and the people thereof, are not then in rebellion against the United States. . . .

And by virtue of the power, and for the purpose aforesaid, I do order and declare that all persons held as slaves within said designated states, and parts of states, are, and henceforward shall be free; and that the Executive Government of the United States, including the military and naval authorities thereof, will recognize and maintain the freedom of said persons.

And I hereby enjoin upon the people so declared to be free to abstain from all violence, unless in necessary self-defense; and I recommend to them that, in all cases when allowed, they labor faithfully for reasonable wages.

And I further declare and make known, that such persons of suitable condition, will be received into the armed service of the United States. . . .

And upon this act, sincerely believed to be an act of justice, warranted by the Constitution, upon military necessity, I invoke the considerate judgement of mankind, and the gracious favor of Almighty God.

▲ Abraham Lincoln

► Members of the 4th Infantry

The Gettysburg Address

On November 19, 1863, President Abraham Lincoln gave a short speech at the dedication of a national cemetery at Gettysburg. His simple yet eloquent words expressed his hopes for a nation divided by civil war.

Four score and seven years ago our fathers brought forth on this continent, a new nation, conceived in Liberty, and dedicated to the proposition that all men are created equal.

Now we are engaged in a great civil war, testing whether that nation or any nation so conceived and so dedicated, can long endure. We are met on a great battle–field of that war. We have come to dedicate a portion of that field, as a final resting place for those who here gave their lives that that nation might live. It is altogether fitting and proper that we should do this.

But, in a larger sense, we can not dedicate—we can not consecrate—we can not hallow—this ground. The brave men, living and dead, who struggled here, have consecrated it, far above our poor power to add or detract. The world will little note, nor long remember what we say here, but it can never forget what they did here. It is for us the living, rather, to be dedicated here to the unfinished work which they who fought here have thus far so nobly advanced. It is rather for us to be here dedicated to the great task remaining before us—that from these honored dead we take increased devotion to that cause for which they gave the last full measure of devotion—that we here highly resolve that these dead shall not have died in vain—that this nation, under God, shall have a new birth of freedom—and that government of the people, by the people, for the people, shall not perish from the earth.

Soldier's kit, Civil War ▼

▲ **Gettysburg Memorial**

I Will Fight No More

▲ Shield made of buffalo hide

In 1877 the Nez Perce fought the government's attempt to move them to a smaller reservation. After a remarkable attempt to escape to Canada, Chief Joseph realized that resistance was hopeless and advised his people to surrender.

Tell General Howard I know his heart. What he told me before, I have it in my heart. I am tired of fighting. . . . The old men are all dead. It is the young men who say yes or no. He who led on the young men is dead. It is cold, and we have no blankets; the little children are freezing to death. My people, some of them, have run away to the hills, and have no blankets, no food. No one knows where they are—perhaps freezing to death. I want to have time to look for my children, and see how many of them I can find. Maybe I shall find them among the dead. Hear me, my chiefs! I am tired; my heart is sick and sad. From where the sun now stands I will fight no more forever.

The Pledge of Allegiance

In 1892 the nation celebrated the 400th anniversary of Columbus's landing in America. In connection with this celebration, Francis Bellamy, a magazine editor, wrote and published the Pledge of Allegiance. The words "under God" were added by Congress in 1954 at the urging of President Dwight D. Eisenhower.

I pledge allegiance to the flag of the United States of America and to the Republic for which it stands, one nation under God, indivisible, with liberty and justice for all.

▲ Students in a New York City school recite the Pledge of Allegiance.

The American's Creed

William Tyler Page of Friendship Heights, Maryland, wrote The American's Creed. This statement of political faith summarizes the true meaning of freedom available to all Americans. The U.S. House of Representatives adopted the creed on behalf of the American people on April 3, 1918.

I believe in the United States of America as a Government of the people, by the people, for the people; whose just powers are derived from the consent of the governed; a democracy in a republic; a sovereign Nation of many sovereign States; a perfect union, one and inseparable; established upon those principles of freedom, equality, justice, and humanity for which American patriots sacrificed their lives and fortunes.

I therefore believe it is my duty to my Country to love it; to support its Constitution; to obey its laws; to respect its flag; and to defend it against all enemies.

The Fourteen Points

On January 8, 1918, President Woodrow Wilson went before Congress to offer a statement of aims called the Fourteen Points. Wilson's plan called for freedom of the seas in peace and war, an end to secret alliances, and equal trading rights for all countries. The excerpt that follows is taken from the President's message.

We entered this war because violations of right had occurred which touched us to the quick and made the life of our own people impossible unless they were corrected and the world secure once for all against their recurrence. What we demand in this war, therefore, is nothing peculiar to ourselves. It is that the world be made fit and safe to live in; and particularly that it be made safe for every peace-loving nation which, like our own, wishes to live its own life, determine its own institutions, be assured of justice and fair dealing by the other peoples of the world as against force and selfish aggression. All the peoples of the world are in effect partners in this interest, and for our own part we see very clearly that unless justice be done to others it will not be done to us. The programme of the world's peace, therefore, is our programme; and that programme, the only possible programme, as we see it, is this:

I. Open covenants of peace, openly arrived at, after which there shall be no private international understandings of any kind but diplomacy shall proceed always frankly and in the public view.

II. Absolute freedom of navigation upon the seas, outside territorial waters, alike in peace and in war, except as the seas may be closed in whole or in part by international action for the enforcement of international covenants.

XIV. A general association of nations must be formed under specific covenants for the purpose of affording mutual guarantees of political independence and territorial integrity to great and small states alike.

Brown v. Board of Education

On May 17, 1954, the Supreme Court ruled in Brown *v.* Board of Education of Topeka, Kansas, *that racial segregation in public schools was unconstitutional. This decision provided the legal basis for court challenges to segregation in every aspect of American life.*

The plaintiffs contend that segregated public schools are not "equal" and cannot be made "equal," and that hence they are deprived of the equal protection of the laws. Because of the obvious importance of the question presented, the Court took jurisdiction. . . .

Our decision, therefore, cannot turn on merely a comparison of these tangible factors in the Negro and white schools involved in each of the cases. We must look instead to the effect of segregation itself on public education.

In approaching this problem, we cannot turn the clock back to 1868, when the Amendment was adopted, or even to 1896, when *Plessy* v. *Ferguson* was written. We must consider public education in the light of its full development and its present place in American life throughout the Nation. Only in this way can it be determined if segregation in public schools deprives these plaintiffs of the equal protection of the laws.

Today, education is perhaps the most important function of state and local governments. Compulsory school attendance laws and the great expenditures for education both demonstrate our recognition of the importance of education to our democratic society. . . . In these days, it is doubtful that any child may reasonably be expected to succeed in life if he is denied the opportunity of an education. Such an opportunity, where the state has undertaken to provide it, is a right which must be made available to all on equal terms.

We come then to the question presented: Does segregation of children in public schools solely on the basis of race, even though the physical facilities and other "tangible" factors may be equal, deprive the children of the minority group of equal educational opportunities? We believe that it does. . . .

. . . We conclude that, in the field of public education, the doctrine of "separate but equal" has no place. Separate educational facilities are inherently unequal. Therefore, we hold that the plaintiffs and others similarly situated for whom the actions have been brought are, by reason of the segregation complained of, deprived of the equal protection of the laws guaranteed by the Fourteenth Amendment.

▲ Troops escort students to newly integrated school.

John F. Kennedy's Inaugural Address

President Kennedy's Inaugural Address on January 20, 1961, set the tone for his administration. In his address he stirred the nation by calling for "a grand and global alliance" to fight tyranny, poverty, disease, and war.

We observe today not a victory of party but a celebration of freedom—symbolizing an end as well as a beginning—signifying renewal as well as change. For I have sworn before you and Almighty God the same solemn oath our forebears prescribed nearly a century and three-quarters ago.

The world is very different now. For man holds in his mortal hands the power to abolish all forms of human poverty and all forms of human life. And yet the same revolutionary beliefs for which our forebears fought are still at issue around the globe—the belief that the rights of man come not from the generosity of the state but from the hand of God.

We dare not forget today that we are the heirs of that first revolution. Let the word go forth from this time and place, to friend and foe alike, that the torch has been passed to a new generation of Americans—born in this century, tempered by war, disciplined by a hard and bitter peace, proud of our ancient heritage—and unwilling to witness or permit the slow undoing of those human rights to which this nation has always been committed, and to which we are committed today at home and around the world.

Let every nation know, whether it wishes us well or ill, that we shall pay any price, bear any burden, meet any hardship, support any friend, oppose any foe to assure the survival and the success of liberty.

This much we pledge—and more.

To those old allies whose cultural and spiritual origins we share, we pledge the loyalty of faithful friends. United, there is little we cannot do in a host of cooperative ventures. Divided, there is little we can do. . . .

Let us never negotiate out of fear. But let us never fear to negotiate.

Let both sides explore what problems unite us instead of belaboring those problems which divide us. . . .

Let both sides seek to invoke the wonders of science instead of its terrors. Together let us explore the stars, conquer the deserts, eradicate disease, tap the ocean depths, and encourage the arts and commerce. . . .

And so, my fellow Americans: ask not what your country can do for you—ask what you can do for your country.

My fellow citizens of the world: ask not what America will do for you, but what together we can do for the freedom of man.

◀ **President Kennedy speaking at his inauguration**

I Have a Dream

On August 28, 1963, while Congress debated wide-ranging civil rights legislation, Dr. Martin Luther King, Jr., led more than 200,000 people in a march on Washington, D.C. On the steps of the Lincoln Memorial he gave a stirring speech in which he eloquently spoke of his dreams for African Americans and for the United States. Excerpts of the speech follow.

There are those who are asking the devotees of civil rights, "When will you be satisfied?"

We can never be satisfied as long as the Negro is the victim of the unspeakable horrors of police brutality. . . .

We cannot be satisfied as long as the Negro's basic mobility is from a smaller ghetto to a larger one.

We can never be satisfied as long as a Negro in Mississippi cannot vote and a Negro in New York believes he has nothing for which to vote. . . .

I say to you today, my friends, that in spite of the difficulties and frustrations of the moment I still have a dream. It is a dream deeply rooted in the American dream.

I have a dream that one day this nation will rise up and live out the true meaning of its creed: "We hold these truths to be self-evident, that all men are created equal."

I have a dream that one day on the red hills of Georgia the sons of former slaves and the sons of former slave-owners will be able to sit down together at the table of brotherhood.

▲ **Dr. Martin Luther King, Jr.**

I have a dream that one day even the state of Mississippi, a desert state sweltering with the heat of injustice and oppression, will be transformed into an oasis of freedom and justice.

I have a dream that my four little children will one day live in a nation where they will not be judged by the color of their skin but by the content of their character. . . .

When we let freedom ring, when we let it ring from every village and every hamlet, from every state and every city, we will be able to speed up that day when all of God's children, black men and white men, Jews and Gentiles, Protestants and Catholics, will be able to join hands and sing in the words of the old Negro spiritual: "Free at last! Free at last! Thank God Almighty, we are free at last!"

◀ **The March on Washington**

Glossary

This glossary includes all the yellow highlighted and boldfaced vocabulary words from your text. Content vocabulary (those words highlighted in yellow in your text) are words that relate to history content. Academic vocabulary (those words boldfaced in your text) are words that will help you understand all of your school subjects. Academic vocabulary is shown with an asterisk (*).

A

*abandon to give up completely or desert (p. 578)

abolitionist a person who strongly favors doing away with slavery (p. 529)

abstain to not take part in some activity, such as voting (p. 542)

*access a way or means of approach (p. 471)

*accommodate make suitable for or to provide help (p. 752)

*accompany to attend as a companion (p. 296)

*achieve to reach an aim or goal (p. 691)

*acquire obtain or take possession of something (p. 676)

*adapt to fit a new situation (p. 128)

*adequate enough to satisfy a particular requirement (p. 201)

*aid to provide with help (p. 626)

alien an immigrant living in a country in which he or she is not a citizen (p. 295)

amendment an addition to a formal document such as the Constitution (p. 223)

amnesty the granting of pardon to a large number of persons; protection from prosecution for an illegal act (p. 625)

annex to add a territory to one's own territory (p. 486)

*annual occurs once a year (p. 472)

*anticipate to look forward to (p. 224)

Antifederalists individuals who opposed ratification of the Constitution (p. 206)

*approach a way to deal with an issue (p. 625)

appropriate to set something aside for a particular purpose, especially funds (p. 227)

*area part of a country (p. 594)

arsenal a storage place for weapons and ammunition (p. 553)

article a part of a document, such as the Constitution, that deals with a single subject (p. 204)

*aspect a certain way something appears or may be regarded (p. 744)

*assemble to collect in one place or group together (p. 354)

assembly line a production system with machines and workers arranged so that each person performs an assigned task again and again as the item passes before him or her (p. 717)

*assign to be given a specific role or responsibility (p. 296)

assimilate to absorb a group into the culture of a larger population (p. 744)

*assist giving help when needed (p. 91)

*assume to take on a special quality or responsibility (p. 231)

astrolabe an instrument used by sailors to observe positions of stars (p. 83)

*authority power of influence over others (p. 180)

*available easy or possible to obtain (p. 322)

B

barrio a Spanish-speaking neighborhood in a city, especially in the southwest U.S. (p. 782)

*benefit something that does good to a person or thing (p. 759)

*bias an attitude that always favors one way of feeling or acting over another (p. 780)

bicameral consisting of two houses, or chambers, especially in a legislature (p. 179)

black codes laws passed in the South just after the Civil War aimed at controlling freedmen and enabling plantation owners to exploit African American workers (p. 630)

blockade cut off an area by means of troops or warships to stop supplies or people from coming in or going out; to close off a country's ports (p. 573)

bond a note issued by the government, which promises to pay off a loan with interest (p. 281)

boomtown a community experiencing a sudden growth in business or population (pp. 503, 668)

border ruffians Missourians who traveled in armed groups to vote in Kansas's election during the mid-1850s (p. 546)

border states the states between the North and the South that were divided over whether to stay in the Union or join the Confederacy (pp. 555, 571)

bounty money given as a reward, such as to encourage enlistment in the army (p. 602)

boycott to refuse to buy items from a particular country (p. 136)

brand a symbol burned into an animal's hide to show ownership (p. 673)

***brief** not very long (p. 636)

bullion gold or silver in the form of bars (p. 94)

bureaucracy system in which nonelected officials carry out laws and policies (p. 449)

burgesses elected representatives to an assembly (p. 119)

cabinet a group of advisers to the president (p. 280)

Californios Mexicans who lived in California (p. 496)

canal an artificial waterway (p. 392)

capital money for investment (pp. 383, 424)

capitalism an economic system based on private property and free enterprise (pp. 91, 383)

carpetbaggers name given to Northern whites who moved South after the Civil War and supported the Republicans (p. 638)

cash crop farm crop raised to be sold for money (pp. 126, 646)

casualty a military person killed, wounded, or captured (p. 579)

caucus a meeting held by a political party to choose their party's candidate for president or decide policy (pp. 293, 449)

cede to give up by treaty (p. 497)

census official count of a population (p. 389)

***challenge** a demanding task (p. 154)

charter a document that gives the holder the right to organize settlements in an area (p. 119)

charter colony colony established by a group of settlers who had been given a formal document allowing them to settle (p. 130)

checks and balances the system in which each branch of government has a check on the other two branches so that no one branch becomes too powerful (p. 205)

circumnavigate to sail around the world (p. 85)

citizen a person who owes loyalty to and is entitled to the protection of a state or nation (p. 236)

civil war conflict between opposing groups of citizens of the same country (p. 547)

coeducation the teaching of male and female students together (p. 410)

***collapse** to fall down suddenly (p. 542)

collective bargaining discussion between an employer and union representatives of workers over wages, hours, and working conditions (p. 727)

colony a settlement of people living in a new territory but controlled by their home country (p. 95)

Columbian Exchange exchange of goods, ideas, and people between Europe and the Americas (p. 95)

commission a group of persons directed to perform some duty (p. 643)

***commit** to perform an action (p. 648)

***communicate** to transmit information, thought, or feeling so it is received and understood (p. 434)

***community** a group of people with common interests, especially when living together (p. 501)

compromise agreement between two or more sides in which each side gives up some of what it wants (p. 199)

***concentrate** giving most attention to one central idea (p. 386)

***concept** principle or idea (p. 491)

***conclude** to come to a final decision (p. 345)

concurrent powers powers shared by the states and the federal government (p. 222)

***conduct** manage or control the direction of relations between two or more parties (p. 205)

Conestoga wagon sturdy vehicle topped with white canvas and used by pioneers to move west (p. 313)

Glossary

confederation a voluntary association of independent states (p. 180)

* **confirm** to support or agree to (p. 280)

* **conflict** a disagreement or struggle (p. 329)

conquistador Spanish explorer in the Americas in the 1500s (p. 86)

conservation the protection and preservation of natural resources (p. 771)

* **consist** made up of (p. 354)

consolidation the practice of combining separate companies into one (p. 707)

* **constant** happening a lot or all the time (p. 433)

constituents people that members of Congress represent (p. 227)

constitution a formal plan of government (p. 121)

* **contract** an agreement between people (p. 103)

* **contrary** the exact opposite (p. 327)

* **contrast** showing the difference between two things when they are compared (p. 292)

* **contribute** help to cause an event or situation (p. 460)

* **controversy** a lot of disagreement or argument about something, usually because it affects something or someone (p. 537)

* **convert** change from one to another (p. 710)

* **convince** make a person believe by arguing or showing facts (p. 136)

* **cooperate** to work with others to get a task done (p. 221)

cooperative store where farmers bought products from each other; an enterprise owned and operated by those who use its services (p. 694)

corporation a business in which investors own shares (p. 719)

* **correspond** to communicate by letters (p. 137)

corruption dishonest or illegal actions (p. 638)

cotton gin a machine that removed seeds from cotton fiber (pp. 384, 423)

court-martial to try by a military court (p. 365)

covenant a formal agreement, or promise, between two or more people (p. 99)

* **create** to make or produce (p. 638)

credit a form of loan; ability to buy goods based on future payment (p. 429)

* **culture** a way of life of a group of people who share similar beliefs and customs (p. 81)

* **currency** money (p. 194)

* **debate** a verbal argument (p. 536)

debtor person or country that owes money (p. 124)

* **decline** to become less in value (p. 695)

decree an order given by one in authority (p. 482)

demilitarize to remove armed forces from an area (p. 363)

* **demonstrate** show by examples (p. 365)

* **deny** refuse to accept (p. 626)

depression a period of low economic activity and widespread unemployment (pp. 194, 460)

* **derive** the origin of something, such as a word, from which another has developed (p. 674)

* **design** the creation of something according to a plan (p. 83)

* **despite** without taking any notice of or being influenced by (p. 686)

* **device** an object or machine which has been invented to fulfill a particular purpose (p. 713)

* **devote** to use space, area, or time for a particular purpose (p. 492)

* **diminish** to be reduced in size or importance (p. 238)

disarmament removal of weapons (p. 363)

discrimination unfair treatment of a group; unequal treatment because of a person's race, religion, ethnic background, or place of birth (pp. 397, 778)

dissenter person who disagrees with or opposes established views (p. 121)

* **distinct** clearly different from one another (p. 291)

* **distribute** to divide among several or many (p. 599)

diversity variety or difference (p. 123)

dividend a stockholder's share of a company's profits, usually as a cash payment (p. 719)

* **document** an important paper (p. 103)

* **dominate** having great influence over all others (p. 636)

draft the selection of persons for military service (p. 602)

dry farming a way of farming dry land in which seeds are planted deep in the ground where there is some moisture (p. 678)

due process of law idea that the government must follow procedures established by law and guaranteed by the Constitution (p. 235)

* **dynamic** to be energetic and forceful in presentation (p. 697)

* **economy** the money system of a country, region, or community (p. 359)

* **eliminate** to remove or get rid of (p. 645)

emancipate to free from slavery (p. 594)

embargo an order prohibiting trade with another country (p. 340)

emigrant a person who leaves a country or region to live elsewhere (p. 474)

emigrate to leave one's homeland to live elsewhere (p. 742)

empresario a person who arranged for the settlement of land in Texas during the 1800s (p. 481)

* **enable** to make possible (p. 634)

encomienda system of rewarding conquistadors with tracts of land and the right to tax and demand labor from Native Americans who lived on the land (p. 88)

* **encounter** an unexpected meeting (p. 580)

* **enforce** to make people obey a law or to accept a new situation (p. 641)

Enlightenment movement during the 1700s that spread the idea that knowledge, reason, and science could improve society (p. 203)

* **enormous** very big (p. 313)

* **ensure** to make sure or certain (p. 309)

entrenched occupying a strong defensive position (p. 605)

* **entrepreneur** someone who starts their own business (p. 93)

enumerated powers powers belonging only to the federal government (p. 222)

* **environment** the combination of the soil, climate and living things that influence the survival of a plant, animal, or human being (p. 239)

* **equip** to supply with necessary tools to work properly (p. 390)

* **establish** to set up (p. 363)

* **ethnic** relating to a large group of people classed according to common racial, national, or cultural origin or background (p. 761)

ethnic group a minority that speaks a different language or follows different customs than the majority of people in a country (p. 742)

* **evaluate** judge the quality or amount (p. 580)

* **eventual** happening or existing at a later time or at the end, especially after a lot of effort or problems (p. 555)

* **exceed** to go beyond the limits (p. 430)

executive branch the branch of government, headed by the president, that carries out the nation's laws and policies (p. 205)

* **expand** open up or spread out in terms of size, number or amount (p. 386)

* **exploit** to use unfairly for one's own advantage (p. 641)

* **export** to sell goods abroad (p. 95)

* **extract** to remove (p. 667)

factory system system bringing manufacturing steps together in one place to increase efficiency (p. 385)

famine an extreme shortage of food (p. 398)

favorite son candidate that receives the backing of his home state rather than of the national party (p. 447)

* **federal** national government (p. 453)

federalism the sharing of power between federal and state governments (pp. 204, 222)

Federalists supporters of the Constitution (p. 206)

* **finance** providing funds or capital (p. 91)

fixed costs regular expenses such as housing or maintaining equipment that remain about the same year after year (p. 429)

* **focus** to concentrate on a central point (p. 405)

forty-niners people who went to California during the gold rush of 1849 (p. 501)

* **found** establish (p. 403)

free enterprise the freedom of private businesses to operate competitively for profit with minimal government regulation (p. 383)

free silver the unlimited production of silver coins (p. 696)

Glossary

freedman a person freed from slavery (p. 626)

frigate warship (p. 355)

fugitive runaway or trying to run away (p. 541)

***function** to work or serve towards a particular goal (p. 221)

***fund** a sum of money saved, collected, or provided for a particular purpose (p. 93)

***generation** individuals born and living at the same time (p. 314)

Gilded Age the name associated with America in the late 1800s, referring to the extravagant wealth of a few and the terrible poverty that lay underneath (p. 752)

***goal** an aim or purpose (p. 413)

grandfather clause a clause that allowed individuals who did not pass the literacy test to vote if their fathers or grandfathers had voted before Reconstruction began; an exception to a law based on preexisting circumstances (p. 648)

***grant** giving consent or permission (p. 122)

***guarantee** a promise that some condition will be fulfilled (p. 341)

guerrilla tactics referring to surprise attacks or raids rather than organized warfare (p. 455)

guerrilla warfare a hit-and-run technique used in fighting a war; fighting by small bands of warriors using tactics such as sudden ambushes (p. 156)

habeas corpus a legal order for an inquiry to determine whether a person has been lawfully imprisoned (p. 600)

homestead to acquire a piece of U.S. public land by living on and cultivating it (p. 676)

horizontal integration the combining of competing firms into one corporation (p. 720)

impeach to formally charge a public official with misconduct in office (pp. 227, 633)

implied powers powers not specifically mentioned in the Constitution (pp. 224, 292)

import to buy goods from foreign markets (p. 136)

impressment forcing people into service, as in the navy (pp. 288, 339)

indentured servant laborer who agreed to work without pay for a certain period of time in exchange for passage to America (p. 126)

Industrial Revolution the change from an agrarian society to one based on industry which began in Great Britain and spread to the United States around 1800 (p. 383)

***inevitable** impossible to avoid (p. 546)

inflation a continuous rise in the price of goods and services (p. 603)

initiative the right of citizens to place a measure or issue before the voters or the legislature for approval (p. 769)

injunction a court order to stop an action, such as a strike (p. 729)

***inspect** to examine closely (p. 771)

integrate to end separation of different races and bring into equal membership in society (p. 638)

interchangeable parts uniform pieces that can be made in large quantities to replace other identical pieces (p. 385)

***interpret** explain the meaning (p. 179)

***intervene** to come between (p. 229)

***invest** to commit money in order to receive a profit (p. 719)

***involve** to contain or include (p. 236)

ironclad armored naval vessel (p. 578)

***isolate** to set or keep apart from others (p. 760)

***issue** a matter that is in dispute between two or more parties (p. 450)

isthmus a narrow strip of land connecting two larger land areas (p. 776)

***item** a good or a product (p. 504)

***job** duty or work done for pay (p. 725)

joint occupation the possession and settling of an area shared by two or more countries (p. 471)

joint-stock company a company in which investors buy stock in the company in return for a share of its future profits (p. 93)

judicial branch the branch of government, including the federal court system, that interprets the nation's laws (p. 205)

judicial review the right of the Supreme Court to determine if a law violates the Constitution (pp. 225, 309)

* **justify** having a good reason for choosing a particular side (p. 556)

* **labor** to work for wages, such as in production of goods and services (p. 725)

laissez-faire policy that government should interfere as little as possible in the nation's economy (pp. 307, 460, 771)

land-grant college originally, an agricultural college established as a result of the 1862 Morrill Act that gave states large amounts of federal land that could be sold to raise money for education (p. 760)

landslide an overwhelming victory (p. 448)

legislative branch the branch of government that makes the nation's laws (p. 204)

* **levy** an imposed tax required to pay off a country, region, or district's loan or debt (p. 194)

literacy test a method used to prevent African Americans from voting by requiring prospective voters to read and write at a specified level (p. 647)

lock in a canal, an enclosure with gates at each end used in raising or lowering boats as they pass from level to level (p. 392)

lode a mass or strip of ore sandwiched between layers of rock (p. 667)

Loyalists American colonists who remained loyal to Britain and opposed the war for independence (p. 153)

lynching putting to death a person by the illegal action of a mob (p. 648)

* **maintain** to keep up (p. 286)

* **major** to be great in size, number, or length (p. 105)

Manifest Destiny the idea popular in the United States during the 1800s that the country must expand its boundaries to the Pacific (p. 474)

* **manual** done by hand (p. 399)

manumission the freeing of some enslaved persons (p. 196)

martyr a person who sacrifices his or her life for a principle or cause (p. 553)

mass production the production of large quantities of goods using machinery and often an assembly line (p. 717)

Mayflower Compact a formal document, written in 1620, that provided law and order to the Plymouth colony (p. 120)

mercantilism the theory that a state's or nation's power depended on its wealth (p. 94)

merger the combining of two or more businesses into one (p. 722)

* **migrate** to move from one country to another (p. 329)

* **military** armed forces (p. 124)

militia a group of civilians trained to fight in emergencies (p. 139)

* **ministry** the office, duties or work of a minister (p. 413)

minutemen companies of civilian soldiers who boasted that they were ready to fight on a minute's notice (p. 140)

mission religious settlement (p. 88)

* **modify** to make changes (p. 777)

* **monitor** to observe for a special purpose (p. 227)

monopoly total control of a type of industry by one person or one company (p. 720)

mountain man a frontiersman living in the wilderness, as in the Rocky Mountains (p. 472)

muckraker a journalist who uncovers abuses and corruption in a society (p. 767)

mudslinging attempt to ruin an opponent's reputation with insults (p. 447)

national debt the amount of money a national government owes to other governments or its people (p. 281)

National Grange the first farmers' organization in the United States (p. 694)

nationalism loyalty to a nation and promotion of its interests above all others (pp. 321, 345)

Glossary

nativist a person who favors those born in his country and is opposed to immigrants (pp. 401, 746)

naturalization to grant full citizenship to a foreigner (p. 236)

*network a system of connected parts (p. 711)

neutral taking no side in a conflict (p. 153)

neutral rights the right to sail the seas and not take sides in a war (p. 339)

neutrality a position of not taking sides in a conflict (p. 288)

*nevertheless despite what has just been said or referred to (p. 606)

nomadic moving from place to place with no permanent home (p. 686)

normal school a two-year school for training high school graduates as teachers (p. 405)

Northwest Passage water route to Asia through North America sought by European explorers (p. 88)

*notion an idea or concept (p. 529)

nullify to cancel or make ineffective (pp. 296, 450, 537)

*obtain to gain (p. 669)

*obvious easily found, seen or understood (p. 573)

*occupy to take possession of (pp. 157, 326)

*occur to happen (p. 603)

offensive position of attacking or the attack itself (p. 573)

oligopoly a market structure in which a few large companies control the prices of the industry (p. 766)

open range land not fenced or divided into lots (p. 673)

ordinance a law or regulation (p. 181)

ore a mineral mined for the valuable substance it contains, such as silver (p. 667)

*outcome result (p. 605)

override to overturn or defeat, as a bill proposed in Congress (p. 630)

overseer person who supervises a large operation or its workers (pp. 127, 430)

*participate to take part in something that others are doing (p. 194)

partisan favoring one side of an issue (p. 291)

patent a document that gives an inventor the sole legal right to an invention for a period of time (p. 384)

Patriots American colonists who were determined to fight the British until American independence was won (p. 153)

*percent one unit of 100 (p. 386)

*period length of time (p. 625)

persecute to treat someone harshly because of that person's beliefs or differences (p. 122)

petition a formal request (p. 150)

philanthropy charitable acts or gifts of money to benefit the community (p. 722)

philosophe French for "philosopher"; during the Enlightenment thinkers, such as writers, teachers, journalists, and observers of society (p. 105)

philosophy a set of beliefs or ideas related to a particular system of cultural values (p. 307)

planter large landowner (p. 326)

plurality largest single share (p. 447)

*policy a plan or course of action (p. 367)

political machine an organization linked to a political party that often controlled local government (p. 765)

poll tax a tax of a fixed amount per person that had to be paid before the person could vote (p. 647)

pool a group sharing in some activity, for example, among railroad barons who made secret agreements and set rates among themselves (p. 711)

popular sovereignty political theory that government is subject to the will of the people (pp. 179, 222); before the Civil War, the idea that people living in a territory had the right to decide by voting if slavery would be allowed there (p. 544)

Populist Party U.S. political party formed in 1892 representing mainly farmers, favoring free coinage of silver and government control of railroads and other monopolies (p. 695)

*pose to put forth; to present (p. 504)

preamble the introduction to a formal document, especially the Constitution (pp. 152, 219)

precedent a tradition (p. 279)

*predominant greater in importance, strength, influence, or authority (p. 424)

prejudice an unfair opinion not based on facts (p. 397)

presidio Spanish fort in the Americas built to protect mission settlements (p. 88)

*primary the main or most important (p. 573); an election in which voters choose their party's candidate (p. 769)

*principle a basic truth that other theories are based on (p. 130)

privateer armed private ship (p. 355)

*process a continuing action or series of actions (p. 743)

*professional engaging in a given activity as a source of support or as a career (p. 752)

*prohibit to forbid (p. 633)

*promote to encourage or contribute to the growth of an idea (p. 203)

proportional to be the same as or corresponding to (p. 199)

proprietary colony colony run by individuals or groups to whom land was granted (p. 130)

*prospect the idea of something that will or might happen in the future (p. 580)

protective tariff tariff that raises the price of goods from other countries (p. 537)

*publication printed material offered for distribution or sale (p. 530)

*publish preparing printed material for public display or sale (p. 407)

pueblo home or community of homes built by Native Americans (p. 88)

*purchase to buy (p. 429)

*pursue strive to gain or accomplish a goal (p. 102)

Ⓡ

radical extreme (p. 625)

ragtime a type of music with a strong rhythm and a lively melody with accented notes, which was popular in early 1900s (p. 762)

ranchero Mexican ranch owner (p. 492)

rancho huge properties for raising livestock set up by Mexican settlers in California (p. 492)

*range series of mountain peaks (p. 501)

ratify to give official approval to (pp. 181, 206, 594)

realism an approach to literature, art, and theater that shows things as they really are (p. 761)

rebate discount or return of part of a payment (p. 710)

Rebel Confederate soldier, so called because of opposition to the established government (p. 574)

recall the right that enables voters to remove unsatisfactory elected officials from office (p. 769)

reconciliation settling by agreement or coming together again (p. 641)

Reconstruction the reorganization and rebuilding of the former Confederate states after the Civil War (p. 625)

referendum the practice of letting voters accept or reject measures proposed by the legislature (p. 769)

*region an area, division, or district (p. 638)

regionalism in art or literature, the practice of focusing on a particular region of the country (p. 761)

*register a written record or list of items (p. 743)

*regulate to govern by rules or laws (p. 199)

*reinforce to provide an army with more soldiers or weapons to make it stronger (p. 577)

*reject to refuse to grant or consider (p. 776)

relocate to force a person or group of people to move (p. 453)

*reluctance an unwillingness to act (p. 593)

*remove take away or dismiss (p. 453)

Renaissance a period of intellectual and artistic creativity, c. 1300–1600 (p. 102)

rendezvous a meeting (p. 472)

repeal to cancel an act or law (p. 136)

republicanism favoring a republic, or representative democracy, as the best form of government (p. 222)

*require to have a need for (p. 307)

reservation an area of public lands set aside for Native Americans (p. 687)

reserved powers powers retained by the states (p. 222)

resolution a formal expression of opinion (p. 139)

*   **resolve** to clear up any unsettled matters (p. 341)

*   **resource** a useful or valuable possession (p. 719)

*   **restrict** to place under limits (p. 550)

*   **reveal** to allow something to be seen that, until then, had been unknown or hidden (p. 544)

*   **revenue** incoming money (p. 284)

revival a series of meetings conducted by a preacher to arouse religious emotions (p. 403)

right of deposit Americans reached an agreement with Spain that would allow free navigation along the Mississippi River (p. 185)

*   **role** a function assigned or taken on (p. 447)

*   **route** an established course of travel (p. 472)

royal colony colony run by a governor and a council appointed by the king or queen (p. 130)

rule of law in ancient Roman law, everyone should be treated equally (p. 99)

S

scalawags name given by former Confederates to Southern whites who supported Republican Reconstruction of the South (p. 638)

scientific method an orderly way of collecting and analyzing evidence (p. 105)

secede to leave or withdraw (pp. 316, 450, 541)

secession withdrawal from the Union (p. 556)

sectionalism loyalty to a region (p. 536)

*   **secure** guarding from danger or loss (p. 155)

sedition activities aimed at weakening established government (p. 295)

segregation the separation or isolation of a race, class, or group (p. 648)

settlement house institution located in a poor neighborhood that provided numerous community services such as medical care, child care, libraries, and classes in English (p. 753)

sharecropping system of farming in which a farmer works land for an owner who provides equipment and seeds and receives a share of the crop (p. 639)

shareholder a person who invests in a corporation by buying stock and is a partial owner (p. 719)

*   **shift** to change from one place or position to another (p. 396)

*   **significant** having a major effect on something (p. 308)

*   **similar** having common qualities (p. 484)

slave code the laws passed in the Southern states that controlled and restricted enslaved people (p. 434)

slum poor, crowded, and run-down urban neighborhoods (p. 752)

smuggling trading illegally with other nations (p. 136)

sodbuster a name given to the Plains farmer (p. 678)

*   **sole** being the only one (p. 474)

sovereignty supreme power (p. 180)

speculator person who risks money in order to make a large profit (p. 282)

spiritual an African American religious folk song (p. 433)

spoils system practice of handing out government jobs to supporters; replacing government employees with the winning candidate's supporters (p. 449)

standard gauge the uniform width of 4 feet, 8.5 inches for railroad tracks, adopted during the 1880s (p. 709)

states' rights rights and powers independent of the federal government that are reserved for the states by the Constitution; the belief that states' rights supersede federal rights and law (pp. 296, 556)

*   **status** position or rank in relation to others (p. 482)

steerage cramped quarters on a ship's lower decks for passengers paying the lowest fares (p. 742)

stock shares of ownership a company sells in its business which often carry voting power (p. 719)

*   **strategy** a careful plan or method of action (p. 341)

strike a stopping of work by workers to force an employer to meet demands (p. 397)

strikebreaker person hired to replace a striking worker in order to break up a strike (p. 727)

*   **structure** an arrangement of parts (p. 279)

subsidy grant of money from the government to a person or a company for an action intended to benefit the public (p. 669)

subsistence farming farming in which only enough food to feed one's family is produced (p. 126)

* **substitute** a person or thing that takes the place of another (p. 602)

suburbs residential areas that sprang up close to or surrounding cities as a result of improvements in transportation (p. 752)

* **sufficient** enough to achieve a goal or fulfill a need (p. 573)

suffrage the right to vote (pp. 409, 449)

* **sum** describe or express briefly the important facts about something or someone (p. 425)

* **survive** to remain alive despite hardships and trauma (p. 119)

sweatshop a shop or factory where workers work long hours at low wages under unhealthy conditions (pp. 725, 744)

* **symbol** a letter, character, or sign used instead of words (p. 461)

tariff a tax on imports or exports (pp. 282, 450)

* **technique** the method or skill used in accomplishing a goal (p. 156)

* **technology** the application of scientific discoveries to practical use (pp. 82, 384, 710)

Tejano a Mexican who claims Texas as his home (p. 481)

temperance the use of little or no alcoholic drink (p. 403)

tenant farmer farmer who works land owned by another and pays rent either in cash or crops (p. 428)

tenement a building in which several families rent rooms or apartments, often with little sanitation or safety (p. 752)

theology the study of religion and religious beliefs (p. 101)

* **theory** an idea that is the starting point for argument or investigation (p. 556)

toleration the acceptance of different beliefs (p. 121)

* **topic** a subject that is discussed, written about, or studied (p. 552)

total war war on all aspects of the enemy's life (p. 609)

trade union organization of workers with the same trade or skill (pp. 397, 726)

transcendentalist any of a group of New England writers who stressed the relationship between human beings and nature, spiritual things over material things, and the importance of the individual conscience (p. 406)

transcontinental extending across a continent (p. 670)

* **transmit** transfer from one person or place to another (p. 713)

* **transport** carrying from one place to another (p. 286)

triangular trade a trade route that exchanged goods between the West Indies, the American colonies, and West Africa (p. 126)

tribute money paid for protection (p. 339)

trust a combination of firms or corporations formed by a legal agreement, especially to reduce competition (pp. 720, 766)

turnpike a road that one must pay to use; the money is used to pay for the road (p. 389)

* **ultimate** the final or extreme result (p. 279)

unconstitutional not agreeing or consistent with the Constitution (p. 282)

Underground Railroad a system that helped enslaved African Americans follow a network of escape routes out of the South to freedom in the North (p. 534)

* **underlie** to be the support or basis of (p. 767)

undertake take on as a duty (p. 389)

* **unify** to unite or bring together (p. 713)

* **unique** being the only one of its kind (p. 325)

utopia community based on a vision of a perfect society sought by reformers (p. 403)

vaquero Hispanic ranch hand (p. 674)

vaudeville stage entertainment made up of various acts, such as dancing, singing, comedy, and magic shows (p. 763)

vertical integration the combining of companies that supply equipment and services needed for a particular industry (p. 721)

veto to reject a bill and prevent it from becoming a law (p. 459)

vigilantes people who take the law into their own hands (pp. 504, 668)

* **violate** to do harm or damage (p. 136)

* **vision** the intellectual ability to think or plan ahead (p. 505)

ward a person under the guardianship of the U.S. government (p. 782)

War Hawks Republicans during Madison's presidency who pressed for war with Britain (p. 343)

Yankee Union soldier (p. 574)

yellow journalism writing which exaggerates sensational, dramatic, and gruesome events to attract readers, named for stories that were popular during the late 1800s (p. 761)

yeoman Southern owner of a small farm who did not have enslaved people (p. 428)

This glossary includes all the yellow highlighted and boldfaced vocabulary words from your text. Content vocabulary (those words highlighted in yellow in your text) are words that relate to history content. Academic vocabulary (those words **boldfaced** in your text) are words that will help you understand all of your school subjects. Academic vocabulary is shown with an asterisk (∗).

A

∗**abandon / abandoner** renunciar o dejar un lugar o a una persona (p. 578)

abolitionist / abolicionista una persona que favorece firmemente suprimir la esclavitud (p. 529)

abstain / abstenerse no tomar parte de una actividad, como de votar (p. 542)

∗**access / acceso** modo de acercarse o entrada (p. 471)

∗**accommodate / acomodar** hacer ajustes o proporcionar ayuda (p. 743)

∗**accompany / acompañar** servir de acompañante (p. 296)

∗**achieve / lograr** alcanzar un objetivo o meta (p. 691)

∗**acquire / adquirir** obtener o tomar posesión de algo (p. 676)

∗**adapt / adaptar** ajustar a una nueva situación (p. 128)

∗**adequate / adecuado** lo suficiente para satisfacer un requisito en particular (p. 201)

∗**aid / ayudar** dar asistencia o socorrer (p. 626)

alien / extranjero una persona inmigrante que vive en un país en el cual no es ciudadano (p. 295)

amendment / enmienda una adición a un documento formal tal como la Constitución (p. 223)

amnesty / amnistía el otorgar perdón a un número grande de personas; la protección del proceso a causa de una acción ilegal (p. 625)

annex / anexar añadir un territorio a su propio territorio (p. 486)

∗**annual / anual** que sucede una vez al año (p. 472)

∗**anticipate / prever** esperar que algo suceda (p. 224)

Antifederalists / antifederalistas personas que estaban en contra de que se ratificara la Constitución (p. 206)

∗**approach / enfoque** método de resolver un asunto (p. 625)

appropriate / destinar apartar para un propósito en particular, dicho especialmente de fondos (p. 227)

∗**area / área** parte de un país (p. 594)

arsenal / arsenal un lugar para el almacenaje de armas y municiones (p. 553)

article / artículo una parte de un documento tal como la Constitución que trata de un solo tema (p. 204)

∗**aspect / aspecto** manera en que algo luce o en que se puede ver (p. 743)

∗**assemble / reunir** acumular en un sitio o agrupar (p. 354)

assembly line / línea de montaje un sistema de producción arreglado con máquinas y trabajadores para que cada persona haga vez tras vez su trabajo designado mientras el artículo pasa por en frente de él (p. 717)

∗**assign / asignar** dar un trabajo o responsabilidad en particular a alguien (p. 296)

assimilate / asimilar introducir a un grupo dentro de la cultura de una población más grande (p. 744)

∗**assist / asistir** dar ayuda (p. 91)

∗**assume / asumir** adoptar una cualidad especial o responsabilidad nueva (p. 231)

astrolabe / astrolabio un instrumento usado por los marineros para observar las posiciones de las estrellas (p. 83)

∗**authority / autoridad** poder o influencia sobre otras personas (p. 180)

∗**available / disponible** fácil o posible de conseguir (p. 322)

B

barrio / barrio una vecindad hispanoparlante de una ciudad, especialmente en el sudoeste de EE.UU. (p. 782)

∗**benefit / beneficio** algo que le hace el bien a alguien o algo (p. 759)

Spanish Glossary

*bias / parcialidad actitud que siempre favorece el mismo modo de pensar o actuar (p. 780)

bicameral / bicameral que consiste de dos cámaras, especialmente dicho en una legislatura (p. 179)

black codes / códigos negros leyes establecidas en el Sur al terminar la Guerra Civil para controlar a los libertos y permitir a los dueños de plantaciones la explotación de los trabajadores afroamericanos (p. 630)

blockade / bloqueo el cerrar un área por medio de tropas o de buques de guerra para prohibir el entrar y el salir de abastos y de personas; cerrar los puertos de un país (p. 573)

bond / bono una obligación hecha por el gobierno la cual promete pagar un préstamo con interés (p. 281)

boomtown / pueblo en bonanza una comunidad experimentando un auge repentino de comercio o población (pp. 503, 668)

border ruffians / rufianes fronterizos hombres de Missouri que viajaban en grupos armados a votar en la elección de Kansas a mediados de los años 1850 (p. 546)

border states / estados fronterizos los estados entre el Norte y el Sur que fueron divididos sobre el problema de quedarse en la Unión o de unirse a la Confederación (pp. 555, 571)

bounty / gratificación dinero dado como recompensa, como para animar el alistamiento en el ejército (p. 602)

boycott / boicotear rehusar comprar artículos de un país en particular (p. 136)

brand / marca a fuego un símbolo quemado en la piel de un animal para mostrar título de propiedad (p. 673)

*brief / breve no muy largo (p. 636)

bullion / lingotes barras de oro o plata (p. 94)

bureaucracy / burocracia sistema en el cual oficiales no elegidos administran las leyes y políticas (p. 449)

burgesses / burgueses representantes elegidos para una asamblea (p. 119)

cabinet / gabinete un grupo de consejeros al presidente (p. 280)

Californios / californios mexicanos que vivían en California (p. 496)

canal / canal vía artificial de agua (p. 392)

capital / capital dinero para inversión (pp. 383, 424)

capitalism / capitalismo un sistema económico basado en la propiedad particular y la empresa libre (pp. 91, 383)

carpetbaggers / carpetbaggers nombre dado a los blancos norteños que se trasladaban al Sur después de la guerra y apoyaban a los republicanos (p. 638)

cash crop / cultivo comercial cosecha cultivada para vender por dinero (pp. 126, 646)

casualty / baja un miliciano muerto, herido, o capturado (p. 579)

caucus / junta electoral una reunión llevada a cabo por un partido político para escoger el candidato a la presidencia de su partido o para decidir políticas (pp. 293, 449)

cede / ceder abandonar por tratado (p. 497)

census / censo registro oficial de una población (p. 389)

*challenge / reto desafío o tarea muy difícil (p. 154)

charter / carta de privilegio un documento que otorga los derechos de organizar establecimientos en una área (p. 119)

charter colony / colonia a carta colonia establecida por un grupo de colonizadores a quienes se les había dado un documento formal permitiéndoles colonizar (p. 130)

checks and balances / inspecciones y balances el sistema en el cual cada rama de gobierno refrena las otras dos ramas para que ninguna rama vuelva a ser demasiado poderosa (p. 205)

circumnavigate / circunnavegar navegar alrededor del mundo (p. 85)

citizen / ciudadano una persona que debe ser leal y tiene derecho a la protección de un estado o nación (p. 236)

civil war / guerra civil conflicto entre grupos opuestos de ciudadanos del mismo país (p. 547)

coeducation / coeducación la enseñanza conjunta de estudiantes hombres y mujeres (p. 410)

*collapse / derrumbarse caer o venirse abajo de pronto (p. 542)

collective bargaining / negociaciones colectivas discusión entre el empresario y los representantes sindicales de los trabajadores sobre salario, horas, y condiciones del taller (p. 727)

colony / colonia asentamiento de personas en un nuevo territorio controlado por su país nativo (p. 95)

Columbian Exchange / Cambio Colombiano el cambio de productos, ideas, y personas entre Europa y las Américas (p. 95)

commission / comisión un grupo de personas dirigidas a hacer algún deber (p. 643)

* **commit / cometer** llevar a cabo un acto (p. 648)

* **communicate / comunicar** transmitir información, pensamientos o sentimientos de manera que se entiendan y comprendan (p. 434)

* **community / comunidad** grupo de personas con intereses en común, especialmente cuando viven en la misma localidad (p. 501)

compromise / compromiso un acuerdo entre dos o más partidos en el cual cada partido abandona algo de lo que quiere (p. 199)

* **concentrate / concentrarse** fijar la atención en una idea central (p. 386)

* **concept / concepto** principio o idea (p. 491)

* **conclude / concluir** llegar a una decisión final (p. 345)

concurrent powers / poderes concurrentes poderes compartidos por los estados y el gobierno federal (p. 222)

* **conduct / conducir** dirigir o controlar las relaciones entre dos o más personas o grupos (p. 205)

Conestoga wagon / conestoga vehículo firme cubierto de lona blanca usado por los pioneros para moverse hacia el oeste (p. 313)

confederation / confederación asociación voluntaria de estados independientes (p. 180)

* **confirm / confirmar** apoyar o consentir (p. 280)

* **conflict / conflicto** desacuerdo o lucha (p. 329)

conquistador / conquistador explorador español en las Américas en los años 1500 (p. 86)

conservation / conservación la protección y preservación de recursos naturales (p. 771)

* **consist / consistir** estar compuesto de (p. 354)

consolidation / consolidación la práctica de juntar compañías particulares en una (p. 707)

* **constant / constante** que ocurre a menudo o todo el tiempo (p. 433)

constituents / constituyentes personas representadas por miembros del Congreso (p. 227)

constitution / constitución un plan formal de gobierno (p. 121)

* **contract / contrato** acuerdo entre personas (p. 103)

* **contrary / contrario** lo opuesto (p. 327)

* **contrast / contrastar** mostrar las diferencias entre dos cosas que se comparan (p. 292)

* **contribute / contribuir** ayudar a causar un suceso o situación (p. 460)

* **controversy / controversia** gran desacuerdo o discusión sobre algo, generalmente porque afecta o les importa a muchas personas (p. 537)

* **convert / convertir** cambiar una cosa en otra (p. 710)

* **convince / convencer** hacer que alguien crea algo por medio de razones o hechos (p. 136)

* **cooperate / cooperar** trabajar con otros para completar una tarea (p. 221)

cooperative / cooperativa una tienda donde los granjeros compraban productos uno al otro; una empresa poseída y operada por los que usan sus servicios (p. 694)

corporation / sociedad anónima un grupo autorizado por ley a montar una actividad pero con los derechos y deberes de una persona particular (p. 719)

* **correspond / corresponder** comunicarse por cartas (p. 137)

corruption / corrupción acciones deshonestas o ilegales (p. 638)

cotton gin / despepitadora de algodón una máquina que sacaba las semillas de las fibras de algodón (pp. 384, 423)

court-martial / formar un consejo de guerra ser enjuiciado por una corte militar (p. 365)

covenant / pacto acuerdo formal o promesa entre dos o más personas (p. 99)

* **create / crear** hacer o producir (p. 638)

credit / crédito una forma de préstamo; la capacidad de comprar productos basada en pagos futuros (p. 429)

* **culture / cultura** la manera de vivir de un grupo de personas que tienen en común sus creencias y costumbres (p. 81)

* **currency / moneda** dinero (p. 194)

D

*debate / debate discusión oral (p. 536)

debtor / deudor persona o país que debe dinero (p. 124)

*decline / decaer perder valor (p. 695)

decree / decreto una orden o decisión dada por alguien de autoridad (p. 482)

demilitarize / desmilitarizar quitar las fuerzas armadas de un área (p. 363)

*demonstrate / demostrar enseñar por medio de ejemplos (p. 365)

*deny / negar no aceptar algo (p. 626)

depression / depresión un período de poca actividad económica y de desempleo extenso (pp. 194, 460)

*derive / derivarse venir de algo, como una palabra que se ha formado de otra (p. 674)

*design / diseño creación de un producto de acuerdo con un plan (p. 83)

*despite / a pesar de sin tomar algo en cuenta o sin ser influido por algo (p. 686)

*device / dispositivo invento o aparato (p. 713)

*devote / dedicar usar un espacio, área o período de tiempo para un propósito (p. 492)

*diminish / disminuir empequeñecer (p. 238)

disarmament / desarme eliminación de las armas (p. 363)

discrimination / discriminación trato injusto de un grupo; trato parcial a causa de la raza, la religión, los antecedentes étnicos, o lugar de nacimiento de alguien (pp. 397, 778)

dissenter / disidente persona que no esta de acuerdo con u opínese a opiniones establecidas (p. 121)

*distinct / bien diferenciados totalmente distintos (p. 291)

*distribute / distribuir dividir entre varios o muchos (p. 599)

diversity / diversidad variedad o diferencia (p. 123)

dividend / dividendo cheque que se paga a los accionistas, por lo general trimestralmente, representa una porción de las ganancias de la corporación (p. 719)

*document / documento escrito importante (p. 103)

*dominate / dominar tener gran influencia sobre todos los demás (p. 636)

draft / reclutamiento la selección de personas a servicio militar requirido (p. 602)

dry farming / agricultura seca una manera de cultivar tierra seca en la cual las semillas se plantan al fondo de la tierra donde hay un poco de humedad (p. 678)

due process of law / proceso justo de ley idea de que el gobierno debe de seguir los procesos establecidos por ley y garantizados por la Constitución (p. 235)

*dynamic / dinámico tener mucho carácter y energía (p. 697)

E

*economy / economía sistema monetario de un país, región o comunidad (p. 359)

*eliminate / eliminar quitar o deshacerse de algo (p. 645)

emancipate / emancipar liberar de la esclavitud (p. 594)

embargo / embargo una orden que prohibe el comercio con otro país (p. 340)

emigrant / emigrante una persona que sale de un país o una región para vivir en otras partes (p. 474)

emigrate / emigrar dejar su patria para vivir en otras partes (p. 742)

empresario / empresario una persona que arregló la coloización de tierra en Texas durante los años 1800 (p. 481)

*enable / posibilitar hacer posible; permitir que algo suceda (p. 634)

encomienda / encomienda sistema de recompensar a los conquistadores con extensiones de tierra y el derecho de recaudar impuestos y exigir mano de obra a los Nativos Americanos que vivían en la tierra (p. 88)

*encounter / encuentro casual hallarse con otras personas inesperadamente (p. 580)

*enforce / hacer respetar hacer que la gente obedezca la ley o que acepte una nueva situación (p. 641)

Enlightenment / Siglo de las Luces movimiento durante los años 1700 que propagaba la idea de que el conocimiento, la razón, y la ciencia podrían mejorar la sociedad (p. 203)

*enormous / enorme muy grande (p. 313)

*ensure / asegurar confirmar o cerciorarse de algo (p. 309)

entrenched / atrincherado que ocupa una fuerte posición defensiva (p. 605)

entrepreneur / empresario alguien que empieza su propio negocio (p. 93)

enumerated powers / poderes enumerados poderes que pertenecen solamente al gobierno federal (p. 222)

* **environment / medio ambiente** combinación de suelo, clima y seres vivos que influyen en la habilidad para sobrevivir de una planta, animal o ser humano (p. 239)

* **equip / equipar** proporcionar los materiales necesarios para hacer un trabajo (p. 390)

* **establish / establecer** fundar, instalar o abrir (p. 363)

* **ethnic / étnico** adjetivo relativo a un grupo grande de personas clasificadas según orígenes o antecedentes raciales, nacionales o culturales comunes (p. 761)

ethnic group / grupo étnico una minoría que habla un idioma diferente o que sigue costumbres diferentes que la mayoría de la gente de un país (p. 742)

* **evaluate / evaluar** juzgar sobre la calidad o cantidad de algo (p. 580)

* **eventual / mucho después** que sucede al pasar bastante tiempo o finalmente, en general después de mucho trabajo o muchos problemas (p. 555)

* **exceed / exceder** sobrepasar los límites (p. 430)

executive branch / rama ejecutiva la rama de gobierno, dirigida por el presidente, que administra las leyes y la política de una nación (p. 205)

* **expand / expandir** abrirse o ensancharse; aumentar en tamaño, número o cantidad (p. 386)

* **exploit / explotar** usar de manera injusta para ventaja propia (p. 641)

* **export / exportar** vender bienes en el extranjero (p. 95)

* **extract / extraer** sacar (p. 667)

factory system / sistema de fábrica sistema que junta en un solo lugar las categorías de fabricación para aumentar la eficiencia (p. 385)

famine / hambre una escasez extrema de comida (p. 398)

favorite son / hijo favorito candidato que recibe el apoyo de su estado natal en lugar del partido nacional (p. 447)

* **federal / federal** gobierno nacional (p. 453)

federalism / federalismo el compartir el poder entre el gobierno federal y los gobiernos estatales (pp. 204, 222)

Federalists / federalistas apoyadores de la Constitución (p. 206)

* **finance / financiar** proporcionar fondos o capital (p. 91)

fixed costs / costos fijos gastos regulares tal como de vivienda o mantenimiento de equipo que se quedan casi iguales año tras año (p. 429)

* **focus / concentrarse** fijar la atención y reflexionar sobre una idea central (p. 405)

forty-niners / forty-niners personas que fueron a California durante la fiebre del oro en 1849 (p. 501)

* **found / fundar** establecer (p. 403)

free enterprise / libre comercio la libertad de empresas privadas para operarse competetivamente para ganancias con la mínima regulación gubernamental (p. 383)

free silver / plata libre la producción sin límite de monedas de plata (p. 696)

freedman / liberto una persona liberada de la esclavitud (p. 626)

frigate / fragata buque de guerra (p. 355)

fugitive / fugitivo evadido que trata de huir (p. 541)

* **function / funcionar** trabajar o servir para alcanzar una meta (p. 221)

* **fund / fondo** cantidad de dinero ahorrada, colectada o proporcionada para algún propósito (p. 93)

* **generation / generación** personas que nacen y viven durante los mismos años (p. 314)

Gilded Age / la Época Dorada el nombre asociado con América al final de los años 1800, referente a la gran riqueza de los tiempos y la terrible pobreza que estaba debajo (p. 752)

* **goal / meta** objetivo o propósito (p. 413)

grandfather clause / cláusula de abuelo una cláusula que permitía votar a las personas que no aprobaron el examen de alfabetismo si sus padres o sus abuelos habían votado antes de que empezó la Reconstrucción; una excepción a una ley basada en circunstancias preexistentes (p. 648)

Spanish Glossary

*grant / conceder** dar el consentimiento o permiso (p. 122)

*guarantee / garantía** compromiso que se va a cumplir una condición (p. 341)

guerrilla tactics / tácticas de guerrilla referente a ataques sorpresas o incursiones en lugar de la guerra organizada (p. 455)

guerrilla warfare / contienda a guerrilleros una técnica de tirar y darse a la huída usada en combates de guerra (p. 156)

habeas corpus / hábeas corpus una orden legal para una encuesta para determinar si una persona ha sido encarcelada legalmente (p. 600)

homestead / homestead adquirir una pieza de tierra pública de EE.UU. por medio de vivir en ella y cultivarla (p. 676)

horizontal integration / integración horizontal la asociación de firmas competitivas en una sociedad anónima (p. 720)

impeach / acusar acusación formal a un oficial público de mala conducta en la oficina (pp. 227, 633)

implied powers / poderes implícitos poderes no mencionados específicamente en la Constitución (pp. 224, 292)

import / importar comprar bienes de mercados extranjeros (p. 136)

impressment / requisición captura de marineros para forzarlos a servir en una marina extranjera (pp. 288, 339)

indentured servant / sirviente contratado trabajador que consiente trabajar sin pago durante un cierto período de tiempo a cambio del pasaje a América (p. 126)

Industrial Revolution / Revolución Industrial el cambio de una sociedad agraria en una basada en la industria que empezó en la Gran Bretaña y se promulgó a los Estados Unidos alrededor del año 1800 (p. 383)

*inevitable / inevitable** que no se puede impedir o escapar (p. 546)

inflation / inflación aumento contínuo del precio de productos y servicios (p. 603)

initiative / iniciativa el derecho de los ciudadanos de poner una medida o tema ante los votantes o la legislatura para aprobación (p. 769)

injunction / amonestación una orden judicial para terminar una acción, tal como una huelga (p. 729)

*inspect / inspeccionar** examinar con cuidado (p. 771)

integrate / integrar suprimir la segregación de las razas diferentes e introducir a membrecía igual y común en la sociedad (p. 638)

interchangeable parts / partes intercambiables piezas uniformes que pueden ser hechas en grandes cantidades para reemplazar otras piezas idénticas (p. 385)

*interpret / interpretar** explicar el significado (p. 179)

*intervene / intervenir** ponerse entre dos cosas (p. 229)

*invest / invertir** gastar dinero en un negocio para sacar ganancias (p. 719)

*involve / envolver** contener, involucrar o incluir (p. 236)

ironclad / acorazado buque armado (p. 578)

*isolate / aislar** separar o mantener separado de otros (p. 760)

*issue / tema** un tema que se disputa entre dos o más partidos (p. 450)

isthmus / istmo una faja estrecha de tierra que conecta dos áreas de tierra más grandes (p. 776)

*item / artículo** una mercancía o producto (p. 504)

*job / trabajo** deber o labor por la cual se recibe pago (p. 725)

joint occupation / ocupación en común la posesión y colonización de un área como esfuerzo compartido por dos o más países (p. 471)

joint-stock company / compañía por acciones una compañía en la cual los inversionistas compran acciones de la compañia a cambio de una porción de las ganancias en el futuro (p. 93)

judicial branch / rama judicial la rama de gobierno, incluyendo el sistema de tribunales federales, que interpreta las leyes de una nación (p. 205)

judicial review / repaso judicial el derecho del Tribunal Supremo para determinar si una ley viola la Constitución (pp. 225, 309)

*****justify / justificar** tener buenas razones para escoger un bando (p. 556)

*****labor / laborar** trabajar por un sueldo, como en la producción de bienes y servicios (p. 725)

laissez-faire / laissez-faire la creencia de que el gobierno no debe de involucrarse en los asuntos comerciales y económicos del país (pp. 307, 460, 771)

land-grant college / colegio de tierras donadas originalmente, un colegio agrícola establecido como resultado del Decreto Morrill de 1862 que dio a los estados, grandes cantidades de tierras federales que podrían ser vendidas para recaudar dinero para la educación (p. 760)

landslide / victoria arrolladora una victoria abrumadora (p. 448)

legislative branch / rama legislativa la rama de gobierno que redacta las leyes de una nación (p. 204)

*****levy / gravamen** impuesto que un país, región o distrito cobra para pagar un préstamo o deuda (p. 194)

literacy test / examen de alfabetismo un método usado para prohibir a los afroamericanos a votar por requerir a presuntos votantes que pudieran leer y escribir a niveles especificados (p. 647)

lock / esclusa en un canal un recinto con puertas en cada extremo y usado para levantar y bajar los buques mientras pasan de un nivel al otro (p. 392)

lode / filón una faja o venero de mena intercalada entre estratos de piedra (p. 667)

Loyalists / lealistas colonizadores americanos que quedaron leales a la Bretaña y se opusieron a la guerra para la independencia (p. 153)

lynching / linchamiento matar a una persona a través de la acción ilegal de una muchedumbre airada (p. 648)

*****maintain / mantener** continuar o sostener (p. 286)

*****major / mayor** importancia que tiene gran tamaño, número o longitud (p. 105)

Manifest Destiny / Destino Manifiesto la idea popular en los Estados Unidos durante los años 1800 de que el país debería de extender sus fronteras hasta el Pacífico (p. 474)

*****manual / manual** hecho a mano (p. 399)

manumission / manumisión el liberar a unas personas esclavizadas (p. 196)

martyr / mártir una persona que sacrifica su vida por un principio o una causa (p. 553)

mass production / fabricación en serie la producción de grandes cantidades de productos usando máquinas y muchas veces una línea de montaje (p. 717)

Mayflower Compact / Convenio del Mayflower un documento formal escrito en 1620 que proporcionó leyes para el mantenimiento del orden público en la colonia de Plymouth (p. 120)

mercantilism / mercantilismo idea de que el poder de una nación dependía de ampliar su comercio y aumentar sus reservas de oro (p. 94)

merger / fusión de empresas la asociación de dos o más negocios en uno (p. 722)

*****migrate / migrar** mudarse de un país a otro (p. 329)

*****military / militares** las fuerzas armadas (p. 124)

militia / milicia un grupo de civiles entrenados para luchar durante emergencias (p. 139)

*****ministry / clerecía** oficio, deberes y labores de un pastor (p. 413)

minutemen / *minutemen* compañías de soldados civiles que se jactaban de que podrían estar listos para tomar armas en sólo un minuto (p. 140)

mission / misión una comunidad religiosa (p. 88)

*****modify / modificar** hacer cambios (p. 777)

*****monitor / observar** seguir de cerca con un propósito en particular (p. 227)

monopoly / monopolio control total de una industria por una persona o una compañía (p. 720)

mountain man / hombre montañés colonizador que vivía en el monte, como en las Montañas Rocosas (p. 472)

muckraker / expositor de corrupción periodista que descubre abusos y corrupción en una sociedad (p. 767)

mudslinging / detractar intentar arruinar la reputación de un adversario con insultos (p. 447)

national debt / deuda nacional la cantidad de dinero que un gobierno debe a otros gobiernos o a su pueblo (p. 281)

National Grange / Granja Nacional la primera organización de granjeros de los Estados Unidos (p. 694)

nationalism / nacionalismo lealtad a una nación y promoción de sus intereses sobre todos los demás (pp. 321, 345)

nativist / nativista una persona que favorece a los nacidos en su patria y se opone a los inmigrantes (pp. 401, 746)

naturalization / naturalización el otorgar la plena ciudadanía a un extranjero (p. 236)

* network / red sistema de partes conectadas (p. 711)

neutral / neutral que no toma partido a ninguna persona ni a ningún país en un conflicto (p. 153)

neutral rights / derechos neutrales el derecho para navegar en el mar sin tomar partido en una guerra (p. 339)

neutrality / neutralidad una posición de no tomar partido en un conflicto (p. 288)

* nevertheless / no obstante sin embargo (p. 606)

nomadic / nómada que se mueve de un lugar a otro sin hogar permanente (p. 686)

normal school / escuela normal una escuela con programa de dos años para entrenar a los graduados de preparatoria para ser maestros (p. 405)

Northwest Passage / Paso Noroeste ruta acuática para Asia por América del Norte buscada por exploradores europeos (p. 88)

* notion / noción idea o concepto (p. 529)

nullify / anular cancelar o hacer sin efecto (pp. 296, 450, 537)

* obtain / obtener conseguir (p. 669)

* obvious / obvio fácil de ver, comprender o hallar (p. 573)

* occupy / ocupar tomar posesión de (pp. 157, 326)

* occur / ocurrir suceder (p. 603)

offensive / ofensiva la posición de atacar o el mismo ataque (p. 573)

oligopoly / oligopolio mercado en que hay pocos productores y cada uno afecta pero no controla el mercado (p. 766)

open range / terreno abierto tierra sin cercas ni dividida en solares (p. 673)

ordinance / ordenanza una ley o regulación (p. 181)

ore / mena un mineral minado por la sustancia valorable que contiene, tal como plata (p. 667)

* outcome / resultado efecto, consecuencias, o producto (p. 605)

override / vencer rechazar o derrotar, como un proyecto de ley propuesto en el Congreso (p. 630)

overseer / capataz persona que supervisa una operación grande o a sus trabajadores (pp. 127, 430)

* participate / participar tomar parte en una actividad con otras personas (p. 194)

partisan / partidario a favor de una parte de un asunto (p. 291)

patent / patente un documento que da al inventor el derecho exclusivo legal de una invención durante un período de tiempo (p. 384)

Patriots / patriotas colonizadores americanos que estaban determinados para luchar en contra de los británicos hasta que se ganara la independencia americana (p. 153)

* percent / por ciento una parte de 100 (p. 386)

* period / período cantidad de tiempo (p. 625)

persecute / perseguir tratar cruelmente a alguien a causa de sus creencias o diferencias (p. 122)

petition / petición una solicitud formal (p. 150)

philanthropy / filantropía acciones caritativas o donaciones de dinero para beneficiar a la comunidad (p. 722)

philosophe / filósofo palabra francesa; durante el Siglo de las Luces, se aplicaba a intelectuales, como escritores, maestros, periodistas y observadores de la sociedad (p. 105)

philosophy / filosofía conjunto de creencias o ideas relacionadas con un sistema de valores culturales (p. 307)

planter / hacendado dueño de muchas tierras (p. 326)

plurality / pluralidad el mayor número de individuos (p. 447)

*****policy / política** plan o instrucciones para lo que se va a hacer (p. 367)

political machine / máquina política una organización aliada con un partido político que muchas veces controlaba el gobierno local (p. 765)

poll tax / impuesto de capitación un impuesto de una cantidad fija por cada persona que tenía que ser pagada antes de que pudiera votar la persona (p. 647)

pool / consorcio un grupo compartiendo de una actividad, por ejemplo, entre barones ferrocarrileros que hacían acuerdos secretos y fijaban tipos entre ellos mismos (p. 711)

popular sovereignty / soberanía popular la teoría política de que el gobierno está sujeto a la voluntad del pueblo (pp. 179, 222); antes de la Guerra Civil, la idea de que la gente que vivía en un territorio tenía el derecho de decidir por votar si allí sería permitida la esclavitud (p. 544)

Populist Party / Partido Populista partido político de los EE.UU. formado en 1892 que representaba principalmente a los granjeros, que favorecía la acuñación libre de plata y el control gubernamental de ferrocarriles y otros monopolios (p. 695)

*****pose / presentar** plantear; causar (p. 504)

preamble / preámbulo la introducción de un documento formal, especialmente la Constitución (pp. 152, 219)

precedent / precedente una tradición (p. 279)

*****predominant / predominante** que tiene mayor importancia, fuerza, influencia o autoridad (p. 424)

prejudice / prejuicio una opinión injusta no basada en los hechos (p. 397)

presidio / presidio un fuerte español en las Américas construido para proteger las colonias misioneras (p. 88)

*****primary / elección preliminar** una elección en la cual los votantes escogen al candidato de su partido (pp. 573, 769)

*****principle / principio** una verdad fundamental en que se basan otras teorías (p. 130)

privateer / buque corsario buque armado privado (p. 355)

*****process / proceso** una acción continua o serie de acciones (p. 743)

*****professional / profesional** que participa en una actividad para su manutención o como carrera (p. 752)

*****prohibit / prohibir** vedar o no permitir (p. 633)

*****promote / promover** alentar o contribuir a la diseminación de una idea (p. 203)

proportional / proporcional que son iguales o que corresponden (p. 199)

proprietary colony / colonia propietaria colonia dirigida por personas o grupos a quienes se les había otorgado la tierra (p. 130)

*****prospect / perspectivas** posibilidad de que algo suceda en el futuro (p. 580)

protective tariff / arancel tarifa que sube el precio de productos de otros países (p. 537)

*****publication / publicación** material impreso que se ofrece para distribución o venta (p. 530)

*****publish / publicar** preparar materiales impresos para exhibición pública o venta (p. 407)

pueblo / pueblo una casa o una comunidad de casas cons-truidas por Nativos Americanos (p. 88)

*****purchase / comprar** obtener por dinero (p. 429)

*****pursue / afanarse** luchar para alcanzar una meta (p. 102)

radical / radical extremo (p. 625)

ragtime / ragtime una clase de música con un ritmo fuerte y una melodía animada con notas acentuadas que era popular al principio del siglo (p. 762)

ranchero / ranchero dueño de rancho mexicano (p. 492)

rancho / rancho propiedades grandísimas para producir ganado establecidas por colonizadores mexicanos en California (p. 492)

*****range / cordillera** serie de montañas (p. 501)

ratify / ratificar dar aprobación oficial para (pp. 181, 206, 594)

realism / realismo una perspectiva de literatura, arte, y teatro que representa las cosas tal como son (p. 761)

rebate / rebaja descuento o devolución de una porción de un pago (p. 710)

Rebel / rebelde soldado confederado, así nombrado a causa de su oposición al gobierno establecido (p. 574)

recall / elección de revocación el derecho que permite a los votantes que despidan de la oficina a los oficiales elegidos que son inadecuados (p. 769)

reconciliation / reconciliación arreglar por acuerdo o por reunirse de nuevo (p. 641)

Reconstruction / Reconstrucción la reorganización y la reconstrucción de los anteriores estados confederados después de la Guerra Civil (p. 625)

referendum / referéndum la práctica de permitir a los votantes que acepten o rechazen medidas propuestas por la legislatura (p. 769)

***region / región** un área, división o distrito (p. 638)

regionalism / regionalismo en arte o literatura, la práctica de enfocar en una región en particular del país (p. 761)

***register / registro** escrito con informes o datos; lista de datos (p. 743)

***regulate / regular** gobernar de acuerdo con reglas o leyes (p. 199)

***reinforce / reforzar** dar más soldados o armas a un ejército para hacerlo más fuerte (p. 577)

***reject / rechazar** negarse a dar o a considerar (p. 776)

relocate / reubicar forzar a una persona o a un grupo de personas a trasladarse (p. 453)

***reluctance / renuencia** desagrado o mala gana de hacer algo (p. 593)

***remove / quitar** sacar, despedir, retirar (p. 453)

Renaissance / Renacimiento un período de creatividad intelectual y artística, alrededor de los años 1300–1600 (p. 102)

rendezvous / rendezvous una reunión (p. 472)

repeal / revocar cancelar un decreto o ley (p. 136)

republicanism / republicanismo que favorece una república, o sea una democracia representativa, como la mejor forma de gobierno (p. 222)

***require / requerir** necesitar (p. 307)

reservation / reservación un área de tierra pública apartada para los Nativos Americanos (p. 687)

reserved powers / poderes reservados poderes retenidos por los estados (p. 222)

resolution / resolución una expresión formal de opinion (p. 139)

***resolve / resolver** solucionar un asunto (p. 341)

***resource / recurso** un bien muy útil o valioso (p. 719)

***restrict / restringir** limitar (p. 550)

***reveal / revelar** descubrir algo que hasta entonces estaba escondido o se desconocía (p. 544)

***revenue / ingresos** entrada de dinero (p. 284)

revival / renacimiento religioso una serie de reuniones dirigidas por un predicador para animar emociones religiosas (p. 403)

right of deposit / derecho de depositar Estados Unidos llegó a un acuerdo con España que le permitía navegar libremente por el río Mississippi (p. 185)

***role / papel** función dada a una persona o de la cual se hace cargo (p. 447)

***route / ruta** camino establecido (p. 472)

royal colony / colonia real colonia administrada por un gobernador y un consejo nombrados por el rey o reina (p. 130)

rule of law / imperio de la ley de acuerdo con la antigua ley romana, todos debían ser tratados con igualdad (p. 99)

scalawags / scalawags nombre dado por los confederados anteriores a los blancos sureños que apoyaban la Reconstrucción republicana del Sur (p. 638)

scientific method / método científico manera ordenada de recopilar y analizar pruebas (p. 105)

secede / separarse abandonar o retirar (pp. 316, 450, 541)

secession / secesión retiro de la Unión (p. 556)

sectionalism / regionalismo lealtad a una región (p. 536)

***secure / salvaguardar** proteger contra el peligro o la pérdida (p. 155)

sedition / sedición actividades con el propósito de debilitar un gobierno establecido (p. 295)

segregation / segregación la separación o aislamiento de una raza, una clase, o un grupo (p. 648)

settlement house / casa de beneficencia institución colocada en una vecindad pobre que proveía numerosos servicios a la comunidad tal como cuidado médico, cuidado de niños, bibliotecas, y clases de inglés (p. 753)

sharecropping / aparcería sistema de agricultura en el cual un granjero labra la tierra para un dueño que provee equipo y semillas y recibe una porción de la cosecha (p. 639)

shareholder / accionista una persona que invierte en una sociedad anónima por comprar acciones y que es un dueño parcial (p. 719)

***shift / mover** cambiar una cosa de lugar o posición (p. 396)

***significant / importante** significativo; que tiene un efecto profundo en algo (p. 308)

***similar / similar** semejante o parecido; con las mismas cualidades (p. 484)

slave code / código de esclavos las leyes aprobadas en los estados sureños que controlaban y restringían a la gente esclavizada (p. 434)

slum / barrio bajo vecindad pobre, superpoblada, y de de vecindades ruinosas (p. 752)

smuggling / contrabandear cambiar ilegalmente con otras naciones (p. 136)

sodbuster / rompedor de césped nombre dado al granjero de las Llanuras (p. 678)

***sole / solo** sin otra cosa o sin compañía (p. 474)

sovereignty / soberanía poder supremo (p. 180)

speculator / especulador persona que arriesga dinero para hacer una ganancia grande (p. 282)

spiritual / espiritual una canción popular religiosa afroamericana (p. 433)

spoils system / sistema de despojos la práctica de dar puestos gubernamentales a los partidarios; reemplazar a los empleados del gobierno con los partidarios del candidato victorioso (p. 449)

standard gauge / medida normal la anchura uniforme de 4 pies, 8.5 pulgadas de las vías ferroviarias, adoptada durante los años 1880 (p. 709)

states' rights / derechos estatales derechos y poderes independientes del gobierno federal que son reservados a los estados por la Constitución (pp. 296, 556)

***status / status** posición o categoría con relación a las demás personas (p. 482)

steerage / entrepuente los cuarteles apretados de las cubiertas bajas de un barco para los pasajeros que pagan los pasajes más bajos (p. 742)

stock / acciones valores de propiedad de comercio que vende una compañía que llevan muchas veces el poder de votar (p. 719)

***strategy / estrategia** plan detallado o método de proceder (p. 341)

strike / huelga un paro de trabajo por los trabajadores para forzar al empresario a satisfacer demandas (p. 397)

strikebreaker / esquirol una persona contratada para reemplazar a un huelguista para suprimir una huelga (p. 727)

***structure / estructura** disposición de las partes de algo (p. 279)

subsidy / subsidio donación de dinero del gobierno a una persona o una compañía para una acción con el propósito de beneficiar al público (p. 669)

subsistence farming / agricultura para subsistencia labranza que produce solamente la comida que se necesita para dar de comer a la familia del trabajador (p. 126)

***substitute / sustituto** persona o cosa que reemplaza a otra (p. 602)

suburbs / suburbios áreas residenciales que brotaron cerca de o alrededor de ciudades como resultado de mejoramientos de transportación (p. 752)

***sufficient / suficiente** bastante para alcanzar una meta o satisfacer una necesidad (p. 573)

suffrage / sufragio el derecho al voto (pp. 409, 449)

***sum / resumir** describir o expresar en breve los datos importantes sobre un tema (p. 425)

***survive / sobrevivir** mantenerse vivo a pesar de dificultades y traumas (p. 119)

sweatshop / fábrica-opresora un taller o fábrica donde se explota a los trabajadores, trabajándolos muchas horas por poco pago y en condiciones malsanas (pp. 725, 744)

***symbol / símbolo** letra, carácter o signo que se usa en vez de palabras (p. 461)

tariff / tarifa impuesto sobre productos importados o exportados (pp. 282, 450)

***technique / técnica** método o destreza que se usa para lograr una meta (p. 156)

***technology / tecnología** el uso de conocimientos científicos para propósitos prácticos (pp. 82, 384, 710)

***Tejano* / tejano** un mexicano que reclama Texas como su patria (p. 481)

temperance / templanza el uso de poca o de ninguna bebida alcohólica (p. 403)

tenant farmer / granjero arrendatario un granjero que labra la tierra de otro dueño y paga renta ya sea con la cosecha o al contado (p. 428)

tenement / casa de vecindad un edificio en el cual varias familias alquilan cuartos o apartamentos, a menudo con pocas medidas sanitarias o seguridad (p. 752)

theology / teología el estudio de la religión y las creencias religiosas (p.101)

*__theory / teoría__ idea que sirve de punto de partida para una discusión o investigación (p. 556)

toleration / tolerancia el aceptar creencias diferentes (p. 121)

*__topic / tema__ materia bajo estudio y discusión, y sobre la cual se escribe (p. 552)

total war / guerra total la guerra en todo aspecto de la vida del enemigo (p. 609)

trade union / gremio una organización de artesanos con el mismo oficio o destreza (pp. 397, 726)

transcendentalist / transcendentalista uno de un grupo de escritores de Nueva Inglaterra que acentuaban la relación entre los seres humanos y la naturaleza, asuntos espirituales sobre asuntos materiales, y la importancia de la conciencia particular (p. 406)

transcontinental / transcontinental que se extiende a través del continente (p. 670)

*__transmit / transmitir__ pasar de una persona o sitio a otro (p. 713)

*__transport / transportar__ llevar de un lugar a otro (p. 286)

triangular trade / trato triangular una ruta de comercio para cambiar productos entre las Antillas, las colonias americanas, y África del Oeste (p. 126)

tribute / tributo dinero pagado para protección (p. 339)

trust / cártel una combinación de firmas o sociedades anónimas formada por un acuerdo legal, especialmente para reducir la competición (pp. 720, 766)

turnpike / autopista una carretera que uno debe de pagar para usar; el dinero se usa para pagar el costo de la carretera (p. 389)

*__ultimate / último__ resultado final o supremo (p. 279)

unconstitutional / anticonstitucional no de acuerdo ni consistente con la Constitución (p. 282)

Underground Railroad / Ferrocarril Subterráneo un sistema que ayudó a los afroamericanos esclavizados a seguir una red de rutas de escape afuera del Sur hacia la libertad del Norte (p. 534)

underlie / subyacer estar por debajo, o servir de base o apoyo (p. 767)

undertake / emprender asumir una responsabilidad (p. 386)

*__unify / unificar__ unir o reunir (p. 713)

*__unique / único__ solo en su clase; sin igual (p. 325)

utopia / utopía una comunidad basada en una visión de la sociedad perfecta buscada por los reformistas (p. 403)

vaquero / vaquero trabajador ranchero hispánico (p. 674)

vaudeville / teatro de variedades entretenimiento compuesto de varios actos, tal como baile, canción, comedia, y espectáculos de mágica (p. 763)

vertical integration / integración vertical la asociación de compañías que abastecen con equipo y servicios necesarios para una industria particular (p. 721)

veto / vetar rechazar un proyecto de ley y prevenir que vuelva a ser una ley (p. 459)

vigilantes / vigilantes gente que toman la ley en sus propias manos (pp. 504, 668)

*__violate / violar__ romper la ley o hacer daño (p. 136)

*__vision / visión__ habilidad para pensar en el futuro y planear de antemano (p. 505)

ward / pupilo persona bajo la tutela del gobierno de Estados Unidos (p. 782)

War Hawks / halcones de guerra republicanos durante la presidencia de Madison que insistían en la guerra con la Bretaña (p. 343)

Yankee / yanqui soldado de la Unión (p. 574)

yellow journalism / periodismo amarillista escritura que exageraba acontecimientos sensacionales, dramáticos, y repulsivos para atraer a los lectores, citando historias que fueron populares durante los fines de los años 1800 (p. 761)

yeoman / terrateniente menor dueño sureño de una granja pequeña que no tenía esclavos (p. 428)

A Gazetteer (GA • zuh • TIHR) is a geographic index or dictionary. It shows latitude and longitude for cities and certain other places. Latitude and longitude are shown in this way: 48°N 2°E, or 48 degrees north latitude and two degrees east longitude. This Gazetteer lists most of the world's largest independent countries, their capitals, and several important geographic features. The page numbers tell where each entry can be found in this book.

A

Abilene City in Kansas (39°N/97°W) 673

Africa Continent of the Eastern Hemisphere south of the Mediterranean Sea and adjoining Asia on its northeastern border 27, 87, 96, 100, 558, 776

Alabama State in the southeastern United States; 22nd state to enter the Union 31, 644

Alamo Texas mission captured by Mexican forces in 1836 (29°N/98°W) 483, 485

Alaska State in the United States, located in northwestern North America 26, 31, 32, 776

Albany Capital of New York State located in the Hudson Valley; site where Albany Congress proposed first formal plan to unite the 13 colonies (42°N/74°W) 390

Angel Island Island in San Francisco, California; served as an immigrant processing center (37°N/122°W) 743

Annapolis Capital city of Maryland (39°N/76°W) 31

Antietam Civil War battle site in western Maryland (40°N/78°W) 614

Appalachian Mountains Chief mountain system in eastern North America extending from Quebec and New Brunswick to central Alabama 33, 122, 135

Appomattox Court House Site in central Virginia where Confederate forces surrendered, ending the Civil War (37°N/78°W) 610

Argentina Country in South America 26

Arizona State in the southwestern United States; 48th state to enter the Union 30

Arkansas State in the south central U.S.; acquired as part of Louisiana Purchase 31, 558, 606, 632

Asia Continent of the Eastern Hemisphere forming a single landmass with Europe 26, 776

Asia Minor The peninsula forming western boundary of Asia between the Black Sea and Mediterranean Sea and bordering on the Aegean Sea to form the greater part of Turkey 100

Atlanta Capital of Georgia located in the northwest central part of the state (34°N/84°W) 33

Atlantic Ocean Ocean separating North and South America from Europe and Africa 26, 33, 87, 96, 119, 135, 156

Augusta Capital city of Maine (44°N/69°W) 31

Austin Capital city of Texas (30°N/97°W) 31

Australia Continent and country southeast of Asia 27, 776

B

Baltimore City on the Chesapeake Bay in central Maryland (39°N/76°W) 122

Barbary Coast North coast of Africa between Morocco and Tunisia 339

Baton Rouge Capital city of Louisiana (30°N/91°W) 31

Birmingham City in north central Alabama; scene of several civil rights protests (33°N/87°W) 721

Bismarck Capital city of North Dakota (47°N/101°W) 31

Black Hills Mountains in southwestern South Dakota; site of conflict between the Sioux and white settlers during 1870s 688

Boise Capital city of Idaho (43°N/116°W) 30

Boston Capital of Massachusetts located in the eastern part of the state; founded by English Puritans in 1630 (42°N/71°W) 122

Brazil Country in South America 26

Bull Run Site of two Civil War battles in northern Virginia; also called Manassas (39°N/77°W) 577

C

California State in the western United States; attracted thousands of miners during gold rush of 1849 30, 558, 644

Canada Country in northern North America 26, 31, 32–33

Cape of Good Hope Southern tip of Africa (34°S/18°E) 84

Caribbean Sea Tropical sea in the Western Hemisphere 29

Carson City Capital city of Nevada (39°N/120°W) 30

Caspian Sea Inland salt lake between Europe and Asia 100

Central America Area of North America between Mexico and South America (11°N/87°W) 29

Central Park A municipal park located on Manhattan Island in New York City; designed by Frederick Law Olmsted 755

Chancellorsville Virginia site of 1863 Confederate victory (38°N/78°W) 605, 606

Charleston (SC) City in South Carolina on the Atlantic coast; original name Charles Town (33°N/80°W) 122, 156

Charleston (WV) Capital city of West Virginia (38°N/81°W) 31

Chattanooga City in southwest Tennessee; grew into a center for trade in the South (35°N/85°W) 430

Cheyenne City in southeast Wyoming; became an important rail station for cattle drives (41°N/105°W) 673

Chile South American country (35°S/72°W) 26

China Country in eastern Asia; mainland (People's Republic of China) under Communist control since 1949 27, 776

Cincinnati City in southern Ohio on the Ohio River; grew as a result of increasing steamship traffic during the mid-1800s (39°N/84°W) 387, 390

Cleveland City in northern Ohio on Lake Erie (41°N/81°W) 533

Colombia Country in South America 26

Colorado State in the western United States 30, 644

Colorado River River that flows from the Colorado Rockies to the Gulf of California 32, 316

Columbia Capital of South Carolina; became a center for trade in the South (34°N/81°W) 430

Columbia River River flowing through southwest Canada and northwestern United States into the Pacific Ocean 32

Columbus Capital city of Ohio (40°N/83°W) 31

Concord (MA) Village northwest of Boston, Massachusetts; site of early battle of the American Revolution (42°N/71°W) 140

Concord (NH) Capital city of New Hampshire (43°N/71°W) 31

Connecticut State in the northeastern United States; one of the original 13 states 31, 121, 355, 558, 606

Cuba Country in the West Indies, North America 29, 775

Dakota Territory Included North and South Dakota, most of Wyoming and Montana; this land was created by Congress as Indian Territory 687

Delaware State in the northeastern United States; one of the original 13 states (38°N/75°W) 122, 355, 558, 606

Delaware River River flowing through eastern U.S.; empties into the Delaware Bay 390

Denver Capital city of Colorado (39°N/105°W) 31

Des Moines Capital city of Iowa (41°N/93°W) 31

Detroit City in southeastern Michigan; site of significant battles during the French and Indian War and the War of 1812 (42°N/83°W) 31, 355

Dodge City Kansas cattle town during the 19th century (37°N/100°W) 673

Dominican Republic Country in the West Indies on the eastern part of Hispaniola Island 29

Dover Capital city of Delaware (39°N/75°W) 31

Ellis Island Island in upper New York Bay; served as immigrant station from 1892–1954 (41°N/74°W) 743

England Division of the United Kingdom of Great Britain and Northern Ireland 87

Europe Continent of the northern part of the Eastern Hemisphere between Asia and the Atlantic Ocean 26, 87, 96, 776

Fallen Timbers Site in northwestern Ohio of General Anthony Wayne's victory over Native Americans in 1794 (42°N/84°W) 287

Florida State in the southeastern United States 31, 558

Fort Sumter Union fort during the Civil War located on island near Charleston, South Carolina; site of first military engagement of Civil War (33°N/80°W) 558

France Country in western Europe 30, 87

Frankfort Capital city of Kentucky (38°N/85°W) 31

Fredericksburg City and Civil War battle site in northeast Virginia (38°N/77°W) 605

Freeport City in northern Illinois; site of 1858 Lincoln-Douglas campaign debate (42°N/89°W) 552

Gadsden Purchase Portion of present-day Arizona and New Mexico; area purchased from Mexico in 1853 34, 497

Gaul Ancient country of Europe 100

Genoa Important seaport city in northwest Italy (44°N/10°E) 94

Georgia State in the southeastern United States 31, 119, 355, 558, 632

Gettysburg City and Civil War battle site in south central Pennsylvania; site where Lincoln delivered the Gettysburg Address (40°N/77°W) 605

Great Britain Kingdom in west Europe comprised of England, Scotland, and Wales 100

Great Lakes Chain of five lakes—Superior, Erie, Michigan, Ontario, and Huron—in central North America 33

Great Plains Flat grassland in the central United States 30

Great Salt Lake Lake in northern Utah with no outlet and strongly saline waters (41°N/112°W) 31, 506

Greece Country in southeastern Europe 100

Guam Unincorporated U.S. territory 775, 776

Guatemala Country in Central America, south of Mexico 29

Gulf of Mexico Gulf on the southeast coast of North America 33, 117

Haiti Country on Hispaniola Island in the West Indies 29

Harpers Ferry Town in northern West Virginia on the Potomac River (39°N/77°W) 553

Harrisburg Capital city of Pennsylvania (40°N/77°W) 31

Hartford Capital city of Connecticut (41°N/72°W) 31

Hawaii State in the United States located in the Pacific Ocean 31, 776

Hawaiian Islands Chain of volcanic and coral islands in north central Pacific Ocean; comprised of eight major islands and 114 minor islands 775, 776

Helena Capital city of Montana (46°N/112°W) 31

Hispaniola Island in the West Indies in North America (17°N/73°W) 29

Homestead City in southwest Pennsylvania; the location of Andrew Carnegie's steel plant where workers went on strike in 1892 (40°N/80°W) 729

Honolulu Capital city of Hawaii (21°N/158°W) 30

Hudson Bay Large bay in northern Canada (60°N/85°W) 29, 89, 135

Hudson River River flowing through New York State 390

Idaho State in the northwestern U.S.; ranks among top states in silver production 30

Illinois State in the north central United States; one of the states formed from the Northwest Territory 31, 558, 644

Indian Territory Land reserved by the United States government for Native Americans, now the state of Oklahoma 316, 454

Indiana State in the north central United States; one of the states formed from the Northwest Territory 31, 644

Indianapolis Capital city of Indiana (39°N/86°W) 31

Indonesia Country in Southeast Asia 27

Iowa State in the north central U.S. acquired as part of the Louisiana Purchase 31, 35, 558

Italy Country in southern Europe along the Mediterranean 26, 100

Jackson Capital city of Mississippi (32°N/90°W) 430

Gazetteer

Jamestown First permanent English settlement in North America; located in southeastern Virginia (37°N/77°W) 122

Japan Island country in eastern Asia 27

Jefferson City Capital city of Missouri (38°N/92°W) 31

Judea The south division of Palestine under Persian, Greek, and Roman rule, succeeding the kingdom of Judah 100

Juneau Capital city of Alaska (58°N/134°W) 30

Kansas State in the central United States; fighting over slavery issue in 1850s gave territory the name "Bleeding Kansas" 31, 558, 644

Kentucky State in the south central United States; border state that sided with the Union during the Civil War 31, 558, 644

Lake Erie One of the five Great Lakes between Canada and the U.S. (42°N/81°W) 33, 355

Lake Huron One of the five Great Lakes between Canada and the U.S. (45°N/82°W) 33, 355

Lake Michigan One of the five Great Lakes between Canada and the U.S. (43°N/87°W) 33, 355

Lake Ontario The smallest of the five Great Lakes (43°N/79°W) 33, 355

Lake Superior The largest of the five Great Lakes (48°N/89°W) 33, 355

Latin America Central and South America; settled by Spain and Portugal 26

Lexington Revolutionary War battle site in eastern Massachusetts; site of first clash between colonists and British, April 19, 1775 (42°N/71°W) 140

Lincoln Capital city of Nebraska (41°N/97°W) 31

Little Bighorn River River south of Montana; where Sioux and Cheyenne warriors defeated the United States army 688

Little Rock Capital of Arkansas located in the center of the state; site of 1957 conflict over public school integration (35°N/92°W) 533

Los Angeles City along Pacific coast in southern California; industrial, financial, and trade center of western United States (34°N/118°W) 670

Louisiana State in the south central United States 31, 119, 606

Louisiana Territory Region of west central United States between the Mississippi River and the Rocky Mountains purchased from France in 1803 35, 135, 313, 316, 558, 606

Louisville City in north central Kentucky (38°N/86°W) 387

Lowell City in Massachusetts (43°N/71°W) 385

Maine State in the northeastern United States; 23rd state to enter the Union 31, 122, 558, 644

Mali Country in Western Africa 26

Manhattan Island Island at northeast end of New York Bay; part of New York City between Hudson and East rivers (44°N/76°W) 117

Maryland State in the eastern United States; one of the original 13 states 35, 122, 355, 387, 558, 606

Massachusetts State in the northeastern United States; one of the original 13 states 121, 122, 140, 558, 606

Mediterranean Sea Sea between Europe and Africa 27, 100

Memphis Tennessee city on the Mississippi River near the Mississippi border (37°N/90°W) 429

Mexican Cession Territory gained by the United States after war with Mexico in 1848 497

Mexico Country in North America south of the United States 26, 30–31, 32, 485, 495

Mexico City Capital and most populous city of Mexico (19°N/99°W) 26

Michigan State in the north central United States; one of the states formed in the Northwest Territory 31

Minnesota State in the north central United States; fur trade, good soil, and lumber attracted early settlers 31, 558, 644

Mississippi State in the southeastern United States; became English territory after French and Indian War 31, 558, 606, 644

Mississippi River River flowing through the United States from Minnesota to the Gulf of Mexico; explored by French in 1600s 33, 117

Missouri State in the south central U.S.; petition for statehood resulted in sectional conflict and the Missouri Compromise 31

Missouri River River flowing through the United States from the Rocky Mountains to the Mississippi River near St. Louis 31, 315, 316, 491

Mobile Commercial seaport in southwest Alabama; exported cotton, coal and agricultural products (31°N/88°W) 429

Mobile Bay Boundary of southwest Alabama and the Gulf of Mexico; the Union controlled this area in 1864 609

Montana State in the northwestern United States; cattle industry grew during 1850s 31, 644

Montgomery Capital of Alabama located in the central part of the state; site of 1955 bus boycott to protest segregation (32°N/86°W) 430

Nashville Capital of Tennessee located in the north central part of the state (36°N/87°W) 533

National Road Road from Baltimore, Maryland, to Vandalia, Illinois 389

Nebraska State in the central United States 31, 644

Netherlands Country in northwestern Europe 27, 87

Nevada State in the western United States 30, 644

New Amsterdam Town founded on Manhattan Island by Dutch settlers in 1625; renamed New York by British settlers (41°N/74°W) 117

New England Region in northeastern United States 33

New France French land claims stretching from Quebec to Louisiana 117, 119

New Hampshire State in the northeastern United States; one of the original 13 states 122, 558, 606

New Haven Coastal city in Connecticut; settled by Puritans in 1638 (41°N/73°W) 122

New Jersey State in the northeastern United States; one of the original 13 states 122, 355, 558, 606

New Mexico State in the southwestern United States; ceded to the United States by Mexico in 1848 31, 117

New Netherland Dutch Hudson River colony 117

New Orleans City in Louisiana in the Mississippi Delta (30°N/90°W) 289, 313, 316, 429

New Spain Part of Spain's empire in the Western Hemisphere 35, 119

New York State in the northeastern United States; one of the original 13 states 31, 117, 122, 387, 558, 606, 644

New York City City in southeastern New York State at the mouth of the Hudson River; first capital of nation (41°N/74°W) 117, 122

Newfoundland Province in eastern Canada (48°N/56°W) 29, 87, 119

Norfolk City in southeastern Virignia; Confederate forces seized a naval ship-yard and rebuilt the *Merrimack* and renamed it *Virginia* (37°N/76°W) 578

North America Continent in the northern part of the Western Hemisphere between the Atlantic and Pacific oceans 26, 87, 96, 776

North Carolina State in the southeastern United States; one of the original 13 states 119, 122, 355, 558, 606, 632

North Dakota State in the north central U.S.; Congress created Dakota Territory in 1861 31

North Sea Arm of the Atlantic Ocean and east of Great Britain 100

Northwest Territory Territory north of the Ohio River and east of the Mississippi River 34, 183

Ohio State in the north central United States; first state in the Northwest Territory 31, 341, 389, 644

Ohio River River flowing from Allegheny and Monongahela rivers in western Pennsylvania into the Mississippi River 33, 355, 386

Oklahoma State in the south central United States; Five Civilized Tribes moved to territory in the period 1830–1842 31, 689

Oklahoma City Capital city of Oklahoma (35°N/98°W) 31

Olympia Capital city of Washington (47°N/123°W) 30

Omaha City in east Nebraska where the Populist Party held their presidential convention in 1892 (41°N/96°W) 670, 696

Oregon State in the northwestern United States; adopted woman suffrage in 1912 30, 558, 644

Oregon Country Area that is now Oregon, Idaho, Washington state, and parts of western Montana and Wyoming 363

Oregon Trail Pioneer trail from Independence, Missouri, to the Oregon Territory 474

Pacific Ocean World's largest ocean, located between Asia and the Americas 26–27, 31, 87, 119, 776

Panama Country in the southern part of Central America, occupying the Isthmus of Panama 29, 776

Panama Canal Canal built across the Isthmus of Panama through Panama to connect the Caribbean Sea and the Pacific Ocean (9°N/80°W) 776–777

Pawtucket City in north Rhode Island; location where Samuel Slater opened a cotton mill (42°N/71°W) 385

Pennsylvania State in the northeastern United States 31, 122, 558, 606, 644

Peru Country in South America, south of Ecuador and Colombia 26, 86

Petersburg City in southeastern Virginia; an important railroad city that the Union seized for nine months (37°N/78°W) 608

Philadelphia City in eastern Pennsylvania on the Delaware River; Declaration of Independence and the Constitution both adopted in city's Independence Hall (40°N/75°W) 122, 726

Philippines Island country in southeast Asia 27, 776

Phoenix Capital city of Arizona (33°N/112°W) 30

Pierre Capital city of South Dakota (44°N/100°W) 31

Pikes Peak Mountain in Rocky Mountains in central Colorado 316

Pittsburgh City in western Pennsylvania; one of the great steelmaking centers of the world (40°N/80°W) 387

Plymouth Town in eastern Massachusetts; first successful English colony in New England (42°N/71°W) 120, 122

Portsmouth Seaport city in southeast New Hampshire (43°N/71°W) 122

Portugal Country in southwestern Europe 26, 87

Potomac River River flowing from West Virginia into Chesapeake Bay 307, 390

Princeton City in west central New Jersey (40°N/75°W) 153

Promontory Summit Site where two sets of the transcontinental railroad connected 670

Providence Capital of Rhode Island; site of first English settlement in Rhode Island (42°N/71°W) 31, 122, 670

Puerto Rico United States common-wealth in the West Indies 29

Quebec City in Canada, capital of Quebec Province, on the St. Lawrence River; first settlement in New France (47°N/71°W) 117

Raleigh Capital city of North Carolina (36°N/79°W) 31

Rhode Island State in the northeastern United States; one of the original 13 states 31, 121, 355, 558, 606

Richmond Capital of Virginia located in the central part of the state; capital of the Confederacy during the Civil War (38°N/78°W) 31

Rio Grande River between the United States and Mexico in North America; forms the boundary between Texas and Mexico 32

Roanoke Island off the coast of present-day North Carolina that was site of early British colonizing efforts (36°N/77°W) 119

Rocky Mountains Mountain range in western United States and Canada in North America 32

Rome City in Italy; one of the most ancient of the European civilizations; developed a republic form of government 99

Russia Name of republic; former empire of eastern Europe and northern Asia coinciding with Soviet Union 27, 776

Sacramento Capital of California located in the north central part of the state (38°N/121°W) 670

Salem Capital city of Oregon (45°N/123°W) 30

Salt Lake City Capital of Utah located in the northern part of the state; founded by Mormons in 1847 (41°N/112°W) 474

Gazetteer

San Antonio City in south central Texas (29°N/98°W) 483

San Diego City in southern California (33°N/117°W) 118

San Francisco City in northern California on the Pacific coast (38°N/122°W) 503

San Juan Capital city of Puerto Rico (18°N/66°W) 31

Santa Fe Capital of New Mexico located in the north central part of the state (36°N/106°W) 117, 491, 495

Santa Fe Trail Cattle trail from Independence, Missouri, to Santa Fe, New Mexico 491

Saratoga Revolutionary War battle site in the Hudson Valley of eastern New York State (43°N/74°W) 154

Savannah City in far eastern Georgia (32°N/81°W) 429

Scandinavia Region of north Europe encompassing Denmark, Norway, and Sweden 87

Seattle Washington city bordered by Puget Sound and Lake Washington (47°N/122°W) 30

Sedalia City in Missouri; the nearest trail point for Texas cattle ranchers (39°N/93°W) 673

Seneca Falls Town in New York State; site of women's rights convention in 1848 (43°N/77°W) 409

Shiloh Site of 1862 Union victory in Tennessee (35°N/88°W) 579

South America Continent in the southern part of the Western Hemisphere lying between the Atlantic and Pacific oceans 26, 119, 776

South Carolina State in the southeastern United States; one of the original 13 states 122, 355, 556, 558, 606, 632

South Dakota State in the north central United States; acquired through the Louisiana Purchase 31

Spain Country in southwestern Europe 26, 87, 100

Springfield Capital city of Illinois (40°N/90°W) 31

St. Augustine City in northeastern Florida on the Atlantic coast; oldest permanent existing European settlement in North America, founded in 1565 (30°N/81°W) 117

St. Louis City in Missouri; the invention of the steamboat played an important role in the growth of this city (39°N/90°W) 31, 390

St. Paul Capital city of Minnesota (45°N/93°W) 31

Switzerland European country in the Alps 27

Syria Ancient country in Asia at the eastern end of the Mediterranean Sea 100

Tallahassee Capital city of Florida (30°N/84°W) 31

Tennessee State in the south central United States; first state readmitted to the Union after the Civil War 31, 558, 606, 644

Tenochtitlán Aztec capital at the site of present-day Mexico City (19°N/99°W) 86

Texas State in the south central United States; Mexican colony that became a republic before joining the United States 31, 485, 495, 558, 606, 632

Topeka Capital city of Kansas (39°N/96°W) 31

Toronto City in Canada on Lake Ontario; capital of the province of Ontario (44°N/79°W) 26

Trenton Capital of New Jersey located on the Delaware River in the central part of the state; site of Revolutionary War battle in December 1776 (40°N/75°W) 153

Union of Soviet Socialist Republics See Soviet Union.

United States Country in central North America; fourth largest country in the world in both area and population 26, 495, 776

Utah State in the western United States; settled by Mormons in 1840s 30

Valley Forge Revolutionary War winter camp northwest of Philadelphia (40°N/75°W) 154

Vandalia City in south central Illinois; the National Road reached here (39°N/89°W) 389

Venezuela South American country on the Caribbean Sea 26

Venice Important seaport city in northeast Italy 94

Vermont State in the northeastern United States; 14th state to enter the Union 606

Vicksburg City and Civil War battle site in western Mississippi on the Mississippi River (32°N/91°W) 606

Virginia State in the eastern United States; colony of first permanent English settlement in the Americas 31, 120, 122, 340, 355, 558, 606, 632

Virginia City City in west Nevada; became a Comstock boomtown during the gold and silver strikes of 1859 (39°N/120°W) 668

Waltham City in northeast Massachusetts; Francis Cabot Lowell opened a textile plant in 1814 (42°N/71°W) 385

Washington State in the northwestern United States; territory reached by Lewis and Clark in 1805 30

Washington, D.C. Capital of the United States located on the Potomac River at its confluence with the Anacostia River, between Maryland and Virginia coinciding with the District of Columbia (39°N/77°W) 31, 282, 307

West Indies Islands in the Caribbean Sea, between North America and South America (19°N/79°W) 29

West Virginia State in the east central United States 31

Willamette Valley Valley of the Willamette River in western Oregon 474

Williamsburg City in southeastern Virginia (37°N/77°W) 122

Wisconsin State in the north central United States; passed first state unemployment compensation act, 1932 31, 558

Wounded Knee Site of massacre of Native Americans by soldiers in southern South Dakota in 1890 and of American Indian Movement protest in 1973 (43°N/102°W) 689, 692

Wyoming State in the western United States; territory provided women the right to vote, 1869 31

Yorktown Town in southeastern Virginia and site of final battle of Revolutionary War (37°N/76°W) 156

Italicized page numbers refer to illustrations. The following abbreviations are used in the index:
c = chart or graph, ctn = cartoon, m = map, p = photograph or picture, ptg = painting, q = quote.

Index

Index

Index

Index

Philadelphia (U.S. warship), 339

Philadelphia, Pennsylvania, *p197;* as capital, 282; celebration in, following ratification of Constitution, 207, 279; colonial, 122; Constitutional Convention in, 197, 199–200; education in, 322; First Continental Congress in, 139; growth of, 126, 327, 398; music in, 762; National Municipal League in, 766; Second Continental Congress in, 150; yellow fever epidemic in, 387

Philadelphia Female Anti-Slavery Society, 409

philanthrophy, 708, 722

Philip II of Spain, 89

Philippines, Spanish-American War and, 775

philosophe, 105

phonographs, 715, 716, *p716*

photography in Civil War, 602

physical maps, 44, *m44*

physical systems, 39

Pickens, Francis, 558

Pickett, George, 606

Pierce, Franklin, 841, *p841;* as president, 544, 546

Pike, Zebulon, 316

Pikes Peak, 316, 667

Pilgrims, 120, 133

Pinckney, Charles: in election of 1796, 293; in election of 1800, 307; in election of 1804, 317; in election of 1808, 340

Pinckney, Thomas, 288

Pinckney's Treaty, 288

Pinta (ship), 84, 108

pioneers, amusements of, 394

pirates, Barbary, 339

Pisa, 82

Pitcairn, John, 141

Pitcher, Molly, 154, *ptg154*

Pittsburgh, Pennsylvania: growth of, 387, 389, 398, 751; as steel capital, 721; strikes in, 727; work for immigrants in, 743

Pittsburg Landing, in Civil War, 579

Pizarro, Francisco, 86

places, 39, 55

plantations, *p418;* life on, 386; in the South, 126–27, 326, 429–30

Plattsburgh, in War of 1812, 358

Pledge of Allegiance, 845, 857

Plessy v. Ferguson, 233, 648, 651, 779, 849

Poe, Edgar Allan, 407

point of view, 63

political machines, 765–66

political maps, 44, *m44,* 58

political parties, 239; emergence of first, 291–92; roots of two party system, 238. *See also specific parties*

Polk, James K., 487, 494, 539, 841, *p841;* in election of 1844, 461, 475; Manifest Destiny and, 475; War with Mexico and, 495–96, 514

poll taxes, 647, 812, 817; abolition of, 268

Polo, Marco, 81, *ptg81*

polygamy, 506

Ponce de León, Juan, 86

Pony Express, 478

pools, railroad, 711

***Poor Richard's Almanack* (Franklin),** 151, 161

Pope, John, 580–81

popular sovereignty, 179, *c221,* 222, 544

population: in California, 505; in 1820, *m386, g386;* foreign born, *g778;* Native American, *g686;* in 1900, *m734;* railroads in redistribution of, 711

Populist Party, *p695,* 695–96; in election of 1892, 696; in election of 1896, 696–97; legacy of, 697

Port Hudson, 606

Port Royal Experiment, 627

Portugal: explorations of, 84, *m87;* improved ship design in, 83; monarchy in, 82; slave trade and, 97

postmaster general, 280

poverty level, *c806,* 807

Powderly, Terence V., 726

Powell, Colin, 677

power loom, 384

Powhatan Confederation, 123

Preamble of the U.S. Constitution, 219, 220, 249

prejudice. *See* discrimination

Prescott, William, 150

president: appointments of, 280; disability and succession of, 268–69; election of, 262; powers of, 225; roles of, 229–30; succession of, 266. *See also* executive branch; *specific presidents*

presidential electors, change in selection of, 449

presidential terms: limit on, 267; number of, 291

presidio, 88

press: colonial, 129; freedom of, 240–41, 260. *See also* journalism; newspapers

Prevost, George, 358

primary elections, 697, 769

primary sources, 62

Prime Meridian, 41, 42

Princeton, in American Revolution, 153

Pringle, Catherine Sager, *q473*

prisoners, reforms for treatment of, 405

privateers, 355

Proclamation of 1763, *m135,* 135–36

Proclamation of Neutrality (1793), 288

progressive education, 759

progressive reforms, 799

progressives, 765, 767, 770

Prohibition, 265; repeal of, 266

Promontory Summit, 670

property taxes, 812, 813

Prophet, 342

Prophetstown, 342, 343

proprietary colonies, 130

Prosser, Gabriel, 435

Protestantism, rise of, 102

public schools, 758–59. *See also* education

pueblos, 88

Puerto Rico, representation of, in House of Representatives, 227

Pulaski, Casimir, 155

Pulitzer, Joseph, 761

Pullman, George M., 710, 729

Pullman Strike, 729

Pun Chi, 515

Pure Food and Drug Act (1906), 767, 771

Puritans, 103, 120, 121

push-pull factors, 641

Quadruple Alliance, 367

Quakers: opposition to slavery, 127, 195; in reform movements, 409; settlement of, in Pennsylvania, 122

quinine, 195, *p195*

racial violence, 780

Radical Reconstruction, 626, 627, 631–33

radiocarbon dating, *p49,* 51

ragtime, 762

railroads: cattle drives and, 673–74; Chinese laborers on, 670; competition and, 710–11; cow towns and, 673; economic growth and, 707, 708, 709–11; effects of, 671; expansion of, 707; formation of corporations and, 719; government control of, 766; government subsidies to, 669–70; growth of cities and, 751; impact of, 707, 711; improving, 709; industrial development and, 646; before 1900, *m710;* in the South, 426; technology and, 710; transcontinental, 669–71, 707; in western settlement, 676

Raleigh, Sir Walter, 119

ranchos, 492

Randolph, Edmund, 199; as attorney general,

Index

Index

Index

One-Stop Internet Resources

This textbook contains one-stop Internet resources for teachers, students, and parents. Log on to tajwwI.glencoe.com for more information. Online study tools include Study Central, Chapter Overviews, ePuzzles and Games, Self-Check Quizzes, Vocabulary e-Flashcards, and Multi-Language Glossaries. Online research tools include Student Web Activities, Current Events, Beyond the Textbook Features, Web Resources, and State Resources. Especially for teachers, Glencoe offers an online Teacher Forum and Web Activity Lesson Plans. The interactive online student edition includes the complete Interactive Student Edition along with textbook updates.

Index

Acknowledgements

Text

186 From *Second Daughter: The Story of a Slave Girl* by Mildred Pitts Walter. Copyright © 1996 by Mildred Pitts Walter. Reprinted by permission of Scholastic Inc. **346** Excerpt from *Crossing the Panther's Path* by Elizabeth Adler. Copyright © 2002 by Elizabeth Adler. Reprinted by permission of Farrar, Straus & Giroux, LLC. **507** From *Thunder on the Sierra*, by Kathy Balmes. Copyright © 2001 by Kathy Balmes. Reprinted by permission of Silver Moon Press, New York. **584** From *Rifles for Watie*, by Harold Keith. Text copyright © 1957 by Harold Keith. Used by permission of HarperCollins Publishers. **680** Excerpt from *A Lantern in Her Hand*, by Bess Streeter Aldrich. Copyright 1928 by D. Appleton & Company, renewed © 1956 by Mary Aldrich Beechner, Robert Streeter Beechner, Charles S. Aldrich, and James Whitson Aldrich. Used by permission of Penguin Group (USA) Inc.

Glencoe would like to acknowledge the artists and agencies who participated in illustrating this program: American Artists Rep., Inc.; The Artifact Group; John Brewster Creative Services; Mapping Specialists, Ltd.; Morgan-Cain & Associates; Studio Inklink; WildLife Art Ltd.

Photo Credits

iv Washington University Gallery of Art, St. Louis Missouri, Gift of Nathiel Phillips, 1890.; v (tl)Fort Ticonderoga Museum, (tr)Lexington Historical Society, Lexington, MA, (br)Copyright 1996, Virginia Historical Society, Lora Robins Collection of Virginia Art; vi (tr)Henry Groskinsky/Timepix, (br)Manassas National Battlefield Park/Larry Sherer; vii Courtesy Ford Motor Company; ix (l)Stock Montage, (r)Chester County Historical Society, West Chester, PA; x Fraunces Tavern Museum, New York City; xi Jacob A. Riis Collection, Museum of the City of New York; **38 39 40** Getty Images; **48** (l)Comstock Images, (c)AP/Worldwide Photos, (r)Getty Images; **49** (t)Ron Sheridan/Ancient Art & Architecture Collection, (cl)Katie Deits/Index Stock Imagery, (b)Photo Researchers, Inc.; **50** (t)Scala/Art Resource, NY, (b) Nimatallah/Art Resource, NY; **51** (l)Michel Zabe/Museo Templo Mayor, (r)Kunsthistorisches Museum, Wien oder KHM, Wien; **52** (t)National Portrait Gallery, Smithsonian Institution/Art Resource, NY, (c)Henry Groskinsky, (bl)Mark Burnett, (br)Library of Congress; **54** NASA; **55** (l)Courtesy Denver Public Library Western History Department, (c)Huntington Library/SuperStock, (r)Henry Groskinsky; **56 59 60 62** Getty Images; **57** H. Armstrong Roberts; **60** (t)Will Hart/PhotoEdit, (bl)Massachusetts Historic Royal Palaces, (bc)The Shelburne Museum, (br)Charles & Josette Lenars/CORBIS; **61** (l)Bettmann/CORBIS, (r)Getty Images; **62** (t)Wenham Museum, (bl) Missouri Historical Society, St. Louis, (bc) Thomas Gilcrease Institute of American Art, Tulsa, OK, (br)Collection of David J. & Janice L. Frent; **63** Bettmann/CORBIS; **64** (l)St. Louis Art Museum, St. Louis, Missouri, USA/SuperStock, (r)Bettmann/CORBIS; **65** (l)Private Collection/Picture Research Consultants, (c)New York Historical Society, (r)The Saint Louis Art Museum. Gift of Bank of America; **66** (t)Richard A. Cooke/CORBIS, (b)The City of Plainfield, NJ; **68** (cw from top)Photograph Courtesy Peabody Essex Museum, SuperStock, H. ARMSTRONG ROBERTS, Pablo San Juan/CORBIS, Morgan-Cain, Tim Flach/Getty Images; **69** (cw from top)Dennis Brack/Black Star, Ted Spiegel/CORBIS, Fraunces Tavern Museum, Stock Montage; **70** (cw from top)United States Naval Academy Museum, The J. Paul Getty Museum, Bettmann/CORBIS, Larry Lee Photography/CORBIS, EyeWire Images; **71** (tl)Flip Schulke/Black Star, (tr)Collection of Cheekwood Museum of Art, Nashville, Tennessee, (cl)Library of Congress, (cr)Picture Research Consultants, (bl)Bettmann/CORBIS, (br)Arthur Schatz/TimePix; **72** (t)U.S. Architect of the Capitol, (bl)Scala/Art Resource, (br)Bettmann/CORBIS; **73** (l)Courtesy Pilgrim Society, Plymouth, MA, (t)file photo, (c)National Portrait Gallery, London/SuperStock, (cr)Bettmann/CORBIS, (b)National Portrait Gallery; **74** (t)Charles & Josette Lenars/CORBIS, (c)Giraudon/Art Resource, NY, (bl)Scala/Art Resource, NY, (bcl)National Portrait Gallery, (bcr)Historical Picture Collection/Stock Montage, (br)Mary Evans Picture Library; **74–75** (bkgd)Worldsat International Inc. 2004, All Rights Reserved; **75** (t)Bettmann/CORBIS, (c)Francis G. Mayer/CORBIS, (bl)Independence National Historical Park, (bcl)White House Historical Association, (bcr)National Portrait Gallery, Smithsonian Institution/Art Resource, NY, (br)Stock Montage; **76–77** William S. Helsel/Getty Images; **79** U.S. Architect of the Capitol; **81** (l)Hulton Archive, (r)The Bodleian Library, Oxford, Ms. Bodl. 264, fol.219R; **82** (l)National Museum of American History, Smithsonian Institution, Behring Center, (r)Photograph Courtesy Peabody Essex Museum; **83** (l)National Maritime Museum, (r)CORBIS; **84** Giraudon/Art Resource, NY; **85** Doug Martin; **88** Florida State Archives; **91** Bibliotheque Nationale, Paris; **92** Scala/Art Resource, NY; **93** Réunion des Musées Nationaux/Art Resource, NY; **94** Jack Fields/CORBIS; **99** The Jewish Museum, NY/Art Resource; **101** Archivo Iconografico, S.A./CORBIS; **102** SuperStock; **104** National Portrait Gallery, London, copyright Snark/Art Resource, NY; **106** Stock Montage; **108** The City of Plainfield, NJ; **109** 1997 Suzanne-Murphy-Larronde; **112–113** Owaki-Kulla/CORBIS;

115 Yale University Art Gallery, Bequest of Eugene Phelps Edwards; **117** Bettmann/CORBIS; **118** Robert Holmes/CORBIS; **123** Gibbes Museum of Art/Carolina Art Association; **125** (bl)National Museum of American History/Smithsonian Institution, (br)Bettmann/CORBIS; **127** file photo; **128** (bkgd)Getty, Yale University Art Gallery, Bequest of Eugene Phelps Edwards; **129** National Portrait Gallery, London/SuperStock; **130** Patrick Henry Before the Virginia House of Burgesses (1851) by Peter F. Rothermel. Red Hill, The Patrick Henry National Memorial, Brookneal, VA; **132** White House Historical Association; **133** Bettmann/CORBIS; **136** (tr)Courtesy of the Massachusetts Historical Society, (bl)file photo; **137** (bl)Library of Congress, (br)Kevin Fleming/CORBIS; **138** (tl)The Royal Collection © 2003 Her Majesty Queen Elizabeth II, (t)DAR Museum on loan from Boston Tea Party Chapter, (bl)Stock Montage, (br)Courtesy American Antiquarian Society; **139** Photograph Courtesy Peabody Essex Museum; **142** Museum of Fine Arts, Boston. Gift of Joseph W. Revere, William B. Revere, and Edward H.R. Revere; **148** (tl cl br)Doug Martin, (cr)file photo; **151** (tr)National Portrait Gallery, Smithsonian Institution/Art Resources, NY, (bl)Yale University Art Gallery; **152** Copyright 1996, Virginia Historical Society, Lora Robins Collection of Virginia Art; **153** Bettmann/CORBIS; **154** (tr)Bill Gentile/CORBIS, (bl)Fraunces Tavern Museum, New York City; **155** William T. Ranney, MARION CROSSING THE PEDEE, 1850, o/c, 1983.126; Amon Carter Museum, Fort Worth, Texas; **158 159 160** Bettmann/CORBIS; **161** Stapleton Collection/CORBIS; **165** Francis G. Mayer/CORBIS; **167** Bettmann/CORBIS; **168** (t)Fraunces Tavern Museum, New York City, (bl)Photograph Courtesy Peabody Essex Museum, (br)Courtesy Pilgrim Society, Plymouth, MA; **169** (cl)Hulton-Deutsch Collection/CORBIS, (c)Lexington Historical Society, Lexington, MA, (cr)Fort Ticonderoga Museum, (b)Michael Holford; **170** (t)Library of Congress, (b)Rob Huntley for Chromographics; **171** (t)White House Historical Association, (cl)Bettmann/CORBIS, (cr)Charles E. Rotkin/CORBIS, (b)Giraudon/Art Resource, NY; **172** (t)file photo, (c)Bettmann/CORBIS, (bl)Moorland Spingarn Research Center, Howard University, (bcl)Delaware Art Museum, Wilmington. Gift of Absalom Jones School, Wilmington, (bcr)Burstein Collection/CORBIS, (br)Yale University Art Gallery, gift of Roger Sherman White, B.A. 1859; **172–173** (bkgd)Worldsat International Inc. 2004, All Rights Reserved; **173** (t)SuperStock, (c)David R. Frazier, (bl)Bettmann/CORBIS, (bcl)Museum of Fine Arts, Boston; Bequest of Winslow Warren, (bcr)Mary Evans Picture Library, (br)Getty Images; **174–175** SuperStock; **180** Picture Research Consultants; **181** (b)Minute Man National Historic Park/Rob Huntley for Chromographics; **184** Chicago Historical Society; **192** Doug Martin; **194** Bettmann/CORBIS; **195** Gallo Images/CORBIS; **196** (tr)Moorland Spingarn Research Center, Howard University, (bl)Delaware Art Museum, Wilmington. Gift of Absalom Jones School, Wilmington; **197** Independence National Historic Park; **198** Burstein Collection/CORBIS; **200** (l)Francis G. Mayer/CORBIS, (r)Joseph Sohm; Visions of America/CORBIS; **203** National Portrait Gallery, London, copyright Snark/Art Resource, NY; **204** Fred Maroon/Smithsonian Institution; **205** Richard Strauss, Smithsonian Institution/The Supreme Court Historical Society; **208** Stock Montage; **209** Bettmann/CORBIS; **210** Library of Congress/American Antiquarian Society; **211** Collection of The New York Historical Society; **214–215** Elliot Teel Photography; **217** Jeff Greenberg/Photo Edit; **218** (l) Bettmann/CORBIS, (r)White House Historical Association; **219** David Young-Wolff/Photo Edit; **220** Mary Evans Picture Library; **226** (l) Francis G. Mayer/CORBIS, (c) White House Historical Association (r)Getty Images; **227 229** Courtesy U.S. Congress; **231** Richard T. Nowitz/CORBIS; **232** Getty Images; **233** Carl Iwaski/TimePix/Getty Images; **234 235** White House Historical Association; **237** (l)North Wind/North Wind Picture Archives, (r) Jeff Greenberg/Photo Edit; **240** (t)Getty Images, (b) Bettmann/CORBIS; **241** Glenn Martin/Denver Post/Wide World Photos; **242** The Pierpont Morgan Library/Art Resource, NY; **243** (t)Burstein Collection/CORBIS, (b)Bettmann/CORBIS; **246** (t)Bettmann/CORBIS, (bl)Picture Research Consultants, (br)Courtesy U.S. Congress; **247** (t)Carl Iwaski/TimePix/Getty Images, (cl)Burstein Collection/CORBIS, (cr)Mary Evans Picture Library; **248** (bkgd)Wes Thompson/The Stock Market/CORBIS, (l)Library of Congress; **250** White House Historical Association; **251** Courtesy U.S. Senate; **252** Bettmann/CORBIS; **254** Boltin Picture Library; **255** White House Historical Association; **262** Joseph Sohm; ChromoShom Inc./CORBIS; **266** Bettmann/CORBIS; **267** Nathan Benn/CORBIS; **268** TimePix; **269** Sandy Schaeffer/TimePix; **270** (t)Frank & Marie-Therese Wood Print Collection, Alexandria, VA, (cr)Beinecke Rare Book and Manuscript Library, Yale University, (bl)AKG London, (br)Giraudon/Art Resource, NY; **271** (t)North Wind Picture Archives, (b)Old Dartmouth Historical Society/New Bedford Whaling Museum; **272** (t)Chicago Historical Society, (c)North Wind Picture Archive, (bl)Archivo Iconografico, S.A./CORBIS, (bcl)White House Historical Association, (bcr)Bettmann/CORBIS, (br)E.S. Paxson,"Lewis and Clark at Three Forks," Courtesy of the Montana Historical Society, photograph by Don Beaty; **272–273** Worldsat International Inc. 2004, All Rights Reserved; **273** (t)Western American Prints, (c)Don Troiani, www.historicalartprints.com, (bl bcl)Bettmann/CORBIS, (bcr)Greenville County Museum of Art, (br)Stock

Montage; 274–275 Royalty-Free/CORBIS; 277 Stock Montage; 278 (l r)White House Historical Association, (c)Yale University Art Gallery; 279 Frank & Marie-Therese Wood Print Collection, Alexandria, VA; 280 (l)General Washington on a White Charger, Gift of Edgar William & Bernie Chrysler Garbisch, Image © 2004 Board of Trustees, National Gallery of Art, Washington D.C., (r)Fred Prouser/Reuters/CORBIS; 282 David R. Frazier; 283 Archivo Iconografico, S.A./CORBIS; 286 Courtesy Winterthur Museum; 287 Chicago Historical Society; 291 Museum of the City of New York/CORBIS; 292 Stock Montage; 294 (tr)Stock Montage, (bl)Bettmann/CORBIS; 296 Stock Montage; 298 Bettmann/CORBIS; 299 file photo; 302–303 Joe Sohm/Alamy Images; 305 Stock Montage; 306 (l)White House Historical Association, (r)Duke University Archives; 308 White House Historical Association; 310 Getty Images; 311 Museum of the City of New York/CORBIS; 312 Western American Prints; 314 Brown Brothers; 315 Bettmann/CORBIS; 318 Bates Littlehales, (t)From Curtis's Botanical Magazine, 1863, photo by Volkmar Wentzel, (bl)E.S. Paxson, "Lewis and Clark at Three Forks," Courtesy of the Montana Historical Society, photograph by Don Beaty; 319 (t)Western American Prints, (b)Kevin C. Chadwick; 321 Beinecke Rare Book and Manuscript Library, Yale University; 322 Old Dartmouth Historical Society/New Bedford Whaling Museum; 323 The Wadsworth Atheneum Museum of Art, Hartford, CT. Purchased from the Artist before 1850; 324 Bettmann/CORBIS; 325 Angelo Hornak, CORBIS; 326 327 Getty Images; 328 North Wind/North Wind Picture Archives; 330 Thomas Gilcrease Institute; 331 Missouri Historical Society, St. Louis; 334–335 Mark E. Gibson/CORBIS; 337 340 CORBIS; 342 (Tecumseh) Field Museum of Natural History; 343 Lorence Bjorklund; 344 (tr)Greenville County Museum of Art, (bl)New York Historical Society; 352 Doug Martin; 354 Library of Congress; 357 Stock Montage; 358 Don Troiani, www.historicalartprints.com; 360 (tr)Hulton Getty, (c)TIME Inc. Picture Collection, (bl)Bettmann/CORBIS; 361 (t)National Gallery of Art, (b)NY Public Library/TIME Picture Collection; 364 (l)Library of Congress, (r)Collection of the Boston Public Library, Print Division; 366 file photo; 368 Smithsonian Institution; 369 Brown Brothers; 372 (t)H. Armstrong Roberts, (bl)National Museum of American History, Smithsonian Institution, Behring Center, (br)Western American Prints; 373 (t)Missouri Historical Society, St. Louis, (r)(Tecumseh)Field Museum of Natural History; 374 (l r)Bettmann/CORBIS; 375 (tr)Chicago Historical Society, (cl)Picture Research Consultants, (c)Mongerson-Wunderlich Gallery, Chicago, (cr)Photo Researchers, (b)Harper's Weekly/CORBIS; 376 (t)Joseph Sohm; Chromosohm Inc./CORBIS, (c)SuperStock, (bl)Bettmann/CORBIS, (bcl bcr)National Portrait Gallery, Smithsonian Institution/Art Resource, NY, (br)Stock Montage; 376–377 (bkgd)Worldsat International Inc. 2004, All Rights Reserved; 377 (t)Steve Vidler/SuperStock, (c)Robert Holmes/CORBIS, (bl)White House Historical Association, (bcl)Stock Montage, (bcr)Smithsonian American Art Museum, Washington, DC/Art Resource, NY, (br)file photo; 378–379 David Muench/CORBIS; 381 (l r)Bettmann/CORBIS; 382 (l)Bettmann/CORBIS, (r)Getty Images; 383 Bettmann/CORBIS; 384 Aaron Haupt; 385 Lewis Hine/Museum of Photography at George Eastman House; 388 (l)SuperStock, (c)Stock Montage; 391 Stock Montage; 392 Joseph Sohm; Chromosohm Inc./CORBIS; 395 Howard University; 396 Jack Naylor; 397 Museum of Fine Arts, Boston; Gift of Maxim Karolik 398 National Park Service Collection; 399 (bkgd)(Detail) The Bay and Harbor of New York c. 1953–1855 Samuel B. Waugh (1814–1885) Watercolor on canvas, 99 1/5 X 198 1/4 Gift of Mrs. Robert L. Littlejohn, Museum of the City of New York, 33.169, (inset)Courtesy of The Bostonian Society/Old State House; 400 United States Naval Academy Museum; 402 (c)CORBIS, (r)National Portrait Gallery, Smithsonian Institution/Art Resource, NY; 403 Bettmann/CORBIS; 404 (t)National Portrait Gallery, Smithsonian Institution, Washington, DC/Art Resource, (b)Time Life Pictures/Getty Images; 406 (bl)Brown Brothers, (br)FPG/Getty Images; 408 (r)Chicago Historical Society; 408 (l)Mount Holyoke College Art Museum, South Hadley, Massachusetts; 409 Bettmann/CORBIS; 410 (l)Chicago Historical Society, (r)Meserve-Kunhardt Collection, courtesy Picture History, Mt. Kisco, NY; 411 (tl)Courtesy of Maria Mitchell Association, (tr)National Archives of Canada, (bl)Bettmann/CORBIS, (bc)Hulton Archive, (br)Nebraska State Historical Society Photograph Collections; 412 Robert Jackson; 414 (t)Library of Congress, (b)Old Dartmouth Historical Society/New Bedford Whaling Museum; 418–419 Bob Krist/CORBIS; 421 The J. Paul Getty Museum; 422 Smithsonian Institution; 423 James Randklev/CORBIS; 424 Bettmann/CORBIS, (r)Smithsonian Institution; 428 Jan Butchofsky-Houser/CORBIS; 429 The J. Paul Getty Museum; 430 Bettmann/CORBIS; 432 (l)Picture Research Consultants, (r)Stock Montage; 434 Trustees of the Boston Public Library; 435 (bkgd)Photo Researchers, (tr)John Deere Museum, (c)Adam Woolfitt/CORBIS (bl)Courtesy of The Charleston Museum, Charleston, South Carolina, (br)Valentine Museum; 436 Stock Montage; 438 Bettmann/CORBIS; 439 Photo Researchers; 442–443 Peter Gridley/Getty Images; 442 (l)White House Historical Association, (c)SuperStock, (r)National Portrait Gallery, Smithsonian Institution/Art Resource, NY; 445 Bettmann/CORBIS;

446 White House Historical Association; 447 New York Historical Society; 448 Pat & Chuck Blackley; 449 Library Company of Philadelphia; 450 North Wind Picture Archive; 452 (l)Smithsonian American Art Museum, Washington, DC/Art Resource, NY, (r)SuperStock; 453 Stock Montage; 455 SuperStock; 456 Smithsonian American Art Museum, Washington, DC/Art Resource, NY; 457 Thomas Gilcrease Institute of American Art, Tulsa, OK; 458 (l)Bettmann/CORBIS, (r)National Portrait Gallery, Smithsonian Institution/Art Resource, NY; 459 Bettmann/CORBIS; 460 New York Historical Society; 462 CORBIS; 463 Archives and Manuscripts Division of the Oklahoma Historical Society; 466–467 Steve Vidler/SuperStock; 468 Hulton Archive/Getty Images; 470 (l)Mongerson-Wunderlich Gallery, Chicago, (r)White House Historical Association, (r)Hulton Archive/Getty Images; 472 (l)Joel W. Rogers/CORBIS, (r)Bettmann/CORBIS; 473 (t)Mongerson-Wunderlich Gallery, Chicago, (b)Henry Groskinsky/Timepix; 476 National Portrait Gallery, Smithsonian Institution/Art Resource, NY; 477 Library of Congress, Prints & Photographs Division; 478 (l)Brown Brothers, (r)Bettmann/CORBIS; 479 (br)Northwind Picture Archives, (r)Brown Brothers, (bl)Chicago Historical Society/Photo Researchers Inc.; 480 (l)Texas Department of Highways and Public Transportation, (r)Texas State Library and Archives Commission; 481 (l)Center for American History/Barker Collection/UT-Austin, (r)Texas State Library and Archives Commission; 482–483 (bkgd)Friends of the Governor's Mansion, Austin; 484 Susanna Dickinson by Harry Anthony DeYoung. Alamo Collection. Photograph courtesy the Daughters of the Republic of Texas Library. CT97.9.; 485 Texas State Library and Archives Commission; 486 (l)Texas State Library and Archives Commission, photo by Eric Beggs, (r)San Jacinto Museum History Association; 488 (tr)Jim Corwin/Index Stock Imagery, (bl)Royalty-Free/CORBIS; 489 CORBIS; 490 (l)Chicago Historical Society, (r)California State Library; 491 (tl)Robert Holmes/CORBIS; 492 Thomas Gilcrease Institute of American Art, Tulsa, OK; 493 Arte Publico Press Archives; 494 Courtesy The Bancroft Library, University of California, Berkeley; 496 (l)file photo, (r)California State Library; 498 (l)Gerald French/CORBIS, (r)In house file; 499 Alaska Division of Tourism; 500 (l)Courtesy Wells Fargo Bank, (r)California State Capitol; 501 Courtesy The Oakland Museum; 502 Courtesy The Bancroft Library University of California, Berkeley; 503 (l)Levi Strauss & Company, (r)Syracuse Newspapers/The Image Works; 504 (t)Royalty-Free/CORBIS, (l)Courtesy The Bancroft Library University of California, Berkeley, (r)Monterey Public Library, California History Room Archives; 505 Courtesy Museum of Art, Brigham Young University; 513 Doug Martin; 514 Courtesy Denver Public Library Western History Collection; 515 Bettmann/CORBIS; 518 (t)Henry Groskinsky, (bl)American Antiquarian Society, (br)Collection of David J. & Janice L. Frent; 519 (t)New York Historical Society, (c)Stock Montage, (b)Mary Evans Picture Library; 520 (t)CORBIS, (c)Collection of William Gladstone, (b)Courtesy of the United States Naval Academy Museum; 521 (tl)Michigan Capitol Committee, photography by Peter Glendinning, (tr)Museum of the Confederacy, (c)Getty Images, (b)Image Select/Art Resource, NY; 522 (t)Bettmann/CORBIS, (c)Thad Samuels Abell II/Getty Images, (bl)Chester County Historical Society, West Chester, PA, (bcl)Collection of William Gladstone, (bcr)Missouri Historical Society, St. Louis, (br)CORBIS; 522–533 (bkgd)Worldsat International Inc. 2004, All Rights Reserved; 523 (t)Joseph Sohm; ChromoSohm Inc./CORBIS, (c)Lee Snider/Photo Images/CORBIS, (bl)National Archives, (bcl)CORBIS, (bcr)Hulton Archive/Getty Images, (br)White House Historical Association; 524–525 William A. Bake/CORBIS; 527 Getty Images; 530 Peabody Essex Museum/Mark Sexton; 531 CORBIS; 532 Collection of William Gladstone; 536 New York Historical Society; 537 Bettmann/CORBIS; 538 file photo; 539 The Corcoran Gallery of Art/CORBIS; 540 Gianni Dagli Orti/CORBIS; 541 New York Public Library, print division.; 544 Bettmann/CORBIS; 545 Schlesinger Library, Radcliffe Institute, Harvard University; 548 (l)White House Historical Association, (c)Missouri Historical Society, St. Louis, (r)National Portrait Gallery, Smithsonian Institution; 550 (t)The Supreme Court of the United States Office of the Curator, #1991.402.2, (b)Library of Congress; 551 The Miriam Matthews Collection; 552 Courtesy Illinois State Historical Library; 555 Chicago Historical Society; 557 Bettmann/CORBIS; 560 561 CORBIS; 562 Massachusetts Historical Society/Picture Research Consultants; 563 Bettmann/CORBIS; 560 (cl)Doug Martin; 565–566 Thad Samuels Abell II/Getty Images; 566 (tl)Museum of the Confederacy, (bl)Michigan Capitol Committee, photography by Peter Glendinning, (r)Getty Images; 569 Museum of the Confederacy; 570 Seventh Regiment Fund, New York City; 572–573 (bkgd)Getty Images; 574 Kean E. Wilcox Collection; 575 Royalty Free/CORBIS; 577 Manassas National Battlefield Park/Larry Sherer; 578 Getty Images; 580 (l)Michigan Capitol Committee, photography by Peter Glendinning, (r)Museum of the Confederacy; 582 Medford Historical Society Collection/CORBIS; 590 Doug Martin; 591 (l)Getty Images, (r)McLellan Lincoln Collection, The John Hay Library, Brown University/John Miller; 592 593 Getty Images; 595 file photo; 597 Kean E. Wilcox Collection; 598 (bkgd)Getty Images, (t)Museum of the Confederacy; 599 Library of Congress;

601 Hulton Archive/Getty Images; 602 (l)Brown Brothers, (c)file photo, (r)CORBIS; 607 Lester Lefkowitz/CORBIS; 610 Northwind Picture Archives; 611 (tr)Washington & Lee University, Virginia, (bl)Bettmann/CORBIS; 612 National Archives; 616 Medford Historical Society Collection/CORBIS; 617 Museum of the Confederacy; 620 (tl)Time Life Books, from the series Civil War/Edward Owen, (bl)Illinois State Historical Library, (bc)Bettmann/CORBIS; 620–621 CORBIS; 623 Photographic History Collection, National Museum of American History, Smithsonian Institution, negative number 86-11374; 624 (l)National Museum of American History, Smithsonian Institution, Behring Center, (r)North Wind Picture Archive; 625 Thaddeus Stevens by Edward Dalton, The Library of the Union League of Philadelphia photo by Rick Echelmeyer; 627 Howard University; 629 White House Historical Association; 630 Chicago Historical Society; 631 Collection of Cheekwood Museum of Art, Nashville, Tennessee; 633 Bettmann/CORBIS; 635 636 CORBIS; 637 Chester County Historical Society, West Chester, PA; 639 Photographic History Collection, National Museum of American History, Smithsonian Institution, negative number 86-11374.; 640 White House Historical Association; 641 Stock Montage; 642 (c)file photo; 642–643 (bkgd)CORBIS; 643 (r)Bettmann/CORBIS; 646 Pembroke Herbert/Picture Research Consultants; 647 Amistad Foundation/Wadsworth Atheneum; 648 The Museum of American Political Life, University of Hartford; 649 Brown Brothers; 650 Bettmann/CORBIS; 651 Carl Iwaski/TimePix/Getty Images; 652 Cook Collection/Valentine Museum; 653 Library of Congress/CORBIS; 656 (tl)Michigan Capitol Committee, photography by Peter Glendinning, (tr)Museum of the Confederacy, (bl)Frank & Marie-Therese Wood Print Collection, Alexandria, VA, (br)Getty Images; 657 (tl)Time-Life Books, Inc. from the series Civil War/Edward Owen, (tr)Illinois State Historical Library, (c)Chicago Historical Society, (b)Mary Evans Picture Library; 658 (tl)courtesy Rockefeller Archive Center, (tr)courtesy California History Room, California State Library, Sacramento, (c)Cantor Arts Center, Stanford University, (bl)Museo Civico Modigliana, Italy/Dagli Orti/Art Archive, (br)Mary Evans Picture Library; 659 (t)White House Historical Association, (c)Courtesy Ford Motor Company, (b)Brown Brothers; 660 (t)Wolfgang Kaehler/CORBIS, (cl)CORBIS, (c cr)Worldsat International Inc. 2004, All Rights Reserved, (bl)National Anthropological Archives, Smithsonian Institution (neg. #2906), (bcl)Stock Montage, (bcr)Bettmann/CORBIS, (br)Jane Addams Memorial Collection (JAMC neg. 1003), The University Library, University of Illinois at Chicago; 660–661 (bkgd)Worldsat International Inc. 2004, All Rights Reserved; 661 (t)CORBIS, (c)Bettmann/CORBIS, (bl)Oscar White/CORBIS, (bcl)Archive Photo, (bcr)Oscar B. Willis/The Schomburg Center for Research in Black Culture, New York Public Library, (br)The Schomburg Center for Research in Black Culture, New York Public Library; 662 (l)Library of Congress, (r)Collection of David J. & Janice L. Frent; 662–663 Wyoming Division of Cultural Resources; 665 Photograph from the book The Life and Adventures of Nat Love by himself/Rare Book and Manuscripts, Special Collections Library, Duke University, Durham, North Carolina; 667 CORBIS; 668 Colorado Historical Society; 669 (l)Brown Brothers, (r)L. Berger/SuperStock; 670 From the original painting by Mort Kunstler, The Race, Mort Kunstler, Inc.; 673 Photograph from the book The Life and Adventures of Nat Love by himself/Rare Book and Manuscripts, Special Collections Library, Duke University, Durham, North Carolina; 674 Thomas Gilcrease Institute of American Art, Tulsa, OK; 675 Yale Collection of Western Americana, Beinecke Rare Book & Manuscript Library; 677 United States Military Museum, West Point; 678 (l)Nebraska State Historical Society Photograph Collections, (r)Montana Historical Society, Helena; 684 Doug Martin; 686 Smithsonian American Art Museum, Washington, DC/Art Resource, NY; 687 Courtesy, National Museum of the American Indian, Smithsonian Institution (20/6563). Photo by Carmelo Guadagno.; 688 Denver Public Library, Western History Collection; 690 Bettmann/CORBIS; 691 National Portrait Gallery, Smithsonian Institution/Art Resource, NY; 693 (l)Collection of David J. & Janice L. Frent, (r)White House Historical Association; 694 New York Historical Society; 695 Kansas State Historical Society; 696 AP/Wide World Photos; 698 Amon Carter Museum, Fort Worth, Texas; 699 file photo; 702–703 Huntington Library/SuperStock; 702 (l)Courtesy Rockefeller Archive Center, (r)Photo by Dane Penland, National Air and Space Museum, Smithsonian Institution (SI 79-764); 705 Kansas Collection, Spencer Research Library, University of Kansas Libraries; 707 Michael Masslan Historic Photographs/CORBIS; 708 Getty Images; 712 (l)Electricity Collections, National Museum of American History, Smithsonian Institution, (r)Courtesy Ford Motor Company; 714–715 Brown Brothers; 716 (tl)Electricity Collections, National Museum of American History, Smithsonian Institution, (tc)Picture Research Consultants, (tr)The Queens Borough Public Library, Long Island Division, Latimer Family Papers, (bl)Picture Research Consultants, (br)Courtesy George Eastman House; 718 (l)Courtesy Rockefeller Archive Center, (r)National Portrait Gallery/ Smithsonian Institution/Art Resource, NY; 720 Library of Congress; 721 (l)National Portrait Gallery/Smithsonian Institution/Art Resource, NY,

(r)National Park Service; 722 Courtesy Rockefeller Archive Center; 724 (l)The George Meany Memorial Archives, (r)Library of Congress; 725 Library of Congress; 726 Fine Arts Museums of San Francisco, Gift of Mr. and Mrs. John D. Rockefeller 3rd 1979.7.4 zz; 728 Bettmann/CORBIS; 730 Time Life Pictures/Getty Images; 731 North Wind/North Wind Picture Archives; 732 733 CORBIS; 736–737 Charles O'Rear/CORBIS; 736 (l)Bettmann/CORBIS, (r)Brown Brothers; 738 CORBIS; 739 Picture Research Consultants; 741 Library of Congress; 743 Jacob A. Riis Collection, Museum of the City of New York; 744 (t)National Archives, (b)Brown Brothers; 745 Bettmann/CORBIS; 746 Picture Research Consultants; 748 Rykoff Collection/CORBIS; 749 Austrian Archives/CORBIS; 752 Orchard Films; 753 Jane Addams Memorial Collection (JAMC neg. 1003), The University Library, University of Illinois at Chicago; 754 Brown Brothers; 755 CORBIS; 757 (l)Doug Martin, (c)Courtesy, National Museum of the American Indian, Smithsonian Institution (N36122/3), (r)Harris Ewing; 758 Library of Congress; 759 (bc br)Bettmann/CORBIS, (others)Library of Congress; 760 (t)CORBIS, (bl)Courtesy, National Museum of the American Indian, Smithsonian Institution, (br)Courtesy, National Museum of the American Indian, Smithsonian Institution (N36122/3).; 762 Winslow Homer American, 1836–1910. Girls with Lobster, 1873. Watercolor and gouache over graphite, 24.2 X 32.9 cm. (c) The Cleveland Museum of Art, 2002. Purchase from the J. H. Wade Fund, 1943.660; 764 (l)White House Historical Association, (r)The Ida M. Tarbell Collection, Pelletier Library, Allegheny College; 765 Library of Congress; 766 CORBIS; 768 file photo; 769 Bettmann/ CORBIS; 770 Collection of David J. & Janice L. Frent; 772 Daniel J. Cox/naturalexposures.com; 773 Robin Brandt; 777 (l)Leonard de Selva/CORBIS, (r)Private Collection/courtesy R.H. Love Galleries, Chicago; 779 (l)Bettmann/CORBIS, (r)Private Collection; 781 (t)Oscar White/ CORBIS, (b)The Schomburg Center for Research in Black Culture, New York Public Library; 782 CORBIS; 784 (bl)Harris Ewing; 785 (tr)Schenectady Museum/Hall of Electrical History Foundation/CORBIS, (others)Bettmann/ CORBIS; 786 Underwood & Underwood/CORBIS; 787 Library of Congress; 790 (t)Brown Brothers, (bl)Bob Mullenix, (br)Picture Research Consultants; 791 (t)Courtesy, National Museum of the American Indian, Smithsonian Institution (20/6563). Photo by Carmelo Guadagno., (c)National Portrait Gallery/Smithsonian Insititon/Art Resource, NY, (b)Yale Collection of Western Americana, Beinecke Rare Book & Manuscript Library; 792 Underwood Archives/Index Stock Imagery; 793 Getty Images; 794 (t)Franklin D. Roosevelt Library, (b)Library of Congress; 795 (t)National Archives, (b)US Army; 796 (t)Robert Reiff/MagicLight Productions, (b)Flip Schulke/Black Star; 797 (t)Mike Segar/Reuters/ TimePix, (b)Thomas E. Franklin/Bergen Record/SABA/CORBIS; 798 Bettmann/CORBIS; 799 Underwood & Underwood/CORBIS; 800 Library of Congress; 801 Charles Moore/Black Star; 802 (t)AP/Wide World Photos, (b)Collection of David J. & Janice L. Frent; 804 (t)CORBIS, (c)A.J. SISCO/CORBIS, (b)Bruce Kliewe/Index Stock; 806 (t)Library of Congress; 807 Detroit Publishing Company; 808 Rob Lewine/ The Stock Market; 809 (t)Swim Ink/CORBIS, (b)US Air Force Museum; 810 (t)Bettmann/CORBIS, (b)Getty Images; 812 Christie's Images; 813 Getty Images; 814 Official Senate Photo/CNP/Getty Images; 816 (t)Schlesinger Library, Radcliffe Institute, Harvard University, (b)Joe Raedle/Newsmakers; 817 (l)Bob Daemmrich, (r)AP/Wide World Photos; 818 (t)Tony Freeman/ PhotoEdit, (b)James Shaffer/PhotoEdit; 819 Royalty Free/CORBIS; 820 (tl)Picture Research Consultants, (tr)Peter Turnley/CORBIS, (tcr)file photo, (cl)SuperStock, (cr bcl)Getty (bcr)Brown Brothers, (br)Courtesy Smithsonian Institution, NMAH/Transportation; 823 MAK I; 824 Maritime Museum, Seville/Artephot/Oronoz; 826 file photo; 828 White House Historical Association; 830 National Archives; 831 832 Bettmann/CORBIS; 833 Geoffrey Clements/CORBIS; 834 Library of Congress; 835 US Army Military History Institute; 836 Choctaw Removal, 1966. Valjean McCarty Hessing, Choctaw, B. 1934. Watercolor on paper, Museum purchase, The Philbrook Museum of Art, Tulsa, Oklahoma., 1967.24; 837 The Museum of American Political Life, University of Hartford; 838 Tim Flach/Getty Images, (l)North Wind Picture Archives, (r)Electricity Collections, National Museum of American History, Smithsonian Institution; 840 841 842 843 White House Historical Association; 844 (br)Official White House Photo by Eric Draper, (bcr)White House Historical Association (White House Collection, 6196), (others)White House Historical Association; 845 (bkgd)Getty Images, (tl)CORBIS; 846 Missouri Historical Society, St. Louis; 847 848 Bettmann/CORBIS; 850 North Wind Picture Archive; 851 852 Bettmann/CORBIS; 853 (t)Bettmann/CORBIS, (b)Courtesy, National Museum of the American Indian, Smithsonian Institution (20/1843). Photo by Carmelo Guadagno.; 854 National Portrait Gallery, Smithsonian Institution/Art Resource, NY; 855 (t)National Portrait Gallery, Smithsonian Institution/Art Resource, NY, (b)Mark Burnett; 856 (l)file photo, (r)Mark Burnett; 857 (t)Denver Art Museum, (b)Bettmann/CORBIS; 859 UPI/Bettmann/CORBIS; 860 Bettmann/CORBIS; 861 Flip Schulke/ Black Star.